Peter Mattock

Conceptual Maths

Teaching 'about' (rather than just 'how to do') mathematics in schools

Crown House Publishing Limited
www.crownhouse.co.uk

First published by
Crown House Publishing Limited
Crown Buildings, Bancyfelin, Carmarthen, Wales, SA33 5ND, UK
www.crownhouse.co.uk

and

Crown House Publishing Company LLC
PO Box 2223, Williston, VT 05495, USA
www.crownhousepublishing.com

© Peter Mattock, 2023.

The right of Peter Mattock to be identified as the author of this work has been asserted by him in accordance with the Copyright, Designs and Patents Act 1988.

Illustrations © Les Evans 2023.

The right of Les Evans to be identified as the illustrator of this work has been asserted by him in accordance with the Copyright, Designs and Patents Act 1988.

Protractor image, page 275 © attaphong – stock.adobe.com. Ruler image, pages 287 and 297 © Vlad – stock.adobe.com. Truncated icosahedron image, page 368 © Iricat – stock.adobe.com.

AQA material is reproduced by permission of AQA.

Activities pages 66, 149, 295, 366, 552 © NRICH. Activities pages 71, 72, 79, 95, 100, 103, 134, 144, 191, 192, 207, 242, 244, 249, 290, 300, 352, 371, 373, 462, 465, 522, 551, 609, 628 © Don Steward. Activities pages 72, 144, 187 © Open Middle. Activity page 153 © MathsBot.com. Activity page 154 © 10 Ticks. Graph page 250 produced using Desmos and used with permission. Activity page 279 © Dan Draper. Activities pages 349, 353, 476, 611 © Boss Maths. Activity page 357 © John Mason. Activity page 383 © UKMT. Pencil image page 387 based on original by basic-mathematics.com. Activity page 468 © Craig Barton. Activity page 470 © Math-Aids.Com. Activities pages 473, 612 © Maths Genie. Activity page 475 © Maths is Fun. Activity page 475 © Kangaroo Maths. Activities pages 481, 528 © Corbettmaths. Activities pages 497, 508, 598 © CIMT. Activity page 504 © Mathsprint.co.uk. Activity pages 574-575 © Onlinemathlearning.com. Activity page 604 © JustMaths. Activity page 607 © PixiMaths. Activity page 610 © Go Teach Maths. Activity page 613 © Jo Morgan. For availability please see reference.

All rights reserved. Except as permitted under current legislation no part of this work may be photocopied, stored in a retrieval system, published, performed in public, adapted, broadcast, transmitted, recorded or reproduced in any form or by any means, without the prior permission of the copyright owners. Enquiries should be addressed to Crown House Publishing.

Crown House Publishing has no responsibility for the persistence or accuracy of URLs for external or third-party websites referred to in this publication, and does not guarantee that any content on such websites is, or will remain, accurate or appropriate.

First published 2023.

British Library Cataloguing-in-Publication Data

A catalogue entry for this book is available from the British Library.

Print ISBN 978-178583599-5
Mobi ISBN 978-178583617-6
ePub ISBN 978-178583618-3
ePDF ISBN 978-178583619-0

LCCN 2021950843

Dedication and thanks

My last book was dedicated to the maths teachers and educational professionals that have been part of my career, to my mum, Lesley, and to my partner (now wife), Rowan. All of you remain an important part of my life and work; please do not think you are forgotten.

This book is dedicated in three parts.

First, to my grandparents, Pat, Ted, Alan and June, whom I know would be proud.

Second, to the boys, Chris, John and Paul. Friends for life.

Finally, to my girls, Erin and Mollie. The lights of my world.

A number of people have allowed me to reproduce their material as part of this book. I would like to thank the following for their contribution:

- 10Ticks
- AQA
- basic-mathematics.com
- Boss Maths
- CIMT
- Corbettmaths
- Dan Draper
- Desmos
- Don Steward
- Go Teach Maths
- Jo Morgan
- Jonathan Hall (MathsBot.com)
- JustMaths
- Kangaroo Maths
- Math-Aids.Com
- Maths Genie
- Math is Fun
- NRICH
- Online Math Learning
- Open Middle
- PixiMaths
- Transfinite
- UKMT
- Variation Theory

Contents

Introduction	1
1. Number	5
2. Addition and subtraction	47
3. Multiplication and multiples	81
4. Division and factors	125
5. Equality/equivalence/congruence	165
6. Proportionality	215
7. Functionality	241
8. Measures	271
9. Accuracy	297
10. Shape	329
11. Transformation and vectors	423
12. Chance	477
13. Charting and graphing	511
14. Data handling	591
Glossary	*641*
Bibliography	*643*

Introduction

What is mathematics? Interestingly, although mathematics has been an integral part of the school curriculum for the best part of the last 75 years or so,[1] there is little consensus on the answer to this question amongst teachers of mathematics. Some people will say that mathematics is a body of connected knowledge, others that it is a way of behaving and making sense of the world, whilst others will say it is a collection of theorems based on fundamental axioms. Some may see this lack of consensus as problematic – we can hardly ensure that learners of mathematics are getting a consistent experience if their teachers don't all have the same idea of what they are teaching! However, for me, a consensus amongst maths educators about what mathematics is isn't as important as what mathematics is not. One thing (in my opinion) that mathematics definitely is not, is a collection of procedures.

That is not to say that procedures aren't important in mathematics; simply that if all one learns about mathematics is how to complete procedures, then one hasn't really learnt a lot about mathematics. Primarily this is because there are (nearly always) many different procedures that will accomplish the same result, with the choice of procedure largely dependent on a mixture of efficiency and what the teacher is familiar with or prefers. Jo Morgan's excellent *A Compendium of Mathematical Methods* highlights some of the multitude of procedures that exist for doing things like multiplying large numbers or solving equations.[2] But a pupil could learn every method in the book and still not have learnt much about mathematics. To learn about mathematics, one has to go deeper, beyond the procedures, and into the structure of its different concepts. In *Mathematics Counts*, the Committee of Inquiry into the Teaching of Mathematics in Schools (the Cockcroft Report), states: '*Conceptual structures* are richly interconnected bodies of knowledge, including the routines required for the exercise of skills. It is these which make up the substance of mathematical knowledge stored in the long term memory.'[3]

Concepts are at the heart of the study of mathematics. They are the ideas that remain constant whenever they are encountered but that combine and build upon each other to create the mathematical universe. The structure of each concept is what gives rise to the procedures and processes that are used in calculation and problem solving. In learning about the structure of each concept, a learner of mathematics can make sense of how different processes are doing what they do, using them flexibly as need demands. A simple image to capture this relationship might look like this:

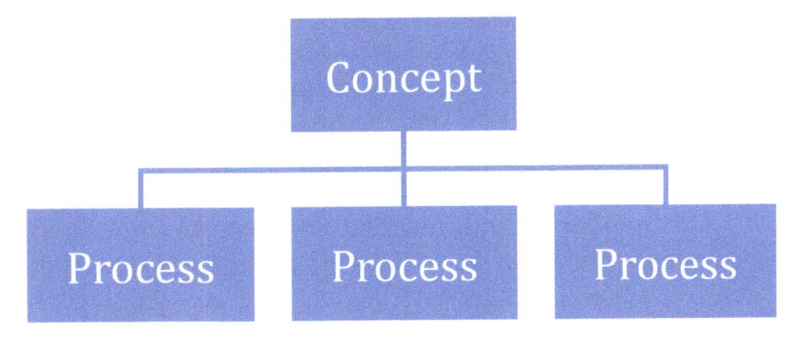

```
           Concept
          /   |   \
    Process Process Process
```

---

1. M. McCourt, A Brief History of Mathematics Education in England, *Emaths* [blog] (29 December 2017). Available at: https://www.emaths.co.uk/index.php/blog/item/a-brief-history-of-mathematics-education-in-england.
2. J. Morgan, *A Compendium of Mathematical Methods* (Woodbridge: John Catt Educational Ltd, 2019).
3. W. Cockcroft, *Mathematics Counts: Report of the Committee of Inquiry into the Teaching of Mathematics in Schools under the Chairmanship of Dr W. H. Cockcroft* [Cockcroft Report] (HMSO, 1982), p. 71. Available at: http://www.educationengland.org.uk/documents/cockcroft/cockcroft1982.html.

However, this model ignores two important aspects of mathematics: the interplay between concepts and overarching themes.

In their fantastic book *Developing Thinking in Algebra*, John Mason, Alan Graham and Sue Johnston-Wilder put forward five mathematical themes:

- Freedom and constraint.
- Doing and undoing.
- Extending and restricting.
- Invariance and change.
- Multiple interpretations.[4]

These themes appear across different mathematical concepts (the last will appear a lot throughout this book) and provide key touchpoints that learners (and teachers) can keep coming back to when they study different concepts. That complicates the model slightly:

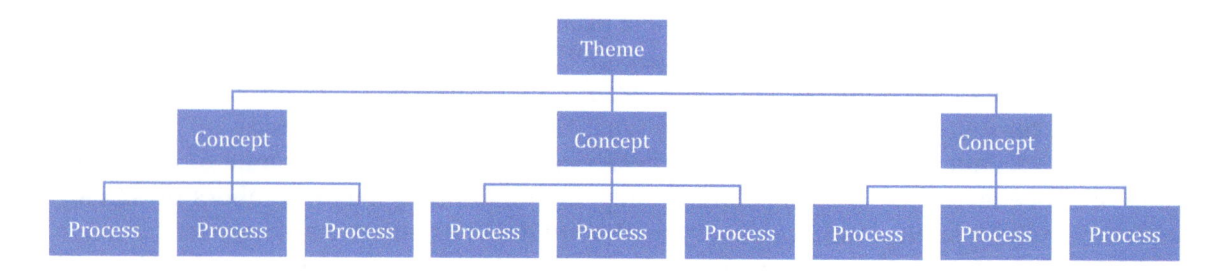

But the flowchart above still doesn't capture the interplay between concepts or how they can come together to build the mathematical universe. One might more accurately adapt the above model to look something like this:

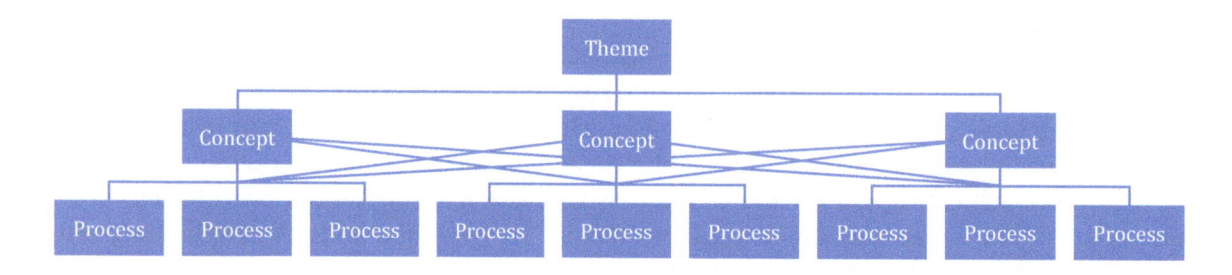

But even this is too simple; some concepts derive from others, some processes bring multiple concepts into play and several themes appear in each concept. The real model is likely to be three-dimensional or higher in order to capture all of the links between all of the themes, concepts and processes. This, of course, explains why it is so difficult to design a curriculum for mathematics even though it is essentially a hierarchical subject – concepts are introduced, then disappear for a while before reappearing in conjunction with other concepts that have been developed in the meantime. It also means that capturing this in text form is incredibly complex, with lots of back and forth between different concepts. In order to support this, each concept will include details such as:

1 Concept – what the concept being explored is.

---

4 J. Mason, A. Graham and S. Johnston-Wilder, *Developing Thinking in Algebra* (London: SAGE Publications, 2005).

2. Prerequisites for each concept – other concepts or parts of a concept that this concept requires to be secure before the given concept is introduced.

3. Linked concepts – other concepts that will come into play with the given concept when developing certain procedures or other aspects of the concept.

4. Good interpretations – good ways of thinking about/representing the given concept.

5. Good questions to ask – questions that can be asked or tasks that can be given to learners to support understanding of the structure of the concept.

6. Procedures – procedures that mainly arise from, or are associated with, the given concept and how to make their link to the concept explicit.

The first three of the above will typically be listed at the start of each section (as well as highlighted when they appear) and the rest will be explored in the main body of the section. It won't be necessary to look at all of these details for all concepts, and for some there may be other details that we will look at, but this will be the essence of what will be addressed for each concept.

In order to try and make the exploration of the mathematical concepts more manageable, we will group them into broader topic areas. These are not necessarily the sort of topic areas we might use with children (although some might be), and as explained there will be plenty of crossover from concepts in one area to concepts in another (there would be no matter how you defined the topic area); however, it will allow for a grouping of broadly similar and strongly related concepts.

We will start with an examination of the concept of number, which will include its generalisation into algebra. We will then move on to looking at the standard numerical operations in three parts: addition/subtraction, multiplication and multiples, and then division and factors. We will follow this with an examination of ideas around equivalence and equality before shifting our attention to proportionality and then functionality. From here we will begin to look at concepts in the realm of geometry, including measures, accuracy, shape and transformation. We will finish in the realms of chance, data and graphing/charting.

In my first book, *Visible Maths*, I concentrated on how the use of representations and manipulatives can provide a window into some of these mathematical structures and can support pupils in creating some of these connections by being able to draw on particular images and tools that could represent mathematical concepts whenever a pupil was working with them. Whilst there will be some crossover in this book, and readers of *Visible Maths* will find some things familiar, my aim with this book is to go broader, but not necessarily as deep, in all areas. *Visible Maths* (I hope) really got into the detail of some very specific concepts, at least in terms of the inherent mathematical structures of those ideas and how they can be manipulated. In this book, I will provide more of an overview of more concepts and include teaching ideas that are not necessarily related to the structure (such as good questions or activities that highlight aspects of the concept). My hope is that people will see *Visible Maths* as a companion to this work, so that in this book they find reference to all the concepts they will be teaching across primary and secondary schools, along with key advice/suggestions for how to ensure they teach this idea in a way that makes its structure explicit so it can be linked with other ideas. In a complementary fashion, in *Visible Maths* they can delve in depth into certain important concepts and look in detail at how good representations and manipulatives can be used to really get into a concept with pupils.

In recent years there has been, in some circles of mathematics education, a strong move back to trying to secure 'procedural fluency' prior to developing 'conceptual understanding'.

Many influential maths teachers are suggesting that learners can gain greater insight into the structure of a concept if they have first reached the point where they are very comfortable with the procedures associated with the concept. However, I am sceptical of this for two reasons:

1   Much of my experience of maths education to date has been of a very instrumental approach in which pupils are often practising procedures for much of the time in the classroom that they don't spend listening to their teacher.[5] Whilst I can see ways to improve this practice so that learners take more from the experience, I don't see it providing the gains in pupil understanding or in their motivation to continue studying mathematics education.

2   As I have intimated, the procedures attached to different concepts actually arise from the structure of the concept itself. To rely on knowledge of the procedure to provide understanding of the concepts seems to be backwards in approach. In addition, because there are many different procedures associated with each concept, it would seem to be time-intensive to have to study many of them to the point of automaticity before being able to use this experience to gain a window into the underpinning structure. Instead, first securing the structure and then exploiting the structure to gain insight into the associated procedures would seem much more logical.

This move back towards procedural fluency is generally attributed to a reaction against the perceived dominance of constructivist approaches to education[6] (which are thought to be linked with a more discovery-based approach to learning) in the late 1990s and first decade of the 21st century. Some feel that this has led to learners being held back as they haven't had their learning directed adequately by a teacher. For me, though, if this is the case, the cure is not to move to teaching procedures. Teaching structure is compatible with both constructivist and didactic approaches to education because it concerns itself with the content to be taught rather than how to go about teaching it. That is what I aim to show in this book: how exposing learners to mathematical structure can ensure they achieve both procedural fluency and conceptual understanding, whether your preferred pedagogy is to teach it explicitly or to offer learners activities to discover this structure through inquiry. Hopefully, in reading this book, teachers will become familiar with the underlying structure for the key concepts in school-level mathematics and will then be able to use this knowledge to support learners in making sense of the content they study. Whether you support learners in constructing that sense for themselves or explicitly teach good ways of making sense of concepts, ensuring learners can make sense of mathematics concepts puts them in a much better place to see the connections between the things they study.

The point about making connections is important. In the last few years, cognitive science has had increasing exposure to teachers and is influencing practice on a larger scale. One of the key ideas in cognitive science is that of a schema. A schema represents our knowledge in a particular area, and how it is connected. If we wish to learn something new in that area, we have to be able to connect it to our existing schema. By teaching about the structure of concepts, these connections become much easier to highlight because the concept is recognisable every time it reappears.[7] What I would hope is that, having read this book, teachers feel able to support learners in recognising the structure behind different mathematical concepts and help them assimilate or accommodate new knowledge of the concept into their schema.

---

5   R. R. Skemp, Relational Understanding and Instrumental Understanding, *Mathematics Teaching*, 77 (1976), 20–26. Available at: https://www.lancsngfl.ac.uk/secondary/math/download/file/PDF/Skemp%20Full%20Article.pdf.
6   Learning Theories, Constructivism (n.d.). Available at: https://www.learning-theories.com/constructivism.html.
7   Learning Theories, Schema Theory (n.d.). Available at: https://www.learning-theories.org/doku.php?id=learning_theories:schema_theory.

Chapter 1
Number

There are many different 'types' of numbers. A common way to view these is as sets, with each set becoming a subset of a further set. Mostly this starts with the natural numbers, which are the whole numbers greater than 0 (also called the positive integers).

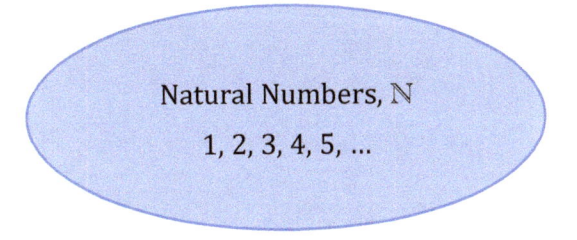

Natural Numbers, $\mathbb{N}$

1, 2, 3, 4, 5, ...

We then extend these to include 0 and the negative integers, creating the set of all integers.

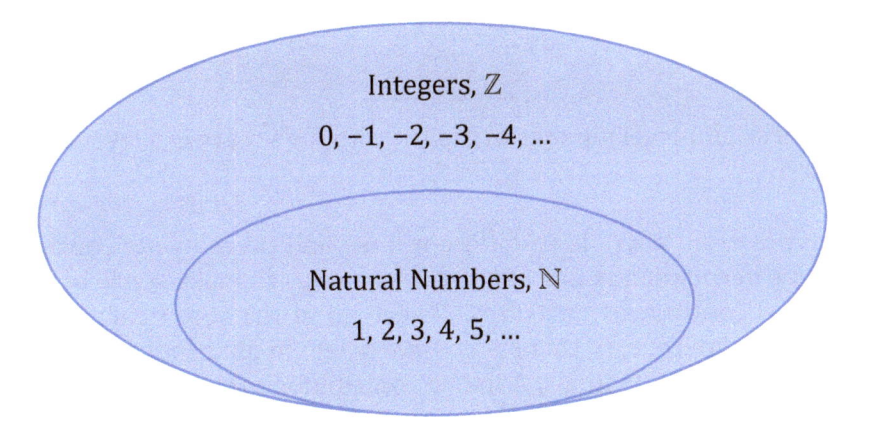

Integers, $\mathbb{Z}$

0, −1, −2, −3, −4, ...

Natural Numbers, $\mathbb{N}$

1, 2, 3, 4, 5, ...

After this we include fractions and decimals, creating a set collectively known as the quotients or rational numbers.

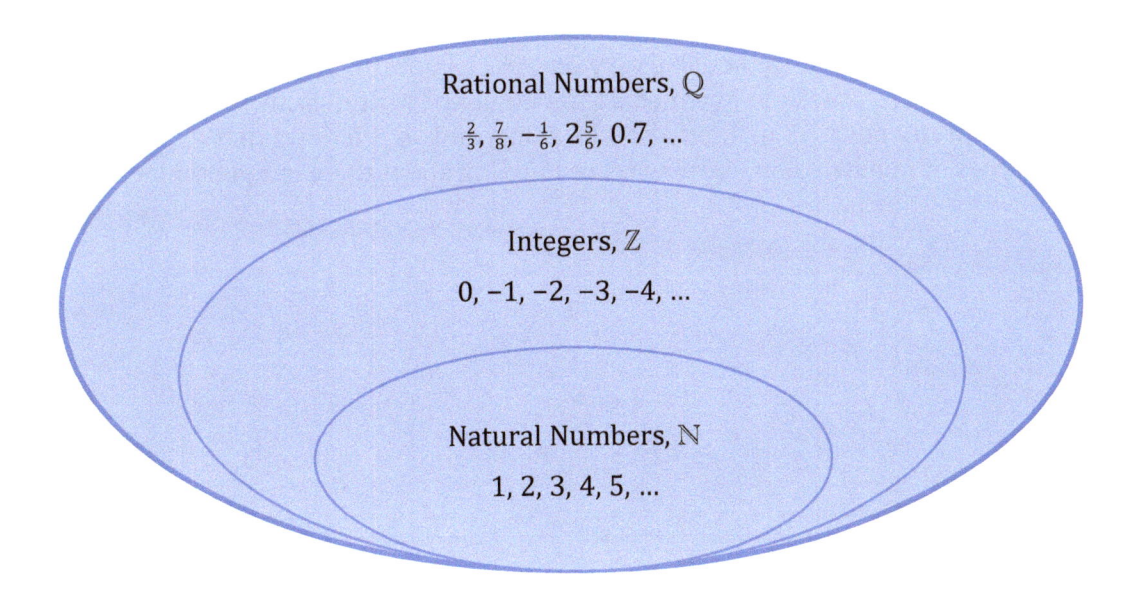

Rational Numbers, $\mathbb{Q}$

$\frac{2}{3}, \frac{7}{8}, -\frac{1}{6}, 2\frac{5}{6}, 0.7, ...$

Integers, $\mathbb{Z}$

0, −1, −2, −3, −4, ...

Natural Numbers, $\mathbb{N}$

1, 2, 3, 4, 5, ...

The next layer includes the irrational numbers, which creates the set of all real numbers.

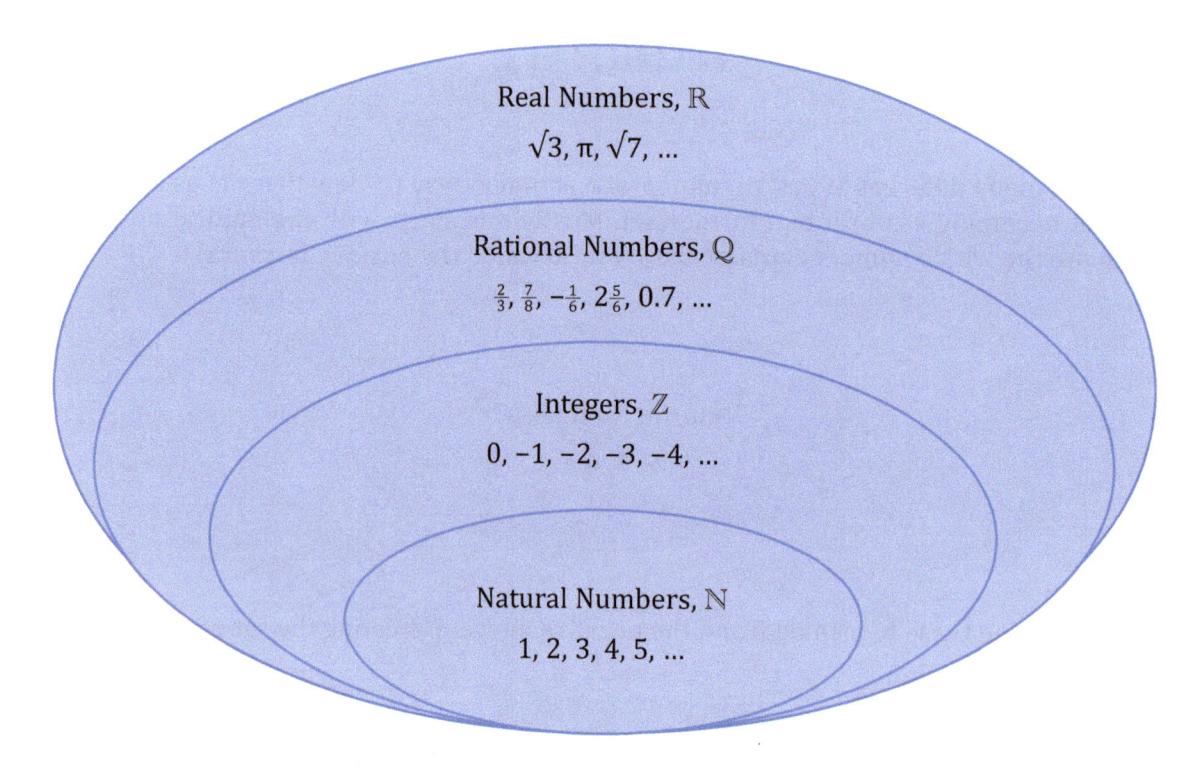

```
Real Numbers, ℝ
√3, π, √7, ...

    Rational Numbers, ℚ
    ⅔, ⅞, -⅙, 2⅚, 0.7, ...

        Integers, ℤ
        0, -1, -2, -3, -4, ...

            Natural Numbers, ℕ
            1, 2, 3, 4, 5, ...
```

This is the limit of school-level number in the UK, although there is a level beyond this that is explored post-16.

Each of these types of numbers have different links and prerequisite concepts; however, what they all have in common is that there are two ways to make sense of them – as **discrete** objects or as **continuous** measures.[1] These go to the very heart of what makes a number. In the early 20th century, there was a movement in philosophy that sought to place mathematics on firm logical footings. A major contributor to this movement was the eminent philosopher Bertrand Russell. In his work *Principia Mathematica* with Alfred North Whitehead, he defined what it means to be a number in terms of all sets of objects that exhibit the same property as that number.[2] So, the number 'four' is defined as all the sets that have four objects, such as the number of prime numbers less than 10 or the number of legs a cat is usually born with, and all of these are associated with the numeral '4'. This was an attempt to put the concept of 'number' on a firm logical footing. Whilst probably overkill for most school-level pupils (although a very interesting question to pose to pupils is 'What is 3?'), it nonetheless speaks to how people *see* numbers. Making sense of numbers is the precursor to pretty much all mathematical learning, and so it follows that exploring these different types of numbers and useful ways of thinking about them is a good place to start.

---

[1] You will notice whilst reading the book that some key mathematical terms are presented in **bold** – for your convenience these terms are defined in a glossary at the back of the book.
[2] See https://www.britannica.com/topic/history-of-logic/Logic-since-1900#ref535751.

Concept: natural number

Prerequisites: None (although some research suggests that informal ideas around spatial reasoning can drastically improve development of early number sense[3]).

Linked concepts: Addition and multiplication are linked directly to the development of the natural numbers, and division will also be important for the development of place value. Virtually all other concepts have natural numbers as a prerequisite.

Children often learn to count prior to starting formal education. Learning to repeat the sequence 'one, two, three' and so on up to 'ten', however, does not imply that a learner has an appreciation of number. What this shows is an appreciation of **order**. The learner that knows that 'three' follows 'two' does not necessarily know that 'three' represents a larger quantity than 'two' or that 'three' is 'one more' than 'two'. What is essential in learning about number is to relate the words 'one', 'two', 'three' with the numerals '1', '2', '3' – and to the actual values that these words/numerals represent.

This process typically starts in early years, with the use of concrete objects. However, as suggested in *Key Understandings in Mathematics Learning. Paper 2: Understanding Whole Numbers*, the relating of number and quantity can take 'three to four years'.[4] This highlights the importance of continuing the use of concrete representations throughout Key Stage 1 and the importance of using them to continue to develop and reinforce learners' knowledge or the links between numerals and quantities. These concrete objects will generally start out as truly representative of the context a learner is working on. For example, if talking about 'How many toys?', the concrete objects will be actual toys. From here, learners will need to make two transitions:

1. The partial abstraction of using standard concrete objects to represent quantities in a one-to-one relationship.
2. The further abstraction of using standard concrete objects to represent quantities in a one-to-many relationship.

Of course, each learner will be ready for these transitions in their own time, and care must be taken not to rush learners through these transitions.

There are many different choices for the 'standard' concrete object to represent quantities in a one-to-one relationship. These can be counters, counting sticks, beads on a rekenrek, cubes; the list is substantial. This object (or objects, as it is a good idea to introduce more than one at different points) becomes the standard to represent a quantity in every situation. If the learner is working on a problem involving toys, one object becomes one toy. If they are working on a problem involving sweets, then one object is one sweet. In this way, the objects *become* the quantity; they represent the quantity in all situations. This is the first step to working with numbers in the abstract, to manipulate them, compare them and operate with them.

The obvious difficulty then arises when pupils start to work with larger and larger values. It is fine to represent 3 as three counters, but to represent 33 in this way is woefully inefficient. Worse, it doesn't actually help in making sense of 33 as a concept – there are simply

---

[3] H. J. Williams, Mathematics in the Early Years: What Matters?, *Impact* (12 September 2018). Available at: https://impact.chartered.college/article/mathematics-in-early-years/.
[4] T. Nunes and P. Bryant, *Key Understandings in Mathematics Learning. Paper 2: Understanding Whole Numbers* (London: Nuffield Foundation, 2009), p. 4.

too many counters for it to be worth it. What is much better for numbers this large is to start to move towards the one-to-many relationship by grouping counters, blocks and so on into groups, usually of 10, to support the beginnings of place value. For example, if using counters these can be arranged in a 10s frame:

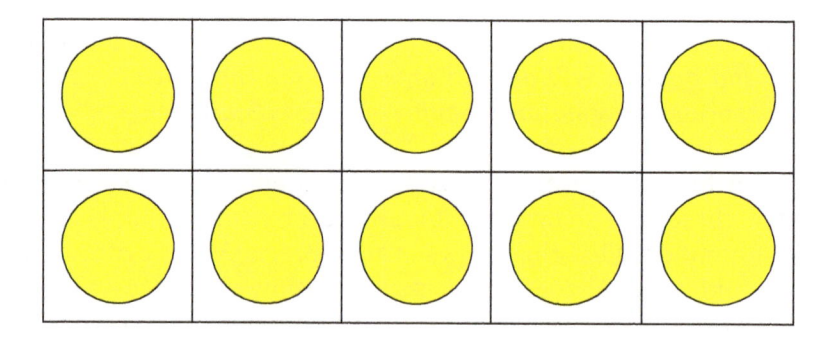

The frame can then act as a unit of counting, so that something like the number 33 can be seen as three of these, plus three further counters – for example:

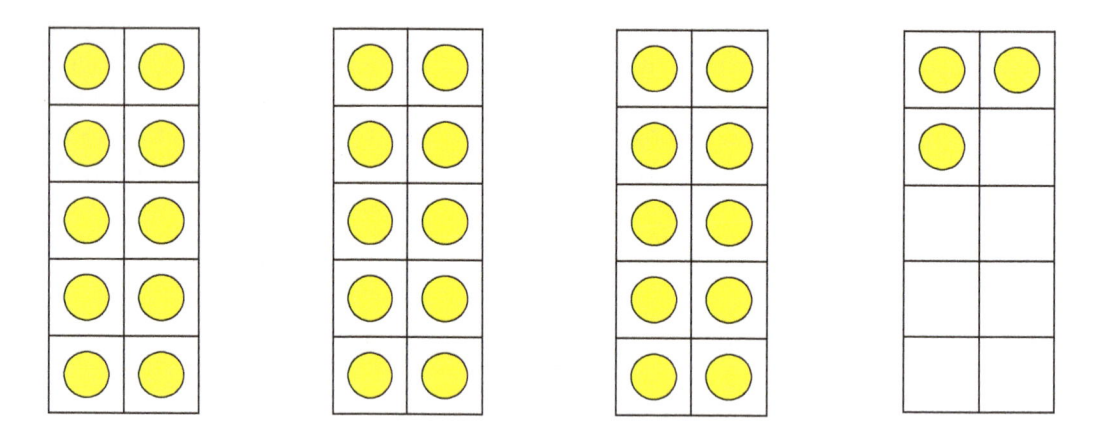

These can help make sense of numbers like 33 as 'three 10s plus three 1s' whilst simultaneously allowing the continued sense of the relationship between a 10 and a 1. Eventually, once pupils are secure on the relationship between a 10 and a 1 and no longer need it to be explicitly present, the whole system can be changed so that a 10 is a single object, which is what happens with place value counters:

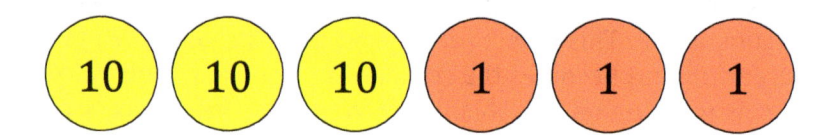

Here, the relationship between a 1 and a 10 is not visible, so this relies on pupils already being secure that a 10 is worth the same as ten 1s, but provided this is clear then this sort of representation can be a real gateway into arithmetic with larger integers.

All of these viewpoints are thinking about numbers as discrete objects. There is also the alternative interpretation of the concept of 'number', namely as continuous quantities. For this, useful manipulatives are Cuisenaire and Dienes. With these representations, 1 can be seen simultaneously as the number of objects but also as the length of the objects. So, three blocks represents 3 both by the number of blocks but also by the length of what is created when these blocks are lined up. Other rods with the same length can then be created to represent that number. For example, in the picture below the green rod represents 3 as it is the same length as a line of three connected 1s.

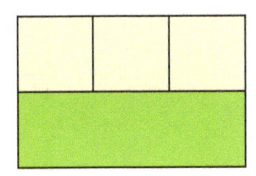

Both Cuisenaire and Dienes then have a rod that is as long as 10 of its unit cubes, allowing the same bridge into place value:

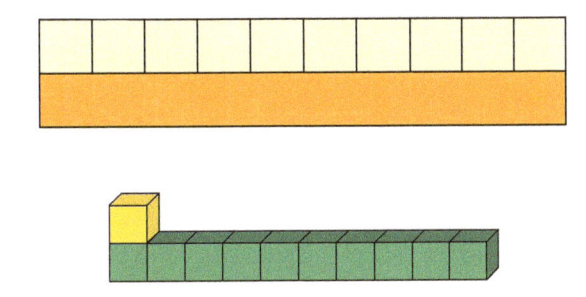

so that larger numbers can be represented continuously as either length:

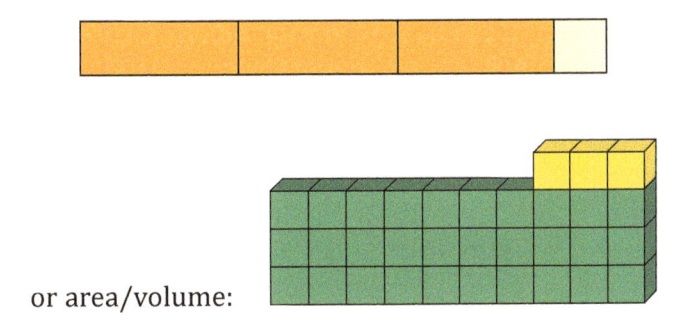

or area/volume:

This area view has very strong links to multiplication and is also what allows the representation of more than two powers of 10 using Dienes blocks, as there are also blocks that can be used to represent ten 10s (100):

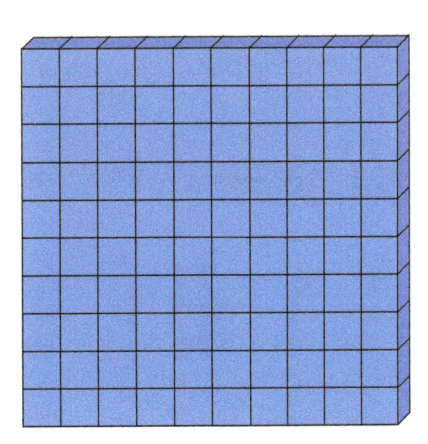

and then, by generalising further into three dimensions, uses volume to represent ten 100s (1000):

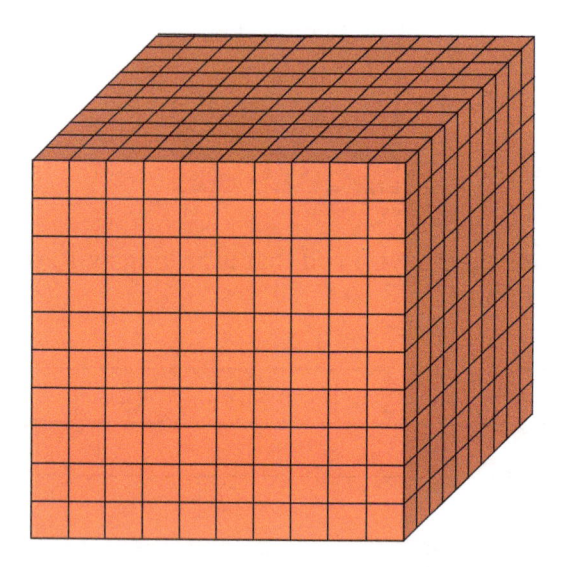

To make this bridge, questions can be asked such as, 'Why is this 3?' (in reference to three blocks) and then, when pupils refer to the number of blocks, showing them that an alternative view is to consider them connected together to create a length. Pupils can then be asked to 'find' different values in the rods. Sentences such as, 'If the length of the white rod is worth one (an important part as the length of the white rod will be changed later), show me the rod whose length is worth …' can be a good way to both secure understanding of number as continuous quantity and also to support gaining familiarity with the concrete resources. This can then later become, 'If the length of the white rod is worth one, show me …' which can allow pupils to use area and volume to show larger values as place value is introduced. Obviously, place value is an important subconcept of number that pupils must secure if they are going to deal with larger numbers. It will be important to make sure pupils recognise the relationship between different place values and multiplication/division by 10.

Subconcept: place value

Prerequisites: Natural numbers.

Linked concepts: Multiplication, division, fractions, decimals, negatives, surds, algebra, indices, equality/equivalence.

Understanding place value rests in recognising the truth in the following question:

What is ρ?

Now, if you put that in front of many English people, they might think you have written a funny-shaped letter 'p'. However, in Greece it would be recognised as the letter 'ro'. If you showed it to a scientist, they might see it as the symbol they use for density (depending on the branch of science). A statistician might think you meant a Spearman's rank correlation coefficient.

The point is that ρ is a symbol and nothing more. The meaning it conveys depends entirely on what we have learnt to associate with it. The same is true of the symbols we use to represent numbers – in our base 10 number system the symbols 0, 1, 2, 3, 4, 5, 6, 7, 8, 9 (usually called digits). These digits can be combined to create **numerals**; 234 is a numeral in that it represents a number in a symbolic form. We are perhaps not used to thinking of things like 234 as numerals, but the idea is no different to writing CCXXXIV – both are numerals designed to represent the same number. The number itself is something abstract – we can represent it symbolically or using different models, but its true existence is in the realms of pure thought. We have already seen that we can choose *how* we think about numbers – they can be thought of as discrete objects, continuous measures or perhaps in other ways not yet thought of (at least by this author!).

The idea of a place value system then, is that it means we can build numerals to represent larger numbers out of relatively few digit symbols. How many digit symbols depends on the **base** of the place value system – we are probably most used to using a denary (base 10) number system, but there are lots of examples of other bases both historical and modern. Computer base language is binary, which is a base 2 number system using only the digits 0 and 1. Colour codings in computers use a hexadecimal number system, which uses the digits 0, 1, 2, 3, 4, 5, 6, 7, 8, 9, A, B, C, D, E, F. In ancient Mesopotamia they used a base 60 (sexagesimal) number system that had a sub-base of 10. What this means is there was a new symbol for 10, and 11 was shown as '10 and 1', 21 was shown as 'two 10s and 1' and so on up to 59 being shown as 'five 10s and nine 1s', and then 60 uses the same symbol as 1, but in the next place:

Source: https://en.wikipedia.org/wiki/Sexagesimal. CC BY-SA 4.0

Now, of course, we may not want to go into this level of detail with young or novice learners when it comes to place value. The important thing for learners to understand is that when writing numbers symbolically, the place that the digit occupies within the numeral is designed to convey the meaning about the size of the number that the digit represents. We can support early understanding of this by using concrete or visual representations alongside the symbolic. Dienes blocks are designed specifically for representing numbers in base 10:

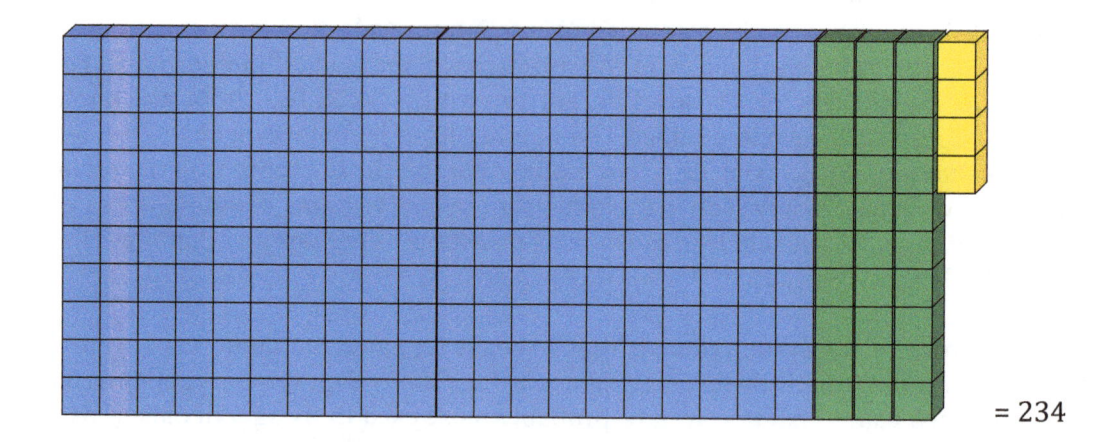

= 234

We can draw further attention to the place value by using a Gattegno chart or place value chart alongside the concrete/visual:

Gattegno chart

100	200	300	400	500	600	700	800	900
10	20	30	40	50	60	70	80	90
1	2	3	4	5	6	7	8	9

Place value chart

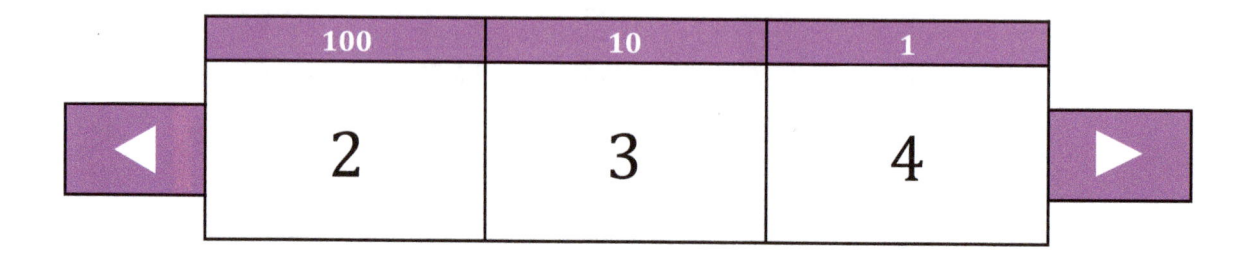

100	10	1
2	3	4

A nice physical version of the place value chart is to use place value cards alongside (and eventually to replace) the Dienes:

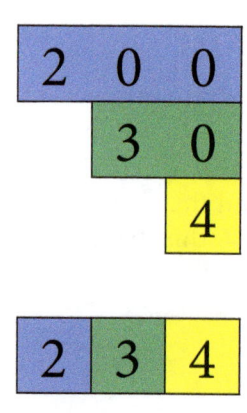

2 0 0
3 0
4

2 3 4

Pupils can be shown numerals on the cards or in the charts and asked to create the number out of Dienes; or they can be asked to do the reverse, given the number in Dienes and asked to build the numeral to represent it. One thing that is important as part of this is to introduce pupils to the use of 0 as a place holder, so using numerals such as 3074 and recognising that there are no hundred squares in that number, but that we can't just write '3 74' as we are likely to misread this as '374'. As pupils progress, questions such as, 'Write down the value of the 5 in the numeral 3578', ordering numbers or converting between numbers written in words and in numerals can reinforce place value fluency, as well as questions such as:

You have cards with the digits 1, 3, 7 and 8 written on them. How would you arrange the cards to create:

1   the largest four-digit number possible?

2   the smallest four-digit number possible?

3   the largest three-digit number possible?

4   the smallest three-digit number possible?

It is really nice with younger learners (and sometimes older ones) to actually give them the cards and ask them to do this physically rather than as a purely written exercise. There is a good opportunity for linking properties of numbers with an activity like this, such as writing the largest even number possible or writing the largest three-digit multiple of 3. The activity 'Four-Digit Targets' from NRICH is a nice stretch to this idea.[5]

As we move to larger numbers, an important aspect of the base 10 number system to draw learners' attention to is the unitary nature of each third column (when reading from right to left). As we read and write larger numbers, we group them into blocks of three places (normally either using a comma or space). This is not just for convenience or ease of reading; this is because each block of three obeys the same unit structure but with a different counting unit.

1000000000	100000000	1000000	100000	10000	1000	100	10	1

We can see here that the right-hand block of three counts 1s, including how many sets of ten 1s and how many sets of one hundred 1s make up the number. However, when we move into the next block of three, our unit changes to thousands and we count how many one thousands, ten thousands and hundred thousands we have. Following this we move onto a unit of millions and we count how many one millions, 10 millions and 100 millions we have. This pattern keeps going as we move up the columns. Alongside this recognition, we will need to introduce learners to the links with multiplication and division. There are two that are really important. The first is that as we move left, the value of the place multiplies by 10, and similarly as we move right, the value of place is divided by 10. It is worth testing, pupils on this aspect of place value specifically; asking questions like, 'If I start in the 100s column and move three columns to the left, what have I multiplied by?' alongside the more usual 'Multiply 23 by 1000'.

---

5   See https://nrich.maths.org/6342/note.

The second important link with multiplication is the building of the number itself. For example, seeing a number like 374 as 3 × 100 + 7 × 10 + 4 × 1. This links to multiplication as unitising – in effect, each column becomes a unit in its own right and the digits tell us how many of each unit. So, 374 can be seen as 3 'hundreds' + 7 'tens' + 4 'ones', and this leads to 3 × 100 + 7 × 10 + 4 × 1. Again, testing pupils on this specifically by asking pupils to write numbers as the sum of multiplications, or filling in blanks such as 5678 = ___ × 1000 + 6 × ____ + ____ × 10 + ____ × ____ is useful.

From here pupils can move on to develop increasing flexibility with the idea of place value by recognising that whilst place helps determine value, it is more about the interplay of value and place. For example, 'one thousand two hundred' is equivalent to 'twelve hundred' – the value '12' and place 'hundred' work together to create a number equivalent to having one thousand two hundreds. It is worth doing this with numbers that are not often read in this way – for example, providing pupils with opportunities to recognise that 'thirty 10s' is another way of saying 300, or 'two thousand four hundred hundreds' is equivalent to 240,000. Questions such as, 'How many ways can you say/write …?', 'What number is equivalent to …?' and so on are good ways to prompt thinking that supports flexibility in place value.

This flexibility is of real help when we eventually come to look at writing numbers in standard form.

Subconcept: standard (index) form

Prerequisites: Natural numbers, multiplication, indices.

Linked concepts: Decimals (which may well be considered prerequisite), fractions, surds, algebra, equality/equivalence, accuracy, measures.

Ultimately, the key to 'unlocking' understanding in standard form is that it is primarily about redefining your counting unit. I tend to start by looking at other units of measurement – when distances (for example) get very big or very small, we tend to change the unit we use to measure with. With very large (or very small) numbers, it doesn't really make sense for '1' to be the main counting unit – it takes an awful lot of ones to make a number like 6,000,000. We can reinforce this point with learners using money: 'Can you imagine how much space 6,000,000 in pound coins would take up?', 'Instead of using £1 coins, wouldn't it be better to use £10 notes? Or even better to use £100 notes?', 'What if there was such a thing as a £1,000 note? Or what if there was such a thing as a £1,000,000 note?'

If we had million-pound notes, we would only need six of them, which makes much more sense (at least in terms of storing the money – I wouldn't want to take it shopping and ask a shop to provide change for it!). What this is showing is the power (no pun intended) of making our counting unit as large as possible, which is what is happening when we write numbers in standard form. So the idea of standard form can be seen as one in which we redefine our counting unit to be that of the largest place digit in the numeral (i.e. the first significant figure). In the number 6,000,000, we are redefining our counting unit to be the 'millions' place and so counting how many millions we have.

Once pupils understand this, it is then about them recognising the place value columns as different powers of 10. Introducing this depends largely on the understanding that pupils already have around indices – if they are already very comfortable with the idea that anything to the power 0 = 1, then we can introduce them to using powers of 10 for place value columns from the 1s column, with $1 = 10^0$, and then $10 = 10^1$, $100 = 10^2$ and so on. If pupils are not yet familiar with an index of 0, then instead we can start with $100 = 10^2$ and build up to $1000 = 10^3$ as well as down to $10 = 10^1$ and $1 = 10^0$. Putting this together gives the process for writing a number in standard form:

Process: converting a denary number into standard form

1 Identify the largest place column to have value (i.e. the first significant figure).

2 Treat that column as the new counting unit, with parts of this unit separated from whole units by a decimal point.

3 Write the unit as a multiplication using the power of 10 that is equivalent to the column place of the unit.

So, something like 6,000,000 would be thought of as '6 million' and then written as 6×10^6. Similarly, something like 320,000 would be thought of as '3.2 hundred thousands' and then written as 3.2×10^5. Very small numbers work in the same way (provided pupils have been introduced to decimals and negative indices), with the number 0.0000435 being thought of as '4.35 hundred thousandths' and then written as 4.35×10^{-5}. This leads to the conclusion that the 'lead number' will always be in the range 1–10 (including 1 but not including 10), as there will only ever be one whole number unit column.

The reverse process can then either be treated as a pure calculation (i.e. treat 6×10^6 as $6 \times 1,000,000$) or by working the steps above backwards.

Process: converting a number from standard form into denary

1 Write the whole part of the lead number in the place indicated by the power of 10, with subsequent digits of the lead number in the following columns.

2 Use place-holding zeroes to return the counting unit to the 1s column.

So, in a number like 4.5×10^7 we might start by identifying that the lead number will need to be in the 10 millions column:

100000000	1000000	100000	10000	1000	100	10	1

and then write the digits of the lead number in the correct columns:

100000000	1000000	100000	10000	1000	100	10	1
4	5						

before filling in the remaining place-holding zeroes.

100000000	1000000	100000	10000	1000	100	10	1
4	5	0	0	0	0	0	0

Similarly, in a number like 4.5×10^{-7} we would have:

1	.	$\frac{1}{10}$	$\frac{1}{100}$	$\frac{1}{1000}$	$\frac{1}{10000}$	$\frac{1}{100000}$	$\frac{1}{1000000}$	$\frac{1}{10000000}$	$\frac{1}{100000000}$
	.								

1	.	$\frac{1}{10}$	$\frac{1}{100}$	$\frac{1}{1000}$	$\frac{1}{10000}$	$\frac{1}{100000}$	$\frac{1}{1000000}$	$\frac{1}{10000000}$	$\frac{1}{100000000}$
	.							4	5

1	.	$\frac{1}{10}$	$\frac{1}{100}$	$\frac{1}{1000}$	$\frac{1}{10000}$	$\frac{1}{100000}$	$\frac{1}{1000000}$	$\frac{1}{10000000}$	$\frac{1}{100000000}$
0	.	0	0	0	0	0	0	4	5

Standard form often comes quite late in a pupil's learning around number because it combines many ideas in number and operation.

Returning to numbers in general, then: length, area and volume are not the only ways that we can see numbers as continuous quantities. Weight is also a possibility. If you have access to a balance scale then, for a good set of rods, the weights of rods with equal values should also balance. So, for example, a rod that is worth 7 should perfectly balance against seven rods that are worth 1. This can be a really nice way to show pupils this aspect of number, although, of course, it is worth checking before you show pupils that the things you think should balance really do!

The discrete/continuous duality of number can then, once a pupil is ready, be captured perfectly on a number line. Consequently, number lines are best introduced once pupils have met numbers in both discrete and continuous form.

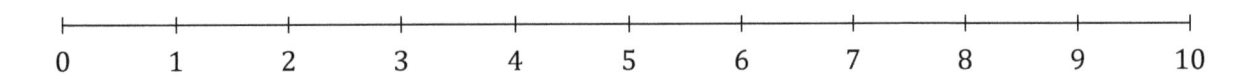

```
├───┼───┼───┼───┼───┼───┼───┼───┼───┼───┤
0   1   2   3   4   5   6   7   8   9   10
```

On the number line above, the natural numbers can be seen as occupying discrete, equally spaced positions along the line. It is worth noting at this point that it is only by convention that number lines increase from left to right, and that in some circumstances we may want to change this. In my opinion, when introducing number lines, it is worth introducing some lines that increase from right to left:

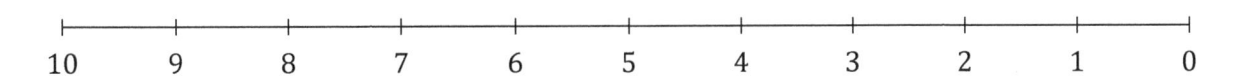

```
├───┼───┼───┼───┼───┼───┼───┼───┼───┼───┤
10  9   8   7   6   5   4   3   2   1   0
```

And also that are orientated vertically, with increases shown both up and down:

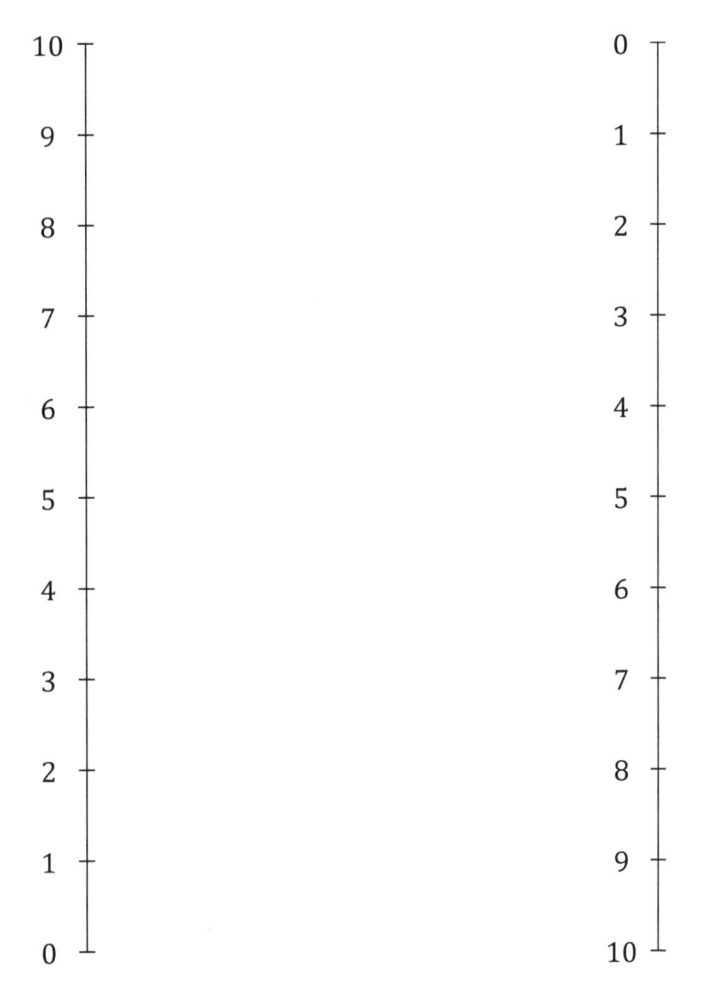

Teachers can then pose problems such as leaving blank spaces and asking for them to be filled in, asking pupils to extend a number line beyond that which is given, and also look at broken number lines once larger numbers are being included, such as 'starting' a number line at 110 and asking pupils to continue from that point. Number lines being graduated in spaces other than 1 are also important, particularly to make the link with place value and separately the idea of 'counting in' a particular jump, such as where the 10s frames/place value counters allowed the counting in 10s:

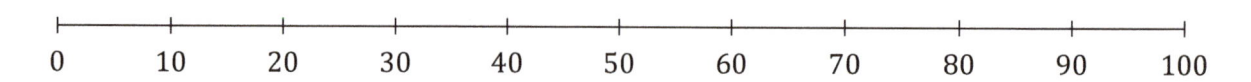

Of course, if this is the number line using discrete positions to represent numbers, the question arises as to where the continuous element is. Part of this can be seen by the lines connecting the values; there is a smooth line from one number to the next. However, to really bring the continuous facet of number to the fore, it is better to bring in an extra representation alongside the number line. We can start by using the same rods we used before to show numbers as continuous:

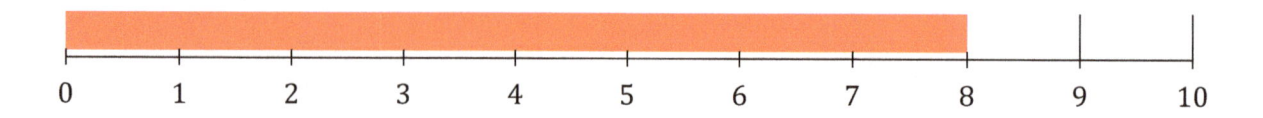

NB. Number lines drawn on centimetre-squared paper so that each value is 1 cm away from the next value will allow rods to take values equivalent to the length of the white rod being 1.

This still requires the use of the concrete manipulative and so, if we are moving from these to a visual representation, then a replacement is required for the rod. The best replacement for this is a one-dimensional **vector**:

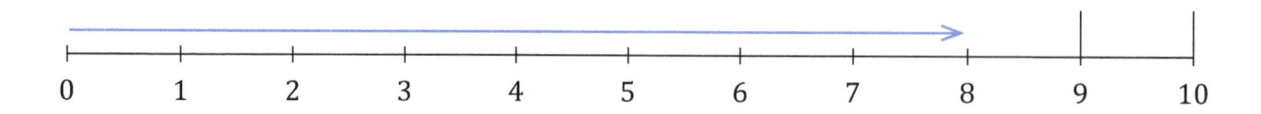

The vector representation of numbers is a great way to transition from using objects where the length represents the quantity, to a purely visual way of representing the quantity. What we are aiming for here is for pupils to see that the dual discrete/continuous nature of number can be seen by simultaneously seeing the number line as both *a representation of the numbers*, and *the scale on which we show the continuous nature of the numbers*. In this way, pupils can see the number '5' both as a discrete point on the number line, and as a vector that is as long as the distance from 0 to 5. Once a pupil understands vectors on the number line, they are in a very powerful position for understanding pretty much all of number and arithmetic. Questions such as 'Draw me the number 5 on the number line' are pretty standard starting points, and then deeper thinking can be prompted by asking pupils things like what number the vector below represents:

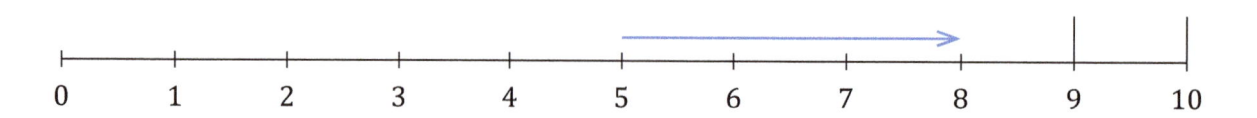

(3, in case you were unsure!) or even to mark the numerals on the number line so that the vector has a value of 2:

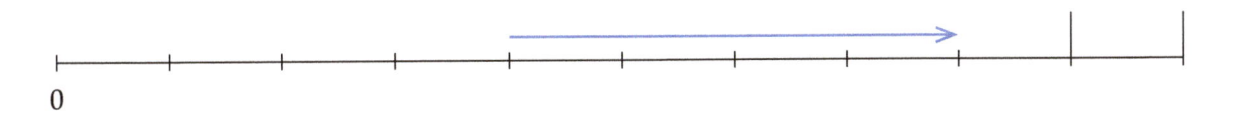

0

This sort of activity also has strong links with measurement, as we will see in Chapter 8.

The importance of developing this view of numbers as continuous cannot be overstated, as it is the natural bridge for when pupils are ready to make the journey from looking at natural numbers to exploring the other sets of numbers outlined at the beginning of this chapter. Although when looking at numbers as subsets of larger sets, we typically follow the natural numbers with the rest of the integers, a more 'natural' extension to the concept of number beyond the naturals comes in the form of fractions. Indeed, certainly in the history of Western mathematics, fractions have been around for a lot longer than 0 or the negative integers.[6]

Concept: fractions

Prerequisites: Natural numbers, division.

Linked concepts: Most concepts that link to natural numbers extend those links to fractions, including all arithmetic operations (particularly multiples and multiplication, as well as factors and division). The concept of equivalence will be used with fractions. Very strong links exist with proportionality, measures, accuracy (typically in the form of decimals), shape (particularly in similarity and trigonometry) and chance.

Once pupils are familiar with continuous representations of numbers, there arises an obvious question: 'What is between … and …?' As a simple start point, this could be having looked at a number line and asking the question, 'What is between 0 and 1?' This opens up the world of proper fractions.

There are a couple of good ways into proper fractions from the continuous view of natural numbers, either using the number line or using length of rods. From a number line perspective, a simple start point might be to look at what number is at this position on the number line:

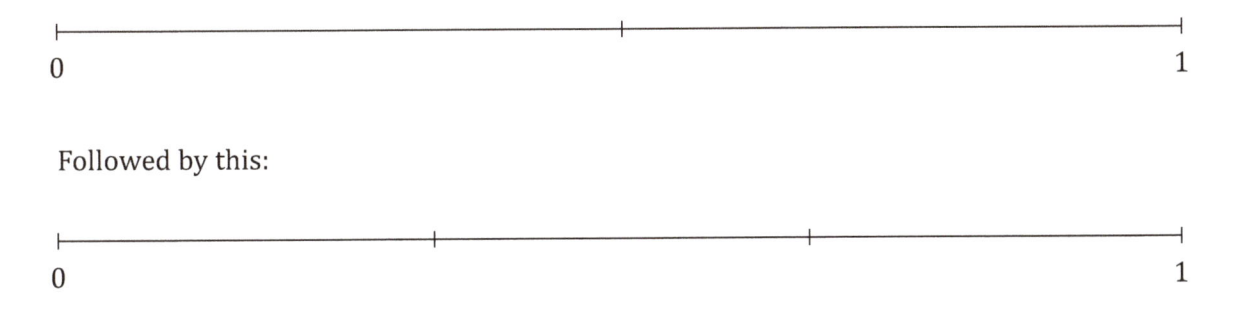

0   1

Followed by this:

0   1

---

6   Story of Mathematics, List of Important Mathematicians (n.d.). Available at: https://www.storyofmathematics.com/mathematicians.html.

And then this:

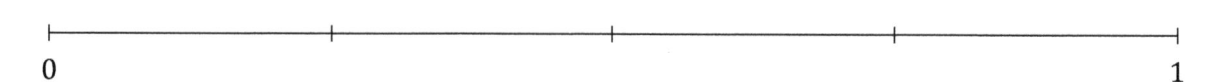

```
├─────────────┼─────────────┼─────────────┼─────────────┤
0                                                       1
```

And so on. This sort of prompt can be used to show that proper fractions exist and can motivate the view of proper fractions as lengths that are a part of 1. The fraction $\frac{1}{2}$ can then be introduced as the fraction that arises from chopping a length of 1 into 2 equal pieces, so that the length of $\frac{1}{2}$ is half of the length of one whole. Similarly, $\frac{1}{3}$ comes from chopping a length of 1 into 3 equal pieces (with $\frac{2}{3}$ being a length equivalent to 2 of those 3 equal pieces) and similarly for quarters and beyond. The roots of equivalent fractions can also be seen here; $\frac{2}{4}$ is the same length as $\frac{1}{2}$. Pupils should draw these number lines on squared paper and should be made to draw them accurately:

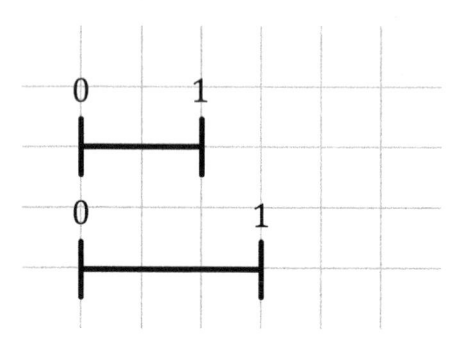

What is important here is to start to ensure that pupils become familiar with the idea of **fraction families**, and the relationship that each family has with the 'length' of one whole. On the first of the two number lines above, I can mark the fraction $\frac{1}{2}$ which is the only proper fraction in the family 'halves'. On the second number line above, I can mark the fractions $\frac{1}{3}$ and $\frac{2}{3}$ which are the only proper fractions in the fraction family 'thirds'. Once pupils become familiar with this idea, we can ask questions like, 'How many squares long would you draw a unit if you wanted to show the family of 'fifths'?' and 'What fraction family would be represented on the number line below?'

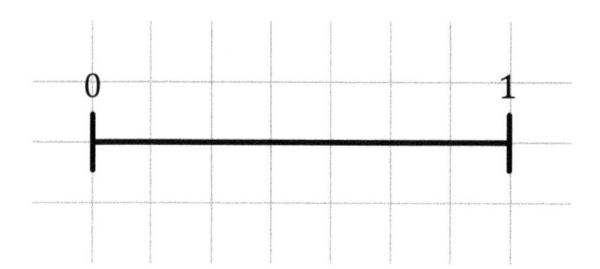

The relationship between equivalence and fractions can then be broached by asking about the *families* that can be shown on this number line:

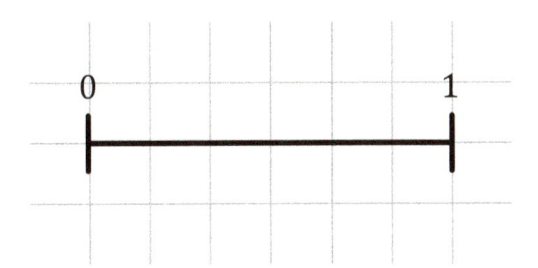

The goal here is for pupils to recognise that as well as showing sixths, this number line can be chopped into two equal pieces (and thus used to show the family of halves) and also into three equal pieces (and thus show the family of thirds). This leads to seeing that every fraction in the families of 'halves' and 'thirds' has an equivalent fraction in the family of 'sixths'. Some of these fractions can be looked at, but the main work here should be in pupils seeing the relationship between the families that have equivalent fractions. Ask pupils things like, 'Which families will have every fraction equivalent to a fraction in the tenths family? The twelfths family?' and get them to draw number lines where necessary to support their work. We can also ask which equivalent fractions are shown here, for example:

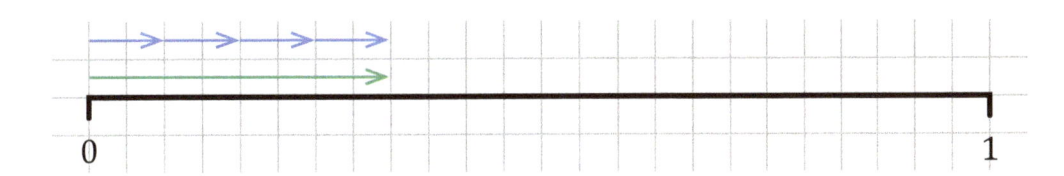

Or even more challenging questions, like where $\frac{1}{4}$ would appear on this number line:

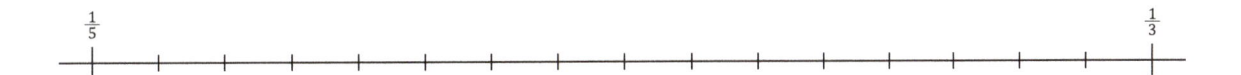

An alternative introduction to fractions takes us back to the rods. Earlier, I highlighted the importance of starting the sentence with, 'If the white rod has a length of 1 …' At this point we can instead start asking questions like, 'What if the red rod had a length of 1?', 'What if the green rod had a length of 1?', etc.

This serves equally well as an introduction into the idea of proper fractions and of fraction families, particularly if pupils have achieved an intimate familiarity of the base values of the rods (i.e. the values of the other rods when the white rod is worth 1). We can ask similar questions to those we used for number lines, such as, 'Which family can be shown if the black rod is worth 1?', 'Which rod would you use to show the family of ninths?', etc.

This way of seeing fractions also leads quite naturally to the introduction of decimals. By setting the orange rod to have a value of 1, or by drawing a number line with 10 hatch marks between 0 and 1, the links can be made between the fraction family tenths and the first place value column after the decimal point (i.e. the tenths column). Dienes can again be used then to explore further place value columns by setting either the square area to have a value of 1 or even the cube to have a value of 1:

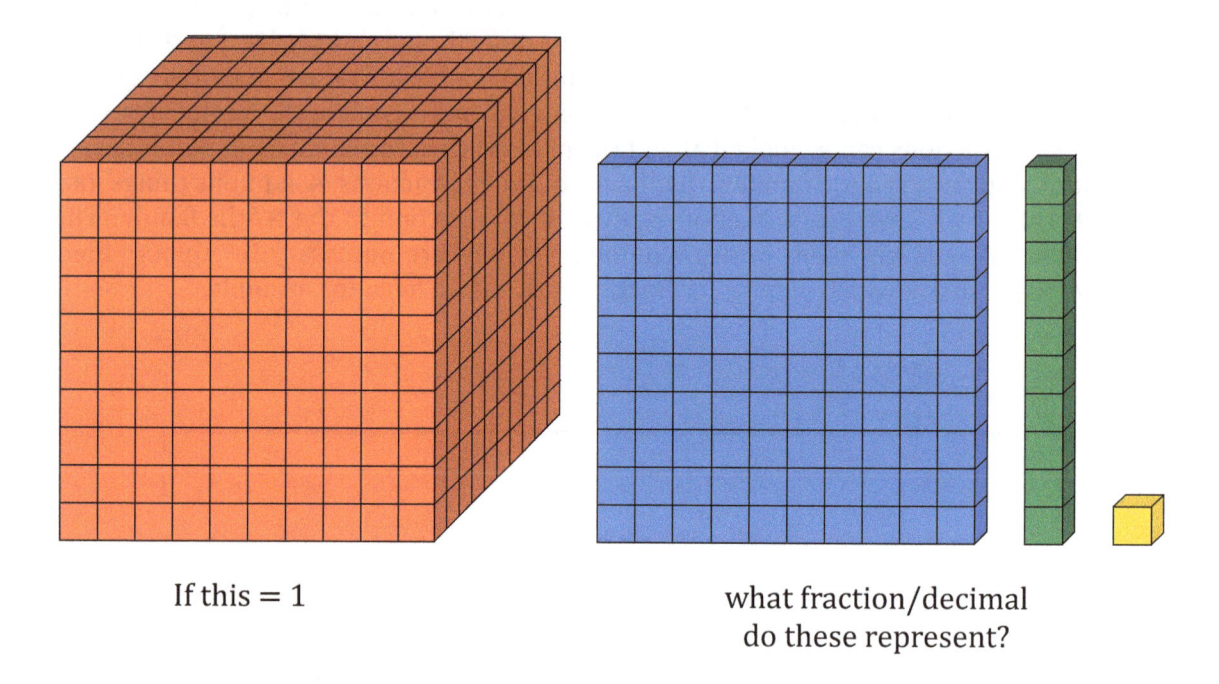

If this = 1   what fraction/decimal do these represent?

Subconcept: decimals

Prerequisites: Natural numbers, division, place value.

Linked concepts: Fractions, standard form, equality/equivalence, accuracy, measures, chance.

Some teachers like to introduce decimals prior to fractions; generally they do this using patterns in place value. If pupils are confident in the idea that places go down by a factor of 10 as the number goes from left to right, then this pattern can be continued beyond the '1s column' to create 'parts of 1'. Typically, we would explain to pupils that the first of these is 1 split into 10 parts, and is therefore called 'tenths' and represented by the numeral 0.1. This is an opportune moment to make sure pupils understand the role of the decimal point: i.e. the decimal point marks the transition between whole values of the unit and part values of the unit (this is important for standard form). From here we can move to splitting a tenth into 10 pieces (or splitting 1 into 100 pieces) to generate 0.01 and so on.

Others prefer to introduce the idea of having part of 1 first (i.e. fractions) and then introduce decimals as equivalent to those fraction families of 10ths, 100ths, etc. However, the extension to the place value columns to include the decimal columns (i.e. the introduction of 0.1, 0.01 in much the same way, and link between the two) will need to be made explicit at some point.

Whether you prefer to introduce decimals prior to fractions or to introduce decimals as equivalent to a particular family of fractions, one thing that is crucial for pupils to understand is the symmetry around the 1s:

10000000	100000	10000	1000	100	10	1	.	$\frac{1}{10}$	$\frac{1}{100}$	$\frac{1}{1000}$	$\frac{1}{10000}$	$\frac{1}{100000}$	$\frac{1}{1000000}$
							.						

The columns to the left of the 1s increase by a factor of 10 – 10 then 100 then 1000 and so on, whilst the columns to the right of the 1s decrease by a factor of 10, becoming tenths, then hundredths, then thousandths, etc. This symmetry helps pupils recognise the correct place in decimal numbers, which is important in concepts like accuracy.

Following this, the same sorts of activities that were used to support pupils' development of place value understanding can be used to extend that understanding to decimals. Of particular import is making sure that pupils recognise relationships like 0.3 = 3 × 0.1, extending to things like 0.37 = 3 × 0.1 + 7 × 0.01 = 37 × 0.01. This last calculation is the extension of the idea of developing flexibility around the places; 3700 can be seen as '3 thousand 7 hundred' or '37 hundred'. In the same way 0.37 can be seen as '3 tenths and 7 hundredths' or '37 hundredths'.

It is also important to develop pupil fluency around counting in decimals. It is a great idea with learners that are relative novices in working with decimals to get them to count in tenths, hundredths or thousandths, and not just from 0. Have pupils do a choral response to sequences like 0.3, 0.4, 0.5, … as well as trickier sequences such as 0.34, 0.35, 0.36, … and 0.34, 0.44, 0.54, … In this last one, make sure you push it past 1 (i.e. to 1.04) to make sure pupils can bridge that gap. It is well worth doing a number of these, where pupils have to count up, count down, start at numbers like 100.1 and count up/down in 0.01s. This sort of thing can also be done on a number line once pupils have had some experience, both on mini whiteboards as a check on understanding and then in independent work. Pupils that need a bit more support can use place value counters to do this sort of counting.

Returning to fractions in general, we have seen that using number lines or rods is a far superior introduction to the concept of fractions than the usual introduction of taking a shape and chopping it into equal parts, such as the image below:

Or worse:

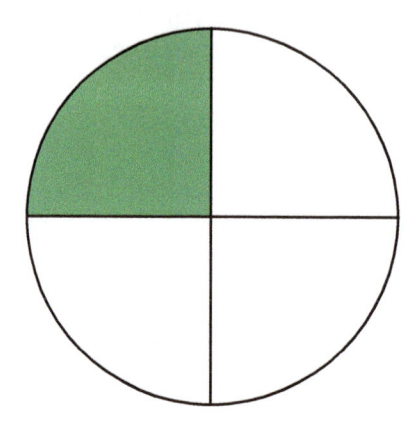

These are fairly typical images that might be used by teachers early in a pupil's experience of working with fractions, and unfortunately are likely to give rise to many of the misconceptions that emerge in pupils' fractional thinking. One of the main issues with these images is that they don't have their roots in pupils' experience of the number 1. The whole (no pun intended) concept of fractions as numbers has to arise from comparison to 1. In looking at pictures like the two above, pupils learn that fractions are simply about counting the number of pieces, and writing the number of shaded pieces over the total. In effect, they are seeing the fraction as two distinct quantities, a total and a subtotal that fit a certain criterion (e.g. a total of four pieces in the circle above, one of which is shaded). Similarly, using concrete objects as an introduction to fractions is also problematic:

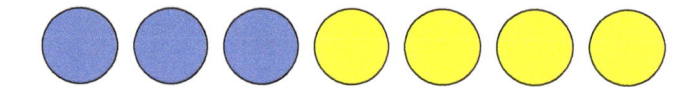

Yes, three out of the seven counters are blue, and so $\frac{3}{7}$ of the counters are blue. However, if this is a pupil's primary mental image for the concept of fractions, then it is easy to see how $\frac{3}{7} + \frac{1}{4}$ erroneously becomes $\frac{4}{11}$. For, of course, if I start with seven counters, three of which are blue, and then I add four more counters, one of which is blue, then what else could I end up with but 11 counters, four of which are blue (which is obviously true, but has little or nothing to do with the fraction addition $\frac{3}{7} + \frac{1}{4}$!)?

The issue in both of these situations is the lack of link back to the value of 1. Having a clear image for 'the whole' (the value of 1) is crucial in understanding fractions as numbers, rather than as the ratio of two separate integers with separate meanings. That isn't to say that this way of seeing fractions isn't important, and pupils should definitely meet fractions as the ratio of two separate integers at some point in their mathematical journey, but it definitely should not be the start point for a pupil's foray into the world of fractions. Pupils' start point with fractions should have a clear relation back to the value of 1, so that pupils understand early on that the value of a fraction is linked to the value of 1, and that representations of fractions have to be linked with the representation of 1 (whole). Once this is clear then we can play with what it means to 'one whole' or 'one unit' and introduce bar models and other shapes as representative of one whole. Lots of questions of the type, 'What fraction of the whole shape is shaded?' or, 'If this rod is one whole, what is the value of this rod (using Cuisenaire rods)?' can help with reinforcing this link back to one whole.

Another representation of one whole that can be important in working with fractions is the unit square. The unit square is obviously the key representation of the value of '1' when it comes to area, but it is also used with manipulatives such as algebra tiles, as well as representations of things like Cuisenaire and Dienes to represent the number 1. The unit square can help support thinking in fraction multiplication, as well as in linking fractions and decimals to percentages. It is definitely a good idea to introduce representing fractions within the unit square at a point when pupils' fractional thinking is reasonably well established, and it can serve as a great vehicle for testing and extending pupils' thinking when it comes to fractions. Broadly speaking, the introduction of the fractions within the unit square can go something like this:

What is the area of this square?

'1 square unit'

So, the value of the area of this square is 1.

Let's consider this square as a representation of 1. What values/fraction family could be represented here?

'Fifths'

What fraction would be represented here?

'One fifth'

What about now?

'One fifteenth'

This last view is particularly important, as pupils need to appreciate that the length and width of the square do not need to be split into the same number of parts, as long as each of the parts is equal in size.

The language in this situation is also important, as it is whenever looking at fractions as a shaded area such as in a bar model or another shape. Attention needs to be carefully drawn to the fact that the pieces have to be equally sized in order for the fraction to be discernible. Language like 'One of 15 *equal* parts of *one whole*' is good to use as it stresses the need for the parts to be equal and that the shape is being used to represent the value of 1. A good idea is to contrast this with non-examples, and make sure that pupils can recognise when a fraction cannot be accurately determined (although it can perhaps be estimated) and when changes to the shape have to be made in order to determine the fraction. Have a look at the images below, where each shape is a representation of 1, and think about whether and how the fraction can be determined.

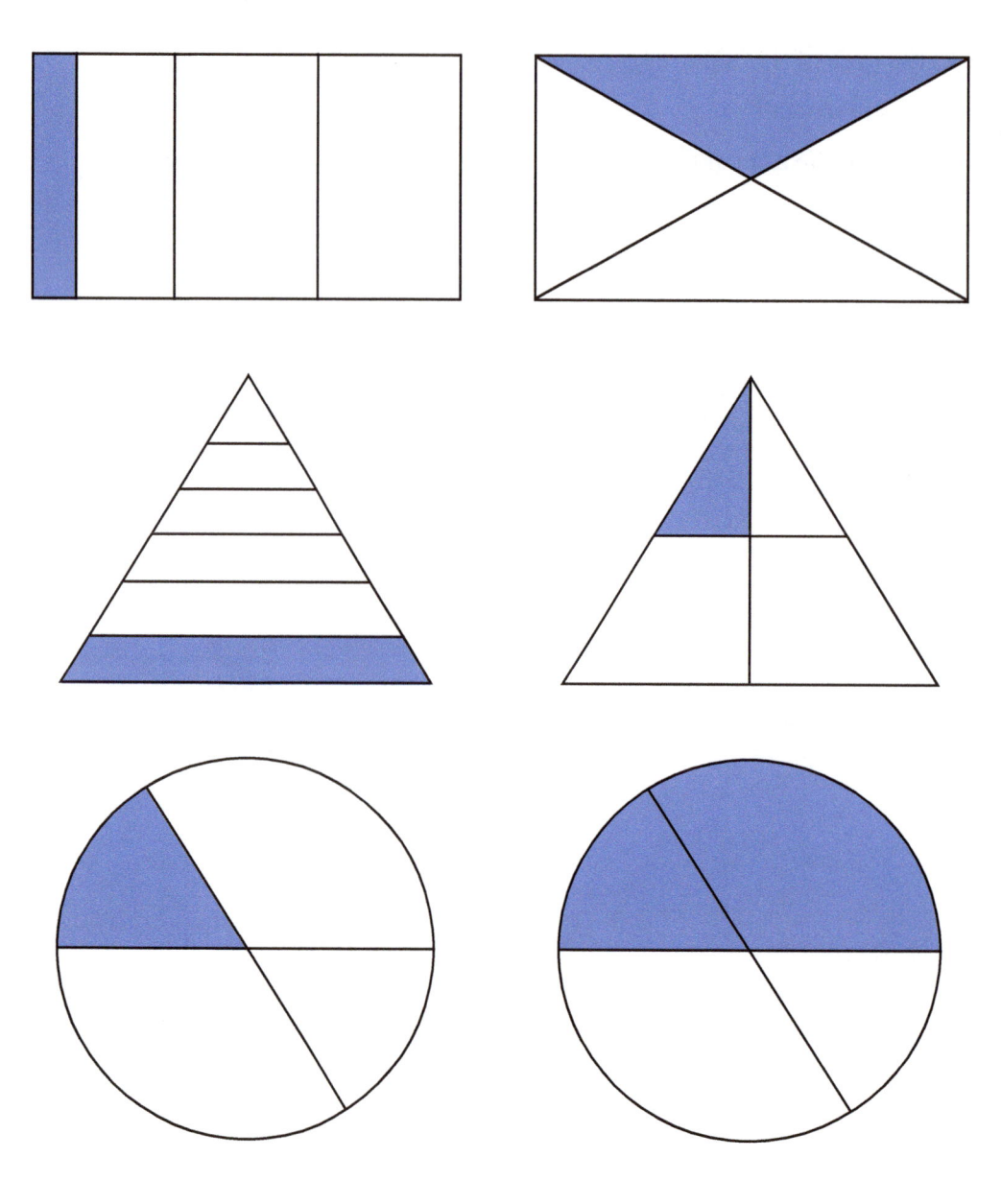

Consider the rectangle and triangle on the right of those images; by adding some extra lines we have:

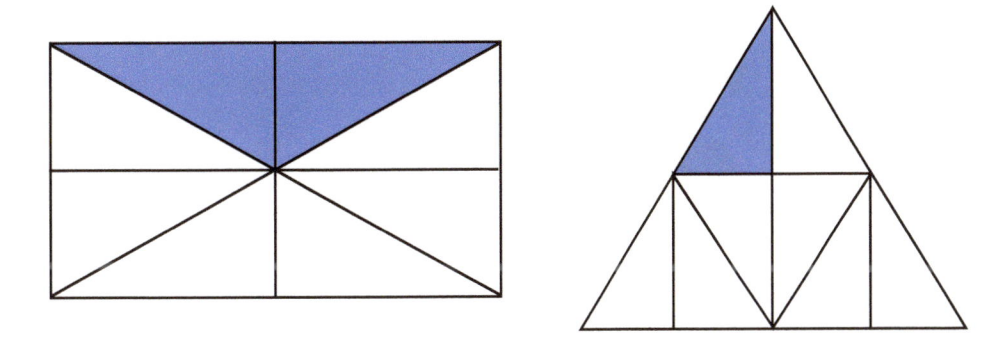

Things like this are nice to stretch pupil thinking around fractions – we could also ask learners to estimate the values of all the fractions before we start and then look at which we can determine precisely and which we can't.

Of course, once pupils are secure in thinking about fractions using continuous representations of number (such as vectors, rods, bars or areas) then discrete representations can be brought back and used. Although it is not recommended to introduce fractions from a discrete representation, once they are introduced then things like counters can take fractional values. A nice way to begin looking at this is with coins, with the idea that because 10 coins with a value of 10p have a total value of £1, each of the 10p coins has a value of $\frac{1}{10}$ of £1. This opens up the idea of counters and other discrete representations for fractions:

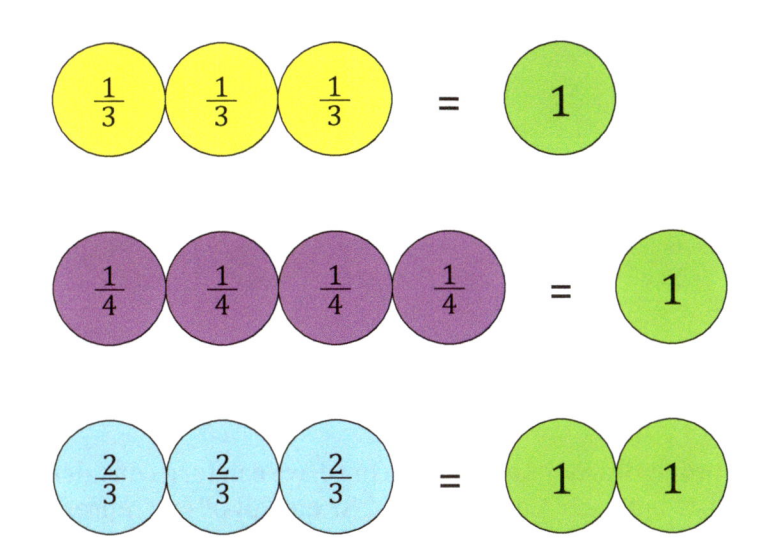

Of course, pupils already need to know about these relationships, as there is nothing in the representation to help make sense of why four of the $\frac{1}{4}$ counters would be equal in value to 1, or why three of the $\frac{2}{3}$ counters would be equal in value to 2. However, this way of thinking about fractions can be useful when examining addition and subtraction of fractions, as well as some multiplications and divisions, so it is worth introducing it to pupils at some stage.

Done well, it can be used as a way to prompt pupils to think differently about equivalent fractions. Have a look at the image below:

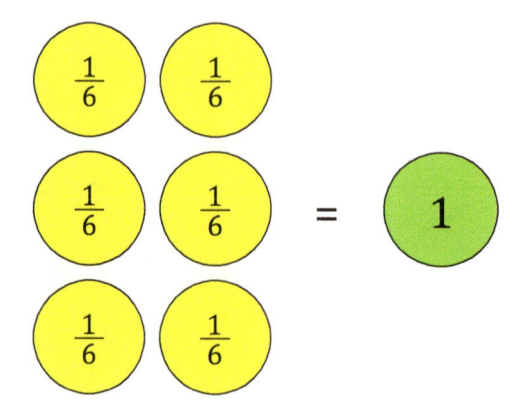

This image can be used as a different way of making sense of the idea that both $\frac{2}{6}$ is equal in value to $\frac{1}{3}$ and $\frac{3}{6}$ is equal in value to $\frac{1}{2}$, by grouping the counters either horizontally or vertically.

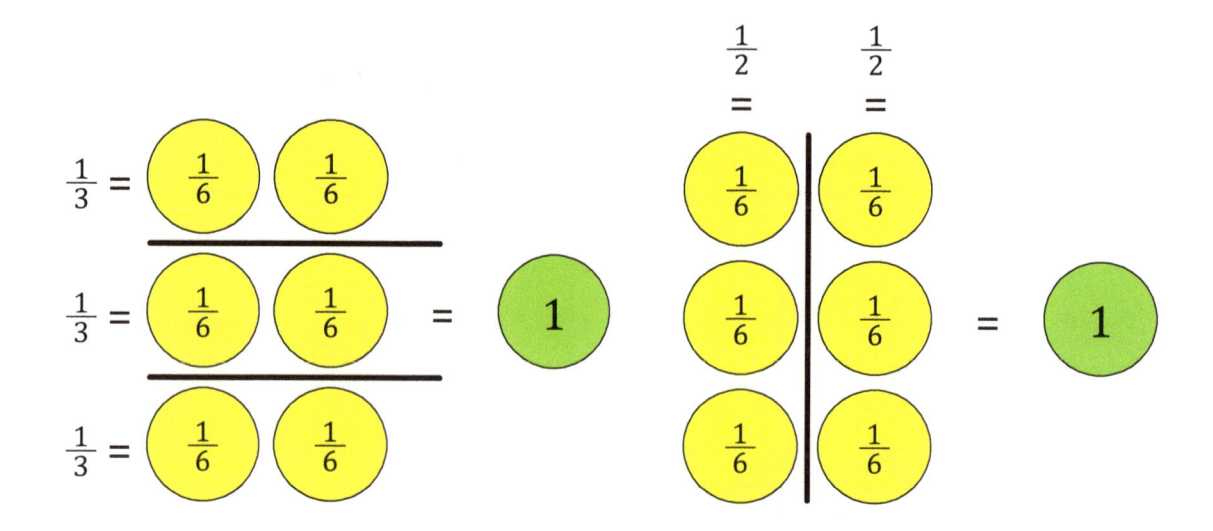

Asking pupils to use the counters to demonstrate why certain fractions are equivalent can be a nice way of reviewing and embedding this knowledge.

Once ideas around proper fractions are well secured, we can turn consideration to improper fractions – what exists between 1 and 2? 2 and 3? etc. All of our representations can help make sense of this:

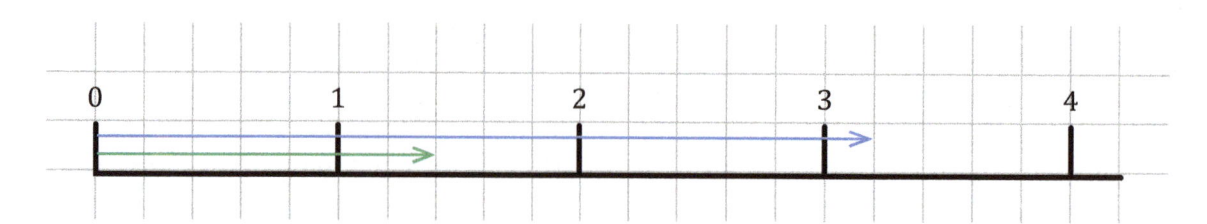

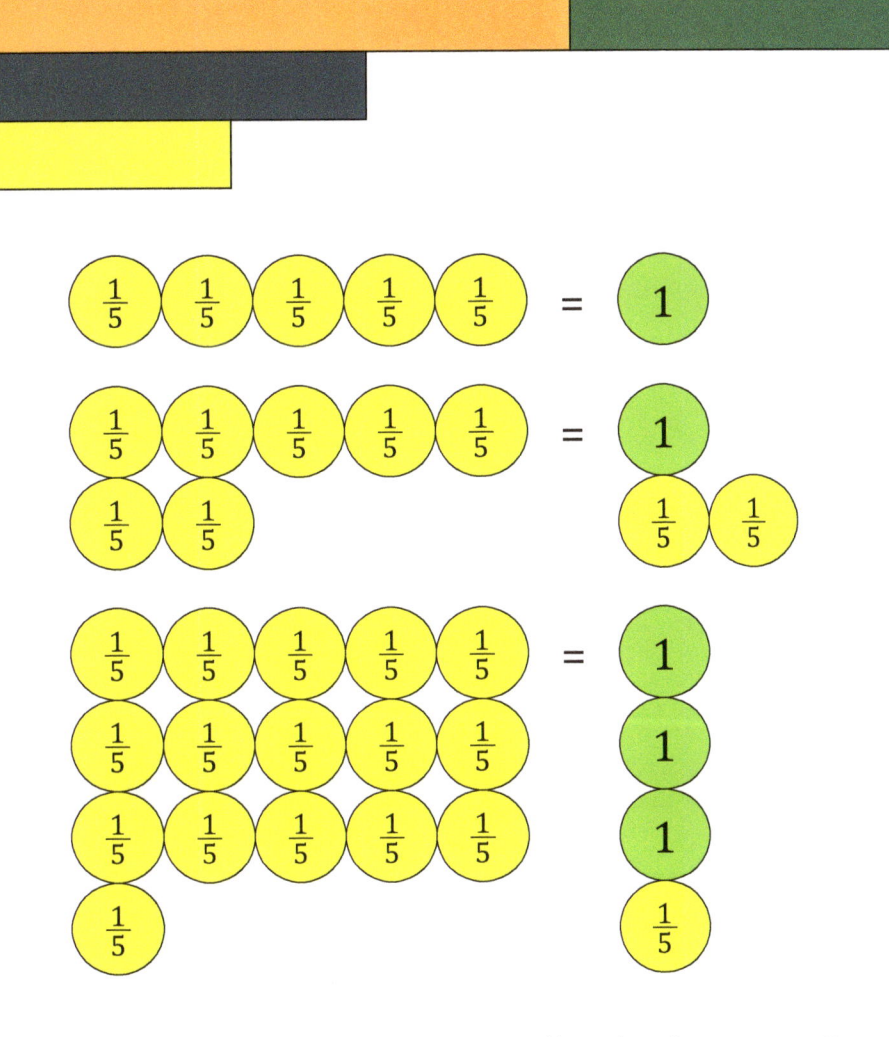

All of these can be used to show that $\frac{7}{5} = 1\frac{2}{5}$ and that $\frac{16}{5} = 3\frac{1}{5}$ and vice versa. Depending on pupils' background knowledge, one or more of these representations can be used to support pupils in making sense of the ideas of improper fractions and mixed numbers, or again can be used to prompt pupils to think in a different way about the same idea.

Once pupils are happy with the idea of converting between equivalent improper fractions and mixed numbers, then we can offer activities such as this:

Convert the following into mixed numbers:

$\frac{7}{2}$ $\frac{7}{3}$ $\frac{7}{4}$ $\frac{7}{5}$ $\frac{7}{6}$

$\frac{8}{2}$ $\frac{8}{3}$ $\frac{8}{4}$ $\frac{8}{5}$ $\frac{8}{6}$ $\frac{8}{7}$

$\frac{9}{2}$ $\frac{9}{3}$ $\frac{9}{4}$ $\frac{9}{5}$ $\frac{9}{6}$ $\frac{9}{7}$ $\frac{9}{8}$

$\frac{10}{2}$ $\frac{10}{3}$ $\frac{10}{4}$ $\frac{10}{5}$ $\frac{10}{6}$ $\frac{10}{7}$ $\frac{10}{8}$ $\frac{10}{9}$

$\frac{1 \times 1}{2}$ $\frac{11}{3}$ $\frac{11}{4}$ $\frac{11}{5}$ $\frac{11}{6}$ ... up to $\frac{11}{10}$

Or this:

Convert each of the fractions below into mixed numbers.

$\frac{5}{3}, \frac{11}{4}, \frac{19}{5}, \frac{29}{6}, \frac{41}{7}$

What do you notice about each answer?

Write down the next improper fraction in the sequence.

Can you write what the numerator would be for a denominator of 21?

Can you write down a rule for improper fractions in the sequence?

Or this:

Find an improper fraction that goes into each section of the Venn diagram. If a section is impossible, say why.

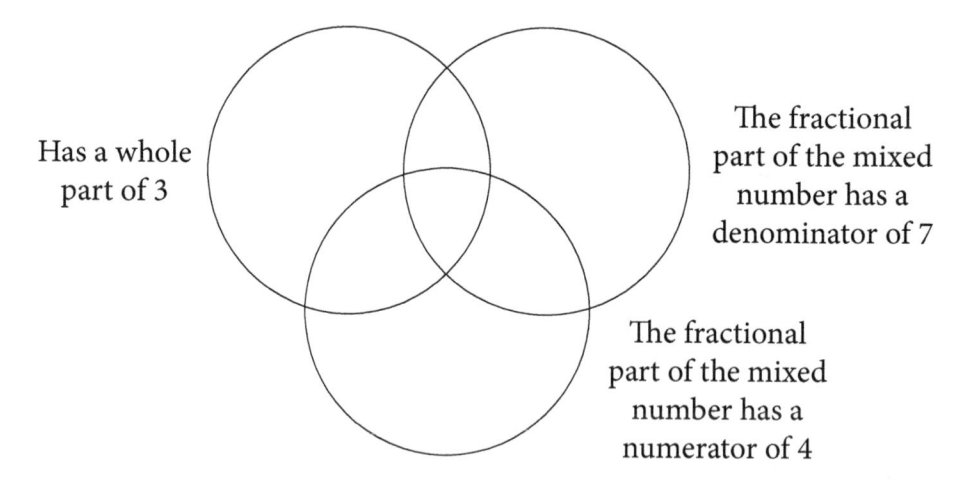

- Has a whole part of 3
- The fractional part of the mixed number has a denominator of 7
- The fractional part of the mixed number has a numerator of 4

In which section does the smallest possible value fit?

All are nice in terms of allowing pupils to see some of the structure underlying conversion between improper fractions and mixed numbers.

When fractions and decimals are introduced in these ways, ordering of fractions and decimals should pose little trouble; however, it is worth highlighting a couple of ways of thinking with pupils:

$\frac{1}{5} < \frac{3}{5}$: We can see that these are in the same fraction family, so the larger numerator will clearly indicate the larger fraction.

$\frac{1}{5} < \frac{1}{4}$: We can see that if we split the same size whole into 5 equal parts or into 4 equal parts, then each part of the first whole will be smaller than each part of the second whole.

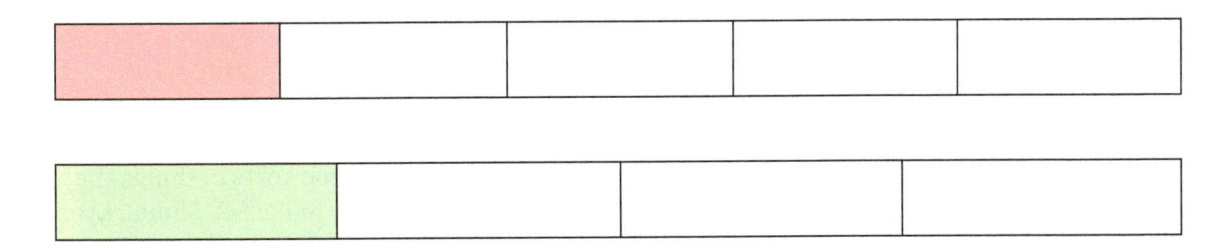

$\frac{4}{5} > \frac{3}{4}$: We can see this as a consequence of the one above – the first of these is $\frac{1}{5}$ less than one whole, and the second is $\frac{1}{4}$ less than one whole. Because $\frac{1}{5}$ is less than $\frac{1}{4}$, we have removed less from one whole, and so we have more.

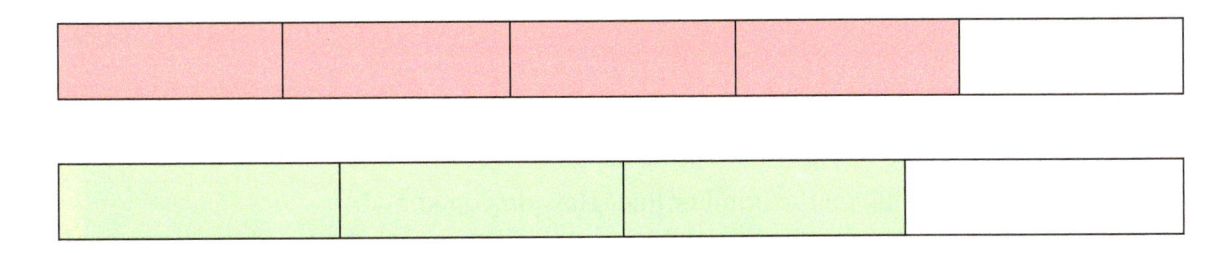

0.3 < 0.257: This is a common misconception, but Dienes can help make it clear for those that do not have the requisite place value fluency.

Concept: negatives

Prerequisites: Natural numbers, addition, subtraction.

Linked concepts: Most concepts that link to natural numbers extend those links to negatives, including all arithmetic operations. Ways of making sense of negatives play an important part in transformations.

Once pupils are familiar with the number line, as well as asking the question, 'What comes between 0 and 1?', another question that can be asked is, 'What happens if we start at 0 and move away from (i.e. subtract) 1?' This is an excellent way to introduce the idea of negative numbers and their relationship to positive numbers as the **inverse** (or, more properly, the additive inverse) of each other.

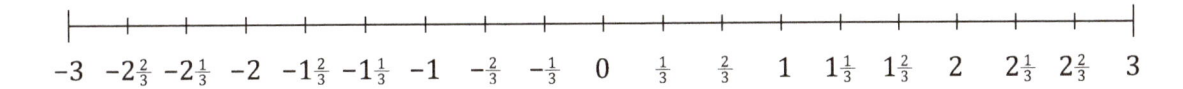

An important idea with negatives is the idea of direction. The idea that the negative direction is the opposite of the positive direction is crucial to working with negatives on a number line. This is true both on the scale and when using vectors:

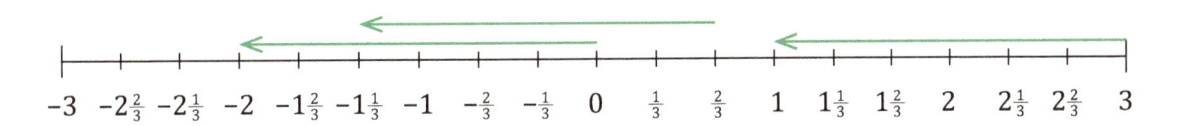

All of these represent the value of −2, being the same length as 2 but in the opposite direction. I like pupils to see this as the vector for 2 rotated through 180°; some people prefer to think of this as a reflection, but I think it links better to vectors in 2 or more dimensions to talk about it as a rotation. However, be clear with pupils that rotating a vector creates its inverse (or more properly, additive inverse), not its 'negative'. This is necessary in order to understand the idea of 2 as the inverse of −2; turning the vector for −2 through 180° creates the inverse of −2, which is 2. It is also worth pupils recognising the same sorts of things they saw in fractions – for example, as described earlier, it takes six $-\frac{1}{3}$ to make −2. Similarly to when number lines were first introduced, activities such as filling in the gaps, extending a number line and broken number lines (where number lines start at a non-zero value and pupils have to continue on) are all useful activities, and something like this can prompt a bit more discussion:

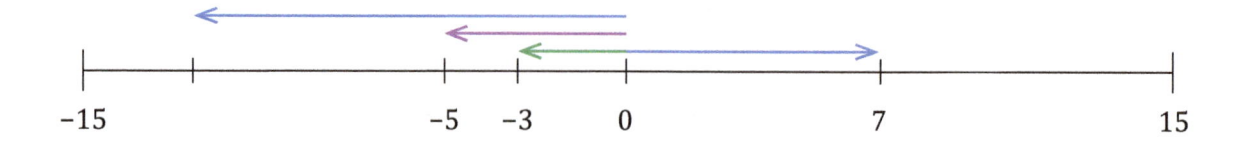

What number is missing on the number line? How do you know?

When introducing negatives, it is a really good idea to show the number lines again increasing both to the left and right, as well as up and down. Certain ways of thinking about division with negatives require the flexibility to redefine the positive direction, and so having seen all four directions being positive at one time or another is incredibly useful.

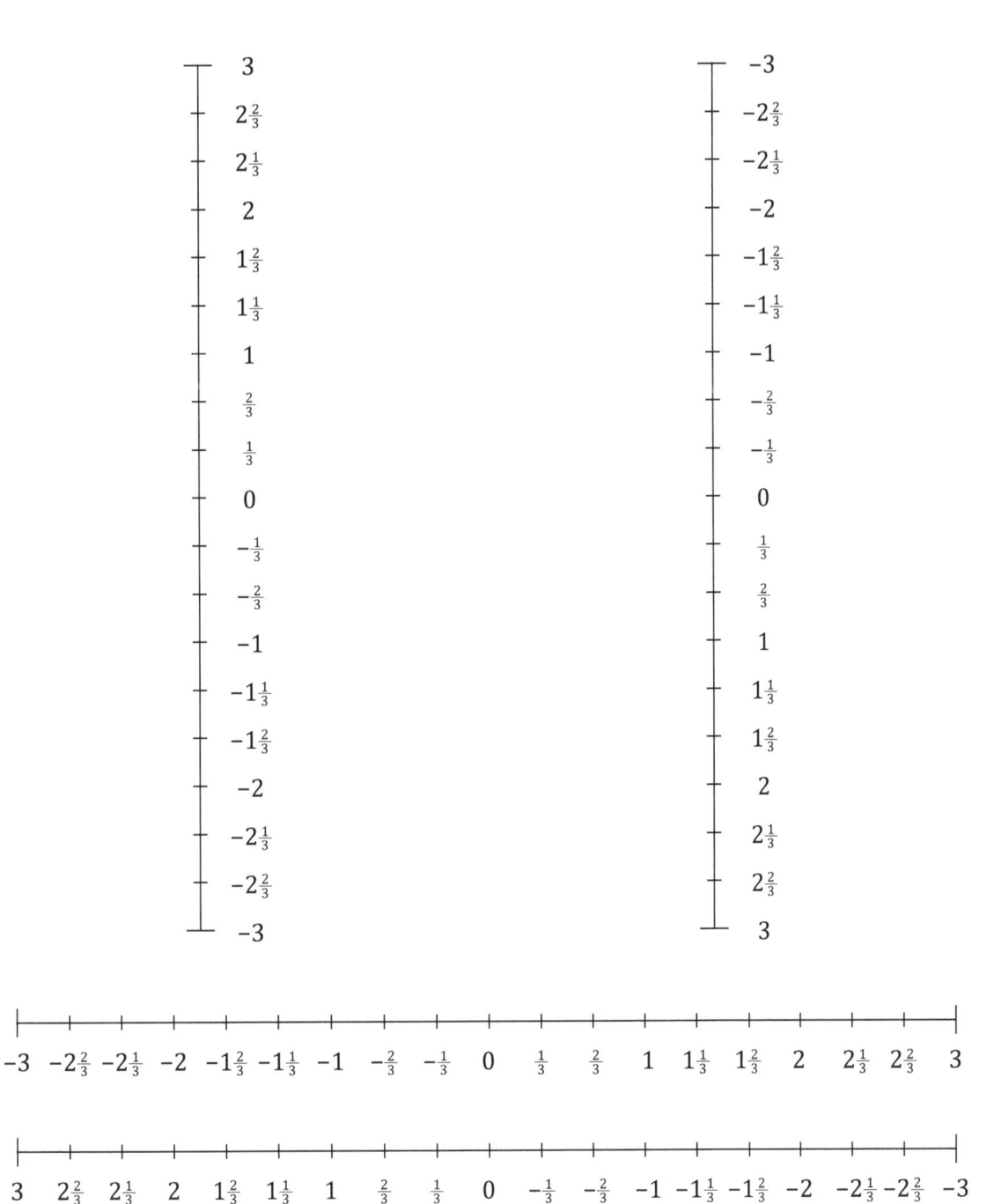

As with other representations of numbers, we can also represent negatives as discrete objects. Typically, this is done using double-sided counters or tiles where one side is defined as 1 and the other side is defined as −1.

Again, it is really important that pupils see this both ways around – although people define the yellow side to be 1 most of the time, we should make sure pupils recognise that this is an arbitrary choice and that what matters is that if one side is defined to be a value, then turning the counter over makes it assume the inverse value. This links nicely with the idea of rotation with vectors as well, as in both cases a 180° rotation creates the inverse.

Integral to using counters for negatives is the idea of **'zero-pairs'**. Pupils need to be taught that any time two counters of opposite colour can be paired, the result is 0. We can use simple activities to help reinforce this, such as asking them to create something that has a value of 5 and uses one red counter (assuming yellow is defined to have a value of 1), or to create something ourselves (as below) and ask pupils what the value is.

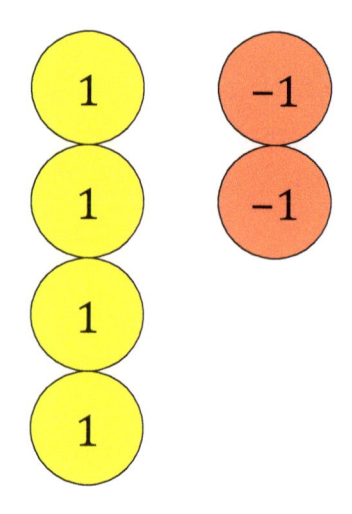

For more involved activities you can ask pupils to create patterns or pictures with the counters (at a professional development session for teachers in Edinburgh, I once had a teacher create a butterfly) and then work out the value/change the value by adding more counters in the same pattern. There are also activities like the ones here, which can prompt pupil thinking around negatives and counters:

Represent the number −1 in as many different ways as you can, using counters. What do your representations have in common?

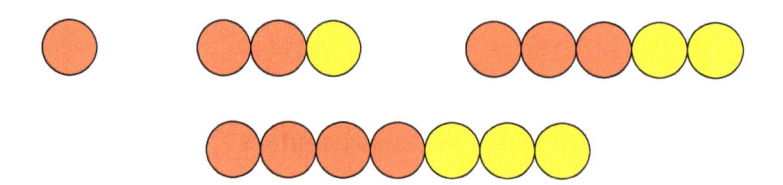

Work out the value of the centre box, assuming yellow has a value of 1. Draw other patterns in each of the boxes which satisfy the conditions. You should aim to make the minimum change possible to the centre box.

Value of the picture

	Less	Same	More
Less			
Same		1 1 1 1 / -1 -1	
More			

(Number of red counters)

Of course, counters don't have to take just integer values – as we have seen, counters can take positive and negative fractional values, and if pupils have already been introduced to fractions, then introducing counters with fractional values can be useful here as well. Pupils can be given similar activities to those above to help make sense of this, with the concept of zero pairs transferring naturally over to rational values.

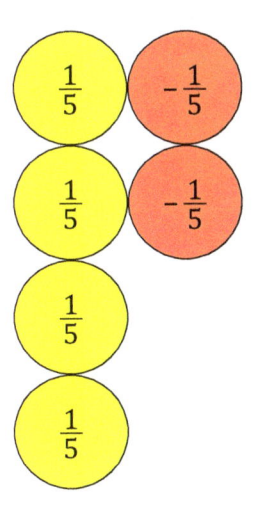

This collection of counters would have a value of $\frac{2}{5}$.

Concept: surds

Prerequisites: Natural numbers, fractions, indices, area, shape.

Linked concepts: Most concepts that link to natural numbers extend those links to surds, including all arithmetic operations. Accuracy plays an important part of thinking about surds, and equality/equivalence is also important in linking with surds.

Once pupils are comfortable with the idea of rational numbers and have experience calculating with and manipulating them, then the next stage of learning about number is to learn about irrational numbers. Depending on the structure of the curriculum, pupils may first meet irrational numbers when introduced to the value of π as part of looking at circle measure; however, π is a type of number called a **transcendental number**, which means there is no easy way to introduce it by looking at calculations that involve whole numbers. Surds have no such issue, being an example of **algebraic** irrational numbers. The natural way to introduce surds is to look at the area of squares. If we consider a square with an area of 9 square units:

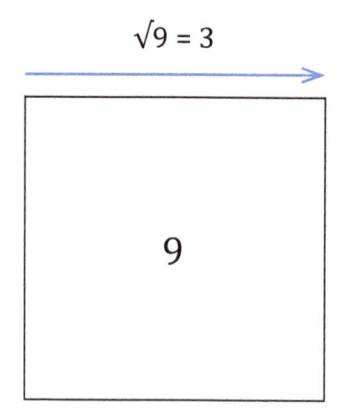

$\sqrt{9} = 3$

9

we can ask pupils what the length of one of the sides of this square is, and provided pupils are already fluent with the idea of square area and its links to indices/roots, then there should be little issue with pupils recognising that the length of one side of this square is three units. We can take this opportunity to reinforce the links between square areas and square numbers/square roots if we need to, by asking about other square areas that would have whole number lengths. If pupils are happy with this, then we can introduce surds by asking about square areas that are not square numbers. An area of 12 can be a nice place to start, particularly if we want to bring in the idea of equivalence of surds.

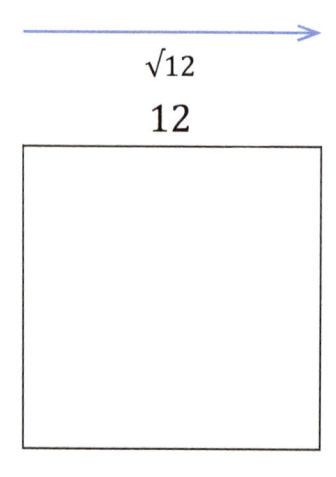

$\sqrt{12}$

12

This allows us to make clear that the length of this square is not an integer but also cannot be a fraction (as whenever we square a non-integer rational the result is a non-integer rational). This means there must be a different type of number that gives the length of this square, and this type of number is called a surd. We can explain to pupils that this type of number is written using the fact that the square root of a square area gives the length of the square, and so the value of the length of this square is $\sqrt{12}$. At a suitable point we can talk about decimal approximations to surd values and using both calculator and non-calculator methods to approximate surd values. Pupils will need a reasonable understanding of the idea of accuracy for this to take hold, however – particularly recognising that even a calculator only gives decimal values to an accuracy of 11 or so decimal places (depending on the size of the number). We should also make it clear here that we can take the square root of any and every (positive, for now) number; what makes square numbers special is not that they have a square root (a common misconception) but rather that their square root is an integer.

One thing it is worth doing is to show these values on a number line as vectors. Although we can't do this exactly (again, the idea of accuracy and decimal approximation being important), it is possible to do this by drawing these squares below the number line. For this to make sense, pupils will need to know roughly the size of these numbers, i.e. if they are between 1 and 2, 2 and 3, 3 and 4, etc.

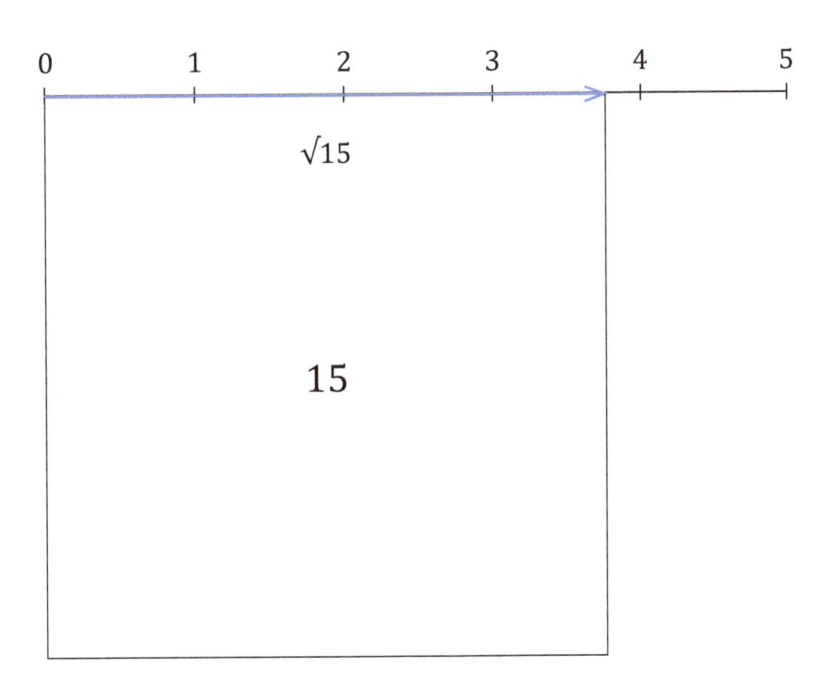

It is important for pupils to know here that because $\sqrt{16} = 4$ and $\sqrt{9} = 3$ that $\sqrt{15}$ is between 3 and 4. It can be a great activity to get pupils to approximate roots of integers/fractions.

Of course, once the idea of the surd is well understood, we can again define discrete objects to be surds. These can be a great representation for manipulating surds and certain arithmetical operations with surds, so they are well worth looking at:

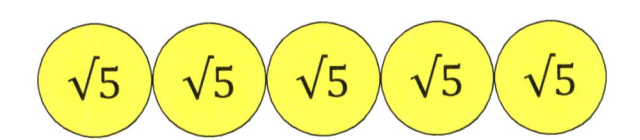

Here we can see 5√5 shown as discrete objects, which is a more compact representation than showing the lengths of 5 squares, each with an area of 5. We can build up to something like this by first defining a single counter as a surd (say √5), and then looking at what the value of two counters is, three counters and so on. This is clearly a way of thinking about multiplication, so pupils will need to have seen multiplication in this way before looking at things like this. The other thing we can introduce nicely with counters is the idea of combinations of two different surds:

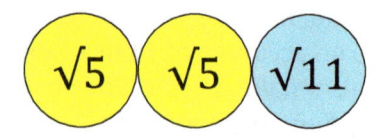

This shows 2√5 + √11, with the important point for pupils being that this is a number, and that there is no simpler way to write this exact number. If needs be, we can go back to squares for something like this:

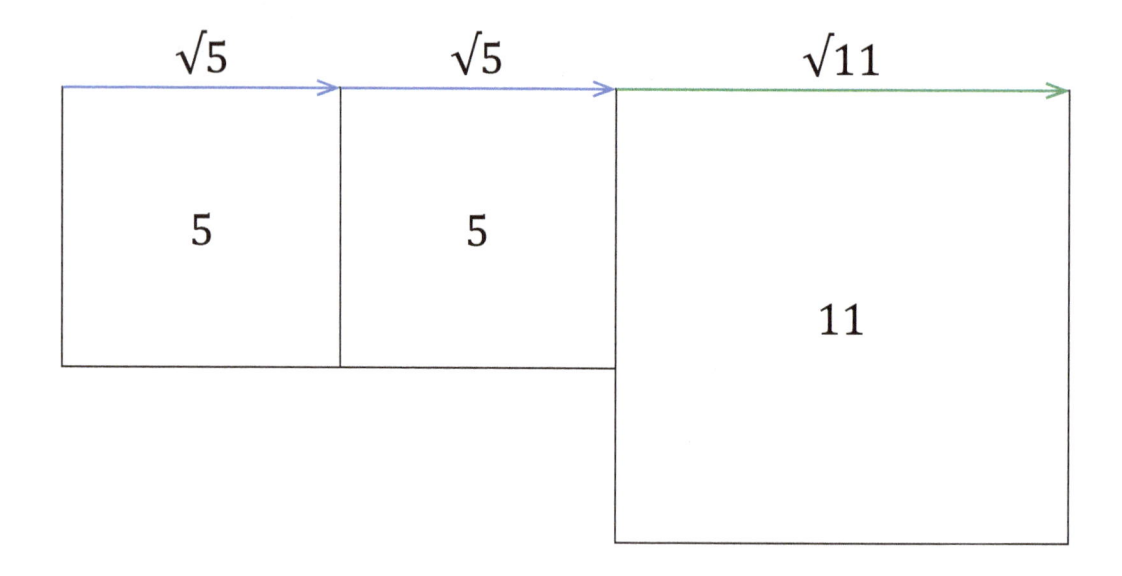

However, most pupils are happy working with counters or even working directly in the abstract once the concept of a number as a surd is well defined.

If we then want to explore equivalence of surds, we can look at an area of 12 in a different way – in this case by splitting the area of 12 into four smaller squares, each with a value of 3:

Of course, √3 is also a surd value; however, what is notable (and what we would want to draw pupils' attention to) is the fact that the length of the original square is twice as long as the length of one of the smaller squares. That is to say √12 = 2 × √3 or 2√3.

Contrast this with a square with an area of 15. A square like this cannot be split into smaller square areas with integer values. This means that √15 has no equivalent surd value.

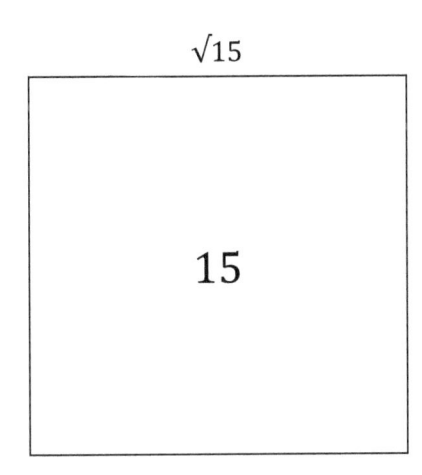

√15

15

At this point it is worth having pupils work with these square areas a little more before drawing attention to the idea of the square factor of 12 (i.e. that 12 = 4 × 3 where 4 is a square number), which is not present in 15. A nice activity is to ask pupils to examine different values for square areas and either physically show which can be broken into smaller squares and which can't, or at least reason which can be split into smaller squares and which can't. This sort of activity is very effective in preparing pupils to see the link between breaking a square into smaller squares and a square factor (having already been exposed to areas of 9, 12 and 15):

Which of the following square areas can be broken into smaller squares each with equal integer areas? How many smaller squares would there be inside each square? What would the value of the area of each smaller square area be?

18, 21, 24, 27, 30, 35, 40, 45, 50

Once pupils have identified that 18 can be split into nine squares of area 2, 24 can be split into four squares of area 6, 27 can be split into nine squares of area 3, 40 can be split into four squares of area 10, 45 can be split into nine squares of area 5 and 50 can be split into 25 squares of area 2, we can then draw attention to the idea that the reason these can be split into smaller square areas is because these numbers have square factors. This could be done through questioning of pupils or explicitly drawing attention to this by the teacher.

In moving towards the abstract, we can mirror what was happening with the squares. Going back to the square with an area of 12:

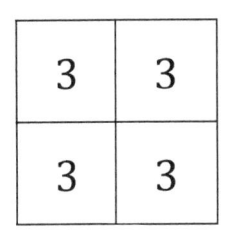

12

3	3
3	3

We started by splitting the area of 12 into four areas of value 3. $12 = 4 \times 3$

We then looked at the length of the square as the square root of the area. $\sqrt{12} = \sqrt{4} \times \sqrt{3}$

(It is worth noting that the roots of 4 and 3 are arrived at slightly differently here – the $\sqrt{3}$ is the length of the square with an area of 3, whereas the $\sqrt{4}$ is because there are $\sqrt{4}$ squares arranged along the length).

This gives the equivalent surd values. $\sqrt{12} = 2 \times \sqrt{3} = 2\sqrt{3}$

A nice link to make here is with indices, and particularly with an index of $\frac{1}{2}$. Provided pupils have previously been introduced to working with fractional indices, then the same results can be arrived at through the application of index laws:

$$\sqrt{12} = 12^{\frac{1}{2}}$$
$$12^{\frac{1}{2}} = (4 \times 3)^{\frac{1}{2}}$$
$$(4 \times 3)^{\frac{1}{2}} = 4^{\frac{1}{2}} \times 3^{\frac{1}{2}} \qquad \text{As powers distribute over multiplication.}$$
$$4^{\frac{1}{2}} \times 3^{\frac{1}{2}} = 2 \times \sqrt{3} = 2\sqrt{3}$$

Personally, I prefer to show pupils both of these approaches at the appropriate times, as it is nice for pupils to recognise that both of these ways of making sense of equivalent surds give rise to the same result.

Concept: algebra

Prerequisites: Natural numbers.

Linked concepts: Most concepts that link to natural numbers extend those links to algebra, including other forms of numbers and all arithmetic operations. Virtually every other mathematical concept can be linked with algebra.

Algebra is probably the most feared area of mathematics for school-age children. Typically, this is because learners have a really poor understanding of what algebra is and what it is for. Algebra is designed to be the general base, to be able to capture those things that are always true in number, no matter what type of number or what number base we are working in. Obviously, this means that in order to make sense of algebra, pupils need lots of experience with working with number, at the very least natural numbers and the laws of arithmetic. I would also recommend a real depth of understanding with fractions and possibly also with multi-base arithmetic.

In beginning to introduce algebra, we can come back to some of the representations we have used throughout number, i.e. as continuous quantities or as discrete objects. We can introduce this idea simply by bringing back rods or counters and asking pupils what the value is:

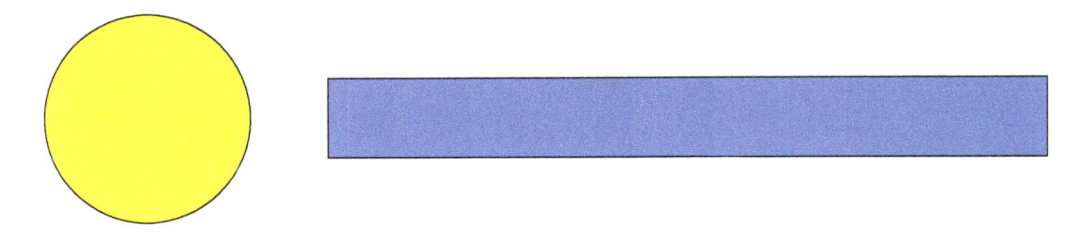

What is the value of this counter/rod?

Of course, the point here is that these counters/rods can take absolutely any value and that what matters more than the actual value is how it interacts with other values, so that something like this:

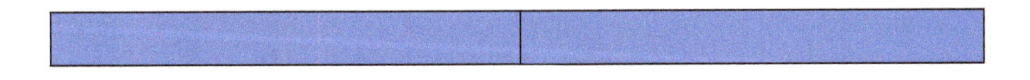

would be double the value of one rod, whereas something like this:

is just two different numbers added together.

The problem with using Cuisenaire rods for something like this is that many of the rods do have relationships relative to each other. The yellow rod is exactly half of the size of the orange rod. The black rod is two white rods less than the blue rod. For this reason, when transitioning to algebra, we tend to use bar models on plain backgrounds for a visual representation, or algebra tiles for a concrete representation (provided the tiles don't have simple ratios between each other). Algebra discs are also useful and popular in certain areas as a way of showing counters transitioning into algebraic variables.

Once pupils understand that a rod/disc can stand for any value, then initial forays into the world of algebra can be made by examining those things that are true for all numbers. This can be simple things such that 1 × any number = that number ($1 \times x = x$) to more complicated relationships such as the distributive law for multiplication over addition ($a(b + c) = ab + ac$). We can ask pupils things like, 'Tell me something that is true for all numbers' and use learner-generated examples to show how algebra can capture those expressions, or we might choose specific relationships to highlight to pupils, such as some of those given below:

How do you find the number that is one more than a given number?

Pupils with even basic familiarity with number should recognise that if we are to find 'one more than' a number, we find this by adding 1 to a number. Depending on how pupils have seen and made sense of addition, we could show this by any of the following:

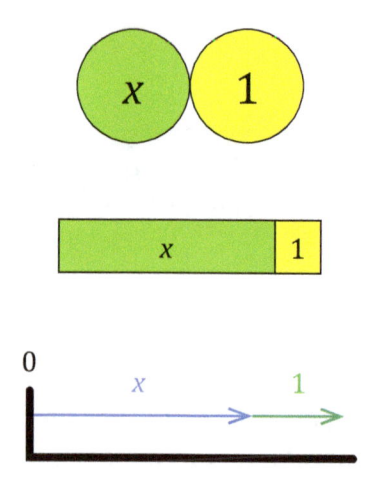

The important thing for pupils to recognise here is that it doesn't matter what the value of *x* is here; *x* could be much, much bigger than 1, it could be smaller than 1, it could be negative, it could be a surd. What is crucial is that this captures the idea that to find 'one more than', we add 1, and that this is true no matter what the value of *x*. We might even want to reinforce this with numerical values (either before or after showing the algebra) and so take pupils through a line of questioning such as:

What is one more than 6? 6 + 1 = 7.

What is one more than 6000? 6000 + 1 = 6001.

What is one more than −6? −6 + 1 = −5.

What is one more than $\frac{6}{11}$? $\frac{6}{11} + 1 = 1\frac{6}{11}$.

What is one more than $\sqrt{3}$? $\sqrt{3} + 1 = \sqrt{3} + 1(!)$.

Of course, the choice of examples will depend on what types of numbers pupils have been introduced to prior to introducing algebra.

When you multiply two numbers, the order of multiplication doesn't matter (the **commutative law** applied to multiplication).

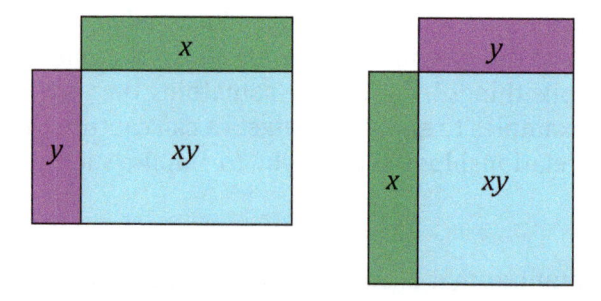

It is more difficult to capture this with algebra discs, and you need two variable algebra tiles in order to capture it concretely, but failing that either vectors or bar models can show this pictorially. Again, pupils need to be familiar with multiplication as a rectangular area to make sense of this model, and be used to seeing multiplications in this way. Numerical examples can once again be used to reinforce this: positive integer multiplication and fractional multiplication can both be captured well by the area model as we will see in Chapter 3.

If we multiply a sum by a number, we can distribute the multiplication over the sum and multiply each part of the sum by the number (the **distributive law**).

Pupils will obviously need to be familiar with using the distributive law with numbers before trying to capture the relationship algebraically. We can draw attention to having used partitioning in the past for multiplication as a way of highlighting this (if we have not taught this law explicitly before), and use this to show that the idea can be generalised:

$7 \times 48 = 7 \times (40 + 8) = 7 \times 40 + 7 \times 8$

$\frac{1}{3} \times 96 = \frac{1}{3} \times (90 + 6) = \frac{1}{3} \times 90 + \frac{1}{3} \times 6$

$4(2 + \sqrt{3}) = 4 \times 2 + 4 \times \sqrt{3}$

Again, in terms of representation, the area model works very nicely for the distributive law:

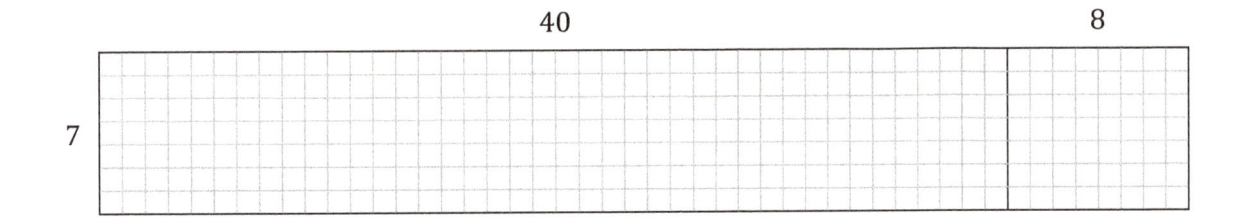

Provided pupils are used to seeing multiplication as area like this (perhaps having partially abstracted this model into a 'grid' multiplication), then we can show the general idea using algebra: $a(b + c) = ab + ac$.

It is also well worth exploring and generalising non-examples using algebra:

Subtracting two non-zero numbers results in different values, depending on which way round you subtract.

Again, numerical examples may be useful, depending on pupils' familiarity with subtraction:

Is 7 − 3 = 3 − 7? No.

Is 1.6 − 2.4 = 2.4 − 1.6? No.

Is $\frac{5}{9} - \frac{1}{4} = \frac{1}{4} - \frac{5}{9}$? No.

Is √7 − √3 = √3 − √7? No.

Representing these will depend on pupils' previous experiences of representing subtraction, but something like this may be appropriate:

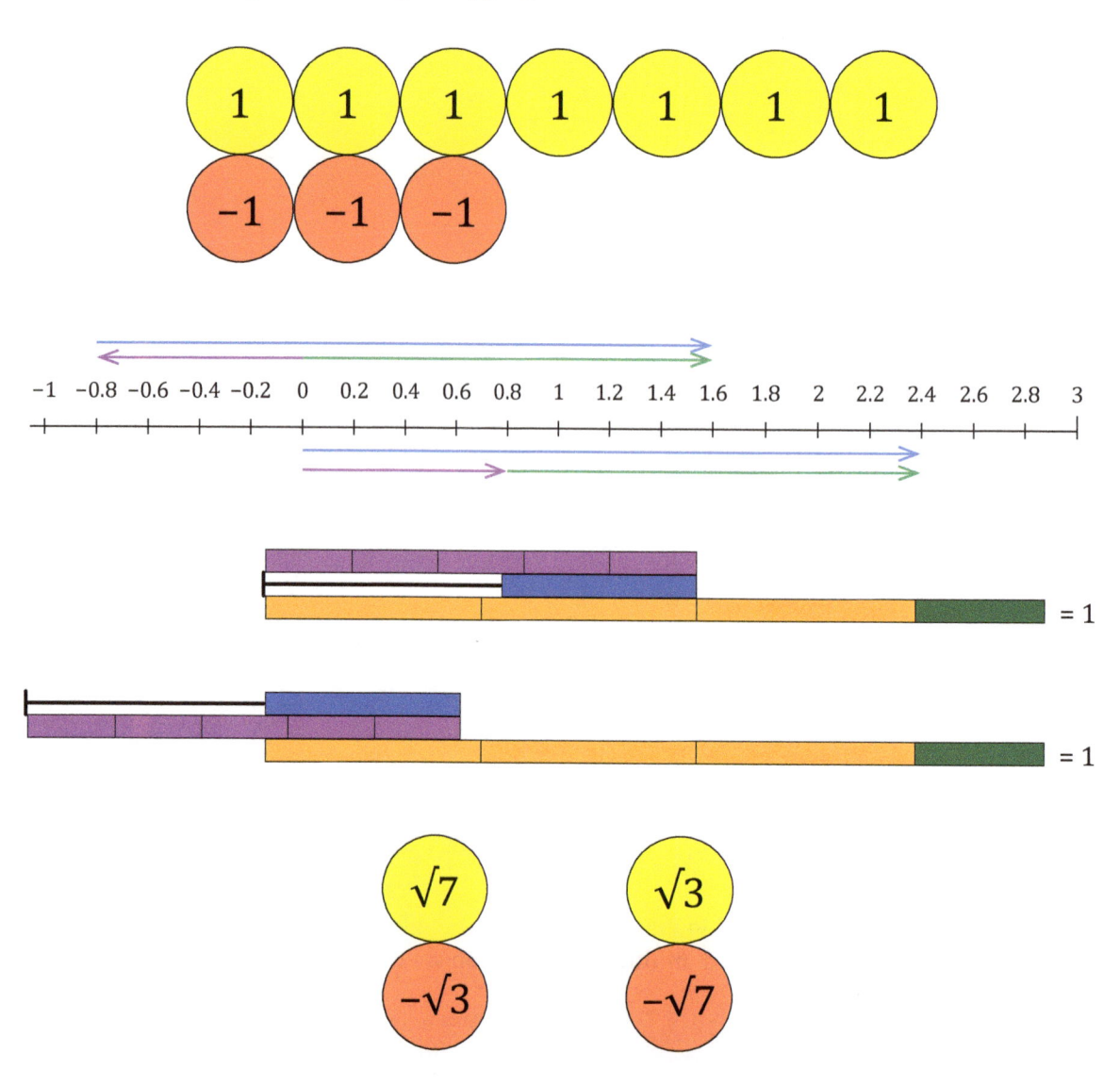

In approaching algebra in this way, as a vehicle for generalising processes, models or concepts that pupils are already familiar with, pupils can make more sense of the idea of letters as **variables**, i.e. that the letter can stand for any number in expressions such as these. Using generalised representations of the manipulatives we have explored number with, either as continuous quantities or as discrete objects, can be helpful.

Chapter 2
Addition and subtraction

Shortly after learning about number, pupils will generally begin to look at operating with numbers. This usually starts with the foundational operations of addition, and its 'inverse' subtraction.

Concept: addition

Prerequisites: Numbers.

Linked concepts: Subtraction, multiplication, equality/equivalence. Many other concepts involve the need to add in some capacity.

The way we make sense of addition is ultimately tied to the way we choose to think about numbers. Choosing to think of the numbers as discrete objects lends itself to thinking of addition as the collecting of objects with the same unit value. So, something like 4 + 5 would look like this:

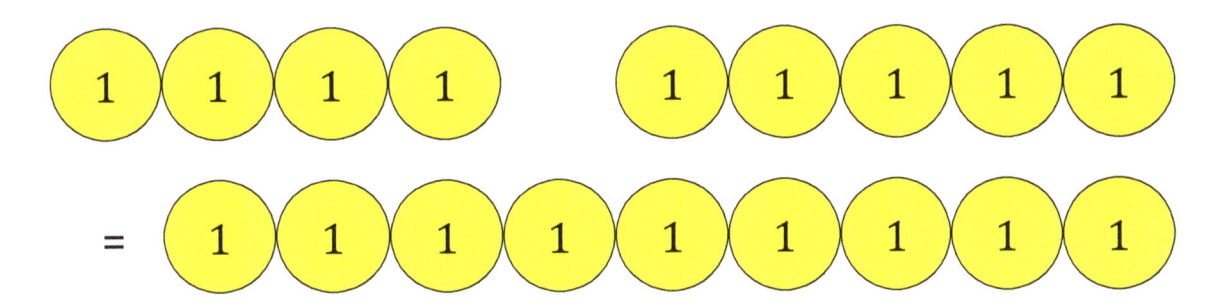

This idea extends to all types of numbers:

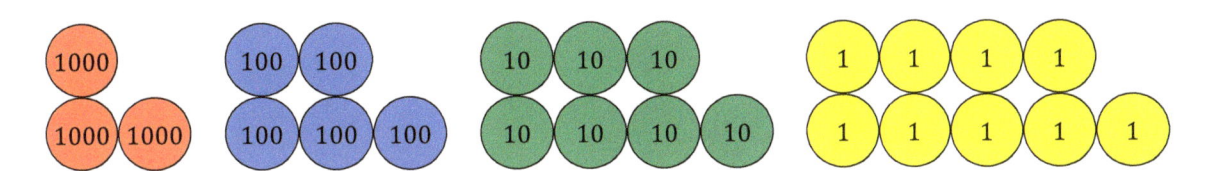

This shows 1234 + 2345, and is one way to see how the column-addition algorithm works. The objects with the same place value are being collected together and when the value of any column is greater than 9, we exchange for an equivalent value in the next column.

Process: column addition

1. Collect together the numbers represented by the digits in the same place value columns.

2 If at any point the resulting number is greater than 9, exchange for the appropriate value in the next place value column.

3 In order to save having to re-evaluate any particular column, it is usual to start with the smallest place value column, unless it is clear that no exchange will be required.

So, as above, if calculating 1234 + 2345, we might notice no exchange will be required – but, if not, we can add the four 1s with the five 1s, the three 10s with the four 10s, the two 100s with the three 100s, and the one 1000 with the two 1000s:

```
  1234
+ 2345
  3579
```

If we have numbers 2345 + 3456, we might notice that there will be an exchange required:

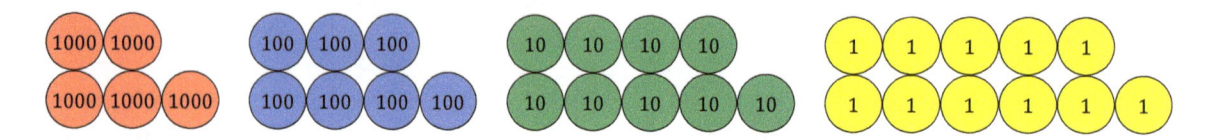

Either way, we add the five 1s and the six 1s, and this makes eleven 1s – which we can exchange for one 10 and one 1.

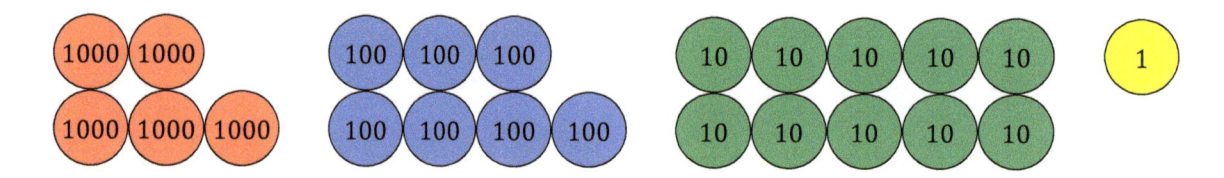

Because we started by collecting the 1s, the extra 10 we gained from the exchange means that when we collect all of our 10s together we have ten 10s, which can be exchanged for one 100.

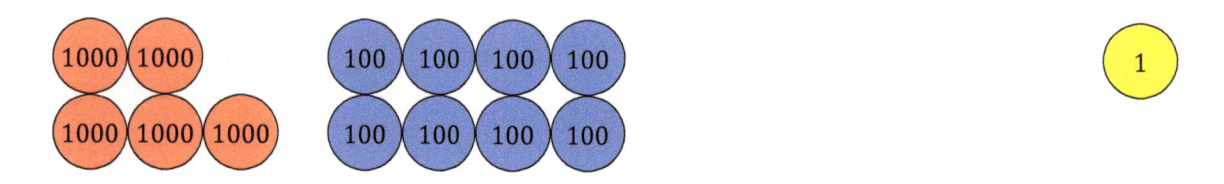

Because we started collecting the 1s, and then the 10s, the extra 10 we gained from the exchange means that we now have 8 hundreds when we collect them together, and then finally 5 thousands. We can show this using digits:

```
              1         11
  2345      2345       2345
+ 3456    + 3456     + 3456
     1        01       5801
```

Exactly the same process can be used for addition of decimals in columns, for example 3.45 + 2.817:

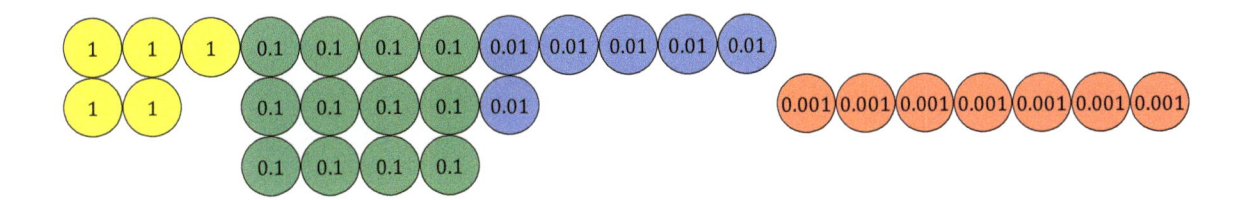

In this case we have 12 tenths, which can be exchanged for 1 one and two tenths.

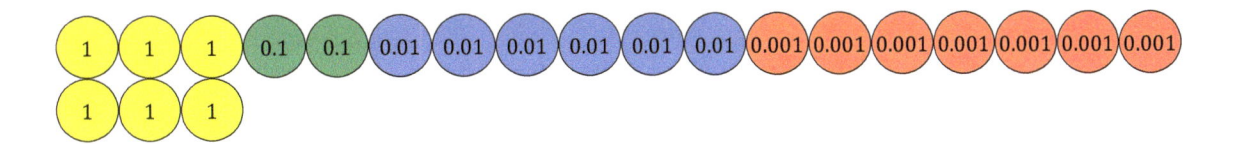

```
              1         1
  3.45       3.45      3.45
+ 2.817    + 2.817   + 2.817
   67        267      6.267
```

Of course, as previously mentioned, pupils need to be secure in place value before they can follow the column-addition procedure when it involves exchange using place value counters, as they need to be comfortable with the idea that 10 of one value will exchange for 1 of the next column.

The simplest activity that can be offered to pupils is practice in adding two or more numbers. This can be straightforward numerical practice, or alternatively questions set in context where a situation arises where pupils have to recognise that they need to add in order to solve the problem. Questions like the one below are important in ensuring that pupils recognise when to add as well as practise adding using columns:

> A school has 243 pupils in Year 7, 245 pupils in Year 8, 237 pupils in Year 9, 252 pupils in Year 10 and 248 pupils in Year 11. How many pupils are in the school in total?

These sorts of questions are best used at two points. The first is when teaching addition so that pupils can make sense of why addition solves these sorts of problems. The second is then later, as part of mixed exercises that are not all about addition, to make sure pupils can correctly identify that addition is required to solve these sorts of problems when they are mixed in with other questions.

In addition to straightforward practice of column addition, and recognising situations where addition is required, activities such as the ones below can prompt deeper thought about addition, particularly using column addition.

> You have cards with the digits 1, 3, 7 and 8 written on them. How would you arrange the cards to create:
>
> a a two-digit number plus another two-digit number with the largest answer possible.

b a two-digit number plus another two-digit number with the smallest answer possible.

Using the digits 0 to 9 only once each, how many ways can you find to complete the calculation below:

☐ ☐ ☐

+ ☐ ☐ ☐ ☐

☐ ☐ ☐ ☐

Using each of the digits 1 to 6 only once each, how many different answers can you get by placing the digits in these boxes?

☐ ☐ ☐

+ ☐ ☐ ☐

Using each of the digits 1 to 6 only once each, how close can you get to an answer of 100 in the sum below?

☐ ☐

☐ ☐

+ ☐ ☐

Column addition is not the only strategy for adding numbers with more than one place value column; other strategies are useful in certain situations, and if pupils are going to become fluent in the idea of addition, then they should be offered the opportunity to recognise when alternative strategies may be of value, such as in the questions below:

1 Calculate 2999 + 2

2 Calculate 2995 + 1002

The first of these is not well modelled using place value counters, so we will leave this for now, but the second can be demonstrated nicely using place value counters:

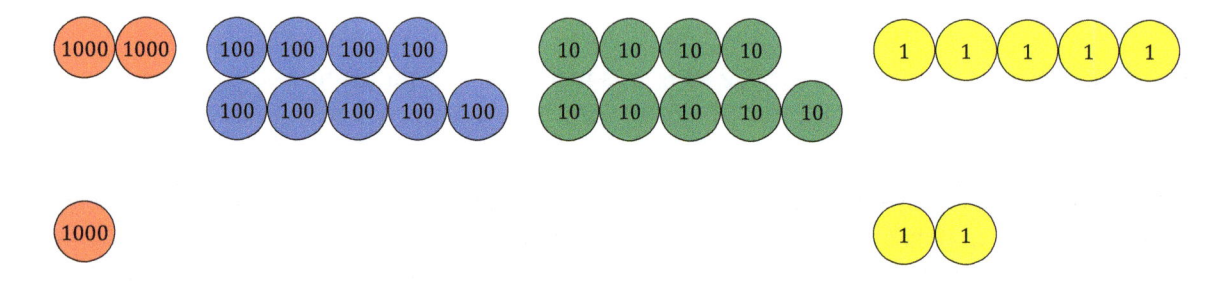

This is, in effect, recognising a situation where addition does not need to start with the 1s column as no exchange will be required, and so it is more straightforward not to go through the process of placing the numbers in columns and adding each column. Instead we can simply add the extra 1000 counter to create 3995, and then add the extra two 1s to give 3997. Learners can be offered activities where they are given different calculations and asked to choose which are best evaluated using column addition and which are best evaluated using a different strategy, such as the one below (although we would need to do a little more on addition to include the strategy for question 1 above):

Decide the best strategy for the following calculations:

1. 9 + 7
2. 29 + 27
3. 29 + 71
4. 92 + 71
5. 902 + 701
6. 942 + 781
7. 992 + 781
8. 992 + 8
9. 999 + 8

Learners should recognise strategies like near doubles, bonds to 10/100, as well as the strategy we would employ for both 2999 + 2 and 999 + 8, i.e. counting on.

As a strategy for addition, counting on makes much more sense when looking at numbers as continuous measures, rather than discrete objects. Indeed, not necessarily all continuous models for numbers easily showcase this strategy. For example, using area with Dienes doesn't really work:

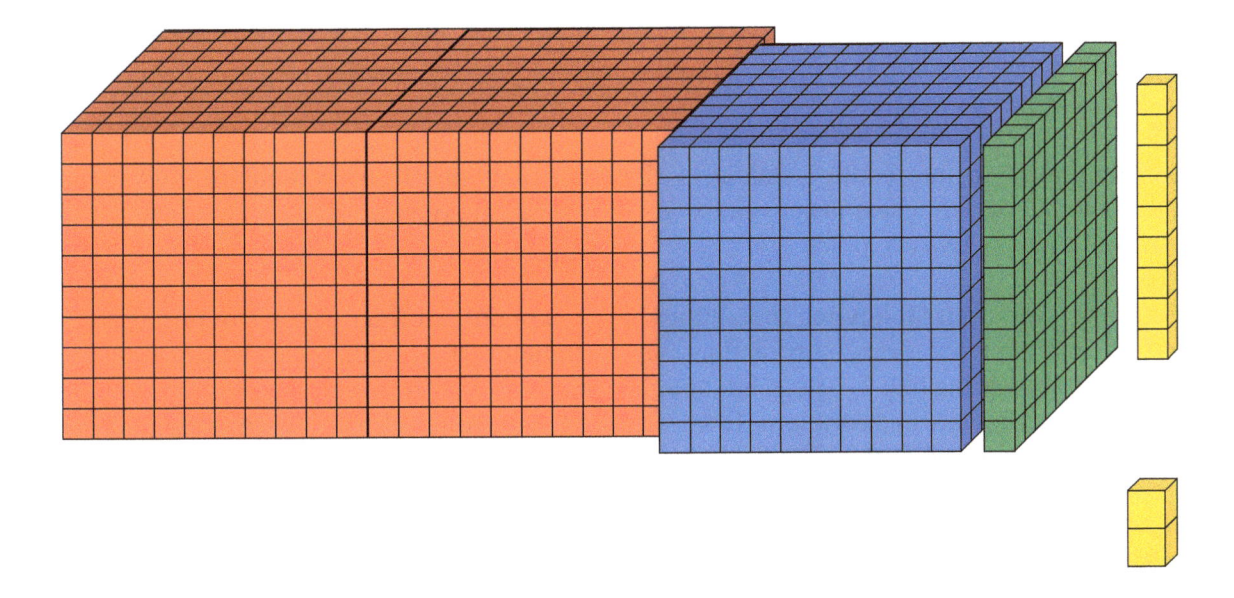

We *can* use this to show that when adding one of the two 1s at the bottom to the row of 1s in the 2999 above, this becomes a row of 10 and can be combined with the other rows of 10 to create a 100 square, which can in turn be combined with the other 100 squares to create a 1000 cube, giving 3001. But this is really only column addition (showing that Dienes can be used nicely instead of place value counters for modelling column addition – particularly for learners whose understanding of place value is still developing). To really see the power of counting on, we need to use a number line, probably with vectors:

We would probably start without the numbers beyond 2999 at first, and maybe even with the 2-vector broken down into two separate one vectors to aid with the counting:

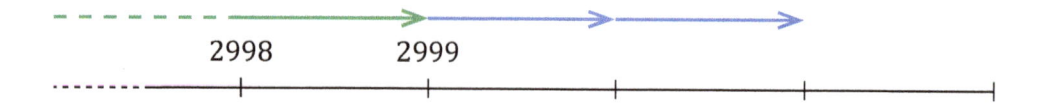

Of course, this is not addition as collection. You cannot 'collect' continuous measures. When we view numbers as continuous, we can think about addition as *connection*. We are connecting one number to the end of the other number. As we can see in the images above, when we show the numbers as vectors, we connect one vector to the end of the next vector to add them. Alternatively (or additionally), we might think about addition as *lengthening/ growing* rather than connecting. If we think about a tree that starts at 40 cm in height and grows by 10 cm, then we can see that to find the new height of the tree, we need to add the 40 and the 10. However, no collection or connection has taken place there.

All other additions can be made sense of in one or more of these three ways. For now though, let us turn our attention to subtraction.

Concept: subtraction

Prerequisites: Numbers.

Linked concepts: Addition, division, equality/equivalence. Many other concepts involve the need to subtract in some capacity.

Subtraction is an interesting concept in that it is mathematically redundant, and yet it speaks to our experience and sensibility from a young age. What makes it even more interesting is that the two are poles apart.

For those who aren't following that, allow me to explain! Subtraction isn't required at all within mathematics. Every subtraction can be thought of as adding the negative of the value. So, something like 7 − 3 can be thought of as 7 + (−3). This makes subtraction redundant as a mathematical operation. However, we tend to meet subtraction very early in our lives as a 'take-away', and very quickly internalise the idea of subtraction with the idea of removal – indeed, for many, the words 'subtraction' and 'take-away' are synonymous. This is what then makes the two seem so separate – as, for many, their idea of addition as collecting or gathering cannot be reconciled with the idea of subtraction as removing things, and so they simply can't accept the idea that subtraction *is* addition. That said, subtraction as the addition of inverses is the simplest and truest model for subtraction. When it comes to making sense of subtraction in a way that dovetails nicely with all types of numbers (as well as when seeing them as either discrete or continuous), there is no other model of subtraction that behaves as consistently. We will look at this again when we come back to addition with negatives, but for now we will turn our attention to other models of subtraction, starting with the one already mentioned – take-away.

Take-away is a reasonable model for subtraction when we limit our attention to positive whole numbers, and it can be extended to other types of numbers (although it requires a bit of creative modelling). However, there is research evidence that suggests that take-away strategies are associated with 'lower ability' and that pupils who are still using take-away strategies for single-digit and double-digit subtractions are likely to struggle with mathematics.[1] In saying that, if this is the model that learners are familiar with, then it can be built upon to explore subtraction with larger numbers.

A take-away model for subtraction works (unsurprisingly) by a reduction of a value (the minuend) by another value (the subtrahend) – for example, 7 − 3 = 4.

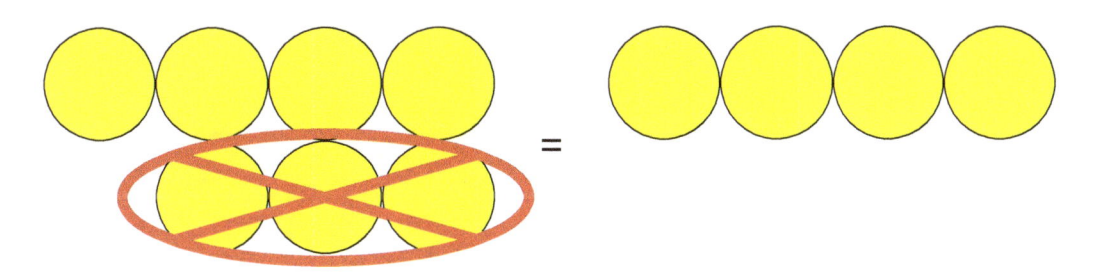

This can then be extended to larger numbers (or smaller numbers, in the case of decimals).

Process: column subtraction

376 − 134

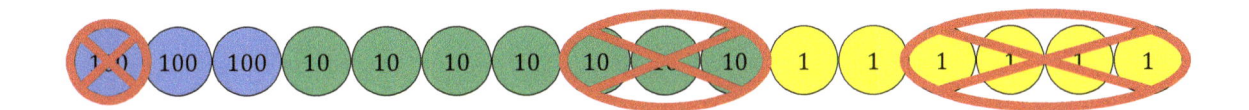

In a take-away of subtraction, the above image shows how the column-subtraction algorithm works. Our minuend is 376 and we remove 134 by removing four 1s from the six 1s to leave two 1s, removing three 10s from the seven 10s to leave four 10s, and then removing one 100 from the three 100s to leave two 100s:

```
  376        376        376
− 134      − 134      − 134
    2         42        242
```

---

1 E. Gray and D. Tall, Duality, Ambiguity and Flexibility: A Proceptual View of Simple Arithmetic, *Journal for Research in Mathematics Education*, 26(2) (1994), 115–141. Available at: https://homepages.warwick.ac.uk/staff/David.Tall/pdfs/dot1994a-gray-jrme.pdf.

Similarly to the column-addition algorithm, it is usual to begin this process with the 1s and work up the columns, but this is not always necessary. The reason why it is usual is that when the value of one or more columns in the subtrahend is greater than the value of the same column(s) in the minuend – for example, 376 – 139:

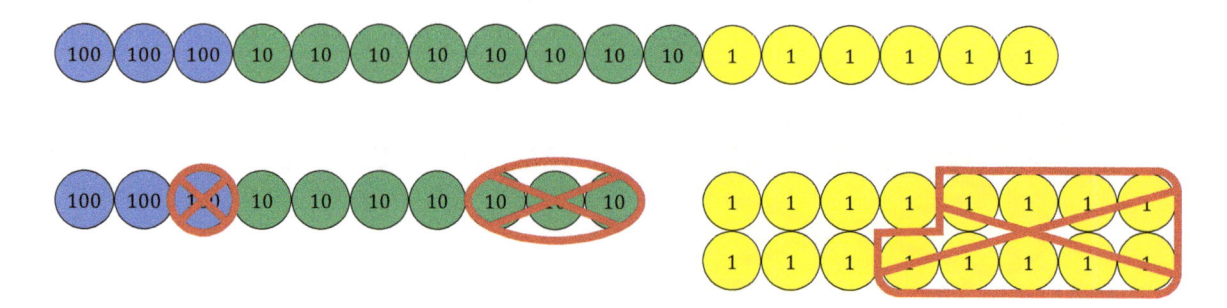

The process here is that I need to remove one 100, three 10s and nine 1s from 376. The issue that arises is that the value of the 1s in the minuend is less than the value of the 1s in the subtrahend. This means I don't have enough 1s to take away nine. The way this is rectified is to exchange one 10 for the equivalent ten 1s in the minuend. This increases the number of 1s available, so that I can remove the required number of 1s. By working from the smallest to largest columns, I can ensure that I don't cause problems by 'taking away' all of one column, meaning I don't have any left if I then need to exchange. The other problem that can be caused is in recording; if I record the result of taking away a number in a higher-valued column and then later find I need to exchange, I will need to edit that recording – for example:

$$\begin{array}{r}376\\-139\\\hline 2\end{array} \qquad \begin{array}{r}376\\-139\\\hline 24\end{array} \qquad \begin{array}{r}3\overset{1}{7}6\\-139\\\hline 247\\3\end{array}$$

In the formal column-subtraction algorithm, it is preferred to exchange from the larger valued column prior to the recording of the subtraction:

$$\begin{array}{r}{}^{6}\\3\overset{1}{7}6\\-139\\\hline 7\end{array} \qquad \begin{array}{r}{}^{6}\\3\overset{1}{7}6\\-139\\\hline 37\end{array} \qquad \begin{array}{r}{}^{6}\\3\overset{1}{7}6\\-139\\\hline 237\end{array}$$

This also means that where a column is empty, meaning there is nothing to exchange, we can carry out multiple exchanges – for example, 306 – 139:

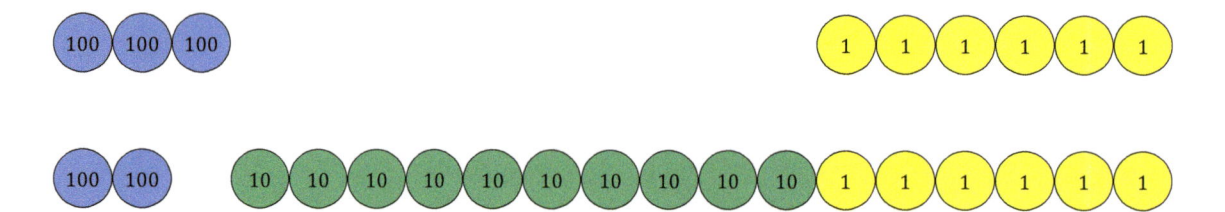

Addition and subtraction

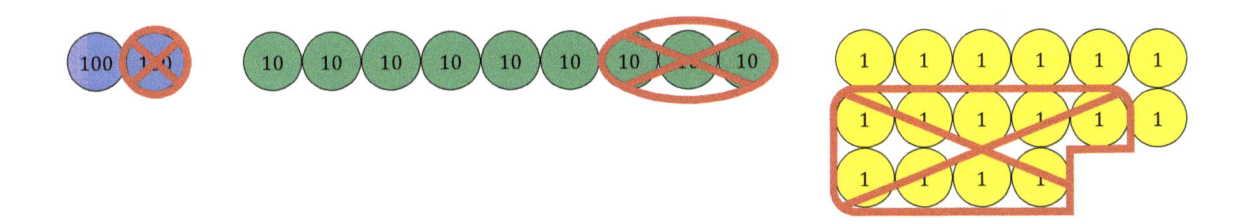

In this we have exchanged one 100 for ten 10s, which then allowed the exchange of one of those 10s for ten 1s. This allowed for the removal of nine of the 1s, as well as three of the 10s.

$$\begin{array}{c} 2 \\ \overset{1}{3}06 \\ -139 \\ \hline \end{array} \qquad \begin{array}{c} 29 \\ \overset{\cancel{1}\,1}{\cancel{3}0\cancel{6}} \\ -139 \\ \hline \end{array} \qquad \begin{array}{c} 29 \\ \overset{\cancel{1}\,1}{\cancel{3}0\cancel{6}} \\ -139 \\ \hline 167 \end{array}$$

A really nice activity for pupils working on column subtraction in this way is to offer a series of subtraction calculations and, before pupils are asked to carry out the calculation, they can first be asked to identify where exchange will be required and where it won't be – even as far as asking pupils to identify which column(s) will require exchange.

There are other models for subtraction, which can suggest other strategies for subtraction calculations. One of these is making sense of subtraction as the difference between two numbers – for example, seeing 7 − 3 as 'the difference between 7 and 3' or 'How much more is 7 than 3?'

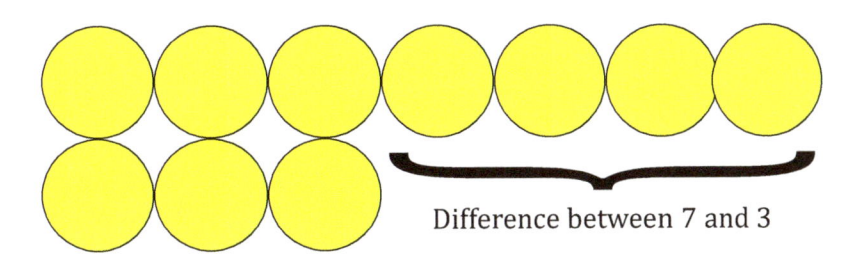

Difference between 7 and 3

One thing that it is definitely worth drawing learners' attention to when looking at subtraction as difference is the fact that difference is maintained when both numbers are increased/decreased by the same amount, i.e. if we take 7 − 3 and increase both values by 2, the difference remains constant:

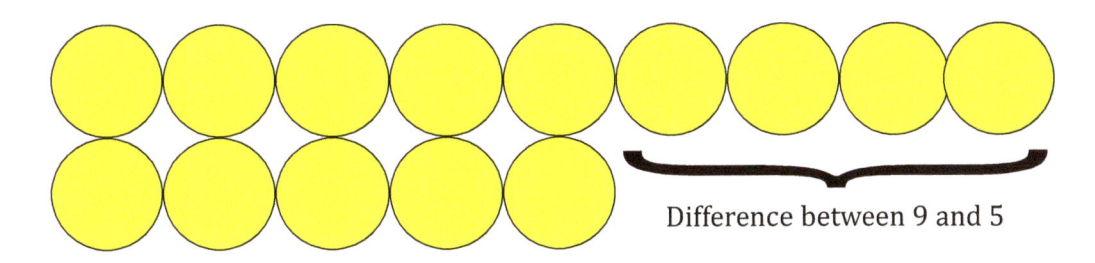

Difference between 9 and 5

This leads to a potentially alternative process for subtraction of larger (or decimal) numbers.

Process: subtraction by equal additions

376 – 139

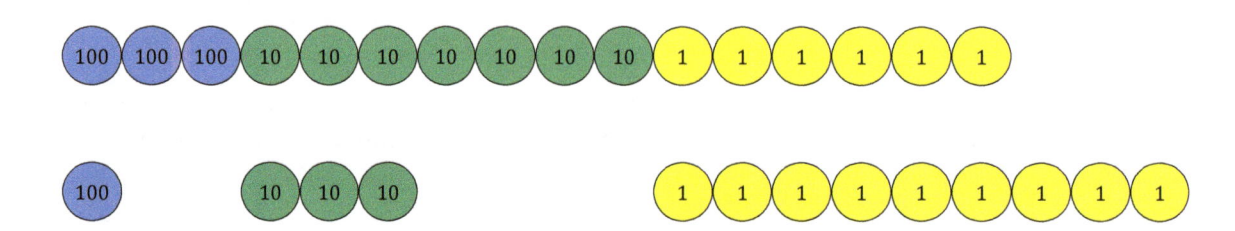

Here we see 376 compared to 139, and we are thinking about, 'How much more is 376 than 139?' Well, we might say, 'there are two more 100s, and four more 10s, but what about the ones?' Of course, we could simply exchange one of the 10s in 376 into 1s – which would be an alternative way of seeing the standard column-subtraction algorithm. However, the fact that we are looking at the difference of two numbers means that we can resolve this situation in an alternative way:

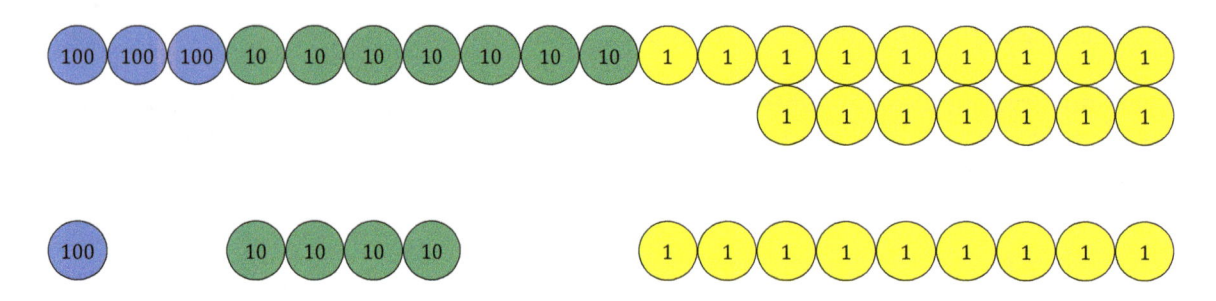

What we see here is that we have increased both values by 10 (so, in effect, changed the calculation to 386 – 149); however, we have added the 10 differently to both numbers. In the upper line we have added ten 1s, but in the bottom line we have added one 10. This allows the question, 'How much more ...' to be answered for each column – there are two more 100s, now only three more 10s and seven more 1s. This can be shown in the numerals as follows:

$$3\ 7\ ^16$$
$$-\ 1\ 4\ 3\ 9$$

$$3\ 7\ ^16$$
$$-1\ 4\ 3\ 9$$
$$2\ 3\ 7$$

The idea of difference can also allow access to other strategies for subtraction. For example, in the subtraction 3002 – 2999, the column-subtraction algorithm often leads to issues, particularly with the need to exchange from the thousands all the way to the ones. Equal additions as a process is also less than ideal, as we end up adding extra 1s, extra 10s and extra 100s. However, we might notice that the numbers simply have a difference of 3:

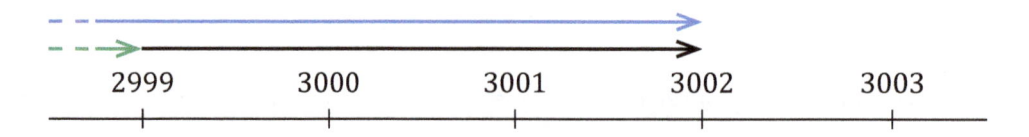

If perhaps our learners don't immediately recognise this, we might suggest simply adding 1 to each number:

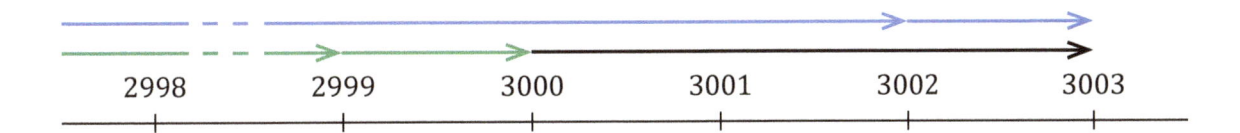

2998   2999   3000   3001   3002   3003

This strategy is typically called 'counting on' and in effect changes the subtraction into an addition, so we answer the question, '2999 add *what* gives 3002?' which we can change into, '3000 add *what* gives 3003?' using the idea of differences remaining constant.

Whilst counting on as a strategy works from the idea of subtraction being the difference between two values, we can also take the opposite approach to recognise a different way of thinking about subtraction, which I call 'counting from' (some call this 'counting back', but this can cause problems when we try and use this strategy with negatives). This model for subtraction shows the subtrahend not as something removed from the minuend but rather as a distance away from the minuend. As a way of making sense of subtraction, counting from is best used in the opposite situation to where we might use counting on, i.e. a question like 3002 − 3. Similarly to counting on, the column-subtraction algorithm and equal-additions algorithm require a lot of work to evaluate this, with multiple exchanges/additions necessary. Instead, seeing the subtraction as 'a distance from' the given value allows us to see something like 3002 − 3 simply as, 'Which number is 3 from 3002?'

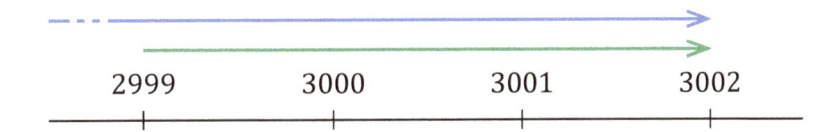

2999   3000   3001   3002

Notice that the 3-vector still points to the right in this subtraction – turning it the other way would mean it represents −3 (although we almost certainly want our learners to appreciate – at some stage – that this is a distinction without a difference).

The final model for subtraction that I want to explore with learners is the idea of 'part-whole'. For something like 7 − 3, this is literally '3 is part of a whole of 7, what is the other part?'

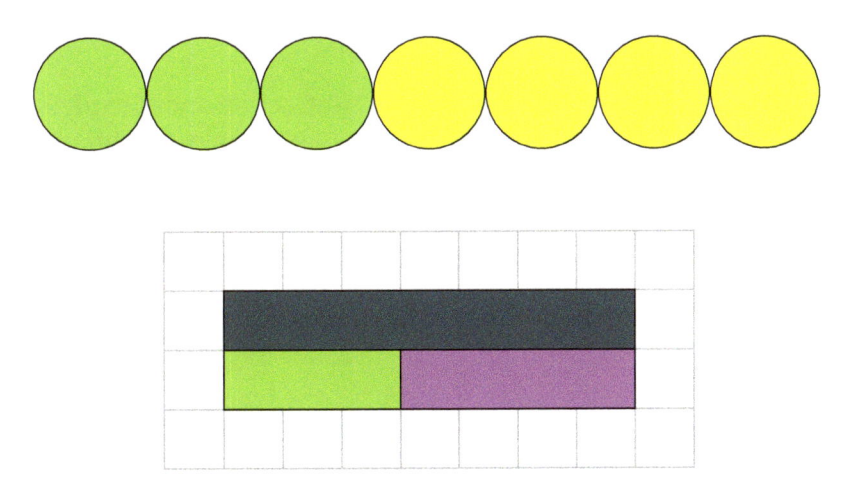

Seeing subtraction as part-whole supports strategies such as 'near-halves' for subtraction, such as for the calculation 72 − 35:

72	
35	?

The logic here is that, by seeing 35 as part of 72, I may notice that 35 is nearly half of 72 (assuming halves are a known fact for pupils). Recognising that the 35 part is one less than half of 72 means I can see that the other part is one more than half of 72, i.e. 37.

Again, a great activity once most/all of these ways of seeing subtraction are secure (or have at least been introduced) is to offer learners different subtractions and ask them to identify suitable strategies before carrying out any calculations:

Write down the strategy you would use to carry out these subtractions:

a   94 − 48   f   904 − 872
b   94 − 88   g   904 − 827
c   94 − 8   h   904 − 897
d   904 − 8   i   940 − 897
e   904 − 800   j   947 − 890

There are also activities that are nice to draw attention to properties of subtraction such as the maintenance of difference:

Given that 87 − 23 = 64, write down:

a   97 − 33   f   94 − 22
b   87 − 33   g   95 − 22
c   97 − 23   h   95 − 23
d   96 − 22   i   950 − 230
e   95 − 21   j   958 − 238

Similar to addition, looking at contexts that lead to subtraction and identifying them with a model of subtraction is also useful, particularly when first exploring different models and then later to test strategy selection:

Steve has 10 sweets. He eats 6 of them. How many sweets does Steve have?

Steve has 10 sweets. David has 6 sweets. How many more sweets does Steve have than David?

Steve runs 10 km in one direction, then 6 km back the way he came. How far is Steve from where he started?

Steve is running a 10 km race. He has run 6 km. How far does he have left to run?

Each of these is solved with the subtraction 10 – 6, but each uses a different model for the subtraction: first take-away, then difference, then counting from, then part-whole.

Having established suitable models for making sense of addition and subtraction, we now need to examine how these work with other types of numbers. These aren't really subconcepts; rather they are the confluence of two concepts – addition with negative numbers or subtraction with fraction, for example. So the rest of the chapter will not so much be looking at subconcepts as much as it will be looking at which models for addition/subtraction work well with which models for numbers.

Concept link: addition of negative numbers

As negatives are best modelled using direction, the combination of vectors for numbers and connection for addition is the model that most closely resembles the one used for positives, with one vector following another:

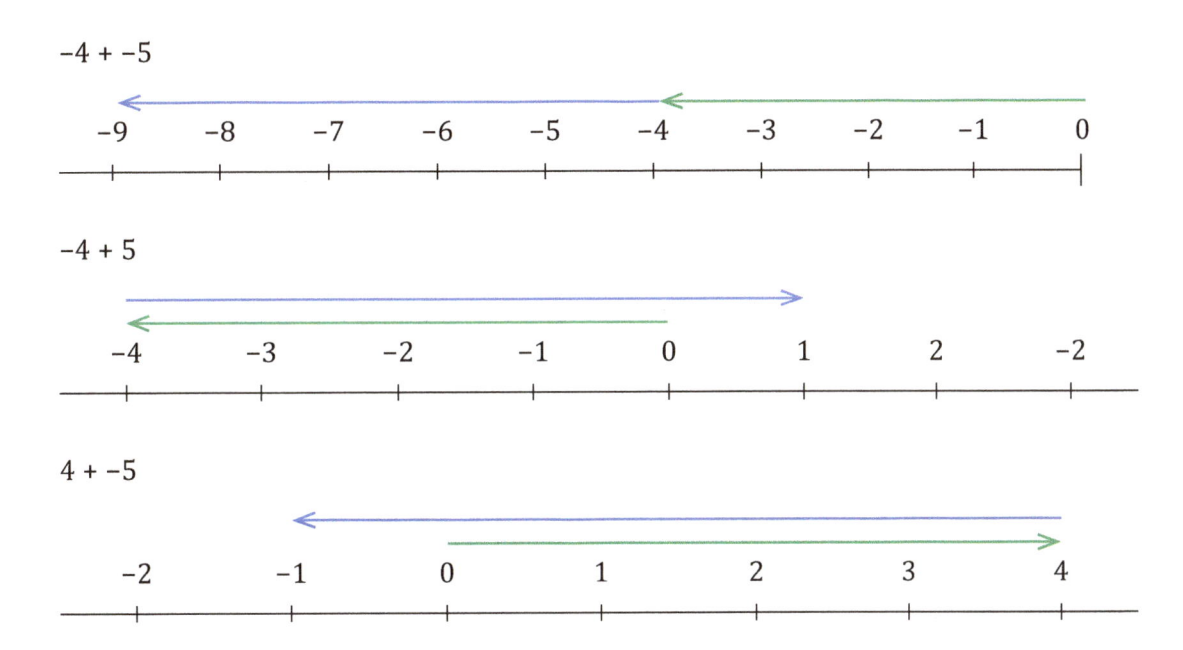

–4 + –5

–4 + 5

4 + –5

Pupils can be encouraged to draw pictures like this, with attention drawn to properties such as –4 + –5 = –(4 + 5), –4 + 5 = 5 + –4 = 5 – 4, and that 4 + –5 = 4 – 5 = –(5 – 4). This is helped a lot if learners are used to seeing number lines in different orientations – we can ask questions like, 'What would the calculation be (in the first picture) if the positive direction was left and not right?' From here we can consider calculations that we wouldn't want to represent on a number line, perhaps with an activity such as this:

Write a different calculation for:

1. 28 + –76
2. –28 + –76
3. 76 + –28
4. 18 + –76
5. –18 + –76
6. 76 + –18
7. –76 + –18
8. –77 + –19

This sort of thing can also be broken down and done using mini whiteboards as multiple-choice questions as well:

Which of these is the same as 65 + −87:

a   −(87 − 65) b   87 − 65 c   (87 + 65)

It is also possible to use a connecting model of addition for negatives when viewing the numbers as discrete objects:

−4 + −5

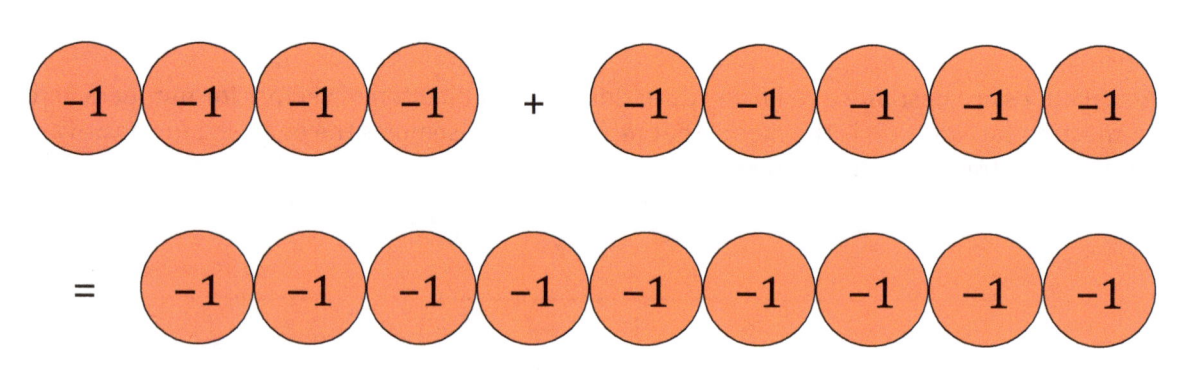

(−1)(−1)(−1)(−1) + (−1)(−1)(−1)(−1)(−1)

= (−1)(−1)(−1)(−1)(−1)(−1)(−1)(−1)(−1)

However, for something like 4 + −5, our idea of collection needs adjustment. Recall that a key point about collection was that the unit had to be the same. At first glance this doesn't appear to be the case:

4 + −5

(1)(1)(1)(1) + (−1)(−1)(−1)(−1)(−1)

= ?

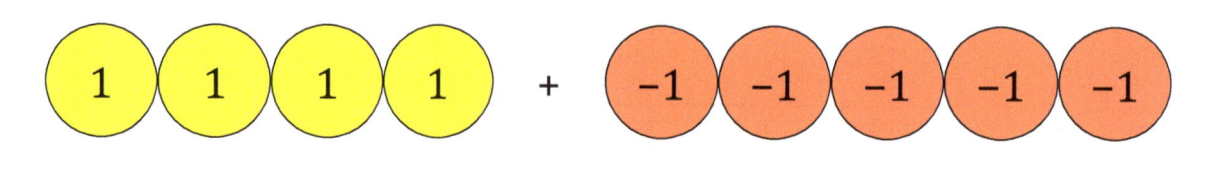

However, we may (and learners may!) remember that when 1s and −1s connect together, they form a zero-pair (page 34). This means we can connect these together!

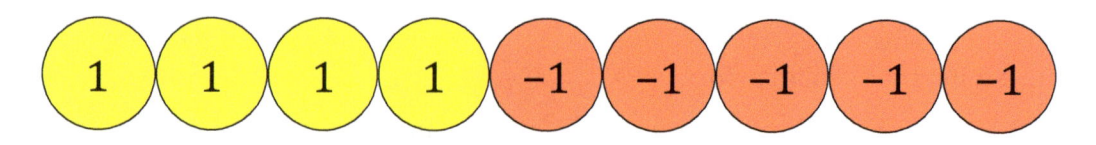

(1)(1)(1)(1)(−1)(−1)(−1)(−1)(−1)

The four 1s will pair with the first four −1s to create four zero-pairs and leave a single −1 counter.

Eventually, we would hope pupils would recognise two generalisations:

1 When adding a positive number and a negative number, if the **magnitude** of the positive number is greater than that of the negative number then the result will be positive. However, if the magnitude of the negative number is greater than that of the positive number, then the result will be negative (and, of course, if the positive and negative numbers are equal in magnitude, the result will be 0).

2 Adding a negative number to any number gives an equivalent result to subtracting a positive number.

In highlighting the first, we might look at vectors of unknown length:

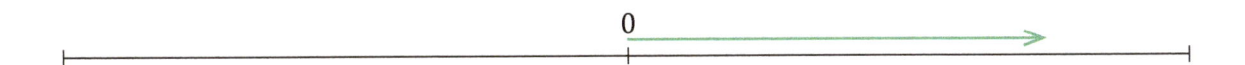

We can ask pupils what must be true about the negative number we would add to this vector if we want the result to be positive, negative or 0, before offering different sums and asking pupils just to identify if the result will be positive, negative or 0 before (or instead of) trying to evaluate the sum. We can do a similar thing starting with a negative vector:

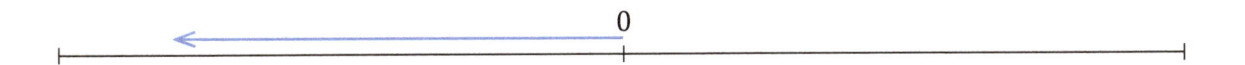

This sort of activity is harder to do with counters, as it is harder to get away from counters taking specific values whilst still justifying needing a certain number of counters. Of course, you can do the same thing with actual values, but then more work is required to see the general idea.

When it comes to the second generalisation that adding a negative number is equivalent to subtracting a positive, this depends, of course, on the model used for subtraction. On page 52 I mentioned that a potential model for subtraction is simply to *define* it as adding the negative. In this case, addition of a negative value would have been tackled before subtraction calculations were considered, and so this generalisation comes as a result of how subtraction has been defined. However, if other models for subtraction have been used, then there will be work to do to ensure pupils become aware of this generalisation. One potential way of highlighting this is to compare additions of negatives with subtractions using vectors:

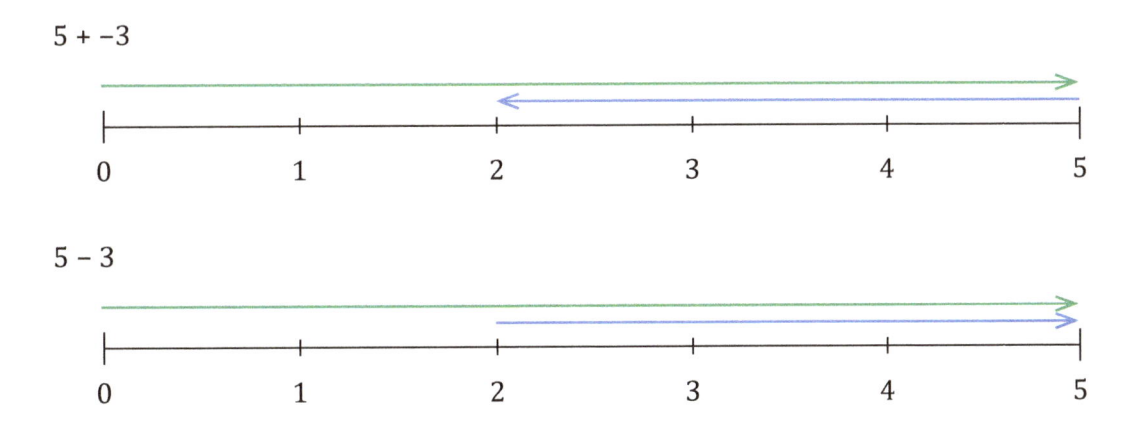

5 + −3

5 − 3

We can ask pupils what is the same and what is different about these two pictures, drawing attention to the fact that although the blue arrows point in different directions, the resultant value is the same in both cases. Of course, this can also be done with vectors of unknown length but it isn't necessary to do this to see the generalisation. In fact, I find that the use of actual values aids pupils in seeing the similarity here in a way that they don't in working with vectors of unknown length.

Ensuring learners recognise this property of addition and its links to subtraction can be very useful prior to exploring the subtraction of a negative number (or subtracting a positive number from a negative). One potential way to introduce these sorts of calculations is to tweak the second generalisation so that instead of it reading 'adding a negative number to any number gives an equivalent result to subtracting a positive number', it reads 'adding the inverse of a number gives an equivalent result to subtracting the number'. Admittedly, this is just a restatement of the idea of using this as a model for subtraction. However, even if pupils haven't been introduced to this as a model for subtraction before now, this may be a good time to introduce it as it significantly simplifies the introduction of subtracting a negative number (or subtraction of a positive from a negative).

Concept link: subtraction and negatives

If pupils are already secure with the relationship between subtracting a number and adding the inverse, then there is little more to do when looking at subtraction than to explore different subtraction calculations, and rewrite them as addition calculations:

Rewrite the following subtraction calculations as additions.

a   5 – –3 (= 5 + 3)

b   –5 – –3 (= –5 + 3)

c   –5 – 3 (= –5 + –3)

d   3 – –5 (= 3 + 5)

e   3 – 5 (= 3 + –5)

f   –3 – –5 (= –3 + 5)

These questions show every possible variation of subtraction involving negatives:

a   Positive minus negative.

b   Negative minus negative (where the result is negative).

c   Negative minus positive.

d   Another example of positive minus negative.

e   Positive minus positive (where the result is negative).

f   Negative minus negative (where the result is positive).

If, however, the link between addition and subtraction of inverse numbers hasn't yet been explored with pupils, then each of these types of calculation will need to be explored within a model for subtraction that pupils are familiar with. The table (on page 64) shows how each might look.

Some notes on these:

1. In the take-away model and part-whole models, all but −5 − −3 require the introduction of zero-pairs.

2. If showing difference using vectors, it is really important to focus on the order of the drawing of the vectors. For example, the vector diagrams for 5 − −3 and −5 − 3 are very similar, and it isn't necessarily clear why one of the orange arrows points to the right, and the other points to the left. The reason is due to the fact that in the diagram for 5 − −3, we draw the 5-vector first and then the −3 vector, and so the resultant takes us from −3 to 5. Contrast this to the −5 − 3 diagram, where we draw the −5 first and then the 3, so the resultant takes us from 3 to −5.

From each of these it is possible to demonstrate why subtraction is the same as adding the inverse. For example, in the take-away or part-whole model for 5 − −3, we might start with 5 and then add 3 zero-pairs. However, because we then remove/compare to the −3, this is just equivalent to adding 3. Similarly, with the difference model, either the vectors or counters can be manipulated by adding the inverse of the subtrahend in to value – in effect, add 3 to both 5 and −3 so that 5 − −3 becomes (5 + 3) − (−3 + 3) = 8 − 0. This is once again using the idea of preservation of difference; by adding (or subtracting when the second number is positive) the same value to both numbers, the difference between them stays the same. Of course, in this case that simply means that we added 3 to the 5! The counting from model is probably the easiest to demonstrate that subtraction is equivalent to adding the inverse. It takes little insight to see that a vector that points one way and ends in the same place as another will leave the same distance as a vector pointing in the opposite direction but that starts where the other ends. In short terms, rotating the subtrahend vector by 180° doesn't affect the result of the calculation.

Conceptual Maths

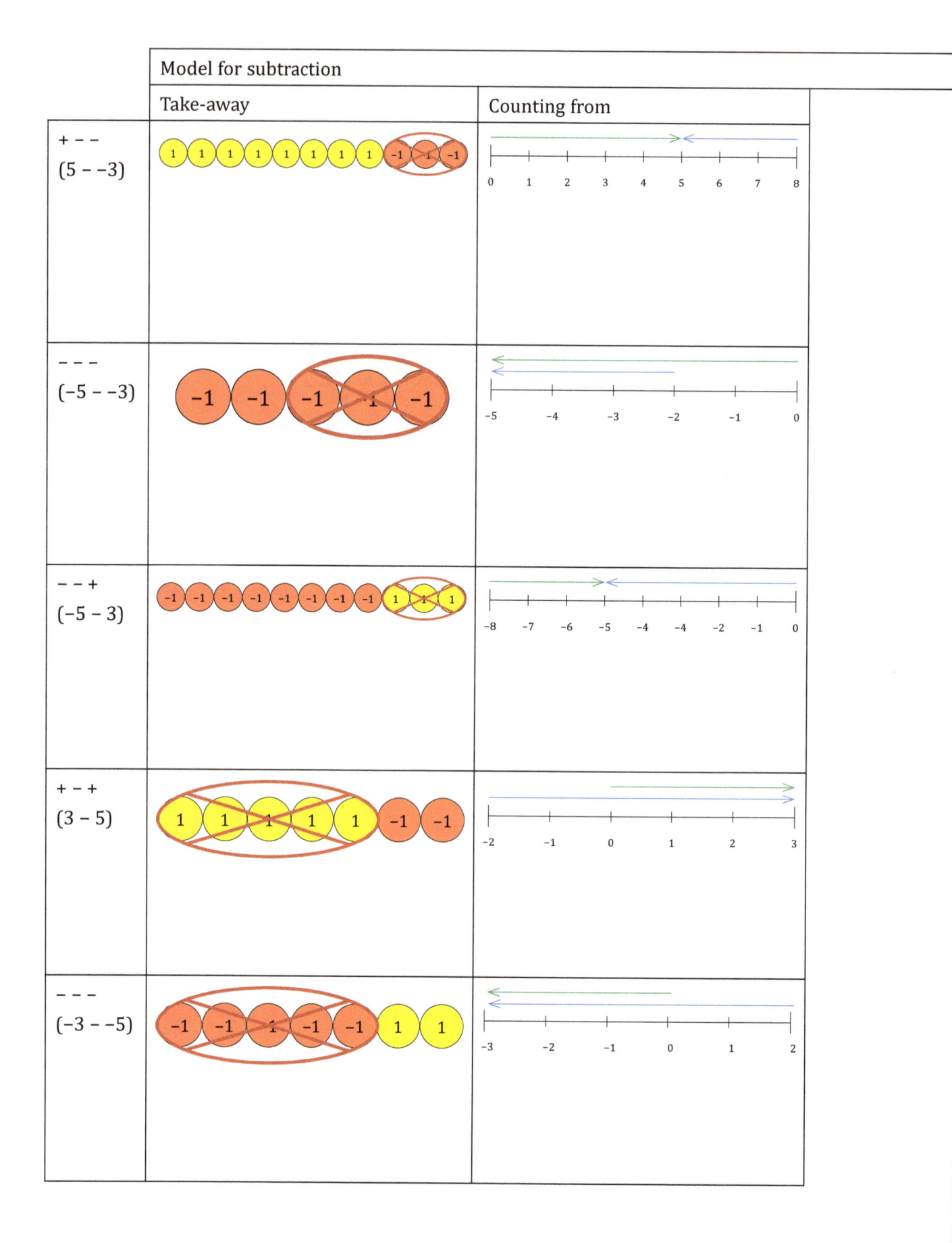

	Model for subtraction	
	Take-away	Counting from
+ – – (5 – –3)	1 1 1 1 1 1 1 1 –1 –1 –1	number line 0 to 8
– – – (–5 – –3)	–1 –1 –1 –1 –1	number line –5 to 0
– – + (–5 – 3)	–1 –1 –1 –1 –1 –1 –1 –1 1 1 1	number line –8 to 0
+ – + (3 – 5)	1 1 1 1 1 –1 –1	number line –2 to 3
– – – (–3 – –5)	–1 –1 –1 –1 –1 1 1	number line –3 to 2

64

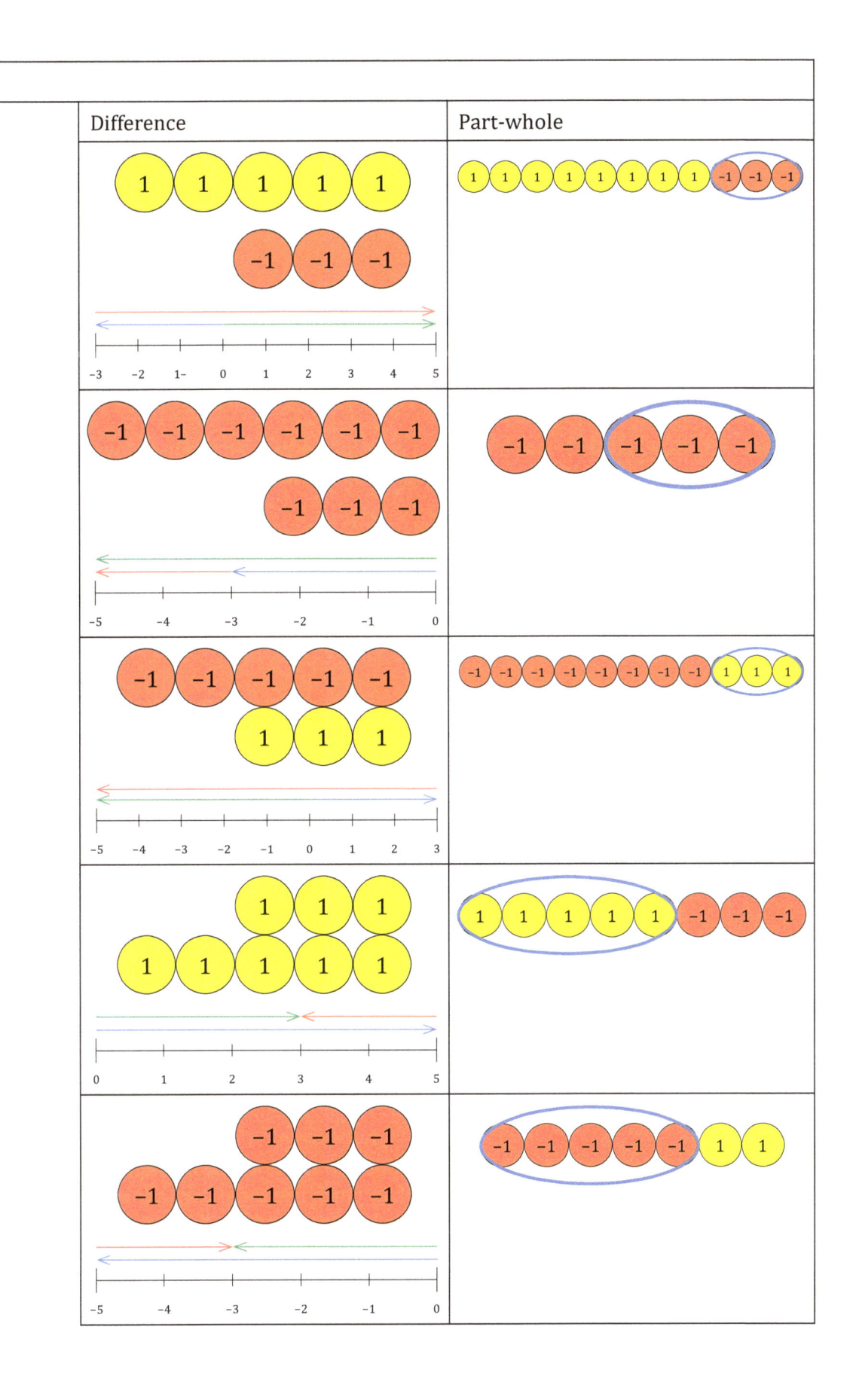

Addition and subtraction

Difference	Part-whole

Practice is then crucial with this idea, from opportunities to rewrite calculations or draw calculations to mixed exercises of addition and subtraction, to working with larger numbers (so that drawing the diagram accurately becomes prohibitive). We can also include questions like those we have seen before – for example:

If −50 − 70 = −120 what is:

a   −51 − 69

b   −51 − 71

c   −71 − 51

d   −73 − 51

e   −73 − 49

Using the numbers −3, −2, −1, 0, 1, 2, 3 at most once each, make each equation below true. How many ways can you find? What do you notice about them?

□ + □ = □   □ − □ = □

Use the numbers 1 to 6 to fill in the boxes so that the first two calculations have the same answer and the last one gives the largest answer.

−□ + □ =   −□ − □ =   −□ − −□ =

How many ways can you find?

Can you do it with the numbers −6 to −1?

There is also a very nice activity from NRICH called 'Negative Dice':[2]

A rather strange dice has normal faces for the even numbers, but the odd numbers are negative (i.e. −1, −3 and −5). Which of these totals cannot be scored from rolling two dice?

a   3   b   7   c   8

And we can add to this with some extra prompts, such as those below:

What other totals can't you get from rolling two of these dice? What about if you have three of these dice? What about if the even numbers are negative but the odd numbers aren't?

From here we can explore addition and subtraction applied to other types of numbers, including algebraic terms and expressions. They all work in much the same way, adhering to the same models depending on whether we choose to view the numbers as discrete or continuous.

---

[2]   See https://nrich.maths.org/2462.

Addition and subtraction

Concept link: adding/subtracting fractions

We can see the addition of fractions in the same way as we have seen addition of whole numbers:

1   If we choose to view the fractions as discrete, then they can be added, provided they have the same unit value.

2   If we choose to view the fractions as continuous, then they can be connected together (or one fraction can be lengthened by another).

If we view the fractions as discrete, then we have this sort of image:

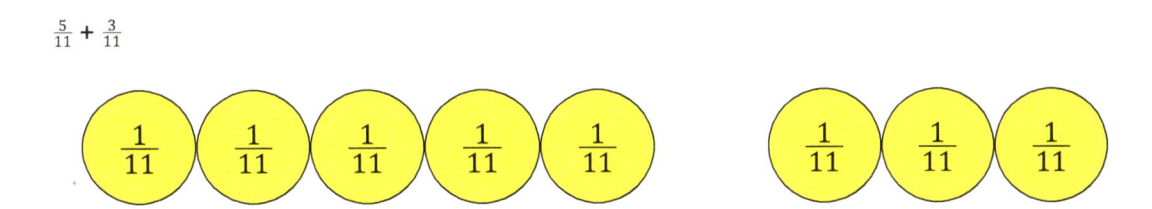

$\frac{5}{11} + \frac{3}{11}$

These have the same unit value, so I can add them together to create $\frac{8}{11}$.

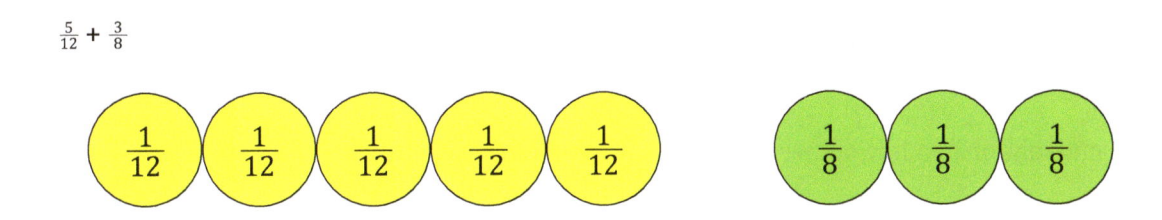

$\frac{5}{12} + \frac{3}{8}$

These do not add in their current form (which is the phrase I use with pupils), because they do not have the same unit value. However, provided pupils have studied equivalent fractions, we can exchange each of the twelfths for $\frac{2}{24}$ and each of the eighths for $\frac{3}{24}$ (as mentioned in Chapter 1, pupils need to know these relationships beforehand, as there is nothing in the representation to suggest it).

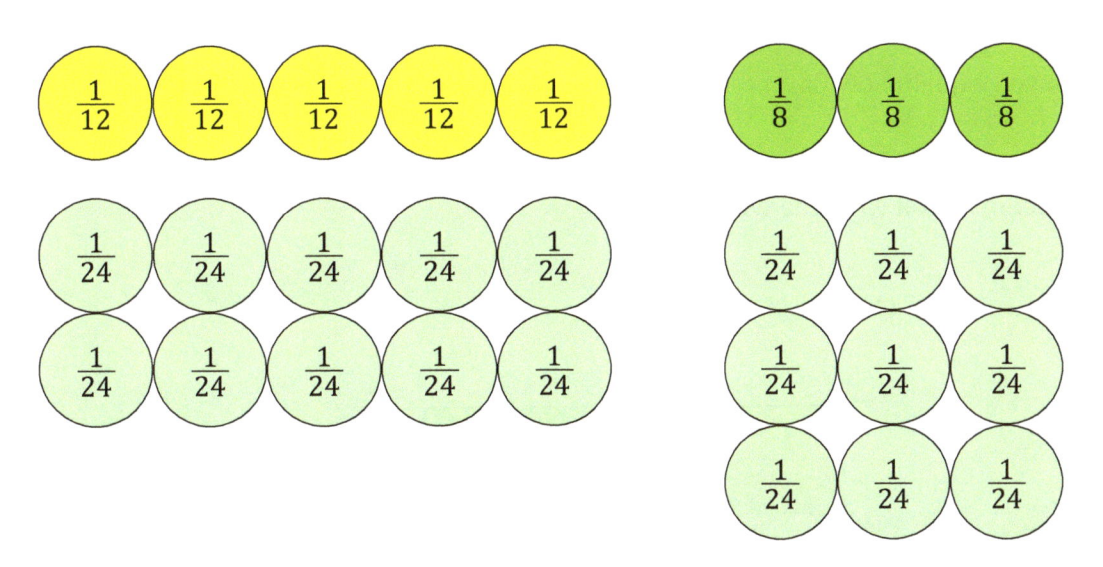

Now we do have objects with the same unit value, so we can add them together.

When it comes to subtraction, if viewing the fractions as discrete objects, then any of the models we have used counters with previously can be made to work here. However, I find the difference model to be the most natural. Looking at the above, we can see a difference model would work nicely – if we changed the calculation from $\frac{5}{12} + \frac{3}{8}$ to $\frac{5}{12} + \frac{3}{8}$ then we can see that the difference between $\frac{5}{12}$ and $\frac{3}{8}$ is $\frac{1}{24}$. The take-away and part-whole model is slightly harder because we don't actually *see* the $\frac{3}{8}$ in this model – it is the amount I remove (in take-away) and isn't obviously part of either $\frac{5}{12}$ or $\frac{10}{24}$, and so I would need to really *know* that $\frac{3}{8} = \frac{9}{24}$.

A great activity once pupils have some experience thinking about addition and subtraction of fractions like this is to get pupils to judge whether a fraction can be evaluated in its current form or not:

State whether each of these calculations can be evaluated fully in its current form. If it can, then evaluate it fully.

a $\quad \frac{4}{13} + \frac{7}{11} + \frac{9}{13}$ d $\quad -\frac{4}{13} + \frac{7}{11} - \frac{9}{13}$ g $\quad \frac{4}{11} - \frac{7}{11} + \frac{9}{13}$ j $\quad -\frac{4}{11} - \frac{7}{11} - \frac{9}{13}$

b $\quad \frac{4}{13} - \frac{7}{11} + \frac{9}{13}$ e $\quad -\frac{4}{13} - \frac{7}{11} + \frac{9}{13}$ h $\quad \frac{4}{11} + \frac{7}{11} - \frac{9}{13}$

c $\quad \frac{4}{13} + \frac{7}{11} - \frac{9}{13}$ f $\quad \frac{4}{11} + \frac{7}{11} + \frac{9}{13}$ i $\quad -\frac{4}{11} + \frac{7}{11} - \frac{9}{13}$

Notice that upon first glance a learner might think that none of the calculations can be evaluated in their current form, but in fact many of them can be, provided pupils understand enough about the relationship between fraction families and 1 that they can immediately recognise that something like $1 + \frac{7}{11} = 1\frac{7}{11}$ and $1 - \frac{7}{11} = \frac{4}{11}$.

Alternatively, or in addition, we can offer learners tasks like this:

Fill in the missing numerators/denominators so that the calculations can be evaluated in their current form. How many different ways can you complete each one?

$\frac{\square}{15} + \frac{\square}{12} + \frac{\square}{\square}$ $\frac{\square}{15} + \frac{\square}{12} + \frac{\square}{\square}$

$\frac{\square}{15} + \frac{\square}{12} + \frac{\square}{\square}$ $\frac{\square}{15} + \frac{\square}{12} + \frac{\square}{\square}$

Mark says '$\frac{1}{5} + \frac{6}{15}$ cannot be evaluated completely in its current form.'

Carol says 'That may be true, but I can still evaluate it, the answer is $\frac{3}{5}$.'

Can you explain how Carol arrived at her answer?

If we choose to view the fractions as continuous, then the real focus when adding/subtracting fractions is on what the whole will be:

$\frac{5}{11} + \frac{3}{11}$

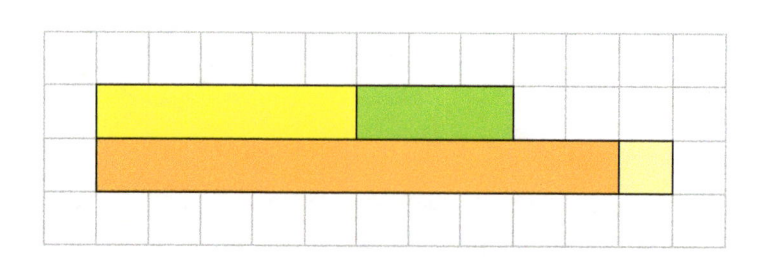

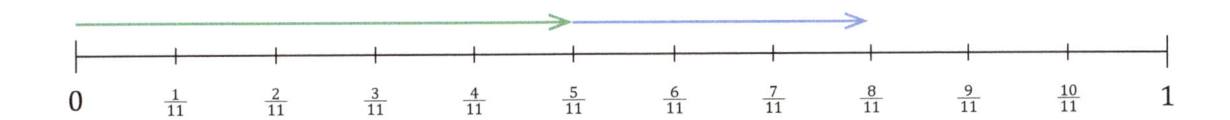

Addition and subtraction

In both cases we can see that a whole that can be partitioned into 11 equal-sized pieces can allow us to show both $\frac{5}{11}$ and $\frac{3}{11}$, and so connect them together.

$\frac{5}{12} + \frac{3}{8}$

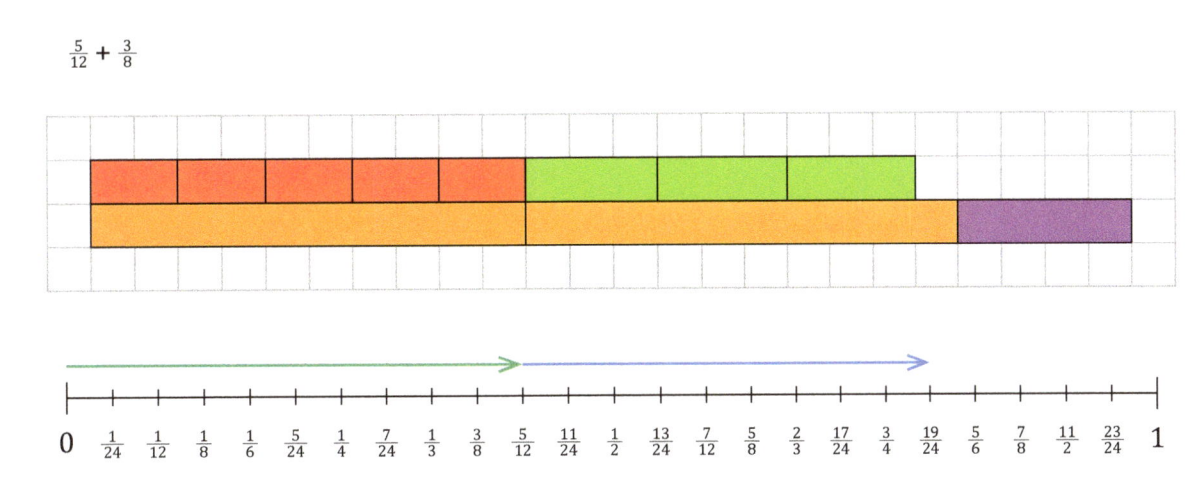

This time a whole that can be partitioned into 24 equal-sized pieces can allow us to show both $\frac{5}{12}$ and $\frac{3}{8}$. It is easier to see in these representations why the useful denominator is 24 – because it is the smallest fraction family that can allow us to represent both twelfths and eighths and so connect a number of twelfths and a number of eighths together. We can then model this as seeing $\frac{5}{12}$ as $\frac{10}{24}$ and $\frac{3}{8}$ as $\frac{9}{24}$. We can see this in the Cuisenaire rods directly, and can see the same thing using vectors by comparing the simplified and unsimplified number line:

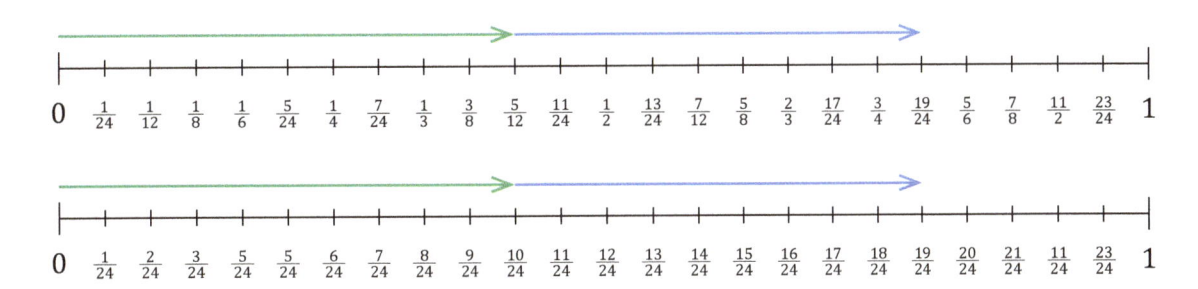

Subtraction, again, is best seen by looking at the difference between two values (or with vectors, counting from):

$\frac{5}{11} - \frac{3}{11}$

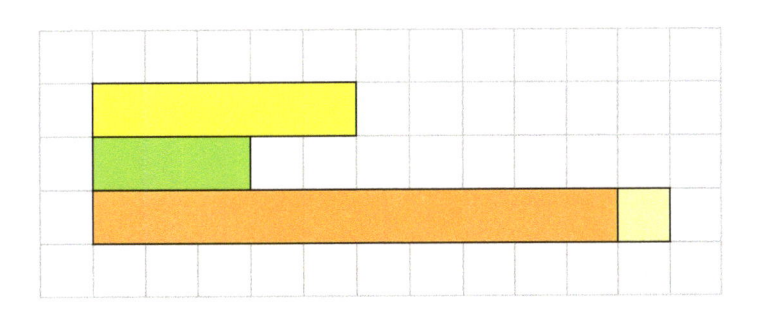

$\frac{5}{12} - \frac{3}{8}$

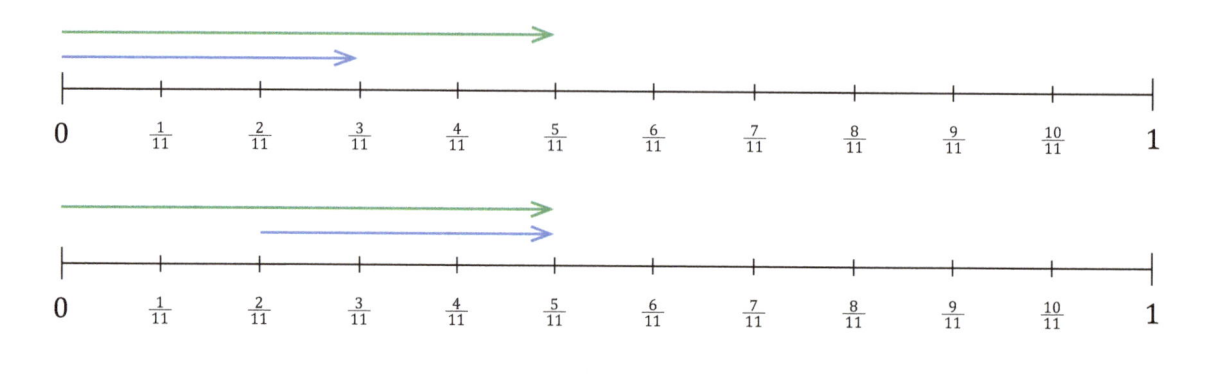

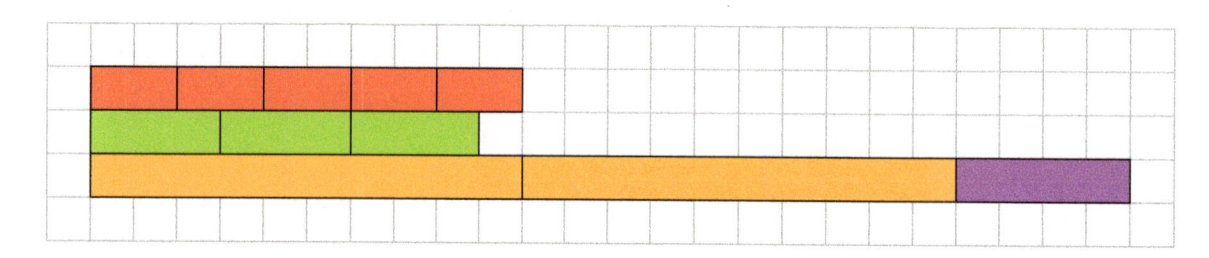

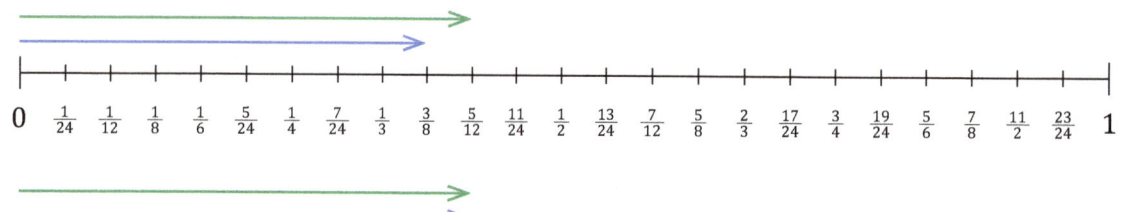

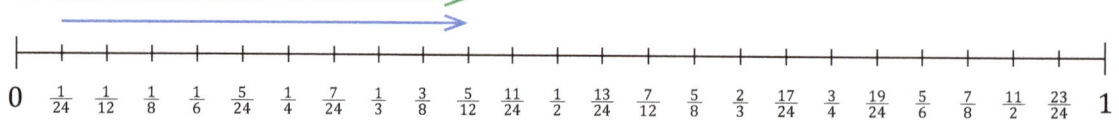

Once learners are beginning to achieve fluency with this using smaller whole numbers, there are lots of ways to mix it up and make the practice something that they have to think about. This will really draw their attention to the multiplicative nature of the relationship between the numerator and denominator:

Work out the following:

a $\quad \dfrac{7}{2001} + \dfrac{3}{10005}$

b $\quad \dfrac{7}{0.3} + \dfrac{3}{0.1}$

c $\quad \dfrac{7}{2^{10}} + \dfrac{3}{2^9}$

d $\quad \dfrac{7}{\frac{3}{5}} + \dfrac{3}{\frac{1}{5}}$

e $\quad \dfrac{7}{\frac{1}{5}} - \dfrac{3}{\frac{3}{5}}$

We can also bring in questions that require a bit of reasoning:

Work out which fractions are missing:

a $\quad \frac{1}{6} + \frac{\square}{\square} = \frac{5}{16}$

b $\quad \frac{5}{6} - \frac{\square}{\square} = \frac{5}{16}$

c $\quad \frac{5}{6} - \frac{\square}{\square} = \frac{7}{16}$

d $\quad \frac{5}{6} + \frac{\square}{\square} = 1\frac{7}{16}$

e $\quad 1\frac{5}{6} - \frac{\square}{\square} = 1\frac{7}{16}$

f $\quad 1\frac{5}{12} - \frac{\square}{\square} = 1\frac{7}{16}$

g $\quad 1\frac{5}{16} + \frac{\square}{\square} = 2\frac{7}{12}$

Fill in the missing boxes so that each block is the sum of the two below it.

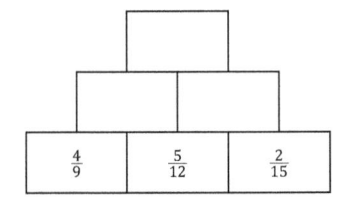

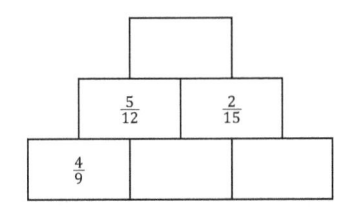

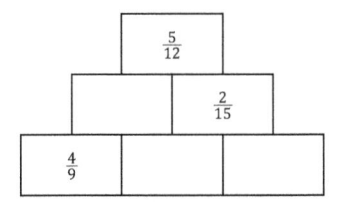

And, of course, situations where a judgement has to be made as to whether we are adding or subtracting (notice the redundant number in the first one):

1. The capacity of the two milk pitchers on the counter is $\frac{9}{10}$ litre each. One pitcher has $\frac{3}{8}$ of a litre of milk in it and the other pitcher has $\frac{5}{12}$ of a litre milk in it. How much milk is there altogether?

2. Each large cookie is $\frac{5}{6}$ oz and each small cookie is $\frac{4}{9}$ oz. What is the total weight of 2 large cookies and 1 small cookie?

3. There is a bag of sugar in the storage room. The bag contained $\frac{9}{10}$ kilograms of sugar. The chef filled up an empty can with $\frac{1}{8}$ kilogram of sugar and then used $\frac{3}{5}$ of a kilogram of sugar for a cake. How much sugar was left in the bag?

There are also some great tasks out there for prompting inquiry into fraction addition, like these from the late, great Don Steward's Median blog:[3]

What is the pattern in the questions?

$$\frac{1}{3} + \frac{1}{6}$$

$$\frac{1}{2} + \frac{1}{?}$$

$$\frac{1}{4} + \frac{1}{12}$$

$$\frac{1}{5} + \frac{1}{20}$$

$$\frac{1}{6} + \frac{1}{??}$$

$$\frac{1}{7} + \frac{1}{??}$$

$$\frac{1}{8} + \frac{1}{??}$$

What is the pattern in the results?

---

3 D. Steward, Fraction Addition Denominators Multiples, *Median* [blog] (12 May 2017). Available at: https://donsteward.blogspot.com/2017/05/fraction-addition-denominators-multiples.html; D. Steward, Four Consecutive Numbers, *Median* [blog] (29 April 2017). Available at: https://donsteward.blogspot.com/2017/04/four-consecutive-numbers.html.

Four consecutive numbers

$\frac{\square}{\square} + \frac{\square}{\square}$ Where would you place the digits 2, 3, 4 and 5 so that the fraction sum has the smallest possible answer?

$\frac{\square}{\square} + \frac{\square}{\square}$ Which four consecutive numbers would you use so that the smallest possible total is greater than 1.5?

$\frac{\square}{\square} + \frac{\square}{\square}$ Which four consecutive numbers would you use so that the smallest possible total is greater than 1.7?

$\frac{\square}{\square} + \frac{\square}{\square}$ Which four consecutive numbers would you use so that the smallest possible total is greater than 1.9?

Or this (based on the type of task available at Open Middle[4]):

Using the digits 1 to 9 at most once each, fill in the boxes to make the equation true.

$\frac{\square}{\square} + \frac{\square}{\square} = \frac{\square}{\square} - \frac{\square}{\square}$

Concept link: adding and subtracting surds

Of course, there are going to be huge similarities between how we think about adding and subtracting surds compared with fractions and even integers. This is because our understanding of 'number' and our understanding of 'addition' (or 'subtraction') doesn't really need to change to accommodate surds. Certain representations have to be used with more care, and certain manipulatives may not be usable in certain circumstances (as we will see), but, ultimately, collecting/connecting/lengthening will work for addition, and our models for subtraction will work equally well with surds as they have previously:

$5\sqrt{2} + 3\sqrt{2}$

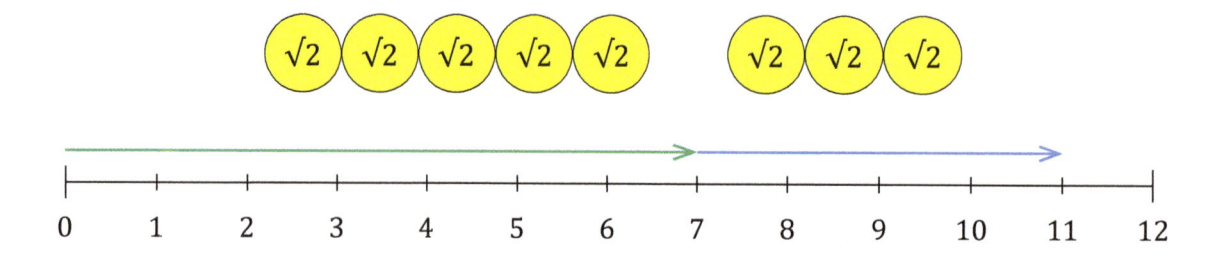

The obvious disadvantage with connecting is that you need to know roughly how the size of each number compares to 1, at least if you want to represent them on a number line scaled in 1s. However, we could change the scale on the number line to $\sqrt{2}$s:

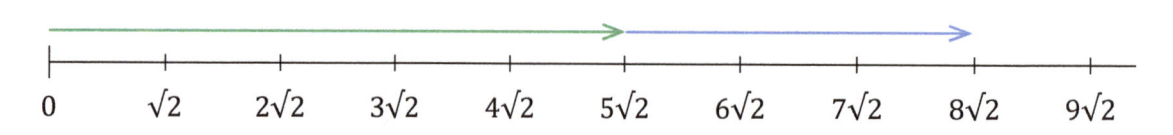

---

4   See https://www.openmiddle.com/.

Or even an unscaled number line:

Although with the number line scaled in 1s, and on the unscaled number line, it isn't clear that the result is $8\sqrt{2}$. For this reason, I prefer using counters to model surd calculations. Number lines also suffer when the surds to be added are different; because there isn't a nice relationship between most surd values, you can't really scale the number line in any useful way:

$5\sqrt{2}+3\sqrt{3}$

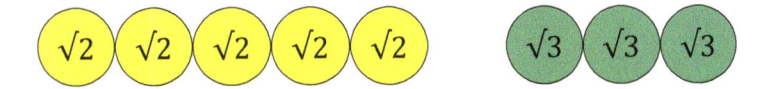

In this representation it is relatively clear that there is no simpler expression than to simply write this number as $5\sqrt{2} + 3\sqrt{3}$; however, if we look at this on a number line, the situation is not so clear:

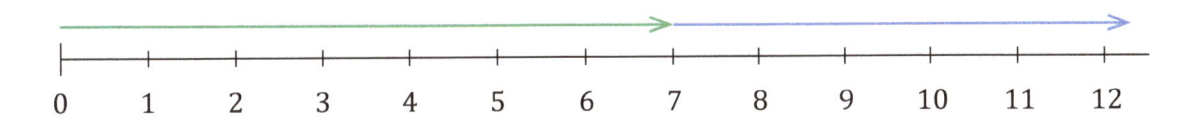

and the situation isn't made better by trying to rescale the number line, because $\sqrt{2}$ and $\sqrt{3}$ are not well related. Cuisenaire rods also cannot be used, as they rely on rational multiplicative relationships between the values, of the rods.

$5\sqrt{2}+3\sqrt{8}$

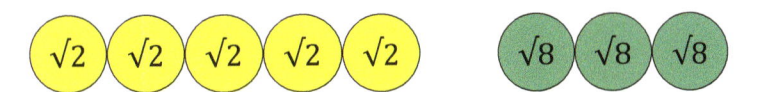

At first glance this looks no better than the previous calculation. However, if pupils have previously studied equivalent surds, we can highlight that $\sqrt{8} = 2\sqrt{2}$, and thus we can exchange each of the $\sqrt{8}$s:

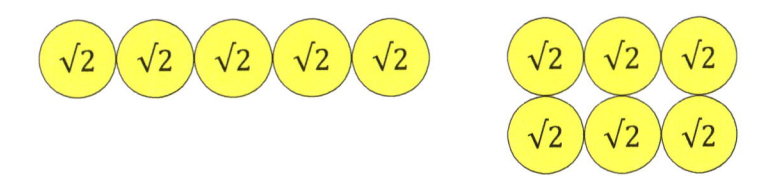

This leads to the conclusion that this sum is $11\sqrt{2}$. It is much more difficult to recognise this on a number line – you basically have to draw the $3\sqrt{8}$ as $6\sqrt{2}$ immediately.

When it comes to subtraction, any of the models that work with discrete representations will work – I can start with 5√2 and 'take away' 3√2, or I can see 3√2 as part of 5√2 (part-whole model) or I can compare 5√2 and 3√2. However, difference is probably the best model here, as we can't really apply the ideas of 'take-away' or 'part-whole' to the calculation 5√2 – 3√3 (although we can with 5√2 – 3√8 with the use of exchange and introduction of a zero-pair).

Once pupils are comfortable simplifying sums and differences of surd expressions (including expressions involving integer/rational numbers and surds), then there are some nice opportunities to practise with surds. One of my favourites is to ask pupils to find the nth terms of linear sequences with a common difference that is a surd value:

Find the nth term of these sequences:
a √5, 2√5, 3√5, 4√5, ...
b 3, 3 + √5, 3 + 2√5, 3 + 3√5, ...
c 3, 5 + √5, 7 + 2√5, 9 + 3√5, ...
d √3, √3 + √5, √3 + 2√5, √3 + 3√5, ...
e 1 + √3, 1 + √3 + √5, 1 + √3 + 2√5, 1 + √3 + 3√5
f 1 + √3, 1 + 2√3 + √5, 1 + 3√3 + 2√5, 1 + 4√3 + 3√5
g 1 + √3, 1 + 2√3 – √5, 1 + 3√3 – 2√5, 1 + 4√3 – 3√5
h 1 + √3, 1 – √5, 1 – √3 – 2√5, 1 – 2√3 – 3√5

Other opportunities to interweave include working with perimeter, finding median or mean, and surd angle values (and pretty much any other mathematical context where addition is used!). Also nice are activities such as these:

In each triangle, the expression on each line is the sum of the expressions in the two red circles at the end of the line.

Find the missing values in these TriProds:

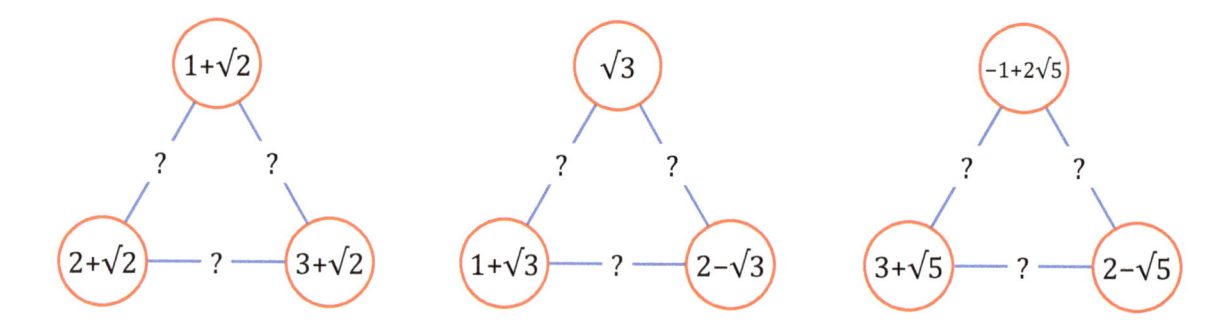

Addition and subtraction

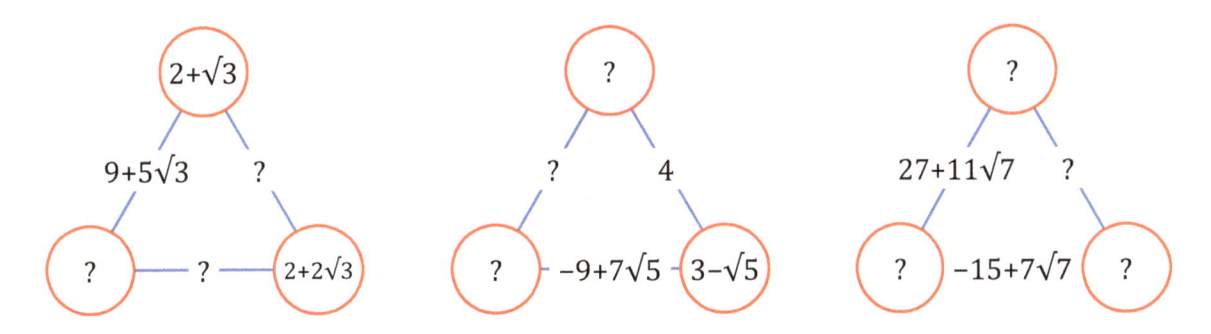

[Triangle puzzle 1: top circle 2+√3; left side 9+5√3; right side ?; bottom: ? — ? — 2+2√3]

[Triangle puzzle 2: top circle ?; left side ?; right side 4; bottom: ? — -9+7√5 — 3-√5]

[Triangle puzzle 3: top circle ?; left side 27+11√7; right side ?; bottom: ? — -15+7√7 — ?]

(This was adapted from the Further Maths resource TriProds: Surds[5])

Concept link: adding and subtracting algebra

As before, the addition and subtraction of algebraic expressions will work in the same way as other additions and subtractions, depending on the way we choose to view the 'numbers', as either discrete objects or continuous measures:

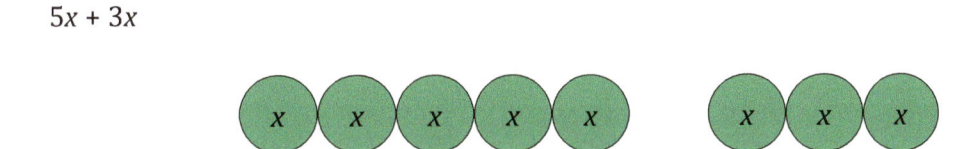

$5x + 3x$

[Five green counters labelled x, then three green counters labelled x]

Of course, this is just showing another example of algebra capturing the general case for what happens with numbers. We have seen counters used to represent 1, 10, 100, 0.1, $\frac{1}{11}$ and even √2, but for all values of the counter, if we have 5 of them, and then add 3 more of them, we end up with 8 of them.

Other representations of the same sum:

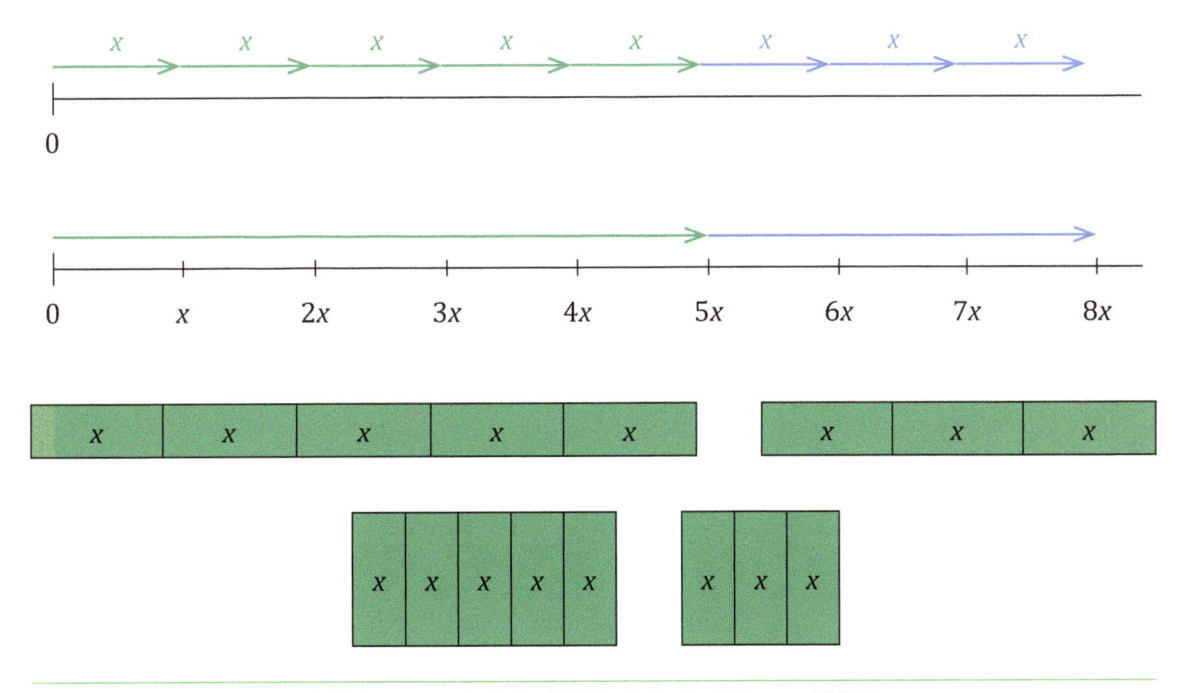

[Number line showing 8 jumps of x from 0]

[Number line marked 0, x, 2x, 3x, 4x, 5x, 6x, 7x, 8x with arrows showing 5x then 3x]

[Bar model: row of 5 x-blocks and row of 3 x-blocks]

[Vertical bar model: 5 x-columns and 3 x-columns]

---
5 See https://www.dropbox.com/s/sh0kaj0wm1u6sbg/TriProds%20Surds_Teacher%20notes.pdf?dl=0#.

The last of these is interesting – they are created using algebra tiles that are like a general base Cuisenaire rod. A typical set includes a 1 tile (where the length of the x tile is not an integer length of the 1 tile) as well as an x^2 tile. There are two ways we can see $5x + 3x$ using these as continuous measures. The first uses the length to represent the value, so we have a length of $5x$ and a length of $3x$ to be connected together. The second uses area as the measure – the first rectangle has a length of 5 and a width of x, whilst the second has a length of 3 and width of x, and when connected together the resulting rectangle has a length of 8 and a width of x. This is a key view of multiplication (as we shall see in the next chapter) and can really help with exploring laws of arithmetic and order of operations (which we will see in Chapter 5).

Different variables can also be added:

$3x + 5y + 2x + y$

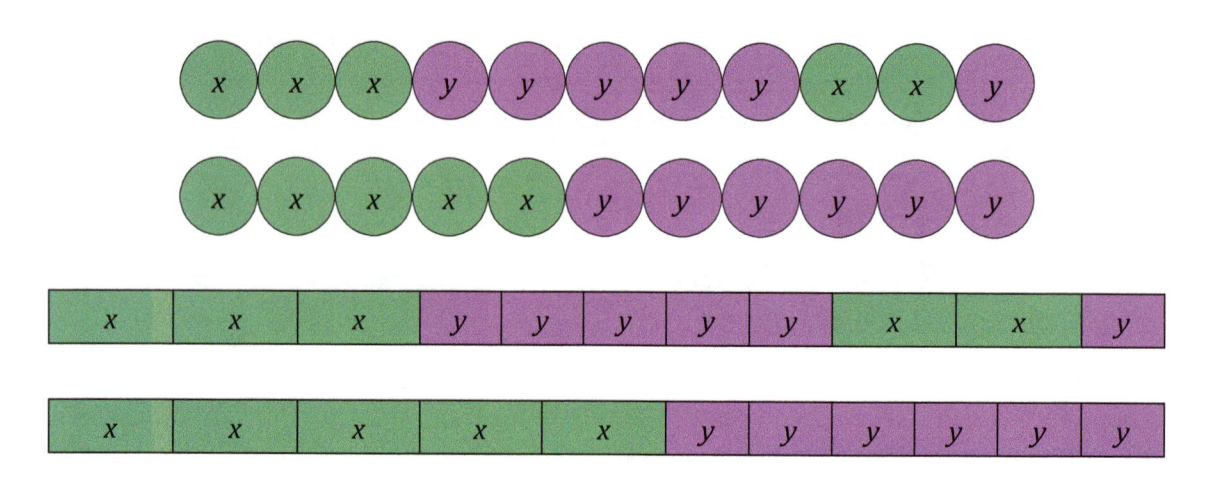

When it comes to subtraction, as always, it depends on the model used. This is an area where seeing subtraction as adding the inverse can be particular helpful:

$5x - 3x$

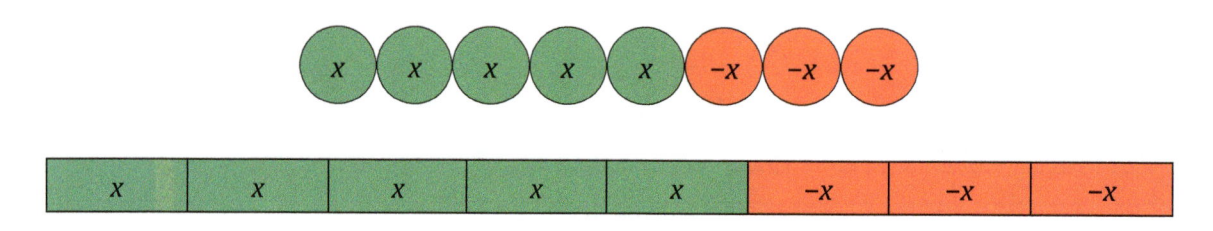

Whilst other models of subtraction will work with simple expressions, seeing $5x - 3x$ as having $5x$ and $-3x$ can be very helpful when it comes to higher operations with algebra.

Similarly to when we looked at adding and subtracting fractions, it is worth bringing in activities here to highlight when expressions will simplify and when they won't:

Will it simplify?

$3p + 3p$	$5y^2 + 2y^2$	$5y^{-2} + 2y^{-3} - y$
$3p - 3p$	$-5y^2 + 2y^2$	$5y^{-4} + 2y^{-4} - y^{-4}$
$3p - 2p$	$5xy + 2yx$	$5y^{-4.7} + 2y^{-4.7} - y^{-4.7}$
$3p - 2y$	$5y^{-2} + 2y^2$	$5y^{\frac{4}{7}} + 2y^{\frac{4}{7}} - y^{\frac{4}{7}}$
$5y - 2y$	$5y^{-2} + 2y^{-2}$	$5x^{\frac{4}{7}} + 2y^{\frac{4}{7}} - z^{\frac{4}{7}}$
$5y^2 - 2y$	$5y^{-2} + 2z^{-2}$	
$5y^2 - 2y^2$	$5y^{-2} + 2y^{-3}$	

As well as looking at carefully sequenced examples.

Simplify the following:

1. $6j + 5k + 4j + 3k$
2. $6j + 5k + 4j - 3k$
3. $6j + 5k - 4j - 3k$
4. $6j - 5k - 4j - 3k$
5. $6j - 5k - 4j + 3k$
6. $6j - 5k + 4j + 3k$
7. $-6j - 5k + 4j + 3k$
8. $-6j - 5k - 4j - 3k$

It is also important, when pupils are learning about general addition and subtraction, to include lots of different variables, including the use of powers, etc.

Simplify the following where possible:

1. $2a + 3a + 7b$
2. $5a + 4b + 3b - 2a$
3. $3c - d + d + 8c$
4. $3w + 6v + 5w - 7w$
5. $4z^2 + 3z$
6. $-4p + q + 7p + 2q$
7. $5x - 4y - 6x - 2y$
8. $8c^2 - c + 2c^2 + 7c$
9. $-3n^2 + 2n^3 + n^3 - n^2$

As well as varying the number of terms and how they appear.

Simplify the following where possible:

1. $7a + 1 + 2a + 3$
2. $5d^2 + 2d + 2$
3. $-3u^2 + 2u^2 + 2u^3 - 7u$
4. $3a + 7b - 6 + 4b - 2c - 8$
5. $3xy + 7x + 2y - xy + 5x$
6. $-7m + 5nm^2 + 2m^2n$
7. $-2u^4 - u^4 - 2 + u^3 + 2u^3$
8. $2f^2 - 8 + 4g - 2h - 9 + 2$

We can also use this as an opportunity to interweave skills with fractions, decimals, etc.

Simplify the following where possible:

1. $2.6r - 2.1r$
2. $1.8x + 4x$
3. $6.3x - 7.015 + 9.9$
4. $1 - 5.18r + r + 0.7$
5. $1.77b - 7.948 + 0.5$
6. $5.2n + 7.5 + n + 7.7$
7. $6.5 - 5.14n + n - 6.6$
8. $-2.8 + 2.4n + 7.8 - 2.8n$
9. $-8.1x - 8.6x$
10. $7.6r + 1.1r$
11. $\frac{p}{2} + \frac{q}{2} - \frac{p}{4} + \frac{3p}{4}$
12. $3x - y + \frac{y}{2} - \frac{5y}{2} + 8y$

Most types of activities that are useful when adding and subtracting other number types can help pupils develop fluency with addition and subtraction of algebra. Indeed, one might argue that this is the ultimate achievement of fluency, provided it is not just taught as a process, as adding and subtracting with algebraic expressions should mean learners can add and subtract with any other type of number. There are some nice opportunities to generalise results of other additions:

Complete the following:

a) i)   Simplify $a - 2a + 3a - 4a + 5a - 6a + \cdots + 49a - 50a$

   ii) What happens if the signs switch?

b) i)   Simplify $a - 2a + 3a - 4a + 5a - 6a + \cdots + 99a - 100a$

   ii) What generalisations can you make for *n* terms?

Arrange these expressions into the magic square:

- $3a + 8b$
- $7b$
- $a + 4b$
- $5a + 2b$
- $6a + 9b$
- $7a + 6b$
- $2a + b$
- $4a + 5b$
- $8a + 3b$

One possible answer

$7a + 6b$	$2a + b$	$3a + 8b$
$7b$	$4a - 5b$	$8a + 3b$
$5a + 2b$	$6a + 9b$	$a + 4b$

Explain Yvonne's mistake in the following problem:

$8x + 6x + 2 = 16x$

And we can keep bringing in other areas of mathematics where addition is used, such as perimeter, arithmetic sequences, mean, etc:

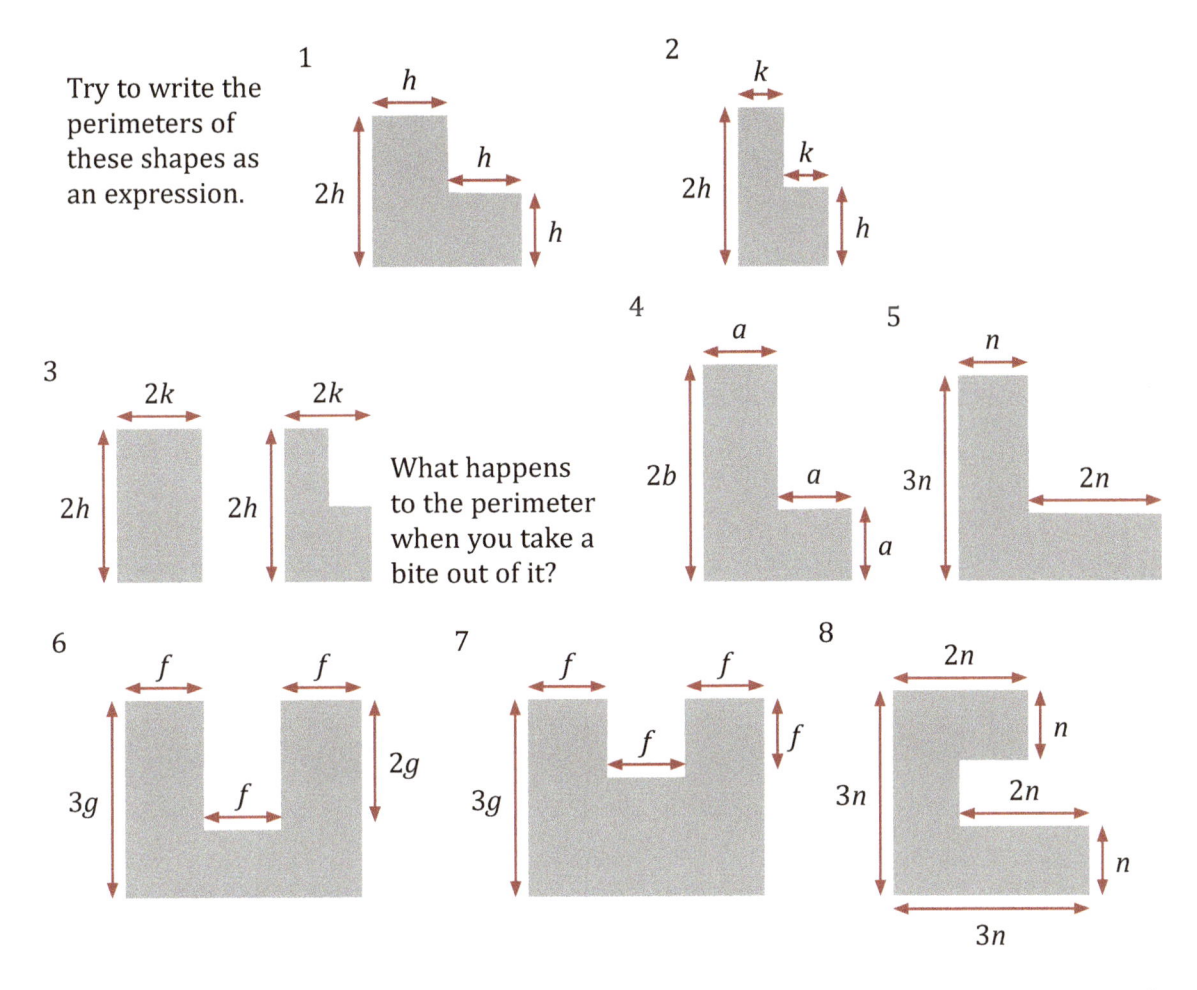

Try to write the perimeters of these shapes as an expression.

1. [shape with labels h, h, $2h$, h]

2. [shape with labels k, k, $2h$, h]

3. [two shapes with labels $2k$, $2h$, $2k$, $2h$] What happens to the perimeter when you take a bite out of it?

4. [shape with labels a, $2b$, a, a]

5. [shape with labels n, $3n$, $2n$, a]

6. [shape with labels f, f, $3g$, f, $2g$]

7. [shape with labels f, f, $3g$, f, f]

8. [shape with labels $2n$, n, $3n$, $2n$, n, $3n$]

(from Don Steward's Median blog[6])

Here are the first and third terms of a different Fibonacci-type sequence.

a _____ b _____ _____

Each term is the sum of the previous two terms.

Work out an expression in terms of a and b for the fifth term.

(Question from AQA Practice Paper Set 3, Paper 1, for the 8300 specification[7])

Of course, we can combine these separate concept links together – for example, the addition/subtraction of algebraic fractions – but these follow exactly the same models and similar activities will prove useful; it is not possible to explore every variant available without significantly extending the length of this book! This will also be true of the other operations.

Let us now turn our attention to the next concept we will consider – multiplication.

---

6   D. Steward, L-Shaped Perimeters, *Median* [blog] (12 February 2012). Available at: https://donsteward.blogspot.com/2012/02/l-shaped-perimters.html.
7   See https://allaboutmaths.aqa.org.uk/8300newpracticepapers3.

Chapter 3
Multiplication and multiples

Having developed an understanding of addition and subtraction, pupils will move on to consider the next 'level of operations'. Whilst, I believe, rules such as 'BIDMAS' are unnecessary if pupils really understand arithmetic and the laws that govern it, I also find it very useful for pupils to appreciate that operations build on each other, starting with addition (and hence subtraction), which leads to multiplication (and hence division) and then, finally, powers (and hence roots). For one thing, these levels of operation link nicely to distributivity – powers distribute over multiplication and multiplication distributes over addition (as we will see in Chapter 5). Fortunately, pupils' early experience of multiplication makes it clear how it develops from addition.

Concept: multiplication

Prerequisites: Numbers, addition.

Linked concepts: Multiple, division/factor, proportionality, measures. Many concepts will require multiplication in some capacity.

The concept of multiplication is probably one of the most researched and explored concepts in school-level mathematics. Reams have been written about teaching multiplication and the difficulties some pupils have in shifting their thinking from additive to multiplicative in nature (just one example from Australia is 'From Additive to Multiplicative Thinking – The Big Challenge of the Middle Years'[1]). In their paper 'Learning Experiences Designed to Develop Multiplicative Reasoning: Using Models to Foster Learners' Understanding' Brown, Hodgen and Küchemann explain that no model gives a complete picture of the nature of multiplication. Rather, a range of models are required to make sense of multiplication, and learners need to develop the ability to move flexibly between them as required. In the same paper, they quote from Anghileri and Johnson's 'Arithmetic Operations on Whole Numbers: Multiplication and Division' which suggests there are six key aspects of multiplication: repeated addition or grouping, arrays and areas, scale factors and enlargements, ratio and proportion, rates, and the Cartesian product.[2]

The initial introduction for most pupils to multiplication is through repeated addition. Unfortunately, this can often be done in the abstract – pupils are simply told that an alternative notation for 5 + 5 + 5 is 5 × 3 (or 3 × 5). I think this probably leads to a lot of the problems that learners end up having with multiplication, for two reasons:

1   This model for multiplication doesn't transfer well beyond the situation where at least one of the numbers is a positive integer.

---

[1] D. Siemon, M. Breed and J. Virgona, From Additive to Multiplicative Thinking – the Big Challenge of the Middle Years, *ResearchGate* (2008). Available at: https://www.researchgate.net/publication/237298794_FROM_ADDITIVE_TO_MULTIPLICATIVE_THINKING_-_THE_BIG_CHALLENGE_OF_THE_MIDDLE_YEARS.

[2] M. Brown, J. Hodgen and D. Küchemann, Learning Experiences Designed to Develop Multiplicative Reasoning: Using Models to Foster Learners' Understanding, *ICCAMS Maths* (2016). Available at: http://iccams-maths.org/wp-content/uploads/2016/01/Brown-Learning-Experiences-Designed-to-Develop-Multiplicative-Reasoning-Using-Models-to-Foster-Learners%E2%80%99-Understanding-1.pdf.

2 By working immediately in the abstract, pupils don't get the chance to see how other models come about from this initial introduction.

Again, it depends on how you are viewing the numbers that are being multiplied as to what the repeated addition model looks like; however, the two are very similar:

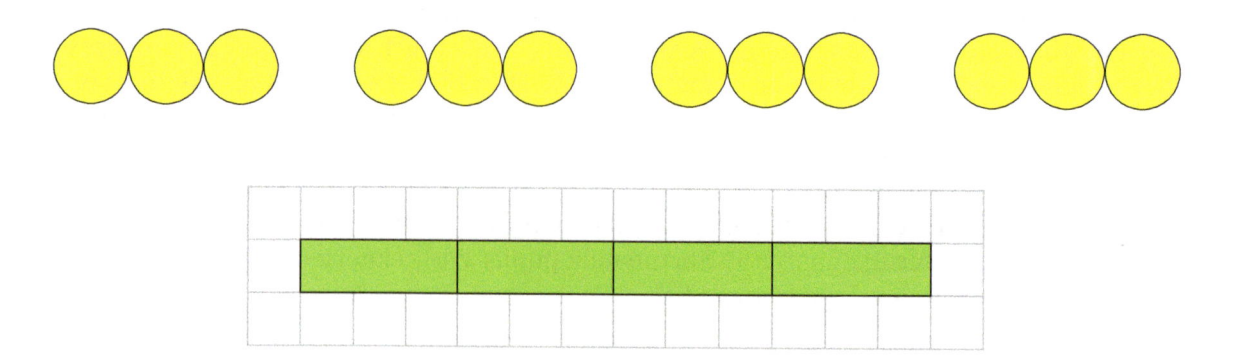

4 × 3:

Both of these are clearly based on an underlying model for addition – in the first image collecting the objects with the same unit values and in the second image connecting the lengths.

By making this explicit with a representation, we can then start to look at alternative ways of arranging these. For example, we might stack the groups of 3 counters on top of each other, or even replace each group of 3 with a single counter worth 3:

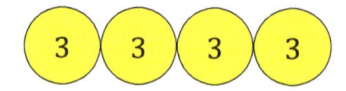

This has clear links with the 'one to many' counting idea from Chapter 1, and shows the idea of grouping or **unitising** with multiplication. Of course, we saw this with numbers in standard form – with something like 4×10^6 being seen as '4 things worth 10^6':

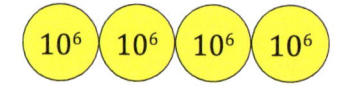

Alternatively, we could rearrange the line of counters/rods into a two-dimensional arrangement:

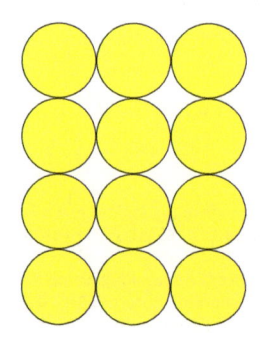

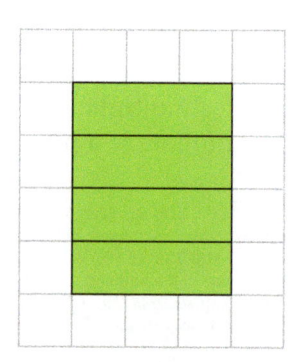

This shows the multiplication as an **array** or **area**, and in general shows the model for multiplication as increasing or changing **dimension**.

When it comes to scaling, we might typically show this on a number line:

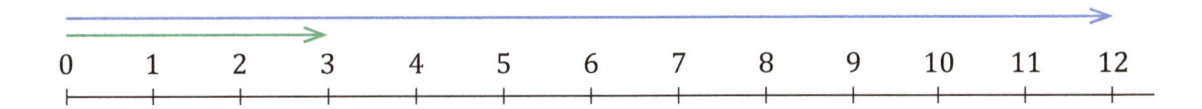

Or potentially over two number lines (which we will see much more of when we come to explore proportionality):

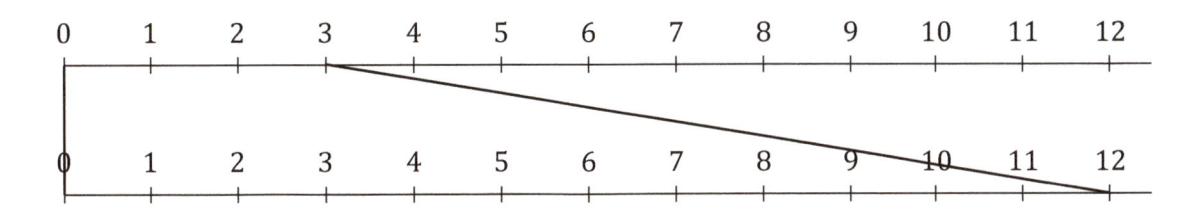

Although the real power of using two number lines is to see what is happening with multiple calculations, so rather than just looking at 4 × 3, we can look simultaneously at 4 × 0, 4 × 1, 4 × 2 and 4 × 3:

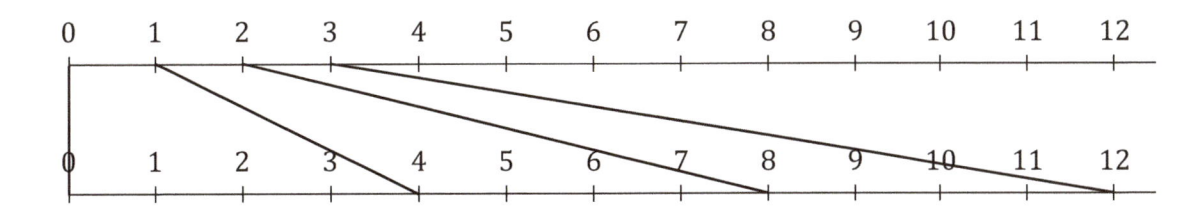

This sort of picture prepares pupils for when we are ready to talk about functionality, as this sort of **mapping diagram** is common when looking at functions (in effect, here we are looking at the 'multiply by 4' function).

Multiplication as a Cartesian product is primarily concerned with combinations of two separate sets of objects. It is heavily linked to using products for counting in probability and statistics. It can be well represented as an array (which shows it is just another facet of the abstract idea of multiplication), but it also can be nicely shown using a tree diagram:

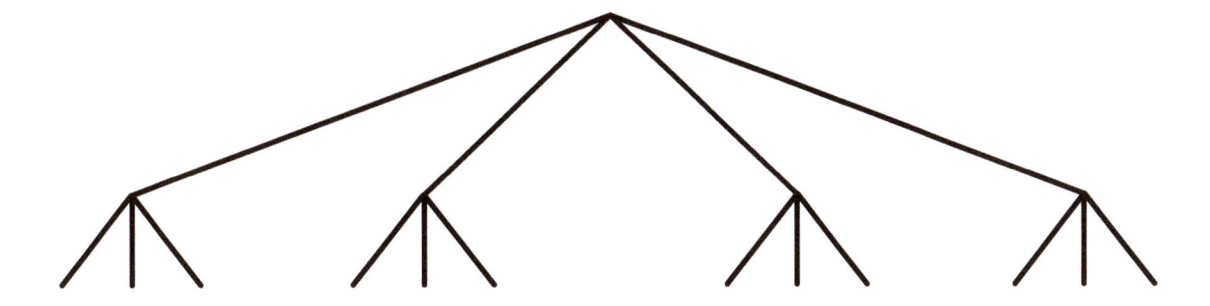

where the first layer of branches shows the number of objects (elements) in the first set, and the second layer of branches shows the number of elements in the second set – in the above picture it is a set of four elements multiplied by a set of three elements where multiplication is being modelled as combining each element in the first set with each of the elements in the second set.

One or more of these models can be used to demonstrate and/or reason the results of pretty much every numerical/algebraic multiplication (although surds takes a bit of doing!). Before we look beyond the positive integers though, let us look at some of the processes/strategies associated with positive integer multiplication.

Process: short multiplication

23 × 7

This is most ordinarily modelled as repeated addition/grouping:

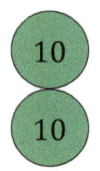

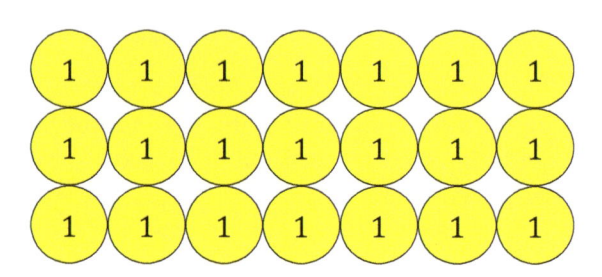

First, we create seven groups of three (because these additions are going to result in exchange, it makes sense to start with the 1s column), which we can then exchange for two 10s and a 1:

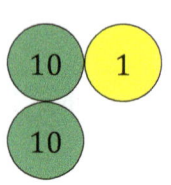

We then proceed with the original two 10s, and add seven sets of those:

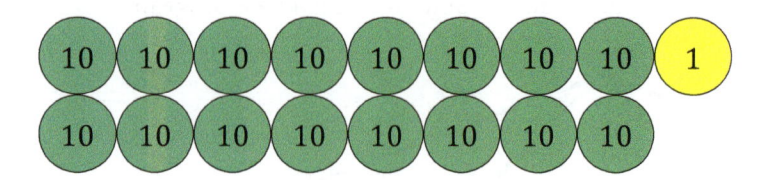

Combining these with the two 10s from the earlier exchange gives sixteen 10s, which can be exchanged for one 100 and six 10s:

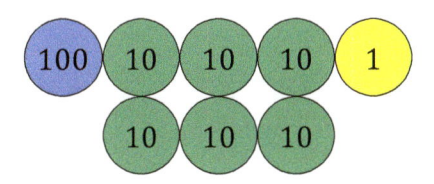

We can model this in the abstract alongside the concrete/visual:

```
  23         23
×  7       ×  7
─────      ─────
   1        161
   2          2
```

Or it can be done in two separate lines:

```
   23
×   7
─────
   21
  140
─────
  161
```

A similar representation leads to the same idea in long multiplication. However, before understanding long multiplication, a learner ideally needs to recognise two things about multiplication:

1. That a multiplication can be decomposed into factors, i.e. multiplication by 20 is equivalent to multiplying by 10 and then multiplying the result by 2 (or vice versa).

2. That multiplication by powers of 10 causes a shift in the place value column.

Pupils should recognise number 2 from the introduction in place value, although they may well have seen it just in reverse (i.e. that shifting the place value is equivalent to multiplying (or dividing) by a given power of 10). As for number 1, well this requires learners to know something about associativity and multiplication – and be fluent enough to be able to recognise the 'undoing' of an application of the associative law (i.e. if $a \times 10 \times 2 = a \times 20$, then $a \times 20$ can be decomposed into $a \times 10 \times 2$). It is worth reinforcing these two ideas with learners separately before embarking on formal long multiplication by getting pupils to write calculations in different ways:

How many different multiplications can you write that give the same result as 40×30?

Fill in the blanks in these calculations:

a $17 \times 30 = 17 \times 10 \times \_\_\_$

b $17 \times 40 = 17 \times \_\_\_ \times 4$

c $17 \times 40 = 17 \times \_\_\_ \times 2 \times \_\_\_$

d $70 \times 40 = 7 \times \_\_\_ \times \_\_\_ \times 4$

e $70 \times 40 = 7 \times \_\_\_ \times 4$

Once pupils have this depth and flexibility of knowledge, they are ready to look at long multiplication.

Process: long multiplication

23 × 27

We first begin in the same way as 23 × 7, resulting in the 161 we had before:

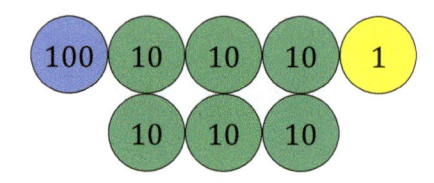

(100) (10) (10) (10) (1)
     (10) (10) (10)

We then have to multiply 23 by 20, which, of course, is the same as multiplying 23 by 10 and then by 2, which means adding two each of the 3 and the 20, and then shifting them up a column:

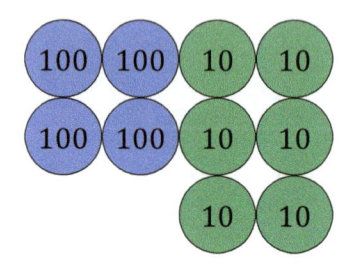

(100) (100) (10) (10)
(100) (100) (10) (10)
            (10) (10)

We can then add these two numbers (including exchanging the twelve 10s for one 100 and two 10s) to give:

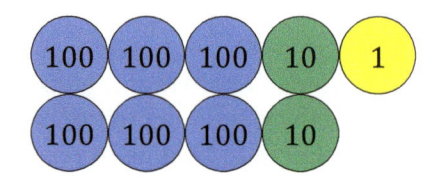

(100) (100) (100) (10) (1)
(100) (100) (100) (10)

Alongside this we can show what it looks like with numerals:

23	23	23	23	23	23
× 27	× 27	× 27	× 27	× 27	× 27
1	1	161	161	161	161
2	2	2	2	2	2
			60	460	460
					621
					1

Process: Gelosia multiplication

The 'Gelosia' method of multiplication (also known as the lattice method, and a host of other names) for larger numbers is based on the same idea, except in this method the results of the multiplication are shown diagonally rather than in columns:

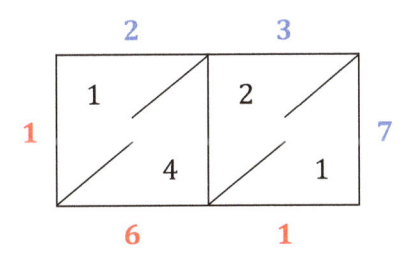

An alternative to short and long multiplication (or Gelosia multiplication) through repeated addition/grouping is the 'grid method' – which isn't really a 'method' as much as it is a partial abstraction of the area model:

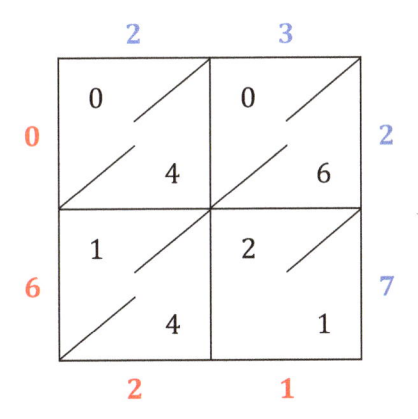

Process: grid multiplication

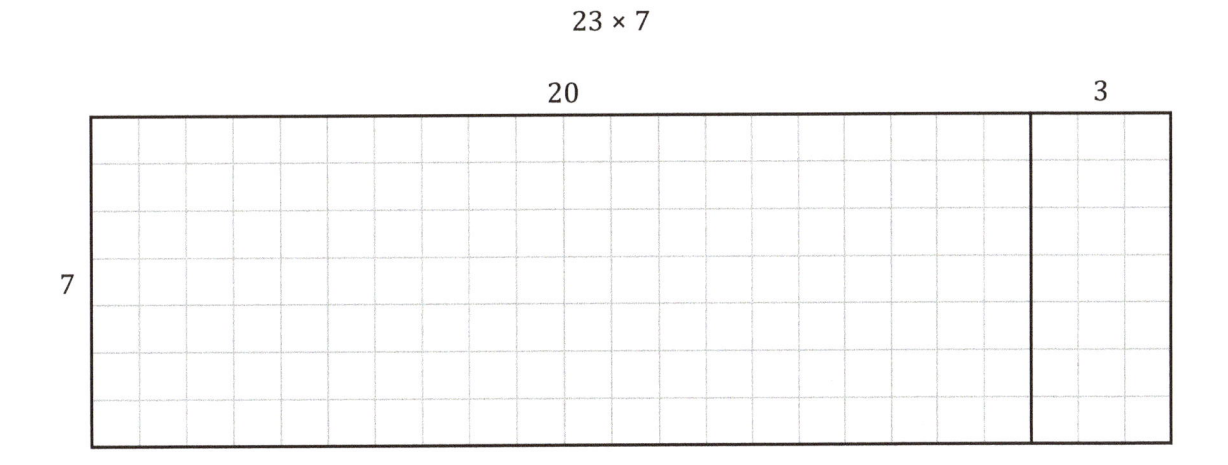

23 × 7

	20	3
7	140	21

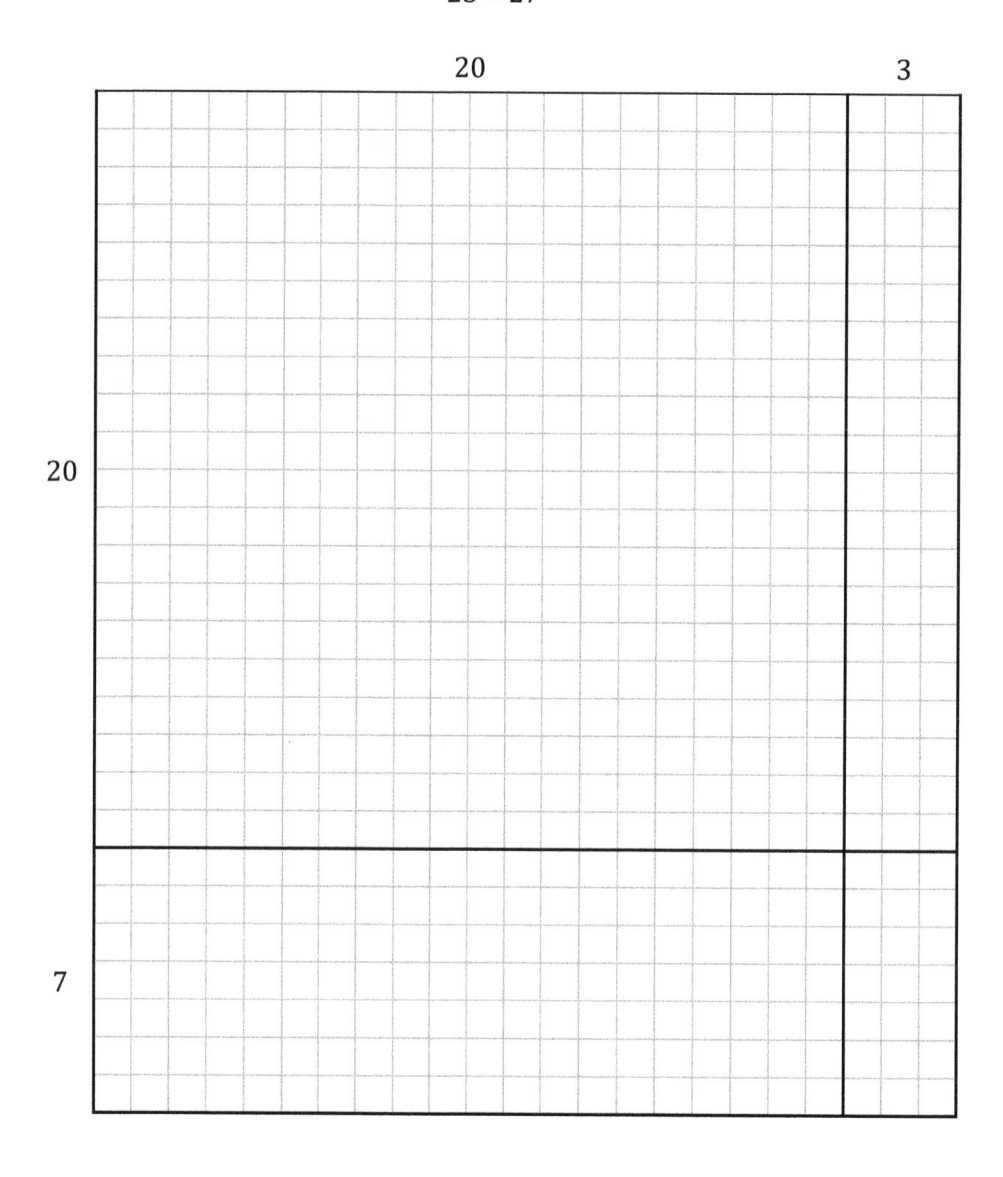

23 × 27

	20	3
20	400	60
7	140	21

Pupils should see the area model used for larger numbers prior to using the 'grid method'; in particular, they should recognise that for larger numbers it is easier to evaluate the area by breaking it into parts corresponding to each place value column. This is the 'process' if you like, the partitioning of the number into its separate 100s, 10s, units, etc.

Other strategies for multiplication follow from other models for multiplication. For example, calculating 99 × 7 can be seen as having ninety-nine 7s, so that if we added one more 7 we would have one hundred 7s – so 99 × 7 = 100 × 7 – 7:

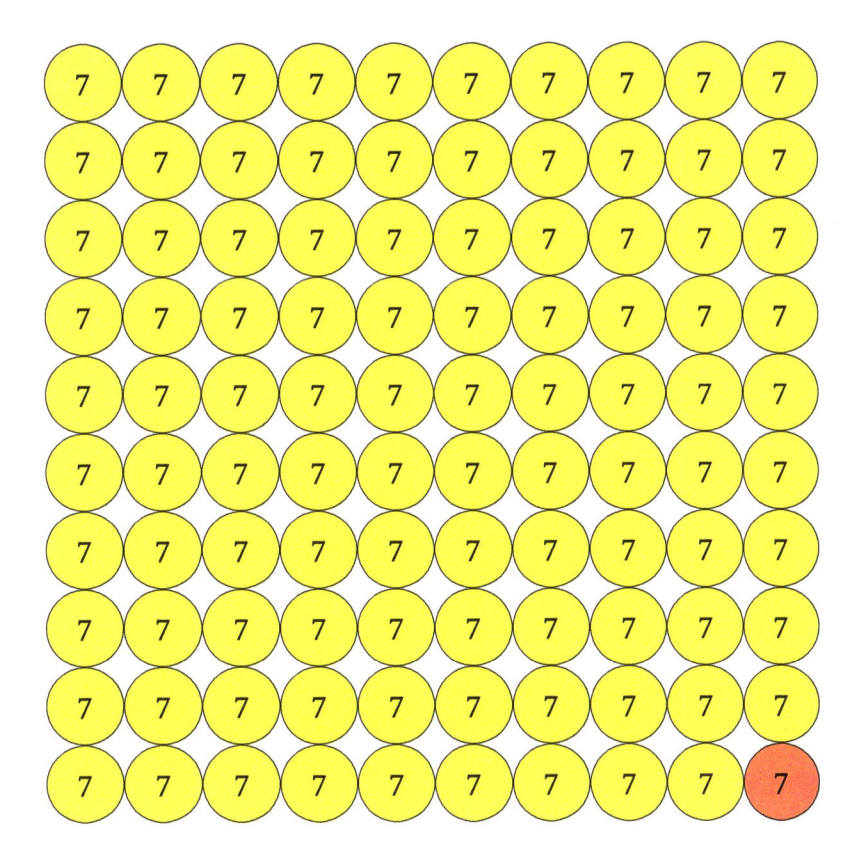

Or alternatively as an area of 100 × 7 with the final column of 7 removed:

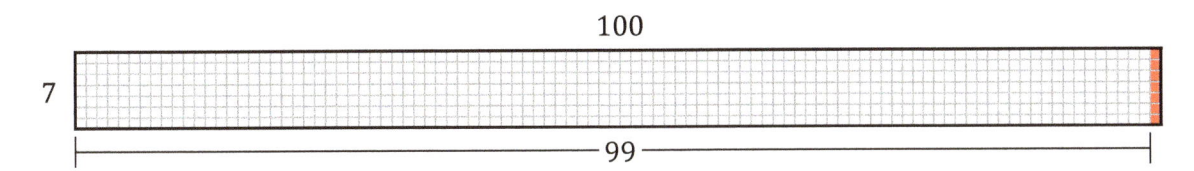

As for addition and subtraction, we can then pose questions to prompt pupils to suggest suitable strategies for multiplication.

Calculate the following:

a 23 × 7

b 27 × 3

c 27 × 30

d 27 × 33

e 27 × 99

f 27 × 101

g 72 × 101

h 72 × 161

i 72 × 27

And we can pose problems that might prompt pupils to think a little deeper about multiplication:

> Use the digits 1, 2, 3, 4, 5 to make two numbers that multiply to make the largest possible answer.
>
> > What happens if you use 2, 3, 4, 5, 6?
> >
> > 3, 4, 5, 6, 7?
>
> What do you notice? What do you wonder?

> Write down any two-digit number. Multiply it by 7. Then multiply your answer by 11. Then multiply your answer by 13. What do you notice? Can you explain it?

And those that interweave previous skills with multiplication:

> > Choose any two-digit number.
> >
> > Reverse the digits.
> >
> > Add the two numbers together.
> >
> > Now take the two digits of your original number, add them together and multiply the result by 11.
>
> What do you notice? Does it always happen? Can you explain it?

Concept link: multiplication of negative numbers

There are two types of multiplication calculation we need to consider when thinking about multiplication of negatives:

1. Multiplying a positive number by a negative number.
2. Multiplying a negative number by another negative number.

The first of these can be made sense of through repeated addition:

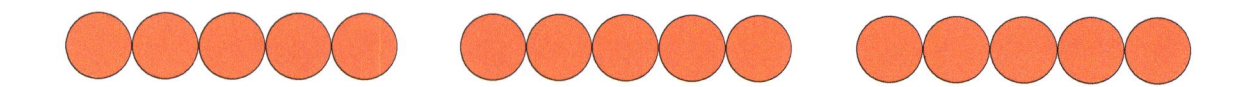

3×-5 (or -5×3)

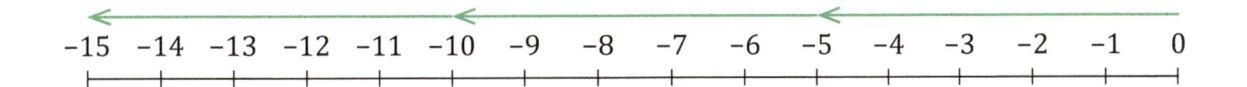

-15 -14 -13 -12 -11 -10 -9 -8 -7 -6 -5 -4 -3 -2 -1 0

However, multiplying two negative numbers is not so straightforward. We cannot make sense of this through repeated addition; for repeated addition to be a usable model for multiplication, then the number of repeats is the value of either the multiplier or multiplicand and so has to be a positive integer. We can adapt this model though:

−3 × −5

One way we can make sense of this is to consider it as 'the negative of 3 × −5'. This means we can take the above representations and think about what the negative of these would be. This is why we were careful when we introduced negatives to talk about rotation and inverse. If we are seeing −3 × −5 as the negative of 3 × −5, then we can simply rotate each of the above representations by 180°:

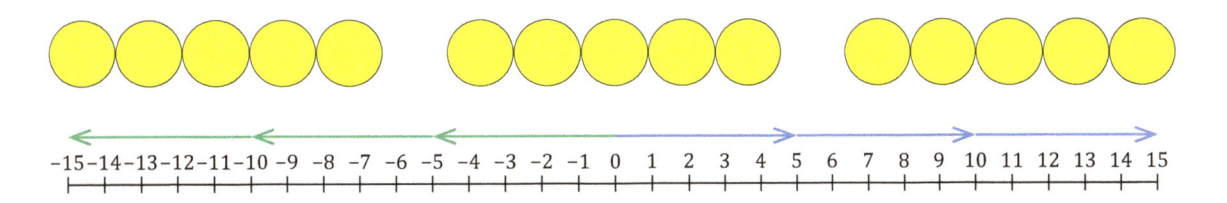

−15−14−13−12−11−10 −9 −8 −7 −6 −5 −4 −3 −2 −1 0 1 2 3 4 5 6 7 8 9 10 11 12 13 14 15

A possible alternative to this is to apply the scaling model of multiplication. If we are going to apply this model, we should also look at a positive multiplied by a negative.

3 × −5

Here we see −5 scaled by a factor of 3:

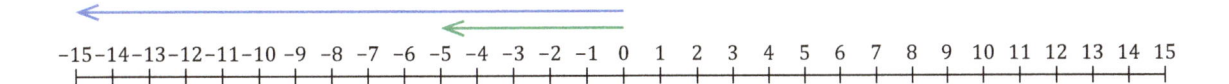

−15−14−13−12−11−10 −9 −8 −7 −6 −5 −4 −3 −2 −1 0 1 2 3 4 5 6 7 8 9 10 11 12 13 14 15

However, this must give the same as 3 scaled by −5:

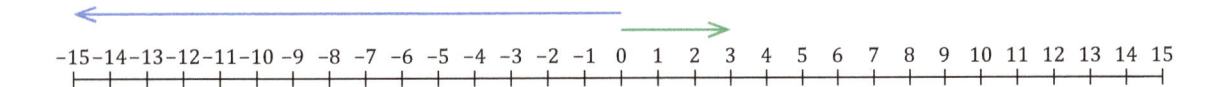

−15−14−13−12−11−10 −9 −8 −7 −6 −5 −4 −3 −2 −1 0 1 2 3 4 5 6 7 8 9 10 11 12 13 14 15

which shows the effect of scaling by −5 is to rotate the vector 180° as well as stretch it. We can now apply the same idea to −3, and scale this by −5:

−3 × −5

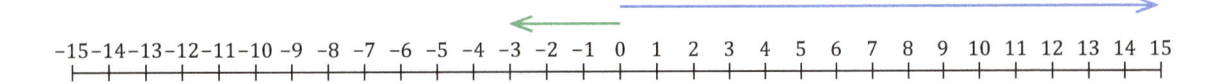

−15−14−13−12−11−10 −9 −8 −7 −6 −5 −4 −3 −2 −1 0 1 2 3 4 5 6 7 8 9 10 11 12 13 14 15

A similar idea to those above can be applied to the array/area, but it is best to build to it from a positive calculation:

[Three arrays shown: 3 × 5 (all yellow +1 tiles), 3 × −5 (length row flipped to −1, interior all −1), −3 × −5 (length and width flipped to −1, interior all +1)]

The idea would be that flipping any tile on the length or width flips everything in the row and/or column. So, having flipped the five tiles along the length, we flip everything in the same column as those five tiles, showing the −15. When we then flip the three tiles along the width, we flip everything in the same row as those three tiles, which reverts the −15 back to 15. Note we could arrive at the same result by making the middle calculation −3 × 5 instead:

[Three arrays shown: 3 × 5, −3 × 5, −3 × −5]

This time, flipping the three tiles down the width has flipped every tile in each row, and then flipping the five tiles along the length flips all the tiles in the five columns.

Of course, the realisation we want from learners is that having a single negative value in the calculation gives a negative result to the calculation, and that having two negative values in the calculation gives a positive result to the calculation. We can quiz this independently of actually calculating:

Will the result of these calculations be negative or positive?

a 3×7

b -3×7

c 3×-7

d -7×3

e -7×-3

f -0.7×-3

g $-\frac{1}{7} \times -3$

h $-\frac{1}{7} \times -\frac{1}{7}$

i $\frac{1}{7} \times -\frac{1}{3}$

j $\frac{1}{7} \times -\frac{1}{3} \times 5$

k $\frac{1}{7} \times -\frac{1}{3} \times -5$

l $\frac{1}{7} \times \frac{1}{3} \times -5$

m $\frac{1}{7} \times \frac{2}{3} \times -5$

n $\frac{1}{7} \times \frac{2}{3} \times -5$

o $\frac{1}{7} \times \frac{-2}{3} \times -5$

p $\frac{-1}{7} \times \frac{-2}{3} \times -5$

We can also bring in similar types of questions to those we have seen before:

Each brick in the pyramid is found by multiplying the two beneath it (see the example). How many ways can you find of completing the pyramid so the top value is −72? Do you notice anything about the solutions?

Example

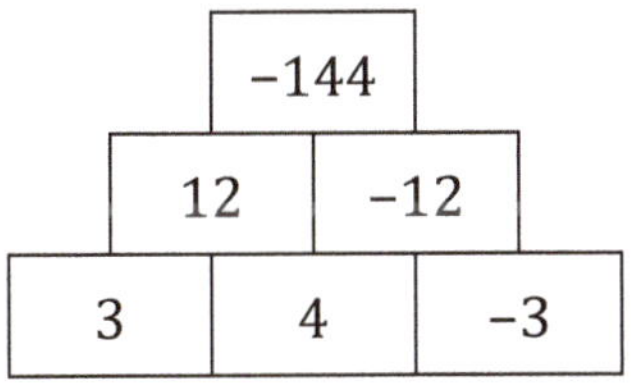

```
        -144
      12    -12
    3    4    -3
```

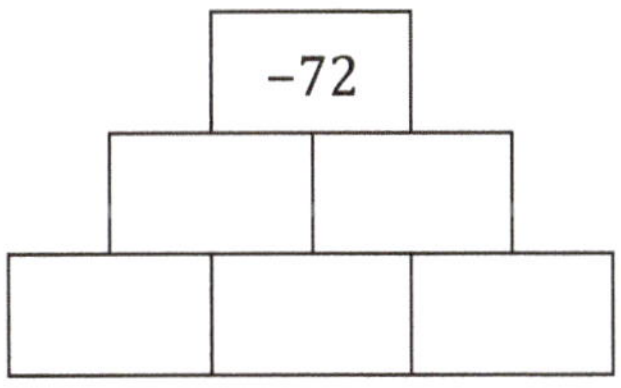

```
        -72
```

Place numbers in the sections to meet the criteria for each section of the Venn diagram. How many ways can you find? What is the greatest number of negative integers you can use?

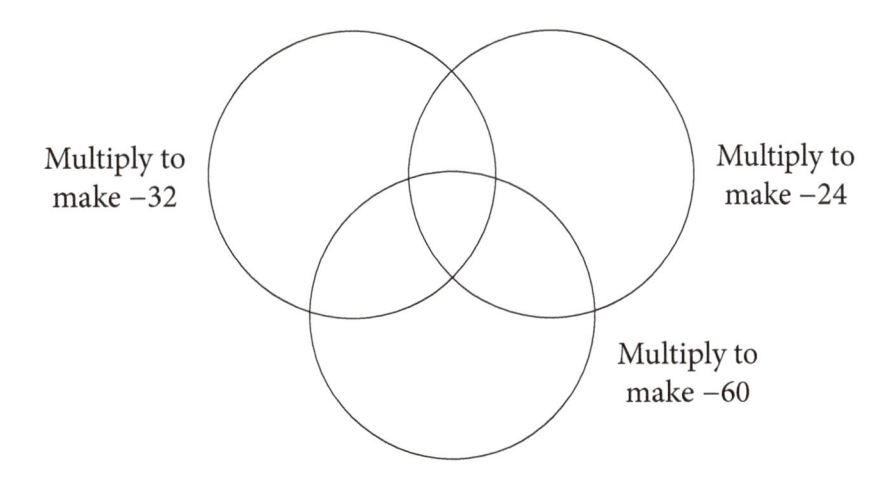

Multiply to make −32

Multiply to make −24

Multiply to make −60

Concept link: multiplying with fractions

Again, we can consider two cases:

1. Multiplying a fraction by an integer.
2. Multiplying two fractions.

Assuming the integer is a positive integer, then we can again look at this sort of calculation as repeated addition:

$8 \times \frac{1}{3}$

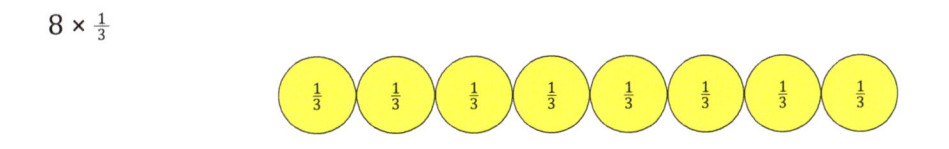

$\frac{1}{3}$ $\frac{1}{3}$ $\frac{1}{3}$ $\frac{1}{3}$ $\frac{1}{3}$ $\frac{1}{3}$ $\frac{1}{3}$ $\frac{1}{3}$

(given the green rod has a value of 1)

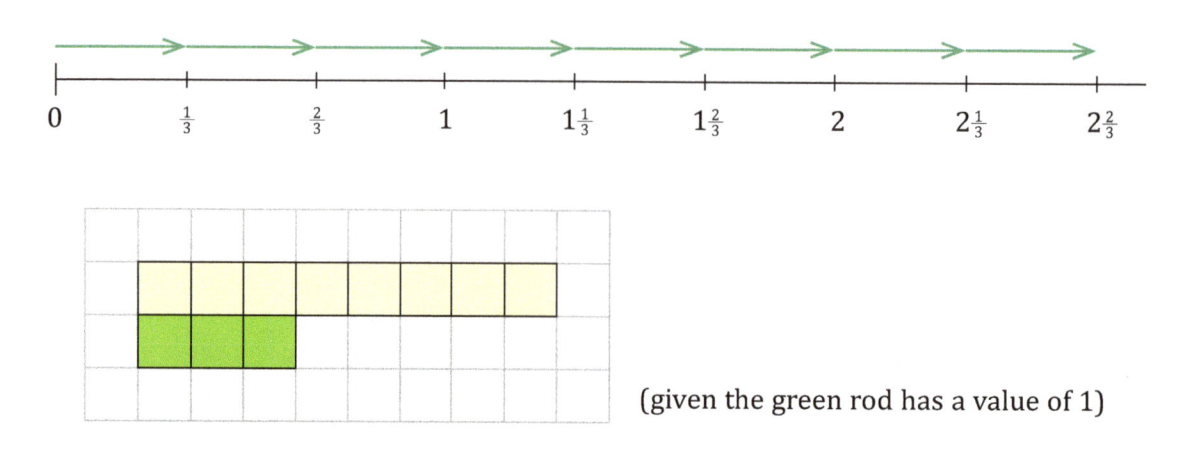

With this we very quickly want pupils to recognise that when multiplying a fraction by an integer, we simply multiply the numerator of the fraction by the integer. However, we should also include non-unit fractions and situations where the result simplifies:

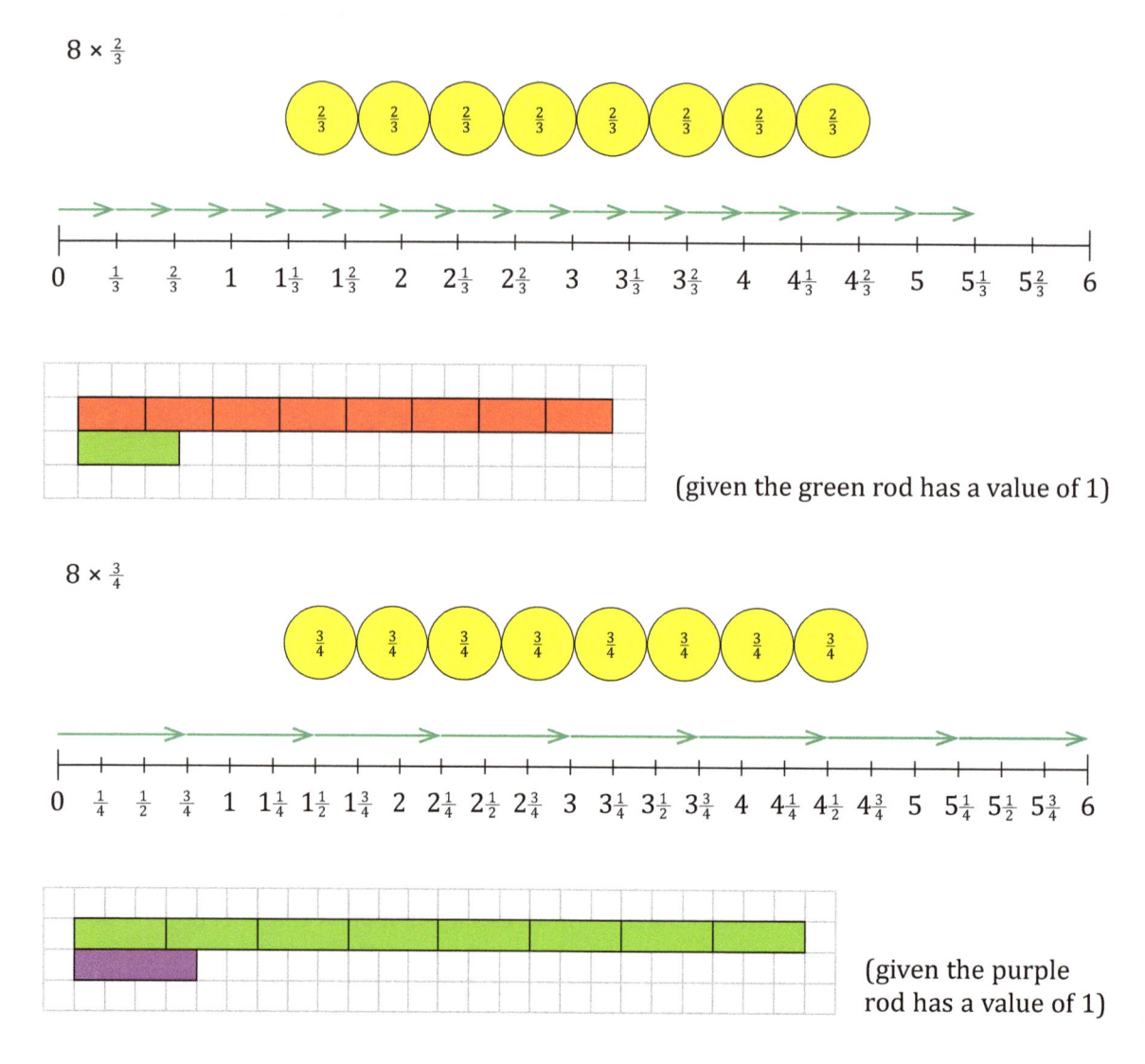

$8 \times \frac{2}{3}$

(given the green rod has a value of 1)

$8 \times \frac{3}{4}$

(given the purple rod has a value of 1)

Another thing it is worth doing is to look at this type of multiplication as an area (although it is best to stick to smaller integers and small denominators to keep the area reasonable):

$3 \times \frac{4}{5}$

Multiplication and multiples

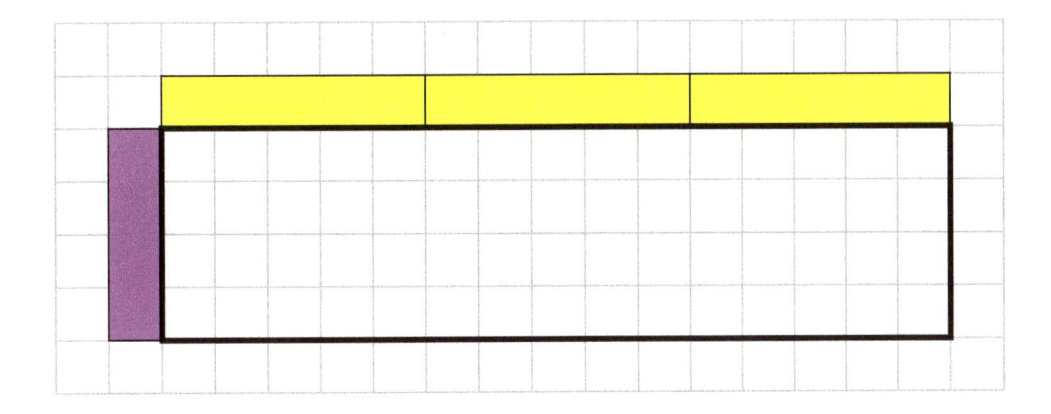

The area diagram needs a little interpreting. In the above diagram, the yellow rod is being defined as having a value of 1. This means the purple rod has a value of $\frac{4}{5}$, and so the area is $3 \times \frac{4}{5}$. The question is, what is the value of this area? To answer this, we need to first consider what an area with a value of 1 would look like:

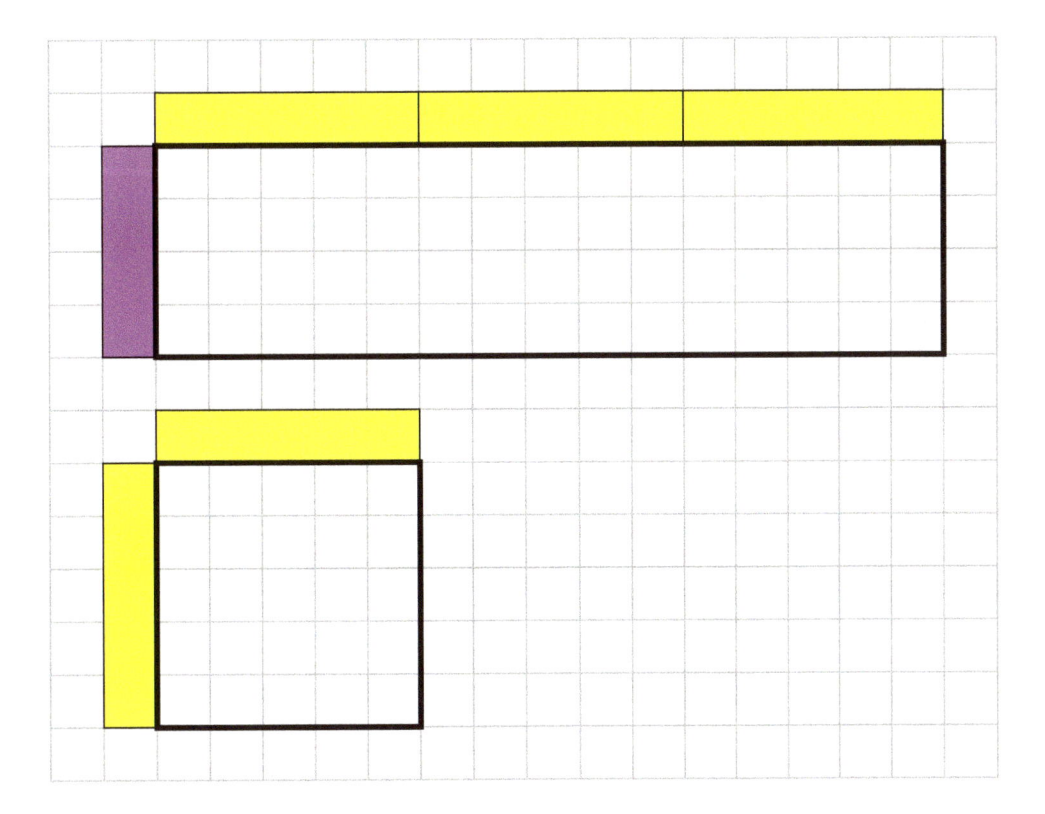

We can see that a 1 × 1 area is made up of 25 of the smaller squares, and so every 25 squares is equivalent to 1. If we look then at the $3 \times \frac{4}{5}$ area, we can see that this is 60 little squares in area, and so the result of the multiplication is $\frac{60}{25} = \frac{12}{5}$.

Of course, this is a great place to bring back (assuming they have previously been taught) skills involving converting between mixed numbers and improper fractions, where pupils can give answers to calculations in either form. There is also a very nice activity from Don Steward's Median blog, where pupils can find missing numbers in fraction and integer multiplications where the answers are all integers:[3]

---

3 D. Steward, Fractions 'of', *Median* [blog] (17 January 2014). Available at: https://donsteward.blogspot.com/2014/01/fractions-of.html.

Conceptual Maths

a

1 $\frac{2}{3} \times \square = 8$ 4 $\frac{3}{8} \times \square = 18$
2 $\frac{3}{5} \times \square = 24$ 5 $\frac{5}{9} \times \square = 40$
3 $\frac{2}{7} \times \square = 12$ 6 $\frac{4}{11} \times \square = 36$

b

1 $\frac{\square}{5} \times 45 = 36$ 4 $\frac{\square}{9} \times 81 = 45$
2 $\frac{\square}{8} \times 48 = 18$ 5 $\frac{\square}{7} \times 56 = 40$
3 $\frac{\square}{7} \times 56 = 48$ 6 $\frac{\square}{13} \times 52 = 28$

c

1 $\frac{2}{\square} \times 28 = 8$ 4 $\frac{6}{\square} \times 84 = 72$
2 $\frac{3}{\square} \times 72 = 27$ 5 $\frac{5}{\square} \times 108 = 60$
3 $\frac{7}{\square} \times 54 = 42$ 6 $\frac{4}{\square} \times 91 = 28$

d

1 $\frac{2}{3} \times \frac{6}{7} \times \square = 20$ 4 $\frac{10}{11} \times \frac{22}{25} \times \square = 20$
2 $\frac{3}{4} \times \frac{8}{9} \times \square = 20$ 5 $\frac{6}{7} \times \frac{35}{48} \times \square = 20$
3 $\frac{3}{5} \times \frac{25}{36} \times \square = 20$ 6 $\frac{14}{15} \times \frac{25}{42} \times \square = 20$

Opening it up a little more is also nice to test the limits of pupil understanding:

Which numbers can you put into the blanks so that the answer is:

a a whole number?

b a proper fraction?

c an improper fraction?

$\frac{\square}{12} \times \square$ $\frac{7}{\square} \times \square$ $\frac{\square}{\square} \times 20$

One of the particular reasons for introducing the area model is that it can really help with multiplying mixed numbers by integers and, ultimately, in multiplying two fractions:

$2\frac{3}{4} \times 3$

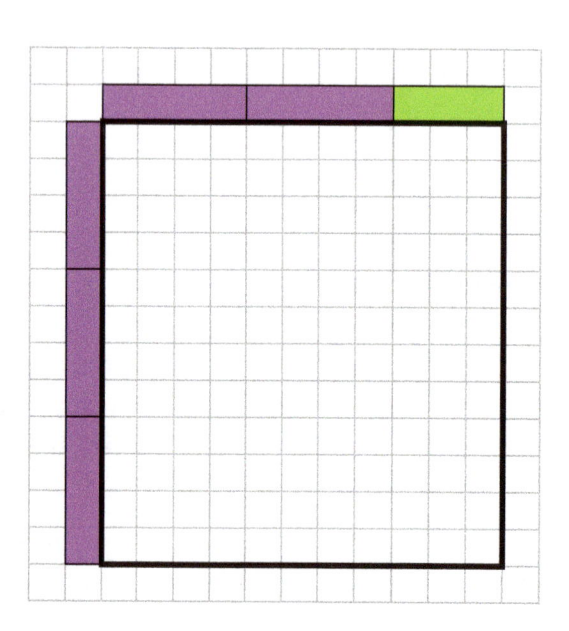

This time the purple rod has a value of 1, meaning that an area of 16 small squares has a value of 1. We can see that part of this area is simply 3 × 2, and the rest is equal to $2\frac{1}{4}$. However, what is important here is that this image can be abstracted into a grid method:

	2	$\frac{3}{4}$
3	6	$2\frac{1}{4}$

This is a potential alternative to evaluating the multiplication by converting $2\frac{3}{4}$ into an improper fraction, particularly if the result is more useful as a mixed number. Again, it might be an idea to present different calculations and examine whether converting the mixed number into an improper fraction is a better strategy or whether keeping the mixed number as a mixed number would make evaluation easier.

Decide which strategy is best for calculating these:

a $1\frac{1}{8} \times 5$

b $4\frac{5}{8} \times 10$

c $3\frac{3}{8} \times 4$

And then again, providing opportunities for thinking more deeply about the structures:

$1\frac{2}{3} \times \square = 1\frac{7}{8} \times \square$

What numbers can you find that will fit into the two different boxes? Is there any pattern you can find?

When we are ready to move on to multiplying two fractions, we are once more in the situation where repeated addition will not help in making sense of the multiplication. Fortunately, the area model will enable us to make sense of such calculations:

$\frac{4}{5} \times \frac{2}{3}$

In the next image we can see a square area, which we will define as having a value of 1. We then have a smaller rectangular area that is $\frac{4}{5}$ long by $\frac{2}{3}$ wide. Again, the question is, what is the value of the smaller rectangular area?

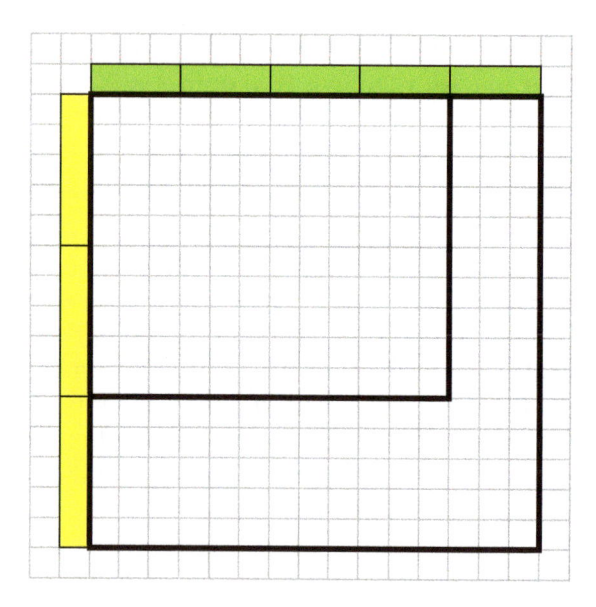

Well, of course, we could work out all of the little squares inside the two shapes. The square is 15 squares long and so contains 225 little squares. The rectangle is 12 squares long by 10 squares wide and so contains 120 little squares. Therefore, the rectangle has a value of $\frac{120}{225}$.

However, alternatively, we can break the entire square into equal-sized rectangles that have a length of one green rod by one yellow rod (the original rectangle is shown in red):

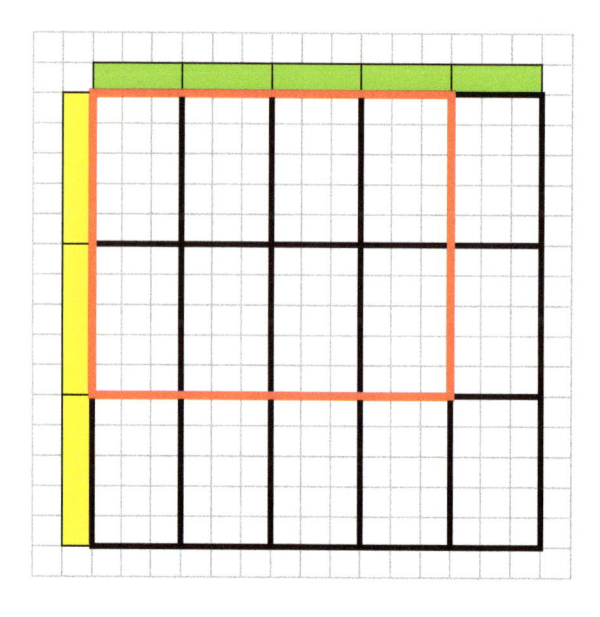

We can see from this that our original rectangular area contains eight smaller rectangles, and the whole square contains 15 of the smaller rectangles, leading to the conclusion that $\frac{4}{5} \times \frac{2}{3} = \frac{8}{15}$.

More importantly, from this we can generalise (although pupils may need more than one example before they can generalise). We can see that the total number of rectangles in our unit square will always be the product of the two denominators, and that the number of rectangles inside the area representing our calculation will be the product of the two numerators. In general, with the product $\frac{a}{b} \times \frac{c}{d}$, the unit square will be split into bd smaller rectangles, and the number of rectangles that make up the required area will be ac, leading to the result that $\frac{a}{b} \times \frac{c}{d} = \frac{ac}{bd}$.

Interestingly, we can also generalise from the original smaller squares picture. We can see that the number of smaller squares will be the square of the product of the denominators, and that the rectangular area will be the product of the diagonal products, i.e. $\frac{a}{b} \times \frac{c}{d} = \frac{ad \times cb}{(bd)^2}$. This simplifies to give the more familiar $\frac{ac}{bd}$. Whilst I wouldn't recommend necessarily introducing this when pupils first meet the multiplication of fractions, it is something nice to come back to when pupils have matured in their knowledge and experience of working with fractions.

There is a minor drawback to the area model in that fractions where 'cross cancelling' might be used to make the multiplication easier to evaluate does not arise from the model, meaning simplification has to be completed after the multiplication. For example:

$\frac{3}{4} \times \frac{5}{6}$

Normally we might 'cross cancel' the 3 and 6 so that we actually compute $\frac{1}{4} \times \frac{5}{2}$. However, the area model won't allow for this:

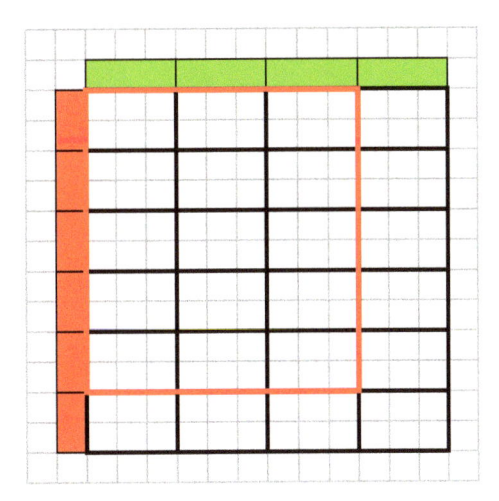

We can see that the required area has 15 rectangles out of 24 but cannot be seen as 5 out of 8 (which would be the result of the cross cancelling). In order to see this, pupils would have to recognise the possibility of breaking this area into eight equal pieces (particularly as the pieces do not have equal length measures but do have equal areas):

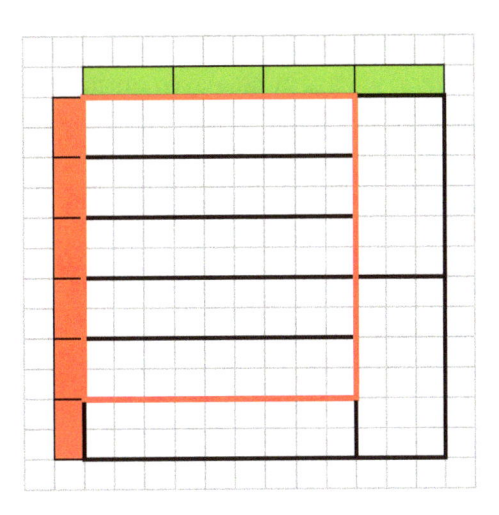

There are lots of opportunities to interweave practice of fraction multiplication with other mathematical skills. Any area of mathematics that requires multiplication can be used with fractions. Calculating area, working with speed and time, enlarging shapes and many other concepts in maths require multiplication to be carried out and can include fractional values. In addition, the usual sorts of questions to prompt thinking about the structures behind fractional multiplication can be used:

Using the numbers 1, 2, 3, 4, write the multiplication calculation with the smallest possible answer in the boxes below.

What if you use 2, 3, 4, 5?

What about 3, 4, 5, 6?

Keep going.

Do you notice anything about:

a   the way you combine the numbers?

b   the answers?

Sum one

Start with two fractions that sum to one.

$\frac{2}{5}$ $\frac{3}{5}$

Square the first and add the second.

Square the second and add the first.

Try this with several pairs of fractions that add up to 1.

Can you find a rule to predict the result(s)?

(from Don Steward's Median blog[4])

From here we can turn our attention in one of two directions:

1   Multiplication of mixed numbers.

2   Multiplication of decimals.

When it comes to mixed numbers, we again have two options:

1   Convert to improper fractions and multiply as we would proper fractions.

2   Consider the mixed numbers as mixed numbers and evaluate the area produced.

Both of these can be seen in the area model:

$2\frac{1}{4} \times 1\frac{2}{3}$

---

[4]   D. Steward, Sum One, *Median* [blog] (22 May 2014). Available at: https://donsteward.blogspot.com/2014/05/sum-one.html?m=0.

Here we see the black area with a value of 1 (it is four quarters long by three thirds wide), and the red area being the one we wish to evaluate.

If we split this into rectangles along each quarter and third we get this picture:

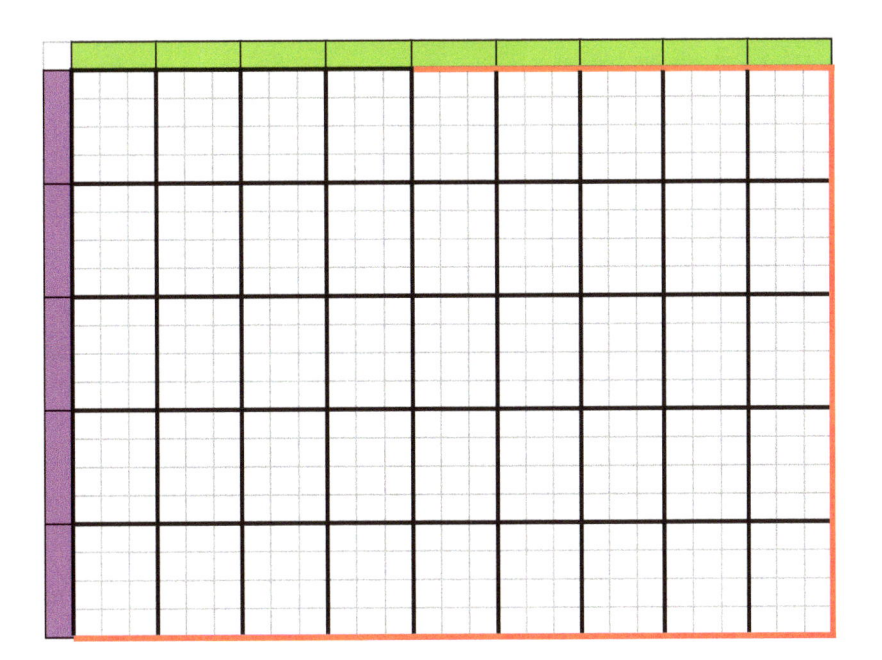

We can see that because there are 9 quarters and 5 thirds, the area required is split into 45 smaller rectangles. If we then look at the unit area, which is 4 quarters by 3 thirds, this is 12 smaller rectangles. Thus the calculation $2\frac{1}{4} \times 1\frac{2}{3}$ becomes $\frac{9}{4} \times \frac{5}{3} = \frac{45}{12}(=\frac{15}{4})$.

Alternatively, if we instead consider the whole parts and the fractional parts separately, the result is this picture:

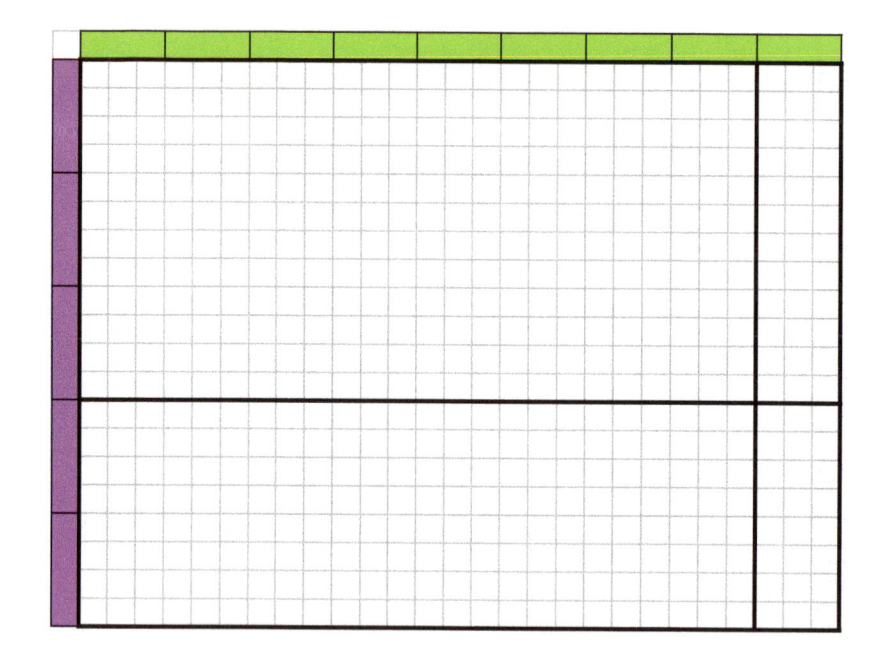

We can see this area is split into four parts. The upper left is a 2 × 1 area, and so has an area of 2. The lower left area is 2 × $\frac{2}{3}$ and so has an area of $\frac{4}{3}$ (or $1\frac{1}{3}$). The upper right area is $\frac{1}{4}$ × 1 and so has an area of $\frac{1}{4}$. Finally, the lower right area is $\frac{1}{4}$ × $\frac{2}{3}$ and so has an area of $\frac{2}{12}$ (or $\frac{1}{6}$). Therefore the total area is the sum $2 + 1\frac{1}{3} + \frac{1}{4} + \frac{1}{6} = 2 + 1\frac{4}{12} + \frac{3}{12} + \frac{2}{12} = 3\frac{9}{12}(=3\frac{3}{4})$.

Of course, this second way of partitioning the image can be partially abstracted into a grid 'method':

	2	$\frac{1}{4}$
1	2	$\frac{1}{4}$
$\frac{2}{3}$	$1\frac{1}{3}$	$\frac{1}{6}$

If pupils learn about both of these ways of viewing the area created by multiplying two mixed numbers (or indeed multiplying a mixed number by a proper fraction), then again the opportunity arises to look at situations where one approach may be preferred to another. Both have drawbacks; converting to improper fractions increases the size of the values that are actually multiplied – $5\frac{7}{8}$ becomes $\frac{47}{8}$ and so we end up having to multiply 47 by something potentially larger, and then, if required, having to re-evaluate the resulting improper fraction as a mixed number. However, leaving as mixed numbers often leads to summing fractions with three different denominators which can also be a lot of work. There are some times where this doesn't come about though:

$4\frac{2}{3} \times 3\frac{3}{5}$

	4	$\frac{2}{3}$
3	12	2
$\frac{3}{5}$	$2\frac{2}{5}$	$\frac{2}{5}$

In this calculation, the resulting fractions only involve fifths, and so arguably this is a much more efficient approach to the calculation than to convert it into $\frac{14}{3} \times \frac{18}{5}$, then having to multiply 14 by 18 (although cross cancelling would make this slightly easier) and then simplify the result – we can clearly see from the grid above that we just have $16\frac{4}{5}$. A nice activity can be to show pupils these two examples and ask them to think about why the only fractional part in this case has a denominator of 5 and to generate other multiplications where this is the case. There are other nice activities to prompt pupil thinking out there as well; as ever, Don Steward has a great one:[5]

Mixed number multiplying:

$$6\tfrac{3}{5} \times 1\tfrac{2}{4} = 9\tfrac{9}{10}$$

- The left-hand side uses all the digits, 1 to 6.
- The two fractions are proper fractions (less than 1).
- One of the fractions cancels down, but that doesn't matter.

Can you find another way to make $9\tfrac{9}{10}$?

Mixed number multiplying:

   6 3
      5
1 4 2

$\square\tfrac{\square}{\square} \times \square\tfrac{\square}{\square} =$

- The left hand side must use all of the digits 1 to 6.
- The two fractions must be proper fractions (i.e. less than 1).
- The fractions could cancel down – that doesn't matter.

1 What is the smallest number that can be made? (smaller than $4\tfrac{1}{2}$)

2 What is the largest number that can be made? (larger than $36\tfrac{1}{4}$)

3 How can these whole numbers be made?

 a $\boxed{1}\tfrac{\square}{\square} \times \boxed{3}\tfrac{\square}{\square} = 6$

 b $\boxed{6}\tfrac{\square}{\square} \times \boxed{1}\tfrac{\square}{\square} = 12$

 c $\square\tfrac{\boxed{2}}{\boxed{6}} \times \square\tfrac{\square}{\square} = 14$

 d $\square\tfrac{\square}{\square} \times \square\tfrac{\square}{\square} = 28$

---

5 D. Steward, Multiplying Mixed Numbers, *Median* [blog] (24 January 2016). Available at: https://donsteward.blogspot.com/2016/01/multiplying-mixed-numbers.html.

4   Can you find two ways to make $20\frac{4}{5}$?

5   Can you find two ways to make $14\frac{17}{20}$?

Having mentioned it a couple of times, I want to touch briefly on this idea of 'cross cancelling'. There is debate in the maths education community (or at least there was at the time of writing!) as to whether this phrase should be used and the process taught. My response to this is that, in common with other processes, it arises from the properties of the concept(s) on which it works – in this case, the properties of fractions and of multiplication. If learners can come to understand how this process arises, then it can be used flexibly and with understanding; if not then it has no business being used. For cross cancelling, pupils need to understand three things:

1   That fraction multiplications can be evaluated by multiplying numerators and denominators separately.

2   That multiplication is commutative (we will see this in Chapter 5).

3   That fractions where the numerator and denominator share a common factor can be simplified into an equivalent fraction (we touched on equivalent fractions in Chapter 1, and will explore simplification more in Chapter 5).

If pupils do understand these things, then they can make sense of cross cancelling:

$$\frac{6}{11} \times \frac{4}{9} = \frac{6 \times 4}{11 \times 9} = \frac{4 \times 6}{11 \times 9} = \frac{4}{11} \times \frac{6}{9} = \frac{4}{11} \times \frac{2}{3}$$

Cross cancelling is simply a recognition that because the numerators and denominators will be multiplied, any factors of either numerator or denominator can be used to simplify the product.

Let us now turn our attention to decimals.

Subconcept link: multiplication of decimals

Some teachers like to introduce decimal multiplication prior to fraction multiplication, others prefer to see decimal multiplication as a specific case of fraction multiplication. It is possible to make sense of decimal multiplication either way round; however, when it comes to multiplying two decimal numbers, we do have a bit of work to do if pupils are not already familiar with fraction multiplication:

7 × 0.21

Similarly to multiplying a fraction by an integer, this can be seen simply as repeated addition (or the creation of an array):

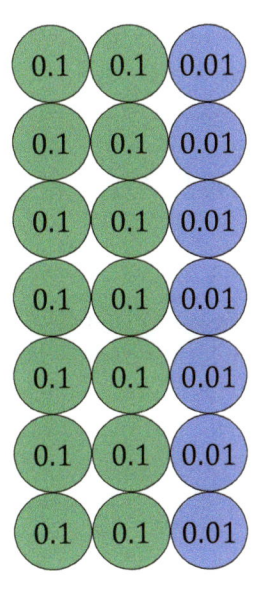

Of course, we would then exchange the 14 tenths for one 1 and 4 tenths:

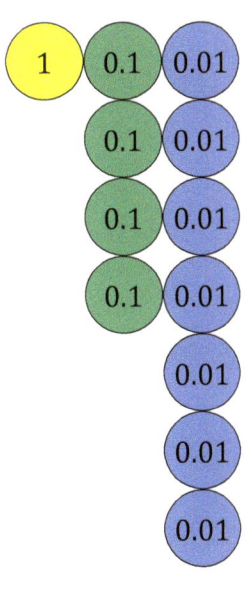

However, once again, when both values are decimal we cannot repeatedly add, and so an alternative model of multiplication will be needed to help make sense:

0.7 × 0.21

We can use an area to model this multiplication; however, the area used to represent a value of 1 would need to be 100 small squares long by 100 small squares wide in order to be able to represent 0.21. This makes the area model a little unwieldy when it comes to decimal multiplication, particularly when more than one decimal place is involved. If pupils already have an understanding of fraction multiplication, then it is a relatively simple matter to convert the two numbers to fractions and multiply them as fractions:

$0.7 \times 0.21 = \frac{7}{10} \times \frac{21}{100} = \frac{141}{1000} = 0.141$

However, if we are choosing to explore multiplication of decimals prior to multiplication of fractions, then how do we make sense of this calculation in a way that actually adds meaning to pupils' experience? Well, some would argue that we can stick to calculations such as 0.7 × 0.2 that can be represented more easily using an area, until pupils have spotted a pattern that can lead to a generalisation that could include 0.21. Personally, I am not satisfied with this: to me, patterns in mathematics are not reasons in themselves, they exist to be made sense of.

A potential alternative is to decompose a number like 0.7 into 7 × 0.1. This is a calculation that has already been made sense of using repeated addition. Similarly, we can decompose 0.21 into 21 × 0.01. This means a calculation like 0.7 × 0.21 can be thought of as 7 × 0.1 × 21 × 0.01. The commutative law allows us to rearrange this calculation to give 7 × 21 × 0.1 × 0.01. We can evaluate 7 × 21. But what about 0.1 × 0.01? Well, these are powers of 10, and we have already seen that multiplying by powers of 10 causes a shift in the place value column. So we can calculate 7 × 21, then shift it down one column, and then shift it down two more columns.

This gives rise to the idea of related calculations. A great reasoning activity is to provide pupils with the result of a calculation, and then ask them to reason the result of other calculations without having to work them out:

Given that 2.7 × 4.8 = 12.96 work out:

a   27 × 4.8   e   0.27 × 0.48

b   2.7 × 48   f   2.7 × 0.48

c   0.27 × 48   g   270 × 0.48

d   0.27 × 4.8

We can also bring in some divisions based on the same relationship:

h   12.96 ÷ 4.8   m   12.96 ÷ 27

i   129.6 ÷ 4.8   n   1.296 ÷ 27

j   129.6 ÷ 48   o   1.296 ÷ 0.27

k   129.6 ÷ 0.48

l   12.96 ÷ 2.7

We can do something similar with a 'fill in the blanks' activity:

Fill in the blanks in these calculations, given that 2.7 × 4.8 = 12.96

_____ × 4.8 = 129.6

_____ × 0.48 = 129.6

_____ × 0.48 = 1.296

2.7 × _____ = 1296

27 × _____ = 12.96

0.27 × _____ = 12.96

And so on.

Before moving on from rational numbers, we need to turn our attention to powers.

Concept: powers

Prerequisites: Number, multiplication.

Linked concepts: The laws of indices will require knowledge of addition, subtraction, division and factors.

The standard introduction to powers is to mirror the introduction to multiplication:

$5 + 5 + 5 + 5 + 5 + 5 = 5 \times 6$

$5 \times 5 \times 5 \times 5 \times 5 \times 5 = 5^6$

So 5 × 6 can be seen as the sum of six 5s, and 5^6 can be seen as the product of six 5s (and definitely not the product of 6 and 5).

This would suggest that our models for multiplication would extend to powers. However, in most cases the exponential nature of the calculations causes difficulties. Consider, for example:

5 × 5 × 5

If thinking about repeated addition, we might think, '5 × 5 = 5 + 5 + 5 + 5 + 5, and so if I multiply by 5 again we have (5 + 5 + 5 + 5 + 5) + (5 + 5 + 5 + 5 + 5) + (5 + 5 + 5 + 5 + 5) + (5 + 5 + 5 + 5 + 5) + (5 + 5 + 5 + 5 + 5)'. Whilst this is technically true, I hope all readers can agree that the potential for confusion here is huge, and if we were to multiply again by 5 (having to repeat that whole set again five times) we are going to start getting so big as to be completely unwieldy. The last thing we want is learners associating powers with addition, and so using repeated addition to model powers is probably not the way to go.

Similarly, unitisation will give rise to the same difficulties. We can have five things worth 5:

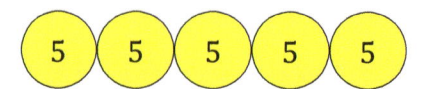

But then we would have to evaluate this to be 25 before then having five things worth 25. Either that or we can put them into an array:

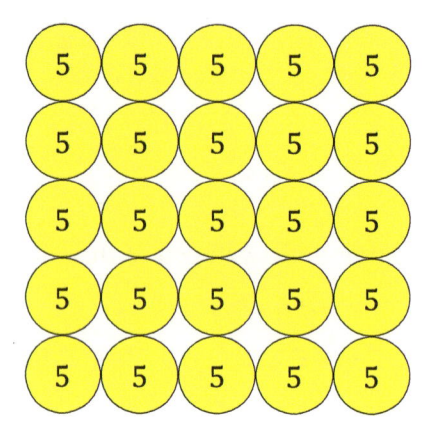

At this point, of course, we are mixing our models for multiplication (which is sometimes not avoidable) but even then, what would happen if we included an extra 5? We might even get away with stacking up piles of 5 on each of the counters in our array, but then one more 5 moves us beyond what we can represent.

Similarly, change of dimension can be used for earlier powers, but once we get beyond power 3, we run out of dimensions:

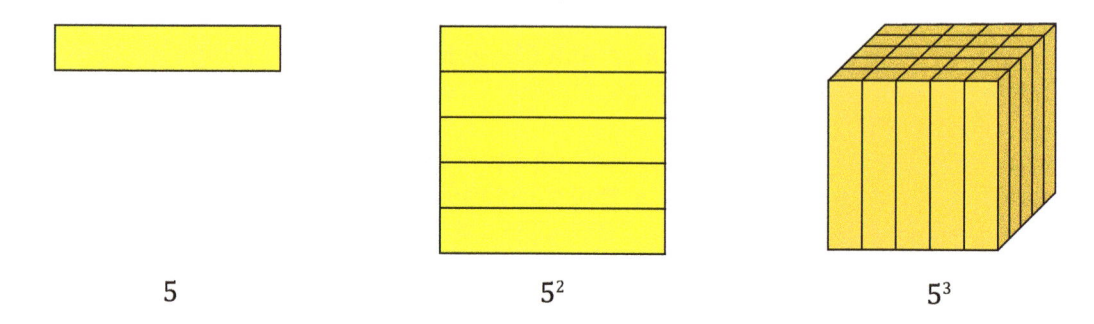

5   5^2 5^3

We can see that we can't represent 5^4 in this way. However, this does at least illustrate why power of 2 is called 'squaring' and power of 3 is called 'cubing'.

Scaling and the Cartesian Product (as represented in a tree diagram) can potentially show higher powers; however, for scaling you would need a very long number line to get into higher powers, which would mean lower values would be difficult to represent. And tree diagrams can get very busy very quickly:

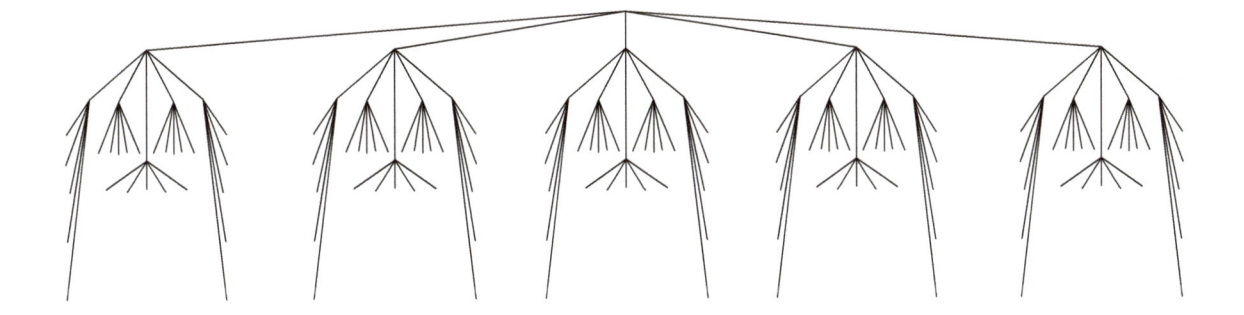

This tree diagram shows 5^3, and we can see that to add five branches to each of the 125 branches that are currently in the third layer of the diagram definitely wouldn't help make sense of what is happening.

Ultimately, I have found that changing dimension communicates enough about smaller powers to allow pupils to see what is going on but that larger powers are probably best handled in the abstract. This is not just because of the difficulties in representing larger powers but also because – like multiplication itself – we want powers to be seen as an operation in their own right. This allows us to explore the inverse operation: roots.

Of course, we have briefly discussed roots in introducing surds; however, these can take on a new 'dimension', so to speak, in that they can be seen as both the inverse of and a type of power (similarly to how subtraction can be seen as a type of addition and division can be seen as a type of multiplication). This is worth exploring explicitly with pupils – many pupils gain a lot of familiarity with square roots but little with higher order roots. We need to make clear to pupils that square roots are the inverse of the square power (i.e. an expression with an index of 2), and then that cube roots are the inverse of the cube power, and so on. Activities like the one below can help make this explicit.

Complete these number sentences:

1. If $x^7 = 2187$ then ...
2. If $x^6 = 2187$ then ...
3. If $x^5 = 2187$ then ...
4. If $x^4 = 2187$ then ...
5. If $x^3 = 2187$ then ...
6. If $x^2 = 2187$ then ...
7. If $x^1 = 2187$ then ...

This last one is, of course, a bit of a trick – there is no root to power 1 as power 1 doesn't have any effect.

Once the ideas of powers and roots are well understood, we can start to explore their properties a little more. I find that this goes easier if we first establish a common language around powers. Jo Morgan and Craig Barton have a great video that explores these in depth, including establishing the necessary language around powers:[6]

Base ⟶ 5^6 ⟵ Exponent/Index

Power

---

[6] J. Morgan, Indices in Depth, *Resourceaholic* [blog] (22 December 2019). Available at: https://www.resourceaholic.com/2019/12/indices-in-depth.html.

Important here is the fact that the whole expression is a 'power', with the expression having two parts, a base and an exponent or index. This, of course, means we can look at what it means to operate on these expressions:

$5^9 + 5^6$

If we look at this in expanded form, this gives:

$5 \times 5 \times 5 \times 5 \times 5 \times 5 \times 5 \times 5 \times 5 + 5 \times 5 \times 5 \times 5 \times 5 \times 5$

Assuming pupils know about order of operations (which we will look at in more detail in Chapter 5), then it is clear that there are only really two things we can do with this calculation:

1. Evaluate it by evaluating both multiplications separately and then adding.
2. Write it with a common unit so that we can add the two expressions, i.e. $125 \times 5^6 + 5^6 = 126 \times 5^6$ (or the same result through **factorisation** using the distributive law).

Of course, subtraction works in the same way as addition (being, at its heart, the same operation) and so replacing the plus sign with the minus sign doesn't change our options, only the result.

$5^9 \times 5^6$

If we look at this in expanded form, this gives:

$5 \times 5 \times 5 \times 5 \times 5 \times 5 \times 5 \times 5 \times 5 \times 5 \times 5 \times 5 \times 5 \times 5 \times 5 = 5^{15}$

This leads to the first index law:

> If two powered expressions with the same base are multiplied, the result is a powered expression with the same base and the sum of the two indices.

This is worth exemplifying with pupils using both examples and non-examples, including non-standard examples:

Write, where possible, as a single power:

a $7^9 \times 7^6$

b $y^9 \times y^6$

c $a^9 \times b^6$

d $(2x + 3)^9 \times (2x + 3)^6$

e $\sqrt{7}^9 \times \sqrt{7}^6$

f $9^7 \times 6^7$

Assuming pupils have learnt about division and its links to fractions (including fraction simplification), then we can also look at dividing powers expressions.

$5^9 \div 5^6$

If we look at this in expanded form, using fraction notation for the division, this gives:

$$\frac{5 \times 5 \times 5 \times 5 \times 5 \times 5 \times 5 \times 5 \times 5}{5 \times 5 \times 5 \times 5 \times 5 \times 5}$$

Assuming pupils are familiar with simplifying fractions, then we can see that this will simplify, resulting in 5^3. This leads to the second index law:

> If two powered expressions with the same base are divided, the result is a powered expression with the same base and the difference of the two indices.

A similar activity to the one above for multiplication helps to make sure pupils can see different examples of this law in operation, as well as when it doesn't work. In addition, if pupils are already familiar with negative indices, we can look at the idea of $5^9 \div 5^6 = 5^9 \times 5^{-6}$, reinforcing the idea that division and multiplication are one and the same.

If we are going to treat powers as an operation in its own right, then we also need to look at what happens when we take a powered expression and raise it to a further power.

$$(5^9)^6$$

To make sense of what is happening here, we simply need to remind learners that whenever something is raised to a power of 6, it can be seen as the product of 6 of those things. This means that:

$$(5^9)^6 = 5^9 \times 5^9 \times 5^9 \times 5^9 \times 5^9 \times 5^9$$

This puts us in a position to apply the first index law five times in succession, so $5^9 \times 5^9 = 5^{18}$, which can then be multiplied again by 5^9 to give 5^{27} and so on. This leads to the realisation that we can simply multiply the indices, giving rise to the third index law:

> If a powered expression is raised to a further power, the result is a powered expression with the same base and the product of the two indices.

So far, we have only examined indices that are positive integers. We can now turn our attention to an index of 0, to negative indices and to fractional indices. All of these can be reasoned from our established index laws:

$$a^0$$

We can begin to consider this by looking at a division that would result in an index of 0:

$$\frac{a^x}{a^x}$$

Applying the second index law would result in a^0. However, we can also see this as the quotient of two identical expression. By this point, pupils should be familiar with the fact that this will produce a value of 1. This leads to the conclusion that $a^0 = 1$. If pupils are not familiar enough with algebra at this point, then numerical examples will do the same job.

We extend this argument to look at negative indices:

$$\frac{a^0}{a^1} \quad \frac{a^0}{a^2} \quad \frac{a^0}{a^3} \quad ...$$

We can choose to see each of these expressions in two different ways:

1. We can apply the second index law to give $a^{-1}, a^{-2}, a^{-3}, ...$
2. We can choose to see a^0 as 1, and so have the unit fractions $\frac{1}{a}, \frac{1}{a^2}, \frac{1}{a^3}, ...$

This allows us to see that negative indices produce unit fractions, in general $\frac{a^0}{a^x} = a^{-x} = \frac{1}{a^x}$.

When it comes to looking at fractional indices, instead of applying the second index law, we apply the third, normally starting with unit fractions:

$$(a^2)^{\frac{1}{2}} = a \quad (a^3)^{\frac{1}{3}} = a \quad (a^4)^{\frac{1}{4}} = a \quad ...$$

This would imply that the unit fractional index is 'undoing' the original index, i.e. that the unit fractional index is the inverse of the positive integer index. However, we have already seen that the inverse of positive integer indices are roots. Logically it follows that:

$$x^{\frac{1}{2}} = \sqrt[2]{x} \quad x^{\frac{1}{3}} = \sqrt[3]{x} \quad x^{\frac{1}{4}} = \sqrt[4]{x} \quad ...$$

I would normally include the '2' in the square root here, just to reinforce the required relationship.

Finally, we can talk about non-unit fractions. Again the third index law is at play:

$$a^{\frac{x}{y}} = (a^x)^{\frac{1}{y}} = \left(a^{\frac{1}{y}}\right)^x$$

This gives us flexibility about how we evaluate powered expressions where the index is a non-unit fraction, and it is worth taking time to look at this with pupils – when is it better to apply the numerator first, and then the unit fraction (and vice versa)?

Rewrite these in the way that would make them easiest to evaluate or simplify:

a $125^{\frac{2}{3}}$ c $5^{\frac{3}{4}}$ e $9^{\frac{5}{2}}$

b $2^{\frac{3}{2}}$ d $10^{\frac{2}{5}}$ f $8^{\frac{2}{3}}$

The reason we looked at powers at this point is because we will find them necessary when we come to think about multiplication and surds:

Concept link: multiplication of surds

This time we have three cases to consider:

1. The multiplication of a positive integer by a surd.
2. The multiplication of rational number by a surd.
3. The multiplication of two surd values.

In common with multiplying positive integers by negatives and fractions, multiplying a surd by a positive integer can be seen as repeated addition:

3 × √2

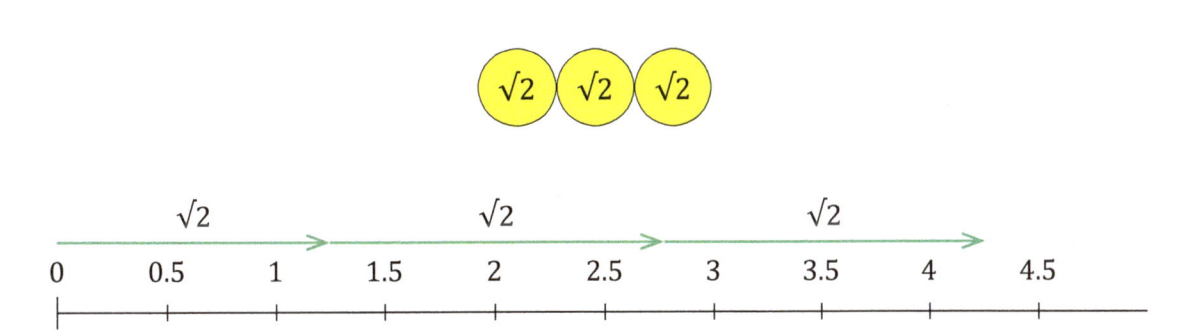

The only thing to really make clear here is that we would normally omit the multiplication sign in this expression, and so would write 3√2 rather than 3 × √2. The really important thing is for pupils to be secure in the knowledge that this is not √6 (a common misconception) – this is not necessarily obvious from the repeated addition (one can be forgiven for thinking that if 2 + 2 + 2 = 6 then √2 + √2 + √2 = √6) but can be made clear by looking at a good approximation of 3√2 (say, on a calculator) and an equally good approximation of √6 (or by noting that √6 is clearly less than 3, as this is √9 – but that 3 × √2 is clearly greater than 3 as it is 3 multiplied by something greater than 1).

In then bridging the gap from multiplication by a positive integer to multiplication by any rational number, we can, if we wish, bring back the ways we have previously looked at multiplication. For example, we can look at multiplication by a negative integer as the rotation of the pictures above. However, I find it is typically a perfectly simple step for pupils to recognise that all rationals work in the same way – i.e. that if 3 × √2 = 3√2 then −3 × √2 = −3√2 and $\frac{1}{3}$ × √2 = $\frac{1}{3}$√2. This includes calculations like 3 × 5√2 = 15√2 and $\frac{2}{3}$ × 6√2 = 4√2.

This leaves us just to examine the product of two surds.

√3 × √2

Now, of course, the temptation here is to simply write √3√2, following the example of multiplying a surd by a rational. So how do we make clear that this is equivalent to √6?

To my knowledge, there is no concrete or visual representation that adequately demonstrates that √3 × √2 is √6. However, we can show this using a bit of extrapolation from the area model (although it doesn't really add a huge amount in terms of making sense of the situation). I will include it below, but can't say I have ever used it with pupils or see that it would be helpful.

To begin, we actually look at $3^2 \times 2^2$ but, in particular, making a 2 × 2 square from 3 × 3 squares:

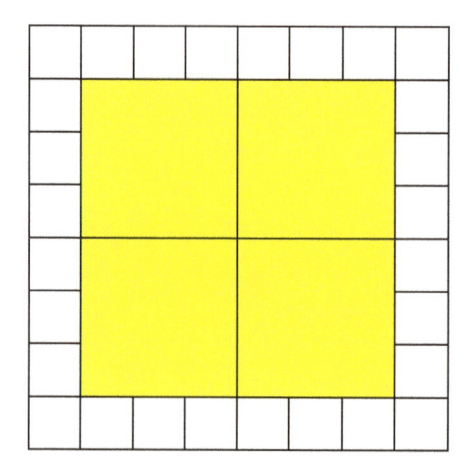

We can use this to see that that $\sqrt{3^2 \times 2^2} = 3 \times 2$, similarly to how we simplified surds. Moreover, we can extrapolate from this that $\sqrt{a^2 \times b^2} = a \times b$:

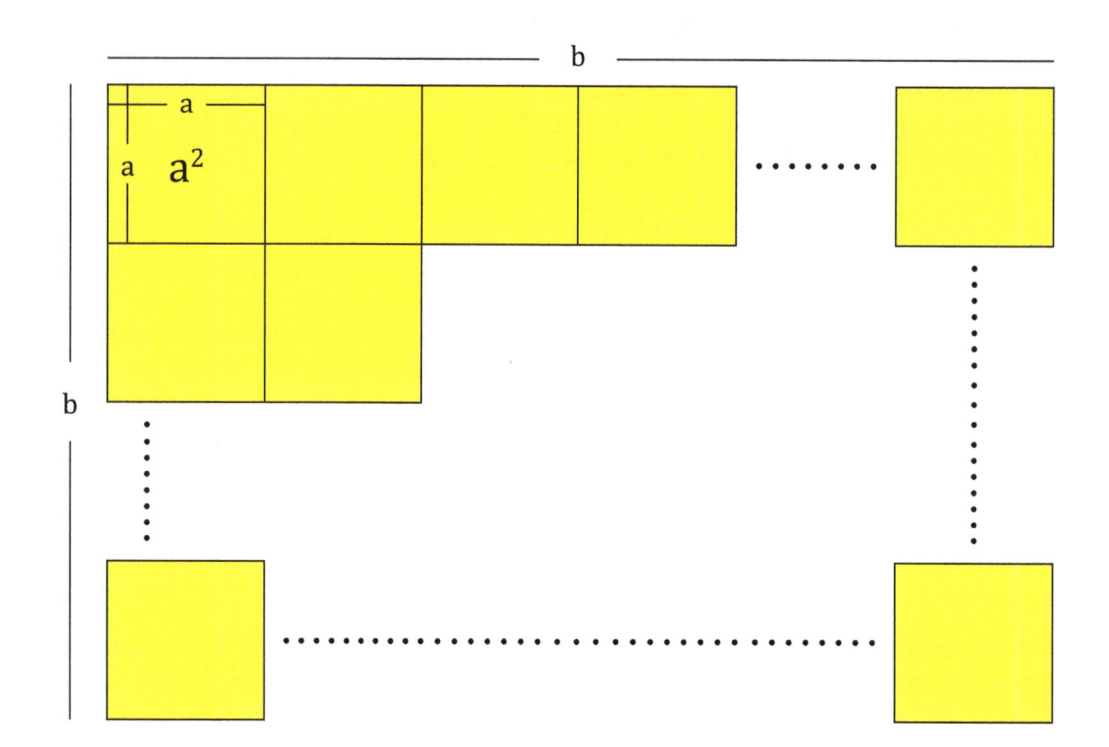

If we then change the area of each square from a^2 to a, and change the number of squares from b^2 to b, then this will change to $\sqrt{a \times b} = \sqrt{a} \times \sqrt{b}$:

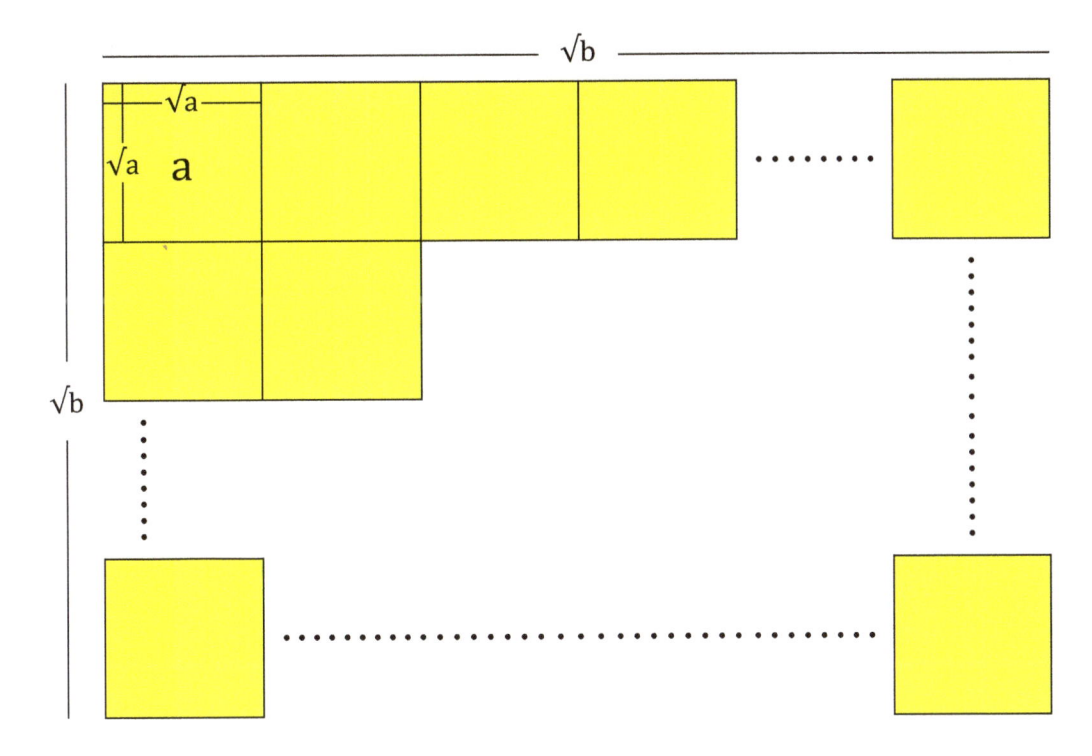

To me, the much better way to explore why $\sqrt{3} \times \sqrt{2} = \sqrt{6}$ (or in general why $\sqrt{a} \times \sqrt{b} = \sqrt{a \times b}$) is to look at the equivalent powers. Provided our learners already understand that powers distribute over multiplication (and this is easily demonstrable for positive integer powers if not – we will look at this in Chapter 5) then we can construct the following logical argument:

$\sqrt{3} \times \sqrt{2} =$
$3^{\frac{1}{2}} \times 2^{\frac{1}{2}} =$
$(3 \times 2)^{\frac{1}{2}} =$
$6^{\frac{1}{2}} = \sqrt{6}$

Of course, this argument is easily generalised by replacing 3 and 2 with a and b respectively.

From here then we can look at multiplying different expressions involving surds and non-surds; multiplications like $\sqrt{3}(\sqrt{2} + 1)$ – assuming distributivity has been learnt by this point – and $(\sqrt{3} + 4)(4\sqrt{2} - 5)$. There are some nice 'Show that' questions as part of N11 of the *Improving Learning in Mathematics* (most commonly known as 'the Standards Unit'), some of which can serve as interesting prompts to jump off into some exploration around surds and multiplication.[7]

---

7   STEM Learning, Manipulating Surds N11 (n.d.). Available at: https://www.stem.org.uk/resources/elibrary/resource/26731/manipulating-surds-n11.

Concept link: multiplication and algebra

As the generalisation of number, we can make sense of multiplying algebraic expressions in the same ways that we make sense of multiplying numbers. Indeed, examining multiplication of algebraic expressions highlights more than anything the need for multiple models for multiplication.

$4 \times b$

This is a situation, similar to those we have seen previously, where, because one of the terms is a natural number, we can model this using repeated addition:

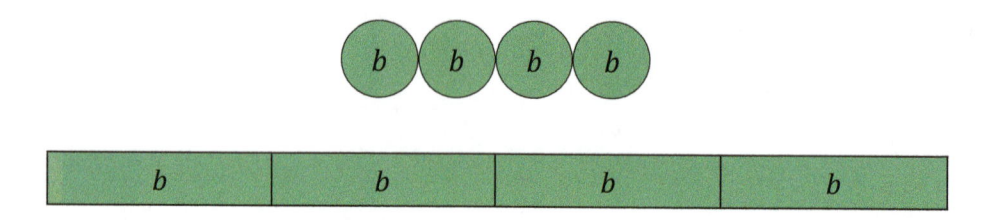

However, from here we can see alternative models for multiplication – in particular the area model:

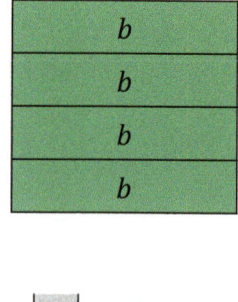

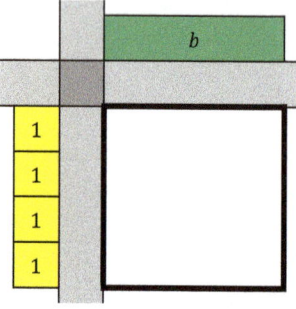

This is particularly important when we look at multiplication of variables by non-natural numbers:

$\frac{1}{2}b$

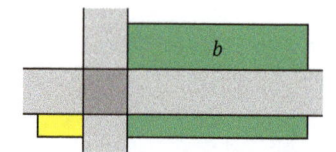

Or two variables:

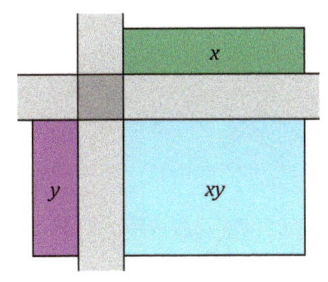

xy

Earlier, I mentioned that sometimes mixing models is unavoidable, and there are potentially a couple of situations here:

3cd

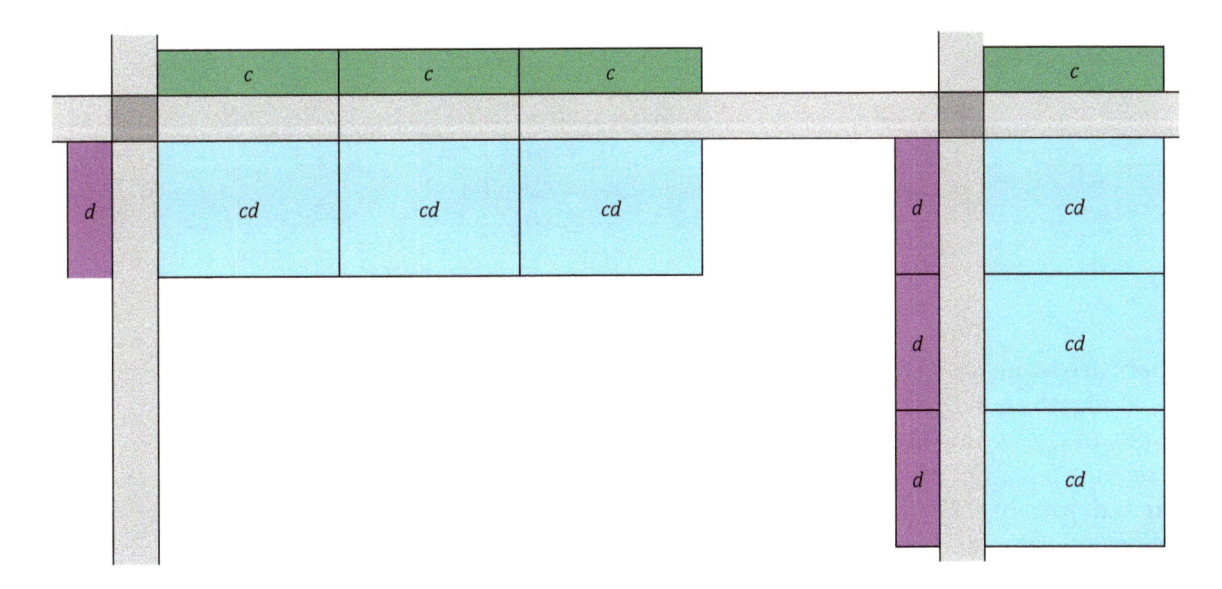

Here we are mixing the models so that either '3c' or '3d' is being seen as repeated addition along the length/width of the area, with the multiplication by the second variable then shown using the area.

abc

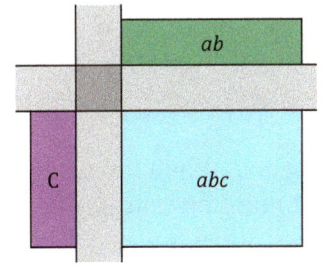

Here we can see one of the lengths being considered the product of two of the variables (indicating that we would need to evaluate this product) and then multiplying by the third variable creates the area. However, I would say that by the time we are getting to this sort of thing, we would ideally be in a position to dispense with the model and work in the abstract.

Spot the mistake:

Identify the errors in these solutions. Can you see how they arrived at their answers? Which one is correct?

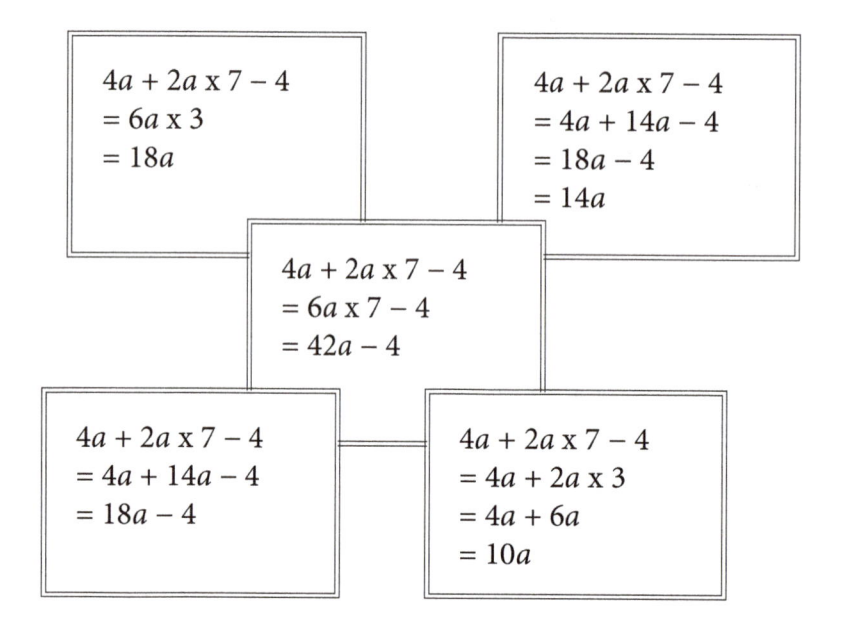

$4a + 2a \times 7 - 4$
$= 6a \times 3$
$= 18a$

$4a + 2a \times 7 - 4$
$= 4a + 14a - 4$
$= 18a - 4$
$= 14a$

$4a + 2a \times 7 - 4$
$= 6a \times 7 - 4$
$= 42a - 4$

$4a + 2a \times 7 - 4$
$= 4a + 14a - 4$
$= 18a - 4$

$4a + 2a \times 7 - 4$
$= 4a + 2a \times 3$
$= 4a + 6a$
$= 10a$

There are some nice activities that can take pupils beyond just multiplying terms or expressions together. Access Maths has some nice True/False grids that can be used to support pupils in deepening their understanding of multiplication of algebraic terms[8] as well as a nice multiplication grid that can prompt pupils' reasoning skills.[9] We can also bring in similar activities to those we have seen throughout; in this activity pupils identify the errors in others' working and explain them (where one contains no errors).

One thing we haven't yet discussed is the idea of 'multiple' in relation to multiplication. We will finish this chapter with a look at this concept.

Concept: multiple

Prerequisites: Natural numbers, multiplication.

Linked concepts: Factor, sequences.

The word 'multiple' is an interesting one. When it was originally conceived, it was probably only meant to be used with natural numbers and probably still works best when we limit our attention to the natural numbers. Since it was originally conceived though, it has morphed in meaning, to a point where the definition is not now clear. A quick search in your favourite search engine will suggest that some define 'multiple' as the product of any two

---

8   See https://www.accessmaths.co.uk/uploads/4/4/2/3/44232537/multiplying_algebra_true_of_false_sheets.pdf.
9   See https://www.accessmaths.co.uk/uploads/4/4/2/3/44232537/_algebra_multiplication_grid_fill_in_the_blanks_with_answers.pdf.

numbers, whilst others specify that one of the numbers in the product must be an integer. However, even this can cause issues: is −24 a common multiple of 8 and 6? −24 can be made by multiplying both 8 and 6 by a number (or indeed, an integer), so it would seem to fit the definition. If −24 is a common multiple of both 8 and 6, does this mean that the 'lowest common multiple' doesn't actually exist? Or does the lowest common multiple have to be greater than zero (and integers) even though multiples don't have to be? Does this also mean that −3 is a factor of −24? If so, is it prime? Or is 3 even prime when it can be written as both 1 × 3 and −1 × −3?

We can see that, potentially, defining multiples outside of the natural numbers may be problematic. Personally, I prefer to keep talk of multiples (and factors – next chapter) to the natural numbers, and talk of other multiplications simply as products. So I would describe −24 as the product of 8 and −3, but I wouldn't describe −24 as a multiple of either 8 or −3. I am sure others will disagree, and that is fine, but I find it keeps a useful distinction.

If for now we limit our attention to natural numbers, then we can talk about the multiples of a number as the product of that number with any other natural number. There are some great activities to support pupils in working with multiples. For example, in the grid below the challenge is to put single digits in each box so that the two-digit numbers created in each row or column are multiples of the values indicated:

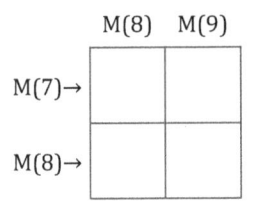

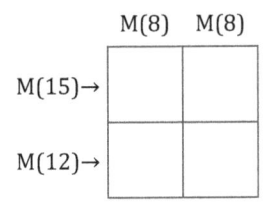

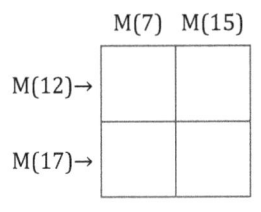

	M(8) M(9)		M(8) M(8)		M(7) M(15)
M(7)→		M(15)→		M(12)→	
M(8)→		M(12)→		M(17)→	

All the 4 digits in each problem should be different.

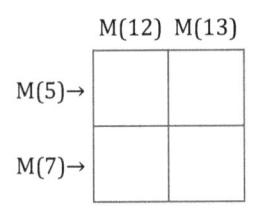

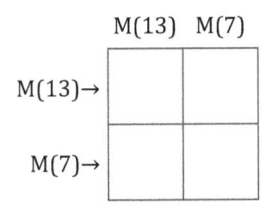

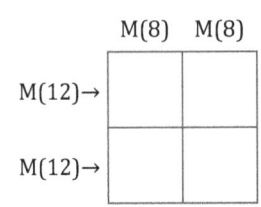

	M(12) M(13)		M(13) M(7)		M(8) M(8)
M(5)→		M(13)→		M(12)→	
M(7)→		M(7)→		M(12)→	

Gabriel's Problem from NRICH is also a really nice problem where pupils have to fill in the digits 1 to 9 so that each row and column create the product given at the end of the row/column.[10]

---

10 See https://nrich.maths.org/11750.

Subconcept: even/odd

Once pupils have begun to explore multiples, they are in a good position to explore even numbers (and then, in contrast, odd numbers). I like the area model/arrays for looking at even numbers – we can simply look at which areas are possible with a dimension of 2/ which numbers of counters can we create arrays with two equal columns:

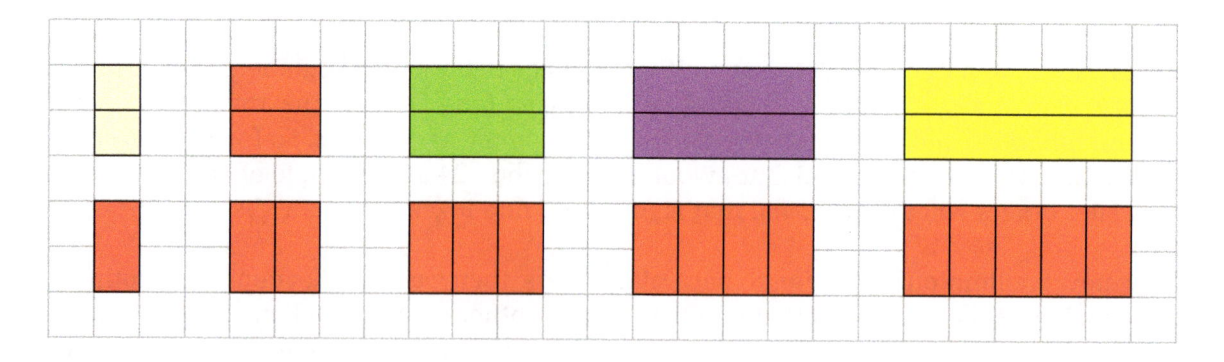

(Two potential area models for even numbers.)

These are clearly the multiples of 2, which highlights the links between multiples, multiplication and 'even-ness'. Odd can consequently be seen as 'those which are not even', i.e. those for which an array/area with a dimension of 2 isn't possible (at least when the other dimension is also an integer). We can then look at properties that even numbers have when written as numerals (i.e. always ending in 0, 2, 4, 6 or 8).

One of my favourite activities for working with odd and even numbers are so-called 'number chains'. I usually start with forming chains in a simple way, such as:

> Start with any number. If the number is even, halve it. If the number is odd, add 1. Keep going to form a number chain. Stop when you reach 1.
>
> What is the longest chain you can find?

This potentially then opens up the Collatz problem,[11] where instead of adding 1 when a number is odd, we first multiply by 3 and then add 1. There is some nice history of maths behind this problem, as well as being (at least to my knowledge at the time of writing) unsolved!

---

11 E. W. Weisstein, Collatz Problem, *Wolfram MathWorld* (n.d.). Available at: https://mathworld.wolfram.com/CollatzProblem.html.

Subconcept: square number

Clearly, as well as being able to explore even/odd with area models that have a dimension of 2 (or use exactly two of a single type of rod), a nice way to introduce the idea of square numbers is to look at those multiples that produce perfect squares:

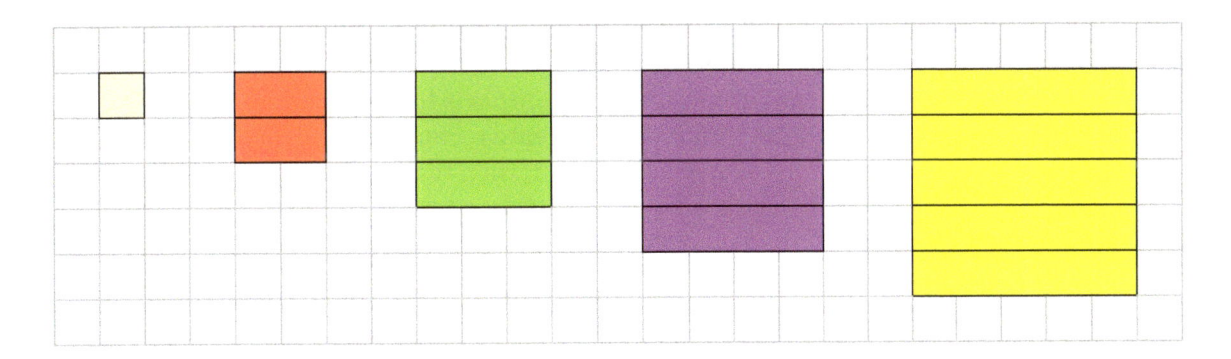

We can then link these with powers, by looking at them as the natural numbers each raised to a power of 2 and to multiples through the use of the same multiplier and multiplicand, i.e. the fourth multiple of 4, or the seventh multiple of 7.

There are some lovely properties to tie in with square numbers, from simple sums of odd numbers creating square numbers (and being able to show geometrically why that is):

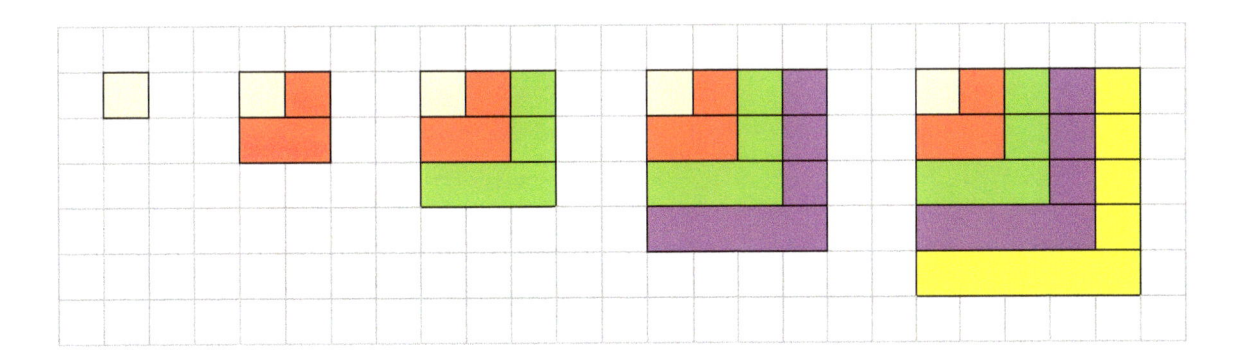

to finding the product of two consecutive even or odd numbers and adding 1, and showing that this will always be square:

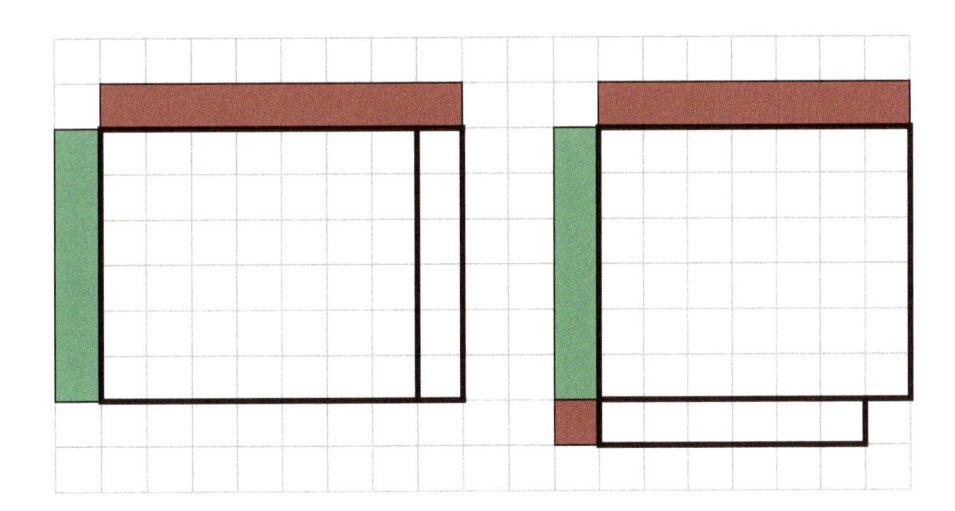

Once again, Don Steward has a great collection of activities that can prompt thinking and exploration about square numbers.[12]

Subconcept: lowest common multiple

When it comes to introducing the lowest common multiple, I find the area model the most useful model (not least because it then translates so nicely to when I want to introduce factors). One way of introducing lowest common multiple is to use Cuisenaire rods; in particular, to take two different coloured rods and to create rectangles with the same area. For example, if I define the white rod to have a value of 1, then the brown rod will have a value of 8 and the dark green rod will have a value of 6, so we can build rectangles out of the 8 rod and the 6 rod that have no gaps and no overlaps that have the same area:

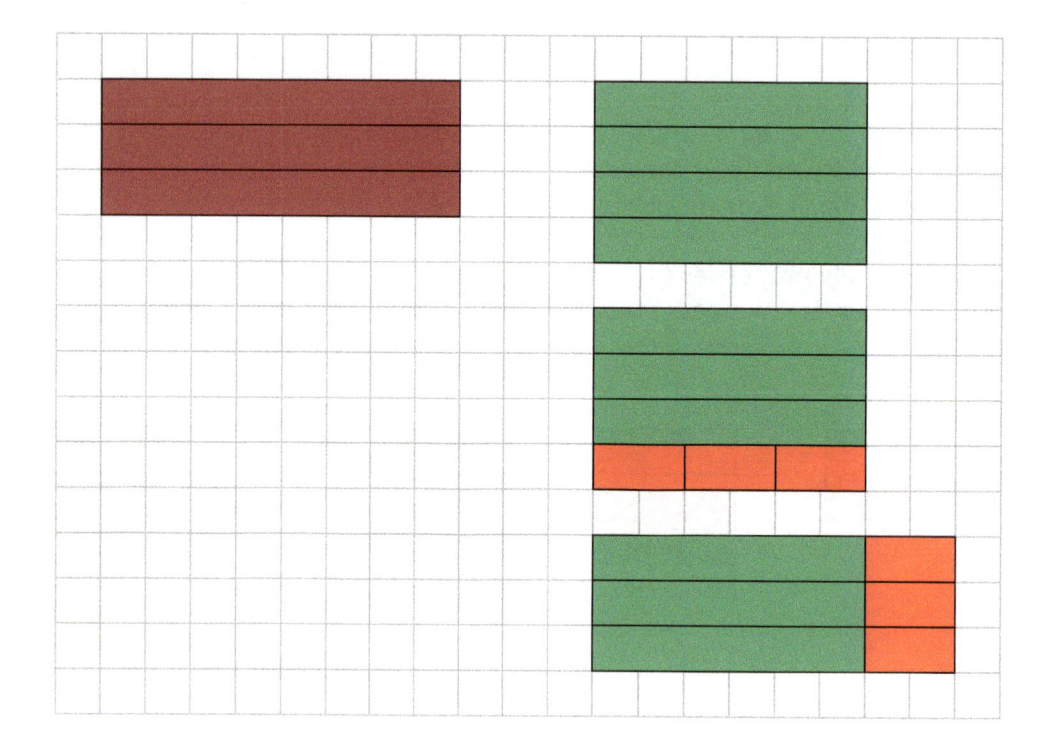

We can see that I can build a rectangle out of three 8 rods, and can build a rectangle out of four 6 rods that has the same area (I can even demonstrate the 'same area' by replacing one of the 6 rods with three 2 rods, and then attaching them to the end of each 6 rod).

There are many different contexts that lowest common multiple skills can be used with. Below is just one example from a set of Corbettmaths practice questions:[13]

Trains leave Bristol

to Cardiff every 15 minutes

to London every 21 minutes

---

12 D. Steward, Square Number Patterns, *Median* [blog] (28 March 2020). Available at: https://donsteward.blogspot.com/2020/03/square-number-patterns.html.
13 J. Corbett, Exam Style Questions: Lowest Common Multiples Highest Common Factors, *Corbettmaths* (2015). Available at: https://corbettmaths.com/wp-content/uploads/2013/02/lcm-hcf-pdf.pdf.

A train to Cardiff and a train to London both leave Bristol at 11 a.m. At what time will a train to Cardiff and a train to London next leave Bristol at the same time?

In addition, good reasoning activities like the one below can prompt deeper thinking around lowest common multiple:

Two different numbers have a lowest common multiple that is nine times bigger than the smallest number. What possible pairs of numbers can you find?

The lowest common multiple of two even numbers is 180. What are the two numbers?

What if the two numbers aren't even, but are multiples of 3?

What about multiples of 4?

Explore further.

Chapter 4
Division and factors

Like subtraction, division is an operation that we could work mathematically without. Every division we would wish to do can be transformed into a multiplication, and eventually this is an important aspect of division that we would want pupils to recognise. This puts division in an interesting position in that it can be seen as the opposite (inverse) of multiplication but also as the same operation (this, of course, is also true of subtraction and addition).

Concept: division

Prerequisites: Numbers, subtraction, multiplication.

Linked concepts: Proportionality, measures. Many concepts will require the need to divide in some capacity.

Of course, whilst division as an operation is redundant, division plays an important role in interpreting situations mathematically. These give rise to some of the ways we might model division – usually this is initially as either grouping or sharing:

$15 \div 3$

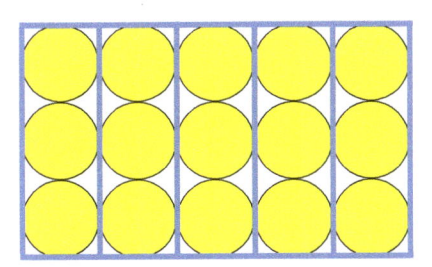

Here we see 15 (the dividend) that has been grouped into groups of 3 (the divisor). The number of groups created gives us the quotient, which in this case is 5. Alternatively, we can take the same underlying array and, rather than create vertical groups of 3, we can create 3 horizontal equal shares:

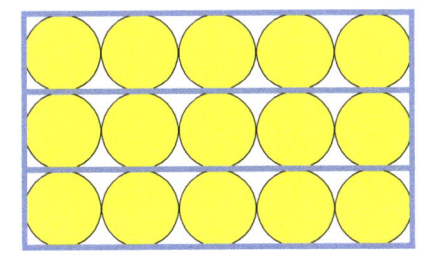

In this case, the divisor (3) is now the number of equal shares that we want to create, and the quotient (5) is the number of counters per share.

Within these two models, we can see lots of links to multiplication, hinting at the inverse nature of multiplication and division. In both pictures we can see an array of 15 counters (although we could create both from a line of counters as opposed to an array), but rather than creating an array by being given the length and width, we are creating the array by being given the total number of objects in the array, and one of the dimensions, and the result of the division is the other dimension.

Other 'inverses' of multiplication can also be seen from these images. We could choose to look at the grouping model as 'how many subtractions of 3 could we do from 15 to get back to 0?' – showing the inverse of the model of repeated addition. We could also choose to see the grouping model as the inverse of unitisation – how many units of 3 could we make from 15?

Of course, these two images only use numbers as discrete objects. But we could also choose to see the numbers as continuous measures. In that case, how can we model division? Well, we can adapt the array images above to a full area image:

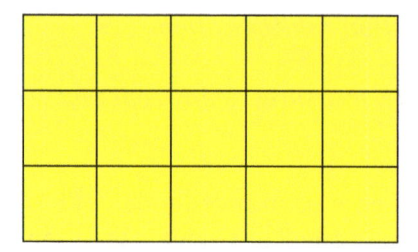

However, it doesn't really make sense to 'group' or 'share' area (unless we are going to physically detach the squares). Instead we would consider 'splitting' this area. Splitting might be seen as the continuous equivalent to either grouping or sharing (or both) – personally it makes sense to me to see it as the equivalent of sharing (i.e. 15 ÷ 3 can be seen as sharing 15 into 3 equal shares when the 15 is discrete, or 15 split into 3 equal parts when the 15 is continuous).

Splitting is also a useful model for division in other continuous representations of numbers:

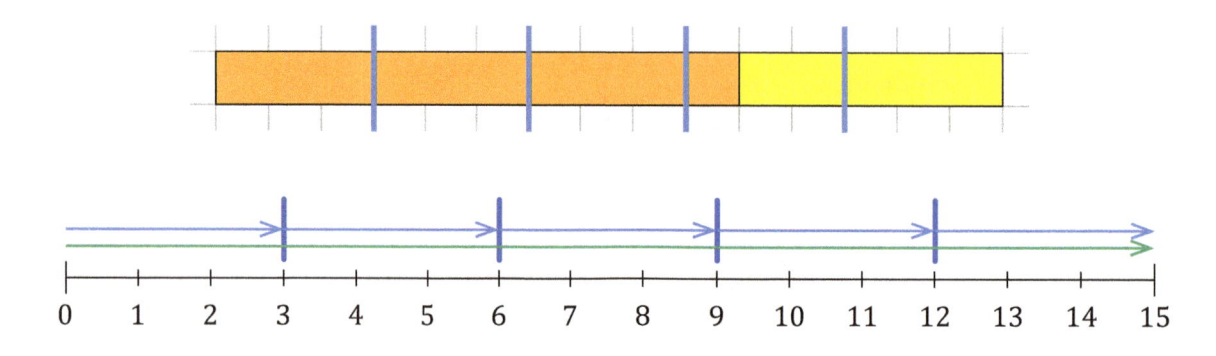

The issue with all of these models of division is that they can be more difficult (and in some cases impossible) to apply when one of either the divisor or the quotient are not a positive integer. For a model that can help with sense-making for any dividend and divisor, we turn to the equivalent to 'difference' for subtraction, typically known as *multiplicative comparison*. The premise here is that, given two numbers, they can be compared in an additive way; 'how much more ...', which is finding the difference (comparing the numbers) as a model for subtraction. Alternatively, we can compare two numbers in a multiplicative way, 'how many times more ...', which is finding the scale as a model for division (indeed, this can be seen as the inverse of multiplication as scaling).

Division and factors

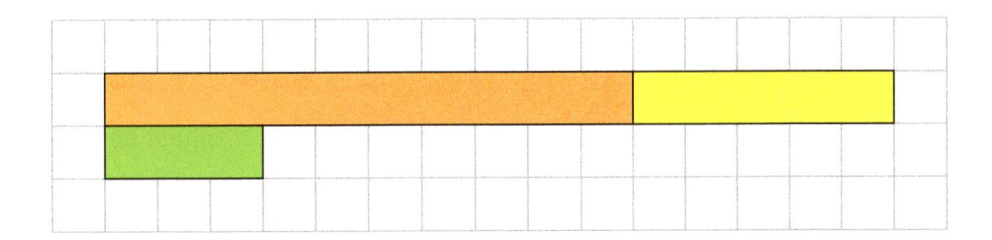

In looking at this image, we could interpret it in two ways:

1   How much longer is the top bar than the bottom bar? This is the difference model for subtraction.

2   How many times bigger is the top bar than the bottom bar? This is the comparison model for division.

A really nice way of thinking about division in this way is to ask yourself the question, 'How is the dividend changed if the divisor is changed to the value of 1?' In this way we can see that this model can also be considered an inverse to a unitising model of multiplication. We can even show this using the rods:

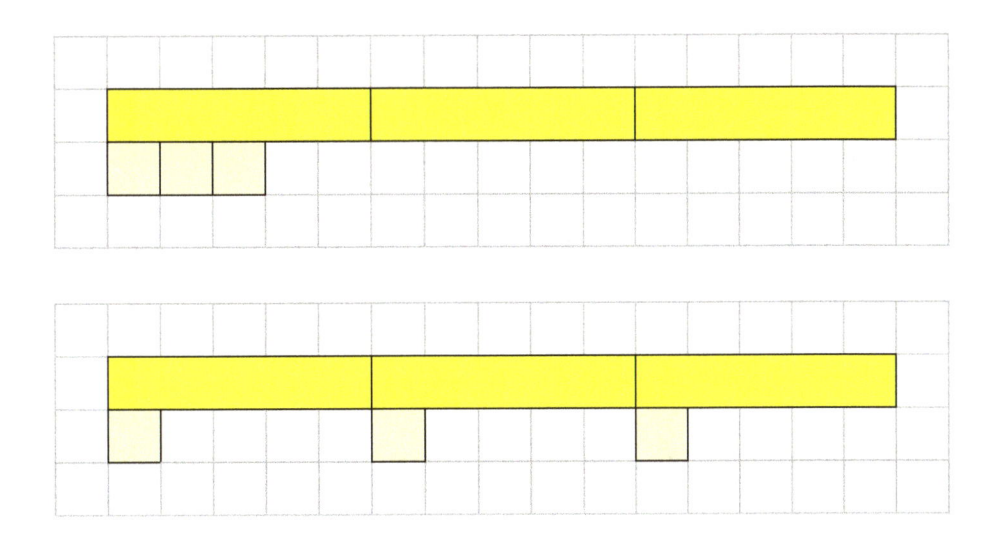

We can see this as '15 is to 3 as 5 is to 1'. This model of division forms the basis of proportional relationships as well as laying the foundations for equivalent fractions. It also allows exploration of strategies for division that involve scaling both the dividend and the divisor – recognising that if both are scaled in the same way that the quotient remains constant:

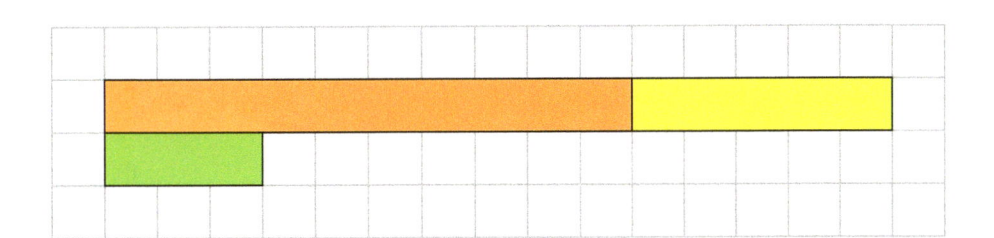

We would normally use this to show 15 ÷ 3; however, we can ask questions such as, 'What if the green rod was worth 6?', 'What if the green rod was worth 10?' This allows pupils to see that this comparison idea leads to families of divisions that result in the same answer. This eventually allows us to look at division of decimals ('What if the green rod was worth

0.2?') as well as motivating division strategies such as calculating 432 ÷ 8 by rewriting it as 216 ÷ 4 and then eventually 108 ÷ 2.

It is worth noting that multiplicative comparison can be used as a model equally well for numbers as discrete objects:

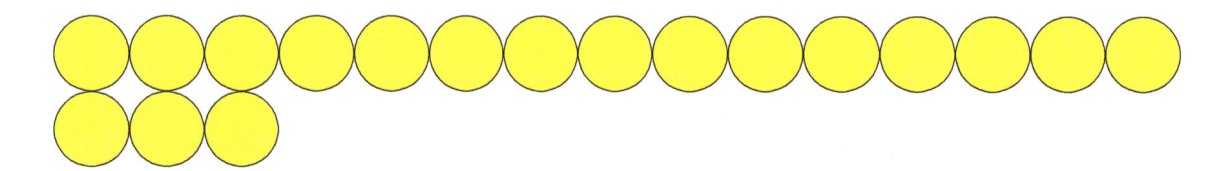

Pupils can show division using these different models and concrete/pictorial representations. We can also offer practical situations where each of these models arises:

Identify which model is being used in each division question:

a A restaurant sold 14 pies last week. How many pies on average were sold each day?

b An industrial machine made 678 shirts. If it takes one minute to make three shirts, how many minutes was it working?

c Sara worked 10 hours in the last five days. Assuming that she worked the same number of hours each day, how long did she work each day?

d There are 666 students going to a trivia competition. If each school van can hold six students, how many vans will they need?

e A vase can hold five flowers. If a florist had 900 flowers, how many vases would she need?

f Joan has 12 violet balloons. She wants to give her six friends the same number of violet balloons, how many will each friend get?

And we can also present different situations involving different operations and ask pupils to identify whether they are addition, subtraction, multiplication or division questions based on the models being used:

Tom wants to buy a saxophone.
The saxophone costs £820.

Tom pays £250 of the cost as a deposit.
He then pays the rest of the cost in 6 equal monthly payments.

There are 150 people on a train.

At the first stop

10 people get off the train
25 people get on the train.

At the next stop

5 people get off the train
16 people get on the train.

The train has 240 seats.
80 of the seats are red.

The diagram shows the distances between some places on a cycle route.

Not drawn to scale

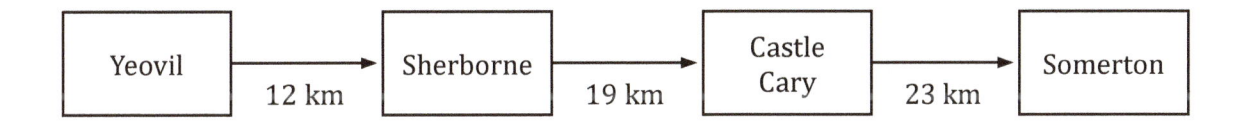

| Yeovil | →12 km→ | Sherborne | →19 km→ | Castle Cary | →23 km→ | Somerton |

We can ask different questions from these sorts of contexts to highlight different operations and model, as well as asking questions to support pupils in developing fluency with division calculations:

A two-digit number is divided by the sum of its digits. How many ways can you do this and get a whole-number answer?

Of course, if not using a calculator, then some of these divisions might be difficult to calculate mentally using known multiplication/division facts. To calculate the results of these divisions, pupils will need to be able to divide larger numbers, using a combination of place value knowledge and division:

Concept link: division and place value

1341 ÷ 3

There are two main processes that combine these two concepts that are taught in schools. The first, and most common, is the use of the short division algorithm.

Process: short division algorithm

This algorithm is best seen as modelling the division as sharing:

3 | 1000 100 10 1
  | 100 10
  | 100 10
  | 10

The goal is to share this number into three shares, using an awareness that we might exchange higher-place value counters when they can't be shared exactly. This means we will start by sharing the highest valued counters. In this case, we cannot share the single 1000 into three shares, so we will exchange it for ten 100s:

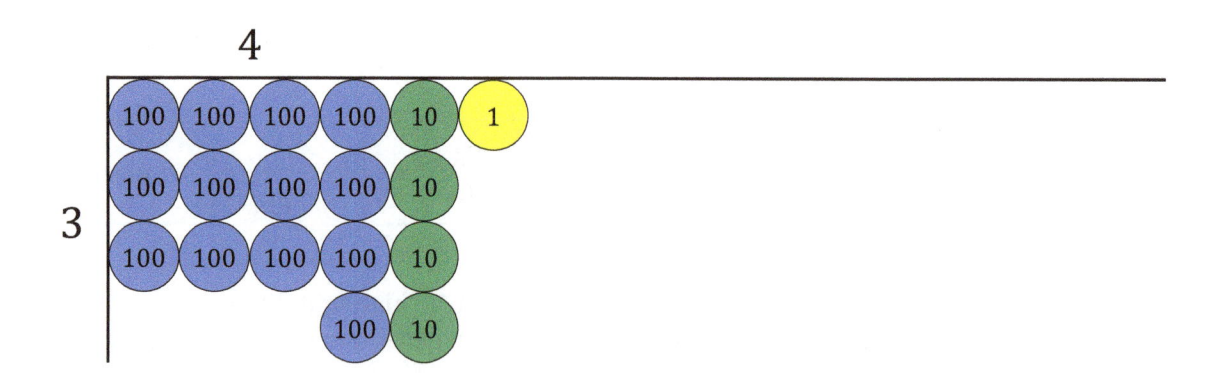

When we complete this exchange, we have thirteen 100s, which when shared into three shares allows us to place four 100s in each share, with a single 100 remaining that doesn't fit into the shares. This single 100 is therefore exchanged for ten 10s:

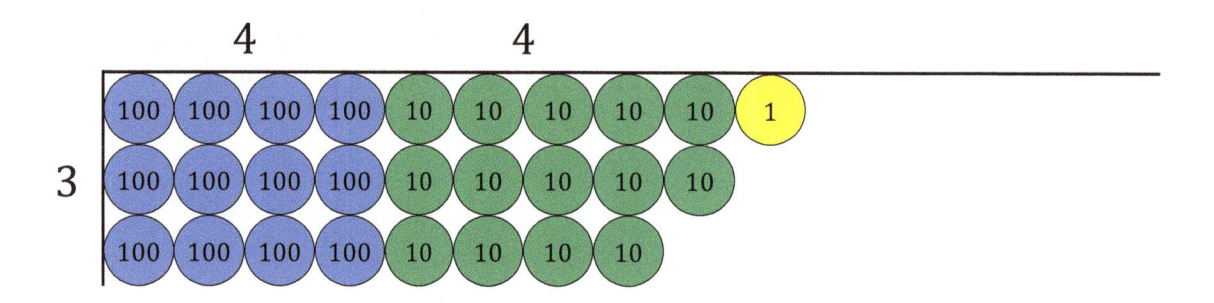

When this exchange is completed, we have fourteen 10s, which when shared into three shares allows us to place four 10s in each share, with two 10s remaining that don't fit into the shares. These two 10s are therefore each exchanged for ten 1s:

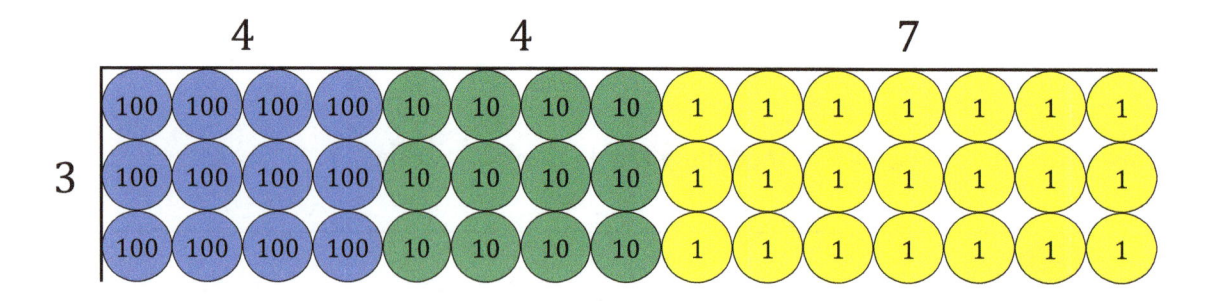

When this exchange is completed, we have twenty-one 1s, which when shared into three shares allows us to place exactly seven 1s in each share. The result is we have placed four 100s, four 10s and seven 1s into each share, meaning the result of the division is 447.

Process: division by chunking

The chunking process is based on repeated subtraction rather than sharing:

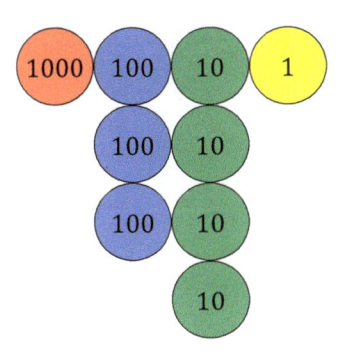

1341 ÷ 3

Of course, we wouldn't want to simply subtract 3 repeatedly from such a large number. Rather we would look to create 'chunks' of 3s, perhaps starting with a chunk of a hundred 3s (so long as we can keep track of how many chunks we are subtracting!).

To continue to subtract chunks of one hundred 3s, we will need to exchange the 1000 for ten 100s:

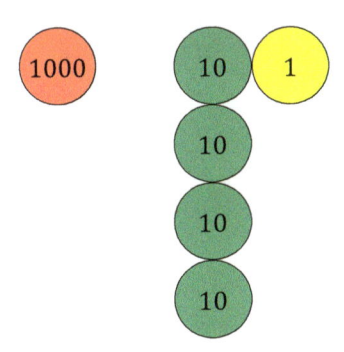

We can now subtract three chunks of a hundred 3s, meaning we will have subtracted four hundred 3s altogether:

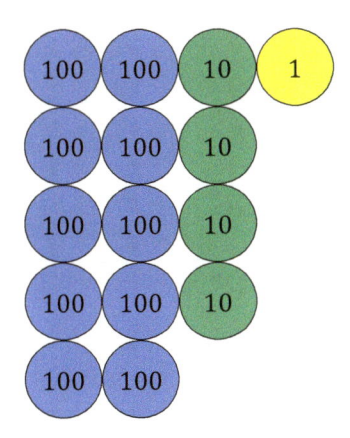

Process: division by chunking

There are no more chunks of a hundred 3s that can be subtracted, so we might move on to subtracting chunks of ten 3s.

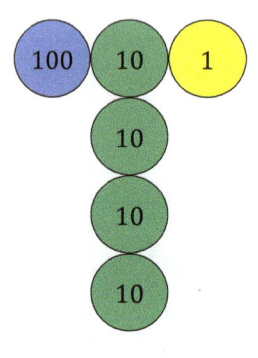

Again, requiring exchange – of the 100 into ten 10s.

We can now subtract three more chunks of ten 3s, which will leave us two 10s and a 1. The two 10s we will exchange for twenty 1s.

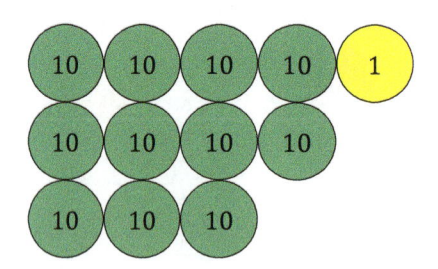

From here pupils may recognise the 21 left as being seven 3s, or we may subtract single chunks of 3, or perhaps even five chunks of 3 and then two chunks of 3. Any which way, eventually we will have subtracted four chunks of one hundred 3s, four chunks of ten 3s and then another seven chunks of 3, meaning altogether 447 chunks of 3.

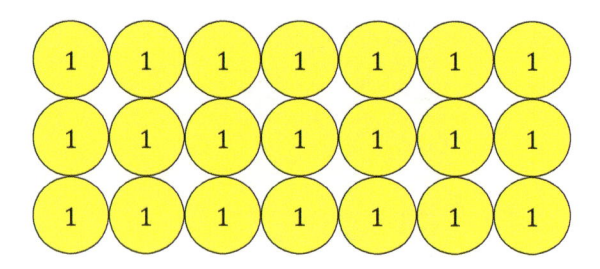

There is a third process associated with division, which seems to come into and out of fashion in maths education – I suspect its use with polynomials keeps it in teacher consciousness – and uses ideas from both the short division algorithm and chunking. This is, of course, the long division algorithm.

Process: long division algorithm

4212 ÷ 12

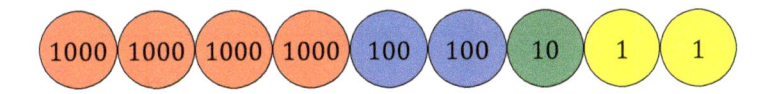

We start by proceeding similarly to short division, i.e. we will exchange the four 1000s for forty 100s and share them into 12 shares:

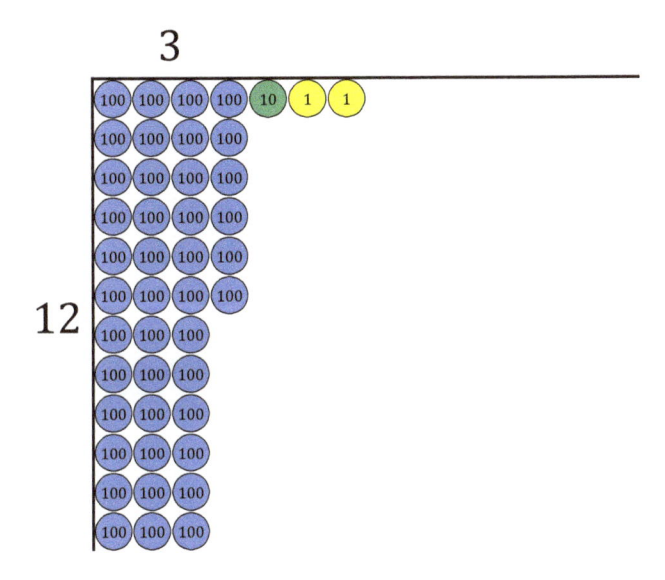

Having worked out that there will be three 100s per share, we then subtract the three 100s from each share (or thirty-six 100s altogether) leaving the number 612. We then begin again with 612, exchanging the six 100s for sixty 10s and creating 12 shares from the resulting sixty-one 10s:

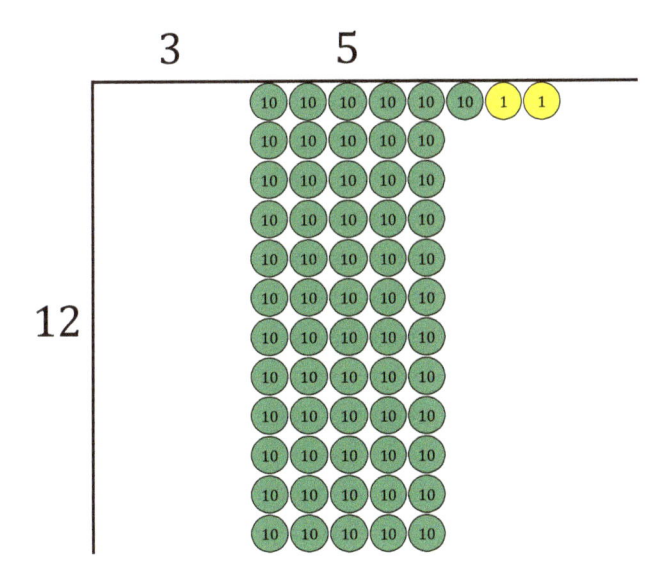

Again, having shown that there will be five 10s in each share, we then subtract the five 10s from each share (sixty of the sixty-one 10s) leaving the value of 112. We then finish by exchanging the single 10 into ten 1s, and then sharing the resulting twelve 1s:

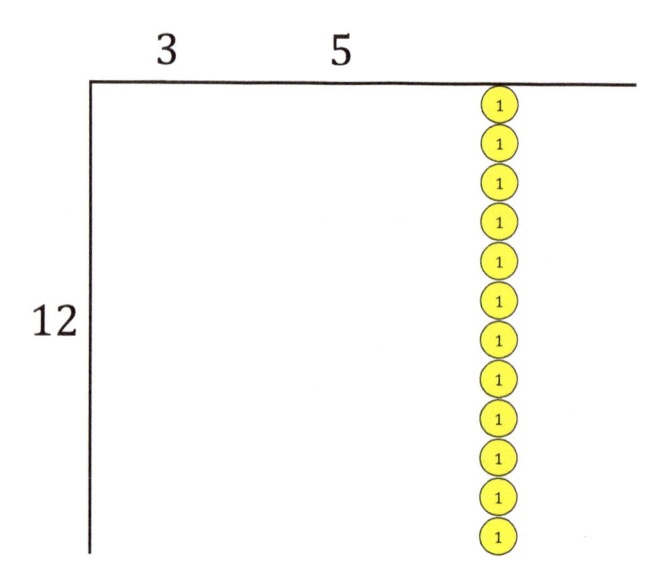

This can also be thought of as grouping and subtracting groups of 12 of each type of counter.

The same strategies can be used for dividing decimals by whole numbers, or dividing two whole numbers where the result is a decimal (although it takes a learner who is very secure in place value to make chunking work for division by a whole number resulting in a decimal). Problems like the one below can then support pupils in developing their understanding of division:[1]

Use the given digits to make the division sums correct

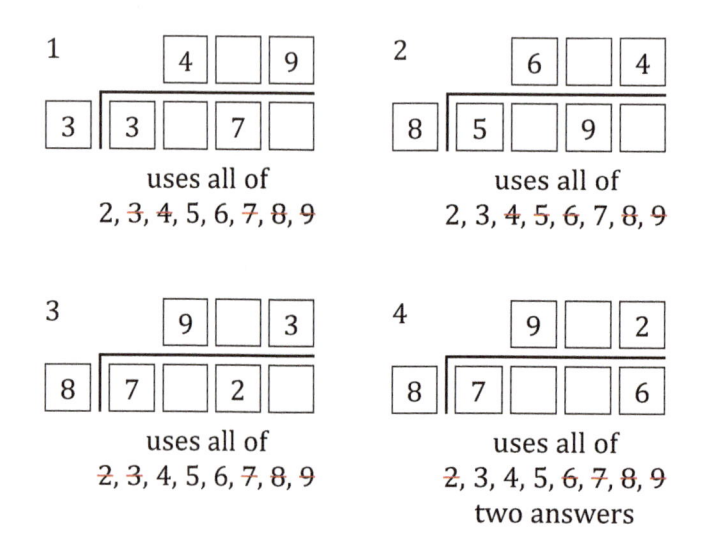

1. 4 ☐ 9 / 3) 3 ☐ 7 ☐
    uses all of
    2, 3, 4, 5, 6, 7, 8, 9

2. 6 ☐ 4 / 8) 5 ☐ 9 ☐
    uses all of
    2, 3, 4, 5, 6, 7, 8, 9

3. 9 ☐ 3 / 8) 7 ☐ 2 ☐
    uses all of
    2, 3, 4, 5, 6, 7, 8, 9

4. 9 ☐ 2 / 8) 7 ☐ ☐ 6
    uses all of
    2, 3, 4, 5, 6, 7, 8, 9
    two answers

---

1 D. Steward, Division, *Median* [blog] (13 February 2019). Available at: https://donsteward.blogspot.com/2019/02/division.html.

Concept link: division and negatives

When it comes to negative integers, sharing and grouping can only really be applied in certain circumstances. For example, the calculation −12 ÷ 3 can be made sense of by sharing:

−12 ÷ 3

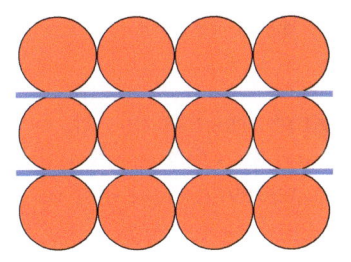

If the red counters are each worth −1, then we can split this into 3 equal shares giving −4 in each share (showing −12 ÷ 3 = −4). However, if we switch the divisor of 3 to a divisor of −3, we cannot really think of this division as sharing – how do we create −3 shares? Rather, in this case, it would make more sense to think about this as creating groups of −3 from −12:

−12 ÷ −3

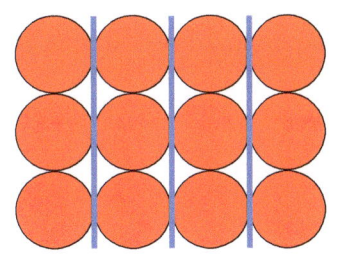

Again, if the red counters are each worth −1, then we can create 4 groups of −3 (showing −12 ÷ −3 = 4). The real challenge comes when the dividend is positive and the divisor is negative – for example, in the following calculation:

12 ÷ −3

The issue here is that we still cannot create −3 shares and so cannot make sense of this as a sharing calculation; however, it isn't straightforward to see how we can create groups of −3 from 12. This leaves comparing the values of 12 and −3 multiplicatively:

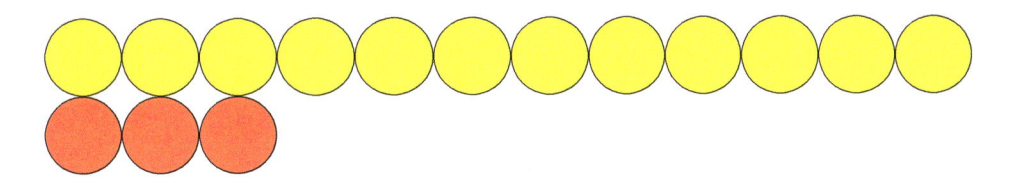

In comparing these we can clearly see that the top line of counters is four times longer than the bottom row of counters; however, they are different colours. We might take this to mean that rather than the result being 4, the result will be −4 (we need to make the bottom line four times longer and turn the counters over to make the top line). However, we can confirm this result by considering the question we often ask in situations of comparison: what if the −3 was redefined to a value of 1? Well if three red counters have a value of 1, it follows that three yellow counters have a value of −1, and so the top line has a value of −4. We can perhaps see this more clearly if we look at the values on a number line:

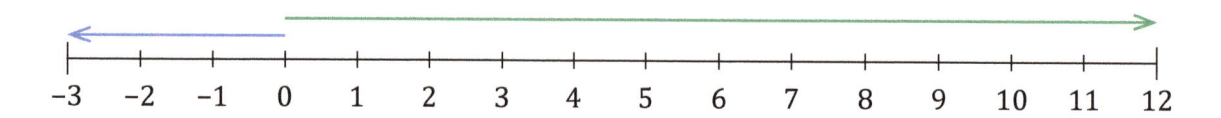

If pupils are used to seeing scaling pictures like this, then this should be clearly identifiable as a picture where −3 has been scaled by a factor of −4, and so comparing 12 and −3 multiplicatively results in −4. This becomes even clearer if we change the scale on the number line so that the −3 becomes 1:

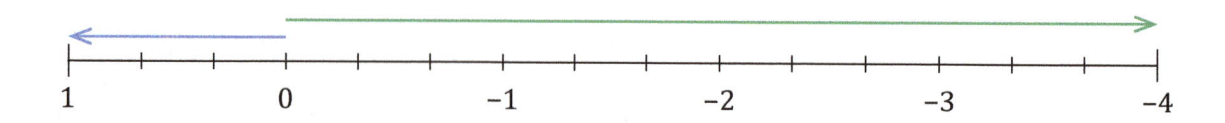

We can see that if left has now become positive then right will be negative, and if the scale changes so that three hatch marks is a unit length, then the lower vector becomes 1 and the upper vector becomes −4 (literally, 12 is to −3 as −4 is to 1). The benefit of this model is that all divisions involving negatives can be made sense of in the same way:

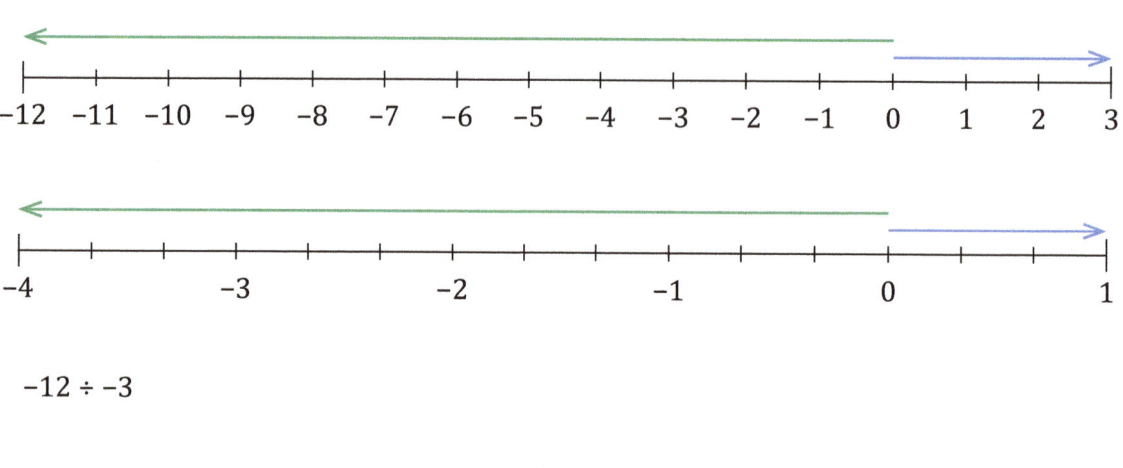

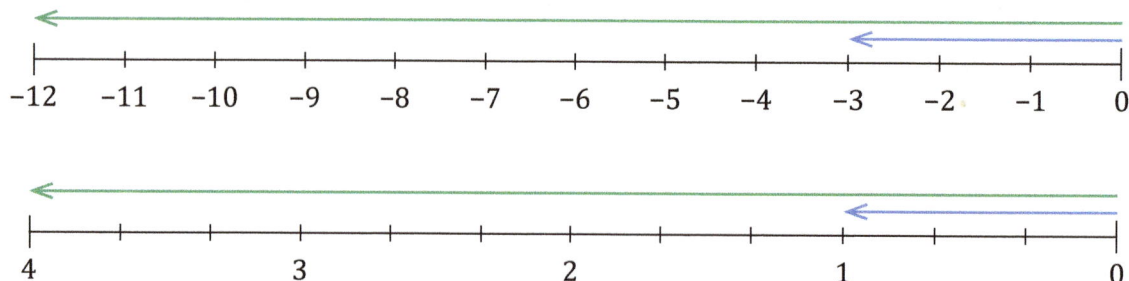

−12 ÷ 3

−12 ÷ −3

Of course, similarly to when we looked at multiplication of negatives, we want that same recognition from pupils that when only one of the dividend or divisor is negative then the result of the calculation is negative, whereas if both are negative then the result is positive. Once again, we can test this independently of calculation:

Will the result of these calculations be negative or positive?

a $15 \div 3$

b $-15 \div 3$

c $15 \div -3$

d $-3 \div 15$

e $-3 \div -15$

f $-0.3 \div -15$

g $\frac{1}{3} \div -15$

h $-\frac{1}{3} \div -\frac{1}{15}$

i $\frac{1}{3} \div -\frac{1}{15}$

j $\frac{1}{3} \div -\frac{1}{15} \div 5$

k $\frac{1}{3} \div -\frac{1}{15} \div -5$

l $\frac{1}{3} \div \frac{1}{15} \div -5$

m $\frac{1}{3} \div \frac{2}{15} \div -5$

n $-\frac{1}{3} \div \frac{2}{15} \div -5$

o $-\frac{1}{3} \div \frac{-2}{15} \div -5$

p $-\frac{-1}{3} \div \frac{-2}{15} \div -5$

Pupils should be able to decide these even if they do not know about how to divide fractions. Of course, if we want learners to actually carry out these calculations, then pupils will also be able to apply the concept of division to the concept of fractions.

Concept link: division and fractions

Similar to the division of negatives, if dividing by anything other than a positive integer, then sharing/splitting are not going to be available as useful models of division. You can't divide something in $\frac{3}{5}$ shares, for example. However, sharing can be a useful model for division of a fraction by a positive integer. Calculations of this type tend to fall into two categories:

$\frac{6}{7} \div 3$

If we model the fraction as a length, then we can consider splitting this fraction into three equal parts:

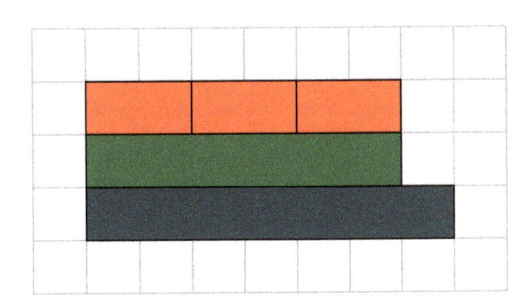

We can see that if we split this fraction into three equal parts, then each part is $\frac{2}{7}$.

We can see the same thing if we model each seventh as an object, rather than modelling as a length:

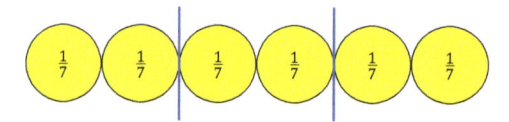

Calculations like this allow us to see that if the numerator of the dividend has a factor of the divisor, then we can simply divide the numerator by the divisor – in this case, because 6 has a factor of 3, I can simply divide 6 by 3. This is an important property of fractions that it is worth pupils being explicitly clear on – although whether we choose to adopt this model of division only for this specific purpose is more debatable as the same result can be arrived at through other models that are more applicable to division and fractions generally.

The second category that sharing could then be applied to is where the numerator of the dividend does not have a factor of the divisor:

$\frac{4}{7} \div 3$

This time, if we model this as a length using a rod that is seven units long for our value of 1, we cannot really see how to split this rod into three equal sections:

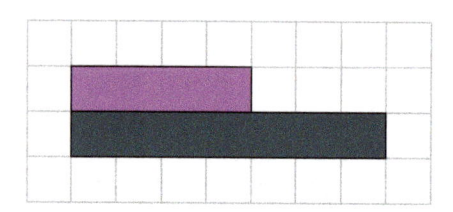

Rather, we would have to choose a different whole that would allow us both to show $\frac{4}{7}$ *and* allow us to split the fraction into three equal pieces. The (semi-)obvious recourse for this is to make our whole three times bigger, and thus make $\frac{4}{7}$ three times bigger:

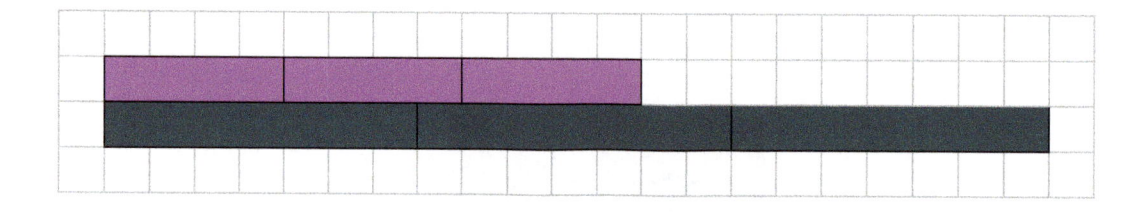

Now we can clearly split this into three equal parts, with the result being $\frac{4}{21}$. We can again model the same idea using objects for our sevenths, requiring an exchange of $\frac{4}{7}$ into $\frac{12}{21}$ before we can complete the sharing:

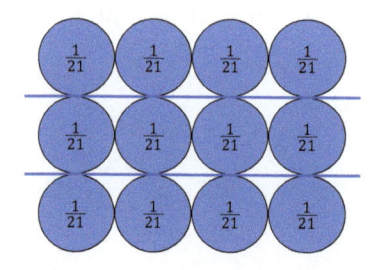

Division and factors

This, of course, is highlighting the idea that we can also multiply the denominator of the dividend by the divisor here, in this case multiplying 7 × 3. A nice thing to do at this point is to show that I could have applied the same logic to $\frac{6}{7} \div 3$; if we multiplied the denominator of the dividend by 3 we would get $\frac{6}{21}$, which, of course, simplifies to $\frac{2}{7}$ because of that factor of 3, which we alluded to earlier. Some people may prefer to do these in the reverse order and prompt pupils to make sense of the 'multiplying the denominator' first, before showing how, in certain cases, this is equivalent to dividing the numerator.

In a similar fashion, there are also certain divisions where a grouping model can support making sense of dividing by a fraction, namely where the result is a positive integer. This is a model often used (at least implicitly) when exploring the important idea of reciprocals (of numbers) with pupils:

$3 \div \frac{1}{4}$

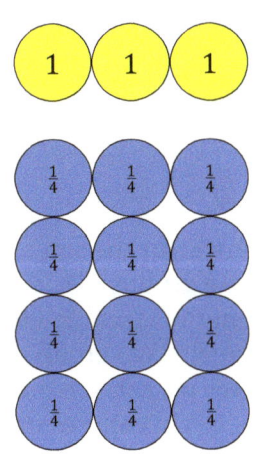

The logic here would be how many 'groups' of $\frac{1}{4}$ we can make out of 3. Clearly there are 12 'groups' of $\frac{1}{4}$, because each of the 1s will exchange for four quarters. This is a great justification for why division by $\frac{1}{4}$ is equivalent to multiplication by 4 – it will take four quarters to make every 1 whole so the number of quarters required to make a value is four times bigger than its whole. Similarly, we can make the same argument for $\frac{1}{3}$, $\frac{1}{5}$, and any other unit fraction. But what about non-unit fractions?

$3 \div \frac{3}{4}$

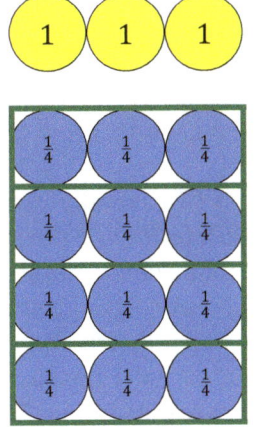

Using the same image, we can see that we can create 4 groups of $\frac{3}{4}$ from 3. We could link this to the above by saying that each whole would create 4 groups of one quarter so we could simply multiply by 4 to find the number of groups of one quarter, and then we need to create groups of 3 quarters and so each of our 4 groups will be divided by 3. We can also potentially apply this idea (with some care) to a division that doesn't result in an integer.

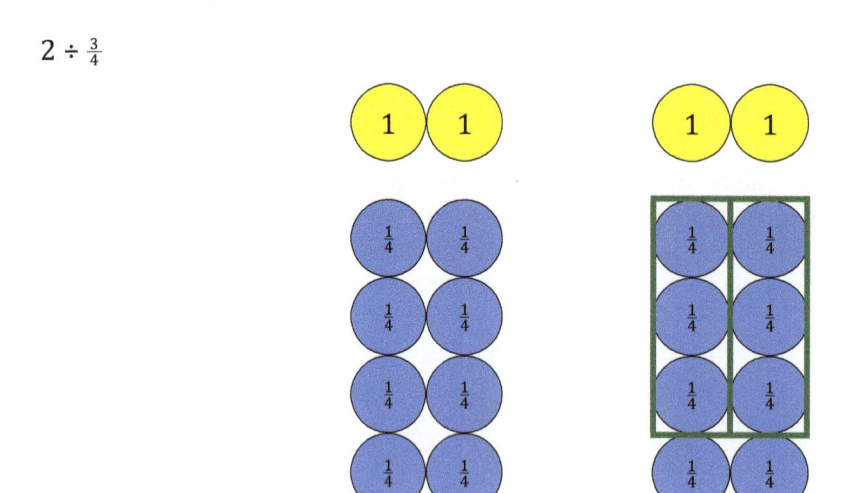

$2 \div \frac{3}{4}$

We can start here by taking the 2 and dividing it by $\frac{1}{4}$; literally how many groups of $\frac{1}{4}$ can be made from 2. This will clearly be 2 × 4 = 8, for the same reasons as above. From here we can reason that if we want to actually create groups of $\frac{3}{4}$, we are going to need to take our eight groups of $\frac{1}{4}$ and create groups of 3 from those, i.e. divide them by 3. We can see in the right-hand image that this means we can create two groups with $\frac{2}{3}$ of the next group left, so the result is $2\frac{2}{3}$. However, more importantly, we can see that the process we have been through is 2 × 4 ÷ 3, which can be seen as 2 × $\frac{4}{3}$. This allows us to show learners that integers and unit fractions are reciprocals, and that fractions of the form $\frac{a}{b}$ have reciprocals of $\frac{b}{a}$. This leads us to the (probably) most usual procedure for division of fractions – converting the division into an equivalent multiplication using the reciprocal.

Process: dividing by a fraction by converting to a multiplication by the reciprocal.

In short this can be summarised as:

$x \div \frac{a}{b} = x \div \frac{1}{b} \div a = x \times b \div a = x \times \frac{b}{a}$

The general logic follows that which is suggested above; we can make b groups of $\frac{1}{b}$ from each whole in x and then break those b groups into a groups, leading to $\frac{b}{a}$.

Pupils tend to be able to see this idea (if carefully presented) with suitable numbers but (perhaps not surprisingly) struggle with following the symbolic argument presented above. In addition, it can be a harder idea to make sense of this when x is a fraction in its own right – it is easy enough to see that we can create eight groups of $\frac{1}{4}$ from 2, but how many groups of $\frac{1}{4}$ can you create from $\frac{2}{5}$? Of course, logically we might know it is $\frac{2}{5}$ × 4 (if 1 whole leads to 1 × 4 quarters, then $\frac{2}{5}$ of 1 whole leads to $\frac{2}{5}$ × 4 quarters) but it is hard to actually see that, particularly with concrete or visual representations. For these reasons grouping is not my preferred way of making sense of dividing fractions but rather using the model of multiplicative comparison.

$\frac{6}{7} \div 3$

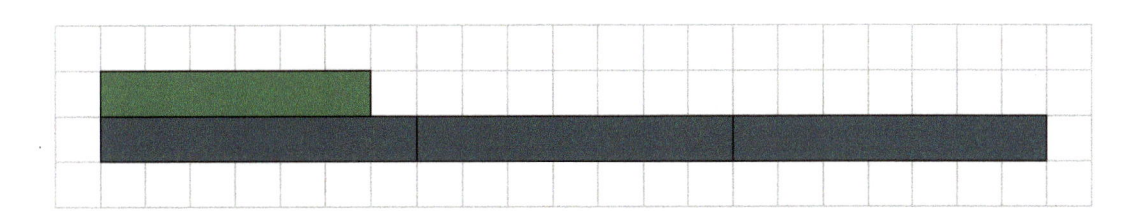

In this image, if a single black rod has a value of 1, then the green rod has a value of $\frac{6}{7}$ and the three black rods clearly have a value of 3. In comparing the length of the two sets of rods, we can see that the green rod is $\frac{6}{21}$ of the length of the total length of the three black rods, i.e. if the total length of the three black rods is redefined to have a value of 1, then the green rod has a value of $\frac{6}{21}$, or alternatively $\frac{2}{7}$:

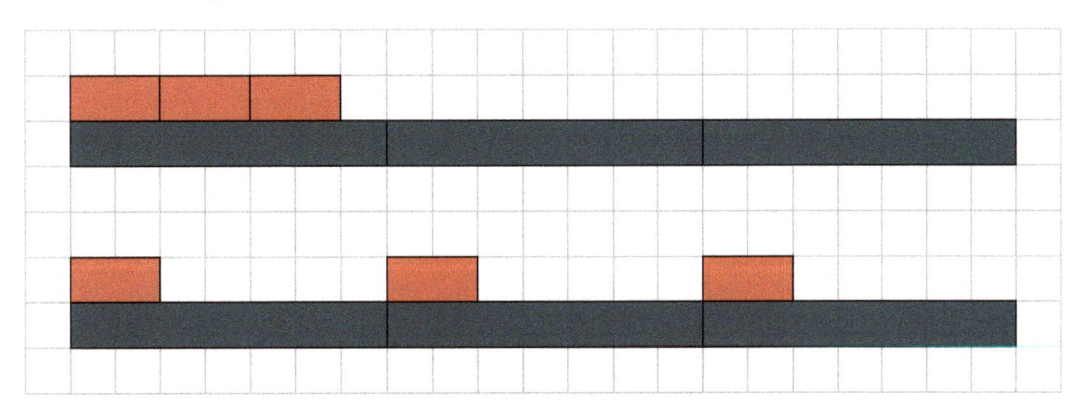

The benefit of using a comparison model for the division is that all of the other divisions we have seen (as well as others) appear in exactly the same way. The potential slight drawback is that we would have to explore the concept of reciprocal (and particularly the property that reciprocals multiply to make 1) separately; although some would argue that this is not a drawback as reciprocals are used with concepts other than division of fractions and, as such, should be explored separately.

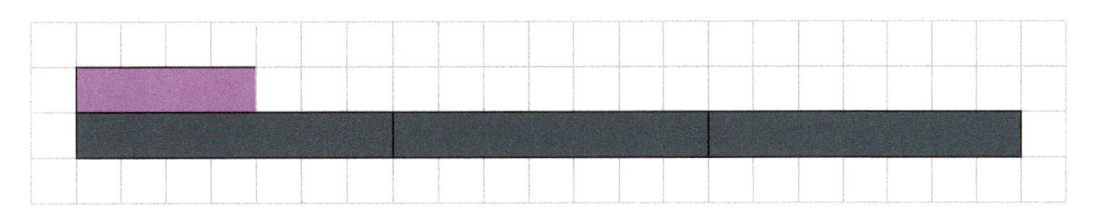

$\frac{4}{7} \div 3 = \frac{4}{21}$

$3 \div \frac{1}{4} = 12$

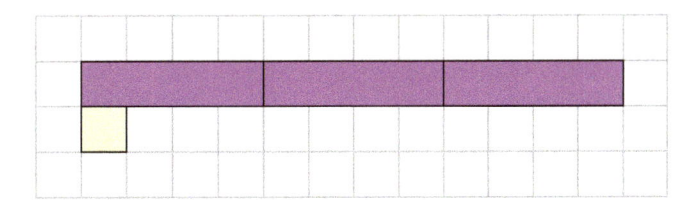

$3 \div \frac{3}{4} = 4$

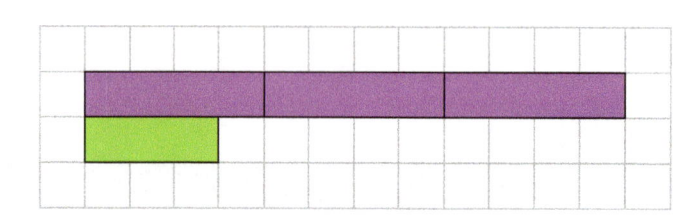

$2 \div \frac{3}{4} = \frac{8}{3} (=2\frac{2}{3})$

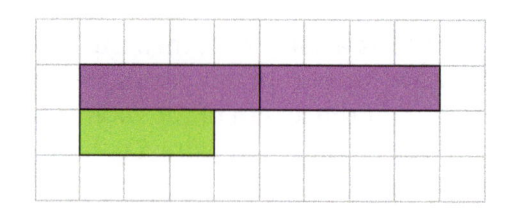

When looking at a division where both the dividend and divisor are fractions, we may need to consider the size of the length we use to represent the value of 1.

$\frac{4}{7} \div \frac{2}{7}$

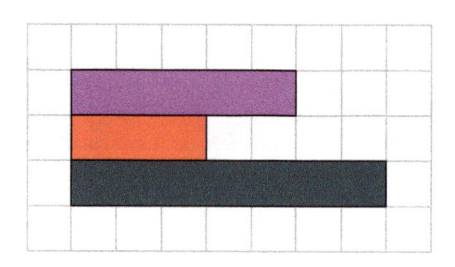

Here the black rod shows a value of 1, and so the purple rod $\frac{4}{7}$ and the red rod $\frac{2}{7}$; and clearly the purple rod is twice the size of the red rod.

$\frac{1}{6} \div \frac{3}{4}$

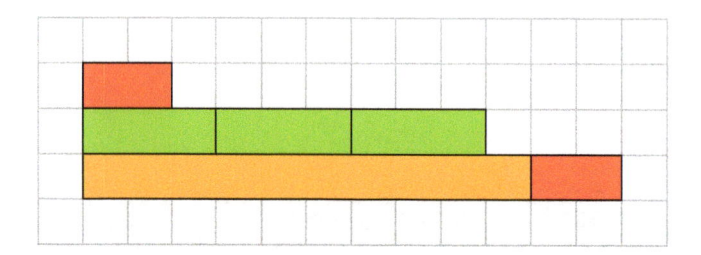

Here the combined length of the orange and red rod shows a value of 1, so a green rod is $\frac{1}{4}$ (and therefore three of them is $\frac{3}{4}$) and a red rod is $\frac{1}{6}$. If we compare $\frac{1}{6}$ to $\frac{3}{4}$ we can see that the red rod is $\frac{2}{9}$ of the length of the three green rods. This view actually gives rise to a couple of different procedures for division of fractions.

Process: dividing by a fraction by converting to a multiplication by the reciprocal

This is my alternative and preferred way of arriving at the process for dividing fractions by converting to a multiplication. In this way of approaching the process, we redefine (as we

Division and factors

have in previous situations) the length of the three green rods to have a value of 1. This means that the red rod now takes on a value of $\frac{2}{9}$. To arrive at the multiplication by the reciprocal, we can rewrite the division as a fraction:

$$\frac{1}{6} \div \frac{3}{4} = \frac{\frac{1}{6}}{\frac{3}{4}}$$

We want the denominator of this fraction to be redefined to a value of 1, and in order to do that we would need to multiply it by its reciprocal. However, we would therefore also need to multiply the numerator by the same value:

$$\frac{1}{6} \div \frac{3}{4} = \frac{\frac{1}{6}}{\frac{3}{4}} = \frac{\frac{1}{6}}{\frac{3}{4}} \times \frac{\frac{4}{3}}{\frac{4}{3}}$$

This changes the denominator into 1, and division by 1 can be ignored:

$$\frac{1}{6} \div \frac{3}{4} = \frac{\frac{1}{6}}{\frac{3}{4}} = \frac{\frac{1}{6}}{\frac{3}{4}} \times \frac{\frac{4}{3}}{\frac{4}{3}} = \frac{\frac{1}{6} \times \frac{4}{3}}{1} = \frac{1}{6} \times \frac{4}{3}$$

However, there is an alternative process that can also be seen from this model.

Process: changing into common denominators

Although we can see the red rod as $\frac{1}{6}$, we can also see it as $\frac{2}{12}$, and the three green rods can be seen as $\frac{9}{12}$. So we can convert the division into a division with common denominators:

The logic here then follows that 2 of anything compared to 9 of that same thing will always result in $\frac{2}{9}$; i.e. for any whole size the red rod would always be 2 units long, and three green rods a total of 9 units long, and so we would always have 2 compared to 9.

$$\frac{1}{6} \div \frac{3}{4} = \frac{2}{12} \div \frac{9}{12}$$

$$\frac{1}{6} \div \frac{3}{4} = \frac{2}{12} \div \frac{9}{12} = \frac{2}{9}$$

Fraction division (ii)　　　　Turning a division into a multiplication

$\frac{5}{7} \times \frac{2}{3} \times \frac{3}{2} = \frac{5}{7}$　Property of reciprocals

$\frac{5}{7} \times \frac{2}{3} = \frac{5}{7} \div \frac{3}{2}$　Equivalent statements

1　$\frac{1}{2} \div \frac{3}{5} =$

2　$\frac{2}{3} \div \frac{3}{4} =$

3　$\frac{3}{2} \div \frac{5}{3} =$

4　$\frac{2}{3} \div \frac{5}{7} =$

5　$\frac{5}{8} \div \frac{2}{3} =$

6　$\frac{3}{2} \div \frac{\square}{\square} = \frac{21}{10}$

7　$\frac{\square}{\square} \div \frac{3}{4} = \frac{16}{30}$

8　$\frac{4}{5} \div \frac{\square}{\square} = \frac{2}{3}$

9　$\frac{3}{4} \div \frac{\square}{\square} = \frac{1}{2}$

10　$\frac{3}{8} \div \frac{\square}{\square} = \frac{3}{4}$

11　$\frac{5}{6} \div \frac{\square}{\square} = 1\frac{1}{4}$

12　$\frac{7}{8} \div \frac{\square}{\square} = 1\frac{1}{4}$

13　$\frac{9}{10} \div \frac{\square}{\square} = \frac{3}{5}$

14　$\frac{2}{9} \div \frac{\square}{\square} = \frac{4}{15}$

15　$\frac{5}{8} \div \frac{\square}{\square} = \frac{2}{3}$

16　$\frac{4}{9} \div \frac{\square}{\square} = \frac{5}{6}$

17　$\frac{4}{5} \div \frac{\square}{\square} = 6$

18　$\frac{3}{4} \div \frac{\square}{\square} = 6$

19　$\frac{2}{3} \div \frac{\square}{\square} = 6$

20　$\frac{9}{10} \div \frac{\square}{\square} = 6$

21　$\frac{1}{4} \div \frac{3}{8} =$

22　$\frac{3}{5} \div \frac{9}{10} =$

23　$\frac{16}{27} \div \frac{8}{9} =$

24　$1\frac{2}{3} \div 2\frac{1}{2} =$

There are some great activities to prompt thought around division of fractions. The activity in the footnote, taken from Don Steward's Median blog, shows a nice further demonstration of the equivalence of division by a fraction and multiplication by the reciprocal.[2] There's also an interesting prompt for pupils to think about division and subtraction:[3]

$4\frac{1}{2} \div 3 = 4\frac{1}{2} - 3$

$4 \div 2 = 4 - 2$

$5\frac{1}{3} \div 4 = 5\frac{1}{3} - 4$

as well as these sorts of problems from Open Middle:[4]

Fraction division

Directions: use the digits 0 through 9, without repeats, to solve the problem below.

$$\frac{\square}{\square} \div \frac{\square}{\square} = \frac{\square\square}{\square}$$

Dividing mixed numbers

Directions: Using the digits 1 to 9 at most one time each, fill in the boxes to make the smallest (or largest) quotient.

$$\square\frac{\square}{\square} \div \square\frac{\square}{\square}$$

The same model of multiplicative comparison is typically the best model for looking at division with surds/algebra.

Concept link: division and surds

As with multiplication, we have a few cases to consider here:

1   Division of a surd by a rational value.
2   Division of a rational by a surd.
3   Division of a surd by a surd.

The first of these has actually already been dealt with in the previous chapter. For example, if we consider something like $\frac{8\sqrt{3}}{4}$, this can be seen as $\frac{1}{4} \times 8\sqrt{3}$, which, of course, is simply $2\sqrt{3}$. Even where we have $\frac{8\sqrt{3}}{5}$, this can be seen as $\frac{1}{5} \times 8\sqrt{3}$, which can be written just as $\frac{8}{5}\sqrt{3}$ (or just left as $\frac{8\sqrt{3}}{5}$).

---

2   D. Steward, Fraction Division, *Median* [blog] (24 May 2011). Available at: https://donsteward.blogspot.com/2011/02/fraction-division.html.
3   D. Steward, Division = Subtraction, *Median* [blog] (27 April 2011). Available at: https://donsteward.blogspot.com/2011/04/division-subtraction.html.
4   S. Errichiello, Fraction Division, *Open Middle* (n.d.). Available at: https://www.openmiddle.com/fraction-division-2/; R. Kaplinsky, Dividing Mixed Numbers, *Open Middle* (n.d.). Available at: https://www.openmiddle.com/dividing-mixed-numbers/.

Division and factors

So what about division by a surd? Well, we don't tend to refer to this as a division at all! This is almost universally referred to as 'rationalising the denominator'.

$$\frac{3}{\sqrt{2}}$$

The language of 'rationalising the denominator' here is an interesting use of the term 'denominator' because in defining fractions it was clear that in a true fraction both the numerator and denominator have to be integers. However, whether we wish to consider this as 'Rationalise the denominator of the expression' or whether we wish to consider it as 'Divide 3 by √2', the way we make sense of it is the same and (as mentioned) revolves around seeing this as a comparison between the two values:

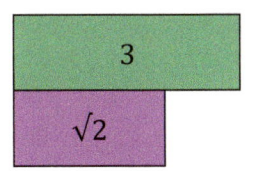

At first glance the comparison here doesn't seem to offer any insight into the division or how we might rationalise the denominator. To gain further insight, we have to become aware of a property of comparisons that has been hitherto overlooked – the fact that the bars have equal width. This is because we want the length to represent the numbers, and so the area of the rectangles need to be proportional to their length. This is only the case if the width is equal. What this means though, is that provided we keep the widths the same, then we can create comparable areas that will have the same result as comparing the lengths. In this case, we can create a rational area by changing the width of both bars to √2:

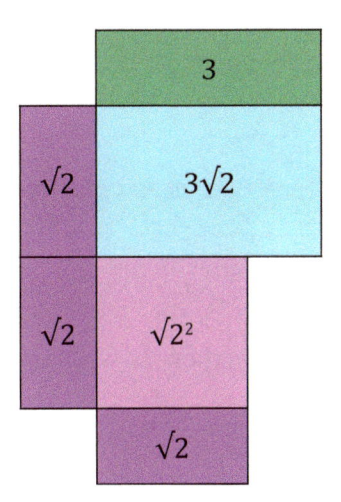

The 'numerator' of the fraction now changes from 3 to 3√2, as it is now represented by the rectangular area with a length of 3 and a width of √2. Similarly, the 'denominator' of the fraction now changes from √2 to √2², as it is now represented by a square area with a length of √2. But this area is actually just 2, and so we have 3√2 compared to 2. Because of the equal widths of the two rectangular areas, this comparison is equal in value to the original comparison, and so we have $\frac{3}{\sqrt{2}} = \frac{3\sqrt{2}}{2}$. This 'fraction' now has a rational denominator, or if we prefer, this is now a division by a rational number, which could be written as $\frac{3}{2}\sqrt{2}$.

Of course, if we consider an example of the third case such as $\frac{\sqrt{5}}{\sqrt{2}}$, then we should be able to see that exactly the same logic applies, with the 'numerator' changing to $\sqrt{5} \times \sqrt{2} = \sqrt{10}$, giving $\frac{\sqrt{5}}{\sqrt{2}} = \frac{\sqrt{10}}{2}$.

Once pupils are happy with this process, we can mix things up by having numerators/denominators that are the product of a rational and a surd – for example, $\frac{4\sqrt{5}}{3\sqrt{2}}$ – recognising that it is only necessary to multiply both numerator and denominator by $\sqrt{2}$ to create the required area, or even having expressions that involve sums/differences of surd and rational values – for example, $\frac{4\sqrt{5}+1}{3\sqrt{2}-7}$ – although these will require further understanding of expansion and factorisation using the distributive law (which we will explore in Chapter 5).

Concept link: division and algebra

$3x \div 3$

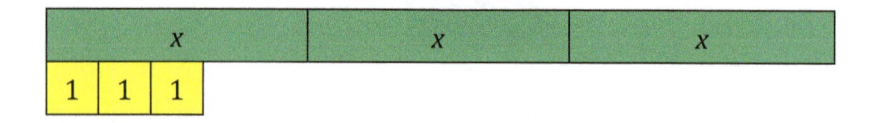

We can see this as $3x$ compares to 3 as what compares to 1, i.e. if the 3 becomes 1, what would $3x$ become?

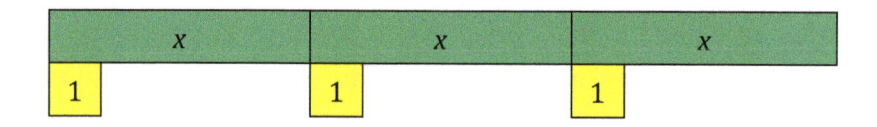

We can see that $3x$ compares to 3 as x compares to 1.

$3x \div 2$

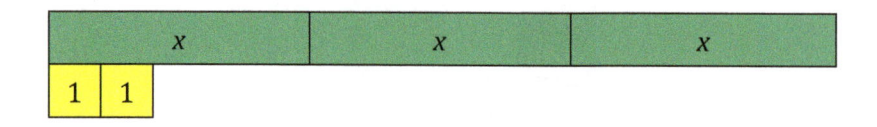

If we redefine the 2 to have a value of 1, then $3x$ will instead have a value of $1\frac{1}{2}x$ (or simply $\frac{3x}{2}$).

$3x \div x$

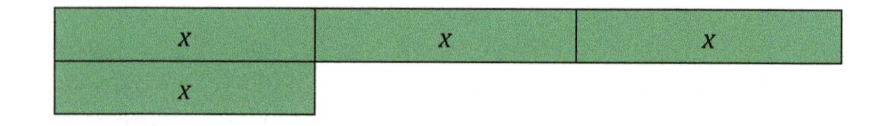

Here we can see that if the x is redefined to have a value of 1, then $3x$ will simply have a value of 3, meaning $3x \div x = 3$.

$x^2 \div 2x$

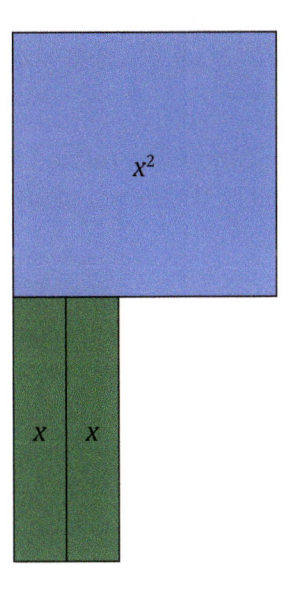

One important thing to note from the above is that the lengths are only comparable as the width of each bar is the same. In the previous cases this was always one unit; however, as long as the width is the same then it doesn't necessarily have to be one unit. What we can see here is that both the x^2 and the $2x$ has a width of x, and so their lengths are the only thing we need to compare. This shows $\frac{x^2}{2x} = \frac{x}{2}$.

There are some nice activities beyond just lists of questions that can support practice for algebraic division. One from Jo Morgan's excellent Resourceaholic website is a resource from the Mathematics in Education and Industry charity and interweaves multiplication, roots and negative powers along with division.[5]

So far, we have used language such as dividend, divisor and quotient in relation to division calculations. A word we haven't used yet is 'factor', and it is to this that we will turn our attention to in the second part of this chapter.

Concept: factors and factorisation

Prerequisites: Numbers, multiplication, division.

Linked concepts: Proportionality, algebra, distributivity.

The words 'factor' and 'product' can really help with tying together the language around multiplication and division. We have previously seen that in a calculation like $5 \times 3 = 15$, we might describe 5 as the 'multiplier', 3 as the 'multiplicand' and 15 as the 'product'. But if we then rearrange this calculation to give $15 \div 3 = 5$, we have described this with a 'dividend' of 15, a 'divisor' of 3 and a 'quotient' of 5. How then do we create the link between 15 being the 'product' in one calculation and the 'dividend' in a different, but clearly related, calculation? This is where the language of 'factor' will be useful. We can instead describe $5 \times 3 = 15$

---

5 Resourceaholic, Alegraic Expressions 1 Maze (n.d.). Available at: https://drive.google.com/file/d/0B9L2lYGRiK2bTlVYMUFWZEJCZ3M/view?resourcekey=0-C9N92eQ2xf9UWLav_eoW9g.

as 'two factors (5 and 3) multiplying results in the product (15)' and then describe 15 ÷ 3 = 5 as 'the product divided by one factor results in the other factor'. We only tend to use the language 'factor' when both factors are positive integers (or, perhaps strangely, algebraic expressions). We wouldn't typically describe −5 as a factor of 15. We also need be careful when a division is not exact – we would not describe 3 or 5 as factors in 16 ÷ 3 = 5 remainder 1; rather we would normally stick with the language of dividend, divisor, quotient and add the word remainder.

As 'factor' and 'product' as language can tie the related multiplication and division calculations together, a great representation to tie these together is the area model:

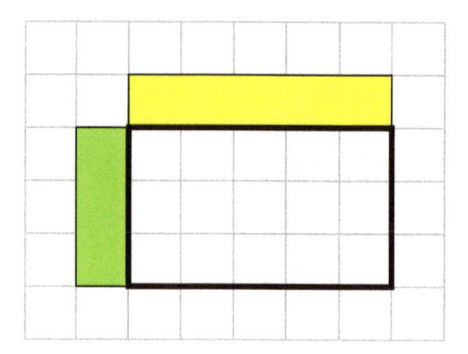

Within this picture we can see 3 × 5 = 15; however, we can also see 15 ÷ 3 = 5 (to me, it even looks a little like the division algorithm picture) and therefore also 15 ÷ 5 = 3. This is a nice way to help pupils make sense of factors – can they build a rectangle with no gaps and no overlaps that has a given area (or if being used prior to pupils learning about areas, that uses rods to a certain value). We can then look at the factors of a number like 15 as per the image below:

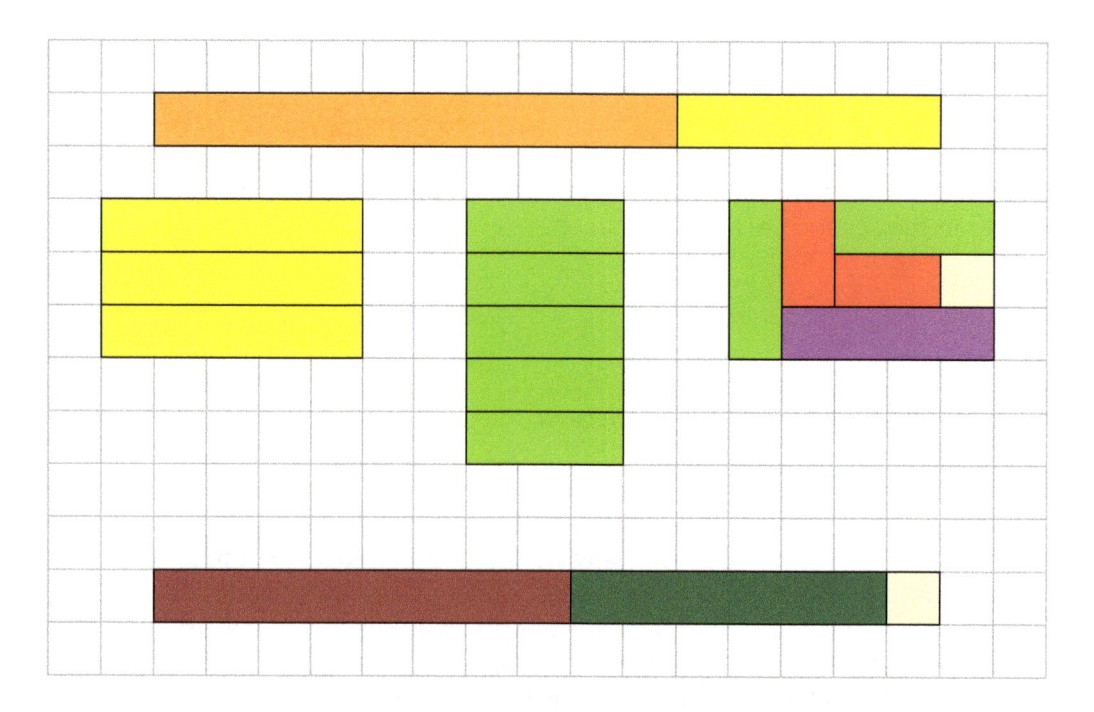

All the rectangles in this picture use rods that sum to a value of 15. However, no matter which rods are used, there are only really two rectangles in the entire picture – a 3 × 5 rectangle and a 1 × 15 rectangle. This shows that there are only two **factorisations** of 15 into factor pairs (namely 3 × 5 and 1 × 15) and therefore that 15 has four unique factors, 1, 3, 5 and 15. This model of factors and factorisation relating to the area model will serve throughout our journey in developing pupils understanding of factors and factorisation – the idea of building rectangles with no gaps and no overlaps can really serve to illustrate the structure of this concept nicely and is always the way I introduce learners to the idea of factors and factorisation.

From here I would normally ask pupils to build these rectangles for the following values:

a   8

b   12

c   9

d   16

e   13

Hence write down all the unique factors of these numbers, and all the different factorisations into factor pairs.

The reason I am choosing these five numbers are:

- 8 – another situation that is similar to 15, where there are four unique factors and two factorisations into factor pairs.
- 12 – a situation where there are more than four (i.e. six) unique factors (to make sure pupils don't get stuck in thinking there are only ever four factors) and more than two (i.e. three) factorisations into factor pairs.
- 9 – a situation where one of the rectangles is a square, leading to a non-unique factor (i.e. 3) but still two factorisations into factor pairs.
- 16 – a mix of the 12 and 9 situations, where there is a non-unique factor from a square but three factorisations into factor pairs.
- 13 – a prime value, where this is only one unique rectangle that can be built (with a width of 1) and hence only two unique factors and one factorisation into factor pairs.

From here we might explore other values, perhaps classifying the numbers from 2 to 30 into those with two, three, four, more than four unique factors before paying special attention to the number 1 and its special case where there is only one rectangle but that there is only one unique factor. A nice thing to add to this is to bring in the idea of deficient, abundant and perfect numbers in an activity such as this one from NRICH, although we would have to introduce the concept of primes to learners before offering this particular activity to them:

> People have been searching for number patterns since ancient times. Mathematicians noticed that some numbers are equal to the sum of all of their factors (but not including the number itself).
>
> 6 is a number that equals the sum of its factors: 1 + 2 + 3 equal 6. Numbers like 6 that equal the sum of their factors are called perfect numbers. 6 is the first perfect number.
>
> 4 is not a perfect number: because the sum of its factors (besides 4 itself), 1 + 2, is less than 4. Numbers like 4 are known as deficient numbers. What does the word deficient mean? Why do you think numbers having factors adding to less than the number itself are called deficient numbers?

12 is not a perfect number because the sum of its factors, 1 + 2 + 3 + 4 + 6 is greater than 12. Numbers like 12 are known as abundant numbers. What does the word abundant mean? Why do you think numbers having factors adding to more than the number itself are called abundant numbers?

Since the time of Pythagoras (about 500 BC), mathematicians have tried to find as many perfect numbers as they can. By 1999 only 38 perfect numbers had been found.

Can you find the next perfect number after 6?

Could a perfect number also be a prime number?

Do you think there are more perfect, deficient or abundant numbers?

Add the factors of all the numbers up to 50. Was your guess correct?

Can you find any patterns in your results?[6]

To me, this is an example of what the eminent Dr Dave Hewitt calls 'subordinating practice'. Although pupils will need to practise finding factors in order to work on the activity, the goal is larger than just 'find some factors'. Instead, pupils have to use their understanding of finding factors to serve the further mathematical aim of classifying numbers as abundant, deficient or perfect and exploring the properties of such numbers. Contrary to what some might intuitively believe, it would appear that this type of practice may support the development of greater fluency as the activity prompts pupils to shift their attention away from just 'doing' to 'using' their knowledge.[7]

Of course, the area model is not the only model for multiplication, and eventually pupils should recognise that any of our models for multiplication can show factors. A simple line of four 5 rods can show us that 4 and 5 are both factors of 20. Once pupils have developed a level of fluency with the ideas of factors and factorisation, we can begin to explore a few different concepts.

Subconcept: highest common factor

If pupils are familiar with the idea of building rectangles (with no gaps and no overlaps) to highlight factors and factorisations, we can introduce common factors (and from there, highest common factors) simply by asking learners to find rectangles for two or more numbers that have a common dimension.

Find rectangles with no gaps and no overlaps that have values of (a) 18 and (b) 24. How many of your rectangles have a length/width in common? What is the highest valued length/width the rectangles can have in common?

---

6   See https://nrich.maths.org/2555.
7   Dr D. Hewitt, Mathematical Fluency: The Nature of Practice and the Role of Subordination, *For the Learning of Mathematics*, 16(2) (1996), 28–35. Available at: https://flm-journal.org/Articles/233DDDC885A730AB6D45226E38BEF.pdf.

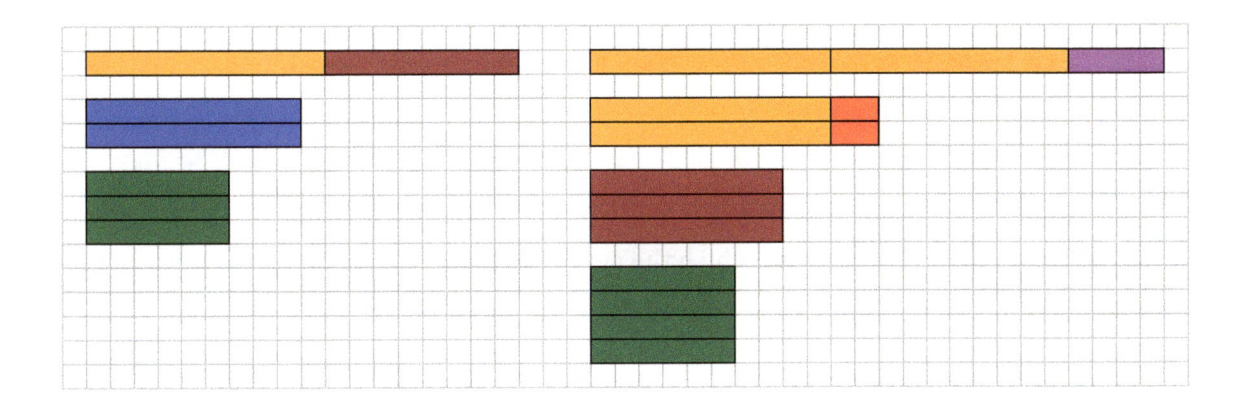

On the left we can see the possible rectangles for 18, and on the right 24. From these we can see that possible common dimensions are 1, 2, 3, and 6, and that 6 is the highest valued dimension. This can be used to define the idea of 'common factors' with learners, including 'highest common factor' (HCF).

An interesting property in the above examples is that the HCF is simply the difference of 24 and 18. A nice activity to prompt practice at finding the HCF is to ask pupils to look at when this is the case, and when it isn't (we can demonstrate it isn't always the case simply by looking at numbers like 2 and 5, which have a HCF of 1).

> Find as many pairs of numbers as you can where the HCF is the difference between the two numbers. Is there any pattern to your numbers? Do they have anything in common?

Pupils can explore what is true about the numbers a, b if HCF(a,b) is equal to $b - a$ (assuming that b is larger than a).

As well as looking at HCF, once pupils are comfortable with factors and factorisation, it is an ideal point to introduce the concept of primes.

Concept: prime numbers

Prerequisites: Numbers, multiplication, division, factors.

Linked concepts: Sequences.

If pupils have seen the idea of building rectangles as a model for factors and factorisation, then the (hopefully) obvious way to begin to explore primes is to ask pupils to focus specifically on those values for which only a single rectangle is possible – this, of course, implies that it will be a rectangle with one dimension of 1 as this is always possible for any positive integer. This leads nicely to a definition of primes as those numbers that have two unique factors – we earlier dealt with 1 as being special in regard to the fact that we can only build one rectangle, but that this rectangle doesn't lead to two unique factors (and hence 1 is not prime!).

There are many classic activities that link to primes. Probably the most classic is the 'Sieve of Eratosthenes' (being over 2,000 years old!). This can be done with any grid of numbers starting at 1 (or adapted for any other grid) but will be shown below with a simple 6 × 6 grid:

Step 1: Cross out 1.

Step 2: Circle the next number that is not already circled or crossed out.

Step 3: Cross out any number for which the circled number is a factor.

Step 4: Continue steps 2 and 3 until all numbers are either circled or crossed out.

1	2	3	4	5	6
7	8	9	10	11	12
13	14	15	16	17	18
19	20	21	22	23	24
25	26	27	28	29	30
31	32	33	34	35	36

The result of those steps on this grid is shown here. A 6 × 6 grid is a nice one to use for this sieve (or any grid with a width of 6) because it highlights an important property for primes, that (with the exception of 2 and 3) all primes are either one more or one less than a multiple of 6 (they all appear in either the first or fifth column). Depending on where pupils are at, we can discuss why this must be the case (simply, any number in the 2nd, 4th and 6th columns are even, and anything in the 3rd column will have a factor of 3, leaving the only possible columns for primes being the 1st or the 5th).

1	2	3	4	5	6
7	8	9	10	11	12
13	14	15	16	17	18
19	20	21	22	23	24
25	26	27	28	29	30
31	32	33	34	35	36

Other nice activities for primes involve highlighting primes on an Ulam spiral[8] (and noticing that primes tend to fall on diagonal lines within the spiral):

400	399	398	397	396	395	394	393	392	391	390	389	388	387	386	385	384	383	382	381
325	324	323	322	321	320	319	318	317	316	315	314	313	312	311	310	309	308	307	380
326	257	256	255	254	253	252	251	250	249	248	247	246	245	244	243	242	241	306	379
327	258	197	196	195	194	193	192	191	190	189	188	187	186	185	184	183	240	305	378
328	259	198	145	144	143	142	141	140	139	138	137	136	135	134	133	182	239	304	377
329	260	199	146	101	100	99	98	97	96	95	94	93	92	91	132	181	238	303	376
330	261	200	147	102	65	64	63	62	61	60	59	58	57	90	131	180	237	302	375
331	262	201	148	103	66	37	36	35	34	33	32	31	56	89	130	179	236	301	374
332	263	202	149	104	67	38	17	16	15	14	13	30	55	88	129	178	235	300	373
333	264	203	150	105	68	39	18	5	4	3	12	29	54	87	128	177	234	299	372
334	265	204	151	106	69	40	19	6	1	2	11	28	53	86	127	176	233	298	371
335	266	205	152	107	70	41	20	7	8	9	10	27	52	85	126	175	232	297	370
336	267	206	153	108	71	42	21	22	23	24	25	26	51	84	125	174	231	296	369
337	268	207	154	109	72	43	44	45	46	47	48	49	50	83	124	173	230	295	368
338	269	208	155	110	73	74	75	76	77	78	79	80	81	82	123	172	229	294	367
339	270	209	156	111	112	113	114	115	116	117	118	119	120	121	122	171	228	293	366
340	271	210	157	158	159	160	161	162	163	164	165	166	167	168	169	170	227	292	365
341	272	211	212	213	214	215	216	217	218	219	220	221	222	223	224	225	226	291	364
342	273	274	275	276	277	278	279	280	281	282	283	284	285	286	287	288	289	290	363
343	344	345	346	347	348	349	350	351	352	353	354	355	356	357	358	359	360	361	362

8 See https://mathsbot.com/activities/ulamSpiral.

as well as a nice grid completion activity that interweaves knowledge of factors, multiples and primes, etc. from 10Ticks:[9]

The factors and multiples game

The playing board

Heading cards

Rules

1 Cut out the heading cards and place one in each of the 10 spaces around the playing board.

2 Cut out the 25 number cards and place each one on the playing board, so that it satisfies the condition given by the heading cards for each.

3 By rearranging the positions of the heading cards and the number cards, try to fill in as many squares on the playing board as possible.

Heading cards

Prime numbers	Square numbers
Factors of 126	Factors of 60
Numbers less than 13	Numbers more than 12
Multiples of 3	Multiples of 5
Odd numbers	Even numbers

Number cards

1	2	3	4	5
6	7	8	9	10
11	12	13	14	15
16	17	18	20	21
24	25	27	30	60

---

9 See https://www.10ticks.co.uk.

If we want to focus more on prime numbers, then a very nice and simple activity is to ask pupils:

> What is the first square number greater than 1 that cannot be formed by the sum of two (not necessarily distinct) primes? Do you notice anything from your search?

This gives some nice insight into square numbers alongside prime numbers.

Once *au fait* with primes, we can then look at linking the concept of primes with the concept of factorisation.

Concept link: prime factorisation

Provided pupils are already familiar with factorisation and its links to the dimensions of rectangles, then we can combine our understanding of primes with our understanding of factorisation:

> Decompose 18 into a prime factorisation.

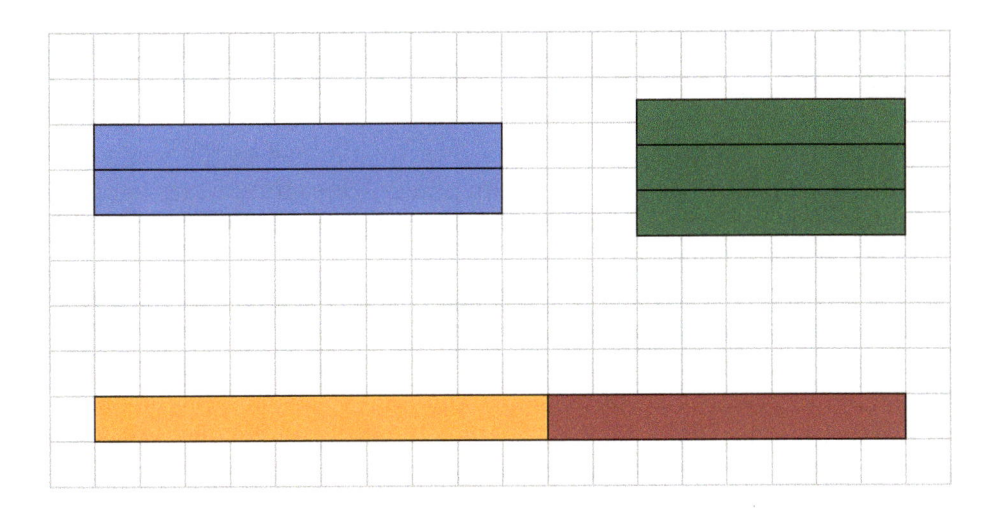

We can see here the possible rectangles that use rods with a value of 18 (of course, we could use different rods but would create the same three shapes). This gives the three decompositions of 18 into a factorisation using factor pairs: 2 × 9, 3 × 6 or 1 × 18. To then link this with the concept of primes, I would ask pupils to find prime valued rods that fit along the length and width, making clear that only a single type of rod can be used along any one dimension. This can be done from the 2 × 9 rectangle:

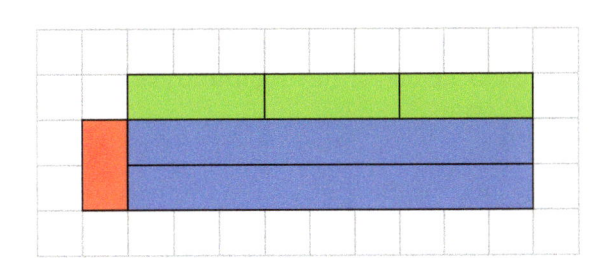

One of the dimensions can be made using a 2-rod, and the other dimension can be made using three 3-rods. This means that, in the factorisation 2 × 9, the 9 has been replaced with 3 × 3 and so the prime factorisation is 2 × 3 × 3. The same can be seen with the 3 × 6 rectangle:

In this case, one of the dimensions can be made using a 3-rod, and the other can be made using either two 3-rods, or three 2-rods. This means that, in the factorisation 3 × 6, the 6 has been replaced with 3 × 2 and so the prime factorisation is 3 × 3 × 2 (which is clearly the same as 2 × 3 × 3).

But what about the 1 × 18 rectangle? Well, clearly in this case we cannot find a prime valued rod that fits along the dimension of 1. This leads us to recognise that a 1 × 18 factorisation is not a useful starting decomposition if we are aiming to decompose the number into a product of its prime factors. This has nice parallels when it comes to algebraic factorisation, where again a rectangle with a dimension of 1 isn't useful in aiming to decompose an algebraic expression involving sums or differences into its algebraic factors.

The fact that both the 2 × 9 rectangle and 3 × 6 rectangle lead to the same prime factor decomposition opens up an obvious activity with pupils – does this always happen? And can we always do this with every non-prime number (clearly, we can't with prime numbers as they can only be factorised into rectangles with a width of 1)? This is a nice exploratory activity for pupils to arrive at the *fundamental theorem of arithmetic*, which I always share with pupils – that every positive integer greater than 1 is either prime or can be decomposed into a unique product of primes. Prompting pupils to explore and confirm this is a great way to get pupils practising factorisation of numbers as well as the full decomposition into a prime factorisation. From here it is worth actually looking explicitly at the relationship between the prime factorisation and other factors of a number:

If 4620 = 2^2 × 3 × 5 × 7 × 11, work out all of the factors of 4620.

What we are aiming for here is pupils recognising that the factors of 4620 come from all of the possible products of the prime factors – in essence, by splitting the prime factorisation into two 'separate' multiplications, we can create every possible decomposition into factor pairs, and hence find every possible factor. For example, we could split the 2^2 × 3 × 5 × 7 × 11 = (2 × 3 × 5) × (2 × 7 × 11), which implies 30 and 154 are both factors, or equally we could split it into (2 × 3 × 5 × 11) × (2 × 7), implying 330 and 14 are factors. Pupils can be asked to find factors of a number given (or having found) their prime factorisation, and we can mix up the skills a little as well.

Fill in the gaps in the prime factorisation, given the information about the factors of the number:

2^3 × 3 × ____ × ____ has factors of 14 and 15

$2^2 \times 3 \times$ ____ $\times$ ____ has factors of 100 and 130

$2^2 \times 5 \times$ ___ $\times$ ____ has factors of 12, 20, 27 and 28

$2^\square \times 3^\square \times 5^\square$ has factors of 100, 200, 300, 400 and 500 (use the smallest values possible)

What is the smallest value we could multiply 72 by to make it into a multiple of:

a 100?
b 110?
c 120?
d 130?
e 135?
f 200?
g 1000?

There are many great applications of prime factor decomposition. Simplification of fractions is an obvious one, which we will explore more in Chapter 5, but some of the ideas we have previously looked at can be pre-examined once prime factor decomposition is well understood.

Concept link: prime factorisation and highest common factor

We have seen the HCF in terms of comparing rectangles and looking for common widths, but it is worth re-examining once pupils have developed a good understanding of primes and prime factorisation.

Given that $4620 = 2^2 \times 3 \times 5 \times 7 \times 11$ and $2376 = 2^3 \times 3^3 \times 11$, find the HCF of 4620 and 2376.

Provided pupils are familiar with finding factors from a prime factorisation, then it is a short step to recognise that $4620 = (2^2 \times 3 \times 11) \times (5 \times 7)$ and $2376 = (2^2 \times 3 \times 11) \times (2 \times 3^2)$, and therefore that the HCF is $2^2 \times 3 \times 11 = 132$. Pupils can be asked to find the HCF of different pairs/groups of numbers either given their prime factorisation or by first finding them. Again, the skills can be mixed:

The HCF of two numbers is 65. One of the numbers has a factor of 35. The other number has a factor of 39. What are the smallest possible two numbers?

This sort of question can be extended further if we combine knowledge of HCF with lowest common multiple.

Concept link: prime factorisation and lowest common multiple

In the previous chapter we saw lowest common multiple in terms of looking at rectangles but once pupils have developed their understanding of prime factorisation and its links to HCF it is worth revisiting lowest common multiple (LCM).

> Given that $4620 = 2^2 \times 3 \times 5 \times 7 \times 11$ and $2376 = 2^3 \times 3^3 \times 11$, find the LCM of 4620 and 2376.

The insight we are looking to support pupils in making here is that any multiple of 4620 will have part of its prime factorisation as $2^2 \times 3 \times 5 \times 7 \times 11$, and similarly that any multiple of 2376 will have part of its prime factorisation as $2^3 \times 3^3 \times 11$. Therefore, if we start with any one of these prime factorisations and multiply it by the fewest number of primes possible until we can form the other prime factorisation, then we must have the LCM:

$$2^2 \times 3 \times 5 \times 7 \times 11 \times 2 \times 3^2 = 2^3 \times 3^3 \times 11 \times 5 \times 7 = 83160$$

So the LCM of 4620 and 2376 is 83160.

Again, pupils can practise finding the LCM of pairs or groups of numbers from the prime factorisation, and can mix the skills (including mixing with knowledge of the HCF).

> The LCM of two numbers is 495. Both numbers are multiples of 5. What are the smallest possible two numbers?

> The LCM of two numbers is 495. The HCF of both numbers is 9. What are the two numbers?

Ultimately this can lead to the very nice relationship that for any two positive integers a and b, then LCM(a, b) × HCF $(a, b) = a \times b$. It is probably easier to see this by examining slightly smaller numbers at first:

> $a = 27 \ (= 3^3)$, $b = 45 \ (= 3^2 \times 5)$

If we examine the HCF and LCM of these numbers, we can see that the LCM is $3^3 \times 5$ and the HCF is 3^2 and so the product of the LCM and HCF is $3^3 \times 5 \times 3^2 = (3^3) \times (3^2 \times 5) = 27 \times 45$. This is generalisable to all pairs of numbers as the LCM will be the product of all of the prime factors of both numbers *except* those they have in common, as we don't need to multiply the prime factorisation of one of the numbers by the common prime factors to get the prime factorisation of the other number (because they are already there!). However, if we then multiply the prime factors that the two numbers have in common, this will end up being all the prime factors of both numbers, and so will be the product of the two numbers.

This relationship actually gives a nice approach to calculating the LCM or HCF of a pair of numbers given information about the other, or even calculating missing numbers given information about both:

> Find the LCM of 2625 and 1100 given that their HCF is 25.

Two numbers have an LCM of 28,875 and a HCF of 75. One of the numbers is 2625. What is the other number?

Concept link: prime factorisation and powers/roots

Another nice link we can make with prime factorisations is the link to powers and their roots. If pupils are familiar with the distributivity of powers over multiplication (which we will look at in Chapter 5), then there is a straightforward general argument that we can make – if a number Q has prime factors $p_1, p_2, p_3 \ldots p_k$ then:

$Q^n = (p_1 p_2 p_3 \cdots p_k)^n$

$Q^n = p_1{}^n p_2{}^n p_3{}^n \cdots p_k{}^n$

which implies that if a number is a power of n, then all of the prime factors will have powers of n (or potentially multiples of n).

If pupils aren't yet familiar with the distributivity of powers over multiplication (or if this sort of argument isn't one that we feel pupils will follow and see the implications of) then we can, of course, explore different square/cube/power numbers and their prime factorisations, and recognise this directly:

$100 = 10^2 = 2^2 \times 5^2$

$216 = 6^3 = 2^3 \times 3^3$

$144 = 12^2 = (2^2)^2 \times 3^2$

etc. ...

We can then use this knowledge to prompt pupils to consider questions like:

Given that $17{,}210{,}368 = 28^5$, write $17{,}210{,}368$ as a product of primes.

What is the smallest number we can multiply 75 by to make it into a square number?

What is the smallest number we can multiply 56 by to make it into a cube number?

What is the smallest number we can multiply 56 by to make it into a square number?

Given that $2304 = 2^8 \times 3^2$, find $\sqrt{2304}$.

This last question requires pupils to understand square roots, either as equivalent to power $\frac{1}{2}$ (and then to recognise the half power can be applied to both prime factors separately), or simply as the inverse of squaring, so that pupils can see we are trying to write 2304 as ___ × ___ where the two gaps are the same (and hence can see that $2^4 \times 3$ is required in each gap).

The same ideas of factors and factorisation *can* be applied to fractions, negatives and surds as well, although, as previously mentioned, the concept of 'factor' doesn't necessarily transfer well to these areas – can 2 be considered prime if −2 and −1 are considered factors? Isn't every number a factor of every other number if we can consider numbers like $\frac{1}{2}$ and $\frac{2}{3}$ to be factors? If $\sqrt{2}$ is a factor of $3\sqrt{2}$, is $\sqrt{2}$ also a factor of $\sqrt{6}$? One place, however, where we might extend the concept of 'factor' and in particular 'highest common factor' is to algebraic terms. We will look at factorisation of expressions involving sums and differences in Chapter 5, after we have looked at the distributive law and its applications, but one area which is perhaps not looked at as explicitly as it might be in some schools is the factorisation of single algebraic terms. We will conclude this chapter with a brief look at this concept link.

Concept link: factorisation and algebra

As we saw earlier in the chapter, when it comes to looking at division of/by algebraic terms, then multiplicative comparison as a model for division is perhaps the most useful. However, when we talk of 'factorisation' it is the area model that has served to best illustrate the concept; although, again, I must say that any model of multiplication can and should be recognised as showing factors and factorisation. We will, therefore, primarily use the area model to make sense of factorisation of algebraic terms, whilst being open to seeing factorisation in other models.

What are the factors of 2x?

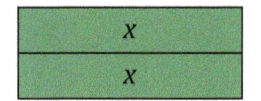

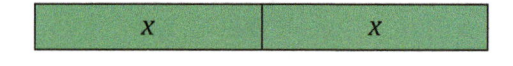

We can see that given two x tiles, we can create two different rectangles – one rectangle with dimensions of 2 and x and one with dimensions 1 and 2x. This suggests four factors of 2x: 1, 2, x and 2x and two decompositions into factor pairs: 1 × 2x and 2 × x.

What are the factors of 4x^2?

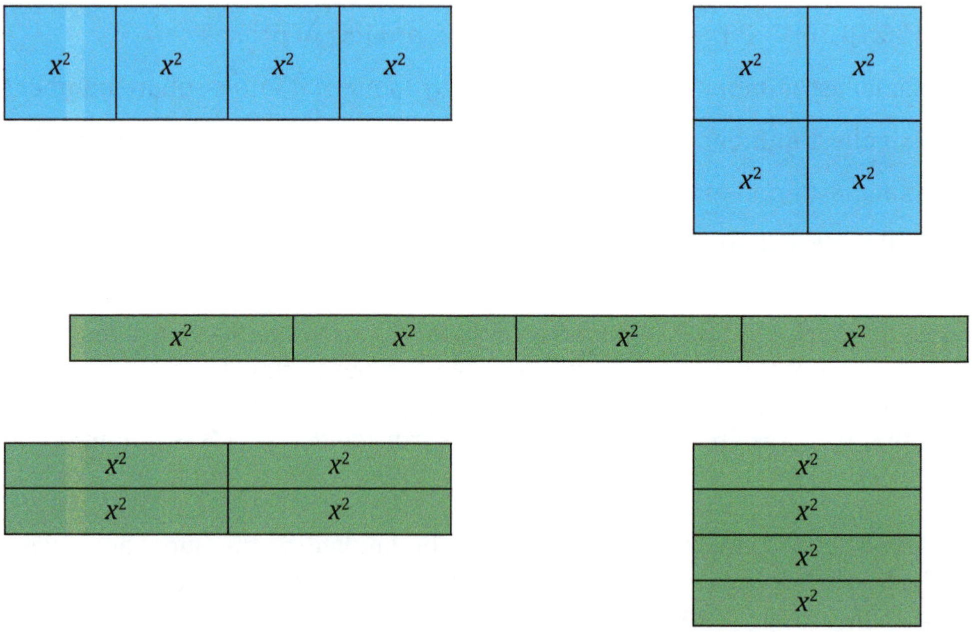

Here is potentially where the area model doesn't show all of the factors of the expression. In the first picture we can see a rectangle that is $x \times 4x$, and in the second a square that is $2x \times 2x$, giving us these four factors. Of course, what is missing are the factorisations involving pure numbers, i.e. $1 \times 4x^2$, $2 \times 2x^2$ and $4 \times x^2$. We can see all of these in the pictures, provided we are willing to shift our model of multiplication – we can see the first picture as 4 things worth x^2, the second as 2 separate rectangles containing $2x^2$, and either picture as 1 group of $4x^2$. Alternatively, we could take a slightly different approach and redefine a length of x^2 rather than our current view of x^2 as an area.

Now we can see that if each rod has a length of 1 and width of x^2, then the first rectangle is $1 \times 4x^2$, the second is $2 \times 2x^2$ and the third is $4 \times x^2$.

What are the factors of $4xy$?

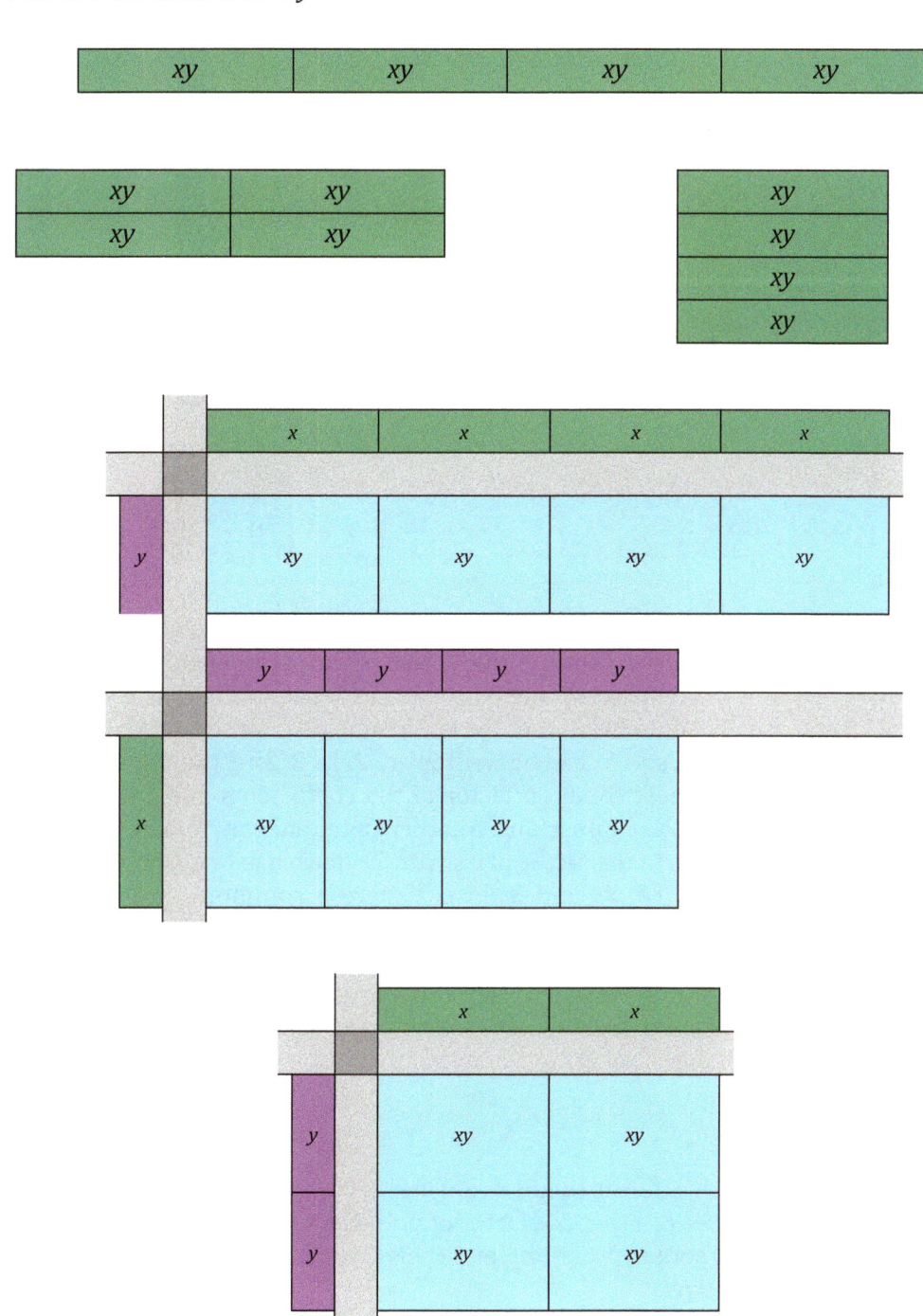

Again, if we treat *xy* as an area, we can see dimensions of $y \times 4x$, $x \times 4y$ or $2x \times 2y$, but those factorisations in which one of the factors involves only a number require us either to change our model to see four things worth *xy*, or two groups of 2*xy* or one group of 4*xy* or to redefine *xy* to be a length, and therefore have 1 × *xy* areas:

where we can see a 1 × 4*xy* rectangle, a 2 × 2*xy* rectangle and a 4 × *xy* rectangle.

Concept link: highest common factor and algebra

In order to tie the idea of highest common factor and the idea of algebra, we need to be clear on how 'highest' applies to variables. Typically, we would consider the highest factor to be the highest power of the variable that is a factor of the expression. This is normally best illustrated with an example:

Find the highest common factor of $4x^2$ and $6x$.

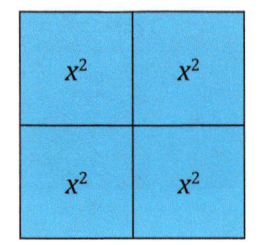

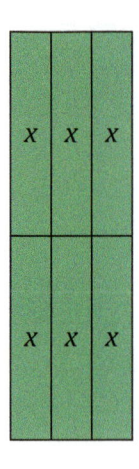

One way of making sense of common factors we have seen is to create rectangles with a dimension in common, and in particular with the largest possible dimension in common for the HCF. In this case, we can create a rectangle for each expression that has a width of 2*x*, and this is the largest possible dimension that the two rectangles can share. We can see that $4x^2$ can be written as $(2x) \times (2x)$ and $6x$ can be written as $(2x) \times 3$. 2*x* is therefore the highest common factor as 2 is the highest common factor of the coefficients and *x* is the highest power of *x* that is a factor of both expressions. Another potential way to explain that 2*x* is the HCF is that the other factors in the factor pairs with 2*x* in each expression do not themselves share a common factor, i.e. 2*x* and 3 do not share a common factor. Due to the variables involved, however, it isn't always possible to represent the two expressions as rectangles with a common width. Pupils will have to be moved to working in the abstract and be comfortable with working systematically though both expressions to identify the HCF in questions like the example below.

Find the HCF of $6x^2y^2$ and $9xy^3$.

We can see that $6x^2y^2$ can be written as $(3xy^2) \times (2x)$ and $9xy^3$ can be written as $(3xy^2) \times (3y)$ and that *x* is the highest power of *x* that is a factor of both expressions and $y2$ is the highest power of *y* that is a factor of both expressions, and so $3xy^2$ would be considered the highest common factor of $6x^2y^2$ and $9xy^3$.

Recognising common factors of algebraic expressions can be a very useful prerequisite to factorisation of expressions involving the sums and differences of algebraic terms, and so the importance in pupils seeing this development of the idea of HCF and having opportunities to practise should not be underestimated. Practice activities can be relatively straightforward – simply take an activity (like this one from Minimally Different) designed to practise factorisation of expressions involving sums and differences of terms and removing the + or − sign to create expressions for which the HCF can be found.

Find the HCF of these expressions:[10]

1   $20x$ 15
2   $20x$ 15
3   $10x$ 15
4   $5x$ 15
5   15 $5x$
6   15 $5x$ $-10y$
7   30 $10x$ $-20y$
8   -30 $-10x$ $-20y$
9   $-20y$ $-10x$
10   $-20y$ $-17x$

11   $13x$ $17x$
12   $26x$ $34x$
13   $26x$ $34x$ x
14   x $26x$
15   x $26x^2$
16   $2x$ $26x^2$
17   $2xy$ $26x^2y$
18   $2xy^2$ $26x^2y$
19   $2xy^2$ $-26x^2y$
20   $2x$ $-26x^2y$

As an alternative/follow-up, pupils can be tasked to create expressions that have a particular HCF.

Write down three algebraic terms that have a HCF of:

1   2
2   $3p$
3   $2b^2$
4   $11a^3c$

Providing further constraints on the terms if you wish to.

We have now finished our exploration of the concepts of addition, subtraction, multiplication and division, which cover the symbols +, -, × and ÷. We will now turn our attention to a symbol even more fundamental to mathematics: =.

---

10 J. Prior, Factorising Linear Expressions 1, *Minimally Different* (22 March 2018). Available at: https://minimallydifferent.com/2018/03/22/factorising-linear-expressions-1/.

Chapter 5

Equality/equivalence/ congruence

The symbol '=' is often (in my experience) misunderstood by learners of mathematics. Many pupils see it is an 'evaluate' instruction; this is probably not helped by the use of the symbol on calculators to evaluate a calculation or by the prevalence of questions in exercises that have the structure 'calculation = ' where pupils have to place the result of the calculation on the right-hand side of the equals sign. Indeed, the paper 'Children's Understanding of Equality and the Equal Symbol' highlights some of the many problems that pupils have with the equals sign, highlighting (for example) that in questions like 4 + 5 = [ ] + 6 that all kindergarten pupils in the study thought that the number 9 was missing from the box because it appears immediately to the right of the equals sign.[1]

The situation is further complicated when we compare notions of equality and equivalence. At this point I suspect most teachers (quite possibly myself included – readers can judge below) are not necessarily clear on the distinction between these two – if indeed a distinction exists! In several places equals and equivalent are treated as synonyms. In the definition of 'equality' from Wolfram MathWorld, it is said that equality is 'a mathematical statement of the *equivalence* of two quantities. The equality "A is equal to B" is written $A=B$.'[2]

The way I tend to think about the distinction between equality and equivalence is that it seems to make sense to say that equality applies to values, and we use the equal sign when we want to draw attention to the fact that two expressions have equal value. Conversely, equivalence seems to make sense when applied to properties. For example, we might write $3(x + 2) = 3x + 6$ when we are drawing attention to the fact that the values these expressions take, for any given value of x, are the same. In contrast, we might write $3(x + 2) \equiv 3x + 6$ if we want to draw attention to the fact that the properties of the expressions are the same (i.e. that $f(x) = 3(x + 2)$ and $f(x) = 3x + 6$ are equivalent functions that will share identical properties such as their graphs, gradients, etc.). This way of looking at equality and equivalence also makes sense when talking about fractions; we often describe fractions like $\frac{3}{4}$ and $\frac{9}{12}$ as equivalent whilst writing $\frac{3}{4} = \frac{9}{12}$. However, if one person takes 3 out of 4 available sweets, and another takes 9 out of 12 available sweets, these people definitely do not have the same number of sweets! The difference here (to me) is how we are viewing the fractions; when we write $\frac{3}{4} = \frac{9}{12}$ we are looking at the fractions as single numbers and stating that these two values are equal (i.e. they are at the same point on the number line). However, when we say '3 out of 4 is equivalent to 9 out of 12' we are describing an equivalence in a property of these fractions – namely their proportions compared to the whole. What is the same as taking 3 out of 4 available sweets and 9 out of 12 available sweets is that in both cases the people have taken *3 out of every 4 available sweets*, which is a subtle shift in the language that highlights an equivalent proportion but not necessarily an equal number of sweets.

If we accept for now that we will treat equality as applying to values, and equivalence as applying to properties, then we can proceed to look at each of these concepts separately and how we might teach what it means to be equal and what it means to be equivalent.

---

1 C. Oksuz, Children's Understanding of Equality and the Equal Symbol, *CIMT* (n.d.). Available at: https://www.cimt.org.uk/journal/oksuz.pdf.
2 E. W. Weisstein, Equality, *Wolfram MathWorld* (n.d.). Available at: https://mathworld.wolfram.com/Equality.html.

Concept: equality

Prerequisites: Numbers.

Linked concepts: Addition, subtraction, multiplication/multiples, division/factors, algebra are important ones, but ultimately most concepts will involve use of equality in one way or another.

How we make sense of equality of values depends, of course, on how we choose to make sense of the values themselves. If we choose to make sense of the values as objects, then two values will be equal if there are the same number of objects when they have the same unit value.

12 = 7 + 5

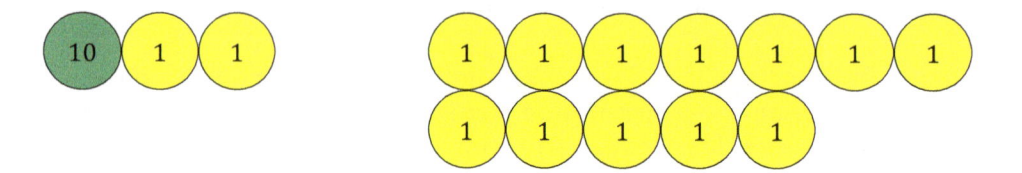

At first these two do not look equal, but that is because they do not have the same unit value. However, when the 10 is exchanged for ten 1s:

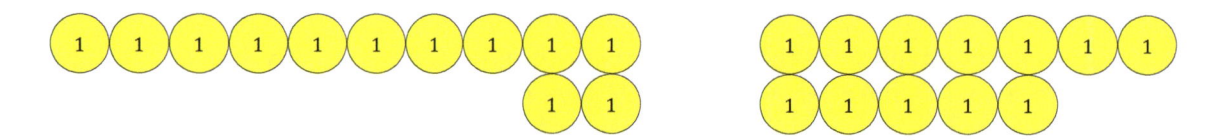

The result is that both sides have an equal number of counters.

What you will notice is that I have deliberately put the 12 on the left-hand side of the equal sign – pupils need to be familiar with working with single values on both sides of the equal sign as well as questions such as the one below:

8 + 4 = 6 + ___ (or 8 + 4 = ___ + 6)

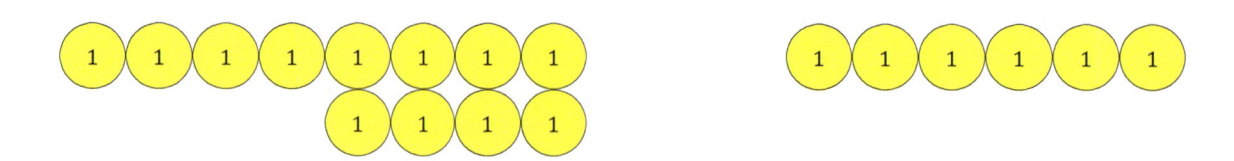

The *Cambridge Mathematics Espresso* article about teaching and learning the equal sign suggests that pupils also need opportunity to encounter three important properties of the equal sign:

- Reflexivity – any mathematical relation where an element will map to itself. Other than equality, other reflexive relationships include 'is divisible by' (any positive integer is divisible by itself), 'congruent to' for shapes (any shape is congruent to itself), 'co-incident' (any line is coincident to itself), etc.

- Symmetry – any mathematical relation where it is true that if $a * b$ then $b * a$. Note this time that 'is divisible by' is not a symmetrical relation (6 is divisible by 3, but 3 is not divisible by 6). However, 'congruent to' is a symmetrical relation (if shape A is congruent to shape B, then shape B is congruent to shape A).

- Transitivity – Any relation where, if $a * b$ and $b * c$ then $a * c$. 'Is divisible by' is a transitive relation (if 12 is divisible by 4 and 4 is divisible by 2 then 12 is divisibly by 2), as is 'congruent to'.[3]

Funnily enough, the fact the 'is equal to' has all three of these properties makes it an **equivalence relation**, implying that 'equality' is potentially a subconcept of the larger concept of 'equivalence'. Pupils can encounter all of these properties through an activity similar to this:

Fill in the missing values in each equation.

1. 367 + 259 = 259 + ___
2. 367 + ___ = 259 + 366
3. 367 + 259 = 366 + ___
4. 259 + ___ = 258 + 366
5. 259 + 366 = ___ + 266 + 100
6. 259 + 466 = ___ + 266 + 100
7. 359 + 366 = ___ + 266 + 100
8. 459 + 266 = ___ + 266 + 100
9. 459 + 266 = 348 + ___ + 100
10. 459 + ___ = 348 + ___ + 100

Of course, in this last question, there are lots of values that could potentially fill the gaps, and this is part of the recognition that we are aiming for. The entire exercise uses numbers that are large enough to make sure evaluation isn't trivial, and so using knowledge of addition and equality to apply/invent alternative strategies is useful for pupils.

As well as the discrete object view of numbers, we also model numbers as continuous measures. When viewing numbers in this way, then the equality can be shown by having the same measure (i.e. the same length, the same area, the same weight, etc.).

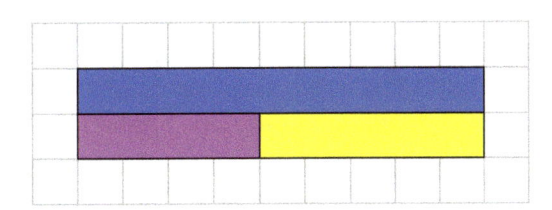

In this picture we can see the length (or area) of 9 is equal in length (or area) to 4 + 5. This sort of picture gives rise to what is often called the *part-part-whole* model for addition,

---

[3] L. Rycroft-Smith and T. Gould, What Does Research Suggest about Teaching and Learning the Equal Sign?, *Cambridge Mathematics Espresso*, 34 (2020). Available at: https://www.cambridgemaths.org/Images/espresso_34_the_equal_sign.pdf.

where the two parts (4 and 5), when added, are equal in length to the whole (9). What follows is that the whole minus one part gives the other part and highlights the relationship between addition and subtraction calculations; in this case that 9 − 4 = 5 and 9 − 5 = 4. This relationship is important for pupils and is worth spending time working on and making explicit.

For each calculation, write down the whole and the two parts and/or write the related calculations.

1   11 + 7 = 18
2   11 − 7 = 4
3   11 = 17 − 6
4   23 = 17 + 6
5   23 + 6 = 29
6   52 = 29 + 23
7   75 − 52 = 23

A similar relationship exists between two factors and a product (as we saw in the previous chapter):

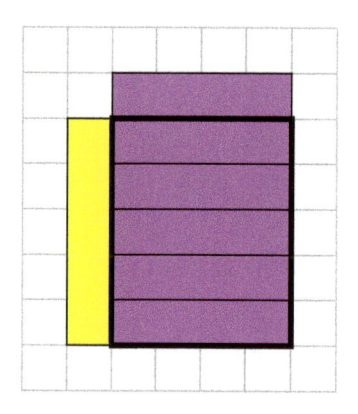

Here we can see 4 × 5 = 20, but also 20 ÷ 5 = 4 and 20 ÷ 4 = 5. A similar activity to the one above for part-part-whole can be offered to pupils to explore the factors and product in different calculations, and/or to write the related calculations.

Once pupils have a good understanding of equality, then we can spend some time exploring properties of arithmetic. Before we turn to equivalence, we will take some time to look at these properties.

Concept: associativity

Prerequisites: Numbers, addition, subtraction, multiplication, division, equality.

Linked concepts: Algebra, commutativity, distributivity, proportion (in particular certain percentage calculations).

Operations are associative when the order of application doesn't affect the end result, i.e. if $(a * b) * c = a * (b * c) = a * b * c$. We can demonstrate that addition is associative:

Equality/equivalence/congruence

(8 + 5) + 3 = 8 + (5 + 3)

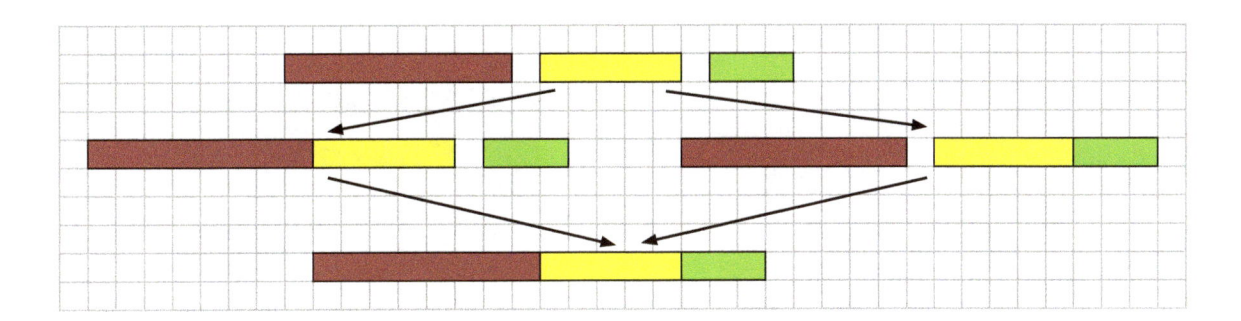

The fact that addition is associative leads to some useful strategies for addition, particularly where different parts of the sum are easier to evaluate and evaluating them makes the whole sum easier to evaluate.

1   Use the associative law to help work out the following:

a   45 + 72 + 28   b   45 + 72 + 18   c   145 + 172 + 18

2   Use the associative law to help work out the following:

a   36 + 57 + 13   b   36 + 47 + 23   c   236 + 47 + 123

3   Use the associative law to help work out the following:

a   153 + 168 + 32   b   153 + 132 + 68   c   153 + 132 + 168

Or we can prompt pupils to think about the structure of calculations where the associative law might be useful.

Fill in a suitable number in the box that would make using the associative law appropriate for completing the addition in each question:

a   92 + 79 + □   c   328 + 165 + □   e   264 + □ + 254
b   56 + 84 + □   d   149 + □ + 187   f   27 + □ + 488

We can also demonstrate the multiplication is associative (we can do this in 3D or using two different models for multiplication:

(2 × 4) × 7 = 2 × (4 × 7)

Here we can see the front-left face is 2 × 4, which is then multiplied by 7. Alternatively, we can see the top face as 4 × 7, which is then multiplied by 2.

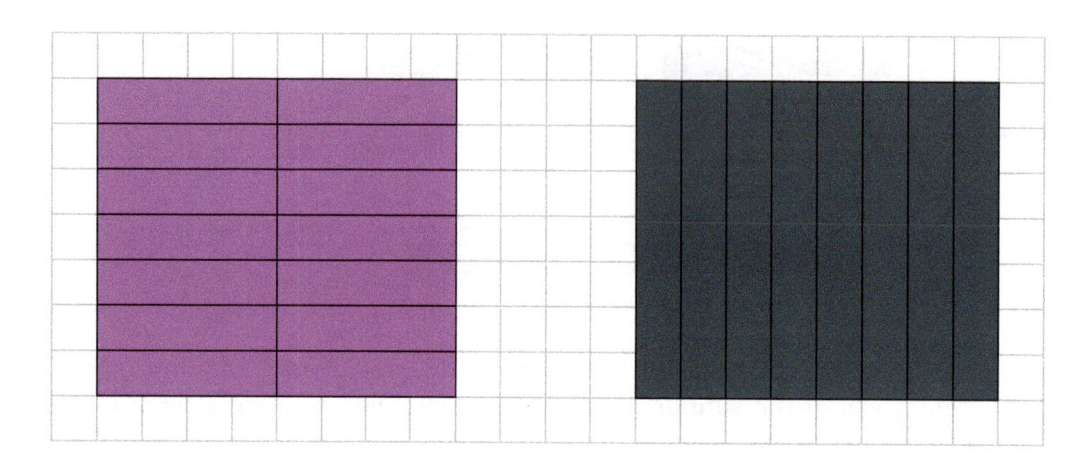

On the left of this picture we see 4 × 2 as the 4-rod repeated twice, and then the area is created by multiplying this by 7. On the right of the picture we can see 4 × 7 as an area, but then the whole area repeated a second time. The fact that the two areas are equal in size (and therefore value) demonstrates the equality between the two and hence that multiplication is associative. Again, this leads to some useful calculation strategies:

1   Use the associative law to help work out the following:

a   17 x 5 x 2   b   17 x 50 x 2   c   17 x 5 x 20

2   Use the associative law to help work out the following:

a   17 x 5 x 4   b   17 x 50 x 4   c   17 x 50 x 40

3   Use the associative law to help work out the following:

a   17 x 25 x 4   b   17 x 4 x 25   c   17 x 40 x 25

Fill in a suitable number in the box that would make using the associative law appropriate for completing the multiplication in each question:

a   29 × 5 × □   c   62 × 50 × □   e   38 × □ × 2

b   87 × 20 × □   d   49 × □ × 4   f   71 × □ × 25

These can be built upon to provide strategies for larger number multiplication (as well as providing the foundation for strategies such as long multiplication) – for example, in calculating something like 47 × 30 by decomposing into 47 × 3 × 10 or calculating 47 × 50 by calculating 47 × 100 × $\frac{1}{2}$.

Equality/equivalence/congruence

We can also demonstrate that subtraction is *not* associative:

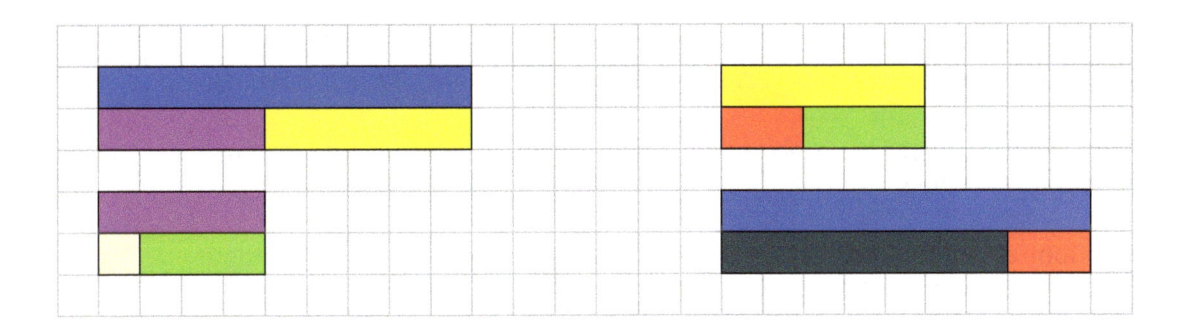

(9 − 5) − 3 ≠ 9 − (5 − 3)

On the left of this picture we can see 9 − 5 giving the result of 4, and then we take the 4 and subtract 3, giving the result of 1. In the second picture we see 5 − 3 giving the result of 2, and then we take 2 and subtract it from 9, giving the result of 7.

Similarly, we can demonstrate that division is not associative:

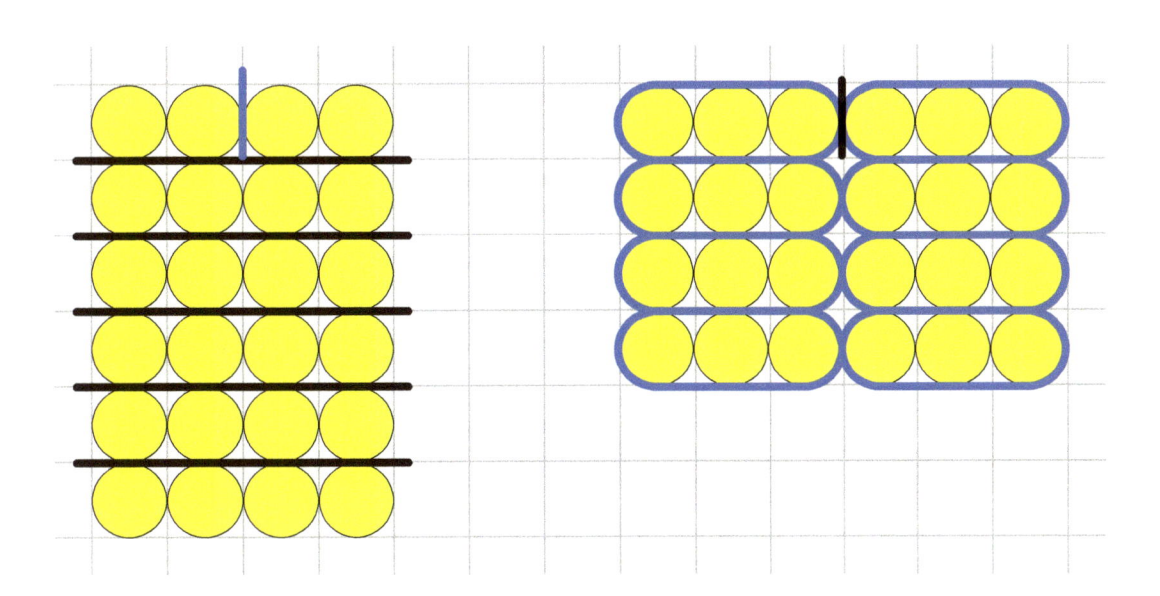

(24 ÷ 6) ÷ 2 = 24 ÷ (6 ÷ 2)

On the left of this picture we see 24 shared into six shares, with a result of four in each share, and then a single four is shared further into two equal shares, with the final result of two counters in that share. On the right we see six shared into two equal shares, with a result of three counters in each share. From here we switch to a grouping model and look at how many of those groups of three are required to make a total of 24, with the result that there are eight groups.

Pupils should also have the opportunity to come back to the associative property of addition and multiplication when exploring the links between these concepts and other types of numbers – for example, fractions, negatives surds and algebraic expressions. Also, when pupils have a bit more familiarity with the idea that subtraction *is* addition, and similarly that division is multiplication, then again we can come back and look at these in a new light.

For example, that 24 ÷ 6 ÷ 2 can be thought of as 24 × $\frac{1}{6}$ × $\frac{1}{2}$, which is why we can't do the '6 ÷ 2' first: it is actually $\frac{1}{6}$ ÷ 2.

Concept: commutativity

Prerequisites: Numbers, addition, subtraction, multiplication, division, equality.

Linked concepts: Algebra, associativity, distributivity, proportion (in particular certain percentage calculations).

Operations are commutative if the order of the values can be reversed without effecting the result, i.e. $a * b = b * a$. We can demonstrate that addition is commutative:

7 + 8 = 8 + 7

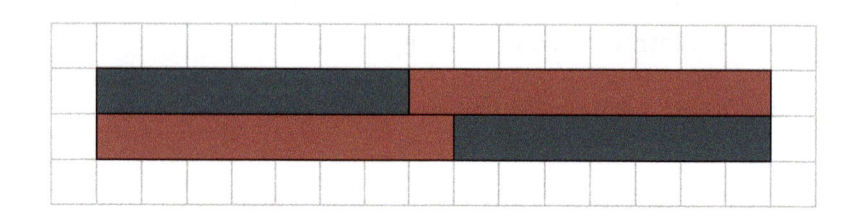

Again, commutativity leads to some useful strategies for addition, particularly when there are sums involving multiple numbers and swapping some of the numbers would make evaluation more straightforward:

1 Use the commutative law to help work out the following:

a 72 + 45 + 28   b 72 + 45 + 18   c 172 + 145 + 18

2 Use the commutative law to help work out the following:

a 57 + 36 + 13   b 47 + 36 + 23   c 47 + 236 + 123

3 Use the commutative law to help work out the following:

a 168 + 153 + 32   b 132 + 153 + 68   c 132 + 153 + 168

1 Fill in a suitable number in the box that would make using the commutative law appropriate for completing the addition in each question:

a 92 + 79 + ☐

b 56 + 84 + ☐

c 328 + 165 + ☐

d ☐ + 187 + 149

e ☐ + 254 + 264

f ☐ + 488 + 27

We can also demonstrate that multiplication is commutative:

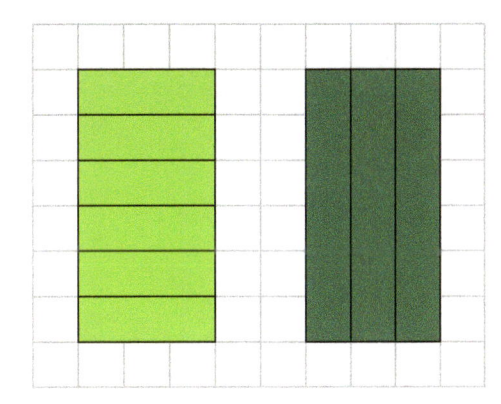

3 × 6 = 6 × 3

Here we can see that the area formed by each calculation is the same in both cases, showing the equality. Once again, similar strategies for multiplication can be shown as a consequence of the commutative law:

1   Use the commutative law to help work out the following:

a   5 x 17 x 2   b   50 x 17 x 2   c   5 x 17 x 20

2   Use the commutative law to help work out the following:

a   5 x 17 x 4   b   50 x 17 x 4   c   50 x 17 x 40

3   Use the commutative law to help work out the following:

a   25 x 17 x 4   b   4 x 17 x 25   c   40 x 17 x 25

4   Fill in a suitable number in the box that would make using the commutative law appropriate for completing the multiplication in each question:

a   5 × 43 × □   c   50 × 51 × □   e   □ × 427 × 2

b   20 × 83 × □   d   □ × 26 × 4   f   □ × 354 × 25

Note that the associative property on its own will not allow us to multiply the first and third values in these calculations (the order of the values remains the same in the associativity, it is only the order of evaluation that changes). However, we can use the commutative property to swap the order of any two of the values, and then, if needs be, use the associative property to calculate: for example, we could either write 5 × 17 × 2 as 5 × 2 × 17 using the commutative property to swap the 2 and the 17 before evaluating, or alternatively we could write 5 × 17 × 2 as 17 × 5 × 2 using the commutative property to swap the 17 and the 5, and then using the associative property to evaluate the 5 × 2 before then evaluating 17 × 10.

As with associativity, we can demonstrate that subtraction is not commutative:

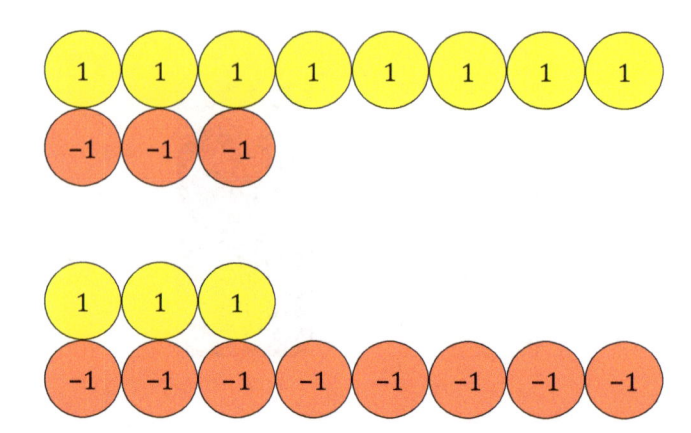

8 − 3 ≠ 3 − 8

Probably the clearest model to see this with is the model where we rewrite the subtraction as an addition (although take-away can also be effective). In the first picture we have 8 + (−3) as 8 − 3; however, in the second picture we can see 3 − 8 as 3 + (−8). Clearly, the two pictures are not the same. Of course, if pupils have already been introduced to this model, along with the fact that addition is commutative, then it is easy to see that the two are not the same, as 8 + (−3) would be equal to (−3) + 8, rather than 3 + (−8).

Similarly, we can demonstrate that division isn't commutative:

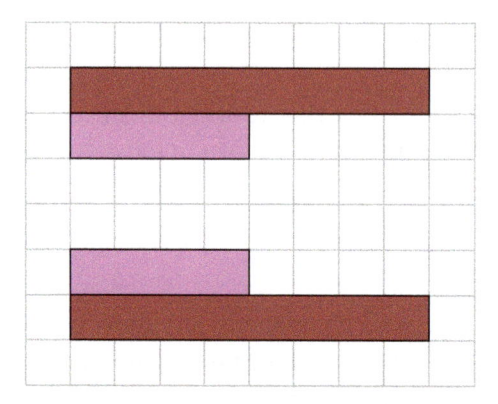

8 ÷ 4 ≠ 4 ÷ 8

Using the comparison model, we can see that if we define the purple rod to have a value of 1 in the upper picture, then the brown rod has a value of 2. However, in the lower picture, as the brown rod is the value of the divisor, if we define this to have a value of 1, the purple rod definitely isn't 2. Again, if pupils are already familiar with the idea that division is multiplication and that multiplication is commutive, then it is straightforward to see that 8 ÷ 4 = 8 × $\frac{1}{4}$, and therefore that a calculation with an equal value would be $\frac{1}{4}$ × 8 and not 4 × $\frac{1}{8}$.

Equality/equivalence/congruence

Concept: distributivity

Prerequisites: Numbers, addition, subtraction, multiplication, division, powers, roots, equality.

Linked concepts: Algebra, associativity, commutativity, factorisation.

Distributivity is fundamentally different to associativity and commutativity in a few different ways:

1. Distributivity works on a combination of two different operations, rather than a single operation.
2. Because of this, the application of the operations matters in applying the distributive property.
3. Distributivity can be applied with both subtraction and division.

Because of these differences, distributivity does require more time for pupils to become familiar with its properties and intricacies, particularly when applying distributivity to numerical calculations. It is also one of the most applied properties of numbers, frequently (although rarely explicitly) being used for several strategies for multiplication and division, as well as for powers and roots. However, it is probably one of the more misused properties as well, with pupils often applying it in situations where it isn't valid to use. Part of the problem is quite possibly that it is rarely taught explicitly, rather its application to multiplying or dividing numbers, expanding expressions, etc. are taught separately instead of being shown as a consequence of what they are – the distributive property at work.

In short, those operations that are at one particular level in the traditional hierarchy of operations will distribute over the operations that are in the level immediately below. So multiplication or division will distribute over sums or differences, and powers or roots will distribute over products or quotients. Some of these are easier to demonstrate/model than others; it is relatively straightforward to model multiplication distributing over a sum or difference:

$3(5 + 2) = 3 \times 5 + 3 \times 2$

We can see in the first picture the sum of 5 and 2 repeated 3 times to create the area of 21. In the second picture we can see the 3 by 5 and the 3 by 2 separately; however, we can see that if we added the two separate areas together, the result would be the same as the picture on the left.

3(5 − 2) = 3 × 5 − 3 × 2

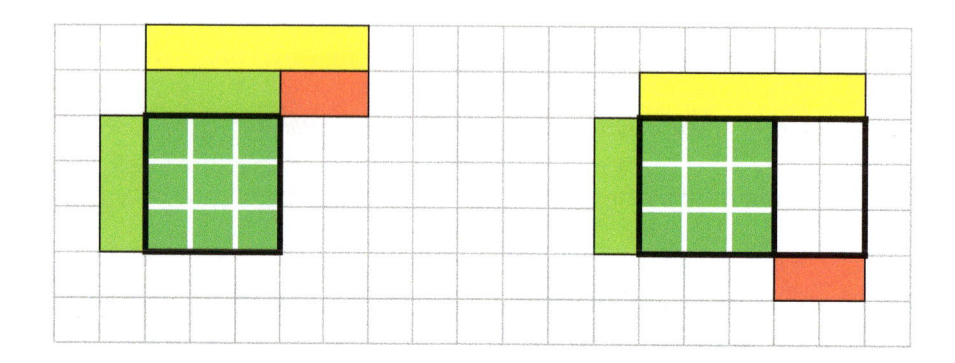

In the left picture we can see 5 − 3, and then the result multiplied by 3. In the right picture we can see the difference between a 3 by 5 area and a 3 by 2 area.

Similarly, we can demonstrate that division will distribute over sums and differences:

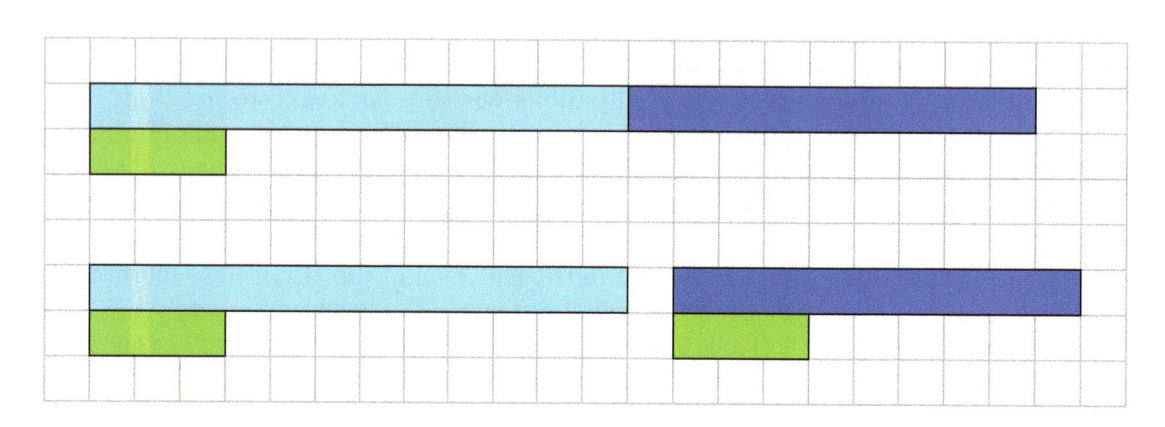

$\frac{12+9}{3} = \frac{12}{3} + \frac{9}{3}$

The comparison model makes this also trivial; in the first picture we can see the sum of 12 and 9 compared to 3. Of course, if we redefine the green rod to be 1, then the sum takes on a total of (4 + 3) = 7. In the second picture we can see the same comparisons carried out separately; however, when we redefine the green rod as 1 we still get values of 4 and 3, which we can then add together.

We can test the writing of this explicitly by asking pupils to rewrite calculations like 5 × (9 + 6) as the sum of two products. However, the real power of the distributive law comes from applying it in situations where the sum is not explicit – for example, in the calculation 8 × 68 or $\frac{84}{3}$. What is particularly nice, having explored both sums and differences, is to prompt pupils to write calculations like this in at least two different ways – one as the sum of two products/quotients and one as the difference of two products/quotients. For example, pupils could write 8 × 68 as 8 × 60 + 8 × 8, but also as 8 × 70 − 8 × 2. Similarly, pupils could write $\frac{84}{3}$ as $\frac{60}{3} + \frac{24}{3}$, or as $\frac{90}{3} - \frac{6}{3}$ (or as many other calculations!). Getting pupils to practise rewriting calculations using the distributive law makes it more likely that they will apply useful calculation strategies for these kinds of calculations. We can extend this by asking pupils to write calculations in as many ways as they can find:

1   How many different ways can you show to complete these calculations:

   a 8 × 47   b 19 × 6   c 13 × 18

2 How many different ways can you show to complete these calculations:

a $\frac{171}{9}$ b 132 ÷ 6 c $\frac{154}{2}$

We can also offer problems like this, to prompt pupils to think more carefully about the structure at play:

6 × (80 + 4) = 504. What numbers would be in the blanks to create the same answer:

1 ___ × (160 + 8)
2 ___ × (40 + 2)
3 ___ × (90 − 6)
4 24 × (___ + ___)
5 24 × (___ − ___)

What other calculations can you come up with that would fit?

Similarly, we can see that powers will distribute over multiplication, although it is better to represent this just with power 2:

$(3 \times 4)^2 = 3^2 \times 4^2$

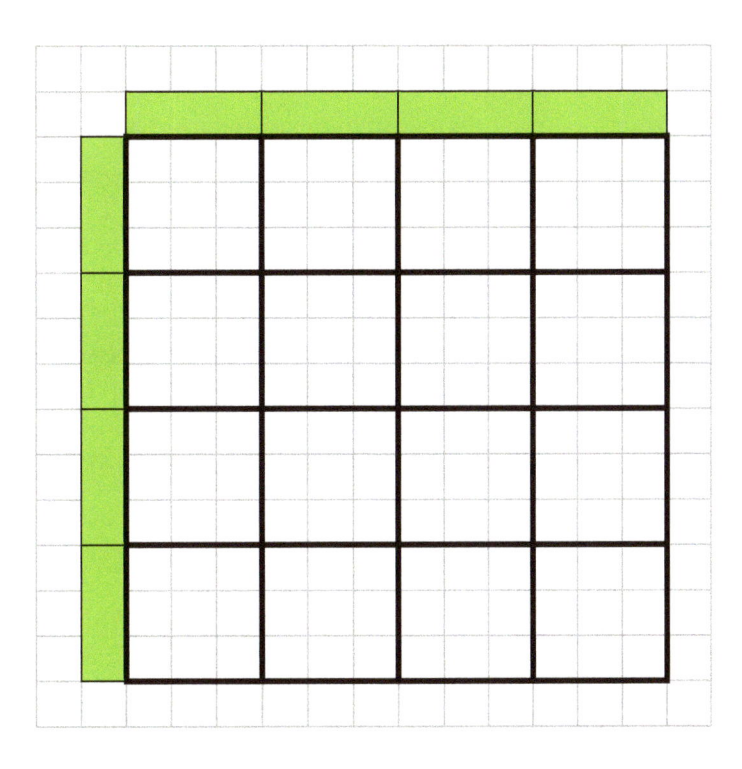

We can see that the length of this square is a 3-rod repeated four times, from where we get $(3 \times 4)^2$. However, this leads to repeated 3 × 3 areas (i.e. 3^2). Further, because each of the 3-rods is repeated 4 times, the 3^2 area is repeated 4^2 times.

$(6 ÷ 3)^2 = 6^2 ÷ 3^2$

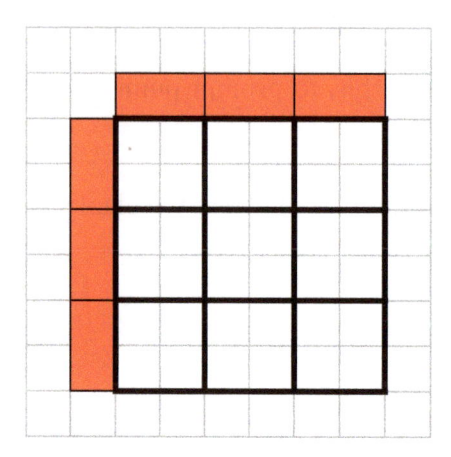

We can see here that a length of 6 has been split into three equal-sized pieces, and then this has been squared. However, within the same picture, we can also see the square of length 6 has been split into smaller squares, and, because there were three rods along each length, this is 3^2 smaller squares, giving $6^2 ÷ 3^2$.

We have already demonstrated the distributivity of roots over multiplication when we looked at multiplication/division with surds.

In addition to be able to demonstrate where distributivity is applicable, we also need to be clear to pupils where it isn't. In particular:

- That addition/subtraction aren't distributive over any other operation.
- That powers/roots don't distribute over addition and subtraction.

We can demonstrate this using representations, but if pupils have some familiarity with these operations, then they are usually fine to work with symbolically:

3 + (4 ± 5) ≠ 3 + 4 ± 3 + 5: This is a direct consequence of the associative property; we already know that 3 + (4 + 5) = 3 + 4 + 5, and similarly that 3 + (4 − 5) = 3 + 4 + (−5).

3 + (4 × 5) ≠ 3 + 4 × 3 + 5: This follows easily from either unitised or area model of multiplication:

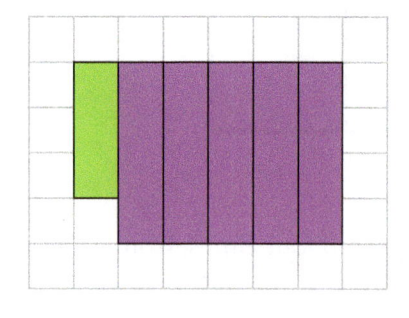

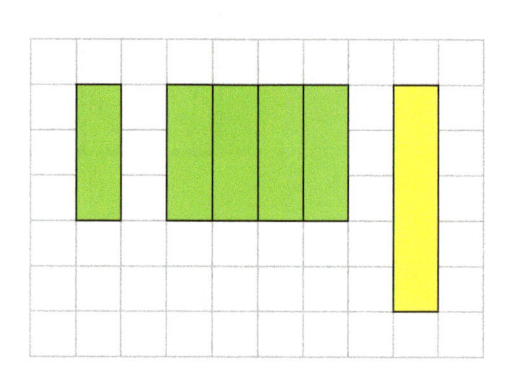

On the left we can see 3 + 4 × 5, and on the right we have 3 + 4 × 3 + 5. It should be clear that these are not equal. Of course, we can work out quite readily that 3 + (4 × 5) = 23, whilst 3 + 4 × 3 + 5 = 20.

$\frac{3}{4+5} \neq \frac{3}{4} + \frac{3}{5}$: This is probably as simple as pointing out that $\frac{3}{4+5}$ is smaller than $\frac{3}{4}$ and $\frac{3}{5}$, and therefore definitely smaller than their sum!

$(3 + 4)^2 \neq 3^2 + 4^2$: Again the area model can be used to demonstrate this quite nicely:

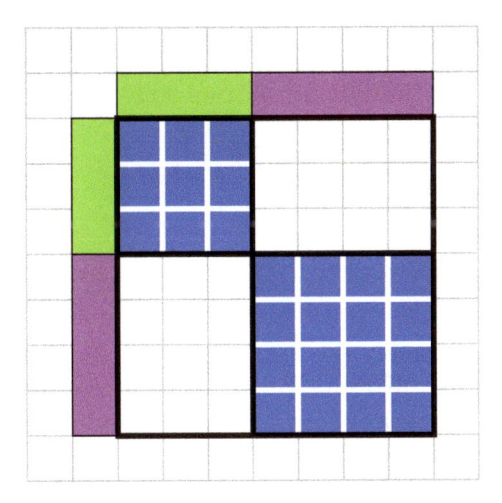

We can see the length of $(3 + 4)$ along each side of this square, giving $(3 + 4)^2$. Within that we can also see an area of 3^2 and an area of 4^2. However, we can see that the sum of the 3^2 and 4^2 areas does not completely fill the $(3 + 4)^2$ space. Indeed, we have seen virtually the same picture when looking at multiplying larger numbers using the area model, leading to the grid method, and so pupils could potentially already be familiar with the idea that multiplying a sum (or difference) by another sum (or difference) that the result requires four separate multiplications to be evaluated (in this case 3×3, 4×3 (twice) and 4×4).

$\sqrt{9 + 16} \neq \sqrt{9} + \sqrt{16}$: We can use the area model to demonstrate these, but they do have to be carefully set up:

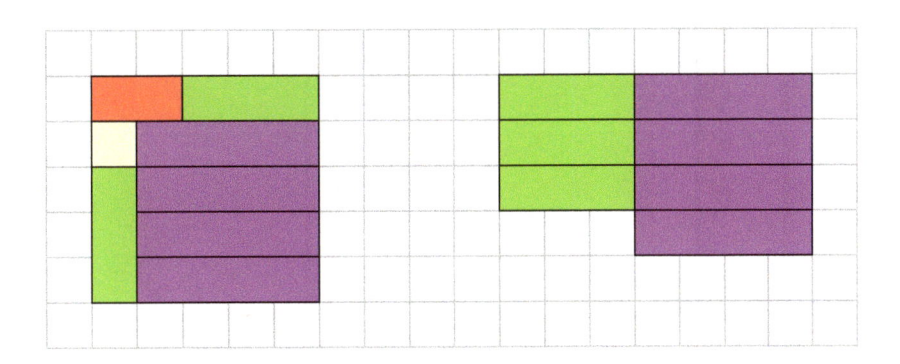

On the left we have $9 + 16$ arranged as a square, so we can see that the length of the square (i.e. $\sqrt{9 + 16}$) is 5. On the right we have 9 and 16 arranged as separate squares, connected edge to edge so we can see the sum of their lengths (i.e. $\sqrt{9} + \sqrt{16}$) across the top. We can see that this is 7; or if we don't want to focus on evaluation we can see that the length across the top of the left-hand square is a green and a red, whereas the length across the top of the right-hand shape is a green plus a purple. Hence, as red and purple are not the same length, these two lengths are not the same.

There are a couple of other aspects to distributivity that we will explore before turning our attention back to equality more generally. One thing to quickly note, however, is that when looking at distributivity, particularly involving multiplication over a sum or difference, pupils should see the sum/difference as both the multiplier and the multiplicand: i.e. calculations like 3 × (4 + 5) and (4 + 5) × 3 so that they don't mistakenly come under the impression that the distributive law can only be applied left to right.

The two aspects to the distributive property that we will explore before going back to more general discussion about equality are:

1   The consequences of the arithmetic properties on the order of operations.
2   Distributivity applied to algebraic expressions.

Subconcept: order of operations

Order of operations is quite possibly the area of mathematics teaching that most needs to be revisited. Typically, rules like BIDMAS, GEMS or PEMDAS pervade the teaching of order of operations teaching. For me, not only are these rules unnecessary, but they are actually incorrect.

Take, for example, the calculation 3 × 14 + 7 × 14: rules like BIDMAS would have us evaluate 3 × 14 and 7 × 14, and then add the results of those two multiplications. Of course, this is patently unnecessary: 3 × 14 + 7 × 14 = 10 × 14. In this case, there is no need to complete the multiplications before the addition. We can either see this as a result of the distributive law:

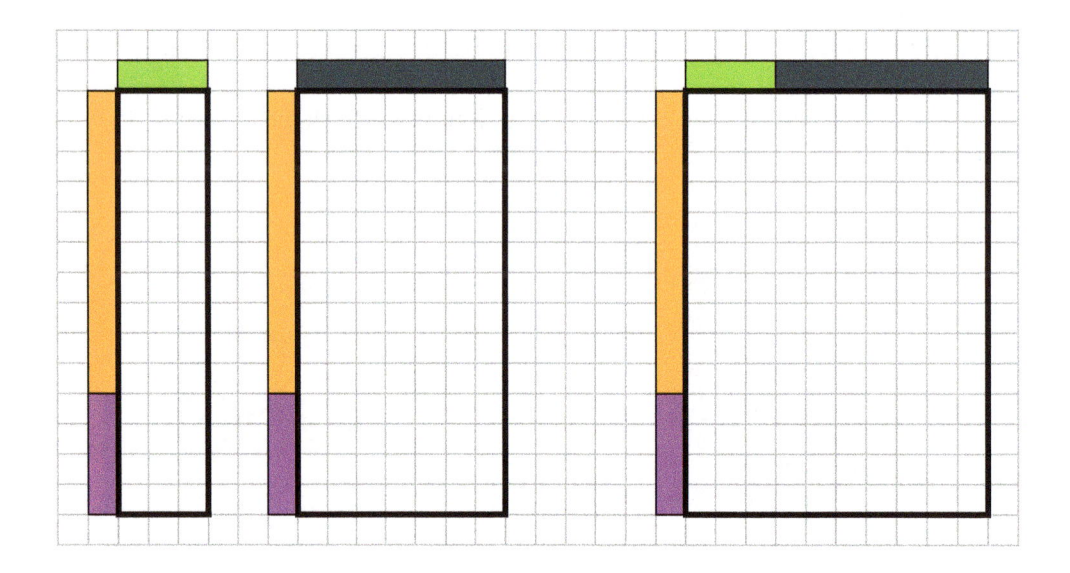

or more fundamentally, a unitising approach to multiplication combined with our pre-existing knowledge of addition when numbers are viewed as discrete objects:

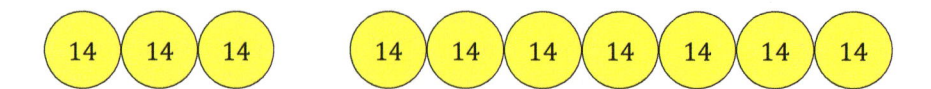

A nice activity to reinforce this use of distributivity with pupils is to look at different calculations and ask pupils to decide whether they can be written as single products (doing so where possible).

Where possible, write each calculation as a single product of two integers greater than 1:

a $2 \times 3 + 5 \times 3$

b $2 \times 7 + 5 \times 7$

c $2 \times 12 + 5 \times 12$

d $2 \times 1000 + 5 \times 1000$

e   2 million + 5 million

f $2 \times 3 + 5 \times 7$

g $2 \times 3 + 5 \times 9$

h $2 \times 3 + 5 \times 6$

i $3^2 + 5 \times 6$

j $2 \times 3 + 5 \times 2$

These start fairly standard, to get pupils tuned into the pattern, but then get more interesting from *f* onwards. In *f* there is no way to write the calculation as the single product of two integers greater than 1. However, it is possible with each of the following questions (indeed in *h* it is possible in two different ways, which can prompt some interesting discussion all on its own). Ashton Coward has a great activity on his website that looks at the same idea and brings in the representations as well.[4]

If we take the time to ensure pupils are fluent in good models of the different operations, alongside the properties of arithmetic, then 'rules' like 'BIDMAS' simply become unnecessary. What can replace them is a real focus on *strategies* for different calculations such as:

$98 \times 18 + 2 \times 18$:   In this case, there is no need to compute the multiplications before the addition, and in fact by adding first we have 100×18, which is easier to evaluate.

$12 \times 11 + 11^2$:   Even if we choose to complete the multiplications first, we can multiply the 12 and the 11 prior to (or at the same time as) we evaluate 11^2 before adding together. Alternatively, we could treat 11 as the unit and show we have 23×11, or potentially even rewrite the whole thing as $11 \times 12 + (12 - 1)^2 = 11 \times 12 + 12 \times 12 - 2 \times 12 + 1 = 21 \times 12 + 1$.

$3 + 5 \times 7$:   In this case, the thing to overcome is the temptation to think that this is 8×7, i.e. that we evaluate left to write. However, as pupils are now fluent in the distributive law, it should already be clear that if we want 8×7 then this would be $(3 + 5) \times 7$ as $8 \times 7 = 3 \times 7 + 5 \times 7$. Without the brackets this cannot be 8×7, and so the addition cannot be evaluated until both parts have the same unit, i.e. 3 ones + 35 ones. We can also justify this (if we choose) by looking at the consequences due to the commutative property: $3 + 5 \times 7$ must have the same result as $3 + 7 \times 5$ (due to the commutativity of multiplication) and this only makes sense if we evaluate the multiplication before adding the 3.

$3 + 9 \times 5 - 8$:   A lovely strategy here is to 'borrow' one of the 5s from 9×5, and add it to the 3, giving $8 + 8 \times 5 - 8$. We can then either treat 8 as the unit, or even more simply, evaluate the $8 - 8$ leaving just 8×5.

$32 - \sqrt{9} \times \sqrt{4} - 5^2$:   Again, what should be clear here is that the subtractions cannot be evaluated with the values in their current form; there is no common unit to be subtracting. Instead, each part must be evaluated first to have all the numbers in 1s. It matters not whether we calculate 5^2 first,

---

[4] A. Coward, Distributive Law – Area model and unit counters, *Mr Coward Maths* (22 February 2021). Available at: https://mrcowardmaths.wixsite.com/website/post/distributive-law-area-model-and-unit-counters.

evaluate the √9 and the √4 first, or even if we combine √9 × √4 into √9 × 4 and then evaluate this. Provided we get to 32 – 6 – 25 before completing any subtraction then there are multiple approaches to the earlier part of this calculation.

There are other great activities that can be used to prompt pupils to consider calculations involving multiple operations. The classic is probably the 'four 4s' – given four 4s and the ability to use any operation (I usually limit this to + - × ÷ and √) and brackets, which different integer values can pupils create? With a potential follow up about different ways to create some of those numbers, and whether those that can't be made have something in common. In addition, activities where pupils have to fill in operations to create certain answers are useful, and often feature in assessments as well.

Fill in the blanks to make these equations true:

1   28 ____ 3^3 _____ 4 = 136

2   7^2 ____ 8 ____ 6 ____ 13 = 84

Etc.

As well as playing a pivotal role in calculations involving multiple operations, being able to apply the distributive property also plays a crucial role in pupils' development of algebraic understanding:

Subconcept: expanding and factorising algebraic expressions

If pupils are familiar enough with the distributive law, and its use in calculating with numbers, then expansion of algebraic terms may well not pose a significant challenge; however, where necessary we can use the same sorts of representations that we have used with numbers to support pupils in sense-making. A nice thing to do is to place these side by side so that pupils can see the relationship with numbers and how it replicates with algebraic expressions:

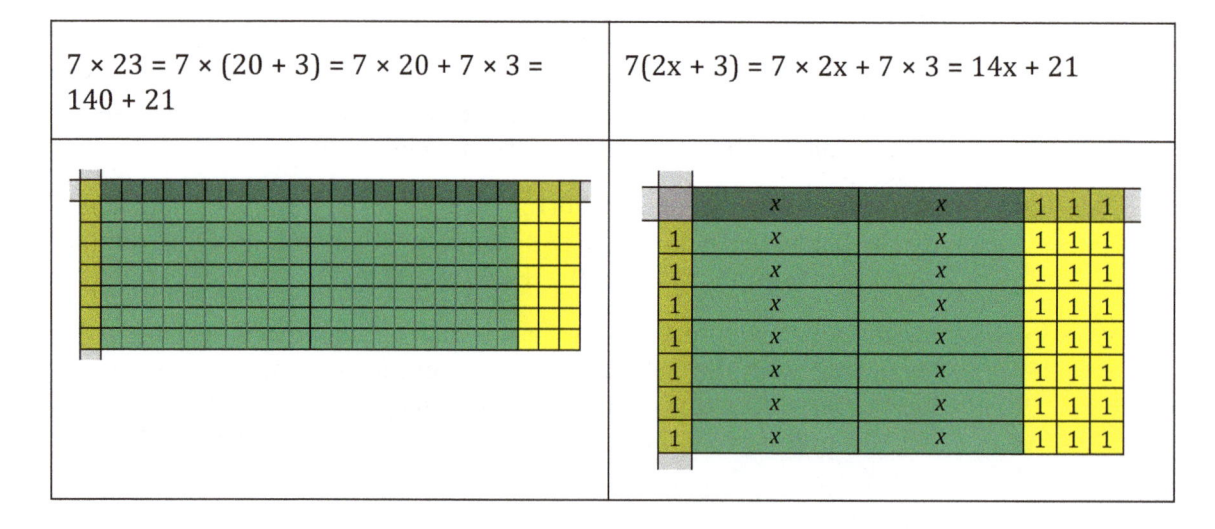

7 × 23 = 7 × (20 + 3) = 7 × 20 + 7 × 3 = 140 + 21	7(2x + 3) = 7 × 2x + 7 × 3 = 14x + 21

Equality/equivalence/congruence

7 × 19 = 7 × (20 − 1) = 7 × 20 − 7 × 1 = 140 − 7	7(2x − 1) = 7 × 2x − 7 × 1 = 14x − 7
17 × 23 = (10 + 7)(20 + 3) = 10 × 20 + 7 × 20 + 3 × 10 + 7 × 3 = 200 + 140 + 30 + 21	(x + 7)(2x + 3) = x × 2x + 7 × 2x + 3 × x + 7 × 3 = 2x² + 14x + 3x + 21
17 × 19 = (10 + 7)(20 − 1) = 10 × 20 + 7 × 20 − 1 × 10 − 7 × 1 = 200 + 140 − 10 − 7	(x + 7)(2x − 1) = x × 2x + 7 × 2x − 1 × x − 1 × 7 = 2x² + 14x − x − 7

There are some lovely activities that can prompt thinking around expansion, including the in the A1 'Interpreting Algebraic Expressions' section of the Standards Unit[5] as well as something like:

> Expand each factor in the top row by each factor in the left-hand column. Do you notice any patterns? Can you explain them?

×	$(x-2)$	$(x-1)$	x	$(x+1)$	$(x+2)$	$(x+3)$
$(x+3)$						
$(x+2)$						
$(x+1)$						
x						
$(x-1)$						
$(x-2)$						

Or simply to ask:

> How many different expressions of the form $(x \pm a)(x \pm b)$ can you find that expand to have a constant term of 24? An x coefficient of 11? Both?

The goal here is to focus pupil attention on to how the changes in a and b affect the constant and the x coefficient, before complicating things by including coefficients on the x terms in the brackets.

It is important that pupils have the opportunity to work with applying distributivity to expressions in lots of different forms, including squaring expressions, simplifying the results of expanding multiple expressions (particularly something like $3(2x + 5) - 4(x - 3)$ as pupils often get mixed up with negatives here), expressions that involve multiple variables and three or more terms (i.e. $(3x + 2y - 7)(4x - 2p)$).

---

5   STEM Learning, Interpreting Algebraic Expressions A1 (n.d.). Available at: https://www.stem.org.uk/resources/elibrary/resource/26952/interpreting-algebraic-expressions-a1.

When it then comes to factorising algebraic expressions, pupils should have more than enough experience to make sense of these very quickly, having seen factorisation of numbers and having used the distributive property 'in reverse'. Again though, where required, we can use representations to support pupils that need it in order to make sense of the idea, using the area model similarly to how it worked with factorising numbers:

Factorise $6x + 9$

We create a rectangular area without gaps or overlaps and then look at the length and width of the expression. As mentioned in the previous chapter, we need to steer pupils away from rectangles of width 1 and towards creating the largest width possible.

Factorise $x^2 + 5x + 6$

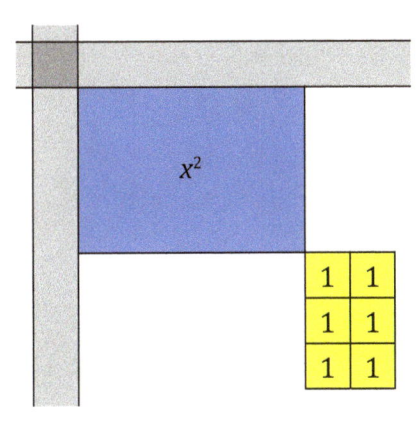

Key to this is recognising that the 1-tiles cannot line up with the x^2 tile, and so must form their own rectangle that joins corner to corner with the x^2 tile. The goal then is to arrange the 1-tiles in such a way as to leave the right space for the x-tiles – in this case as a 3 × 2 rectangle leaving space for the five x-tiles.

Factorise $2x^2 + 7x + 6$

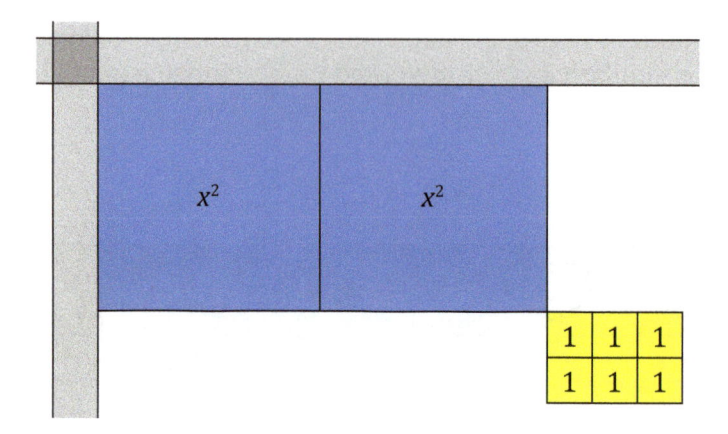

This is the same idea as the previous example; however, what is key to recognise in this case is that the arrangement of the 1-tiles into a rectangle causes more potential permutations in the spaces left for the *x*-tiles, as the shape that the 1s rectangle is attached to is no longer a square. This means that the length of width of the $2x^2$ rectangle will mean a differing number of *x*-tiles depending on how the 1s rectangle is arranged. In this case, we can see that this is to arrange the 1-tiles as a 2 × 3 rectangle to create the right space for the seven *x*-tiles.

Something we may wish to highlight to pupils at this point is the fact that the original quadratic has been changed into $2x^2 + 3x + 4x + 6$, and that 2 × 6 = 3 × 4. This is useful if we are going to move on to more abstract methods involving multiplying the coefficient of x^2 and the constant term, as it provides the justification for why we multiply these together and then look for two factors that add to make the total of our *x* coefficient. An interesting challenge is to prove that it will always be the case that if $ax^2 + (b+c)x + d$ factorises then $ad = bc$.

Again, there are great activities to prompt thinking around factorisation. One of my favourites, which is lovely to work on with the tiles, is simply to ask pupils to find as many expressions that fit certain criteria as possible, for example:

How many different ways can you fill in the blank so that the expression is factorisable?

1 $x^2 + \_\_\_ x + 4$

2 $x^2 + \_\_\_ x - 12$

3   $3x^2 + $___$x + 8$

4   $2x^2 + 3x + $___

Or something like this (based on an Open Middle task):

Use the digits 1 to 9 at most once each to fill in the boxes and make the equation true. Which digits cannot be used?

□x + □ = □ (□x + □)

There is also a specific strategy for factorisation that is worth exploring with pupils; the factorisation of expressions that are the difference of two squares:

Factorise $4x^2 - 25$.

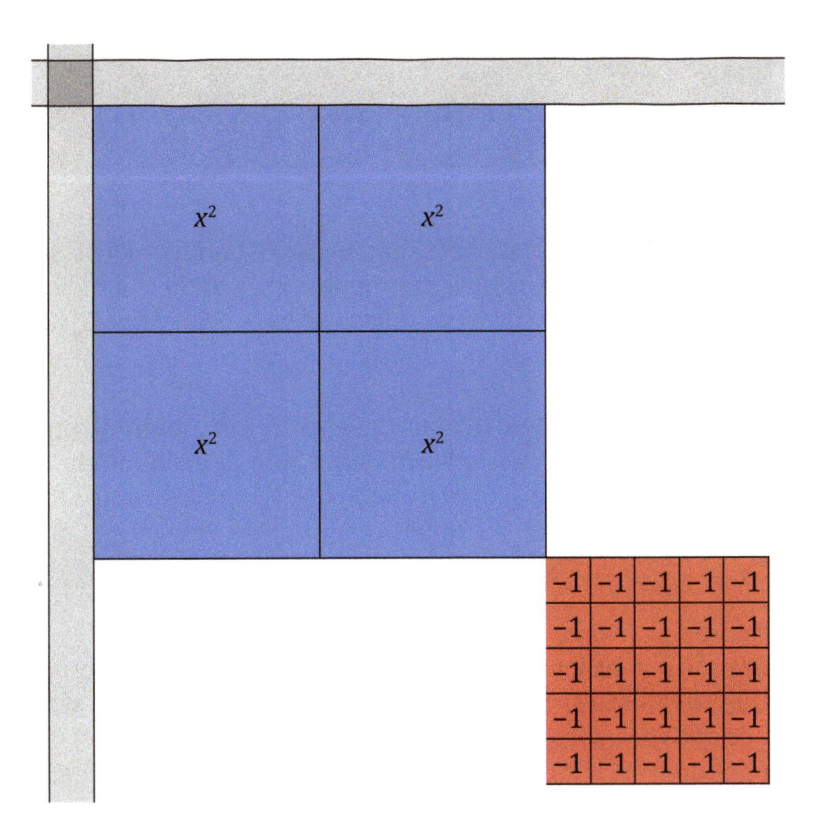

The same logic follows as per the previous factorisations: that the spaces must be right to allow the correct number of x-tiles. In this case, of course, the number of x-tiles has to be '0', meaning in reality that there must be the same number of x-tiles and -x-tiles. The only way this can happen, though, is if both the x^2-tiles and the negative 1-tiles are arranged as perfect squares, so that the spaces in the rectangle are the same size. These can then be filled with x and -x tiles.

[Algebra tiles diagram showing a 2×2 arrangement of x^2 tiles with x-strips on the right and -x strips/-1 tiles at the bottom, illustrating $4x^2 - 25$.]

Pupils' attention should be drawn to the fact that, because both the x^2-tiles and the -1-tiles form squares, the factorisation will involve the square roots of the coefficients of x^2 and the constant term (not including the sign). So, in this case, $4x^2 - 25 = (2x + 5)(2x - 5)$ as 2 is $\sqrt{4}$ and 5 is $\sqrt{25}$.

The difference of two squares is a particularly useful factorisation for numerical calculations. There are two particular types of problems that are definitely worth exposing pupils to:

Calculate $8.9^2 - 1.1^2$

This can potentially form another part of pupils' exposure to multi-operation calculations (again showing the utter uselessness of rules like BIDMAS). A better strategy here is to apply the difference of two square factorisation, giving $(8.9 + 1.1)(8.9 - 1.1)$. The benefit in this case to using this approach is that the first bracket sums to 10; the calculation becomes 10×7.8, which is much easier to evaluate.

Which is greater: 78 × 76 or 77 × 77?

Again we can apply a difference of two squares argument: if we treat 78 × 76 as $(77 + 1)(77 - 1)$ then we can see this becomes $77^2 - 1$, i.e. 78 × 76 is one less than 77 × 77.

Now that we have thoroughly explored the properties of arithmetic and their consequences, we return our attention back to equality to examine algebraic equation manipulation/solving.

Equality/equivalence/congruence

Subconcept: manipulating/solving algebraic equations

Having explored equality in some detail, the representations for equations should already be well understood:

$2x + 3 = 19$

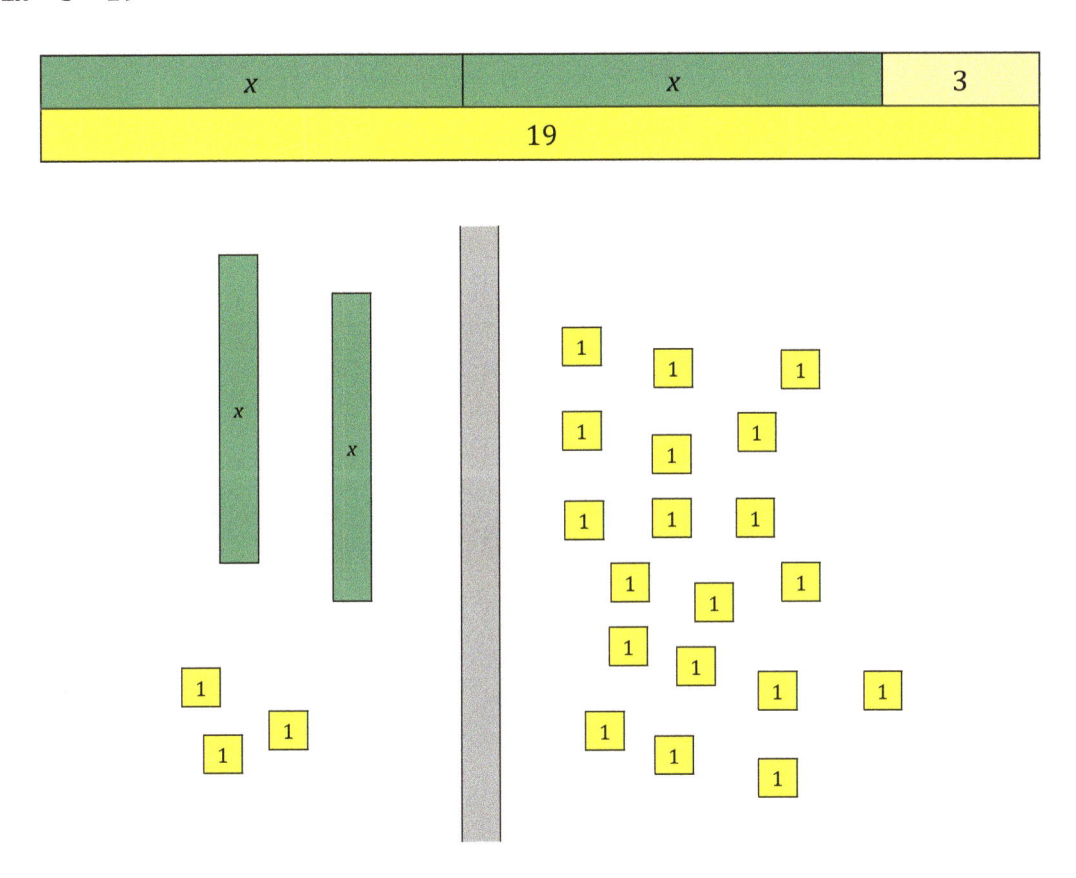

We can either see the equality in the lengths/area above or we can set the equality by saying the number of objects to the left of the line is equal to the number of objects on the right of the line when measured with the same unit value.

The natural question that arises in this scenario is what is the value of x? That could be, 'What is the length of x?' (if looking at the picture above) or 'how many 1s is an x worth?' if looking at the object view. However, this is not where I would start with algebraic equations. Rather I would start with simply manipulating equations, getting pupils used to the logical deductive process that holds with equations, such as in the activity below.

If $2x + 3 = 19$, then write down an expression/value that is equal to:

a $2x + 4$ e $5x$ i $x + 60$

b $2x + 2$ f   95   j $60 - x$

c $4x + 4$ g   57

d $5x + 4$ h   60

How many more equations can you write down based on the original equation?

We can bring lots of different equations into this sort of activity – equations with unknowns on both sides of the equal sign, even equations with more than one unknown such as $3x + 2y = 17$. This eventually can lead to discussions about solvable equations, and the conditions upon which equations can be solved.

Once pupils have experience manipulating equations, that is the point I will steer more towards manipulating the equation until the value of x is known, i.e. until the equation is of the form x = value. This comes with the same sort of logical deduction that we saw in the activity above – it doesn't need a special process. Logically we can deduce that if $2x + 3 = 19$, then $2x = 16$, therefore $x = 8$. We can see this through either the length/area view of the equality:

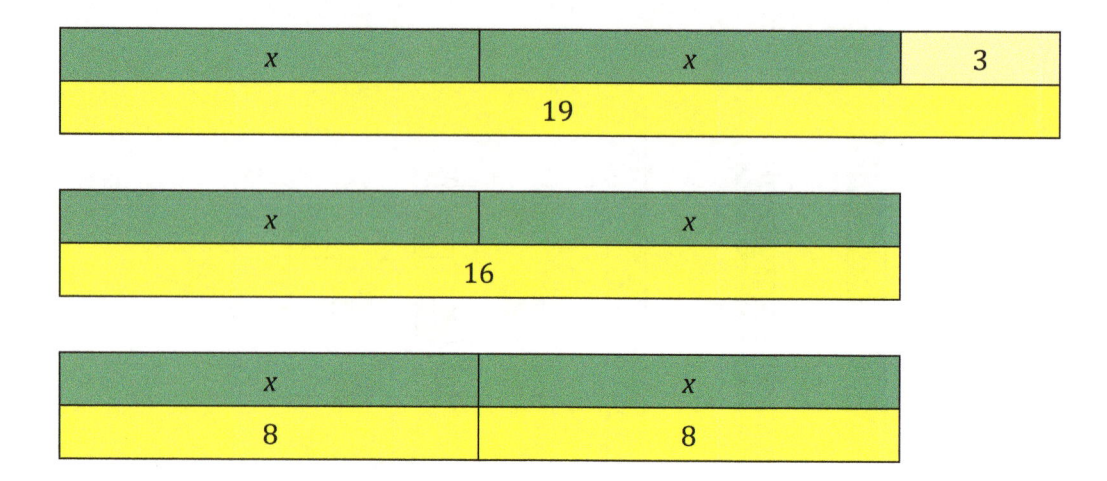

Alternatively, if using the object view:

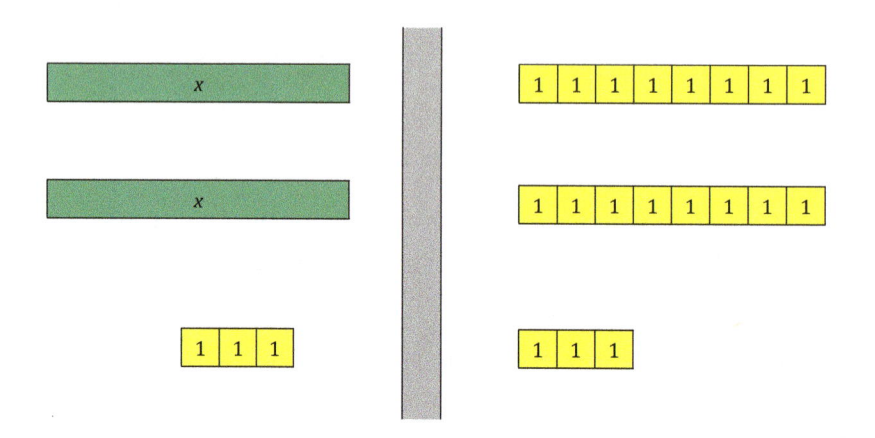

The same sort of logic can be used to solve all linear equations and can be transferred nicely into solving two equations in two unknowns:

$3x + 2y = 23$

$4x - 2y = 12$

Equality/equivalence/congruence

x	x	x	x	$-y$	$-y$
12					

Adding these two together gives:

x	x	x	y	y	x	x	x	x	$-y$	$-y$
23						12				

which leads to:

x	x	x	x	x	x	x
35							

giving $x = 5$, which further gives $y = 4$.

When offering activities to support pupils in practising solving simultaneous equations, it is important that pupils can first identify when equations can be solved and when they cannot be. Pupils should be familiar with the fact that there are only a finite number of roots of a single equation when it involves a single unknown. This can then be extended to being able to recognise a finite number of roots of a system of equations when the number of equations matches the number of unknowns. This may accompany looking at degrees of freedom in equations (which we will talk about in Chapter 7 when looking at formulae). Once pupils can recognise when equations/systems of equations are solvable, there are some excellent tasks that can focus pupils' attention on key structures, such as this one from Don Steward:[6]

Simultaneous equation generalisations:

i $2x + y = 9$
     $x - y = 3$

ii $2x + y = 18$
     $x - y = 6$

iii $2x + y = 27$
     $x - y = 9$

iv $2x + y = 36$
     $x + y = 12$

v   What pattern is there in these equations?

     Try two or three more examples.

     Try to state a general rule.

     Try to establish that it always works.

i $2x + y = 4$
     $3x + y = 9$

ii $5x + y = 25$
     $2x + y = 4$

iii $4x + y = 16$
     $6x + y = 36$

iv $5x + y = 25$
     $9x + y = 81$

v   What pattern is there in these equations?

     Try two or three more examples.

     Try to state a general rule.

     Try to establish that it always works.

---

6   D. Steward, Simultaneous Equations Generalising 1 (out of 6), *Median* [blog] (20 February 2019). Available at: https://donsteward.blogspot.com/2019/02/simultaneous-equations-generalising-1.html.

as well as setting the questions in some interesting contexts:[7]

What are the lengths and widths of the congruent rectangles for each question?

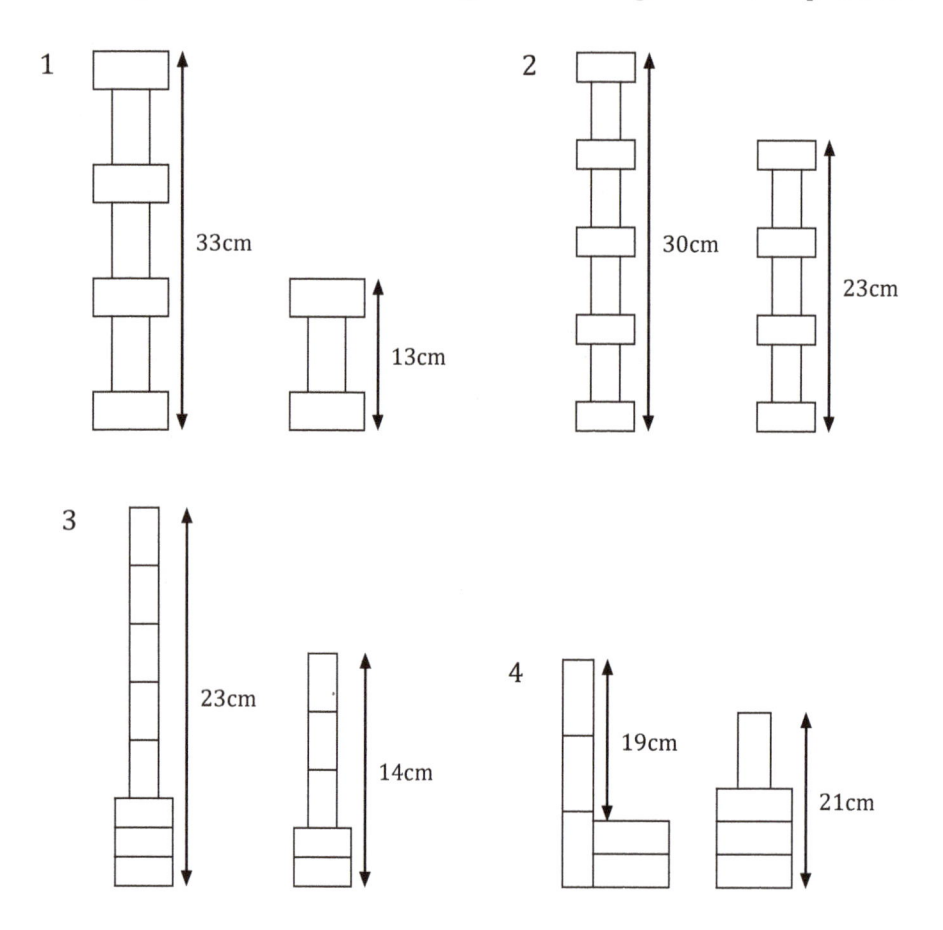

1. 33cm, 13cm

2. 30cm, 23cm

3. 23cm, 14cm

4. 19cm, 21cm

When it comes to quadratic equations, they can be solved in a similar way with some additions to the deductive process using factorisation:

$x^2 - 5x - 6 = 0$

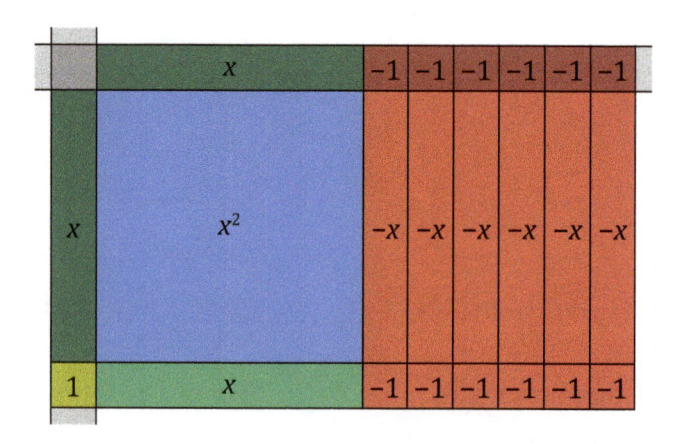

---

[7] D. Steward, Simultaneous Equation Tasks, *Median* [blog] (14 July 2013). Available at: https://donsteward.blogspot.com/2013/07/simultaneous-equation-tasks.html.

Here we see $x^2 - 5x - 6$ factorised to give $(x - 6)(x + 1)$. The logic goes that if this area is to take a value of 0, then either the length or the width of the rectangle has to take a value of 0.

We can make the length take a value of 0 by making $x = 6$, which leads to the following picture:

We can see that the 6 × 7 [$x \times (x + 1)$] rectangle is perfectly balanced by the −6 × 7 rectangle, resulting in areas of 42 and −42, which will combine to give an area of 0.

Alternatively, to make the width 0, we need to make x have a value of −1, which leads to this picture:

Again, we get the two rectangles with the same physical size, but opposite sign, resulting in the area of 0.

A similar process can yield the solution to a quadratic equation through use of the completed square form. We haven't yet explored this explicitly, so we will take a moment to show what this might look like.

Subconcept: completed square form of a quadratic expression

The goal in completed square form is to write the general quadratic in the form $a(x + b)^2 + c$. There are two important things pupils should recognise about completed square form:

1 Unlike factorised form, every quadratic expression can be written in completed square form.

2 Both the x^2 term and the x term in the expanded form are contained within the square bracket, so the focus needs to be on making sure the coefficients of x^2 and x are

correct. The constant term can be adjusted by choosing a suitable positive or negative value of c. Take, for example:

$x^2 + 4x - 5$

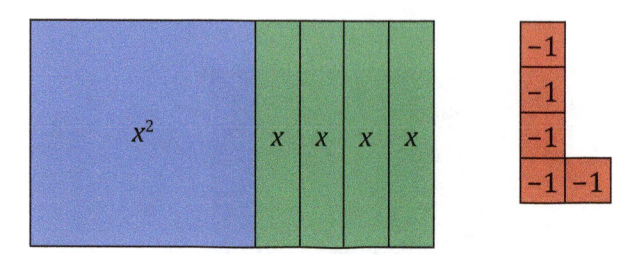

We start by considering the x^2 and the x terms, and arranging these to be as close as possible to a completed square:

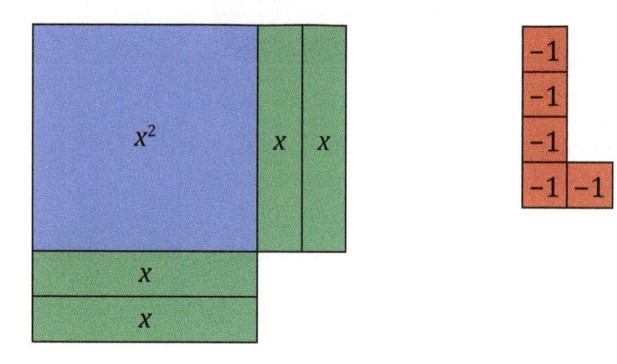

At this point we can either say that the shape we have is 4 less than a complete square (we cannot place the negative tiles in the space as clearly the length of the square is positive as both sets of x-tiles are positive). So we would have $(x + 2)^2 - 4 - 5$. This leads to $(x + 2)^2 - 9$.

Instead, we might actually complete the square by putting four 1-tiles into the space. However, in order to place four 1-tiles into the space, we will need to balance them with four −1-tiles:

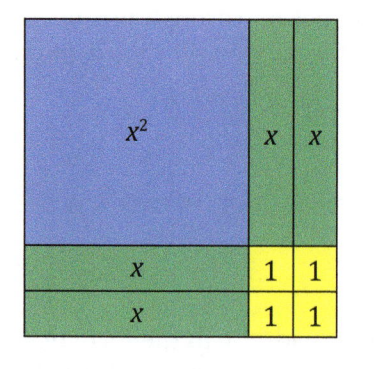

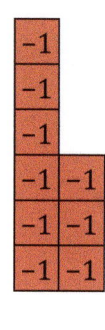

Here we can now see a complete $(x + 2)^2$, with the extra −9 that is not part of the square, which leads directly to the expression $(x + 2)^2 - 9$.

One key factor in this representation is that we can see properties such as why the constant term in the square bracket is always half of the coefficient of x; because half of the x-tiles are arranged vertically on the sides of the square, and the other half of the x-tiles are arranged horizontally. What should be clear is that this will always need to be the case for us to get as close as possible to a complete square.

From here we might look at making multiple squares, where the coefficient of x^2 is greater than 1, which leads to having the a in front of the bracket, and shows us why the value of a in the expanded form and the value of a in the completed square form will always be the same:

$2x^2 + 4x + 9$

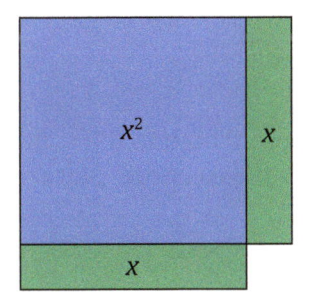

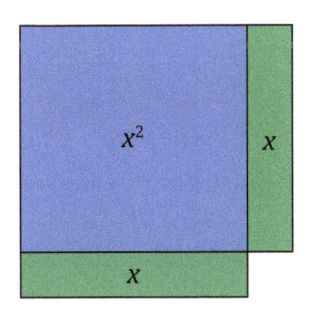

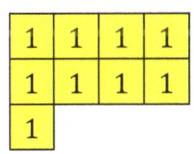

We can see that the formation of the squares has already started, by rewriting the expression as $2(x^2 + 2x) + 9$. From here we can complete each square by introducing two extra 1-tiles, and pairing them with two −1-tiles outside of the squares (or we could say that each square is one less than a complete square, so altogether that is two less than our complete squares):

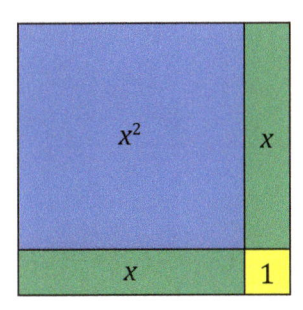

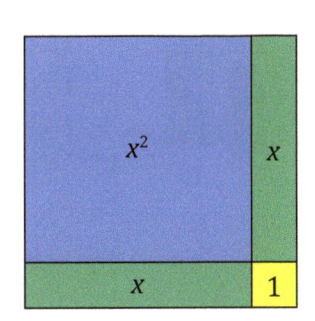

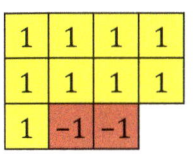

We now have $2(x + 1)^2 - 2 + 9$, from which we can create two zero-pairs to leave $2(x + 1)^2 + 7$.

Returning then to equations, we can see how completed square form can be helpful in solving equations:

$x^2 + 4x - 5 = 0$

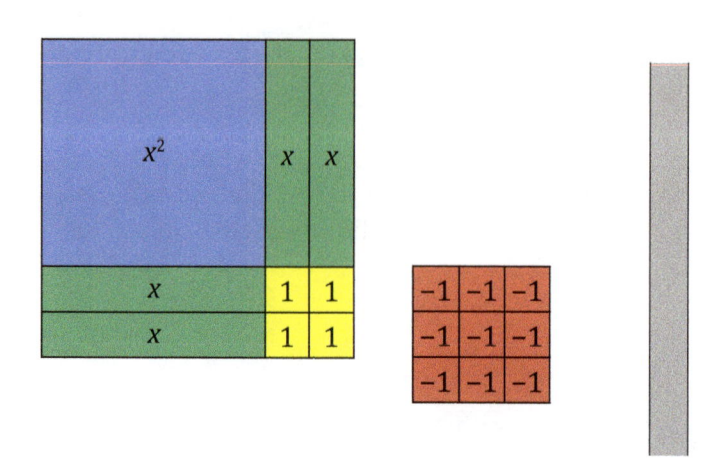

Here we see the completed square form of $x^2 + 4x - 5$, with it being set equal to 0 (i.e. nothing). We can deduce that the $(x + 2)^2$ must have a value of 9 (we can, if we choose, physically add 9 to each side of the line):

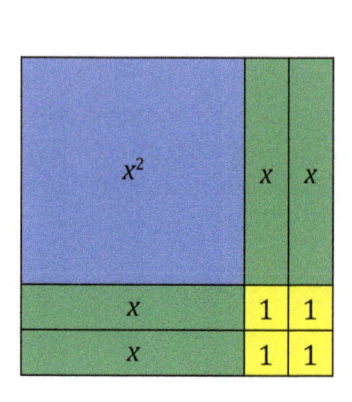

Further, the deduction goes that there are two ways we can make these squares equal in area, and that is to make their length either 3 or −3. Given that part of the length of the (x + 2)² is 2, we can make x + 2 = 3 by making x = 1, or we can make x + 2 = −3 by making x = −5:

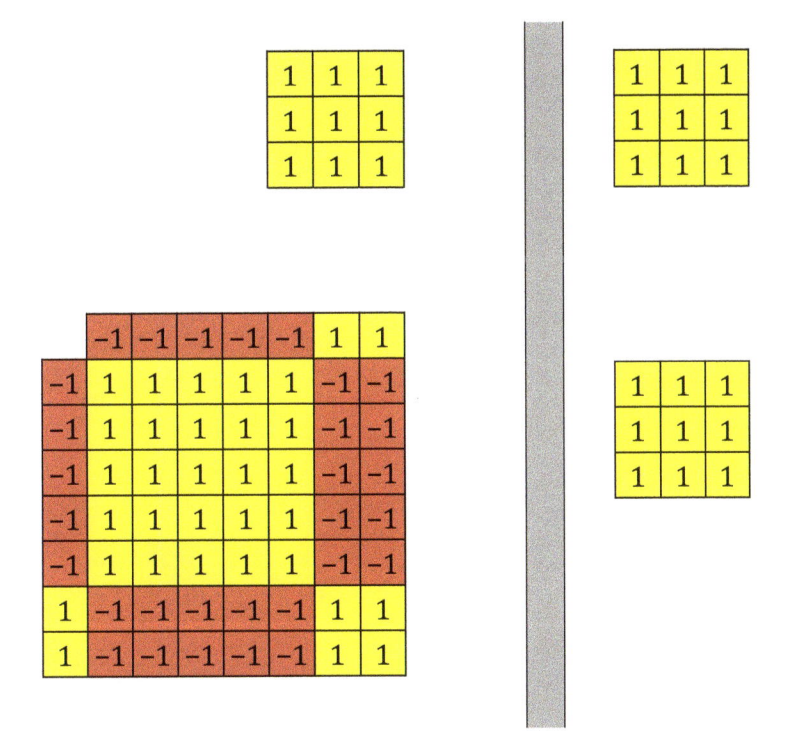

Here we can see that in both cases, the resultant area has a value of 9 (the length and width when x = −5 have been shown explicitly to aid visualisation of where the different positive and negative areas come from).

The other approach that pupils often study for solving quadratic equations is the use of the quadratic formula. Of course, the quadratic formula can be derived by completing the square on the general expanded quadratic, $ax^2 + bx + c = 0$. It is possible to show this visually, but it isn't particularly easy and it may well be better to wait until pupils are comfortable working purely in the abstract before trying to derive this formula with them.

Activities for prompting pupils to think about the structure underlying completing the square are very similar to those for factorisation. Things such as filling in the gaps at different places in the expression are useful, particularly where there is potentially more than one solution to the problem. What will also be important is to relate both the factorised and completed square form to the graph of a quadratic function – we will explore these points further in Chapter 13.

Whilst this is a reasonably thorough examination of the notion of equality and how we can use properly introduced models for equality to examine some further properties of arithmetic, the heading of this chapter also alluded to equivalence and congruence. We will finish the chapter by looking at these concepts; however, prior to this we have one more stop. Having examined equality, we should now take the time to contrast it properly with the concept of 'inequality'.

Concept: inequality

Prerequisites: Numbers, equality.

Linked concepts: Addition, subtraction, multiplication, division, algebra, measurement, transformations, data analysis, graphing, probability.

Inextricably linked to the concept of equality is the concept of inequality. In fact, the symbols for inequality and equality can be demonstrated nicely as arising from similar places:

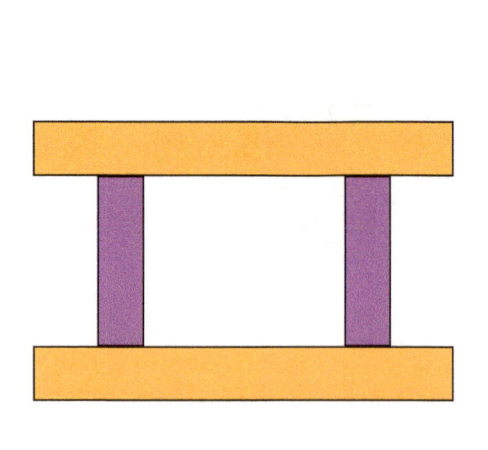

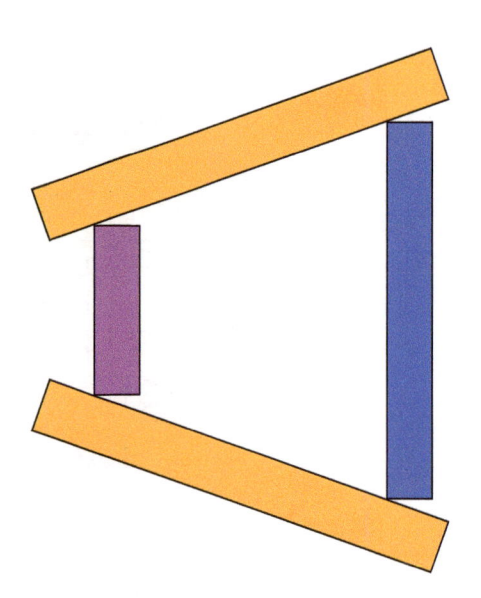

On the left we can see two numbers that are equal in length, which means that two parallel lines can show the relationship between their heights. On the right we can see two numbers that aren't equal in length, so the lines that show the relationships between their heights are no longer parallel, but form the basis of the inequality symbol: <.

Pupils can work with inequality alongside their work on equality. One of the most straightforward activities is to offer pupils different expressions and ask them to select the correct symbol to connect them.

Write either =, > or < between these expressions:

a $7 + 4$ ___ $7 + 5$

b $7 + 4$ ___ $6 + 5$

c $7 + 5$ ___ $6 + 4$

d 7×5 ___ 6×4

e 7×4 ___ 6×5

f $7 \div 4$ ___ $6 \div 5$

g $7 \div 6$ ___ $5 \div 4$

h $7 - 6$ ___ $5 - 4$

i $7 - 6 - 5$ ___ $5 - 4 - 3$

j $7 - 6 + 5$ ___ $5 + 4 - 3$

Notice that we are working on pupil understanding of the four main operations alongside understanding of equality and inequality, and pupils should be encouraged where possible to complete these questions without formal evaluation of the expressions. We can use inequalities repeatedly throughout our curriculum to work on classic misconceptions around ordering of numbers – for example, in this activity on decimals (we could do a similar thing with fractions as well):

Write the correct symbol of <, = or > between the numbers.

a 7.6   7.7   f 3.45   3.54
b 2.85   2.850   g 6.70   6.07
c 4.7   4.701   h 0.1   0.1000
d 2.93   2.925   i 23.8   28.3
e 9.76   9.725   j 1.01   10.1

Notice also that we haven't yet introduced the symbols ≤ or ≥ – it doesn't really make sense to introduce these until we are working on accuracy or with variables (in short with unknown values). We will look at the use of inequalities and accuracy in Chapter 9, but we can look at the use of inequalities and a single variable now (we will save two variables for Chapter 13).

When introducing variables within inequalities, my preferred approach is to tie language, symbolic representation and number-line representation together:

Numbers that are no less than 5 $x \geq 5$

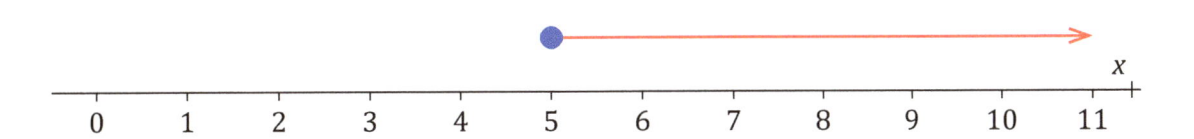

This allows us to be playful with language, introducing language like 'at least' and 'at most' at appropriate points. This is also the natural point to introduce 'between' inequalities, unless they have been introduced previously in work around data-handling or probability (for example).

Numbers between 3 and 10 (including 3 but not 10) $3 \leq x < 10$

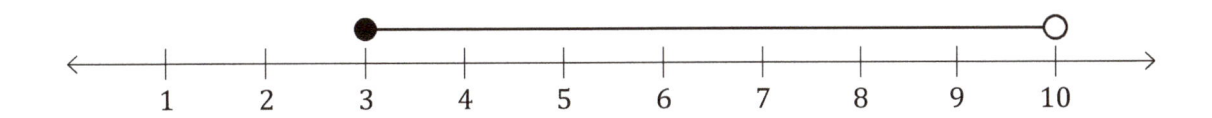

What is also nice is to also give examples of lists of numbers that fit the inequalities, so pupils can match those as well. The matching activity in the footnote gives a flavour of the sort of activity that can be useful with pupils to support their developing understanding.[8]

A key property of inequalities is what happens when we multiply them or divide them by a negative value. Before moving on to look at solving inequalities, it is worth taking some time looking at manipulating inequalities, and the results of those manipulations. This can include adding and subtracting a value as well as multiplication and division. When it comes

---

8 See https://onedrive.live.com/view.aspx?resid=AC85973C4EE44325!129549&ithint=file,docx&wdLOR=c0AA28375-C746-4961-BD96-6C5181424C58&authkey=!AMoiO4Lx6rgGKvI.

to multiplying or dividing by a negative number, a key representation is the idea of rotating the inequality through 180° about 0, as we saw with vectors:

$x > 3$ when both sides are multiplied by -2 becomes $-2x < -6$

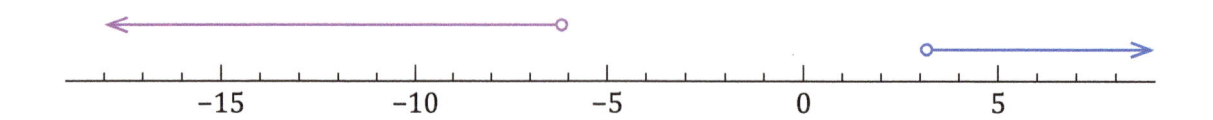

The original inequality is shown in blue here, and we can see that when this is multiplied by −2, the new inequality (purple) not only moves twice as far from 0 (is scaled by a factor of 2) but also rotates 180° around 0. We can also make sense of this in terms of thinking about the numbers; if I choose a number greater than 3 and multiply it by −2, all of those bigger positive numbers are going to become 'larger' (in terms of magnitude) negative numbers. I can't generate small (in terms of magnitude) negative numbers without choosing small positive numbers, i.e. numbers that are smaller than 3.

Once pupils have worked with manipulating inequalities, the obvious next step is into solving inequations – provided pupils are already familiar with solving for missing values in an equation. I am not going to go into a huge amount of detail here – the logic and activities mirror those that we use with solving equations. The one thing that it is worth taking time to explore with pupils is the idea that the solution to an inequality is itself an inequality: any complete solution to an inequality (i.e. not only wanting integer solutions) will be a range of values. Pupils can have difficulties with this, particularly if their only prior experience of 'solving' is to solve linear equations (or potentially quadratics as well) where there is only one (or two at most) roots. If this is pupils' only prior experience then it may be worth putting in a quick activity that just focuses on whether the solution set is empty, a single value, two values or infinite in size (which could just be one value or infinite in size, if quadratics haven't been looked at yet).

Speaking of quadratics, we can, of course, adapt our sense of quadratic equations to quadratic inequalities as well. Personally, I find linking to the graph the most straightforward to make sense of quadratic inequalities, and would always start there with pupils, but at some point would like to tie this in with the other work done on quadratic equations, as per the examples below:

Solving by factorisation

$x^2 + 4x - 5 < 0$

$(x + 5)(x - 1) < 0$ implies each bracket has opposite signs, i.e. $+ \times -$ or $- \times +$.

$x + 5 > 0 \Rightarrow x > -5$ and $x - 1 < 0 \Rightarrow x < 1$.

$x + 5 < 0 \Rightarrow x < -5$ and $x - 1 > 0 \Rightarrow x > 1$.

The second of these is impossible as there is no value of x that is simultaneously less than −5 and greater than 1, so the solution comes from the first condition, where $x > -5$ and $x < 1$, i.e.

$-5 < x < 1$.

Solving by completing the square

$x^2 + 4x - 5 \geq 0$

$(x + 2)^2 - 9 \geq 0 \Rightarrow$

$(x + 2)^2 \geq 9 \Rightarrow$

$x + 2 \geq 3$ AND $x + 2 \leq -3 \Rightarrow$

$x \geq 1$ AND $x \leq -5$

The completed square form is clearly a more straightforward analytical approach to solving quadratic inequalities, provided pupils are clear at the point where we want to take the 'square root' of 9, and can see how to arrive at the two separate inequalities at that point. The factorisation approach does serve to re-highlight the relationships between positive and negative numbers, and the results of multiplying positives and negatives, and so is also worth exploring with pupils at some point (although it will probably not be the 'go-to' method for solving quadratic inequalities).

Let us now finish the chapter with a look at equivalence and congruence.

Concept: equivalence

Prerequisites: Numbers.

Linked concepts: Virtually every concept in mathematics has equivalencies within them or between them.

As mentioned at the beginning of the chapter, the line I am taking on equivalence is that it draws attention to properties rather than values. However, as we have seen, it is probably not going to be possible (and potentially not even desirable) to separate completely the concepts of equivalence and equality; not least because equality is a kind of equivalence relation. In addition, the equal sign is sometimes used to indicate equivalence, as well as the symbols $\cong$, $\equiv$ and even $\Leftrightarrow$. For example, teachers will often write $20\% = \frac{1}{5}$; however, '20%' is not a value, and so can't really be equal in value to $\frac{1}{5}$. However, 20% is an equivalent proportion to $\frac{1}{5}$, which is what we really mean – that 20% of a number is equal in value to $\frac{1}{5}$ of the same number. Similarly, we will often write that 3:5 = 9:15, but we mean that the ratio 3 to 5 is equivalent to 9 to 15.

An important set of equivalencies that it is important for pupils to recognise are the equivalencies between fractions, decimals and percentages. A nice representation that can be a start point for this is the use of the 100-square:

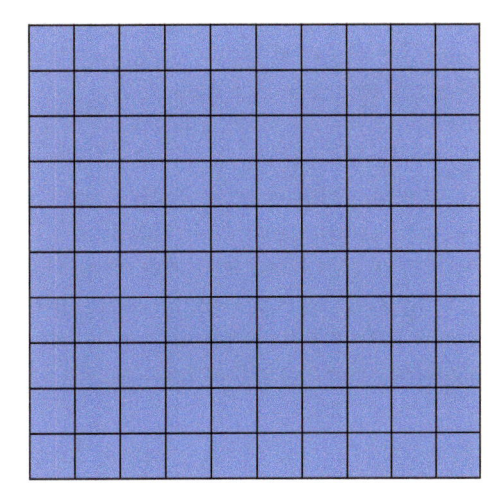

We have seen already that this can take the value of 1, and when it does, each single square is a representation of $0.01 = \frac{1}{100}$. We can extend this to include percentages by saying that each square is 1% of the whole. This creates the equivalence between the values of 0.01 and $\frac{1}{100}$ and the proportion 1%. From there we can explore other equivalences between percentages and decimals/fractions (as well as different equalities between fractions and decimals).

When exploring these equivalencies, it is important to provide opportunities to look at a wide variety of different percentages, including:

- Integer percentages between 0 and 100, e.g. 58%.
- Decimal percentages both smaller than and greater than 0, e.g. 0.4%, 78.24%.
- Percentages greater than 100 (including much bigger than 100), e.g. 100.2%, 120%, 210%, 2100%.
- Percentages that relate to important fraction families, e.g. 25%, 50%, 66.6̇%, 80%.

Of course, as decimals and fractions can both be considered values, we can say these are equal (although we often still describe a fraction as being equivalent to a decimal of equal value – I told you separating these would probably not be possible!). When looking specifically at decimal and fraction equivalencies, we can add a couple more important items to the list:

- Recognising when a fraction will convert to a terminating decimal or a recurring decimal.
- Converting from terminating decimals to fractions using the place value relationships.
- Converting from a fraction into a decimal (either terminating or recurring).
- Converting from a recurring decimal into a fraction.

The first of these can be explored simply by offering different fractions to pupils (or pupils creating their own) and converting these to decimals (which can be a calculator activity or an equivalent fraction/division activity, if useful). It is quite straightforward to show that terminating decimals will only ever be equivalent to fractions that have denominators that only have prime factors of 2 and/or 5, as these are the prime factors of 10 (and therefore 100, 1000 and all other powers of 10). Any simplified fraction with a denominator that has a prime factor other than 2 or 5 will never be able to made into an equivalent fraction with a denominator that is a power of 10. This leads immediately into being able to convert terminating decimals into fractions by writing the decimal as a fraction whose denominator is a power of 10, and converting a fraction into a decimal by first writing the fraction as an equivalent fraction with a denominator that is a power of 10.

When it comes to converting a fraction into a decimal where it not possible to write the denominator as a power of 10, the most typical strategy would be to use the formal division algorithm, and extend it to decimal columns in a similar way as you might when dividing a decimal value by an integer value, so this can be modelled in the same way that it has been previously. This leaves converting from a recurring decimal into a fraction. The main strategy that would work in all cases is to create a situation where subtraction eliminates the recurring part of the decimal, as per the examples below:

Convert 0.25̇ into a fraction.

$x = 0.25555555\ldots$

$10x = 2.555555555\ldots$

$10x - x = 9x = 2.3$

$x = \frac{2.3}{9} = \frac{23}{90}$

Convert 0.2̇5̇ into a fraction.

$x = 0.252525\ldots$

$100x = 25.252525\ldots$

$100x - x = 99x = 25$

$x = \frac{25}{99}$

There are potential alternatives. The first relies on pupils recognising the decimal equivalents to the fraction family of ninths, i.e. $\frac{1}{9} = 0.\dot{1}$, $\frac{2}{9} = 0.\dot{2}$ and so on. This means we can separate the decimal into a sum of two decimals, and then write the equivalent fraction for each decimal before summing the fractions – for example:

$0.2\dot{5} = 0.2 + 0.0\dot{5}$

$\quad = \frac{1}{5} + \frac{5}{90}$

$\quad = \frac{23}{90}$

Technically, we can carry out something similar with the second, if we recognise the decimal equivalents to the elevenths family and their 'divisibility' by 9, i.e. $\frac{4}{11} = 0.\dot{3}\dot{6}$ and therefore $\frac{4}{99} = 0.\dot{0}\dot{4}$. That allows:

$0.\dot{2}\dot{5} = 0.\dot{1}\dot{8} + 0.\dot{0}\dot{7}$

$\quad = \frac{2}{11} + \frac{7}{99}$

$\quad = \frac{25}{99}$

However, extending these strategies require pre-existing knowledge of an increasing number of decimal and fraction equivalencies, and so the general algebraic strategy is worth pupils becoming fluent in.

Of course, in some cases the resulting fraction will simplify to an equivalent fraction. I have already mentioned equivalent fractions briefly in Chapter 1, but we are now in a position to explore further the idea of equivalent fractions and simplifying fractions.

Subconcept: equivalent fractions

The equivalence of two or more fractions comes from the choice of the value of 1. We saw in Chapter 1 that if I want to represent the family 'quarters', then we can define a suitable value of 1:

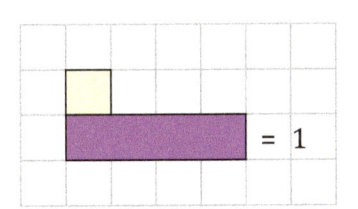

In this case, if the purple rod represents 1, then the white rod represents $\frac{1}{4}$. However, the purple rod is not the only choice for the value of 1 that can be used to represent quarters:

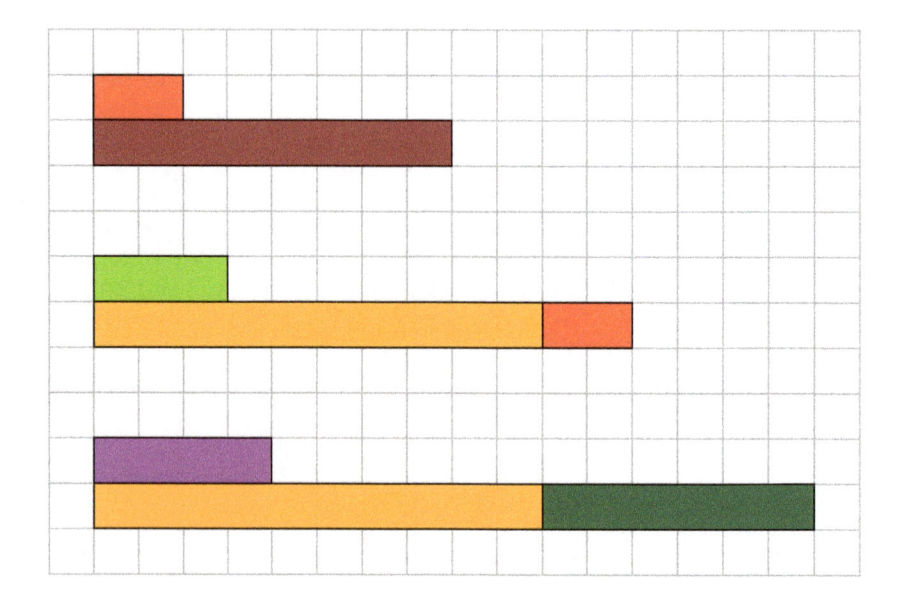

In each of these cases, if the larger rod represents 1, then the smaller rod represents $\frac{1}{4}$. Of course, each of these can also represent their own family: the brown rod can represent the eighths family, the orange and red together can represent the twelfths family, the orange and green rod can represent the sixteenths family and so on. This leads us to the conclusion that $\frac{1}{4} = \frac{2}{8} = \frac{3}{12} = \frac{4}{16}$ and so on. This has strong ties to the multiplicative comparison model from division – if the lower bar in each picture has a value of 1, what is the upper bar? Indeed, this is a great way for pupils to see that division and fraction are the same idea. Pupils can be offered different lengths to represent 1 and can find equivalent fractions, or alternatively can be asked to choose suitable representations of 1 that can demonstrate fraction equivalencies.

Care needs to be taken representing these relationships, however, as even in the line above, the eye is naturally drawn to the additive relationship (the numerator increases by 1, the denominator increases by 4), where ideally we would want to be drawing attention to the multiplicative relationships (the denominator is four times bigger than the numerator; the numerator and denominator have been scaled by the same factor). An activity like the one below can help to draw more attention to this sort of structure.

Fill in the blanks to make these fractions equivalent:

$\frac{2}{3} = \frac{\square}{9}$ $\frac{2}{3} = \frac{22}{\square}$

$\frac{2}{3} = \frac{\square}{12}$ $\frac{2}{3} = \frac{20}{\square}$

$\frac{2}{3} = \frac{\square}{21}$ $\frac{2}{5} = \frac{20}{\square}$

$\frac{2}{3} = \frac{\square}{6}$ $\frac{2}{5} = \frac{\square}{30}$

Find the numerator of the fraction equivalent to $\frac{2}{3}$ with a denominator of 15.

Which of these numbers could be the denominator of a fraction that is equivalent to $\frac{1}{4}$? Justify your answer.

8, 12, 15, 19, 22, 24, 30, 32, 35, 40

Equality/equivalence/congruence

This can be followed up with activities like this:

A   Circle any correct equivalent fraction in each problem.

1   $\frac{1}{3}$ = ?   a $\frac{3}{15}$ b $\frac{2}{14}$ c $\frac{8}{24}$ d $\frac{5}{10}$

2   $\frac{3}{5}$ = ?   a $\frac{6}{30}$ b $\frac{7}{9}$ c $\frac{4}{15}$ d $\frac{12}{20}$

3   $\frac{3}{4}$ = ?   a $\frac{9}{16}$ b $\frac{4}{5}$ c $\frac{15}{20}$ d $\frac{12}{20}$

4   $\frac{5}{8}$ = ?   a $\frac{10}{16}$ b $\frac{2}{16}$ c $\frac{20}{32}$ d $\frac{30}{42}$

5   $\frac{2}{9}$ = ?   a $\frac{4}{15}$ b $\frac{6}{27}$ c $\frac{16}{72}$ d $\frac{4}{18}$

6   $\frac{10}{7}$ = ?   a $\frac{9}{9}$ b $\frac{14}{20}$ c $\frac{30}{18}$ d $\frac{60}{42}$

7   $\frac{4}{12}$ = ?   a $\frac{14}{6}$ b $\frac{3}{18}$ c $\frac{1}{2}$ d $\frac{6}{18}$

B   Write any 3 equivalent fractions.

1   $\frac{1}{6}$ = _____

2   $\frac{2}{5}$ = _____

3   $\frac{7}{4}$ = _____

Or this:

Where on this number line would you place all the fractions that have:

a   a numerator of 1?

b   a denominator of 6?

c   either a numerator or denominator of 2?

|—+—+—+—+—+—+—+—+—+—+—+—+—+—+—+—|
0   1

When it comes to simplifying a fraction, we can see this as the reverse idea:

Simplify $\frac{6}{15}$

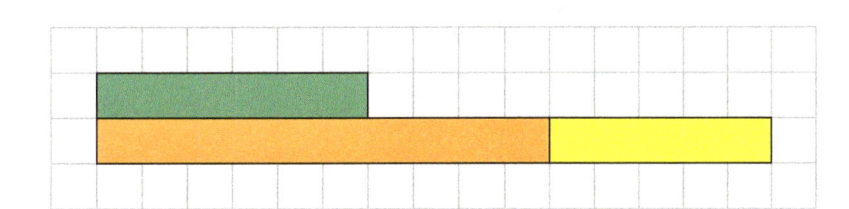

In this picture we can see the fraction $\frac{6}{15}$. We can then show the simplification in a few of different ways:

1   Replace each of the bars with different bars, all the same colour, that are equal in length.

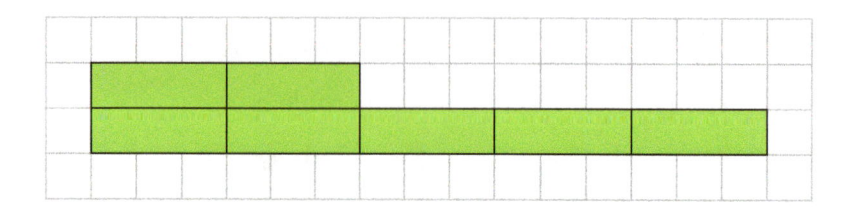

We can see that we can use the green bar to recreate the same model. The numerator uses two rods, and the denominator uses five rods, and so we can see the simplification of $\frac{6}{15}$ to the equivalent fraction $\frac{2}{5}$.

2. Replace the numerator and the denominator with the same number of smaller bars.

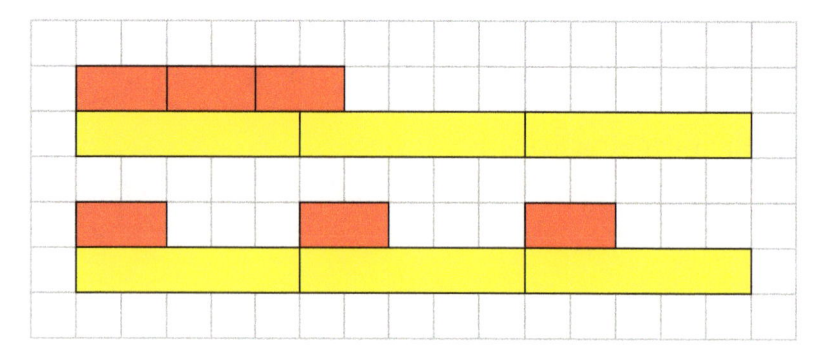

We can recreate the model using three red bars for the numerator, and three yellow bars for the denominator. We can then see that if we define a single yellow bar to represent 1, then the red bar represents $\frac{2}{5}$.

3. Build $\frac{6}{15}$ using two rectangles, each with the same width:

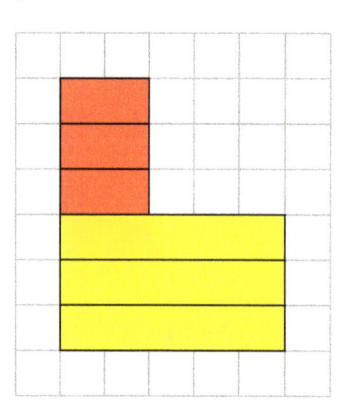

We can create a rectangle of 6 with a width of 3 and a length of 2, and then the rectangle of 15 with a width of 3 and a length of 5. Each of these has a width of 3. Because they both have the same width, their areas compare in the same way as their lengths (we have met this idea previously when looking at surds, but this could be an ideal place to introduce it), so the lengths of the rectangles being 2 and 5 leads to the simplified fraction of $\frac{2}{5}$.

What is clear in all of these representations is the factor of 3. In the first case it was the green rod being 3 squares long, in the second it was using 3 of each rod, and in the third it was the common width of 3. In each case this leads to the same symbolic representation:

$$\frac{6}{15} = \frac{2 \times 3}{5 \times 3} = \frac{2}{5}$$

I much prefer using the factorised form of the values rather than talking about 'dividing the numerator and denominator by 3'. This mirrors much more closely how we might work with algebraic fractions, and if we wish we can insert the intermediate step to actually separate out the factors into two separate fraction multiplications (although this does require pupils to recognise that this is the result of a fraction multiplication and be comfortable with 'undoing' this multiplication, as well as recognising the value of 1):

$$\frac{6}{15} = \frac{2 \times 3}{5 \times 3} = \frac{2}{5} \times \frac{3}{3} = \frac{2}{5} \times 1 = \frac{2}{5}$$

Beyond simple practice, activities such as these can be useful in focusing pupil attention on the importance of factors and factorisation when simplifying:

> Which numbers can you write in the missing spaces so that the fractions simplify? Find all the numbers you can.
>
> $\frac{\Box}{15}$ $\qquad$ $\frac{35}{\Box}$ $\qquad$ $\frac{\Box}{77}$ $\qquad$ $\frac{65}{\Box}$

Fraction sequences:

1. $\quad \frac{2}{3}, \frac{3}{7}, \frac{4}{11}, \frac{5}{15}, \frac{6}{19}, \frac{7}{12}, \frac{8}{27}, \frac{9}{31}, \frac{10}{35}, \frac{11}{39} \ldots$

   > In this fraction sequence there are various patterns. Some of the fractions will cancel down. Which?
   >
   > What would the next fraction to cancel down be?
   >
   > What is a rule for the cancelled-down fraction sequence?

2. $\quad \frac{1}{4}, \frac{3}{7}, \frac{5}{10}, \frac{7}{13}, \frac{9}{16}, \frac{11}{19}, \frac{13}{22}, \frac{15}{25}, \frac{17}{28}, \frac{19}{31} \ldots$

   > In this fraction sequence there are various patterns. Some of the fractions will cancel down. Which?
   >
   > What would the next fraction to cancel down be?
   >
   > What is a rule for the cancelled-down fraction sequence?

3. $\quad \frac{3}{4}, \frac{5}{9}, \frac{7}{14}, \frac{9}{19}, \frac{11}{24}, \frac{13}{29}, \frac{15}{34}, \frac{17}{39}, \frac{19}{44}, \frac{21}{49} \ldots$

   > In this fraction sequence there are various patterns. Some of the fractions will cancel down. Which?
   >
   > What would the next fraction to cancel down be?
   >
   > What is a rule for the cancelled-down fraction sequence?

(from Don Steward's Median blog[9])

> Write integers that could go into each section of the Venn diagram. If any region cannot be filled in, say why. How many different numbers can go into each region? Assume all fractions formed are proper fractions.

---

[9] D. Steward, Fraction Cancelling, *Median* [blog] (12 May 2017). Available at: https://donsteward.blogspot.com/2017/05/fraction-cancelling.html.

Simplifies over a denominator of 24.

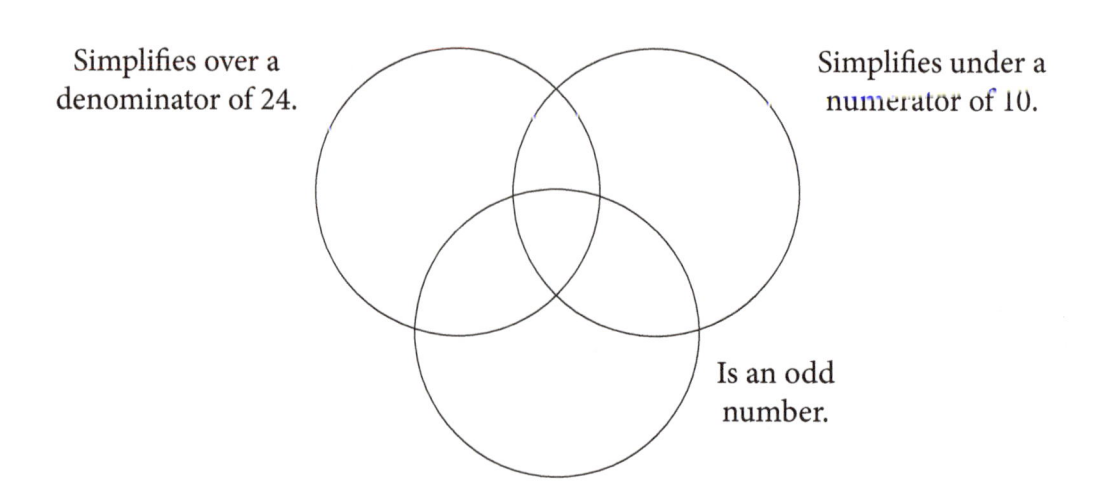

Simplifies under a numerator of 10.

Is an odd number.

In a similar way to the four main operations, we can, of course, link this subconcept to other forms of numbers; we have seen simplifying surds and algebraic expressions but we can look at simplifying algebraic fractions. It is worth seeing one of these to appreciate that the third of the three models for simplifying is the one that most usefully applies:

Simplify $\frac{x^2 + 5x + 6}{2x^2 + 7x + 3}$

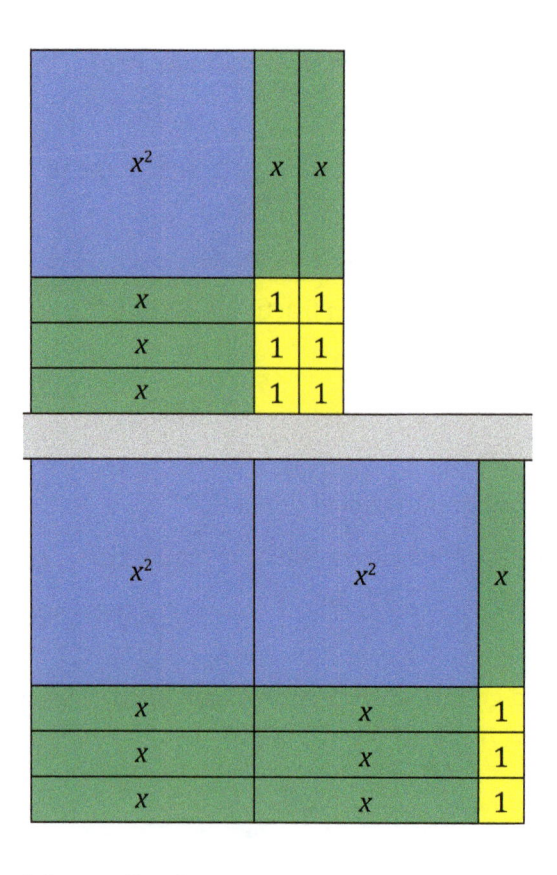

We can see the factorised form of both expressions in this image; at the top $x^2 + 5x + 6 = (x + 2)(x + 3)$ and at the bottom $2x^2 + 7x + 6 = (2x + 1)(x + 3)$. They both have a width of $(x + 3)$, so their lengths compare in the same way as their areas (as per the previous model). The length of the numerator is $(x + 2)$ and the length of the denominator is $(2x + 1)$. This leads to $\frac{x^2 + 5x + 6}{2x^2 + 7x + 3} = \frac{x + 2}{2x + 1}$.

Of course, there are lots of variants we might use of algebraic fractions, from simple ones like $\frac{3}{3a}$ to the more complicated examples like the one above; however, if pupils have a full understanding of factorisation of algebraic expressions and simplifying fractions, then there should be no situation that pupils cannot handle. Where pupils tend to make the most mistakes is through not properly recognising factors: things like trying to simplify $\frac{x+2}{x+3}$ by 'cancelling' the x to give $\frac{2}{3}$ – where necessary, using the tiles should illustrate the mistake sufficiently.

Where we tend to see the ≡ symbol more is when we are talking about equivalent algebraic expressions. Again, this is a situation where, for me, the choice of using the equal sign or the equivalent sign should highlight whether we are drawing attention to equal value or to equivalent properties. For example, we have previously written that $(x + 2)(x + 3) = x^2 + 5x + 6$, but we could equally write $(x + 2)(x + 3) \equiv x^2 + 5x + 6$. It would seem to make sense that in the first case, we are drawing attention to the fact that the values obtained from each expression are equal. In the second case, it is more about seeing the two as equivalent expressions with the same properties, i.e. the same graphical properties, the same order, etc. Of course, we do therefore need to be clear with pupils the difference between writing $(x + 2)(x + 3) = x^2 + 5x + 6$, and $(x + 2)(x + 3) = 0$ (and I know some people that advocate for only ever writing $(x + 2)(x + 3) \equiv x^2 + 5x + 6$).

When we do write things like $(x + 2)(x + 3) \equiv x^2 + 5x + 6$, we usually refer to the relationship as an identity. Taken together, this means an identity is an equivalence between two expressions. It is definitely a good idea for pupils to work on determining between solvable equations, identities, formulae, functions, etc. There is a nice activity on TES that provides different types of expressions, equations, etc. and prompts pupils to sort them under the correct heading.[10]

Pupils can be offered the opportunity to prove different identities such as that $\frac{x}{x+1} - \frac{x-1}{x} \equiv \frac{1}{x(x+1)}$ as well as to solve equations created using identities, such as the example below:

If $ax(x + b) + c \equiv 3x^2 + 15x - 11$, then work out the values of a, b and c.

The symbol ≡ is also used in geometry to denote congruence. It is with an examination of this concept that we will complete this chapter.

Concept: congruence

Prerequisites: Equivalence, measurement, shape.

Linked concepts: Transformation.

Congruence in shapes is another example of an equivalence relation (i.e. the relationship between congruent shapes is reflexive, symmetrical and transitive). In common with equivalence in numbers/expressions, congruent shapes are shapes that have identical properties. When we talk about shape properties though, we are talking about length, angle, area, etc.

Pupils can identify congruent shapes by measurement in simple cases, or by sight when shapes are drawn on square or isometric grids. Pupils should be clear that translations,

---
10 Chu96, Algebraic Vocabulary Match-Up Cards (Term, Expression, Equation, Identity, Formula, Function), *TES* (22 February 2018). Available at: https://www.tes.com/teaching-resource/algebraic-vocabulary-match-up-cards-term-expression-equation-identity-formula-function-11584496.

reflections or rotations have no effect on the properties of the shape, and so the image and object under any of these transformations are automatically congruent.

Of special interest in congruence are the minimum conditions required to determine that two shapes are congruent (or alternatively, the minimum conditions required to determine uniqueness of a shape). For example, if we know that a quadrilateral has two opposite equal lengths and three right angles, then that quadrilateral must be a rectangle. The question is, are these four criteria the minimum number of criteria that uniquely define a rectangle? Or can we say for sure that two rectangles are identical or not with less information?

At school-level mathematics we tend to limit discussions of this type to triangles. Many pupils learn the rules for congruence, but relatively few appreciate their purpose. When congruence in triangles is introduced, it should be in the way I have just introduced congruence above: 'Given two triangles, what is the least I can get away with demonstrating in order to prove they are actually the same triangle?' Ultimately, congruence proof is about efficiency; we do not have to prove every single property is the same before we can say two shapes are congruent, but once we have established that two triangles are congruent, then we do know for sure that every property of the two triangles is the same.

Potentially, this could be offered to pupils with little else in the way of guidance; simply, 'What are the minimum number of properties we have to demonstrate are the same before we can say for sure that every property is the same?' However, pupils might struggle with the lack of structure here. I tend to offer different prompts, some of which are sufficient to prove congruence and others not, and get pupils to either confirm or provide a counter-example. The sorts of prompts I would offer to pupils might be:

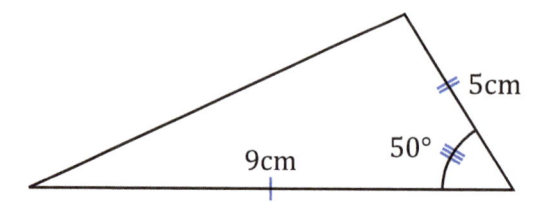

Side-angle-side

My question would be something like, 'Is there any way we could draw another triangle that has the same marked properties as this one but that looks different?' Of course, in this case there isn't, so therefore any two triangles that have these properties are congruent triangles.

Side-side-angle

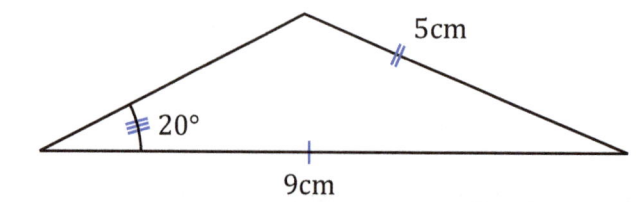

The same question would follow (or be asked about all the prompts simultaneously). However, in this case, there is an alternative triangle that has the same properties but looks different:

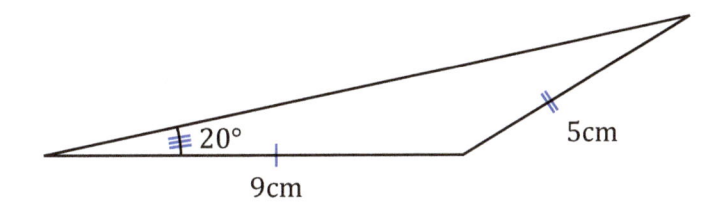

We can see that all of the same properties appear in this second triangle, but the third lengths are clearly not the same, and the other two angles are not the same (this also very nicely sets up the ambiguous case when using the sine rule).

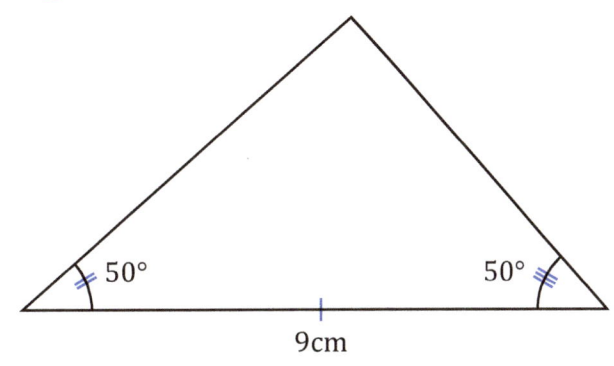

Angle-side-angle

This is another case where this is sufficient information to prove congruence, and so any two triangles with these properties are congruent.

Angle-angle-side

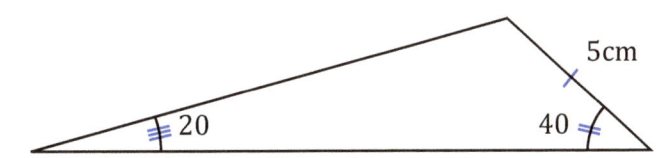

These criteria do prove congruence; however, there is a clear link to the criteria above, and so they are not counted as a separate set of criteria (although it is worth offering this to pupils and making sure that they see that because we can calculate the third angle, this will become angle-side-angle).

Angle-angle-angle

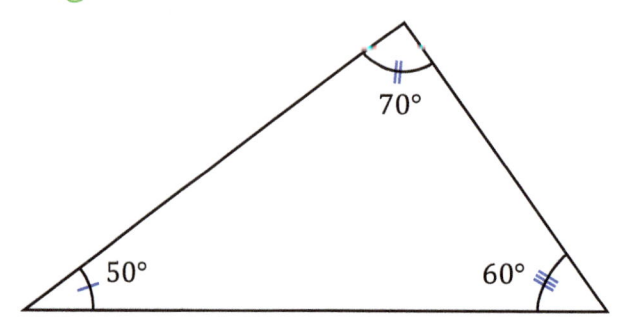

This is the one that pupils tend to eliminate quite early, recognising that we could produce smaller triangles and larger triangles that have these three angles.

Right angle-hypotenuse-side

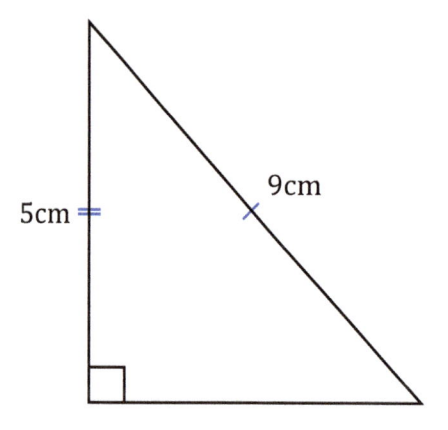

Again, pupils will often pick this one out as it is a departure from the others but should be able to show that the right angle fixes the third side, and so any two triangles with these three properties will be congruent.

Right angle-hypotenuse-angle

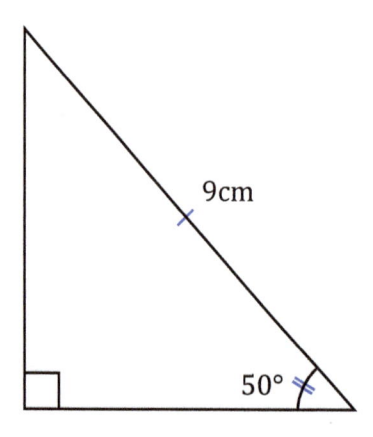

This is another situation that can be shown to be the same as angle-side-angle, although it is one that pupils often miss (they see a right angle and automatically think 'right angle-hypotenuse-side') so it is worth exploring this one explicitly with pupils so they are familiar with it.

Side-side-side

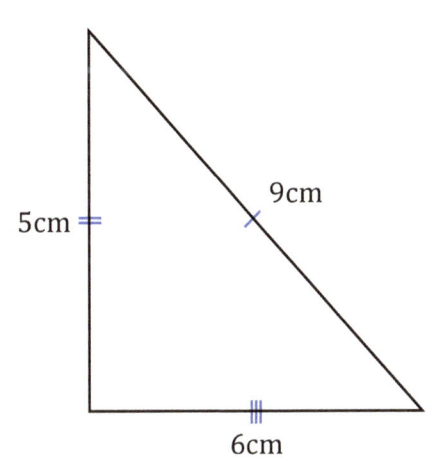

Pupils recognise quite quickly that this is sufficient to establish congruence, as any two triangles with three sides the same have all other properties identical.

Again, the point here is to impress upon pupils that we don't need to establish every property is the same before we can say two triangles are identical; simply three well-chosen properties will be sufficient and at that point we know all of the other properties must be the same.

Once pupils are familiar with the different properties that establish congruence, we can introduce the formal notation, i.e. given triangles ABC and DEF that both have three of the required properties, we can write that $\triangle ABC \equiv \triangle DEF$.

Pupils can then be offered activities where they have to identify congruent triangles from groups of triangles, or be given two congruent triangles and be asked to identify which three properties they share that will establish the congruence. Eventually, this will lead to proving the congruence of two triangles using angle facts and shape properties.

One of the properties I have mentioned a lot in this chapter is that of proportion, and having equivalent proportions. It is now time to turn our attention more fully to the concept of proportion, as it is one of the more important concepts in school-level maths.

Chapter 6

Proportionality

The shift from additive to multiplicative thinking is an important one for pupils to make and can be a significant barrier to learning school-level mathematics if pupils fail to make the transition. We have already seen a number of models that can support the development of multiplicative thinking, including modelling multiplication as unitisation and as area/volume. Issue 28 of the *Cambridge Maths Espresso,* looking at proportional reasoning, makes clear that the development of proportional reasoning needs to be connected across mathematical strands, and that it is a particularly important step into algebraic thinking.[1] There are some excellent representations that can help with connecting proportional reasoning across different strands of mathematics.

Concept: proportion

Prerequisites: Numbers, multiplication, division, equality, equivalence, potentially ratio.

Linked concepts: Functionality, measures, similarity, trigonometry, transformation, chance, graphing, data analysis.

Two quantities are said to be in proportion if there exists a constant multiplicative relationship between those quantities. Take, for example, the relationship between the number of feet and the number of yards that measure a given distance. As a yard is three times longer than a foot, then the number of feet used to measure a given distance will always be three times greater than the number of yards, i.e. 1 yard = 3 feet, 2 yards = 6 feet, 10 yards = 30 feet, etc.

A nice way to introduce this idea is physically with Cuisenaire rods:

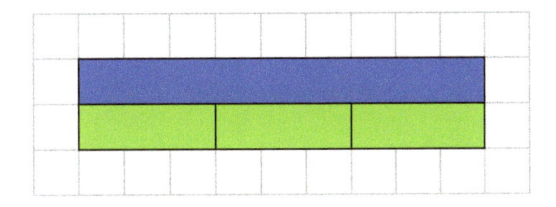

I would normally start by asking pupils to find combinations of a single colour rod that is the same length as a blue rod, before looking at the combinations they have found – such as the one in this picture. We would look at the idea that the number of green rods will always be three times bigger than the number of blue rods for the same distance. Questions like the ones below will prompt pupils to utilise this relationship:

The number of blues = _____ × the number of greens.

84 blues are the same length as _____ greens.

84 greens are the same lengths as _____ blues.

---

1 L. Rycroft-Smith, D. Macey, R. Horsman and T. Gould, What Does Research Suggest about the Development of Proportional Reasoning in Mathematics Learning?, *Cambridge Maths Espresso,* 28 (February 2020). Available at: https://www.cambridgemaths.org/Images/espresso_28_proportional_reasoning.pdf.

After exploring several relationships that have an integer multiplier, we will introduce a relationship like this:

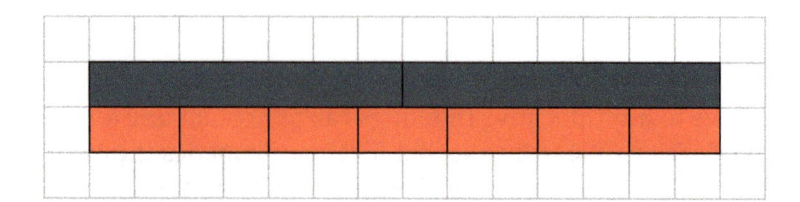

Here the number of reds is 3.5 × the number of blacks, which we can see because 2 blacks = 7 reds (as well as being able to see that the end of the first black rod is exactly halfway along the fourth red rod). The links to division can be explored here as well; using the comparison model that has featured heavily up to this point. We can ask things like, 'If the green rod has a value of 1, what value is the blue rod?' or, 'If the red rod has a value of 1, what is the value of the black rod?'

We will also bring in relationships that have other fractional values:

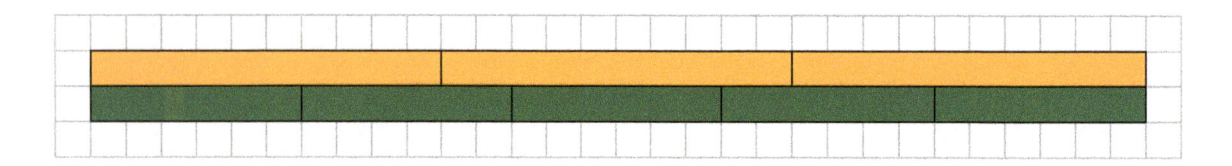

In this case, we have that the number of dark greens = $1\frac{2}{3}$ × the number of oranges, or alternatively that if the dark green rod has a value of 1, then the orange rod has a value of $1\frac{2}{3}$.

Once pupils have met and worked with a few different proportional relationships, we will look to draw out a couple of key features:

1. Scaling – that if one of the values is scaled by a scale factor, then the other will be scaled as well (i.e. if 3 oranges = 5 dark greens, then 30 oranges = 50 dark greens).

2. Zeroes – that if one of the values becomes 0, the other also becomes 0 (i.e. if we have 0 orange rods, we will also have 0 dark green rods).

Once pupils are familiar with these properties, we will mix problems where the multiplicative relationship or the scaling relationship will be the most beneficial to use. The two problems below are prime examples of these:

1. If 11 pencils costs 26 pence, what is the cost of 55 pencils?
2. If 11 pencils costs 55 pence, what is the cost of 26 pencils?

Clearly, in the first question, using the fact that the number of pencils has been scaled by a factor of 5 is the most efficient way to solve the problem, whilst in the second, recognising that the cost in pence is 5 times greater than the number of pencils is a better strategy.

Similar questions were asked in one of the lessons during the ICCAMS project. where pupils had to complete a mini-test featuring one of two questions about spicy soup.[2] Interestingly, in the review of this mini-test, 91% of the (approximately) 75 pupils answering the

---

2 See http://iccams-maths.org/.

question where the number of people was scaled by an integer value answered it correctly, compared to only 51% of those (again approximately 75) pupils who were given the alternative question where the amount of tabasco is an integer multiple of the number of people.[3] It would appear that pupils tend to more readily identify simple integer scalar multipliers than simple integer functional multipliers (the multiplicative relationship between two different quantities). It is primarily for this reason that I prefer to start pupils' exploration of proportionality by looking at the functional multiplicative relationship and only move on to scaling the relationship when pupils have the necessary fluency in identifying and using the multiplicative relationship.

Of course, there are many proportional relationships that are difficult (if not impossible) to represent using Cuisenaire rods. The Cuisenaire can serve to bridge towards visual, and then ultimately more abstract representations of proportional relationships:

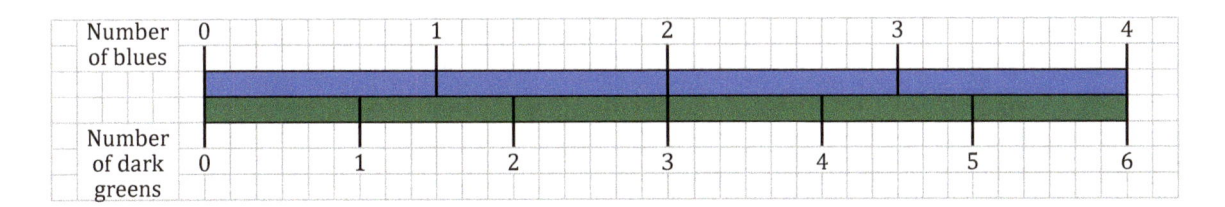

This representation is a dual or double number line. It creates two scales from the proportional relationship between the two quantities that can be used to work with the multiplicative relationships that exist between them.

If we really want to focus pupils' attention on the relationship, then a potential strategy here is to use nonsense words to form the relationship. The question below gives an example of this:

7 bimps = 2 bamps

a In your book, draw a dual number line to show this relationship.

b How many bamps is 35 bimps?

c How many bimps is 42 bamps?

d How many bamps is 60 bimps?

e How many bimps is 28 bamps?

f How many more bimps is 11 bamps than 9 bamps?

g How many more bimps is 25 bamps than 8 bamps?

h How many less bamps is 9 bimps than 10 bimps?

i How many less bamps is 3 bimps than 17 bimps?

Care must be taken with parts (f) through (i), however, as they may turn pupils thinking back towards additive thinking, so should only be included if pupils have achieved the necessary fluency that this temporary shift back to additive thinking will not be destructive to their developing multiplicative thinking skills.

---

3 ICCAMS Maths, Mini Ratio Test (Versions A and B) (2013). Available at: http://iccams-maths.org/wp-content/uploads/2015/11/MR-2AB-2013z.pdf.

From the dual number line we can further abstract the relationship by condensing the dual number line down into a ratio table:

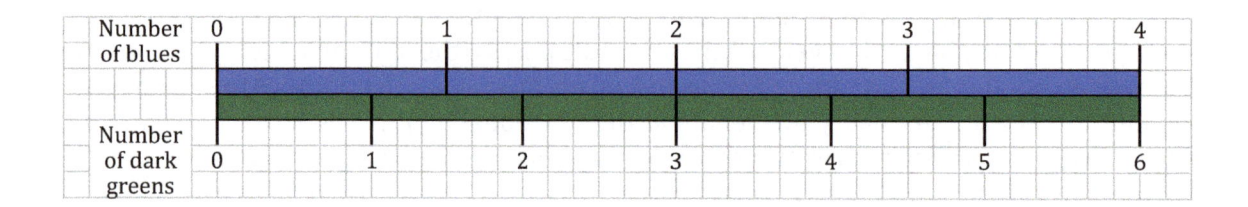

Number of blues	0	1	2	3	4
Number of dark greens	0	1	2	3	4	5	6

Number of blues	2	4	6	24		33	
Number of dark greens	3	6	9		33		50

Because the table removes the scaled part of the number line, leaving only the equivalent values, it can be significantly shortened, making it easier to pose multiple problems within the table structure (as I have done by leaving the blank cells in the table – the implication being that these are values to be found).

Some people prefer to set their ratio table up vertically (of course, the dual number line will work equally well vertically), or to use ratio boxes rather than a table:

Number of blues	Number of dark greens
2	3
4	6
6	9
24	
	33
33	
	50

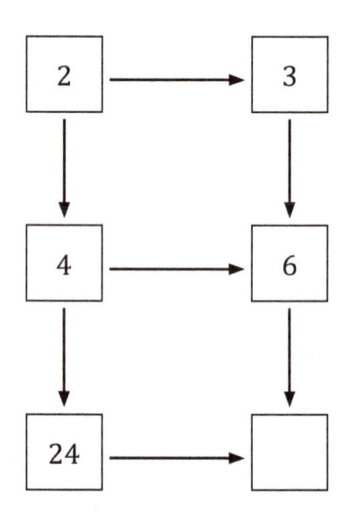

2 → 3
↓   ↓
4 → 6
↓   ↓
24 → ☐

As well as finding missing values in a proportional relationship, we should ensure pupils can establish whether a relationship is proportional. There are different approaches that might be taken to this:

1. Establish the functional multiplier for each pair of values (what is normally referred to as the 'exchange rate' or occasionally 'conversion factor' depending on the context) and show that it is the same in all cases.

2. Establish that both quantities are zero at the same time, and both scale in the same way.

3. Establish that the ratios between the values in both quantities are equal (provided pupils are familiar with ratios, in particular writing and simplifying).

Proportionality

Let us take the following example:

> A four-pack of toilet tissue costs £1.24 and a six-pack costs £1.86. Is the cost of toilet tissue proportional to the number of rolls in the pack?

1. We can establish the exchange rate using a ratio table or similar:

Number of rolls		Cost in pence
4	× 31 →	124
6	× 31 →	186

The exchange rate is 31 pence per roll in both cases, which means that the cost is proportional to the number of rolls (we can challenge pupils to see why, if cost in pence is proportional to the number of rolls, then the cost in pounds must be as well).

2. We can establish that 0 rolls would cost 0 pence (trivially true) and the scale factor from one value to another:

Number of rolls	Cost in pence
4 ↓ × 1.5	124 ↓ × 1.5
6	186

Both values have been scaled by 1.5, so they scale the same and have the same zeroes, so the cost is proportional to the number of rows.

3. The number of rolls is in the ratio 4:6 = 2:3. The cost in pence is in the ratio 124:186 = 2:3. The fact that the ratio is the same means that the cost is proportional to the number of rolls (this is actually the formal definition of a proportion – if two ratios are equal then there exists a proportion between their quantities).

Another aspect of proportion that should be explored is the strong links between proportional relationships and fractional relationships:

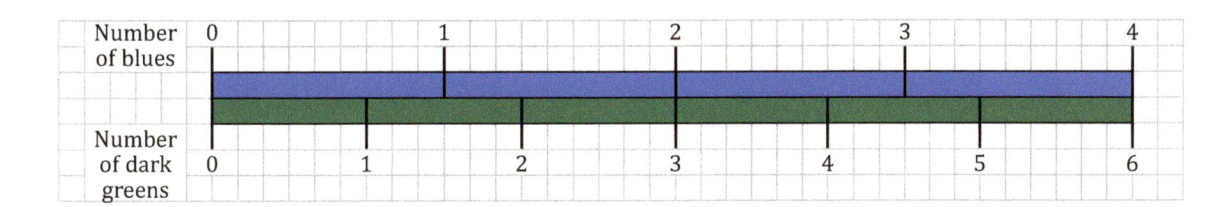

Number of blues	Number of dark greens
2	→ 3

We can see that as well as the number of dark greens being 1.5 times the number of blues, we also have that the number of blues is $\frac{2}{3}$ of the number of greens. Alternatively, we could be saying that the length of a dark green is $\frac{2}{3}$ that of blue. Of course, this is a great point at which to reinforce (or introduce) the notion of the reciprocal: the number of dark greens = $\frac{3}{2}$ × the number of blues and the number of blues is $\frac{2}{3}$ × the number of greens.

Recognising fractional relationships is a useful step in then exploring problems involving fractional changes, such as the problems below:

> A cereal box holds 300g. A special box holds an extra $\frac{1}{4}$. Work out the amount of cereal in the special box.
>
> A mint-condition toy cost £60 when new. It is now worth £85. By what fraction has the value of the toy increased?
>
> The number of birds living on an island in 2020 has increased by $\frac{3}{10}$ since 2015. If there are 2600 birds on the island in 2020, how many were there in 2015?

The ratio tables below show how proportion can help with both of these types of problem:

Fraction	Weight (g)
1	300
$1\frac{1}{4}$	?

Fraction	Cost (£)
1	60
?	85

OR

| ? | 25 |

Fraction	Number of birds
$1\frac{3}{10}$	2600
1	?

Notice, in the first question, the new fraction is $1\frac{1}{4}$ rather than just $\frac{1}{4}$. One potential issue with this is pupils thinking this means simply '300 + $\frac{1}{4}$'. Pupils need to be clear that the units of these two values are not the same; the first has a unit of 'grams' whilst the second does not. We need to be clear with pupils that '300g plus an extra $\frac{1}{4}$' means '300g plus an extra $\frac{1}{4}$ of 300g' so that the value we add to 300g also has a unit in grams.

There are many other areas of maths that show proportional structure, and we will encounter many of those in the forthcoming chapters, but it is worth highlighting some of them now:

> The currency used in Croatia is Kuna (Kn). £1 is worth 8.75 Kn. Work out the number of Kuna that is worth the same as £656.

This sort of problem is relatively straightforward to model with a ratio table:

£	Kn
1	8.75
656	?

This is suggestive of what is commonly termed the 'unitary method' for solving proportion problems, which basically amounts to first reducing one of the values to 1.

> A large box of tea costs £3.50 and contains 240 tea bags. A smaller box contains 180 tea bags and costs £2.75. Which box is better value?

There are a number of different ways of demonstrating the better value product, a few of which are given below:

1   Work out the cost for a unit number of bags; whichever costs least is better in value.

2   Work out the number of bags for a unit cost; whichever gives more bags is better in value.

3   Establish the exchange rate from number of bags to cost; whichever has the smaller exchange rate is better in value (this is equivalent to number 1).

4   Establish the exchange rate from cost to number of bags; whichever has the larger exchange rate is better in value (this is equivalent to number 2).

5   Work out the scale factor or fractional increase/decrease for one quantity and apply the same change to the other. If the provided value is less than the worked-out value, then this is the better value.

The major difference between 1 and 3 (and 2 and 4) is that 3 (4) fixes the unit to 1, whereas 1 (2) allows more flexibility as to the choice of unit – we could set the unit per 10 tea bags, for example, or per 25 pence.

For pupils who are confident enough, it is a great activity to offer this as a 'How many different ways can you come up with...' or even getting pupils to come up with their solution and then inviting pupils to share the different solutions they come up with. This is a strategy that is often used in places like Japan and Singapore with great effect and can open up lovely discussions about efficiency of strategy, ease of calculation, etc.

> A cake recipe calls for 150 grams of sugar and for 200 grams of flour. Phillipa wants to bake a bigger cake that uses 300 grams of flour. How much sugar should she use?
>
> A fire engine can hold 3000 gallons of water. A firefighter can deliver 160 gallons of water every 2 minutes. How long will it take for the firefighter to empty the tank?
>
> Derek uses a 52-inch flat steel bar that weighs 10.4 lb to make a rack in his workshop. Find the weight of a 67-inch steel bar.

All of these are fairly straightforward proportion questions that are set in some sort of context. When exploring context-based proportion, it can be a good idea to include some situations where the relationship between the quantities is not in proportion, such as the examples below:

If the diameter of a 1 pence coin is 20 mm, what is the diameter of a 5 pence coin?

A stone falls 144 feet in 3 seconds. How far will it fall in 6 seconds?

It takes 3 minutes to soft boil an egg. How long will it take to soft boil 10 eggs?

Eventually, we would want pupils to recognise that the constant exchange rate between two quantities in proportion means we can express the relationship algebraically, i.e. in the form $y = kx$ where y and x represent the values of the two quantities and k is the exchange rate between them (normally called the constant of proportionality when the relationship is expressed algebraically). We can pose similar problems to those we have seen before when looking at proportion – problems involving finding the exchange rate/constant of proportionality, and then having found the constant (or having been given it), finding missing values of either one variable or the other.

An avenue that pupils often find easier to explore once proportion is represented algebraically is proportion between different powers of the variables. Usually, the relationship $y = kx$ will be referred to as 'direct proportion' because the proportion exists directly between the variables, and then other proportions relating to the powers are simply described as proportions. For example, we could have $y^2 = kx^3$ as 'y squared is proportional to x cubed' (symbolically we could write that as $y^2 \propto x^3$), whereas if we have $P = kN$ we might say 'P is directly proportional to N' (although we would still represent this symbolically as $P \propto N$). Pupils should recognise the language (both spoken and symbolic) as indicative of the equality relationship and so it is important to mix up the use of these to ensure pupils engage with them all; although without a strong grounding in proportional relationships prior to the introduction of algebra, then all of the symbology is likely to make little sense to pupils.

One proportion (which I have already briefly mentioned in the previous chapter) is of particular importance in the mathematics curriculum, and that is the proportion in relation to 100 – better known as percentage.

Concept: percentage

Prerequisites: Numbers, addition, subtraction, multiplication, division, equality, equivalence, associativity, commutativity, distributivity, proportion.

Linked concepts: Fraction, decimal, ratio. Most concepts can utilise percentage within problems.

We have already seen percentage and its links to decimals and fractions using the 100-square. However, to grasp percentage as a concept, pupils need to a couple of things about percentage and its symbol, %:

1. The use of % as a unit – particularly important for addition and subtraction of percentages.

2. The use of percentages as proportion – particularly important for calculating with percentages.

Taking the first of these, if pupils are already familiar with percentages and their relation to fractions in the hundredth family, then it is a small transition to see the % symbol as a unit for counting, in the same way we might see any other fraction family. What is important here is for pupils to recognise things like 30% + 15% = 45%, with '%' serving as the unit (provided they are percentages of the same whole value). This allows pupils to see that percentages can be added and subtracted to/from each other but not to other units. Another important aspect here is for pupils to recognise that if we write something like 30 + 15%, we rarely (if ever) mean $30 + \frac{15}{100}$. Rather, we mean 30 + 15% of 30 and that the 'of 30' part of this sentence is often implied rather than explicitly written (perhaps similarly to when we looked at fractional increase). For pupils encountering increase and decrease by a percentage of the given value for the first time, there might be some mileage in actually making this explicit in early questions, i.e. writing questions as, 'Increase 30 by 15% of 30' before making the transition to simply writing, 'Increase 30 by 15%'.

This, of course, leads us to the second point – calculating with percentages. For this, pupils need to recognise that the percentage is forming a proportional relationship with the value in the other unit, and that our different strategies for calculating with percentages come from our pre-existing understanding of the nature of proportional relationships.

Calculate 10% of £70.

Leaving aside for a minute any consideration of the context from which such a calculation might arise, we can use the same sort of proportional representations to help make sense of different strategies we might use for this calculation.

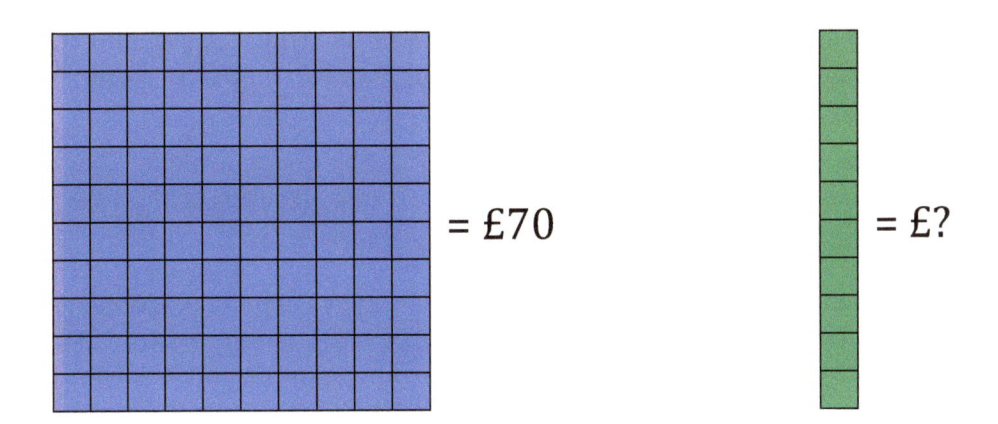

Being already familiar (hopefully) with the 100-square, one way of representing this is to show that the total value of the 100-square is £70, and that the calculation requires the value of 10 squares (i.e. 10%).

This can also be shown on a dual number line:

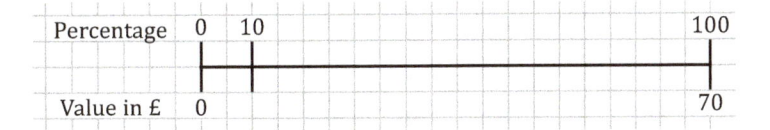

Ideally though, if pupils have already transitioned in their understanding of proportion to using ratio tables, then we would go straight into using a ratio table to model this problem:

Percentage	Value in £
100	70
10	

Note that implicit in all of these is a recognition that £70 represents the whole quantity that we have, and therefore is related to 100%. Again, this is important to highlight to pupils, as it will not always be the case.

From the ratio tables we can potentially explore the three most common strategies for calculating with percentages:

1. Scaling the percentage value by a factor of 0.1, and so scaling the value in £ by the same factor (i.e. 70 × 0.1). This can lead in time to recognising that the 'multiplier' for calculating 10% of a whole quantity (i.e. a quantity equivalent to 100%) will always be 0.1, and further into the general strategy for calculating multipliers for any percentage calculation.

2. Calculating the exchange rate between the percentage value and the value in £; in this case 0.7. Because the relationship between percentage value and value in £ is proportional, this will mean that any value in £ will be 0.7 times the percentage value, and so lead to the calculation 10 × 0.7. This is an often overlooked strategy that is particularly useful in certain percentage calculations, as well as laying the groundwork for pupils to see relationships like x% of y = y% of x (which we will look at in more detail shortly).

3. Scaling the percentage value not by multiplication by 0.1 but by the equivalent division by 10 (which is the most common introductory strategy for calculating 10% of a value).

Pupils should have the opportunity to work with many different types of percentage values, including integer values, decimal values, values greater than 100 and values less than 1. The following gives a flavour of the range of values we should encourage pupils to work with:

Calculate each of the following:

a 74% of 765 Newtons
b 47% of 765 Newtons
c 94% of 765 Newtons
d 9.4% of 765 Newtons
e 0.94% of 765 Newtons
f 9.04% of 765 Newtons
g 904% of 765 Newtons
h 904.904% of 765 Newtons
i $\frac{9}{4}$% of 765 Newtons
j $\frac{9}{40}$% of 765 Newtons

We may also wish to include negative percentage values and percentages of negative values.

It may be worth, prior to something like this activity, to build confidence in identifying the scale multiplier that transforms 100% into other percentages. Hopefully, if pupils have a strong enough understanding of place value and division by 100, this should be a relatively straightforward step. Nonetheless it is a step some pupils find beneficial to work on in isolation.

Find the multiplier that:

a   turns 100% into 30%

b   turns 100% into 35%

c   turns 100% into 53%

d   turns 100% into 50.3%

e   turns 100% into 5.03%

f   turns 100% into 503%

g   turns 100% into 500.3%

h   turns 100% into 530%

i   turns 100% into 0.53%

j   turns 100% into 0.5%

It may be worth modelling this using part of the dual number line or ratio table:

Examples:

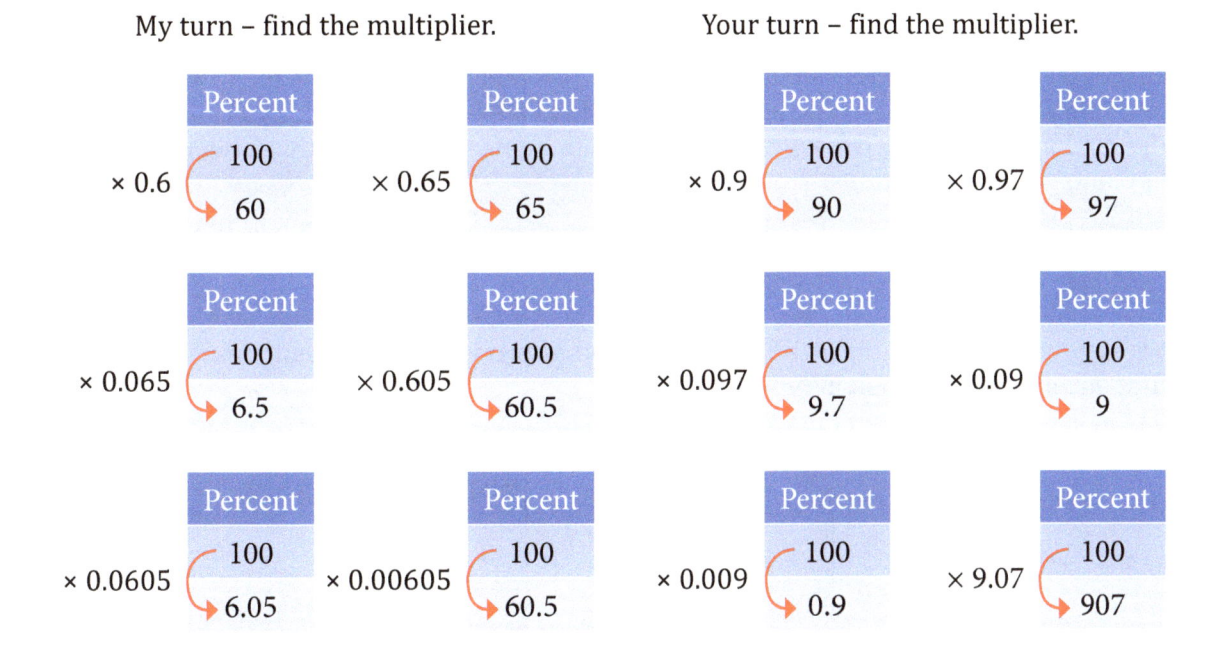

My turn – find the multiplier.

Percent
100
60

× 0.6

Percent
100
65

× 0.65

Percent
100
6.5

× 0.065

Percent
100
60.5

× 0.605

Percent
100
6.05

× 0.0605

Percent
100
60.5

× 0.00605

Your turn – find the multiplier.

Percent
100
90

× 0.9

Percent
100
97

× 0.97

Percent
100
9.7

× 0.097

Percent
100
9

× 0.09

Percent
100
0.9

× 0.009

Percent
100
907

× 9.07

As well as calculating percentages of quantities using the scale multiplier, there are often cases where using the functional multiplier (the exchange rate) is a much more straightforward approach. Consider this question:

Calculate 7.2% of £300.

In this case, whilst we could simply multiply 300 by 0.072, it is more efficient to recognise that £300 is 3 times bigger than 100%, and so we can simply multiply 7.2 by 3:

Percent	Value in £
100	×3 → 300
7.2	×3 →

Ultimately, recognising both approaches to percentage (as in all proportional structures) opens up the possibility for deeper insight into the percentage calculations, and true fluency in working with percentages. If, having calculated percentages of values using both scale multipliers and functional multipliers, we draw pupils' attention to how these multipliers are calculated, it is relatively easy to see the equivalence in both calculations:

1. To use the scale multiplier:

    $7.2 \times \frac{1}{100}$ (calculates the scale multiplier) $\times 300$

2. To use the functional multiplier:

    $300 \times \frac{1}{100}$ (calculates the functional multiplier) $\times 0.72$

This leads to further strategies being available to pupils for calculating percentages, such as in this example:

Calculate 0.32% of 25.

Seeing this first as $0.32 \times \frac{1}{100} \times 25$, we can apply the associative and commutative properties to rewrite this as $25 \times \frac{1}{100} \times 0.32$, which can then be reimagined as 25% of 0.32. If pupils are already aware of the equivalence of 25% to the fraction $\frac{1}{4}$, then this calculation becomes almost trivial. Please note, I am not saying pupils should go through the full rewriting of the multiplication every time they wish to apply this strategy, but seeing it as a consequence of the dual approaches to working with proportion helps to reinforce that understanding of percentages as proportions.

If 30% of a value = 45, what is 25% of the same value?

We may wish to model this in a ratio table or other proportion representation when pupils first encounter this problem type:

Percent	Value
30	45
25	

(×$\frac{5}{6}$ from 30 to 25; ×1.5 from Percent to Value; ×$\frac{5}{6}$ on Value side)

Of course, we do not need to scale immediately by $\frac{5}{6}$ here, and strategies such as dividing by 6 (× $\frac{1}{6}$) and then multiplying by 5 can also be explored and encouraged, alongside recognising that the value is 1.5 times bigger than the percentages, and that this will hold for any other percentage value.

In addition to these types of problems, pupils will also need to work with values that are being changed by a given percentage or have been changed by a given percentage.

Increase £75 by 65% (of £75).

Generally pupils' starting strategy here is to find 65% of 75, and then add the result to £75. There is nothing necessarily wrong with this strategy; however, it doesn't transfer well to other problems involving percentage change. Ideally pupils should be encouraged to see percentage calculations as multiplicative in nature (again, reinforcing the proportional nature of percentage and value) and so be moved towards seeing this question as akin to calculating 165% of £75. This is one of the reasons why it is useful for pupils to already have experience of adding/subtracting percentage values and of calculating with percentage values greater than 100%. Alternatively, the distributive property can also be used to demonstrate why we can calculate 165% of £75; 100% × 75 + 65% × 75 = (100% + 65%) × 75. Conversely, this can serve as a reminder to pupils of the distributive property once they are already secure in calculating percentage changes by finding the changed percentage value.

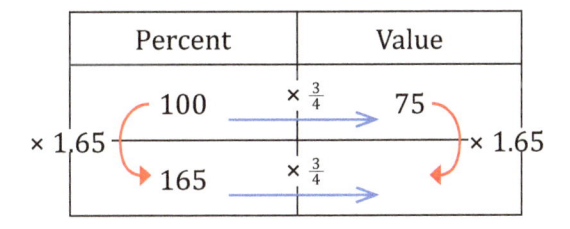

Percent	Value
100	75
165	

× $\frac{3}{4}$ (both rows); × 1.65 (left, between rows); × 1.65 (right, between rows)

A value is decreased by 40%. The decreased value is £420. What was the value before the decrease?

Here is the first situation where the sort of additive thinking that pupils may default to will lead them astray. The most common misconception in this calculation is to find 40% of £420 and add it on, thereby 'undoing' the process of finding 40% of £420 and then subtracting. Of course, the issue here is that it wasn't 40% of 420 that was taken off, and therefore we can't 'undo' this by adding on 40% of 420. However, if we model this using percentage values in a ratio table:

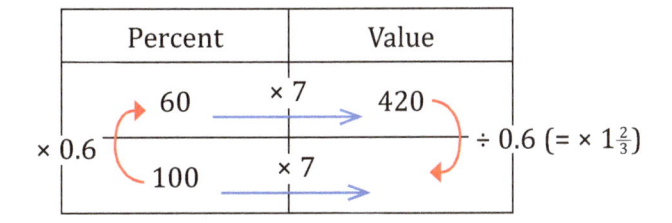

Percent	Value
60	420
100	

× 7 (both rows); × 0.6 (left, between rows); ÷ 0.6 (= × $1\frac{2}{3}$) (right, between rows)

Again, it is worth noting here that the functional multiplier is very straightforward and is by far the most efficient way of arriving at the correct original value. However, we could also recognise that the scale multiplier from 100% to 60% (i.e. 0.6) would take us from the unknown original value to the known changed value, then dividing by the scale multiplier (or multiplying by the reciprocal of the scale multiplier) will calculate the original value. The benefit of this approach is that it can be generalised – given the relative ease of finding the scale multiplier from 100% to any other percentage value then we can 'undo' the application of the scale multiplier to an unknown original value by dividing by the scale multiplier (or multiplying by its reciprocal).

The selling price of goods in a shop is 75% on top of their purchase price to make a profit. In a sale, the shop reduces the selling price by 25%. What percentage profit will they make on the goods sold in the sale?

The realisation we are aiming for here is that the actual purchase price of the goods doesn't matter, all that matters is the combined effect of the two percentage changes. The classic misconception in this case is for pupils to say 50%, this time caused by neglecting that the 75% increase is applied to the purchase price but the 25% is taken off the sales price. Many people find a bar-model representation useful here; not necessarily to aid in calculation, but simply as an illustration that the problem is not so straightforward:

In the upper box we are seeing a bar representing the purchase price, which is then increased by 75%, and then this selling price is reduced by 25%. In the lower box we can simply see the purchase price increased by 50%. The clear indication is that the bottom bar in the first box is not equal to the bottom bar in the second box. In terms of calculation then, we could use the bars above (as they are properly scaled) but we might well just use a 'ratio table' with the value left completely blank:

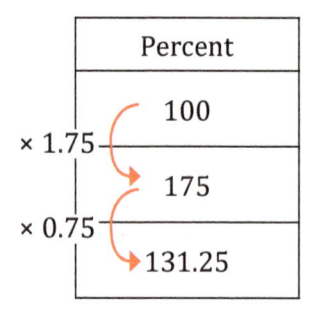

Percent
100
175
131.25

× 1.75
× 0.75

This time we are applying the scale multiplier that we already know calculates 175% of any quantity (to increase by 75%) and then applying the scale multiplier that calculates 75% of any quantity (to decrease the result by 25%), and this produces a final result of 131.25%, which can be interpreted as only a 31.25% profit on the original purchase price.

The massive benefit that this multiplicative thinking produces is the ability to become aware that the order of these calculations will not affect the result, i.e. I could reduce the original by 25% and then increase that value by 75% and I would get the same final result (provided, of course, that commutativity of multiplication is well understood). This leads eventually to the idea that we can find the overall percentage change of several different percentage changes simply by multiplying each of the scale multipliers by each other (a result very commonly exploited when looking at repeated percentage change, which we will examine in the next chapter as part of the wider idea of growth and decay functions).

A value increases from 25 to 40. What is the percentage increase in the original value?

There are two potential approaches to this:

1   Set 25 equal to 100% and then find the percentage value of 40, and then subtract 100% from this value.
2   Find the actual increase from 25 to 40; set 25 equal to 100%, and then find the percentage value of the increase.

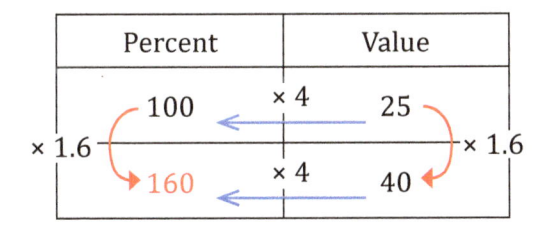

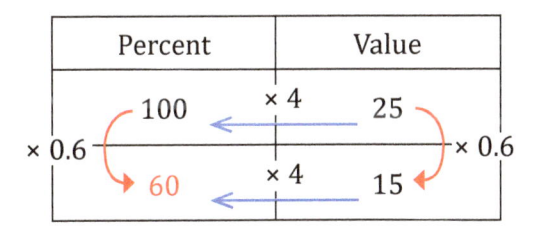

Percent	Value
100	25
160	40

×1.6 ×4 ×4 ×1.6

Percent	Value
100	25
60	15

×0.6 ×4 ×4 ×0.6

Probably the most straightforward calculation strategy in this particular case is to recognise that the percentage value is 4 times greater than the actual value, and to apply this exchange rate to the final value (either 40 if using approach 1, or 15 if using approach 2). Alternatively, we can find the scale factor to take the value before the change to the changed value and apply this same scale factor to the percentage value. In general this second strategy is more accessible as we simply divide one value by another, and then multiply the result by 100. However, in my opinion, this shouldn't just be offered to pupils without looking at something like the above representations to make sense of the idea that the division tells us the scale factor, and then multiplication by 100 is applying the same scale factor to 100%. The most common misconception in this approach is likely to be dividing the values the wrong way around, and if this approach is taught very instrumentally, this misconception is likely to be more prevalent.

Concept: ratio

Prerequisites: Number, multiplication, division, equality, equivalence, potentially proportion.

Linked concepts: Percentage, measures, similarity, trigonometry.

Personally, I think ratio deserve more consideration than they often have in the English curriculum. Very often they are limited to being a vehicle for unequal sharing, with a nod to their use as a scale in maps or scale drawings. There might be a bit of simplifying going on ('They simplify like fractions') or writing in different forms (1:*n*, for example). Recently, more problem types have appeared, partially driven by the refocus on ratio and proportion in qualifications at 16. What is often missing though is a look at what ratios *are*. What are they for? What do they show? This is further complicated by the English (perhaps Western?) oddity where the main focus of ratio is often the relationship with each part to the whole. As mentioned earlier, in most other areas, the relationship shown in a ratio focuses on the two parts (which makes sense if you think about it; if you list the two parts, it would make sense for them to be the focus). For me, the entire point of a ratio is to record and highlight the multiplicative relationship between the two values. When we write the ratio 1:5 (for example) we are wanting to highlight that the second value is 5 times greater than the first (and therefore conversely that the first is $\frac{1}{5}$ of the second). What is perhaps less in focus is the fact that each part represents $\frac{1}{6}$ and $\frac{5}{6}$ of some whole. Of course, this might depend on how you represent the ratio:

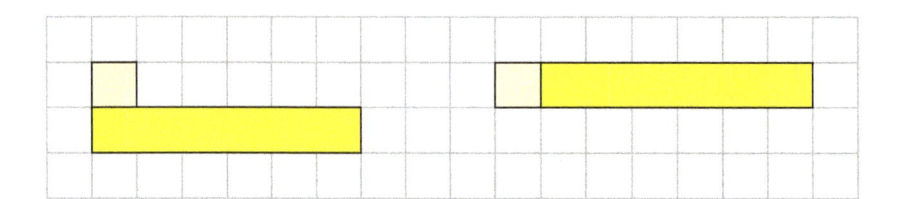

In the left-hand image the bars for the two parts of the ratio are shown one above the other, where the natural thing to do is to compare the two parts, seeing the lower as 5 times larger than the higher, or seeing the upper as $\frac{1}{5}$ of the lower. Conversely, in the right-hand image the two bars are shown attached to each other, which brings more into focus a whole of 6 (or that is 6 times larger than the first part), and therefore each part representing $\frac{1}{6}$ or $\frac{5}{6}$ of the whole.

Personally, I think this choice of what to highlight through our choice of representation is where we should start teaching with ratio. This would naturally highlight both the multiplicative relationships between the values (particularly if pupils have already modelled fractions in this way) and between each value and the whole. But more than that, it adds some weight to what the ratio notation is for – the purpose it serves; that it allows for the multiplicative comparison between these different parts and between each part and the whole. This also creates the strong link between ratio and division, as multiplicative comparison is a model we have used for division.

This is a much stronger foundation on which to place ratio if we are wanting to then progress to simplifying, rewriting, and ultimately assigning values to different aspects of the ratio.

Process: simplifying ratio

Simplify 6:9.

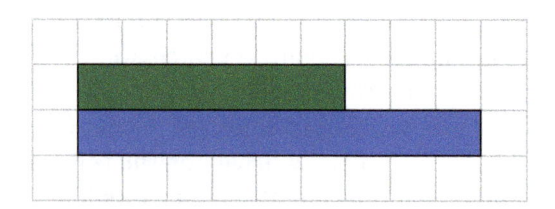

There are a few potential ways to make sense of what it means to simplify this ratio, and it doesn't make much in the way of difference if we look at the ratio with one bar under the other, or the bars side by side (and it could be argued that we should look at them in both ways to keep both models in mind). The models for simplifying the ratio are identical to those for simplifying fractions, which, of course, we would expect if we are seeing the fractional relationships:

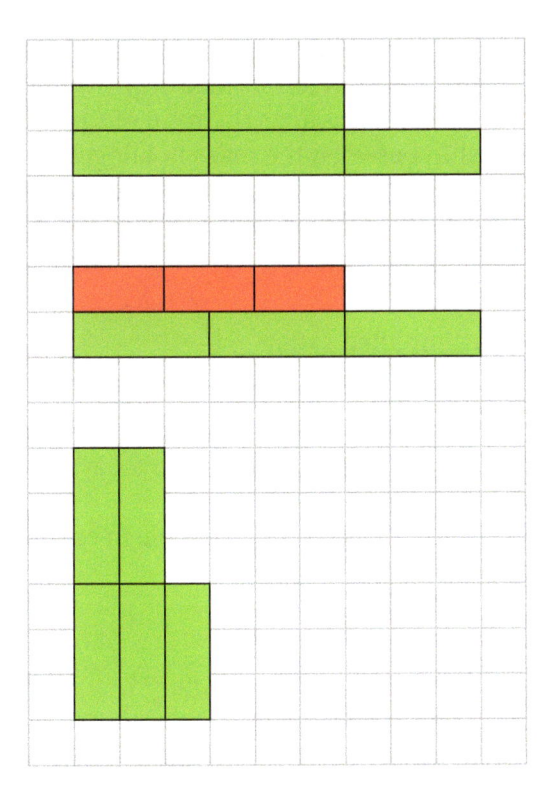

In the first model we replace both rods with a single colour rod, with the simplification being the number of rods used in both lines; i.e. we can replace both the dark green and blue rods with a number of green rods, and if the green rod is worth 1 then this is the ratio 2:3.

In the second model we replace both rods with the same number of rods, with the simplification being the value of the rods used: i.e. we can replace the dark green rod with three red rods and the blue rod with three green rods. The red rod has a value of 2 (if each square is 1), and the green rod has a value of 3, so we have the ratio 2:3.

In the third model we tie in the idea of factorisation by creating an area for both the 6 and 9, with the idea being that we attempt to create areas that have the same width. So with the 6 we can create a 3 × 2 area and for the 9 we can create a 3 × 3 area. Because the areas have the same width, their lengths will compare as their areas do, so the 6:9 becomes 2:3. This third model, in particular I feel, captures the idea of simplifying as reducing the values in the ratio until the numbers are integers with no common factor without altering the multiplicative relationships that exist between them.

Ratio simplifying is an ideal opportunity to interweave different factorisations/division, particularly once pupils have moved beyond the concrete/pictorial. This can include multiple factorisations, even decomposition into products of prime factors for ratio involving larger numbers:

Simplify the ratio 8000: 275.

as well as practising working with decimals:

Simplify the ratio 2.25:4.95.

Another nice opportunity is to look at units and unit conversion. Before doing this, it is worth making clear that a ratio can only be formed from values that measure the same quantity with the same unit, so we cannot form the ratio of £1 to 1.2 kg (although there can exist a multiplicative relationship between the mass in kilograms and the number of GBP). Similarly, we cannot form the ratio 8 hours to 3 days until the two measures of time are both in the same unit. It is in this second type of question that the opportunity exists for unit conversion:

Write 8 hours to 3 days as a simplified ratio.

This question in particular has a nice discussion point as to whether to employ the strategy of writing 3 days as 72 hours, or writing 8 hours as $\frac{1}{3}$ of a day.

As we have seen, simplifying ratio can also play a key role in establishing whether a proportion exists between two quantities.

Process: writing ratio in the form 1:n

Again, a key focus here is the purpose – namely to make clear the multiplicative relationship that exists between the two parts of the ratio.

Write the ratio 4:7 in the form 1:n.

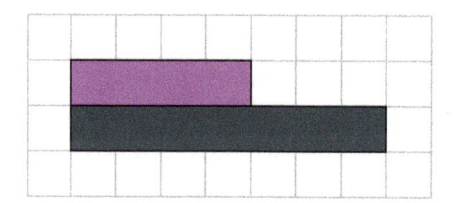

If pupils are used to representing fractions with Cuisenaire, and a comparative model for division, then this becomes so simple as to almost be trivial. Pupils should be very at home in defining a value of 1 at this point and being able to decide what the other value is. In this case, if the purple rod takes a value of 1, then the black rod has a value of $1\frac{3}{4}$. Because pupils are then used to the 'What if this is 1' question being linked to the comparative model for division, it should be relatively clear that we are dividing both sides of the ratio by 4.

Again, we can bring other types of numbers at this point, as well as unit conversion prior to the writing of the ratio in the required form. We should also make sure pupils have to work with ratios where the first number is the larger number, and so when written in the form 1:n the value of n is less than 1. Another nice thing to do is to switch the terms of the ratio around and look at writing them in the form 1:n both ways round, and so reinforce the idea of reciprocal – for example:

Write 2:5 and 5:2 in the form 1:n.

2:5 = 1:$\frac{5}{2}$ and 5:2 = 1:$\frac{2}{5}$

Of course, alternatively we could simply reverse the form:

> Write 2:5 in the form 1:n and n:1.

This, of course, would use the same values as the above, i.e. 1: $\frac{5}{2}$ and $\frac{2}{5}$: 1. For pupils this is important as it highlights the two multiplicative relationships that exist between the two parts of the ratio; that the right is $\frac{5}{2}$ of the left (i.e. 2.5 times bigger) and the left is $\frac{2}{5}$ of the right. This can lead to strategies for solving problems with ratio, as well as offering a pupil the opportunity to work with ratios already in this form.

> Find as many different ratios as you can that can be written in the form 1:$2\frac{2}{3}$. What do they have in common? How are they different?

When introducing ratio problems, often the first type of problem pupils are introduced to is sharing when the whole of the ratio is known. However, for me, these are the last type of problem that should be introduced: particularly if pupils' experience of ratio up to this point has been more focused on the relationship between the two parts. This is where we should start looking at ratio problems:

> Persons A, B and C share money in the ratio 2:3:5. Work out how much each of the others gets and/or the total amount of money shared if:
>
> i   A gets £180   ii   B gets £180   iii   C gets £180

If pupils have become fluent with the multiplicative relationships between the parts of the ratio, then they should have little problem in writing this ratio in the form 1:$1\frac{1}{2}$:$2\frac{1}{2}$, or $\frac{2}{3}$:1:1$\frac{2}{3}$, or $\frac{2}{5}$:$\frac{3}{5}$:1 and then find the required fractions of the given value. To me, this is a much preferable strategy to the common strategy of breaking down the value into the requisite number of parts as it focuses attention on the important thing in the ratio, i.e. the multiplicative relationships between the parts. A potential alternative, though, is to look at it in a ratio table:

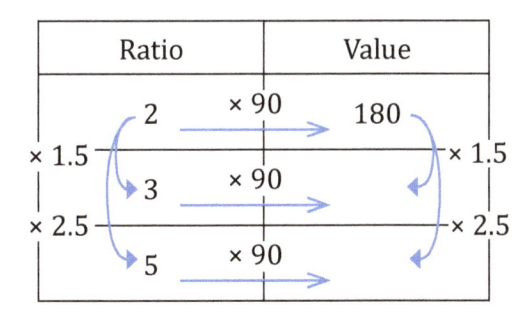

Ratio	Value
2	180
3	
5	

(× 90 between Ratio and Value; × 1.5 from 2 to 3 and from 180 down; × 2.5 from 2 to 5 and from 180 down)

Here we can see the scaling of the ratio by the same multiplicative relationships that we highlighted earlier between the parts of the ratio being applied to the value of £180. However, in this form, we can see that an exchange rate of £90 per part also exists between the parts of the ratio and the values in pounds (this is, of course, equivalent to the strategy of sharing the money between the given number of ratio parts, in that case £180 into 2 parts giving £90 in each part).

If needed, we can also bring back the Cuisenaire rods, either as a physical bar model or as a pictorial version to highlight the same relationships:

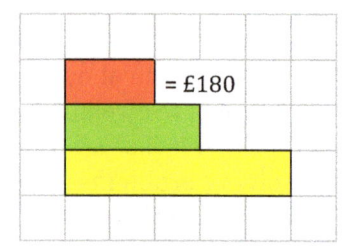

We can see the same relationships here, with the green rod being $1\frac{1}{2}$ times greater than the red rod, and the yellow rod is $2\frac{1}{2}$ times greater than the red rod. Alternatively, we can see the value of the red rod as 90 times greater than its length in units, and so each of the other rods must have a value 90 times greater than their lengths in units.

There are many problems like this, and similarly to proportion, we can involve too many different other areas of maths to make it worthwhile exploring them all now. However, one area that is worth highlighting is that this problem type is very typically used in map and scale diagram problems:

> A map has a scale of 1:50000. On the map two points are 9 cm apart. Work out the distance between the two points in real life. Give your answer in metres.

This is exactly the same problem type, only complicated by the fact that the numbers are perhaps a little larger than pupils are used to (unless we have deliberately included values of this size prior to looking at map scales to help prepare pupils), but it should be quite clear that in this case we are going to calculate 9 × 50,000 = 450,000 cm, which we will then need to convert into metres. This conversion is in itself a proportional relationship (as we will see in Chapter 8), with the conversion resulting in a final value of 4,500 metres.

Once pupils are clear solving ratio problems where one part has a known value, we can turn to other types of ratio problem. Again, I would not yet be looking at problems where the whole is known at this point; rather I would turn at this point to problems where the difference between two parts is known. There are a number of different ways that this problem type can be communicated:

> Persons A, B and C share money in the ratio 2:3:5. The difference between person B's amount and person C's amount is £180. Work out the amount of money each person gets and/or the total amount of money shared.

> Persons A, B and C share money in the ratio 2:3:5. Person C gets £180 more than person B. Work out the amount of money each person gets and/or the total amount of money shared.

> Persons A, B and C share money in the ratio 2:3:5. Person B gets £180 less than person C. Work out the amount of money each person gets and/or the total amount of money shared.

> Persons A, B and C share money in the ratio 2:3:5. If person B was given £180 more they would have the same as person C. Work out the amount of money each person gets and/or the total amount of money shared.

Persons A, B and C share money in the ratio 2:3:5. If person C gives £90 to person B they would have the same amount of money. Work out the amount of money each person gets and/or the total amount of money shared.

All of these questions are really the same type of problem; namely that the difference between the parts of the ratio allocated to person B and person C is £180. We can make sense of this in the ratio table by including a fourth part to the ratio, which is the difference between person B and person C:

	Ratio	Value
Person A	2	× 90
Person B	3	× 90
Person C	5	× 90
Difference between B and C	2	× 90 180

We can see that the same multiplicative relationships that exist between the parts assigned to the different people also exist between the parts and the differences between parts. The differences can be scaled in the same way, and there is the same exchange rate between them and the values assigned. If needed, of course, we can bring back the Cuisenaire rods again, this time to look at the difference between parts:

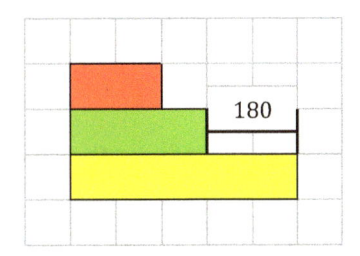

We can see the same things again that we saw in the ratio table; the scaling of this difference by 1, 1.5 and 2.5 to find the values of the red, green and yellow rods. The Cuisenaire rods can also potentially help pupils see why each of the problem types above result in this same picture.

Once pupils are familiar with this, I would then look to include problems where the sum of the parts is known.

Persons A, B and C share money in the ratio 2:3:5. If they share £180 in total, how much does each get?

This time, rather than looking at the difference between two parts, we will instead look at the total of all the parts:

	Ratio		Value
Person A	× 0.2 → 2	× 18 →	
Person B	× 0.5 → 3	× 18 →	
Person C	× 0.3 → 5	× 18 →	
Total of A, B and C	× 0.5 → 10	× 18 →	180

In a similar way to the difference between parts, we can see that the total can be scaled in the same way as any of the parts, and the same exchange rate exists between the total number of parts of the ratio and the total value as between the number of parts and the value of each part.

This is, of course, akin to bringing back the Cuisenaire representation with the rods in a line, as we are more concerned with the value of each part in relation to the whole:

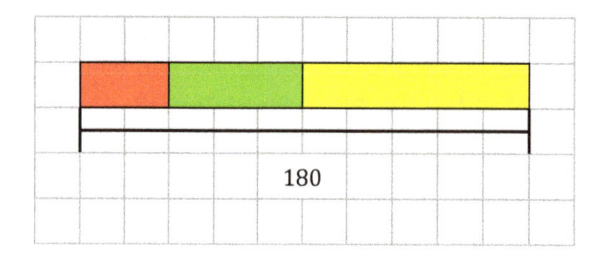

Again, we can see all the same relationships here that we saw in the ratio table, both in terms of the fractions that each part represents of the whole and the exchange rate between the size of the whole in the ratio and the value of the whole. Hopefully, pupils should be familiar with pictures like this from their work with fractions and so should have little problem in recognising that each part is given by a certain fraction of £180.

One problem type that is structurally identical to this one but can appear different to pupils is problems involving a hidden whole. These commonly occur in geometric situations where information is already known about the sum of sides or angles – for example:

The three interior angles of a (planar) triangle are in the ratio 2:3:5. Find the size of each angle.

In this problem no mention of the total is given; however, it is expected that pupils working with this problem would bring knowledge of interior angles of a triangle summing to 180°. It is a good idea for pupils to work with problems where they have to bring previous knowledge from other mathematical areas and combine it with ratio so that they get used to recognising when we might have hidden wholes (or potentially parts/differences between parts).

Proportionality

Once pupils have studied the three basic problem types, it is potentially a worthwhile activity for them to be given mixed questions where they have to determine whether the information they are being provided about the ratio is about a part, the difference between parts or the whole.

We can also bring in slightly more challenging ratio questions, such as the one below:

> There are blue and green counters in a bag in the ratio 3:8. I add 12 blue counters to the bag. The ratio of blue to green counters is now 3:4. Work out the number of green counters in the bag.

We might look at this using Cuisenaire/a bar model:

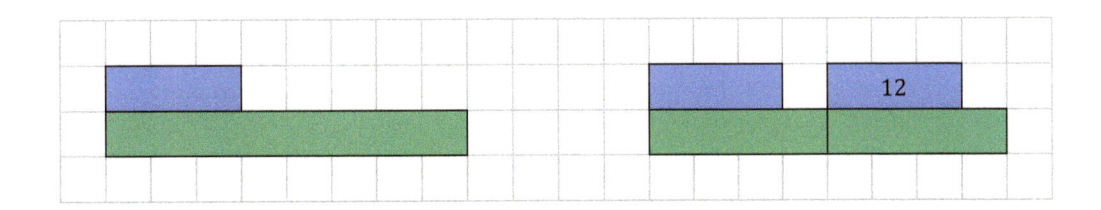

The key to this problem is that the number of green counters doesn't change, so the '4' in the ratio 3:4 that shows the relationship between final number of blue and green counters must be the same as the '8' in the original ratio. This should make it clear that, effectively, adding 12 blue counters has doubled the number of blue counters. This means that the original number of blue counters was 12, and therefore the number of green counters is $\frac{8}{3}$ of 12, which equals 32 green counters.

The same can be seen with a ratio table:

	Original ratio	New ratio	Value
Original blue	3 ← × 0.5	1.5	
Green	8 ← × 0.5	4	
New blue	6 ← × 2	3	
Difference between original blue and new blue	3	1.5	12

This can then be finished off by establishing either of the exchange rates from the original ratio to the value or the new ratio to the value and using those, or scaling either of the differences into the other parts.

The idea of a key part of the ratio staying the same is also an important part of questions like the following:

> The ratio a:b = 3:8 and the ratio b:c = 10: 17. Find the ratio a:c in its simplest form.

The fact that *b* appears in both ratios is the important factor here, as this provides the relationship that can connect *a* and *c*. Some pupils may see this purely through the use of the multiplicative relationships, i.e. $b = \frac{8}{3}a$ and $c = \frac{17}{10}b$ so $c = \frac{17}{10} \times \frac{8}{3} \times a$ giving $a:c = 1:\frac{68}{15} = 15:68$. For others, using a ratio table will help in seeing the structure:

	First ratio	Second ratio
a	3	
b	8 × 1.25 →	10
c		17

Many may well add a third column that shows *b* having been changed to 40, so that the multiplicative relationships are integer relationships rather than rational ones.

Whilst the majority of ratio problem types can be accessed in this sort of way, there are some for which the use of symbolic algebra is the most efficient approach:

> There are blue and green counters in a bag in the ratio 3:8. I add 12 blue counters to the bag and 12 green counters to the bag. The ratio is now 1:2. How many counters were originally in the bag?

If we let the number of blue counters be *x* then the number of green counters is $\frac{8}{3}x$. Adding 12 to both of these gives $x + 12$ and $\frac{8}{3}x + 12$. The ratio 1:2 means there are now twice as many green as blue, so $2(x + 12) = \frac{8}{3}x + 12$. Solving this gives $x = 18$, so there were 18 blue counters originally. The total number of counters is $\frac{11}{3}$ of this number, giving 66 counters in total.

Now that we have explored the important proportional structures, we will finish the chapter with a look at inverse proportion.

Concept: inverse proportion

Prerequisites: Number, multiplication, division, equality, equivalence, proportion, potentially ratio.

Linked concepts: Measures, shape, graphing.

Like proportion, there are a couple of different ways you might introduce the concept of inverse proportion. What they have in common is they are the 'inverse' of how we might introduce proportion. So, if we introduced proportion using ratio and *a:b* = *c:d*, then inverse proportion might be introduced as *a:b* = *d:c*, i.e. if two quantities are inversely proportional then taking two values *a* and *b* from the first quantity and taking the two corresponding quantities (*c* and *d*) from the second quantity, then the two quantities are inversely proportional if *a:b* = *d:c*.

However, if we have introduced proportion as the constant multiplicative relationship between two quantities, we may have a slight risk of a misconception that inverse proportion is a constant division between the two quantities. This risk can be allayed if pupils already have an understanding that division is a multiplicative relationship, but still needs watching for.

So, what is the inverse of a constant multiplicative exchange rate? The way I tend to introduce this is as a *constant multiplicative result*, i.e. multiplying a value of the first quantity by the corresponding value of the second quantity will always produce a constant result. This is potentially the most useful introduction for inverse proportion in terms of its utility – it allows a wide range of inverse proportion problems to be solved. We may also play a bit with the language here and unpack the phrase 'inversely proportional' into its full meaning; namely proportional to the multiplicative inverse (i.e. the reciprocal), which leads more to the standard $y = k \times \frac{1}{x} = \frac{k}{x}$. Of course, we would still have the constant multiplicative result, as $y = \frac{k}{x}$ can be rearranged to give $yx = k$.

In addition to the constant multiplicative result, there are a couple of properties of inversely proportional quantities that are important to explore with pupils (in a similar vein to the properties of proportional relationships we saw earlier in the chapter):

1. Inverse scaling: This is probably where pupils will see the most direct example of the 'inverse' relationship. Given a value from the first quantity and the related value from the secondary quantity, if one value is scaled by a certain scale factor, then the other value is scaled by the multiplicative inverse (i.e. the reciprocal).

2. Non-existence of zeroes: When two quantities are inversely proportional, then neither quantity can become 0 – there is no value of the quantity y that will satisfy $y \times 0 = k$ unless k is zero. In practical situations it normally leads to an absurd situation if either one of the quantities becomes 0. Establishing these two properties is also enough to demonstrate that the relationship between two quantities is inversely proportional.

So, if we look at the following:

> Three pumps will empty a tank in 8 hours and 5 pumps will empty the same size tank in 4.8 hours. Show that the number of pumps and the time taken are inversely proportional.

1. We could show that the number of pumps has been scaled by a factor of $\frac{5}{3}$, and the number of hours has been scaled by $\frac{3}{5}$, which means that the second quantity is scaled by the multiplicative inverse of the first. Similarly, zeroes don't make sense in the context of the question – the tank cannot be emptied in 0 hours no matter how many pumps (it will take at least some time), and if we have 0 pumps then the tank will never be emptied.

2. We can calculate the number of 'pump hours' for each pair of values. 3 pumps × 8 hours = 24 pump hours. 5 pumps × 4.8 hours = 24 pump hours. The fact that the number of pump hours is constant suggests that the number of pumps and the number of hours are inversely proportional.

3. The ratio of the number of pumps is 3:5. The corresponding ratio for the time in hours is 8:4.8 simplifies to 5:3. The fact that these ratios are the reverse of each other shows the two are inversely proportional.

In a very similar way, we can then solve inversely proportional problems involving missing values:

> Three pumps will empty a tank in 8 hours. How long will it take 10 pumps to empty the tank if they all pump at the same rate?

1. The number of pumps has been scaled by $\frac{10}{3}$. This means that the number of hours will be scaled by $\frac{3}{10}$ and $\frac{3}{10} \times 8 = 2.4$ hours.

2. From the first pair of values, the number of pump hours = 3 × 8 = 24. As the number of pump hours will have to stay 24, we can calculate the number of hours by $\frac{24}{10} = 2.4$ hours.

3. The ratio of the number of pumps is 3:10. This means the ratio for the number of hours needs to be 10:3. So we need to solve 10:3 = 8:?, which can be solved to give 2.4 hours.

Many different situations can give rise to inversely proportional situations; in many cases there are relationships involving three variables where if one variable is fixed, the other two are inversely proportional and if either of the other two variables is fixed, that the remaining two are proportional. Many of these will come up in measures or shape, and we will examine them when we come to these areas.

In common with proportion, once pupils attain a measure of fluency in working with inverse proportion, we can begin to examine inverse proportion between powered variables, i.e. relationships like $y = \frac{k}{x^n}$. These will proceed in a very similar way to the above problems – being able to demonstrate an inversely proportional relationship exists or using the fact that a relationship is inversely proportional to find missing values. One particular type of relationship that is worth spending some time on is $y = \frac{k}{x^2}$ as there are many relationships in the physical sciences that have an inverse square relationship.[4] Newton's law of gravitation, the electrostatic attraction or repulsion between two charged particles, and the intensity of light all exhibit an inversely proportional relationship to the square of the distance between the two masses/particles/the light source to the object. This makes the physical sciences a rich vein of practical questions that involve inversely proportional relationships.

When we start to consider proportion and inverse proportion with respect to powers of variables, we are beginning to move beyond the direct multiplicative relationship into a more functional relationship between the two variables. It is to the broader idea of functionality that we now turn our attention.

---

4   Wikipedia, Inverse-Square Law (7 October 2021). Available at: https://en.wikipedia.org/wiki/Inverse-square_law#Occurences.

Chapter 7

Functionality

One could argue that the ultimate goal in number/algebra instruction is to move pupils' thinking through additive thinking to multiplicative thinking and then ultimately to functional thinking – a place where they can experience and appreciate the vast array of potential types of relationships that can exist between different values and variables.

Before introducing different types of functions, it is worth introducing the idea of related variables, namely introducing formulae.

Concept: formulae

Prerequisites: Number/algebra, addition, subtraction, multiplication, division, equality, equivalence, proportion, inverse proportion.

Linked concepts: Measures, shape, chance, graphing.

In terms of school-level maths, a formula is usually treated like a type of equation where the degree of freedom is greater than 0, and in particular where the number of degrees of freedom is one less than the number of variables (although the true definition is a little more general). This may be an opportune time to introduce the idea of 'degrees of freedom' in an equation to learners: if they have experience in solving equations (particularly linear equations) then it may well be that we can look again at the idea that all of those equations had 0 degrees of freedom, and it is this that makes equations solvable. Of course, this will need adapting for looking at systems of equations, where they are 'solvable' providing the degree of freedom across the system is 0, even if it wouldn't be for any single equation within the system.

Although algebra tiles might seem the natural way to introduce formulae, my preference is actually to use Cuisenaire rods to introduce formulae. The reason for this is that, by this point (provided pupils have had repeated exposure to them), pupils are already familiar with the rods taking many different values (including fractional/decimal values) and are also familiar with the relationships between rods (including the additive and multiplicative relationships). The fact that there aren't the same additive and multiplicative relationships between algebra tiles gives them their great utility in modelling other situations that can be represented symbolically, but not necessarily well suited to formulae (although we might transition to them at some point).

Find as many different combinations of rods as you can that are equal in length to the blue rod:

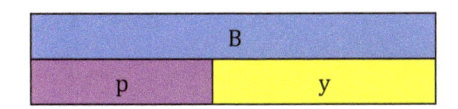

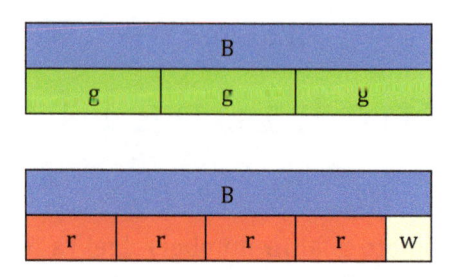

Three potential responses to the above task can be seen in this image. In each case we are replacing the length of the rod with a variable to stand for the length of the rod, so B is the length of the blue rod, p is the length of the purple rod and so on. We can introduce this to pupils by reminding them that at different points in their learning these rods have taken many different values, but what has always been true are the relationships between the rods – the blue rod has always been the same length as the purple rod and the yellow rod combined. From this we can create a formula, namely $B = p + y$.

The major benefit in this approach is that, because the equal lengths are representing the equality, it is relatively straightforward to see other ways of writing this formula (particularly if pupils are familiar with good models for the different operations). In the first formula, as well as seeing $B = p + y$, we can also see $y = B - p$ as y being the difference between B and p. Similarly, we can see $p = B - y$ as p being the result of counting y from B. In the second formula, we can see $B = 3g$, and we can see additive relationships such as $B - g = 2g$ but we can also see $\frac{B}{3} = g$ (either as B split into three equal parts, or via a comparison between B and g). This is taken further in the third formula, where we can start to mix additive and multiplicative views. In this formula we can see $B = 4r + w$ but we can also see all of the following:

- $B - 4r = w$
- $B - w = 4r$
- $B - 2r = 2r + w$
- $\frac{B - w}{4} = r$

and many more. From here we can start to think about recording how we can manipulate each of these formulae to create the others, and consider the **subject** of a formula, i.e. the dependent variable (where it exists).

The Don Steward task 'Cuisenaire Equations' contains further examples of using Cuisenaire rods to support pupils in making sense of formulae. An example of one slide is given below:[1]

$p + \square = b$

$2p + \square = \odot$

$3y - \square = B$

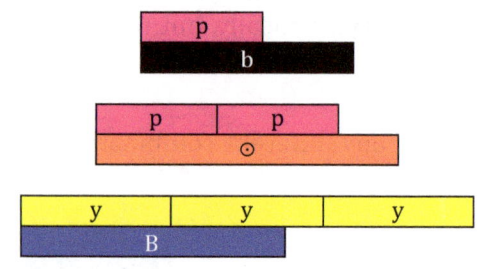

---

1 D. Steward, Cuisenaire Rod Equations, *Median* [blog] (30 March 2013). Available at: https://donsteward.blogspot.com/2013/03/cuisenaire-equations.html?m=0.

$\frac{1}{2}\odot + \square = t$

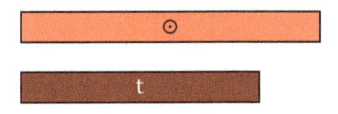

The minor drawbacks to introducing formulae using Cuisenaire rods are:

1. If we introduce values for the rods (i.e. to look at substituting into formulae) then we may well end up destroying the relationships between the rods.
2. It is very difficult to represent formulae involving additive constants, as once we assign a constant value to one rod, the other rods naturally take related constant values.

When we want to look at substitution and/or formulae involving additive constants, there are (broadly speaking) two other representations we might use:

1. Algebra tiles/discs.
2. A bar-model visual representation.

Both of these have pros and cons. The pro with algebra tiles/discs is that pupils can continue to manipulate them physically; however, the same use of length to enable seeing the formula in different ways will usually not be available. The length view can be maintained with a bar model, but then we lose the ability for pupils to physically manipulate the formula.

What is the value of $z = 3x - 2y + 8$ when $x = 5$ and $y = 7$?

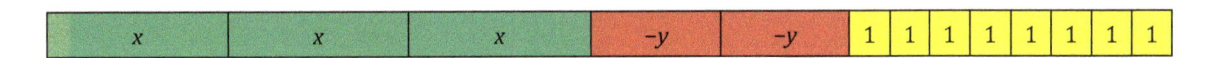

Here we see the expression $3x - 2y + 8$. Unfortunately, the algebra tiles do not have a third variable counter to show this being 'equal' to z.

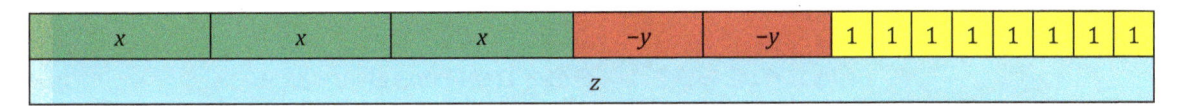

In the bar model we can draw in the third variable, but pupils cannot physically build the formula.

In both cases the substitution comes from simply removing the letter and replacing with the given value:

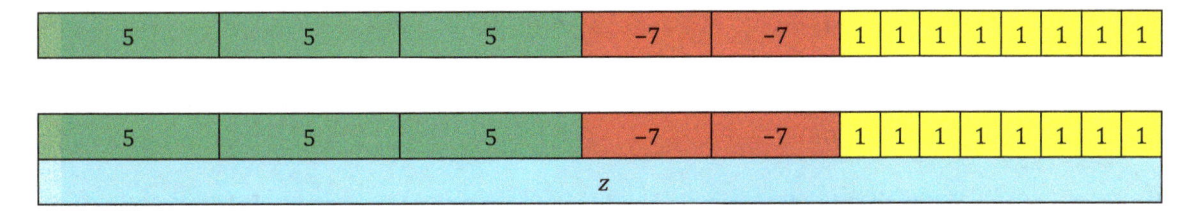

which can be evaluated to give a value for $z = 9$.

There are, of course, a huge array of practical formulae available to maths teachers to support pupils in developing fluency around substituting into formulae, both from maths and other curriculum areas. Once again, Don Steward has an excellent activity on his Median blog, although this would only really be suitable once pupils are comfortable working in the abstract:[2]

$$n = 10$$

$$5n =$$

$$5n + 2 =$$

$$\frac{5n + 2}{4} =$$

$$3\left[\frac{5n + 2}{4}\right] =$$

$$3\left[\frac{5n + 2}{4}\right] + 6 =$$

$$\frac{3\left[\frac{5n + 2}{4}\right] + 6}{5} =$$

$$7\left[\frac{3\left[\frac{5n + 2}{4}\right] + 6}{5}\right] =$$

$$7\left[\frac{3\left[\frac{5n + 2}{4}\right] + 6}{5}\right] - 1 =$$

$$\frac{7\left[\frac{3\left[\frac{5n + 2}{4}\right] + 6}{5}\right] - 1}{2} =$$

Pupils' exposure to functions rarely begins with the introduction of symbolic function notation (although we may not always use this language). One of the first places that pupils encounter functional relationships is in studying sequences.

Concept: sequences

Prerequisites: Number/algebra, addition, subtraction, multiplication, division, equality, equivalence.

Linked concepts: Formulae, functions, measures, shape, chance, graphing.

In primary/secondary school a sequence is often introduced as a list of numbers that obey a given rule. However, a potentially better way of thinking about sequences is as the result of a function applied to the domain of natural numbers. Although we might not use this language with pupils, this is almost certainly the view of sequences that we want to highlight and promote long term.

One type of sequence that is often overlooked is a sequence of constants. It is worth including examples of these throughout work on sequences. Although the properties of constant sequences aren't particularly exciting (at least in some people's opinion!); constant

---

2   D. Steward, To and Fro, *Median* [blog] (10 July 2019). Available at: https://donsteward.blogspot.com/2019/07/to-and-fro.html.

sequences do form the foundation of all other polynomial sequences, as well as linking to graphs and potentially even post-16 mathematics in calculus.

Subconcept: constant sequences

There are two important aspects of constant sequences that pupils should become aware of:

1   That the arithmetic difference between any two consecutive terms is 0, and the common ratio is 1.
2   That every term is the same.

These may seem obvious, but the first is important in then building to sequences where the arithmetic or common ratios are constant (i.e. arithmetic or geometric sequences), and the second is important in supporting the development of the functional view of sequences that is so important. In particular, we can direct attention to being able to find terms further in the sequence than the first few, i.e. finding the 37th term of the sequence, so that pupils are used to this sort of thinking when we want to explore it with other types of sequence. We might even begin to introduce symbolic notation for sequences, such as $T_n = 7$. However, one major reason for exploring constant sequences is so that pupils can see them as the building block for arithmetic sequences.

Subconcept: arithmetic sequences

In introducing the concept of an arithmetic sequence, provided pupils have been introduced to constant sequences, the introduction can simply be that arithmetic sequences are those whose differences form a constant sequence. Pupils can use this knowledge to identify arithmetic sequences and non-arithmetic sequences. A nice activity to offer pupils here is the creation of sequences that meet particular constraints, even adding constraints as we go:

> Write down an arithmetic sequence whose differences are the constant sequence 4, 4, 4, 4, … Write down another such sequence. And another.

> Write down an arithmetic sequence whose differences are the constant sequence 4, 4, 4, 4, … where the first term of the sequence is negative. Write down another such sequence. And a harder example.

> Write down an arithmetic sequence whose differences are the constant sequence 4, 4, 4, 4, … where the first term of the sequence is a negative fraction. Write down another such sequence. And a harder example.[3]

One thing that we might highlight from this is the fact there are a lot of arithmetic sequences based on any one constant sequence. Whilst this doesn't sound like much, it has nice links to integration in calculus – in integrating the constant function $f(x) = a$ we get a whole family of linear functions $F(x) = ax + b$ and what we are seeing here is the same idea applied to only discrete numbers. By highlighting this now, we can potentially redraw this parallel when pupils study integration. It also makes clear why, when writing a term-to-term rule for a

---
3   Question sequence adapted from J. Mason, A. Graham and S. Johnston-Wilder, *Developing Thinking in Algebra* (London, SAGE Publications, 2005) p. x.

sequence, we must define at least one of the terms of the sequence (normally the first). Pupils may well start by writing these term-to-term rules in words, such as, 'Start at 3 and add 8 each time', before eventually moving onto writing recurrence relations (which we will look at later). Of course, term-to-term rules are not specific to arithmetic sequences, and pupils can work with lots of different types of sequences to generate them from term-to-term rules given in words, or to write in words term-to-term rules for a given sequence. In addition, pupils can invent different rules for a short sequence, and explore the consequences of those rules – for example:

> A sequence starts 2, 6, ... Find as many different term-to-term rules for this sequence as possible. Which rules produce the same sequences. Can you see why?

When it comes to studying the functional relationships underpinning sequences, a lot depends on whether pupils are already familiar with the form of a linear function ($f(n) = an + b$). If they are, then we might expect pupils to recognise the values of an arithmetic sequence as fitting a linear function. Assuming for now that arithmetic sequences are being introduced before pupils have achieved the required fluency with linear functions (and in fact exploring arithmetic sequences will likely be part of developing this fluency with linear relationships) then there is one crucial arithmetic sequence that pupils need to be intimately familiar with – namely the natural numbers starting at 1. A nice way to introduce these in a way that can support further work with arithmetic sequences is using algebra tiles:

The reason this sequence is so important is that the ordinality and cardinality of each term are equal, i.e. the 1st term is 1, the 2nd term is 2, the 3rd term is 3 and, in general, the nth term is n. This sequence is particularly important because where we can create relationships between the values of n and the values of the terms of a given sequence, this can be seen as a position to term rule for the sequence: i.e. if we can write $T_n = f(n)$ for some sequence then we have a function linking the position of a term in the sequence with its value.

Once pupils recognise the importance of this particular arithmetic sequence, we can begin to look at other arithmetic sequences. I would suggest that the first we might look at are sequences that are an additive transformation of n, for example:

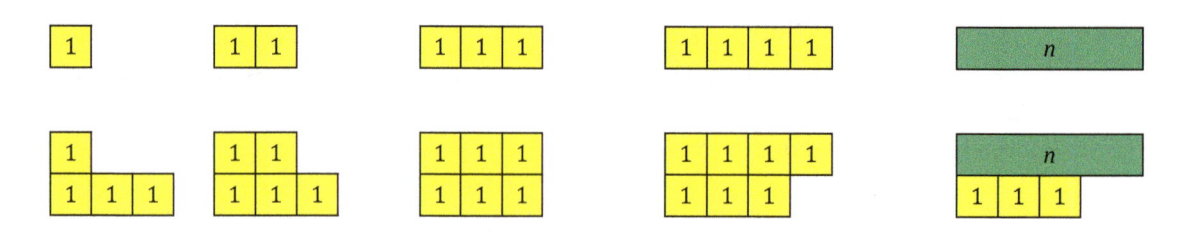

We might offer pupils the first four of each of these diagrams and ask them to decide how the natural numbers have been transformed to give the sequence underneath and then apply the same change to the n-tile. From here we might encourage pupils to write down symbolically what the position to term rule is: i.e. $T_n = n + 3$, and to predict the longer-term behaviour of the sequence, i.e. what would the 69th term be?

We can include subtraction as an additive transformation using the negative tiles; I find it best not to actually combine them and remove them as zero-pairs so that we can still discern the relationship back to *n*.

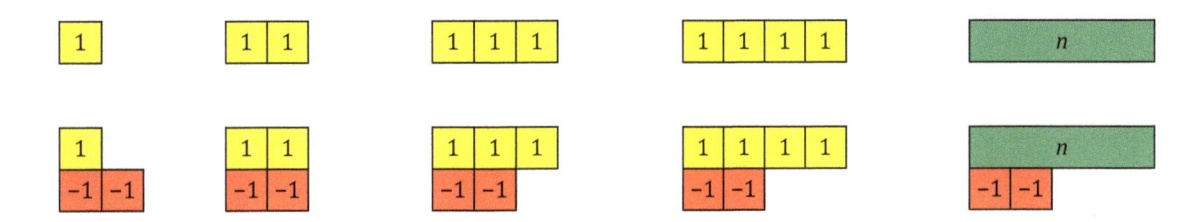

Once again, we can prompt pupils to write down the position to term rule/nth term, in this case $T_n = n - 2$, and predict long-term behaviour.

The next logical step from here is to look at sequences formed from multiplicative transformations of *n* – for example:

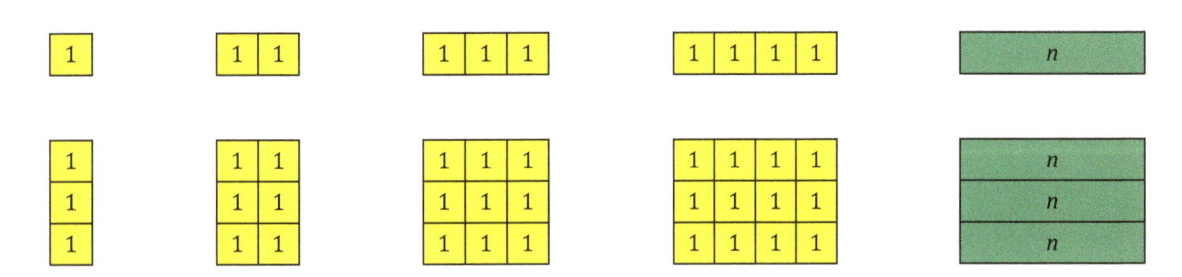

Again we could perhaps offer pupils only the first three or four of these pictures, asking them to build (potentially) the next one and the general case as well as prompting symbolic writing of the function $T_n = 3n$ and, once more, long-term prediction.

The final step is to then combine these two types of transformation:

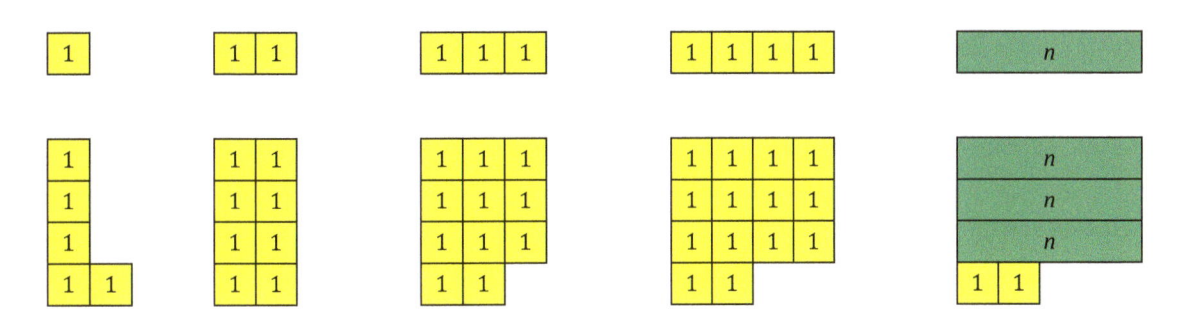

When then looking at these numerically, we can support pupils in tying together the idea that the values in the constant sequence underpinning the arithmetic sequence inform us about the multiplicative transformation on *n*. For example:

> Find the position to term rule for the sequence 7, 13, 19, 25, ...

The fact that this arithmetic sequence is based on a constant sequence of 6s indicates that the sequence is based on transforming *n* through multiplication by 6, because as *n* increases by 1 the sequence increases by 6: i.e. every time we add 1 in our sequence of *n* we add an extra column of 6 to our set of tiles. This can be helpful in modelling the sequence using tiles:

Pupils can then look at finding the *n*th term of other arithmetic sequences. In particular, it is worth making sure to include adequate experiences for pupils in working with three types of arithmetic sequences:

1   Sequences where the coefficient of *n* is negative.
2   Sequences where the coefficient of *n* is positive but start with a negative value.
3   Sequences where the coefficient of *n* is fractional.

These all tend to be sources of difficulty/misconception with pupils, potentially due to pupils' lack of familiarity with negative/fractional multiples and working with negative/fractional values in general. This can be seen as an ideal opportunity to revisit these types of numbers and operating with them, although examples will have to be chosen carefully to allow the algebra tiles to continue to be useful. Another common misconception is pupils thinking that things like the 100th term is 10 times bigger than the 10th term, so opportunities for examining this sort of fallacy should also be planned.

In addition, pupils will benefit from having opportunity to apply their understanding of arithmetic sequences in several different ways. Examples of this include examples of sequences where not all terms are given.

Find the nth term of the following arithmetic sequences:

a   4, 9, ... , ... , ... ,
b   ... , 4, 9, ... , ... ,
c   4, ... , 9, ... , ...
d   4, ... , ... , 9, ...
e   4, ... , ... , ... , 9
f   9, ... , ... , ... , 4
g   9, ... , ... , 4, ...

as well as solving problems with sequences:

> Explain why 458 is not in the arithmetic sequence 4, 9, 14, 19, ...
>
> Explain why 458 is not in the arithmetic sequence 4, 7, 10, 13, ...
>
> Is 458 in the arithmetic sequence 4, 10, 16, 22, ...? Explain your answer.
>
> Find an arithmetic sequence that 458 is in. And another, and a harder one.
>
> Find the first term of the arithmetic sequence 4, 10, 16, 22, ... that is greater than 100.
>
> Find the first term of the arithmetic sequence 111, 102, 93, 84, ... that is negative.

including these problems from Don Steward's blog:[4]

> Arithmetic sequences
>
> Find the value of 'n' that makes these four expressions the consecutive terms in an arithmetic sequence:
>
> a $2n + 1$ $4n - 1$ $5n$ 19
>
> b $n + 1$ $4n$ $7n - 1$ $9n$

These last two problems in particular really reinforce the underpinning constant sequence behind the arithmetic sequence.

Another nice opportunity to offer pupils is to make the link to other visual patterns:

> How many lines will be drawn in the 100th pattern?

Pupils can, of course, write out the number of lines in the first, second, third pattern and then analyse the sequence, but beyond this pupils can be prompted to try and make sense of the pattern directly, potentially in many different ways. For example, pupils might notice that we are continually adding 3 lines, from a start point of 1 (two horizontal and one vertical) and so arrive at $3n - 2$ and hence 298. Alternatively, pupils might see that the number of vertical lines is always the same as the pattern number, whilst the number of horizontal lines is double the previous number of vertical lines, which leads to having 100 vertical lines and 2 × 99 horizontal lines (or in general $n + 2(n - 1) = 3n - 2$). Or pupils might see 1, then 1 + 2 + 1, then 1 + 4 + 2 and so on and so the 100th would be 1 + 198 + 99 (in general $1 + 2(n - 1) + (n - 1)$). There are, of course, other ways pupils could make sense of this pattern, but one thing we might want to draw attention to (particularly if pupils are finding the nth term as $3n - 2$) is the 'three-ness' in the pattern – the recurrence of the pattern of two horizontal lines and one vertical as being integral to the structure.

---

4   J. Steele, Equations with Arithmetic and Quadratic Sequences, *Median* [blog] (23 May 2018). Available at: https://donsteward.blogspot.com/2018/05/equations-with-arithmetic-and-quadratic.html.

One more thing that it may well be worth introducing pupils to is the relationship between arithmetic sequences and linear graphs. Whether pupils have actually studied linear graphs in any great detail by this point is not hugely important – indeed, this can serve as a nice introduction into linear graphs. Once again, algebra tiles can support this introduction:

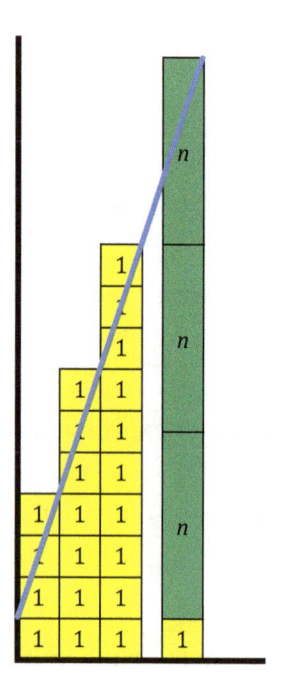

We can see that one of the properties of this arithmetic sequence (and arithmetic sequences in general) is that the values lie on a straight line. We can prompt pupils to think about why this must be the case for all arithmetic sequences, linking to the underpinning constant sequence and the gradient of the line. This allows us to link the language of 'linear' with 'arithmetic', and so pupils can understand why arithmetic sequences can be referred to as linear sequences. Dynamic graphing and geometry software can also be useful here, plotting $T = an + b$ and allowing for varying values of a and b.[5]

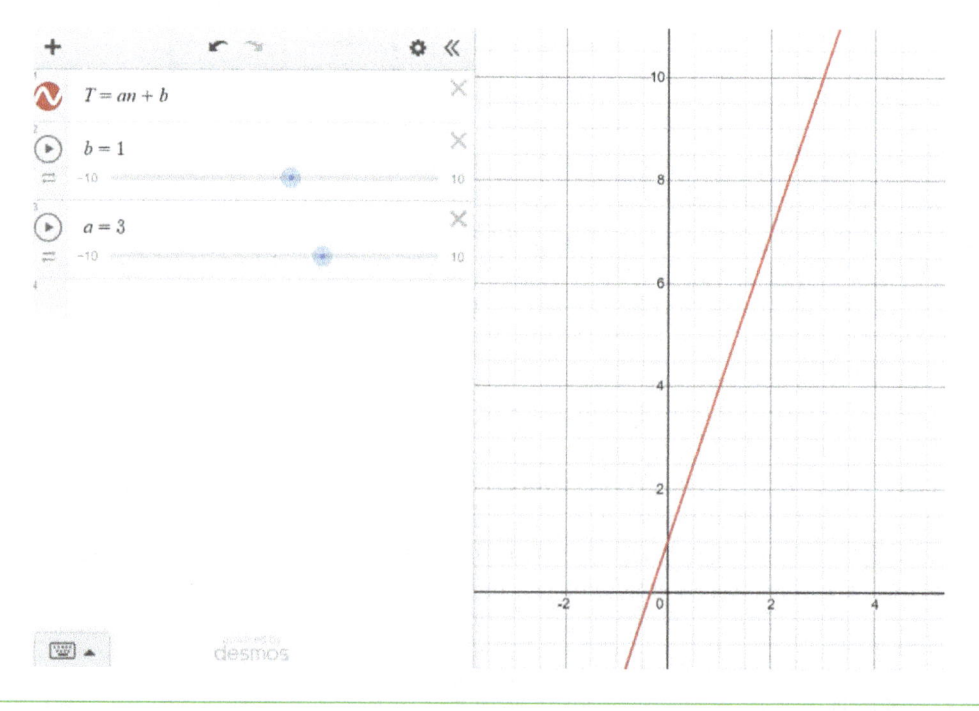

---
5   See https://www.desmos.com/calculator.

Pupils can use this to explore the linearity of different arithmetic sequences, reinforcing the idea that linearity is a property of all arithmetic sequences.

Arithmetic sequences also become a useful vehicle for supporting practice in other areas of mathematics that are typically studied (or become more mature) at some point after arithmetic sequences are introduced. The following are examples of areas that might allow for interweaved/interleaved practice:

> A set of 5 values forms an arithmetic sequence with a mean of 8 and a range of 10. Work out the 5 values.
>
> Find the nth term of the sequence $\sqrt{3} + 5, 2\sqrt{3} + 2, 3\sqrt{3} - 1, 4\sqrt{3} - 4, \ldots$
>
> Find the nth term of the sequence $p + q, 2p + 4q, 3p + 7q, 4p + 10q, \ldots$
>
> Find the nth term of the sequence $\frac{4}{7}, \frac{6}{11}, \frac{8}{15}, \frac{10}{19}, \ldots$
>
> Find the nth term of the sequence $\frac{4}{7}, \frac{3}{5}, \frac{8}{13}, \frac{5}{8}, \ldots$

There are, of course, other areas that can be drawn on to prompt pupils to apply their knowledge of arithmetic sequences combined with other concepts in mathematics.

From the study of arithmetic sequences, we can proceed in two directions. We can look to continue layering sequences additively, or return to a sequence of constants and look to layer them multiplicatively. The first of these leads to sequences that can be described by a quadratic function.

Subconcept: quadratic sequences

As a family of arithmetic sequences is underpinned by a single constant sequence, so each family of quadratic sequences is underpinned by an arithmetic sequence. Pupils can use this relationship to identify whether sequences are quadratic or not, as well as to conjecture about the further layering of sequences (i.e. that a quadratic sequence will underpin a cubic sequence and so on).

When it comes to a term-to-term rule, these can be trickier for pupils to write and invariably pupils will fall back on 'Add the next odd/even number'. This can make quadratic sequences a really nice motivator for looking at recurrence relations (which we will come to later); potentially more so than the Fibonacci sequence and other Lucas sequences.

In common with arithmetic sequences, there is a potential choice of approach to introducing the functional relationship with n depending on whether pupils already have the necessary fluency with quadratic functions. If pupils already have quite a depth of knowledge of quadratic functions, then we might be able to immediately introduce the idea that any quadratic sequence will be described by the function $T_n = an^2 + bn + c$ and then explore this in relation to each particular sequence. If pupils potentially don't have this fluency with quadratic functions yet, we can use algebra tiles to support this development with regards sequences.

If using tiles then the obvious first choice for exploring quadratic sequences is to look at the square numbers:

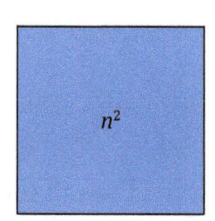

We are looking to highlight here the 'squareness' in this pattern so that we can recognise other patterns based off it:

Here we see $T_n = n^2 + 3$.

Here we see $T_n = n^2 + n$

Here we see $T_n = 2n^2$

If we use enough of these examples, we can potentially motivate the structure that is $T_n = an^2 + bn + c$, which is so crucial in generalising a process in finding the *n*th term. Even if pupils were already familiar with quadratic functions, it is still worth offering some of these so that pupils can physically see the 'squareness' in the sequences. The reason the symbolic structure is so crucial is the relationship between the value of *a* and the constant sequence that underpins the linear sequence, which in turn underpins the quadratic sequence; namely that the values in the constant sequence are twice the values of *a*. Once pupils understand the quadratic structure, we can create a logical argument as to why this is, which might go something like:

If all quadratic sequences have nth term of the form $T_n = an^2 + bn + c$ then the general form of the first three terms are $T_1 = a + b + c$, $T_2 = 4a + 2b + c$, $T_3 = 9a + 3b + c$. If we then examine the difference between these terms, we have $D_{1,2} = 3a + b$ and $D_{2,3} = 5a + b$, which would be the first two terms of the linear sequence that underpins the quadratic sequence. If we then examine the difference between these 2 we have $DD = 2a$. What is more, we can reason that this must always be the case because we can reason that there will only ever be a single occurrence of '*c*' in each term, and so this will always disappear when any two terms are subtracted. Similarly the coefficients of '*b*' in consecutive terms will themselves be consecutive integers, as they increase by 1 as *n* increases, and so any two differences will have a single occurrence of '*b*' each, which will then disappear when the differences are subtracted. Finally the coefficients of '*a*' in consecutive terms will be consecutive square numbers. The differences between consecutive square numbers are consecutive odd numbers, so in the linear sequence there will be consecutive odd coefficients of *a*, which will then lead to a constant sequence of $2a$.

We can also formally prove this algebraically:

Let $T_n = an^2 + bn + c$ then $T_{n+1} = a(n + 1)^2 + b(n + 1) + c$ and $T_{n+2} = a(n + 2)^2 + b(n + 2) + c$.

Expanding T_{n+1} and T_{n+2} and finding the differences between the terms gives $D_{n, n+1} = 2an + a + b$ and $D_{n+1, n+2} = 2an + 3a + b$. These are consecutive terms of the linear sequence that underpins the quadratic sequence written in terms of a and b. If we then subtract these, we will have the value of the constant sequence underpinning the linear sequence, and $DD = 2a$.

Recognising this relationship between the constant sequence that underpins the linear that underpins the quadratic and the value of the coefficient of n^2 in the nth term of the quadratic is, as I have said, crucial in forming a process for finding the nth term of a quadratic sequence, as it allows us to see how many 'squares' the sequence is based on. This can lead to an approach for finding the nth term of any quadratic sequence:

Find the nth term of the quadratic sequence 3, 7, 13, 21, 31, ...

We can see that the linear sequence underpinning this quadratic sequence is 4, 6, 8, 10, and therefore the constant sequence underpinning both sequences is 2, 2, 2, 2. This further implies that the coefficient, 'a', of n^2 is 1. This means that the nth term of this sequence is based on a single square, so we can create a sequence of squares and look at how we build from there to create the given sequence:

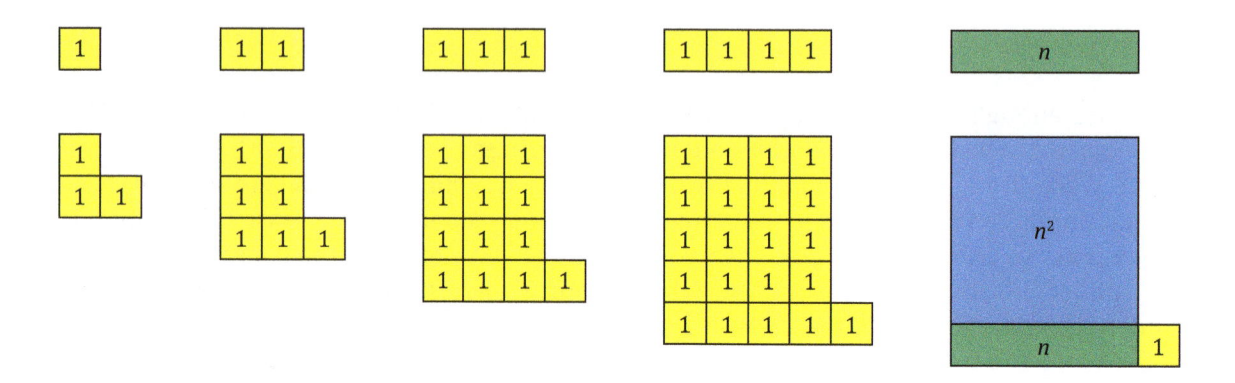

We can see that we are adding one more than the length of the square in each case, leading to the nth term $T_n = n^2 + n + 1$. Numerically, this could be seen as:

1	2	3	4	5	n
1	4	9	16	25	n^2
2	3	4	5	6	$n + 1$
3	7	13	21	31	$n^2 + n + 1$

Provided we can identify the coefficient of n^2 then the nice thing is that we can reduce the problem into that of finding the nth term of a linear sequence.

Find the nth term of the quadratic sequence 1, 2, 7, 16, 29, ...

In this case, the underpinning linear sequence is 1, 5, 9, 13, ... and so the constant sequence underpinning both is 4, 4, 4, ... This leads to the conclusion that the original quadratic is based on $2n^2$:

1	2	3	4	5	n
2	8	18	32	50	$2n^2$
−1	−6	−11	−16	−31	$-5n + 4$
1	2	7	16	29	$2n^2 - 5n + 4$

A major benefit of this approach is that it can potentially be generalised to sequences whose position to term rules are given by any polynomial function. Pupils who quickly grasp this sort of idea can be offered the opportunity to confirm this sort of conjecture.

A different possible approach is to use the algebraic relationships found in the argument/proof that the terms of the constant sequence are equal to half the coefficient of n^2. If we have already shown that the difference between the first two terms of any quadratic sequence is $3a + b$ and we already know the value of a, then we can find the value of b (technically we can use the difference of $2an + a + b$ between any two terms to find the value of b if we know the value of a). Similarly, once we have worked out the values of a and b we can use $an^2 + bn + c$ to find the value of c by equating to any specific term (i.e. $a + b + c$ is equal in value to the first term, or $4a + 2b + c$ is equal in value to the second term, etc.)

Once pupils are comfortable in identifying the nth term of a quadratic sequence we can offer pupils very similar problems to those we offered for linear sequences; remembering that rather than only providing two values, we will need to provide a minimum of three for pupils to establish the quadratic nature. There are plenty of practical problems or visual patterns that give rise to quadratic sequences such as the number of cubes in each row (not the number of cubes in total!):

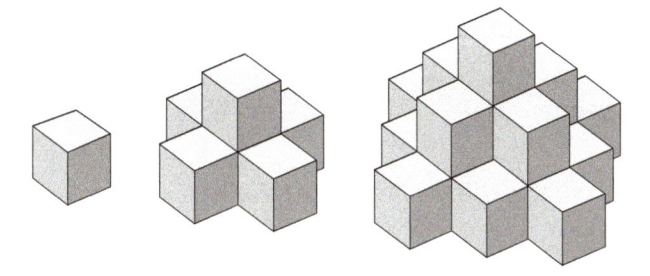

One of the images that can again support bridging from sequences into graph work is the arrangement of tiles to create the quadratic graph:

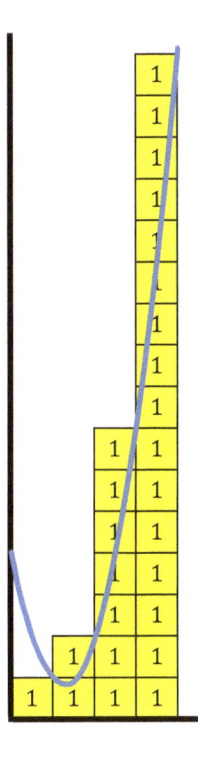

Of course, there are potentially different curves that could be fit to these values, and so knowing something about the parabolic shape of quadratic curves and things like the *y*-intercept of the curve and its links to the given quadratic function will be required to help support pupils in making the link more directly – this can once again be followed up with using dynamic geometry/graphing software to allow for further exploration. Following this, the same sort of interweaving/interweaving of other subject content that we saw with arithmetic sequences can be brought in to help pupils in reviewing and applying their knowledge both of sequences and of other concepts in mathematics.

As previously indicated, we could at this point continue to 'layer' sequences on top of the quadratic, leading to cubic, then 4th power and so on polynomial functions; and indeed pupils may be prompted to explore this as an extension to their work on arithmetic and quadratic sequences. However, another tack we could take here is to return to a sequence of constants and use them, not in an additive way to build a new sequence, but rather in a multiplicative way: i.e. rather than building a sequence with a common difference, instead building a sequence with a common ratio. This gives rise to the idea of a geometric sequence.

Subconcept: geometric sequences

Assuming pupils are comfortable with linear/arithmetic sequences prior to the introduction of geometric sequences, then a nice way to introduce geometric sequences is in contrast to arithmetic sequences.

What is the same and what is different about these two sequences?

2, 5, 8, 11, 14, ...

2, 6, 18, 54, 162, ...

This can serve to highlight to pupils that, whilst arithmetic sequences are built by taking a constant sequence as a common difference between terms, a geometric sequence is built by taking a constant sequence as a common ratio, i.e. $\frac{6}{2} = 3$, $\frac{18}{6} = 3$, $\frac{54}{18} = 3$, etc.

The creation of/use of term-to-term rules for geometric sequences is pretty much as straightforward as for arithmetic sequences (provided pupils are fluent with multiplication/division) and decidedly simpler than writing down term-to-term rules for quadratic sequences. However, creating the functional relationship between *n* and a geometric sequence is a little more problematic because *n* is fundamentally an additive sequence. Strictly, this is not necessary in the English compulsory curriculum (at least at the time of writing), but it has such strong links to other areas that are included that it makes perfect sense to explore at least a little way into the concept of the *n*th term of a geometric sequence.

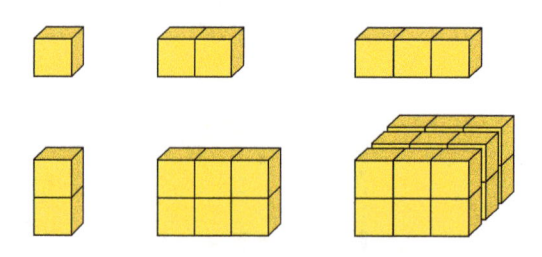

What we might be able to see here is that the relationship between n and the terms of the sequence comes from the number of **dimensions** that form the term; i.e. the first term is just shown by the height of the tower, the second by the area of the face, the third by the volume. Indeed, this links to why these sequences are known as geometric, as the increase in dimension caused by the repeated multiplication has geometric implications as we consider geometry in 1, 2, 3 (and more) dimensions.

What this, of course, leads to is the idea that the value of n will be reflected in a power for the position to term rule. This makes perfect logical sense as well – when looking at arithmetic sequences, the repeated additive change from term to term was reflected in the multiplicative coefficient of n, and so we might expect that a repeated multiplicative change would reflect in the base for a power of n. This means that it would be sensible to start any real exploration of geometric sequences with a look at different powers sequences.

1	2	3	4	5	n
$3^1 = 3$	$3^2 = 9$	$3^3 = 27$	$3^4 = 81$	$3^5 = 243$	$T_n = 3^n$

Here we can see the common ratio of 3 and its links to the base of the power sequence – although we are no longer representing this using tiles/blocks as we lack the required number of dimensions (at least in our area of the universe!). Once pupils are familiar with this link, we can explore multiplicative transformations of power sequences – perhaps starting with integer multiplications before looking at fractional one:

Find the nth term of the geometric sequence 12, 36, 108, 324, 729, ...

The fact that these terms still have a common ratio of 3 leads to the conclusion that this sequence is a multiplicative (not additive, as we shall see) transformation of the powers of 3:

1	2	3	4	5	n
$3^1 = 3$	$3^2 = 9$	$3^3 = 27$	$3^4 = 81$	$3^5 = 243$	3^n
12	36	108	324	729	$T_n = 4 \times 3^n$

We can see that if we create an additive transformation of a powers sequence, then we actually destroy the geometric nature (this is potentially worth exploring with pupils but only perhaps briefly to highlight why geometric sequences are multiplicative transformations of power sequences):

Find the terms of the sequence $T_n = 1 + 3^n$

1	2	3	4	5	n
$3^1 = 3$	$3^2 = 9$	$3^3 = 27$	$3^4 = 81$	$3^5 = 243$	3^n
4	10	28	82	244	$T_n = 1 + 3^n$

What we can see from this is that there is no longer a common ratio between the terms; instead there is a common ratio in the differences (which is what suggests this is an additive transformation of a powers sequence, as finding the difference would remove the additive transformation – exploring this might be an exercise for the very interested teenage learner; particularly the general idea that $b + a^{n+1} - (b + a^n) = a^{n+1} - a^n = a^n(a - 1)$ and what this means for the structure of the differences of sequences such as this). There is a nice link here to the fact that distributivity applies between powers and multiplication, and between multiplication and addition, but not between powers and addition.

We will also need to explore sequences that are a fractional transformation of a powers sequence:

Find the nth term of the geometric sequence 2, 6, 18, 54, 162.

Again, the common ratio of 3 leads to the conclusion that this is a multiplicative transformation of the powers of 3:

1	2	3	4	5	n
$3^1 = 3$	$3^2 = 9$	$3^3 = 27$	$3^4 = 81$	$3^5 = 243$	3^n
2	6	18	54	162	$T_n = \frac{2}{3} \times 3^n$

What this allows is to highlight the fact that $\frac{2}{3} \times 3^n = 2 \times 3^{n-1}$. We can also then reference this back to the sequence, demonstrating it from the fact that the sequence can be written as 2, 2 × 3, 2 × 3 × 3, 2 × 3 × 3 × 3 and so on. This can lead to the general symbolic structure $T_n = a \times r^{n-1}$. This has nice links to general exponential functions (which we will see later) but care must be taken to ensure pupils are clear that the exponent of $n - 1$ comes from the fact that we are starting with the first term, and so there is one less multiplication by 3 than there are terms. Otherwise, there is a potential confusion when introducing growth and decay.

Although representing geometric sequences beyond power 3 is difficult using increasing dimension, in common with other sequence types there is a nice tie in to graphical representation:

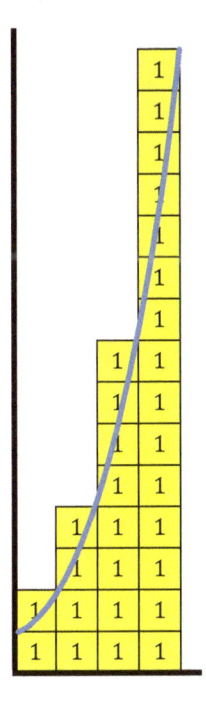

Of course, superficially this can look similar to a parabolic curve, so attention will need to be drawn to the difference between this type of graph and the graphs of quadratic functions.

Once more we can interweave a whole array of further maths concepts, including surds, algebraic manipulation, data handling, even probability (e.g. the probabilities of the four possible outcomes of an event form a geometric sequence with common ratio 2. Work out the probability of the most likely outcome – this can lead to a nice exploration for different numbers of possible outcomes and different common ratios).

Throughout exploring sequences, we have talked briefly about term-to-term rules, which are often written in words when pupils are first beginning to look at sequences. At some point in the learning journey, we will look to transfer this into a more symbolic notation, often called a recurrence relation.

Subconcept: recurrence relations

When introducing pupils to recurrence relations, there are often some issues around notation that pupils struggle with. It is worth spending time with pupils actually making sense of the notation before trying to use it to make sense of sequences. In particular, the mix of using letters a, u, t as well as using k and n:

> If a_1 is the first term of the sequence, what would be the third term of the sequence?
>
> If u_5 is the fifth term of the sequence, what would be the 11th term of the sequence?
>
> If t_n is a term of the sequence, what would be the next term of the sequence?
>
> If a_k is a term of the sequence, what would be the previous term of the sequence?

These do not need to be formal written questions, nor do they require formal written responses. We could simply put the first part on a board – for example, 'If u_n is a term of the sequence, what would be ...' and then prompt verbally for call and response or for mini-whiteboard response. The aim is to allow pupils to become comfortable with the notation so that when it comes to using it with recurrence relations, pupils are in a position to correctly 'decipher' the notation used in the recurrence relation. We can then move on to defining sequences using a recurrence relation:

> Write down the first five terms of the sequence defined by the recurrence relation $u_1 = 4$, $u_{n+1} = u_n + 7$.
>
> Write down the first five terms of the sequence defined by the recurrence relation $a_1 = 4$, $a_{n+1} = a_n + 2n$.
>
> Write down the first five terms of the sequence defined by the recurrence relation $t_1 = 4$, $t_{n+1} = 3t_n$.

Of course, what is nice here is that the first of these generates an arithmetic sequence, the second a quadratic and the third a geometric – pupils can be prompted to recognise this about these sorts of recurrence relation and potentially even be able to convert between a sequence defined recursively and a sequence defined directly in terms of n. However, we don't need to stop at these previously studied sequences (assuming they are all previously studied) and can define a wide array of different sequences using different recurrence relations. One that might appear obvious to teachers of mathematics are Fibonacci-style sequences.

Subconcept: Fibonacci-style sequences

The original Fibonacci sequence was created by Leonardo De Pisa (at least in Western mathematics) – nicknamed Fibonacci – in the late 12th or early 13th century. As many will know, the sequence arose from a problem involving rabbit breeding in one of Fibonacci's books. The sequence can be defined recursively as:

$u_1 = 1$, $u_2 = 1$, $u_{n+1} = u_n + u_{n-1}$

(Many define the first term of the sequence to be 0, but apparently Fibonacci himself did not include 0 in the sequence.[6])

In words, this is simply 'Every term is the sum of the previous two terms', which is why the first two terms of the sequence need to be defined explicitly. Other Fibonacci-style sequences are typically defined with the same recursive definition, but with different starting numbers, and are a particular case of the more general 'Lucas sequences' defined as $u_{n+1} = Pu_n + Qu_{n-1}$ for given constants P and Q as well as the first two terms being defined. Once pupils have been introduced to the original Fibonacci sequence, there are a multitude of ways to prompt exploration, from changing the first two terms to create other Fibonacci-style sequences, to defining sequences as each term being the sum of 3, 4, 5, etc. previous terms, or the difference between terms. It is nice just to allow pupils to follow up one or more of these different lines of enquiry and see what interesting sequences they can generate, particularly if they (prompted where necessary) remember to consider the use of negative and/or fractional values.

---
6 See https://www.britannica.com/science/Fibonacci-number.

One property that is nice about Fibonacci-style sequences is the ratio of the terms tending to the **Golden Ratio**, which ultimately becomes useful in finding a position to term rule for the Fibonacci sequence (the proof of which is beyond most school-age pupils) as well as occurring in a lot of other places to do with nature, beauty, music, etc.

Returning to recurrence relations in general, once pupils have gained familiarity with using them, we can then progress to writing them for given sequences, as well as solving problems with them.

A sequence is defined by the recurrence relation:

$u_1 = 2$, $u_{n+1} = au_n + b$

Given that $u_2 = 8$ and $u_3 = 26$, find the values of a and b.

(It would be beneficial for pupils to have already looked at simultaneous equations before solving this problem.)

A recurrence relation is (potentially) the first example that pupils will work with of an iterative process in maths. We will look at using iteration to find approximate solutions to equations in Chapter 9, but it may well be worth introducing the term when looking at recurrence relations (assuming these come before using iteration to solve equations).

Sequences might well be the first time that pupils encounter functional thinking explicitly (or it may not be); however, at some point we will want to introduce pupils to the formal concept and notation of functions.

Concept: functions

Prerequisites: Number/algebra, addition, subtraction, multiplication, division, equality, equivalence, proportion, inverse proportion.

Linked concepts: Formulae, sequences, measures, shape, chance, graphing.

At school-level maths, a function and a formula can seem very similar in nature, although they appear differently on the surface. Both tend to involve a relationship between a starting value/values and a final value. Formally, a function is a relationship between two sets, a domain and a co-domain, where the values the functions act on are values in the domain, and the values the function produces are the range. What is important here is that pupils recognise two aspects of functions:

1   They can be seen as transformative: One way of seeing functions is to see them as the action behind a change or transformation from one variable to another.

2   They can be seen as covariant: A different way of seeing functions is to see them as relations where changing one value changes the other in a predictable fashion. This is in contrast to the first view which is much more uni-directional.[7]

---

[7]   M. Ayalon, A. Watson and S. Lerman, Students' Conceptualisations of Function Revealed Through Definitions and Examples, *Research in Mathematics Education*, 19(1) (2017), 1–19. DOI: 10.1080/14794802.2016.1249397

There are different ways of 'seeing' functions, each of which draws attention to one of the two different aspects. For example, a mapping diagram is suggestive of the first aspect:

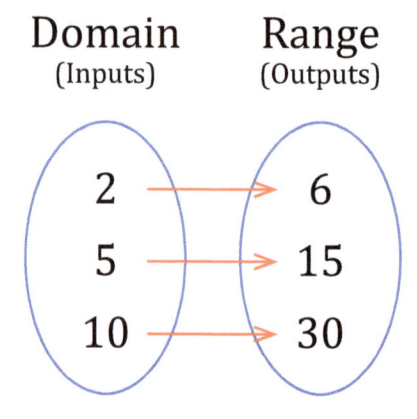

Domain (Inputs) **Range** (Outputs)

2 → 6
5 → 15
10 → 30

This function takes an input value and multiplies it by 3.

In this picture there is a strong implication of the values on the left being transformed to the values on the right. A function machine provides a similar view:

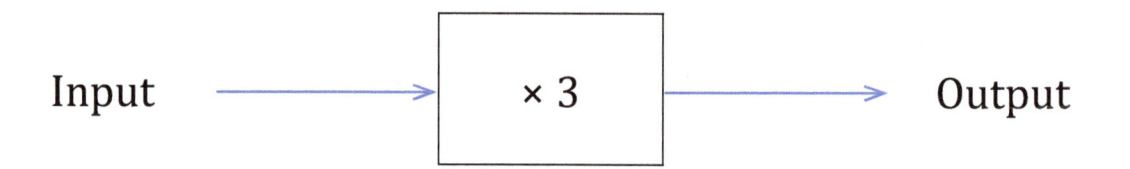

Input → × 3 → Output

Whereas if we look at a table of values, we can perhaps see more of the covariation:

x	y
2	6
5	15
10	30

Here we can see the same relationship, but perhaps more readily in both directions. It is also potentially more natural for us to notice how changing one value would change the other. For example:

1. What happens to y if x changes from 1 to 2?
2. What happens to y if x changes from 8 to 9?
3. What happens to y if x changes from 8 to 10?
4. What happens to x if y changes from 1 to 10?
5. What happens to y if x changes by 10?
6. What happens to x if y changes by 10?

7   What happens to y if x changes from 10 to 1?

8   What happens to y if x changes from $\frac{1}{2}$ to 1?

9   What happens to y if x changes by a?

10 What happens to x if y changes by a?

11 What happens to y if x changes from a to b?

The other representation that highlights the covariation between the two variables is a graphical representation plotted on a Cartesian axis. We will look at this more in Chapter 13.

What is important across all three of these views is that pupils recognise that the 'function' is the word we use for the connection between the variables (in this case it might be considered the 'multiply by 3' function or '3 of' function). When pupils begin to represent functions algebraically, their focus is often incorrectly around the variable used for the 'input' rather than the more important aspect that is the relationship connecting the 'input' and 'output'. As teachers, we can support directing pupil attention to the relationship by using the different representations and highlighting the connection over the values/variables. In addition, once pupils are beginning to represent functions algebraically, we can potentially use different variables/values to highlight the invariant nature of the relationship.

Given $f(x) = (2x - 1)^2 + 7$, write down in similar form:

1   $f(y)$

2   $f(a)$

3   $f(5)$

4   $f(1000)$

5   $f(-8)$

6   $f(\frac{3}{4})$

7   $f(x + 1)$

8   $f(y + 1)$

9   $f(2x)$

10 $f(px)$

The idea here is that pupils have a clear understanding of the role of f in this situation, and the fact that it is f that performs the transformation/creates the relationship. In this context pupils should be seeing f as the name of the relationship between the 'input' and 'output' values – the series of operators that transforms the input into the output. When f is expressed algebraically, x is just a convenient variable to apply f to in order to communicate what f does. This is what we should be trying to make clear to pupils with a combination of activities like this combined with representing functions in different forms (including algebraically). Each opportunity should be used to draw attention to what the function is doing in each case – the relationship it is creating between variables and how this can be interpreted as transforming one variable to another. This includes using alternative notation for defining functions algebraically, i.e. $f:x \rightarrow (2x - 1)^2 + 7$, which arguably highlights the transformative role of f more fully than the alternative $f(x) =$ notation, which could be seen to highlight the covariance.

Once pupils have a clear idea about what functions are, we can move on to looking at important aspects of functions, in particular the creation of composite and inverse functions.

Subconcept: composite functions

The classic issue pupils have with composite functions is the order of composition, i.e. with the composite fg, recognising that this is f applied after g. Part of this issue can be alleviated by the sort of activity that we looked at above, which included substitution of other functions into the given function f. Before looking at the notation for formal composition, it is potentially worth reinforcing this just by looking at 'composite' functions, and prompting pupils to identify the simpler functions that have been used and the order in which they are used, perhaps with an activity like the following.

Each of the following functions has been built using '×3', '+2' and/or '²'. Write down which of these has been used *and* in what order.

a $f(x) = 3x + 2$
b $f(x) = 3(x + 2)$
c $f(x) = x^2 + 2$
d $f(x) = 3x^2$
e $f(x) = (3x)^2$
f $f(x) = 3x^2 + 2$
g $f(x) = 3(x^2 + 2)$
h $f(x) = 9x^2 + 2$
i $f(x) = x^2 + 4x + 4$
j $f(x) = 3x^2 + 12x + 12$
k $f(x) = 9x^2 + 12x + 4$

From here we might bring in function notation for each part but retain the separation of the functions.

If $f(x) = 3x$, $g(x) = x + 2$ and $h(x) = x^2$, write down:

a $f(x + 3)$
b $g(5x)$
c $h(2x + 1)$
d $f(g(x))$
e $f(h(x))$
f $f(f(x))$
g $g(f(x))$
h $g(h(x))$
i $g(g(x))$
j $h(f(x))$
k $h(g(x))$
l $h(h(x))$
m $f(g(h(x)))$
n $h(g(f(x)))$
o $f(f(g(g(h(h(x))))))$

From here it should be a relatively short step to go from $f(g(x))$ to $fg(x)$, which can be reinforced with some further questions like the ones above without the brackets separating the functions, potentially with well-chosen multiple-choice answers to help assess pupil understanding – bringing back the mapping diagrams and/or function machines to help visualise the order of composition. It is also worth changing up the variables at certain points (perhaps even defining one of the functions using a different variable (see below for an example). An activity like the one below might be beneficial:

Given $f(x) = 2x$, $g(y) = 4 - y$ and $h(z) = z^2$, build as many different functions as you can in terms of the variable w.

As well as identifying the composition.

If $f(x) = x^2$ and $g(x) = x - 2$ write each of the functions h below as a composite of f and g:

a $h(x) = (x - 2)^2$ c $h(x) = x - 4$ e $h(x) = x^4 - 4$

b $h(x) = x^2 - 2$ d $h(x) = x^4$ f $h(x) = (x - 2)^2 - 2$

Question 3 in the document linked in the footnote is also relatively nice for prompting thinking about composite functions. Although the context is somewhat oversimplified, it does at least provide some opportunity for thinking about interpretation of composites.[8]

Alongside composition of functions, we will also want to explore inverse functions with pupils.

Subconcept: inverse functions

Technically, in order for an inverse 'function' to exist, we need to place certain constraints on certain functions. This tends to be explored more beyond compulsory mathematics study at 16, so we will not say more about it here. In terms of school-level mathematics, the inverse function can be seen as the function that 'undoes' another function, i.e. the function f^{-1} such that $ff^{-1}(x) = f^{-1}f(x) = x$.

A function machine is often used to introduce inverse functions:

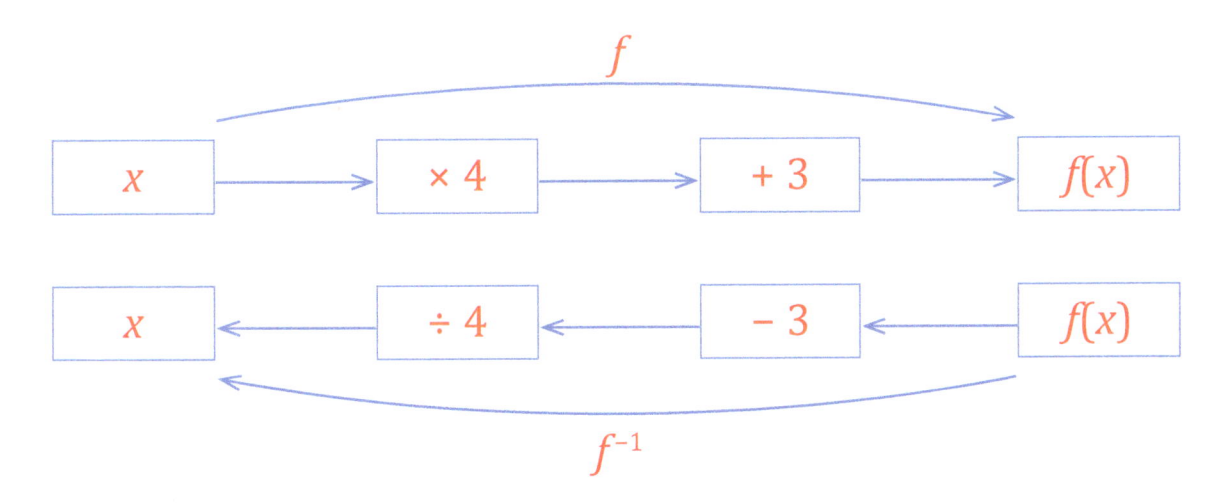

However, care should be taken as, at some point, we will want to draw pupil attention to the fact that inverse functions and transposition of formulae are the same underlying idea. The function machine highlights the transformative nature of functions, whereas the transposition of formulae requires a recognition of the relationship between the variables. In addition, functions like $f(x) = \frac{3x}{x-1}$ are difficult to make sense of using a function machine, and so we can't really use a function machine to make sense of the inverse function. As an alternative, we might use the function machine to highlight an alternative way of seeing the inverse function is that if $f(x) = y$ then $f^{-1}(y) = x$. What follows is if we let $y = \frac{3x}{x-1}$ then transpose this formula to give $x = \frac{y}{y-3}$, then this implies $f^{-1}(y) = \frac{y}{y-3}$, which we can then write using any variable we like, including $f^{-1}(x) = \frac{x}{x-3}$.

---

8 See https://www.austincc.edu/lochbaum/08-1%20Composition%20of%20Functions.pdf.

One thing that we should draw pupil attention to when looking at functions like the one above is the need to go from *x* (or whichever variable we use) appearing more than once, to *x* appearing only once. We can then highlight the two potential ways that this can happen (at least in school-level maths); namely factorisation provided the powers of *x* are the same or completing the square. This becomes a nice opportunity to interweave completing the square:

If $f(x) = 2x^2 - 8x + 7$ then find $f^{-1}(x)$.

$y = 2x^2 - 8x + 7$

$y = 2(x^2 - 4x) + 7$

$y = 2[(x - 2)^2 - 4] + 7$

$y = 2(x - 2)^2 - 1$

$y + 1 = 2(x - 2)^2$

$\frac{y+1}{2} = (x - 2)^2$

$\pm \sqrt{\frac{y+1}{2}} = x - 2$

$2 \pm \sqrt{\frac{y+1}{2}} = x$

$2 \pm \sqrt{\frac{y+1}{2}} = x$

$2 \pm \sqrt{\frac{y+1}{2}} = f^{-1}(y)$

$2 \pm \sqrt{\frac{x+1}{2}} = f^{-1}(x)$

Another thing to consider when looking at inverse functions with pupils is how we want pupils to make sense of functions like $f(x) = 4 - x$ and $f(x) = \frac{1}{x-4}$. With the first of these, pupils can, of course, rewrite this as $f(x) = -x + 4$, which would lead to $f^{-1}(x) = \frac{x-4}{-1} = 4 - x$, which is identical to $f(x)$. This could lead to us talking about the idea of 'self-inversing', and potentially viewing this as a 'subtract from' function, whose inverse is also the 'subtract from' function. If we apply the same idea to $f(x) = 4 - 3x$ we get:

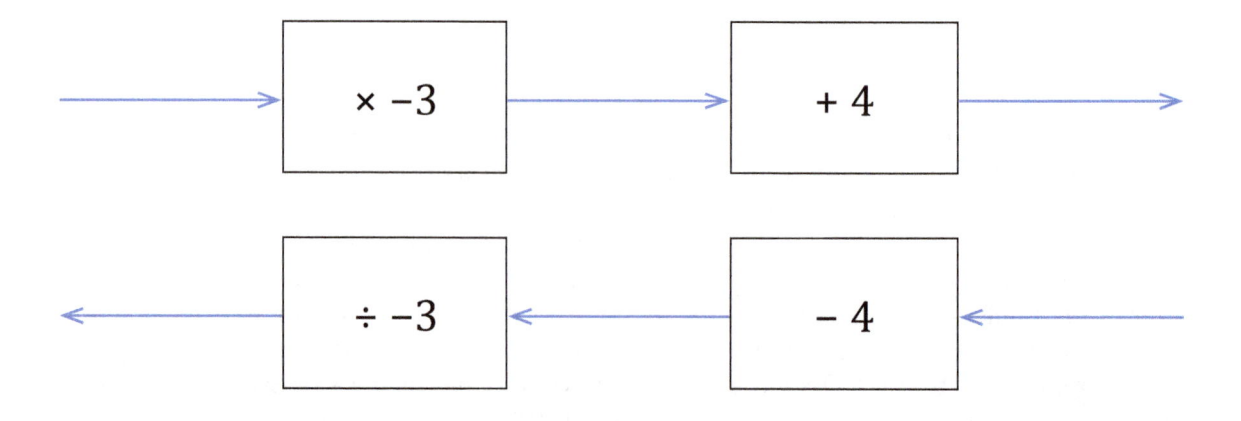

⟶ [× −3] ⟶ [+ 4] ⟶

⟵ [÷ −3] ⟵ [− 4] ⟵

Or

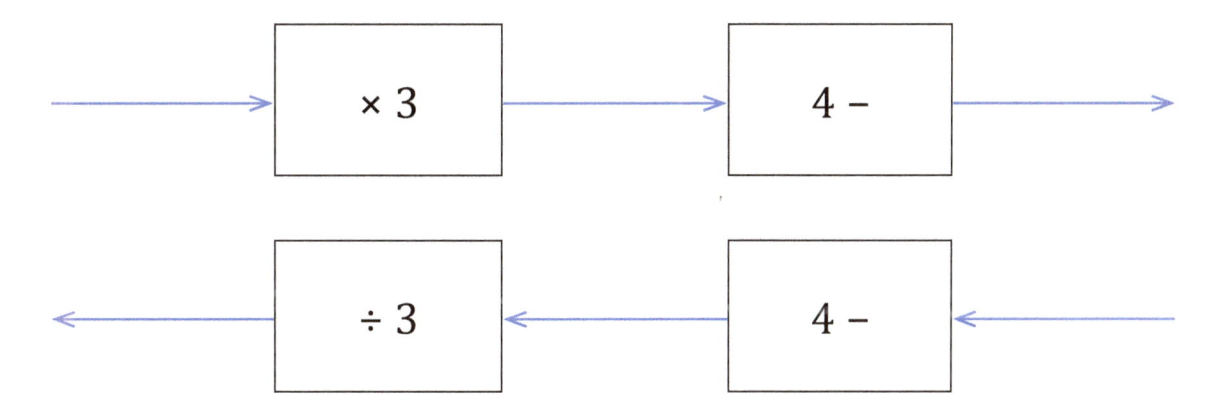

[Flow diagram: forward arrow → ×3 → 4 − → ; reverse arrow ← ÷3 ← 4 − ←]

In both cases the result ends up as $f^{-1}(x) = \frac{4-x}{3}$.

Similarly, in the case of $f(x) = \frac{1}{x-4}$, we will want to introduce pupils to the 'reciprocal' function. Of course, pupils should already be familiar with the idea of reciprocals from working with fractions, so the jump to apply a function called 'reciprocal' (shown as $\frac{1}{x}$) should be a small one. Pupils can then explore the idea of the inverse of the reciprocal function, and meet the idea that the reciprocal function is also self-inversing so that finding $f^{-1}(x)$ can be seen as:

$y = \frac{1}{x-4}$

$\frac{1}{y} = x - 4$

$\frac{1}{y} + 4 = x$

$\frac{1}{y} + 4 = f^{-1}(y)$

$\frac{1}{x} + 4 = f^{-1}(x)$

or

$y = \frac{1}{x-4}$

$y(x - 4) = 1$

$x - 4 = \frac{1}{y}$

which then proceeds as above.

There are many different classes of function that pupils will be introduced to during compulsory school mathematics. We have already seen things like the reciprocal function as well as seeing things like '× 3' or 'square' as functions. At some point pupils will also meet trigonometric functions (we will look at those in Chapter 10) and potentially things like statistical functions. One class of functions I do want to look at before the end of this chapter is exponential functions.

Subconcept: exponential functions

Pupils may well have met specific examples of exponential functions in two places:

1   Geometric sequences.
2   Repeated percentage change.

We have looked at geometric sequences already but have not yet explored percentages beyond proportion. Part of a pupil's journey in learning about percentages should ideally involve making the transition from seeing percentages proportionally into seeing percentages functionally using a multiplier. So pupils see 'increase by 13%' as synonymous with the function $f(x) = 1.13x$. This significantly increases the efficiency of pupils' percentage calculations, as well as allowing access to problems that are more difficult to solve using proportional structures, for example:

> A population starts the decade at 20 million and increases by 2.5% every year for 10 years. What is the population at the end of the decade?

Whilst this can be solved using proportional structures, those tend to be longer and require more effort (in this case repeated redefinition of the whole). Instead, approaching this problem functionally leads relatively smoothly to the calculation 20×1.025^{10} (at least, provided pupils are clear and comfortable with the idea of multipliers).

To support pupils generalising this sort of idea, we might offer two related problems:

> What is the same and what is different about each of these?
>
> Find the remaining amount when 1000 is reduced by 10% every year for 10 years.
>
> A geometric sequence has first term 900 and common ratio 0.9. Find the 10th term of the sequence.

This gives us an opportunity to look at why 1000×0.9^n and $900 \times 0.9^{n-1}$ give the same result, not just when $n = 10$ but for any value of n. We can also highlight that this sort of structure applies in more than one situation, and is, in fact, a general mathematical function called an exponential (pupils will hopefully have already met the language of 'exponent' as an alternative to 'index' when looking at powers). Pupils should be introduced to the general functional form of an exponential $f(x) = Ab^x$, and come to understand that A is the initial value of function (i.e. the value of $f(0)$) and b is the growth or decay factor. We can offer pupils activities to prompt both of these separately – for example, by asking pupils to reason why $f(0)$ will be equal to A no matter what the value of b, presenting problems in different contexts and asking for 'initial values', given a value of b asking how many times bigger/smaller the value of $f(x)$ gets when x goes from 0 to 1, 1 to 2, 2 to 3, 10 to 11, 174 to 175, etc. Activities like the one below are also useful:[9]

> State whether each of the following represent growth or decay.
>
> | | | |
> |---|---|---|
> | $y = 50 \times 2^x$ | $M = 0.5 \times 3^n$ | $H = k \times \left(\frac{1}{2}\right)^t$ |
> | $A = 25 \times 0.7^b$ | $K = 3 \times 5^t$ | $M = a \times \left(\frac{a}{b}\right)^n$ |

---

[9] See https://allaboutmaths.aqa.org.uk/attachments/7453.doc.

$$A = 2b \times 4^t \qquad Y = 0.5z \times 2^x$$

Of course, a big part of studying exponential functions at school level is in studying the graphs produced by plotting exponential functions; we will look at this in more detail in Chapter 13.

There are many practical situations that give rise to exponential functions – many phenomena in the physical sciences (radioactive half-life, cooling, etc.) behave exponentially. Exposing pupils to questions in these contexts will help firm up the links across the curriculum. In addition, we can interweave other maths areas, particularly the solution of simultaneous equations:

> $f(x) = A \times B^x$. Given that $f(1) = 27$ and $f(3) = 546.75$, find the values of A and b.

Formally this gives rise to the equations $Ab = 27$ and $Ab^3 = 546.75$, which can be solved by dividing the second equation by the first to give $b^2 = 20.25$ and therefore $b = 4.5$ (pupils may reason this less formally by making the link to geometric sequences and recognising $27 \times b^2 = 546.75$). Note b cannot be -4.5 as in exponential functions b has to be a positive number not equal to 1. Once the value of b is established, A can be determined from either equation (although the first is clearly more straightforward).

As growth and decay are ultimately about a repeated multiplicative function, we can also interweave other ways of communicating multiplicative relationships. We have seen already examples that use percentages, fractions and decimals, but haven't yet seen ratio used to communicate the growth/decay factor:

> A website is increasing its number of visits in the ratio 20:23 each month. If the website was getting 10,000 hits a month initially, how many hits will it be getting a year later?

Throughout the earlier chapters we have sometimes modelled numbers as continuous measures. However, we are yet to put the concept of 'measure' and 'measurement' on a secure footing. This is where we will turn our attention in Chapter 8.

Chapter 8

Measures

In my experience, pupils are often taught to measure quantities in a very instrumental way. They are taught some units of measure, shown them on a scale, and told to read numbers from the scale. Most of the teaching is around being able to read different scales, or the units used for different quantities. Both of these are important but, for me, premature. The key idea in 'measuring' is quantification. Pupils will have early developed notions of measurement, in terms of being able to see more or less (for example). The understanding we want pupils to gain in teaching measurement explicitly is that we are trying to actually assign a value to the quantity, so these comparisons can go from 'this is more' to 'this is x amount more' or 'this is x times greater than'. Whenever we want to talk about measuring with pupils, our first question (in my opinion) should be, 'How can we assign a value to this quantity?' For pupils to understand the idea of measures, they need to be able to see what different measurable quantities have in common, what is needed to be able to assign a value to a physical quantity, and this typically starts with the definition of a unit.

Concept: units of measure

Prerequisites: Numbers, subtraction, division, algebra.

Linked concepts: Equivalence, proportionality, shape, transformation, graphing, data analysis. Also depending on exactly how the idea of measures and measuring is to be approached and at what point pupils are at, accuracy can be seen either as a prerequisite or as a linked concept.

There are thousands of units both modern and historical that humans have used in different cultures for every imaginable physical quantity. It is always worth taking some of these and actually looking at their definitions (the cubit and the yard were two of my favourites when 'dabbing' was popular):

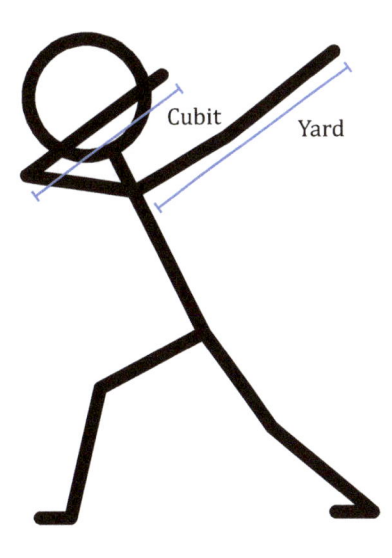

The goal here is not necessarily that pupils will remember lots of different definitions for different units, rather that pupils recognise that before a quantity can be measured, a unit must be defined for it to be measured against. Another activity I often use in the classroom is to define nonsense units and measure things against a nonsense unit (this can be as simple as defining myself as a 'Mattock' and measuring other pupils' heights against me roughly as, say, 0.8 Mattocks). Pupils can use their own hands to measure the lengths of things, or other objects such as pencils. This understanding of choosing a unit is invaluable when we look at measuring things that pupils tend to struggle with, such as measuring turn or compound measures.

So, having looked at the importance of defining a unit when it comes to measurement, we can then move on to looking at how we use these units to actually measure a quantity. A good idea is to look at length initially, and to have pupils estimate the length of objects compared to the length of 1 metre. We can simply hold up a metre stick and ask pupils how many of those it would take to reach the ceiling, to be as tall as a house, to fit across the length of the room, etc. Accuracy is not necessarily the goal here; rather the goal is to highlight to pupils that they are making a comparison between the defined unit length and the length to be measured. The same thing can be done with in-class objects and the length of a single centimetre or decimetre. These lengths can be drawn on the board (as accurately as possible) and pupils can compare the lengths of objects in the room to this length.

This sort of comparison is precisely the same type of multiplicative comparison that we saw in division, i.e. a multiplicative comparison. The act of redefining the divisor to have a value of 1 is akin to defining the unit of measure, and then the measuring of the object is evaluating how the object compares to the unit in a multiplicative way. Making this link explicit with pupils can be really helpful in supporting pupils' sense-making when it comes to working with units of measure. This can be made explicit by a teacher drawing attention to it; usually by having the idea of measuring side by side with a comparative division:

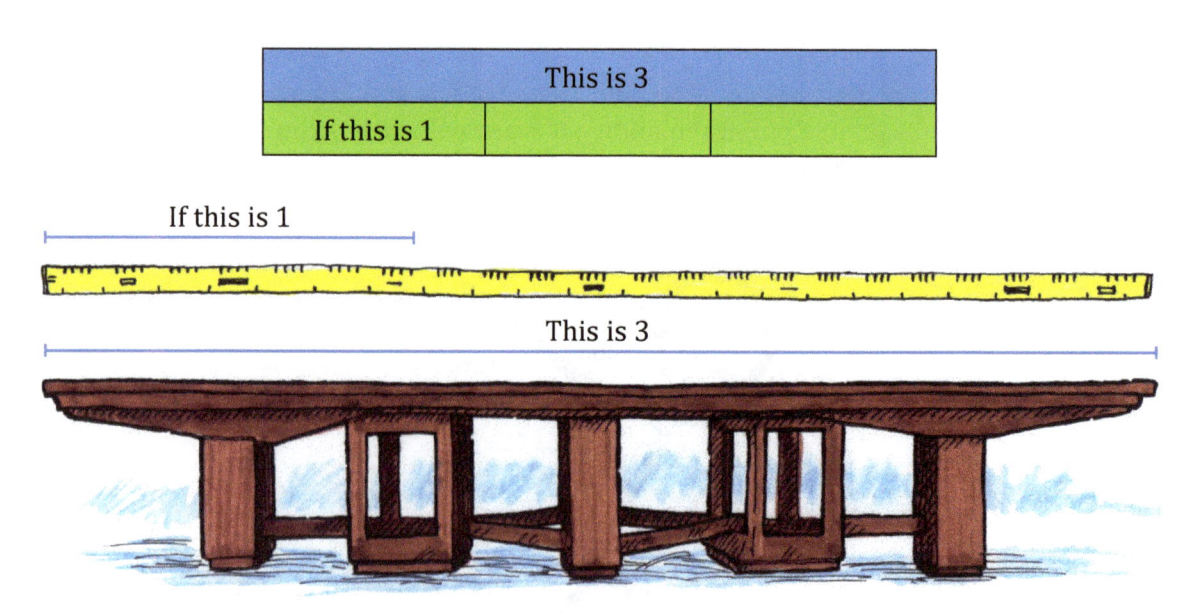

Alternatively, a questioning activity can be set up to draw attention to the comparative nature of measurement and the same nature of division whereby a teacher offers questions either to the whole class, groups of pupils or individual pupils that prompt them to recall this way of making sense of division and consider it compared to unit measure.

Having seen this with length, it is then a good idea to offer further opportunities with different units of measure. Getting pupils to compare the weight of different objects against the weight of a kilogram (or gram) mass can be a nice activity to further illustrate the concept. Again, this can be done informally at first by pupils holding a kilogram mass in one hand and an object in the other (provided they are strong enough!) and then more formally using a balance scale. A similar illustration can be done with a bucket scale and capacity, by filling one of the buckets from an unmarked bottle or pitcher, and then adding water from a measuring jug or cylinder until it balances.

A nice one to look at following this is time. Obviously, time can't be 'weighed' using a comparison scale, but we can compare times with a unit time – probably a second, unless you are going to spend a significant part of the lesson on the activity. I like to have pupils try and time 100 seconds in their head (I don't use a minute to avoid confusion with units) before standing up to show they think the correct time has elapsed. I then record the times of the pupil who is first to stand, last to stand and closest to the correct time. This is just to reinforce again the comparative nature of such a measurement – just make sure you remember to take your clock down first!

So where does this leave the use of the scale then? Well, the scale is a tool to make the comparison easier. Instead of having to compare the size of an object to a single unit, we can place multiple units along the scale to allow for a more straightforward comparison. However, care must still be taken when introducing pupils to these comparisons. Consider the picture below:

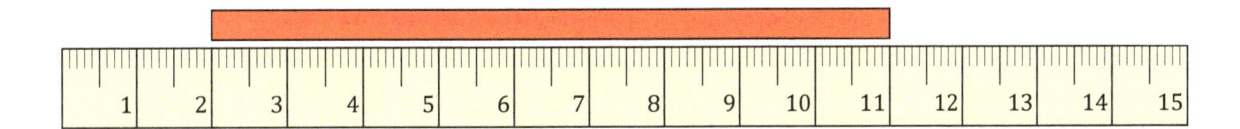

A classic mistake in this situation is for pupils to read this as 11 cm long, because they are looking at the final value rather than how many centimetres long the object is. It is important to ensure that when pupils are first using a scale for measuring that they recognise that there is still a comparison to the size of the unit going on, and so the object is 9 cm long because it is 9 times longer than a single centimetre.

This sort of activity works really well for length, as different objects can be started at different points along the ruler. For something to prompt pupils to think a little more, we can offer something like this:

> The red bar is a whole number of centimetres long. What is the smallest length the bar could be? What is the largest length the bar could be?

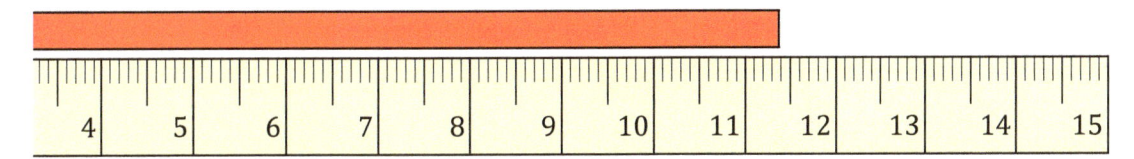

It is harder to create activities like this with other measures as starting the measuring at anywhere other than 0. One possibility (once suitable units for weight/mass and capacity are defined) is to use weighing scales with one object already on the scale and then adding another, or to use a measuring cylinder/jug with some liquid already in, and then adding more, as per the pictures below:

Activities such as these can then prompt an interesting discussion about when the measure can simply be read directly from the scale and when it can't. This will bring into focus the importance of starting from the 0 on the scale. Most of the above activities will actually be solved by subtracting one value from the other, and we draw pupils' attention to the fact that what this subtracting is doing is translating this scale back to a start point of 0. This is made easier if pupils have learnt that the idea of 'difference' in subtraction is intimately related to the idea of changing the subtrahend to 0 and applying the same change to the minuend. Recognising the importance of the scale having an initial value of 0 is important when pupils then meet more unfamiliar measures, such as measures of turn.

Subconcept: measuring turn

Measuring turn is something that pupils struggle with much more then measuring length, mass and capacity. There are two big contributors that mean pupils can struggle with this more than other measures:

1   Pupils are not clear on what an angle is and how it is created.

2   Pupils do not appreciate the commonalities between using a protractor to measure an angle and the general practice of using a scale to measure a quantity.

When introducing the idea of measuring turn, it is important that pupils understand what an angle is and how it is created. An angle is the name given to the measure of turn from one straight line to another, i.e. how much you would need to turn one line through so that it is coincident with another line. Angles are created when two lines meet at a point, and pupils need to appreciate this so that they can appreciate the importance of the 'hinge point' when using a protractor.

The second issue arises when pupils don't have an explicit idea of what it means to use a scale to help with measuring. If pupils are already familiar with the idea that we start measuring from the 'zero' on the scale, and that we are using the scale to see how many times bigger than a single unit the quantity we are trying to measure is, then we can draw attention to these when showing pupils how to measure turn, and highlight how we are doing this when we demonstrate measuring turn. Of course, before pupils actually measure angles, we will need to define the unit of measure (again, highlighting the commonalities between measuring turn and measuring other quantities). In school-age maths, the unit pupils will use is the degree (not to be confused with degrees centigrade, Fahrenheit or Kelvin in measuring temperature). The degree is a relatively arbitrary unit for turn, but we can introduce it in terms of its historical links[1] to Babylonians in order to help motivate why there are defined to be 360° in a full turn. It is also then worth making sure pupils understand at least that, as a consequence of this, there will 180° in a half turn (as most protractors are 180° protractors) and 90° in a right-angle/quarter turn (as this is often a key point on a protractor).

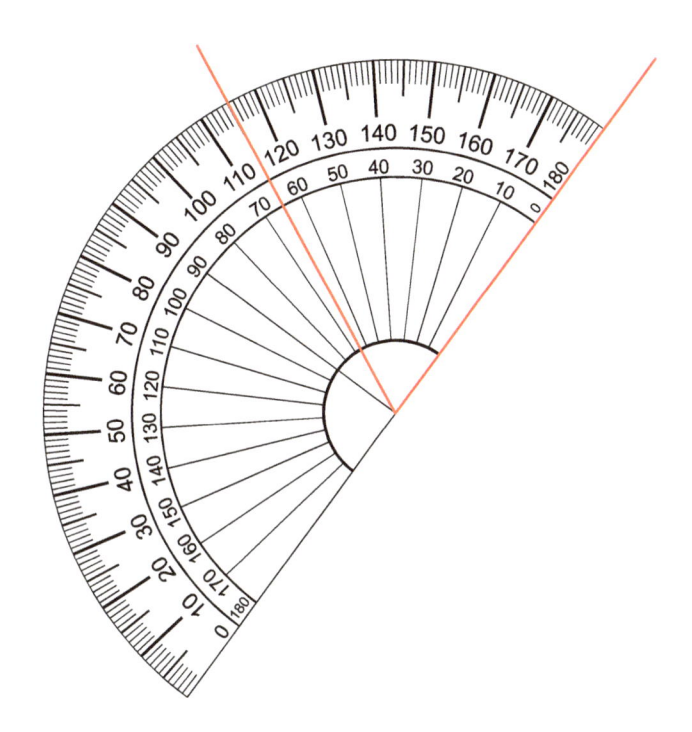

When showing pupils measuring turn using a protractor, we can point out to pupils that the reason we are lining up one of the lines that creates the angle with the bottom of the protractor is because that is the 'zero' on the scale (in common with using scales in other scenarios), and that the reason the point at the centre of the base of the protractor is placed on the point where the lines meet is because that is the hinge point that creates the angle.

One of the big problems that pupils have with physically using a protractor is that protractors often come with two scales so that angles can be measured both clockwise and anticlockwise. Again, it is worth being explicit with pupils as to why this is, and so we can identify which scale to use by identifying whether the 'turn' from the zero through the angle we are measuring is a clockwise turn or an anticlockwise turn. We can also draw attention to the 'degree' as a unit of measuring turn, in the same way that 'metre' or 'centimetre' are units for measuring length. Measuring this turn then, in the same way as measuring any other physical quantity, is about establishing how many times bigger this turn is than a single degree worth of turn. We can physically count this round from the zero to see how many times bigger this is, and when stating our answer can say things like 'This angle 65 times bigger than a single degree, so it is 65°.' I wouldn't recommend doing this every time – pupils need to be clear that the last part of this sentence communicates the first part – but initially this can bring pupils' attention to the similarity this process has with measuring other quantities.

---

1 M. Ronan, Full Circle, *History Today* (4 April 2020). Available at: https://www.historytoday.com/history-matters/full-circle.

This doesn't mean pupils won't still make mistakes with measuring turn, but it does mean that we have established a common thought process that we can utilise when pupils do. We can remind pupils about the importance of starting the measuring process on a scale at zero and check that pupils have done that and remembered the importance of that. We can remind pupils that an angle is created by two lines meeting at a point and check that pupils have paid attention to the point where the lines meet when using their protractor. We can remind pupils that one scale on the protractor measures clockwise and the other anticlockwise, and check that they have identified whether the line they have set as 'zero' is being turned clockwise or anticlockwise. Another thing that I often do is get pupils to check whether the angle they are measuring is acute, right, obtuse or reflex, and then to check whether the value they have measured makes sense in that context.

Another misconception that pupils can have around angle measurement is thinking that this:

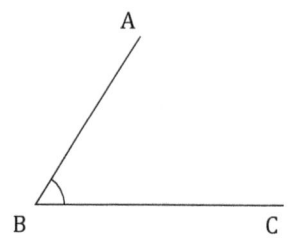

Is a smaller angle than this:

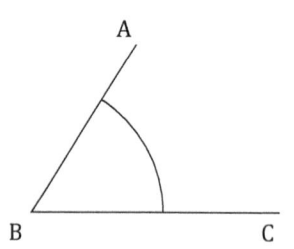

One thing I find quite useful in looking at this misconception is my classroom door! By opening my classroom door to a certain amount, I can ask pupils if different points on the door have turned by different amounts. Pupils are much happier to accept that the amount of turn is equal when they can physically see that there is only one turn going on.

When pupils are measuring angles, it is important for these angles to appear in lots of different diagram types. It is very common for pupils to only be asked to measure angles where the hinge point is at the end of the two lines, like the point B in the diagrams above. This can lead to pupils not being comfortable with angles that don't look like this, particularly when it comes to calculating angles in different diagrams (which we will look at in Chapter 10). As a good rule of thumb, a diagram that can be used for angle calculation can also be used for angle measurement simply by removing the values of any given angle and the words 'not drawn to scale' where they appear.[2]

---

2   Adapted from Tristanjones, Maths GCSE worksheet: Using Angle Facts, *TES* (20 January 2015). Available at: https://www.tes.com/teaching-resource/maths-gcse-worksheet-using-angle-facts-6159350.

Measure all the angles in these diagrams:

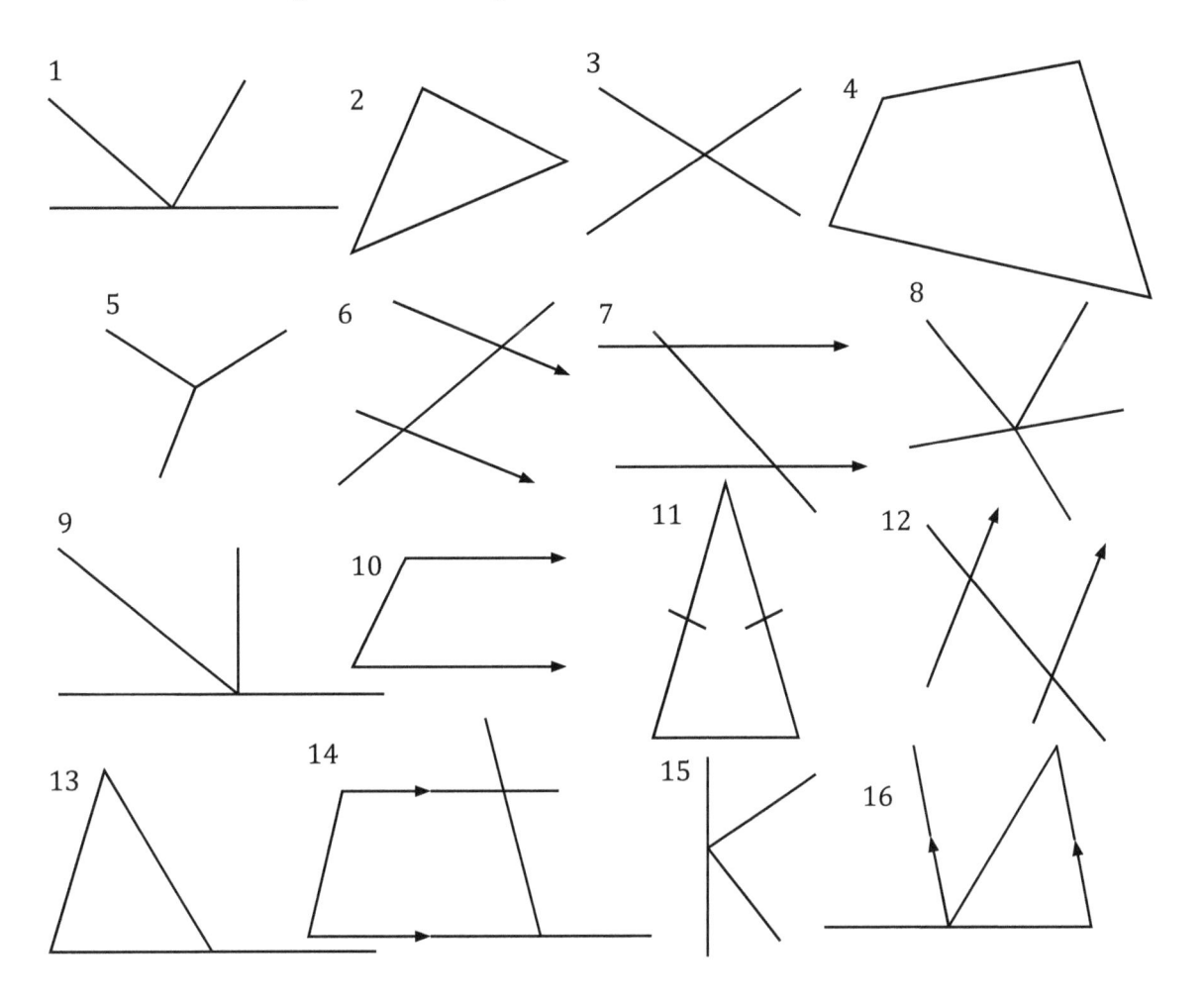

1 2 3 4
5 6 7 8
9 10 11 12
13 14 15 16

When it comes to measuring angles, pupils can have particular difficulties with measuring reflex angles, especially if using a 180° protractor. There are a couple of different strategies pupils could use for this, and it may well be worth offering reflex angles to pupils and looking at the strategies they invent to measure the reflex angles. One strategy that we might want to point pupils towards is to measure the size of the non-reflex angle in the diagram and then calculate the size of the reflex angle, using the fact that a full turn is defined to be 360°. We might look at this calculation skill specifically with pupils, using activities like the ones below:

If the angles given are measured in a diagram, work out the size of the reflex angle in each diagram.

a	40°	h	160°	o	18°
b	65°	i	95°	p	106°
c	80°	j	115°	q	158°
d	35°	k	27°	r	99°
e	55°	l	62°	s	124°
f	110°	m	79°	t	171°
g	135°	n	33°		

If these are the size of the reflex angles, what is the size of the angle you would measure?

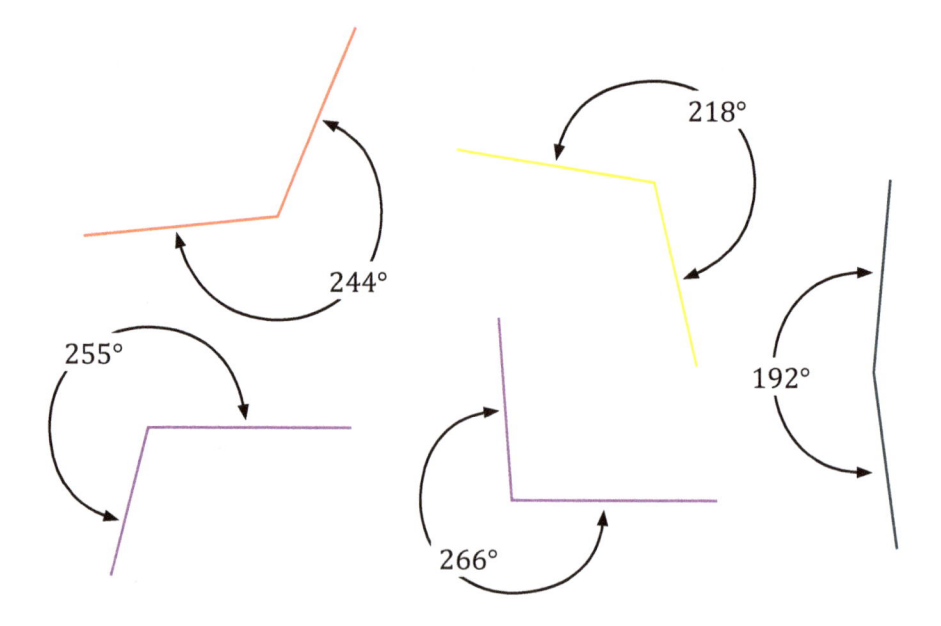

[Diagram showing five angles with reflex measurements labelled: 244°, 218°, 255°, 192°, 266°]

One specific application of angle measure is within bearings. There is a little way around pupils being introduced to the 'rules' for bearings – these are practical in nature rather than particularly mathematical.

Bearings are angles:

1. measured between north and the direction of travel.
2. measured in a clockwise direction.
3. given using three figures.

In introducing bearings, pupils can simply be offered different diagrams showing straight-line travel between two points and an appropriate North line and asked to measure the required bearing. Calculations will naturally follow (we will see examples of these in Chapter 10). However, there are some excellent reasoning activities that pupils can work with prior to getting into calculation. The following from Dan Draper are some of the best out there (at least at the time of writing!):[3]

---

3   D. Draper, Reasoning with Bearings, *Opinions Nobody Asked For* (n.d.). Available at: https://mrdrapermaths.wordpress.com/2020/02/23/reasoning-with-bearings/.

Measures

1   The bearing of A from B is 180°. Sketch the north line.

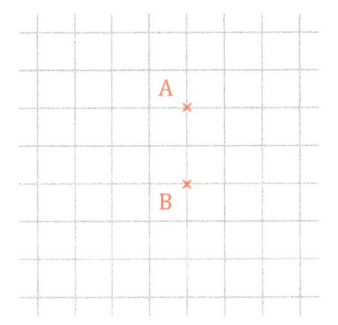

3   The bearing of A from B is 180°. Sketch a different north line.

5   The bearing of A from B is 180°. Sketch a different north line.

2   Point C is on a bearing of 045° from B and lies on a gridline intersection. Sketch C.

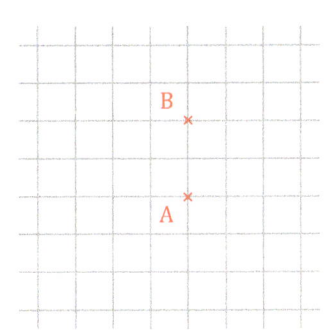

4   Point C is on a bearing of 045° from B and lies on a gridline intersection. Sketch C.

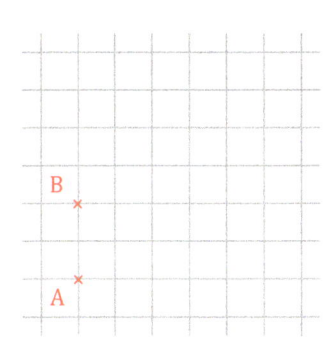

6   Point C is on a bearing of 045° from B and lies on a gridline intersection. Sketch C.

1   The bearing of A from B is 180°. Sketch A and B.

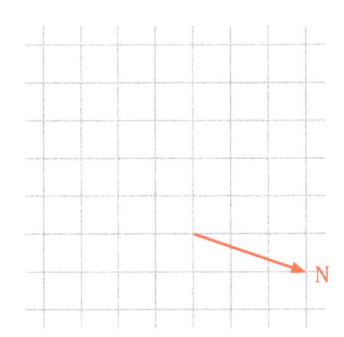

3   The bearing of A from B is 180°. Sketch A and B.

5   The bearing of A from B is 180°. Sketch A and B.

2   Point C is on a bearing of 045° from B and lies on a gridline intersection. Sketch C.

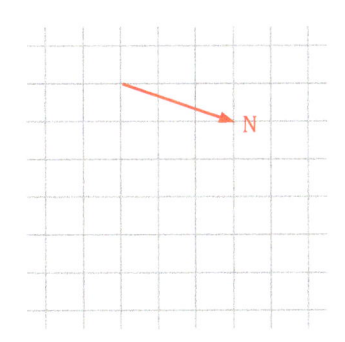

4   Point C is on a bearing of 045° from B and lies on a gridline intersection. Sketch C.

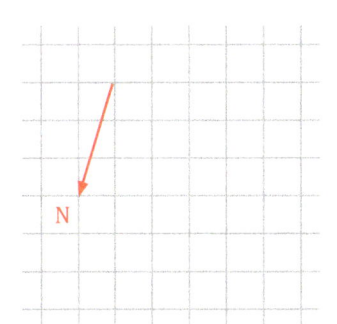

6   Point C is on a bearing of 045° from B and lies on a gridline intersection. Sketch C.

1. The bearing of A from B is 180°. Sketch a north line and B.

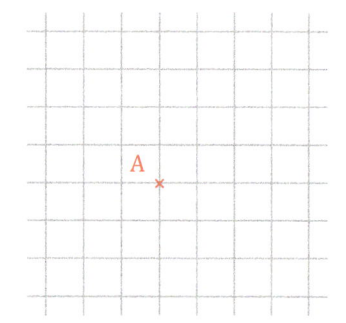

2. Point C is on a bearing of 045° from B and lies on a gridline intersection. Sketch C.

3. The bearing of A from B is 180°. Sketch a different north line and B from question 1.

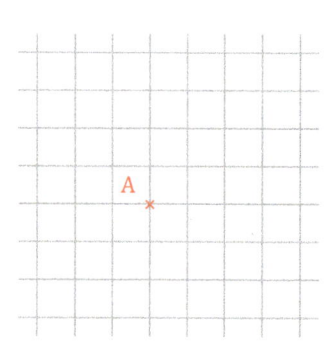

4. Point C is on a bearing of 045° from B and lies on a gridline intersection. Sketch C as such that AC>AB>BC.

5. The bearing of A from B is 180°. Sketch a north line and B.

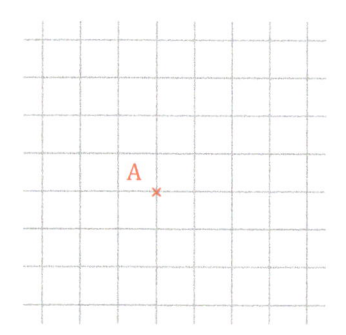

6. Point C is on a bearing of 045° from B. Sketch C as such that ABC is an isosceles triangle (with compass/ruler).

One really nice aspect of the above is that, due to the numbers chosen, pupils can actually complete these without using a protractor, potentially giving them a new insight into angle drawing and measuring.

There are, of course, other quantities we wish to measure that we don't tend to use a scale for. The ones that pupils will encounter most commonly at school level are measuring area and volume. In Chapter 10 we will look in more detail at the importance of defining these quantities so that when pupils are attempting to measure them, they understand what it is they are trying to measure. However, once they begin to look at measuring these quantities, it is useful to bring pupils back to what it means to measure, starting with defining the appropriate unit.

Subconcept: measuring area

When it comes to area, pupils need to recognise that because we are measuring a two-dimensional space, we need a two-dimensional unit space. Before just revealing that this is a square, I like to ask pupils to think about what space would make a good unit space. Pupils are often stumped by this, and so most of the time I have to show pupils that we use a square with a length of one unit, and define this space to have an area of one unit. Having done this though, I will then prompt pupils to think about why this makes a good unit for measuring space. Pupils typically focus on the right angles in this situation, and I will either explain that this is part of it – that because we tend to build and create shapes with right-angles in, it makes sense to use a square to measure a two-dimensional space, or question them as to why right angles might be useful. However, that isn't the only reason that a square makes a good unit area; the property often missed by pupils is that it tessellates.

Pupils appreciating that tessellation is a good property of an area unit opens up the possibility of considering which other shapes might make good units of area. If pupils have previously studied tessellation then they may be aware that equilateral triangles and regular hexagons will also tessellate – I always make the point with pupils that if we were bees, we would likely define a hexagon with side length of 1 unit to have an area of 1 unit 'hexagoned'. Activities like the following can be interesting to prompt pupils to consider what would happen if a shape other than a square is used as the unit area:

If the blue triangle has an area of 1 unit, what other areas can you find in this picture?

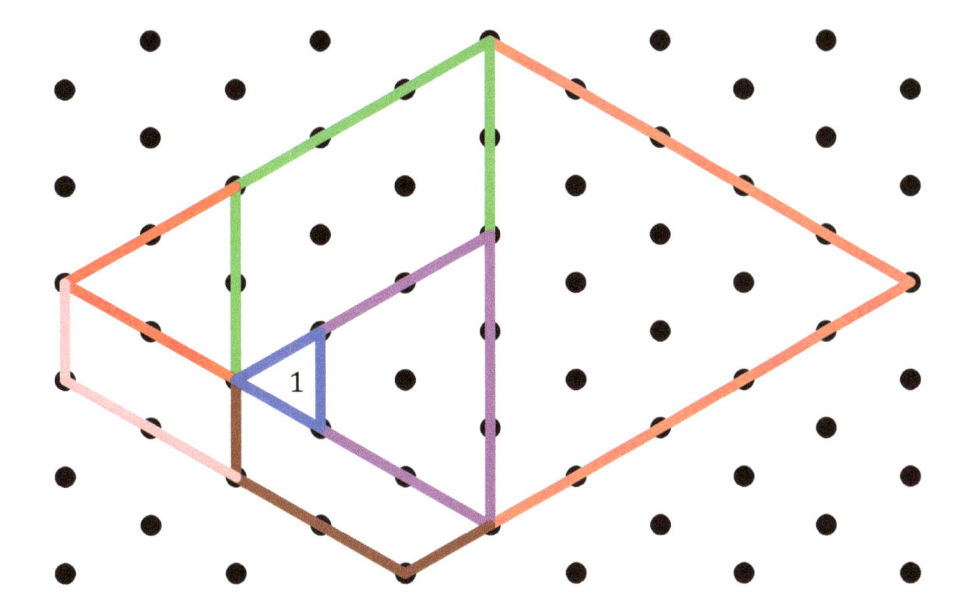

However, it might be preferable for pupils to actually have some experience of measuring area with squares before offering something like this:

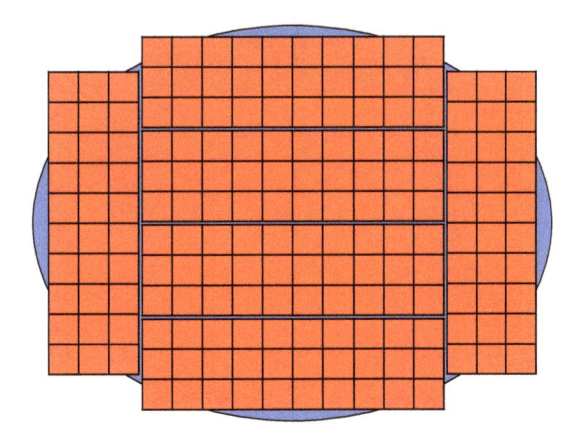

To further reinforce the core ideas of measurement, I like to take pupils through the same processes as I do for length, i.e. having them compare area to a single unit and estimate the area before constructing an 'area scale' out of centimetre-squared paper and asking pupils to try and measure the area of certain spaces using their scale.

This shows an attempt to measure the area of an ellipse using an 'area scale' of 30 cm². The key learning point here is that using a scale separate to the shape is not as effective for measuring area as it is for measuring, say, length, mass or volume. This motivates the far better approach of actually drawing the shape onto a grid of unit squares or eventually using a formula/calculation strategy to work out the area of different shapes.

I like to present pupils with different shapes drawn on centimetre-square grids and rather than getting them to find the area, getting them to articulate their strategy for counting the number of squares inside the boundary of the shape. For the shape below, this might be recognising that the left-hand half of the shape has one row of 3 at the bottom, and then if we take the half of a square at the top and combine it with the half square on the left, we can create six groups of 2. This would lead to half of the shape having an area of 15 cm², and therefore the whole shape has an area of 30 cm². Alternatively, if we took the two half squares at the top of the shape and combined them with the halves at the sides of the shape, we could create seven groups of 4 squares with the two extra squares sticking out at the bottom of the shape so that we have 4 × 7 + 2 = 30 cm². This conservation of area when shapes are cut and recombined is an important property, and one that we should highlight to pupils, perhaps giving them the opportunity to physically cut up shapes and move the pieces around, whilst recognising the area stays constant. Prompting pupils to consider more than one calculation strategy is a great way to get them thinking about area calculations, and leads very nicely into formalising approaches to calculating the area of shapes such as rectangles, parallelograms, triangles, kites, rhombi and trapezia (as we will see in Chapter 10).

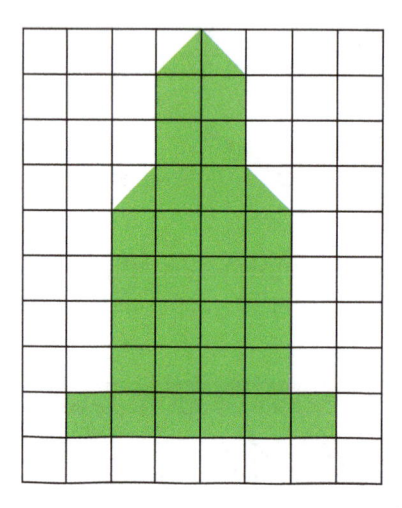

Subconcept: measuring volume

When it comes to volume, the idea is very similar to area. Instead of defining a two-dimensional unit space, we now need to define a three-dimensional unit. Instead of a square fitting the criteria for a good space unit, it is now a cube (although the idea of three-dimensional tessellation is one that pupils will perhaps be less familiar with – and one that can add some lovely depth to the idea). We can make comparisons to a single centimetre cube or a single metre cube; pupils are always amazed at how big a metre cube is compared to a centimetre cube – well worth building one out of metre rulers or at least outlining the size of the length, width and depth using three rulers if you don't have enough for the full cube. Pupils can recognise that this comparison process isn't particularly accurate, and they are much better off actually building the shape out of cubes. And then, pupils can start looking at calculation strategies for certain three-dimensional shapes:

Find the volume of each of these shapes if each cube has a length of 1 cm.

Notice there are half cubes in these pictures as well, which adds something nice to pupils' counting strategies, which we can then use to support the introduction of formulae for volume calculations (which we will look at in Chapter 10).

At this point we may well want to make the link between measuring volume and measuring capacity. This usually comes in the form of pupils learning that 1 cm^3 of volume is equivalent to 1 ml of capacity, i.e. a hollow cube of length 1 cm would hold 1 ml of liquid. This can be challenging to demonstrate physically, as the cube is very small (as is a single ml of liquid); however, alternatively we can use a cube of length 10 cm (hence having a volume of 1000 cm^3) and show that it holds precisely 1000 ml of liquid (as in the video linked in the footnote[4]).

We could then come back to shapes previously looked at and ask pupils to decide how much liquid they could hold if hollow, particularly if pupils are already proficient in converting units so we could ask them to give answers in centilitres or even litres. Another nice activity to do at this point is the 'Archimedes' experiment.[5] By submerging objects in water and looking at the change in the amount of liquid, we can determine the volume of the object (as shown in the video linked below[6]).

Subconcept: measuring temperature

Another quantity that pupils may well be familiar with measuring is temperature. This is an opportune time to return to the concept of measurement and see how measuring temperature conforms to the same ideas. Before measuring temperature, we define the unit of measurement; in Europe this is usually degrees Celsius/centigrade. We can look with pupils at how a single degree centigrade is defined, as $\frac{1}{100}$th of the temperature change required to change the state of water from solid to gas (i.e. 0°C is the freezing point of water and 100°C is the boiling point of water). Of course, comparison to a single unit is very challenging here,

---

4 S. Milam, 1mL = 1cm^3 [video] (2017). Available at: https://www.youtube.com/watch?v=028tWJGCSdM.
5 R. Ross, Eureka! The Archimedes Principle, *Live Science* (26 April 2017). Available at: https://www.livescience.com/58839-archimedes-principle.html.
6 Sabins, Understanding Archimedes' Principle, [video] (2020). Available at: https://www.youtube.com/watch?v=XfkJ7wBT-PA.

as it isn't really possible for a human to discern a change in air temperature by a single degree. This leads us naturally to want to define a scale for such changes and using a thermometer to measure change in temperature.

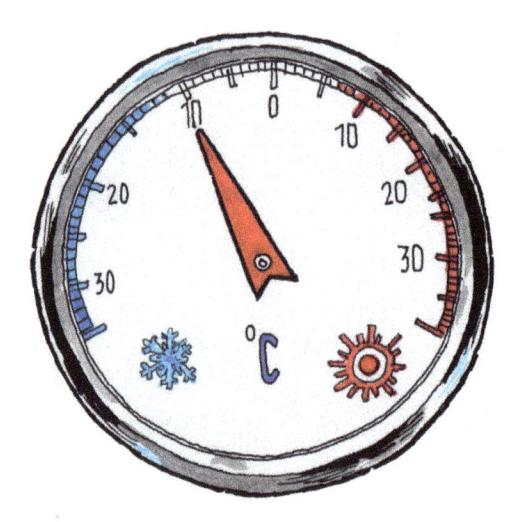

This is a nice place to interweave work on negative numbers, as this is potentially the first quantity that will naturally have negative values (the concepts of negative angle or displacement using negative 'distances' are not normally introduced until much later in school learning, if at all). We can provide pupils with start and finish temperatures on a scale and look at what the change in temperature has been between the two readings, using different scales to make sure pupils have to apply knowledge of scales as well. Of course, if the equipment is available, pupils can actually physically measure temperature of different substances. This is more likely to be available in science than in the mathematics classroom, but it might be worth talking to the science team about borrowing equipment and lab space or tying together learning around this concept between the departments (as would be possible to do in primary schools – using knowledge of measurement studied in maths when studying science).

Subconcept: measuring time

The final quantity I want to touch on again briefly when looking at scales is time. Telling the time is a rather interesting idea from the point of view of using a scale, as it would appear fewer and fewer pupils are now exposed to the scale for time-telling outside of school: i.e. the analogue clock. The prevalence of digital devices for telling the time means that pupils often only encounter analogue clocks in the classroom. However, time works like any other quantity in terms of measurement. We define a unit for time which is the second, with every other unit of time defined in terms of the second. I love sharing the definition of a second with pupils, as it is so technical as to make no sense to pretty much anyone who isn't a theoretical physics professor:

> The second is defined by taking the fixed numerical value of the caesium frequency Δv, the unperturbed ground-state hyperfine transition frequency of the caesium 133 atom, to be 9 192 631 770 when expressed in the unit Hz, which is equal to s^{-1}.[7]

---

7   NPL, SI Units Second: (s) (n.d.). Available at: https://www.npl.co.uk/si-units/second.

Obviously, I am not expecting pupils to remember this, but it serves nicely to illustrate the need for and search for ever more accurate definitions of units.

When it comes to the analogue clock, the same ideas of using a scale apply. The 'zero' at the scale is at 12. The scale is graduated in 5s for minutes, and 1s for hours. One difficulty pupils tend to have is identifying the difference in time, which is in part because the scale goes around and uses the same values. We can mitigate against this by looking at this sort of thing when we look at weighing objects and using a mechanical scale:

If pupils are familiar with using a scale like this with objects weighing 7 kg, 13 kg, etc. then we can draw attention back to this when looking at the clock ticking around.

Because of the lack of exposure to analogue clocks in the real world these days, when pupils start secondary school, it is not uncommon to have pupils that cannot read the analogue clock. If your curriculum then requires this to be taught, it may well be necessary to have some extension and enrichment available for pupils. The classic enrichment here involves using angles on the clock, with questions like these:

1   What is the acute angle between two lines drawn from the centre of the clock to consecutive numbers on the clock?

2   How many degrees does the minute hand turn through in one minute?

3   How many degrees does the hour hand turn through in one minute?

4   How many degrees is the obtuse between the minute hand and the hour hand at 12:30?

5   How many different times can you find where the angle between the hour hand and the minute hand is a right angle?

When it comes to larger spans of times such as using a calendar, learning about leap years, etc., NRICH have some fantastic activities to support teaching. Two of my favourites are 'Calendar Sorting'[8] and 'A Calendar Question'.[9]

---

8   See https://nrich.maths.org/10322.
9   See https://nrich.maths.org/1064.

Concept: converting between units of measure

Prerequisites: Numbers, multiplication, division, proportionality, functionality (for some unit conversions).

Linked concepts: Equivalence, shape, graphing. Interestingly, whilst it is clearly inadvisable for pupils to explore converting between units of measure without having first looked at units of measure, it is theoretical possible to learn about conversion without having encountered the units previously.

Nearly all units for the same measurable quantity (i.e. all units of length, or units of weight, etc.) have a directly proportional relationship to each other. This is typically due to the nature of the quantity. Recall the key properties of a directly proportional relationship are:

1   Scaling: Scaling one quantity will scale the other by the same scale factor.

2   Exchange rate/conversion factor: There is a constant multiplicative conversion factor between the two quantities.

3   Zeroes: Because of the constant conversion factor, when one quantity has a value of zero, so does the other.

Typically, most measured quantities automatically fulfil these criteria. If you have zero length, zero area, zero time, then you will have zero, no matter what unit you choose to measure with. Similarly, if the quantity is doubled, trebled, or scaled up/down by any factor, all units used to measure it will be scaled in the same way. These two together will actually imply the existence of the conversion factor – any relationship between two quantities that has zeroes in the same place and scales will maintain a constant conversion factor between the quantities. Of course, in many cases one unit is defined in terms of another, and this is invariably in the form of a conversion factor. However, even when one unit isn't defined in terms of the other, the scaling and zeroes will still guarantee the exchange rate exists.

We can make it explicit to pupils that proportional relationships exist between units of measure by using the same sorts of representations to explore unit comparison as we used to introduce and explore proportionality. Indeed, many of the scales we use to measure quantities are set up to measure in more than one unit, which makes them perfect dual number lines.

In this picture we can see that there are two scales, the red one in pounds and the black in kilograms.

Unrolling this scale produces this dual number line:

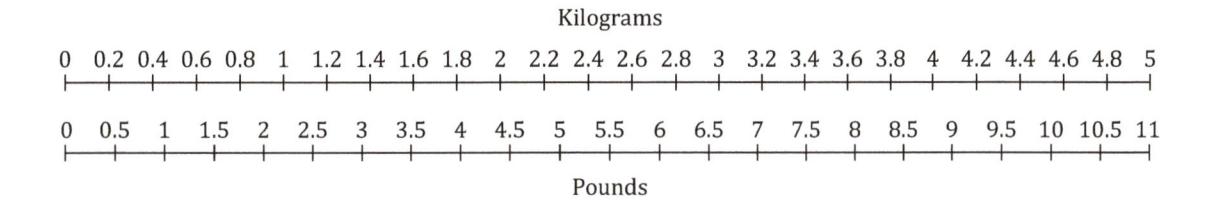

Kilograms
0 0.2 0.4 0.6 0.8 1 1.2 1.4 1.6 1.8 2 2.2 2.4 2.6 2.8 3 3.2 3.4 3.6 3.8 4 4.2 4.4 4.6 4.8 5

0 0.5 1 1.5 2 2.5 3 3.5 4 4.5 5 5.5 6 6.5 7 7.5 8 8.5 9 9.5 10 10.5 11
Pounds

This is immediately recognisable as the same sort of dual number line that we saw when looking at proportionality. Indeed, many of the length scales are much more closely linked to dual number lines:

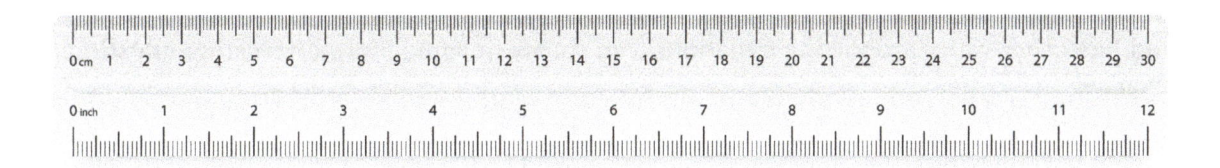

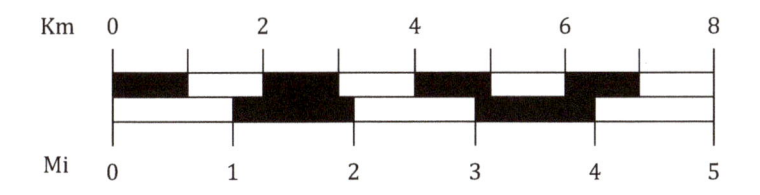

These are all scales that are in common use that serve as perfect dual number lines. It is always nice to bring these sorts of practical examples into the classroom, either as physical tools (most pupil rulers are graduated in centimetres and millimetres, which gives one immediate possibility) or at least as images.

From the dual number line, the partial abstraction to the ratio table is fairly straightforward:

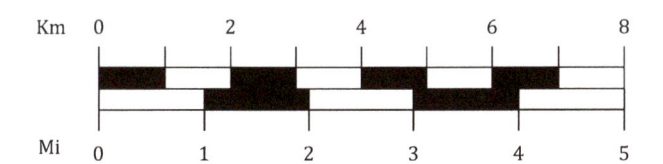

Km	Mi
8	5

which can then be used to solve problems involving either scaling both values by the same amount:

Km	Mi
8	5
24	15

× 3 ... × 3

or by using the conversion factor between the two quantities:

Km		Mi
8	× 0.625 →	5
30	× 0.625 →	18.75

and like other ratio/proportion situations, can throw in some more interesting questions, such as:

- Dion travels from his home to a holiday cabin. The distance in kilometres has a value that is 180 more than the value of the distance in miles. Work out the distance in miles.

- Dion travels from his home to a holiday cabin. When he travels back home he takes a different route that is 20 miles longer. This means his total distance travelled is 352 km. Work out the number of miles Dion travelled on his journey to the holiday cabin.

- Dion and Deena arrange to meet at a holiday cabin. Deena lives 40 miles closer to the cabin than Dion. If Dion were to drive and pick up Deena before travelling to the holiday cabin it would mean his total journey would be double the distance. Dion lives 160 km from Deena. How far does Deena have to travel to get to the cabin?

Measures

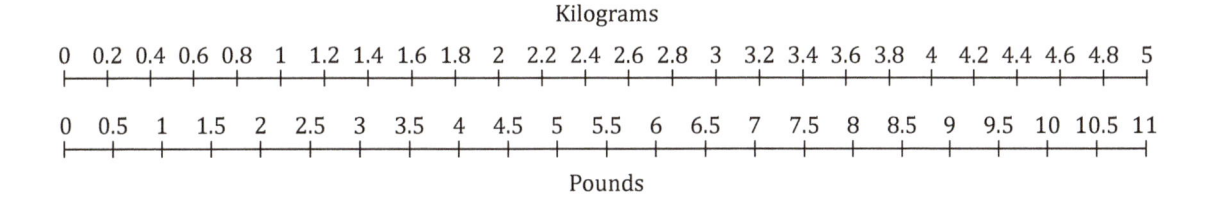

```
         Kilograms
0  0.2 0.4 0.6 0.8  1  1.2 1.4 1.6 1.8  2  2.2 2.4 2.6 2.8  3  3.2 3.4 3.6 3.8  4  4.2 4.4 4.6 4.8  5
├──┼───┼───┼───┼───┼───┼───┼───┼───┼───┼───┼───┼───┼───┼───┼───┼───┼───┼───┼───┼───┼───┼───┼───┼──┤

0  0.5  1  1.5  2  2.5  3  3.5  4  4.5  5  5.5  6  6.5  7  7.5  8  8.5  9  9.5  10  10.5  11
├───┼───┼───┼───┼───┼───┼───┼───┼───┼───┼───┼───┼───┼───┼───┼───┼───┼───┼───┼───┼───┼───┤
                              Pounds
```

A very common thing to do with unit conversion (which will actually work with all other proportional relationships) is to take the dual number line and rotate one of the lines to create a conversion graph:

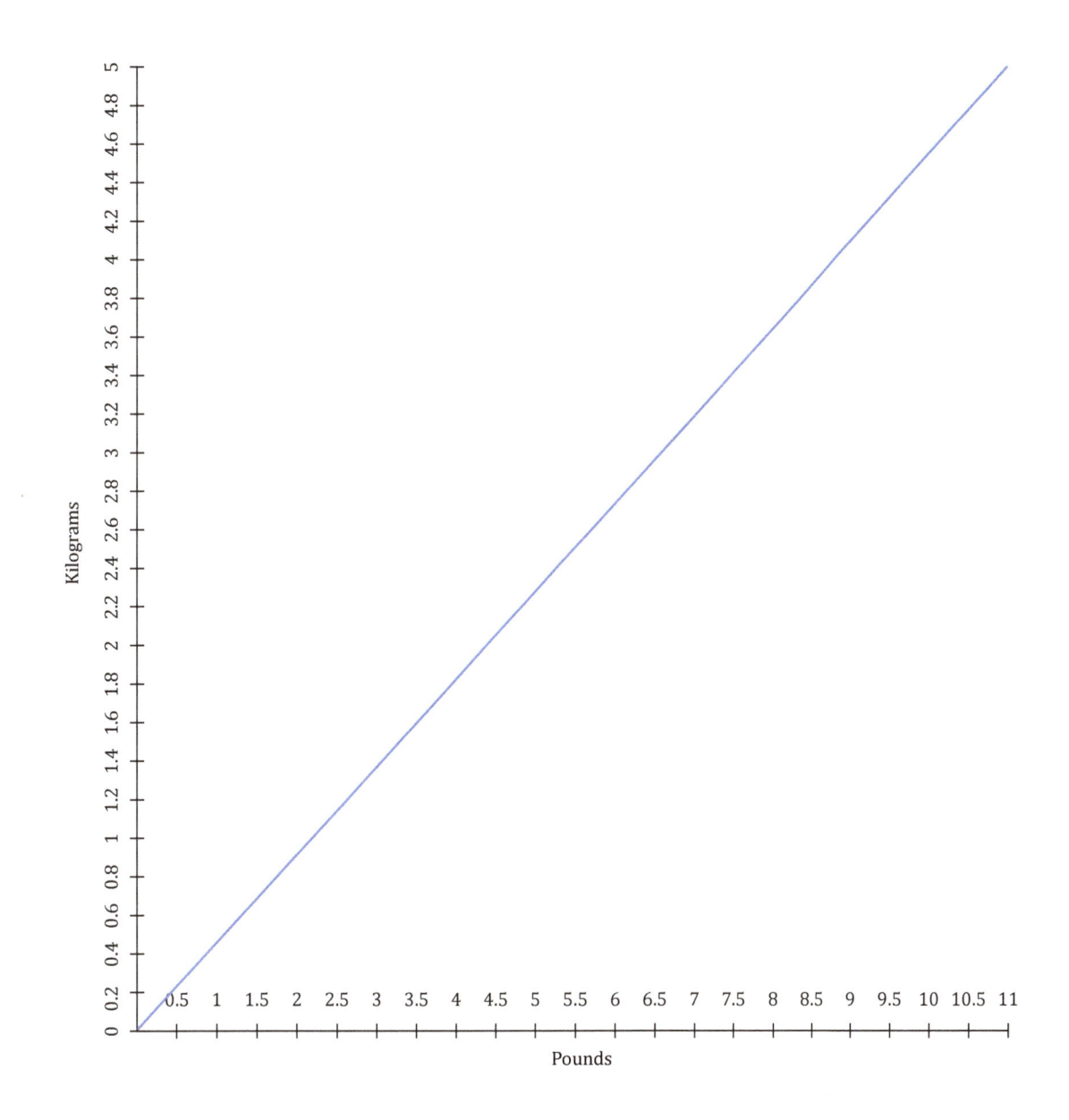

We will look at graphs for proportional relationships in more detail in Chapter 13.

The major unit conversion that isn't a proportional relationship is the conversion between Celsius and Fahrenheit temperature. This is because, unlike quantities like length, mass and time that have a state of 'nothing' from which to start their scale, neither the Celsius or Fahrenheit scale start at the 'nothing' for temperature, i.e. absolute zero. Instead, both of these units base their scale on relatively arbitrary points; in the case of Celsius this is the

289

freezing and boiling point of water and for Fahrenheit the zero was originally set as the freezing point of a brine solution and the average temperature of the human body (at the time set to be 96°F). Since Fahrenheit originally set his scale, it has been recalibrated to also use the freezing and boiling point of water at 32°F and 212°F respectively, meaning there is 180°F between the two (a nice link that a circular temperature scale with the freezing point and boiling point of water at either end of a diameter has 1°F = 1° of turn).

Converting between Celsius and Fahrenheit is an example of a functional relationship between the two units. How we want to introduce this functional relationship depends on pupils' previous learning around functionality. It is possible to derive the functional relationship from a graph – the graph can either be provided or generated from measuring different temperatures using a thermometer showing both Celsius and Fahrenheit (or just using the scale on the thermometer), although if measuring temperatures teachers need a plan to deal with the inherent accuracy issues.

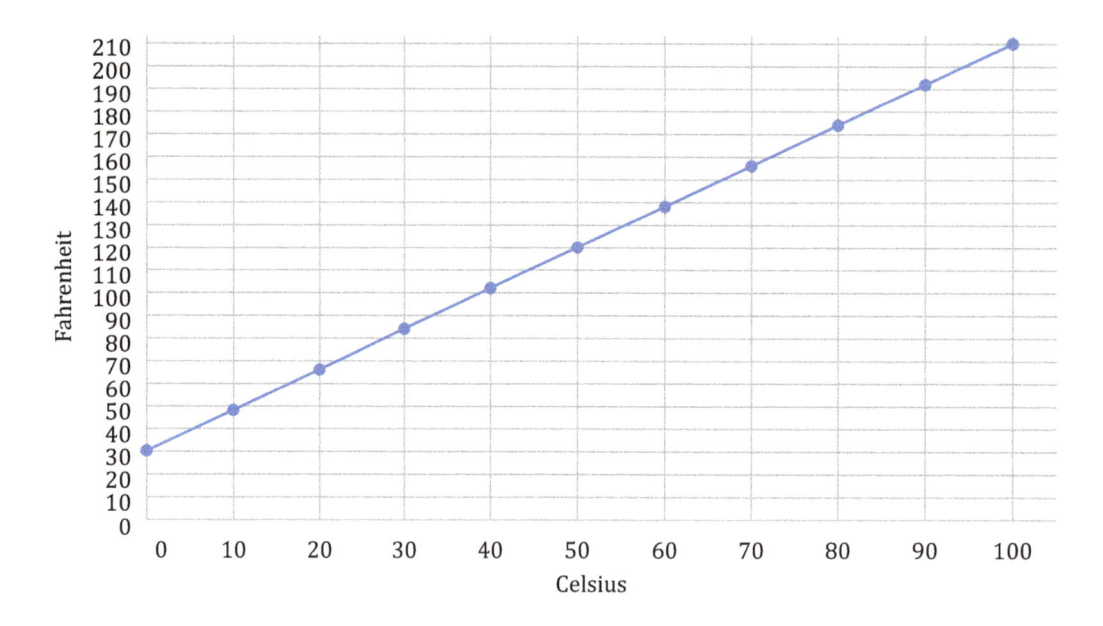

If deriving the formula, two potentially key points are that 10°C = 50°F and that 60°C = 140°F as these could be used to derive the relationship, and importantly to show they are not proportional.

Alternatively, many people simply like to introduce the formula, either as $F = 1.8C + 32$ or as $C = \frac{5}{9}(F - 32)$, and simply use it as a vehicle to practise working with functions/formulae. There are opportunities within this formula to work with negatives, fractions/decimals or even percentages (if we change the formula to this one given in the Don Steward activity[10]).

An accurate conversion rule:

	90
	180
× 2	180 – 18
– 10%	162
+ 32	194

Find the values °C to °F.

Starting at 0 and increasing by 10 (up to 100°C).

---

10 D. Steward, Temperature Conversion, *Median* [blog] (1 March 2011). Available at: https://donsteward.blogspot.com/2011/03/temperature-conversion.html.

100
200
200 − 20
180
212

Concept: compound measures

Prerequisites: Numbers, multiplication, division, proportionality.

Linked concepts: Equivalence, functionality, graphing.

There are lots of different approaches to working with compound measures that are used by teachers, and not just in mathematics. Learners will also meet compound measures in science, in geography (population density) and possibly in subjects like design and technology. Very possibly, these subjects will use an approach like the formula triangle:

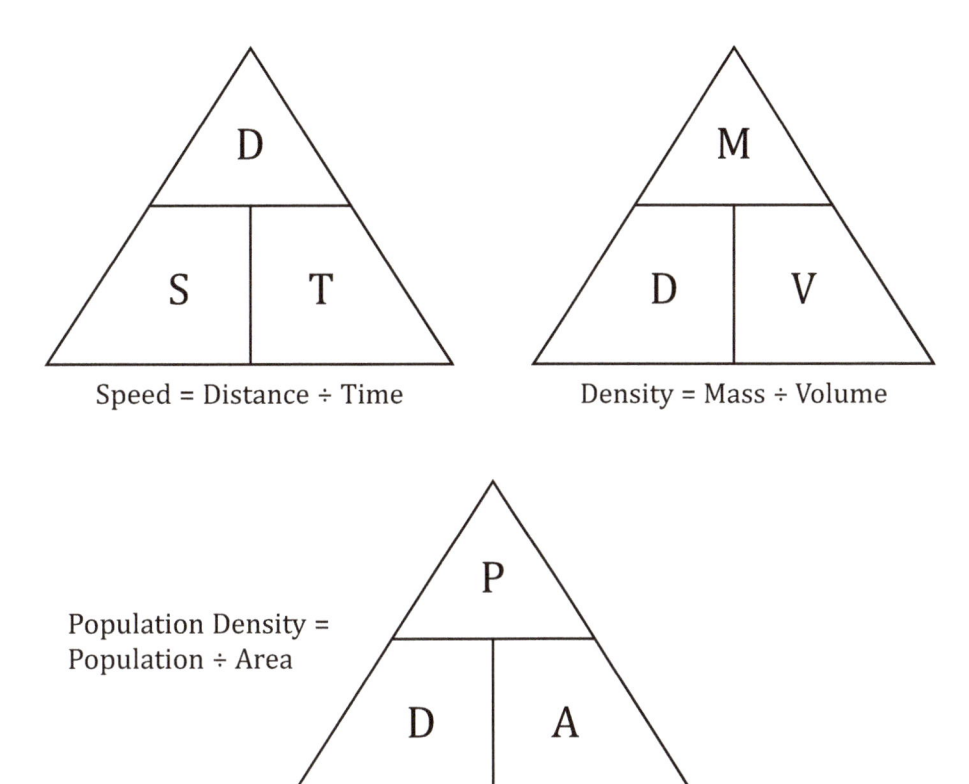

Speed = Distance ÷ Time

Density = Mass ÷ Volume

Population Density = Population ÷ Area

However, whilst these can be effective in supporting pupils to solve certain problems involving compound measures, it perhaps isn't the best representation for getting at the heart of the concept of compound measures. For this, pupils need to understand compound measures as arising from a proportional relationship between simpler units. For example, constant/average speed is distance travelled in a defined unit of time, (constant) density is the mass of material in a given unit of volume and population density is the number of people living on a defined unit of area. This has clear links to the unitary idea in proportion and allows us to use proportional reasoning to make sense of compound measures and to solve problems with compound measures. Professor John Mason suggests introducing compound measures using density (it is perhaps most common to introduce them using speed) as there are physical quantities pupils can see and handle as well as density being more likely to be constant (provided no large changes in temperature).[11]

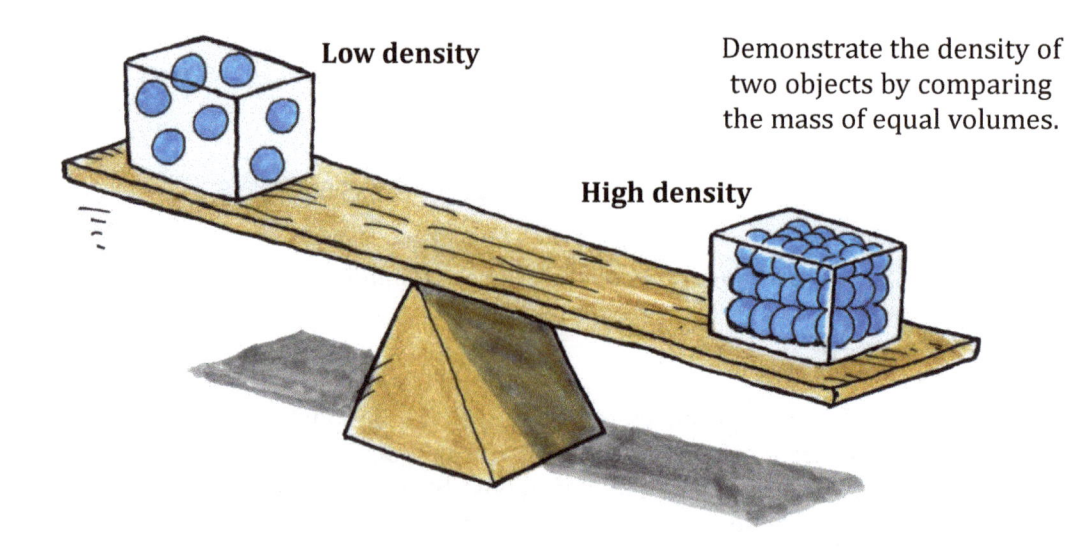

Low density

High density

Demonstrate the density of two objects by comparing the mass of equal volumes.

We can support pupils developing this view by using the same sorts of representations as we used to support the development of proportional reasoning. When introducing speed, we can show this on a dual number line:

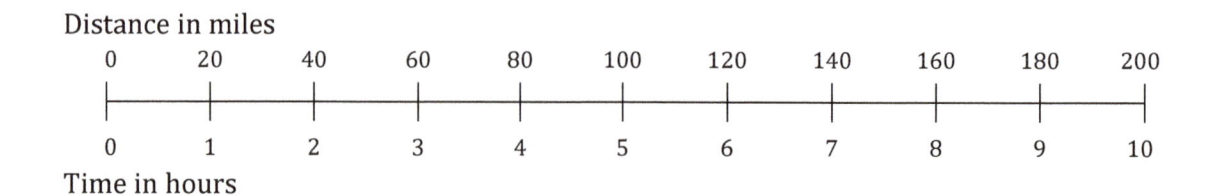

Distance in miles
0   20   40   60   80   100   120   140   160   180   200
0   1   2   3   4   5   6   7   8   9   10
Time in hours

with the idea being that we can draw learners' attention to the fact that the speed is the exchange rate/conversion factor between the distance and the time, or alternatively the distance travelled when the time has a value of 1 (which creates a nice link back to defining units of measure and division as comparison). Other compound measures can be approached in a very similar way (in fact, using the very same dual number line!).

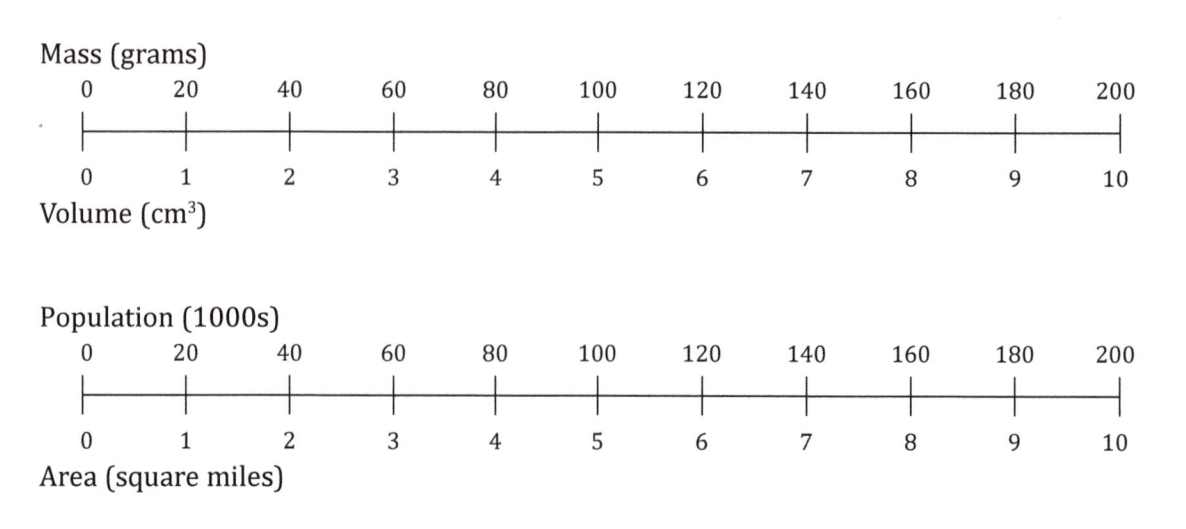

Mass (grams)
0   20   40   60   80   100   120   140   160   180   200
0   1   2   3   4   5   6   7   8   9   10
Volume (cm^3)

Population (1000s)
0   20   40   60   80   100   120   140   160   180   200
0   1   2   3   4   5   6   7   8   9   10
Area (square miles)

---

11 Personal correspondence.

From here we can continue onto representations like ratio tables, which are a much more concise representation to support problem-solving:

An object travels at an average speed of 30 mph for 4.5 hours. Work out the distance travelled.

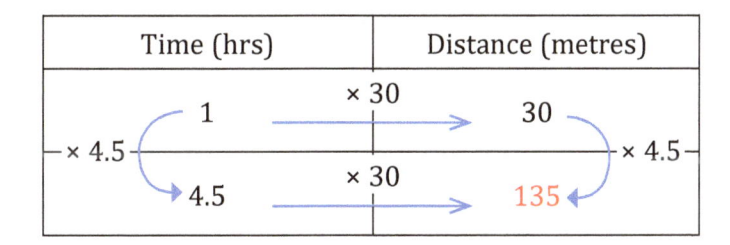

Time (hrs)	Distance (metres)
1	30
4.5	135

(× 4.5 on time, × 30 across, × 4.5 on distance)

The proportional structure here makes it clear that to find the distance travelled, I have two ways of thinking about the problem (which admittedly amounts to the same calculation):

- The speed, as the exchange rate between the time and the distance, means that the distance will always be 30 times bigger than the time.

- The fact that the time has increased by a factor of 4.5 means that the distance will also increase by a factor of 4.5.

An object travels at an average speed of 30 mph and covers 75 miles. Work out how long the object travels for.

Time (hrs)	Distance (metres)
1	30
2.5	75

(× 2.5 on time, × 30 across, ÷ 30 back, × 2.5 on distance)

In this case, the same proportional ideas can help us work with this situation. The ratio table makes it clear that division by 30 (or alternatively × $\frac{1}{30}$) is a potential way to find the time required. Another approach would be to identify that the distance has increased by a factor of 2.5, and therefore the time will do the same.

An object travels 75 miles in 4.5 hours. Work out the average speed of the object.

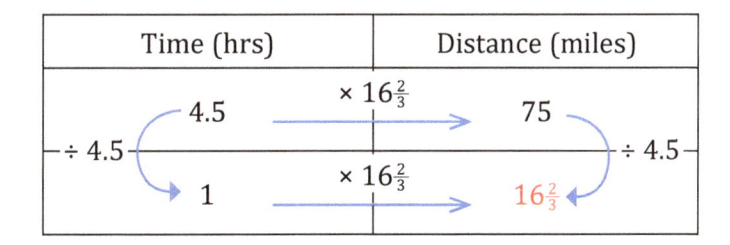

Time (hrs)	Distance (miles)
4.5	75
1	$16\frac{2}{3}$

(÷ 4.5 on time, × $16\frac{2}{3}$ across, ÷ 4.5 on distance)

Again, recognising the proportional nature of this problem, we can potentially proceed in two ways: either by identifying the exchange rate between the time and the distance as $16\frac{2}{3}$ mph, or by scaling the time to a single hour and then applying the same scale to the distance.

Understanding that time and distance are directly proportional when speed is constant (or considering average speed) opens up much more flexibility for solving problems involving speed.

An object travels 9 km in 2 minutes. Work out the average speed of the object. Give your answer in m/s.

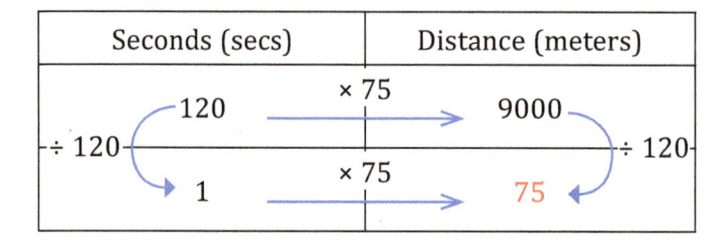

Seconds (secs)	Distance (meters)
120	9000
1	75

(÷120 on time, ×75, ÷120 on distance, ×75)

An object travels at 9 km/h. How far does the object travel in 1 hour 20 minutes?

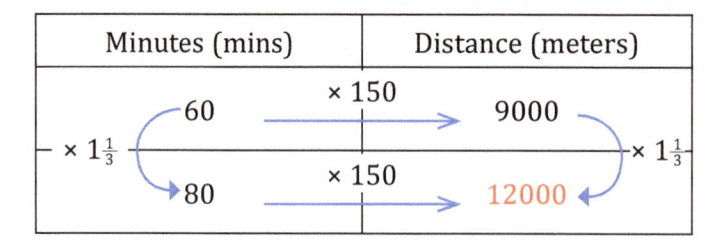

Minutes (mins)	Distance (meters)
60	9000
80	12000

(×$1\frac{1}{3}$, ×150, ×$1\frac{1}{3}$, ×150)

The object travels 12 km.

I drove from Cambridge to Cardiff at an average speed of 50 mph (it was heavy traffic) but I managed to drive back at an average speed of 70 mph. Why wasn't my average speed for the round trip 60 mph? What average speed for the return journey would make the round trip average 60 mph?

Outward Journey

Time (hrs)	Distance (miles)
1	50
D/50	D

Return Journey

Time (hrs)	Distance (miles)
1	70
D/70	D

Total Journey

Time (hrs)	Distance (miles)
$\frac{12D}{350}$	2D
1	$58\frac{1}{3}$

(×175/3)

(This is the NRICH problem 'An Average Average Speed'.[12])

---

12 See https://nrich.maths.org/5988.

Of course, you might not expect pupils to work algebraically with this problem straightaway. We could suggest pupils measure the distance from Cambridge to Cardiff on a map, perhaps first in a straight line and then to add some distance due to having to travel by road. We could even simply suggest pupils make up a distance and try it. No matter what pupils set the distance to be, the speed will come out to be a little more than 58 mph.

Outward Journey

Time (hrs)	Distance (miles)
1 $\xrightarrow{\times 50}$	50
D/50 $\xrightarrow{\div 50}$	D

Total Journey

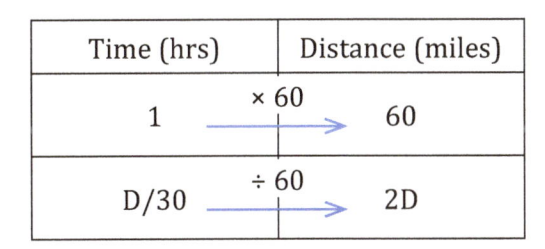

Time (hrs)	Distance (miles)
1 $\xrightarrow{\times 60}$	60
D/30 $\xrightarrow{\div 60}$	2D

Return Journey

Time (hrs)	Distance (miles)
$\frac{D}{30} - \frac{D}{50} = \frac{D}{75}$ $\xrightarrow{\times 75}$	D
1 $\xrightarrow{\times 75}$	75

All other compound measures work in precisely the same way – we could change each of these questions to involve density, mass and volume – pressure, force and area or speed, acceleration and time. Even frequency density (when it comes to drawing histograms and working with unequal class-widths) can be treated as a compound measure and worked with in exactly the same way as speed, density, pressure, etc. can be.

Once again, another aspect to the concept we can explore is the rotation of one of the number lines (or one of the scales, depending on how we draw them) to create axes, and then plot a graph.

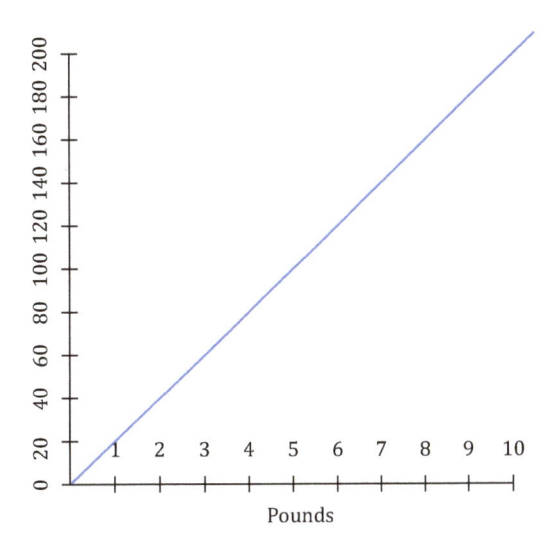

This will eventually lead to drawing piece-wise graphs to represent journeys and other real-life situations (explored in Chapter 13).

There are a number of other quantities we might want to measure throughout compulsory schooling in mathematics. Notably absent at this point are measures of slope (we will see in Chapter 10), measures of 'average' (Chapter 14) and measures of chance (Chapter 12). One area that is inextricably linked with physical measurement, however, is accuracy. It is to this that we now turn our attention.

Chapter 9

Accuracy

Unusually for me, I am firmly of the opinion that the idea of accuracy needs to be broached with pupils from a practical context. I say unusually because I generally feel that one of the nicest things about studying mathematics is the fact that most of it exists in the realm of pure thought – that mathematics doesn't rely on context to make sense. However, in this case, I make an exception. To me, it simply doesn't make sense to talk about accuracy, and in particular reducing the accuracy of values, without a context underlying why we would need to. Whilst it may be possible to use the decimal equivalents to irrational numbers to motivate the need for statements about accuracy, in most cases teaching about accuracy is looked at prior to irrational numbers. Whilst the argument can be made that estimation can serve as a vehicle for motivating conversations about accuracy, for me estimation is something that should happen less formally, and be part and parcel of carrying out calculations.

This is not to say that, once introduced, the idea of accuracy cannot then be generalised into the abstract; indeed it should absolutely be a goal of teaching and learning about accuracy to understand that these ideas apply across multiple contexts and can therefore be modelled without context at all.

Concept: rounding to a given place value

Prerequisites: Numbers, place value, measurement.

Linked concepts: Equivalence.

At some point in learning about the use of numbers to quantify measurements, pupils should become aware of the inherent inaccuracy in using tools and scales to measure with. A simple example might be something like:[1]

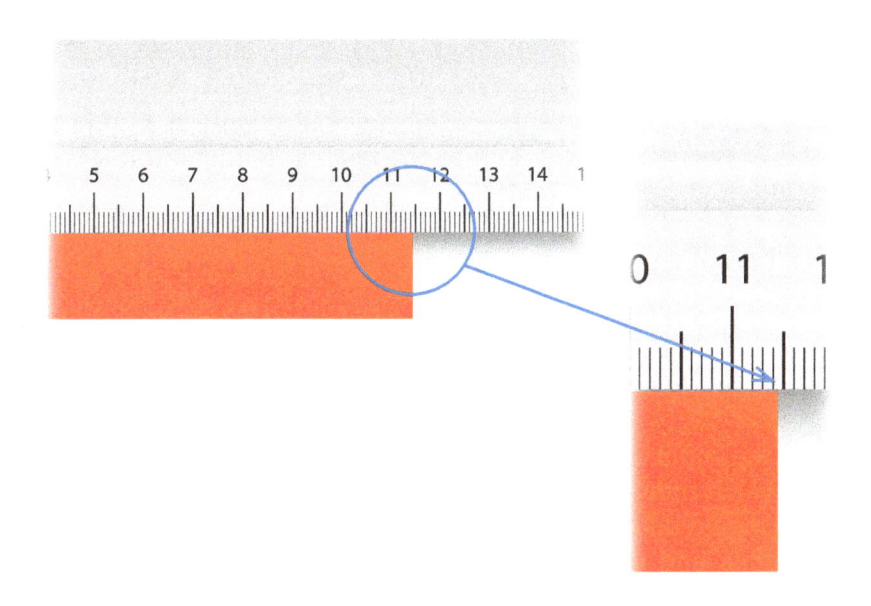

---

1 Image based on http://stonecoldhands.com/articles/MeasurementExample.html (now inactive).

Pupils measuring this object might first suggest the length is 11.4 cm; however, if we look closer we can see that the object is actually somewhere between 11.4 and 11.5 cm, but because of the inaccuracy of the tool we cannot be sure exactly how much longer than 11.4 cm the object is. This leads to us having to qualify our measurement – and a lot of the accuracy studied at compulsory school level is ultimately about being able to better qualify the measurement. At this introductory stage this is simply being able to state that this length is 11.4 or 11.5 cm accurate to the nearest tenth of a centimetre.

The question then naturally follows: which is it? And how do we decide which to say? Rather than introduce rounding 'rules' at this point, we might offer pupils an activity that allows a bit more of an intuitive sense of the rounding:

Would you say this length is 11.4 cm or 11.5 cm to the nearest tenth?

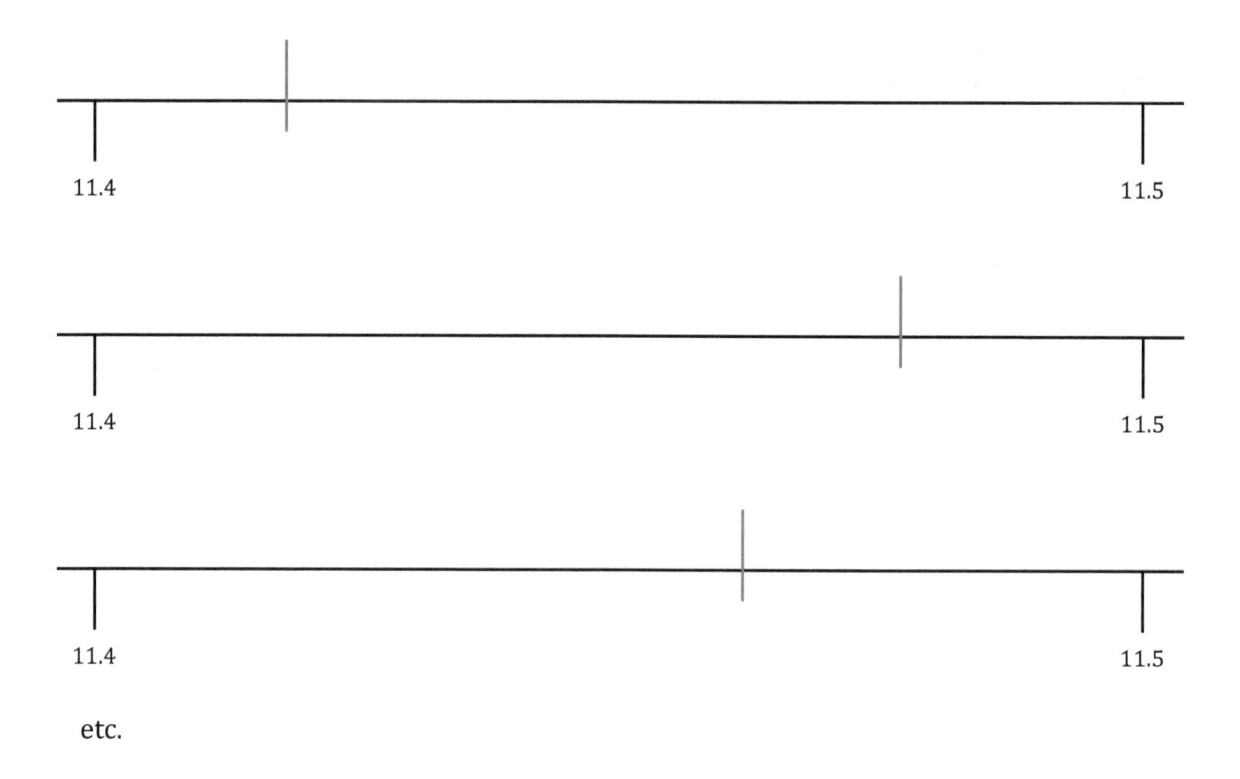

11.4   11.5

11.4   11.5

11.4   11.5

etc.

This should begin to allow pupils to see that the 'crunch' point will come at 11.45 cm, and that if a value is below 11.45 we will say it is 11.4 to the nearest tenth, and if it is above 11.45 we would say it is '11.5 to the nearest tenth'.

At this point I can imagine that you might have a couple of queries:

1   Would you go straight in with looking at decimals for this?

2   Would you say 'to the nearest tenth' or 'to the first decimal place'?

To the first I would say that the important understanding is around place value, and if pupils understand decimal place value then wherever we start should be fine – one of the key learning points that pupils should take from learning about accuracy is that rounding ultimately transcends place value and works the same no matter how many place value columns a number has, or to which place we choose to round to. It is also slightly more difficult to motivate scales that would be ambiguous at the 10s or 1s place, meaning that we might lose something in introducing the need to consider accuracy. However, if decimal place value is less secure than integer place value, we may wish to introduce rounding using integer place value columns before moving to decimal place value.

As for the second query, I would always start by saying 'nearest tenth' in order to tie it in to how we describe rounding to places greater than 1. However, I would then talk about how this is normally called 'the first decimal place' and that this language is used interchangeably with 'nearest tenth'.

The previous activity, of course, speaks to using a number line to support making sense of rounding, and equating the scale used for measurement to the number line. In this way we can make clear to pupils that the unit we are measuring in doesn't affect the rounding. We can reinforce this by potentially offering something like the following:

Round the following to the nearest whole number:

a   53.75 cm

b   53.75 kg

c   53.75 miles

d   53.75 seconds

etc.

Pupils should quickly spot that these are all the same, and therefore all that needs to be considered is the value, not the actual quantity being measured or the unit of measurement, and so we can consider rounding purely as a numerical exercise. From here, if needed, we can also use concrete apparatus to support making sense of rounding:

How close can you get to building this number if only using blue and green rods?

= 257

This can help support pupils in making sense of rounding to a less accurate value.

Of course, the one aspect of rounding that neither the number line or the Dienes blocks can settle is the rounding of the midway point – for example, 11.45 or 255. This is because both the number line and the Dienes blocks use a continuous measure view of number, and on a continuous scale the midway is not 'nearer' to either the upper or lower value in the next larger place.

Ultimately, the choice of rounding the midway values to the larger value in the next place is a relatively arbitrary one and there are different rounding conventions that round a '5' differently depending on whether the number to the left is even or odd (round half even, for example[2]). The general choice to round half up may come from a kind of symmetry in that if the digit following the place to be rounded to is a 0, 1, 2, 3, or 4 we round down, so if what follows is a 5, 6, 7, 8, 9 we round up, which can be seen using place value counters:

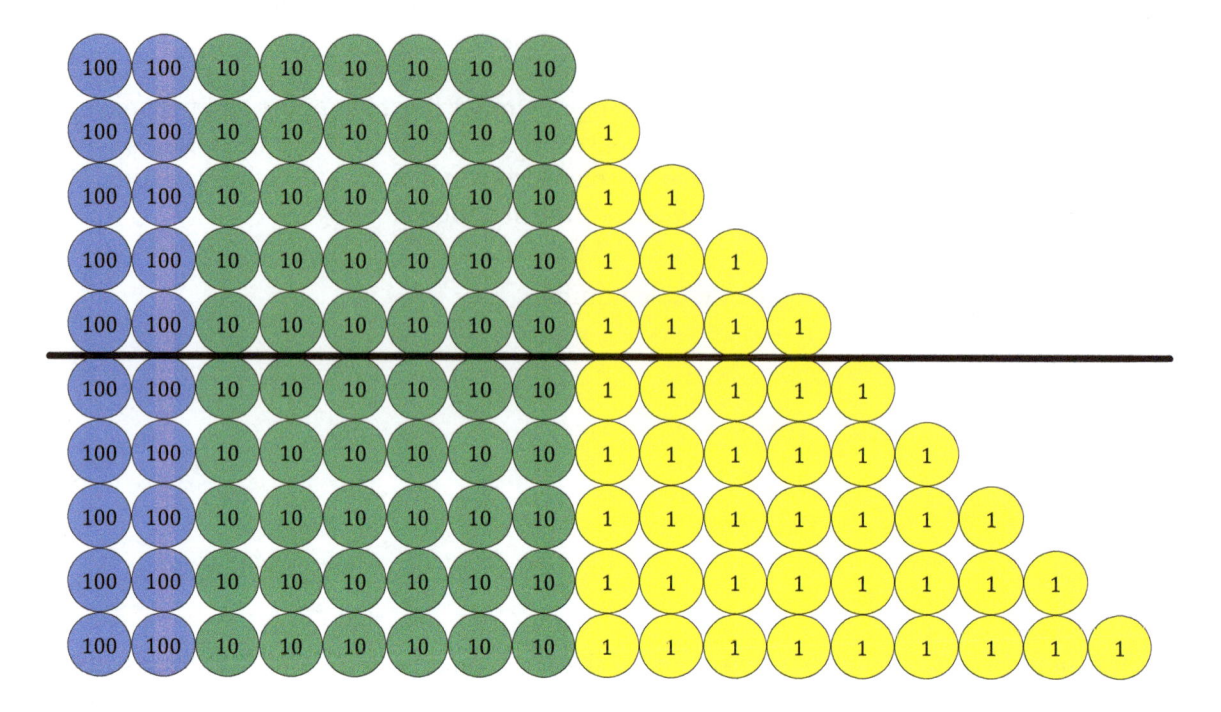

Once pupils have started to develop their understanding of rounding, there are many ways to support practice and to prompt thinking. A simple activity is one like the below:

Roll three dice. Use the three values given to create as many three-digit numbers as you can. Round each number to the nearest 10.

This activity can be adapted to then create decimal numbers, once again highlighting the parity between rounding for different place value columns. More dice can be added if required or virtual dice can be used if it is necessary to make sure all pupils are working on the same values. Following up with an activity like this one may also prompt more thinking about rounding.[3]

---

2 Everything2, Round Half to Even (11 January 2016). Available at: https://everything2.com/title/Round+half+to+even.
3 D. Steward, Rounding to Powers of 10, *Median* [blog] (20 August 2017). Available at: https://donsteward.blogspot.com/2017/08/rounding-to-powers-of-10.html.

Where we are eventually leading to is to be able to judge the relative accuracy of two measurements. For example, we might ask pupils:

Which of these has been measured more accurately?

a   2.37 metres

b   1.8 metres

Of course, this is fairly straightforward to judge as both numbers are of the same order of magnitude. However, the next is potentially not so simple:

Which of these has been measured more accurately?

a   2.37 metres

b   51.8 metres

In this case, the second number is one order of magnitude higher than the other, making it more difficult to judge – this illustrates that judging accuracy is not as simple as just looking at the number of decimal places/the number of columns used. We can further illustrate this:

The mean diameter of the Sun is 864,938 miles. The mean distance from the Earth to the Sun is 92,955,800 miles. Which of these is measured more accurately?

What we are illustrating here is that we can't really judge the relative accuracy of two measurements with different orders of magnitude by examining their place value columns. This motivates the introduction of the concept of significant figures.

Concept: significant figures

Prerequisites: Numbers, place value, measurement, rounding to a given place.

Linked concepts: Standard form, calculations completed on measured quantities (i.e. shape calculations, compound measure calculations).

The fundamental idea behind significant figures are those figures that are required to convey accurate information about the value and accuracy of a number. This implies automatically that all non-zero digits in a numeral will automatically be significant, as they tell us about the size of the part of the number indicated by the particular place value column in which that digit resides. This leaves the skill in identifying significant figures being ultimately tied up with being able to identify if any zero digits in the numeral are significant. To determine this, pupils need to be able to identify three of the roles that zero plays in any numeral:

1   Unit counting place holding.

2   Column separating place holding.

3   Accuracy place holding.

Accuracy

Complete the table:

The difference is:
nearest 100
− nearest 10

number	nearest 100	nearest 10	difference
174	200	170	+ 30
438			
563			
218			
35			
923			
263			
871			

Why are some differences the same?

What could the numbers be?

The difference is:
nearest 100
− nearest 10

number	nearest 100	nearest 10	difference
			− 30
			− 50
			+ 50
			+ 10
			− 10
			+ 20
			0
49			
51			

What type of number has a difference of −40?

Tara and Kieran start with
exactly the same number

Tara rounds this number
to the nearest 10

Kieran rounds the number
to the nearest 100

Kieran's number is now
double Tara's number

How can that happen?

To understand these three roles, we might consider something like the following:

> A quantity is measured and given the value 0.003300330 correct to the ninth decimal place. How many significant figures does it have?

What we can see here is that the first three zeroes (when reading from left to right) are only required because we have chosen our counting unit to be the 1s; they convey information about how the other columns relate to our counting unit but do not in and of themselves convey information about either the value or the accuracy of the number. Zeroes that place hold to convey information about the counting unit are not significant, as ultimately the choice of counting unit is arbitrary.

The next two zeroes (between the two sets of two 3s) play a different role. These are also place holders, but their job is to tells us about how many place value columns there are between the second and third 3. Without these zeroes we could not be sure about the place value that the third and fourth 3 are indicating. Any zeroes that separate the columns containing two other significant figures in this way are considered significant.

The final zero again plays a slightly different role again. This zero is not required to convey how the other digits relate to the counting unit, nor how their place value relates to each other; rather this zero is required to convey accurate information about the accuracy the value is being given to. This only really applies to values that have been rounded, as accuracy considerations only apply to inexact values. This makes this final zero significant.

One way we might support learners in making sense of this is to use a place value chart. However, rather than showing all columns, we only show the columns required to convey accurate information about the value and accuracy of the number.

> Write down the number of significant figures in the number 0.05020.

0.01s	0.001s	0.0001s	0.00001s
0.01		0.0001	
0.01		0.0001	
0.01			
0.01			
0.01			

We can see that in order to actually model this number (using place value counters in this case), I can start with the hundredths column, as the ones and the tenths are not needed to communicate anything about either value or accuracy. However, I do need the thousandths column as it separates the hundredths from the ten-thousandths (on MathsBot.com this appears automatically because there is a need for the ten-thousandths column).[4] The ten-thousandths column is required as there are 2 ten-thousandths as part of this number, and then the hundred-thousandths column is also required because the value has been given to that level of accuracy. This indicates that there are four significant figures as part of this numeral.

A potential alternative to this is to write the number in standard form. Because standard form can be seen as redefining the counting unit to be the largest column that holds value, this will automatically remove any unit-counting place holders, leaving only those that are column separating (although pupils still need to be clear to leave any accuracy place holding zeroes). If we consider the same value of 0.05020 written in standard form, this would be 5.020×10^{-2}. We can see that the lead part of this numeral contains the four significant figures, and so writing a number in standard form provides a mechanism by which we might identify significant figures (provided we have broached the issue of accuracy place holders with pupils). This, of course, requires pupils to be proficient in writing numbers in standard form and so would make standard form a prerequisite to teaching about significant figures. The relationship between significant figures and standard form is almost symbiotic in nature, with understanding of one being able to inform the other, whichever way around they are explored, and so the choice as to which to explore first is largely down to teacher/school preference (there is no research that I am aware of that suggests there is a benefit to teaching about one before the other). However, both concepts are used outside of maths, particularly in science, and so it may be that this also needs to be taken into account when deciding which concept to teach first. Either way, it would seem sensible to use one to inform and support the other, and the links between the two should definitely be highlighted once both have been examined by pupils.

It is important when teaching significant figures to consider the range of examples that pupils will need to have been exposed to in order to fully comprehend the concept.

Identify the number of significant figures in each of the following:

a	3200		k	30.02
b	32_0_0		l	3.002
c	320_0_		m	3.020
d	3020		n	0.320
e	302_0_		o	0.302
f	3002		p	0.032
g	300.2		q	0.32
h	302.0		r	0.0302
i	30.20		s	0.0320
j	30.2		t	1.0320

One thing to draw explicit attention to here is the underline notation used on some of the zeroes in questions b, c, and e. This is a notation that can be used to indicate that a zero is being used to show accuracy rather than being a unit-counting place holder. For example, in

---

4 J. Hall, Place Value Counters, *MathsBot.com* (n.d.). Available at: https://mathsbot.com/manipulatives/placeValueCounters.

(b) there are considered to be three significant figures, and in (c) there are four significant figures (as the first zero now also becomes significant as it is place holding between two other significant figures).

In addition to identifying significant figures in a numeral, a nice activity is to prompt pupils to write numerals that contain given significant figures. This can again be done as an activity that introduces constraints or using an activity like the 'Particular, Peculiar, General' sequence described in the book *Thinkers* from the Association of Teachers of Mathematics:[5]

Write down a number that has:

a   4 significant figures

b   and is greater than 10000

c   and only contains 2 non-zero digits

d   and contains exactly one zero that shows accuracy

Write down an example of a number that has 4 significant figures.

Write down a peculiar example.

Write down some general examples.

Developing pupils' understanding of what significant figures are, and how to identify them, brings several advantages. The first is that it resolves the issue around identifying the level of accuracy within measurements that have different orders of magnitude. If we now return to these questions:

Which of these has been measured more accurately?

a   2.37 metres

b   51.8 metres

The mean diameter of the Sun is 864,938 miles. The mean distance from the Earth to the Sun is 92,955,800 miles. Which of these is measured more accurately?

we can see that in the first question, both values have been measured to three significant figures, and therefore both might be considered equally accurate. In the second question, the diameter of the Sun and the distance from Earth to the Sun are both given to six significant figures, again suggesting they are equally accurate. The use of significant figures rather than place value columns to measure the given accuracy of a measured value gives a much greater sense of the accuracy of the measurements, although in failing to take account of the actual size of the values being measured still is not perfect (we will explore better ways of judging relative accuracy later in the chapter).

---

[5] C. Bills, L. Bills, J. Mason and A. Watson, *Thinkers: A Collection of Activities to Provoke Mathematical Thinking* (Derby: Association of Teachers of Mathematics, 2004), p. 9.

A second advantage to the use of significant figures is the flexibility they give in being able to express the desired accuracy for values that have very different orders of magnitude. Consider the following question.

Round each of the following to 1 significant figure:

320,000

32,000

3200

320

3.2

0.32

0.032

0.0032

To achieve the same result in reference to place value columns, we would have to specify a different place value column for each value. By communicating the desired accuracy using significant figures rather than place value columns, we can simplify the communication significantly. In carrying out the rounding required, pupils will, of course, consider the place value column that the first significant figure is in, and round to that place accordingly – pupils should be clear that using significant figures does not change the process or thinking underpinning the act of rounding, rather simply how we communicate it.

Significant figures can also be used to provide a 'rule of thumb' for judging the appropriate accuracy to give results to calculations that involve measured or inaccurate values. For example:

A rectangular field is measured as having dimensions of 3.24 metres by 6.87 metres. Give a suitable value for the area of the field.

If we simply calculate the area of the field using the given values, we arrive at a value of the area of 22.2588 m^2. However, it should be clear that this value does not take into account any error in the measurement of the dimensions of the rectangle. This would suggest that the true value of the area may well be something other than precisely 22.2588 m^2. We can judge what might be a 'suitable value' for the area of the field by considering the accuracy of the values used to calculate the area – in this case both were measured to three significant figures. The good rule of thumb for judging a suitable accuracy for the result of this calculation is to use no more than the same level of accuracy for the result than is used in the initial measurements, and potentially one figure less. In this case, that would suggest that either 22.3 m^2 or simply 22 m^2 is a suitable value for the area of the field.

A rectangular field is measured as having dimension of 3.247 metres by 6.87 metres. Give a suitable value of the area of the field.

In this case, the result of calculating the area with the given numbers is 22.30689 m^2. However, this time the dimensions have been given to different levels of accuracy, the first given to four significant figures and the second only to three (why this might be is open to guess!). In this case, the 'rule of thumb' would still suggest giving the final value to either three or two significant figures, taking the level of accuracy from the least accurate measurement provided, i.e. the fact that one value has been provided to four significant figure accuracy does not mitigate against the issues arising from the fact that the other has only been given to three.

Similarly to using significant figures to compare the level of accuracy different measurements have been given to, there are more robust ways to decide what is a suitable value for the result of calculations based on inaccurate values. However, the use of significant figures can provide a start point for the journey towards these more robust methods, as well as serving as an excellent vehicle for revisiting calculations based on measured quantities that pupils may have worked on in previous concepts such as area, volume, compound measures, etc. To work towards more robust approaches pupils will need to consider the actual sizes of the errors involved in these measurements and how these errors propagate in calculations.

Concept: errors, error intervals, error bounds

Prerequisites: Numbers, place value, measurement, rounding to a given place, inequalities.

Linked concepts: Significant figures, calculations completed on measured quantities (i.e. shape calculations, compound measure calculations).

At first glance these might seem like three different concepts, and in a way they are, but they are so closely related that it will not be detrimental to examine them together, or at least in close proximity to each other. Once pupils are introduced to the idea of error in measurement, then we can talk about how we might quantify that error. There are different possible approaches that can be taken:

1. To write the size of the error as an absolute possible difference to the given quantity.
2. To write an interval showing the possible values the measurement might take, bounding the measurement between its smallest and largest possible values.
3. To write the size of the error relative to the size of the measurement (usually as a percentage).

Let us consider the following:

> A length, l, is measured as 4.28 metres to three significant figures. What is the largest possible error in this measurement? What are the bounds on the size of this measurement? Write an interval for all possible values that l could take. What is the relative percentage error in this measurement?

A nice way to visualise this is on a scale or number line:

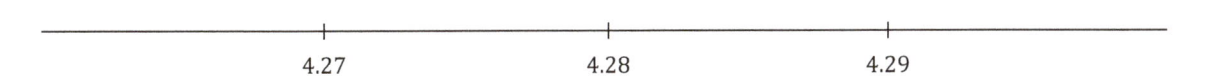

```
─────────────┼──────────────┼──────────────┼─────────────
           4.27           4.28           4.29
```

On the line we can see the given value for the length of 4.28 and also the two closest values that have the same level of accuracy. We are interested in the maximum distance we could be away from 4.28, and still give a value of 4.28 rather than 4.27 or 4.29 when rounded to three significant figures. Pupils should have little trouble in seeing the similarities between what we are considering here and how we approached introducing rounding; indeed we could phrase the previous statement as, 'We are interested in the maximum distance we could be away from 4.28 and still have a value that rounds to 4.28 rather than 4.27 or 4.29 when rounded to three significant figures.' If pupils have been properly introduced to rounding in this way, then it should not be a huge leap to arrive at the conclusion that the furthest away we could be is a distance of 0.005 metres – any further below 4.28 and the values would round to 4.27, and if we were this far above 4.28 then we would potentially round to 4.29 (depending on the rounding convention used). This gives the absolute possible error as 0.005 metres, and so we could more accurately write that the given length is 4.28 ± 0.005 metres. Pupils should be clear that this represents the maximum absolute error in this measurement; it is physically the furthest we could be from 4.28 metres and still be correct in giving the value as 4.28 metres when rounded to three significant figures.

To go a little further, we could then state the value of this measurement is bounded by the values 4.275 and 4.285 – these are the actual values that mark the points where the true value of the length would be closer to 4.28 than to either 4.27 or 4.29. We can inform pupils that 4.275 would be considered the lower bound for this measurement, and 4.285 would be considered the upper bound for this measurement. Of these, it is generally the upper bound that causes the most consternation, and pupils correctly identify that if the true length was 4.285 this would actually be rounded to 4.29 (given the standard rounding convention of round half up that is used in compulsory school mathematics). Pupils are often tempted instead to think the upper bound would be 4.284 – if pupils are making this mistake then it suggests they are stuck in thinking about numbers in a discrete fashion rather than the necessary continuous fashion for this case. A good idea in this instance is to remind pupils about the existence of numbers such as 4.2849 and potentially to push them towards recognition that, when treating values as continuous there is no 'last number' before 4.285 – the concept of 'next' and 'last' don't really exist without a discrete counting unit. This means that 4.285 is the upper bound for the length, but we can acknowledge that this behaves slightly differently to the lower bound in that the length cannot actually take the upper bound value, whereas it can take the lower bound value. A further confusion then arises when we consider bounds for discrete valued variables (as we will see shortly).

Having established the upper and lower bound values, we can then write an interval for all possible values of l, namely $4.275 \leq l < 4.285$.

This interval takes into account the issue surrounding the different natures of the lower and upper bounds by using inequalities symbols to make clear the value of l could be 4.275 but cannot actually be 4.285. This should go some way towards supporting pupils in seeing why 4.285 is a valid upper bound.

The absolute error of ±0.005 does not, however, take into account the size of the measurement itself. In order to do this, we need to look at assigning a value to the error, which is relative to the size of the measurement itself. This is normally given as a percentage:

$\frac{0.005}{4.28} \times 100 = 0.117\%$ (given to 3 significant figures (s.f.))

Relative percentage error gives a much more robust way of comparing the accuracy in measurement of two values, particularly when the measurements have different orders of magnitude. Coming back again to this question:

> Which of these has been measured more accurately?
>
> a   2.37 metres
>
> b   51.8 metres

We can see that in the first measurement the absolute error is 0.005 metres, and so the relative percentage error would be $\frac{0.005}{2.37} \times 100 = 0.211\%$ (3 s.f). In the second measurement the absolute error is only 0.05 metres, but the relative percentage error is $\frac{0.05}{51.8} \times 100 = 0.0965\%$ (3 s.f.) suggesting the second measurement is somewhere near twice as accurate as the first, even though both have been given to three significant figures – the logic here being that it is much more difficult to measure such a comparatively large distance as 51.8 metres to the given level of accuracy, compared to the much smaller measurement of only 2.37 metres. However, it should be noted that it is unusual to see relative percentage error calculated based on the maximum possible error (although it is, of course, possible). Instead, relative percentage error tends to be used to compare a measured value with a 'true value'; often a value generated from experimentation compared to the value provided by a theoretical model:

> In an experiment the time taken for a ball to fall from a height of 2 metres to the ground is measured to be 0.78 seconds. A model for the falling ball gives a 'true' value for the fall of 0.75 seconds. Work out the relative percentage error of the experimental value from the true value.

This would be calculated as $\frac{0.03}{0.75} \times 100 = 4\%$ relative percentage error.

Although relative percentage error is not part of compulsory school mathematics (at least at the time of writing), it may be used in science and other curriculum areas, and is a great way to interweave percentage calculation with error and uncertainty.

Returning to the issue with discrete values, the fact that 'next' and 'last' do exist for discrete data means that we can treat the bounds slightly differently. It should be noted, however, that the sorts of situations in which these issues arrive are almost always somewhat contrived as discrete values are rarely (if ever) the subject of measurement error – it is almost always possible to assign a value to a discrete value that is exact. The following, then, might be considered for the sake of completeness or interest, but pupils should be clear it is unlikely to be a useful real application of the idea of error:

> A bank account promises to pay £10.00 interest (I) per quarter, to the nearest 10p. Find the upper and lower bounds of this value, and express the error as an interval.

In this case, the number line is less helpful, as it is a continuous scale, but can still support pupils in visualising the situation:

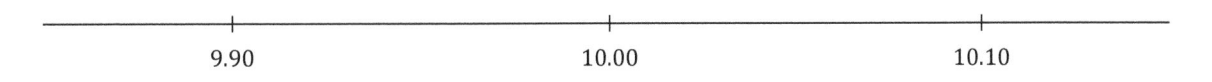

```
─────────────┼─────────────────────┼─────────────────────┼─────────────
           9.90                  10.00                 10.10
```

Here we see the monetary values scaled in 10 pence increments, focussed around £10. What the number line doesn't convey as well in this case is that not all values between those given exist – there is no 10.007, for example. We could, of course, amend the number line to show only the values that exist:

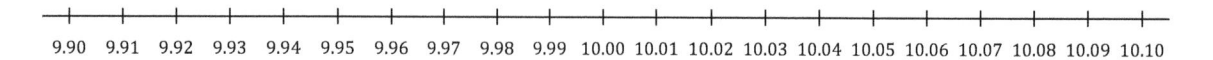

|—+—
9.90 9.91 9.92 9.93 9.94 9.95 9.96 9.97 9.98 9.99 10.00 10.01 10.02 10.03 10.04 10.05 10.06 10.07 10.08 10.09 10.10

However, the number line still doesn't (for me at least) adequately capture the discrete nature of this problem. An alternative could be to use place value counters; however, we would need a lot of them to create the 21 different values between £9.90 and £10.10 (inclusive). Whatever we decide, the important point for pupils to recognise here is that, because £10.05 would round to £10.10 to the nearest 10 pence, then whilst the lower bound is still £9.95, the upper bound is now £10.04, as that is the last possible value that would round to £10.00 to the nearest 10p. If we were to express this using inequalities, we would write $9.95 \leq I \leq 10.04$. Although it would equally be true that $9.95 \leq I < 10.05$, the first inequality is completely equivalent to this as no value exists between 10.04 and 10.05, and in writing the second we are treating a discrete quantity as if it were continuous.

As previously mentioned, this sort of thing is rarely (if ever) something that needs to be considered for errors and measurement; however, it can be useful to consider such scenarios to reinforce the differing nature of discrete and continuous quantities, and may be useful when considering writing ranges of values more generally – for example, in writing constraints for integer programming problems or when grouping discrete valued data variables.

One of my favourite activities to offer pupils to support practice around errors and bounds is the table on page 4 of the Nuffield Foundation 'Errors' document. What is nice about this activity is that, whilst the values and units change, the degree of accuracy given remains the same for each bank of three to four questions. The first four questions are all values provided to the nearest whole number, then to one decimal place, then two, then to the nearest 10. This aspect of the task uses **variation** to support pupils in discerning the underlying structure of the ideas around error and bounds by varying the non-essential features. Then, in the last four questions, the same value is repeated twice whilst the given accuracy changes, which means that the task reinforces with pupils how changing the given accuracy changes the error and bounds.[6]

In addition, questions such as this are great to prompt thinking about bounds:

> The length of the River Thames is 300 km when rounded to 1 significant figure and is 350 km when rounded to 2 significant figures. Find the upper and lower bounds.

Returning to this question:

> A rectangular field is measured as having dimensions of 3.24 metres by 6.87 metres. Give a suitable value for the area of the field.

---

[6] Nuffield Foundation, Errors (2011). Available at: https://www.nuffieldfoundation.org/sites/default/files/files/FSMA%20Errors%20student(1).pdf.

A classic misconception once pupils have studied bounds is to think that we can bound the area of this field by calculating the area using the given values, and then considering the bounds on the result, i.e.:

3.24 × 6.87 = 22.2588

Therefore the lower bound is 22.25875 and the upper bound is 22.25885.

What this fails to take into account is the way that errors propagate in calculation. It may be simpler to actually consider perimeter before area when beginning to look at bounds on calculated values, as pupils can see the effect of the error propagating due to the addition much more straightforwardly than they can through multiplication:

> A rectangular field is measured as having dimensions of 3.24 metres by 6.87 metres. Give a suitable value for the perimeter of the field.

When looking at this with pupils, it is highly recommended to look at a picture of the rectangle:

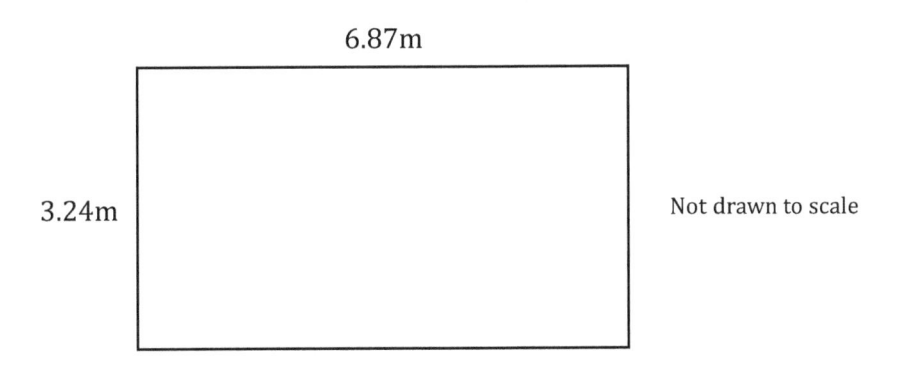

```
                6.87m
        ┌──────────────────┐
        │                  │
3.24m   │                  │   Not drawn to scale
        │                  │
        └──────────────────┘
```

These values give a perimeter of 20.22 metres and would suggest (erroneously) that the bounds might be 20.215 metres and 20.225 metres. Of course, the values provided are not necessarily the true values of the dimensions. The smallest possible dimensions the rectangle could have are:

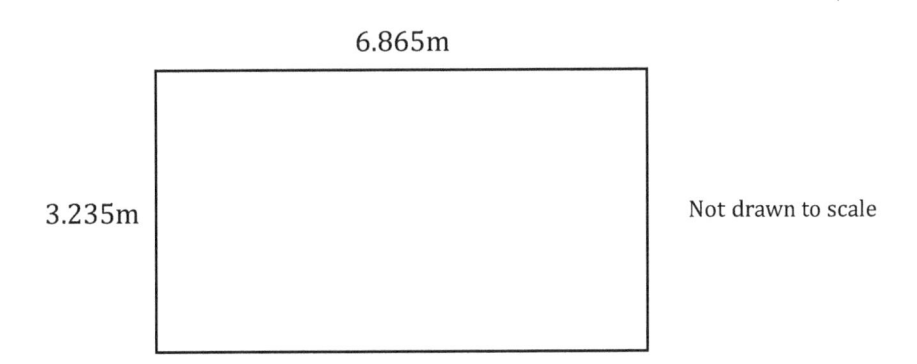

```
                6.865m
        ┌──────────────────┐
        │                  │
3.235m  │                  │   Not drawn to scale
        │                  │
        └──────────────────┘
```

This would mean the perimeter could actually be as low as 20.2 metres. Similarly, the largest possible dimensions the rectangle could have are:

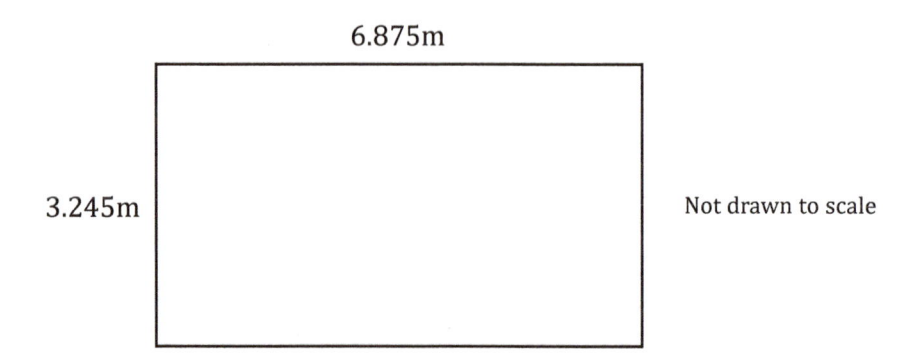

6.875m

3.245m   Not drawn to scale

Giving a maximum perimeter of 20.24 metres. These are very different lower and upper bounds to those that would be given from calculating the perimeter using the given values. It is worth asking pupils to reason why this would be, prompting them to recognise that the erroneous bounds are only 0.005 different from the calculated perimeter, whereas the correct bounds are 0.005 × 4 = 0.02 metres from the calculated perimeter, and that this is precisely because each length contributes 0.005 to the overall error. This shows pupils that the errors in the original values propagate in calculations – and serves as a stark warning to pupils about the dangers of using inaccurate values in further calculations.

Of course, what we have avoided at this point is a more rigorous analysis of how different operations affect the bounds on the result when calculations are completed using inaccurate values. It is quite intuitive that combining bigger lengths will give bigger results, and combining smaller lengths will give smaller results. However, this can lead to a misconception that we always choose the upper bounds of the measured values to calculate the upper bound of the result, and the lower bounds of the measured values to calculate the lower bound of the result. We need to dispel this misconception early with pupils if it arises. There are a couple of approaches that we can take to this, the first of which is to represent the calculations on a number line (it might be easier to start with whole numbers with pupils, but the sorts of pictures will be the same):

$(0.3 \pm 0.05) + (0.4 \pm 0.05)$

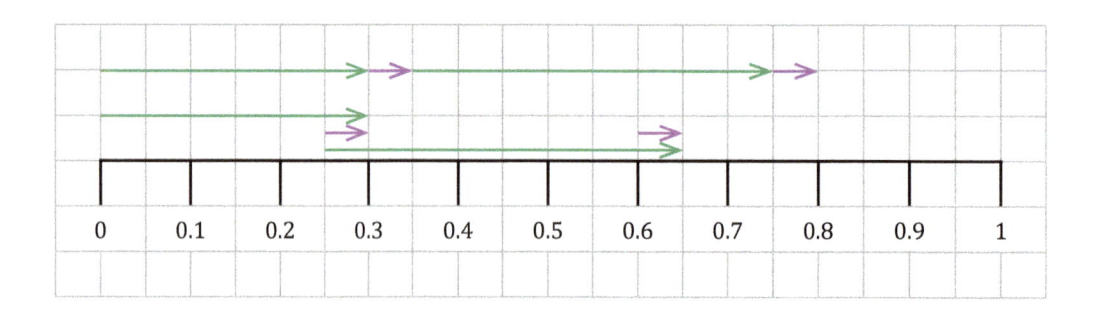

What is happening here is that we are trying to combine the four vectors in such a way as to create the longest length possible, and the shortest length possible, where the green vectors have to be added but the purple vectors can either be added or subtracted. We might offer this as a set of instructions to pupils (provided they are well versed in modelling addition and subtraction using vectors), although it can be difficult for some pupils to make sense of these as instructions. This can be supported by actually providing physical apparatus for the vectors – pencils and erasers can work well if there isn't time to create actual models of the arrows, and similar things can be modelled with Dienes blocks by choosing a suitable whole (here the square block would be the most suitable whole). In this case, we can see that the longest length it is possible to create is a value of 0.8 (0.3 + 0.05 + 0.4 + 0.05) and the shortest length it is possible to create is a value of 0.6 (0.3 – 0.5 + 0.4 – 0.5). A similar diagram arises from considering subtraction:

(0.4 ± 0.05) – (0.3 ± 0.05)

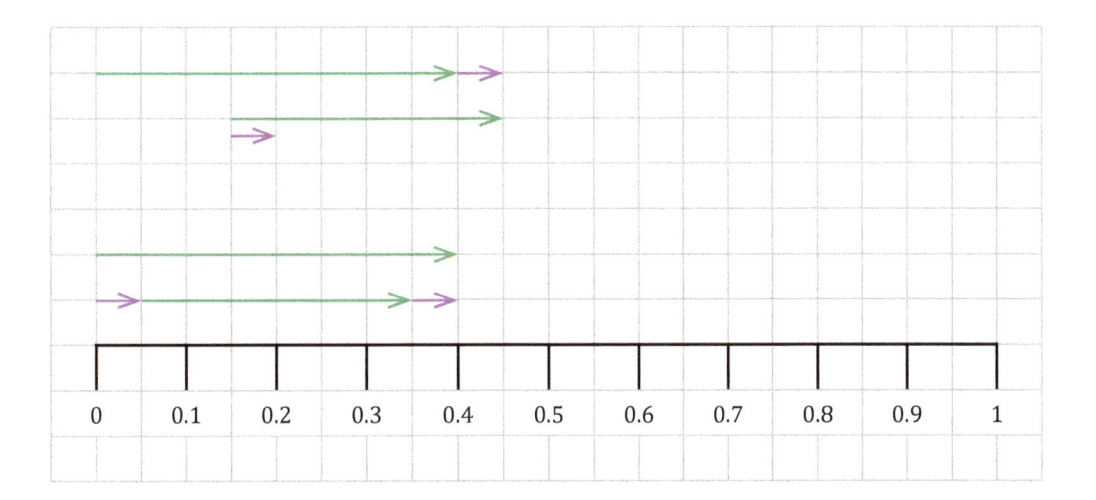

Now, of course, we are trying to create the largest and smallest possible values when the smaller green vector has to be subtracted from the larger, but the purple vectors can still be added or subtracted. This time the largest possible value is 0.2 (which properly is the result of the calculation 0.4 + 0.05 – (0.3 – 0.05) but can equally be seen as 0.04 – 0.03 + 0.05 + 0.05) and the smallest is actually 0 (again, properly this is from 0.4 – 0.05 – (3 + 0.05) but can equally be seen as 0.4 – 0.05 – 0.3 – 0.05).

This hints at a general approach for finding the upper and lower bounds of an addition or subtraction calculation, where the upper bounds are found by doing the minimum number of subtractions possible (in the case of an addition calculation this is 0, and in a subtraction calculation this is 1), or conversely the maximum number of additions possible, and where the lower bound is found by doing the maximum number of subtractions possible (for addition, 2; for subtraction, 3) or conversely the minimum number of additions.

When it comes to multiplication, the area model is probably the best model to the show how the upper and lower bound is calculated; however, it isn't particularly helpful to support evaluating the result of the calculations:

(0.4 ± 0.05) × (0.3 ± 0.05)

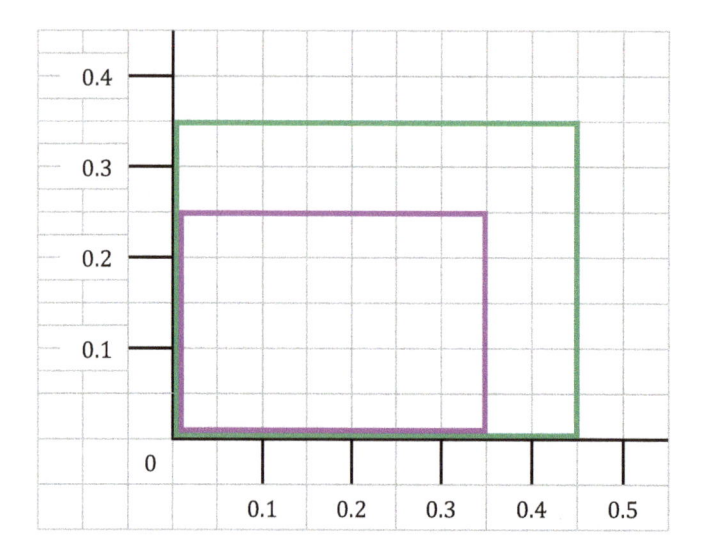

Because we are using an area model, the question becomes reasonably straightforward – 'How do we create a rectangle with the smallest/largest possible area?' Pupils should quite readily identify that the upper bound will come from having the largest possible dimensions, and the lower bound will come from having the lowest possible dimensions.

Finally, when it comes to division, the most applicable model is the comparison model. In a similar vein to the area model, the question becomes 'How can we make the comparison, between the first and second number as large/small as possible – i.e. how do we make the first number as large/small as possible compared to the first?'

$(0.4 \pm 0.05) \div (0.3 \pm 0.05)$

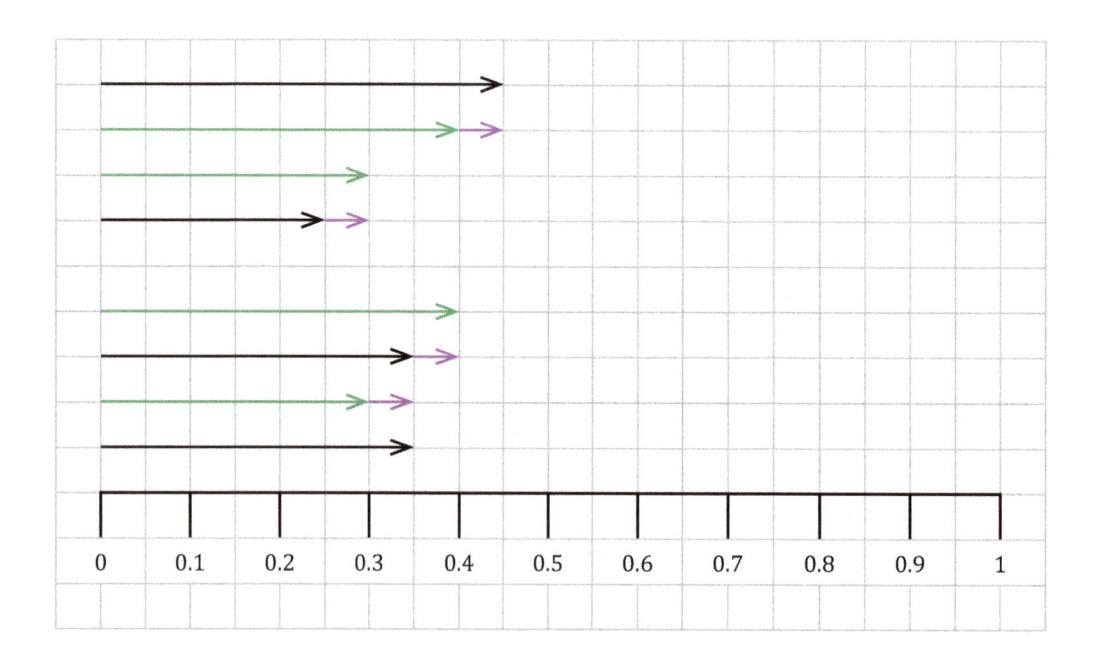

The comparison here is between the black vectors, which are the resultants. In the top picture we make the upper vector compare as largely as possible to the lower vector by making the upper vector as large as possible, and the lower vector as small as possible. In the bottom picture we do the reverse – make the upper vector as small as possible and the lower vector as large as possible. This gives the upper bound as 1.8 and the lower bound as 1.

Some find that these pictures, particularly for multiplication and division, don't really add a huge amount to pupils making sense of the concept. As mentioned, Dienes blocks might be an alternative:

| (0.4 ± 0.05) + (0.3 ± 0.05) |
| (0.4 ± 0.05) − (0.3 ± 0.05) |
| (0.4 ± 0.05) × (0.3 ± 0.05) |
| (0.4 ± 0.05) ÷ (0.3 ± 0.05) |

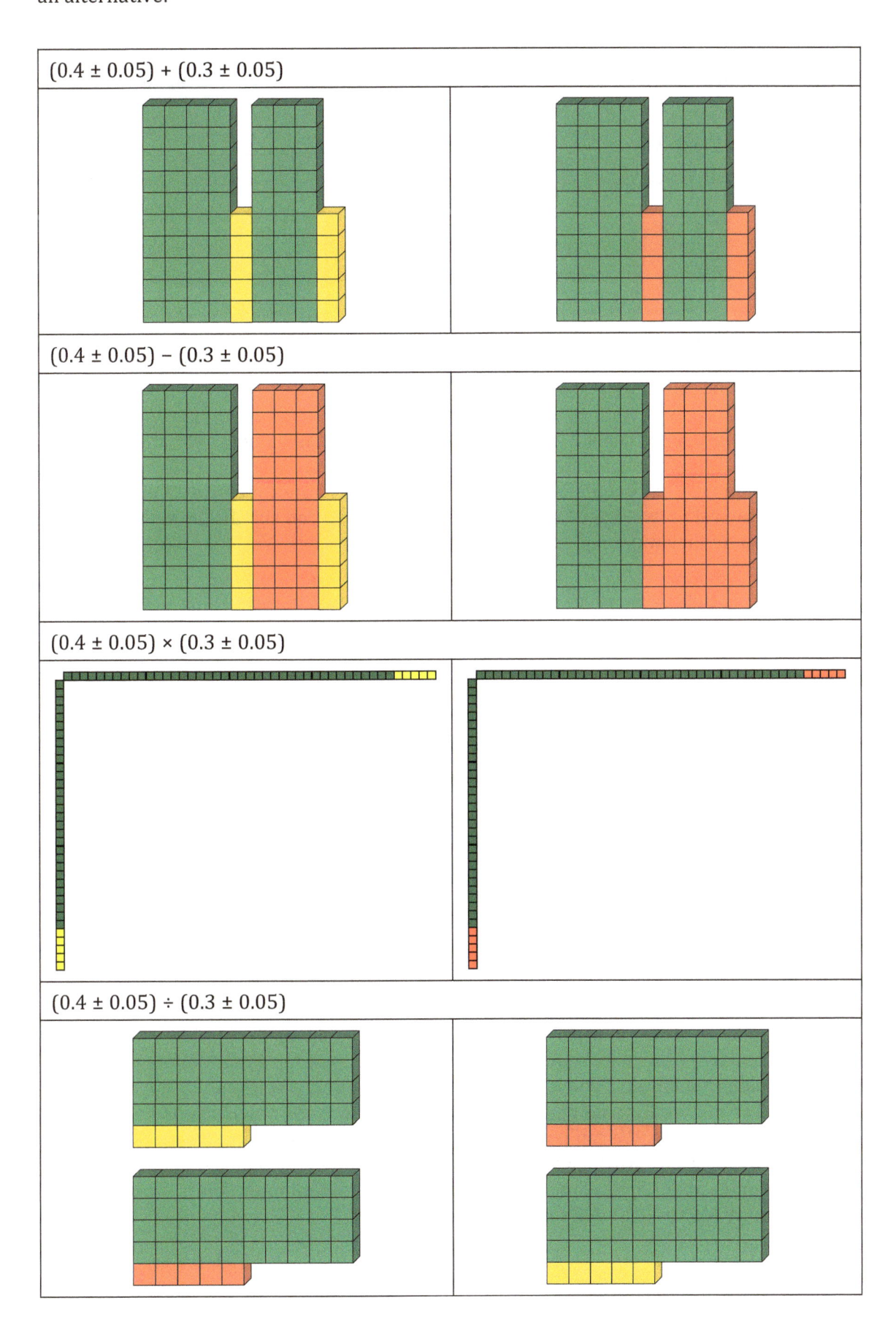

However, again, one might question the usefulness of this, particularly for multiplication and division.

A nice activity that can support or replace the above use of visuals is something like:

Choose any two numbers from the list below and fill in the blanks to create an answer that is:

a   the largest possible.

b   the smallest possible.

$$2, 5, 7, 11, 16, 28$$

___ + ___   ___ − ___   ___ × ___   ___ ÷ ___

This activity might prompt reinforcing when we might choose the upper bound, and when we might choose the lower bound – particularly recognising that 5, 7, 11 and 16 will not be used in any of the calculations.

We can offer many practical situations where errors in measurement will affect calculations. In fact, what I find nice here is to revisit those practical situations that we originally looked at when we were judging suitable accuracy using significant figures. This allows us to compare the values we judged to be 'suitable' when based on significant figures and see how appropriate they were. For example, in this question:

A rectangular field is measured as having dimensions of 3.24 metres by 6.87 metres. Give a suitable value for the area of the field.

Originally, when using significant figures to judge suitable accuracy, we suggested that either 22.3 m^2 or simply 22 m^2 were suitable based on the calculated value of 22.2588 m^2 and an accuracy of either 2 or 3 significant figures. If we now calculate the bounds on the area we find that:

Lower bound: 3.235 × 6.865 = 22.208275 m^2

Upper bound: 3.245 × 6.875 = 22.309375 m^2

From the bounds we can see that the value of the area could actually be low enough that it would round to 22.2 m^2 if we were to round it to three significant figures. This means we cannot actually claim for sure that the area of this rectangle is 22.3 m^2. In fact, the highest level of accuracy we can be sure of is that the true value of the area rounds to 22 m^2. This provides the more robust approach for deciding what the most appropriate value is for a measure calculated from inaccurate values. By revisiting the same situations we used when looking at using significant figures to judge accuracy, we can see when our earlier rule of thumb worked and when it didn't, as well as being able to write down a properly rounded value for each situation. We can potentially also link this to solving equations by trial and improvement (which we will look at later) – the establishment of bounds that allow a judgement to be made about a value to a particular accuracy is common to both concepts, even though the way we arrive at those bounds is different.

In offering pupils situations in which to consider the bounds on calculation, it is important that we consider calculations that involve exact values, such as $A = \frac{3\sqrt{3}}{2} s^2$ as the formula for the area of a regular hexagon or $C = 2\pi r$ as the circumference of a circle so that pupils have to consider for which values bounds are needed (i.e. the measured ones) but also have to consider the implications of using rounded versions of irrational numbers like $\sqrt{3}$ and π. In addition, problems such as the one below are also useful:

> A solid cube has a length of 16.2 cm to the nearest mm. When the cube is weighed the scale reads 3.27 kg to 2 decimal places. An object can float in water if its density is less than the water. The density of water is 1 g/cm³. Is it possible the cube will float?

There is a lot for pupils to unpick in this question: 'How do I calculate the density?', 'Do I need maximum or minimum density?', 'How does this affect the mass I use?', 'What about using the length of the cube to get the volume?' There are lots of different problem-solving strategies out there that teachers can use to support pupils with interpreting what is required from problems like this. Two strategies that I have found successful for this sort of problem with different pupils are to work the problem through first without considering the bounds – just find the volume of the cube, use this with the mass to find the density, then compare the density to the given one – and then once this process is clear, consider how we need to adapt it to take into account the measurement inaccuracy. Alternatively, for some pupils I find it more useful to work backwards along the chain: to answer the question we need the minimum density, and as long as this is less than 1 then it is possible the cube will float. To find density I divide mass by volume, so to find minimum density I need the minimum mass (in grams) and the maximum volume. The maximum volume will be found by cubing the maximum length. We can then run this forward with the actual values: $\frac{3265}{12.25^3}$ = 0.7608 ... < 1 so yes the cube could float.

Potentially, the 'ultimate' version of a question like this (at school level anyway) would involve the cosine function (which we will discuss when considering shape in the next chapter) so that pupils have to consider the effect that taking the upper bound on an angle will give the lower bound of the cosine of the value and vice versa. Of course, a lot depends on the curriculum structure we are working with as to whether pupils have sufficiently studied the cosine function to recognise this property as it applies to bounds.

So far, we have only looked at the idea of errors, intervals and bounds applied to rounded values. However, rounding is not the only way that we commonly reduce accuracy of values to make them more appropriate. We will continue this chapter with a look at truncation.

Concept: truncation

Prerequisites: Numbers, place value, division, measurement.

Linked concepts: Significant figures, rounding to a given place, calculations completed on measured quantities (i.e. shape calculations, compound measure calculations), inequalities.

The use of the word 'truncation' was first introduced in school-level maths in England in 2015, but the idea has been used a lot more informally for a lot longer. What is important in teaching about truncation is that we recognise situations where it arises, and ensure pupils recognise and use the language explicitly. What this means is that, rather than teaching a block on 'truncation' (although we will want to teach about it explicitly – perhaps in comparison to rounding), it is often the approach (and in my view a perfectly sensible one) to make sure opportunities to identify, name and exemplify truncation occur throughout the teaching of other concepts (including error, as we shall see). Take, for example, this question:

> Seven people want to share £223 equally between them. How much should each person get?

This is the sort of question that primary age pupils might be offered, and we would certainly expect secondary pupils to recognise the steps required to solve the problem even if they don't immediately understand and respect the nuance involved in providing a satisfactory solution to the question. Clearly, the calculation required is 223 ÷ 7, which gives a result (as a decimal) of 31.857142. This is, of course, not an appropriate answer to this question as it is not a valid amount of money. Pupils might be tempted to round this to £31.86; however, this is not a correct answer as 7 × 31.86 = £223.02 and we do not have that amount of money. In this case, the most money that each can receive is actually £31.85, and if we are further limited to only being able to share whole pounds (perhaps the lowest denomination of coin we have is a £1 coin) then we can only give each person £31, even though the result of the division is clearly nearly £32. Now, of course, we could discuss the practical implications of this problem – giving two people a single penny less, or what to do with the extra 5p/£6 (depending on whether we are limited to sharing whole pounds or not) that we are not able to share equally, but one thing that mustn't be overlooked in this situation is that we have truncated the value of 31.857142 to either 31.85 or just 31. It is opportunities like these that must be planned for and seized upon to exemplify what truncation is and where it is used. Pupils should be taught that the name for this removal of all value after a certain place value column is called truncation, and they should be prompted to properly name it whenever it occurs. Pupils could even be asked to design scenarios where truncation will be preferred or required rather than rounding – many of these will undoubtedly involve division and so it is when teaching concepts that rely heavily on division as a part of them that we should plan for and seize upon situations where truncation will arise.

As part of exploring truncation as and when it arises, we should spend some time on it when looking at errors and intervals. A typical practical situation where we might look at truncation is in looking at age:

> A person gives their age on a form as '15 years old'. Write an interval showing the possible error in the age of the person.

Unlike most other measured quantities, age in years tends not to be given as a rounded value. If a person is 14.5 years old, we wouldn't say they are 15 years old. Indeed, we wouldn't say they are 15 even if they are $14\frac{364}{365}$ years old. We wouldn't, in fact, say the person is 15 years old until the day they turn 15 (it gets a little more interesting if we start to consider time of day). Similarly, six months after a person's 15th birthday, they don't suddenly start referring to themselves as 16 – they won't do so until their 16th birthday. This, of course, is indicative of truncation – if a person's age is 15.anything, they will say it is 15.

In writing the error interval, we therefore have to take the age from the day of turning 15, right up until just before the day they turn 16, i.e. $15 \leq A < 16$.

A nice activity to explore errors due to truncation is to look at covered calculators. Because truncation is about removal of digits, covering the end of a calculator display can be seen as truncating the value. This can be described in words:

A calculator display has a 9 in the hundred-thousands column and a 6 in the ten-thousands column. The rest of the digits are hidden. Write down an interval to show the range of values that could be displayed on the calculator.

Or shown as an image:[7]

Use inequalities to show the range of values that could be displayed on this broken calculator screen:

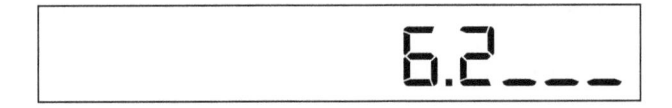

[calculator display: 96____]

It is worth noting that the inequalities from each of these questions would be slightly different; in the first it would be $960000 \leq x < 970000$, whereas in the second, because we know it is an integer (there is no decimal point) the range of values would be a little more limited to $960000 \leq x \leq 969999$. What is nice about this second type of question, though, is that we can prompt a lot more thinking about range of values, for example:

Use inequalities to show the range of values that could be displayed on this broken calculator screen:

[calculator display: 6.2___]

Because these values are effectively discrete, we are using discrete bounds to show the range of values. In this case, the number cannot actually be 6.2000 as this wouldn't be displayed in this way on the calculator, so the correct inequality would be $6.2001 \leq x \leq 6.2999$.

Once pupils have explored writing error intervals from both rounding and truncation then it is definitely worth offering a mix of situations so that pupils have to consider whether the value has been rounded or truncated before writing the interval.

At the beginning of the chapter, I said that estimation should be a skill that is used throughout pupil work in mathematics, and I stand by that statement. The ability to informally estimate and judge whether results are sensible is something that should constantly be expected of pupils, and pupils should be supported in achieving it. There are, however, explicit situations in school-level maths where values are required to be rounded in order to estimate the result of a calculation. We will now look at the teaching of estimation.

---

7   P. Mattock, Errors in Truncation, *TES* (7 May 2016). Available at: https://www.tes.com/teaching-resource/errors-in-truncation-11271966.

Conceptual Maths

Concept: estimation

Prerequisites: Numbers, operations.

Linked concepts: Measurement, significant figures, rounding to a given place, calculations completed on measured quantities (i.e. shape calculations, compound measure calculations).

As previously stated, pupils should be introduced to the idea of estimation very early, at or shortly after the point where they start looking at calculations large enough that a simple representation won't immediately make it clear whether the calculated result is correct. Pupils should be encouraged to develop a 'sense' of whether the computed answer makes sense given the order or magnitude of the numbers involved. For example:

Rosie says that 700 ÷ 5 = 35 because 700 ÷ 10 = 70 and 5 is half of 10. Is Rosie's answer sensible?

We are not looking here for pupils to take any real formal approach, and in offering pupils this sort of question, the focus should be on the strategies pupils use to make decisions; including those who erroneously agree with Rosie and buy into her incorrect argument. We might have pupils suggesting that because 700 ÷ 10 is 70, that 700 ÷ 5 must be 'larger than' 70, and should push at this point for pupils to quantify how much 'larger' or how many times 'larger'. A nice strategy here might be to say 'well 500 ÷ 5 = 100, so 700 ÷ 5 must be bigger than 100', but again we will want to push pupils to quantify further; 'Is it bigger than 200? 150?' Ideally, considering the size of a computed value in terms of the sense it makes should become almost second nature to pupils, with pupils persistently questioning the validity of the results of their calculations.

In addition to developing a sense of whether the results of calculations are correct, pupils should also develop a sense of whether measures are sensible given a measured value. This can be tricky, particularly for larger measures where pupils might have limited conception of the size – is 1000 km for the distance between London and Edinburgh sensible? What about 500 km? 100 km? It is harder for pupils to judge these sorts of values. However, judging whether London to Edinburgh is 3 km, or that we might travel this distance in 25 minutes, should be easier for pupils to identify as erroneous. Also, smaller values should be easier to consider – does it make sense for a classroom to be 30 metres long? Does it make sense for an apple to weigh 5 grams? Or 5 kg? Again, when working with measures we should look for opportunities to get pupils to question both the values given and in particular the results of any calculations – does this make sense for the given context?

At some point we will want to look explicitly at the links between rounding, significant figures and estimation – again as a 'rule of thumb' that if we want to produce an estimate of the result of a calculation, we often find it easiest to round every value to one significant figure. It should be noted though that this is only a rule of thumb; it is by no means the hard and fast rule that some pupils seem to think it is and in some cases is definitely not appropriate. Consider four simple cases:

Use approximations to estimate the result of calculating:

a   207 ÷ 5.13   c   207 ÷ 6.13

b   207 ÷ 7.13   d   207 ÷ 10.13

In the first case it is entirely sensible to round both values to 1 s.f. to generate the estimate, and to calculate 200 ÷ 5. However, in the second case it is still not straightforward to get a sense of the size of 200 ÷ 7. If instead we round 207 to the nearest 10, then getting a sense of the size of 210 ÷ 7 is significantly easier provided pupils have some underlying knowledge of place value and the relationship between multiplication and division. When it comes to the third, it isn't really straightforward to get an immediate sense of either 200 ÷ 6 or 210 ÷ 6 (although if we spot something about 210 being even and a multiple of 3, then we might make some headway). So, in this case it may well be that we approximate this by actually calculating 210 ÷ 7, or potentially by using two calculations, such as saying it will be about halfway between 210 ÷ 7 and 200 ÷ 5. This type of estimation by bounding the calculation clearly has strong links to things we have looked at earlier in this chapter, but it is not often something that is explored with pupils in great detail and I think that is to pupil detriment when it comes to estimation. Finally, when it comes to the last of the four questions, it doesn't really matter (from the point of view of ease of calculation) whether we approximate the calculation as 200 ÷ 10, 210 ÷ 10 or 207 ÷ 10, and it might be at this point that we want to consider the fact that we have rounded the 10.13 down, and so it might be beneficial to round the dividend down as well. A curveball we might even throw in is to suggest rounding to the nearest 5, and calculating 205 ÷ 10 (indeed, of the four suggested calculations, this gives the closest estimation to the true value of the calculation).

One specific case where rounding to one significant figure is rarely the best approach to approximation is for calculations involving roots. A simple scenario would be something like:

A square has an area of 62 cm². Use approximations to estimate the length of the square.

62cm²

Rounding this value to 60 cm² and then trying to find the length is actually no easier than trying to find the length given the original value of 62 cm². What makes much more sense in this case is to approximate the 62 cm² to 64 cm², as we know that the length of a square with an area of 64 cm² is 8 cm. This suggests that the length of a square with an area of 62 cm² will almost certainly be close enough to 8 cm that it would round to 8 cm to the nearest whole number, and so 8 cm would be a reasonable estimate of the length of this square.

As I have said multiple times, pupils should have the opportunity to estimate throughout the curriculum; however, when it comes to potentially studying estimation as a separate mathematical concept, it is definitely worth offering pupils a range of problem types, including estimating the result of numerical calculations and estimating the result of calculations set in mathematical and non-mathematical contexts – things like shopping lists and bills as well as measures calculations all work well for setting up questions or tasks that focus explicitly on pupils developing understanding of estimation.

As well as estimating the results of calculations, there is also an important aspect of estimation, which pupils will almost certainly have to come first, and this is estimating physical quantities. This is different (although related) to estimating sensible measures of quantities but actually being able to look at something and estimate how many there are or how much there is. This is crucial in developing that early number sense that we would need pupils to bring when estimating calculations later on and would hopefully be well covered by pupils in primary school. The site WeAreTeachers provides some great ideas for physical estimation activities, such as the one linked below.[8]

One final aspect of estimation that we are yet to touch on is using graphs to estimate. We will tackle this when we look at graphing in Chapter 13, but for now we will finish this chapter by looking at accuracy and equations.

Concept: approximating solutions to equations

Prerequisites: Numbers, operations, equations, substitution, rounding, significant figures.

Linked concepts: Error intervals and bounds, graphs. There are lots of mathematical concepts that can be used to form equations, which can be visited at appropriate times.

In Chapter 5 we looked at solving equations by being able to equate either the number of objects or a measure like length or area. However, we know that there are many equations that cannot be solved analytically (or that an analytical solution is overly difficult and not really necessary). We might offer such an equation to pupils, for example:

Can you find the value of x such that $x^4 - 3x = 2$?

Pupils may well try some form of manipulation (look out for invalid manipulations) or some informal version of trial and improvement, but will not be able to find a value that gives exactly 2 (although they may eventually land on a value that their calculators can only approximate to 2 if given long enough). We can say to pupils here that the approach to determine the exact solutions to this equation (as in this case it is actually possible) is beyond the scope of school-level maths (although we might invite pupils to try and reason/research it if they wish). However, if we change the question to:

Given $f(x) = x^4 - 3x$, can you find the value of x that satisfies the equation $f(x) = 2$ to 1 decimal place?

then it isn't actually necessary to solve the equation fully, we just need to establish the closest value having 1 decimal place (d.p.) to the true value. What pupils can have trouble understanding is that it isn't necessary to actually know the true value in order to establish the closest value to 1 d.p. We will often need to make explicit and reinforce with pupils that we will never know the true value that satisfies the equation. What we can do (and what is

---

[8] J. Staake, 18 Estimation Activities That Take the Guesswork Out of Teaching Math, *WeAreTeachers* (17 July 2019). Available at: https://www.weareteachers.com/estimation-activities/.

necessary for all approaches we might take) is to establish bounds on the solution. In this case, we have that $f(1) = -2$ and $f(2) = 10$, implying that there must be a value of x such that $f(x) = 2$ between $x = 1$ and $x = 2$. Pupils may well need support in following the logic here, as it isn't necessarily straightforward – a graph sketch may offer some help:

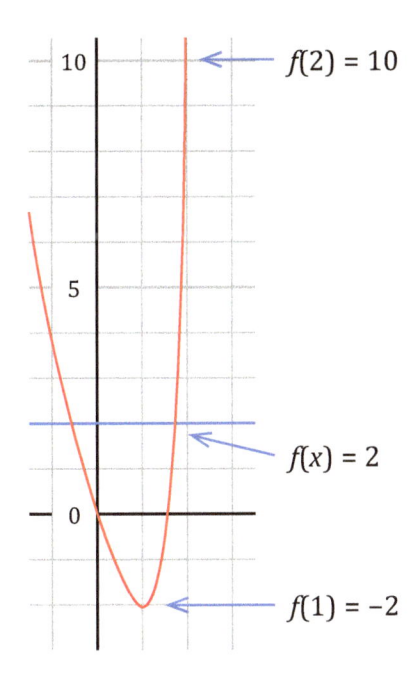

And in general to solve $f(x) = b$ we start by establishing a value w where $f(w) < b$ and another value y where $f(y) > b$ which tells us *x is between w and a.*

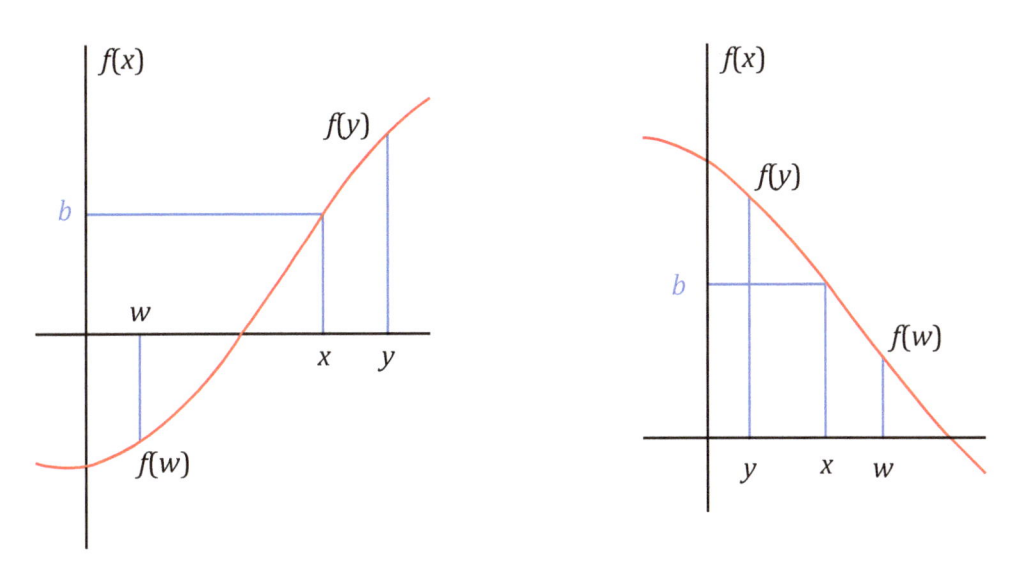

From here there are different processes we might go through in order to establish the approximate solution, probably the most straightforward of which is trial and improvement.

Process: trial and improvement

Trial and improvement is one of a number of interval dissection strategies that can be used to establish an approximate solution to an equation, but it is the only one taught in compulsory school mathematics. The process can be summarised as dissecting and reducing the solution interval until the distance between the bounds on the solution is equal in size to the required level of accuracy, and then using an interval bisection to determine which end of the interval is closest to the true value:

> Given $f(x) = x^4 - 3x$, use trial and improvement to find the value of x that satisfies the equation $f(x) = 2$ to 1 decimal place.

We have already established that the true value of x lies between 1 and 2, so we would choose a value of x between 1 and 2 to evaluate, such as $f(1.5)$.

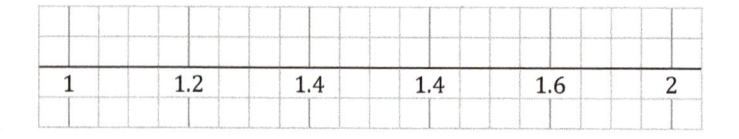

$f(1.5) = 0.5625$, which is lower than 2, so we can reduce the interval to $(1.5, 2)$. From here we choose another value in this new interval, keeping to values with only 1 d.p. A nice choice here would be $f(1.7)$.

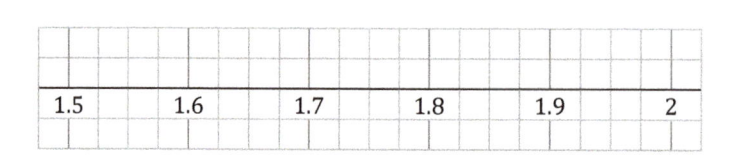

$f(1.7) = 3.2521$, which is greater than 2, so we can reduce the interval in which the true value of x lies to $(1.5, 1.7)$, which means the next value we would choose would have to be $f(1.6)$.

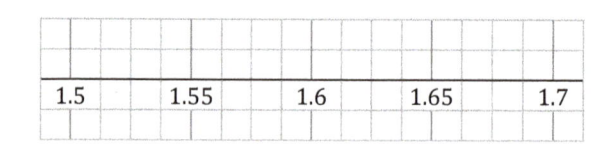

$f(1.6) = 1.7536$, which is smaller than 2, and so this reduces the interval further to $(1.6, 1.7)$. This interval is equal in size to the required accuracy (i.e. one tenth), and so we will do one final evaluation by bisecting the interval, namely $f(1.65)$.

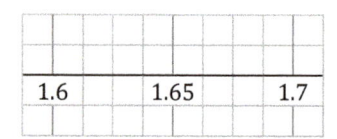

$f(1.65) = 2.46200625$, which is greater than 2. This reduces the interval to $(1.6, 1.65)$. What is key about this interval is that every possible of x in the interval, when rounded to 1 d.p. gives a value of 1.6, and so we do not need to know the true value of x to know that it must round to 1.6 to 1 d.p.

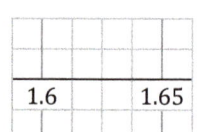

It is the last point that pupils often don't appreciate and therefore omit, but it is potentially the most crucial part of the whole process as it is the part of the process where the interval becomes small enough that we can say for sure what the value of x will round to. It is worth spending more time on this final part; the rest may appear different for different pupils and there is a relative freedom as to how the pupils go about establishing the solution is between 1.6 and 1.7, but once established, this final step is fixed if our statement that x = 1.6 (1 d.p.) is actually going to be mathematically justifiable.

There are many scenarios that we can use to form equations that can be solved by trial and improvement. Most areas of mathematics can have problems set that would lead to equations that pupils then wouldn't solve analytically. One of my favourites is:

> An event has four possible outcomes. The probability of the second is the square of the probability of the first. The probability of the third is the square of the probability of the second. The probability of the fourth is the square of the probability of the third. Find the probability of the first outcome.

Pupils may well be used to these sorts of problems when probabilities are multiples of each other, but rarely where they are powers of each other. Pupils also rarely have to work with 8th powers in a way that arises quite naturally from a situation.

Probably the biggest issue with interval dissection and reduction approaches is the need for both evaluation and determination at each stage, i.e. we evaluate the function for a certain value and then have to determine what the next good value will have to be. Other dissection and reduction methods allow for this process to be more automated, but ultimately a determination still has to be made at each stage as to what the correct reduction of the interval will be. The (perhaps) better alternative is to not have to establish an interval, but rather to establish a value for the solution to some degree of accuracy, and then use this value directly to produce a better value. This removes the 'determination' that is required at each stage of interval dissection methods and allows us to arrive at a solution via only repeated evaluation. This is the essence of using an iterative method to solve equations.

Process: using iteration to solve equations

There are many different iterative processes that can be used to solve equations. In compulsory school-level mathematics, pupils don't really have to be able to create the iterative formula for themselves. The exception is that pupils may need to apply rearranging skills to derive an iterative formula; however, because pupils are not required to know differentiation, they will not be able to determine whether a formula they have derived themselves from rearrangement will work to solve the given equation. This necessarily means that if pupils are asked to derive an iterative formula, they will be given the final formula and the question will be of the 'show that' form. Of course, this doesn't mean that these need to be the only type of question that pupils see in studying the use of iterative formulae to solve equations. This can be an ideal time to interweave rearrangement skills – so long as we keep the rearrangement suitably separate to the actual solving:

> Rearrange the equation $x^4 - 3x = 2$ into the form $x = f(x)$ in as many ways as possible.

Alternatively (or alongside) we might offer something like this:

> Show how the equation $x^4 - 3x = 2$ can be rearranged to give the following:

a $x = \sqrt[4]{3x+2}$

b $x = \frac{x^4-2}{3}$

c $x = \frac{2}{x^3-3}$

d $x = \sqrt[3]{3+\frac{2}{x}}$

e $x = \sqrt[3]{\frac{3}{x}+\frac{2}{x^2}}$

When it comes to solving equations using an iterative formula, the best tool I have found is actually a spreadsheet. A spreadsheet allows the capturing of one value being based on a previous value quite nicely:

Use the iterative formula $x_{n+1} = \sqrt[4]{3x_n + 2}$ to find a solution to the equation $x^4 - 3x = 2$ correct to 4 decimal places.

n	xn	xn+1
0	2	1.681793
1	1.681793	=(3*B3+2)^($\frac{1}{4}$)
2	1.629206	1.620008
3	1.620008	1.618383
4	1.618383	1.618096
5	1.618096	1.618045
6	1.618045	1.618036
7	1.618036	1.618034
8	1.618034	1.618034

What is important for pupils to recognise is that in order to be sure of the value of x correct to four decimal places, we will need to make sure that there is no change in the fifth decimal place. Pupils should understand that because an iterative formula generates a progressively better approximation to the true value of the solution, this means that once the values of x settle down to the fifth decimal place, this allows us to confirm the value of x correct to four decimal places.

Of course, pupils will not have access to a spreadsheet when being assessed, so they will also need to be able to use a calculator to carry out such iterations. The use of the 'answer' button on calculators here is a real benefit in automating the iteration. We can simply type '2 =' into our calculator to put the value of 2 into our calculator's output display, and then type the formula in as '$\sqrt[4]{3 \times Ans + 2}$' and each time we press the 'equal' button we will generate the next value of x_n.

An important aspect of working with iterative formulae is to work with different ways of communicating the process; we have seen the formula communicated algebraically, but a good alternative is to communicate it using a flow chart.

We can also set problems in mathematical and non-mathematical contexts so that pupils have to interpret the solution to the equation:[9]

> A scientist is measuring tidal patterns and records the height of the sea above or below a fixed point on the harbour wall. During a particular period, the height (in metres) can be modelled by the function $x^3 - 5x^2 + 3x - 2$ where x represents the time (in hours) after the tidal patterns started to be measured.
>
> 1 The scientist wants to find the time at which the height of the tide is 3 metres above the point on the harbour wall. Show that a suitable iterative formula would be $u_n + 1 = \sqrt[3]{5u_n^2 - 3u_n + 5}$ and use this with $u_1 = 0$ to find to one decimal place the required time.
>
> 2 The scientist also wants to find the time at which the height of the tide is 2 metres below the point on the harbour wall.
>
> Show that a suitable iterative formula would be $u_n + 1 = \sqrt{\frac{u_n(u_n^2 + 3)}{5}}$ and use this with $u_1 = 1$ to find to two decimal places the required time.

Solving equations, along with estimation, will make a reappearance in Chapter 13 when we look at graphs, but for now we will turn our attention to geometry.

---

9 AQA, Bridging Units: Resource Pocket 4, Iterative Methods for Solving Equations Numerically (2015). Available at: https://allaboutmaths.aqa.org.uk/attachments/5309.pdf.

Chapter 10

Shape

Shape and space is probably one of the earliest mathematical areas that humans begin to develop and explore. From infants playing with blocks and sorters to beginning to name shapes and draw patterns with symmetry, people have a natural curiosity when it comes to shape and space. This can bring both benefits and drawbacks when it comes to the formal study of geometry: benefits in that we can build on that natural interest and curiosity as well as pupils prior experience with shape, but drawbacks in that the scope for pupils to have developed misconceptions prior to formal study are higher. As teachers working with pupils on developing understanding of geometry and geometrical reasoning, we need to be acutely aware of pupils' prior experience of shape and space (perhaps more so more than other areas of mathematics).

One thing that we might consider is how quickly we introduce the study of two- and three-dimensional shape when teaching geometry. Formal study of properties of two-dimensional and three-dimensional shapes begins in Year 2 of formal schooling in England, but study of line properties (which could be considered a prerequisite of properties of higher dimensional shapes) is not really introduced until Year 3.[1] Whilst opportunities to work with space and spatial reasoning are important for the development of number, it is perhaps questionable as to what extent we need to formalise that study into directed attention to particular properties. This would potentially mean more time available to properly embed the study of line properties.

Concept: lines

Prerequisites: Numbers, measures, operations (note, these are not prerequisite to the introduction of lines, but are to all of the properties we will wish to look at).

Linked concepts: Proportion, shape, transformation, graphing, data analysis.

In my experience as a secondary teacher, pupils come to secondary school without a clear understanding of what it means for lines to be 'straight', 'parallel' or 'perpendicular' in that they can struggle to identify lines that exhibit these properties. It is important that we spend enough time looking at these, what might be considered, more straightforward properties so that they are properly embedded in pupil understanding. An important part of this is exposing pupils to a wide array of examples and non-examples, including boundary examples:

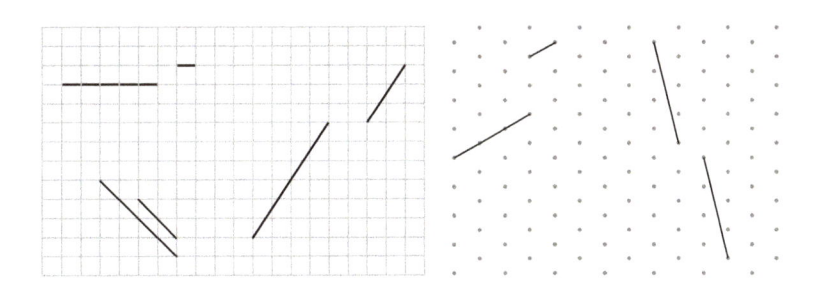

---

[1] Department for Education, *Mathematics Programmes of Study: Key Stages 1 and 2 National Curriculum in England* (2013). Reference DFE-00180-2013. Available at: https://assets.publishing.service.gov.uk/government/uploads/system/uploads/attachment_data/file/335158/PRIMARY_national_curriculum_-_Mathematics_220714.pdf.

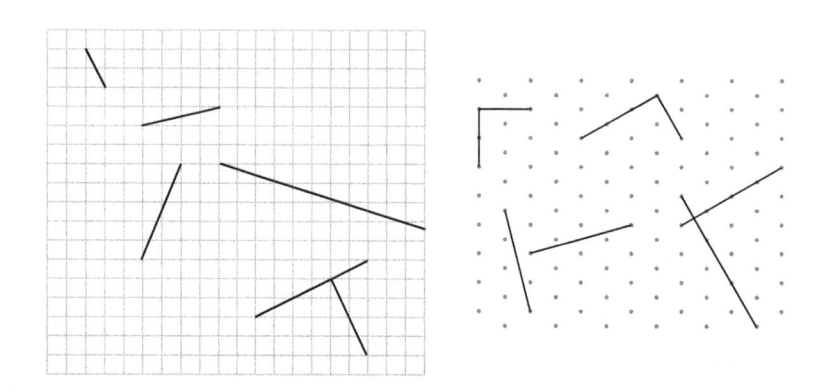

What are straight lines?

Examples

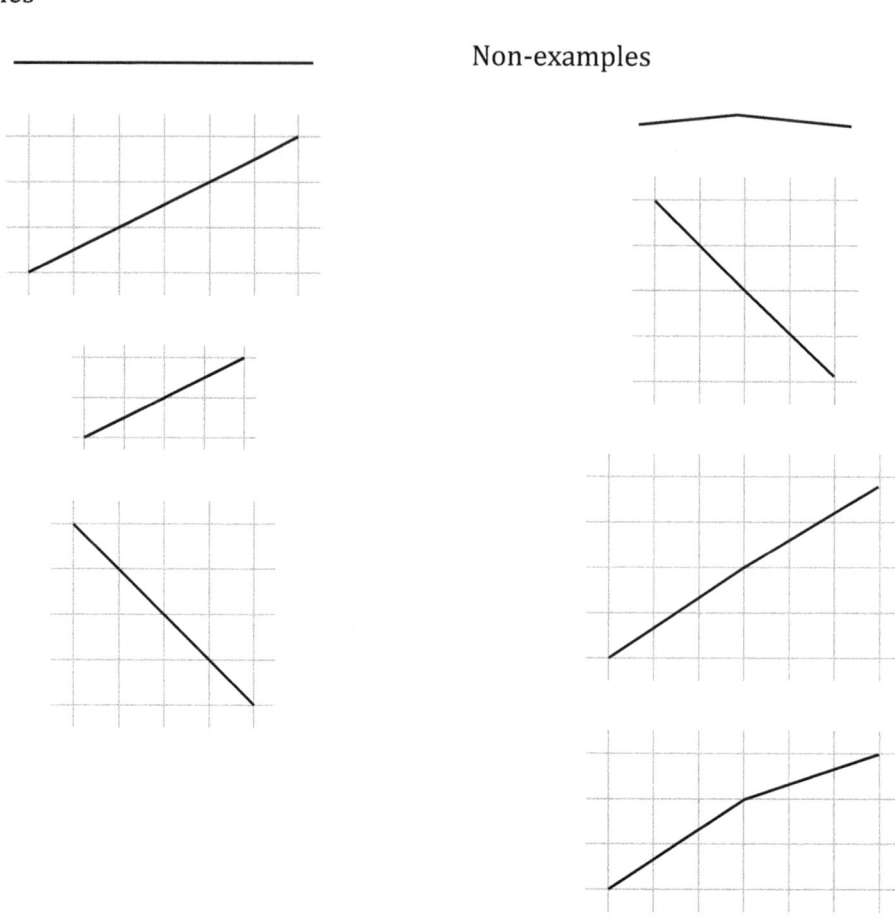

Non-examples

Using different backgrounds, directions, etc. is important in supporting pupils to make sense of these properties of lines. From here we might ask pupils to define what it means to be a straight line, or for straight lines to be parallel, or perpendicular. Activities like this can then help reinforce the ideas:

On the grid below, draw:

a   A line that is parallel and twice as long as the given line.

b   A line that is twice as long and perpendicular to the given line.

Shape

    c   A line that is the same length as the given line but neither parallel or perpendicular.

    d   A horizontal line the same length as the given line.

On the grid below:

a   Circle the straight lines.

b   Mark with an arrow > any lines that are parallel.

c   Join up any lines that are perpendicular.

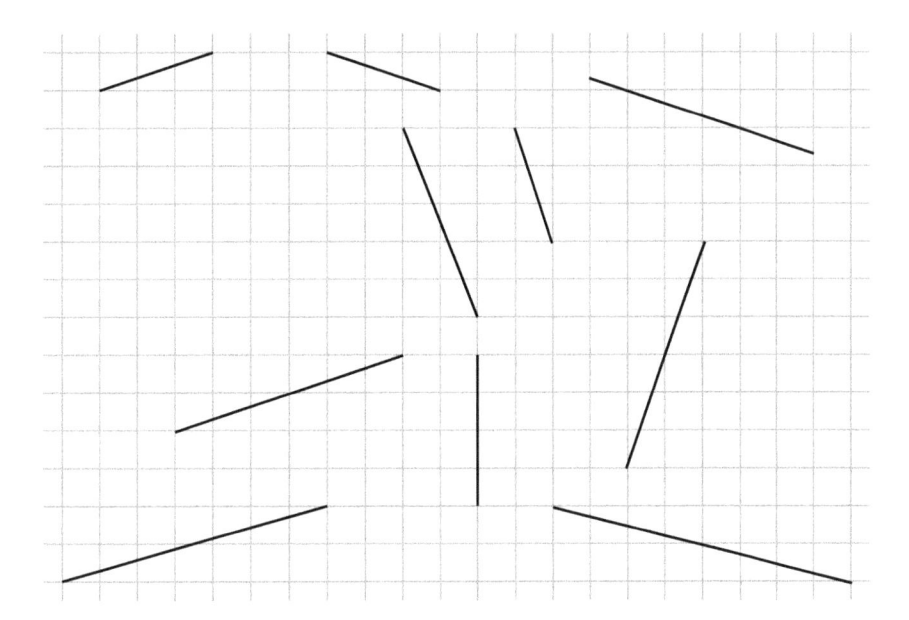

Notice here the introduction of the arrow notation for parallel lines; we may also introduce the use of the right-angle notation for perpendicular lines – making the link to pupils' previous use of the notation for right angles in angle measure.

In addition, we should look explicitly at approaches for determining whether lines are parallel or perpendicular, including use of a protractor, measuring distance from each other at different points, etc. as well as being able to identify directly from the different backgrounds.

An interesting activity is to then ask pupils to define what it means to be a 'straight' line, or for lines to be parallel/perpendicular. One way to do this is to use a Frayer model:[2]

---

2   See https://www.frayer-model.co.uk/geometry-and-measure.

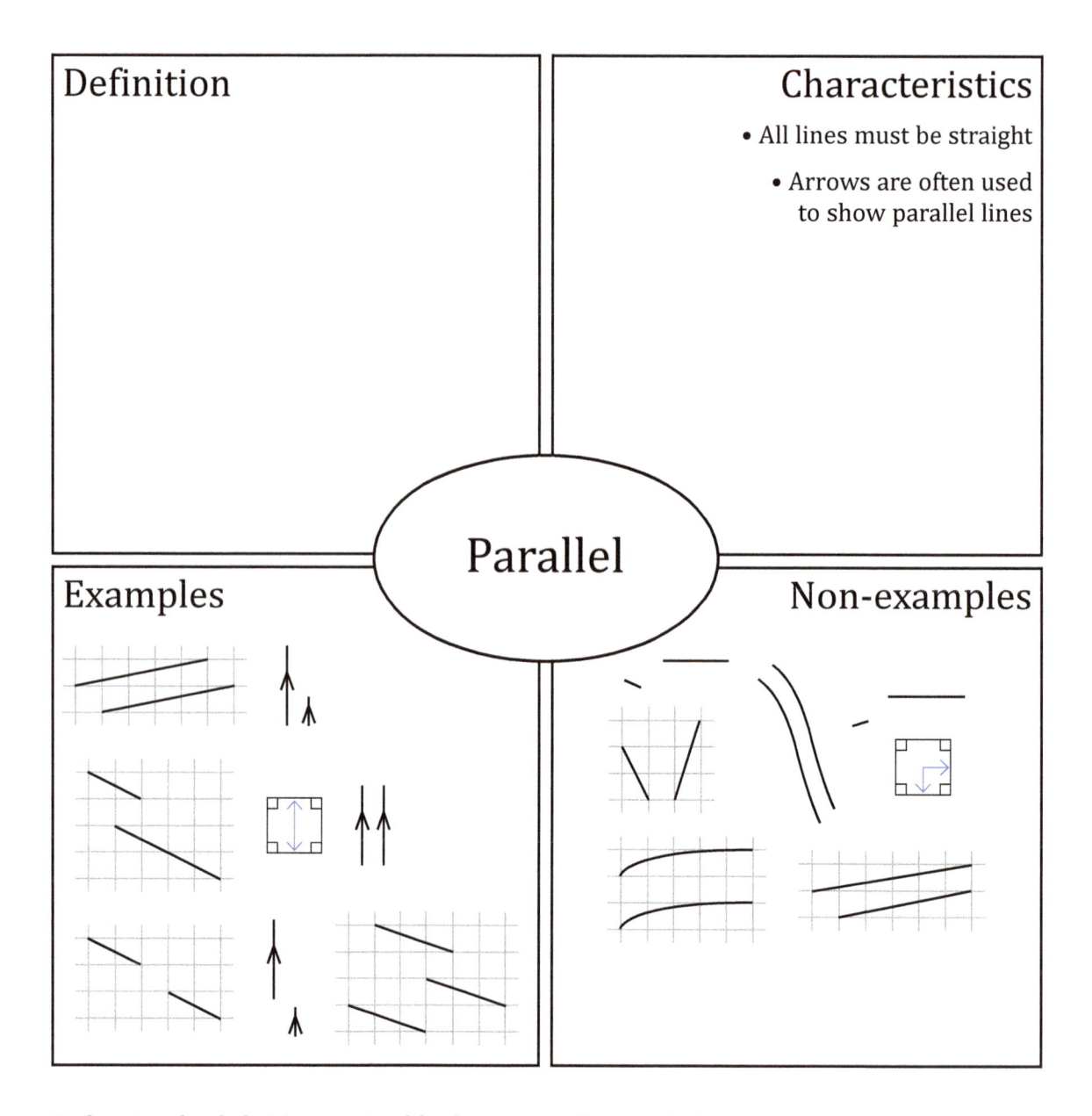

Definition	Characteristics
	• All lines must be straight • Arrows are often used to show parallel lines
Examples	Non-examples

Parallel

By leaving the definition section blank, we can offer pupils the opportunity to write in their own or to suggest definitions that are refined as a class before adding the same definition to every model. Pupils can also be asked to add their own example or non-example, the characteristics section could be left blank instead (or as well) for pupils to complete or we could simply quiz from a completed model.

One important property of lines that pupils will become increasingly familiar with as they think about lines being straight, parallel and perpendicular is slope. Indeed, we might define straight lines/line segments as lines of constant slope (with a special case for vertical lines) and parallel lines as lines that have the same slope at all points. Once we start looking at slope though, it makes sense to compare the slope of lines (not just to see if they have the same slope, but to see which has greater slope):

Which line is steeper? OR put the lines in order of steepness from least steep to most steep.

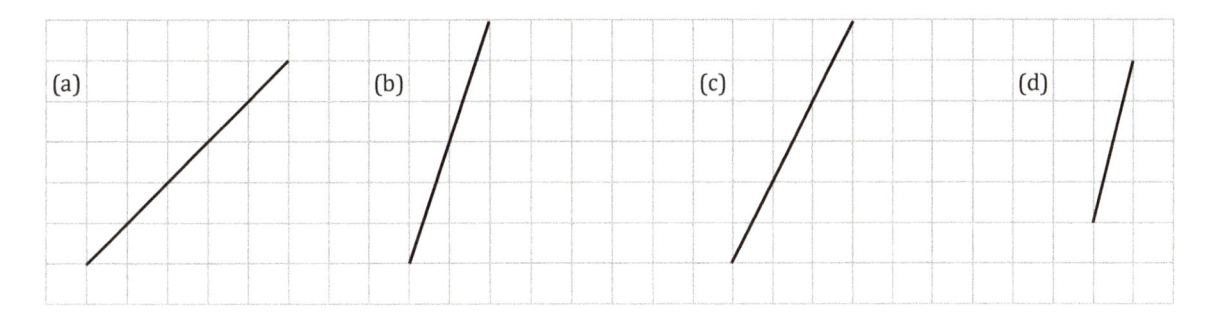

Many pupils will mistakenly identify (b) as the steepest, as it is relatively easy to confuse length with steepness. This, of course, prompts a need to measure slope.

Concept link: measuring slope

There are two main ways to measure slope. Pupils can be offered the opportunity to try and reason these – it may be a great opportunity to prompt them to consider again the key things required to measure a quantity (i.e. definition of a unit, multiplicative comparison to the unit, etc.). Pupils may well suggest the use of angle, and we might well choose to explore this with pupils (it helps create nice links with gradient and tangent function in later learning), defining slope as the number of degrees anticlockwise from the horizontal. However, whether suggested by pupils or not, at some point we will want to introduce the idea of using the vertical change for a unit horizontal change to measure slope, along with the name 'gradient' to describe this measure.

Subconcept: gradient

A nice way to introduce the idea of gradient is to look at two pairs of lines, like the ones below:

Which line is steeper in each pair? How can you tell?

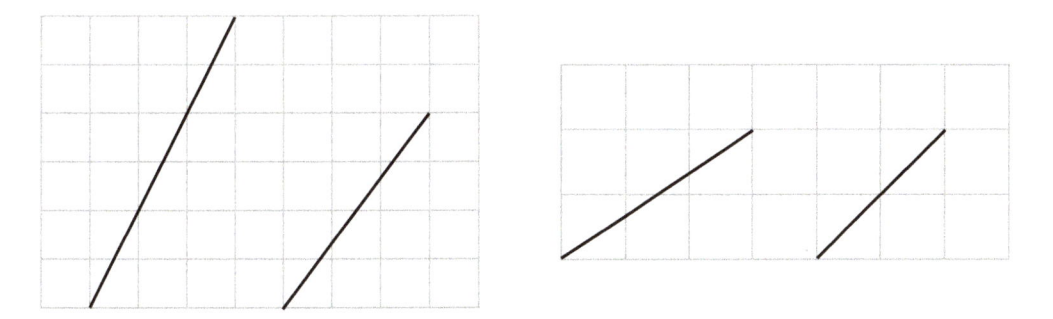

With the first, pupils will probably focus on the fact that the first 'goes up more', which is where we can direct attention to the second pair. For this pair both 'go up' the same, so which is steeper here? In this case, pupils will usually reason that the second is steeper because it goes across less for the same vertical change. We can then direct back to the first pair and highlight the fact that these both go across the same, i.e. have the same horizontal change. This should draw pupils' attention to the fact that both horizontal and vertical change need to be considered if we want to measure steepness in this way. We could then change the second line in the first pair to something like the pair below:

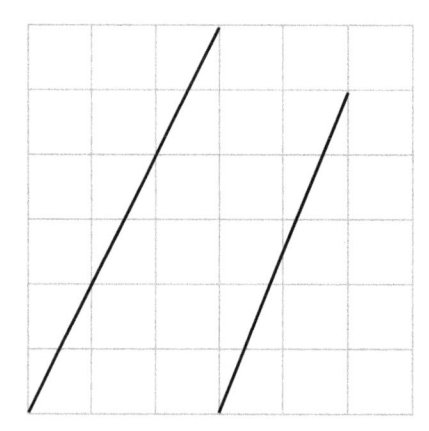

We can look at this pair of lines now and reason that if we look at a horizontal distance of 2 squares, the first line goes up by 4, where the second line goes up by 5, so the second line is steeper. This begins to highlight that if we consider the same horizontal change, then whichever has the greater vertical change would be steeper. We can then look at a pair of lines like the ones below:

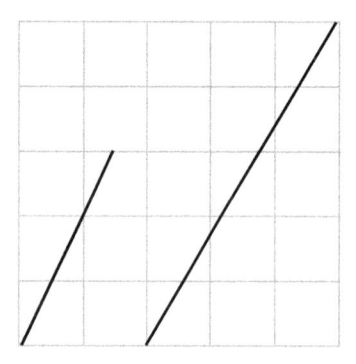

If we now look at which is steeper, pupils might reason that if we made the first line twice as long, it would go up 6 squares for a horizontal change of 3. If they do, we should probe this a little more – how do they know this? We might get responses about it going across 1.5 squares; but how do we know that is precisely 1.5? Our goal, of course, is to focus attention on the unit horizontal change: the first line goes up 2 for a unit horizontal change whilst the second line goes up less than 2 for a unit horizontal change, so the first line is steeper. From here, it is a good idea to offer more lines, some of which have integer gradient and some that don't, and ask pupils to focus on a unit horizontal change to determine steepness.

By looking at a unit horizontal change, put these lines in order of steepness:

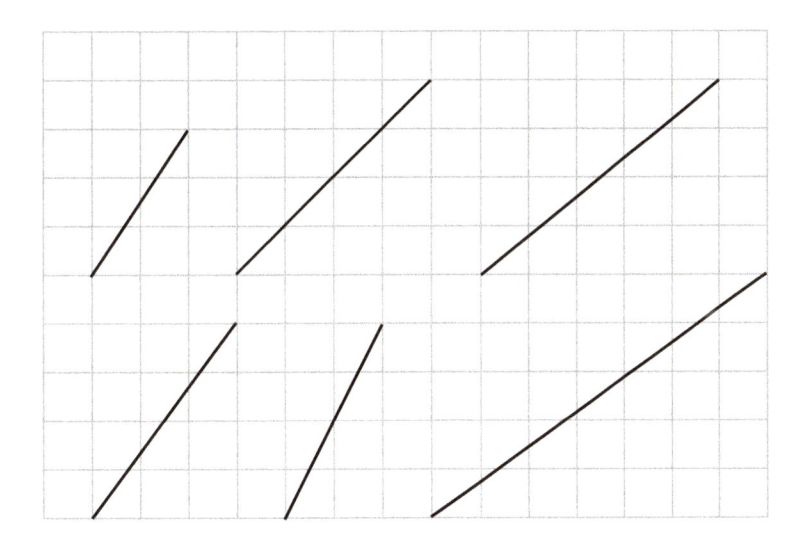

From here we can introduce and define the term **gradient** as being the value of the vertical change for a unit horizontal change. Teachers often use lots of lines of integer or unit fractional gradient to introduce gradient, but there is a danger in limiting pupil experience too early, which means they might struggle to apply the idea more widely. Potentially a better approach to exploring gradient, following activities like those above, is to then take these lines and link the gradient to a ratio/proportional idea through a suitable representation. This is the approach taken in places like Singapore and South Korea.[3] Provided pupils have previously studied proportion, then we might look at gradient using a dual number line or eventually a ratio table:

Horizontal	Vertical
2	× 1.5 → 3
× ½ ↓ 1	× 1.5 → 1.5 × ½

Alternatively, we could write the ratio of horizontal:vertical and then make the link to writing the ratio in the form 1:n, i.e. 2:3 = 1:1.5. In both cases we want pupils to be clear that the value of the vertical when the horizontal is 1 is how we define gradient, and that this value can act as a measure of steepness as it fixes the horizontal to a value of 1, meaning the vertical will tell us the steepness.

Pupils can then use their ratio/proportional reasoning skills to determine the gradient of the other lines as 1, $\frac{4}{5}$, $\frac{4}{3}$, 2 and $\frac{5}{7}$ and confirm their original ordering. An important thing to then look at with pupils is the idea that because the lines are straight, the gradient is constant for all points on the line – the second and fifth lines above are useful for this as we can consider different approaches to the calculation of the gradient. For example, in the fifth

---

[3] B. L. Choy, M. Y. Lee and A. Mizzi, Insights into the Teaching of Gradient from an Exploratory Study of Mathematics Textbooks from Germany, Singapore, and South Korea, *International Electric Journal of Mathematics Education*, 15(3) (2020). Available at: https://files.eric.ed.gov/fulltext/EJ1254836.pdf.

line we could look at these three different horizontal changes and show that they all produce a gradient of 2:

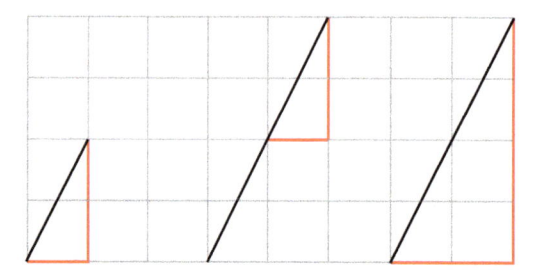

Once pupils are comfortable with this idea, we can introduce the idea of negative gradients, potentially by comparing a positive and negative gradient with the same magnitude:

What is the gradient of these lines? What is the same and what is different?

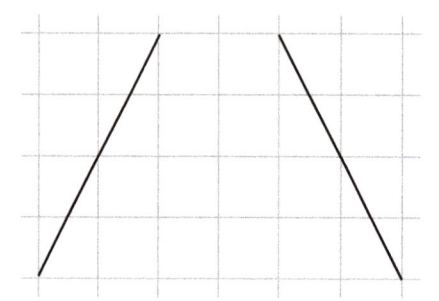

From here we might want to take lines onto an *x–y* axis so that we can explore the effect of different scales in calculation of gradient.

Find the gradient of these lines:

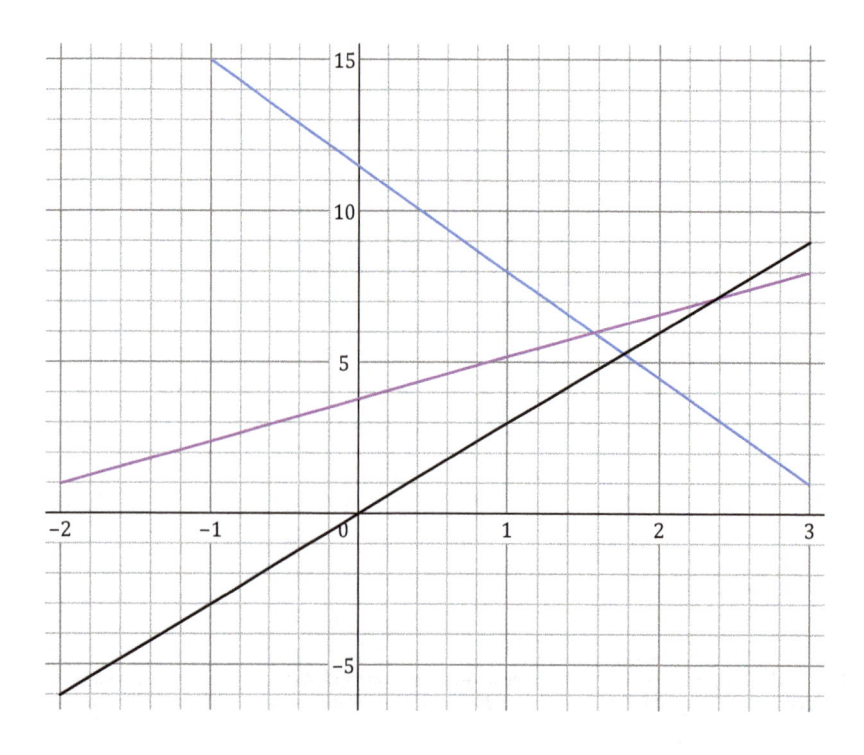

The other benefit that this gives is to immediately get pupils used to looking at changes in values, rather than the values themselves, by making sure not all lines go through (0, 0).

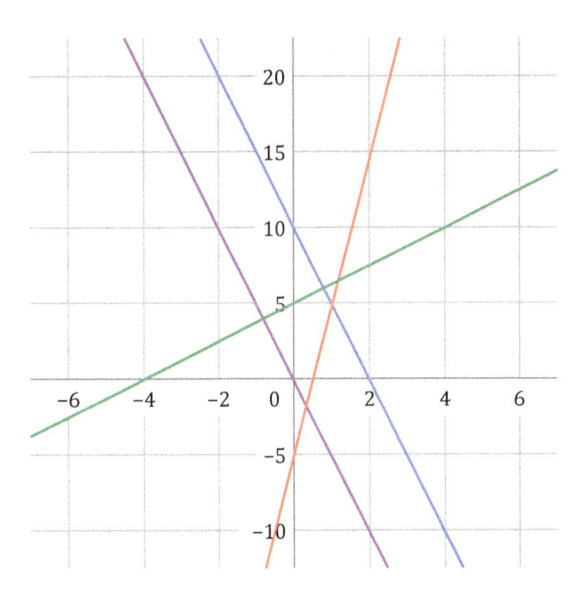

Having established the concept of gradient, we can then revisit the ideas of 'parallelness' and perpendicularity. Pupils with a secure understanding of what it means to be parallel and with the idea of gradient rarely have problems identifying that straight lines/line segments will be parallel if their gradients are the same, and if pupils are having difficulty with this link then it suggests that one or more of these concepts is not secure. When it comes to perpendicularity, it might be beneficial to have explored rotation with pupils prior to exploring the links between gradients of perpendicular lines; however, if pupils are already used to drawing perpendicular lines, then we might simply offer pupils some lines and ask them to draw perpendicular lines and then find the gradient of these lines and compare to the gradients of the original lines. Pupils will usually then have little difficulty in identifying the relationship as the negative reciprocal (although they may need reminding of the language) and may be able to go some way towards recognising that this relationship will always hold:

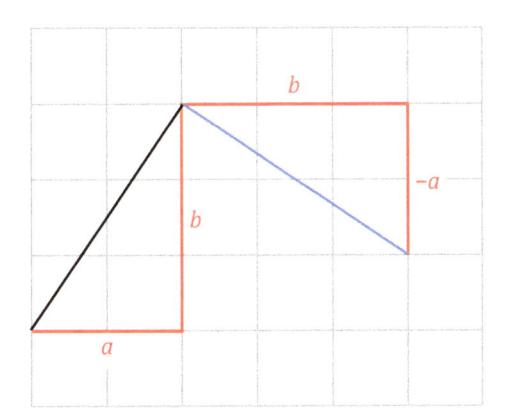

This relies on pupils recognising that, although a line might look like its horizontal change is 2 and its vertical change is 3, this depends entirely on the scale used – provided pupils have already met gradients on differently scaled axes then they should be clear on the fact that something that appears to be a change of 2 may not actually be a change of 2, and that these could actually be any two values, hence the use of variables to show the changes.

Pupils will eventually move to looking at the links between the value of the gradient and the equation of a linear graph (linking, of course, to sequences and linear functions generally), and also to the rate of change of real-life functions when plotted graphically. We will explore this further in Chapter 13 when we look more at charting and graphing.

Understanding parallel and perpendicular lines is crucial in understanding the properties of several two- and three-dimensional shapes. Before we explore these though, we will look at the angle properties of line diagrams.

Concept link: angles and lines

One of the things pupils should have already seen with regard to lines is that they can be turned around a hinge point. When these diagrams are drawn accurately, we can measure the amount of turn in degrees. However, there is a huge amount of reasoning we can do with inaccurate diagrams with relatively little information given. This is the idea we need to convey to pupils; that in many situations an inaccurate sketch of a diagram is all that is required to represent a situation for which we have limited information, and then we can reason the rest if we know something of the properties. Pupils should understand that this often presents a choice in how we might solve a geometrical problem – either draw it accurately and measure or sketch inaccurately and reason (it is also possible, of course, to reason within accurately drawn diagrams).

As a simple example of this, we might remind pupils of the reasoning we did when looking at measuring reflex angles – measuring the acute angle and subtracting from 360°. We might then offer further examples:

A nice alternative is to use dynamic geometry software, such as GeoGebra, in order to vary aspects of the diagram:[4]

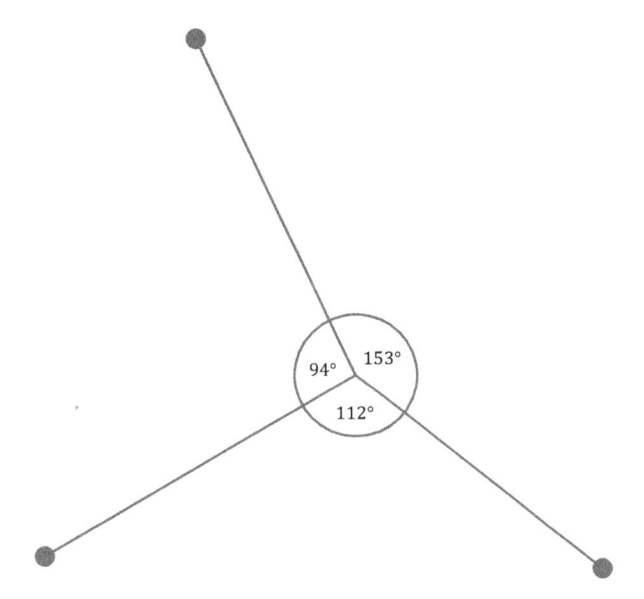

Using a dynamic image such as this, we can remove the angle labels and ask pupils to reason what the missing angle is, but we can also vary things like then making one angle 10° larger and asking pupils to reason the effect on another angle. We can also do things like lengthen lines and show that this has no effect on the amount of turn. Of course, technically these diagrams are accurate diagrams, and so pupils could measure angles here if they wish, but a big point is that they don't have to – we can figure this out without measuring. We can also add more lines to the diagram (although we have to delete and redo the angle measures) and if required change the accuracy of the angle values to include decimal values.

Once we have developed further pupils angle reasoning around a hinge point, we can then move on to explore further diagrams from which we might reason. The usual next step here would be to look at angles at a point that form a straight line. Pupils should readily be able to reason that when angles at a point form a straight line, the amount of turn is half of a full turn, and therefore 180°. This sort of opportunity needs to be offered to pupils, as it is the precursor to forming full geometric proofs.

In exploring angles at a point on a line, there are actually two key skills we would look to develop with pupils:

1 Identifying when angles that are at a point form a line.

2 Applying the fact that the angle sum is 180° to solve problems.

---

4 Applet created by Peter Mattock using https://www.geogebra.org/.

With the first of these, the use of examples and non-examples are once again helpful, both to exemplify the idea and to test pupils in identifying correct diagrams from incorrect diagrams:

Angles on a point on a straight line   Not angles at a point on a straight line

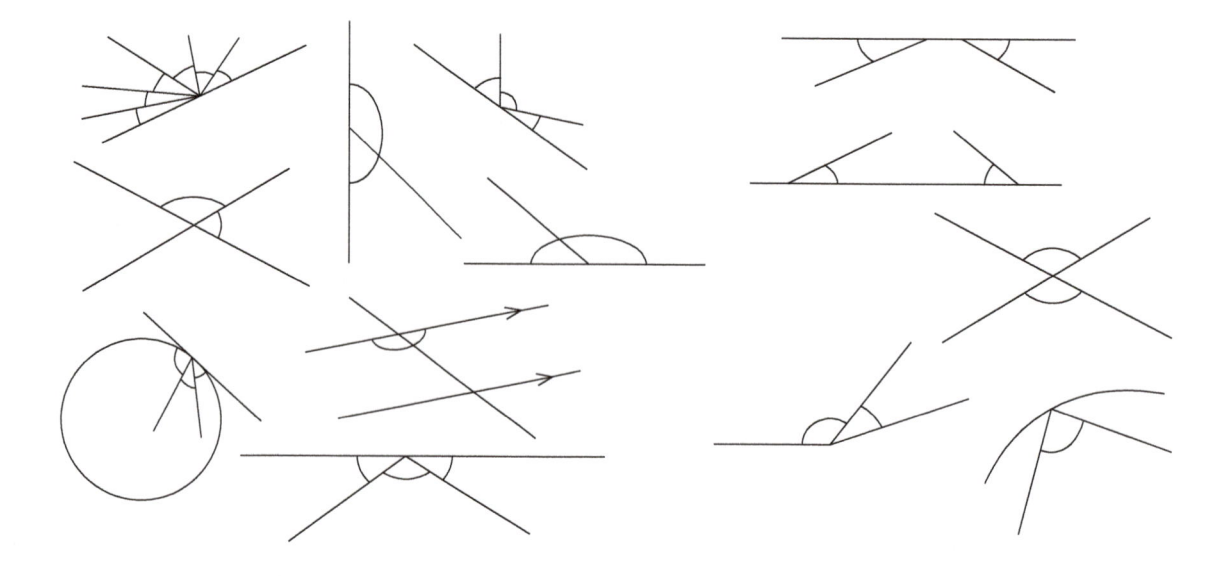

We will notice there are many examples of diagrams that will potentially involve much later angle reasoning, but we can introduce these now so that pupils are used to seeing them and associating them with angles at a point forming a line as well as the later properties. We should also do similar things when asking pupils to work out missing angles; include things like redundant information and use a wide range of diagrams:

Work out the angles marked by a letter in each diagram.

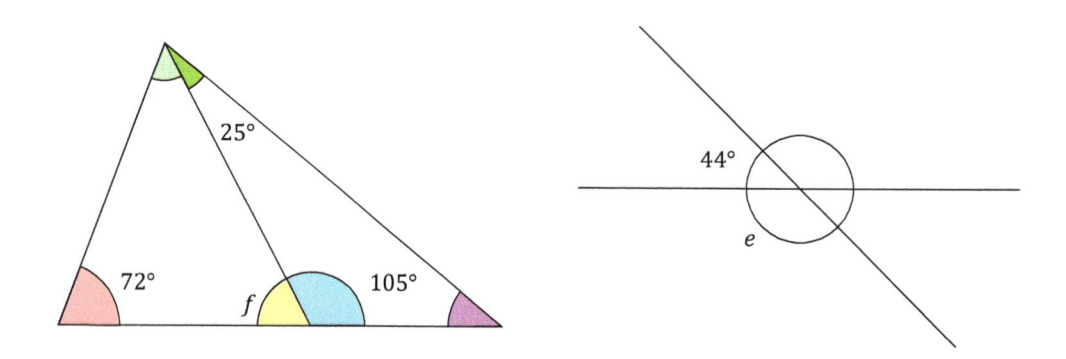

Shape

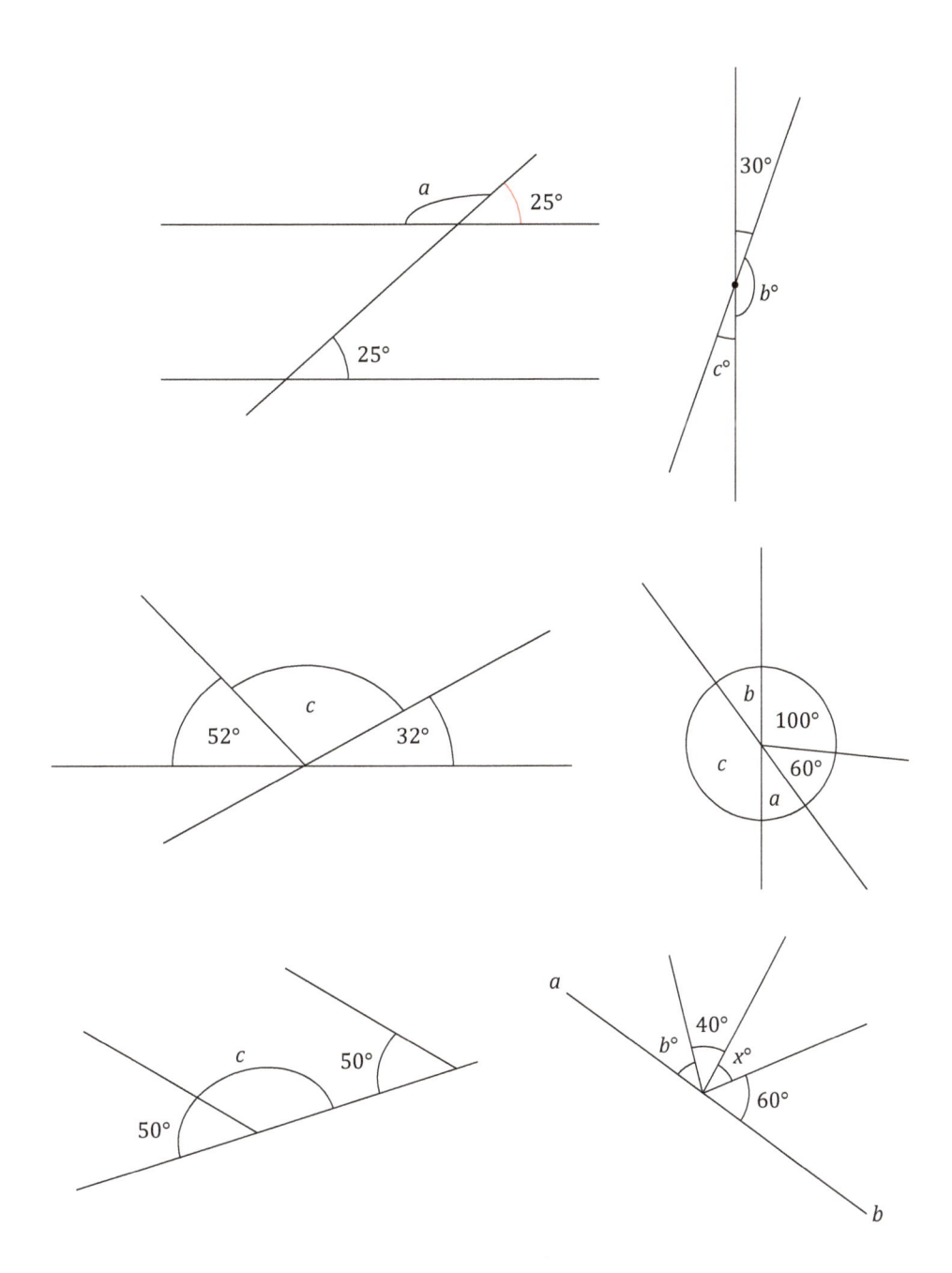

When introducing further angle-reasoning diagrams, we will typically mirror the development of the same two key skills: first being able to identify when diagrams exhibit a certain property (and importantly, when they don't) and then being able to apply reasoning skills with those diagrams to work out missing angles. From straight lines, pupils can reason that the vertically opposite angles where two straight lines meet are equal in size:

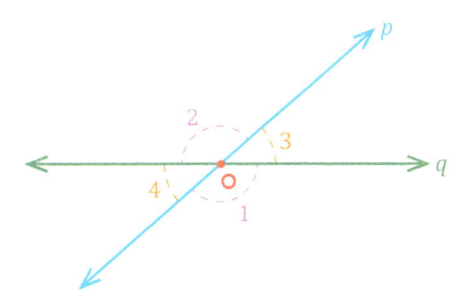

The logic pupils can potentially use (or at least follow) is that angles 1 and 4 form a straight line at the point O, but so do angle 1 and 3. It follows that angles 3 and 4 must be the same size (we might show this in calculation):

$\angle 1 + \angle 4 = 180°$

$\angle 1 + \angle 3 = 180°$

$\angle 1 + \angle 4 = \angle 1 + \angle 3$

$\angle 4 = \angle 3$

Another good reason to make this explicit is that pupils often miss the straight line in reasoning with vertically opposite angles (called so, because two non-adjacent angles in polygons are called opposite angles). For example, in a question such as this:

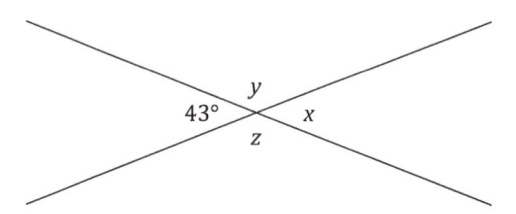

pupils will often reason that x is 43° because the vertically opposite angles are equal, but then work out y and z by subtracting two 43° angles from 360° and then dividing by 2, rather than seeing y and z as both forming a straight line with the 43° at the point the two lines cross. Potentially, pupils that have engaged with a straight-line argument to reason why opposite angles are equal may well be more open to seeing the straight lines in this sort of diagram.

Once again, examples and non-examples are useful in supporting pupils in identifying vertically opposite angles:

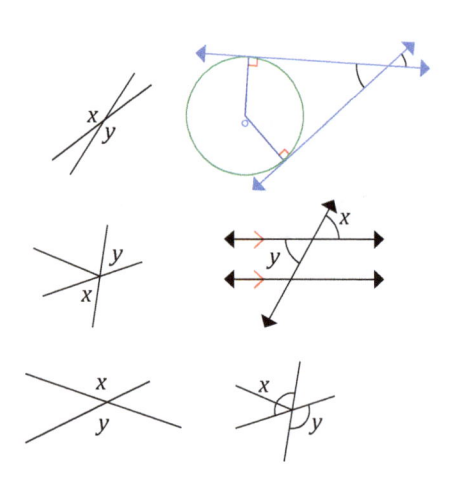

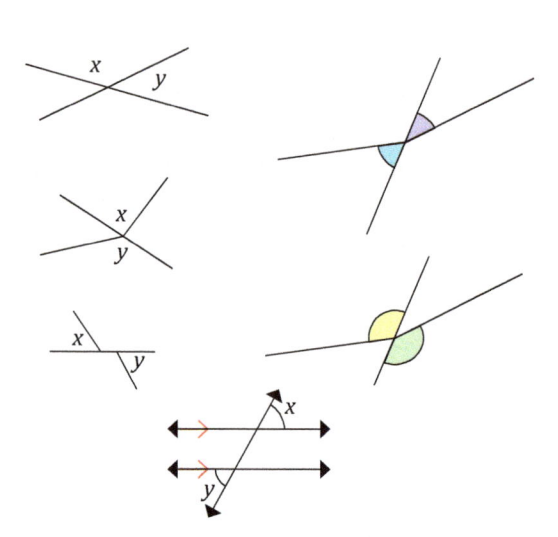

Examples   Non examples

When moving to application, once pupils are used to identifying vertically opposite angles and finding values in simple cases, it is definitely worthwhile presenting pupils with diagrams where they have to select the appropriate strategy from those learnt so far. This could be questions where only one skill is required but mixed up so pupils have to identify the appropriate skill or alternatively questions like the one below where multiple properties can be applied.

Pupils can find different ways to find the values of the missing angles, even being prompted to find them in different orders:

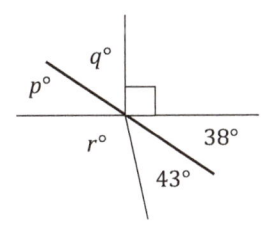

Show how we could find the value of each angle in the following orders:

i   p, q, r

ii   r, p, q

iii   p, r, q

iv   q, p, r

v   r, q, p

The natural extension to looking at the angle properties of two straight lines crossing each other is to look at when one straight line crosses two or more other lines:

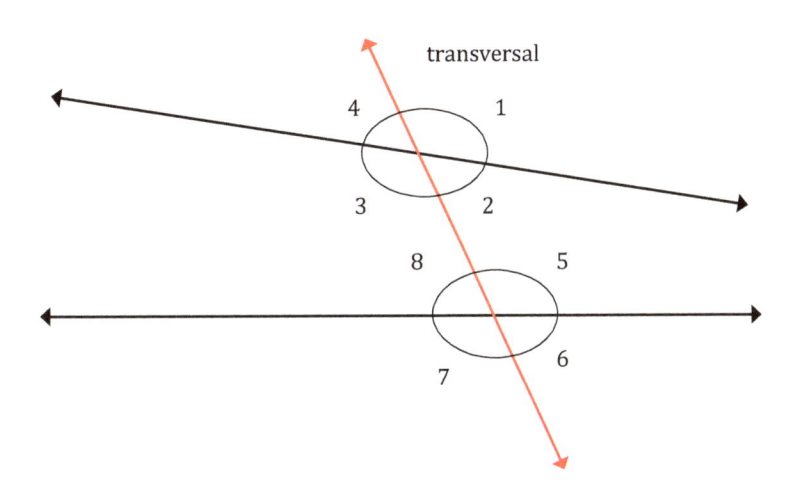

We should still take the opportunity to highlight the angles that form straight lines at the points where the transversal crosses each of the other two lines. However, we can now introduce pupils to the idea of corresponding and alternate angles.

Corresponding angles are relatively straightforward – the word corresponding here takes the same meaning in general English as it does in this context (i.e. angles in the corresponding or 'same' position in relation to the transversal and other lines are corresponding angles). In this case, this means that angles 1 and 5 are corresponding, as are 2 and 6, 3 and 7, and 4 and 8.

When it comes to alternate angles, a nice way to tie these into previously learnt angle properties is to show them as corresponding to the opposite angle; for example, if looking for the alternate angle to angle 3, we first identify angle 1 as the opposite angle and then identify angle 5 as corresponding to angle 1. This gives angle 5 as the alternate angle to angle 3. This situation is slightly complicated (particularly in the UK) in that angles 1 and 7 are not generally considered to be alternate angles – in contrast, in the USA angles 1 and 7 would be called 'exterior alternate angles' (and angles 3 and 5 would be interior alternate angles) – so in the UK we would have to add the condition that alternate angles would have to be 'interior' to the two lines (i.e. in the space 'between' the two lines).

Of course, the main utility in defining corresponding and alternate angles is to utilise their special properties when the two lines crossed by the transversal are parallel. Interestingly, proving this is the case historically relies on the fifth of Euclid's five postulates, which can be seen as the axioms of Euclidean geometry in the same way as there are axioms of arithmetic, i.e. results that reason allows us to state as true without proof.[5] Euclid's fifth postulate states that if the two interior angles between two lines on the same side of a transversal (what we now call co-interior angles) sum to less than 180°, then the two lines will meet at some point if they are extended far enough. It then follows that if the two co-interior angles sum to 180° then the lines will never meet no matter how far they are extended, i.e. they are parallel. From here follows both properties that when lines are parallel the corresponding angles are equal and the alternate angles are equal. Indeed, non-Euclidean geometries can be created in which the fifth postulate isn't true.

If pupils have been introduced to the 'field axioms' for arithmetic, then it may well be that introducing the equivalent axioms for (Euclidean) geometry will be considered a worthwhile exercise. What is clear is that without the fifth postulate we cannot 'prove' that corresponding or alternate angles are equal when parallel lines are crossed by a transversal – although we can demonstrate the property using dynamic geometry software or use reasoning starting with two crossing lines and 'imagining' sliding a copy of one line down the other, recognising that the angles are unchanged (indeed it is possible to combine these two and physically do this using dynamic geometry software).

However we decide to introduce pupils to the properties of corresponding and alternate angles when parallel lines are crossed by a transversal, it will again be useful to examine examples and non-examples of each (only equal corresponding angles are shown here):

---

[5] E. W. Weisstein, Euclid's Postulates, *Wolfram MathWorld* (n.d.). Available at: https://mathworld.wolfram.com/EuclidsPostulates.html.

Examples of equal corresponding angles   Non-examples of equal corresponding angles

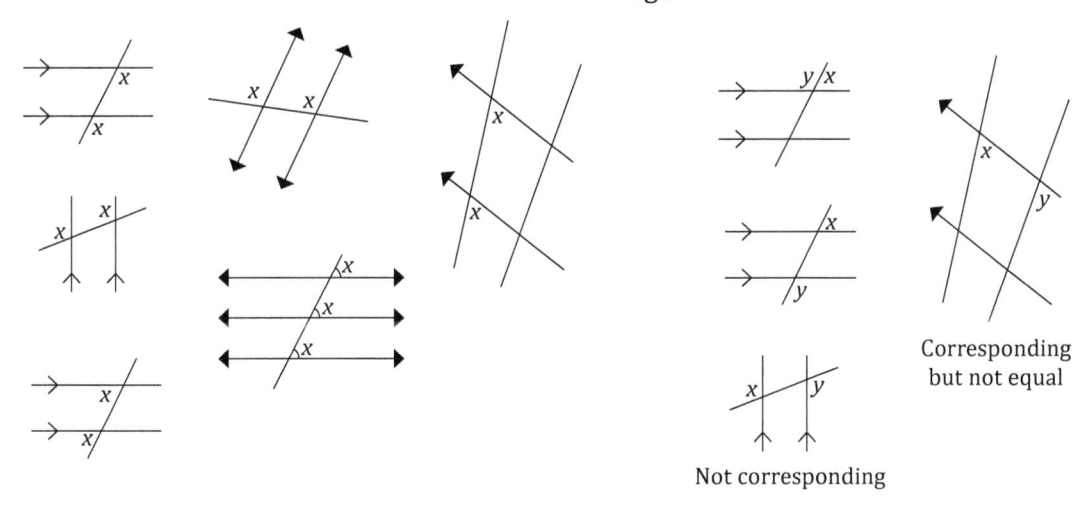

Corresponding but not equal

Not corresponding

When it comes to practice in applying the properties to solve missing angle problems, it may well be beneficial to offer practice working with equal corresponding angles and equal alternate angles in isolation and well-separated, as the two are prone to confusion. In addition, offering practice where pupils use the properties in reverse is also important, i.e. deciding whether lines are parallel using their angle properties.

Decide whether the two lines that are crossed by the transversal are parallel or not:

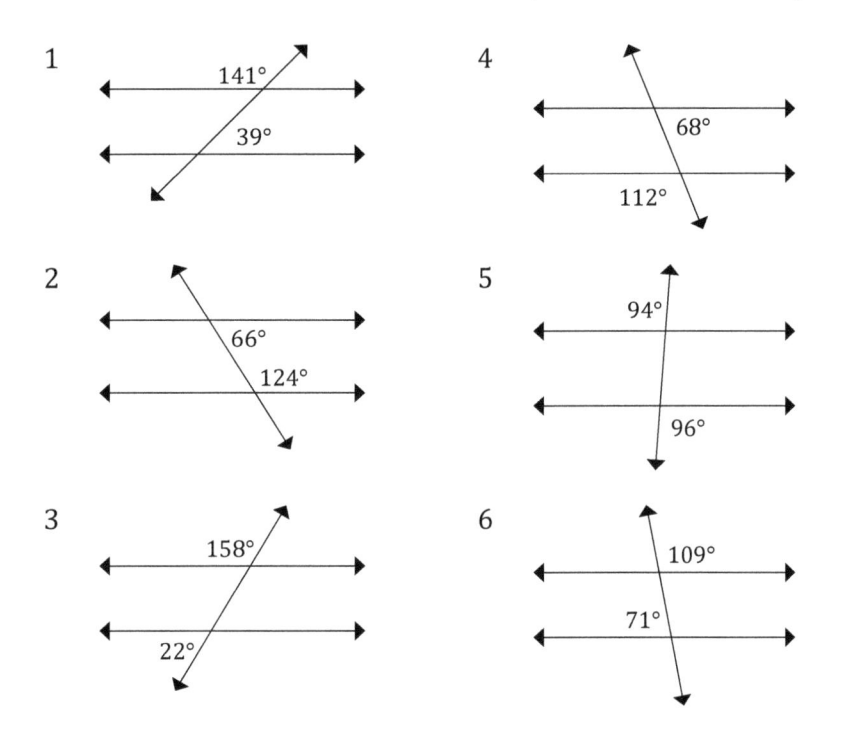

1. 141°, 39°
2. 66°, 124°
3. 158°, 22°
4. 68°, 112°
5. 94°, 96°
6. 109°, 71°

Eventually, of course, we will want to offer practice that combines these angle properties of line diagrams, and potentially many/all of the others. Simple bearings problems (such as calculating a 'back' bearing) can be included at this stage, as can problems such as:

Find the value of all the angles in this diagram that are marked with a letter.

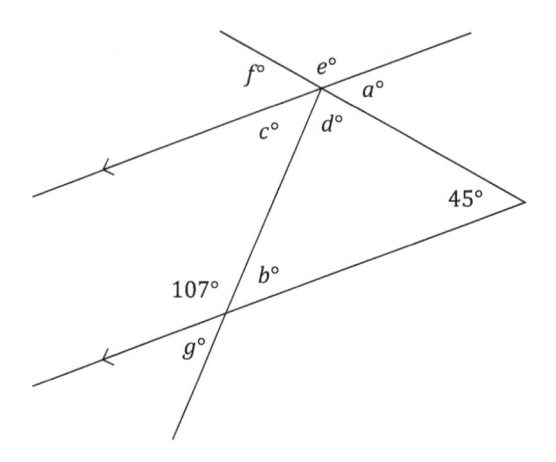

One nice thing about this question is that pupils might notice angles *b* and *c* being equal, and *a* being equal to 45°. This might highlight a property of the sum of the interior angles in a triangle, which leads very nicely into the study of angle properties in polygons.

Concept: polygons

Prerequisites: Numbers, measures, addition, subtraction, multiplication and division will all be requisite to some properties of polygons we will wish to explore.

Linked concepts: Shape, transformation, graphing.

Pupils may well have met the language of 'polygon' when being introduced to measures, in particular measures of area. The literal translation comes from the Greek meaning 'many angles' – which implies the use of straight lines (as it takes two straight lines to create an angle). In order to make full sense of the concept, examples and non-examples will again be useful:

What are polygons?

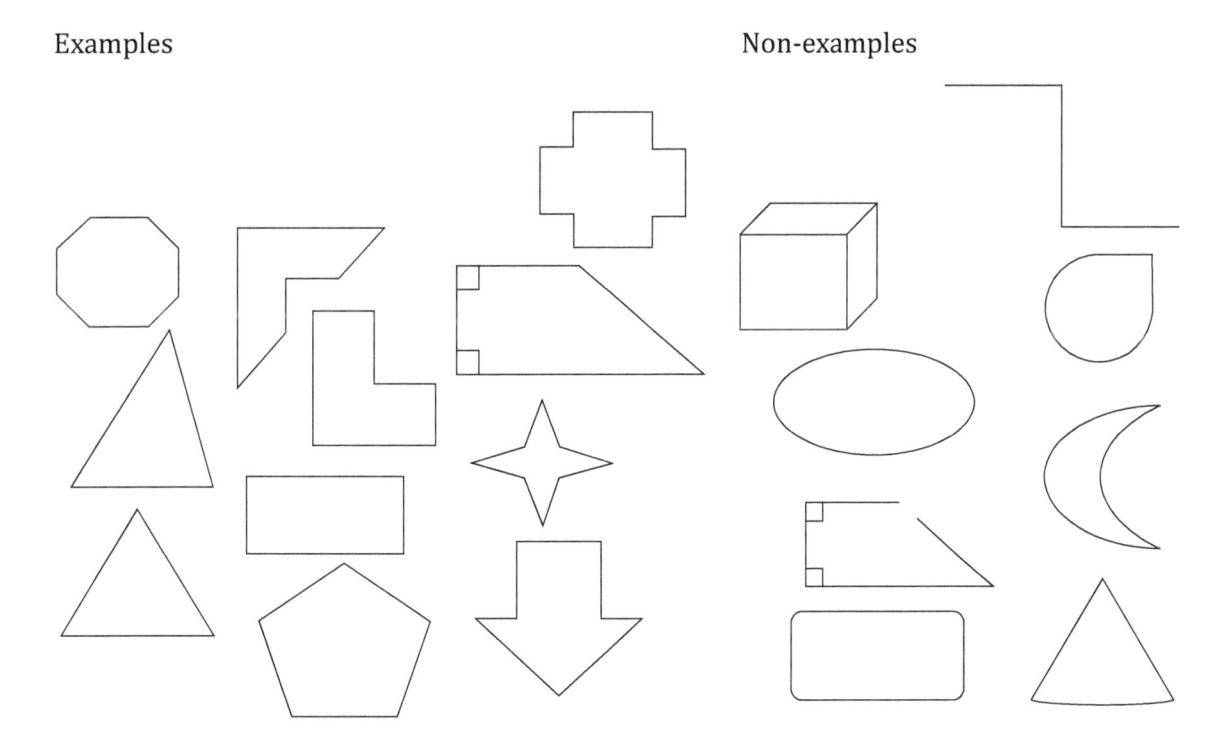

Examples   Non-examples

It may well be that we wish to explore specific examples of polygons before introducing the general term, in which case examples and non-examples of each specific polygon/sub-type of polygon can be useful in supporting pupils to make sense each type or sub-type. For example, we may use examples and non-examples to exemplify what it means to be a triangle, and then further examples and non-examples of what it means to be an isosceles triangle. The goal in each case is to try and ensure that pupils form a full understanding of the concept or subconcept, so as always, care needs to be taken with the examples so that they provide full exposure to the concept and also with the non-examples so that they cover the common misconceptions that pupils may form around identifying when the idea does/ does not apply. For example, when looking at triangles, pupils often assume a triangle is equilateral because 'it looks like it'. Making it explicitly clear when a triangle can be taken to be equilateral and when it can't is extremely useful, using the common hatch mark notation to denote equal-sized measures:

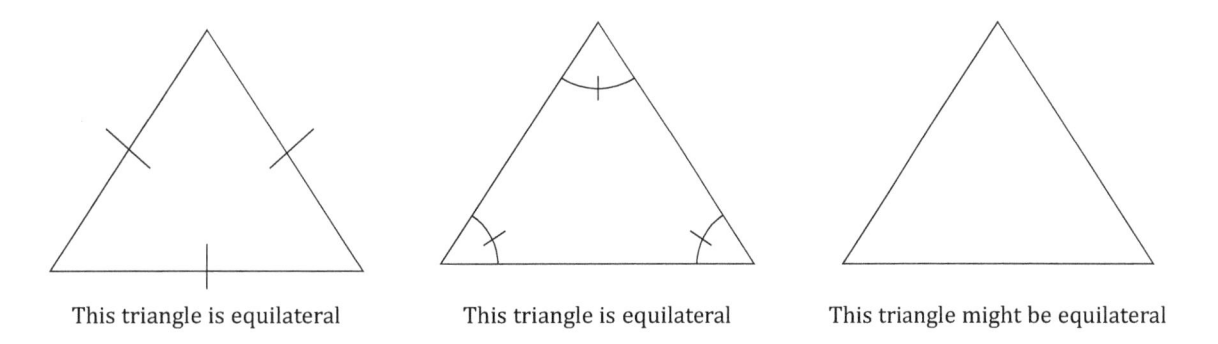

This triangle is equilateral   This triangle is equilateral   This triangle might be equilateral

Of course, we would want to look at equilateral triangles of different sizes and different orientations. Even if we choose not to use examples and non-examples to support in every case, we should take care with the examples we use throughout teaching of a concept to make sure they appear in as many different ways as is practicable.

Once pupils have a clear idea of what we are talking about, whether it is polygons in general or a specific type/sub-type, we can then look at properties of these polygons. For the vast majority of polygons studied at school level, this will be limited to perimeter, area, symmetry and angle properties of single polygons.

Concept: perimeter

Prerequisites: Numbers, measures, addition, subtraction, multiplication and division.

Linked concepts: Shape, transformation.

The word 'perimeter' is literally a translation (from Greek, through Latin) of 'around measure'. We can introduce this to pupils using simple polygons either drawn or cut from paper and ask pupils to 'measure around' them. This should allow pupils insight into the idea that we are summing the lengths of the polygon, either summing as they are measured or measuring each length separately and then summing them all.

From here we can transition to drawing polygons onto centimetre-squared paper, and pupils being able to find the perimeter by using the squares to 'count' the length, rather than having to measure it with a ruler, and then eventually to sketches where the lengths are provided:

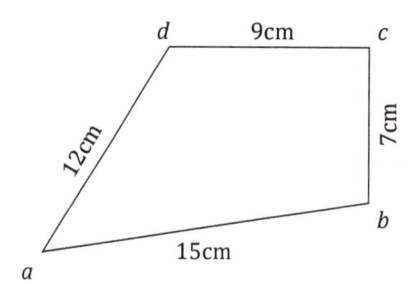

Once pupils are comfortable with the idea of perimeter, both in terms of measuring and calculation, the big transition to lead them towards is in situations where not all lengths are given and some have to be reasoned. This can start with very simple reasoning, using lengths that are the same:[6]

---

[6] S. Gokarakonda, G17a – Perimeter of Polygons, *Boss Maths* (n.d.). Available at: https://www.bossmaths.com/g17a/.

Gamma exercise

Find the perimeter of each of these shapes:

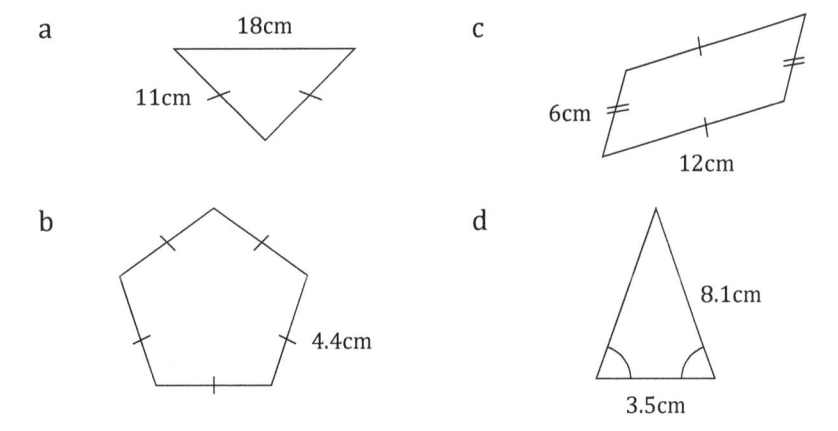

a) triangle with sides 18cm, 11cm, and a marked equal side

b) regular pentagon with side 4.4cm

c) rhombus with sides 6cm and 12cm marked

d) isosceles triangle with equal sides 8.1cm and base 3.5cm

Before moving on to situations where lengths can be reasoned in comparison to other lengths. It may well be worth actually drilling down into this step and offering pupils shapes instructing them to find the missing lengths before shifting back to then finding after pupils have practised this skill. As well as the more standard L-shaped hexagons, we can offer shapes that are a little more challenging where appropriate.

Find the missing side-lengths in these shapes (all sides are either vertical or horizontal):

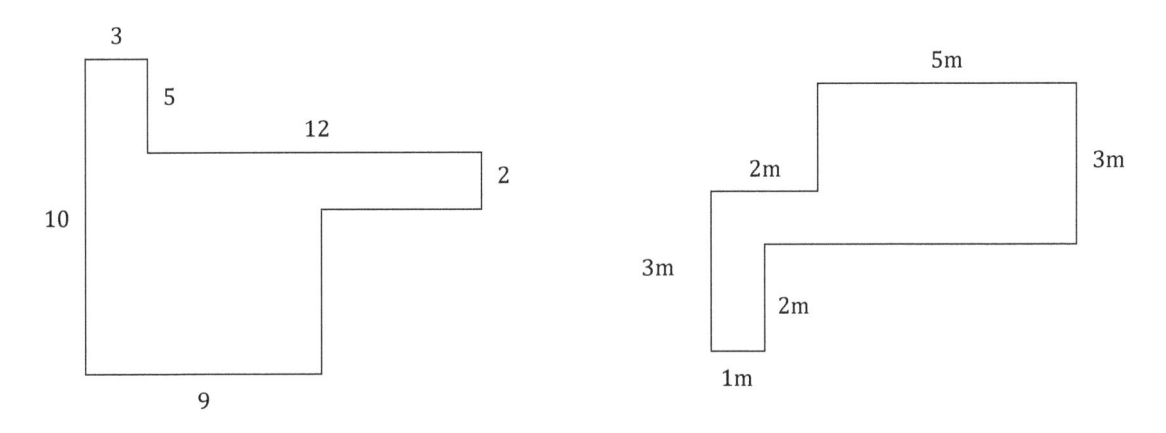

Shape 1: sides labelled 3, 5, 12, 2, 10, 9

Shape 2: sides labelled 5m, 3m, 2m, 3m, 2m, 1m

The next big transition is then towards pupils recognising that they don't necessarily need to know all the lengths of every side of a polygon in order to calculate perimeter, provided they know what the lengths sum to. There are a number of different ways we might introduce this sort of problem:

349

Conceptual Maths

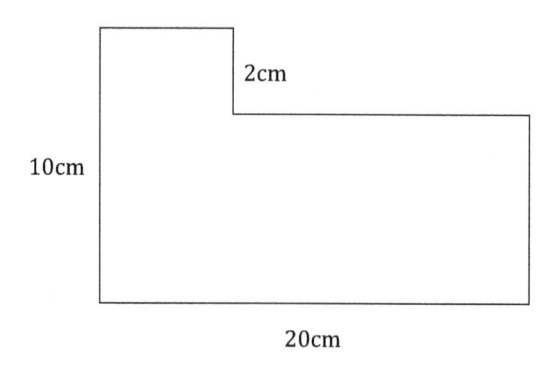

In this case, although pupils can work out the missing vertical length, they cannot say for sure what each of the missing horizontal lengths are. However, if we are interested in the perimeter, we do not actually need to know the lengths individually, we only need to know that they sum to 20 cm. This should lead (perhaps through some strategic prompting) to the understanding that the perimeter of this shape has the same value as the perimeter of a 10 cm by 20 cm rectangle. From here we might offer something like this:

Which shapes have the same perimeter as the rectangle in the top left picture? Try to decide without calculating the perimeter of each shape.

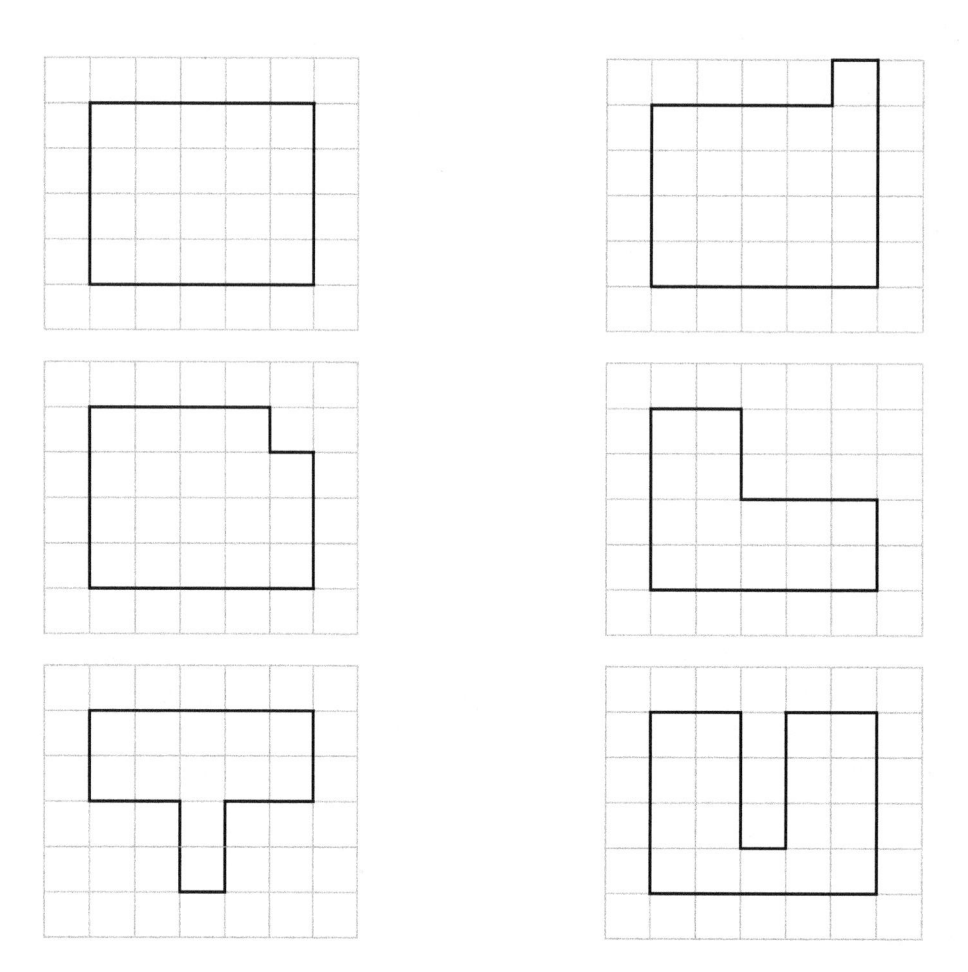

Shape

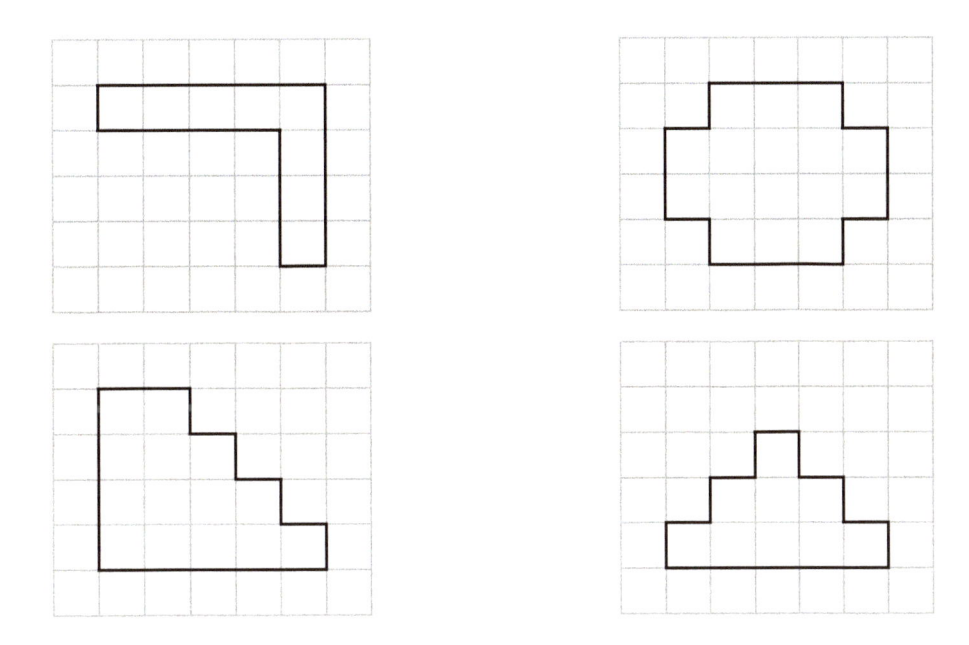

Alternatively, we might offer something like this:

If possible, find the perimeter of these shapes. If not, state which lengths can be found and which cannot.

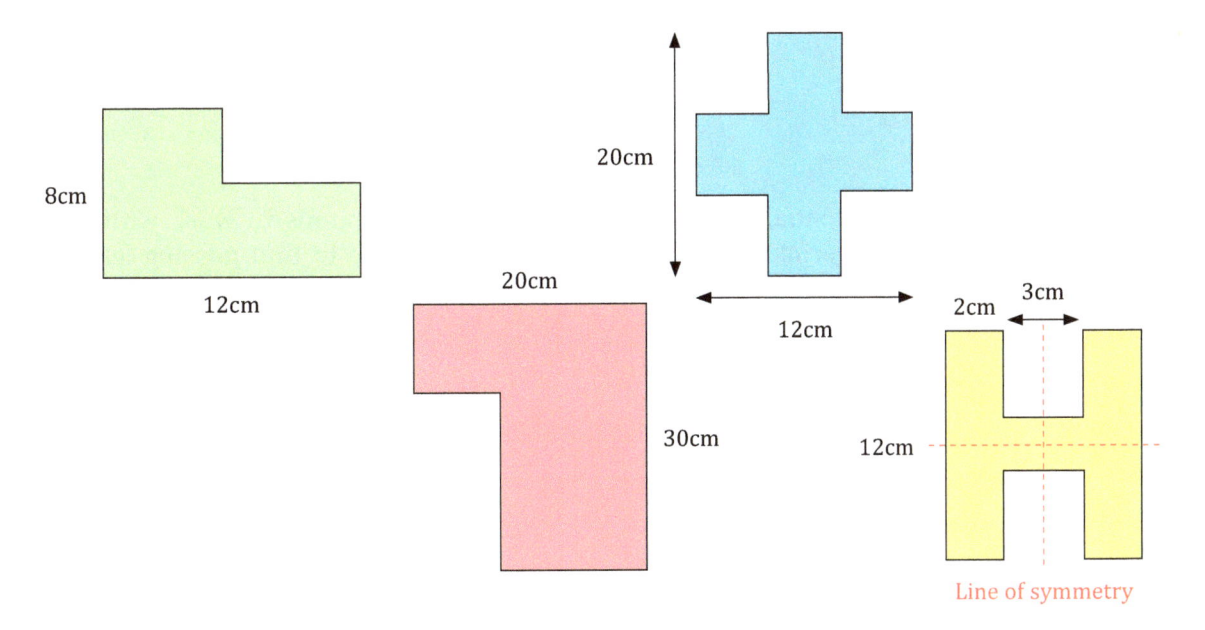

351

Or this activity from Don Steward's Median blog:[7]

What are the perimeters of the overall shapes?

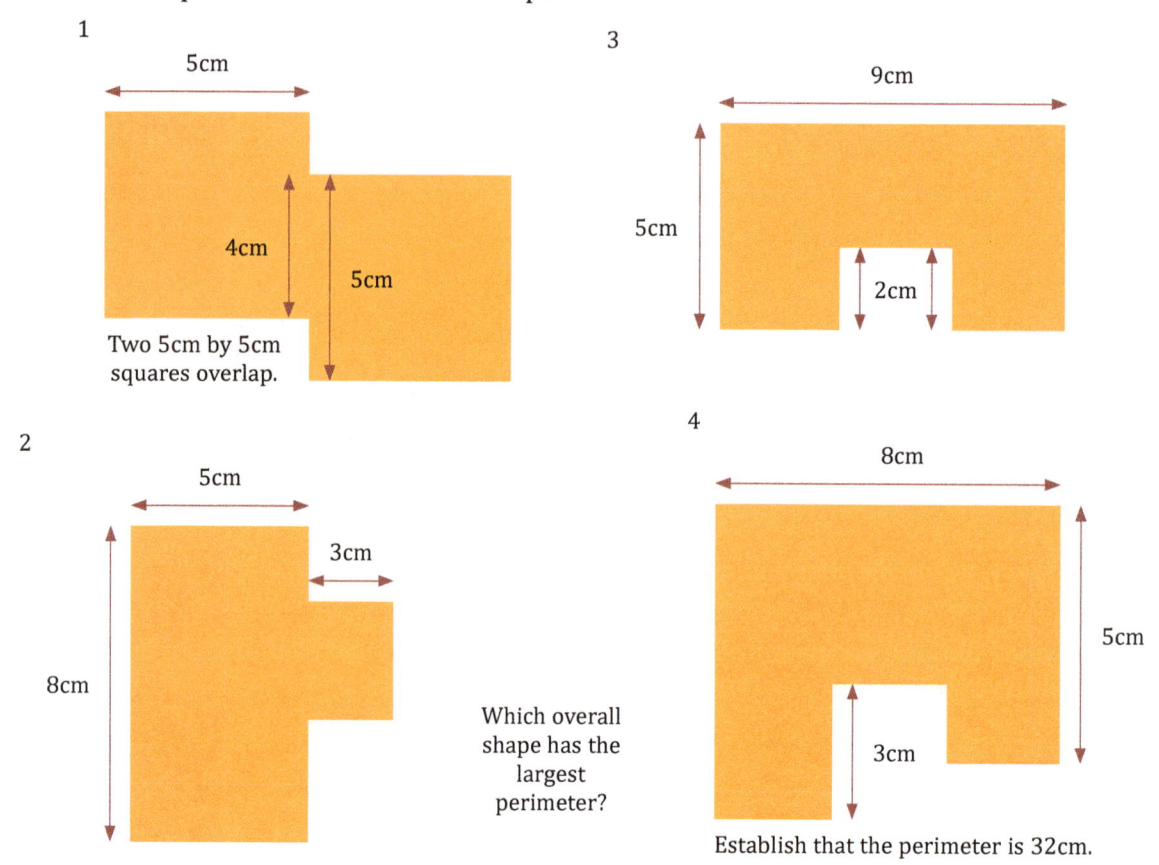

1
5cm, 4cm, 5cm
Two 5cm by 5cm squares overlap.

2
5cm, 3cm, 8cm

3
9cm, 5cm, 2cm

4
8cm, 5cm, 3cm
Establish that the perimeter is 32cm.

Which overall shape has the largest perimeter?

There are many other potential activities that we might want pupils to work with that require reasoning about perimeter. The classic activity might be to find missing lengths given perimeter:

Find the missing lengths of these shapes, given the perimeter. If it isn't possible, explain why not.

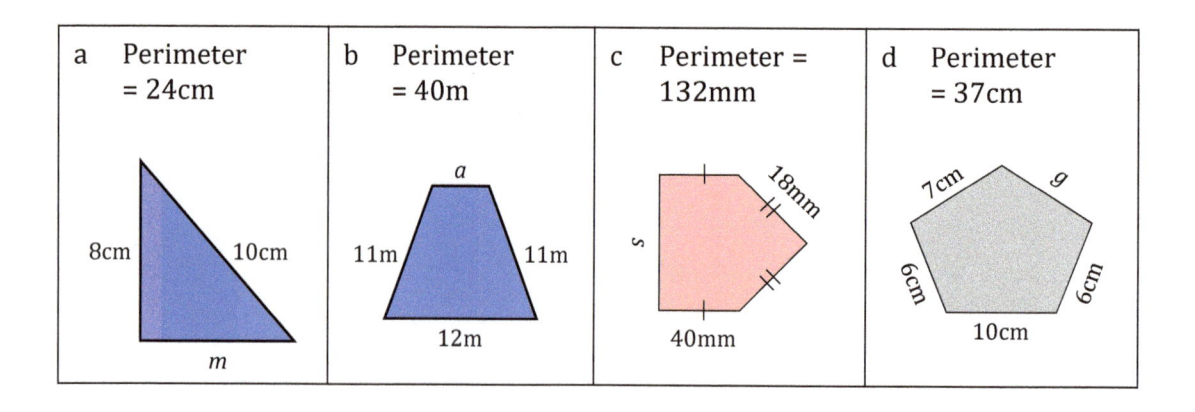

a Perimeter = 24cm	b Perimeter = 40m	c Perimeter = 132mm	d Perimeter = 37cm
triangle: 8cm, 10cm, m	trapezium: a, 11m, 11m, 12m	18mm, s, 40mm	pentagon: 7cm, g, 6cm, 10cm, 6cm

---

7 D. Steward, Obloidal Perimeters, *Median* [blog] (22 February 2012). Available at: https://donsteward.blogspot.com/2012/02/obloidal-perimeters.html.

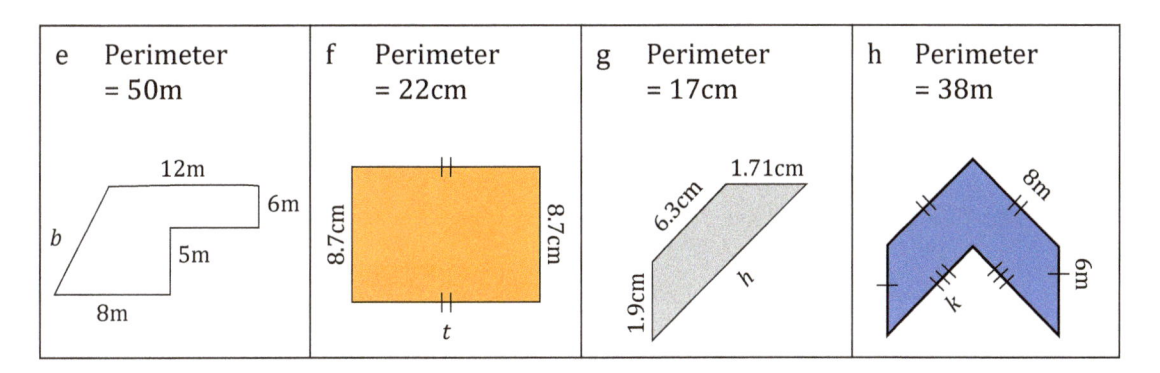

e Perimeter = 50m	f Perimeter = 22cm	g Perimeter = 17cm	h Perimeter = 38m
12m, 6m, b, 5m, 8m	8.7cm, t, 8.7cm	1.71cm, 6.3cm, 1.9cm, h	8m, 6m, k

One of my favourite reasoning problems is this one from Boss Maths:[8]

Exam-style question 4

The diagram shows a star shape made up of a regular pentagon and 5 isosceles triangles.

The perimeter of the pentagon is 40 cm.

The perimeter of the isosceles triangle is 28 cm.

Find the perimeter of the star shape.

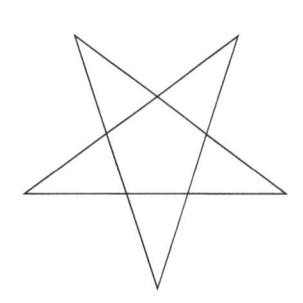

as well as this exam question from AQA:[9]

A triangle has perimeter 32 cm.

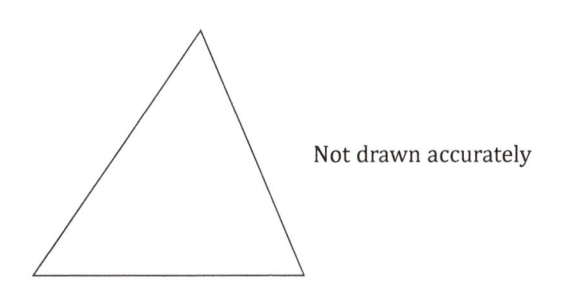

Not drawn accurately

A square has perimeter 40 cm.

Not drawn accurately

---
8 S. Gokarakonda, G17A – Perimeter of Polygons.
9 See https://filestore.aqa.org.uk/sample-papers-and-mark-schemes/2017/june/AQA-83001F-QP-JUN17.PDF.

Two sides of the shapes are put together to make a pentagon.

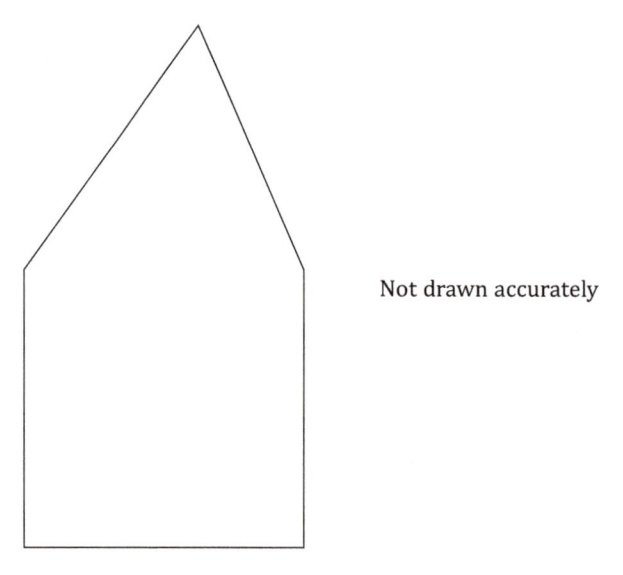

Not drawn accurately

Work out the perimeter of the pentagon.

Of course, eventually we will look to combine perimeter with other concepts in mathematics; often algebra in forming algebraic expressions or equations is a popular pairing. Another popular pairing is with the concept of area.

Concept link: area of polygons

Pupils will (hopefully) have met area as use of a square unit and found the area of shapes (including polygons) using square-counting strategies (we examined these in Chapter 8). When we are ready to then move towards using formulae for calculating the area of different polygons, we may well offer pupils a simple square:

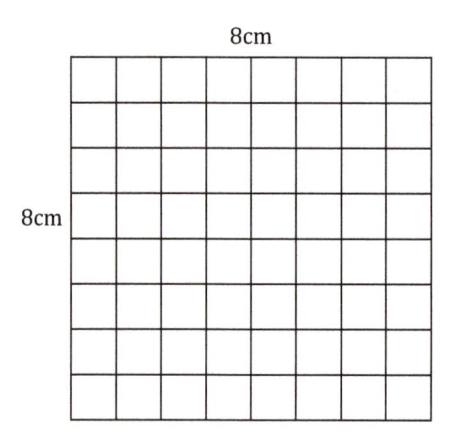

8cm

8cm

Of course, we would want to perhaps steer pupils towards the fact that an efficient strategy in this case is simply to 'square' the length of 8 cm and, more importantly, that this strategy will generalise to any square. Indeed, this allows us to make the link with values to a power of 2 being described as being 'squared'. Before moving on to other polygons, it is definitely worth then looking at the reverse calculation – given the area of the square finding the length. This is crucial when we come to look at things like Pythagoras' theorem, and so needs proper attention here.

From squares we will inevitably move on to look at other triangle and quadrilaterals; this may be in quick succession or over a longer period of time. Regardless of the time scale, a potential route through these polygons that should make sense to pupils is given below, starting with moving from squares to rectangles.

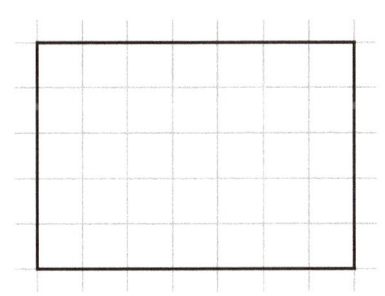

Pupils can approach this in the same way as above, by articulating their strategy for calculating the number of squares contained within the boundary. Invariably, this leads to pupils noticing that we can calculate this by considering it as 5 rows of 7, or 7 columns of 5, leading to the calculation 5 × 7. Following this, we can draw attention to the idea that this strategy will work for any rectangle, and so we can generalise this strategy. At this point pupils may or may not have been formally introduced to algebra – if they have, this is a great link back to the fact that algebra captures relationships that are always true, and so this is a perfect candidate. By defining variables such as l for length, h for height and A for area, we can write a formula to capture this calculation strategy: namely $A = l \times h$ (or $A = lh$). If pupils haven't yet been introduced to algebra, we can still write this as a word formula rather than defining the variables.

From here the other shapes are relatively straightforward to make sense of in terms of the strategies for calculating their area. Area of parallelograms can be seen as moving a right-triangular slice from one end of the rectangle to the other (which is one reason why the 'conservation of area' idea was important when mentioned in Chapter 8):

Triangle area can be seen as half that of a parallelogram:

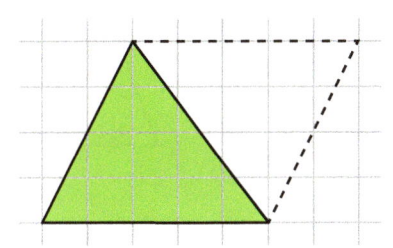

whilst the area of a kite can be seen as the area of two congruent triangles:

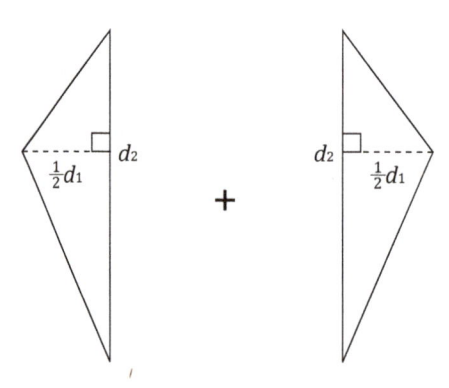

and a rhombus can be seen both as a kite and a parallelogram:

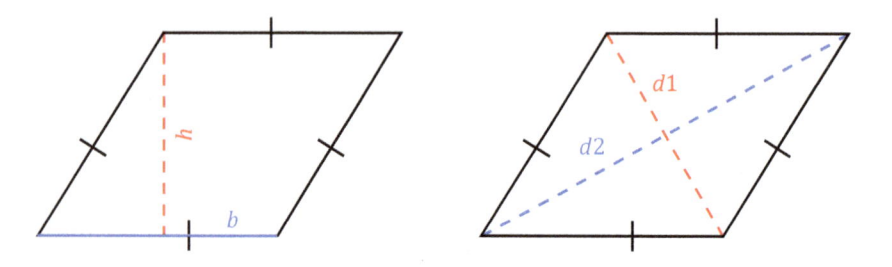

As for a trapezium, well there are many different ways to show why the formula for the area of a trapezium is given by $\frac{1}{2}(a + b)h$, where a and b are the parallel sides and h is the perpendicular distance between the parallel sides. The website Boss Maths has interactive demonstrations of five different ways (at the time of writing),[10] and there are plenty more besides – indeed, if you have a group of pupils who are confident in other areas and possibly a bit of algebraic manipulation, it may be worth setting them the challenge to prove the formula for the area of a trapezium in as many different ways as they can find.

Just because pupils can see how all of these polygons follow from looking at calculation strategies for working out the number of squares, it doesn't necessarily mean they will automatically remember all of them and keep them separate in their heads. Pupils will need the opportunity to revisit and reinforce their memory of using these formulae. A nice little activity that takes pupils beyond basic regurgitation and calculation is something like this:

> The triangle, parallelogram and the two trapezia below each have the same base and the same height. Place them in order from largest to smallest area. Explain your order. Can you prove it?

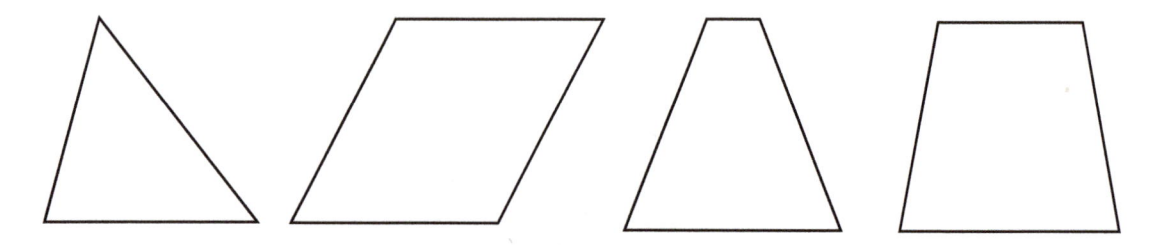

---

10 S. Gokarakonda, G16d – Area of a Trapezium, *Boss Maths* (n.d.). Available at: https://www.bossmaths.com/g16d/.

When it comes to other polygons, we will come to the point where pupils recognise that all polygons can be built from combinations of each of these. This might be looking at the area of L-shaped hexagons by breaking them into rectangles in the early stages, right up to looking at all sorts of regular and irregular polygons using trigonometry (which we will explore later in the chapter).

At the end of the last section, we mentioned the idea of looking at area and perimeter. Care must be taken, however, as these are two concepts that pupils will often confuse. In his blog, Bruno Reddy, the former head of mathematics at the high-performing King Solomon Academy in London, advocates teaching these concepts separately – by a significant amount of time.[11] I think it is important for them to be brought together at some point but can see the benefits of initially exploring them separately. One of my favourite activities to do with pupils when I am ready to bring them together is this excellent one I first saw from Professor John Mason, based on something similar from Pessia Tsamir and Dina Tirosh:[12]

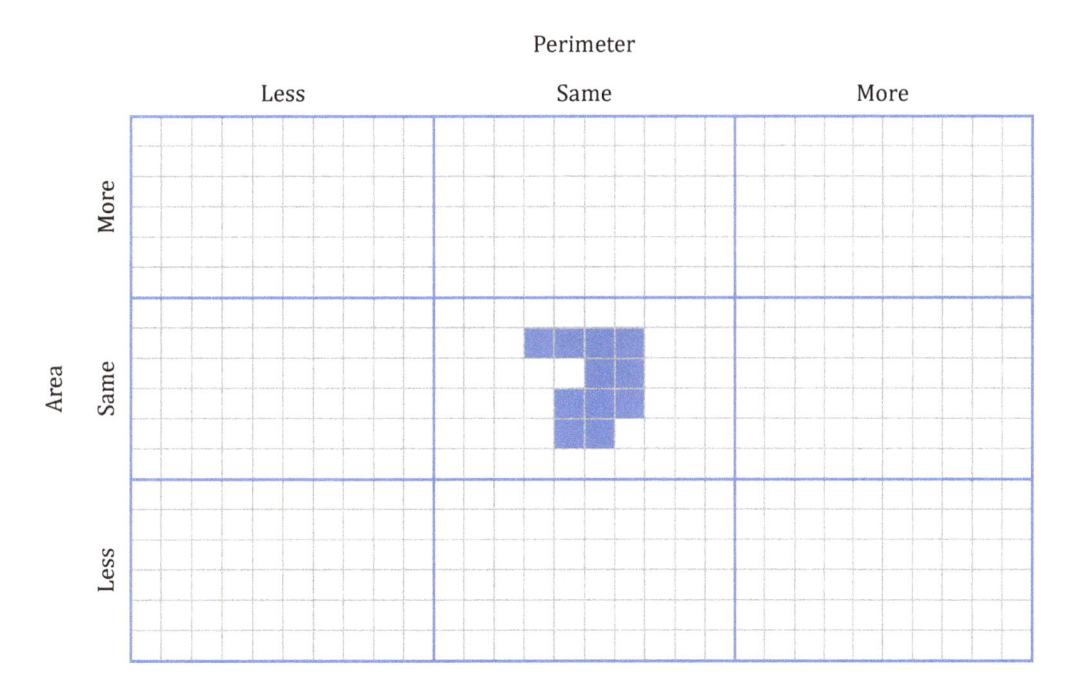

The key instruction here is that pupils should populate the other spaces in the grid by making the minimum change possible to the shape in the centre space (as we saw in Chapter 1 with representing negative integers).

---

[11] B. Reddy, Design Your Own Mastery Curriculum in Maths, *Mr Reddy Maths* [blog] (29 March 2014). Available at: http://mrreddy.com/blog/2014/03/design-your-own-mastery-curriculum-in-maths/.

[12] J. Mason, Perimeter and Area: More, Same, Less grid (based on an idea by P. Tsamir and D, Tirosh), *More Same Less* (n.d.). Available at: https://www.more-same-less.co.uk/grid-collection/Shape?lightbox=comp-k8x2n8zb2_da541e74-d546-4e7d-9053-26507cb6dc35_runtime_dataItem-k8x2n8ze.

Concept link: angle properties of polygons

Unlike area, where potentially starting with squares and rectangles is the most 'natural' path to the other polygons, when it comes to angles, all other polygons stem from triangles. Provided pupils have a secure understanding of corresponding and alternate angles, and the fact that they are equal when lines are parallel, then the proof that the interior angles of a planar triangle sum to 180° is quite an accessible proof for pupils:

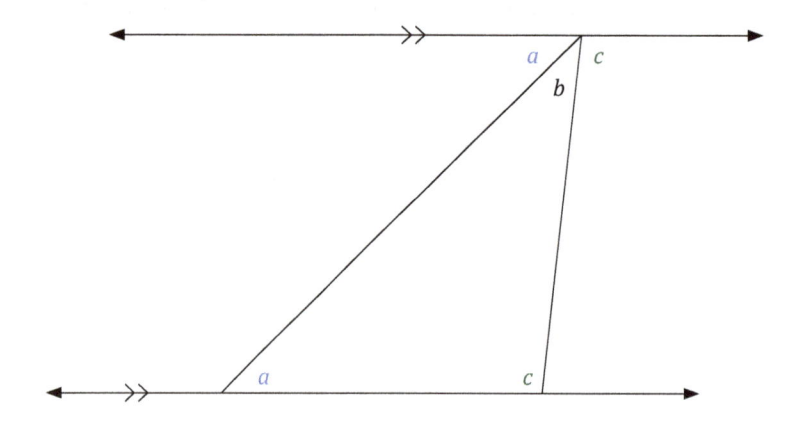

Angles *a*, *b* and *c* clearly sum to 180°, as they form a straight line at a point. However, the bottom-left angle interior to the triangle is also equal to *a*, and the bottom-right angle interior to the triangle is also equal to *c* as they are alternate angles and the lines are parallel. This clearly implies that the three interior angles in the triangle sum to 180°.

Pupils can add this property of planar angles to the other properties they have studied, using them to find missing angles in increasingly complex pictures, from simple triangles to diagrams such as:

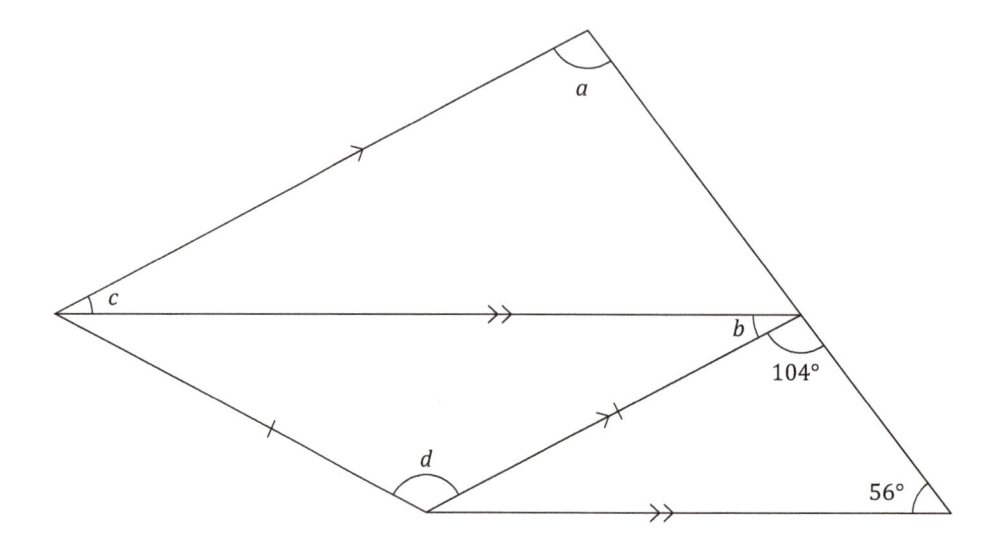

We can see in this diagram as well that pupils should have the opportunity to reason with isosceles triangles, as well as right-angled and equilateral triangles, from being able to justify their angle properties to using them in diagrams like the one above.

Once pupils are secure with angles in triangles, we can begin to build polygons with more sides, starting with quadrilaterals:

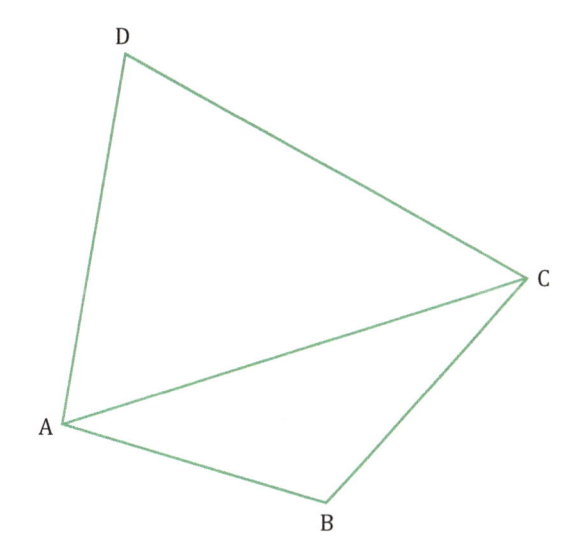

Pupils can reason (or we can highlight, if necessary) that the sum of the four angles interior to the quadrilateral ABCD is equal to the sum of the angle interior to each of the triangles ABC and ACD. Given that pupils are clear that the interior angles of each triangle sum to 180°, this leads to the conclusion that the sum of the angles in the quadrilateral sum to 360°. Further, pupils should be quite happy that this argument will generalise to any quadrilateral – drawing in a single diagonal will split any quadrilateral into two triangles whose angle sum is the same as the angle sum of the original quadrilateral (or alternatively that any quadrilateral can be made by combining two triangles along a common length).

When we get to quadrilaterals, it is worth spending some time with pupils reasoning out the specific angle properties of the different quadrilaterals. All of these are a direct consequence of the fact that the angles sum to 360°, along with properties such as corresponding and alternate angles, but they are important for pupils to have experience working with and solve as an excellent vehicle for reprising and reasoning with these properties. For example, even the fact that a square has to have four interior right angles can be seen as a consequence of the fact that the four interiors angles simultaneously have to sum to 360° and have to be equal in size. The angle properties of shapes like kites, rhombi, parallelograms and trapezia can all be reasoned from their parallel lines (except the kite, which has none) and the angle sum of 360° (with a kite it is helpful to highlight the two isosceles triangles created by a diagonal to reason the two equal angles).

As well as reasoning the angle properties of different names quadrilaterals, we should also offer opportunities for pupils to use angle properties to reason which quadrilateral is being shown. For example:

Which of these are definitely trapezia?

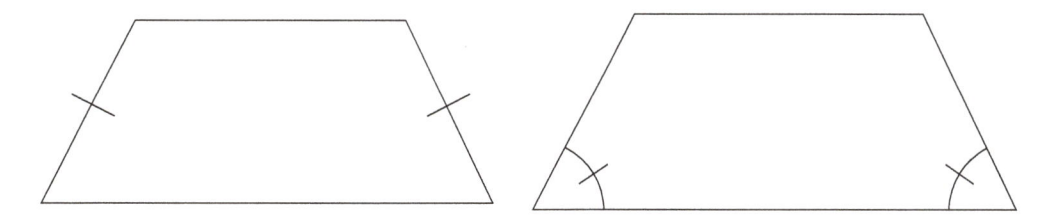

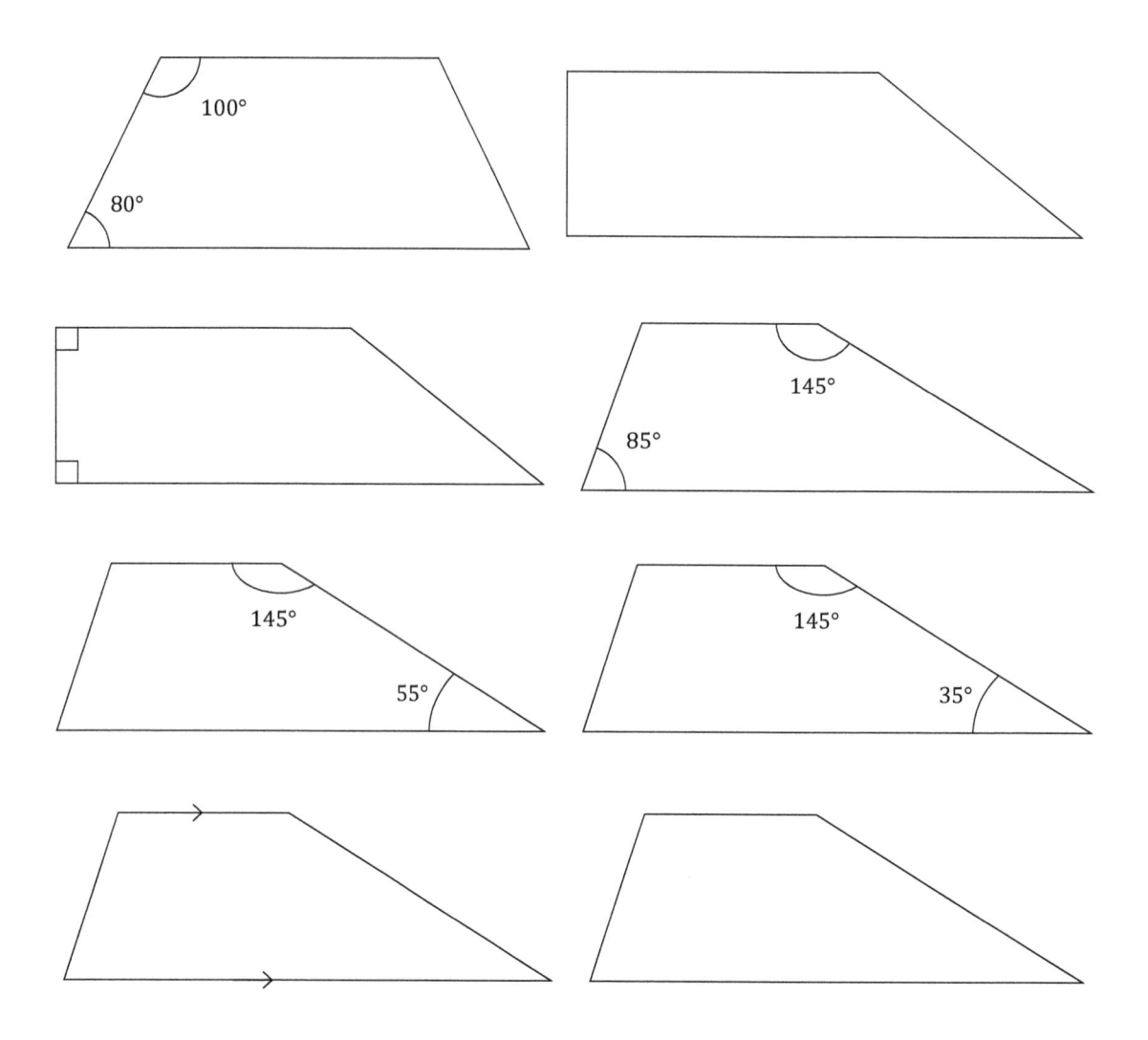

There are many good practice activities out there for angle-reasoning calculations based on the angle properties of quadrilaterals, one of the better ones being from Maths4Everyone.[13] A nice alternative is to use exam questions in a goal-free approach:

Work out everything you can about this diagram.

ABDE is a parallelogram.

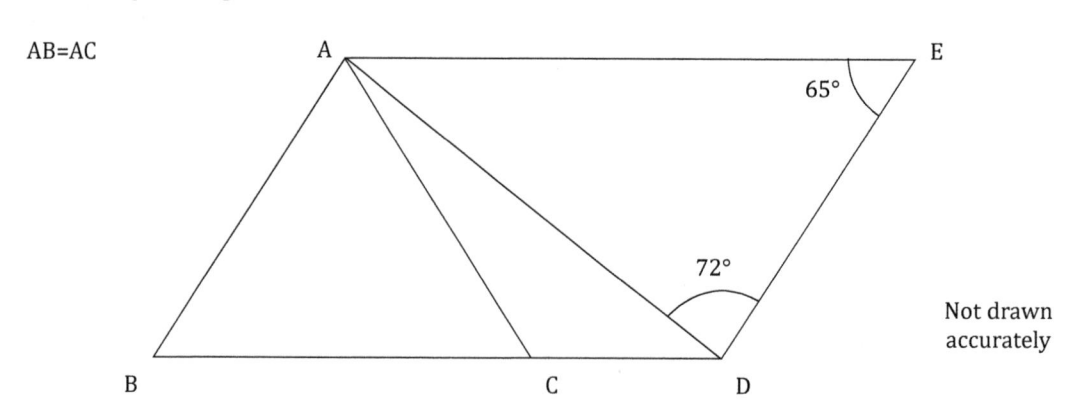

AB=AC

Not drawn accurately

(Question image from AQA GCSE Mathematics 8300F1 Practice Paper Set 3.)

---

[13] D. Morse, Angles in Quadrilaterals (Worksheets with Solutions), *TES* (16 September 2021). Available at: https://www.tes.com/teaching-resource/angles-in-quadrilaterals-worksheets-with-solutions-12208149.

There is evidence from cognitive science that removing the goal of finding a given angle means learners (particularly so-called 'novice' learners) learn more from the experience of working with the diagram as they are not wasting working memory keeping the goal state and progress towards the goal state in mind.[14] These work best where there is a finite and relatively clear amount of information that can be reasoned from a situation; sometimes pupils can struggle to decide what information they can even generate from a given prompt if the prompt is too open. There is a large selection of goal-free problems covering many different mathematical concepts on the Goal Free Problems website.[15]

From quadrilaterals the natural extension is to look at angles in polygons with a greater number of sides, i.e. pentagons, then hexagons, then heptagons and so on. This might be by offering something like this:

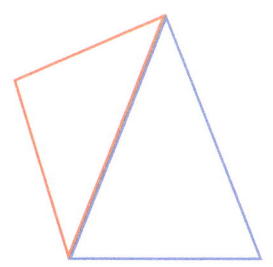

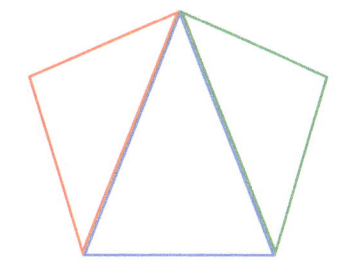

where pupils can see that a pentagon can be created by adding two lines (or an 'extra' triangle) to the side of a quadrilateral, and can continue this process to create further polygons with more sides.

From here we would ideally look to bring in the relationship between the number of sides and the sum of the interior angles in a planar polygon. We might approach this similarly to approaching the *n*th term of a sequence (indeed, pupils should understand that the generalisation thought process is very similar) by asking pupils to try and consider what the sum of the interior angles for a polygon with a reasonable large number of sides (say 40 or so) is. Pupils might reason a polygon with 40 sides will have been built from 38 triangles, and therefore the sum will be 38 × 180°. Pupils should be able to see that this idea will generalise to the formula $S = 180(n = 2)°$, where S is the sum of interior angles and n is the number of sides. Pupils can then work with this to reason missing angles in different polygons when given information about other angles. This can be by providing sketches of the quadrilaterals with sufficient angle information.

Find the angle labelled x in this hexagon:

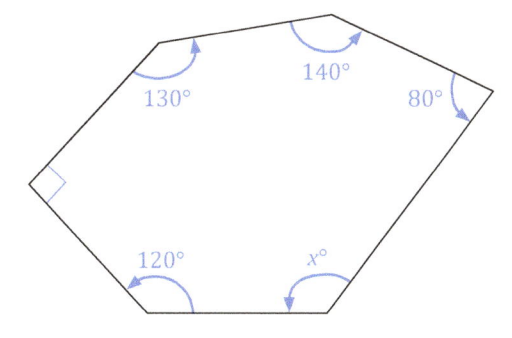

---
14 J. Sweller, Cognitive Load During Problem Solving: Effects on Learning, *Cognitive Science,* 12 (1988). Available at: https://onlinelibrary.wiley.com/doi/pdf/10.1207/s15516709cog1202_4.
15 See http://goalfreeproblems.blogspot.com/.

Or it might be presented purely in words:

A hexagon has angles of 97°, 97°, 97°, 97°, and 97°. Find the size of the 6th angle.

A nice activity is to then get pupils to try and sketch the hexagon in question, and to make up other combinations of angles that will form a polygon and sketch those.

In introducing polygons with more than three or four sides, we will also want to introduce the idea of a **regular** polygon. For a pupil that understands polygons in general, the definition of a regular polygon being a polygon where every side has the same length and every interior angle the same size is usually well understood, but needs exemplifying to be well secured and remembered. The choice of non-examples to support understanding is also important here; the use of polygons like rhombi and rectangles to show that just equal sides or equal angles is not enough on its own to ensure regularity, as well as including polygons with a greater number of sides that are either equilateral or equiangular:

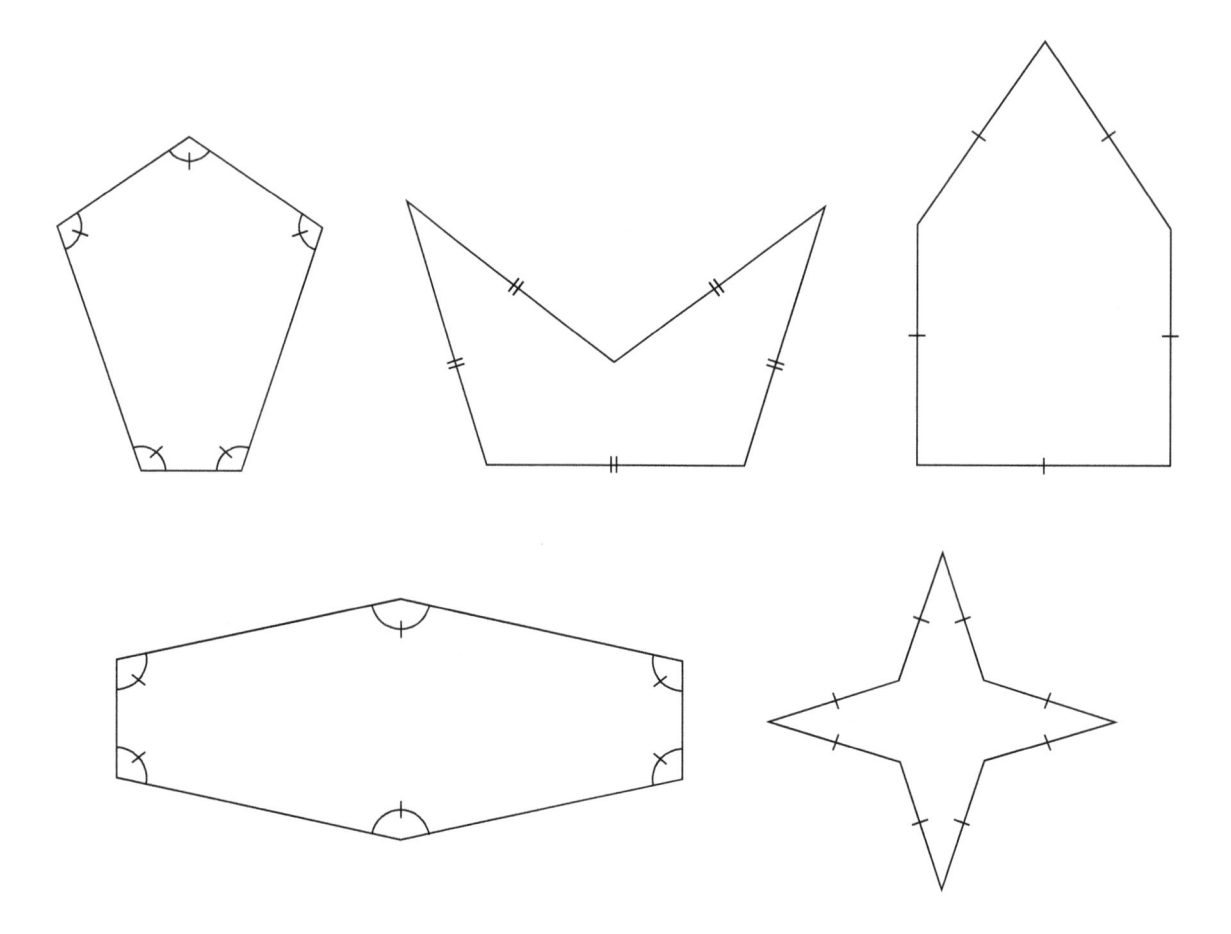

Potentially a nice thing to explore once pupils are clear on regularity is why equilateral implies equiangular for triangles (i.e. why an equilateral triangle must have three equal interior angles) when this is not the case for any other regular polygon (i.e. that a polygon having more than 3 equal sides does not imply that the interior angles will be equal in size).

Of course, hand in hand with examining interior angles for polygons is to examine exterior angles. Here we meet a potential 'misconception'. The 'natural' idea that often comes to mind to pupils that have met interior angles when the discussion moves on to exterior angles is something like the picture below:

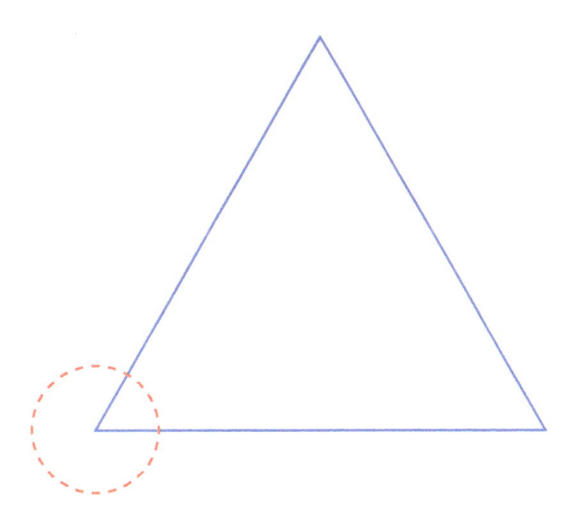

The reason the word 'misconception' appears in inverted commas in the previous paragraph is that thinking of this as a misconception is a little different to other misconceptions, in that it would actually (at least at first glance) make perfect sense to define this as the exterior angle. The only reason this isn't considered an exterior angle is because part of the angle is redundant in terms of how its value changes when the number of sides increases.

Let us suppose, for a moment, that we did define exterior angles in the way the above image suggests, and then examine the 'exterior' angles for the 'first' three regular polygons:

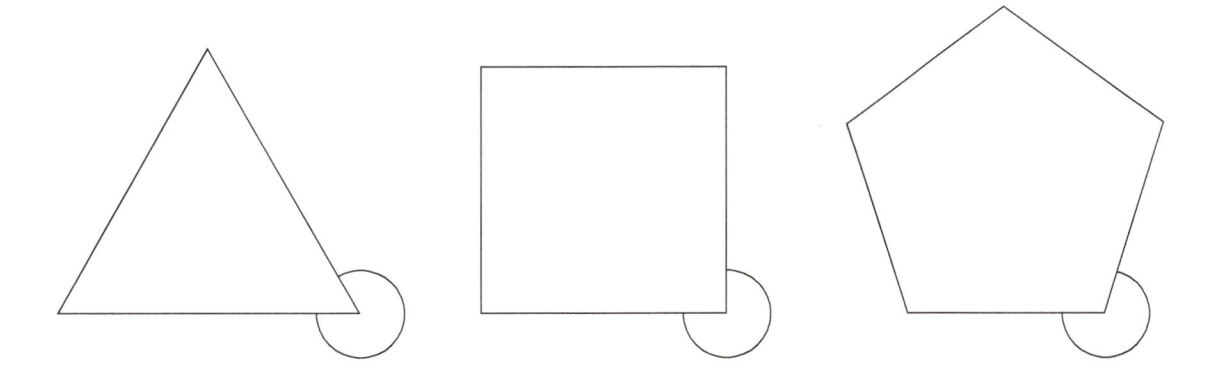

We can see that increasing the number of sides decreases the size of the angle; however, if we focus on what actually changes about the size of the angle, we can see that the bottom 'half' of the turn (below the line in the next image) doesn't change.

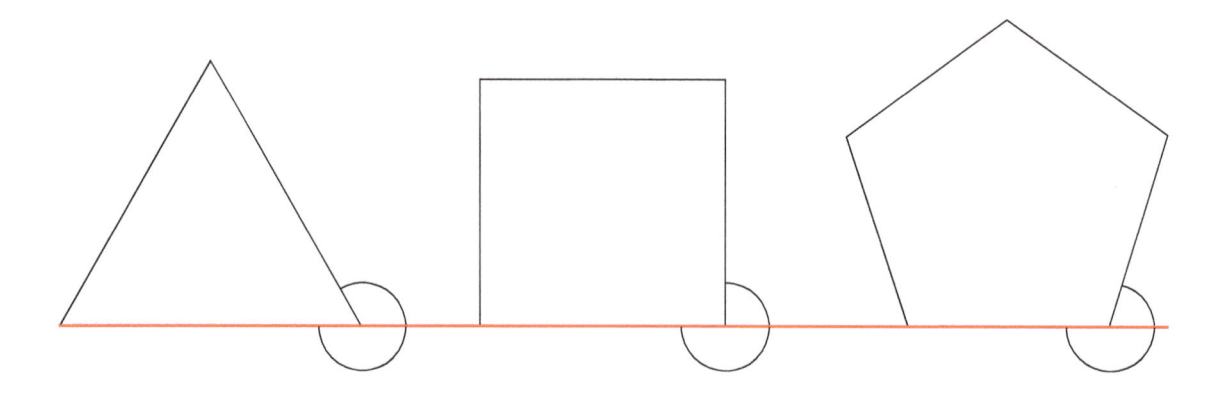

Further, we can reason that this 'half' of the turn will never be impacted no matter how many sides we increase the polygon by, as we would need to make the interior angle a reflex angle in order to impact on that part of the angle. This means it make sense to define an exterior angle to always be the part that is less than 180°. This leads to the idea of defining the exterior angle to be the angle between one side and an extension of the other side, with the further implication that the interior angle and exterior angle meeting at a point are supplementary.

In addition to the property that exterior and interior angles at any vertex of a polygon are supplementary, there is another important property of exterior angles of polygons: namely that the sum of the exterior angles in a single direction is always 360°. This property is nicely provable with regular polygons:

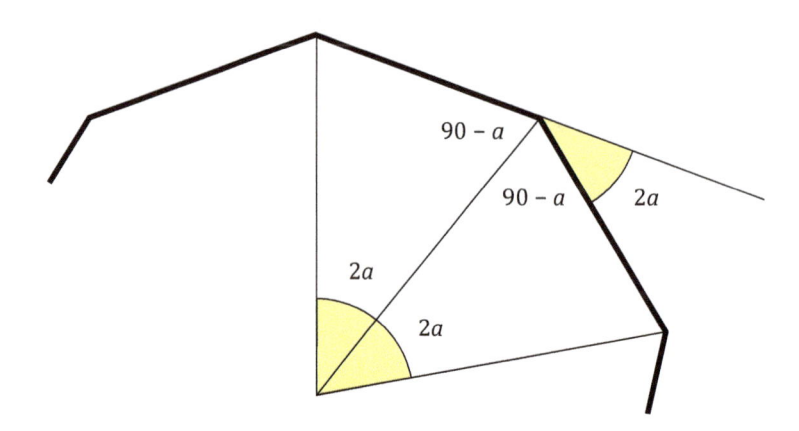

The logic being that because the angles around the centre point of the polygon will sum to 360°, then so will the exterior angles. More generally, there is a relatively straightforward algebraic proof that uses the fact that each pair of interior and exterior angles will sum to 180°. This means that, given a polygon with n sides, there will be n pairs of interior and exterior angles, which will sum to $180n°$ (as each pair sums to 180°). We already know that the sum of the interior angles is given by $180(n - 2)°$, and so the sum of the exterior angles is $180n - 180(n - 2) = 180n - 180n + 360 = 360°$.

A common alternative to the formal algebraic proof of exterior angles summing to 360° in a single direction is to demonstrate that moving round the polygon is equivalent to a full turn:

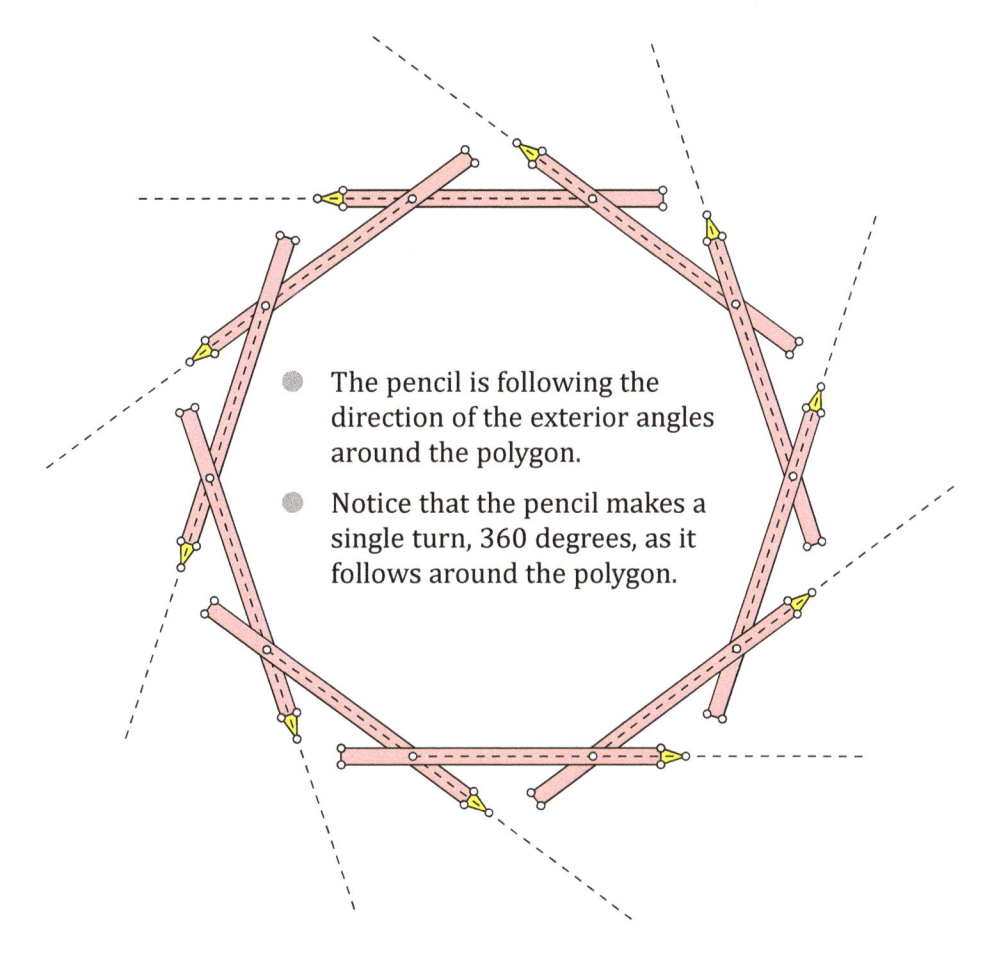

- The pencil is following the direction of the exterior angles around the polygon.
- Notice that the pencil makes a single turn, 360 degrees, as it follows around the polygon.

There is a nice animation that demonstrates a similar approach on the Resourceaholic website.[16]

Similarly to the interior angle sum, we can offer pupils opportunities to use the exterior angle sum to calculate missing angles:

Find the value of the exterior angle labelled y in this diagram.

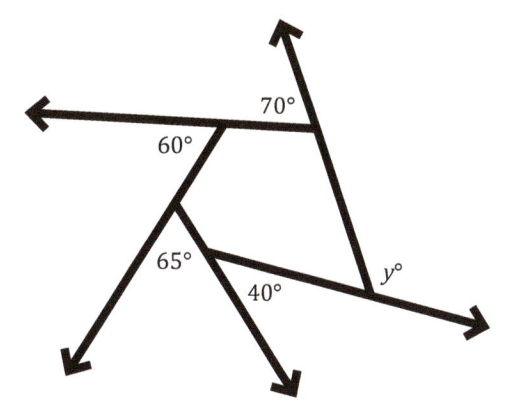

---

16 J. Morgan, Animations and Simulations, *Resourceaholic* [blog] (7 August 2014). Available at: https://www.resourceaholic.com/2014/08/gifs.html.

One of the biggest advantages of the exterior angle sum being fixed at 360° for all polygons is that it creates a very simple relationship for regular polygons, namely that the size of a single exterior angle is equal to 360° ÷ the number of sides of the polygon. Pupils can use this relationship to find the size of both exterior and interior angles in regular polygons (as interior and exterior angles are supplementary) and can use their knowledge of multiplication and division families to reason that this will also imply that the number of sides can be found by dividing 360° by the size of a single exterior angle, provided the polygon is regular. We might offer pupils a question like this to prompt pupils' reasoning:

> A regular polygon has a single interior angle of 156°. Work out the number of sides of the regular polygon.

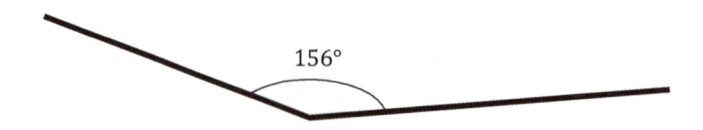

Another very nice opportunity to offer pupils when looking at angles and polygons is to look in more detail at tessellations, and which shapes can tesselate. Pupils will need to understand that the key requirement in tessellation is the angles at the meeting point summing to 360°, which they may reason or need to be prompted to see:

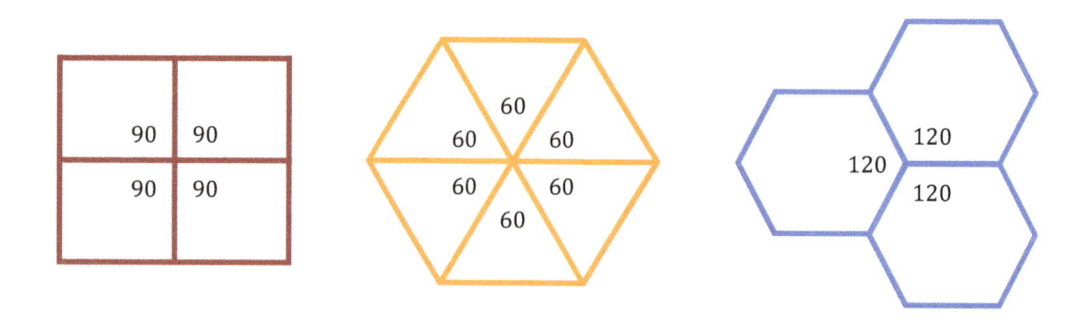

Pupils should then be able to reason why the only regular polygons that will tessellate on their own are squares, equilateral triangles and regular hexagons, as well as potentially being prompted to find pairs (or more) of polygons that will tessellate. There are nice interactive applets that pupils can use to explore tessellations. NRICH has a nice one for regular polygons.[17]

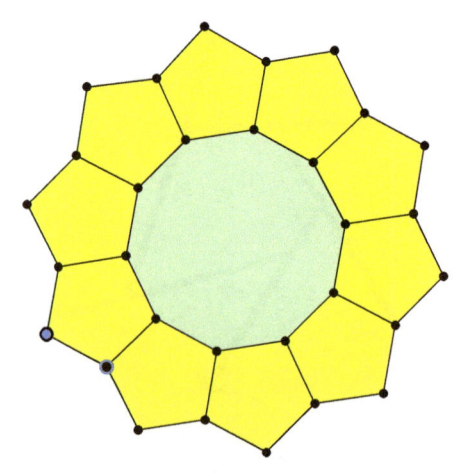

---

17 See https://nrich.maths.org/6069.

From two-dimensional polygons the natural transition is to increase to three dimensions and into polyhedra.

Concept: polyhedra

Prerequisites: Numbers, measures, addition, subtraction, multiplication and division will all be requisite to some properties of polyhedra we will wish to explore.

Linked concepts: Shape, transformation, graphing.

Having introduced the language of 'polygon' to pupils previously as meaning 'many angles', pupils will generally be quite accepting of 'polyhedron' as meaning 'many faces'. Of course, we will have to introduce pupils to the language of 'face' as being the two-dimensional shapes that make up the surface of the polyhedron (pupils should already be familiar with the language of 'edge' and 'vertex' from polygons). As with polygons, examples and non-examples will be useful in making the concept clear:

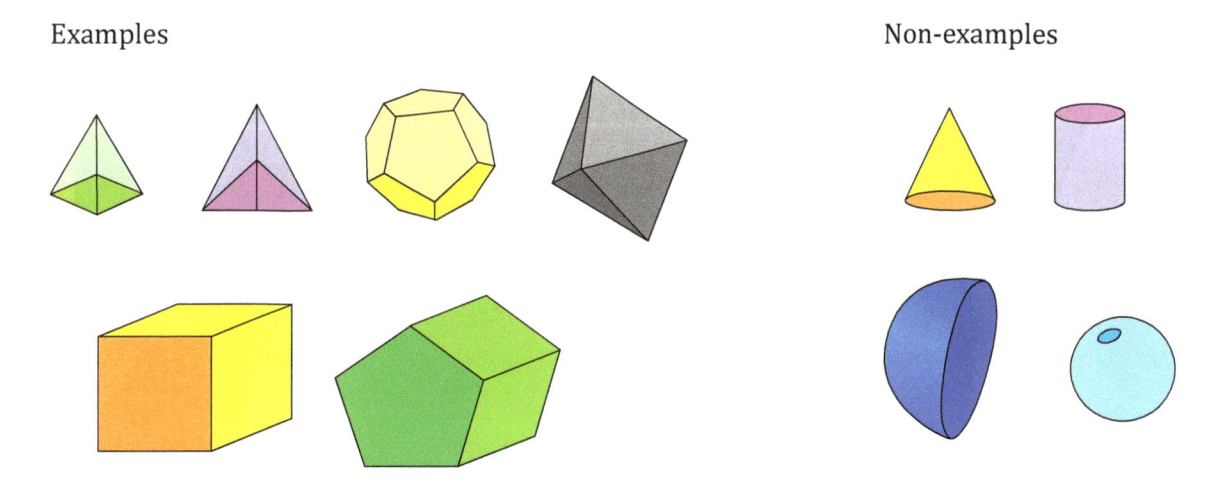

Examples   Non-examples

as they will in exemplifying the sub-categories of polyhedral such as prisms, pyramids and the five Platonic solids.

There are a number of really nice activities that we can offer pupils to allow them to gain familiarity with polyhedra. Exploring nets with Polydron, trying to find different nets of a given polyhedron (such as the 11 nets of a cube or an octahedron):

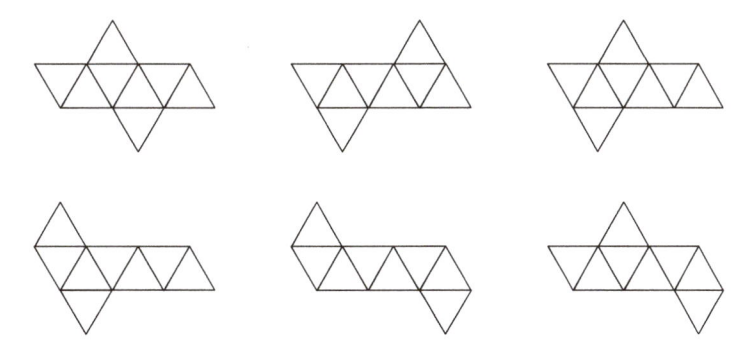

Conceptual Maths

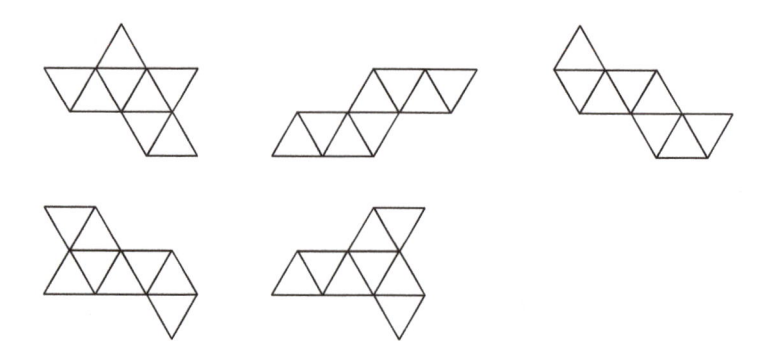

or combining polyhedra together to create new shapes (such as the cuboctahedron or the gyrobifastigium):

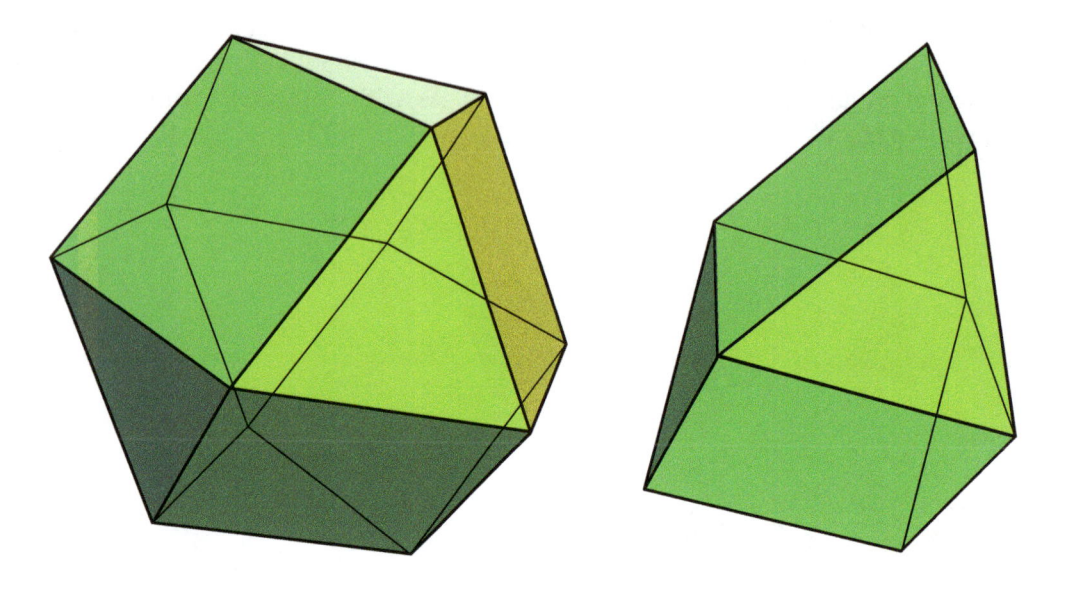

or, of course, the ever-popular original football shape – the truncated icosahedron:

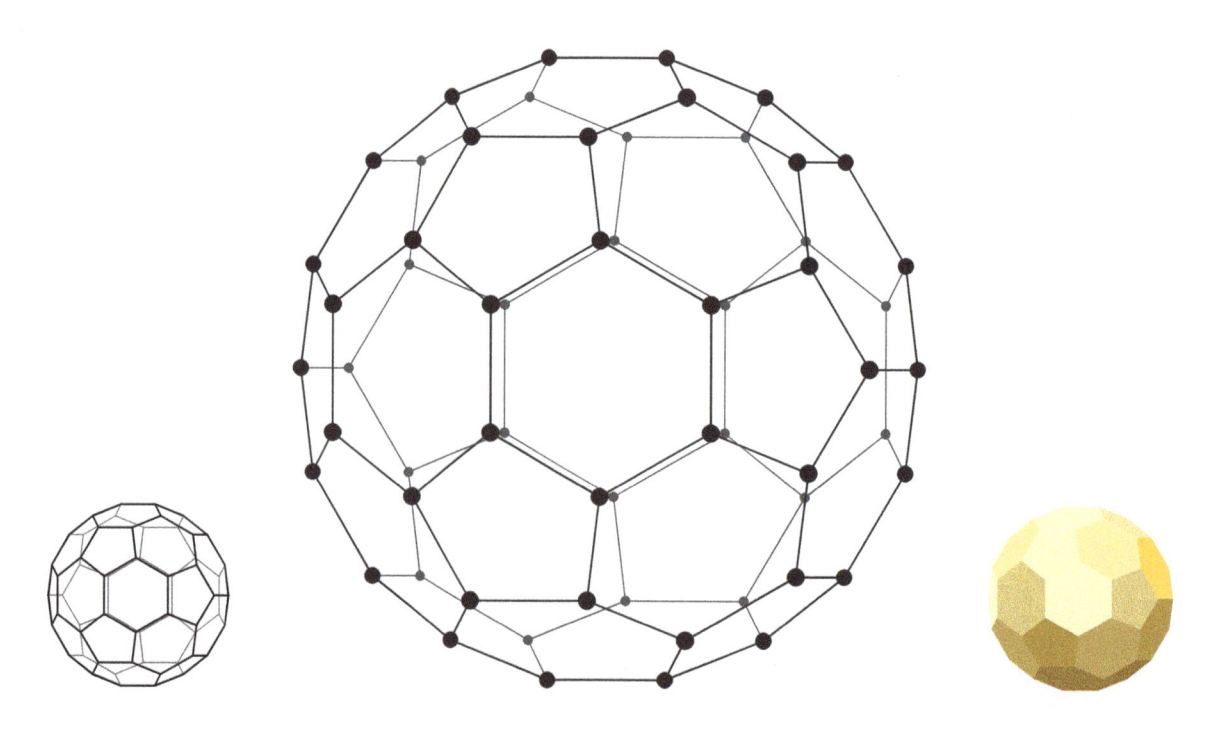

Another potential activity is to explore Euler's formula for polyhedra. This can be a discovery-based activity, where pupils explore different polyhedra and have the opportunity to notice the relationship between the number of faces, edges and vertices. Alternatively, we can challenge pupils to build polyhedra with a given number of faces, edges and vertices:

Which of these polyhedra can you build?

i   6 faces, 8 vertices, 12 edges

ii 5 faces, 5 vertices, 8 edges

iii 8 faces, 12 vertices, 16 edges

iv 12 faces, 8 vertices, 16 edges

If you are building a polyhedron with 8 faces and 6 vertices, how many edges does it have? What about 5 faces and 6 vertices? What about 5 faces and 8 edges – how many vertices will it have?

The idea with these questions is not necessarily that pupils should learn Euler's formula prior to answering them, but that they might attempt to build these shapes and use the act of building them to help reach a deeper understanding about the relationships between the faces, edges and vertices.

Nets are not the only representation of polyhedra that pupils will be introduced to during school mathematics. Pupils will also need to develop skills in orthogonal drawing, usually on isometric paper (although it is worth noting that in design and technology pupils may well actually have to create their own orthogonal grids). One thing that pupils should come to appreciate when being introduced to orthogonal drawing is that the figure below is not a 'true' representation of a cube, in that any view that would lead to the front face appearing square would mean the other two faces wouldn't actually appear as they do in this image.

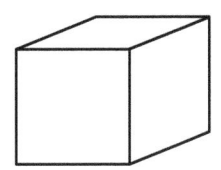

Contrast this with a 'true' orthogonal representation like the one below, where the view is shifted so that the front edge and top-front vertex is furthest forward, and we see a view of a cube that can actually appear in real life.

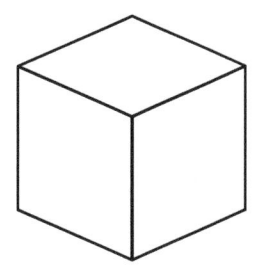

Multilink or Unifix cubes can be great for working with orthogonal drawing; pupils can build shapes out of cubes for each other and then attempt to draw them at different orientations. Pupils can also move beyond shapes built from cubes, so that they can appreciate the difficulties in trying to represent certain polyhedra orthogonally.

The other representation that pupils will learn about are the different projections of a three-dimensional shape. We can use architectural drawings or similar to make clear what we mean by 'plan', 'front elevation', etc. before pupils practise drawing different views from a given three-dimensional shape. The most common misconception here is for pupils to try and still give a sense of the '3D-ness' of the shape in the projection:

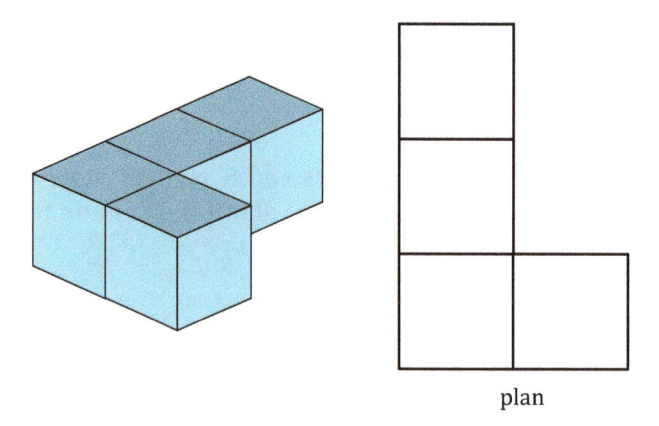

plan

Pupils will need to be clear that these projections do need to be two-dimensional representations, but once that is clear then a nice activity is for pupils to move between these two views, taking shapes drawn orthogonally and drawing the different projections, and also taking a combination of projections and drawing an orthogonal picture of the solid shape (potentially having built the shape from cubes before drawing it).

Having looked at basic properties and representations of polyhedra, pupils will (at some point) move on to looking at measures involving polyhedra.

Concept links: surface area of polyhedra

I always prefer to start exploring measures of polyhedra with surface area rather than volume, for three reasons:

1. Pupils will already be familiar with area calculation, so surface area presents an ideal opportunity for interweaving of previously understood knowledge.

2. There is a natural extension of measurement, starting from distance to measure space in a single dimension, to area measuring space in two dimensions, and then to volume measuring space in three dimensions. I want pupils to understand this progression, which means I don't want to cause potential confusion in pupils by talking about extending space measure to three dimensions and then muddling the situation by looking at two-dimensional measure of a three-dimensional shape.

3. Related to the second point, there are natural parallels in the relationship between perimeter and area of two-dimensional shapes, and surface area and volume of three-dimensional shapes, with perimeter/surface area forming the boundary of the space and area/volume being the measure of the space inside the boundary, with the measure of the boundary being a dimension less than the measure of the space. Again,

there is potential confusion if we introduce the idea of measurement of a three-dimensional space before making secure the idea of what bounds it.

A standard approach to introducing the surface area of different polyhedra is to consider the nets of those polyhedra. The nets clearly form a two-dimensional shape, and so it makes sense to look at what the area of the net will be, and what this will mean when the net is folded up to create the polyhedron. This might include pupils actually building nets and measuring the required lengths in order to calculate areas (either out of paper or Polydron) and/or being given a combination of shapes represented on paper both as nets and in an orthogonal (or other three-dimensional) representation (such as the ones shown on the worksheet from MathWorksheets4Kids linked below[18]).

This is also a great point to bring back ideas like conversion of units by providing values measured in different units for different edge lengths, so that pupils have to convert these into a common unit before calculating the surface area.

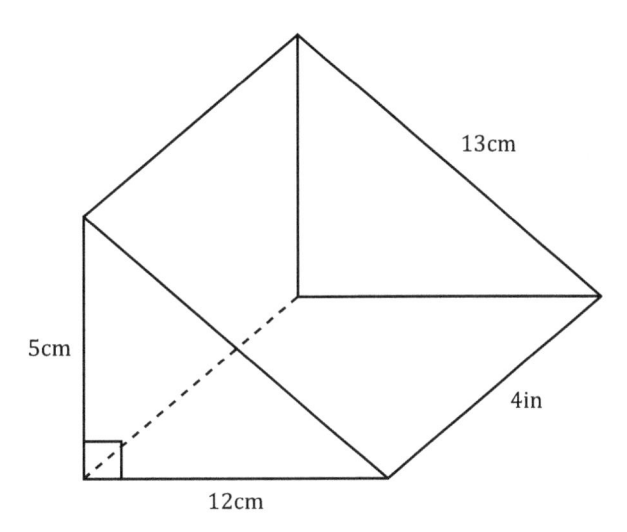

In addition, we can use surface area as a vehicle to revisit forming and solving equations, particularly quadratic equations.[19]

Surface areas of cuboids

1   A cuboid has a square for two of the faces. The length is 1 cm longer than the height (and the width).

    The surface of the cuboid is 66 cm².

    What are the dimensions of the cuboid?

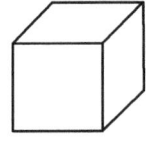

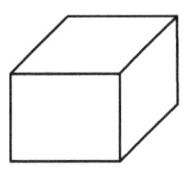

2   A cuboid has dimensions (height, width and length) that are consecutive numbers.

    The surface area of the cuboid is 214 cm².

    What are the dimensions of the cuboid?

---

[18] Math Worksheets 4 Kids, Surface Area of Solids Using Nets (n.d.). Available at: https://www.mathworksheets4kids.com/surface-area/nets/metric/total-surface-area-1.pdf.

[19] D. Steward, Surface Area and Factorizable Quadratics, *Median* [blog] (6 December 2018). Available at: https://donsteward.blogspot.com/2018/12/surface-area-and-factorisable.html.

3 A cuboid has a square base. The height is 1 cm less than the length (and width).

   The surface of the cuboid is 80 cm².

   What are the dimensions of the cuboid?

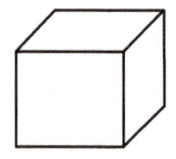

4 A cuboid has a height that is 1 cm more than the width and the length is double the height.

   The surface area of the cuboid is 72 cm².

   What are the dimensions of the cuboid?

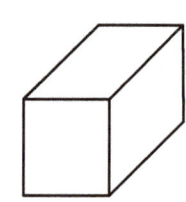

Once we have thoroughly examined the idea of surface area, we can then move onto looking at measuring the volume of space inside different polyhedra.

Concept link: volume of polyhedra

Pupils should already be familiar with the idea of using cubic units to measure three-dimensional space, and of considering calculation strategies for counting cubes (as outlined in Chapter 8). The journey for introducing the calculations for volumes of different polyhedra then mirrors that which we have seen for area and polygons. Cubes and cuboids are natural extensions of squares and rectangles:

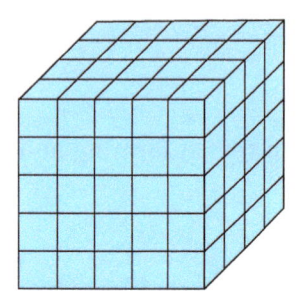

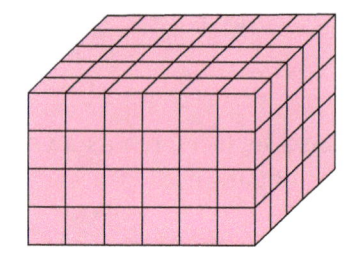

The key thing here is to draw attention to the rows of cubes on any face, and that we can know this simply by calculating the area of this face. If you are wanting to break this skill down, you can actually offer pupils shapes like this:

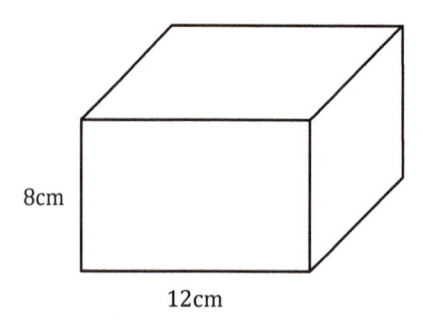

8cm

12cm

and ask pupils how many cubes in the shape are attached to the front face of the shape. We can then add the third dimension, linking to the number of 'strips' of cubes. This leads us nicely to the volume of a prism and the formula for calculating:

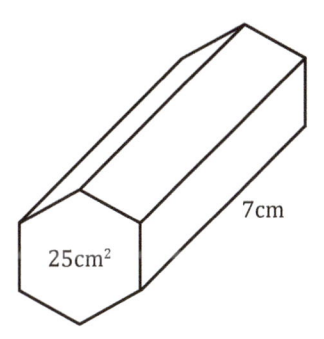

In this prism the area of 25 cm² at the front tells us how many squares make up the area of the hexagon, but it also tells us how many cubes are in the first row of cubes in the prism. Pupils can then recognise this leads us to the formula for calculating the volume of the prism by calculating the area of the cross-section and multiplying by the depth. This can lead to calculating the volume of different prisms, including prisms that have irregular cross-sections.

Find the volume of this prism:

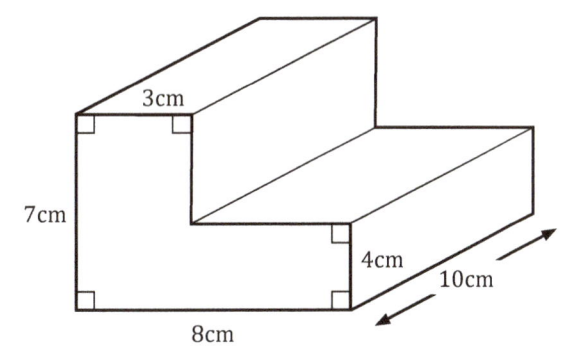

From this we can explore pyramids – there are some great animations out there that show that the volume of a pyramid is one third the volume of a prism; this image below from Don Steward comes from a blog post that contains a Geogebra applet that allows the user to edit the dimensions of the cuboid and then split it into three pyramids, rotating them so they can clearly be seen.[20]

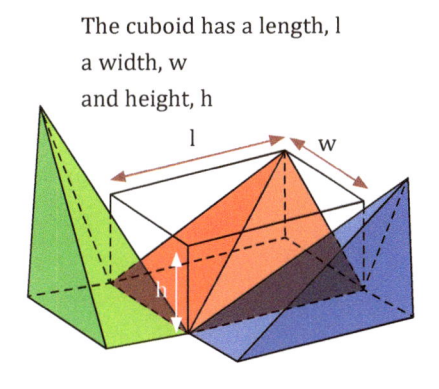

The cuboid has a length, l
a width, w
and height, h

---

20 D. Steward, Volume of a Pyramid, *Median* [blog] (29 September 2012). Available at: https://donsteward.blogspot.com/2012/09/volume-of-pyramid.html.

From here we can make the link between the base area of a pyramid and the area of cross-section (we can see in the image above that any of the faces of the cuboid could be considered the 'base' of the pyramid). This leads us to the formula for calculating the volume of a pyramid as $\frac{1}{3}$ × base area × height, as well as being equal in value to $\frac{1}{3}$ that of the encompassing prism. This relationship can be reinforced by offering pupils questions like the one below, potentially as part of a larger exercise in finding pyramid volume:

The triangular prism below has a volume of 369 cm³. Work out the volume of the pyramid.

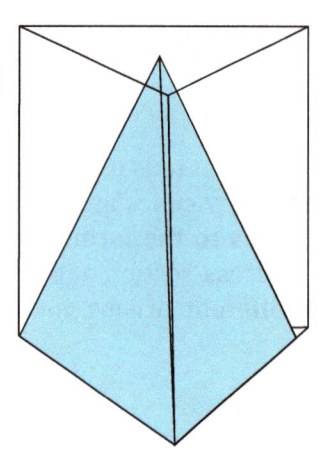

Other polyhedra can then be dealt with in the same was as compound two-dimensional shapes, by breaking the shape down into simpler pyramids and prisms.

Find the volume of this shape:

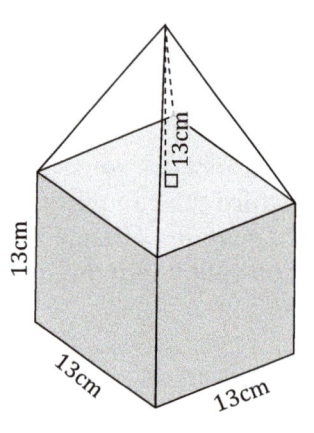

Of course, every shape we have considered to this point has straight edges, being either a polygon or a polyhedron. At some point pupils are going to begin to include shapes that have curved lengths, starting with the circle.

Concept: circles

Prerequisites: Numbers, measures, addition, subtraction, multiplication and division will all be requisite to some properties of circles we will wish to explore. We may also want loci to be a prerequisite, or we may want to introduce the idea of loci through introducing circles.

Linked concepts: Similarity, angle, area, graphing.

Pupils will no doubt have been introduced to circles in terms of linking a shape that looks like this:

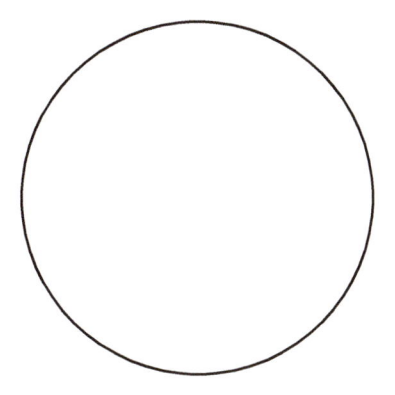

with the word 'circle'. When we start to study circles in a bit more detail, we should ideally begin with a focus on two key areas:

1. The nomenclature used in studying circles, and how it is different to that of polygons.
2. What is/are the defining feature(s) of the circle?

The first of these is important, and often overlooked, as the terminology associated with circles is entirely different to that used with polygons. Language such as 'edge', 'angle', 'diagonal' that are used in defining different polygons and their properties simply don't exist in the circle. Instead, pupils need to be introduced to words like 'radius', 'diameter', 'circumference'. This is best done using circle diagrams:

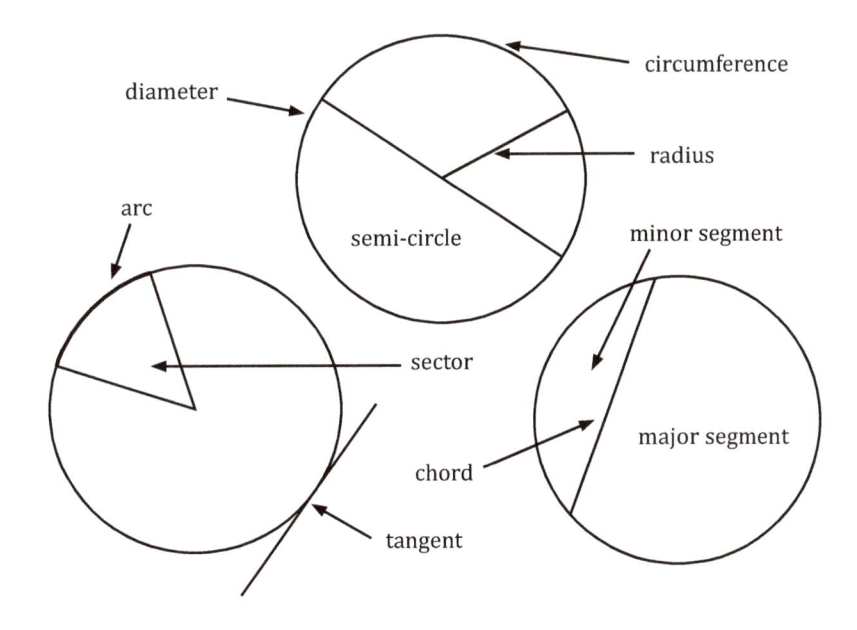

There are a number of nice activities that can prompt pupils to use this language correctly and consider the connections between some of the lengths and areas highlighted. There is an excellent activity in the *Year 9: Measures, Shape and Space* book from the 'Key Stage 3 Developing Numeracy' series called 'Round in Circles' that offers pupils different opportunities to work with different lines and parts of circles.[21] I also designed this CLOZE activity to prompt pupils to reason with these terms:

Circle Terms

Use each of the following words to fill in the sentences below. Some of the words may be used more than once.

       diameter   radius   circumference   chord   tangent   arc

       sector   major segment   minor segment   radii

1   A line that goes from the centre of the circle to the edge is called a ....

2   The distance around the edge of a circle is called the ....

3   Any line that touches the circumference of a circle on the outside once is called a ....

4   A .... cuts the circle into 2 parts the .... and the ....

5   An .... is the distance between the points where 2 .... meet on the circumference.

6   2 .... cut out a .... of the circle

7   The .... is twice the ....

8   A .... is a .... if it passes through the centre of the circle.

9   The area of the .... plus the area of the .... is equal to the area of the whole circle.

10 A line that goes from one point on the .... to another is called a ....

Once pupils are familiar with the correct terminology to use with circles, we can consider how we even define a circle. Examples and non-examples may be helpful here, with non-examples particularly useful; however, there is only really one example that can be shown (although pupils appreciating this is perhaps useful in and of itself).

An alternative (or potentially complementary) approach to defining the circle is to have pupils draw circles using a pair of compasses, whilst asking pupils to be aware of what it is about, what they are doing that results in a perfect circle. Pupils should realise it is the fact that the pencil always stays the same distance away from the centre of the circle that is the key to producing a perfect circle, which can be translated into the definition of a circle being the locus of all points of constant radius from the fixed centre. This approach might also be a great introduction to constructions and loci, from which other loci can be explored.

Once pupils are clear on what a circle is, we can begin to explore measures of different properties of the circle, starting with its circumference.

---

21 H. Koll and S. Mills, *Year 9: Measures, Shape and Space; Activities for Teaching Numeracy* (New York: A&C Black Children's & Educational, 2004).

Concept link: circumference of circles

The proof of the ratio of the lengths of the circumference and diameter being equal to π is much too complicated for pupils at school level. However, there are things that can be demonstrated about the circle that can enable an understanding of why π makes sense to be the ratio of the lengths of the circumference and diameter:

1. If pupils have previously learnt about similarity, then they should be happy that all circles are similar regardless of size. This implies that the ratio of the circumference to the diameter is the same of all circles.

2. That the circumference of the circle is a little more than three times bigger than the diameter:

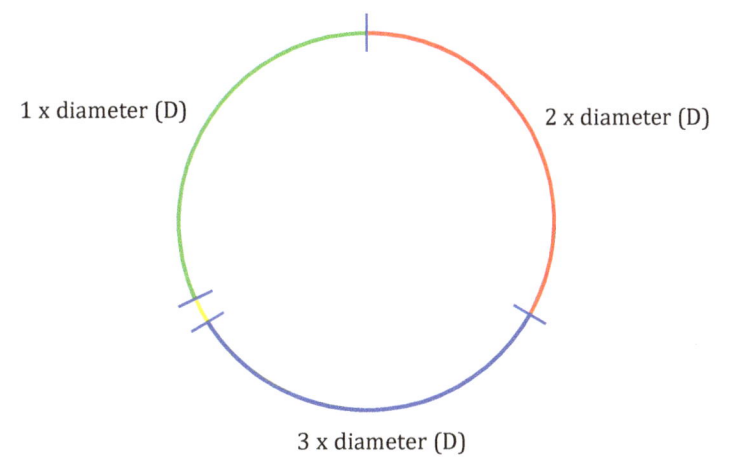

1 x diameter (D)   2 x diameter (D)

3 x diameter (D)

3. That if the diameter of the circle is a whole number, then the circumference can't be a rational number.

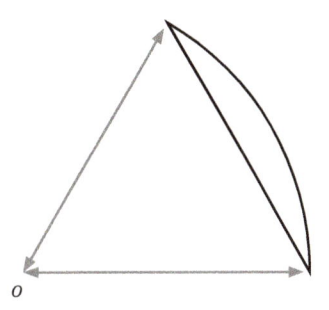

0

This is a bit trickier to see, but it boils down to the idea that if we keep trying to fit lengths of one unit along the curve, the length will only be a chord to the curve, and if we then continue to break into smaller and smaller units (i.e. cm, then mm, then μm, etc.) there will always be a small difference between the curved length and the unit length. This (kind of) suggests the decimal continuing forever (the 'without repeating pattern' bit is a little more of a leap of faith). I am aware this is not a proper and complete mathematical justification, and if anything is rather suggestive than definitive, but nonetheless when the three are combined, they can go some way to helping pupils understand why $\frac{C}{D}$ = π and that π is an irrational number.

This sort of thing might follow a measurement-type activity, where pupils are measuring the diameter and circumference of circles (normally on the end of cylinders using string – things like plastic cups, Pringles tubes, etc. are good for this sort of thing) or might be followed by it. The measurement activity might be the way pupils come to see part 2 of the above (that the circumference is broadly three times longer than the diameter), or might be a way of pupils engaging further with π as the ratio of circumference and diameter after having it introduced through alternative means – such as a video or dynamic geometry software.[22]

Once pupils are happy with the relationship then they will need practice in using it, both to find circumference given diameter and to find diameter given circumference. In addition, there are two further relationships that pupils should be introduced to:

1   The fact that when a circle completes one revolution (without slipping), it travels forward a distance equal in length to the circumference.

2   That, due to the diameter being twice the length of the radius, the ratio of the length of the circumference to that of the radius is equal to 2π.

The first is quite straightforward to demonstrate either physically (using a cylinder wrapped around once with paper or simply using pen to mark the initial point of contact between the circle and the surface). The second is a relatively simple logical argument – doubling the radius gives the diameter so the ratio of circumference to radius must be double that of the ratio between circumference and diameter.

There are many questions that can be set in practical contexts involving wheels or conveyor belts on cylindrical runners that can support pupils in applying these relationships to different problems:

> The conveyor belt below is turned as the cylinders rotate. The cylinders have a diameter of 60 cm. The conveyor belt is 10 metres long in total. How many times do the cylinders rotate so that the belt does one complete revolution?

This mixed in with general practice that involves providing pupils with information about one of the circumference, diameter or radius and asking for information about at least one of the other values should allow pupils to reach a measure of fluency with circumference that can be reinforced as we look at other situations where calculations involving the circumference will be used. It is worth highlighting though that, in my opinion, getting pupils to memorise the 'formula' $C = \pi D$ or $C = 2\pi r$ is potentially unhelpful, as it sets up a 'one-way' relationship that leads from diameter/radius to circumference. Keeping the ratios of $\frac{C}{D} = \pi$ and $\frac{C}{r} = 2\pi$ allows for more flexibility in terms of which information we are given and which we are attempting to find, as well as reinforcing key skills around transposition of formulae (particularly in this case as this structure of relationship is found in places such as proportion and inverse proportion and trigonometry, and so the more practice manipulating this structure, the better).

---

22 teachMathematics, Circle Circumference, (n.d.). Available at: https://www.teachmathematics.net/page/11010/around-circles.

From here the obvious extension is to look at the relationship between the diameter/radius and the length of an arc as a fraction of the whole circumference. A unitary approach can work well here; with first looking at the length of the arc represented by 1° worth of circumference, before scaling up to whichever angle we are interested in. Alternatively, the use of a ratio table can help pupils see the proportional nature of the relationship:

Distance	Angle
πD	360°
s	θ

This leads nicely to seeing the relationship $\frac{s}{D} = \frac{\theta \pi}{360}$ or $\frac{s}{r} = \frac{2\theta \pi}{360}$ $(=\frac{\theta}{180})$, where s = length of the arc and θ = the angle at the centre of the sector. This form of the relationship is particularly nice as when pupils move to post-16 mathematics and are introduced to radian measure it is quite easy to see where $\frac{s}{r} = \theta$ comes from.

Again, a mix of practice is useful in securing the use of this relationship, where pupils are provided with the value of any two of s, r/D or θ and finding the third, is important in pupils developing fluency with arc length. In addition, questions where pupils have to find the perimeter of sectors of shapes combined with sectors can prompt application of these skills.

Find the perimeter of these shapes:

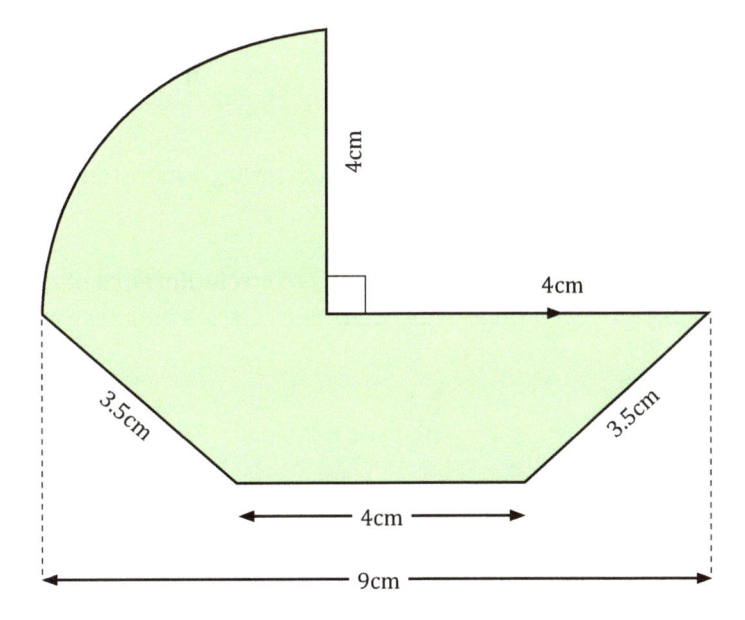

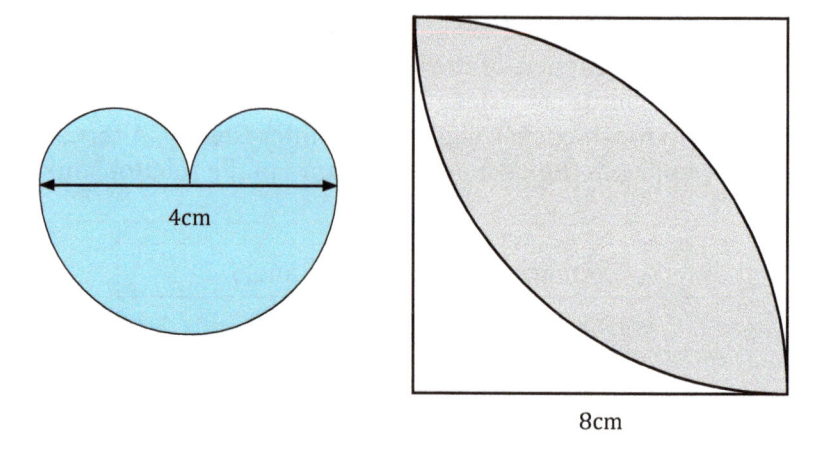

A particularly nice result for pupils to arrive at as part of this is that the following shapes all have the same perimeter:

and to reason that this will always be the case, no matter how many smaller semi-circles are placed along the diameter of the largest semi-circle.

Having explored problems and relationships linked to circumference of circles and arcs, the next stage will be to explore area measures relating to circles and sectors.

Concept link: area of circles

Again the formal proof of an area of a circle is beyond the realms of school-level mathematics (at least compulsory mathematics pre-16 in the UK). However, we can offer pupils some justification for the relationship between the area of a circle and the square of the radius also being equal to π. This potentially comes in two parts:

1 We can demonstrate that the area of a circle is between three and four times larger than the area of a square with a length equal to the radius of the circle:

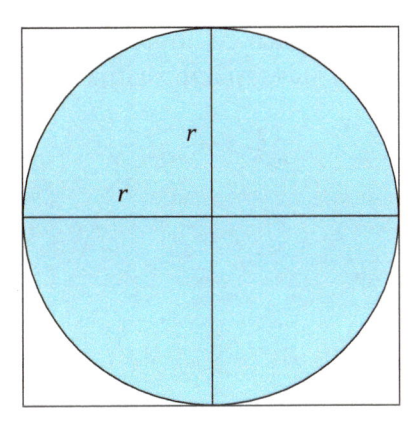

Clearly, the area of the circle is less than that of the area of four squares, with length equal to the radius of the circle (we need to trust a bit more to faith that three of the white areas are less than the area of the quarter circle to believe that the area of the circle is more than that of three of the squares).

2   That, if the length of the radius is a whole number, then the area of the square cannot be rational. This follows a very similar argument to that used for the circumference, in that if we break the square down into smaller squares, we will always have a fraction of the larger square, but will never be able to fit the side of the square perfectly against the curve; there will always be a small area outside of the squares.

Again, this is suggestive of π as a candidate for the ratio of the area of the circle to the square of the radius. An alternative approach, given pupils have worked with circumference, is to break the circle down into sectors:

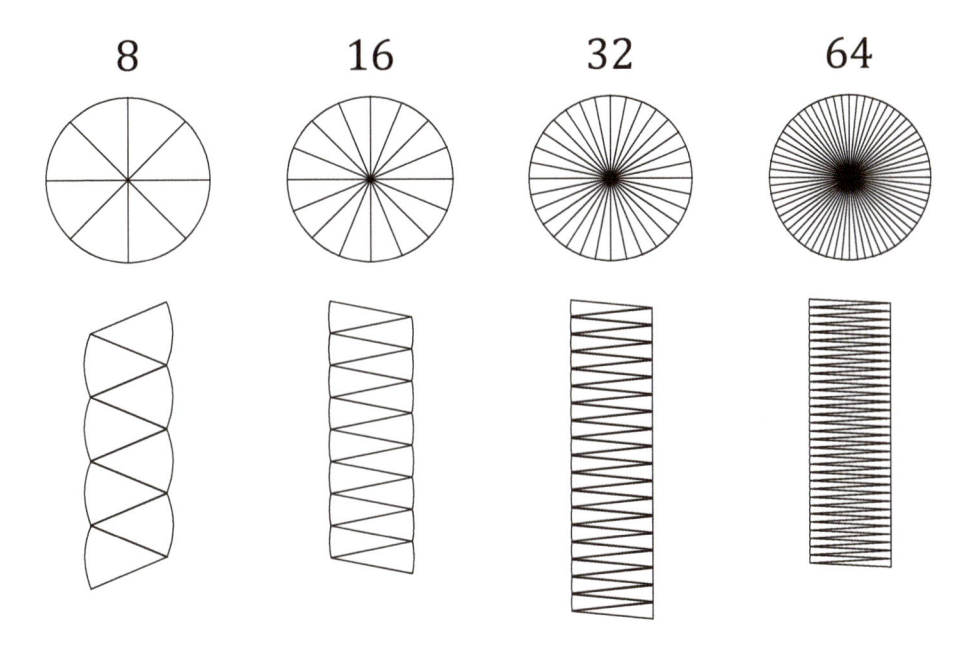

Recombining the sectors creates a shape that is nearly equal in area to a parallelogram with length equal to πr, half the circumference of the circle, and height r. This leads to the area being approximately equal to πr^2, with this being a better approximation the more sectors we create. It isn't (typically) hard for pupils to imagine that in the limiting case the value of the area will be equal to πr^2.

The approach I haven't mentioned to both circumference and area introduction is the use of polygons of increasing number of sides to approximate the area of the circle:

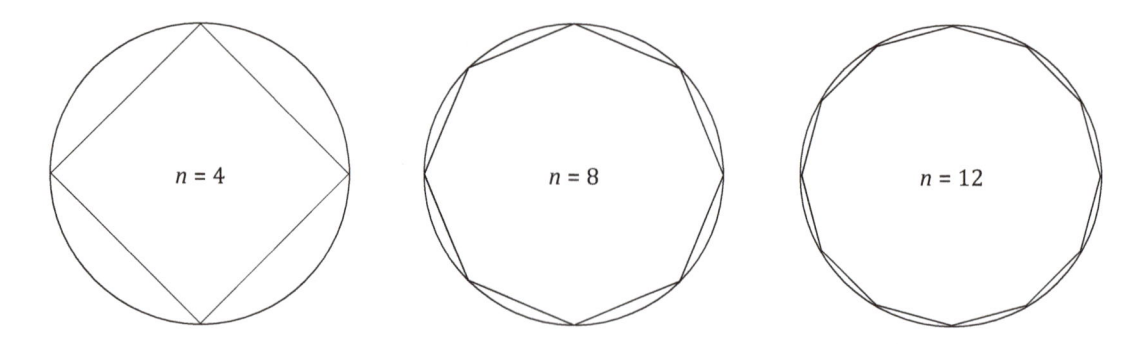

$n = 4$ $n = 8$ $n = 12$

The reason I haven't included these is because finding the area of these requires some quite involved trig work, which is typically introduced after circles. I see this as potentially something that those studying advanced mathematics at post-16 level might like to come back to and explore, rather than a way of introducing the area of circles with pre-16 learners.

From here the path in exploring area of circles will be very similar to that of exploring circumference, where first pupils should be offered the opportunity to work with the relationship $\frac{A}{r^2} = \pi$, given the radius and finding the area, as well as finding the radius given the area. Questions like the one below are also useful in ensuring pupils retain understanding of the relationship between the area of the circle and the square of the radius:

The area of the circle is 45 cm², find the area of the square:

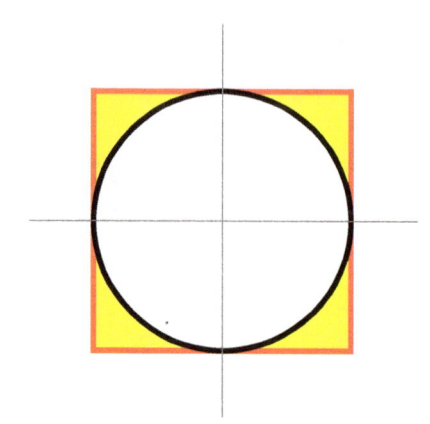

before looking at adapting the relationship to include that between the area and the diameter, leading to $\frac{A}{d^2} = \frac{\pi}{4}$. This relationship is a particularly nice one to use when calculating area with an odd diameter without a calculator, as the division can be completed after the squaring:

Find the area of a circle with diameter 11 cm in terms of π.

In this case, it is much easier to first square the diameter and then give the area as $\frac{121}{4}\pi$, as opposed to first calculating the radius as 5.5 cm and then trying to square 5.5 (at least for most pupils). We can then offer problems, potentially involving practical contexts, that require circle area.

Shape

We will then continue on to consider sector area, potentially using the same unitary approach or ratio table that we used for examining arc length:

Area	Angle
πr^2	360°
S	$\theta°$

This leads nicely to $\frac{S}{r^2} = \frac{\theta \pi}{360}$, where again, once pupils understand this relationship, this can be used by pupils to find any one of S, r or θ given the other two. Add to this pupils finding the area of compound shapes involving sectors (such as the shapes we found the perimeter of earlier), and they should develop a strong level of fluency involving area calculations involving circles.

Assuming pupils have then studied circumference and area of circles in relative isolation, there will be a need for pupils to be offered opportunities for deciding whether circumference/arc length, sector area or neither are required to solve problems. These may be problems set in practical contexts but three of my favourite problems to offer pupils are from the UKMT maths challenges (from the sorting on the Mathsduck website[23]).

In the diagram, the smaller circle touches the larger circle and also passes through its centre. What fraction of the area of the larger circle is outside the smaller circle?

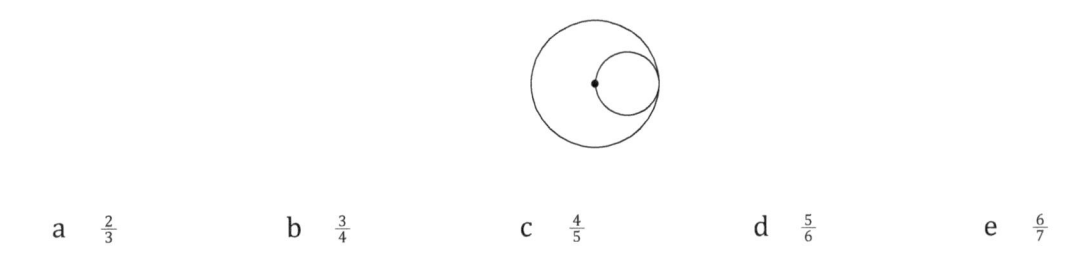

a $\frac{2}{3}$ b $\frac{3}{4}$ c $\frac{4}{5}$ d $\frac{5}{6}$ e $\frac{6}{7}$

The perimeters of the three shapes shown are made up of straight lines and semi-circular arcs of diameter 2. They will fit snugly together as in a jigsaw.

What is the difference between the total perimeter of the separate three pieces and the perimeter of the shape formed when the three pieces fit together?

a 0   b $2 + 2\pi$ c $8 + 4\pi$ d $22 + 2\pi$ e $30 + 6\pi$

---

23 See https://mathsduck.co.uk/ukmt/.

The diagram on the right shows a rectangle with sides of length 5 cm and 4 cm. All the arcs are quarter-circles of radius 2 cm. What is the total shaded area in cm²?

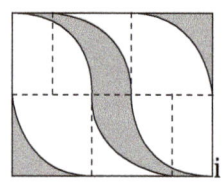

a   12 − 2π   b   8   c   8 + 2π   d   10   e   20 − 4π

A nice thing about these particular questions is that the first doesn't actually require any calculation of circumference or area, whilst the second and third require circumference/area respectively. This means pupils have to think about what properties of a circle they are going to need to use before they attempt the question.

One final nice thing that pupils can potentially explore is a direct relationship between the arc length and the sector area. We know that the arc length of a given sector can be found as $s = \frac{\theta}{360} \times 2\pi r$ and the sector area can be found as $S = \frac{\theta}{360} \times \pi r^2$. The first of these can be transposed to give $\frac{s}{2} = \frac{\theta}{360} \times \pi r$, which can then be combined with the second to give $S = \frac{sr}{2}$. This can potentially be offered to pupils as a 'show that' style question or simply as a prompt to find a formula for S in terms of s and r.

Of course, once pupils are secure in measures involving circles in two dimensions, we will generally move on to look at three-dimensional shapes involving circles.

Concept link: surface area of 3D curved shapes

In a similar way to polyhedra, we can introduce surface area of curved shapes by examining the nets of shapes:

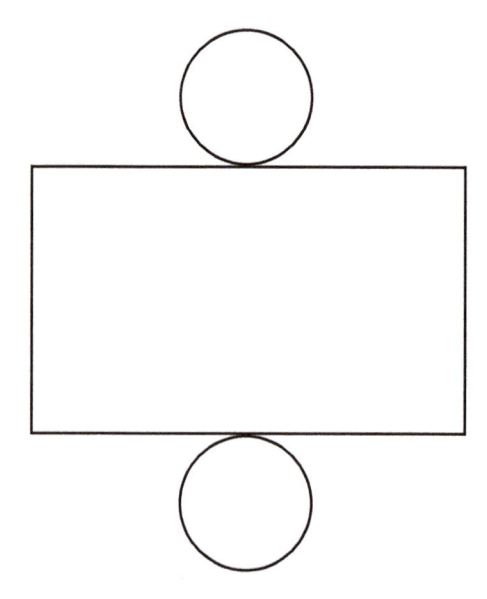

Pupils can see from this that part of the surface area is the area of the two circles, and the remaining part is a rectangle that is curved around the circumference of the circles. This leads quite naturally to the formula for the surface area of a cylinder as $2\pi r^2 + 2\pi r h$, where r is the radius of the circle and h is the height of the cylinder (which corresponds to the 'width' of the rectangle). What is important here is that pupils recognise that some cylinders are not closed, and so one or more of the circles may not be part of the net. This is why it is important for pupils to understand how the different parts of the surface area formula are arrived at, so that they can be flexible in approaching surface area calculations. Offering pupils different cylinders, some closed at both ends, some only closed at one end, and some open at both ends will allow pupils to develop this flexibility.

Following on from cylinders, the net of a cone can also provide insight into the surface area of the cone.

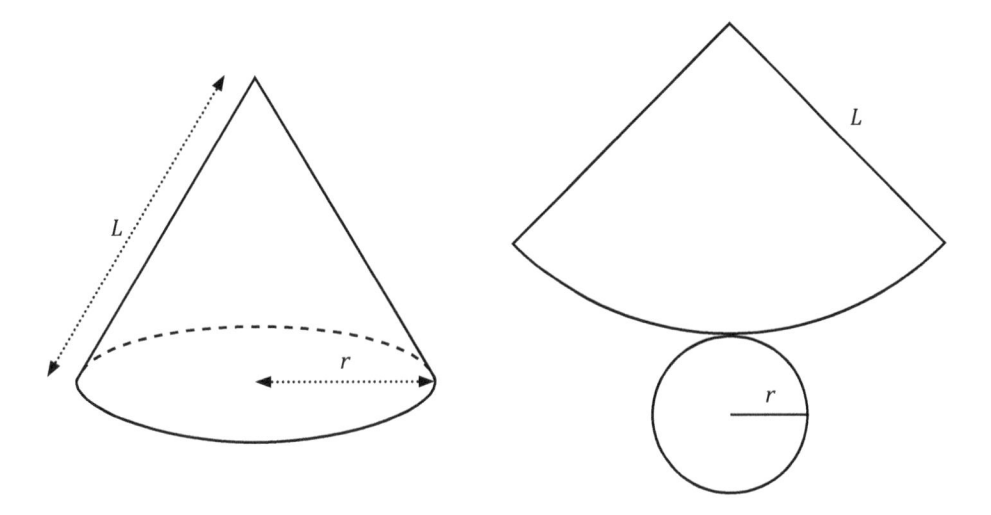

One thing that pupils potentially won't have considered before is having to work with the slant height, L, of the cone. Pupils' experience to this point is likely to have been centred around perpendicular height of different shapes when calculating area or volume, so make sure pupils are clear on the difference between slant height and perpendicular height. Once pupils are clear on this, we can use the net to see why the slant height is important in this case, the net of the curved surface is a sector of a circle with radius L and arc length equal to the circumference of the base circle, $2\pi r$. Using the relationship we found earlier between the arc length and sector area, this gives the area of this sector as $S = \frac{2\pi r L}{2} = \pi r L$, which provides the value of the area of the curved surface of the cone (as well as demonstrating why the slant height is important, as it is equal to the radius of the sector in the net). Combining the curved surface with the base circle area of πr^2 gives a formula for the total surface area of $\pi r^2 + \pi r L$. Again, though, it is important that pupils understand both parts of this formula and how they arrived at it, so that they can work with 'open' cones that have no base (such as cone-shaped water cups), and pupils should be offered the opportunity to work with both closed and open cones and find their surface area.

A nice opportunity to include when looking at surface area of cones and cylinders is the use of factorisation to rewrite the formulae in different ways. For a closed cylinder the formula can be factorised to give $2\pi r(r + h)$; a cylinder only closed at one end can have it surface area formula written as $\pi r(r + 2h)$ and the closed cone surface area formula can be written as $\pi r(r + L)$. What I particularly like to do is to offer these formulae pre-factorised (once pupils are familiar with their expanded forms) and ask them to identify which shape each formula will provide the surface area for.

From cones the natural place to move on to is to consider spheres. However, this is where the net of the shape will start becoming less useful in providing insight into how we might calculate the surface area:

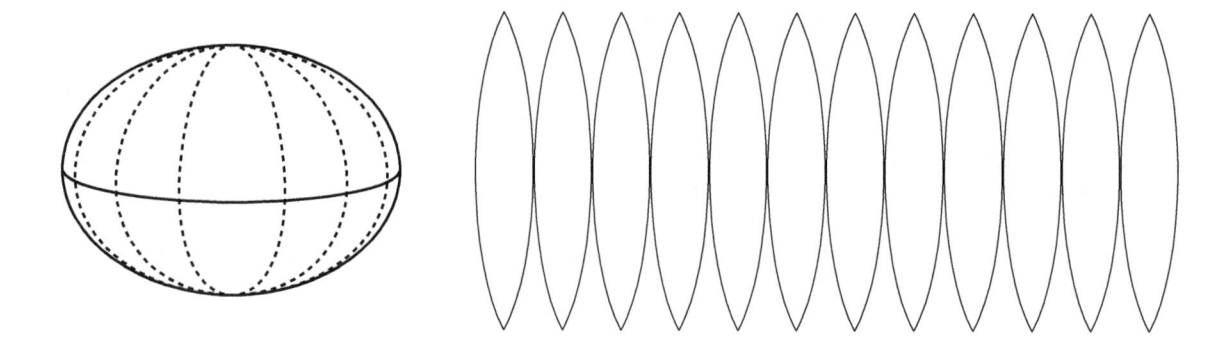

As we can see, the area of the net is not particularly easy to calculate (or even to see how we might calculate) and so we are going to have to approach the sphere differently. Personally, I would still show this to pupils, so that they can appreciate that our previous approaches involving finding the area of nets will not be applicable in this case.

So if the net won't allow that insight, how might we approach finding a way of determining that the surface area of a sphere is equal to $4\pi r^2$? One potential approach is to use a wrapped sphere, showing that the area of the wrapping is four times greater than the area of the circle around the equator (BBC Bitesize has a nice video that arrives at the formula using orange peel[24]).

There are alternatives to this that are a little more rigorous, for example the approach outlined on the website basic-mathematics.com,[25] although this requires pupils to have prior knowledge of the volume of the sphere formula. Ultimately, calculus is required to give a direct fully rigorous demonstration of the surface area of the sphere formula.

However we arrive at it (including potentially just providing the formula directly), one important aspect of the surface area formula that pupils should appreciate (either through their own insight or having been explicitly taught it) is that the surface area of the sphere is four times bigger than that of the circle created by the equator of the sphere. Offering pupils a question like the one below might prompt this awareness or might be used to reinforce it if the relationship has been explicitly taught:

> A sphere is cut into two pieces along the equator to form two hemispheres as shown. Each hemisphere rests on the circular base with an area of 200 cm². Find the surface area of the original sphere.

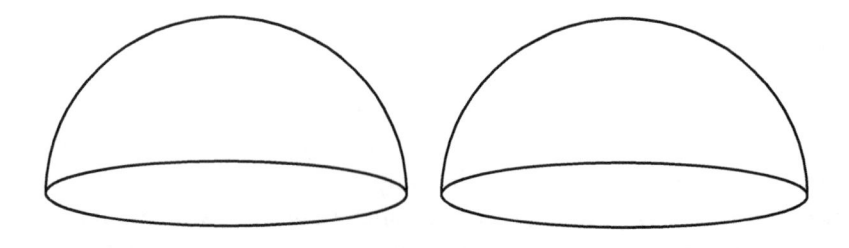

---

24 See https://www.bbc.co.uk/bitesize/topics/zrf3cdm/articles/ztgdsrd.
25 See https://www.basic-mathematics.com/surface-area-of-a-sphere.html.

Of course, this question can be adapted to ask for things like the difference between the surface area of the original sphere and the two hemispheres, or even the ratio of the surface area of the original sphere to the two hemispheres. This sort of question can be combined with more traditional questions that provide the radius of the sphere for direct surface area calculations.

As with circles, there are lots of directions pupils can take the study of surface area of curved shapes. All three formulae involve the radius of the sphere in the calculation of surface area; pupils could rewrite these using diameter or even circumference (although care should be taken here not to confuse measures of length with measures of area). The surface area of a cylinder is particularly nice when written in terms of the circumference of the base circles, being just $Cr + Ch$ (where C is the circumference), whilst the sphere might prove slightly more challenging – particularly if we ask pupils to demonstrate that it can be written as $\frac{c^2}{\pi}$. In addition, the usual part shapes or combined shapes can provide further practice whilst forcing pupils to consider how to adapt the formulae to correctly calculate the surface area; the classic of these is the pencil modelled as a combination of the cone, cylinder and hemisphere:

A pencil is modelled as a cone, cylinder and hemisphere joined together. Find the total surface area of the pencil.

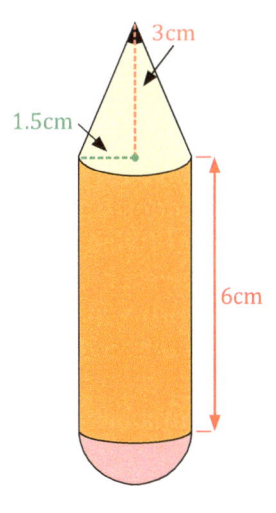

In this case, of course, pupils would need an understanding of Pythagoras' theorem to calculate the slant height of the cone.[26] This might mean that teachers want to explore Pythagoras' theorem before looking at surface area, or it might be that this provides an opportunity to interweave surface area calculations when looking at Pythagoras' theorem at a later time. It is also true that pencils are, in the main, not cylindrical in nature, and so teachers might prefer a more realistic example to provide more of a pressing reason why a surface area calculation might be important – these types of problems are often linked to volume calculations, such as trying to maximise volume for a given surface area or to minimise surface area for a given volume in order to spend as little as possible on packaging. This would mean we would also have to have introduced pupils to calculations for finding the volume of curved shapes.

---

26 Image from https://www.basic-mathematics.com/volume-of-solids.html.

Volume of 3D curved shapes

In the same vein as surface area, inspiration for the calculations for finding volume of curved shapes can draw from the same sources as their polyhedral counterparts. The calculation for volume of a cylinder mirrors that for the volume of prisms:

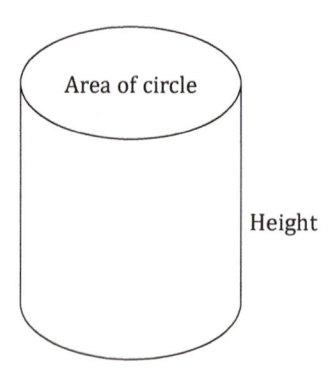

The area of the circle will provide a value for the number of cubes in a slice of height 1 unit, and then multiplication by the value of the height will calculate the total number of cubes in all of the slices. Pupils will already know that the area of a circle can be found using the formula πr^2, and so this leads to the volume of the cylinder calculation being $\pi r^2 h$. Alternatively, the area of the circle can be found using the formula $\frac{\pi d^2}{4}$, and so the volume of the cylinder can also be calculated as $\frac{\pi d^2 h}{4}$.

Similarly, the volume of a cone can be found by treating it as analogous to a pyramid, being a third of the volume of the containing cylinder. However, it is more difficult to visualise this than with a square or rectangular pyramid (where we can show pyramids attached to the side of the prism as well as the base); however, there are nice video demonstrations that involve filling a cone-shaped container with water and pouring it into a cylindrical container with the same base circle (as demonstrated in the video linked below[27]).

This leads to the volume of the cone formula being equal to $\frac{1}{3}\pi r^2 h$, or alternatively $\frac{1}{12}\pi d^2 h$. One thing that pupils need to be clear on here is the use of the vertical height when calculating the volume of a cone, which is in contrast to the use of the slant height when calculating the curved surface area. Offering pupils opportunities to work with both of these is important to make sure pupils use the correct lengths in the correct situations.

When it comes to finding the volume of the sphere, again typically calculus would be used to derive the formula; however, there are similar demonstrations to the one above: particularly showing that the sphere of radius r (and therefore diameter $2r$) can be filled with a cone with height $2r$ (and therefore volume of $\frac{2}{3}\pi r^3$) twice over leading to the conclusion that the volume of the sphere can be calculated by $\frac{4}{3}\pi r^3$.[28] There is also a derivation of the formula that doesn't require calculus, but does require Pythagoras' theorem and a reasonable amount of geometric knowledge and insight. The proof rests around demonstrating that when a hemisphere is placed inside a cylinder with the same height and radius (as per the next image) it is possible to show that the space inside the cylinder outside of the hemisphere is equal to the space taken up by a cone with the same radius and height as the cylinder.

---

27 MooMooMath and Science, Demonstration: Volume of a Cone and Cylinder [video] (2015). Available at: https://www.youtube.com/watch?v=yfuHUBDH2T0&list=RDCMUCE_WiQFez8FZcICpbwblyyg&start_radio=1&rv=yfuHUBDH2T0&t=92.
28 K. Pearce, Cones and Spheres [ACT 3]: How Many Cones Does It Take To Fill a Sphere? [video] (2014). Available at: https://www.youtube.com/watch?v=PaA-g_z_E2E.

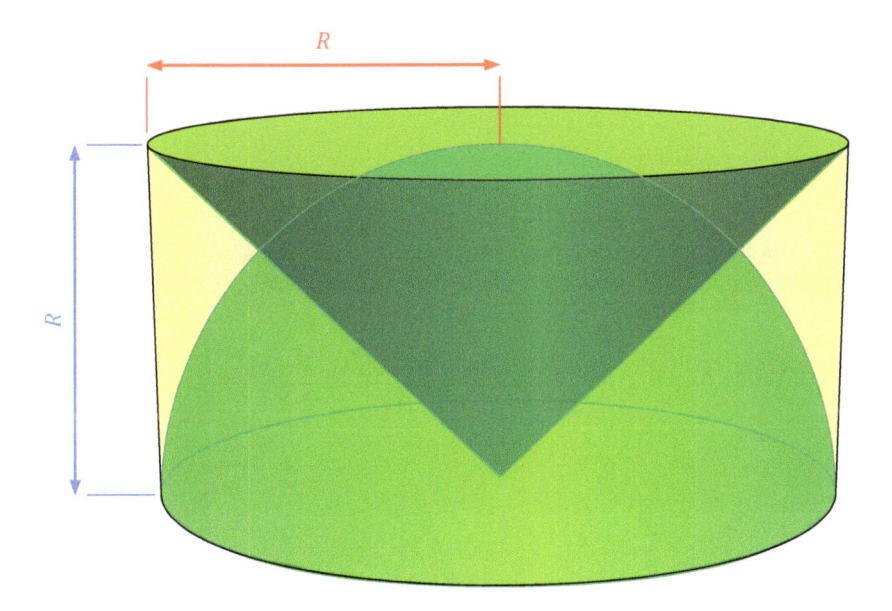

As the cylinder's volume can be calculated by πr^3 (as $h = r$) and the volume of the cone can be calculated by $\frac{1}{3}\pi r^3$, then the volume of the hemisphere must be $\frac{2}{3}\pi r^3$ (and therefore the full sphere would be $\frac{4}{3}\pi r^3$).[29]

It is worth noting that at the current time of writing, pupils only need to remember or derive the formula for surface area and volume of cylinders (at least in the English curriculum pre-16); the formula for curved surface area and volume of a cone and sphere will be provided if required in examinations. For some teachers, this will mean that some will decide there is no need to go through all of this derivation or demonstrations – I have sympathy with this viewpoint but I do believe there are relationships here that are worth taking the time to explore and that it is important pupils retain a sense of what it is they are calculating – how many square units can be placed on the surface of a shape or how many cubic units can fit inside a space.

Practice applying these formulae to different shapes will be useful for pupils to further cement their developed understanding, alongside the usual compound shapes. Again, the inimitable Don Steward has some great stuff for this, including activities prompting the comparison of a sphere, cone and cylinder, a lovely animation showing how a cone and hemisphere can be combined to create a cylinder, and a video showing the derivation above.[30]

Before leaving behind curved shapes, one area that pupils may study in pre-16 mathematics will be angle diagrams involving circles. It is to these that we turn next.

---

29 GINGERSNAPSMATH, The Volume of a Sphere (without Calculus) (24 April 2016). Available at: https://gingersnapsmath.wordpress.com/2016/04/04/the-volume-of-a-sphere-without-calculus/comment-page-1/.
30 D. Steward, Cone, Sphere, Cylinder, *Median* [blog] (25 July 2013). Available at: https://donsteward.blogspot.com/2013/07/cone-sphere-cylinder.html.

Concept link: angle diagrams involving circles (circle theorems)

Before embarking on more complicated angle diagrams involving circles, an oft-overlooked skill to develop with pupils is to identify isosceles triangles created by a chord and two radii within a circle. This skill is regularly required in reasoning and proof with more complicated angle diagrams, and so it is worth taking the time to explicitly explore this with pupils:

Identify the isosceles triangles in the diagrams below.

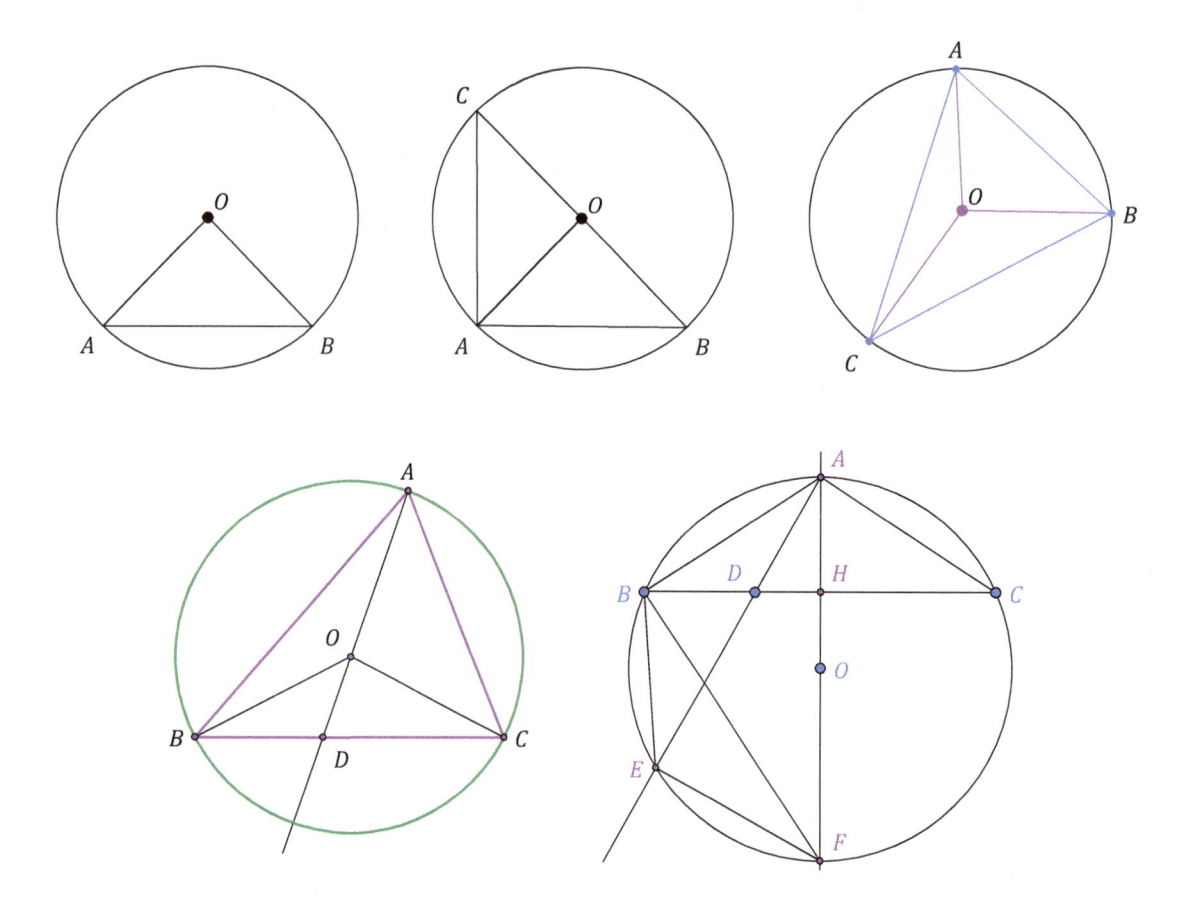

We could, of course, adapt this by providing angles and asking pupils to find other angles or to state whether angles are possible to find.

When it comes to introducing further properties, my preference is to group these properties together. The first two I tend to introduce are what I collectively refer to as 'Inscribed angle' diagrams, starting with the angle at the centre being twice the measure of the angle at the circumference when inscribed from the same arc:

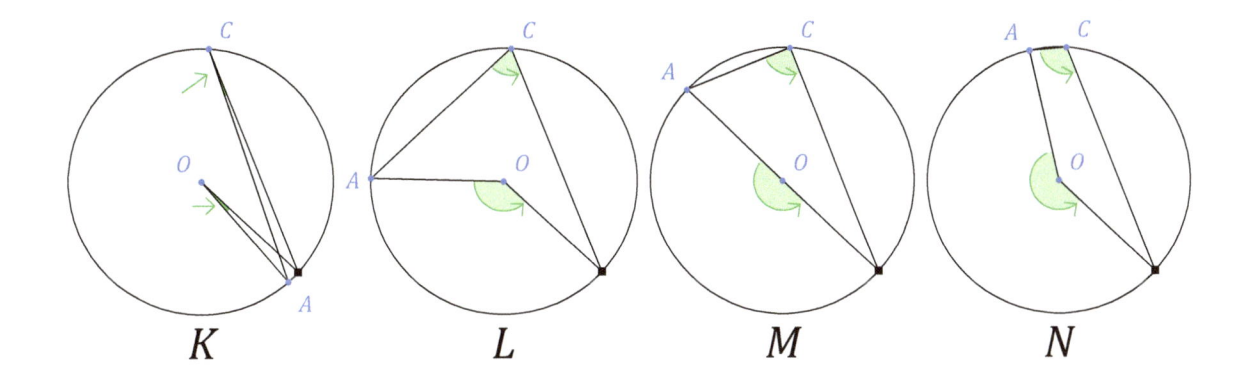

K   L   M   N

The reason I start with this property is that it is quite straightforward to prove using isosceles triangles:

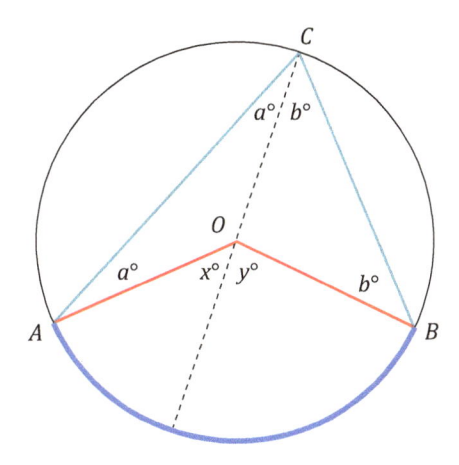

The angle COA is equal to $(180 - 2a)°$, and similarly COB is equal to $(180 - 2b)°$. This gives $x + y = 360 - (180 - 2a) - (180 - 2b) = 2a + 2b = 2(a + b)°$, completing the proof.

Following this, it is almost trivial to show that inscribed angles subtended by the same arc are always equal, as they are all half the size of the angle at the centre.

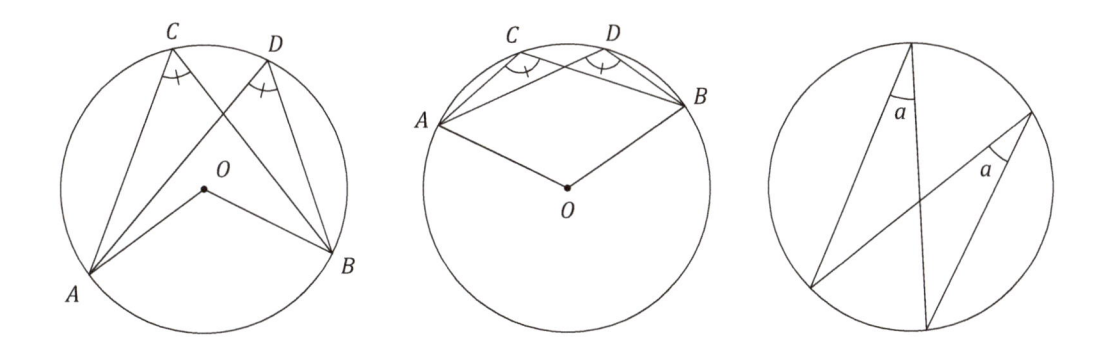

Pupils can practise identifying these properties and then using them to find missing angles in different angle diagrams.

From here I will introduce what I term the 'Shape' circle theorems, with the first being any triangle based off a diameter is a right-angled triangle, with the right-angle at the circumference:

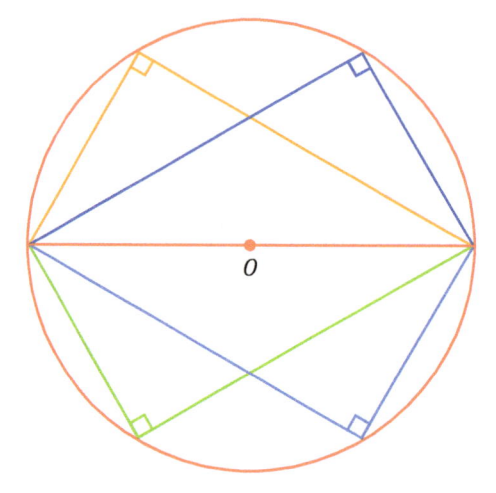

This, of course, is just a special case of the angle at the centre theorem, and pupils should understand it as such. Following this I will introduce the cyclic quadrilateral:

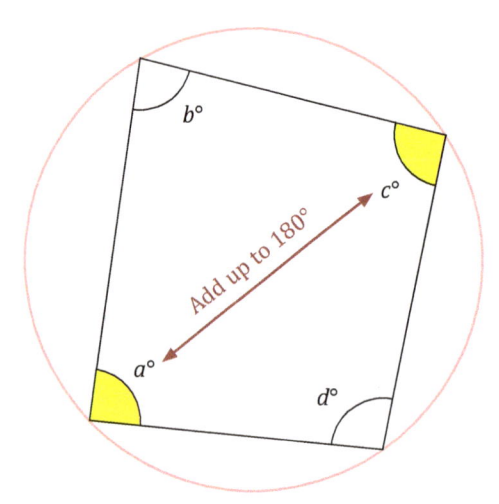

This can also be seen as a consequence of the angle at the centre theorem:

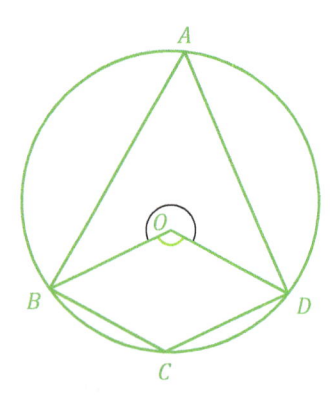

Angle *BAD* is half of the value of the obtuse angle *BOD*, and similarly angle *BCD* is half of the value of the reflex angle *DOB*. However, the two centre angles clearly sum to 360°, leading to the conclusion that the two inscribed angles sum to 180°.

Once again, pupils should be offered opportunities to practise identifying these properties in different diagrams, and using these properties combined with earlier explored properties to solve angle problems. We can also interweave areas like equation-solving into these sorts of questions:

Find the value of x.

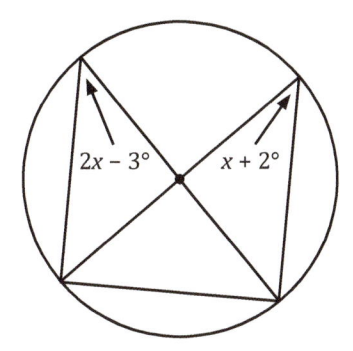

2x − 3°   *x + 2°*

The next set of circle theorems I will typically introduce are the tangent circle theorems, starting with the fact that a radius and tangent will always meet at right angles:

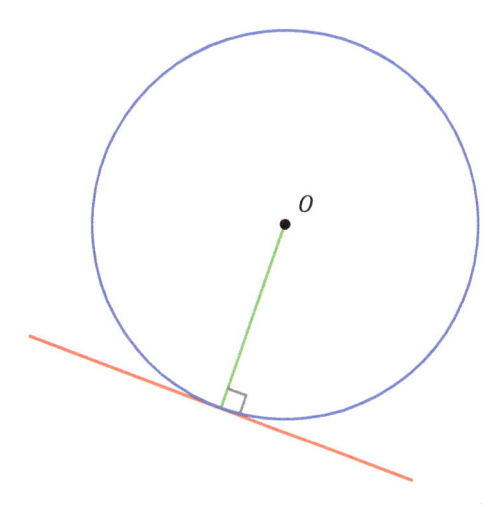

O

There are different proofs of this theorem, the simplest probably being the use of proof by contradiction. We start by assuming that the radius is not at right angles to the tangent, so we draw a line from the centre that is at right angles to the tangent:

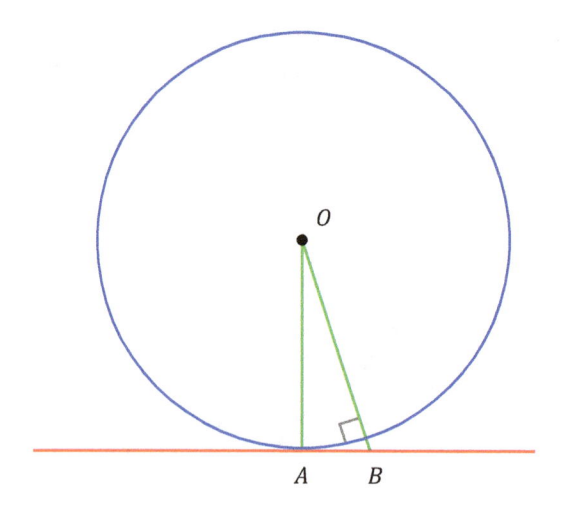

However, this implies that the length OA is greater than OB, as OA is the side opposite the right angle in a right triangle is the longest side. This is a contradiction as OB is clearly bigger than OA (it goes from O beyond the circumference of the circle, and therefore is longer than the radius). The only conclusion is that the right angle must be at A.

Alongside this I will introduce the theorem that two tangents that meet are equal in length from their points of contact with each other to their points of contact with the circle (and the related theorem that the line from the centre to the contact point bisects the angle at the centre and at the point of contact between the tangents).

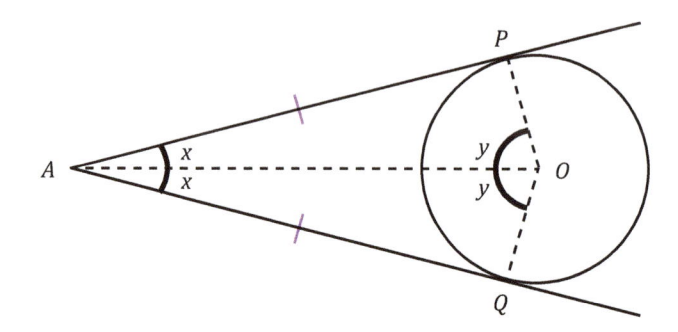

A standard proof of this follows from the tangent and radius meeting at a right angle, in that the line OA creates two congruent triangles (each triangle has a right angle, a common hypotenuse of OA, and a third side equal to the radius of the circle).

The fact that both of these theorems produce right angles or right-angled triangles make them an ideal opportunity to interweave questions involving Pythagoras' theorem or right-angled trigonometry. Once pupils have studied all of these concepts, it is definitely worth offering pupils questions that link these ideas together.

The final class of circle theorems we will typically look at are what I tend to call 'chord and segment theorems'.

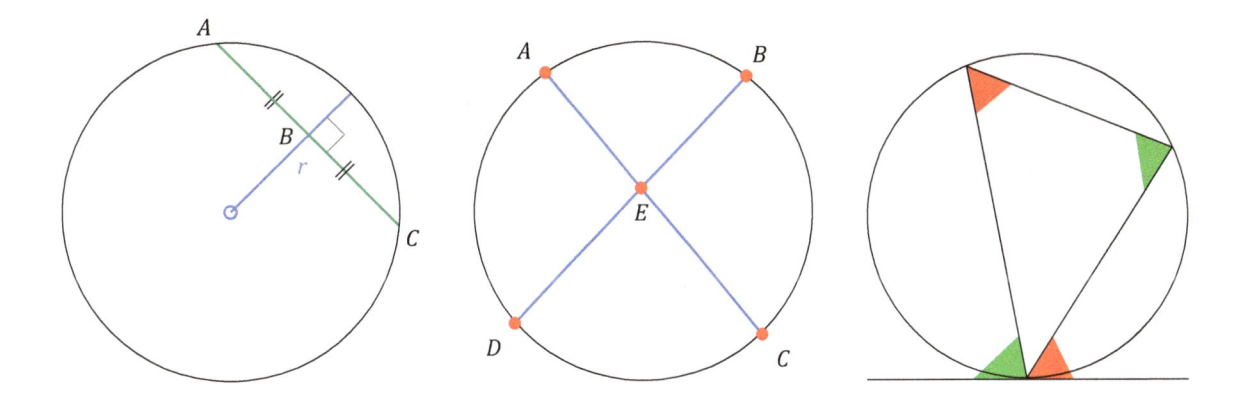

The first of these states that any radius that bisects a chord does so at right angles (or alternatively that if a radius meets a chord at right angles then it bisects the chord). The second states that the products of the lengths of two chords to their points of intersection are equal (i.e. in the second diagram $|AE| \times |EC| = |EB| \times |ED|$). The final one is the alternate segment theorem, indicating the green angles in the right-hand diagram are equal in size, and that the red angles are similarly equal.

The first of these theorems follows quite naturally from the tangent and radius meeting at right angles, with the chord AC being parallel to a tangent. The intersecting chords theorem is a direct consequence of the fact that triangles AEB and EDC are similar triangles. The alternate segment theorem is provable using the angle at the centre combined with a chord and radius meeting at a tangent, as per the image below:

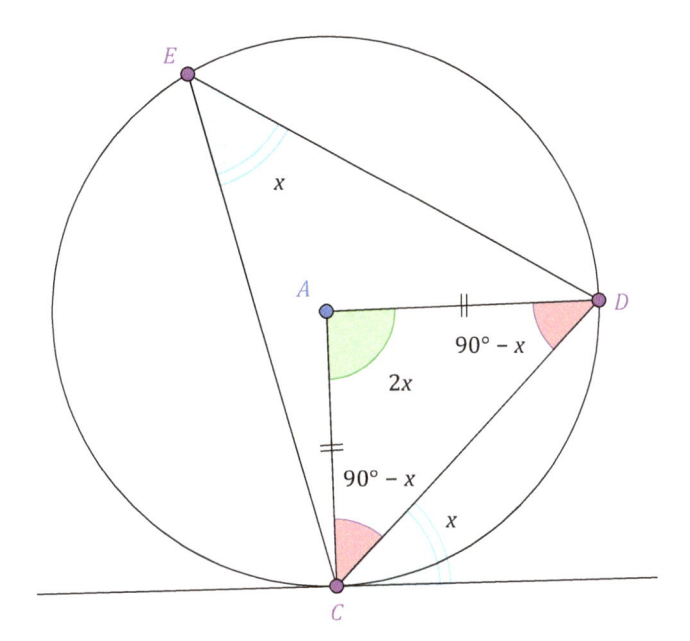

As we introduce these theorems, pupils should work with increasingly complex angle diagrams, requiring reasoning with the use of multiple theorems to find missing angles, as well as proof of other geometrical properties using these circle theorems as a base, for example:

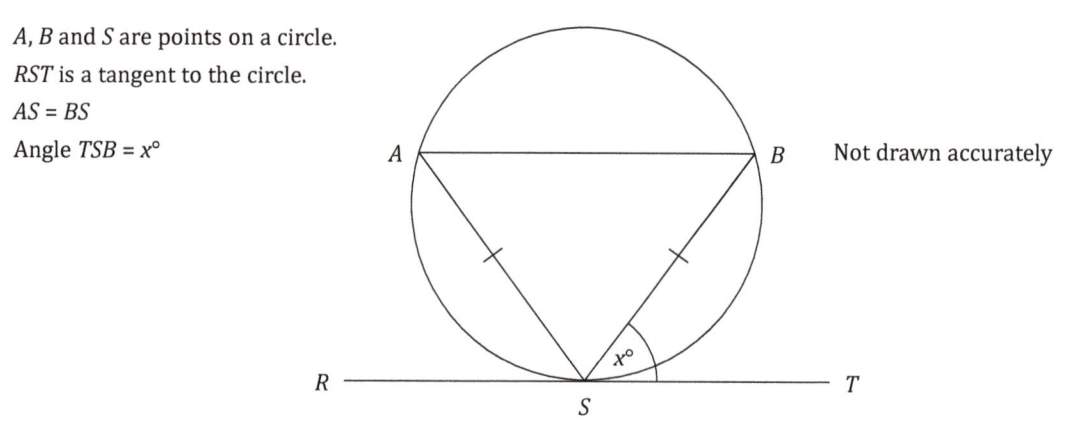

A, B and S are points on a circle.
RST is a tangent to the circle.
AS = BS
Angle TSB = x°

Not drawn accurately

Prove that AB is parallel to RT.

Concept: constructions and loci

Prerequisites: Shape (particularly properties of polygons).

Linked concepts: Angle, graphing.

Constructions and loci are somewhat lambasted by some mathematics teachers as no longer relevant to pupils. With the advent of computer software that can achieve accurate constructions in a fraction of the time of hand-drawn diagrams, some feel that constructions involving a straight edge and a pair of compasses don't have a place in the mathematics curriculum for pre-16 pupils. For me though, ruler and compass constructions are a great place to revisit properties of different polygons.

Construct an angle of 60°.

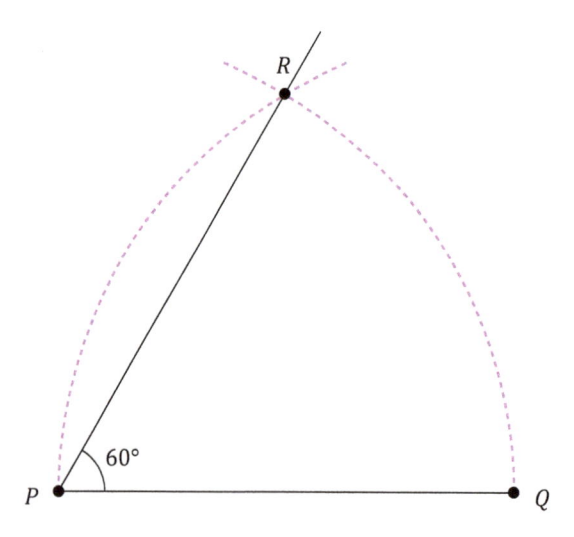

This allows pupils to revisit the property of an equilateral triangle that each of its interior angles are 60°. By drawing the straight line *PQ*, and then drawing two arcs of radius equal to *PQ* (one centred on *P* and the other on *Q*) we identify the position of the third vertex of an equilateral triangle (as the others are *P* and *Q*). Joining either *P* or *Q* (in this case *P*) to *R*, we create another side of the equilateral triangle, which produces the angle of 60°. If required, we can, of course, complete the third side and produce the equilateral triangle.

Construct a rhombus using the two given lines as sides:

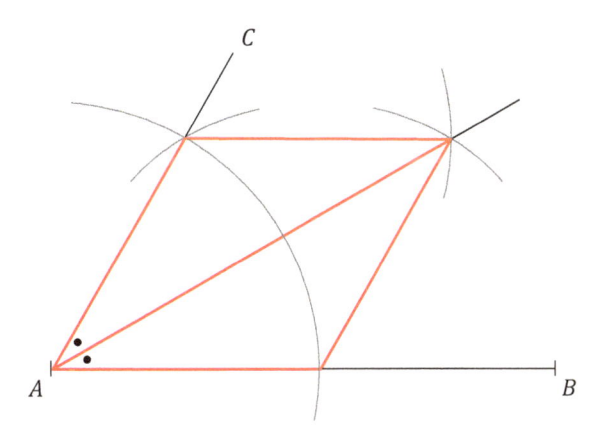

The two lines given are *AB* and *AC*. Producing an arc centred on *A* that crosses both lines produces two sides of the rhombus. Provided we then keep the radius of the arc the same, we can create two further arcs centred on the ends of the two sides already constructed. This produces the fourth vertex of the rhombus, allowing us to complete the shape. This reinforces the property that a rhombus has four equal sides.

Construct a kite using the two given lines as sides:

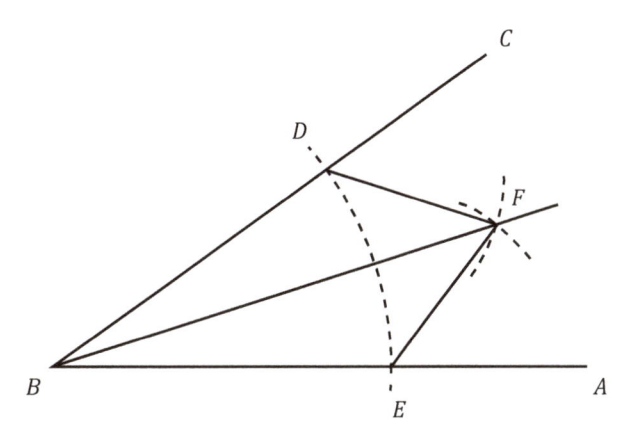

The given lines are *AB* and *BC*. Producing an arc centred on *B* that crosses both lines produces two sides of the kite, with the two vertices *D* and *E*. Then creating two arcs centred on both *D* and *E* (of a different radius to the first arc but both of equal radius to each other) produces the fourth vertex of the kite, *F*, which when joined to *D* and *E* completes the kite. This reinforces the property of the kite that the adjacent sides are equal.

Of course, the reason for focusing on these two shapes is the fact that their diagonals bisect their interior angles (in the case of the kite only the diagonal that joins the vertices connect to the equal sides). As I am sure we can appreciate, either of these diagrams would be a standard diagram that would create the angle bisector between the original two lines (minus the final two sides).

Construct a rhombus with opposite vertices *A* and *B*:

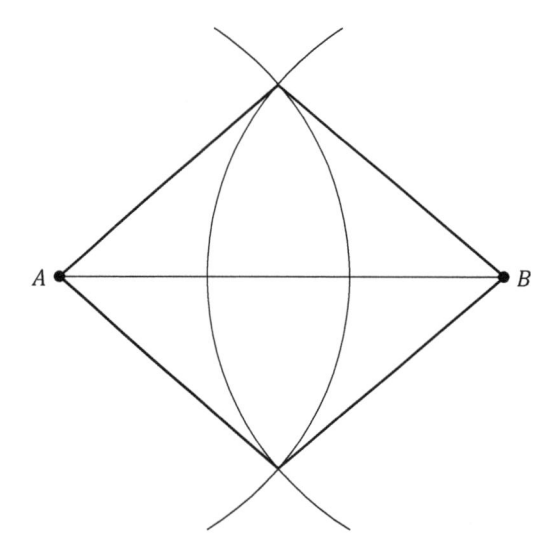

In this case, we can create an arc centred on *A*, and another of the same radius centred on *B*, so that the arcs intersect at two points (meaning the radius of these arcs must be over half the distance *AB*). These two points are the remaining two vertices of the rhombus, each being equidistant from both points *A* and *B*. Of course, this is the precursor diagram to the creation of the perpendicular bisector of the line connecting *AB*. If instead of drawing the sides of the rhombus, we were to connect the two points of intersection of the arcs with a single straight line, then this line would bisect the line connecting *AB* at right angles. This is reinforcing the property that the diagonals of a rhombus are perpendicular bisectors of each other.

With these basic constructions understood, we can then branch out into other constructions:

Construct an angle of 75°.

There are potentially three ways pupils could approach this: the first is that pupils could create an angle of 60°, bisect it twice to go from 60° to 15°, and then construct another angle of 60° on top of the 15° to give a total of 75°.

The second would be to create a right angle (following the same sort of process as a perpendicular bisector) and then create an angle of 60° inside the right angle. This leaves an angle of 30°, which can be bisected to create the extra 15°.

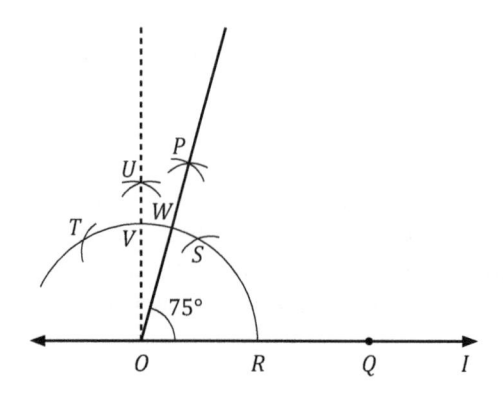

The third shows a little more insight, and starts with the creation of an angle of 60°, followed by an angle bisection to produce an angle of 30°. Pupils may then recognise that an isosceles triangle with an angle of 30° will have base angles of 75°.

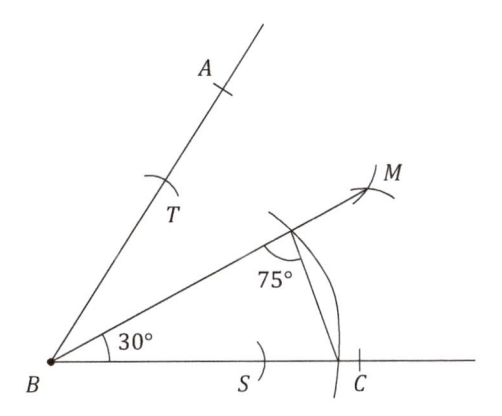

Pupils can create all manner of shapes and angles, including squares and other regular polygons (using a circle as a guide). Of particular interest are creating the circumcircle of a triangle, using perpendicular bisectors of the sides of the triangle and also the incircle of a triangle using angle bisectors of the angles of the triangle. The blog from Galway Maths Grinds has some simple information for each of these,[31] and there are interesting properties pupils can explore.

Once pupils are practised at construction, we can introduce loci. Pupils might already be familiar with a circle as the locus of all points a fixed radius from a single point (it was mentioned as a possible way we can define the circle). We can build on this understanding to develop pupils' sense of loci as all points that obey specific conditions or criteria. Broadly speaking, these will fall into two categories: fixed distance loci (of which the circle has already been introduced) and equidistant loci.

The locus of points a fixed distance from a line *AB*.

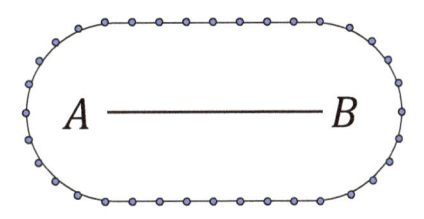

The locus of points a fixed distance from a shape (note that there may be points inside the shape depending on the distance).

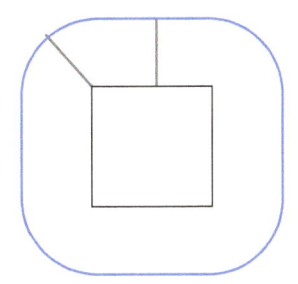

---

31 Galway Maths Grinds, Circumcircle and Incircle (n.d.).Available at: https://galwaymathsgrinds.wordpress.com/maths-topics/circumcircle-and-incircle/.

The locus of points equidistant from a single line.

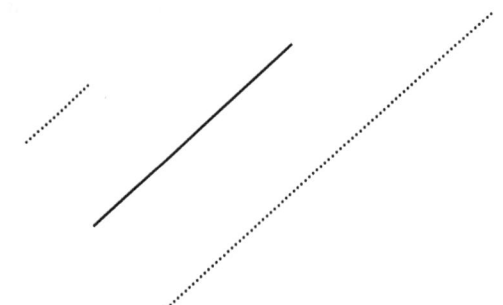

The locus of points equidistant from two points (which is the perpendicular bisector of the line connecting the two points).

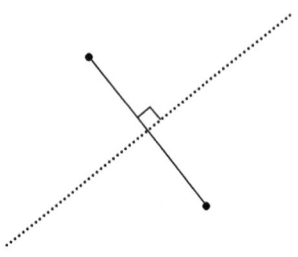

The locus of points equidistant from two intersecting lines (which is the angle bisector of the two lines).

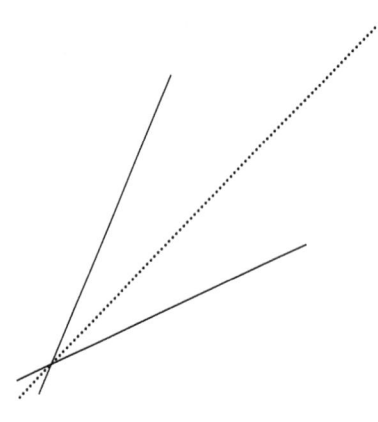

The locus of points equidistant from two parallel lines (l and m).

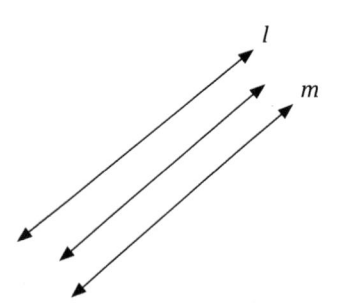

Pupils can work with a number of different situations where they have to construct loci, both set in practical context or as a pure mathematics exercise. The website MME Revise has a large collection of material that can support pupil practice in construction and loci.[32]

Concept: Pythagoras' theorem

Prerequisites: Shape, area, similarity, angle.

Linked concepts: Surds (may be considered prerequisite), circle theorems, volume and surface area calculations, graphing.

We have mentioned Pythagoras' theorem a few times in connection to other concept areas, and have seen that potentially the Pythagorean formula might be taught much earlier than some of these, or after.

There is some debate about whether Pythagoras' theorem is a theorem that primarily concerns lengths or areas. This is probably because, in higher mathematics, the Pythagorean theorem is definitely about length (the response to the question on Stack Exchange makes the point clear, although it might be difficult to follow[33]). However, probably the best way for school-age pupils to make sense of the Pythagorean formula is to consider it as a relationship between areas, and rudimentary dimensional analysis would seem to suggest this view as well. Personally, I am of the opinion that at school level, it is fine to consider Pythagoras' theorem as a relationship between areas; it is just another model that eventually becomes superseded by a more exact and correct version (not unlike the Bohr model of the atom).

The statement of Pythagoras' theorem relates to right-angled triangles, like the one below:

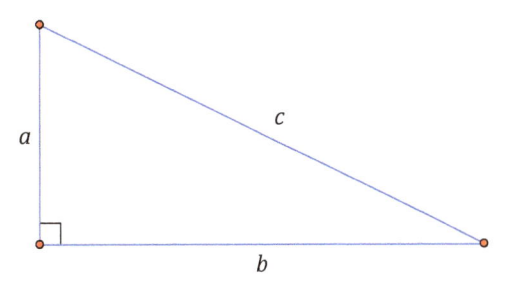

With the theorem stating that $a^2 + b^2 = c^2$. This is where the area interpretation usually comes from, in seeing a^2, b^2 and c^2 as representing the areas of squares attached to the three sides of the triangle:

---

32 MME Revise, Loci and Construction Worksheets, Questions and Revision (n.d.). Available at: https://mathsmadeeasy.co.uk/gcse-maths-revision/loci-and-construction-gcse-revision-and-worksheets/.
33 Stack Exchange, Is Pythagoras' Theorem about Distances or Areas? (2017). Available at: https://math.stackexchange.com/questions/2359457/is-pythagoras-theorem-about-distances-or-areas.

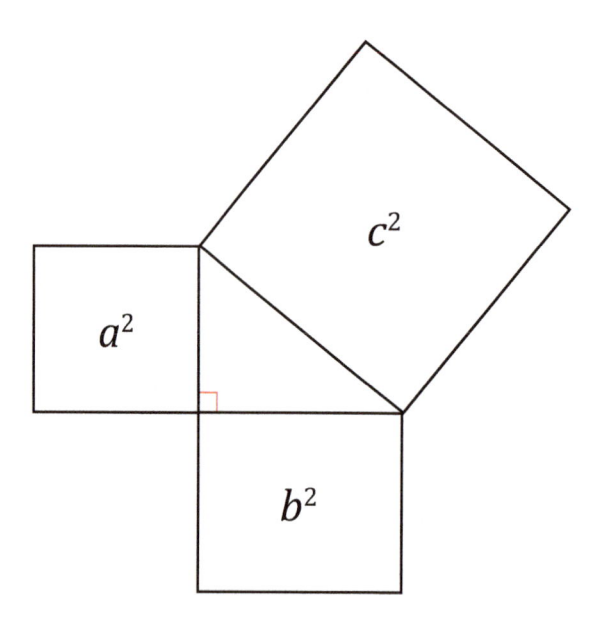

This is therefore often seen as the sum of the areas of the squares attached to the legs of the right triangle is equal to the area of the square attached to the hypotenuse. In reality, any shapes can be attached to the triangle, provided they are similar to each other.

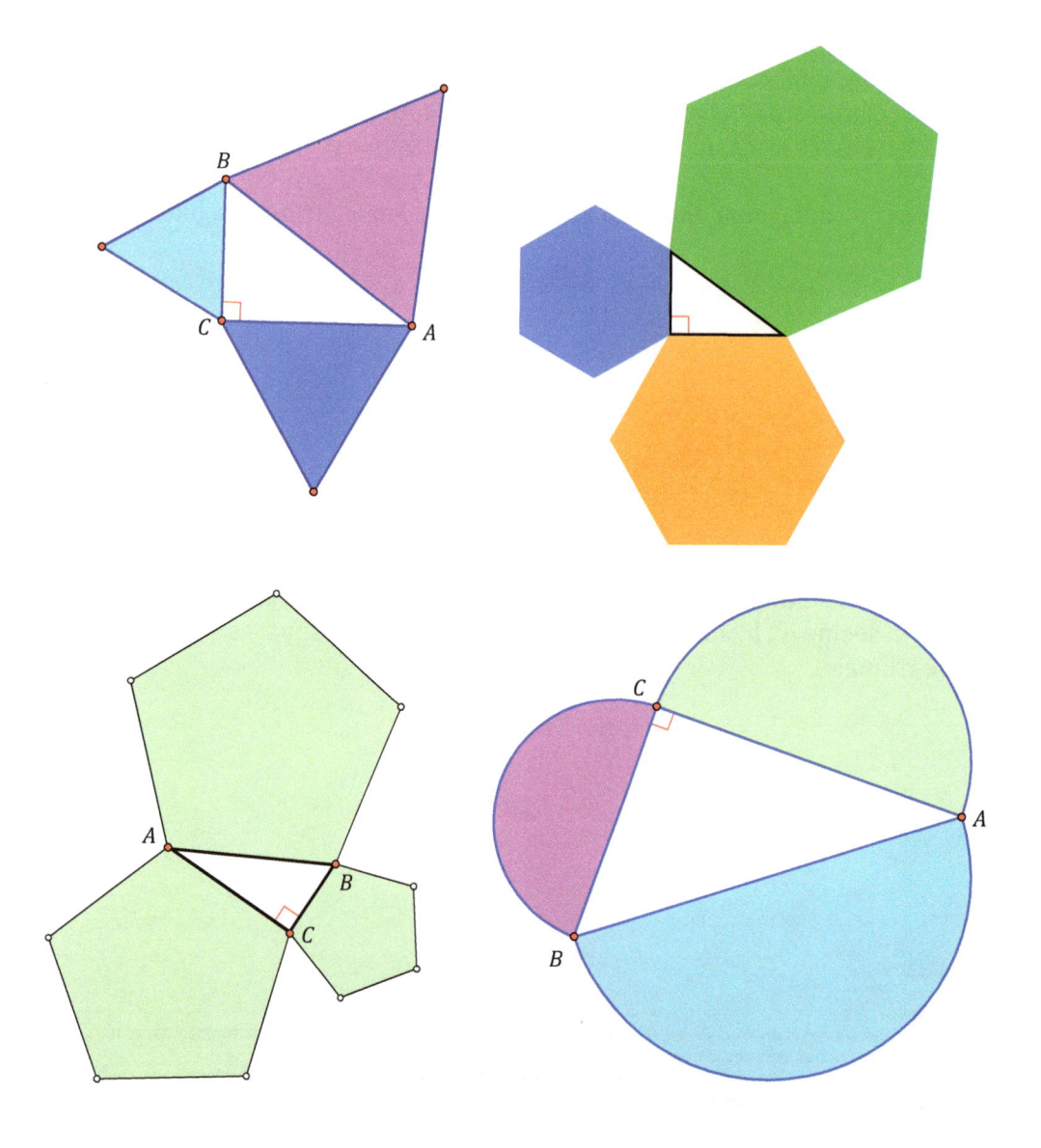

There are many different proofs of Pythagoras' theorem (Alexander Bogomolny lists 54 proofs and references a book that contains 367 proofs[34]). It might be worth showing pupils some of these, or asking them to try and find them, and many of them utilise other properties of shapes (for example, former President of the USA James Garfield derived a proof in 1876 that requires the use of the area of a trapezium). However, it may well be that a formal proof is not the best approach to introducing pupils to the formula. Some prefer a more discovery-style activity, where pupils draw triangles on squared paper and then draw the squares leading off each side. The nice thing about this activity is that it allows interweaving of perpendicularity – pupils having to draw squares of different lengths at different slopes having to revisit the properties of perpendicular lines. However, care does need to be taken as it can be difficult for pupils to accurately count the number of unit squares in each area and so the activity is sometimes not as illuminating as it might be. Other demonstrations are available, such as using dynamic geometry software or even videos/animations (one of my favourite ones is the water demonstration mentioned on Jo Morgan's Resourceaholic blog post about Pythagoras' theorem[35]).

When it comes to applying the formula, many teachers do a lot of work with pupils to secure finding the hypotenuse of the right triangle given the length of the two legs before moving on to finding the length of one of the legs given the length of the hypotenuse and the other leg. I prefer to mix problems where pupils have to find the length of the hypotenuse with those where they have to find the length of a leg. This tends to help avoid the common misconception that pupils continue to add even when presented with information regarding the length of the hypotenuse; if pupils haven't yet got into a fixed routine about adding the areas of squares together then this misconception doesn't arise. For me, the modelling and practice of a mix of problems from early stages after introduction to the formula is a much more fruitful approach. Like with area calculation this should definitely include triangles in many different orientations so that pupils have to recognise the hypotenuse in many different places.

One of the most accessible early enigmas that knowledge of Pythagoras' theorem allows access to is that of Pythagorean triples. Pupils can be shown one or two sets of three integers that fit Pythagoras' theorem, and then be challenged to find others. Eventually, we might want to introduce Euclid's formula[36] for calculating triples, encouraging pupils to prove that it is true.

As well as finding missing lengths using Pythagoras' theorem, pupils should also become aware of and utilise the contrapositive result for the theorem, namely that if $a^2 + b^2 = c^2$ for some triangle, then the triangle is definitely right-angled (and therefore if $a^2 + b^2 \neq c^2$ the triangle is not right angled). Further to this, Pythagoras' theorem can provide further information about the triangle – in particular whether it is an acute- or obtuse-angled triangle:

---

34 A. Bogolmony, Pythagorean Theorem, *Cut the Knot* (n.d.). Available at: https://faculty.umb.edu/gary_zabel/Courses/Phil%20281b/Philosophy%20of%20Magic/Arcana/Neoplatonism/Pythagoras/index.shtml.html.
35 J. Morgan, Pythagoras' Theorem, *Resourceaholic* [blog] (2 September 2014). Available at: https://www.resourceaholic.com/2014/09/pythagoras.html.
36 M. Molony, Generating Pythagorean Triples, *Dreamshire* [blog] (14 November 2012). Available at: https://blog.dreamshire.com/generating-pythagorean-triples/.

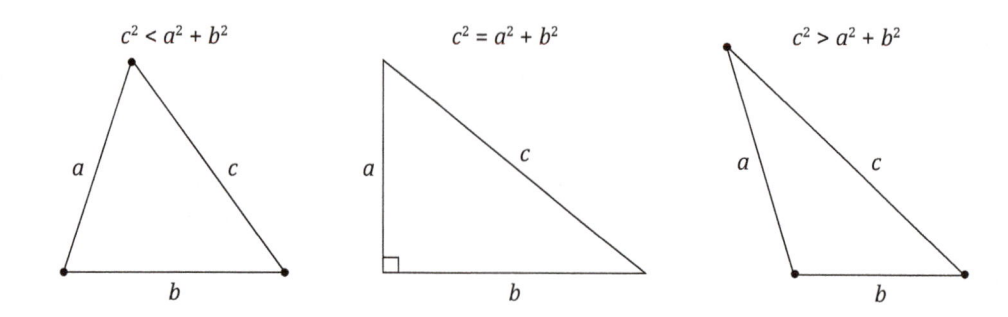

The area idea can be helpful in seeing why this is the case: if the angle opposite c grows smaller than a right-angle, then the length of c will shrink, and therefore so will the area of the square (or other shape) attached to it. However, if the angle opposite c grows larger than a right angle, the length of c will grow and therefore so will its square. Something like this can be modelled nicely using dynamic geometry software such as Geogebra,[37] with pupils and teachers being able to manipulate the size of the angle and examine the resulting change on the area. Of course, we have to take care that c remains the longest side of the triangle, particularly in the case of $c^2 < a^2 + b^2$; if a or b becomes the biggest side then we might have $c^2 < a^2 + b^2$ whilst the triangle is still obtuse.

Pythagoras' theorem can be applied in many different contexts, both mathematical and non-mathematical. Some of these will come up in later chapters, but this is an opportune moment to interweave some of those pupils have already seen:

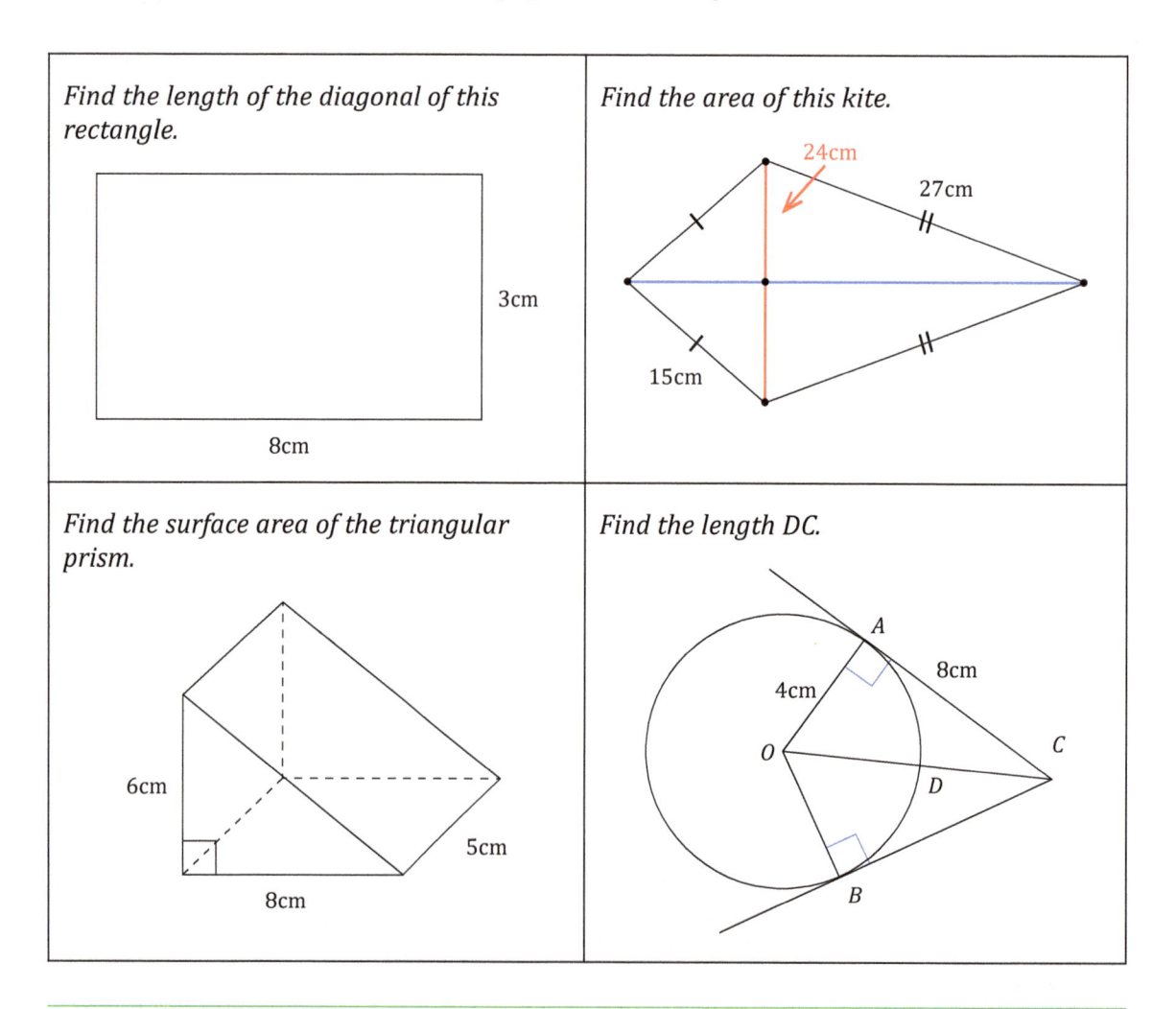

Find the length of the diagonal of this rectangle. 	*Find the area of this kite.*
Find the surface area of the triangular prism. 	*Find the length DC.*

---

37 See https://www.geogebra.org/calculator/vjvb6cjc.

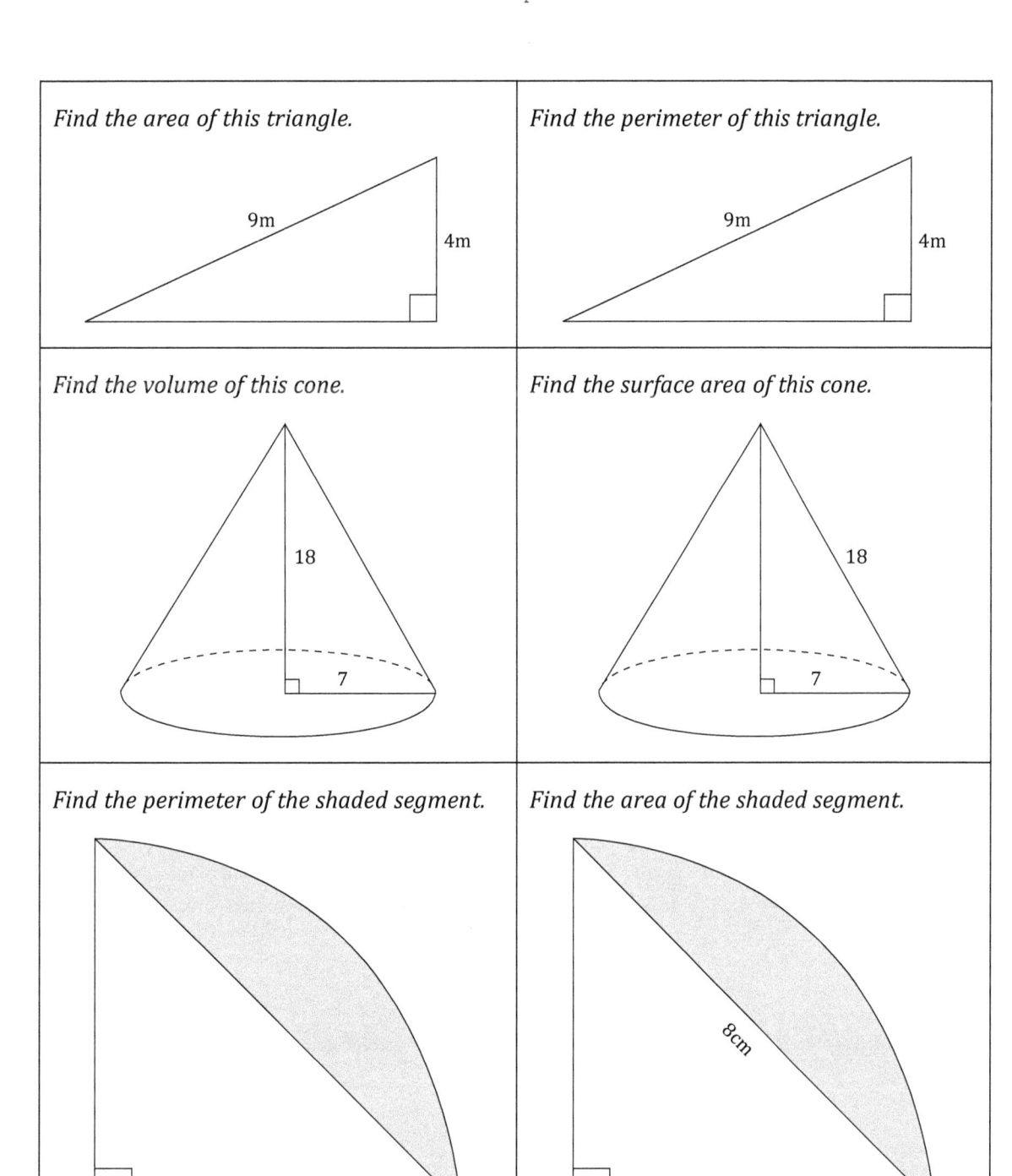

Find the area of this triangle. 9m, 4m	*Find the perimeter of this triangle.* 9m, 4m
Find the volume of this cone. 18, 7	*Find the surface area of this cone.* 18, 7
Find the perimeter of the shaded segment. 8cm	*Find the area of the shaded segment.* 8cm

One of my favourite problems is to ask pupils to find the diagonal of a parallelogram, given only its side lengths and vertical height.

Find the lengths of both diagonals of the parallelogram below:

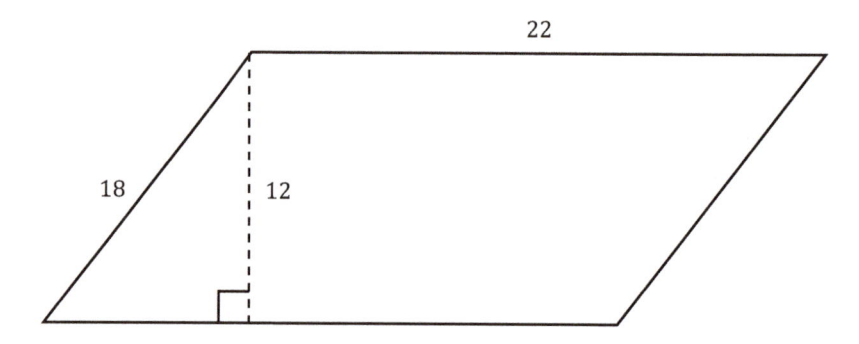

Of course, not all of these will necessarily be taught before Pythagoras' theorem is taught (although technically they all could be) so it may be that we are using questions like this when we are exploring applications of Pythagoras' theorem or it could be that we are using these questions to interweave Pythagoras into these areas when they arise in the curriculum.

In all likelihood, we will also want to explore Pythagoras' theorem in three dimensions. This doesn't just mean applying Pythagoras to two-dimensional triangles that happen to be part of a three-dimensional shape (as is the case of the cones and triangular prism in the previous questions) but applying Pythagoras' theorem to finding the lengths of lines that actually move through all three dimensions. The usual way to introduce this to pupils is to consider the line across a cuboid:

Find the length of the line EC.

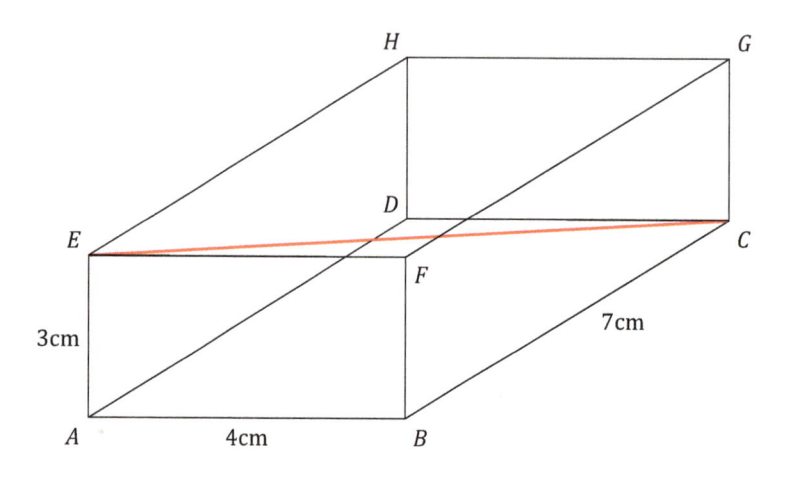

Pupils typically bump into two issues when first exploring application of Pythagoras' theorem to three dimensions:

1   They will struggle to identify the right-angled triangle(s) that the line EC is part of.
2   They might think that length of the line can be found using just one application of Pythagoras (usually in this picture using the 3 cm and 7 cm length).

I think something that can help with both of these issues is not to immediately focus on the line, and instead focus on identifying the rectangle the line goes across:

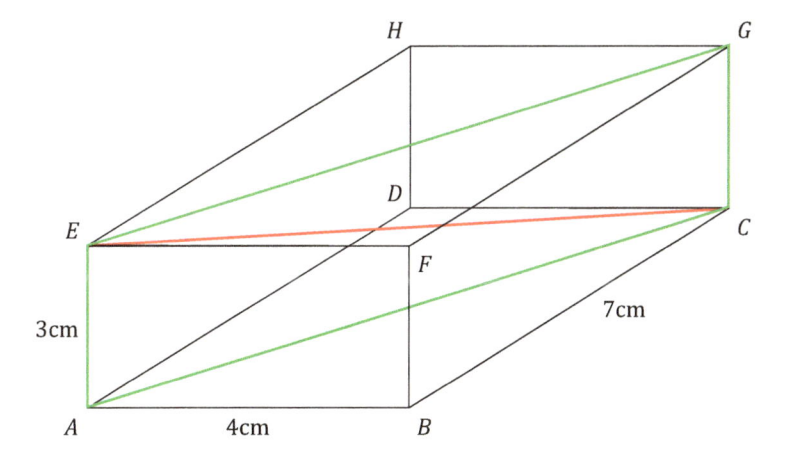

Pupils seem to be happier identifying something like *EGCA* as a rectangle than seeing either *EGC* or *EAC* as a right-angled triangle.

We can then draw out the rectangle, rather than immediately trying to draw out the triangle:

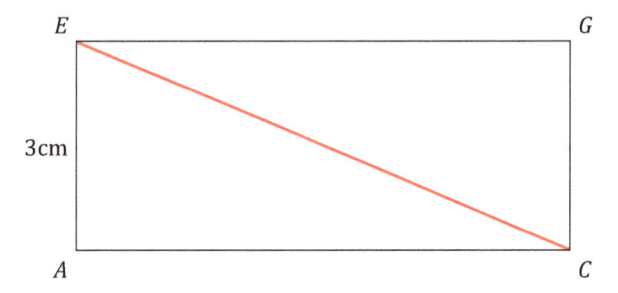

This also helps pupils see that we only actually know one length in the rectangle (the 'height' of 3 cm), and so attention can be turned to how we can find the length *AC*. Pupils are generally happier in identifying right-angled triangles like *ABC* directly from the diagram; however, if necessary we can go through the same sort of process – identify a rectangle for which *AC* is the diagonal, draw the rectangle and then use the marked lengths. Some would use this as a vehicle to introduce a generalisation of Pythagoras' theorem to three dimensions – $d^2 = a^2 + b^2 + c^2$, where a, b and c are all at right angles to each other. However, I would caution against this, particularly if using an area interpretation of Pythagoras theorem. It is difficult to show this directly as the sum of three areas (although not impossible) but can also lead to issues when pupils try and apply this to shapes other than cuboids. It may be that some pupils can extend their understanding to apply this correctly directly into three dimensions, but for most I don't necessarily think it is a problem to stick with multiple applications of Pythagoras' theorem in two dimensions. Indeed, it may well be that pupils will see the generalisation for themselves once they start to apply Pythagoras' theorem in three dimensions.

Again, pupils can be offered a number of different scenarios and contexts in which Pythagoras' theorem might be required in three dimensions, although generally this will be finding lengths within different three-dimensional shapes no matter what the context the shape is set in. The 'rod in the box' question is always a nice one, asking pupils to determine the longest rod that can be places into different shaped boxes.

Of course, rarely is Pythagoras' theorem mentioned without close proximity to the wider study of trigonometry. It is with this area that we will conclude the shape chapter.

Concept: trigonometry

Prerequisites: Shape, similarity, angle.

Linked concepts: Surds (may be considered prerequisite), area, circle theorems, volume and surface area calculations, graphing.

In my opinion, trigonometry is an area of mathematics in which teachers often try and move pupils towards a very functional view too quickly, without taking the time to draw attention to and embed key ideas that underpin the formulae we eventually want pupils to use. Even in introducing trigonometry through a 'measurement' activity where pupils measure lengths and angles within different right triangles the awareness we want pupils to achieve is often missed (as well as being fraught with danger itself due to the inherent inaccuracies in measurement of these quantities).

The teaching of trigonometry truly begins when teachers work with pupils on the idea of similarity (which we will explore more in the next chapter). In particular the two key ideas that:

1 The ratios of any two lengths in similar shapes are equal.
2 Angles in similar shapes are equal.

For example, if we consider these two triangles:

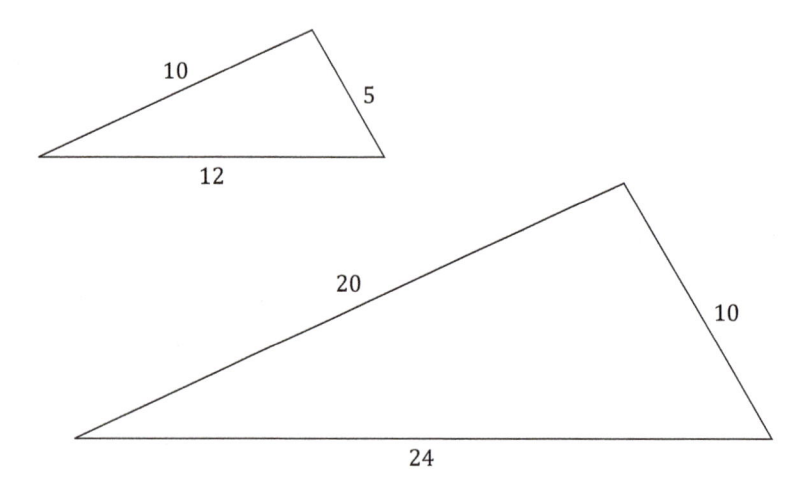

pupil attention might immediately go to the fact that every length in the larger triangle is double the size of the corresponding length in the smaller triangle, but in addition pupils would also need to recognise that the angles in both triangles are equal, and that the ratio of any two lengths in the smaller triangle is equal to the ratio of the corresponding lengths in the larger triangle – for example, 10:5 = 20:10 or even 27:12 = 54:24 (the ratio of the perimeter to the longest side).

The reason that we need pupils to have intimate familiarity with these two properties of similar shapes is because then the natural question arises – surely the two properties are related? If angles are equal, and also ratios of sides are equal, surely knowing the value of one should allow us to work out the value of another. This realisation is what gives birth to trigonometry, with the justification that we only need consider triangles because all other polygons can be made from triangles (and we can create triangles inside polyhedra when it comes to examing three dimensions). Further, every triangle can be split into two right-angled triangles, and right triangles are useful because if we fix one angle as 90° then we only need one other angle to know that two triangles are similar (because, of course, if we know two angles in a triangle are equal, then so must the third be). Yes, I would take pupils through all of this logic when introducing trigonometry – a pupil that can't follow it isn't in a position where they are ready to study trigonometry and, for me, pupils seeing these as links in the chain will gain a deeper appreciation of trigonometry. That isn't to say I will lecture pupils through these points; rather offering prompts and images, questions such as, 'What can you tell me about …', 'Why might triangles be important/a good start point?' and then perhaps asking different pupils to take me through a step at a time in the logic, as a summary will draw the necessary attention to how the study of trigonometry arises. It is at this point that I will introduce the first (what I term) 'base triangle':

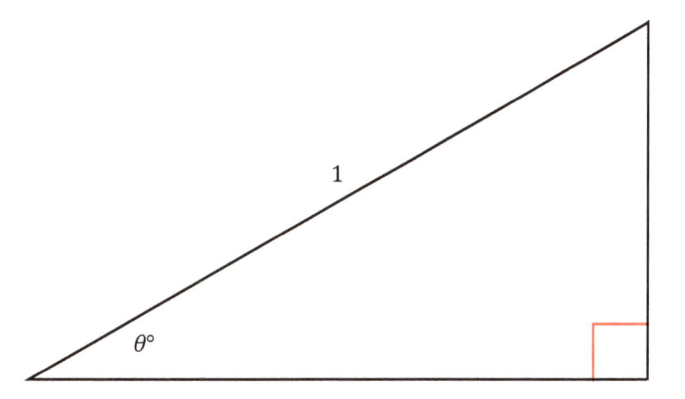

The discussion we will have here is that every right-angled triangle is similar to this triangle for a given value of θ, so if θ is, say, 42°, then this triangle is similar to all other right triangles with an angle of 42° as one of the interior angles. It is at this point that we will introduce the first two trigonometric functions that pupils will meet; sine and cosine:

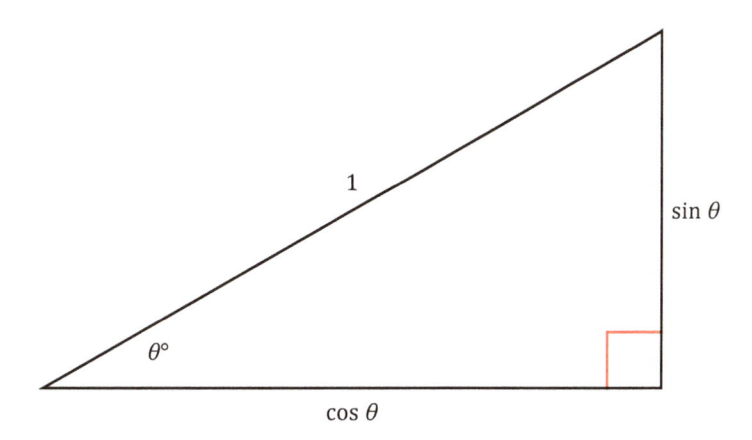

Pupils should be clear that applying the sine/cosine functions to the given angle will tell us the value of opposite/adjacent sides in a triangle with a hypotenuse of 1 (we might need to spend some time making sure pupils are secure on the language of hypotenuse, adjacent and opposite before proceeding). At this point, pupils should spend some time using their calculator simply to find lengths in this triangle for a given angle. This could be done as a class, potentially using whiteboards, with just a picture of the first triangle and the teacher replacing θ with a numerical value and pointing to a particular side for pupils to find. When pupils are secure with this, we can then introduce the idea of being given the side and finding the angle, using the inverse trig functions arcsine and arccosine (to understand these terms pupils need to know about radian measure, so teachers may prefer to use the $^{-1}$ notation that pupils should have seen when working with inverse functions). Again, pupils can be provided with a value for the length of a side in the base triangle and asked to find either of the angles.

It is only once pupils have a secure grasp of this that we would introduce triangles with a length other than 1, usually starting with introducing triangles with a different value of the hypotenuse.

Find the value of the length marked x in this triangle:

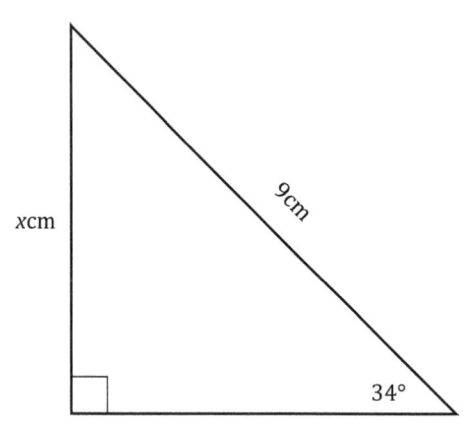

At this point pupils might well immediately spot that they can scale the original base triangle (with a value for θ of 34) by a factor of 9 to create this triangle, and this recognition should be acknowledged and applauded. It may be that we are happy with pupils solving problems using a scale factor for a while; however, we should explain to pupils that it will be beneficial long term to consider the ratios between lengths within each shape, as this will allow us to move towards a functional view of trigonometry rather than being kept at a more proportional view. In this case, that would mean being able to write down:

$\frac{\sin 34}{1} = \frac{x}{9}$ or just $\sin 34 = \frac{x}{9}$

which we might first use a ratio table to support with.

Base triangle	Given triangle
1	9
sin 34°	x

Pupils should work with a number of problems of this type using both sine and cosine, including problems where the hypotenuse is the unknown:

Find the value of the length marked *x* in this triangle.

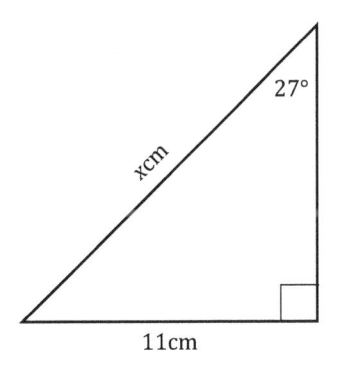

as well as finding missing angles when given two sides when one is the hypotenuse.

Find the value of the angle marked *x* in this triangle.

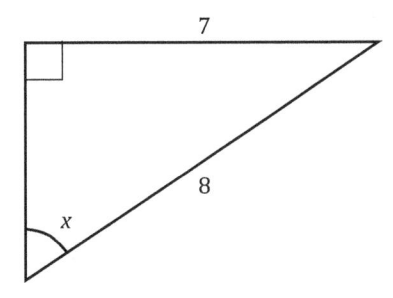

It is only at this point that we might prompt pupils with a triangle like this:

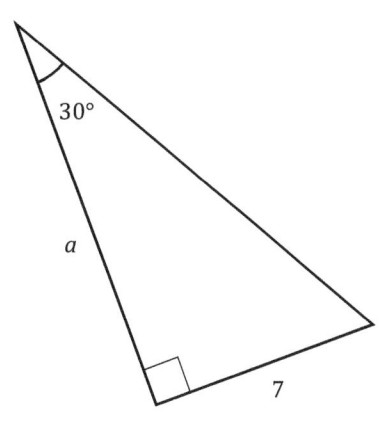

Find the value of the length marked *a* in this triangle.

Pupils can actually solve for this length using what they know already if they think carefully, and may eventually arrive at something like this:

$\frac{\cos 30}{\sin 30} = \frac{a}{7}$

Of course, we will use this prompt to introduce the tangent function, with a second base triangle:

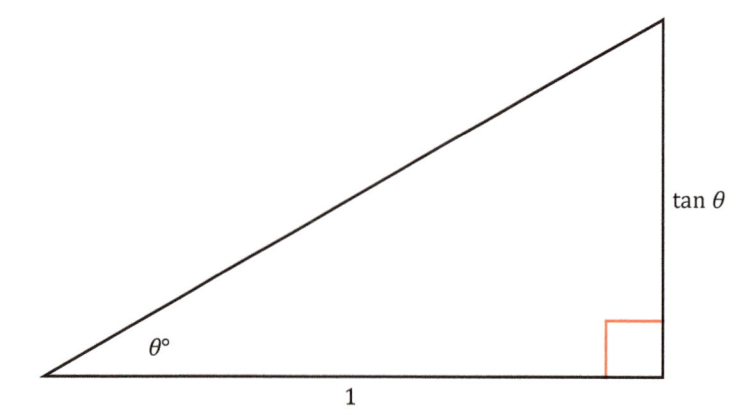

[Right triangle with angle θ° at bottom left, horizontal base of length 1, vertical side on the right labelled tan θ, and right angle at bottom right.]

By this point pupils are very used to working with trigonometric functions, so the introduction to using the tangent function should be quite smooth and can probably be accelerated compared to the initial introduction of sine and cosine. Still, it is worth spending some time working with this new base triangle, giving values of θ so pupils can find side lengths and giving values of the side length so that pupils can find angles. From here we will build up to looking at 'scaled up' versions of the triangle, finding missing sides and angles, making sure that pupils can solve problems like this:

Find the value of the length *AC* in this triangle.

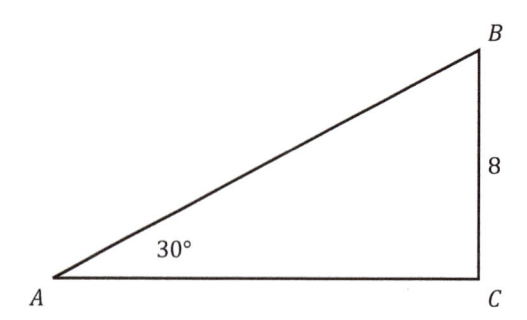

[Right triangle with vertices A (bottom left), C (bottom right), B (top right). Angle at A is 30°, side BC = 8.]

This requires pupils to recognise that the equal ratios are:

$\frac{8}{AC} = \frac{\tan 30}{1}$ *or just* $\frac{8}{AC} = \tan 30$

It also allows them to potentially recognise an alternative, namely:

$\frac{AC}{8} = \frac{1}{\tan 30}$

Although by this point, pupils (hopefully) have enough experience in solving equations of the type $\frac{k}{x} = c$, where *k* and *c* are constants, that this alternative would primarily be for interest in linking back to reciprocals, rather than as a necessary part of the strategy for solving this type of trigonometric equation.

One aspect of right-angled trigonometry that we will want pupils to explore (although potentially not until they have considerable experience solving for missing sides in right triangles) are the values of sine, cosine and tangent for 30°, 45° and 60°. However, I would caution against approaching this from the point of view of the angles – from introducing this to pupils as, 'Now we are going to find the values of sine 30°, 45° and 60° because they are special angles.' With this approach, the natural question arises, why are they special? What is special about them? It is difficult to answer this question before pupils actually see the results, which means we have to give an almost 'wait and see' type response that can be frustrating for pupils (although others will potentially enjoy the tension it creates).

The alternative is to ask what would seem a perfectly reasonable question about the initial base triangle: are there values for θ that make the opposite side simple fraction? We can focus on the opposite side as if we find one that makes the adjacent side a simple fraction, we can just subtract it from 90° and this value will make the opposite side a simple fraction (an argument that we might offer to pupils if they can't see it for themselves when questioned as to why the focus on the opposite sides is justified).

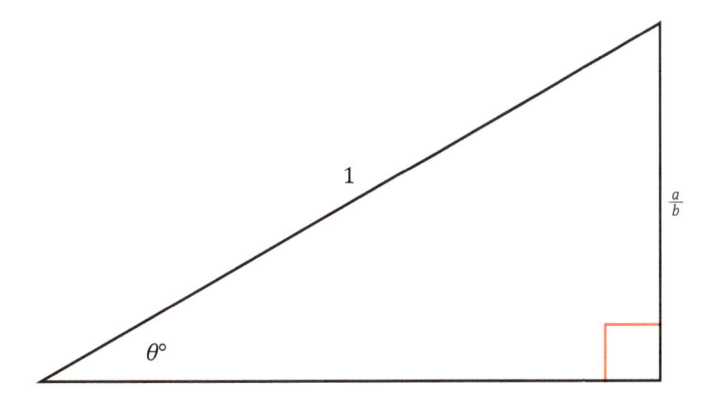

We might let pupils explore this a little with their calculators, creating simple fractions and using the arcsine function to find the value of the angle. If they do explore this a little, they will, of course, realise that the vast majority of simple fractions come from irrational (or at least very complicated) values of the angle, except for when the side length has a fraction of $\frac{1}{2}$. If we don't want pupils exploring, we might offer the fraction of $\frac{1}{2}$ as a start point, and then prompt reasoning as to why an angle of 30° leads to an opposite side length of $\frac{1}{2}$. To start with, we might need to offer pupils this diagram:

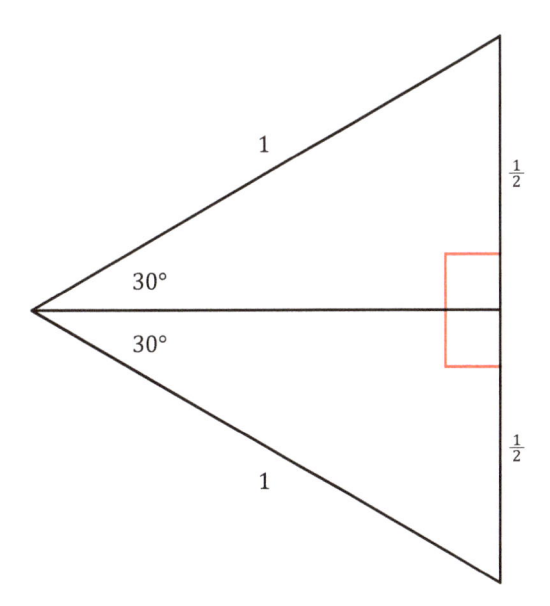

Pupils at this point will normally reason that this is an equilateral triangle, and it therefore makes sense for sin 30° to equal $\frac{1}{2}$. Of course, once this is established, then clearly the logical thing is to ask – what else can this triangle tell us? From here, with a bit of Pythagoras' theorem use we will get the exact values of cos 30°, sin 60° and cos 60°.

From here, of course, we can look at tan 30° and tan 60° – the easiest way to do this is to double the size of the original base triangle so that one of the legs takes a value of 1:

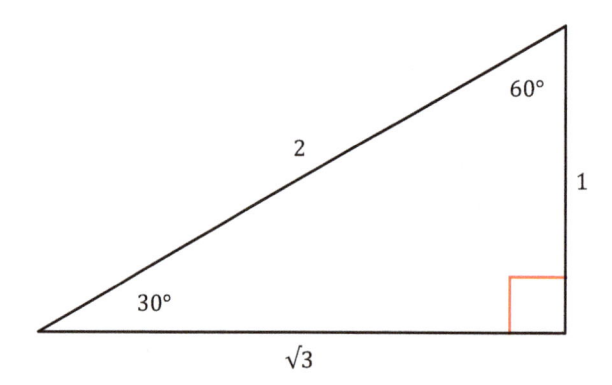

This allows us to recognise tan 60° = √3 and tan 30° = $\frac{1}{\sqrt{3}}$, and it is also worth highlighting to pupils that we can see the values of sine/cosine of 30°/60° that we found earlier.

Finally, we can ask the question, 'What about the other base triangle? What can this tell us about exact values in trigonometry?'

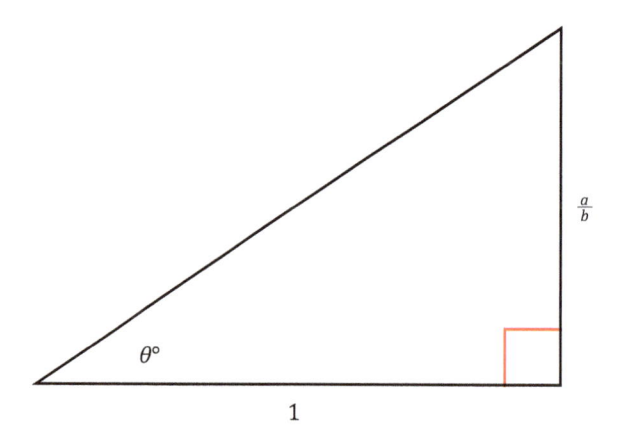

Again, we might offer this as an investigation to begin with, or we might simply ask for suggestions about what fractions might arise from a nice angle (potentially reminding pupils that this fraction can now be a whole number or improper fraction). Whichever approach, pupils should come to realise that if the side opposite the angle is also 1, then this will become an isosceles triangle and so θ will take a value of 45°. This leads nicely to the conclusion that tan 45° = 1, which, of course, begs the question, what about sin 45° and cos 45°? A small application of Pythagoras in this triangle will allow pupils to see that both sin 45° and cos 45° are equal to $\frac{1}{\sqrt{2}}$.

Trigonometry is one of the key ideas in post-16 maths, and so plenty of time to embed key ideas and apply them to a variety of contexts will be required, both immediately upon study and throughout the remainder of the pre-16 course of study. The contexts we might use will be similar to those we highlighted in the Pythagoras' theorem section, including finding lengths that will allow us to find areas, or finding angles that will allow us to find other angles in diagrams involving circles. The three-dimensional work will also be very similar, finding angles and sides in the same sorts of diagrams as we did for Pythagoras (and approaching the teaching of it in much the same way). Another nice type of question is to provide a fractional value of any one of the trigonometric functions, and ask pupils to sketch a right triangle that could produce it, for example:

Sketch a right triangle that has an angle θ such that $\cos \theta = \frac{3}{11}$.

Further applications of right-angled trigonometry will be to establish how we can widen the scope of trigonometry to non-right triangles. This will require us to define the trig functions for angles greater than or equal to 90°, which will require the unit circle.

Technically, the unit circle is not explicitly part of the pre-16 mathematics curriculum in England; however, trigonometry for triangles with angles beyond 90° and trigonometric graphs are both part of the curriculum for some pupils, and it seems difficult to see how we would introduce these in any meaningful way without the unit circle.

Assuming pupils have a strong grasp of how the trigonometric functions are defined in terms of the base triangles, then the extension to the unit circle should be relatively straightforward. Again, we will begin with the first base triangle:

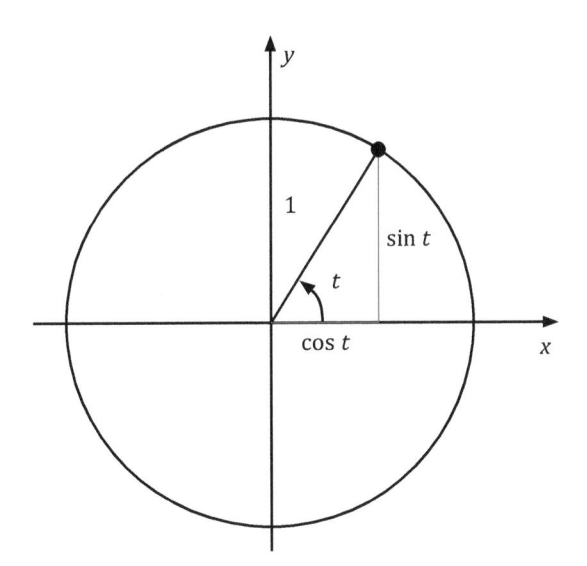

This shows pupils that superimposing this base triangle on the unit circle allows us to stretch the definition of the sine and cosine functions to any angle, measured anticlockwise from the positive horizontal. We can also see immediately why the maximum and minimum values of these functions are 1 and −1, and the exact values of sin 0°, sin 90°, cos 0° and cos 90°, which are all part of the pre-16 curriculum. We can also see why things like sin $t°$ = sin(180 − t) are true. It is worth allowing pupils to explore this circle a little, and come up with some more relationships between values of sin and cosine of different angles.

When it comes to the tangent function, there are different ways to define it in terms of the unit circle.

Fixing the adjacent side to have a value of 1 can actually lead to problems:

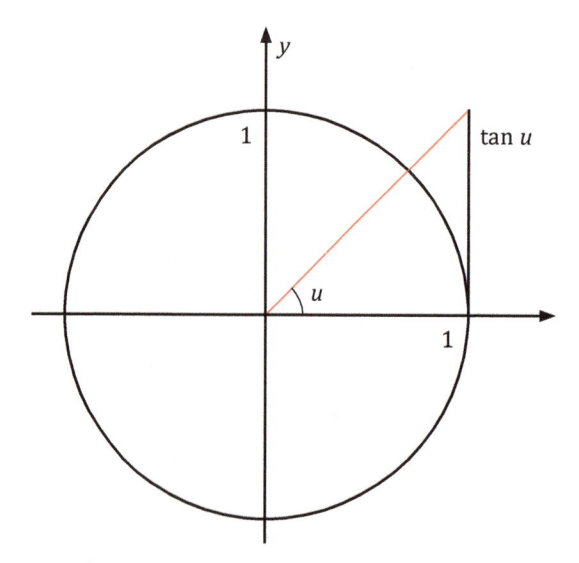

There are no issues for angles smaller than 90° or even in seeing that tan 90° cannot be defined (as we can't increase θ to 90 whilst maintaining the value of 1 on the adjacent side). The issue comes when we try and increase θ beyond 90°. At first glance, it might appear that this will continue quite nicely, with the value of, say tan 91° being equal to tan 89°. However, we have to account for the fact that the adjacent will not strictly be 1, but will actually be −1. We can account for this simply by telling pupils that this means we need the negative of the value when the horizontal is −1, but this seems a little contrived.

My preferred approach to introduce the tangent function with the unit circle is to take a closer look at the normal base triangle:

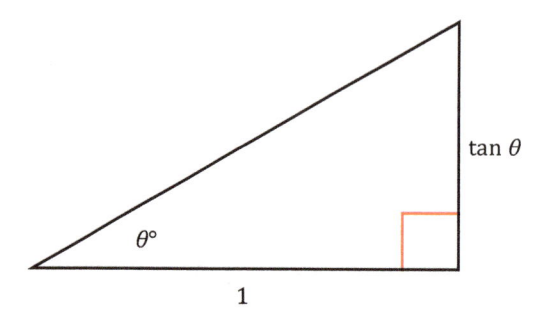

The hypotenuse of this triangle travels 1 unit horizontally from start to end, and tan θ vertically. This, of course, is exactly the value of the gradient of the line (we could have helped pupils make this connection earlier in their studies). If we then define tan θ to be the value of the gradient of the radius in the unit circle, this solves the issues around when tan θ is postive or negative, and also allows us to make sense of why tan 0° = 0, but why tan 90° is undefined (a vertical line doesn't have gradient).

Once pupils are clear as to how the trigonometric functions are defined for angles beyond 90°, then we can start to explore trigonometry for non-right triangles, most likely starting with the sine rule. There are different ways of approaching the sine rule with pupils. We might prompt a full proof:

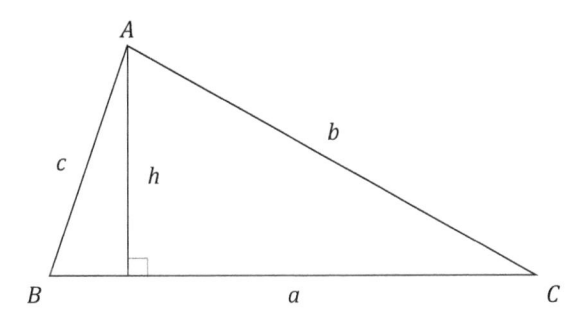

$h = b \sin C$ (from the right-hand triangle)

$h = c \sin B$ (from the left-hand triangle)

So $b \sin C = c \sin B$ which can be rearranged to give $\frac{c}{b} = \frac{\sin C}{\sin B}$.

This is my preferred way to state the sine rule, whether we introduce it through proof or not. The reason for this is because, for me, it relates most directly to the use of the sine function for right-angled triangles, i.e. when angle B is 90°, this form of the sine rule degenerates to the relationship that we are familiar with from right-angled triangles. In this way, we can see the division by $\sin B$ as the adjustment required to go from the standard right-angled relationship to the non-right relationship.

Pupils should use the sine rule to find both missing sides and missing angles. An important part of working with the sine rule to find angles is recognising the so-called 'ambigious case', which arises when we are finding a missing angle opposite a side and the given angle is an acute angle. Take, for example, the situations below:

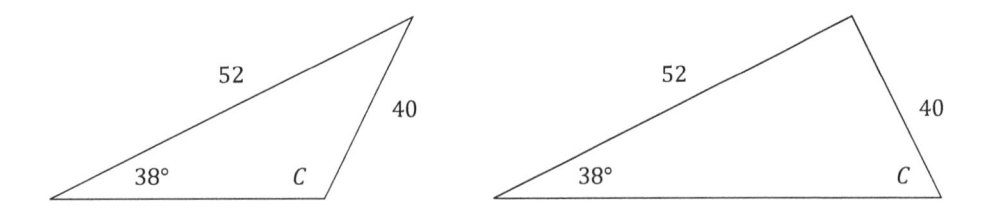

We can see that there are two possible angles that could be opposite the side of 52 when an angle of 38° is opposite the side of 40. A calculator will only return the acute angle of 53.2°, so how do we find the obtuse angle? There are two potential approaches: the first is to refer back to the unit circle to find the other value less than 180° that has the sine value as 53.2° (which will be 180 − 53.2), or we can show that the two possible values of C will add to 180° by joining the two triangles along the common side to 40:

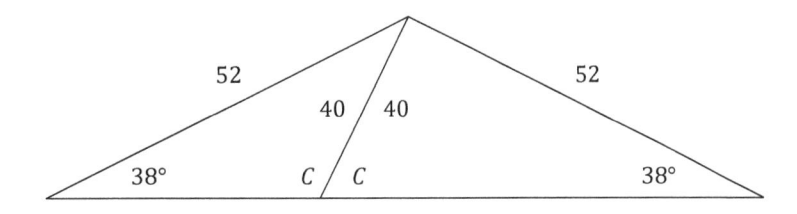

Pupils can practise applying the sine rule to find sides and angles in many different contexts, potentially including contexts similar to those we have seen previously (to find perimeter, area or volume; to find angles in circle diagrams so that other angles can be found; in three dimensional shapes) both with and without a calculator (using the exact values we have previously discovered). As usual, Don Steward has good examples of the sort of thing we might offer pupils.[38] Once the sine rule is well understood by pupils, we can turn our attention to the cosine rule. Again, this may or may not start with prompting a proof from pupils:

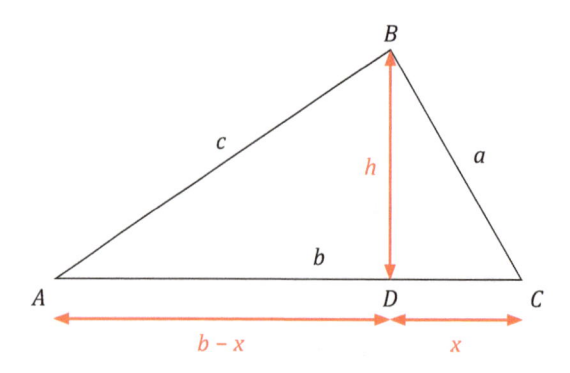

$h^2 = a^2 - x^2$ and $x = a \cos C$ from the right-hand triangle.

$h^2 = c^2 - (b - x)^2$ from the left-hand triangle.

So $a^2 - x^2 = c^2 - (b - x)^2$

$a^2 - x^2 = c^2 - b^2 + 2bx - x^2$

$a^2 = c^2 - b^2 + 2bx$

$a^2 + b^2 - 2bx = c^2$

$a^2 + b^2 - 2ab \cos C = c^2$

Whether we introduce the cosine rule with a proof or not, we want pupils recognising the similarity between this and Pythagoras' theorem. Indeed, if we compare the above triangle to the one below:

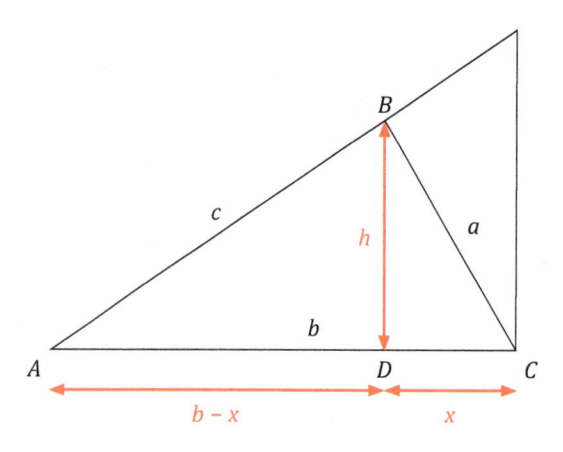

---

38 D. Steward, Sine Rule, *Median* [blog] (19 November 2013). Available at: https://donsteward.blogspot.com/2013/11/sine-rule.html.

we can see that if we made the angle at *C* into 90° then *c* (and therefore c^2) would be longer than in the previous triangle. Therefore, the '$-2ab \cos C$' can be seen as 'adjusting' Pythagoras' theorem for the fact that the angle at *C* is no longer a right angle. This also holds when the angle at *C* is greater than 90°, as we have seen from the unit circle that applying the cosine function to an angle greater than 90° gives a negative value, and so in the cosine rule when *C* is greater than 90°, the '$-2ab \cos C$' will become a positive value, and so will add extra to the the value of *c* (and therefore c^2).

Pupils should be offered opportunities to use the cosine rule to find missing lengths and missing angles in a variety of contexts. Bearings calculations can give rise to some interesting questions that can require pupils to use a combination of the sine rule and the cosine rule to find different values in the situation, as well as many of the contexts we have seen previously around circle theorems, perimeter, area and volume calculations, calculations of diagonals in different shapes, etc. and, of course, practical contexts. In particular, pupils should be faced with scenarios where they have to decide whether use of the sine rule or the cosine rule will be useful in solving the problem, once they have a firm grasp of both separately. In addition, an important question type are triangles that require a choice between a non-straightforward application of the cosine rule, or use of the sine rule followed by the cosine rule. Consider, for example, the question below:

Find the length of the side marked *x*.

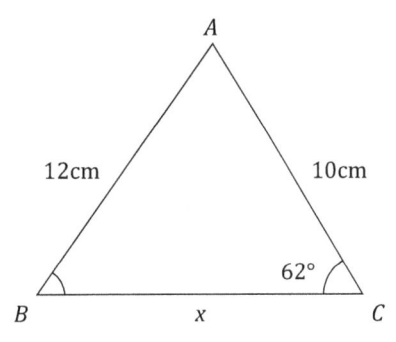

A

12cm   10cm

               62°

B   *x*   *C*

Pupils can use the cosine rule directly here, but in doing so they will form a quadratic equation in *x*:

$12^2 = x^2 + 10^2 - 20x \cos 62$

In this case, only one of the solutions to the quadratic is a valid length, as the other is negative.

An alternative approach to the solution would be to first use the sine rule to calculate the angle at *B*. This looks like it could be the ambiguous case (if the angle at *B* wasn't clearly acute), but the possible obtuse angle for *B* is actually a little over 132°, and we can't have a triangle with an angle of 132° and 62° (which is why the quadratic equation above only produces one valid solution). We can then work out the angle at *A* using the fact that angles in a planar triangle sum to 180°. This allows a more straightforward application of the cosine rule using the value of the angle at *A*.

It may be that we simply offer pupils problems of this type and see what strategies they try and employ, or it may be that it is preferred to have a discussion with the class about why this isn't a straightforward application of the cosine rule, and then to collectively discuss alternative strategies. It may even be worthwhile assigning the different strategies to different people/groups in the room: 'This half of the room solve the quadratic equation, and this half of the room find the angle at A using the sine rule and angles in a triangle before using the cosine rule', before having each half confirm they get the same result. Or it may be that we want to highlight both potential strategies to pupils and then allow them the choice as to which they apply.

The final application of trigonometry to non-right-angled triangles is in links to area calculation. Again we might choose to start with either demonstrating or using questions to prompt a proof:

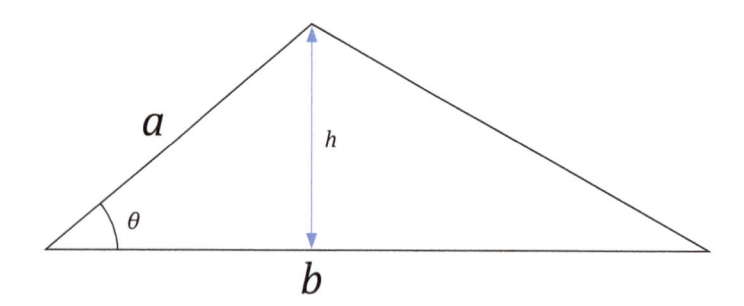

Pupils should already know that the area of the triangle can be calculated as $\frac{1}{2}bh$. However, h can be replaced here with $a \sin \theta$, leading to an alternative calculation for area of $\frac{1}{2}ab \sin \theta$. Whether we choose to use this proof or not, what pupils should be clear on in using this alternative calculation is that this can always be separated into a $\frac{1}{2} \times$ a side $\times$ the perpendicular height; so if we write it as $\frac{1}{2} \times a \times b \sin \theta$ then $b \sin \theta$ is the value of the perpendicular height from side a to vertex A. Similarly, writing the calculation as $\frac{1}{2} \times b \times a \sin \theta$ gives $a \sin \theta$ as the perpendicular height from side b to vertex B. As with the sine and cosine rules, pupils should be offered different contexts and situations to apply this calculation. One of my favourite contexts is in calculating the area of shapes like parallelograms, as this can lead to the nice generalisation that the area of a parallelogram is simply $ab \sin \theta$, where a and b are the two sides of the parallelogram and θ is either the acute or the obtuse angle between the sides (further reinforcing that $\sin \theta = \sin(180 - \theta)$). One important context for use of both cosine rule and the area calculation is in use with circular segments.

For the shaded segment below, find:

a   the perimeter

b   the area

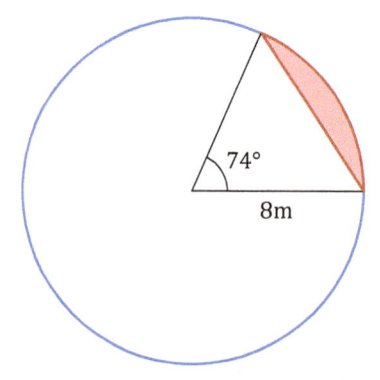

This gives a nice opportunity to interweave the calculation of arc length with the use of the cosine rule, as well as calculation of sector area with triangle area using trigonometry.

Pupils can then potentially play around with this sort of situation, posing questions like, 'What if we knew the perimeter of the segment and the radius? Could we work out the angle?', 'What if we knew the segment area and the angle? Could we work out the radius?' which in some cases lead to some significantly challenging problems.

Chapter 11

Transformation and vectors

To complete our study of geometry, we will now turn our attention to spatial relationships – how objects and shapes relate to each other in two (or higher) dimensional spaces. And for me, the key to this is an understanding of vectors.

In 2015 the English GCSE was redesigned and the basics of vector diagrams and notation were included as content for all learners, where previously they had been reserved only for pupils on the 'Higher' tier. For me this is a very positive move, as it opens up the opportunity for all pupils to really understand spatial relationships and what happens when spaces are transformed. Vectors really underpin all of this and can act as the central representation that allows pupils to connect their understanding of all school-level transformations. So even though vectors (at least in two or more dimensions) are often introduced towards the end of a pupil's school-level maths journey, I am going to start this chapter by looking at vectors.

Concept: vectors

Prerequisites: Number (particularly negatives), addition, subtraction, multiplication, line properties (particularly parallel and perpendicular).

Linked concepts: Gradient, translation, rotation, reflection, enlargement, symmetry, graphing.

If pupils have used vector representations for numbers, then the transition to vectors in two dimensions is relatively straightforward. We can start by highlighting the importance of magnitude and direction with negative numbers – for example, the fact that −8 is a greater magnitude number than 5 but points in the opposite direction, is why the result of adding −8 and 5 is a negative number (i.e. points in the same direction as the −8 and not the 5). We can then draw attention to the comparison between vector representations of numbers with vectors in two dimensions; this is generally enough for pupils to get the idea of using a column representation for the vector:

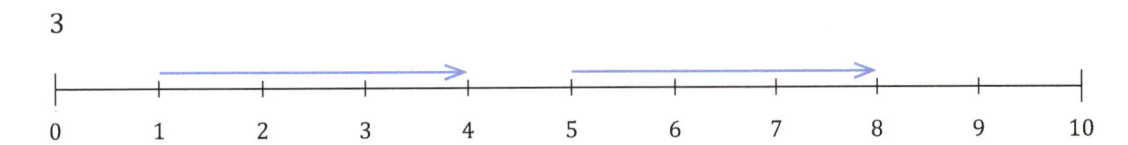

3

$\begin{pmatrix} 3 \\ 2 \end{pmatrix}$

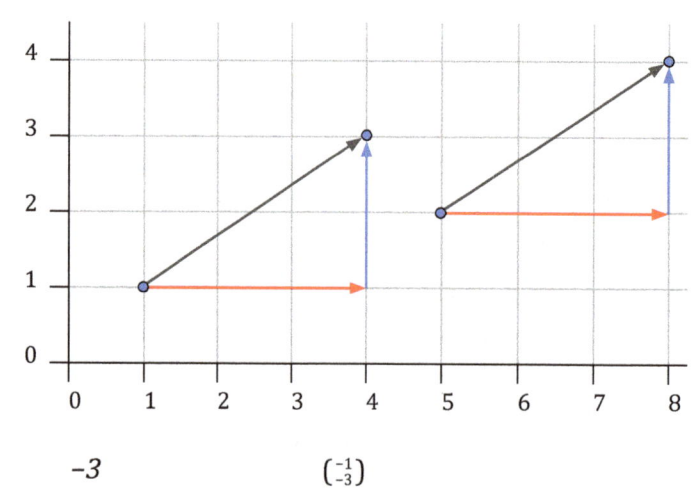

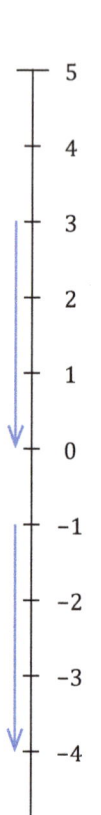

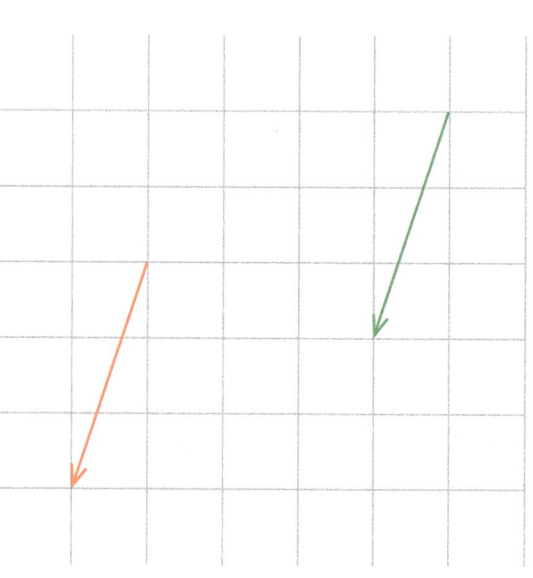

−3 $\begin{pmatrix} -1 \\ -3 \end{pmatrix}$

Using examples like this, tying the two-dimensional vector to the column representation and highlighting the similarity between this and vector representations in one dimension to model numbers, usually leads to pupils quickly gaining a secure grasp of how we represent vectors in two dimensions, particularly if we use a few non-examples (such as straight lines without a specified direction, or curved lines). This could simply be through an activity where pupils have to write down the column representation for vectors that we show to the class (perhaps using mini whiteboards or a digital alternative) and then have some of the pictures show the non-examples to prompt the discussion around why these objects are not vectors. Alongside these we can introduce the underline and bold notation for vectors, so writing $a = \begin{pmatrix} 3 \\ 2 \end{pmatrix}$ if handwriting or $b = \begin{pmatrix} -1 \\ -3 \end{pmatrix}$ when typing.

Once pupils are happy with the links between column representation and the vector diagram, then we can start to explore some of the relationships between vectors. For example, we can explore what happens when we keep the magnitude of the vectors the same but reverse their direction:

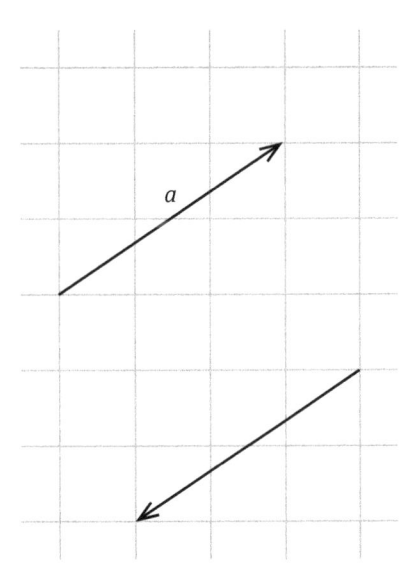

Pupils who have a secure grasp of directed number generally have little trouble seeing that this is the vector −a and that this leads to the values in the column representation changing sign, i.e. if $a = \binom{3}{2}$, then $-a = \binom{-3}{-2}$. It is worth exploring a few examples to embed the mechanics (no pun intended) of this, being sure to include some initial vectors where either one or both of the values in the column representation is already negative so that we reinforce with pupils that the additive inverse of a negative value is a positive value.

We can also offer pupils vectors that are parallel to a but are a different length – probably an integer multiple until pupils get used to the idea:

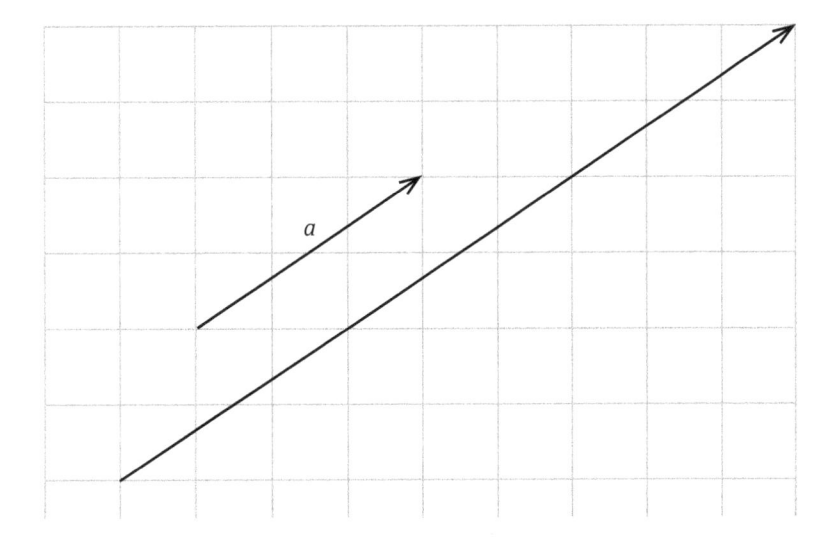

Again, pupils will generally have little trouble in seeing this as three times bigger than a, and so can be written as 3a, with the numbers in the column representation both being multiplied by 3. At this point again, it is worth offering a few of these to pupils to be able to work with, both giving the column vector and asking how it is related to a, and also offering diagrams that pupils can interpret in terms of a. One of my favourite activities to ask pupils to complete is known as a 'Vector hunt', where pupils have to find occurrences or multiples of a given vector:

Given the red vector a, find all the occurrences and multiples of a in the diagram.

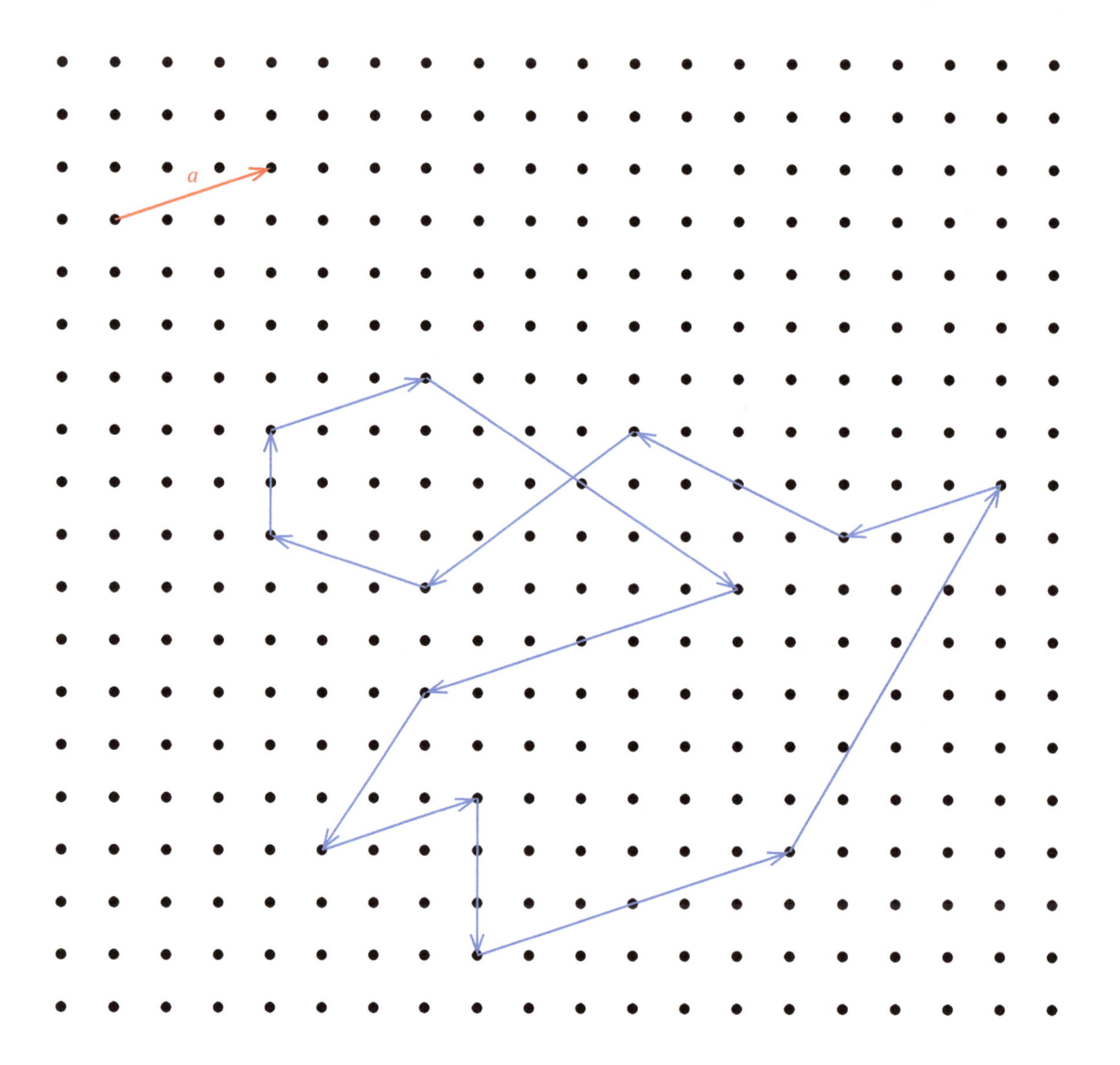

One thing this activity often throws up is the vector $\binom{-3}{1}$ (in the upper left portion of the diagram); pupils often want to say that this is in some way related to a. Of course, it is the same length as a, but not related to a in any other way. This is an important learning point for pupils and it is worth spending some time reinforcing – how vectors with column representations that use values of the same magnitude are related to each other. An activity such as this might be helpful:

Draw each of the vectors $\binom{4}{1}$ $\binom{-4}{1}$ $\binom{4}{-1}$ $\binom{-4}{-1}$ $\binom{1}{4}$ $\binom{-1}{4}$ $\binom{1}{-4}$ $\binom{-1}{-4}$

What do you notice?

Or potentially something like this:

Given $a = \binom{4}{1}$ state which of these vectors are (i) parallel to a (ii) perpendicular to a. Explain why they are all the same length as a.

$\begin{pmatrix}-4\\1\end{pmatrix} \begin{pmatrix}4\\-1\end{pmatrix} \begin{pmatrix}-4\\-1\end{pmatrix} \begin{pmatrix}1\\4\end{pmatrix} \begin{pmatrix}-1\\4\end{pmatrix} \begin{pmatrix}1\\-4\end{pmatrix} \begin{pmatrix}-1\\-4\end{pmatrix}$

This should ideally lead to pupils generalising these relationships:

Given the vector $p = \begin{pmatrix}a\\b\end{pmatrix}$ write down how each of the following relate to p geometrically:

$\begin{pmatrix}-a\\b\end{pmatrix} \begin{pmatrix}-b\\a\end{pmatrix} \begin{pmatrix}b\\-a\end{pmatrix} \begin{pmatrix}-b\\-a\end{pmatrix} \begin{pmatrix}-a\\-b\end{pmatrix}$

There is a strong link here to gradients of lines – pupils may well spot on their own that a vector like $\begin{pmatrix}4\\1\end{pmatrix}$ will have a gradient of $\frac{1}{4}$, and so if pupils have studied gradients, and how the gradients of perpendicular lines relate to each other, then they might reason why the switching of the horizontal and vertical components along with changing the sign of a single component produces a perpendicular vector (for example).

Pupils should also be familiar with representing the addition and subtraction of vectors from vector representations of numbers:

4 + 3 = 7

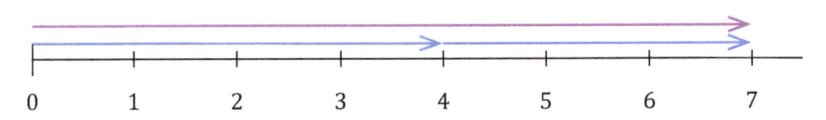

$\begin{pmatrix}4\\1\end{pmatrix} + \begin{pmatrix}1\\2\end{pmatrix} = \begin{pmatrix}5\\3\end{pmatrix}$

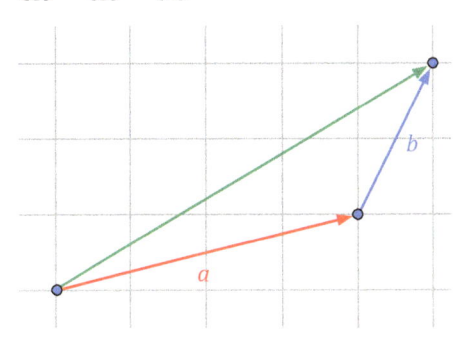

4 + -3 = 1

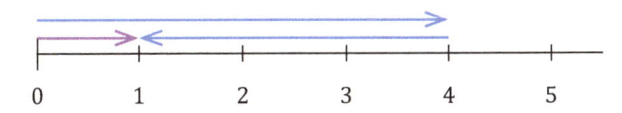

$\begin{pmatrix}4\\1\end{pmatrix} + \begin{pmatrix}-1\\-2\end{pmatrix} = \begin{pmatrix}3\\-1\end{pmatrix}$

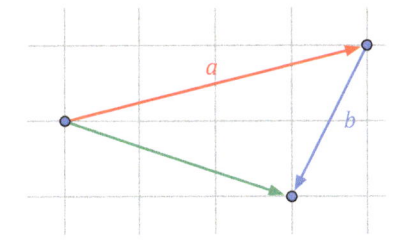

When it comes to subtraction, there are two models that we may have used with pupils:

4 − −3 = 7

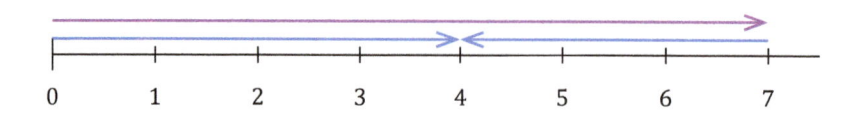

OR

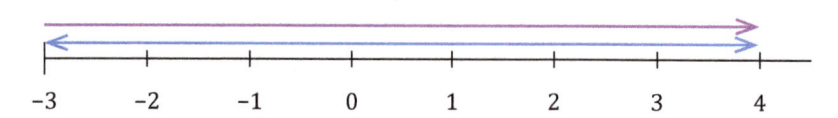

These generalise perfectly to vectors in two dimensions:

$\binom{4}{1} - \binom{1}{2} = \binom{3}{-1}$

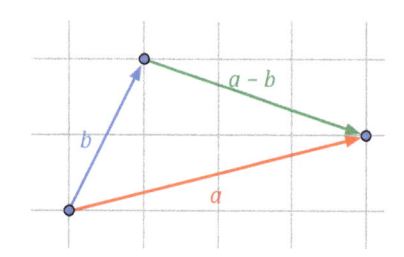

OR

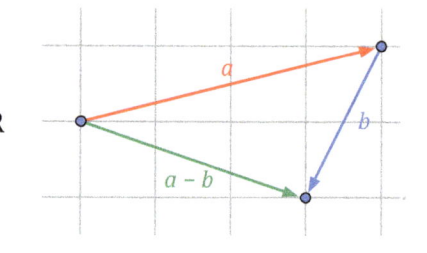

Of course, what we will want pupils to recognise about vector subtraction (which they may already be familiar with from working with numbers) is that $a - b = a + -b$. This is why we used $-b$ when modelling vector addition, so that we can draw the parallels with vector subtraction:

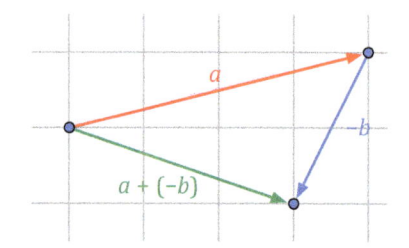

$\binom{4}{1} + \binom{-1}{-2} = \binom{3}{-1}$ $\binom{4}{1} - \binom{1}{2} = \binom{3}{-1}$

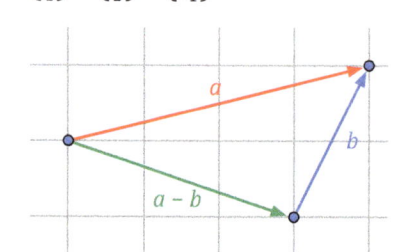

A nice activity to prompt pupil thinking here is the vector addition and subtraction matching activity. In this activity pupils are provided pictures of vector diagrams, some involving a and b, with others involving a and $-b$.

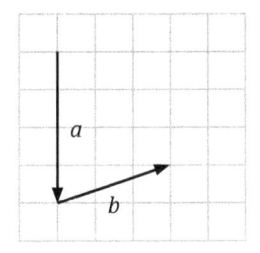

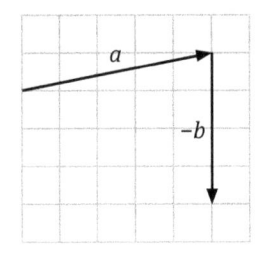

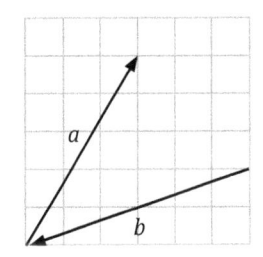

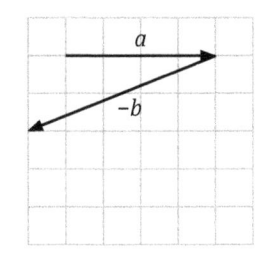

Pupils are then provided with cards that show the column representations of the vectors a and b (causing them to have to think again about how a picture of $-b$ relates to the column vector of b).

$$a = \begin{pmatrix} 0 \\ -4 \end{pmatrix}$$
$$b = \begin{pmatrix} 3 \\ 1 \end{pmatrix}$$

$$a = \begin{pmatrix} 5 \\ 2 \end{pmatrix}$$
$$b = \begin{pmatrix} 0 \\ 4 \end{pmatrix}$$

$$a = \begin{pmatrix} 3 \\ 5 \end{pmatrix}$$
$$b = \begin{pmatrix} -6 \\ -2 \end{pmatrix}$$

$$a = \begin{pmatrix} 4 \\ 0 \end{pmatrix}$$
$$b = \begin{pmatrix} 5 \\ 2 \end{pmatrix}$$

$$a + b = \begin{pmatrix} 3 \\ -3 \end{pmatrix}$$

$$a - b = \begin{pmatrix} 5 \\ -2 \end{pmatrix}$$

$$a - b = \begin{pmatrix} 3 \\ -3 \end{pmatrix}$$

$$a - b = \begin{pmatrix} -1 \\ -2 \end{pmatrix}$$

Finally, pupils are given cards showing the calculations from the pictures, with $a + (-b)$ being given as $a - b$.

Pupils, of course, have to match the picture to the two separate vectors, and then to the vector calculation.[1]

Up to this point, all of the vectors we have looked at have been on square grids, so that we can represent them using column vectors. Once pupils are secure and practised with how vector addition and subtraction pictures appear in two dimensions (as well as scalar multiplication and the like from earlier), then we are in a position to take the vectors off a square grid, and to use them in geometrical situations. A nice bridge into geometry is to look at either a triangular or rhomboid grid:

---

[1] P. Mattock, Adding and Subtracting with Vectors Matching Cards, *TES* (8 October 2015). Available at: https://www.tes.com/teaching-resource/adding-and-subtracting-with-vectors-matching-cards-11132334.

Given that the shape below is a regular hexagon, write each of the following in terms of x and y.

Write down each of the following in terms of p and q.

i	$\overrightarrow{AB}$	iii	$\overrightarrow{AC}$	v	$\overrightarrow{CD}$	vii	$\overrightarrow{AE}$	ix	$\overrightarrow{EC}$	xi	$\overrightarrow{FE}$
ii	$\overrightarrow{FC}$	iv	$\overrightarrow{EB}$	vi	$\overrightarrow{AD}$	viii	$\overrightarrow{FB}$	x	$\overrightarrow{FD}$	xii	$\overrightarrow{DB}$

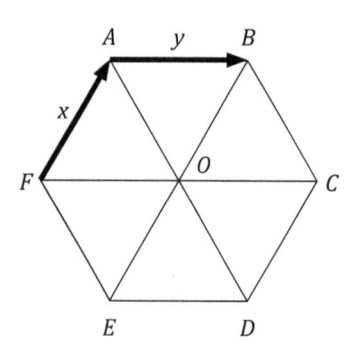

Two vectors p and q are shown on the grid.

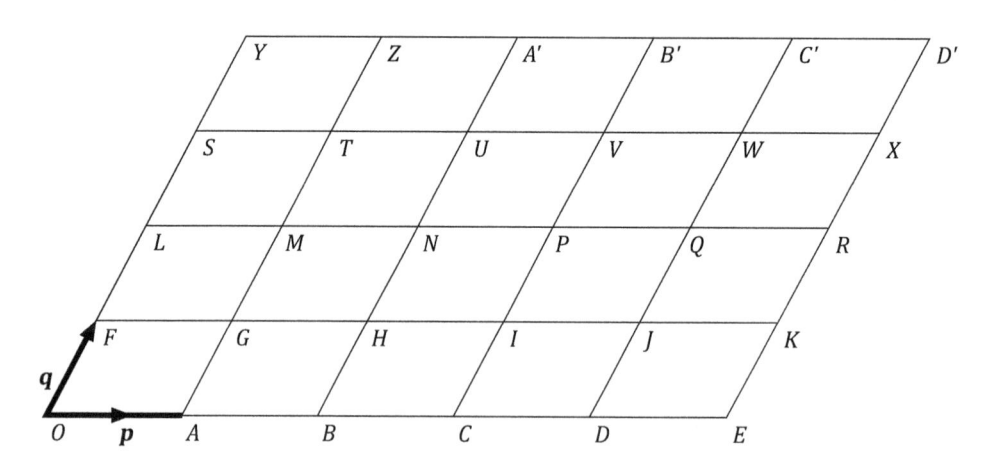

Write down each of the following in terms of p and q.

i	$\overrightarrow{GP}$	ii	$\overrightarrow{MV}$	iii	$\overrightarrow{VM}$	iv	$\overrightarrow{QY}$	v	$\overrightarrow{RM}$	vi	$\overrightarrow{CD}$

Write down, using letters, any vector equal to:

i $2p + 3q$ iii $2p - 3q$ v $3q - 2q$
ii $3p + 2q$ iv $3q - 2p$ vi $-2p + 3q$

From here we can offer pupils potentially more challenging scenarios, where geometric reasoning has to play a part in pupils working out how to represent paths using vectors:

ACPM is a rectangle. Every other point is either the midpoint of a line segment (e.g. *B* is the midpoint of *AC*) or a point of intersection between two line segments (e.g. *G* is the point of intersection between *KB* and *FH*). $\overrightarrow{HL} = a$ and $\overrightarrow{GD} = b$. Write every other possible vector in terms of a and b.

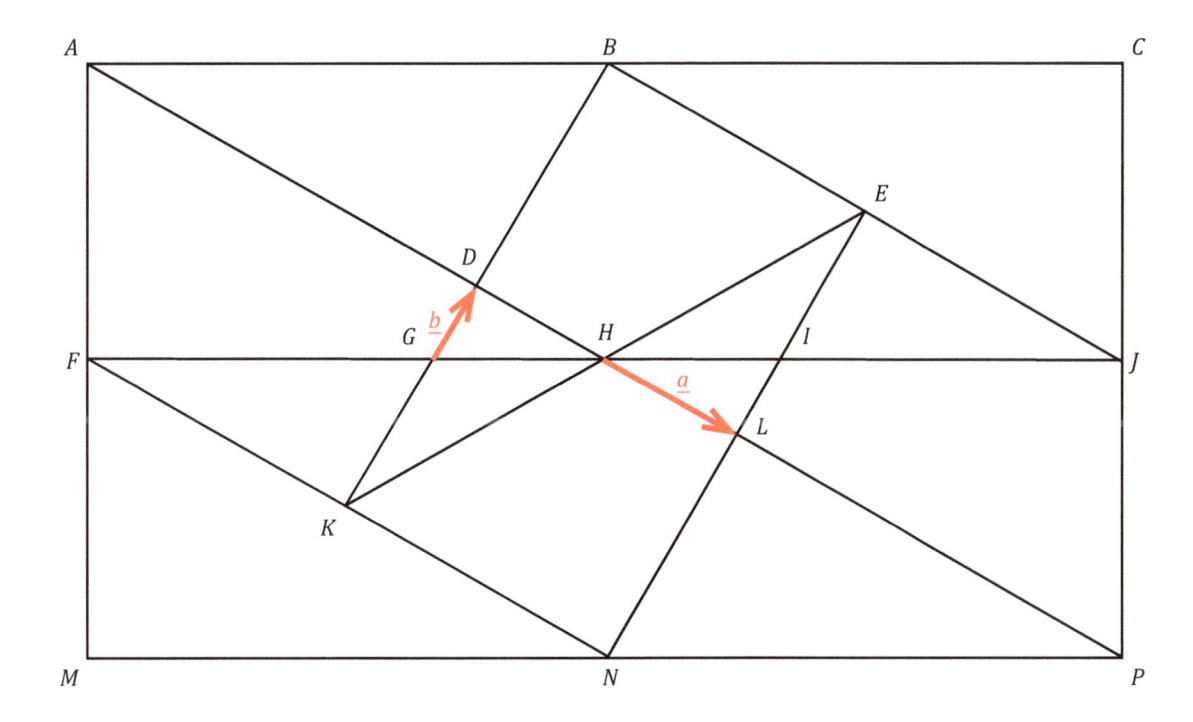

Once pupils are finding vector expressions like these, it is important to highlight or prompt recognition of certain key features – for example, in the diagram above, $\vec{AB} = 3a + 3b$ and $\vec{FG} = 2a + 2b$. Pupils should realise that this implies that $\vec{AB}$ and $\vec{FG}$ are parallel but that $\vec{AB}$ is 1.5 times longer than $\vec{FG}$ (or conversely that $\vec{FG}$ is $\frac{2}{3}$ of $\vec{AB}$).

These sorts of properties are important when it comes to pupils proving geometrical relationships using vectors. A nice follow-on to the above activity is this:[2]

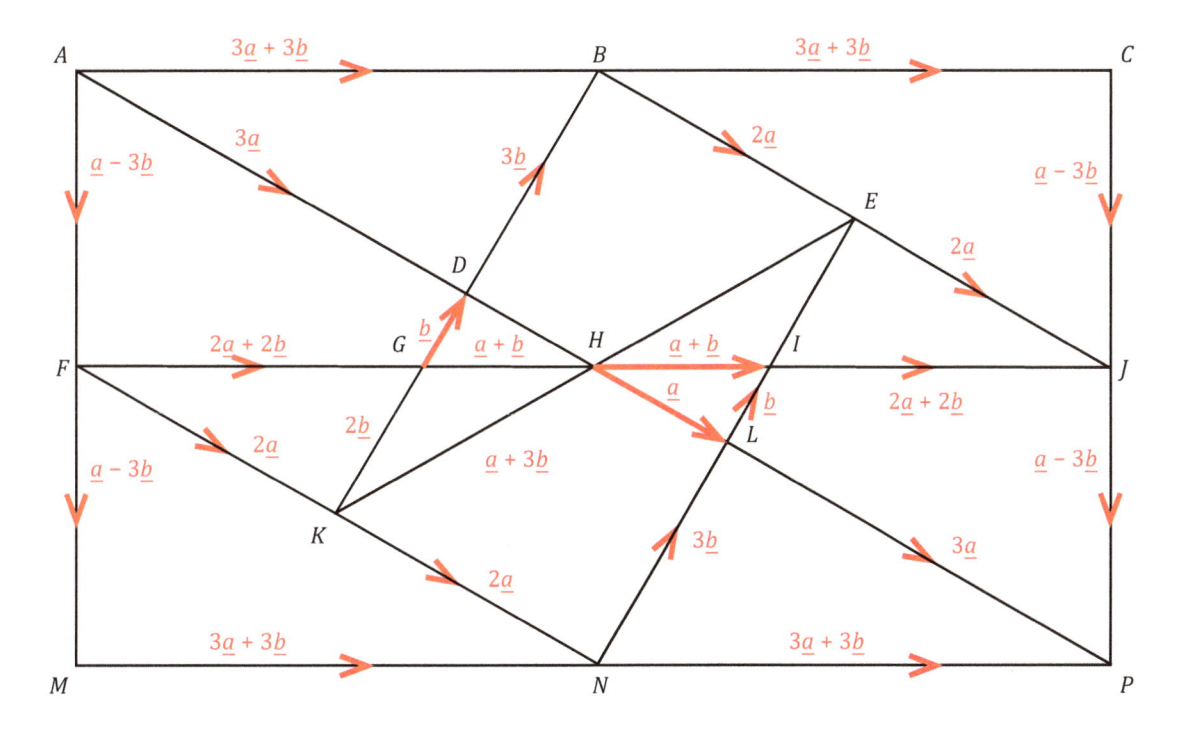

---

2   P. Mattock, Vector Proof, *TES* (17 November 2015). Available at: https://www.tes.com/teaching-resource/vector-proof-11138743.

Which of these points lie on straight lines? Prove your answers.

a *HEC*   b *FDE*   c *MKI*   d *BIP*   e *BHN*   f *AGN*

Work out the ratio of the lengths of the line segments:

a *AL:LP*   b *KG:GB*   c *FI:IJ*   d *KL:LJ*   e *KE:EC*

The point *X* is between *A* and *B* so that *XDN* is a straight line. Find the ratio *AX:XB*.

Past exam questions on geometrical proof using vectors are quite plentiful, and there are lots of different diagrams that vector proof questions can be designed as part of. DrFrostMaths has a 'Full Coverage' paper that includes multiple questions for vector proof, as well as other area of vectors.[3]

It may well be that we will not transition from introduction to vectors all the way to geometrical proof using vectors in quick succession, and there may be months or even years between them. However, if we are going to study the mathematical properties of transformation, then at least a secure understanding of the basics of vectors will be critical.

Concept: translation

Prerequisites: Number, basic direction.

Linked concepts: Vectors, rotation, reflection, enlargement, congruence, graphing.

When it comes to teaching translations at school level, one thing that pupils often don't appreciate is that every point in the two-dimensional space is translated. We often focus our attention on the effect of a translation on a particular set of points that form the vertices, perimeter or area of a given shape, but pupils should ideally understand that this is just the effect we choose to focus on. In fact, when introducing translations, it may well be more useful for pupils' long-term learning to focus on a single point rather than a whole shape:

Show the position of the image when the point *A* is translated 8 units right and 5 units down.

---

3   DrFrostMaths, Full Coverage: Vectors (n.d.). Available at: https://www.drfrostmaths.com/resource.php?rid=341.

State the coordinates of the image point when the point (3, 2) is translated 2 units left and 4 units down.

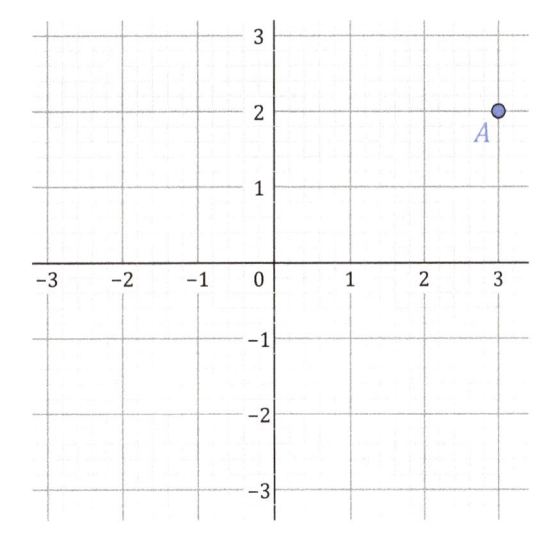

As well as carrying out a translation on a point, pupils should be asked to describe a translation:

The object point *P* is translated so that its image is *P'*. Describe the translation.

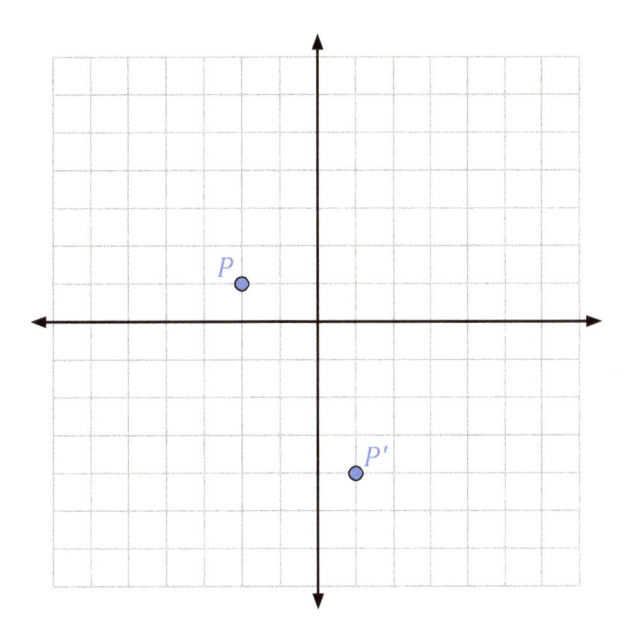

We could also use a 'fill in the blanks' style response as part of this question:

___ right and ___ down   OR

3 ___ and 5 _____

Introducing translation in this way will help pupils make sense of what is happening when we then examine translation applied to shapes and/or graphs – seeing it as the movement of a collection of points.

Show the position of the image when the shaded triangle is 3 units right and 2 units up.

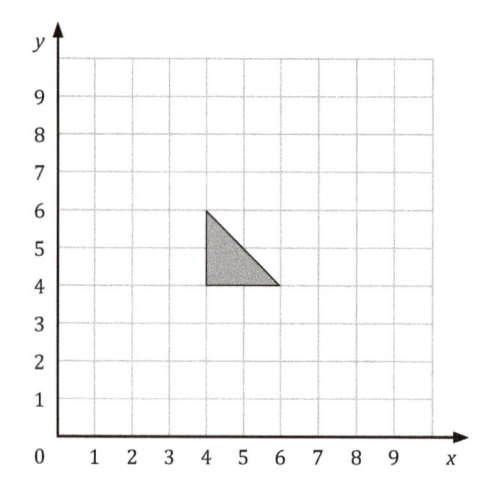

Another potential mistake that teachers might make here is to focus too early on the vertices of a triangle. Although eventually we will want pupils to understand that one of the easiest ways to find the image of a translated shape is to examine the image of the vertices, we don't want to lose the idea that a translation affects every point. In early explanations it is worth choosing points along edges as well as at the vertices, and potentially even inside the perimeter of the shape. In this case, we could use the points (4, 5); (5, 4); (5, 5) or even (4.5, 4.5) in addition to points (4, 4); (4, 6) and (6, 4).

The triangle ABC is translated to give the triangle $A'B'C'$. Describe the translation.

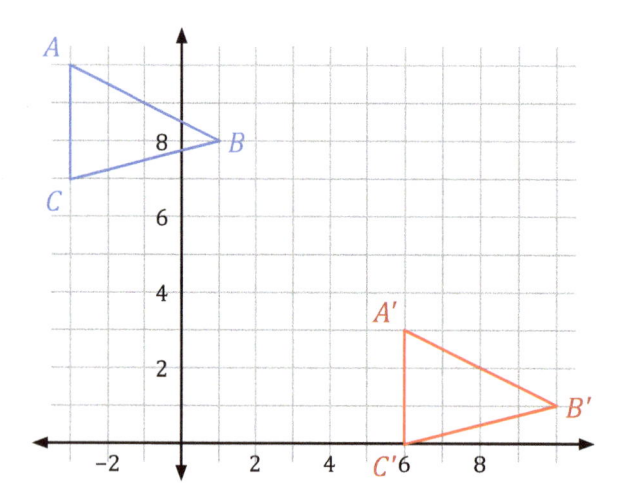

Having used a coordinate grid, we can also then begin to examine the numerical effect of the translation on the coordinates – that the image of, say, (5, 4) in the first question will become (8, 6) as it increases the x ordinate by 3 and the y ordinate by 2. Eventually, this will lead into the use of position vectors as part of a vector sum, but initially this will help with the introduction of using vectors to describe the translation. Again, I personally think that when introducing vectors to describe a translation, it is worth going back to a single point:

The point P is translated so that it follows the path of the vector $\binom{6}{-7}$. Mark the position of the point P', the image of P.

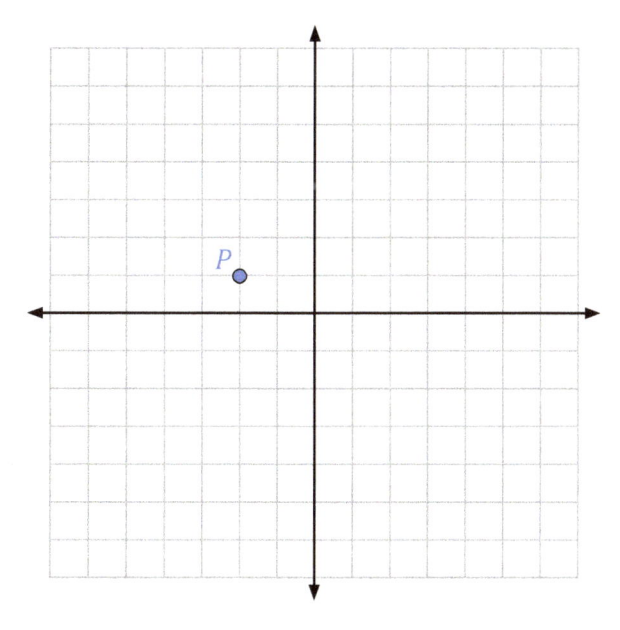

Pupils should also be asked to write down the column representation of the vector that describes how an object point translates to an image point, before graduating to doing the same thing with shapes.

The triangle IRT is translated to give the triangle I'R'T'. Use a vector to describe the path each point takes under the translation.

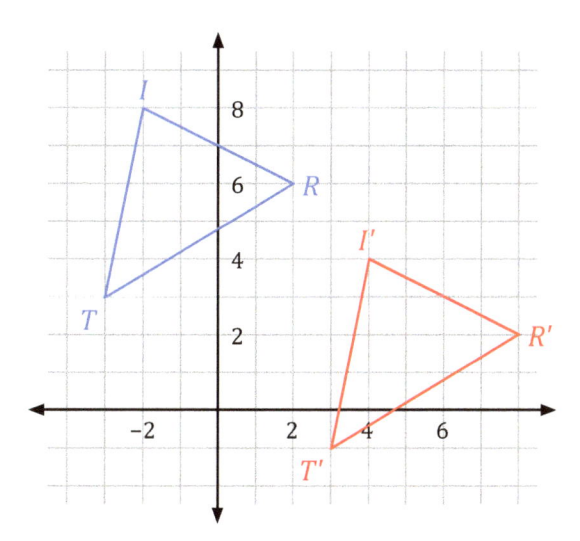

Eventually, we would look to simplify the language a little in these questions, but in early examples I want to make sure pupils are reminded that every point moves, as well as the vector being a vehicle to describe the path that the point follows (which will basically become the 'translation vector'). We will also want pupils to carry out the translation of multiple points using a vector to describe the translation.

The triangle ABC is translated so that every point follows the vector $\binom{4}{-1}$. Show the image A'B'C' of triangle ABC.

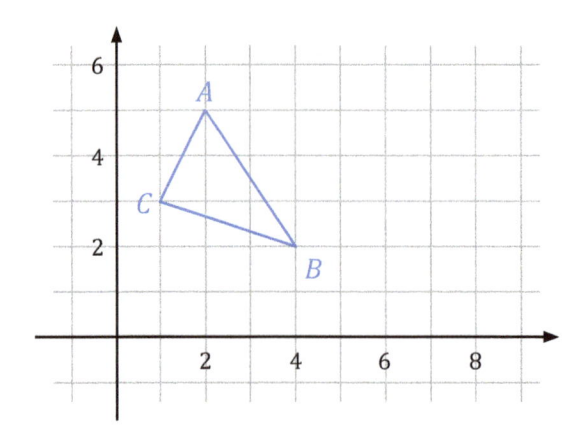

Often, this is as far as pupils go with using vectors to complete or describe translations. However, there are many more questions or activities we might offer that reinforce knowledge and understanding of both concepts. For example, once pupils have moved to summing vectors, we might offer simple questions that link this to repeated translation, such as:

The point P is translated to the point P' using vector $\binom{5}{-2}$. P' is then translated to P" using the vector $\binom{2}{7}$. Give the vector that would translate P directly to P".

Going forward, once pupils have been introduced to vectors on shapes other than rectilinear spaces, we might even offer pupils the opportunity to link this use of vectors with transformation.

Given the vectors *a* and *b* as marked, translate the shaded triangle using the vector:

i   2*a*   ii   2*a* − *b*   iii   2*a* + *b*   iv   *a* + 2*b*

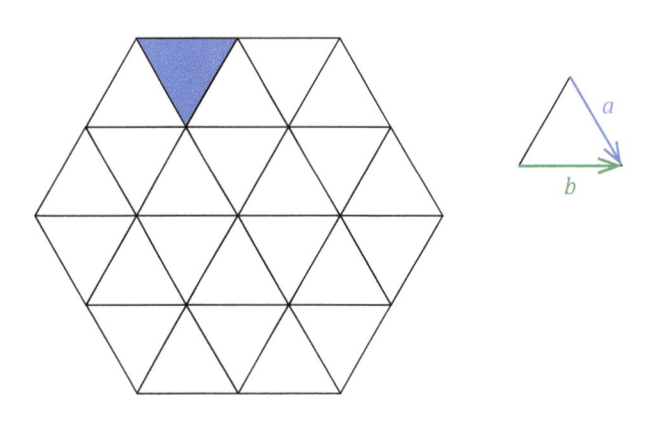

This sort of activity allows for greater interweaving of the higher end vector work with translation, providing greater insight into both concepts.

Although translation is the transformation most closely associated with vectors, all transformations benefit from an understanding of vectors. We will see this as we now begin to explore reflection.

Transformation and vectors

Concept: reflection

Prerequisites: Number (particularly negatives), line properties.

Linked concepts: Vectors, rotation, translation, enlargement, congruence, graphing.

Reflection is introduced very early in pupils' learning about geometry. This is often in creating symmetrical pictures: I think we have all done the activity where we fold a piece of paper in half, paint a picture in one half of the paper and then fold it over to create the other half of the picture. This will often then become using a mirror to identify lines of symmetry within different shapes.

These early introductions to reflection and reflective symmetry are nice, and they give a reasonable basis for later exploration of reflection and reflective symmetry. However, what this tends to develop is a more intuitive approach to reflection, which can sometimes mean pupils struggle to apply techniques to even the smallest increase in difficulty. I am sure we have all seen pupils make this mistake:

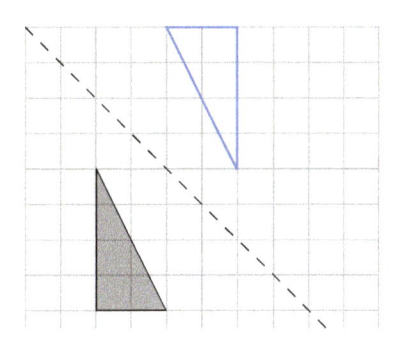

Often the solution to this is to bring in the use of tracing paper to help assist with completing the reflections. However, whilst this might help pupils carry out the reflection, or see that their initial attempt is incorrect, it doesn't really help pupils see the key idea underlying reflection – perpendicularity. For this, we can employ vectors.

If we first start with reflections in horizontal or vertical lines, pupils' intuitive ideas will initially serve them well, which we can build on. For example, offering pupils things like this:

Reflect these shapes in the given mirror lines.

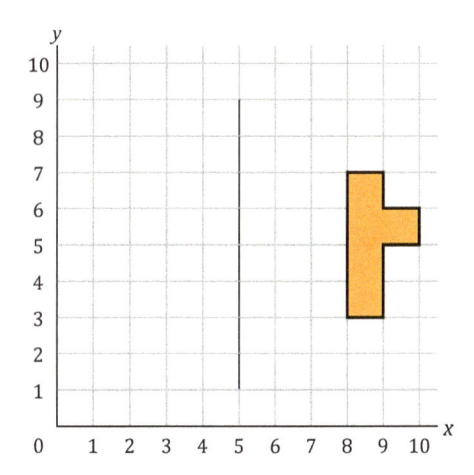

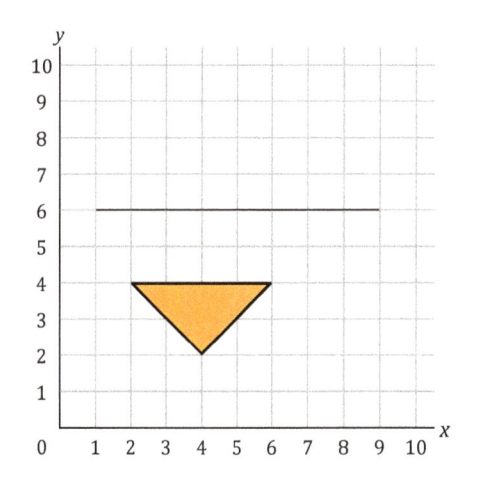

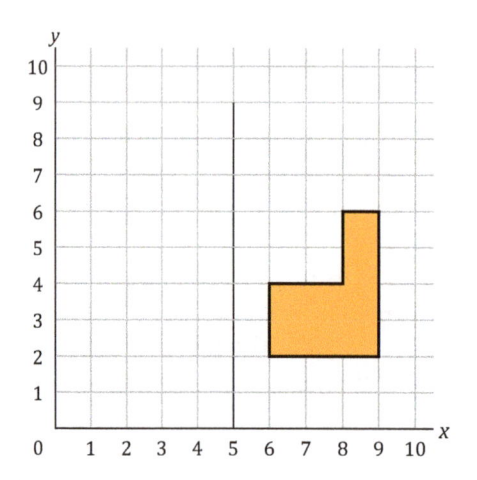

We can then use these as a vehicle to highlight some key ideas to pupils:

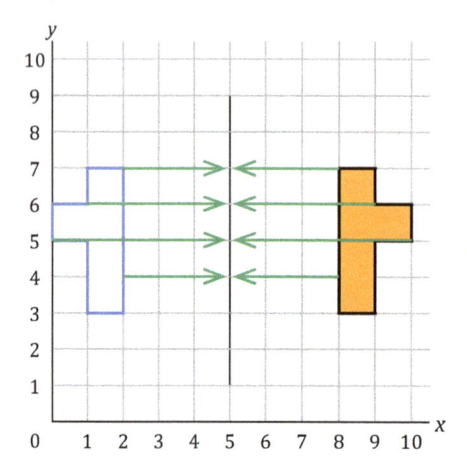

In particular, we want pupils to see that the vectors from the points on the object shape to the mirror line and the vectors from the image shape to the mirror line are the negative of each other, as long as the vectors are perpendicular to the mirror line. Pupils recognising this means they can then apply the same idea to finding mirror lines for shapes that have already been reflected (noticing the inclusion of mirror lines that are not perfectly along the grid lines).

Find the mirror line that would mean shape *B* is a reflection of shape *A*:

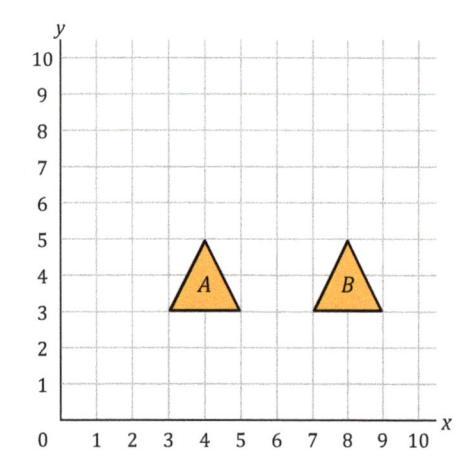

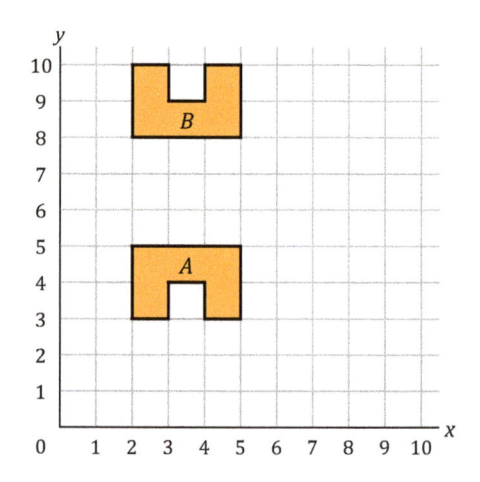

Pupils should recognise that if they identify the vectors connecting object points to image points, then the perpendicular bisector of these vectors (there should, of course, only be one) will be the mirror line:

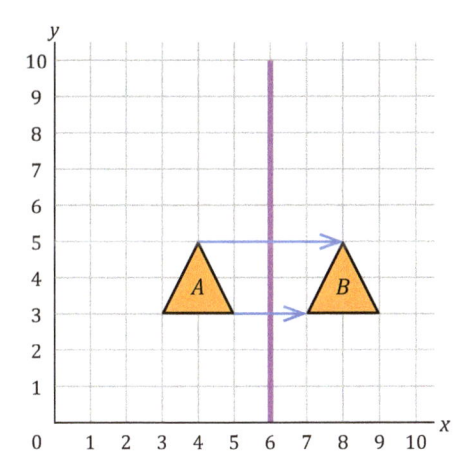

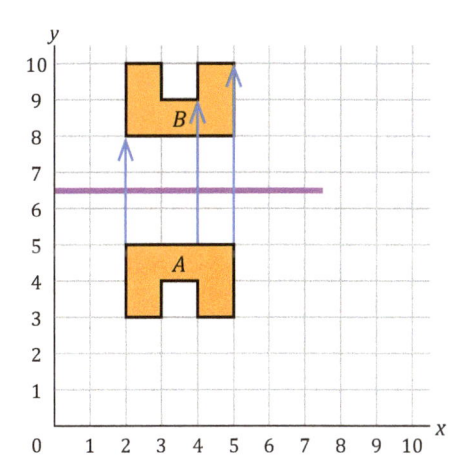

Importantly though, these ideas can also be applied when mirror lines are not horizontal or vertical, particularly if we support pupils in recognising that the fact that the perpendicular vectors from the object and image to the mirror line are the negative of each other means that whatever the perpendicular vector from the object to the mirror line is, we can simply repeat this to find the position of the image point. When first exploring reflection with straight lines that are not horizontal or vertical, we should approach it by looking at a single point in a similar way to our initial introduction of translation:

Find the position of the image point when the point P is reflected in the given line.

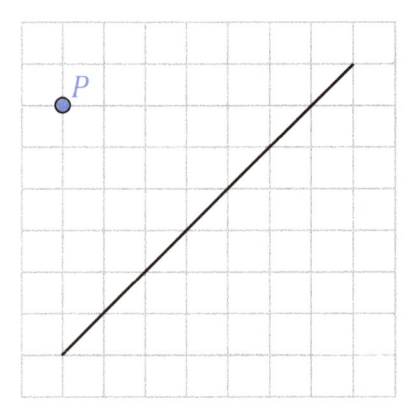

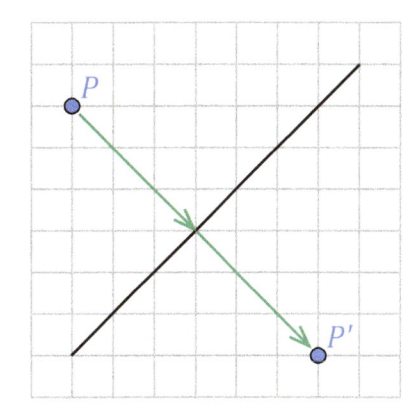

before progressing on to reflecting shapes in sloped lines:

Reflect the shaded triangle in the given mirror line.

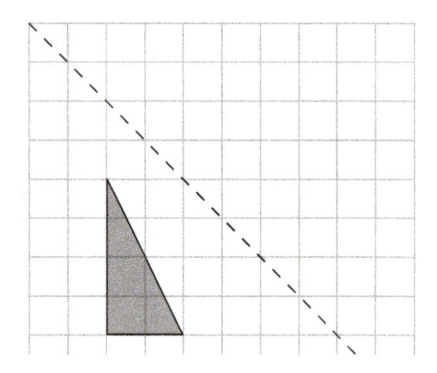

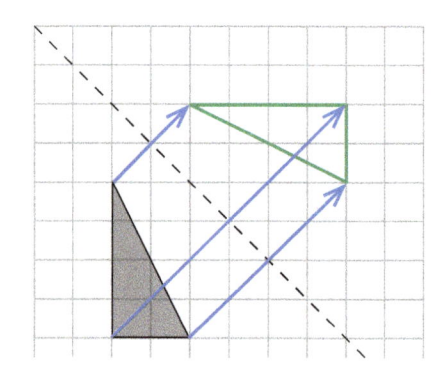

including lines that are not sloped at 45°.

Reflect the point *P* in the given mirror line:

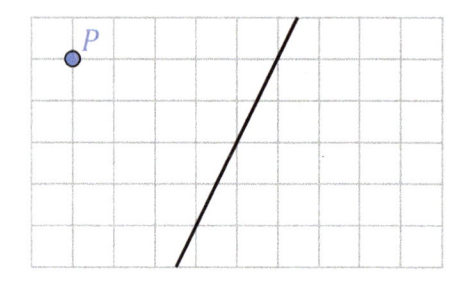

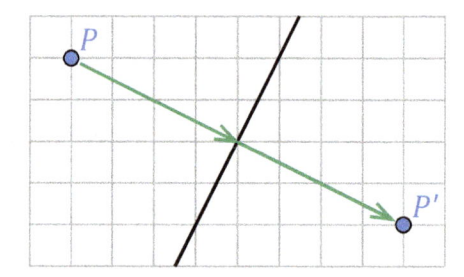

However, it is worth noting that asking pupils to reflect shapes in a line that isn't horizontal, vertical or sloped at 45° can be difficult, particularly if the vectors don't meet the mirror lines at the corner of a square. Tracing paper can help with this a little or very careful question choosing.

Find the mirror line that will reflect the point *P* onto the point *P'*.

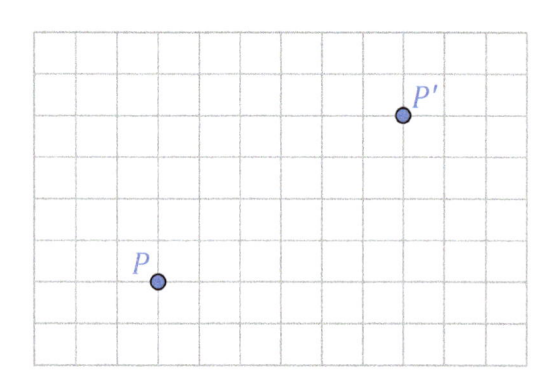

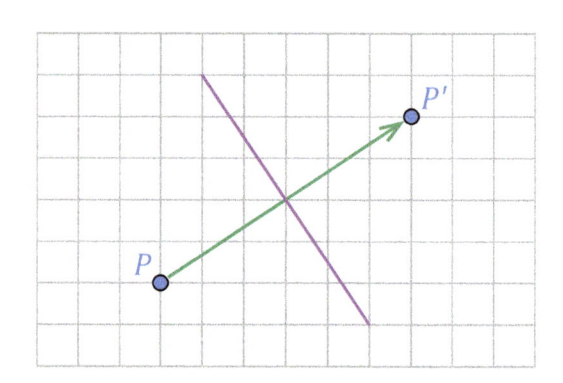

In the same way as vectors, we should also offer pupils the opportunity to reflect points/shapes in lines that don't appear on a rectilinear grid:

Show the position of the shaded triangle when it is reflected in the line.

   i   *AE*   ii *JB*   iii *IJ*   iv *CJ*

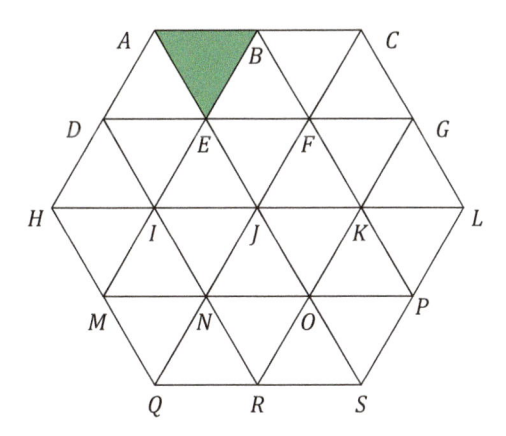

There will be further opportunities to interweave other skills with reflection. We will see in Chapter 13 how reflections can be linked to finding or using the equation of a straight line, and how it links to changes in the algebraic definition of a function. For now though, we will progress on to looking at rotation.

Concept: rotation

Prerequisites: Number (particularly negatives), angle, time.

Linked concepts: Vectors, reflection, translation, enlargement, congruence, graphing, trigonometry.

Similarly to reflection, rotation will be introduced in a basic way through talking about quarter turns, half turns, three-quarter turns, etc. Again, this gives a reasonable basis for exploring rotation but can lead to misunderstanding if we then don't reintroduce the concept carefully, in particular the importance of the centre of rotation.

Pupils will already have experience of the idea of orbit, being aware of things like the Moon orbiting the Earth and the Earth and other planets orbiting the Sun. I find this an invaluable 'hook' in introducing the study of rotation and the role of the centre of rotation. Pupils should come to understand that when we rotate, we rotate all points around the centre (except for the centre itself, of course) in the same way that all planets orbit the Sun. Again, this is best introduced by starting with a single point:

Rotate the point P through 90° clockwise centre O.

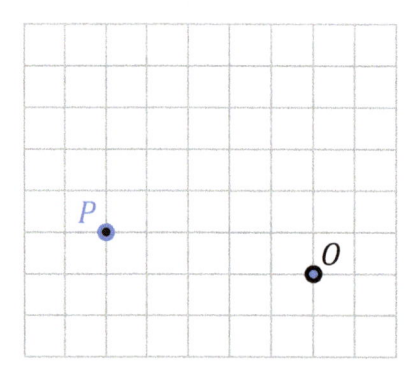

Pupils may use tracing paper to help with this, but if pupils have previously studied vectors, then an understanding of vectors can help pupils see what is happening when they rotate a shape (as well as supporting when the rotations are not so straightforward). In this case, the vector $\vec{OP} = \begin{pmatrix} -5 \\ 1 \end{pmatrix}$ and when the vector is rotated 90° clockwise it becomes $\begin{pmatrix} 1 \\ 5 \end{pmatrix}$. This means the vector $\vec{OP'} = \begin{pmatrix} 1 \\ 5 \end{pmatrix}$.

If pupils are familiar with perpendicular gradients/vectors then rotation through 90° is a nice place to bring back those skills. If pupils are studying rotations before looking at vectors/perpendicular gradients, then we should come back to rotation when exploring these concepts and use them as a vehicle for revisiting and creating connections with rotation.

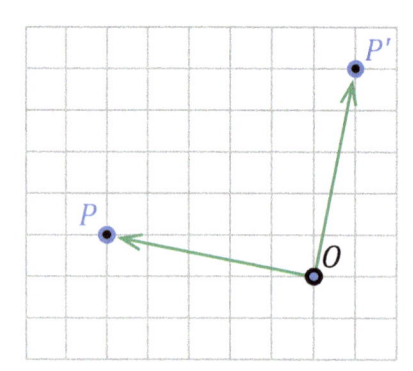

A rotation of 180° can be dealt with in a very similar way: if pupils have already studied vectors (as suggested) then they may well already be familiar with the idea that a 180° rotation creates the negative of a vector and be able to apply this to a rotation of 180°:

Rotate P through 180° centre O.

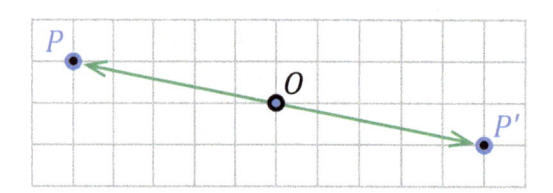

It is always worth asking pupils why a rotation of 180° doesn't require a direction with it, just to make sure they recognise the reason. We can then start to develop this to include rotating on shapes:

Rotate the shaded shape through each of the given instructions.

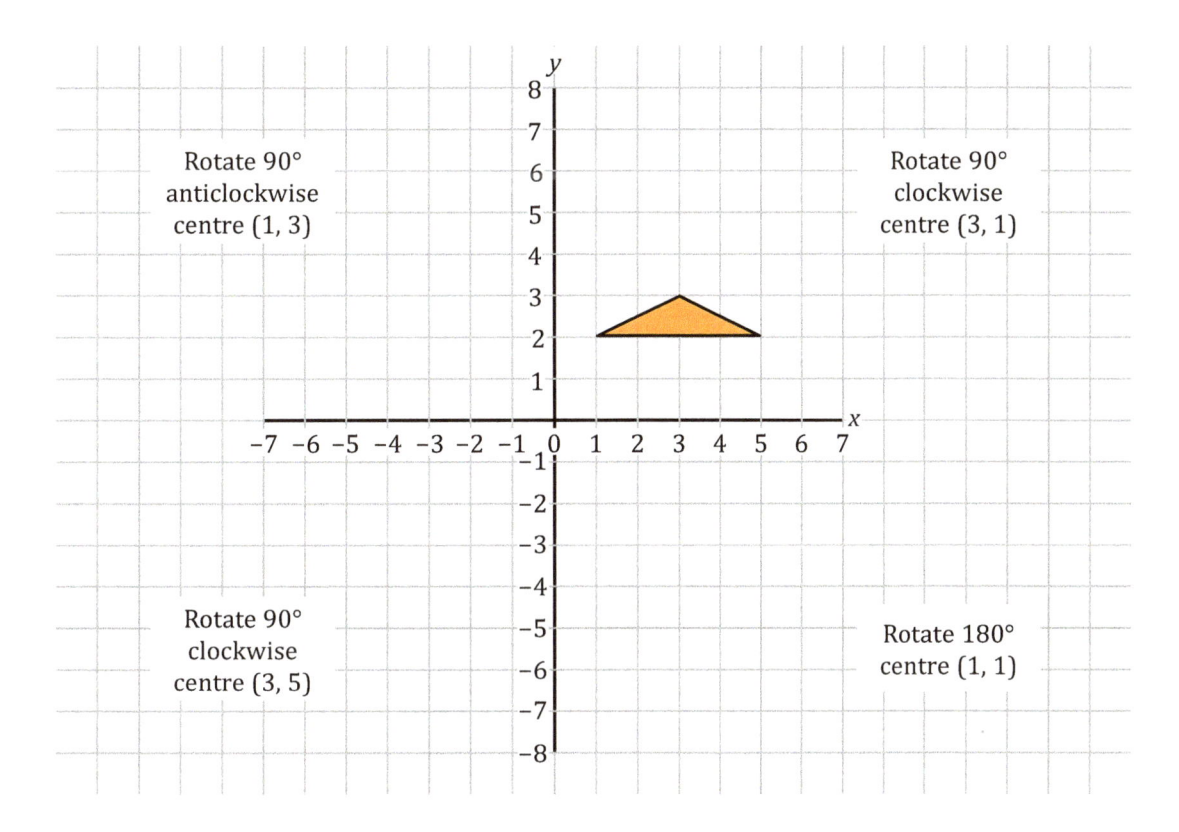

Rotate 90° anticlockwise centre (1, 3)

Rotate 90° clockwise centre (3, 1)

Rotate 90° clockwise centre (3, 5)

Rotate 180° centre (1, 1)

When it comes to working out what rotation has taken place, the often difficult part is establishing the centre of rotation. There are potentially two ways we can approach this:

1. Look at individual points, recognising that there are infinitely many rotations that could take one point to another. Then use the understanding developed to support working with rotated shapes.

2. Start with shapes, using the change in orientation to determine the angle and direction, and then use strategies to find the centre of rotation.

Take points *P* and *P'* as an example of the first approach:

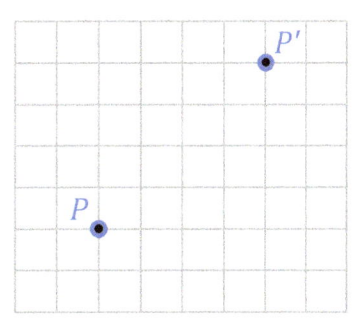

There are some potentially more obvious rotations that could map P to P':

Rotation of 180° centre O.

Rotation of 90° clockwise centre O.

Rotation of 90° anticlockwise centre O.

There are others beside these three, but for now, pupils will likely only be able to identify 90° or 180° rotations. Pupils can then take this understanding into identifying the centre of rotation when one shape has been rotated to another:

Describe the rotation that takes rectangle ABCD to A'B'C'D'.

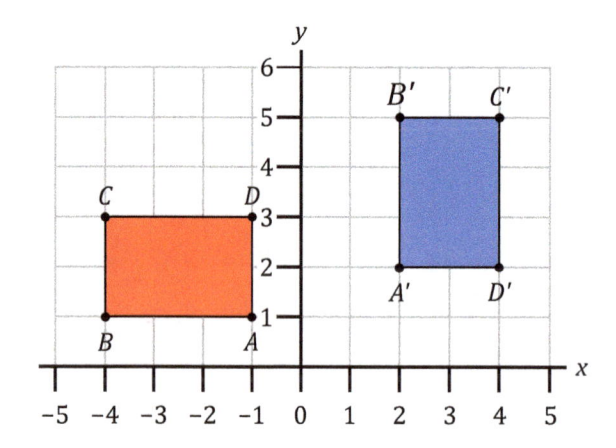

Looking first at A to A', we can potentially identify three rotations that would complete the transformation:

1. Rotation of 180°, centre (0.5, 1.5).
2. Rotation of 90° clockwise, centre (1, 0).
3. Rotation of 90° anticlockwise, centre (0, 3).

Of these, the only one that works for the other points is the second, and so this is the correct rotation.

Alternatively, there are different strategies to determining the centre of rotation if we already know the angle a shape has been rotated through. In a 180° rotation, the vectors connecting object and image points will intersect at the centre of rotation:

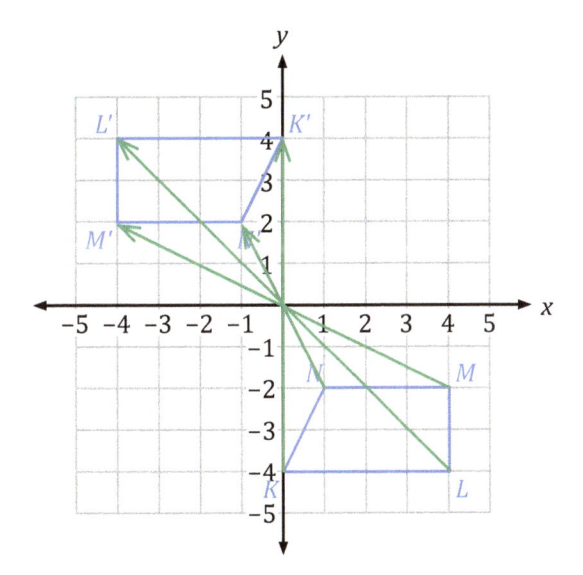

In this case, we can see that the rotation is 180° centre (0, 0). The reason this works (as you will have noticed) is that not only do all the vectors intersect, but they all bisect each other. In effect, what this does is create two vectors each of the same length that are the negatives of each other, i.e. at 180° to each other.

If we then consider a 90° rotation (either clockwise or anticlockwise):

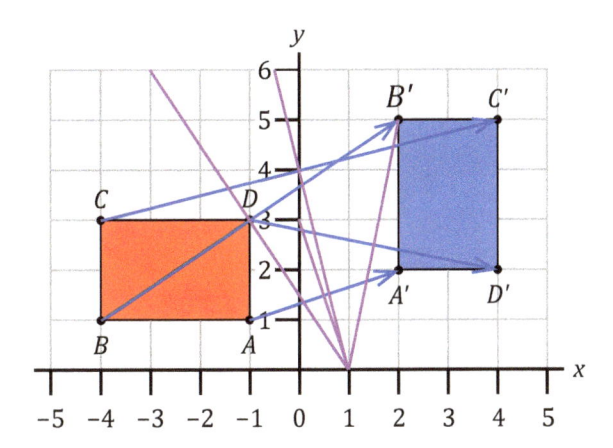

We can see that initially we create the vectors from the object points to the image points (which don't bisect each other as there isn't a 180° rotation). We then create the perpendicular bisector of each vector, with the centre of rotation being the point of intersection of the perpendicular bisectors. However, we can see this is quite a complicated and messy diagram, which may not add much in the way of insight into the concept.

In addition to creating and describing rotations of 90° or 180° on a rectilinear grid, we can bring in other shapes on which to complete rotations. These tend to be where the use of vectors helps more than the use of tracing paper – turning paper through 90° or 180° is more rooted in pupils' early experience (quarter turns, half turns) than say a 60° angle on a triangular space:

Rotate each shaded shape 60° clockwise about the marked centre.

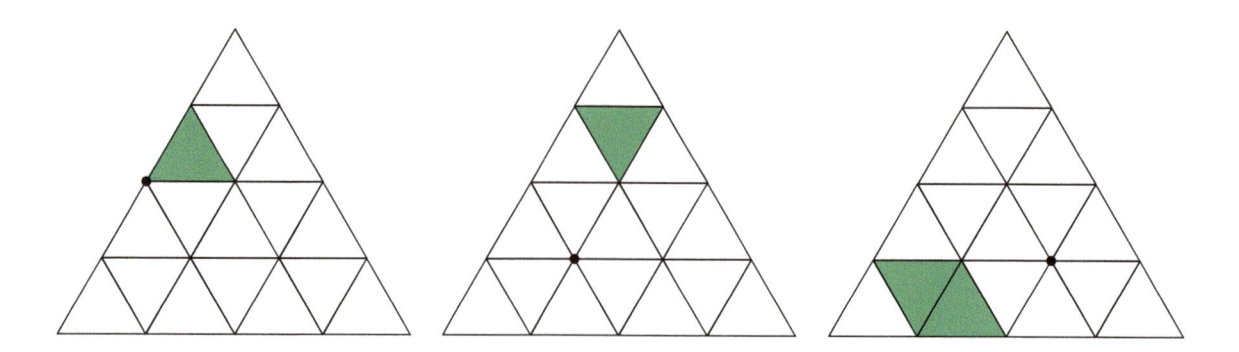

I created an activity that has a few examples and questions of this type to stretch pupil understanding and experience of rotation.[4]

A further nice link to make is the link with trigonometry, and using trigonometry to work out coordinates of points rotated through angles other than 90° and 180°:

The point (2, 0) is rotated by 70° anticlockwise about centre (0, 0). Work out the coordinates of the image point.

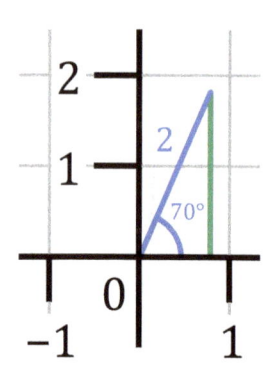

Pupils might need the sketch (either by being provided it or being prompted to draw it themselves if necessary) and occasionally will need to be reminded that the coordinate is made up of the horizontal and vertical distance from the origin. This, and questions like it (including increasing difficulty by making the angle greater than 90° or moving the centre of rotation away from the origin), serve as a really good way of interweaving knowledge of rotation and knowledge of trigonometry – potentially increasing the depth of understanding of both concepts.

Before we move on to the final transformation that is studied pre-16 (at least in England), we need to examine a concept with links to both reflection and rotation, but that is rarely re-examined as pupils learn more about these concepts.

---

[4] P. Mattock, Rotations on a Triangular Grid, *TES* (12 May 2021). Available at: https://www.tes.com/teaching-resource/rotations-on-a-triangular-grid-12528910.

Transformation and vectors

Concept: symmetry

Prerequisites: Numbers (particularly fractions), shape (particularly polygons).

Linked concepts: Vectors, reflection, rotation.

Subconcept: line symmetry

Symmetry is one of the first geometrical properties that pupils are introduced to – in English schools this is as early as Year 2 (as young as 6 years old).[5] This is often in the context of folding paper – folding shapes in half so that both halves overlap. This is a reasonable basis for a more thorough exploration of symmetry; however, there is a danger that pupils will confuse 'folding in half' with 'cutting in half' – this is something we need to be very aware of as it is very typical for pupils to confuse these two, particularly when it comes to rectangles, parallelograms and scalene triangles:

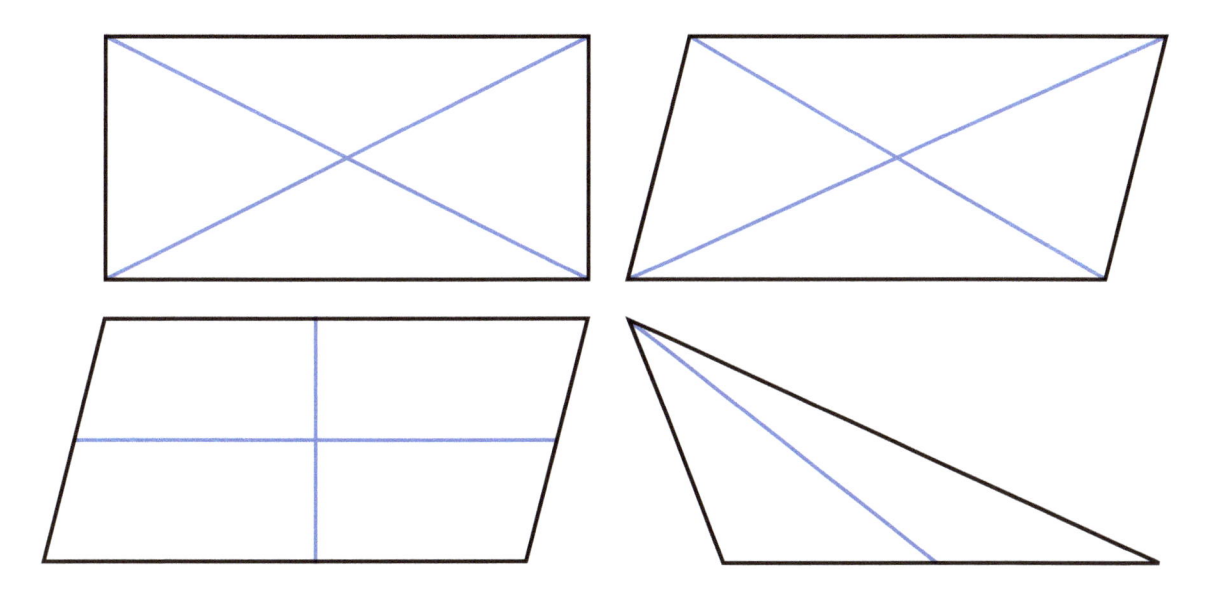

Pupils will often mistake the blue lines in these pictures as lines of symmetry, as they do cut the shape into two equal pieces, but the two pieces will not fold along those lines so that the two pieces overlap. This is something that needs to be explicitly examined with pupils repeatedly throughout their learning around symmetry and reflection.

One place where we should prompt pupils to revisit line symmetry is when exploring polygon properties. There are some nice links to be made with diagonals:

> For which quadrilaterals is at least one diagonal also a line of symmetry? Which quadrilaterals have both diagonals as lines of symmetry. Do you notice anything about the quadrilaterals that have one/two diagonals as lines of symmetry?

In addition to exploring the links between diagonals and symmetry, an obvious relationship to prompt pupils to explore is the link between number of sides and polygons (especially

---

[5] Department for Education, *Mathematics Programmes of Study: Key Stages 1 and 2 National Currciulum in England.*

regular polygons). I particularly like to get pupils drawing (or at least sketching) shapes that have certain numbers of lines of symmetry:

Draw shapes to complete each section of the grid. If a section can't be filled in, say why.

	Number of sides			
Lines of symmetry	3	4	5	6
0				
1				
2				
3				
4				

Pupils should start to recognise the fact that in regular polygons, the number of sides is equal to the number of lines of symmetry, but also that the number of lines of symmetry is either 0 or a factor of the number of sides. This can open up opportunities for pupils to try and reason why this might have to be the case.

In addition to identifying lines of symmetry, pupils should also be offered the opportunity to complete pictures so that they are symmetrical. These can start as relatively simple polygons:

Complete this picture so that the red dotted line is a line of symmetry.

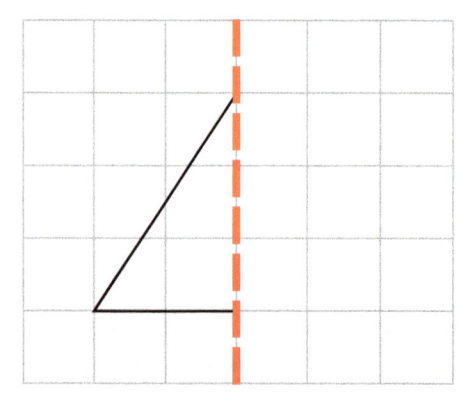

to more complicated polygons (or even curved shapes):

Complete this picture so that the red dotted line is a line of symmetry.

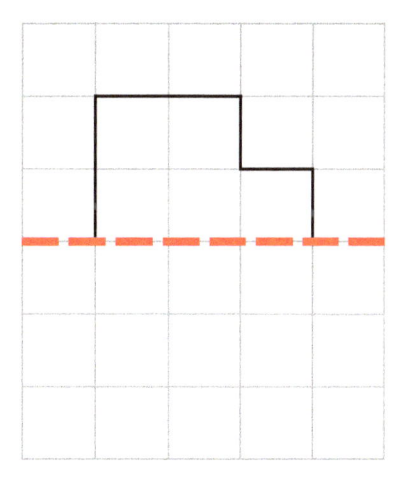

This experience will be crucial in the beginning to explore reflection with pupils more generally, making the link between the last question and this question:

Reflect the given shape in the mirror line.

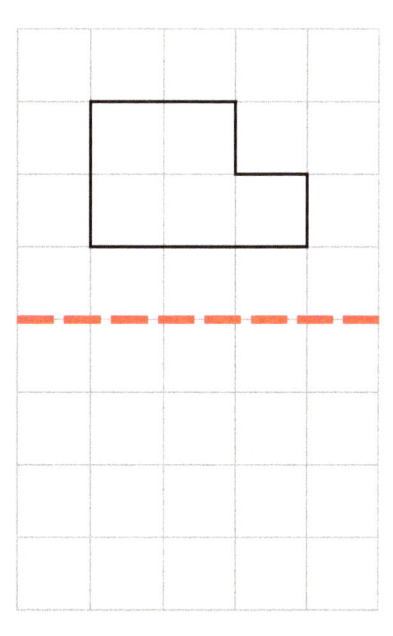

Once pupils start exploring reflection, it is worth coming back to the idea of symmetry again, and reinforcing the line symmetry of different shapes. This activity is a nice one to reinforce why some lines are lines of symmetry, and others aren't:

Reflect each shape in the given line. What do you notice?

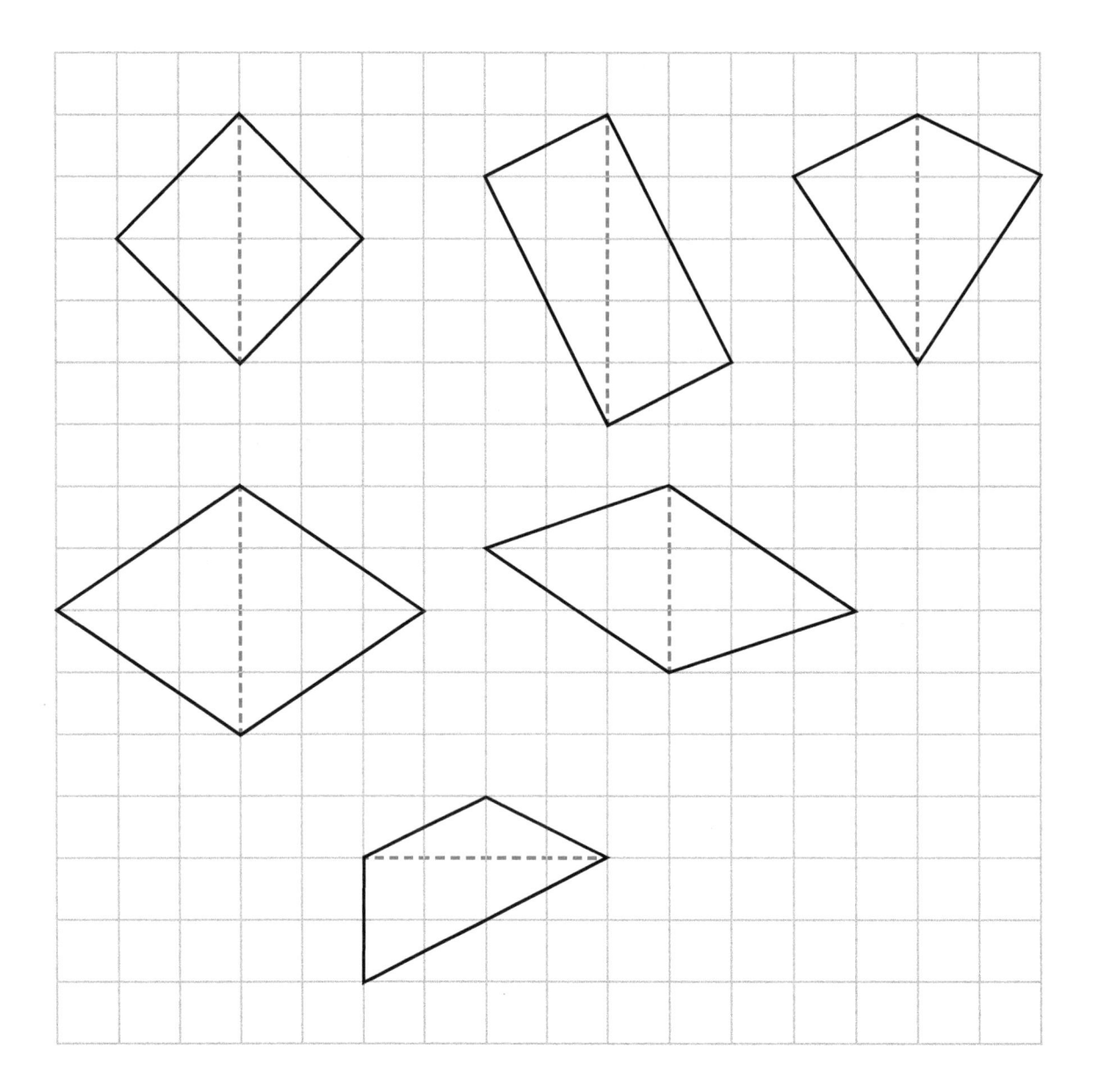

This sort of activity can also be adapted to make the diagonals sloped lines if we want to bring this in when pupils are looking at reflection in sloped lines.

The links between reflection and symmetry can (and should) continue to be reinforced when we make the transition to looking at non-rectilinear grids.

Shade three more triangles so that the hexagon has exactly three lines of symmetry.

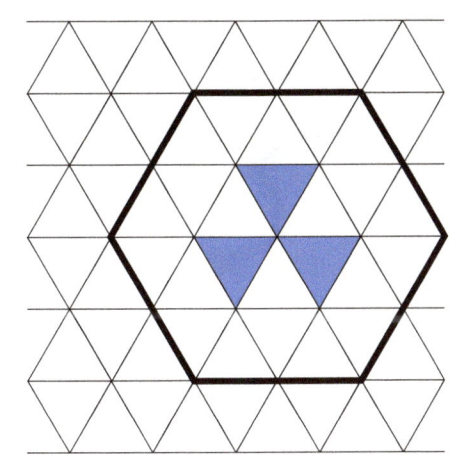

Pupils have to be careful here not to create a shape with six lines of symmetry, which is something teachers need to be on the lookout for, but if pupils make the mistake then pointing this out and prompting them to look again can actually be a great thinking and learning process as it is often something they have overlooked.

Once pupils have gained a depth of fluency with reflection, it is worth then returning full circle and considering how we define line symmetry. This can be offered directly to pupils, with a prompt suggesting that the folding definition is perhaps a little impractical and imprecise, and that we might come up with a better one. This might be done as a paired/grouped activity to begin with, before perhaps combining the best of these as a class definition. We would potentially be looking for something along the lines of, 'A mirror line is a line of symmetry for a shape when every image point following the reflection coincides with an object point of the original shape.' As well as really focusing pupil attention on what it means to be a line of symmetry, and how it links to reflection, this also allows us to link together the definitions of reflection symmetry and rotation symmetry.

Subconcept: rotational symmetry

For me, the study of rotational symmetry gives a measure of closure and satisfaction to the study of symmetry. There are lots of shapes that pupils will encounter at primary level that look or feel like they should have line symmetry but, in fact, don't. The most obvious of these is the parallelogram:

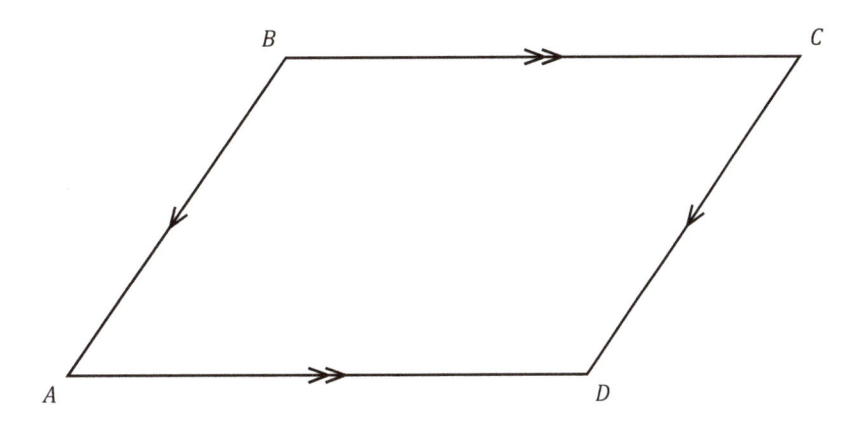

but also more interesting polygons like this dodecagon:

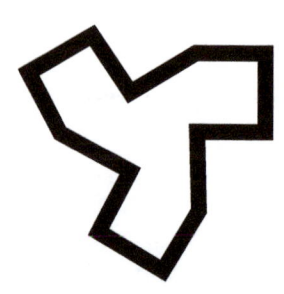

or even shapes that are not polygons at all:

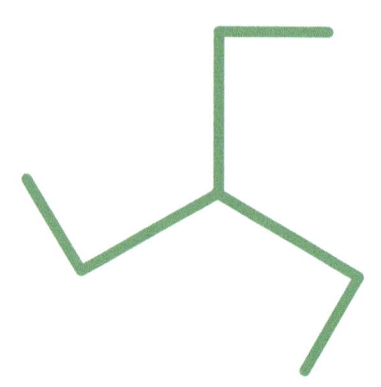

Being able to give a name to the 'symmetry' that these shapes exhibit is, I think, an important step for pupils to take, as well as opening up the study of rotation more generally. We might start to talk about rotational symmetry in terms of turning a shape around its own centre. Of course, this opens up potential debate about what is considered the 'centre' of the shape, which we may actually want pupils to consider and arrive at some conclusion, even if it is not fully mathematical at this point (it may well help when we come to talk about the centre of rotation later on). There are good links to make here between the number of times during a complete turn that the shape appears identical to its original orientation – the order of rotational symmetry – and the fraction of a full turn that the shape turns through before its orientation looks identical to its initial orientation. This then ties further to the concept of the reciprocal – pupils can consider why it would make sense for these two to be the reciprocals of each other.

A common misconception that pupils will form is that the number of lines of symmetry and the order of rotational symmetry is always the same (despite having seen shapes like a parallelogram). A nice activity to offer pupils to reinforce the differences is similar to the one we used to support pupils in making connections between the number of lines of symmetry and the number of sides:

Draw shapes to complete each section of the grid. If a section can't be filled in, say why.

		Order of rotational symmetry			
		1	2	3	4
Lines of symmetry	0				
	1				
	2				
	3				
	4				

In common with line symmetry, it will also be useful for pupils to complete drawings so that they have a given rotational symmetry:

Shade six squares so that this shape has rotational symmetry of order 4.

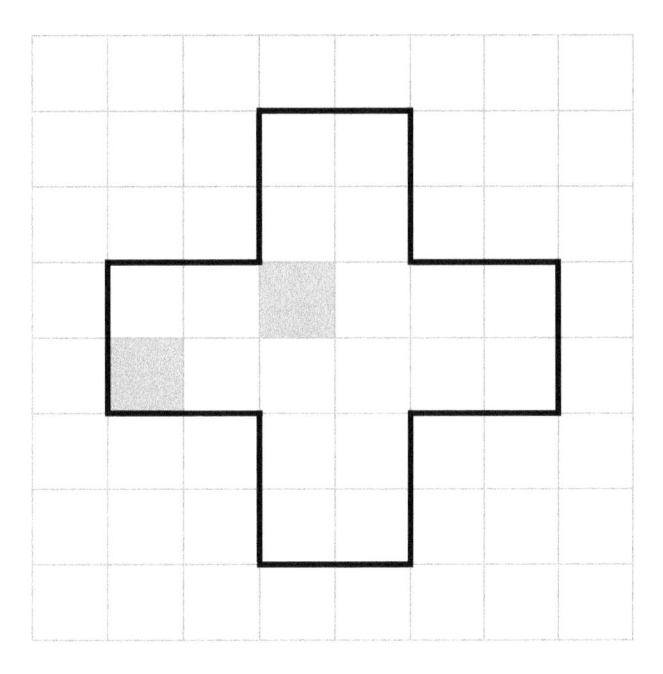

In further parallels to line symmetry, when it comes to introducing the relationship between the transformation rotation and rotational symmetry, we might want to offer something like this so that pupils can see the underlying identical structure:

Shade squares so that the 6 by 6 grid has rotational symmetry of order 4.

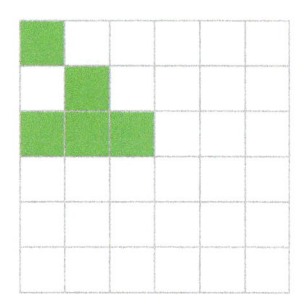

Rotate the shape

a   90° clockwise about the marked centre.

b   180° clockwise about the marked centre.

c   90° anticlockwise about the marked centre.

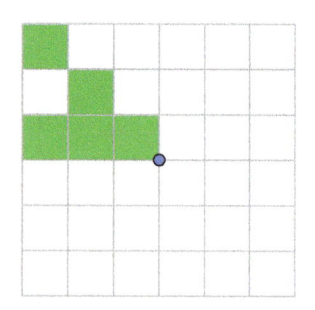

which should also (eventually) involve non-rectilinear grids:

Shade five triangles to give this shape rotational symmetry of order 3.

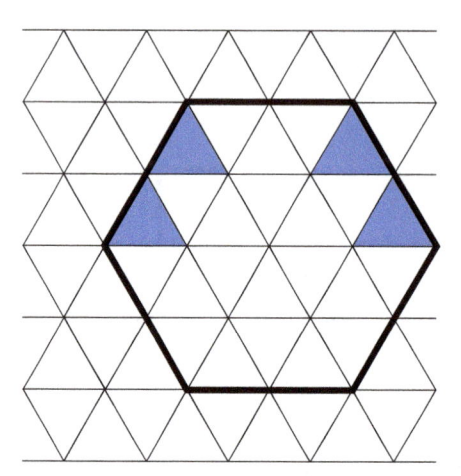

and at a suitable point may then include looking at defining rotational symmetry (in a similar way to line symmetry), which would be something along the lines of, 'The order of rotational symmetry of a shape is the number of times that all image points coincide with object points when the shape is rotated through 360° about a given centre.'

This sort of definition ties nicely with pupils' learning about rotational symmetry and transforming a shape through rotation. It also mirrors (no pun intended) the definition of line symmetry that we prompted earlier.

Having explored the links between symmetry and reflection/rotation, we will continue on to the final transformation studied at school level: enlargement.

Concept: enlargement

Prerequisites: Number, multiplication.

Linked concepts: Vectors, reflection, translation, rotation, ratio/proportion, congruence, similarity, area, surds.

Enlargement is, for me, probably the transformation where the premature focus of its effect on a particular shape is the most detrimental to pupil long-term learning. In many cases, pupils are introduced to enlargement in a way similar to this:

Enlarge the given shape by a scale factor of 3.

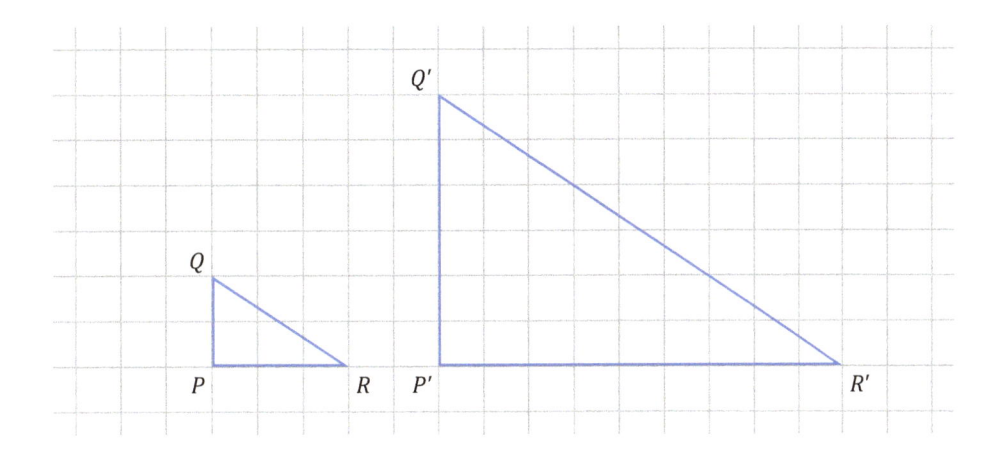

What this approach may lead to is pupils struggling when we introduce the idea of enlarging using a centre of enlargement. In my experience, the most common problem with enlargement seems to be when pupils begin to look at enlargement using a centre, with pupils misunderstanding the role of the centre and either centring the shape directly on the centre of enlargement or using the centre of enlargement incorrectly to place the shape in a different position to that which it should be. In the Cambridge Assessment article 'Common Errors in Mathematics' Nicky Rushton suggests that with IGCSE, the most common error in describing enlargements is omitting the centre of enlargement altogether.[6]

Instead of introducing enlargement in this way, a potential approach that would mitigate against these misconceptions is focusing on enlarging a single point away from a given centre, in a manner similar to how we might introduce translation, reflection and rotation. This approach would be greatly benefitted if pupils already have a working knowledge of vectors.

---

6   N. Rushton, Common Errors in Mathematics, *Research Matters: A Cambridge Assessment Publication*, 17 (2014), 8–17. Available at: https://www.cambridgeassessment.org.uk/Images/466316-common-errors-in-mathematics.pdf.

Enlarge the point P using a scale factor of 3 from centre O.

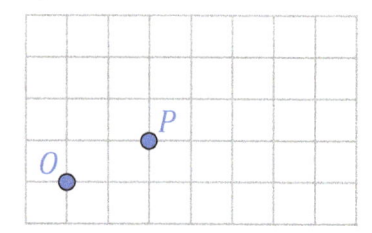

Because it is a single point that is being enlarged, this will focus pupil attention on the movement of the point, rather than the changing size, highlighting the key feature of enlargement that the centre represents.

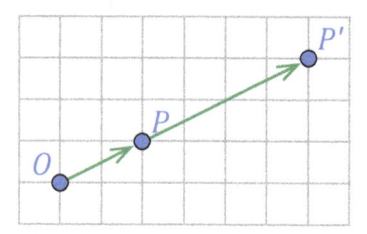

Using vectors, we can see that the vector $\vec{OP} = \begin{pmatrix}2\\1\end{pmatrix}$. Because the scale factor is being applied to the vector, this means the vector $\vec{OP'} = 3 \times \begin{pmatrix}2\\1\end{pmatrix} = \begin{pmatrix}6\\3\end{pmatrix}$. This allows us to place the point P' in the correct position.

Once pupils have worked with enlarging single points, then we can turn our attention to applying the same idea to multiple points in a shape.

Enlarge triangle ABC by scale factor 3 centre (−1, 2).

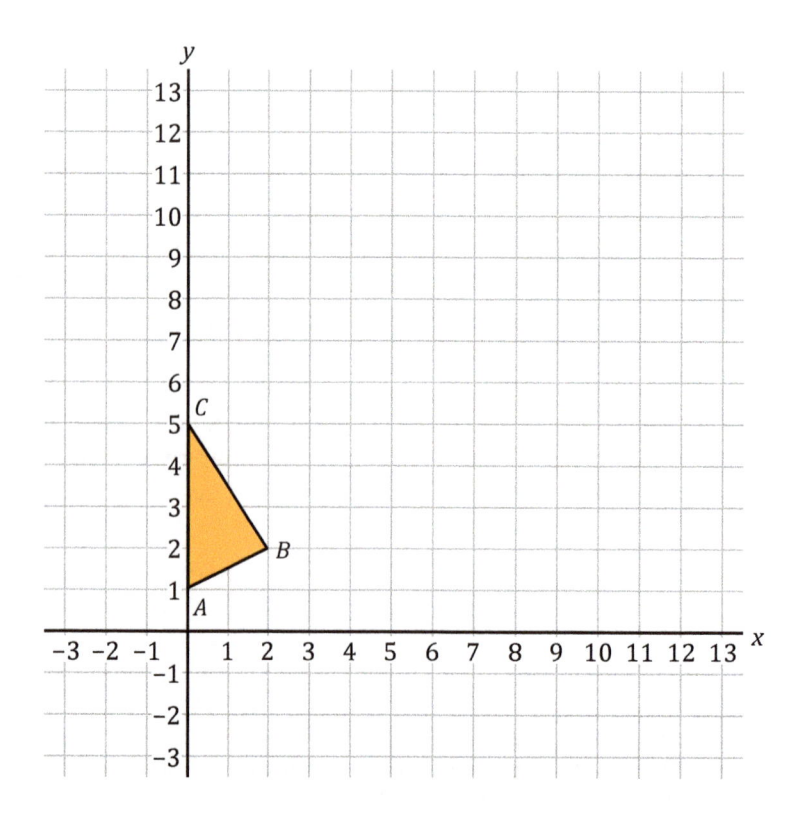

The big point to make to pupils here is that it is still about points moving relative to the centre. The obvious points to find are *A', B'* and *C'*, as these would be the vertices of the enlarged shape. However, we should also make clear that it is not just these points that move; every point is moving. It may be worth actually picking one of the points along the length *AC* and showing how that is enlarged as well as the vertices, just so pupils are clear that choosing the vertices is a good strategy but not a property of the enlargement itself.

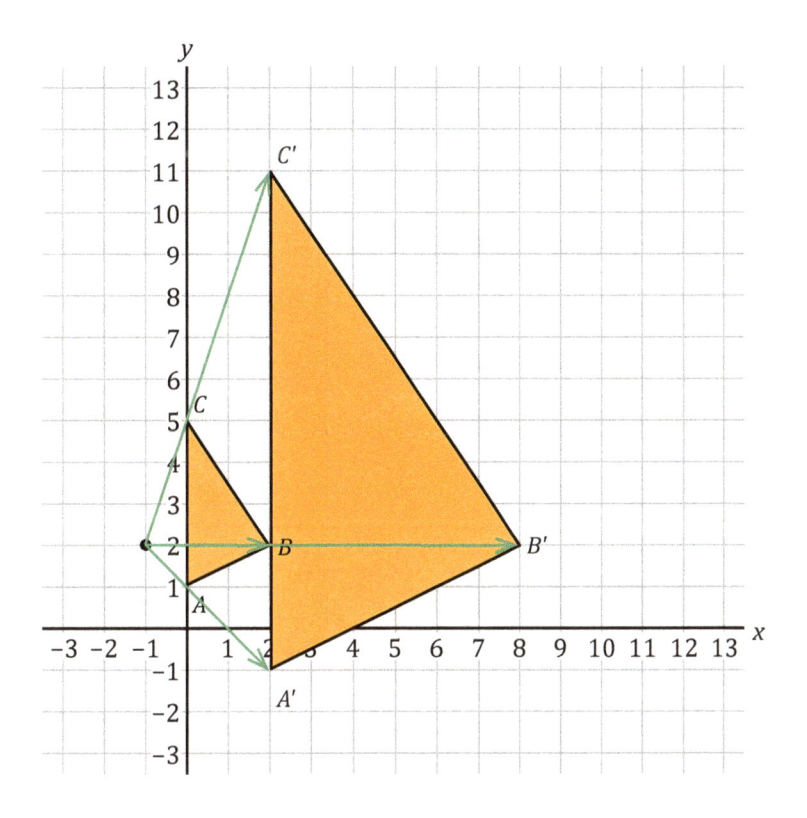

The increase in the length of each side can then be seen as almost a by-product of the enlargement; indeed, pupils can be challenged to explain why it happens (because the points are all moving three times further from the centre, they also move three times further from each other).

A further benefit to this approach is that when we consider enlargement using fractional or negative scale factors, no adaptation of the 'method' is required; primarily because it isn't a method, but a way of making sense of enlargement. We may wish to go back to enlarging a point when introducing these, but it shouldn't really be necessary if pupils have understood the idea fully.

Enlarge triangle *ABC* by scale factor of $\frac{2}{3}$, centre (1, 0).

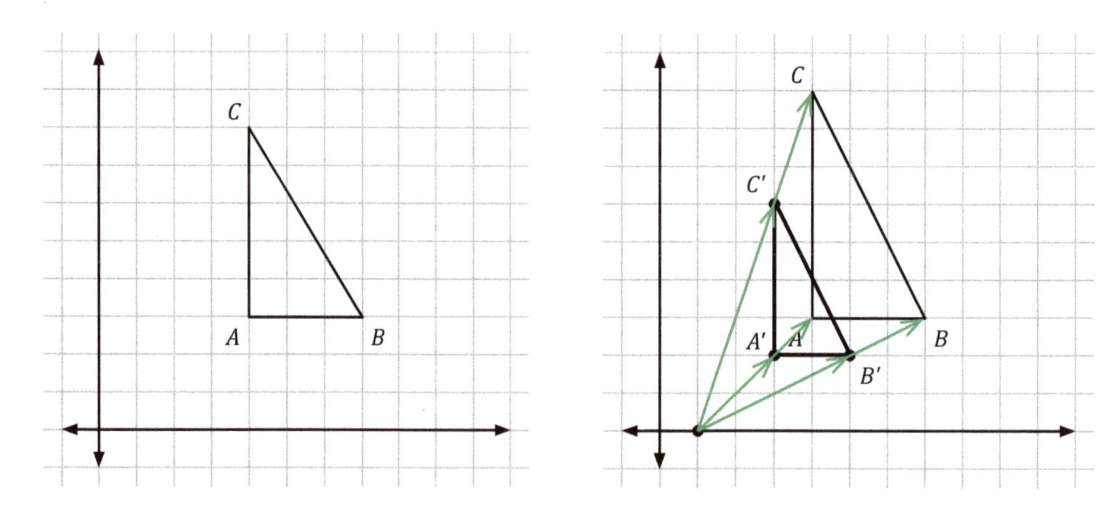

Enlarge trapezium *ABCD* by scale factor −2, centre *O*.

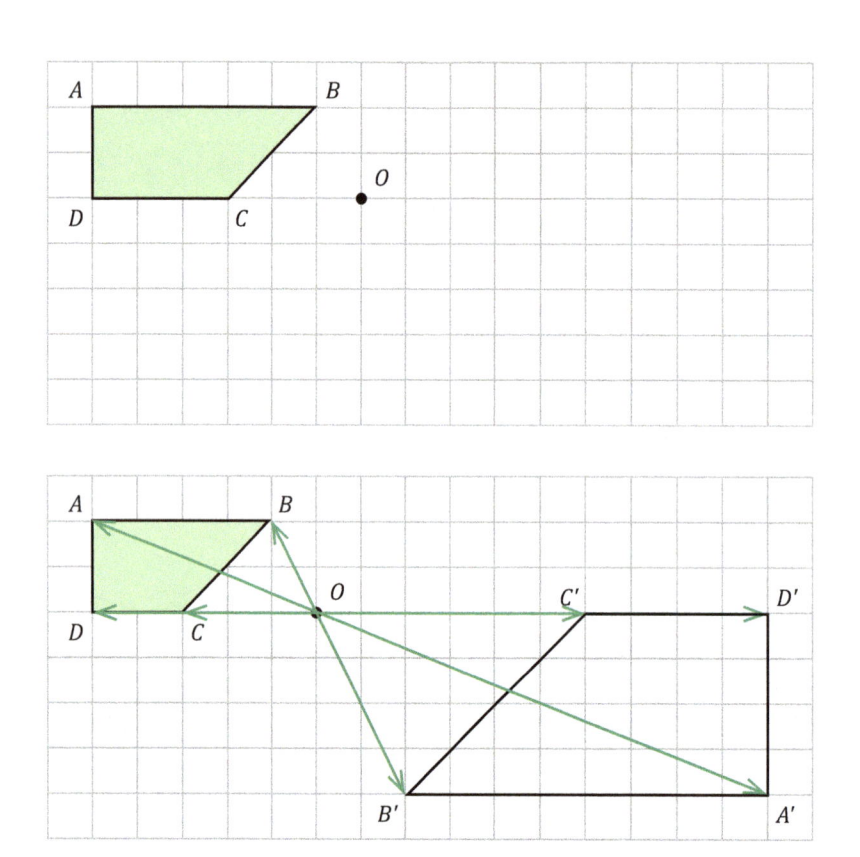

It is worth noting that it may not be necessary to keep drawing the vectors onto the diagram if pupils reach the point where they can operate directly on the column representation vectors and visualise the result.

When it comes to identifying and describing an enlargement, the key thing that pupils have to have recognised is that the vectors connecting the centre of enlargement to both the object and image points are parallel. This allows us to find the direction of the vector from the centre to either the object or image points, by looking at the vector directly connecting the object and image:

Transformation and vectors

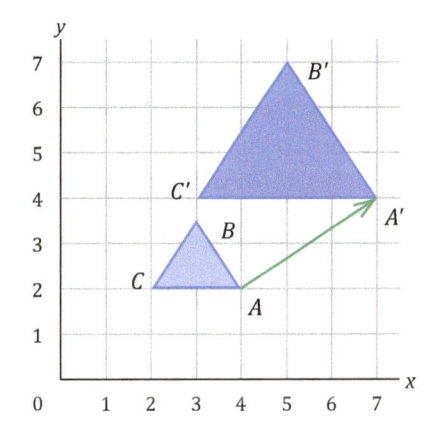

What pupils should be clear on here is that, given the unknown centre of enlargement O, the vectors $\vec{OA}$ and $\vec{OA'}$ must be parallel (and coincident) to $\vec{AA'}$. This means that if we extend the line connecting A and A', then the centre O must be somewhere along the line.

Pupils should then potentially appreciate the different strategies that we might use to find the centre of enlargement, the most obvious one being that if the centre of enlargement lies on the line connecting A and A', then it must also lie on the line connecting B and B' and the line connecting C and C'.

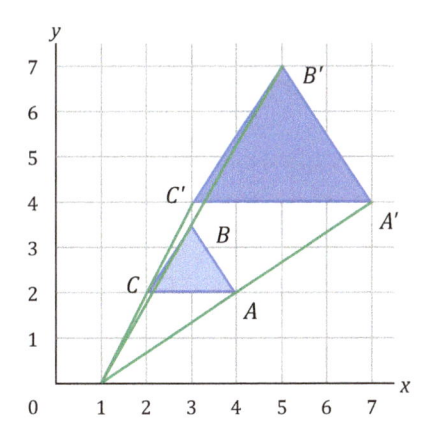

As these straight lines can only intersect at a single point, that point must be the centre of enlargement.

A possible alternative approach is to use knowledge of the scale factor of the enlargement to identify how far along the line connecting A and A' the centre of enlargement is. In this case, we can identify the scale factor is 2 by examining the lengths associated with each of the triangles ABC and $A'B'C'$. Knowing that the scale factor is 2 then turns the finding of the centre of enlargement into a ratio problem, which can be shown using a ratio table or similar:

$\vec{OA}$	$\vec{OA'}$	$\vec{AA'}$
1	2	1
$\begin{pmatrix} 3 \\ 2 \end{pmatrix}$	$\begin{pmatrix} 6 \\ 4 \end{pmatrix}$	$\begin{pmatrix} 3 \\ 2 \end{pmatrix}$

the logic here being that the scale factor of 2 implies that the vectors $\vec{OA}$ and $\vec{OA'}$ are in the ratio 1:2; and therefore that $\vec{AA'}$ (the difference between $\vec{OA}$ and $\vec{OA'}$) is equivalent to 1 part in the ratio. Knowing that $\vec{AA'}$ is the vector $\binom{3}{2}$ allows us to work out $\vec{OA}$ and $\vec{OA'}$ as column vectors, and therefore work out $\vec{AO}$ or $\vec{A'O}$ (as the negative of $\vec{OA}$ or $\vec{OA'}$), which will allow us to find O. This strategy is particularly useful when we are identifying the enlargement that has happened to a single point:

> The point A' is an enlargement of point A of scale factor 4 from centre O. Find the position of O.

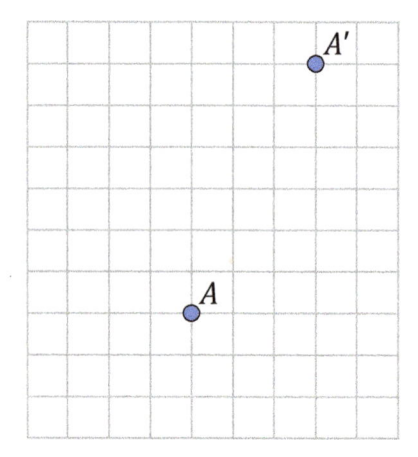

The ratio table that helps make sense of this problem looks like this:

$\vec{OA}$	$\vec{OA'}$	$\vec{AA'}$
1	4	3
$\binom{1}{2}$	$\binom{4}{8}$	$\binom{3}{6}$

Given that $\vec{OA}$ and $\vec{OA'}$ are in the ratio 1:4, this gives $\vec{AA'}$ as 3 parts of the ratio. Given that the vector $\vec{AA'} = \binom{3}{6}$, this gives $\vec{OA}$ and $\vec{OA'}$ as $\binom{1}{2}$ and $\binom{4}{8}$ and hence allows us to find O (either using the vector $\vec{AO}$ or $\vec{A'O}$. The same approach can be used with fraction scale factors:

> The point A' is an enlargement of point A of a scale factor $\frac{3}{4}$ from centre O. Find the position of O.

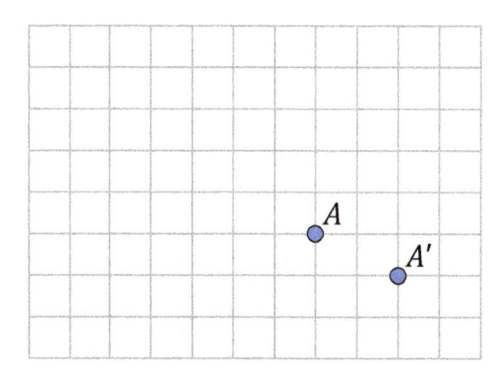

$\vec{OA}$	$\vec{OA'}$	$\vec{AA'}$
4	3	1
$\binom{8}{4}$	$\binom{6}{3}$	$\binom{2}{1}$

This time the ratio table looks like this:

allowing us to find O. The use of fractional scale factors in identifying enlargement is particularly important as pupils often misidentify the scale factor when dealing with fractionally enlarged shapes:

Describe fully the single transformation that maps shape A onto shape B.

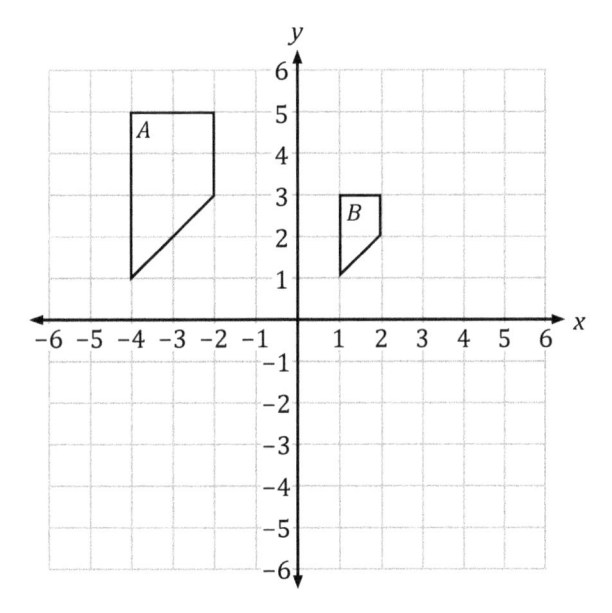

Pupils are usually fine with identifying this as an enlargement; however, what is quite likely is that they will identify it as an enlargement of scale factor 2, rather than scale factor $\frac{1}{2}$. This may or may not have a knock-on effect on pupils' ability to identify the centre of enlargement, depending on their approach, but either way, pupils should be exposed to this type of problem, and if any are mistakenly identifying the scale factor from the image to the object rather than the object to the image, then this will need addressing directly with them.

One further thing pupils will need to recognise is that when a point is enlarged using a negative scale factor, $\vec{OA}$ and $\vec{OA'}$ point in opposite directions, so one of the values in ratio will be negative:

The point A' is an enlargement of point A of scale factor −3 from O. Find the position of O.

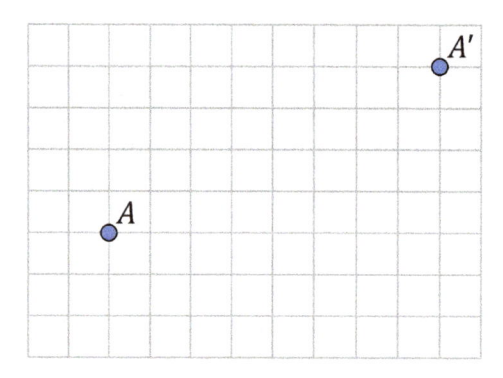

This time the ratio table would look like this:

$\vec{OA}$	$\vec{OA'}$	$\vec{AA'}$
1	−3	−4
$\begin{pmatrix} -2 \\ -1 \end{pmatrix}$	$\begin{pmatrix} 6 \\ 3 \end{pmatrix}$	$\begin{pmatrix} 8 \\ 4 \end{pmatrix}$

which allows us to pinpoint O.

This approach to identifying enlargement gives us a nice opportunity to interweave use of ratio problems and may lead to greater understanding when applying vector ideas to prove geometrical relationships.

Another nice opportunity to offer pupils is to explore the result of combining different enlargements together. Don Steward has a wonderful activity for this, which can prompt pupils to consider the result of multiple enlargements:[7]

The brown triangle is enlarged by scale factor 2 using the blue dot as a centre to give the blue triangle. The blue triangle is enlarged by scale factor 2 using the red dot as a centre to give the red triangle. What do you notice?

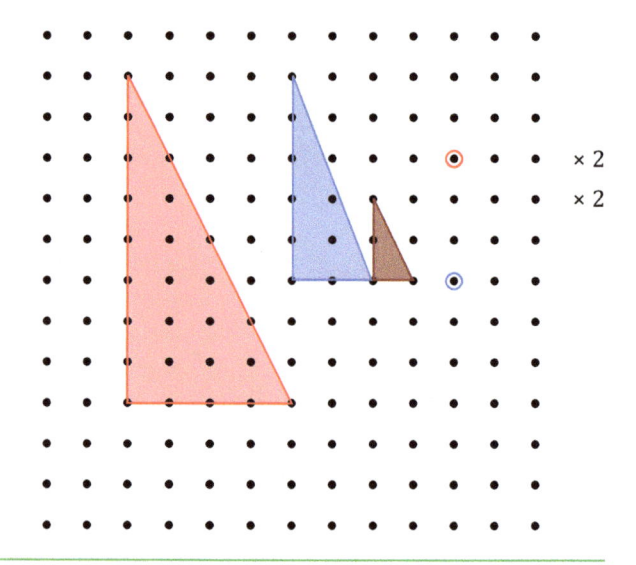

× 2
× 2

---

7   D. Steward, Combined Enlargements, *Median* [blog] (24 April 2016). Available at: https://donsteward.blogspot.com/2016/04/combined-enlargements.html.

In the activity, pupils have the chance to explore different enlargements with different scale factors. Most pupils will recognise quite quickly that the resulting scale factor is the product of the two separate scale factors, but it is the resulting centre of enlargement that provides an interesting problem for pupils to consider.

The final aspect of enlargement that is worth exploring with pupils is the effect of enlargement of a shape on the area of the shape. It is another classic misconception that pupils will carry over from working with enlargements of shapes that the area scale factor is equal to the length scale factor. This can be somewhat mitigated by introducing pupils to scale factors as operating on the vectors connecting points to the centre of enlargement, rather than operating directly on the shapes themselves, but not completely eradicated. The use of enlarged squares and rectangles is usually a nice way into exploring the area of enlarged shapes:

> The diagram shows a rectangle ABCD enlarged using centre O to give A'B'C'D'.
>
> a   Write down the scale factor of the enlargement.
>
> b   Work out the area of rectangle ABCD.
>
> c   Work out the area of rectangle A'B'C'D'.
>
> What do you notice? What might you conjecture? Explore further.

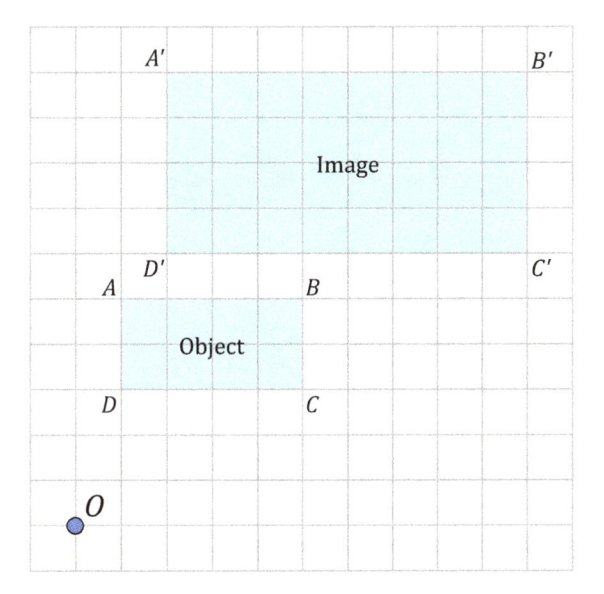

Pupils can go on to consider different shapes, and different scale factors, arriving at the conclusion that the area scale factor is the square of the length factor. We can then offer pupils the opportunity to work with length and area scale factors, finding areas of images and objects when given the length scale factor (and vice versa), culminating in questions such as:

> A shape A is enlarged to give shape A'. The area of shape A is 5 square units and the area of shape A' is 405 square units. The coordinate (3, 2) is part of shape A, which maps to the coordinate (11, 18) on shape A'. Find the centre of enlargement.

When and if pupils have worked with surds, we can further adapt questions of this type to deal with area scale factors that lead to surd scale factors, and so require manipulation of surds to find missing lengths or coordinates.

We will see this idea again, and its extension to three dimensions and volume, when we examine similarity with pupils.

Concept: similarity

Prerequisites: Number, multiplication, ratio/proportion.

Linked concepts: Vectors, enlargement, congruence, angle, area, volume, surds.

Similarity is often introduced to pupils in links to enlargement, i.e. that when one shape is enlarged to give another shape, the two shapes are similar. Whilst this is not necessarily problematic, care needs to be taken with this approach, as the converse is not true: i.e. if two shapes are similar, one is not necessarily an enlargement of the other. Take, for example, these two shapes:

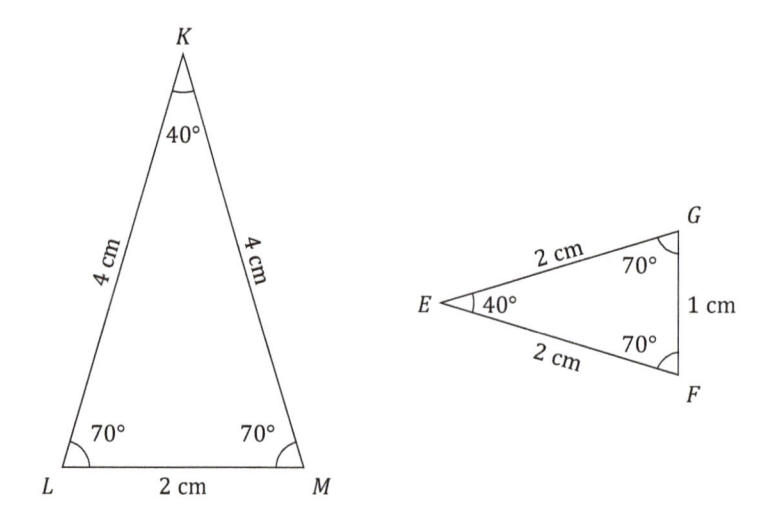

These two shapes are similar shapes, but *EFG* is not a simple enlargement of *KLM*. Indeed, the definition of similarity in Euclidean geometry is given with regards to one shape being an enlargement of the other, potentially with further reflections or rotations.

When it comes to introducing similar shapes, there are three key properties pupils should recognise and apply:

1. A constant scale factor between any corresponding lengths on the shapes.

2. A constant ratio between any two lengths on one shape and the corresponding lengths on the other shape.

3. The equivalent angles in each shape being equal (with a further recognition that this both implies and is implied by the other two only for triangles – this is the basis for trigonometry).

These properties allow pupils to identify when two shapes are similar, which is always worth exploring with pupils before any application of properties to find missing side lengths or other measures. An activity like the one below can help pupils focus their attention on both of the length properties (once again from the Don Steward blog[8]).

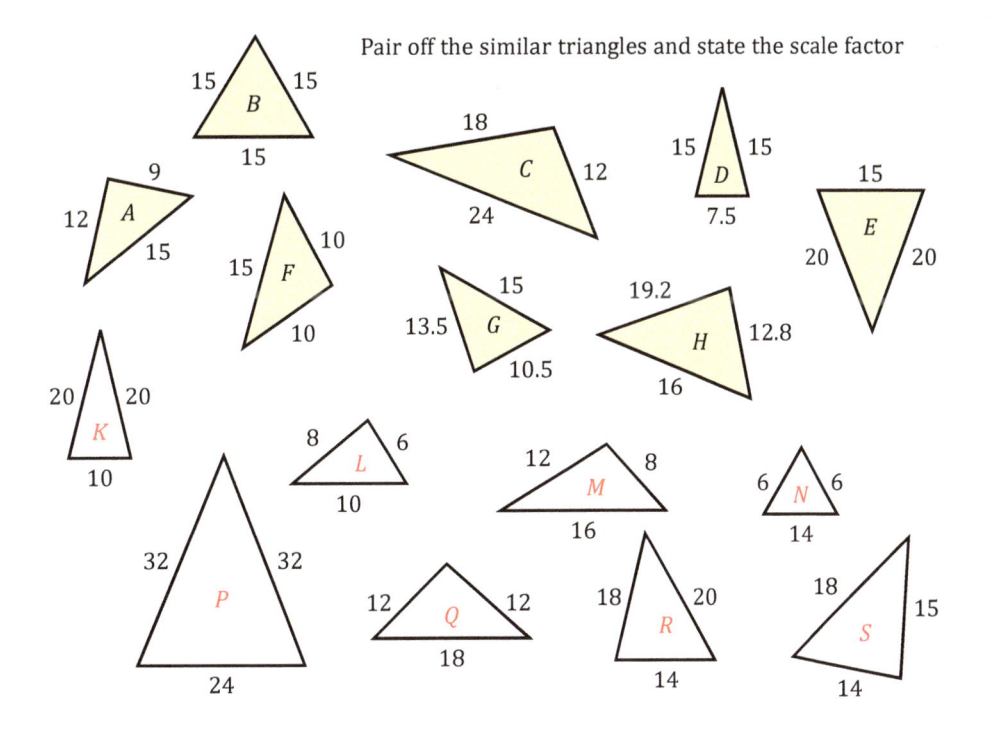

Pair off the similar triangles and state the scale factor

I will often remove the requirement to state the scale factor here, so as not to lead pupils to focus on the scale factor – they ratio of sides is a much more profitable focus for many of these triangles. The equal angles property is particularly useful when combined with parallel line angle properties – again it is worth examining this separately and well prior to actually finding missing sides in these sorts of diagrams:

Explain why each pair of triangles is similar.

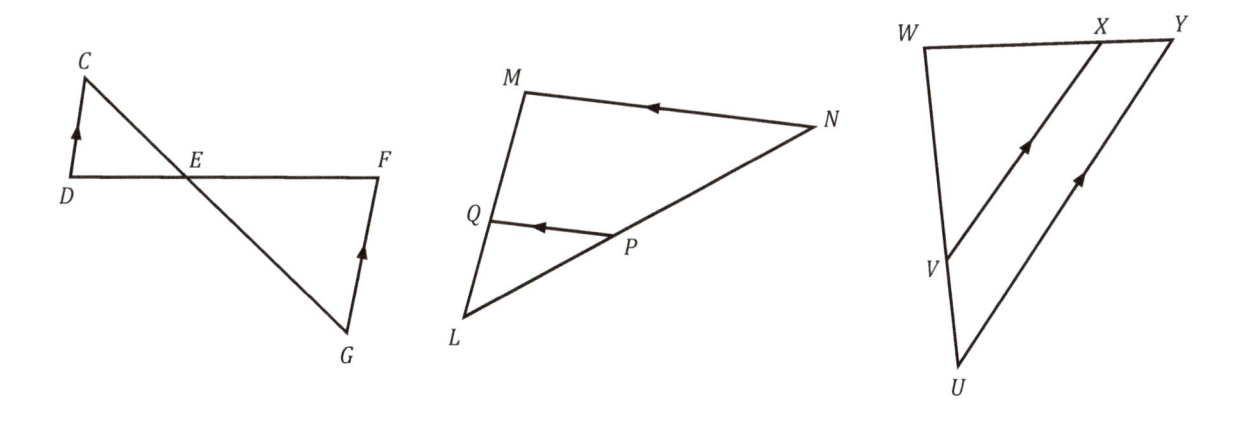

---

8   D. Steward, Similar Pairs, *Median* [blog] (14 September 2012). Available at: https://donsteward.blogspot.com/2012/09/similar-pairs.html.

and if/when pupils study circle theorems, we can throw in this pair of triangles as well:

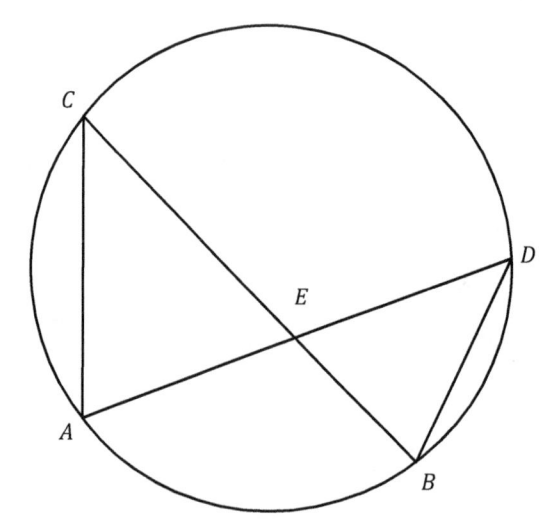

We shouldn't, of course, just focus on triangles; pupils will benefit from working with a wider array of shapes, including examples of shapes that are not similar but share equal angles:

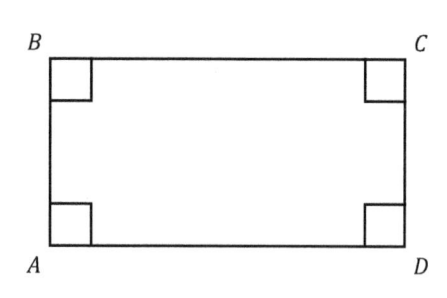

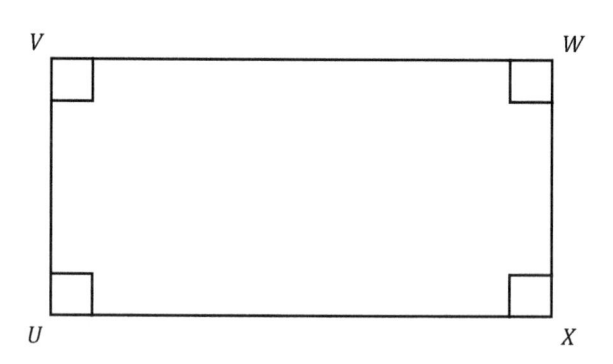

These rectangles may or may not be similar, but the fact that all their angles are equal are not enough to be certain they are similar. This is also true of these parallelograms:

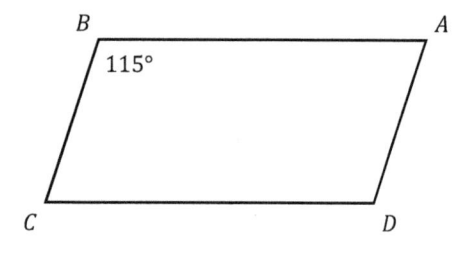

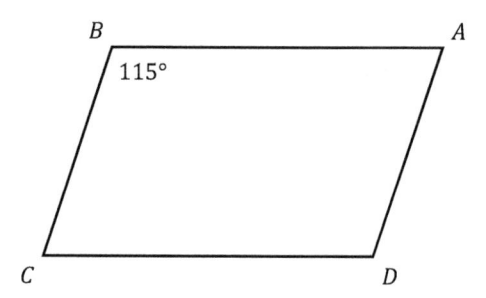

and these hexagons (for example):

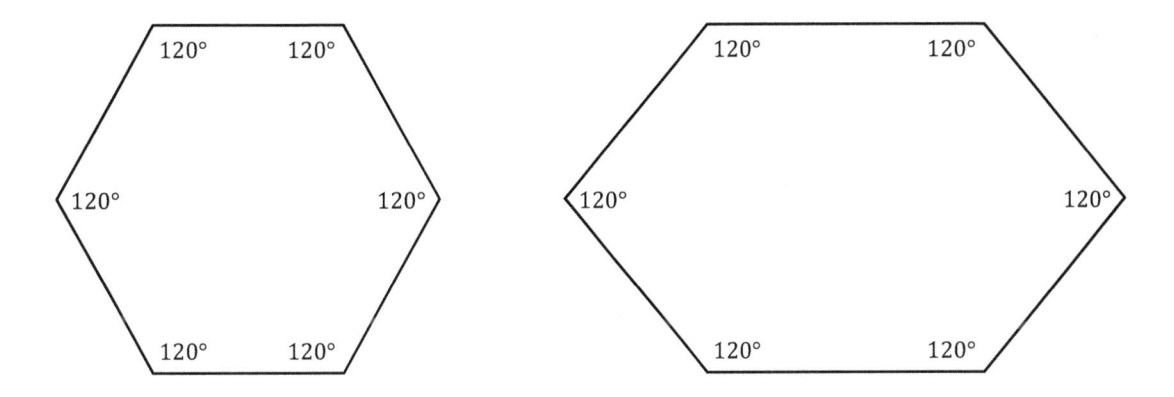

Pupils should also identify whether shapes other than triangles are similar or not:

Are these quadrilaterals similar? Justify your answer.

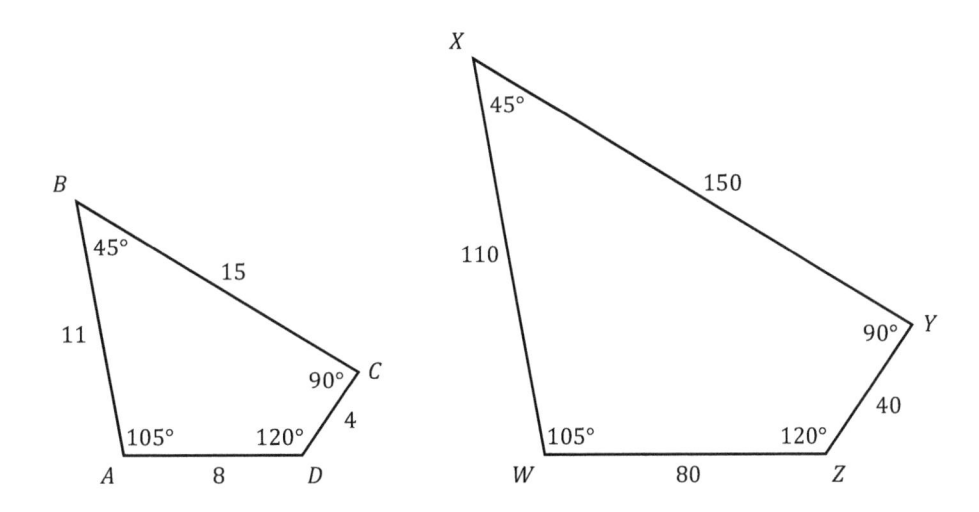

including three-dimensional shapes:

Are these cuboids similar? Justify your answer.

This should lead to pupils recognising that all regular polygons and polyhedra of the same type are similar (and, in fact, that this generalises to all shapes that can be defined in terms of a single length). This recognition can be highlighted to pupils, or offered to them to reason:

> Explain why all squares are similar. Explain further why this also applies to equilateral triangles. What about regular pentagons? What other shapes would this apply to?

Once pupils have had experience in identifying similar shapes, we can then offer opportunities for solving problems with similar shapes such as finding missing length, which pupils should be encouraged to solve using both a scaling and side-ratio approach. These sorts of questions can be offered using diagrams:

> Each shape in the pair is similar. Find the value of the marked missing length.

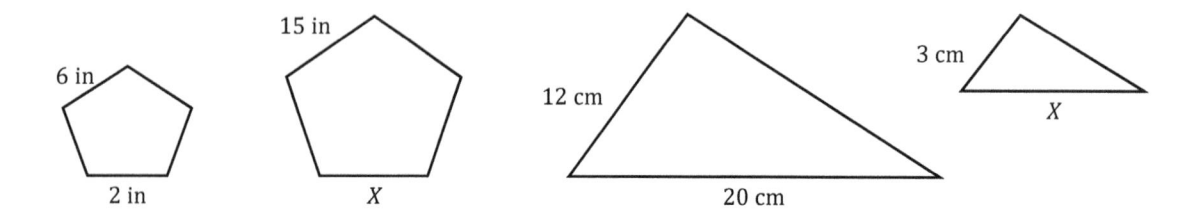

Or simply in words:

> Two rectangles, A and B are similar. Rectangle A has lengths of 8 cm and 15 cm. Rectangle B has a length of 10 cm. Work out the two possible values of the other length of rectangle B.

The website Variation Theory has a nice activity that focuses on triangles, with pupils having to use the marked angles to identify which sides are equivalent in each pair of shapes (provided you don't mind triangles that aren't even close to accurately drawn!).[9]

Intelligent practice – find the length of every missing side.

Triangles not drawn to scale.

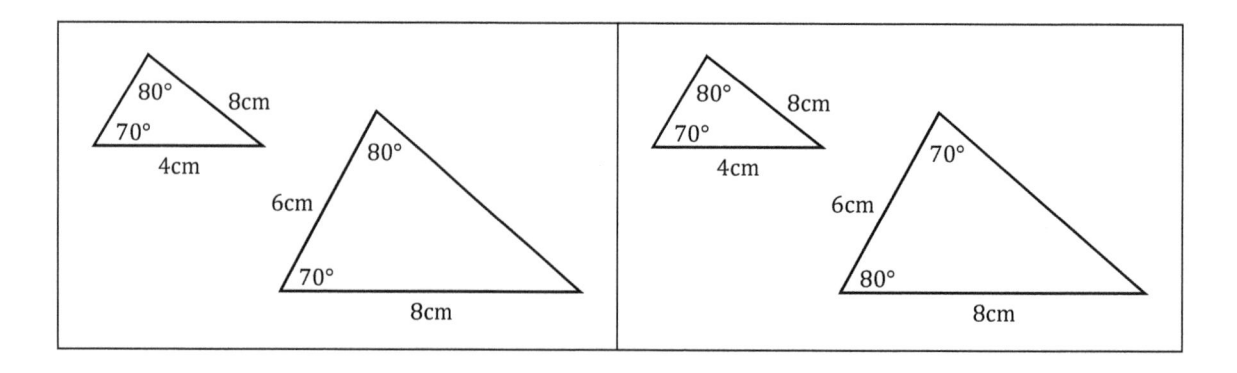

---

9 P. Aldridge, Similar Triangles: Missing Sides, *Variation Theory* (3 May 2019). Available at: https://variationtheory.com/2019/05/03/similar-triangles-calculating-the-length-of-missing-sides/.

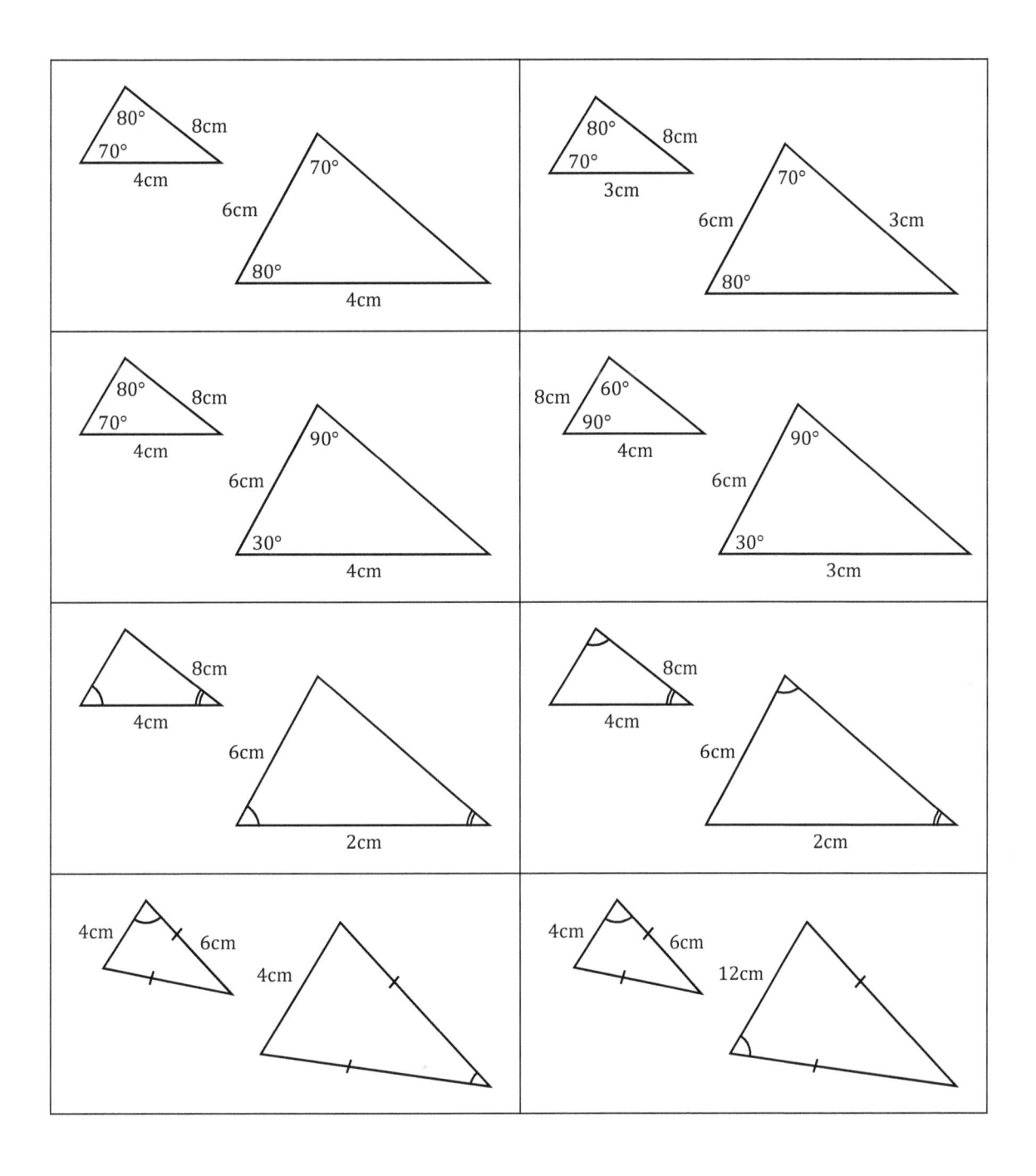

Again though, pupils shouldn't only be exposed to triangles – the website Math-Aids.Com can provide a few nice questions that mix up the information provided for pupils to work with:[10]

Each polygon is similar. Find the missing side length.

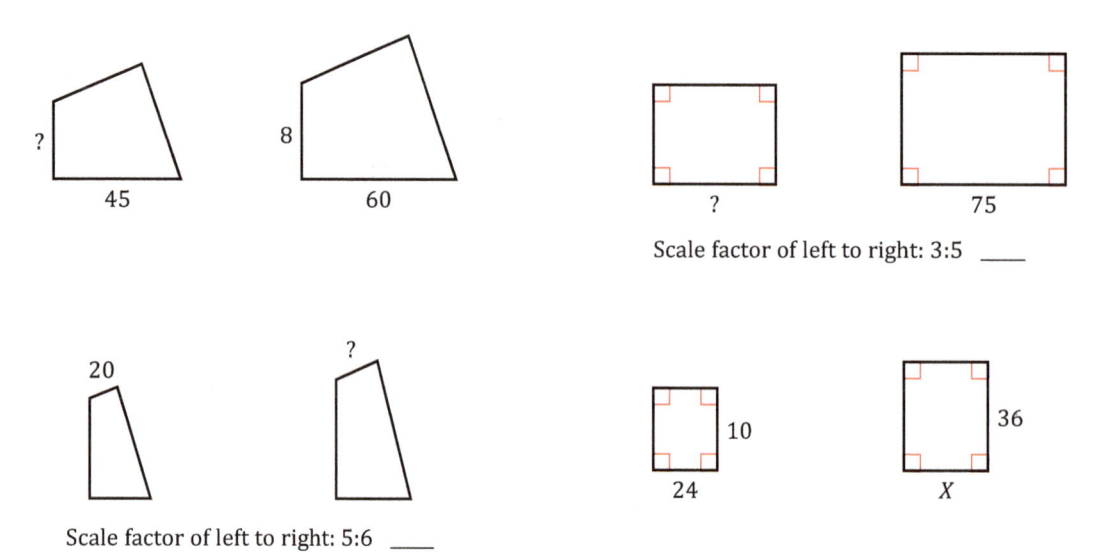

Scale factor of left to right: 3:5 ____

Scale factor of left to right: 5:6 ____

The use of ratio to show the scale factor here is particularly nice as it links well to pupils looking at the relationship between length ratios, area ratios and volume ratios. The same site also has some nice questions involving triangles that are embedded within each other:

Find the value of x in each triangle.

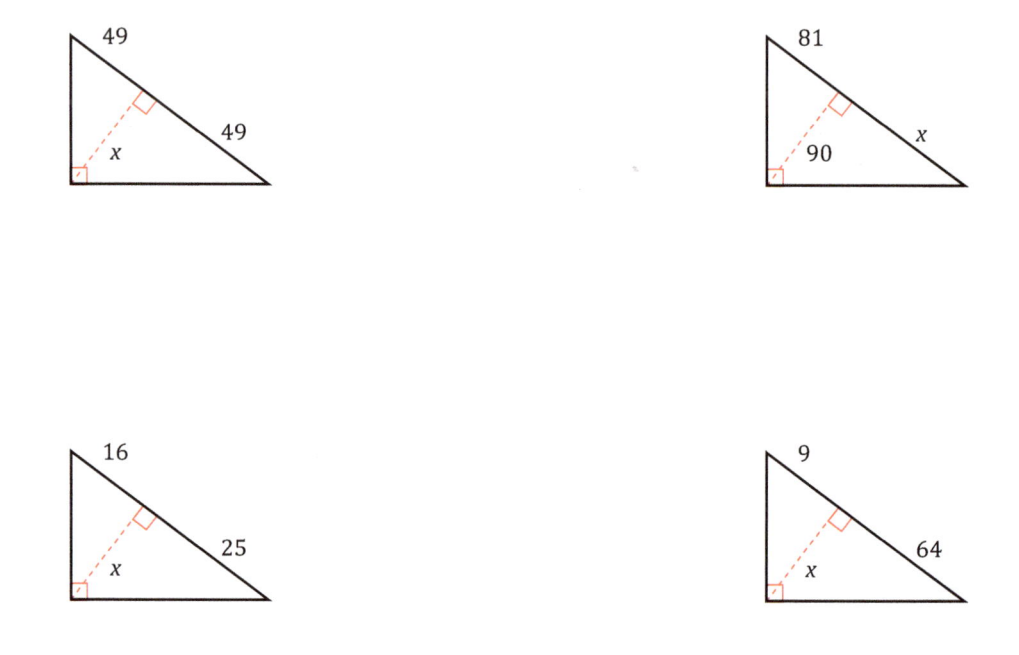

---

10 M. Theodore, Similarity Worksheets, *Math-Aids.Com* (16 November 2022). Available at: https://www.math-aids.com/Geometry/Similarity/.

Pupils typically struggle with embedded triangles when it comes to finding missing sides. A good strategy to explore with pupils is to draw the triangles out separately and in the same orientation, which makes it easier for pupils to recognise where the equivalent sides are.

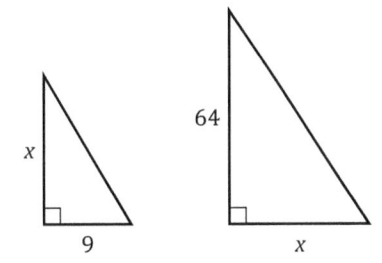

It can be hard for pupils to even spot that these two triangles are similar (it takes a little insight into the angles to recognise this) so it may be worth offering pupils these sorts of triangles and starting with identifying the similar triangles rather than going straight into problem-solving and finding missing sides. We can also offer other types of embedded triangles:

Find the value of x in each of these triangles.

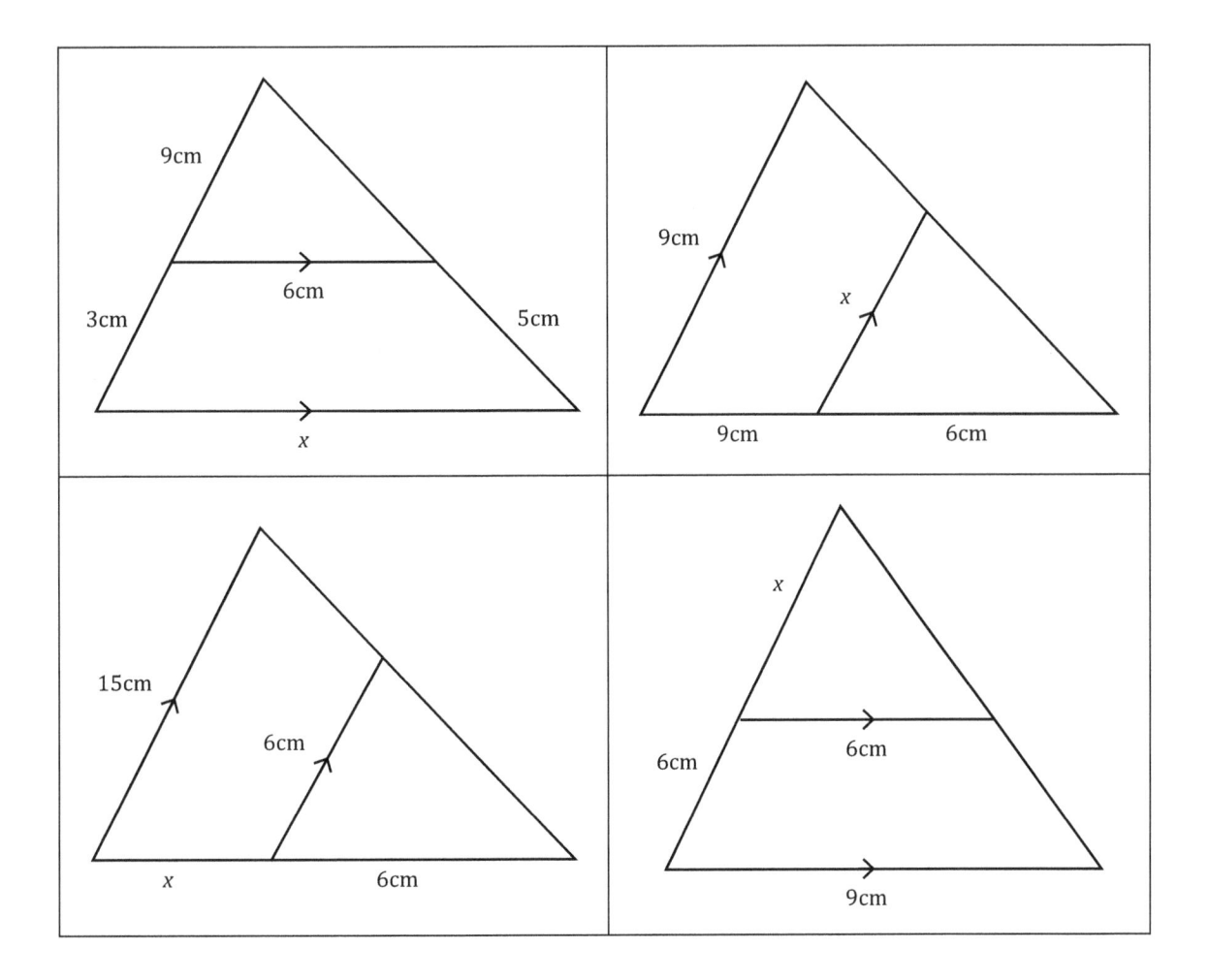

Once again, we want to move beyond triangles for embedded shapes:

Rectangles *ACDF* and *EBCD* are similar. Find the value of *x*.

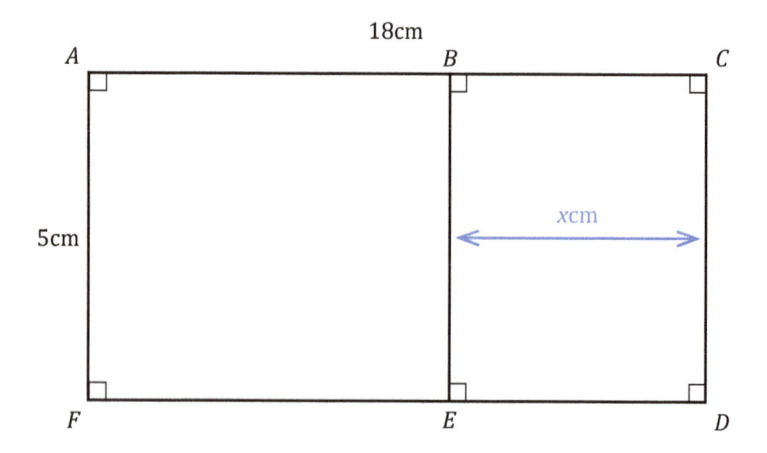

Trapezia *BCFE* and *BCDA* are similar. Find the value of *x*.

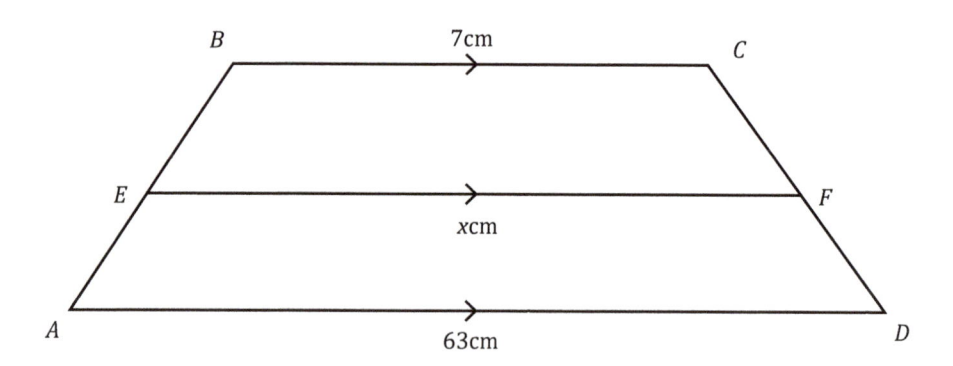

Another aspect of similar shapes that pupils can explore is the relationship between the areas (and volumes for three-dimensional shapes) of similar shapes. The most straightforward shapes to begin this exploration with are squares and cubes:

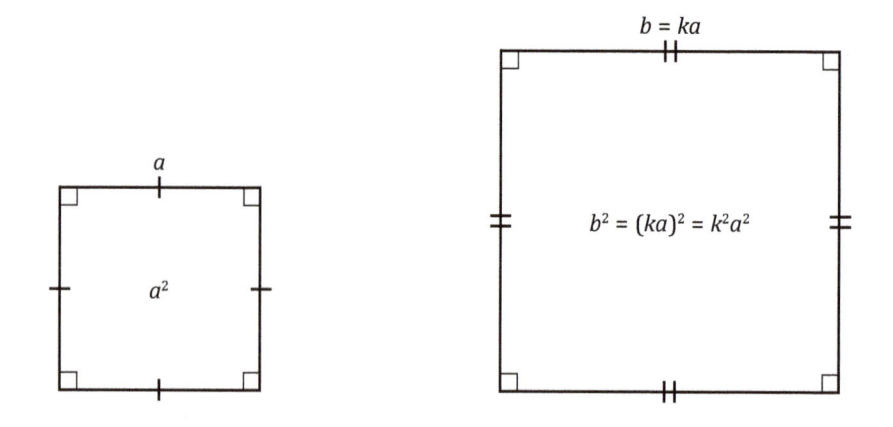

We can look at this either as the scale factor for the lengths being $\frac{b}{a} = k$ and the scale factor for the areas being $\frac{b^2}{a^2} = k^2$. Alternatively, we can look at the ratio of the lengths of the two shapes being $a : b$, and the ratio of the areas being $a^2 : b^2$. Pupils can then go on to demonstrate that this is true for other shapes and potentially to reason that this is true for all similar shapes (including the surface area of three-dimensional shapes). We can also turn to cubes to look at the analogous relationship with volume:

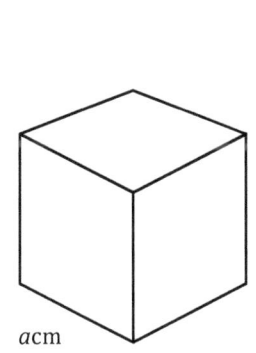

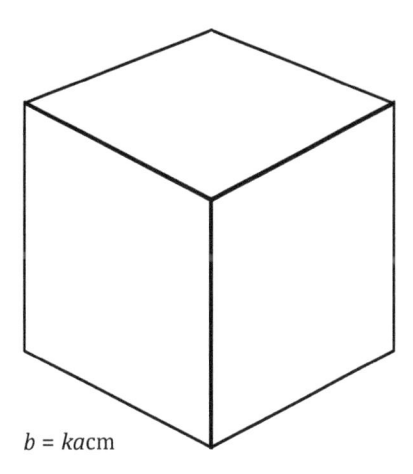

*a*cm

b = *ka*cm

We can again approach this similarly to either of the two above; the volume scale factor being $\frac{b^3}{a^3} = k^3$ or the ratio of the volumes being $a^3 : b^3$. Again, pupils can then demonstrate this for other shapes and reason why it must be true for all three-dimensional shapes. Pupils can then be offered the opportunity to solve problems involving finding missing area or volumes, like the ones created by the Centre for Innovation in Mathematics Teaching for their Mathematics Enhancement Programme (MEP), [11] and the exam-style questions from Maths Genie:[12]

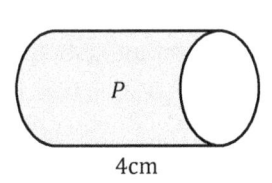

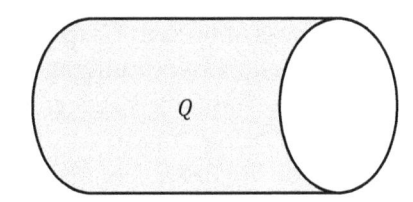

Not drawn accurately

P

Q

4cm

Two cylinders, *P* and *Q*, are mathematically similar.

The total surface area of cylinder *P* is 90πcm².

The total surface area of cylinder *Q* is 810πcm².

The length of cylinder *P* is 4cm.

a   Work out the length of cylinder *Q*.

The volume of cylinder *P* is 100πcm³.

b   Work out the volume of cylinder *Q*. Give your answer as a multiple of π.

---

11 CIMT, MEP Y8 Practice Book 8 Chapter 19: Similarity (n.d.). Available at: https://www.cimt.org.uk/projects/mepres/book8/bk8_19.pdf.
12 J. Yusuf, GCSE (1–9) Similar Shapes (Area and Volume), *Maths Genie* (n.d.). Available at: https://www.mathsgenie.co.uk/resources/similarshapes2.pdf.

A particularly nice application of this is to look at frustra:

> A frustrum is created by chopping a cone with a circular base of radius 5 ft from the top of a large cone with a circular base of radius 7 ft. The volume of the smaller cone is 1200 ft³. Work out the volume of the frustrum.

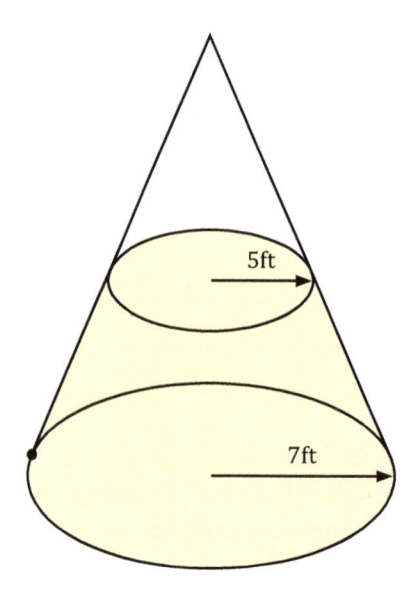

The final aspect of similarity we will want to examine with pupils is the use of maps and scale diagrams (although we may not necessarily want to leave it until the end of a pupil's journey). We may have perhaps used map scales when looking at ratio and/or proportion problems (indeed, a simple example was shared in Chapter 6); however, it is worth reviewing maps/scale diagrams/blueprints, etc. when studying similarity. One thing that pupils should be clear on is that a map/scale diagram is designed to be similar to the real plan view or elevation of the shape or space being drawn. It then becomes natural to start bringing our understanding of similarity to our use of maps/scale diagrams. This might be in simple ways, such as using the scale factor from the map to real life to find real-life distances or areas:

> A scale diagram of a park uses a scale of 1 cm = 10 m.
>
> a A park is 15 cm across on the diagram. Work out the equivalent distance in real life.
>
> b A playground in the park as an area of 4.3 cm² on the diagram. Work out the area the playground takes up in real life.

One of my favourite stimuli for working with pupils on this is the Nuffield Foundation 'Plans' resource. This resource includes different scale diagrams that pupils can measure and then convert using the provided scale (I often just use the diagrams and invent my own questions for pupils rather than use the tables provided).[13]

---

13 Nuffield Foundation, Plans (2011). Available at: https://www.nuffieldfoundation.org/sites/default/files/files/FSMA%20Plans%20student.pdf.

In addition to using scale diagrams on paper, we can work with pupils to support them in using skills learnt about similarity to solve real-life problems, like this one from Maths Is Fun:[14]

> Sam is trying to measure the height of tree. He puts a stick in the ground so that it stands 2.4 metres above the ground (as shown). Sam then measures the length of the shadow that the stick casts as 1.3 m, and the length of the shadow that the tree casts as 2.9 m. Use this information to work out the height of the tree.

This, of course, can actually be done practically with pupils provided schools have space, which gives a lovely experience of pupils practically applying their maths. What is important if we are undertaking this activity practically is that pupils understand that we are creating a 'scale diagram' of the tree using the stick in the ground – scale diagrams don't only work on paper in this sense. Pupils may then wish to represent the problem on paper:

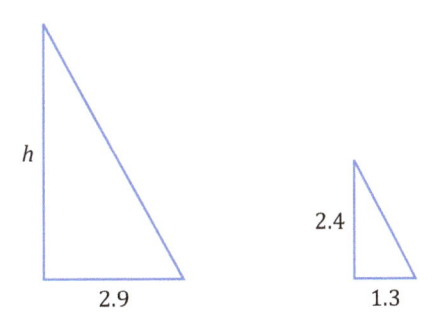

Looking at maps in more detail also provides excellent opportunities for interweaving other previously studied concepts, such as bearings and accurate constructions (from Kangaroo Maths[15]).

> An aeroplane leaves an airport and flies 500 km on a bearing of 078°. It then changes to a bearing of 245° and flies 1000 km.

---

14 R. Pierce, Proportions, *Maths Is Fun* (5 June 2022). Available at: https://www.mathsisfun.com/algebra/proportions.html.
15 Kangaroo Maths, Bearings and Scale Drawings (2011). Available at: https://kangaroomaths.co.uk/wp-content/uploads/2019/11/Bearings-and-Scale-Drawing.pdf.

a   At the point where the aeroplane was due south of the start, how far was it from the airport?

b   What is the straight-line distance between the start point and end point of the flight?

eChalk have some nice problems that link bearings and map scale together[16] or we can offer pupils more loci-based questions involving scale, like this one from Boss Maths:[17]

Exam-style question 2:

A fighter pilot wishes to fly from P to Q.

The pilot must remain closer to point B than point A at all times.

The pilot must also stay at least 30 km away from point C.

On the diagram, accurately shade the region that the pilot must avoid.

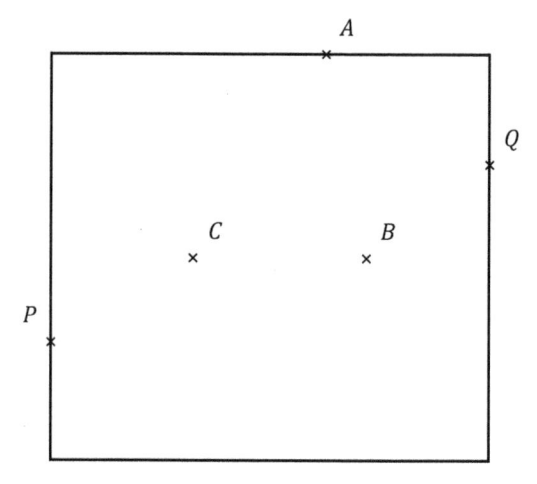

Scale: 1 cm represents 10 km

This concludes our examination of vectors, transformations and related concepts, and with it, our focus on geometry. We will now move on to consider teaching the concepts underpinning chance.

---

16 eChalk, Bearings: Maps and Scale Drawings (n.d.). Available at: https://www.echalk.co.uk/Maths/bearings/mapReading/bearingsWorksheet.pdf.
17 S. Gokarakonda,, G2c – Mixed Loci Problems, Boss Maths (n.d.). Available at: https://www.bossmaths.com/g2c/.

Chapter 12

Chance

When it comes to the study of chance, we should not rush to provide 'measures' of chance, be they words like 'certain' or 'unlikely', indications on a scale or numerical values. The first key point that pupils should consider when it comes to chance is that we are trying to decide the probability of a particular event out of all the possible outcomes of an experiment, and that there are a couple of possible ways we might go about this, namely:

1. If we know all possible outcomes, we might be able to determine the relative likelihood of a particular event happening in the experiment.

2. We can look at evidence gathered, either historically or in a properly designed fair experiment to help determine the likelihood of a particular event, appreciating that this will only allow us to estimate the probability and that the more trials of the experiment that are considered, the better our estimate will be.

Concept: probability

Prerequisites: Number (particularly fractions/decimals), measures, percentage.

Linked concepts: Ratio/proportion, graphing, frequency.

Before we then consider what a measure of this probability might be, we might start by examining how we might determine probability from a given situation (including situations where there is no need to determine probability because the situation is controlled).

> Consider in each situation how we might determine the probability of the particular event:
>
> a Drawing an ace from a full deck of cards.
>
> b Determining the probability of a green car passing the front of a building in a 30-minute time span.
>
> c A roulette wheel landing on the number 27.
>
> d Picking out a particular colour of pencil crayon from a drawer full of crayons whilst looking.
>
> e Picking out a particular colour of pencil crayon from a drawer full of crayons with eyes closed.
>
> f A field in a farm producing more than a tonne of vegetables in a harvest.
>
> g The weather being dry tomorrow.
>
> h Winning a lottery jackpot.

There should be good discussion around prompts like this, which should start to bring in the need for randomness (particularly when comparing the events from (d) and (e) above) as an important consideration when considering the probability of a particular outcome when knowing all possible outcomes. In addition, this is a good time to secure important language around probability, particularly words like **event, outcome, experiment** and **trial**.

For each situation above:

a   Describe the experiment.

b   Suggest those experiments that may benefit from more than one trial in determining the probability.

c   List at least three possible outcomes from the experiment.

d   State the particular event and whether it consists of just one of the outcomes or many outcomes.

Once pupils are clear on how the language associated with the study of probability and what we might consider when trying to determine probability, then we can go on to look at how we can attempt to measure the probability. Normally this would start with ascribing a simple word to the probability of different events. An oldie, but goodie, for this is the activity 'What are the chances?' from the *Year 7: Handling Data* book in the 'Key Stage 3 Developing Numeracy' series.[1]

One thing to watch out for here is pupils having differing views on whether some events are likely or not and saying things like, 'It is just random, isn't it'. These sorts of views must be challenged – it is entirely the point of studying probability that we are trying to find a way to describe and measure just how 'random' a particular event is. Pupils often confuse randomness with 'equally likely', and we will often need to reinforce the idea that whilst experiments may have random outcomes, that doesn't mean all events are equally likely.

Of course, the issue with using words is it is very difficult to distinguish between the relative likelihood of different events whose probabilities are close in value. For example, if two events A and B are both 'likely' to occur from a given experiment, which is more likely? Now, we can compare them (e.g. 'A is more likely than B'), but the entire point of (effective) measurement (as we have seen) is to provide comparable values. This leads to the idea of using a scale (in common with other measurement) to show a measure of the probability of a particular event happening, first using words to show the ends of the scale:

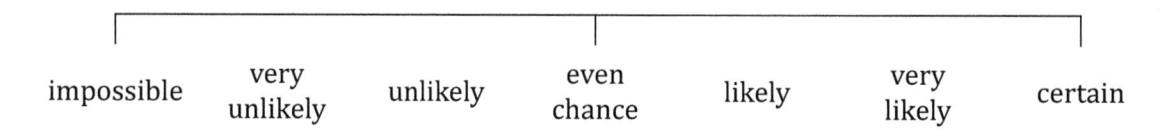

| impossible | very unlikely | unlikely | even chance | likely | very likely | certain |

where similar events to those from the activity above can be placed on the scale, before then considering how we can turn this into a numerical scale. Percentages are a good bridge to this, with things like '100% certain' and 'zero chance' being language that pupils will perhaps have met in different contexts. This can then allow the transition to the more usual probability scale starting in 0 and ending in 1.

---

1   H. Koll and S. Mills, *Year 7: Handling Data; Activities for Teaching Numeracy* (New York: A&C Black Children's & Educational, 2004).

Impossible	Unlikely	Equally unlikely as likely	Likely	Certain
0	$\frac{1}{4}$	$\frac{1}{2}$	$\frac{3}{4}$	1
0	0.25	0.5	0.75	1
0%	25%	50%	75%	100%

(Although we need to be clear that 'likely' and 'unlikely' are not directly equivalent to 75% and 25% respectively but rather span the whole space between either end and the middle).

This then leads to the idea that probabilities can be written as fractions.

When it comes to writing probabilities as fractions, pupils should understand that one way the fraction can be arrived at is simply by taking the possible outcomes for an event and writing it as a fraction of the total number of possible outcomes from an experiment. This, however, is only the case when each possible outcome has an equal chance of happening. A nice way to highlight this is to use these two spinners:

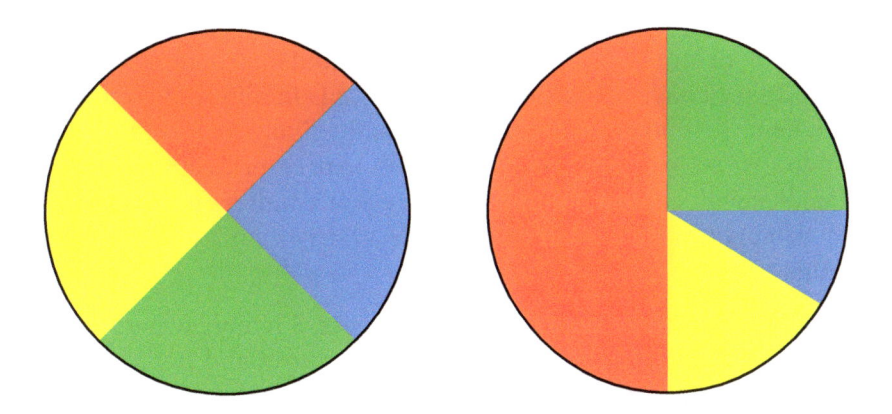

Both spinners have the same four colours; however, only in the first is each colour equally likely to happen. This means that if we consider an event such as 'spinner lands on red' or 'spinner lands on a primary colour of light', then in the case of the first spinner we can write that, in theory, P(red) = $\frac{1}{4}$, or P(primary colour of light) = $\frac{3}{4}$ (in each case the possible outcome(s) for the event written as a fraction of the total number of possible outcomes from spinning the spinner). What we must impress upon pupils is that, when we write something like this, we are still assigning a measure to the chance of a particular event happening *the next time* the spinner is spun; it is easy for pupils to get bogged down in just looking at outcomes to write probabilities as fractions and lose sight of the idea that we are measuring chance of future events.

In the case of the second spinner, the point to be made is that whilst there are four possible outcomes from spinning the spinner, they are not all equally likely, and so if we want to examine something like P(red) or P(primary colour of light), we cannot simply say, 'There are four possible outcomes from this experiment.' However, we might encourage pupils to redefine the possible outcomes from the experiment, either into 1° sections or potentially into sections equal in size to the blue:

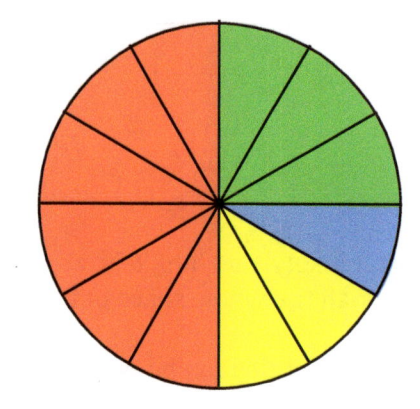

Pupils should understand that we are now considering each section as a separate outcome to the experiment 'spinning the spinner', so that when evaluating P(red), we can see that the event 'lands on red' can occur from six different equally likely outcomes, out of a possible 12 different equally likely outcomes.

This reimagining and redefining of outcomes from an experiment so that each outcome is equally likely is an important idea for pupils to understand in probability, and pupils should be given opportunities to have to consider how to do this in different circumstances, alongside questions where the outcomes are already equally likely. Spinners that can be broken into different equal-sized sections are an obvious source of questions, such as the one above, as well as dice with repeated numbers, sweets or counters in a bag or jar, etc. Sweets are particularly useful because we can offer pupils a fairly innocuous-looking sweets question similar to this:

> In a jar there are 4 strawberry sweets, 5 apple sweets, 3 lemon sweets and 8 blackcurrant sweets. Ellis reaches into the jar with his eyes closed and pulls out a sweet. Ellis says he as a $\frac{1}{4}$ chance of picking an apple sweet because there are four flavours and apple is one of them. Comment on Ellis' reasoning.

This question gives us an opportunity to explore pupils' thinking around probability a little more closely, making sure they understand that each separate sweet is a separate outcome to the 'experiment' regardless of the flavour, but then we might prompt pupils to consider what happens if the sweets are different shapes or sizes, if the sweets are randomly distributed throughout the jar (are you more likely to take a sweet from the top or the bottom of the jar?) and other complicating situations that mean that each sweet is not equally likely to be chosen.

Another important aspect to writing probabilities that pupils should appreciate is the link to expectation. Pupils should understand that when we say P(apple) = $\frac{1}{4}$ in the above question, then we are saying there is a $\frac{1}{4}$ or 25% chance that a sweet chosen at random (assuming this is possible) will be an apple-flavoured sweet, but we are also saying that if we were to take four sweets at random, then we would expect to get one apple sweet in the four. Of course, this may or may not actually happen; we may get two, three or four apple sweets, or we may get none at all, but the most reasonable expectation is that we will get one sweet. We can then offer pupils the opportunity to reason further: what if there were 40 strawberry sweets, 50 apple sweets, 30 lemon sweets and 80 blackcurrant sweets, and we were to take 20? Or 30?

There are plenty of different questions that can form basic practice with these ideas, as well as questions that can prompt pupils to think and apply the ideas alongside others, such as this question from Corbettmaths:[2]

Elliott has eight numbered cards.

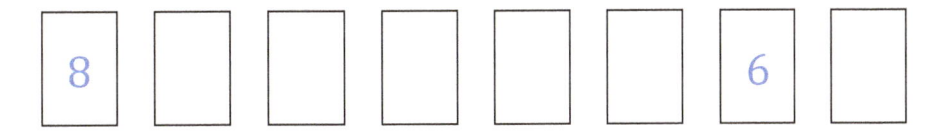

[8] [ ] [ ] [ ] [ ] [ ] [6] [ ]

One of the cards is chosen at random. Elliott says:
- The probability of an 8 is $\frac{1}{4}$.
- The range of the numbers is 5.
- The probability of a number greater than 10 is 0.
- The probability of a 7 is $\frac{1}{2}$.

Fill in the six missing numbers.

Once pupils are used to measuring chance using fractions, we can then go back to the idea of measuring chance using historical data or a carefully designed experiment using the **relative frequency** of the outcomes for an event compared to the total number of outcomes (or the number of times the experiment is performed). There is a wealth of historical data that we can offer to pupils to examine the probability of future events (we still shouldn't lose sight of the fact that this is what we are trying to achieve); a nice source is the historical England census data found on the Office of National Statistics website.[3] As well as historical data, pupils can be actively involved in generating data for estimating probability by conducting different statistical experiments. These can range from simple biased die experiments (create die using nets and cubes and weight them towards whichever value you like, or you can purchase loaded dice online) to experiments based on interesting historical problems such as the Monty Hall Problem.[4] One of my personal favourites is the paving slabs investigation in Colin Foster's *Data, Numeracy and ICT* book (from the 'Instant Maths Ideas for Key Stage 3 Teachers' series).[5] One key outcome from these experiments should be that pupils appreciate that the value of the estimate of the probability produced by experimental data will tend towards the theoretical or 'true' value of the probability as the number of trials increases.

---

2 J. Corbett,, Probability, *Corbettmaths* (2021). Available at: https://corbettmaths.com/wp-content/uploads/2021/03/Probability-2.pdf.
3 Office for National Statistics, Census (n.d.). Available at: https://www.ons.gov.uk/census#censusdataandbackground.
4 K. M. Ellis, The Monty Hall Problem, *Monty Hall Problem* (1995). Available at: https://www.montyhallproblem.com/.
5 C. Foster, 3.5 Probability, *Foster77* (2003), p. 4. Available at: https://www.foster77.co.uk/3.05%20Probability.pdf.

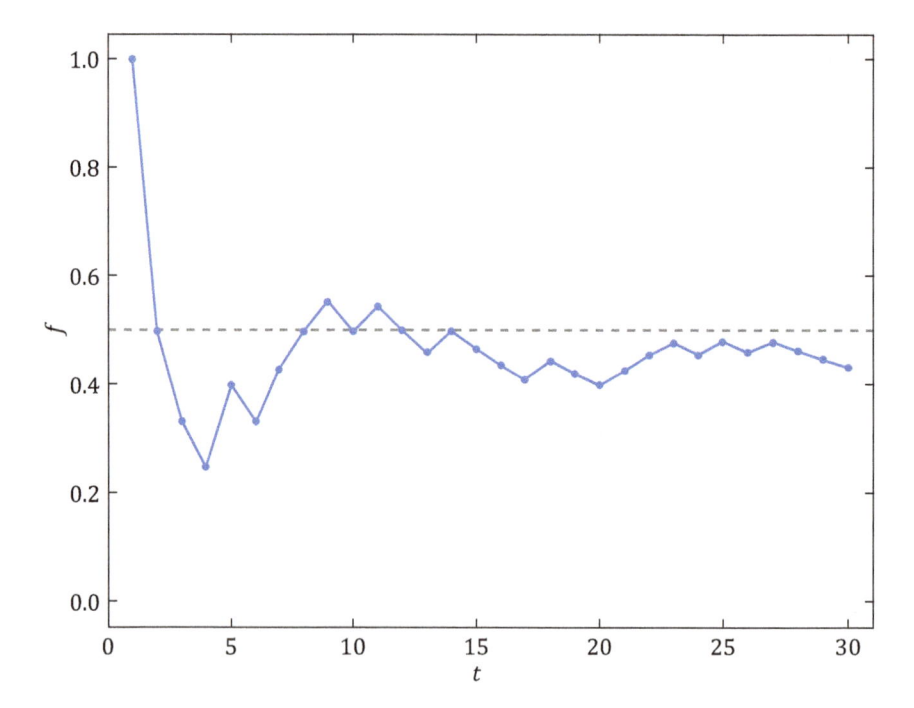

There are a multitude of different problems that pupils can be offered around single-event probability. Many of these involve some form of proportional or algebraic thinking, such as:

> The ratio of red counters to yellow counters in a bag is 3:2. The probability of choosing a red counter from the bag is $\frac{1}{8}$. Work out the probability of choosing a yellow counter from the bag.

> A bag contains different coloured counters. The probability of choosing a red counter is $\frac{3}{11}$. The probability of choosing a blue counter is $\frac{2}{5}$. If there are 15 red counters, work out the number blue counters.

> A bag contains different coloured counters. The probability of choosing a red counter is double the probability of choosing a blue counter. The probability of choosing a yellow counter is $\frac{1}{2}$. The difference between the probability of choosing a red and yellow counter is $\frac{1}{3}$. Work out the smallest possible number of counters in the bag.

One problem type inextricably linked to considering probability is the idea of 'fairness'. Pupils should understand that probability can help identify whether a situation is fair in two different ways:

1. That every person involved has an equal chance of achieving an equally valuable 'reward'.

2. If a person involved has a smaller chance of achieving the reward, then the value of the reward changes to reflect this.

A simple situation that most pupils will understand is a two-player game. A game like the one below can help illustrate the different ways a situation can become fair:

> Two players are playing a game where they flip a coin onto the grid of boxes below so that the coin lands completely inside one of the boxes at random. If the coin lands in a

blue box, player 1 gets a point. If the coin lands in a white box, player 2 gets a point. The first player to get to 20 points wins. Is this game fair? Justify your response.

Pupils can play this game; however, it ideally needs to have three-dimensional boxes (or at least raised lines) so that coins flipped onto the grid do have to fall inside a single box. If pupils do play the game (particularly if they play a reasonable number of times), then they might come to recognise that player 1 and player 2 broadly win an equal number of times. Whether pupils play the game or not, we can reason that the game is fair because the chance of either player winning a point is $\frac{10}{20} = \frac{1}{2}$. We can then begin to complicate this into three-person games, etc. and even questioning pupils as to what the chance of each person winning would have to be for fair games involving different numbers of people (leading to the relatively straightforward idea that if there are n people playing that each needs a $\frac{1}{n}$ chance of winning a point/round, etc. for the situation to be fair). We can then potentially return to a scenario similar to the above, with a prompt such as:

Two players are playing a game where they flip a coin onto the grid of boxes below so that the coin lands completely inside one of the boxes at random. If the coin lands in a blue box, player 1 gets four points. If the coin lands in a white box, player 2 gets one point. The first player to get to 20 points wins. Is this game fair? Justify your response.

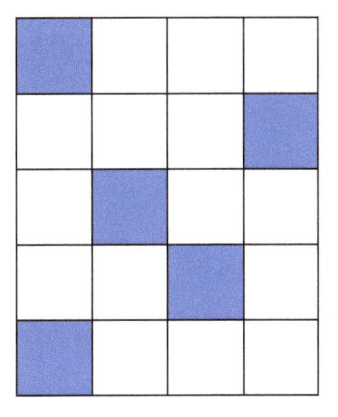

In this case we can clearly see that the chance of player 1 scoring is less than the chance of player 2 scoring; however, the scenario is complicated by the fact that when player 1 does score, they score more. I find pupils are more clearly able to see that this game is fair if we examine what is expected when a number of turns are taken – in this case, five (or a multiple of). As the probability of player 1 scoring is $\frac{1}{5}$, we would expect player 1 to score on one in every five flips. Similarly, we would expect player 2 to score on four in every five flips.

This means we expect player 1 to score 1 × 4 points in every five flips, and player 2 to score 4 × 1 points in every five flips. This leads to the conclusion that both players are expected to score the same number of points in every five flips, and therefore the game is fair. This further leads to the idea that the probability of winning and the reward for winning for each player should be inversely proportional for a game to be fair (assuming pupils have studied inverse proportionality by this point; if not then it is a good thing to come back to when inverse proportionality is studied). When we then study further situations involving reward, pupils can use inverse proportion to demonstrate whether games are fair or not:

A spinner has 5 equal sectors numbers 1 to 5, it is spun many times.

If the spinner stops on an even number, team A gets 3 points.

If the spinner stops on an odd number, team B gets 2 points.

The probability of an even number is $\frac{2}{5}$ and the reward is 3 points, and $\frac{2}{5} \times 3 = \frac{6}{5}$. The probability of an odd number is $\frac{3}{5}$ and the reward is 2 points, and $\frac{3}{5} \times 2 = \frac{6}{5}$. The fact that these results are the same shows that the probabilities and rewards are inversely proportional; and so the game is fair.

As well as deciding whether games are fair, pupils can, of course, design their own fair games. Care must be taken so that pupils' attention is on the mathematics underpinning their game, rather than the game concept, etc. but it can be an opportunity that pupils can access at a range of points, from designing simple games where probabilities are kept equal and rewards are equal, to more complicated games where unequal probabilities are balanced by unequal rewards. This may also lead into (or conversely be better left until) looking at events that require combining outcomes as it creates a good motivation for examining more complex probabilities to create more involved games.

When it comes to combined-event probability, what pupils should appreciate is that the actual act of arriving at the measure of chance is not different to what we have already seen. The added complexity comes from the increased difficulty in evaluating what the outcomes are when they come from combining events together. The study of combined-event probability therefore typically has to begin with different ways of working out the outcomes.

Concept: combined events

Prerequisites: Number (particularly fractions/decimals), operations, measures, percentage, probability.

Linked concepts: Data analysis.

If I roll two fair dice, what is the probability at least one of them lands on a 6? This is the sort of question that we might offer pupils to prompt them to think about more complicated situations where either the number of outcomes for an event or the total number of possible outcomes is not immediately obvious due to the fact that the outcomes are being combined from separate experiments. It is worth offering something like this without teaching around sample spaces or other approaches to combining events first, so that we can examine pupils' informal approaches to thinking about these sorts of problems. Pupils may well attempt some sort of listing strategy or thought process, which we can acknowledge (listing strategies are useful in many circumstances), but rarely are these informal strategies complete or efficient. This provides a platform to offer some ways to represent combined events, starting with a sample space:

		Second dice					
		1	2	3	4	5	6
First dice	1	(1,1)	(1,2)	(1,3)	(1,4)	(1,5)	(1,6)
	2	(2,1)	(2,2)	(2,3)	(2,4)	(2,5)	(2,6)
	3	(3,1)	(3,2)	(3,3)	(3,4)	(3,5)	(3,6)
	4	(4,1)	(4,2)	(4,3)	(4,4)	(4,5)	(4,6)
	5	(5,1)	(5,2)	(5,3)	(5,4)	(5,5)	(5,6)
	6	(6,1)	(6,2)	(6,3)	(6,4)	(6,5)	(6,6)

Pupils rarely need too much help in seeing the benefits of this sort of representation once they have tried their own listing strategies (particularly when – as often happens – these do not lead to easy evaluation of the possible outcomes). Re-posing the question once pupils have seen this sample space will normally lead to correct identification of the fraction $\frac{11}{36}$, which it normally helps pupils to conceptualise if we talk about it as a little more than 30% probability (some pupils might be able to see it as a little under $\frac{1}{3}$ but not necessarily all of them).

Pupils should have the opportunity to construct their own sample spaces and to interpret sample spaces that have been pre-constructed. Important amongst these are when combining different outcomes leads to the same result – for example, when summing the results of two dice roles:

	+	Second dice					
		1	2	3	4	5	6
First dice	1	2	3	4	5	6	7
	2	3	4	5	6	7	8
	3	4	5	6	7	8	9
	4	5	6	7	8	9	10
	5	6	7	8	9	10	11
	6	7	8	9	10	11	12

Pupils really need to understand that, although some of the results are the same, all 36 entries represent the same different outcomes that they did in the first table. In this way, each of the outcomes can be considered equally likely, and we can evaluate probabilities like $P(5)$ or $P(Prime)$ in the same way we did for single-event probabilities.

As well as highlighting the advantages of a sample space, we should also highlight the drawbacks; in particular, the fact that a sample space can only handle combing the outcomes of two experiments, and will only inform us about probabilities if each outcome of the separate experiments are equally likely (although sample spaces can be adapted to allow examination of outcomes that are not equally likely).

One representation that tends not to be introduced until significantly later, and potentially unnecessarily late, is that of a tree diagram. I do not mean tree diagrams with probabilities attached that lead to calculations, but simple tree diagrams showing outcomes that are equally likely.

The use of tree diagrams in mathematics teaching in England has probably been coloured by their use in end of Key Stage 4 examinations, which typically involves using them as a vehicle for probability calculation. However, pupils should be exposed to tree diagrams well before their use for probability calculations as a way of representing combined events. A nice early example of this is representing the possible outcomes from flipping three fair coins (or a single fair coin three times):

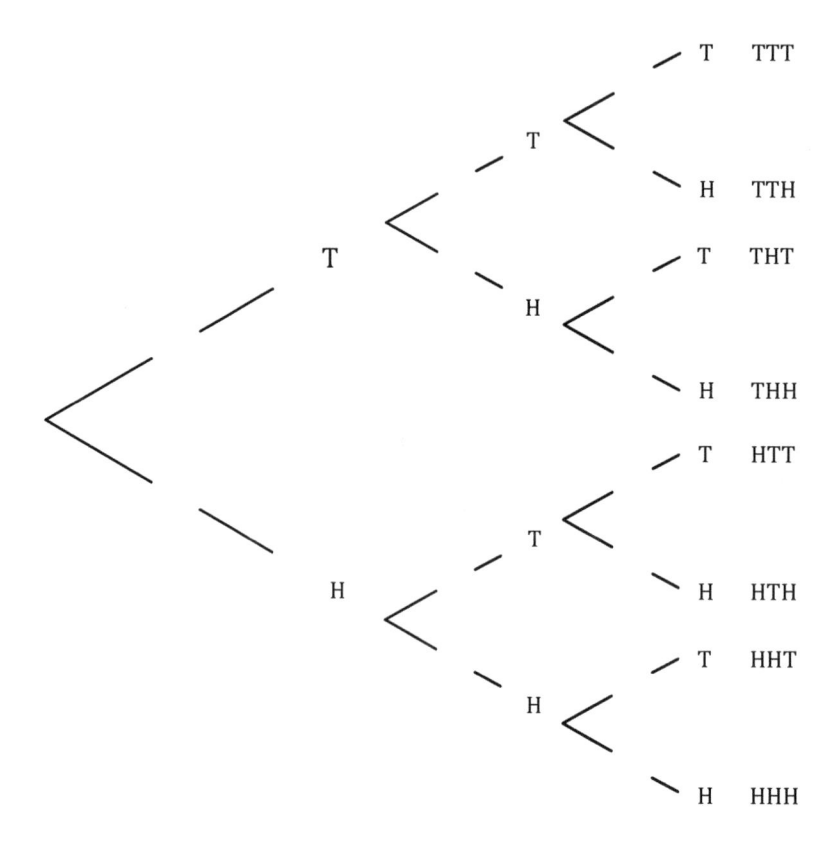

```
                                    T   TTT
                            T <
                                    H   TTH
                T <
                                    T   THT
                            H <
                                    H   THH
        <
                                    T   HTT
                            T <
                                    H   HTH
                H <
                                    T   HHT
                            H <
                                    H   HHH
```

We can see, if the outcomes of each coin flip are equally likely, then there are eight equally likely outcomes from the combined events. Pupils should appreciate the relative strengths and weaknesses of tree diagrams with respect to sample spaces; in particular that tree diagrams can represent the result of combining more than two experiments but work best if there are a relatively small number of outcomes in each experiment. It may be worth, for example, showing pupils a tree diagram for the rolling of two dice so that they can compare directly to the sample space:

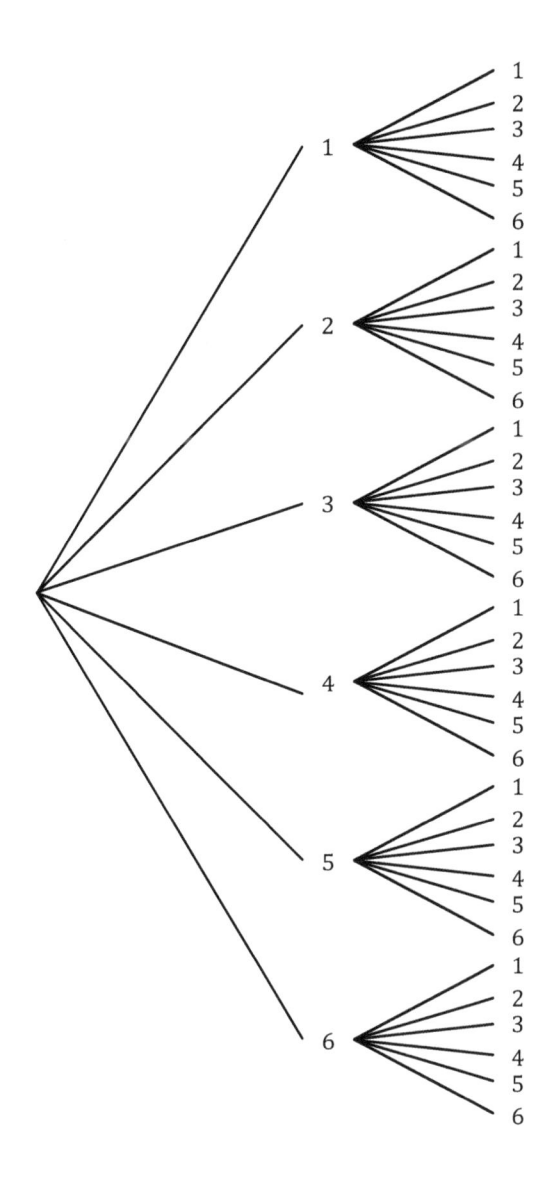

Pupils can appreciate that this is much more time- and space-consuming than the sample space because there are too many possible outcomes at each event. Of course, if we were to add a third die, then neither the sample space nor the tree diagram will be a particularly useful representation – in fact, this will be one of the primary motivations to allow us to leave representations behind and rely simply on the product rule and probability calculation. However, before we examine probability calculations, we should examine a third approach to combining events – using systematic listing.

We mentioned earlier that pupils may try and utilise listing strategies when faced with more complicated probability scenarios. One big reason why these strategies are often not successful is that there is little in the way of strategy in pupils' informal listing approaches. An important thing we need to explore with pupils is a pre-planned system for generating lists, to ensure that we identify all possible outcomes without duplicating any outcome. As a start point we might go back to the tree diagram showing three coin flips and talk about how the tree diagram imposes a structure on how the final outcomes are displayed: first outcomes TTT and TTH (that start with TT), then THT and THH (that start with TH), then HTT and HTH (that start with HT), and finally HHT and HHH (that start with HH). We can discuss with pupils alternative strategies we could use to list all of these outcomes whilst ensuring we continue to list all outcomes with no duplicates. We can then offer other scenarios; the classic is the race final:

> There are six runners in a 100-metre final race, numbered 1 through 6. The three quickest runners win medals – gold (G), silver (S) and bronze (B). List all the different possible combinations of medal winners.

The obvious strategy here is an ordered list, either low to high or high to low:

G	S	B
1	2	3
1	2	4
1	2	5
1	2	6
1	3	2
1	3	4
1	3	5
1	3	6
1	4	2
1	4	3
1	4	5
1	4	6
2	6	1
2	6	3
2	6	4
2	6	5
3	1	2
3	1	4
3	1	5
3	1	6
3	2	1
3	2	4
3	2	5
3	2	6
3	4	1
3	4	2
3	4	5
3	4	6
3	5	1
3	5	2
3	5	4
3	5	6
3	6	1
3	6	2
3	6	4
3	6	5
4	1	2
4	1	3
4	1	5
4	1	6

G	S	B
1	5	2
1	5	3
1	5	4
1	5	6
1	6	2
1	6	3
1	6	4
1	6	5
2	1	3
2	1	4
2	1	5
2	1	6
4	2	1
4	2	3
4	2	5
4	2	6
4	3	1
4	3	2
4	3	5
4	3	6
4	5	1
4	5	2
4	5	3
4	5	6
4	6	1
4	6	2
4	6	3
4	6	5
5	1	2
5	1	3
5	1	4
5	1	6
5	2	1
5	2	3
5	2	4
5	2	6
5	3	1
5	3	2
5	3	4
5	3	6

G	S	B
2	3	1
2	3	4
2	3	5
2	3	6
2	4	1
2	4	3
2	4	5
2	4	6
2	5	1
2	5	3
2	5	4
2	5	6
5	4	1
5	4	2
5	4	3
5	4	6
5	6	1
5	6	2
5	6	3
5	6	4
6	1	2
6	1	3
6	1	4
6	1	5
6	2	1
6	2	3
6	2	4
6	2	5
6	3	1
6	3	2
6	3	4
6	3	5
6	4	1
6	4	2
6	4	3
6	4	5
6	5	1
6	5	2
6	5	3
6	5	4

Whilst this is a long list, there are a couple of nice directions we can take this in:

1   We can talk about whether all of these outcomes are equally likely – in real racing, those with the quickest times in the heats are the favourites and tend to start in the middle lanes, so those involving lanes 3 and 4 in the gold and silver positions are potentially more likely.

2   If we assume that each outcome is equally likely, then a lovely event to explore is 'the numbers appear in either ascending or descending order'; so 3, 4, 6 and 5, 2, 1 are both outcomes for the event, but 5, 1, 6 is not.

There are lots of simpler listing activities out there (fixed price menus are a popular context to place listing in). The Centre for Innovation in Mathematics Teaching created a nice exercise as part of their MEP Year 8 textbook,[6] but lists like this reinforce the idea that ideally we would like to go beyond the need to list or represent all possible outcomes – it shouldn't be necessary if what we really want to know is how many there are, rather than what each one of them is. This is the perfect bridge into probability calculations.

Concept link: operations and probability

The calculation that arises most naturally from the representations and listing strategies above is the product rule for counting. Highlighting these previous representations, we can ask questions like, 'Why did rolling two dice produce 36 different outcomes?', 'Why did flipping three coins result in eight different outcomes?' Many pupils will then reason the multiplicative nature of the process; particularly if pupils have seen area or tree diagrams linked in general to multiplication. We can then explore the race situation and understand why there are 120 different outcomes in that list: there are six people that could take the gold medal, and then once one person gets gold there are five that could take silver, and then once gold and silver are fixed, there are four people left that could take bronze. This means the number of possible combinations are 6 × 5 × 4 = 120 outcomes. We can then take this a step further and consider the outcomes for a particular event, like the one suggested earlier about having values in ascending or descending order (to be fair, this is relatively complicated to consider with the product rule, so we might need to build up to it!).

Pupils should work with different scenarios for the product rule, including independent events that lead to powers, ordering scenarios that lead to factorials (I always introduce pupils to factorials and factorial notation at GCSE for the product rule) and then general scenarios that lead to more general multiplication. The three of these can be highlighted with these three related examples:

> A bag contains four colours of counters: red, blue, green and yellow. A counter is removed from the bag, its colour noted, and then the counter is replaced. This is repeated four times. How many different possible colour combinations could be written down?

> A bag contains four colours of counters: red, blue, green and yellow. One of each colour counter is removed from the bag and placed in one of four spaces. How many different combinations of counters could be made?

---

6   CIMT, MEP Y8 Practice Book 8A Chapter 10: Probability – Two Events (n.d.). Available at: https://www.cimt.org.uk/projects/mepres/book8/bk8_10.pdf.

A bag contains a large number of four colours of counters: red, blue, green, yellow. Four counters are removed from the bag, one after the other. No two consecutive counters are the same colour. How many different combinations of colours could be taken out?

In the first case, we have $4^4 = 256$ different colour combinations, compared to the second scenario where there are $4! = 4 \times 3 \times 2 \times 1 = 24$ colour combinations. In the third scenario there are $4 \times 3 \times 3 \times 3 = 108$ different colour combinations: the first counter could be any of the four colours, but there are only three possible colours for the second (it can't be the same as the first), then only three possible colours for the third (it can't be the same as the second) and then finally, only three possible colours for the fourth (it can't be the same as the third). In my blog from 2015, I talk about how questions of each type can be created easily by tweaking questions that originally asked for lists or listing strategies, including my personal favourite multiplicative counting scenario:[7]

Anne, Barry, Colin and Damien book four seats next to each other in the cinema as shown.

Seat 1	Seat 2	Seat 3	Seat 4

a How many different ways can they sit?

b What is the probability that Anne and Barry sit next to each other?

c How is your answer to part (b) affected if the four seats are not next to each other in a cinema, but around a table on a train as shown?

Seat 1	Seat 2

Seat 4	Seat 3

This opens up many lines of enquiry, including extra people, extra seats, different arrangements of seats, etc.

Because of the quick growth of repeated multiplication, the product rule for counting is a great place to interweave writing numbers in standard form. Excellent scenarios to offer pupils here are combination padlocks:

A padlock uses a five-digit code. Each digit can be any of the digits 0, 1, 2, 3, 4, 5, 6, 7, 8, or 9. Work out the number of possible combinations. Give your answer in standard form.

---

[7] P. Mattock, Multiplicative Counting – The Different Types, *Educating Mr Mattock* [blog] (17 August 2015). Available at: https://educatingmrmattock.blogspot.com/2015/08/multiplicative-counting-different-types.html.

Bingo cards:

On a 75-ball bingo card, each column has five numbers except the middle one which has four. The first column picks from the numbers 1 to 15, the second column from 16 to 30, the third from 31 to 45, the fourth from 46 to 60 and fifth from 61 to 75.

Work out the number of cards it is possible to create. Give your answer in standard form.

B	I	N	G	O
2	17	31	48	63
6	20	38	51	68
7	22	FREE	54	69
12	23	39	57	72
15	27	44	60	75

and different vehicle number plates:

In each number plate below, the letters can be anything from A to Z, and each digit from 0 to 9. Work out how many number plates are possible in each case. Give each answer in standard form, rounded to 3 significant figures.

Conceptual Maths

The product rule for counting is one potential way to then move onto multiplying probabilities; however, a really nice way to begin with this is to revisit some of our earlier representations and consider how we might adapt them to deal with the following situation:

A coin is biased so that it has a $\frac{3}{5}$ probability of heads. If I flip the coin twice, what is the probability that:

a   the coin lands on heads twice?

b   the coin lands on heads then tails?

c   the coin lands on tails then heads?

d   the coin lands on tails twice?

The issue here is that the representations we used earlier do not factor in the bias:

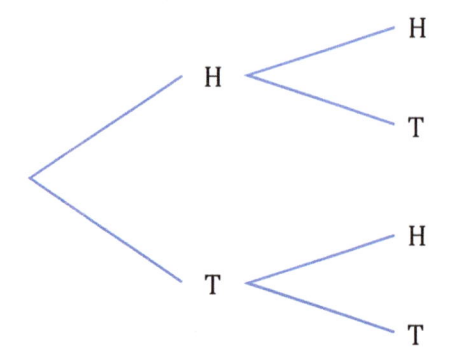

	Coin 1		
Coin 2		H	T
H		HH	HT
T		TH	TT

We can, however, modify both of these to take into account the bias by representing the probabilities as five different outcomes in a modified sample space or graph:

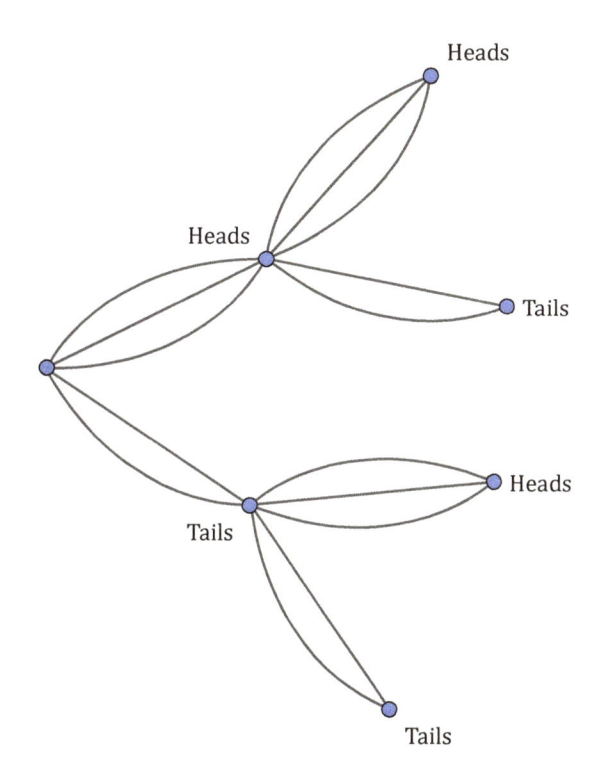

	H	H	H	T	T
H	HH	HH	HH	TH	TH
H	HH	HH	HH	TH	TH
H	HH	HH	HH	TH	TH
T	HT	HT	HT	TT	TT
T	HT	HT	HT	TT	TT

Either of these show why the probabilities are multiplied to find the probability of the combined event; for example, getting two heads. If pupils have used area models to multiply fractions, then the sample space should be immediately recognisable as being akin to an area model where we multiply $\frac{3}{5} \times \frac{3}{5}$; we can see the 'HH' section is a 3 × 3 part of the 5 × 5 whole.

The graph shows the same: for two heads there are 3 × 3 routes we could follow (3 to the first heads, and then for each of these, 3 for the second) and 5 × 5 routes in total (or alternatively $\frac{3}{5}$ of the routes take us to the first heads, and then $\frac{3}{5}$ of the routes following this lead to the second heads). This graph in particular is then a very short step to a tree diagram with probabilities attached – this can be seen as a partial abstraction of the graph above:

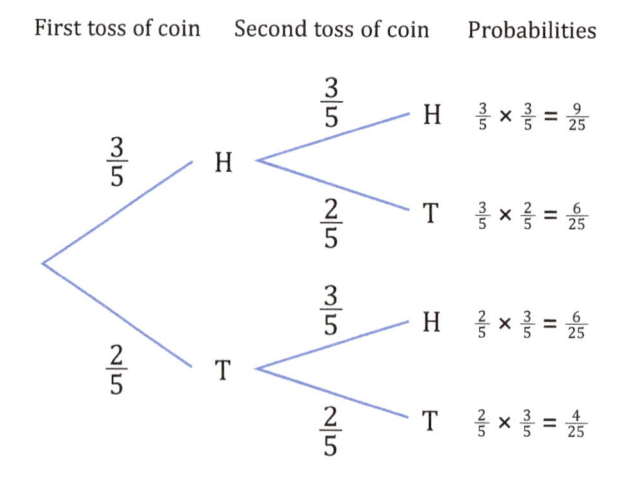

First toss of coin   Second toss of coin   Probabilities

$$\frac{3}{5} \text{ H} \begin{cases} \frac{3}{5} \text{ H} \quad \frac{3}{5} \times \frac{3}{5} = \frac{9}{25} \\ \frac{2}{5} \text{ T} \quad \frac{3}{5} \times \frac{2}{5} = \frac{6}{25} \end{cases}$$

$$\frac{2}{5} \text{ T} \begin{cases} \frac{3}{5} \text{ H} \quad \frac{2}{5} \times \frac{3}{5} = \frac{6}{25} \\ \frac{2}{5} \text{ T} \quad \frac{2}{5} \times \frac{3}{5} = \frac{4}{25} \end{cases}$$

Of course, in this case, the results of the two flips are independent of each other (i.e. the result of the first flip does not affect the probabilities of each result on the second flip). Pupils will have to apply tree diagrams to both situations where outcomes are independent, but also where probabilities of outcomes of later experiments are affected by results of earlier experiments – usually referred to as either dependent or conditional probability calculations. Again, the MEP has some lovely questions on this, both in the book I referenced on page 489 and in the 'Probability' chapter of their 9A Practice Book[8] including this reproduction of a wonderful question from the 1996 Key Stage 3 Maths English SATS extension paper:

On a tropical island the probability of it raining on the first day of the rainy season is $\frac{2}{3}$. If it does not rain on the first day, the probability of it raining on the second day is $\frac{7}{10}$. If it rains on the first day, the probability of it raining more than 10 mm on the first day is $\frac{1}{5}$ If it rains on the second day but not on the first day, the probability of it raining more than 10 mm is $\frac{1}{4}$.

You may find it helpful to copy and complete the tree diagram before answering the questions.

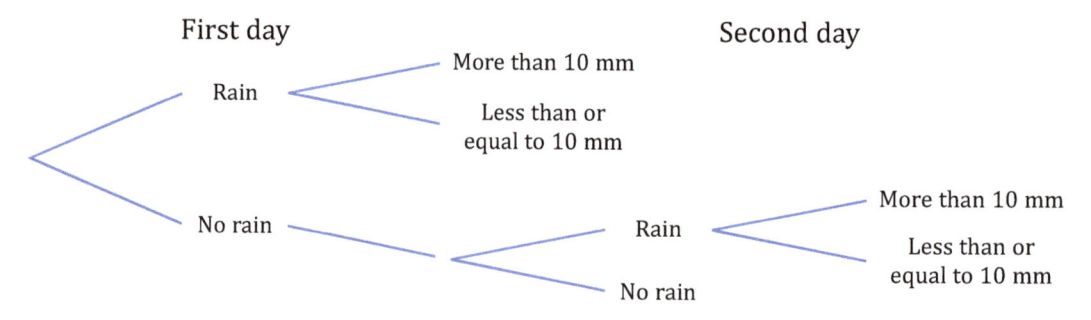

First day

Rain — More than 10 mm
     — Less than or equal to 10 mm

No rain — Rain — More than 10 mm
              — Less than or equal to 10 mm
       — No rain

Second day

a   What is the probability that it rains more than 10 mm on the second day, and does not rain on the first? Show your working.

---

8 CIMT, MEP Y9 Practice Book 9A Chapter 6: Probability (n.d.). Available at: https://www.cimt.org.uk/projects/mepres/book9/bk9_6.pdf.

b   What is the probability that it has rained by the end of the second day of the rainy season? Show your working.

c   Why is it not possible to work out the probability of rain on both days from the information given?

One thing that is particularly notable about this question is that the tree diagram does not grow in a symmetrical manner – most tree diagrams that pupils encounter have the same number of branches at all points so it is important that pupils also see imbalanced tree diagrams like this. Another example of this is in the question below, also from MEP:

Alex takes a driving test. The probability that he will pass on his first attempt is 0.4. If he fails, then the probability that he will pass the test on any subsequent attempt is 0.7.

a   Copy and complete the tree diagram to show the possible outcomes for the first two attempts.

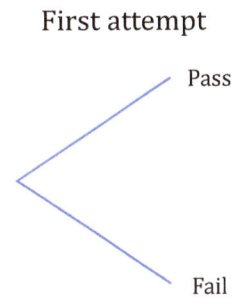

First attempt

Pass

Fail

b   Calculate the probability that Alex needs two attempts, and passes on his second attempt.

c   Calculate the probability that he passes the test after three or four attempts.

Another thing to note in part (b) of the rainfall question on page 495 and also in part (c) of the driving test question, is that there is a requirement to combine the probabilities at the end of different branches through the tree diagram. This requires pupils to understand when probabilities of different events can be combined, and how to combine them. This means exploring the ideas of mutually exclusive events, and the effect that being mutually exclusive has on probability calculations.

Subconcept: mutually exclusive events

Prerequisites: Addition, probability.

Linked concepts: Exhaustivity, algebra, equations, Venn diagrams, set notation.

Although we are only just coming to explore mutual exclusivity now, in reality, due to the lack of prerequisite knowledge required, it is usually the case that mutual exclusivity of events is first examined when pupils are looking at single-event probability. There are two separate strands that pupils need to learn about when it comes to mutually exclusive events:

1   Identifying when events are mutually exclusive and when they are not.

2   Understanding that only when events A, B, C, ... are mutually exclusive does P(A or B or C or ...) = P(A) + P(B) + P(C) + ...

With the first of these, examples and non-examples are particularly useful in highlighting when events are mutually exclusive and when they are not.

A coin comes down heads/ A coin comes down tails	Rolling an even number on a die/ Rolling an odd number on a die
Getting a red card/ Getting a king	Rain during a day/ Sun during a day
Passing an exam/ Failing an exam	Watching the TV/ Listening to music
Being in a maths lesson/ Being in an English lesson	Winning a game/ Losing a game
The sun being visible/ The moon being visible	Being a vegetarian/ Being a vegan
Being summer/ Being winter	Studying/ Reading a book

We can discuss these pairs of events with pupils, deciding which are mutually exclusive and which aren't. We must be careful, however, not to imply that mutually exclusive events only come in pairs, so we should also offer collections of three or more events, and also ask pupils to provide lists of two, three or more than three mutually exclusive events. A good example is traffic lights: using three events – red, amber, green – then red and green are mutually exclusive, amber and green are mutually exclusive, but red and amber are not. However, if we define four states – red, red-amber, amber, and green – then these four events are all mutually exclusive.

Once pupils are familiar with identifying mutually exclusive events (at least through experience, we will get to a more rigorous approach to identification later) then we can introduce the addition law. Again, in single events this can be relatively intuitive to start with.

> A bag contains 3 red counters, 4 green counters, and 6 yellow counters. A counter is picked from the bag at random. Write down the probability that the counter is:
>
> a   red
>
> b   green
>
> c   either red or green

We can answer part (c) in that there are 7 counters that are either red or green, out of 13 counters, and so the probability is $\frac{7}{13}$. But we can also see that this is the sum of the answers to (a) and (b); $\frac{3}{13} + \frac{4}{13} = \frac{7}{13}$.

If introducing the idea that P(A or B) = P(A) + P(B) for mutually exclusive events in this way, then again highlighting non-examples can be useful in making sure pupils understand when this applies and when it doesn't:

> In a class of 30 pupils, 15 of them study history and 14 of them study geography. A pupil is to be picked at random. Frank says that the probability that pupil studies either history or geography is $\frac{29}{30}$, because $\frac{15}{30} + \frac{14}{30} = \frac{29}{30}$. Marie says Frank is wrong. Who do you agree with and why?

If pupils struggle to see why Frank is wrong, then perhaps ask pupils what would happen if, instead of 14 pupils studying geography, 16 pupils studied geography.

Pupils should then be given the opportunity to work directly with probabilities, deciding whether events are mutually exclusive or not and finding probabilities of more than one of the events happening when they are (this is an excellent opportunity to interweave practice for addition of fractions and decimals). The Year 7 MEP book on probability has some nice questions where the events are mutually exclusive, but for best effect they need to be mixed up with occasions where the events are not mutually exclusive – fortunately, there are a few questions later in the same book where events are not mutually exclusive that can be adapted to prompt pupil thinking.[9] These questions relate to the general addition law for probability, which we will explore a little later in the chapter.

Having studied the addition property for the probabilities of mutually exclusive events, we can then start adapting scenarios to allow pupils to solve problems. These can include simple problems such as:

> There are counters in a bag, some of which are red and some green. A counter is chosen from the bag at random. The probability of choosing a red counter is 0.17. The probability of choosing a red or green counter is 0.43. Work out the probability of choosing a green counter.

To those that may benefit from algebraic interpretation:

> There are counters in a bag, some of which are red, some are green and some are yellow. A counter is chosen from the bag at random. The probability of choosing a red or green counter is 0.4. The probability of choosing a red or yellow counter is 0.6. The probability of choosing a yellow counter is 5 times greater than the probability of choosing a green counter. Show that there must be at least 1 more colour of counter in the bag.

A natural place for mutually exclusive events to progress into is looking at exhaustive lists of events.

Subconcept: exhaustive lists

Prerequisites: Addition, subtraction, probability, mutually exclusive.

Linked concepts: Equations, proportion.

---

9 CIMT, MEP Y7 Practice Book 7B, Chapter 21: Probability of One Event (n.d.). Available at: https://cimt.org.uk/projects/mepres/book7/bk7_21.pdf.

The introduction to exhaustive lists of events mirrors very closely the introduction to mutually exclusive events, in that pupils need to learn to identify whether lists are exhaustive or not before then understanding how this affects calculations with probabilities. In identifying, examples and non-examples are again important; in particular, pupils recognising the key difference between these two phrases:

> A bag contains red, yellow, blue and green counters ...
>
> A bag contains only red, yellow, blue and green counters ...

Again, we can offer pupils different lists of events to decide whether they are exhaustive (things like win/lose are nice, where draw may or may not be an option) and/or ask pupils to create exhaustive lists. One important aspect to then link to this is whether a list is also mutually exclusive. For example, consider the two lists of events below in reference to rolling a single six-sided die.

> Are the lists below exhaustive? Are they also mutually exclusive?
>
> Rolling a prime number, rolling a square number, rolling a 6.
>
> Rolling an even number, rolling a prime number, rolling a 1.

Pupils appreciating that lists of events can be mutually exclusive and not exhaustive, exhaustive and not mutually exclusive, both mutually exclusive and exhaustive, and neither mutually exclusive nor exhaustive, is important if they are then going to move onto using exhaustivity in probability calculations; in particular that if $A_1, A_2, A_3, ... A_n$ are mutually exclusive events that form an exhaustive list, then $P(A_1) + P(A_2) + \cdots + P(A_n) = 1$. This can be easily justified in that the probability of one or another of these events happening is found by their sum (because they are mutually exclusive) and that it is 'certain' that one or another of these events will happen (as it is an exhaustive list). As 'certain' is denoted by a probability of 1, this means the list of events must sum to 1.

Having met this calculation, one opportunity that is often not focused on enough is simply using it to determine whether events form an exhaustive list or not:

> Events A, B, C and D are mutually exclusive events. $P(A) = \frac{1}{8}$, $P(B) = \frac{1}{4}$, $P(C) = \frac{2}{5}$, $P(D) = \frac{9}{40}$. Work out if A, B, C and D are an exhaustive list.

When pupils have worked with this, we might then offer them the opportunity to solve problems such as finding missing probabilities:

> Events A, D, C and D are mutually exclusive events that form an exhaustive list. $P(A) = \frac{1}{5}$, $P(B) = \frac{1}{4}$, $P(C) = \frac{1}{3}$. Work out $P(D)$.

These sorts of questions are often given in table form, and can link to other areas of mathematics, such as equation solving or ratio/proportion:

> An experiment has possible outcomes A, B, C and D, with probabilities shown in the table below.

$P(A)$	$P(B)$	$P(C)$	$P(D)$
x	$2x$	$3x$	$4x - 0.05$

Work out the probability of the most likely event.

An experiment has possible outcomes A, B, C and D. The ratio of P(A):P(B) = 2:3. The ratio of P(C):P(D) = 4:5. The ratio (P(A) + P(B)) : (P(C) + P(D)) = 11:9. Complete the table below:

$P(A)$	$P(B)$	$P(C)$	$P(D)$

Given that pupils may initially meet mutually exclusive and exhaustive events relatively early on in their study of probability, it may well be that these sorts of questions will be offered when pupils are revisiting the concepts (or possibly as interweaved content when studying other mathematical concepts). We can also revisit and develop both concepts using a Venn diagram representation, coupled with the use of set notation.

Venn diagrams are a very versatile representation for sorting and classifying values or objects. A nice way to introduce pupils to these is sorting a mixture of physical objects and numbers according to property:

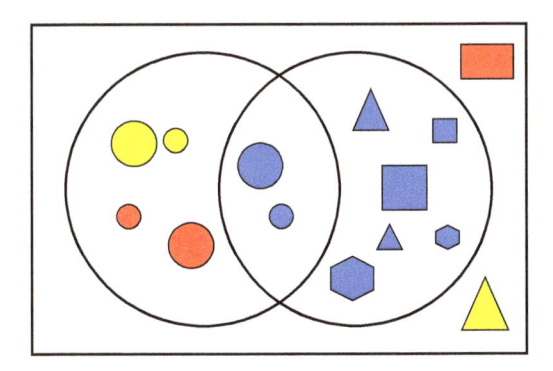

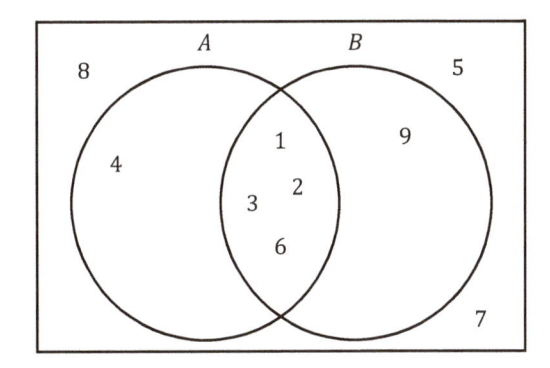

As well as asking pupils to sort objects or information, we can also ask pupils to identify what criteria has been used to sort the objects or numbers in the Venn diagram.

In addition to sorting objects or values, Venn diagrams are a great tool for pupils to work out the frequency of people or objects that satisfy a given criteria – for example:

100 pet owners were asked if they own a dog or a cat. 34 of them owned a cat, 60 owned a cat or a dog, 14 owned a cat and a dog. Fill in the Venn diagram and find the probability that a pet owner chosen at random owns:

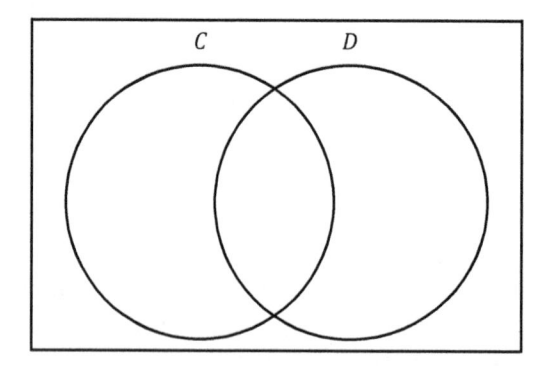

a   neither a cat nor a dog.

b   a dog.

c   a dog but not a cat.

One style of question like this that tends to test pupil thinking a little more are those where they have to work out how many people or objects fit both criteria – for example:

In a group of 100 students, 50 study physics, 29 biology and 33 study neither. Find the probability that:

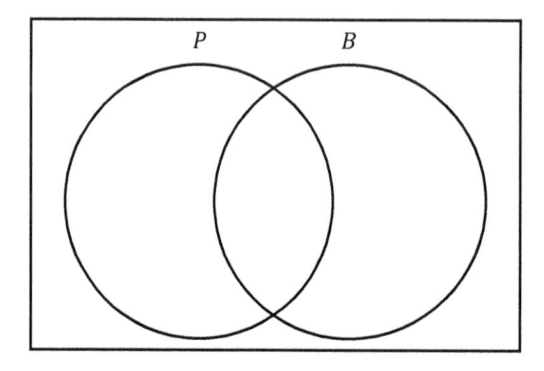

a   if we went to the biology department and picked a student at random, they would study physics.

b   if we went to the physics department and picked a student at random, they would study biology.

Pupils can also solve problems involving Venn diagrams with three (or more) criteria, with the information already sorted:

In a health club, 224 members were surveyed to see what facilities they use. The Venn diagram below shows the results:

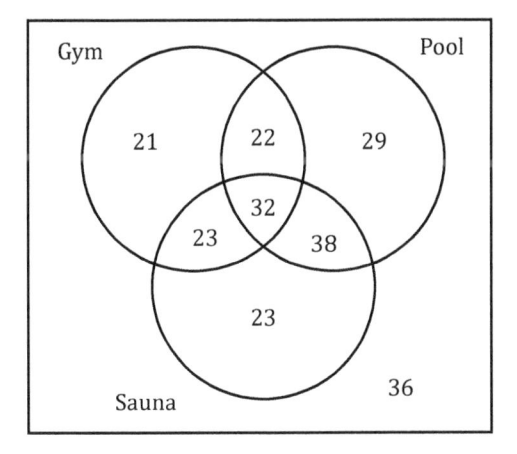

```
Gym                    Pool
    21   22   29
        32
      23   38
         23
                  36
   Sauna
```

Find the probability that:

a   the member only used the gym.

b   the member used the gym.

c   the member did not use the gym.

d   the member did not use any facilities.

e   the member used the gym and the pool but not the sauna.

f   given we know it is someone who used the gym, the probability that they also used the pool and sauna.

Or have to sort it themselves:

A survey of some adults who enjoy at least one of the activities art, music and drama gave the following information:

55% enjoy art; 6% enjoy art and music, but not drama; 27% enjoy art and drama; 22% enjoy music and drama; 10% only enjoy drama; 15% enjoy all three activities.

Find the percentage of the people who:

a   enjoy only music.

b   enjoy exactly one activity.

c   enjoy exactly two activities.

d   enjoy music and drama but not art.

We can also offer opportunities for pupils to problem-solve by bringing in other areas of maths. We have previously seen how Venn diagrams can be used to promote mathematical thinking and reasoning with other areas of maths; they can also be used to interweave other mathematical knowledge like in this exam question from the AQA practice exam Set 3:[10]

In this Venn diagram

ξ = 295 students in the college

H = students who take history

E = students who take English

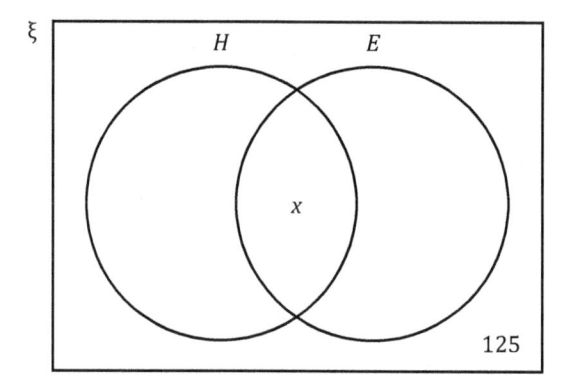

One half of the students who take history also take English. The number who take English is twice the number who take history.

Work out the value of x.

As mentioned, Venn diagrams are crucial in supporting pupils to develop an understanding of set notation. At the time of writing in England, pupils need to recognise the following:

- ∪ being the union of two sets.
- ∩ being the intersection of two sets.
- ' being the complement of a set.
- ξ being the universal set.

and may also benefit from knowing:

- ∅ being the empty set.
- | being the symbol for 'given'.

Pupils should also recognise the use of braces {} to show members of a set (i.e. if A = {1, 2, 3, 4, 5} then these five elements are the members of set A).

A classic approach to the symbols involved in set notation is to provide rough English translations. The ones that I have found most powerful are:

- union being loosely equivalent to 'either ... or ...'
- intersection being loosely equivalent to 'both ... and ...'
- complement being loosely equivalent to 'not in ...'

---

10 See https://allaboutmaths.aqa.org.uk/attachments/8465.pdf.

- the universal set being loosely equivalent to 'all ...'

A classic mistake in teaching pupils about set notation is to teach them with these words applied to particular example sets, i.e. teachers don't just introduce the symbol '∪' as being 'union' and translating to 'either ... or ...' but instead introduce it as '$A \cup B$' being the union of A and B and translating to 'either A or B'. The issue with this is that pupils don't just apply union, intersection and complement to sets A and B but rather apply them much more widely:[11]

Students should know the following notations and the associated shaded area on a Venn diagram:

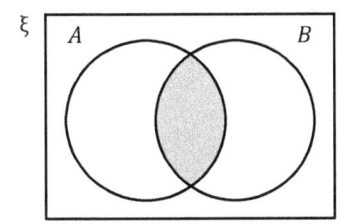

$A \cap B$ to mean the intersection of A and B

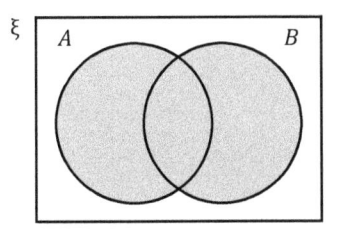

$A \cup B$ to mean the union of A and B

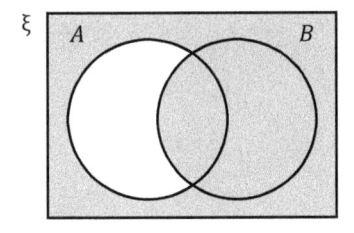

A' to mean everything not in A

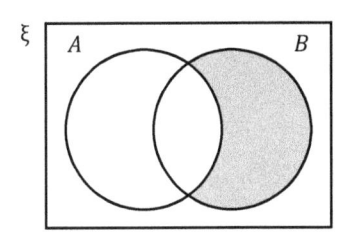

$A' \cap B$ to mean everything not in A that is in B

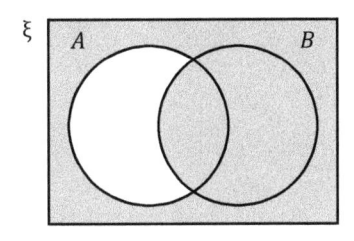

$A' \cup B$ to mean the union of A' and B

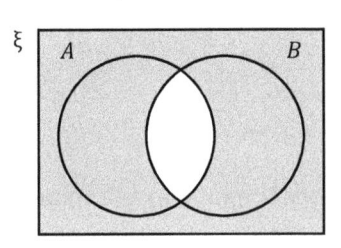

$(A \cap B)' = A' \cup B'$ to mean everything not in the intersection

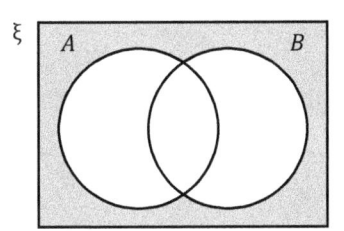

$(A \cup B)' = A' \cap B'$ to mean everything not in the union

---

[11] See https://allaboutmaths.aqa.org.uk/teachingguidance8300.

In my experience, pupils that have been introduced to the union, intersection and complement notation being immediately applied only to *A* and/or *B* will often struggle to mix these together and apply more than one at once whereas, those pupils that are introduced to the words more generally before having them applied to specific examples including all those above find the mixing of the different notations easier. The last two of the previous image are particularly worth noting as well, as they start to lay the foundation for what it might mean to 'expand a bracket' in set notation and ultimately the study of things like Boolean logic.

Basic practice with shading and identifying shaded regions in a Venn diagram will almost certainly be required for pupils to become comfortable with using and apply set notation, such as this excellent worksheet from MATHSprint.[12]

1 Shade the following regions:

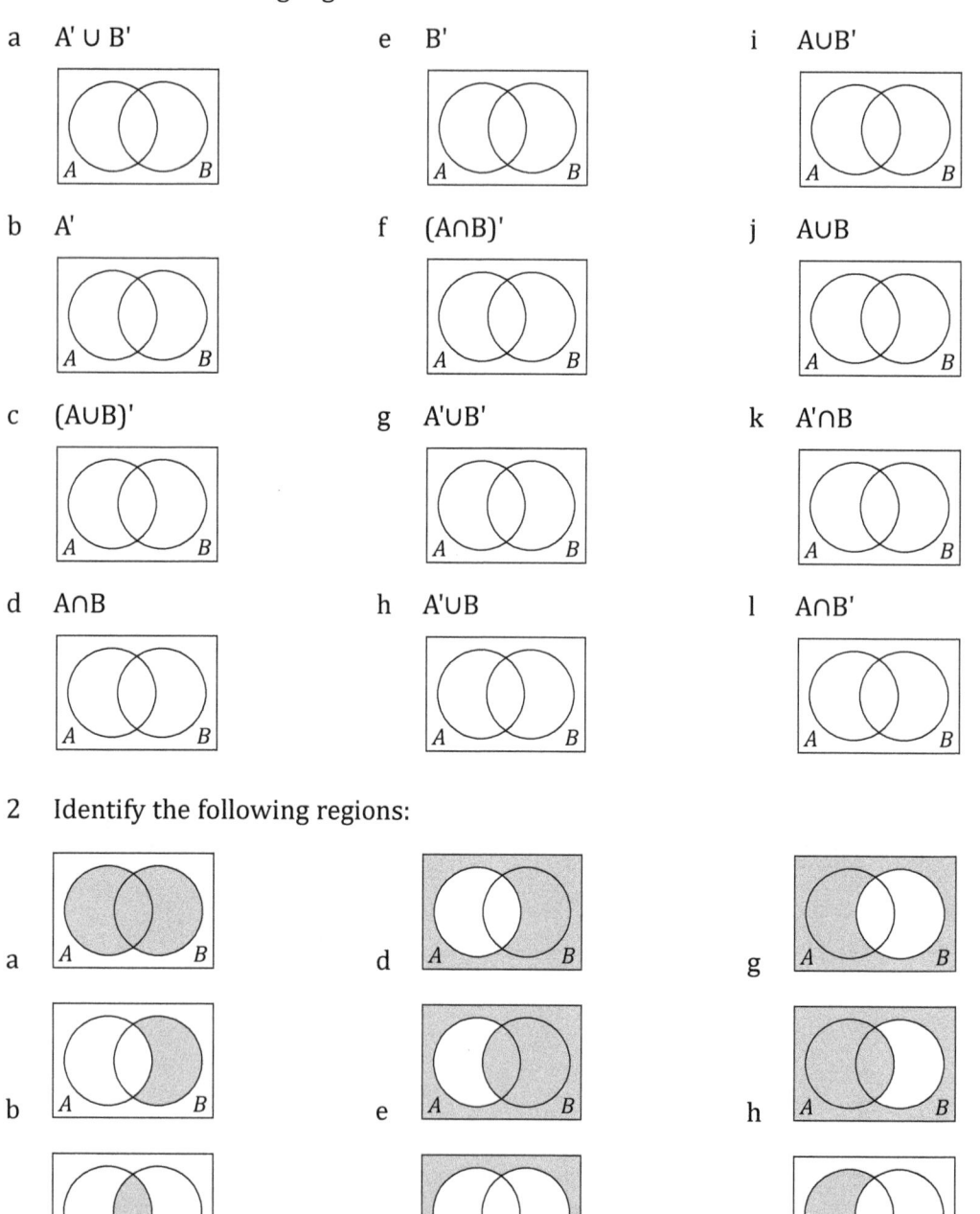

a $A' \cup B'$

b A'

c $(A \cup B)'$

d $A \cap B$

e B'

f $(A \cap B)'$

g $A' \cup B'$

h $A' \cup B$

i $A \cup B'$

j $A \cup B$

k $A' \cap B$

l $A \cap B'$

2 Identify the following regions:

---

[12] Transfinite, Venn Diagrams Practice Questions + Solutions, *TES* (14 April 2015). Available at: https://www.tes.com/teaching-resource/venn-diagrams-practice-questions-solutions-6330738.

One strategy that can be very helpful, particularly with questions like those in activity 1 above, is to draw Venn diagrams for each separate part (where there are separate parts). For example, when trying to shade $A' \cup B$, we can start by shading A' and shading B separately:

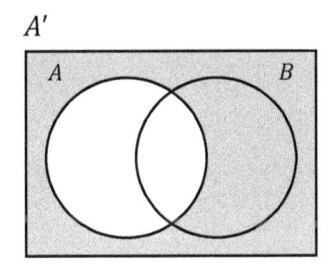

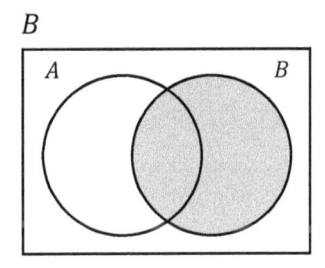

A'

B

We can then say that to shade $A' \cup B$ we shade anything that is shaded 'either in the first picture or in the second picture' (using the 'either ... or ...' translation).

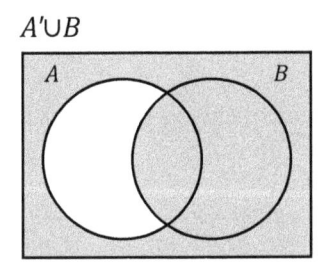

A'∪B

Similarly, if trying to shade $A \cap B'$ we shade A and B' separately:

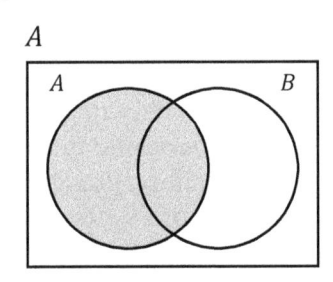

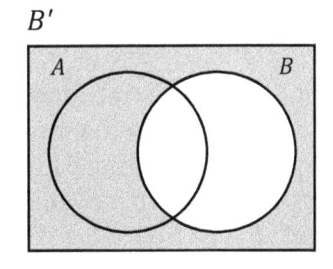

A

B'

And then shade anything that is shaded both in the first picture and in the second picture.

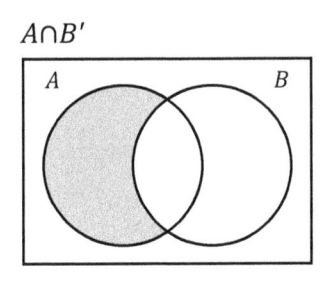

A∩B'

Provided we introduce the use of the symbols ∪, ∩ and ' more generally than to immediately apply them only to A and B, and then follow this up using the strategy of shading separate criteria before using the translations to combine them, then pupils will normally achieve a good level of fluency with what can be a very tricky set of notation for pupils to learn about.

Once pupils are working well with the set notation, then we can revisit the ideas of mutual exclusivity and independence in light of learning about Venn diagrams and combining them with our understanding of probability. Mutually exclusive events are probably simpler to interpret in terms of a Venn diagram:

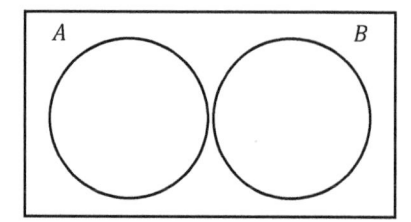

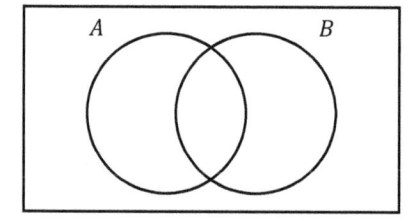

A and B are mutually exclusive.

A and B are not mutually exclusive.

This naturally leads to two ways to then arrive at a more formal definition of mutual exclusivity, one involving set notation and one involving probability:

1 Two events, A and B, are mutually exclusive if and only if $A \cap B = \emptyset$

2 Two events, A and B, are mutually exclusive if and only if $P(A \cup B) = P(A) + P(B)$

Another key result that can come out of this re-examination of mutually exclusive events is the more general addition law for probability:

$$P(A \text{ or } B) = P(A \cup B) = P(A) + P(B) - P(A \cap B)$$

Probably the best way to explore this with pupils is to highlight that if we simply add $P(A)$ and $P(B)$ together, then we will add the probability of the intersection twice (once because it is part of A and once because it is part of B). This means if we subtract the probability of the intersection once, we will have one left.

A classic mistake that pupils will often make is to think that independent events need to also have no intersection in their Venn diagrams. In fact, it is virtually impossible to spot just from looking at a Venn diagram that two events are independent. Pupils need to understand that either of the above two pictures could show independent events – that for events to be independent they don't have to be separate. What needs to happen for independent events is that $P(A)$ needs to not be affected by B. This is probably most easily stated as $P(A|B) = P(A)$, i.e. the probability of event A doesn't change even if B happens. We have also seen from our earlier work with tree diagrams/sample spaces that if we want to find the probability of one event and the other happening (i.e. $P(A \cap B)$), then we multiply the probabilities together. When the events were independent, the probabilities associated with the second event were always the same, whereas when one event depended on the other, the probabilities changed in the second event. This leads to the results:

1 for independent events $P(A \cap B) = P(A) \times P(B)$.

2 for conditional events $P(A \cap B) = P(A) \times P(B|A)$.

In fact, since $P(B|A) = P(B)$ when events are independent (as we noted above), then the result for independent events can be seen as a special case of the more general result for conditional events.

Knowledge of these results allows pupils to work with a wider array of probability problems, including those where events are not mutually exclusive but are independent:

The table below shows pupils who study English and history.

	History	Not history	Total
English	9	21	30
Not English	6	14	20
Total	15	35	50

a   Show that the events 'Pupil studies English' and 'Pupil studies history' are independent.

b   Work out the probability that a pupil studies English or history.

For part (a) we can see from the table that the probability a pupil studies both English and history is $\frac{9}{50}$. We can also see that the probability that a pupil studies English is $\frac{30}{50} = \frac{3}{5}$ and the probability that a pupil studies history is $\frac{15}{50} = \frac{3}{10}$. Multiplying these together gives $\frac{3}{5} \times \frac{3}{10} = \frac{9}{50}$. This demonstrates that the two are independent.

For part (b), we can use $\frac{3}{5} + \frac{3}{10} - \frac{9}{50} = \frac{36}{50}$; which also happens to be $\frac{21+6+9}{50}$.

Again, it is worth pupils working with questions of this type, such as the ones contained within the worksheet listed in the footnote:[13]

In a group of 15 boys, 10 like apples, 8 like bananas and 6 like both apples and bananas.

Let A = a boy likes apples and B = a boy likes bananas.

a   Show that A and B are not independent.

b   Find the probability that a boy likes apples or bananas.

Of the 26 cars on a garage forecourt, 12 had ABS brakes, 16 had a CD player, 6 had neither ABS brakes nor a CD player.

Let A = has ABS and B = has CD player.

a   Show that A and B are not independent.

b   Find the probability that a car has ABS or a CD player.

In a group of 20 boys, 8 have blue eyes, 10 have fair hair and 4 have both blue eyes and fair hair.

Let A = has blue eyes and B = has fair hair.

a   Show that A and B are independent.

b   Find the probability that a boy has either blue eyes or fair hair.

---

13 P. Mattock, Independence, Dependence, Mutually Exclusive or Not?, *TES* (6 November 2016). Available at: https://www.tes.com/teaching-resource/independence-dependence-mutually-exclusive-or-not-11413604.

There were 38 books on a shelf: 17 had large print, 12 were novels with large print, 10 were not novels and did not have large print.

Let A = is large print and B = is a novel.

a   Show that A and B are not independent.

b   Find the probability that a book is either large print or is a novel.

In a group of 24 girls, 18 like oranges, 8 like bananas and 4 like neither oranges nor bananas.

Let A = likes oranges and B = likes bananas.

a   Show that A and B are independent.

b   Find the probability that a girl either likes oranges or bananas.

In a group of 40 people, 24 played cricket and 30 played tennis. The events 'played cricket' and 'played tennis' are independent. Find the probability that a person plays either cricket or tennis.

In a group of 30 people, 10 read books and 24 read newspapers. The events 'read books' and 'read newspapers' are independent. Find the probability that a person either reads books or newspapers.

Eventually then, we should be aiming for pupils to reach the point where they can interpret scenarios and calculate with them without the need for representation (although representation is still an option when it is necessary). For example, if we come back to an earlier question:

Alex takes a driving test. The probability that he will pass on his first attempt is 0.4. If he fails his first test then the probability that he will pass the test on any subsequent attempt is 0.7.

a   Copy and complete the tree diagram to show all the possible outcomes for his first two attempts.

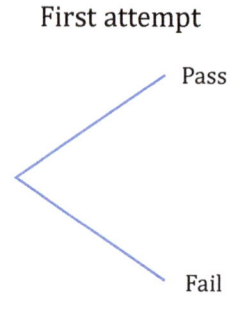

First attempt

Pass

Fail

b   Calculate the probability that Alex needs two attempts, and passes on his second attempt.

c   Calculate the probability that he passes the test after three or four attempts.

and adapt it to:

> Alex takes a driving test. The probability that he will pass on his first attempt is 0. 4. If he fails his first test then the probability that he will pass the test on any subsequent attempt is 0. 7.
>
> Calculate the probability that he passes the test after three or four attempts.

Pupils should be able to follow the logic that in order to pass on the third or fourth attempt, we would need the following:

Fail first attempt AND fail second attempt AND pass third attempt.

OR

Fail first attempt AND fail second attempt AND fail third attempt AND pass fourth attempt.

which, if we consider 'pass on first attempt' as event A and 'pass on subsequent attempt' as event B, then we can interpret this as:

$P((A' \cap B' \cap B) \cup (A' \cap B' \cap B' \cap B)) = P(A') \times P(B') \times P(B) + P(A') \times P(B') \times P(B') \times P(B) = 0.6 \times 0.3 \times 0.7 + 0.6 \times 0.3 \times 0.3 \times 0.7 = 0.1638$

(taking advantage of the fact that passing on the third attempt and passing on the fourth attempt are mutually exclusive)

One important approach to solving probability problems is using the fact that A and A' always form an exhaustive list and for pupils to recognise when one event is the complement of another:

> A bag contains 6 red balls and 4 green balls. 3 balls are to be taken from the bag, one after the other. Work out the probability there are:
>
> a No green balls removed.
>
> b Exactly 1 green ball removed.
>
> c At least 1 green ball removed.

For part (a) pupils should be able to reason here that the only way no green balls are removed is if all three balls removed are red, i.e. the first ball is red AND the second ball is red AND the third ball is red. This gives $\frac{6}{10} \times \frac{5}{9} \times \frac{4}{8} = \frac{1}{6}$.

Part (b) is one that pupils often don't consider well enough without representation, but reminding them of a tree diagram is normally enough for them to realise that getting exactly one green ball requires either green AND red AND red, OR red AND green AND red, OR red AND red AND green, which gives $\frac{4}{10} \times \frac{6}{9} \times \frac{5}{8} + \frac{6}{10} \times \frac{4}{9} \times \frac{5}{8} + \frac{6}{10} \times \frac{5}{9} \times \frac{4}{8} = \frac{1}{2}$.

Part (c) is the scenario that pupils struggle with most. Some might recognise that one way to approach this may be:

green AND red AND red OR red AND green AND red OR red AND red AND green OR

green AND green AND red OR green AND red AND green OR red AND green AND green OR

green AND green AND green.

However, they will then baulk at the amount of calculation required. What pupils will less often see is that the event 'at least one green ball removed' is the complement of 'no green balls removed' and so these two will form an exhaustive list. This means that P(at least one green ball removed) = 1 − P(no green balls removed) and so we can simply work out $1 - \frac{1}{6}$ = $\frac{5}{6}$. So P(at least one green ball removed) = $\frac{5}{6}$.

When we are ready to work with these sorts of problems with pupils, it is worth examining this complement identifying separately and explicitly; offering pupils different events and getting them to identify the complement. These events can be taken from all the contexts pupils will have previously met with probability. What is important in doing this is that pupils work with 'at least' and 'at most' events, as these are the ones where the complement will typically be most useful in calculating with probabilities, such as:

Identify the complement of:

1 rolling at least 3 on a die.

2 rolling at most 5 on a die.

etc.

Pupils being able to interpret and calculate with probabilities in these ways will have a secure foundation with which to move onto post-16 study.

We have seen how powerful different representations can be in helping pupils gain insight into mathematical ideas both in this chapter and in previous chapters. We will now turn our attention to how different graphical representations can help support similar and deeper insights.

Chapter 13

Charting and graphing

Pupils meet many different charts and graphs throughout their school lives: graphs based on statistical data, graphs based on measured values, graphs based on algebraic relationships and more besides. This is not to mention the study of 'graph theory', which pupils may encounter post-16, in which pupils' prior understanding of what a 'graph' is can be challenged significantly. This is in part because, whilst pupils often learn about different graphs and charts, what is rarely highlighted is what connects these different representations – why is it that we draw graphs and charts? And no matter what type of graph and chart we select, what is it we are trying to achieve? This should very much be at the forefront of pupil learning about graphing, both initially and as new graphs are introduced.

So what, fundamentally, is a graph or chart? There are different definitions out there, but what they all have in common is that they are a visual/pictorial representation that represents related (at least potentially) things in an organised fashion. We draw graphs and charts to gain an insight into the (potential) relationship; what form does it have? Does it follow a trend? As teachers, we can get bogged down in making sure pupils draw different graphs and charts correctly, without really focusing on their intended use or even if they are useful at all. Ideally, as pupils learn to draw different graphs and charts, they should also be learning about why we have chosen to draw that particular graph and chart in that context. In addition, when interpreting different graphs and charts, it is important that the questions we ask tie in with the intended use – many activities ask questions that are easy enough to answer but that would have been just as easy to answer provided we had access to the data, measures or relationship from which the graph or chart was drawn, rather than actually needing the graph or chart itself! If we are not careful, this can create an unrealistic impression of what graphs and charts are for.

So, whenever we introduce a new chart or graph type to pupils, the sorts of initial questions we might be asking/things we should be highlighting are:

- What are the related or potentially relatable things?
- How does the nature of the (potential) relationship inform the features of the graph or chart?
- Are there any other influences on the features of the graph or chart (e.g. the intended audience)?
- What sort of insight into the relationship is the graph or chart going to provide?

This will ensure pupils are learning about the different graphs or charts they come into contact with through school maths, rather than just learn the mechanics of drawing them and answering basic questions from them.

Conceptual Maths

Concept: pictograph/pictogram

Prerequisites: This is open to some debate – at their simplest, only a general sense of quantity is truly prerequisite.

Linked concepts: Number, multiplication, proportion, data (particularly categorical data), tally chart/data collection sheet, average.

Pictograms are likely to be the first graphical representation that many pupils encounter, potentially without even realising it. Any child that has used, or is part of, a sticker-based reward chart has technically interacted with data arranged in a pictogram. Indeed, many pupils will be familiar with this sort of system even if they have never been a part of it, and so this sort of context may well be the ideal introduction to the idea of representing data using objects.

In terms of the questions from the beginning of the chapter, there is a slight disconnect between the use of pictograms at school-level mathematics and some of their more general usage. At school level, pictograms are almost exclusively used to represent categorical data using pictures to show the relationship between the frequency of people or objects in a category and the different categories chosen/available. This may be using a one-to-one relationship between picture and frequency (i.e. a frequency of 12 being shown using 12 pictures) or a proportional relationship between the frequency and the number of pictures (e.g. a single picture is representative of a frequency of 3), where the relationship between the picture and the frequency it represents is normally made clear using a key rather than using a numerical scale, such as in the example below:

Number of donuts baked:

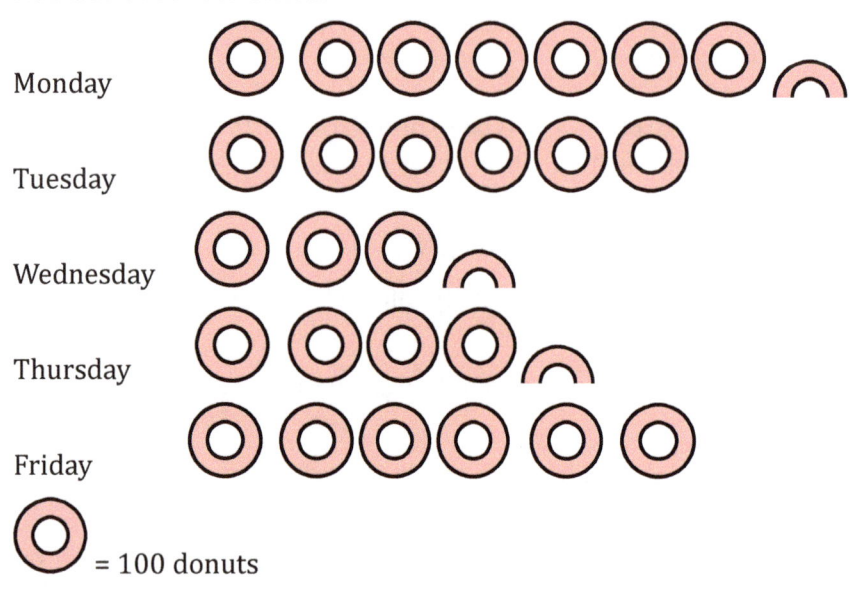

Monday: ⊙ ⊙ ⊙ ⊙ ⊙ ⊙ ⊙ ⌒
Tuesday: ⊙ ⊙ ⊙ ⊙ ⊙ ⊙
Wednesday: ⊙ ⊙ ⊙ ⌒
Thursday: ⊙ ⊙ ⊙ ⊙ ⌒
Friday: ⊙ ⊙ ⊙ ⊙ ⊙ ⊙

⊙ = 100 donuts

In contrast, most pictograms that are in more general use typically do not have any sort of relationship between the frequency and the number of pictures; rather the number of pictures stays fixed and shading or values are used to indicate either a measure of average or the total frequency. The most common examples of these are found in ratings (for example, Amazon ratings use a number of filled stars out of 5 to indicate the average rating given to a product by all reviewers) and in social media (the number of likes and dislikes on YouTube are represented by a single thumb up and thumb down, with the frequency of each provided as a value next to the pictures).

If, for now, we stick to pictograms as they are generally encountered in the maths classroom, then it should be clear to pupils that the pictogram is less concerned with communicating the actual values of the frequencies than showing how the different categories compare to each other, using a visual that makes the context clear. For example, in the pictogram above, communicating the fact that there were 750 donuts baked on Monday and only 350 baked on Wednesday is not the primary goal of the representation – rather it is showing that Monday has a much higher frequency than Wednesday, and that this data relates to donuts.

Because the primary purpose of a pictogram is to give a visual comparison of the frequencies of the different categories, it is clearly important that pictures are equal in size (or at least close to equal in size) and lined up with each other. The pictogram above might be a good example of a poorly drawn pictogram – although the pictures are the same size, they are not well lined up. A particular part that can be drawn attention to in this pictogram is how Tuesday compares to Friday. The two categories should actually have the same frequency, but it is not apparent from the pictogram; the Friday row starts further to the left than the Tuesday row and finishes further to the right because of different spacing. This is the sort of thing that should be avoided, as it undermines the purpose of the chart.

One factor that motivates the design and use of a pictogram is the intended audience. Typically, a pictogram might be used for a juvenile or uneducated audience (at least uneducated in the medium that the categories are drawn from). Pictograms can also be useful if language could be a barrier to understanding the context, as the pictures can support making sense of the context. This potentially means that pictograms can allow insight into how categories compare to each other for a wider audience than if the raw or processed data is all that was available or a different graph/chart is produced.

Pupils should have the opportunity to draw and interpret pictograms. When it comes to drawing, it is important to make the contexts authentic so that they would actually be scenarios where pupils should be drawing pictograms. This should include after pupils have studied other graphs/charts so that pupils have the opportunity to decide which chart/graph to draw for a given scenario.

A nice activity to prompt thinking when interpreting pictograms (and other graphs/charts) is to hold a game of 'Pointless'. This involves pupils (often in groups) having to write down as many mathematical facts/interpretations from a given pictogram that they can find. Pupils then select one thing they have seen in the pictogram to offer as an 'answer', and score points for any other pupil/group that also has the same thing written down. The goal is to score the lowest number of points by finding something that no other pupil/group thinks of. It is important to make sure that the pupils are considering mathematical facts/interpretations, otherwise we end up with answers such as 'the pictures are blue', which, whilst it may be true, does not particularly show insight into the pictogram.

In graphing frequencies of separate categories, a pictogram is very closely related to a bar chart. Indeed, very often the choice is between drawing a bar chart and drawing a pictogram.

Concept: bar chart
=================

Prerequisites: Number (particularly bar model representation), categorical data, tally chart/ data collection sheet, scale.

Linked concepts: Pictogram, pie chart, vertical line chart, frequency chart, histogram.

In common with a pictogram, the purpose of a bar chart is to show how values (normally frequencies) change for different categories. Pupils should already be very familiar with the use of bars to model numbers by the time we are ready to explore bar charts, and so they should be an almost intuitive representation for categorical frequency data. Indeed, it may well be that if we simply say to pupils 'how might we represent this set of data?', that the idea of using bars to represent the numbers arises early in that discussion.

Choice of colour	Frequency
Blue	20
Brown	6
Green	18
Orange	9
Purple	11
Red	28
Yellow	8
Total	100

From here it is a short hop to get to one of these:

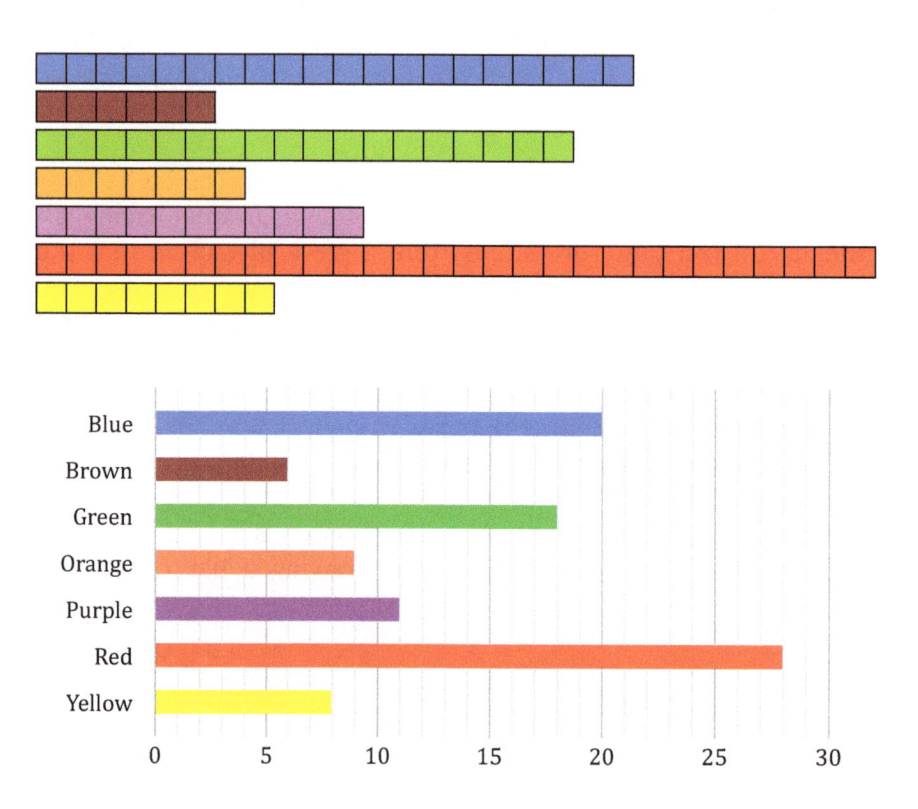

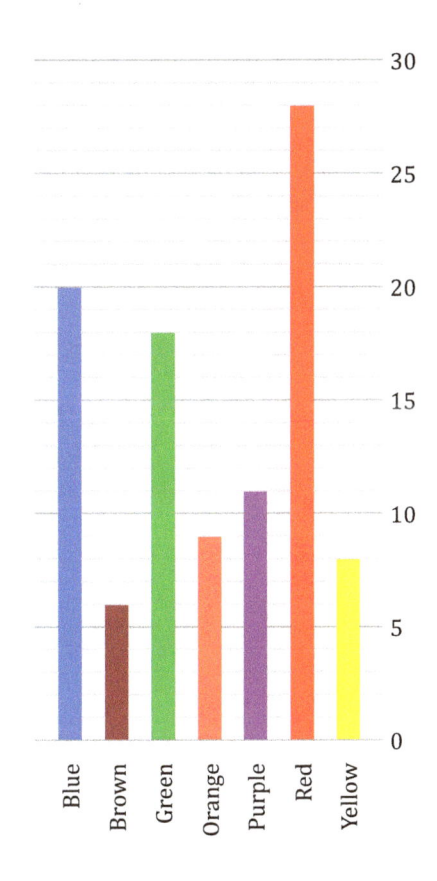

Opinion is divided about the use of bar charts compared to pictograms. There is a nice article from Forbes that references a couple of contrasting opinions, including a great quote from Gregor Aisch, former graphics editor with *The New York Times*:

> A plain bar chart, praised a lot for its efficiency in communicating numbers, also has the potential of scaring people away because it's also a very abstract representation. We should be aware that some people are not able to connect emotionally to highly efficient charts, but do feel attracted to, and understand, displays that include little pictograms, icons, and illustrations.

However, the same article points out that lengths are more natural to compare than icons, where counting is potentially required (although keeping all pictures the same size and in line would mitigate against this).[1] A big part of this depends (as for pictograms) on the audience. An audience that is more mature in terms of the subject matter would likely be more comfortable comparing categories using a bar chart than a pictogram, which they may see as condescending to their expertise or experience.

---

1   N. Robbins, Two Opinions on the Usefulness of Pictographs, *Forbes* (12 October 2012). Available at: https://www.forbes.com/sites/naomirobbins/2012/10/10/two-opinions-on-the-usefulness-of-pictographs/?sh=7d9b583623dd.

An important aspect of bar charts that pupils need to appreciate is that the lengths are only the natural comparison because each bar is equal width. If we contrast this with the bar chart below:

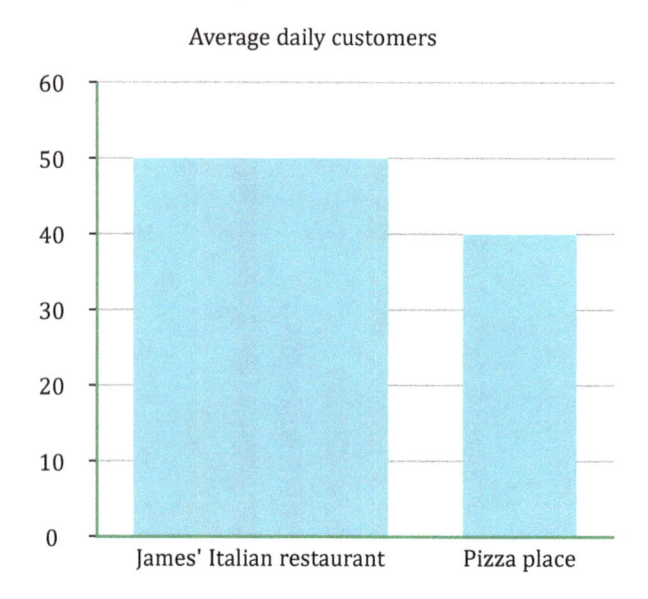

Average daily customers

(Bar chart showing James' Italian restaurant at 50 with a wider bar, and Pizza place at 40 with a narrower bar)

we can see that the first bar is wider; the person drawing this has made the bar wide enough to stretch over the name of the category. The effect of this is to make the left-hand bar appear significantly larger than the right-hand bar, even though it is actually supposed to represent only 10 more customers. This is because, with bars of different widths, the brain adjudges size by area and naturally compares areas rather than lengths or heights. It is only when the bars are the same width, and so length and area are proportional, that the brain is free to focus on length as representative of value. In general, pupils should be aware that when we construct charts that use rectangles to represent values, then the width of each rectangle should be constant unless there is a good mathematical reason for them not to be.

There are other ways that bar charts can be misleading to their audience. Pupils should be made aware of the different ways that bar charts could be misleading, and how the normal design of a bar chart mitigates against these:

1   Frequency starting at 0:

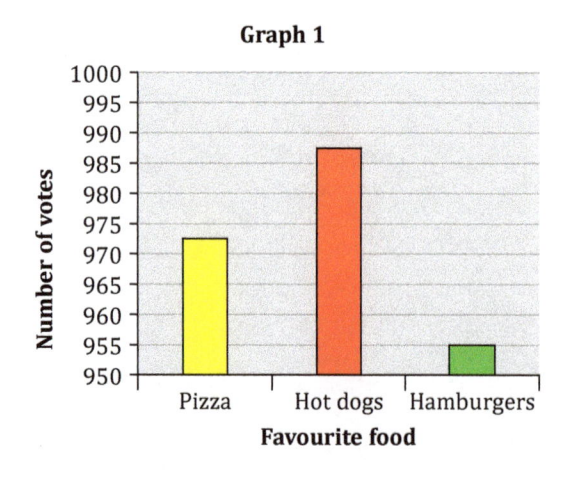

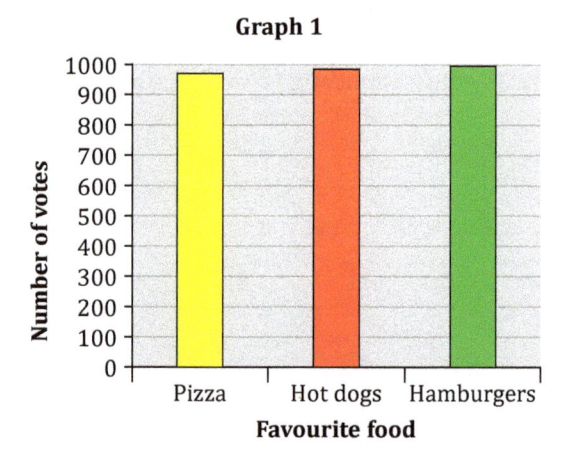

Graph 1 (left: y-axis 950–1000, showing Pizza ~972, Hot dogs ~987, Hamburgers ~955)

Graph 1 (right: y-axis 0–1000, showing Pizza, Hot dogs, Hamburgers all near 1000)

In general (again unless there is a good reason not to), any chart or graph that represents frequency (or a value calculated from frequency) should start the frequency axis from 0, even if all frequencies are significantly larger than 0. If not starting the frequency axis at 0, the differences between frequencies are exaggerated, which can be potentially misleading. For example, in the bar charts above, the Hot dogs bar in the left chart is significantly larger (more than six times bigger) than the Hamburgers bar, whereas in reality it only represents a difference of little over 30. In the right-hand chart we can see a truer picture of how the two categories compare, which is to say there are virtually the same number of choices for both.

2 Spacing of bars:

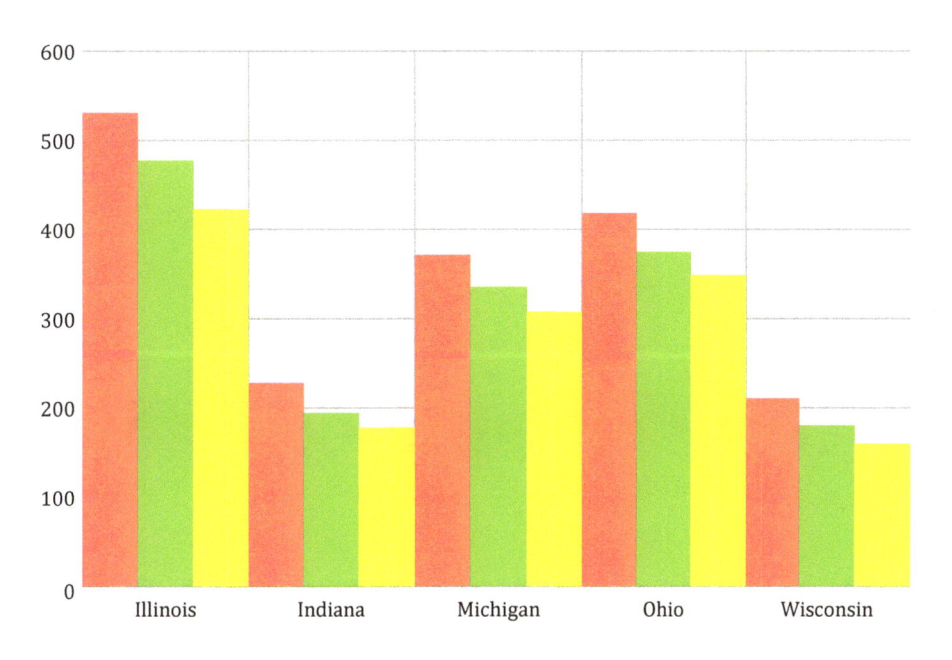

As we can see, the lack of spacing between the bars makes this bar chart particularly hard to read. Pupils should understand that, in part because we are representing data in separate categories, the bars for each of those categories should be separate and that, in general, if bars are connected, this is to show a mathematical connection, such as in this bar chart:

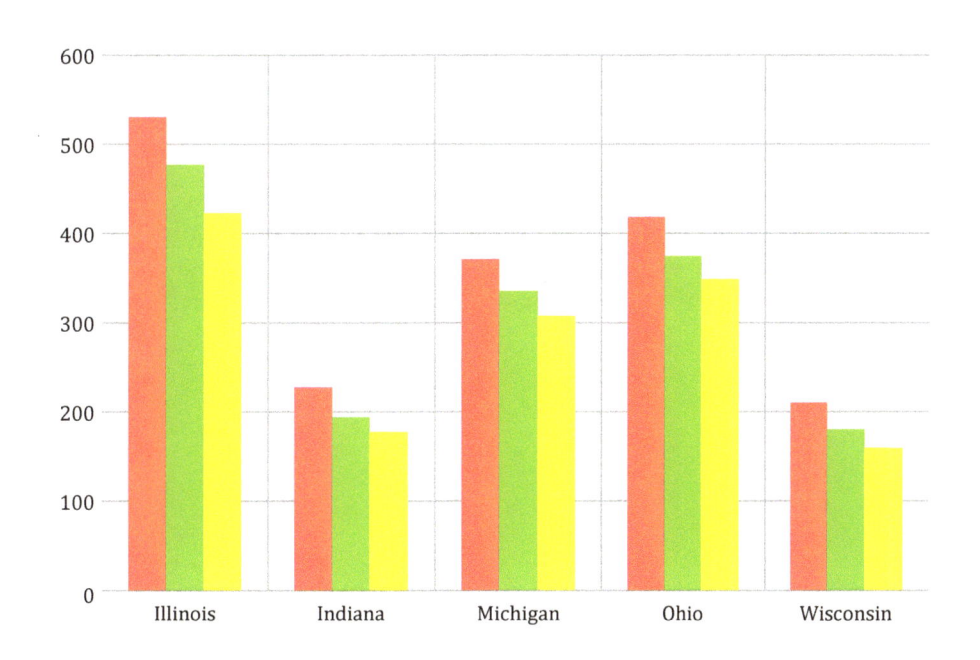

In this case, the red, green and yellow bars for each state are rightly connected, as they represent different aspects within the same category, but then the bars for each state are separated from each other as they are separate states, making them easier to compare. Further, the spacing is equal between each set of bars – similar to the connection having mathematical significance, a difference in spacing would also imply a mathematical reason to have different spacing.

Pupils should be offered the opportunity to interpret and construct bar charts. A really nice application that pupils can access for practice in this area is decoding ciphers by using relative letter frequency:

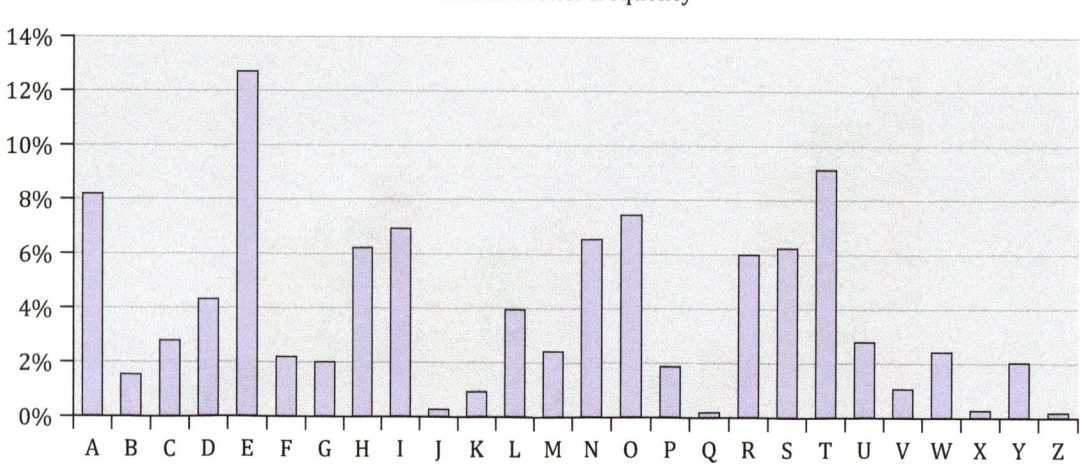

Relative letter frequency

Pupils can take enciphered text and draw bar charts showing the frequency of each letter and then compare their bar charts to the one above to try and decide how the message was encoded. The website Crypto Corner has some good examples of codes and codebreaking, including a message that pupils can decode.[2]

Pupils can, of course, encode messages for each other to try and break; however, it requires a message of significant length for frequency analysis to work, so this may be considered too time intensive.

Pupils might also benefit from the opportunity to move between pictograms and bar charts, constructing one, given the other. This may give pupils a better appreciation of how these two charts are related, although we do need to make sure that this doesn't undermine the different scenarios where one is more suitable than the other.

Although having a simple visual representation for how categories compare to each other is often useful, of potentially equal use is how the size of each category compares to the whole. The chart best suited to allowing this comparison is a pie chart.

---

2 Crypto Corner, Cryptography Worksheet – Breaking the Code (n.d.). Available at: https://crypto.interactive-maths.com/uploads/1/1/3/4/11345755/breaking_the_code.pdf.

Charting and graphing

Concept: pie charts

Prerequisites: Number, angle, proportion, categorical data, tally chart/data collection sheet.

Linked concepts: Pictogram, bar chart, vertical line chart.

As mentioned, the primary purpose of a pie chart is to give a visual representation of how different categories relate to some whole of which they are part. Unlike with a bar chart where we want to keep the frequencies/values intact so as to make them more comparable to each other, with a pie chart the important aspect is what proportion of the whole each category represents. This means that we very often won't show the actual frequencies/values – more often we might add detail like percentages (this is very common when pie charts are used in other subjects) of the whole that each category represents (although we may well just leave the chart to communicate the proportions):

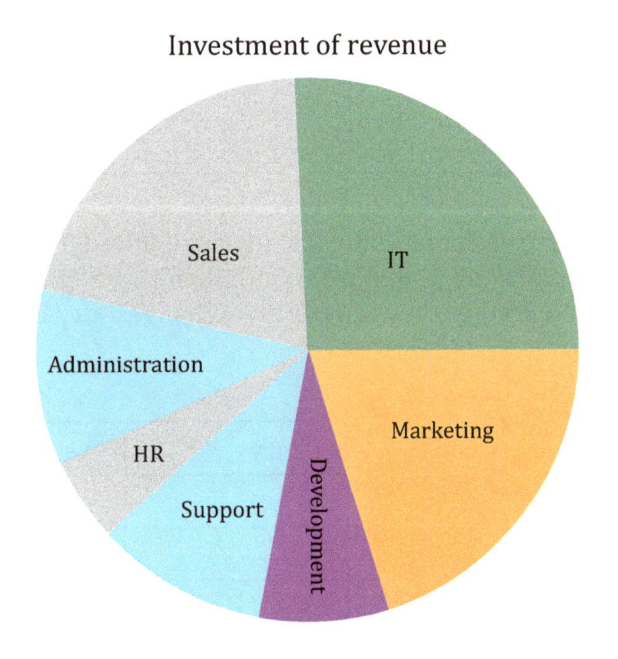

Investment of revenue

Pupils should understand how this use contrasts with bar charts; a nice thing to do is to use non-examples for situations where pie charts have been drawn that weren't appropriate to the situation. Take, for example, the situation below:

Name	Defence
Charizard	78
Blastoise	100
Venusaur	83
Meowth	35
Arcanine	80
Alakazam	45
Horsea	70

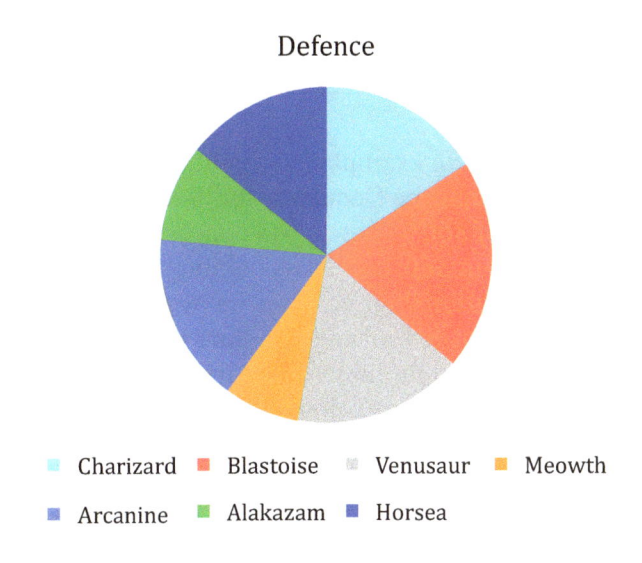

Defence

This table and pie chart refer to a well-known (at least of the time of writing!) TV show and card game, where fictional creatures battle against each other. The table shows the defence ratings for some of the fictional creatures, from which a pie chart has been created. However, in this case, there is no 'whole' of which each of these are part; they are all separate ratings for separate creatures. This data would be much more suited to a bar chart so that the ratings for each creature are compared directly to each other, rather than to the (non-existent) whole. Pupils should appreciate that there will be some scenarios where bar charts will be suitable and pie charts will not be, as well as the opposite, and also where both could be suitable depending on which type of comparison we wish to highlight.

When it comes to constructing pie charts, the important thing is for pupils to appreciate that the relationship between frequency/value and the angle drawn is a proportional relationship. We can help to reinforce this if we have used good representations when introducing and working with proportion:

Number of rolls	Cost in pence
4	124
6	186

Frequency	Angle
4	124
6	186

Pupils can use a unitary approach to finding the angles required for the pie charts, working out how many degrees a value of '1' will have (although this is generally better when the total frequency is less than 360) or they can use an exchange-rate/scaling approach to finding the required angles.

Choice of colour	Frequency	Angle
Blue	20	
Brown	6	
Green	18	
Orange	9	
Purple	11	
Red	28	
Yellow	8	
Total	100	360

In this case, for example, we might work out that each angle will be the frequency multiplied by 3.6, or that the frequency for 'Blue' is $\frac{1}{5}$ of the total frequency, and so the angle required will be $\frac{1}{5}$ of 360°. These sorts of approaches can be more useful when the total frequency is greater than 360, as well as helping to reinforce that this is one more example of a proportional relationship. It may be worthwhile having pupils work with a few of these relationships to find angles before they actually start drawing the pie charts themselves – it would depend on how long it has been since pupils have practised working with proportional relationships using ratio tables or similar.

Obviously, the construction of the pie chart itself is an excellent opportunity to bring back and practise construction skills (using the pair of compasses to draw the circle) and angle drawing. Pupils often find it difficult to draw the angles in a pie chart – in all likelihood this is because they are used to constructing single angles on a line, rather than multiple angles in a turn. This, in part, can be mitigated by making sure that pupils use pie-chart templates when they are first beginning to draw angles. If not, then it may well be worthwhile getting pupils to practise this independently simply by getting pupils to draw one, two and then more angles of given size inside the template (this may well be done before the calculation step above). Pupils can then be offered the opportunity to put both skills together and calculate the necessary angles from a given set of data, and then draw the required pie chart. Again, it is important that these contexts are authentic for the need to draw a pie chart.

When it comes to interpreting pie charts, the obvious sort of activity for pupils to engage in is to work out frequency from given angle – what is important here is that pupils have the opportunity to do this from both total frequency and from the frequency of a given category, i.e. questions like:

> 120 people were asked to rate their experience of a hotel from 1 to 5 stars. The frequency of each rating is then displayed in a pie chart. The angle used for the frequency of 5 stars is 210°. How many of the 120 people rated the hotel 5 stars?

> Some people were asked to rate their experience of a hotel from 1 to 5 stars. The frequency of each rating is then displayed in a pie chart. 56 people rated the hotel 5 stars, and this was represented by an angle in the pie chart of 210°. Work out the number of people that were asked to rate their experience.

> Some people were asked to rate their experience of a hotel from 1 to 5 stars. The frequency of each rating is then displayed in a pie chart. 56 people rated the hotel 5 stars, and this was represented by an angle in the pie chart of 210°. The angle in the pie chart for those that rated the hotel as 4 stars was 120°. Work out the number of people that rated the hotel as 4 stars.

Questions can be offered purely in text (like these) or with pupils actually given pie charts where they have to measure angles in order to work out missing frequencies.

As well as working out missing frequencies when interpreting pie charts, pupils should be given the opportunity to compare pie charts, as there are a number of misconceptions that can arise when looking at two pie charts simultaneously. A 'true or false' activity like the one below is a good way to get at the heart of some of the possible misconceptions pupils may come to:

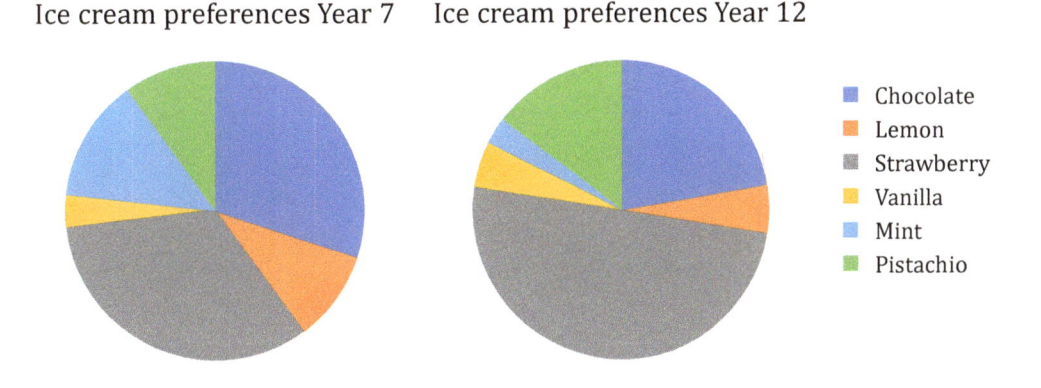

Ice cream preferences Year 7   Ice cream preferences Year 12

- Chocolate
- Lemon
- Strawberry
- Vanilla
- Mint
- Pistachio

Answer 'True', 'Maybe' or 'False' to each of the following questions concerning the two pie charts above:

1   Out of the five flavours, vanilla was the least chosen.

2   Four times as many Year 7 pupils chose chocolate than Year 12 pupils.

3   Year 12 chose strawberry more than any other flavour.

4   More than 1/4 of the pupils chose strawberry.

5   Fewer Year 12 pupils chose lemon than Year 7 pupils.

As well as comparing pie charts to each other, a nice activity to get pupils thinking about the different representations is to prompt pupils to compare pie charts with bar charts, like in this task adapted from Don Steward:[3]

Match the pie chart and the bar chart that show the same data.

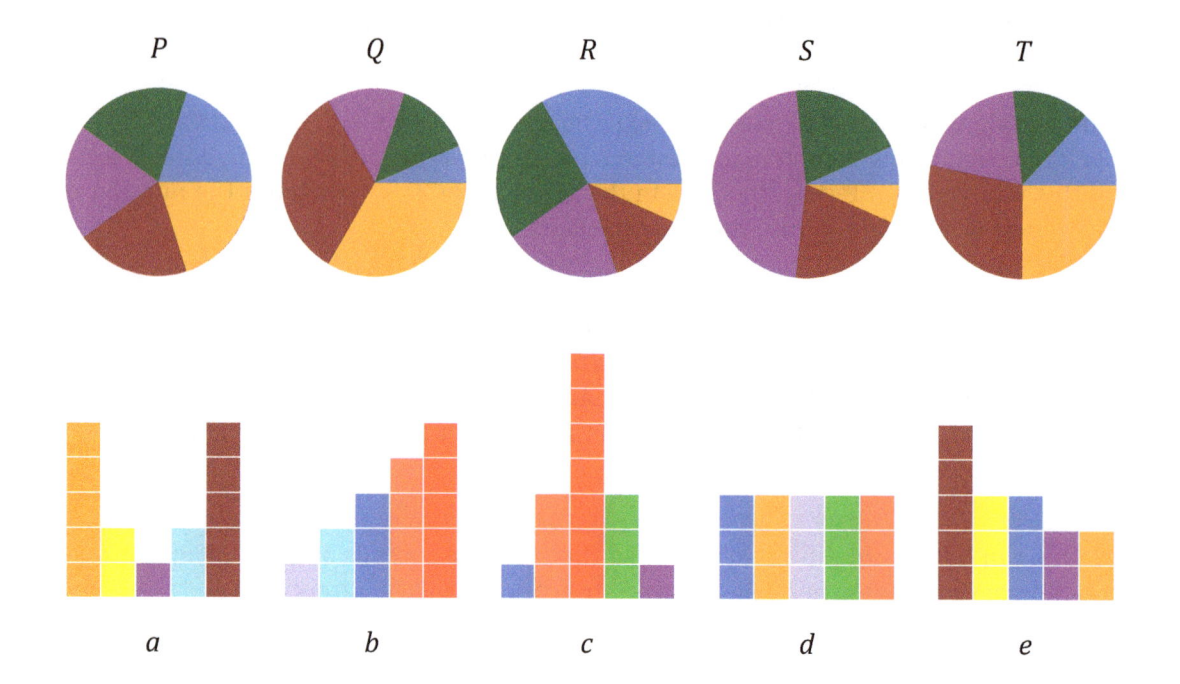

P   *Q*   *R*   *S*   *T*

a   *b*   *c*   *d*   *e*

Pictograms, bar charts and pie charts are generally used with categorical data. Pie charts are also used for discrete and even continuous data (although more rarely) when comparing parts to a whole. If, however, we want to compare frequencies of numerical data or grouped numerical data, there are other charts that pupils will need to be familiar with. The first of these is a vertical line chart.

Concept: vertical line chart

Prerequisites: Number, discrete data, tally chart/data collection sheet, scale.

Linked concepts: Pictogram, bar chart, pie chart, frequency chart, histogram.

---

[3]   D. Steward, Relating Charts to Data Sets, *Median* [blog] (20 March 2011). Available at: https://donsteward.blogspot.com/2011/03/relating-charts-to-data-sets.html.

A vertical line chart is basically the equivalent of a bar chart, but for discrete numerical data instead of categorical data. Often, people will simply draw a bar chart for discrete numerical data, treating the data as separate categories. For all practical purposes there is nothing really wrong with this; the same comparisons arise well out of either chart. The reason for the vertical line chart is more for technical reasons than practical. Because the data is numerical, it should be displayed on a numerical scaled axis rather than on an axis showing different categories. And on a numerical scaled axis, width implies a range of values. For example:

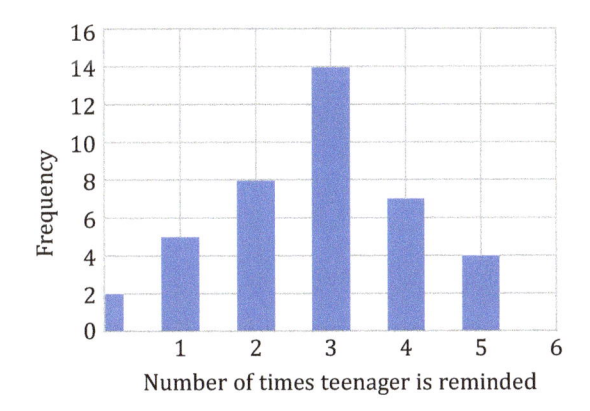

In this bar chart, drawn on a scaled axes, the width of the bar around 3 (say) means that bar actually covers a space on the horizontal axis between roughly 2.8 and 3.2, and, technically, these values do not exist for this data set. This is why a vertical line chart should be drawn for discrete numerical data, as the line (being one-dimensional) shows the frequencies only for the specific values that are in the data set:

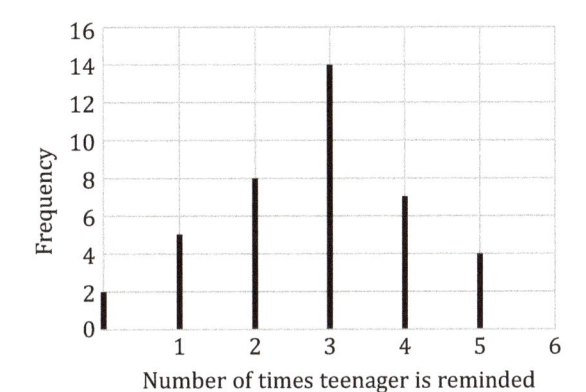

The activities that pupils undertake in working with vertical line charts will be very similar to working with bar charts – construction and interpretation. Unfortunately, at the time of writing, there are relatively few resources for teachers that involve interpreting vertical line charts where the chart is actually drawn correctly. The MEP books referenced earlier contain some questions that prompt pupils to construct vertical line graphs and then follow up with questions about them,[4] but if we want to provide pupils with a vertical line chart in order to just focus on prompting pupils to gain insight from the graph, then we will likely have to create our own or adapt the questioning from the examples provided in the aforementioned book.

---

4   CIMT, MEP Y8 Practice Book 8A Chapter 5: Data Analysis (n.d.). Available at: https://www.cimt.org.uk/projects/mepres/book8/bk8_5.pdf.

One important property of numerical data that it is worth starting to explore with vertical line charts is the idea of **distribution**: the shapes associated with different distributions and comparing distributions. In particular, pupils should recognise the 'normal' distribution, along with positive and negative skew.

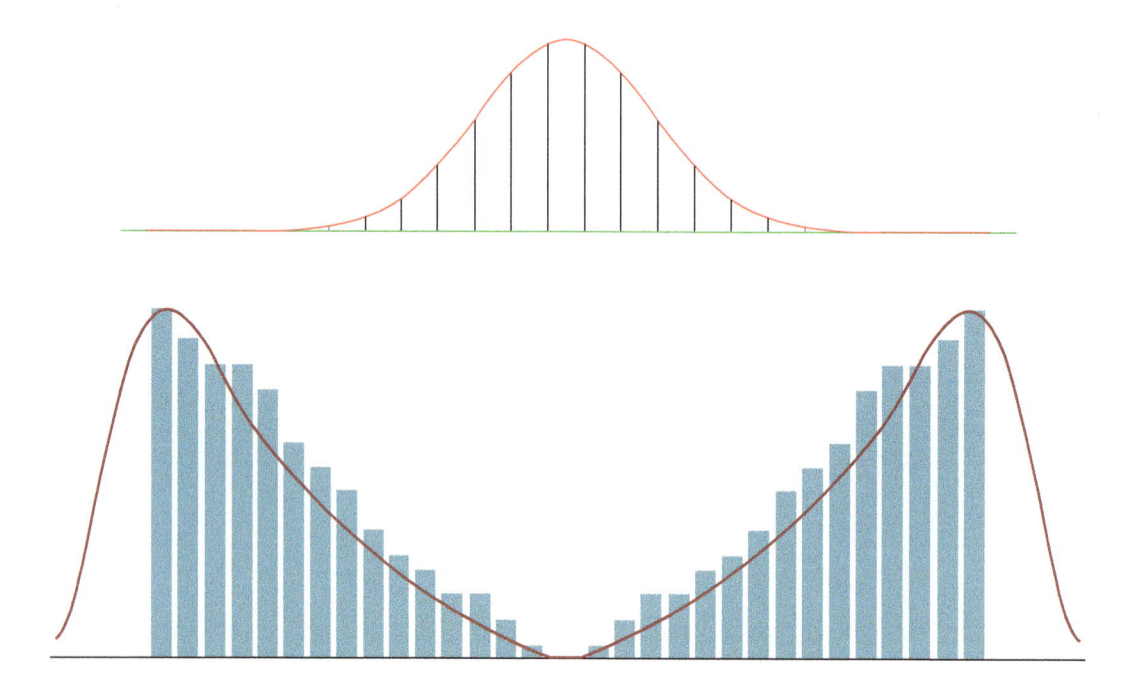

Vertical line charts are also a great opportunity to interweave understanding of things like probability. This can be simple questions like:

> What is the probability that the next time the teenager is asked to complete a task, they have to be reminded twice?

to more complicated questions such as:

> For the next two tasks the teenager is given, what is the probability they have to be reminded a total of six times?

We need, of course, to ensure these sorts of questions don't detract from the key purpose of the vertical line chart, but there may well be suitable points where we can offer pupils questions like this, provided we make it clear that this is more about pupils having to interpret the chart to find the required information than the typical sort of use that we might put a vertical line chart to.

Having examined bar charts for categorical frequency data and vertical line charts for discrete frequency data, the obvious question is: how does this extend to continuous data? And so we introduce frequency charts.

Concept: frequency charts/histograms

Prerequisites: Number, proportion, continuous data, grouped data table, scale.

Linked concepts: Errors, inequalities, pictogram, bar chart, vertical line chart, frequency polygon, mean.

When it comes to continuous data, pupils should already have understood that we cannot collect data about frequencies unless the data is grouped. The fact that the data is grouped therefore affects how we would chart the frequencies, and indeed *how* the data is grouped affects whether we would chart the frequencies. This is why I have referred to this section as 'frequency charts/histograms' – some people use the term 'histograms' to refer only to those charts that do not plot frequency data and frequency charts for those that do, whereas others use the term 'histogram' to refer to any chart that is used to chart grouped data.

Pupils should understand that, because continuous data is numerical in nature, it will be plotted on a numerical axis (similarly to a vertical line chart), and that, in contrast to a vertical line chart, the width will now show the range of values over which the frequency is distributed. For example:

Time, t, (minutes)	Frequency
$0 \leq t < 10$	3
$10 \leq t < 20$	6
$20 \leq t < 30$	9
$30 \leq t < 40$	10
$40 \leq t < 50$	7
$50 \leq t < 60$	5

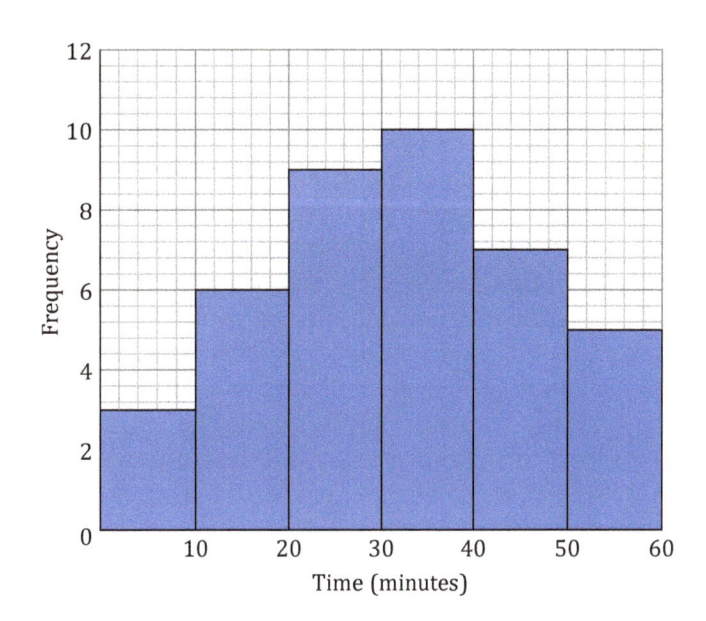

The first bar has a width of 10 (from 0 to 10 on the Time axis) that shows the class width, and a height of 3 to represent the frequency. This then continues on through the rest of the chart.

Once pupils understand why frequency charts have the structure they do, then we can work on construction and interpretation in the same way we did for bar charts and vertical line charts. Once again, the idea of distribution is a key one to explore with pupils (the frequency chart above shows roughly a normal distribution, with perhaps a slightly negative skew), including comparing distributions and comparing groups within a distribution.

Once pupils have worked with frequency diagrams with equal class widths, we can then start to explore unequal class widths. Key to this is pupils recognising that, as with bar charts, if the widths of the bars aren't equal, then the height of the bar will no longer be a good representation of the frequency; the area will automatically be what draws the eye and how the brain interprets the relative sizes of the bars. It may be worth actually giving an example of this, like the one below:

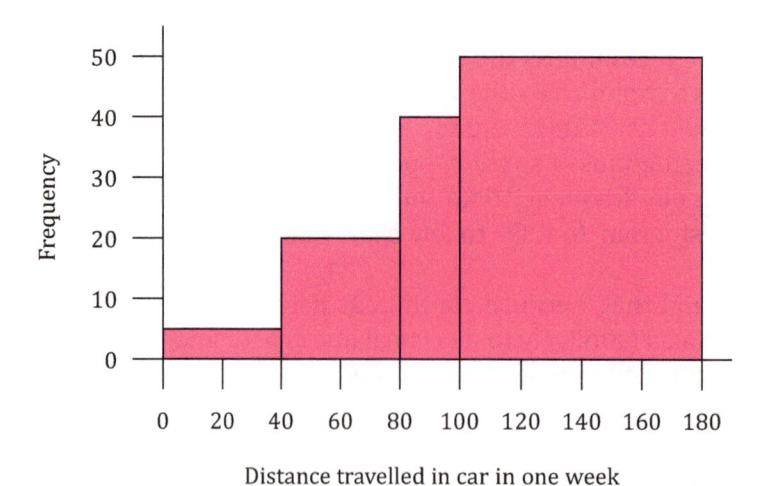

[Histogram: Frequency vs Distance travelled in car in one week. Bars: 0–40 at frequency 5; 40–80 at 20; 80–100 at 40; 100–180 at 50.]

We can see in this diagram that, at first glance, the final bar looks bigger than the other three put together (because it is), but in reality it is only supposed to represent 10 more people than the previous bar. Pupils can then discuss how we solve that problem so that we see the correct distribution – pupils may then come up with 'averaging' the frequencies out across the class width (and if they don't, we can steer things that way!). Pupils should recognise that this has links to density – taking a measure of quantity and dividing it into unit spaces (again, this recognition can either be spontaneous from the pupil or highlighted by the teacher). If pupils study geography, they may also have come across population density and we can highlight the link here as well – the measure of the quantity of the population divided into a unit area. Pupils should then be introduced to the term 'frequency density' as the correct term for averaging out the frequencies – giving the frequency per unit width of class. Indeed, we can use the same sort of proportion structures here to make clear the links between these concepts:

Mass (g)	Volume (cm³)
5	40
0.125	1

Density

Frequency	Class width
5	40
0.125	1

Frequency density

If pupils have already studied mean, then they might also recognise the links to mean – sharing the total equally over the space. We might highlight how this links to the idea of 'averaging' the frequency over the class width.

The frequency densities for each class can then be calculated, and a histogram (this is where we would introduce the word if we have previously been using 'frequency chart') that plots frequency density against class width can be drawn:

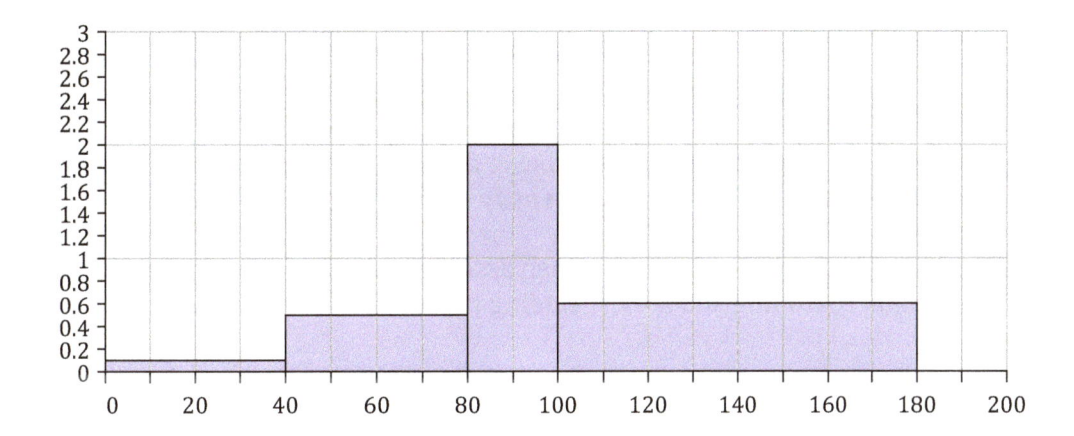

Pupils should be able to see that this gives a much truer picture for the distribution of these people than the original frequency chart – the people are much more normally distributed than the original chart would suggest because the 50 people in the last group are spread over a much greater space than any of the other people.

There is some debate as to how useful histograms that plot frequency density are, with some favouring ensuring that class widths should always be equal so that height can always be used for frequency. However, there are situations where unequal class widths make sense; wage structures in companies are rarely equally spaced. When we look at grade distribution, we may well want to look at unequal-sized groups, and performance data may be grouped for greater focus around certain key boundaries; there are many scenarios that can give rise naturally to unequal groups. For example, in this histogram that shows the distribution of calls in a customer service centre, the unequal groups make perfect sense; the first group looks at calls that are dealt with quickly (inside of 10 minutes) and then the next groups would all be 30 minutes long, except the group that spans the hour is split so that we can see those calls that only just lasted over an hour compared to those dealt with just before (perhaps there is a target to deal with a certain proportion of calls inside an hour).

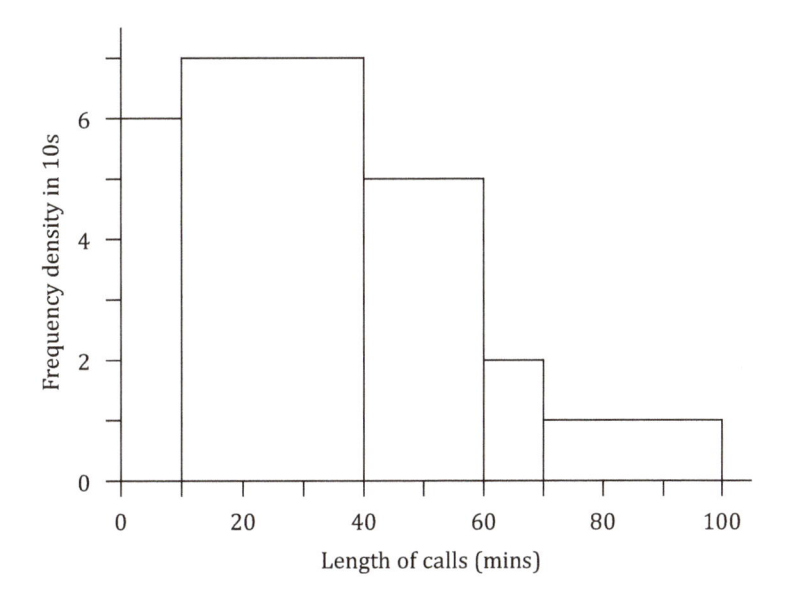

When it comes to interpreting histograms, the key idea that pupils need to become aware of is that it is the area that now represents the frequency. This will be in part be supported by the introduction above – pupils should be able to see that if it was the area that we used to judge the 'size' of each class in relation to each other, then the area relates to the frequency of each class in a proportional way (for the vast majority of histograms, area of a bar is equal to frequency but, for example, in the histogram above, this depends on the vertical scale used). We can reinforce this by examining the calculation for frequency density: if frequency density has been calculated by frequency ÷ class width, then frequency = class width × frequency density (or in the case above, frequency density in 10s = frequency ÷ class width ÷ 10, so frequency = frequency density in 10s × 10 × class width).

There are many problem types that we can then associate with histograms that nicely interweave proportional reasoning and area, including problems like the one below:[5]

The histogram shows the speeds in miles per hour of 82 cars on a road.

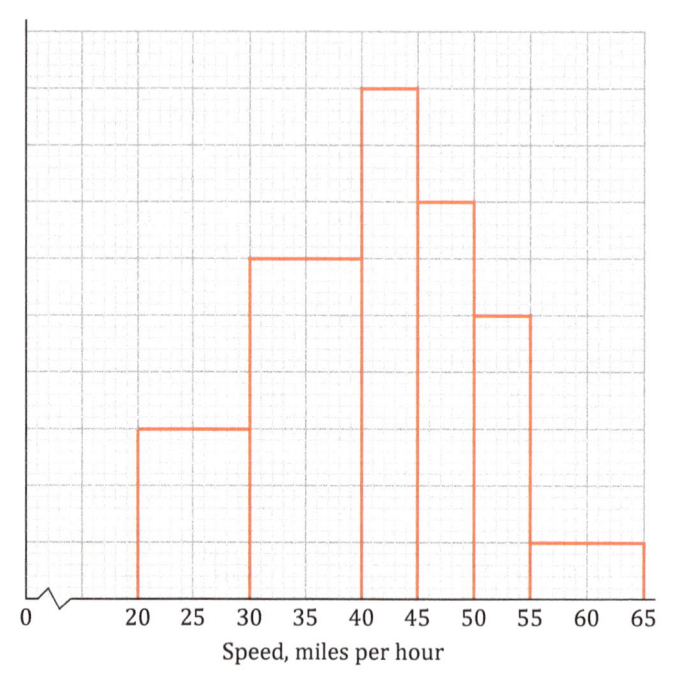

14 cars were travelling over 50 mph.

Calculate an estimate of the number of cars that were travelling between 42 and 49 mph.

So far we have only dealt with continuous data, as we had vertical line charts for discrete data. However, there are times when we group discrete data, and we may want to then look at the distribution of the data when grouped. For example, if we look at the table:

Class interval	Frequency f
30–39	3
40–49	1
50–59	8
60–69	10
70–79	7
80–89	7
90–99	4

---

5   J. Corbett, Exam Style Questions Histograms, *Corbettmaths* (2013). Available at: https://corbettmaths.com/wp-content/uploads/2013/02/histograms-pdf2.pdf.

we can see the difficulty with this is that there would be gaps between the bars – for example, between 39 and 40. We can ask pupils about how we might rectify this – some might suggest leaving the gaps, or changing the class intervals so that the end of each interval matches the start of the next (as for continuous data). Eventually, we can turn this to the idea that we can make the change from one bar to the next at the point halfway between the end of one class and the start of the next (e.g. the end of the 30–39 bar will be at 39.5, as will the start of the 40–49 bar). We can then highlight that this will stretch the classes between the first and last by 1, but that the first and last classes will only be stretched by 0.5. This motivates why we would also move the start of the first class to 29.5 and the end of the last class to 99.5 so that each bar is stretched by 1.

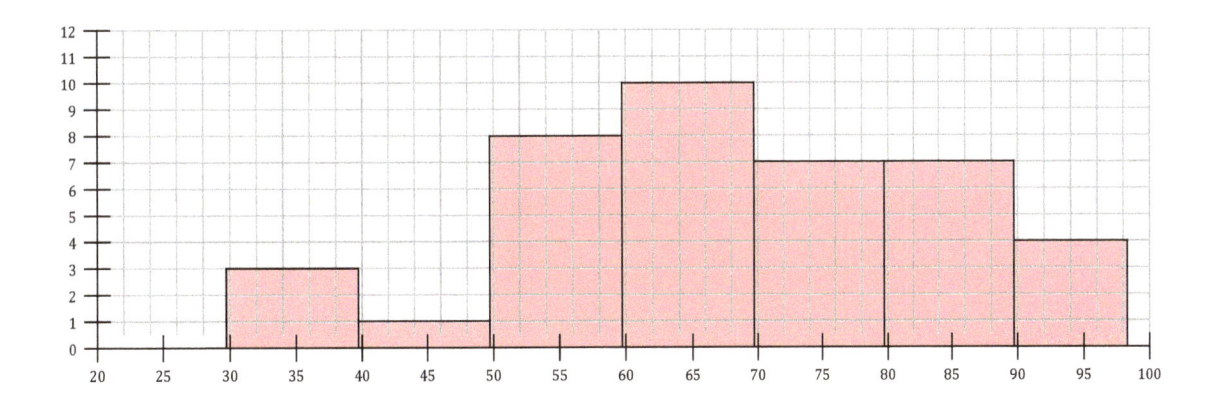

This, of course, has strong links to upper and lower bounds, and this is an ideal point to remind pupils of these ideas. In effect, what is happening here is that the ends of the class intervals are being treated as rounded continuous values rather than discrete values, and we are drawing the bars to show the full range that each member of the class could take prior to the 'rounding'. Pupils should appreciate this and draw histograms for data that is grouped in this way.

Whilst frequency charts/histograms are a nice way to see the distribution of frequencies within a single scenario, it can be more difficult to compare two distributions. For this, we would typically draw frequency polygons.

Concept: frequency polygons

Prerequisites: Number, polygon, numerical data, grouped data table, scale, coordinates.

Linked concepts: Pictogram, bar chart, vertical line chart, frequency chart/histogram, cumulative frequency graph, line graph, median/mean.

A frequency polygon is an alternative approach to showing frequencies for numerical data (generally grouped data). Arguably, it is a better approach to showing distribution than a frequency chart when data is grouped into equal width classes, although they wouldn't necessarily give an accurate distribution for data grouped in classes with unequal widths. However, the main advantage is that it is much easier to superimpose two frequency polygons on the same scaled axes, and so directly compare their distributions.

	120 ≤ h < 130	130 ≤ h < 140	140 ≤ h < 150	150 ≤ h < 160	160 ≤ h < 170	170 ≤ h < 180	180 ≤ h < 190	190 ≤ h < 200
Class A	0	2	1	9	5	5	2	1
Class B	0	1	4	8	11	1	0	0

Pupils should recognise that if we are going to represent all the values possible in a class by a single point, then the midpoint is a good point as it is both the median and mean of the two values at each end of the class, i.e. for the class 150 ≤ h < 160 above, the median and mean of 150 and 160 is 155. In effect, what we are saying here is that we expect the 9 pupils from Class A in that group to roughly average out to a height of 155, so we can effectively plot a frequency of 9 at a value of 155. The same argument works for the other height classes (although pupils should appreciate that the greater the frequency in each group, the more robust the assumption is) and leads us to be able to plot the values.

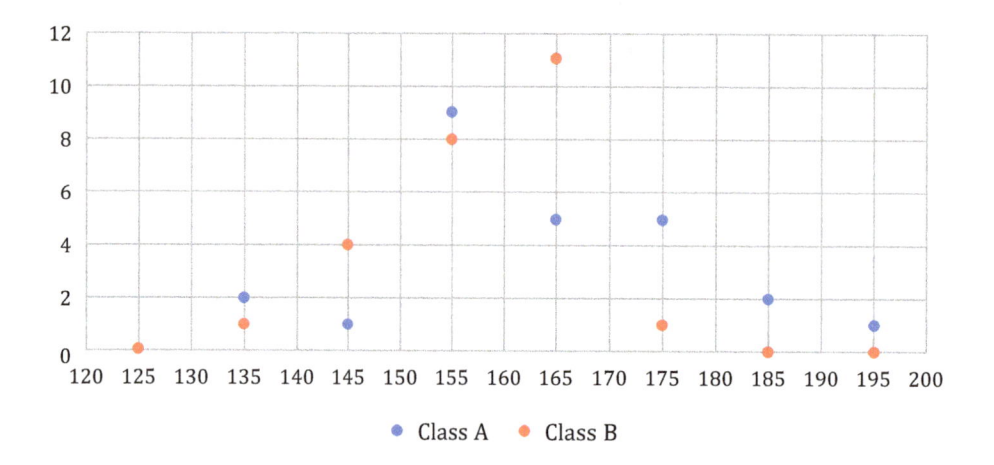

Of course, this doesn't help us actually see the distributions particularly well, until we connect the points. There is a worthwhile discussion here as to whether we join these dots with a smooth curve or with line segments. Of course, to create a 'polygon', pupils should already be aware that we will need to use straight-line segments – although in doing so, pupils should understand that we are, in effect, predicting that the frequencies follow a broadly linear relationship from one group to the next, which may or may not be accurate.

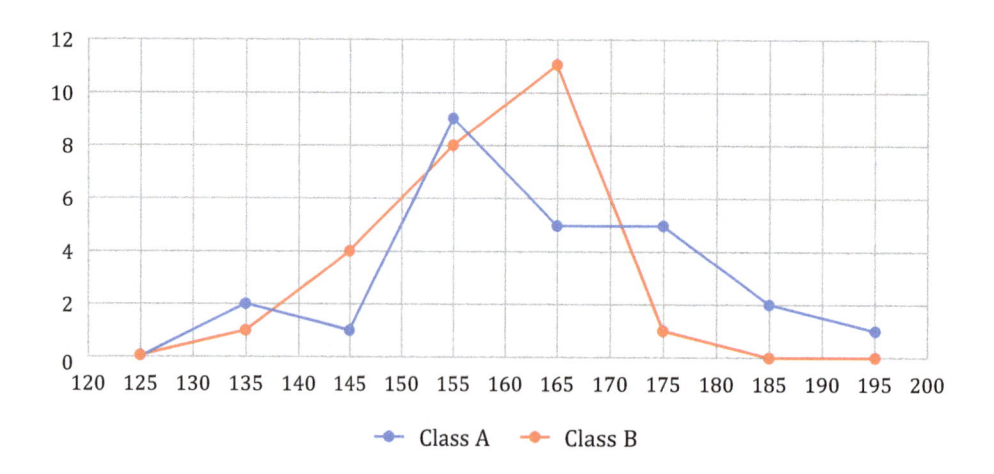

We can now see much more clearly how the distributions compare between the two classes, with Class A having the taller pupils, with broadly the reverse being true for Class B. Of course, one might query the need to compare these distributions at all: why do we need to analyse and compare the heights of these two classes? This potentially highlights again the importance of using data that actually serve a real purpose in comparison – for example, comparing number of sales of two products over different quarters, or how pupil performance for different groups compares to each other.

However, when we compare performance, we are often interested in the number of people that score above, below or between different performance thresholds. For this it would be better to look at a cumulative frequency graph.

Concept: cumulative frequency

Prerequisites: Number, numerical data, grouped data table, scale, coordinates.

Linked concepts: Frequency polygon, line graph, box plot, median, quartiles.

As mentioned, pupils should understand that if we are interested in different thresholds for performance, then looking at and graphing cumulative frequency will be useful in analysing how many people or items hit targets. The obvious example that will probably resonate with pupils is analysing how many pupils in a class/group/school achieve grade 4, 5, etc. in GCSE exams. Indeed, it may well be useful to provide data on frequency of pupils scoring between 0–10%, 10–20% and so on, and then looking at the grade boundaries (also given as percentages) to see how many (or what percentage) of pupils are attaining at different thresholds.

Percentage	Frequency
$90 \leq p < 100$	3
$80 \leq p < 90$	5
$70 \leq p < 80$	17
$60 \leq p < 70$	28
$50 \leq p < 60$	32
$40 \leq p < 50$	45
$30 \leq p < 40$	30
$20 \leq p < 30$	21
$10 \leq p < 20$	9
$0 \leq p < 10$	4

Grade							
9	8	7	6	5	4	3
86%	71%	57%	44%	31%	18%	11%

We can then explore how many pupils scored each grade. Pupils can actually do this informally first of all, just by looking at the data table and estimating how many they think would get each grade. We can then explore the approaches pupils use, which will most likely be trying to estimate the number of pupils up to or between the given percentage values. This leads nicely into the idea of cumulative frequency. We can then compare the values pupils estimate to the ones we eventually get from a cumulative frequency graph.

The first things pupils should be introduced to is the idea of using the end point of each class alongside the cumulative frequency; the idea being that we are counting how many people have scored up to a certain percentage and then plotting this against the upper percentage value:

Percentage	Cumulative frequency
$p < 100$	194
$p < 90$	191
$p < 80$	186
$p < 70$	169
$p < 60$	141
$p < 50$	109
$p < 40$	64
$p < 30$	34
$p < 20$	13
$p < 10$	4

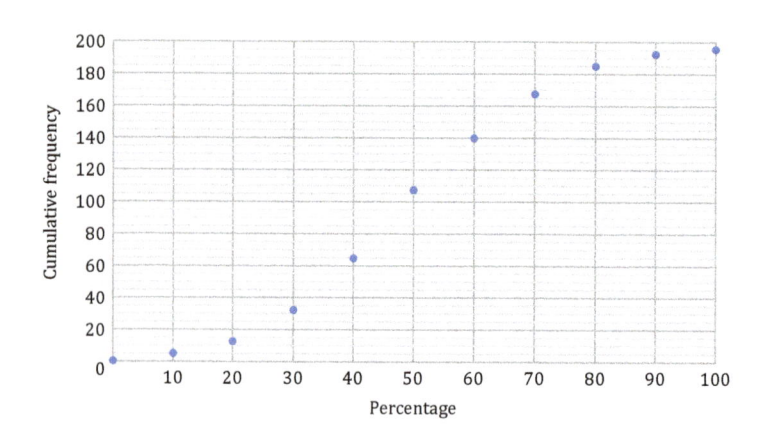

Again, we can then have the same discussion as we had with frequency polygons around whether to connect these points with straight lines or a smooth curve; with the same implication that if we use straight lines, the frequencies progress in a broadly linear fashion. Indeed, we can use technology to look at how drawing straight lines and drawing a curve compare to each other, and alter any result we find when looking at pupils achieving the different grades:

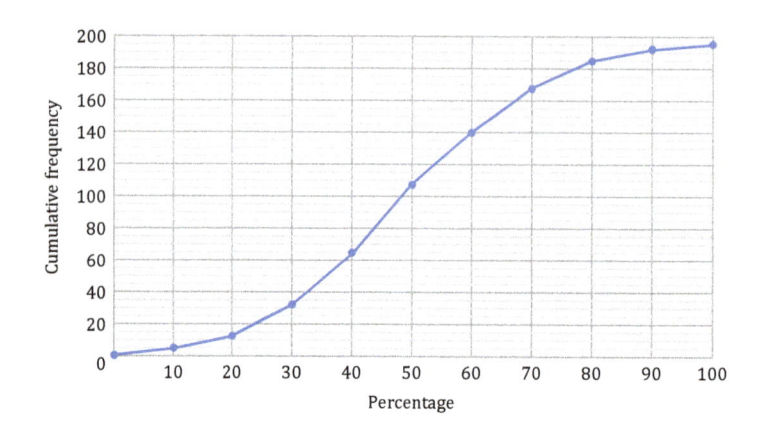

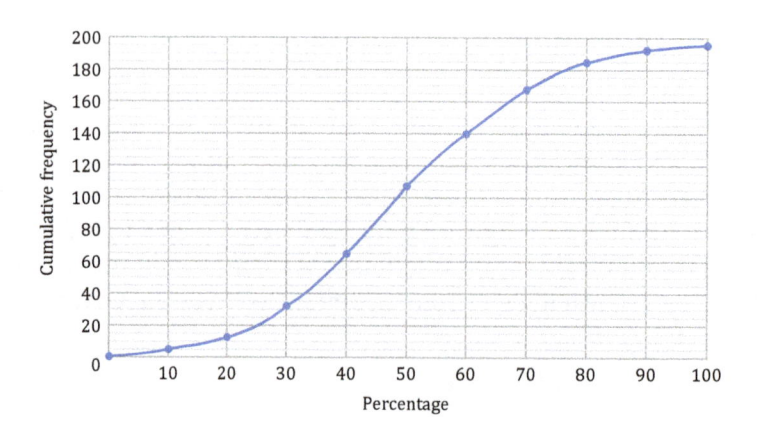

We can see that there is very little difference between the two graphs, and so we may as well join up the points with line segments rather than trying to fit a smooth curve if drawing graphs by hand.

Once the graphs are drawn, we can start to look at how many pupils achieved at each grade. This provides a great model for ensuring pupils understand that when we read values from a cumulative frequency graph, it tells us how many of our data items are below a given value. So, for example, if reading 57% to see how many pupils achieved grade 7, the value we get of approximately 135 tells us that 135 pupils scored below the level required to achieve grade 7. If we then look at 71% being approximately 170 pupils (being the cut-off for grade 8) we can see that this means approximately 35 pupils achieved grade 7.

We can pose different questions about this graph, where pupils have to find those achieving below, above, and between different percentages, and then present other scenarios where pupils have to draw or interpret cumulative frequency graphs. It is worth noting that when drawing graphs, pupils should be faced with the table in different formats so they have to adapt to ensure they identify the required information correctly, i.e. the end of the class interval and the cumulative frequency up to that end value.

Concept: line graphs

Prerequisites: Number, numerical data, scale, coordinates.

Linked concepts: Measures (particularly gradient), area calculations, frequency polygon, cumulative frequency graph, scatter graph, tangent.

A line graph is designed to allow us to track how changes in one variable affect a second variable. Often this second variable is time (in which case the line graph is typically called a time series graph). A key property of this is that the changes in the first variable are controlled, so it may be how temperature changes for differences in altitude:

Altitude (km)	Temperature (°C)
0	20
5	−12
10	−45
12	−60
20	−53
30	−38
40	−18
50	−2
60	−26
80	−87

This gives us data that we can plot on a scaled Cartesian axis:

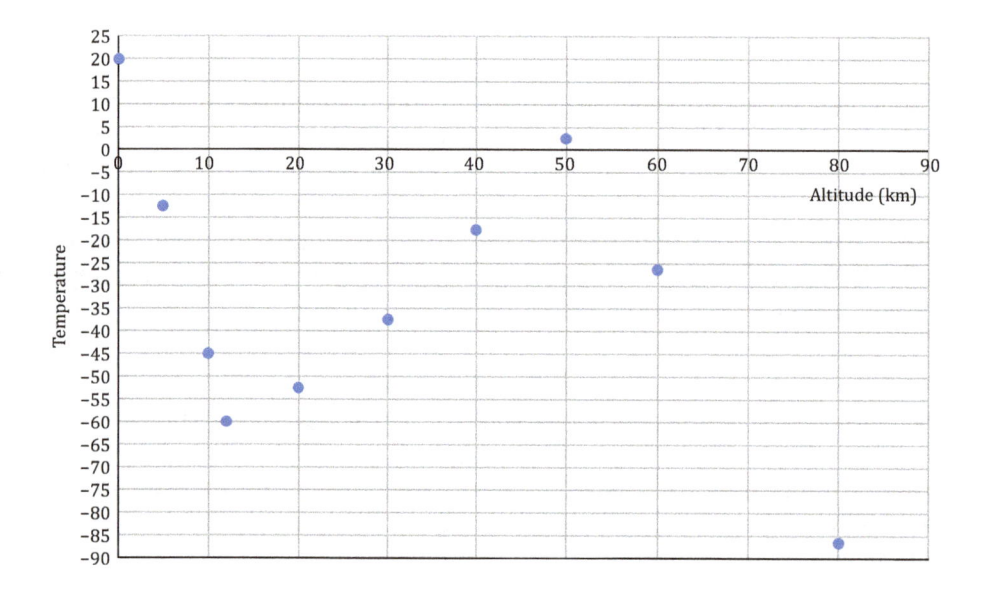

which enables us to see the broad shape of the relationship between altitude and temperature (we still need to remember that the key idea behind any charting or graphing is to gain insight from the visualisation of the relationship). The decision we now need to make (with our pupils) is whether we join these with straight line segments or attempt a smooth curve, recognising that we may do either, but line segments are easier as it is not too inaccurate to assume a linear transition between points (again, we may wish to demonstrate this using technology to show both). This produces the finished graph:

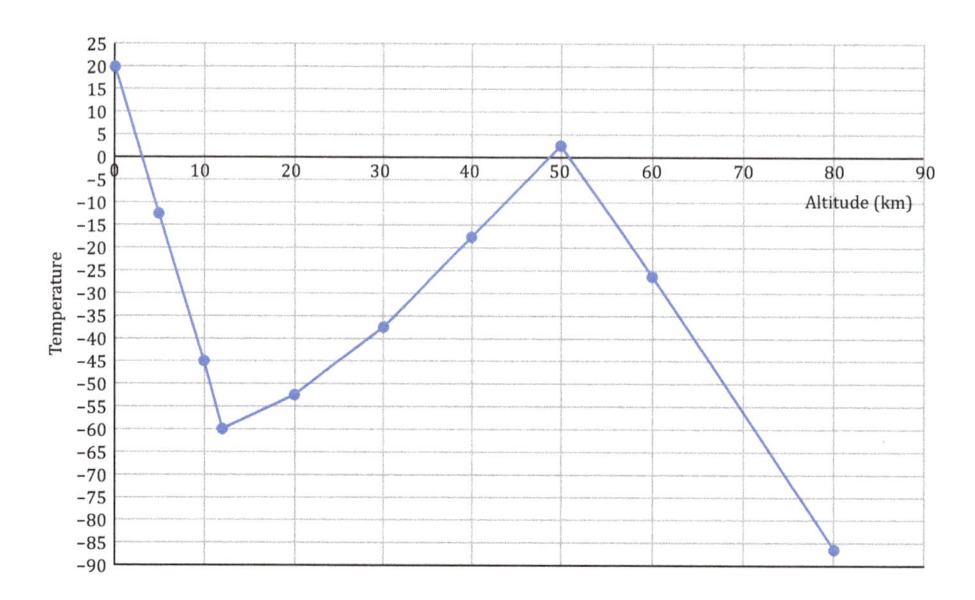

It is worth noting that if using Microsoft Excel, then we have to use the 'X Y (Scatter)' graph to produce this picture unless the controlled variable is graduated in equal increments. This potentially creates a misconception if we allow pupils to use Excel for creating line graphs, unless we choose the data very carefully, so it may be better to have alternative software available, such as Autograph from La Salle Education.[6] Pupils can then be offered different

---

6   See https://completemaths.com/autograph.

sets of data or generate their own from experimentation (either in maths lessons or in a combined effort with the science) in order to plot line graphs.

When it comes to interpretation of line graphs, one of the key things that pupils should be looking for is **trend**. Trend can come in many forms, but it basically refers to underlying and explainable pattern. This might be a seasonable trend (although this may be considered a pattern):

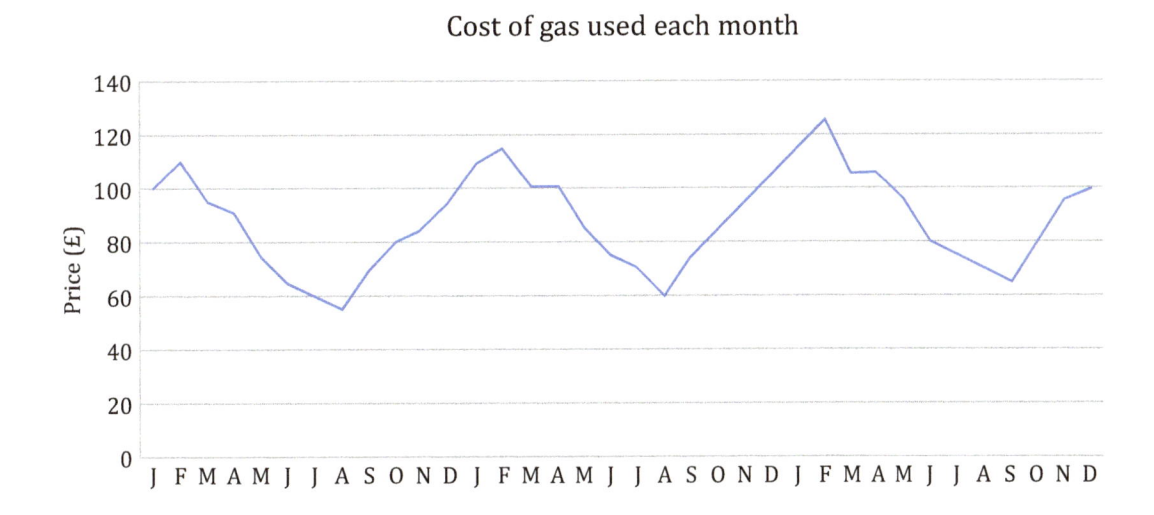

Cost of gas used each month

or increasing/decreasing trends over time:

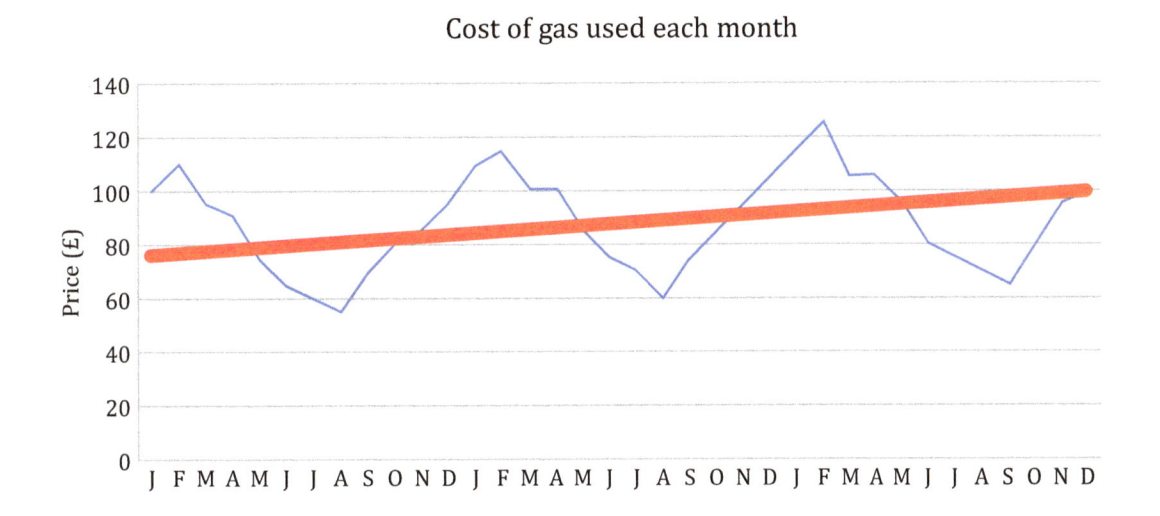

Cost of gas used each month

One of my favourite sets of line graphs to offer pupils to consider patterns/trends is this one:

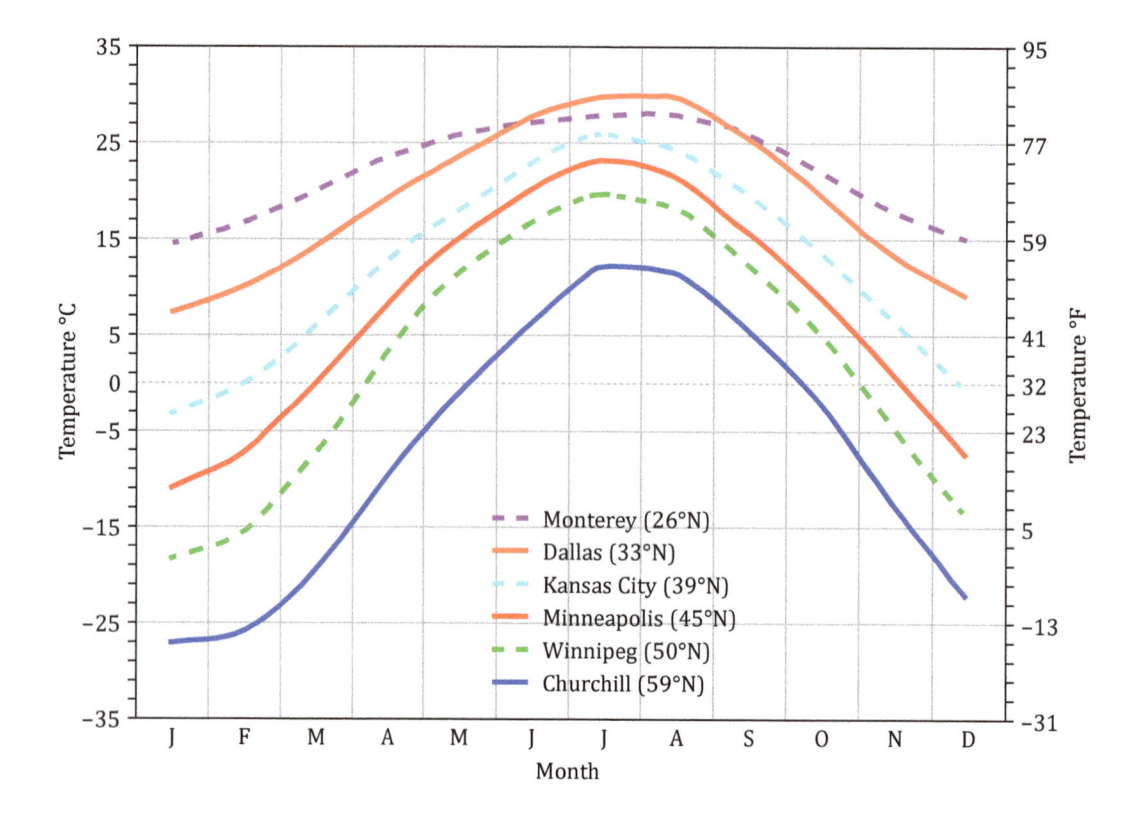

[Graph showing average monthly temperatures in °C and °F across the year for Monterey (26°N), Dallas (33°N), Kansas City (39°N), Minneapolis (45°N), Winnipeg (50°N), and Churchill (59°N)]

There are several trends we can see across these different graphs:

- Temperatures start colder at the beginning of the year, get warmer to a maximum in the middle of the year, and then colder again as we move towards the end of the year.
- Temperatures tend to be lower the further north a place is at most points in the year.
- The range of temperatures tends to be higher the further north a place is.

Pupils will work with a huge number of line graphs over the course of school-level maths, including graphs such as distance–time or speed–time graphs, water flow graphs, tariff graphs/financial graphs, even conversion graphs. In my experience though, many pupils don't appreciate that these graphs are all effectively line graphs showing how one variable changes with respect to another. When we look at these graphs, we really need to reinforce that these are line graphs. It is a good idea to include graphs from these contexts in the teaching of line graphs, providing data on distance travelled at certain points that pupils can graph:

Time (mins)	Distance (km)
0	0
20	5
45	15
70	30
80	30
100	40
120	60

Charting and graphing

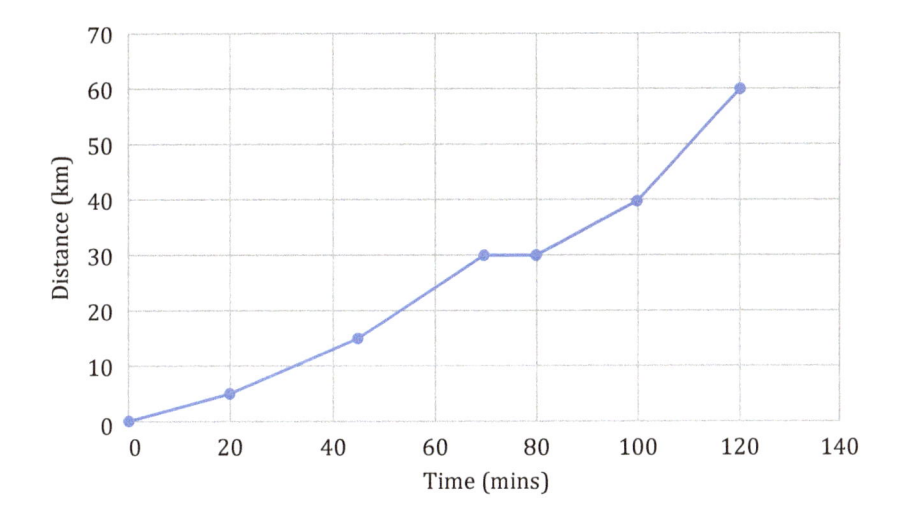

as well as providing the graph and asking pupils to recreate the data table that was used to plot it:

Fill in the blanks in this table that was used to plot the line graph.

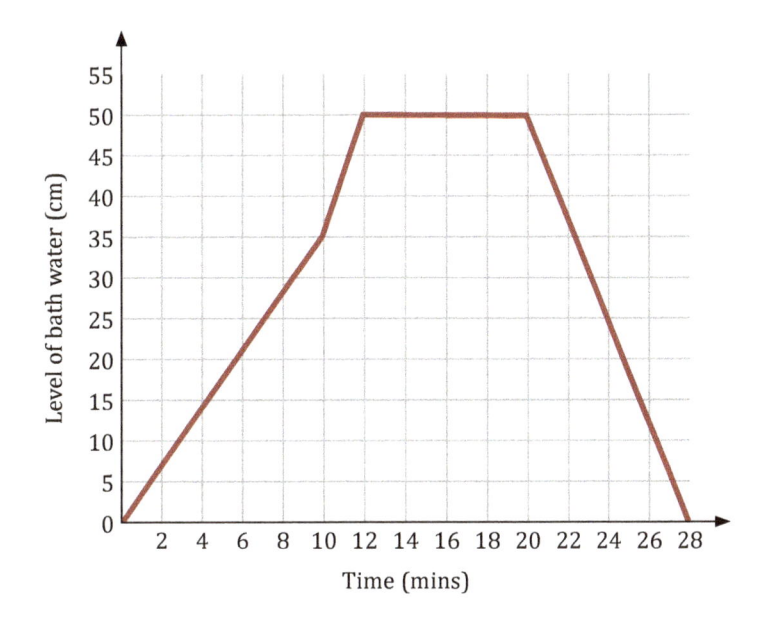

Time (min)	Level (cm)
0	
10	
12	
20	
28	

Once pupils are used to seeing line graphs linked to tabular data in many different contexts, then we can introduce pupils to other ways to communicate the relationship between the two variables. This might include the use of a conversion factor that pupils can use to create a data table:

Given that 5 miles = 8 km, fill in the gaps in the table, and hence draw the conversion graph.

Miles	5	10	15	20	25	30	35	40
Km	8							

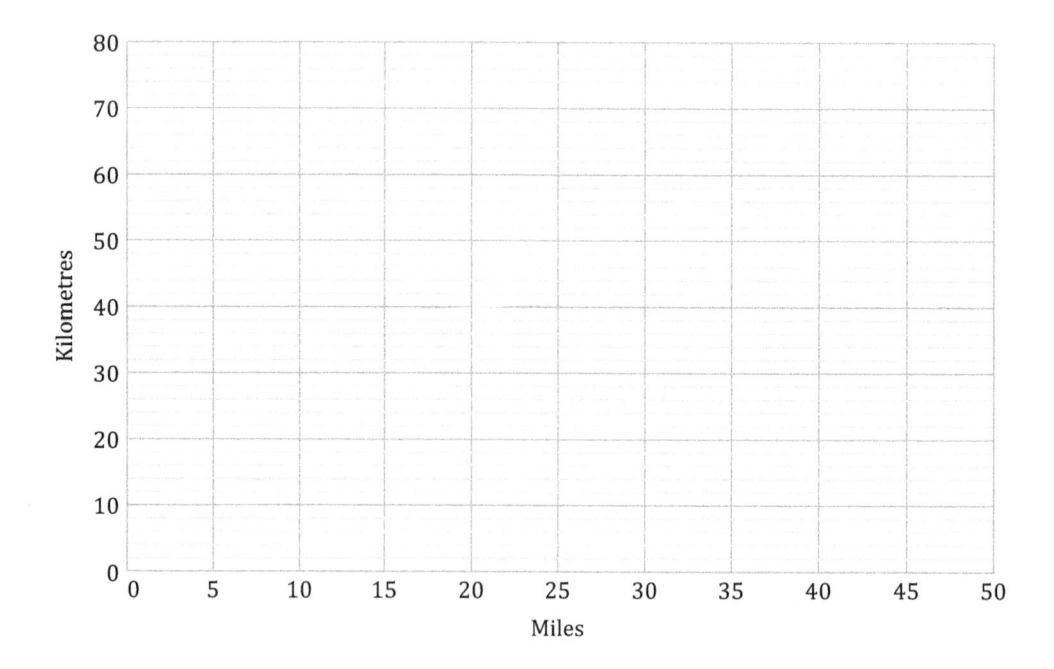

Or it might include information given in words rather than as a data table that pupils have to interpret:

I walk at 5 km/h to a bus stop that is 2 km away. I wait 12 minutes for a bus. I am on the bus for 24 minutes, riding to a shopping centre that is 20 km away from the bus stop. I shop for 3 hours, and then take a taxi home, which travels at a constant speed of 40 km/h. Plot a graph to show my journey.

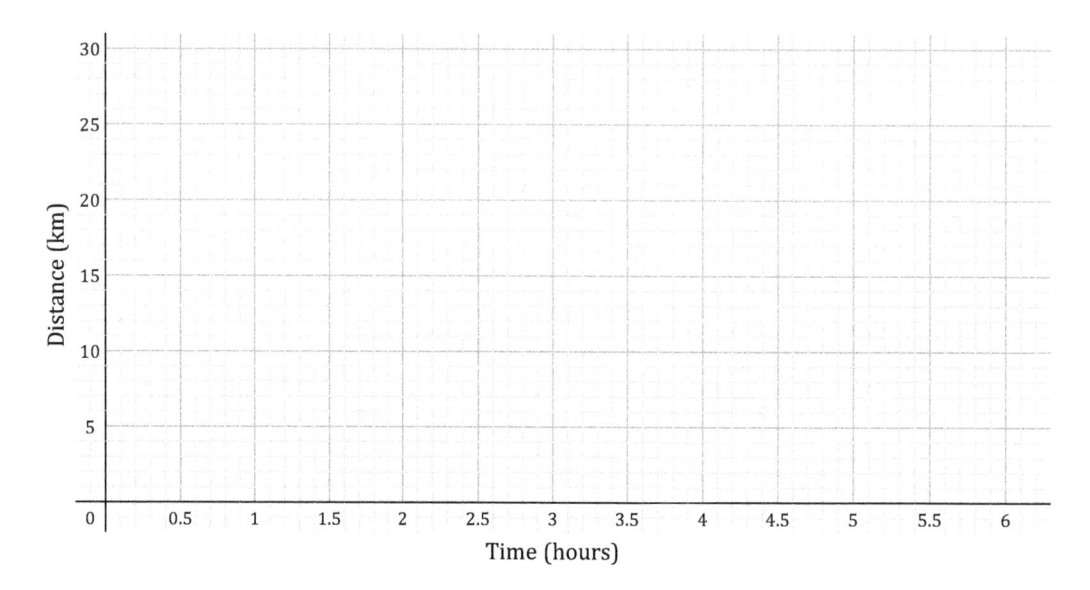

This sort of question can then prompt the consideration of gradient of line graphs and its link to the quantities involved in the graph. In particular, pupils should recognise that:

- The gradient of a distance–time line graph at any point/between any two points gives the speed at that point/average speed between the two points.

- The gradient of a speed/velocity–time line graph at any point/between any two points gives the acceleration at that point/average acceleration between the two points.

- In general, the gradient of line graph at any point/between any two points gives the rate of change of the vertical variable with respect to the horizontal variable.

Charting and graphing

This may well start with the exploration of piecewise linear graphs, such as the line graph below:

This graph shows the cost in dollars of a ticket to the Superbowl each year. Find:

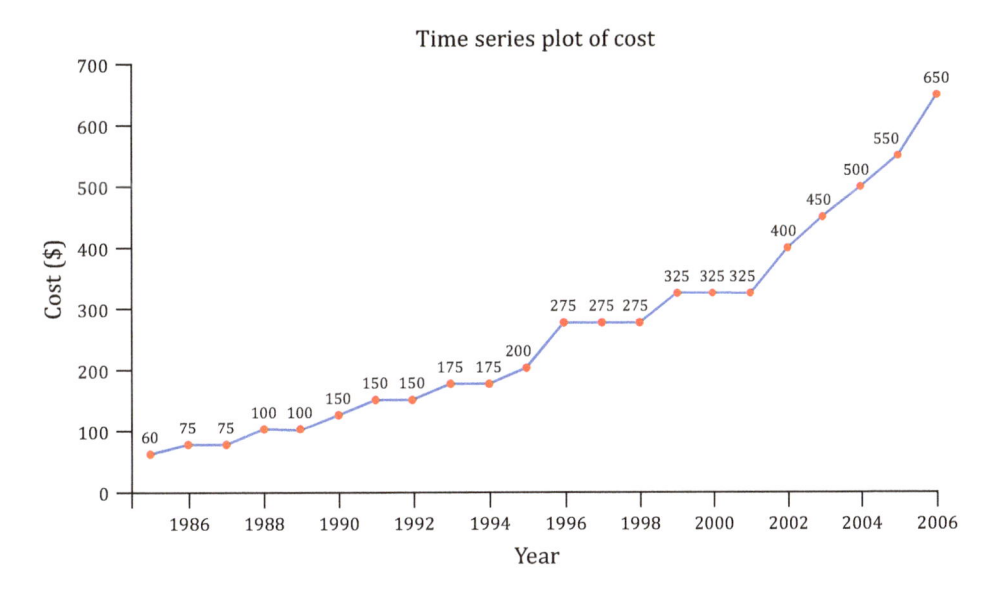

Time series plot of cost

i   The gradient of the line between 2001 and 2002. State the units of your answer.
ii The average rate of change from 1985 to 2006. State the units of your answer.

and eventually to the use of tangents and chords to work with curved line graphs:

The graph shows the time taken for a hot object to cool.

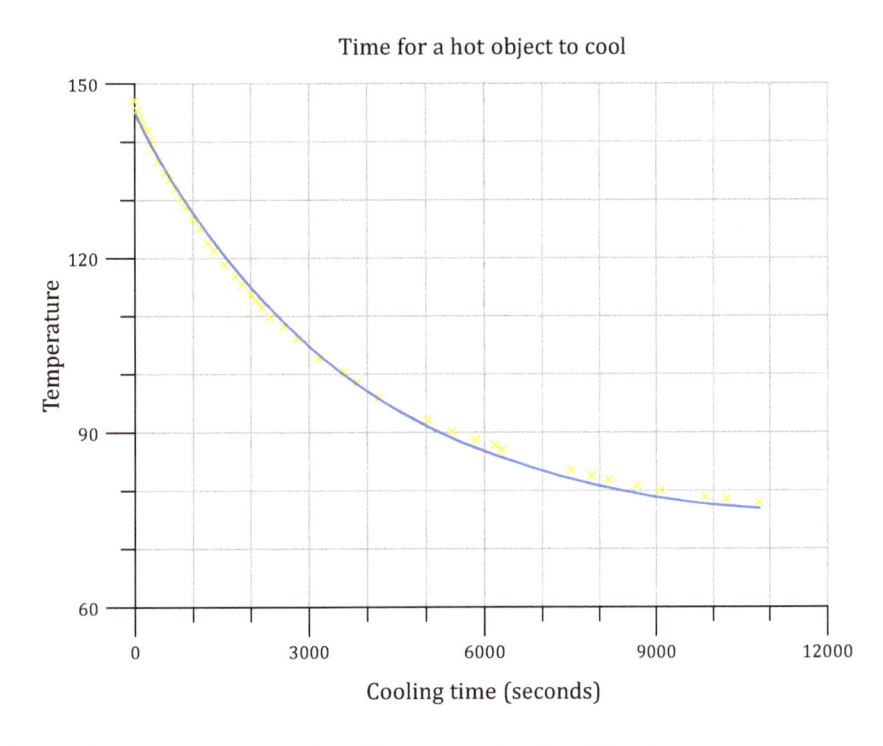

Time for a hot object to cool

a   Work out the average rate of cooling over the first 50 minutes.

b   Estimate the rate of cooling at 4000 seconds.

c   Work out the average rate of cooling over the measured time of 10,800 seconds.

d   Compare your answers to parts (b) and (c). What does this tell you?

Having looked at the links between gradient and line graphs, the other property we will want to examine with pupils is the area under different line graphs (laying the way, eventually, for the study of calculus). This might start with simple line segment graphs, probably involving speed or velocity:

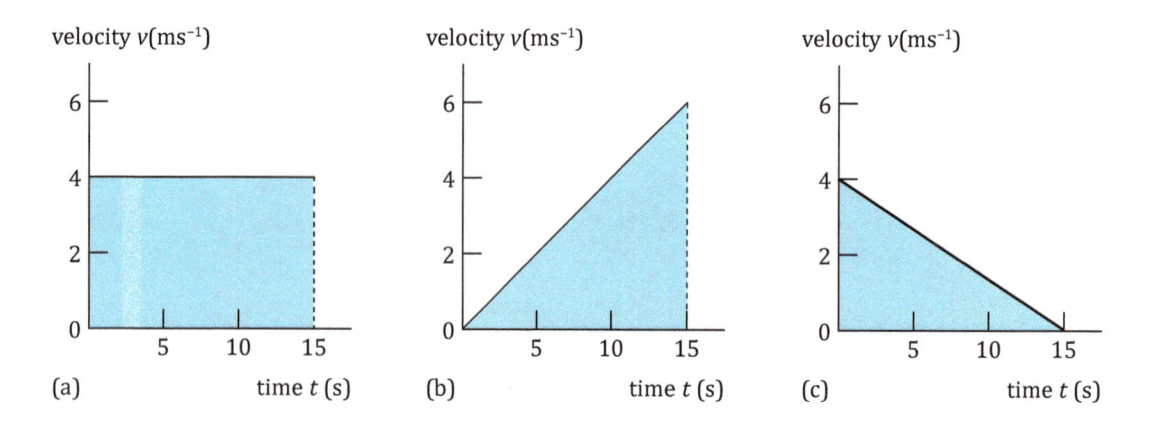

Graph (a) allows us to make the link back to distance, as pupils should already be aware that the distance travelled by an object travelling at constant speed is equal to speed × time, which in this case works out the area of the rectangular area highlighted. This can then be generalised into area under a velocity/speed–time graph calculating distance through the use of graphs (b) and (c), which clearly gives an opportunity to interweave area calculations for well-known shapes:

Find the distance travelled by the object represented in this velocity–time graph.

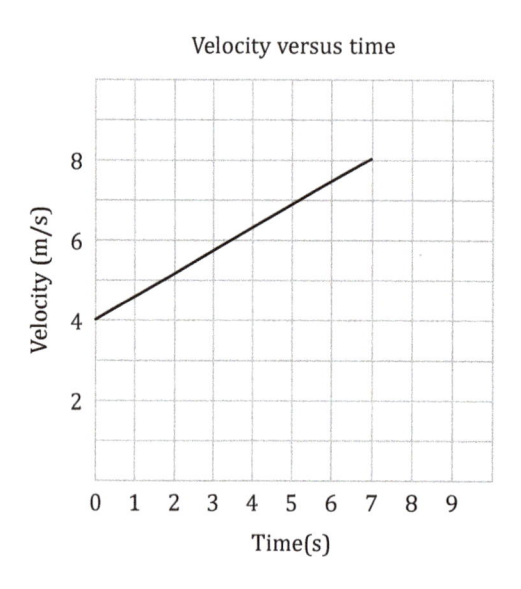

The nice thing about this graph is that its general case can allow the derivation of the kinematics formulae for an object with constant acceleration that pupils meet during school-level maths and science (at least in England).

If we first look at the connection between v and u: we know the gradient of the velocity–time graph gives acceleration, which gives

$\frac{v-u}{t} = a$

which can be rearranged to give

$v = u + at$

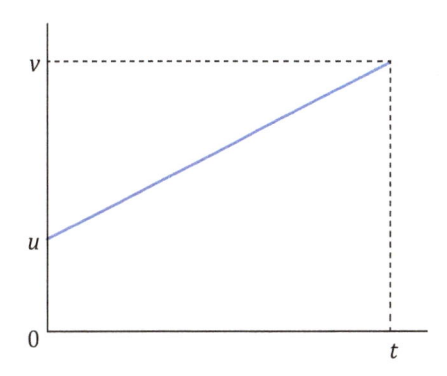

(this form can also be derived directly from the graph: if the gradient of the line is a, then difference in height between v and u is at, and so the height v is equal to $u + at$).

If we then consider the area under the graph using the area of the trapezium formula, knowing the area gives the distance, s, travelled by the object, we have:

$s = \frac{1}{2}(u + v)t$

However, we already know that $v = u + at$, so

$s = \frac{1}{2}(u + u + at)t = \frac{1}{2}(2u + at)t$

expanding the bracket gives

$s = ut + \frac{1}{2}at^2$

(this can also be found by considering the area as two separate areas, a ut rectangular area and a $\frac{1}{2}at^2$ triangular area).

The same trapezium area formula also gives rise to a third formula, provided we rearrange the gradient equation $\frac{v-u}{t} = a$ to give $\frac{v-u}{a} = t$. We can then take:

$s = \frac{1}{2}(u + v)t = \frac{1}{2}(u + v) \times \frac{v-u}{a} = \frac{(u+v)(v-u)}{2a}$

Expanding the brackets gives:

$s = \frac{v^2 - u^2}{2a}$

which can be rearranged to give

$v^2 = u^2 + 2as$

if required.

Pupils may well have used these formulae before as examples of formulae into which values can be substituted or rearranged, but this is an excellent time at which to show where they come from.

We can also stretch this idea to finding and interpreting the area under piecewise linear graphs by treating it as a compound area:

Find the area under this graph (shaded). What does it tell you? OR Water flows through a pipe at a rate shown by the line graph below. Work out the total volume of water that flows through the pipe.

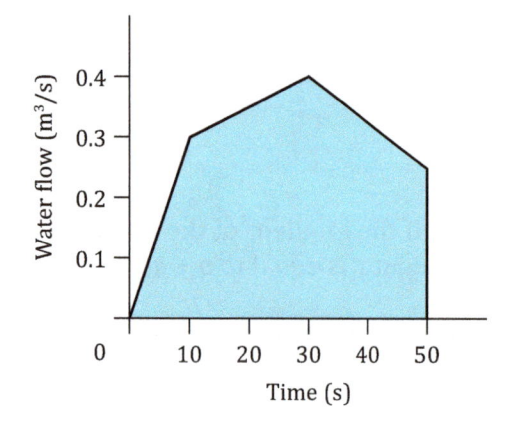

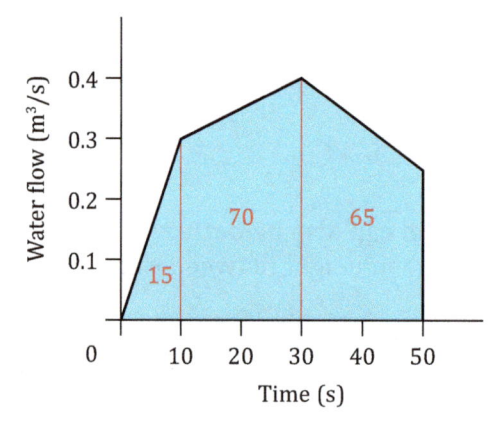

and then eventually to estimating and interpreting the area under curved line graphs:

The graph shows the electricity usage in kilowatts of a church hall during part of a day. Estimate the energy used in kilowatt hours. Explain whether your value is an overestimate or an underestimate.

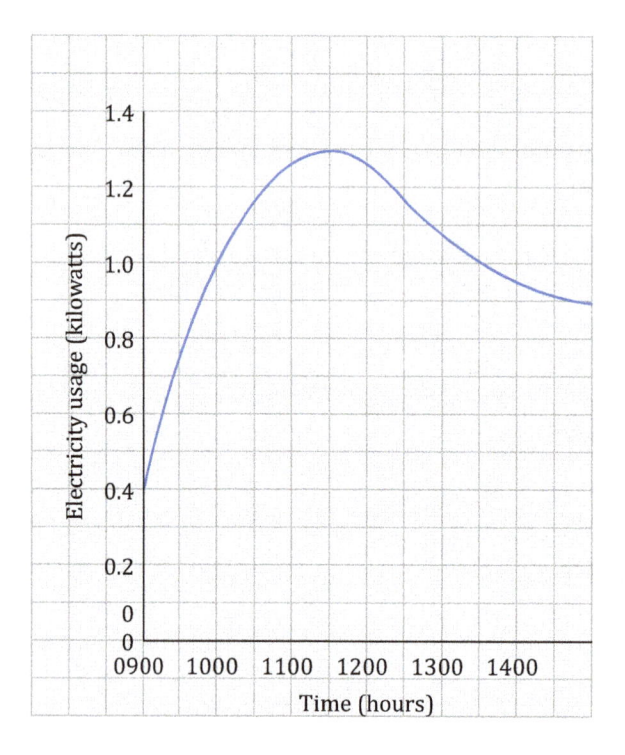

Situations like this will typically be approached by breaking the area up into compound shapes that approximate the given area, although in this case it is also possible (and potentially a nice follow-up) to ask pupils to find the energy usage represented by one small square, and then to estimate the number of small squares under the graph.

Another type of graph that is related to the line graph, to the point where the English school-level science curriculum doesn't distinguish between them, is the scatter graph.

Concept: scatter graph

Prerequisites: Number, numerical data (particularly bivariate data), scale, coordinates.

Linked concepts: Frequency polygon, cumulative frequency graph, line graph, linear graph, correlation, causation, interpolation, extrapolation, mean.

Pupils should understand that the prime difference between a line graph and a scatter graph (at least in maths) is that a scatter graph is plotted from data where both variables can change in an uncontrolled way. This can be linked to work pupils may have done on data collection (which we will look at in Chapter 14), in particular the use of data collection sheets and two-way tables to collect data or tally charts and two-way tables to process data already collected. We might start with some simple examples of scatter graphs compared to line graphs to illustrate the difference to pupils:

Hours of sunshine	Visitors
6	300
0.5	475
8	100
3	390
8	200
10	50
7	175
5	220
3	350
2	320

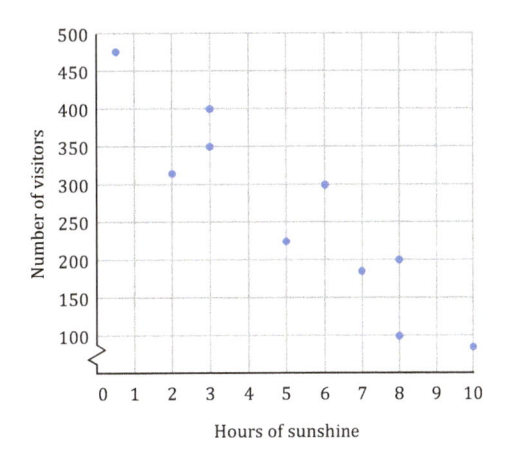

Date	High (°F)	Low (°F)
1/3/12	43	34
2/3/12	44	39
3/3/12	54	44
4/3/12	51	44
5/3/12	46	34
6/3/12	44	32
7/3/12	48	29
8/3/12	60	33
9/3/12	49	41
10/3/12	45	43
11/3/12	44	37
12/3/12	47	33
13/3/12	42	33
14/3/12	46	34

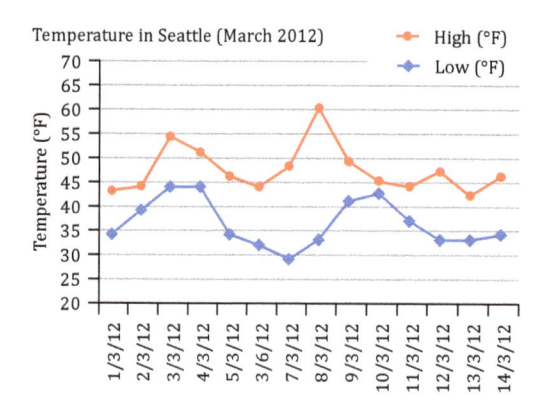

We can see in the first scenario that we are recording two different but related values, neither of which we control. Contrast this in the second scenario, where we have date against temperature, where we are 'controlling' the date (i.e. we decide to record the highest/lowest temperature each day) and track how the temperatures change with respect to date. It is worth noting as well (once pupils are clear on the difference) that we *could* plot a scatter graph of High temperature against Low temperature from the data in the second scenario, which would tell us whether the two were correlated (co-related):

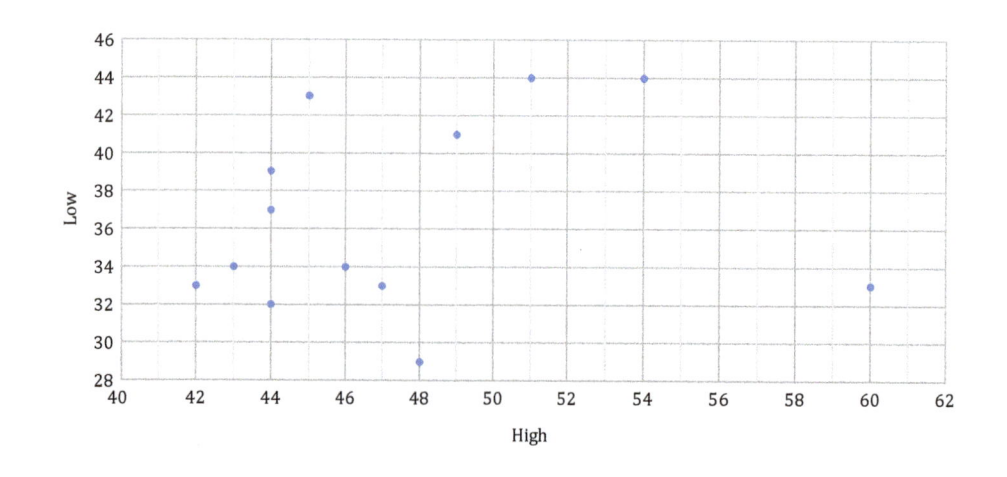

In this case, there doesn't appear to be much in the way of correlation between the highest and lowest temperature across the days where the temperatures were recorded.

It may well be of benefit for some pupils to look at different scenarios and decide what sort of graph we might draw. There is a nice chapter on bivariate data from Hawker College in Australia, which includes a list of different scenarios on page 2 (Exercise 2A, Question 1).[7] Whilst the offered question is around dependent and independent variables, I prefer to ask pupils to choose whether a line graph or a scatter graph (or neither) is the most appropriate graph to plot for each scenario.

Pupils should be able to plot scatter graphs from given data, and identify specific data values plotted on a scatter graph, such as in the question below:

The scatter graph shows the age and monthly salary of a sample of eight teachers in a large school.

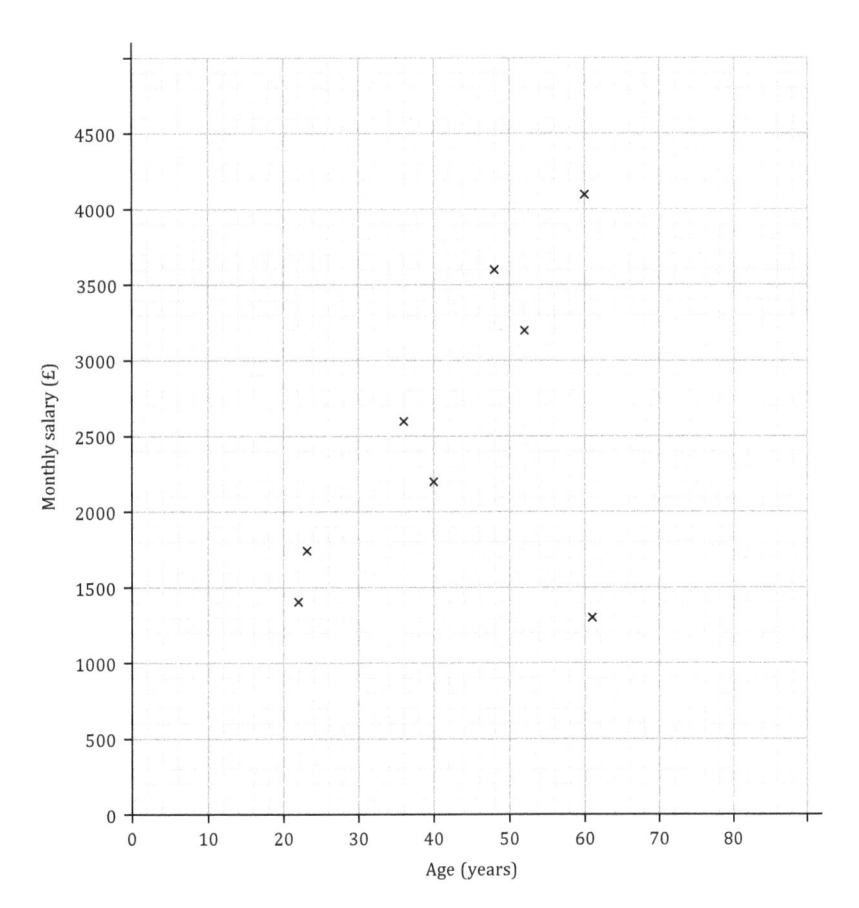

Albert was recently made redundant after working in a factory for 30 years.

He has only been teaching for two years and is part time.

Circle the point on the graph that represents Albert's data.

---

7   A. Novak, R. Bakogianis, K. Boucher, J. Nolan and G. Phillips, *Maths Quest 12: Further Mathematics* (London: Jacaranda, 2009). Chapter available at: https://www.hawkermaths.com/uploads/7/7/3/8/77386549/bivariate_data_chap_2.pdf.

Pupils should also recognise the different types of linear correlation that a scatter graph can show, and what these mean for the relationship between the variables:

Positive correlation

Negative correlation

No correlation

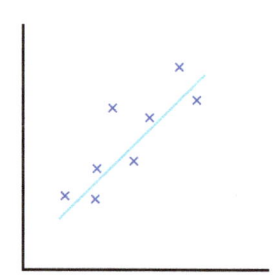

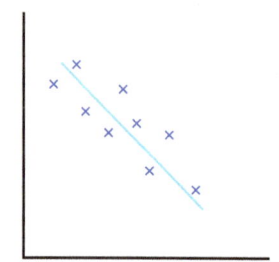

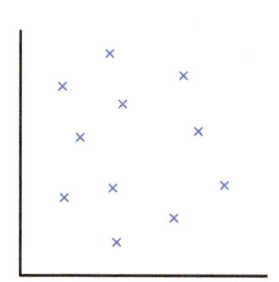

The points lie close to a straight line, which has a positive gradient.

This shows that as one variable increases the other increases.

The points lie close to a straight line, which has a negative gradient.

This shows that as one variable increases, the other decreases.

There is no pattern to the points.

This shows that there is no connection between the two variables.

One thing we should draw attention to here is that, whilst positive and negatively correlated variables are clearly related, the relationship is not necessarily causal in nature, i.e. whilst, for positive correlation, as one variable increases the other increases, this doesn't mean the increase in one variable causes the increase in the other. As pupils look at different scatter graphs, this is something we should continually revisit – whether the relationship is a causal relationship or a correlated relationship.

Pupils should know that the line that positive and negative correlation lie close to is called the line of best fit, and its role is to model the relationship between the variables. Pupils should understand that, in drawing a line of best fit, the goal is to minimise the distances of the points from the line.

When drawing lines of best fit, a common mistake pupils make is trying to force the line of best fit to go through the origin. This should be explicitly tackled with pupils to make sure they recognise that linear relationships do not have to go through the origin, and so don't draw lines of best fit through the origin unless it makes sense to do so.

A common use for a line of best fit is to allow us to **interpolate** values – pupils should be clear that without a line of best fit to model the relationship between the variables, we should not attempt to predict values from the scatter graph. Pupils should understand that the individual data points are subject to experimental error, and that the line of best fit is what we are saying is the true picture of how the variables are related, and so without it we cannot predict. Pupils can be asked to interpolate values from a scatter graph once a line of best fit is drawn, and should recognise this as equivalent to solving an equation graphically (more on this later in the chapter).

The scatter graph below shows the amount of money spent in an ice cream shop for different temperatures. Use the line of best fit to estimate the amount of money spent on a day when the temperature is 21°C.

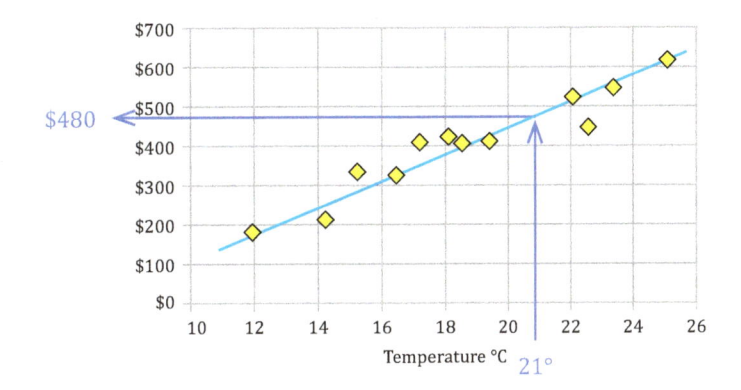

Whilst pupils should be happy with interpolating values from a line of best fit, pupils should also be very aware of the dangers of **extrapolation**; in particular, that unless there is strong reason to believe that a relationship will continue outside of the range of the data used to draw the scatter graph, then we should not be trying to extrapolate.

The scatter graph below shows the amount of money spent in an ice cream shop for different temperatures. Use the line of best fit to estimate the amount of money spent on a day when the temperature is 29°C. Explain why this figure may not be accurate.

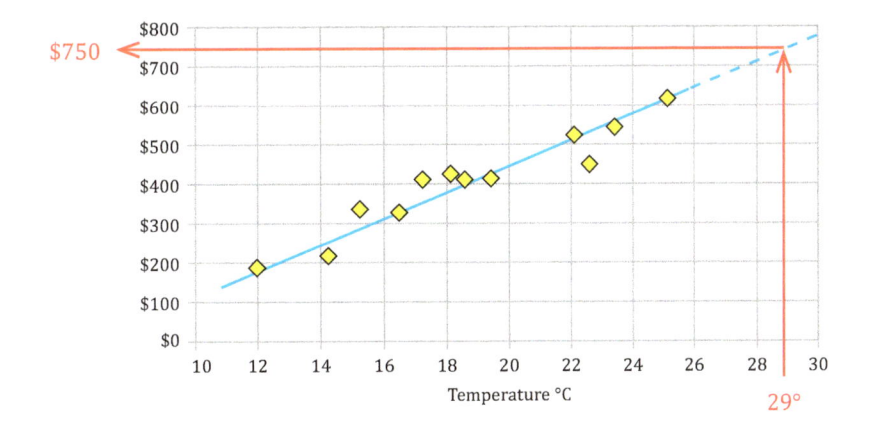

There is one more type of graph/chart that school-level pupils will be required to utilise in pre-16 mathematics (at least at the time of writing), which relies heavily on ideas we will develop in the next chapter. As such, we will include the basics of the representation here but leave further development until the appropriate point in Chapter 14.

Conceptual Maths

Concept: box plots

Prerequisites: Number, median, lower quartile, upper quartile, scale.

Linked concepts: Cumulative frequency graph, range, average.

Pupils should understand that a box plot (also called a 'box and whisker diagram') is a representation designed specifically to highlight and allow comparison of the distribution of numerical data. The way it does this is to break the data into four equal-sized groups, and to show the range of values spanned by each of these four groups.

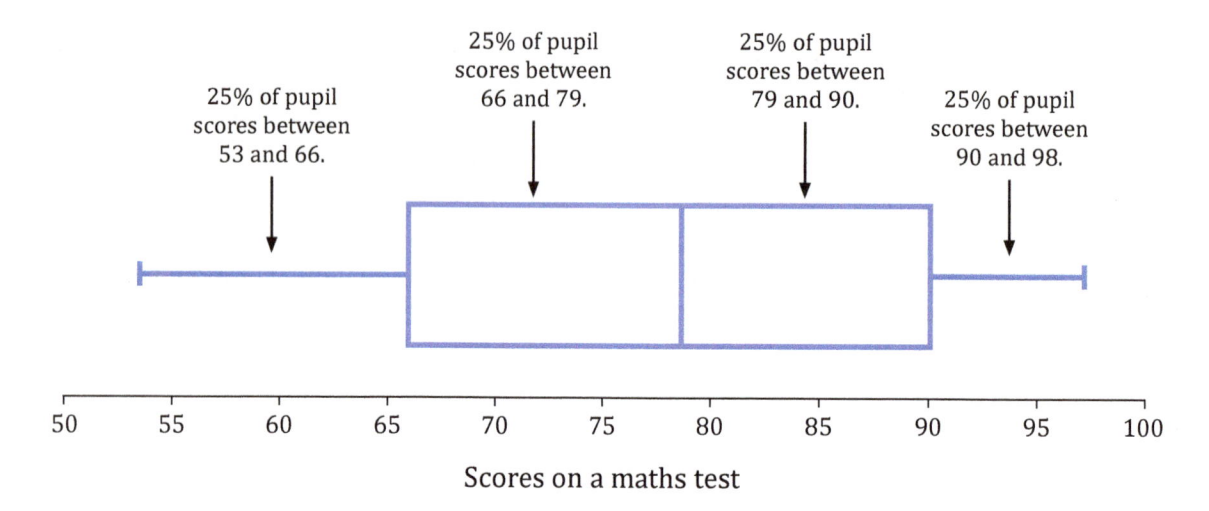

[Box plot showing: 25% of pupil scores between 53 and 66. 25% of pupil scores between 66 and 79. 25% of pupil scores between 79 and 90. 25% of pupil scores between 90 and 98. Scale from 50 to 100. Label: Scores on a maths test]

Pupils should know that the point of transition between the first and second quarter is the lower quartile or $Q1$, the point of transition between the second and third quarter is the median or $Q2$, and the point of transition between the third and fourth quarter is the upper quartile or $Q3$ (we will look at actually identifying these values for data sets in Chapter 14).

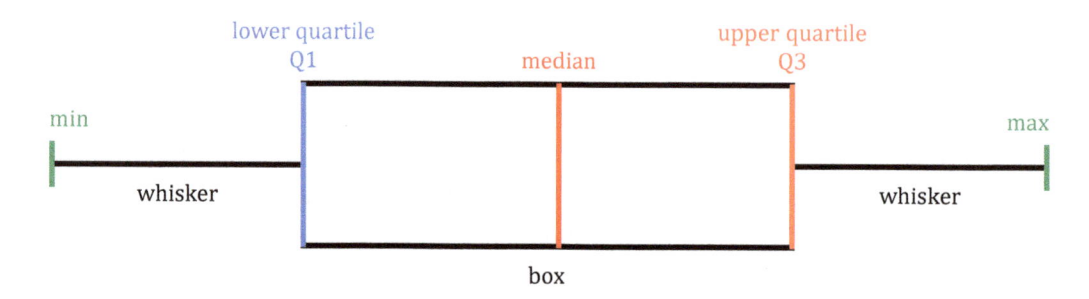

[Labelled box plot showing: min, whisker, lower quartile Q1, median, upper quartile Q3, whisker, max, box]

Pupils should be able to draw box plots, including the scale on which they are drawn when given the different values of the transition points and end points.

Here are the number of goals scored by the 11 members of a football team in 2001:

	Least goals	Most goals	Q_1	Median	Q_3
2001	0	11	2	5	6

On graph paper, mark a scale from 0 to 12. Draw a box plot.

Pupils should also recognise that the distances between the quartiles give us a very quick and easy way of recognising and comparing distribution of values.

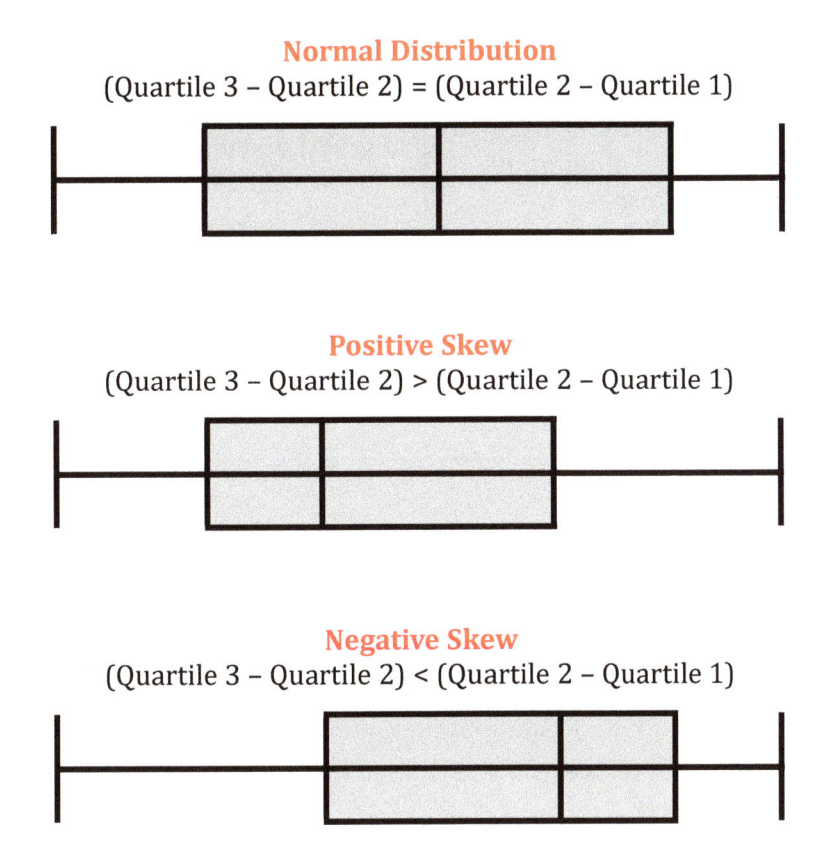

Normal Distribution
(Quartile 3 − Quartile 2) = (Quartile 2 − Quartile 1)

Positive Skew
(Quartile 3 − Quartile 2) > (Quartile 2 − Quartile 1)

Negative Skew
(Quartile 3 − Quartile 2) < (Quartile 2 − Quartile 1)

Of course, in a perfectly normal distribution $Q3 - Q2 = Q2 - Q1$; however, provided $Q3 - Q2 \approx Q2 - Q1$ then the distribution will be broadly normal, whereas if $Q3 - Q2$ is much greater than $Q2 - Q1$ then there is a definite positive skew and similarly if $Q3 - Q2$ is much less than $Q2 - Q1$ then there is a definite negative skew.

The Standards Units has a truly excellent resource in its statistics section that prompts pupils to compare frequency line graphs, cumulative frequency graphs and box plots to match those that show the same distributions. What is more, there is also a set of cards to match a description of the scenarios that could rise to that distribution. To use this fourth set of cards, pupils will need to have studied mean and mode and how these relate to each other for different distributions, so if pupils have not yet learnt these things then we will need to leave this set of cards out and just provide pupils with the different graphs/charts to match.[8]

---

8   STEM Learning, Interpreting Frequency Graphs, Cumulative Frequency Graphs, Box and Whisker Plots S6 (n.d.). Available at: https://www.stem.org.uk/resources/elibrary/resource/26994/interpreting-frequency-graphs-cumulative-frequency-graphs-box-and.

This was the sort of exam where you could either do everything or you couldn't get started.	This exam did not sort out the better-performing candidates from the poorer-performing ones. They all got similar marks.
Two groups of candidates sat the exam. One group had studied the work for two years. The other group had only just begun.	This exam resulted in a huge spread of marks. Everyone could do something but nobody could do it all.
In this exam, the mean mark was greater than the modal mark.	In this exam, the mean mark was smaller than the modal mark.
In this exam, the median and the modal marks were the same. There was a very wide range of marks.	This exam was much too difficult for most candidates.

Up to this point we have focused very much on graphs that we draw to show relationships based on gathered data, either provided or as a result of experimentation. In the second part of this chapter we will look at graphs that we draw to show relationships that are defined algebraically. Before we explore these, however, we need to formally look at how we define a coordinate system.

Concept: coordinates

Prerequisites: Number, measures.

Linked concepts: Graphing/charting, vectors, Pythagoras theorem, ratio/proportion, median/mean, angle, circles, bearings, gradient.

The story of Descartes' invention of the rectilinear coordinate system is one of my favourite stories to tell pupils and even to mimic with pupils when first introducing coordinates.[9] Ultimately, the prompt is a good one to get kids considering: how do we define location on a two-dimensional surface (and eventually a three-dimensional space)?

The first thing that pupils should understand is that key to any coordinate system is its initial reference point – the origin. All coordinate systems have an origin, from which all other positions are referenced. In fact, even the number line can be considered a one-dimensional coordinate system with an origin at 0 and all other positions located by the distance from 0 in either a positive or negative direction. It is worth highlighting this to pupils so that they see the similarities between this and when we then introduce the two-dimensional rectilinear coordinate system designed by Descartes.

There are many different ways that pupils might suggest to provide a position or location on a two-dimensional surface – pupils may have heard of latitude and longitude, using polar coordinates (typically through suggesting radar) or even distance and bearing. We can acknowledge these things and help pupils to see that the key thing they have in common is that they use two values to reference location in relation to their origin. For polar coordinates, the origin is the centre of the concentric circles of different radii (called the 'pole'), and the

---

[9] Wild Maths, Rene Descartes and the Fly on the Ceiling (n.d.). Available at: https://wild.maths.org/ren%C3%A9-descartes-and-fly-ceiling.

two values are the straight-line distance from the pole and the angle measured anticlockwise from a horizontal line connected to the pole. For latitude and longitude the origin is the point where the equator crosses the prime meridian, and the two values being the number of degrees north and east from there (with the angle measured from the line that connects the origin to the centre of the Earth and the line that connects the centre to the point on the surface). For distance and bearing, the origin would be the point that we draw the north line from, and the two values would be distance from the bottom of the north line and the bearing.

The final thing we will want to perhaps highlight to pupils is that in all of these systems we will need to be consistent about which value comes first and which comes second. We can't give a polar coordinate of (43, 56) if we don't know if this means 43 km away at an angle of 56° or 56 km away at an angle of 43°! Pupils should understand that this is likely to be decided by convention – people agree that a coordinate system will be used a certain way (always latitude before longitude, for example), as there will rarely be a mathematical reason to put one value before the other.

Once pupils appreciate these key components of a two-dimensional coordinate system, we can introduce the Cartesian coordinate system and show how it meets the criteria – with the convention that we give the horizontal distance from the origin first, and then the vertical distance. Notice, I have not used the variables x and y here; x and y are often used as a shorthand to reference the horizontal and vertical axis, but there may well be situations in the future that pupils come across where y is the variable we place on the horizontal axis, or x on the vertical (for example, when plotting (t, x) for movement along a line with respect to time). Pupils should be clear that the axes are only an x and y axis when these are the variables attached to the axes, but they could equally be a t and d axis (if plotting time and distance) or any other combination of variables. What will continue to be the case is that the value of the horizontal ordinate will be given first, and then the value of the vertical ordinate, no matter what the variable labels are. We may also at this point want to explore the convention that the positive directions are generally defined to be to the right and up from the origin, and the negative directions to the left and down (although, as with number lines, this is a convention that we will change if it makes the maths easier – such as defining down as positive when we are considering gravity near the Earth's surface).

Once pupils have been introduced to the Cartesian coordinate system, they should have a chance to work with it, identifying coordinate pairs and plotting points for given coordinates. There are a number of resources available where pupils plot coordinates or join up pre-plotted coordinates to create a 'join the dots' picture, and these are fine provided they do not detract attention away from the key things we want pupils to remember – the order of the ordinates and the positive and negative directions. There are also things like Connect 4 or Battleship-style games that pupils can play in pairs to get used to drawing and identifying coordinates. An important part of this is pupils having the opportunity to create their own scaled axes – this is something a lot of pupils struggle with and needs careful attention alongside the use of pre-drawn axes. There is an excellent resource, free on *TES*, that highlights specific mistakes that pupils make when drawing axes.[10]

The Cartesian coordinate system also provides an excellent opportunity to interweave properties of shapes (particularly polygons) provided pupils have previously studied these (of course, if not, then introduction of shape properties can serve as a nice point to interweave working with coordinates). This might include activities like the one from Don Steward:[11]

---

10 Dave314, Common Mistakes Drawing Axes, *TES* (2018). Available at: https://www.tes.com/teaching-resource/common-mistakes-drawing-axes-11069060.
11 D. Steward, Rectangles on a Grid, *Median* [blog] (16 July 2011). Available at: https://donsteward.blogspot.com/2011/07/rectangles-on-grid.html.

Conceptual Maths

Rectangles on a grid:

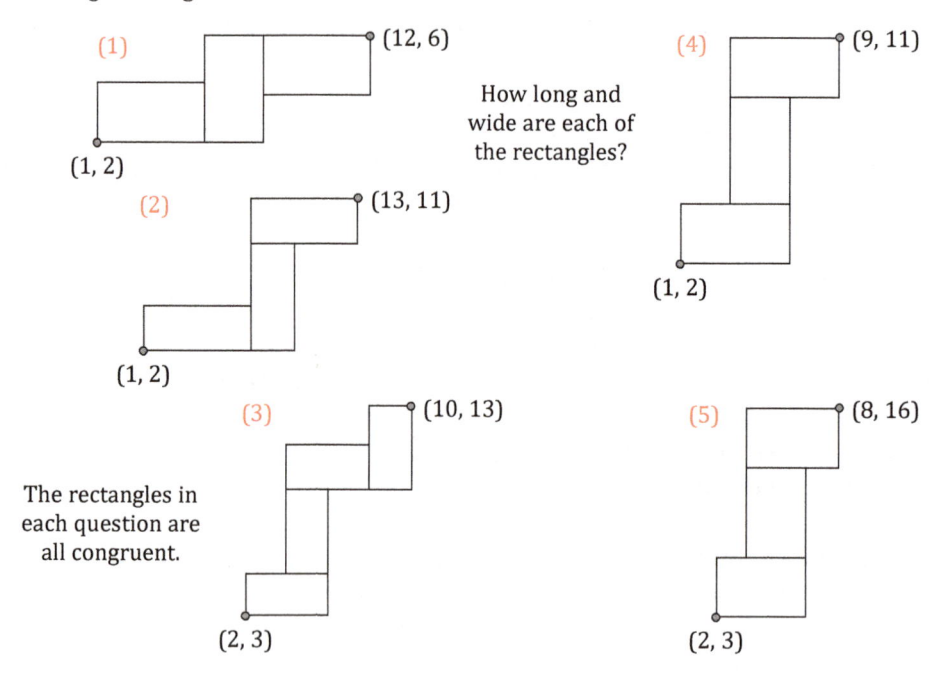

(1) ●—————● (12, 6)
●
(1, 2)

How long and wide are each of the rectangles?

(4) ●————● (9, 11)

●
(1, 2)

(2) ●————● (13, 11)

●
(1, 2)

(3) ●————● (10, 13)

The rectangles in each question are all congruent.

●
(2, 3)

(5) ●————● (8, 16)

●
(2, 3)

Or this from NRICH (particularly if adapted so that pupils have to write down the coordinates of each square they find):[12]

On the axes there are 28 marked points.

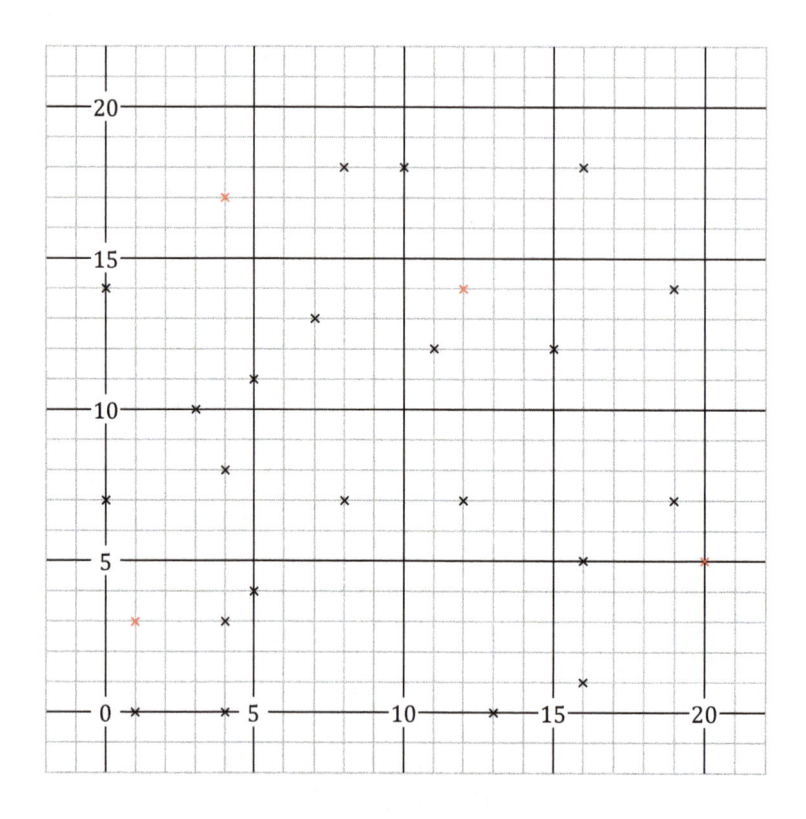

These points all mark the vertices of eight hidden squares.

Each of the four red points is a vertex shared by two squares.

---
12 See https://nrich.maths.org/6280.

The other 24 points are each a vertex of just one square.

All of the squares share just one vertex with another square.

All the squares are different sizes.

There are no marked points on the sides of any square, only at the vertices.

Can you find the eight hidden squares?

or can include finding coordinates that fit given geometric criteria:

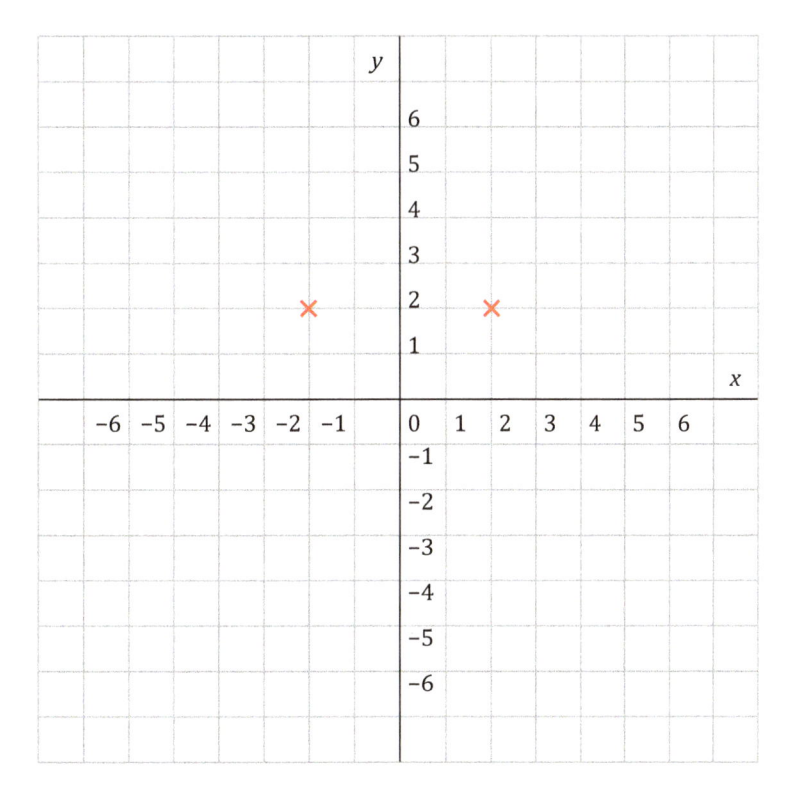

These are two vertices of a square.

There are three squares that can be plotted when starting with these two points.

Can you find all three?

Can you create all four different types of triangle (equilateral, isosceles, scalene, right-angled)?

When pupils have learnt about ratio and proportion, a nice activity to link this to coordinates is to ask pupils to think about finding the coordinate that lies along a line so that the distances between points are in a given ratio. It may be better to start with coordinates on a horizontal or vertical line to begin with so that pupils make sense of how this links to ratio work they have previously done – for example:

A is the point with coordinates (3, 8) and B is the point with coordinates (3, −4). C is a point on the line AB and between A and B such that the ratio of the distances $AC:BC$ = 1:3. Find the coordinates of the point C.

We can then complicate things a little:

> A is the point with coordinates (3, 8) and B is the point with coordinates (11, −4). C is a point on the line AB such that the ratio of the distances AC:BC = 1:3. Find the coordinates of the two possible positions of the point C.

A special case of this link is to find the midpoint of two points, which pupils should see as the ratio 1:1, and also the links to mean/median:

> i   A is the point with coordinates (3, 8) and B is the point with coordinates (11, −4). M is the point on the line AB such that the ratio of distances AM:BM = 1:1. Find the coordinates of the point M.
>
> ii Plot A, B and M on an axis. What do you notice about the position of M compared to A and B?
>
> iii Find the median and mean of 3 and 11, and also the median and mean of 8 and −4. What do you notice about your values compared to the values in the coordinates of M?
>
> iv Can you generalise what you have found to the points with coordinates (x_1, y_1) and (x_2, y_2)?

Admittedly, there may need to be more work on midpoints and coordinates before pupils can go to step 4 independently.

As well as finding coordinates based on geometric or proportional reasoning, an important idea for pupils to consider is finding the distance between two points. It may be helpful here to use units of distance that pupils are more familiar with before moving to the more general 'units'. Again, we might want to start this with points lying on horizontal or vertical lines to begin with:

> A and B are points plotted on a square-centimetre grid with coordinates (3, 8) and (3, −4), respectively. Find the distance AB.

before moving on to the use of Pythagoras' theorem to find distances:

> A and B are points plotted on a square-centimetre grid with coordinates (3, 8) and (12, −4), respectively. Find the distance AB.

and even combining the distance and ratio problems:

> A is the point with coordinates (3, 8) and B is the point with coordinates (12, −4). C is a point on the line AB such that the ratio of the distances AC:BC = 1:3.
>
> i   Find the coordinates of the two possible positions of the point C.
>
> ii Find the distances AC and BC in each case and verify that they are in the ratio 1:3.

Many ideas in measures and geometry can be combined with the use of coordinates, including ideas of gradient, perimeter, area and angle. Indeed, one of the key properties of the Cartesian axis is that it allows for the worlds of algebra and geometry to be connected. As pupils study different ideas in geometry and measure, we should take the opportunity to tie these back to coordinates:

1. Work out the gradient between the points (4, 9) and (7, −3).

2. The points (0, 0); (2, 4); (6, 4) and (0, −8) form a quadrilateral.

    i   Show that this quadrilateral is a trapezium.

    ii Find the perimeter of the trapezium.

    iii Find the area of the trapezium.

3. For the triangle below, find:

    i   the size of angle CAB.

    ii the area of the triangle.

4. A circle has points $A = (5,1)$, $B = (7,-3)$, $C = (2,-8)$ and $D = (-2,0)$ on its circumference.

    i   Find the angle ACB.

    ii Hence find the angle ADB.

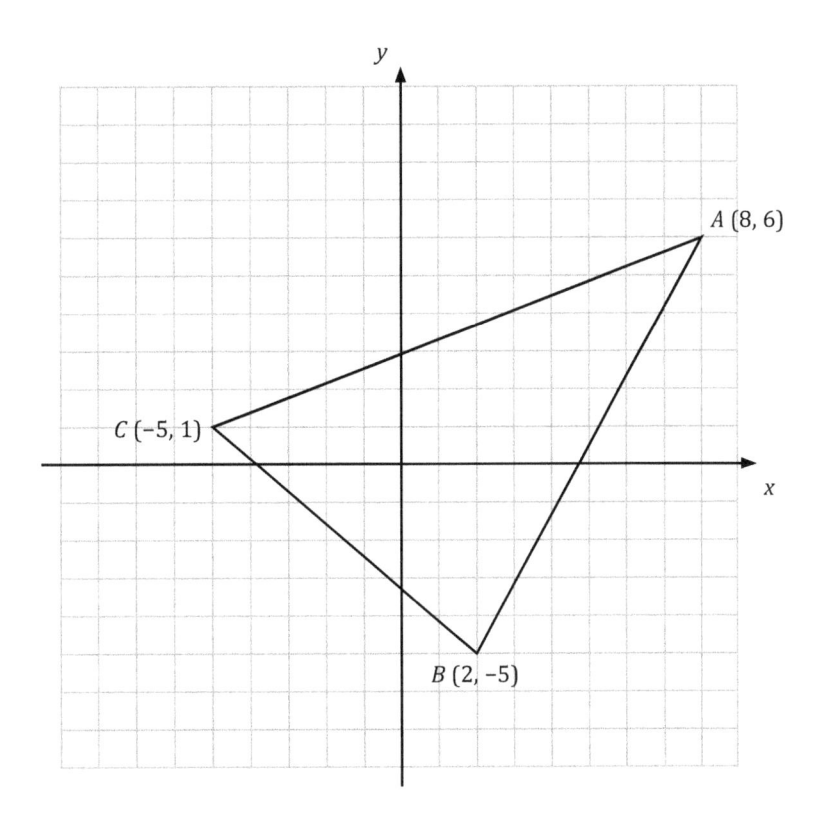

Once pupils have begun to explore coordinates, and in particular started to make the link between coordinates and shape, then we can start to explore with them the relationships between coordinates that make up different shapes, starting with simple lines.

Conceptual Maths

Concept: linear graphs

Prerequisites: Coordinates, graphing/charting, equations.

Linked concepts: Arithmetic sequences, gradient, rearranging formulae.

There are two broad approaches that one might take to introduce the graphs of linear equations, depending on pupils' previous experience of coordinates and graphing:

1. Pupils investigate coordinates that form a straight line, looking for a relationship that links the horizontal ordinate and the vertical ordinate.

2. Pupils explore different equations, looking at the coordinates that fit the relationships and what it is about them that produces a straight line.

Both approaches have merit: the first potentially allows the form of the linear equation to be discerned more directly, although it tends to be slower as pupils have to examine many different sets of coordinates before a fully generalised equation for the line can be found:

What do we notice on each line about the second ordinate compared to the first?

What is always true about coordinates on lines that are vertical?

By looking at the coordinates on each line, decide which of these lines are vertical.

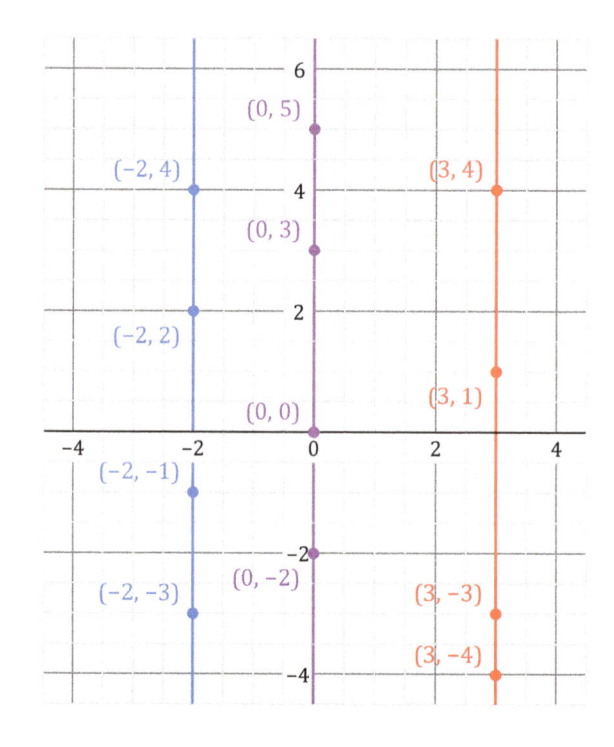

Line 1: (18, 5); (18, 8); (18, 28); (18, −18)

Line 2: (5, 18); (8, 18); (28, 18); (−18, 18)

Line 3: (−27, 5); (−27, 8); (−27, 80); (−27, 500)

Line 4: (−9, −9); (−9, −32); (−9, −11); (−9, −2.3)

What do we notice on each line about the second ordinate compared to the first?

What is always true about coordinates on lines that are horizontal?

By looking at the coordinates on each line, decide which of these lines are horizontal.

Line 1: (18, 5); (18, 8); (18, 28); (18, −18)

Line 2: (5, 18); (8, 18); (28, 18); (−18, 18)

Line 3: (−27, −5); (−7, −5); (80, −5); (500, −5)

Line 4: (−9, −9); (−9, −32); (−9, −11); (−9, −2.3)

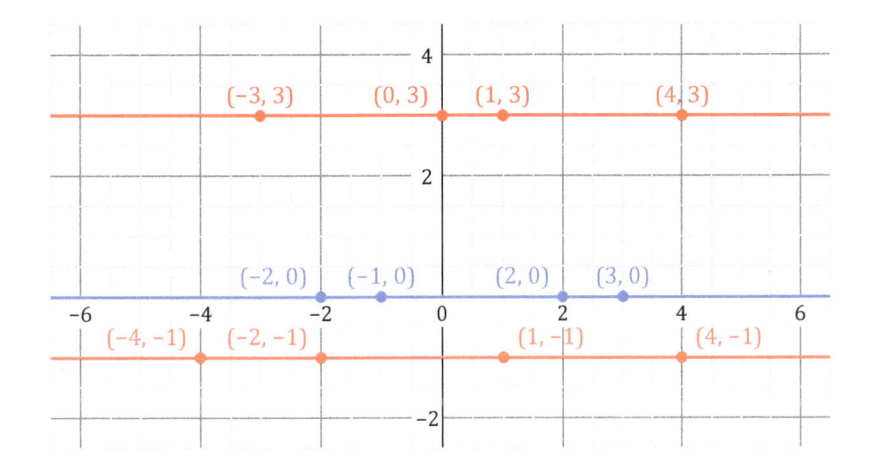

What do we notice on each line about the second ordinate compared to the first?

What is always true about coordinates on lines that slope at 45°?

By looking at the coordinates on each line, decide which of these lines slope at 45°:

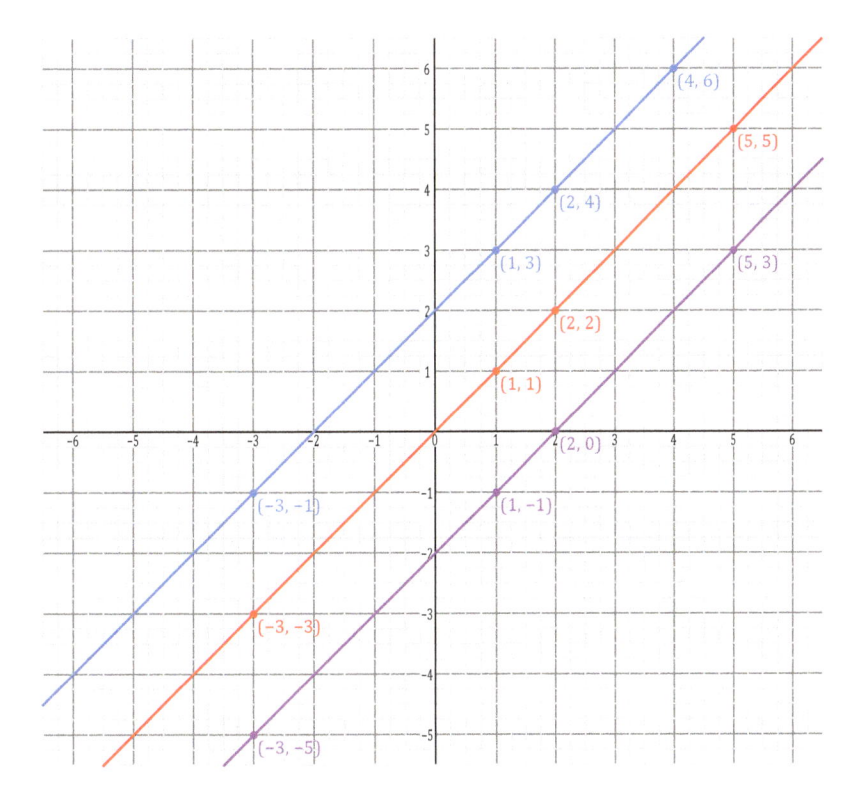

Line 1: (0, 5); (3, 8); (23, 28); (−23, −18)

Line 2: (0, 5); (3, 8); (23, 28); (−23, −28)

Line 3: (0, 5); (3, 8); (30, 80); (100, 500)

Line 4: (5, 0); (8, 3); (28, 23); (−23, −28)

What do we notice on each line about the second ordinate compared to the first?

What is always true about coordinates on lines that slope through (0, 0)?

By looking at the coordinates on each line, decide which of these lines slope through (0, 0).

Line 1: (5, 30); (6, 31); (7, 32); (8, 33)

Line 2: (5, 30); (−5, −30); (50, 300); (19, 114)

Line 3: (5, 30); (−5, −30); (30, 5); (−30, −5)

Line 4: (5, 30); (10, 60); (−5, −30); (−10, −60)

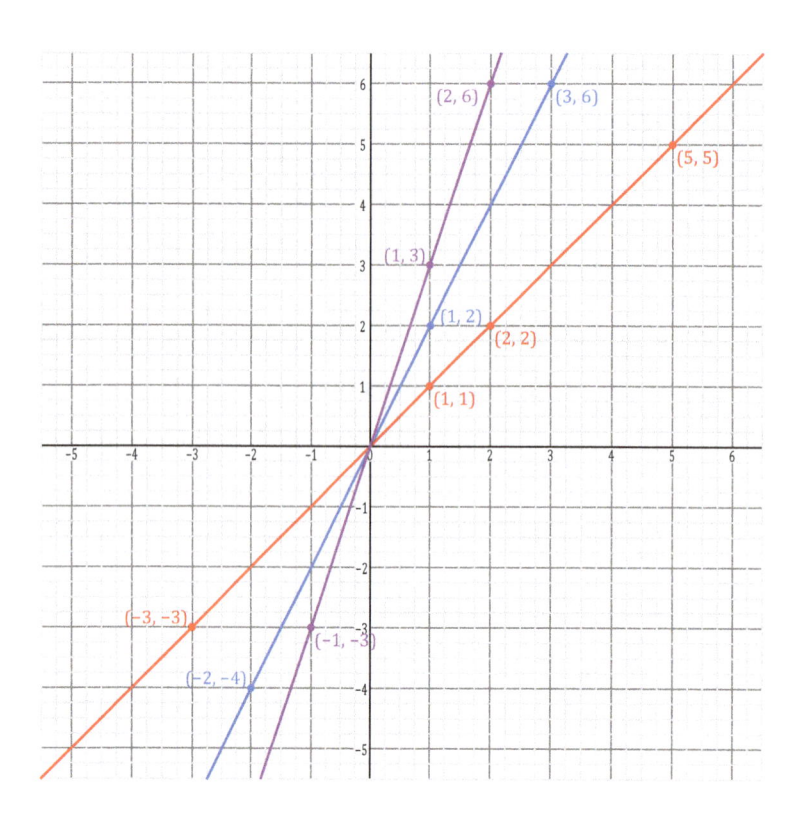

The first two of these can be generalised into capturing the relationship $y = c$ and $x = a$, and the last two can be generalised into $y = mx + c$, with the additive element coming from the first and the multiplicative from the second.

The alternative to this is to offer the algebric relationships immediately, highlighting to pupils that we can use substitution to generate values that can be plotted – drawing the links to other graphs such as line graphs or frequency polygons:

Given $y = 3x - 1$ complete the table of values to show how y varies with x, and then plot the graph of $y = 3x - 1$.

x	−3	−2	−1	0	1	2	3	4
y								

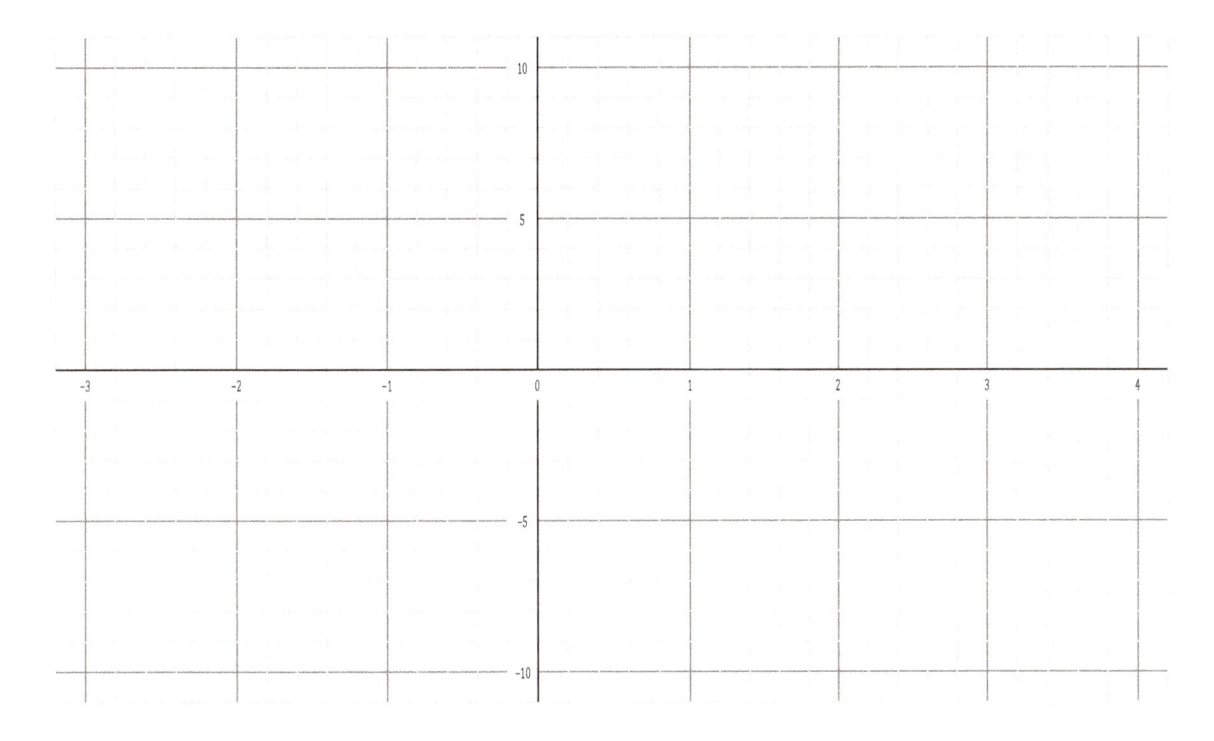

We can explore different equations, as well as potentially some non-linear equations, and can then explore why certain equations produce linear graphs. This is usually more successful if pupils have already met linear/arithmetic sequences or linear functions because we can draw the parallels between the growth of linear sequences/functions and the linear nature of the graph (i.e. every time x goes up 1, y goes up by the same amount – in the above case, 3). This, of course, then carries naturally into the idea of gradient, and the fact that when an equation is in the form $y = mx + c$, then m is the value of the gradient of the line. With this approach, lines of the form $x = a$ and $y = c$ generally have to be explored separately, either before or after sloped lines.

Whichever approach is taken, once pupils are aware that equations of the form $y = mx + c$ produce graphs that are perfect straight lines, then we can start to tie this to properties of straight lines that we have previously met, in particular the idea of gradient – which pupils should definitely explore as a measure of slope well prior to linking it to linear equations. Providing pupils are clear on gradient as the vertical change for a unit horizontal change, then the idea that y will increase by m when x increases by 1 is one that follows quite naturally both algebraically:

$y = mx + c$

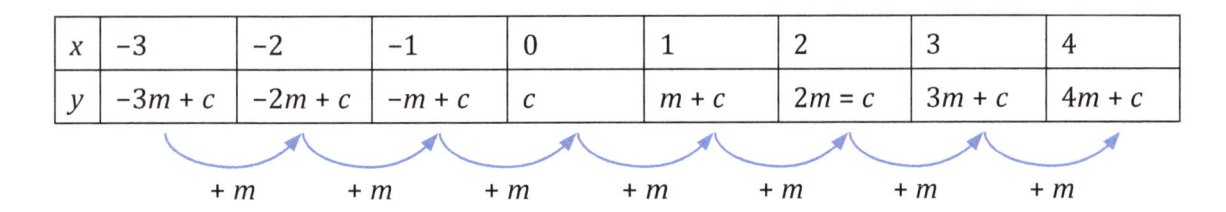

x	−3	−2	−1	0	1	2	3	4
y	$-3m + c$	$-2m + c$	$-m + c$	c	$m + c$	$2m = c$	$3m + c$	$4m + c$

$+ m \quad + m \quad + m \quad + m \quad + m \quad + m \quad + m$

or graphically:

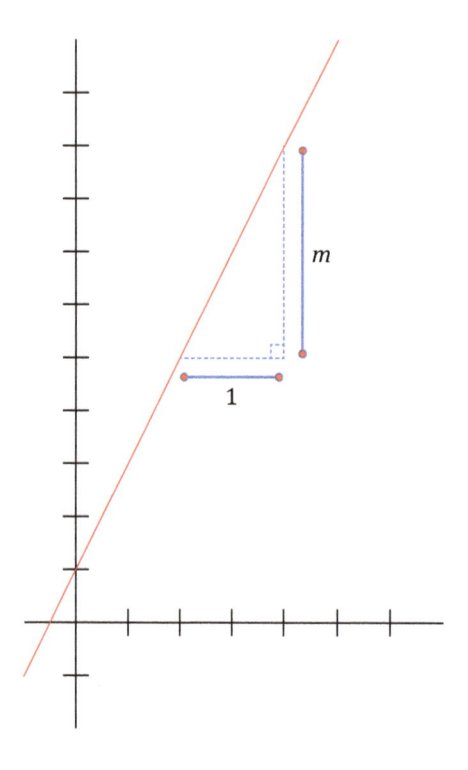

The algebraic view above also shows the other key value when working with linear equations in the form $y = mx + c$, namely that the value of c is the y-intercept. Pupils can then use this understanding to plot graphs of linear equations, by first plotting the value of c on the y-axis and then using m to find other points. Pupils should be introduced to this as the 'gradient intercept' form of the equation precisely because the values of the multiplicative and additive constants are equal to the gradient and y-intercept when an equation is in this form. A nice activity is then to offer pupils linear equations, and ask them to identify gradients and y-intercepts of the graphs without plotting:

What would the gradient and y-intercept be of the graph of each equation?

a $y = 3x + 8$
b $y = -2x + 5$
c $y = 6x - 3$
d $y = 0.5x + 1$
e $y = 4x$
f $y = 3 + 8x$
g $y = \frac{1}{3}x + 4$
h $y = 7 - 3x$
i $y = \frac{x}{2} + 2$
j $y = \frac{1}{4} - \frac{2}{3}x$

including those that require rearrangement:

What would the gradient and y-intercept be of the graph of each equation?

a $x + y = 10$
b $2x + y = 8$
c $y - x = 2$
d $y - 4x = \square 3$
e $2y - 6x = 7$
f $3x + 2y = 10$
g $3x - 2y = 14$
h $3y - 2x + 3 = 0$
i $4x - y = 2$
j $5y - 8x = 15$
k $6x - 2y + 8 = 0$
l $3y - 2x + 3 = 0$

Charting and graphing

This allows us to introduce the standard form of a linear equation:

ax + by = c

Pupils should recognise that this form allows us to represent all linear equations by choosing suitable values of *a*, *b* and *c*. This includes horizontal lines (with *a* = 0 and '*c*' = $\frac{c}{b}$), sloped lines (with *m* = $-\frac{a}{b}$ and '*c*' = $\frac{c}{b}$) and, importantly, vertical lines (with *b* = 0 and '*a*' = $\frac{c}{a}$). As part of this, pupils should become aware that whilst the gradient-intercept form of a line can also include horizontal lines, as when *m* = 0 the equation degenerates to *y* = *c*, we cannot represent vertical lines in any way that derives from *y* = *mx* + *c* because vertical lines have no gradient. As such, *y* = *mx* + *c* is really only a form of a linear equation for sloped lines (including a slope of 0), whereas *ax* + *by* = *c* is a suitable form for all possible straight-line graphs.

Pupils should also recognise that this form potentially opens up an alternative approach to plotting the graph of a linear equation. With this (or prior) comes the realisation that a straight line is uniquely defined by two points. This means that if we can find two points that fit the equation of the line, we can simply plot those two points. With equations in the form *ax* + *by* = *c* we can highlight to pupils that if we set *x* = 0, then the equation degenerates to *by* = *c*, of which the solution *y* = $\frac{c}{b}$ is relatively easy to find. Similarly, setting *y* = 0 gives *x* = $\frac{c}{a}$. This implies that two points on any line given in this form are (0, $\frac{c}{b}$) and ($\frac{c}{a}$, 0), and so plotting these two points will allow us to draw the line. This is sometimes called the 'cover-up method', as if we cover the *x* term we can solve for the *y* value, and vice versa. There are two things to be careful with here though:

1. that pupils understand how this 'method' relates to the standard form of the equation and the values when *x* = 0 and *y* = 0.

2. that when the two points are close together, although they still define the line, they may make it practically difficult to draw the line – as a small inaccuracy in drawing a ruled line through two points close together will become a larger inaccuracy the farther from the two points we travel.

In addition to identifying gradient and *y*-intercept, pupils should also be given the opportunity to identify the equations of lines drawn. This can include lines drawn accurately on a scaled axis (again, making sure we use different scales so pupils have to think about the value of the gradient):

Find the equation of each line:

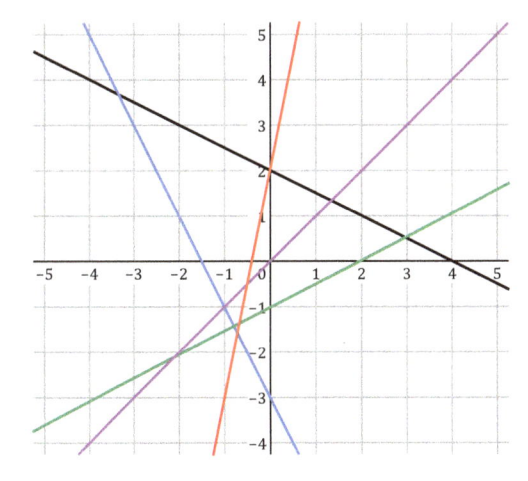

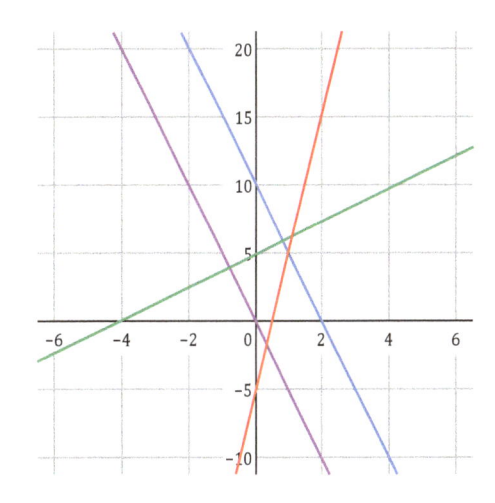

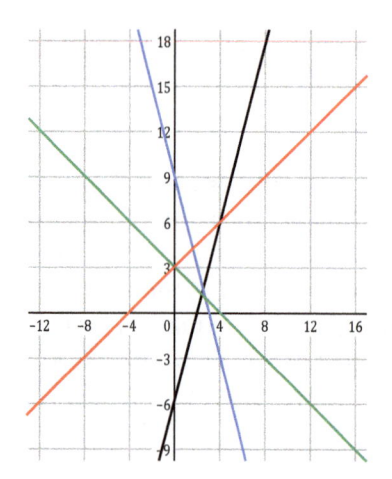

with sketches that include key information:

Find the equation of these straight lines:

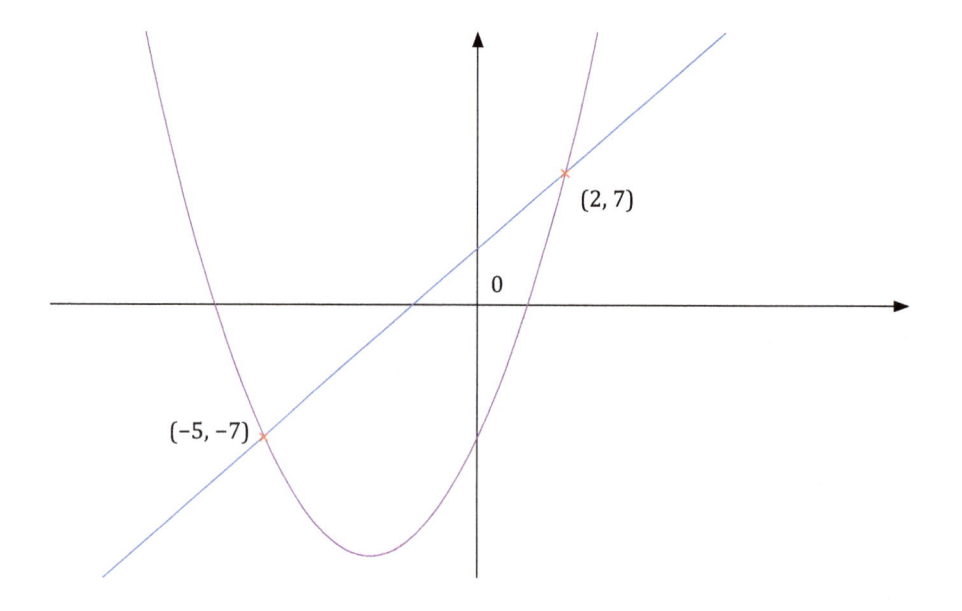

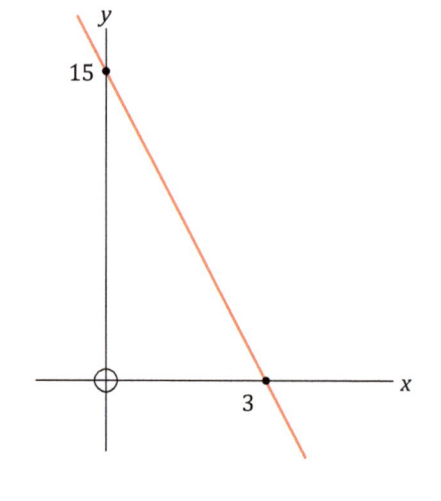

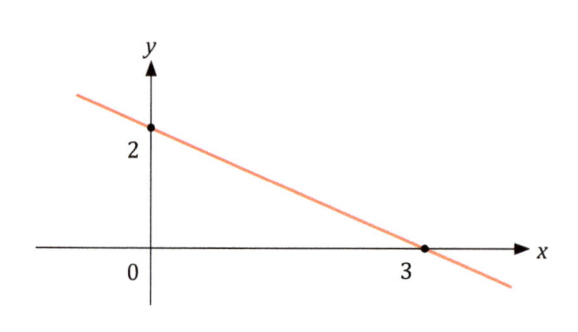

and even just with the key information in words:

In each case, use the information given to find the equation of the straight line described below.

1. Gradient 3 and passes through (0, 5).
2. Gradient 0.5 and passes through (0, −3).
3. Gradient 8 and passes through (0, $\frac{1}{2}$).
4. Gradient 7 and passes through the origin.
5. Passes through (0, 5) and (1, 8).
6. Passes through (0, 2) and (2, 8).
7. Passes through (0, −4) and (1, 0).
8. Passes through (0, −3) and (4, 17).
9. Passes through (0, 4) and (−1, 0).

The table gives two points on a line. Use the two points to find the equation of the straight line passing through both points.

Point 1	Point 2
(0, 0)	(2, 2)
(1, 3)	(3, 7)
(0, 5)	(4, 25)
(2, 2)	(−1, 5)
(4, 3)	(10, 6)
(7, 8)	(−4, −3)

Point 1	Point 2
(7, 1)	(−1, 5)
(6, 5)	(8, 1)
(1, 3)	(5, 10)
(−1, 4)	(9, −5)
(1, 0)	(−2, −4)
(1.5, −6.5)	(−1.75, 4.3)

Which line has the greater gradient, $4x - 5y = 1$ or $5x - 4y = 1$?

It is worth noting here that in some cases point 1 is to the left of point 2, and in some cases it is to the right of point 2. This is important because it is easy to fall into the trap of always working from left to right – many resources out there fall into this trap. This isn't to say pupils shouldn't always work left to right when identifying gradient (in fact, this is eminently sensible when considering gradient), but the points shouldn't always be in given in the order that might seem 'natural' to pupils.

As well as these sorts of activities, there are many practical scenarios that we can offer for pupils to find the equation of a straight line and that tie to other areas of mathematics. Pupils can find the equation of things like lines of best fit from scatter graphs (which links nicely to regression in post-16 maths), line segments from line graphs (including distance–time graphs or velocity–time graphs) and tariff graphs (particularly interpreting graphs with fixed overheads and then a linear increase in costs per unit or similar); the Ms. Bello's

Maths Hub resource on building linear equations has a set of excellent questions that cover a variety of useful scenarios.[13]

Having considered the *y*-intercept as part of finding the equations of lines in the form $y = mx + c$, it is natural to also consider the *x*-intercept when equations are in this form as well as in standard form. Having made the link between the *y*-intercept, 'c', and the value of $y = mx = c$ when $x = 0$, and also that we find a point on the line when in standard form by substituting $y = 0$, pupils should be happy that the *x*-intercept will be the value of *x* when $y = 0$, i.e. the solution to the equation $0 = mx + c$. This understanding that the *x*-intercept(s) of the graph of the function $y = f(x)$ happens when $y = 0$ is an important one for pupils to gain, and the opportunity to introduce this when looking at linear functions should not be overlooked as its extension to other functions will be easier to support if introduced at this point. Pupils can use graphs to identify these points:

The graph below shows the graph of the equation $y = px + q$, where p and q are values to be found.

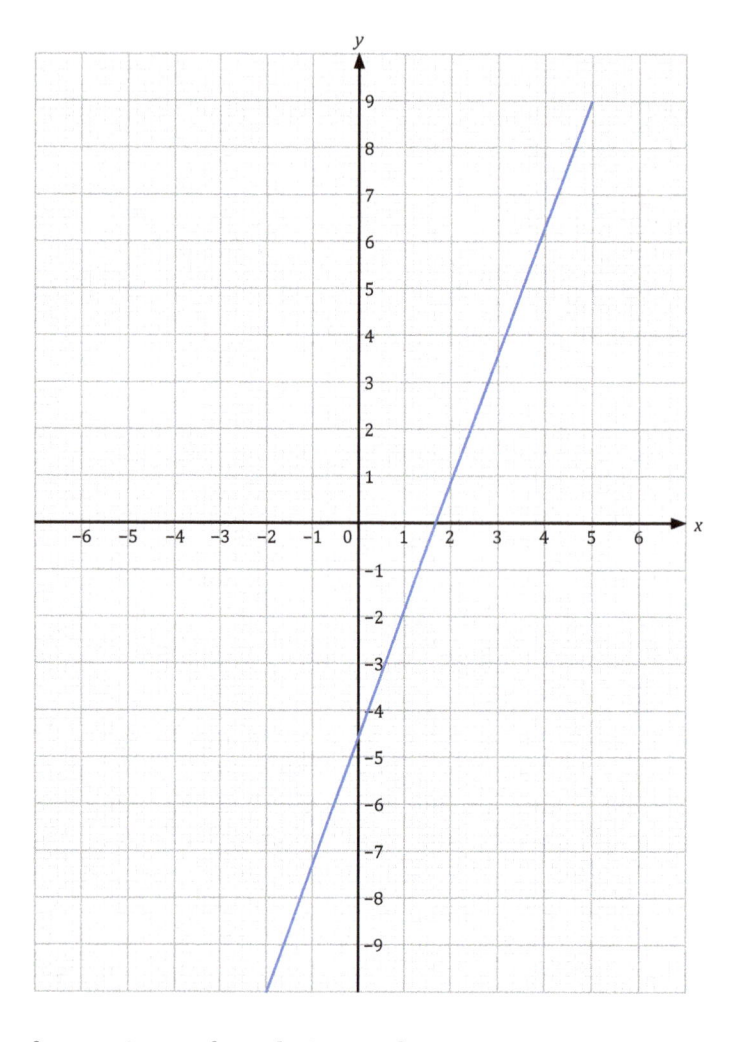

a   Use the graph to estimate the solution to the equation $px + q = 0$.

b   Find the values of p and q.

c   Hence solve $px + q = 0$ algebraically and compare your solution to your estimate in part (a).

---

13 Ms. Bello's Math Hub, Building Linear Equations (n.d.). Available at: http://villanovamath.weebly.com/uploads/1/3/7/8/13787526/building_linear_equations.pdf.

This idea can then be generalised into solving all types of linear equation, linking back to earlier work on reading values from the graph (you will recall we mentioned the importance of making this link earlier).

The graphs below show the equations $y = 3x$, $y = \frac{3}{2}x + 4$ and $2y + 7x = 23$.

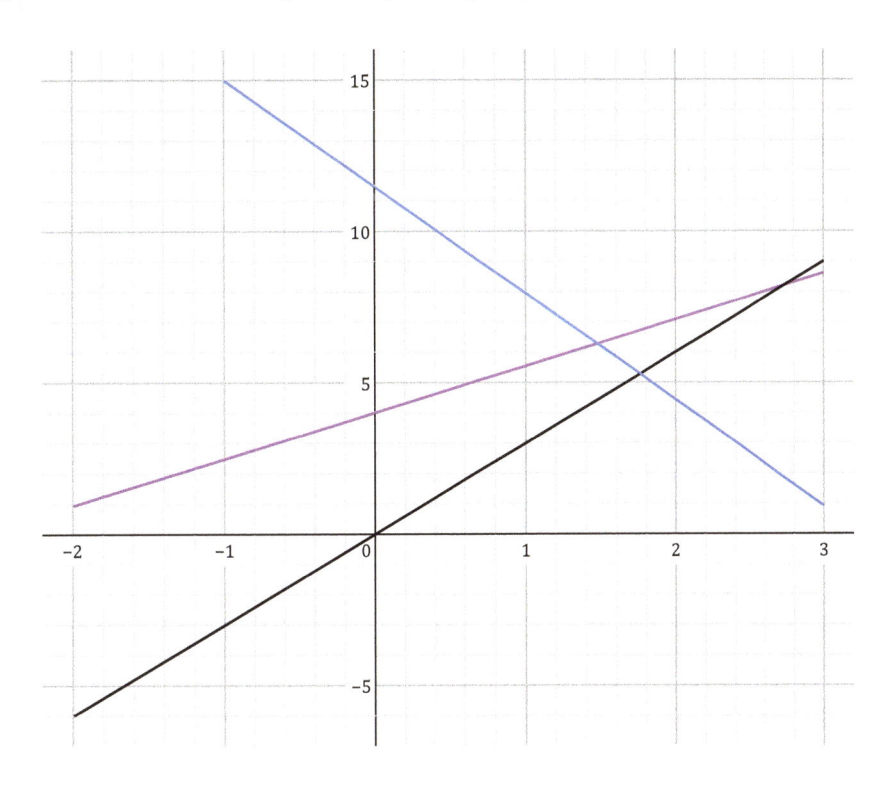

Use the graphs to give approximate solutions to the following:

a $\frac{3}{2}x + 4 = 1$

b $20 + 7x = 23$

c $3x = \frac{3}{2}x + 4$

and even linear simultaneous equations.

Use the graphs to give approximate solutions to the simultaneous equations:

a $y = 3x$ and $2y + 7x = 23$

b $y = \frac{3}{2}x + 4$ and $2y + 7x = 23$

Pupils should also bring their understanding of parallel and perpendicular gradients to their study of linear graphs. Often these are studied in close proximity, i.e. parallel and perpendicular gradients immediately before finding the equation of parallel and perpendicular lines. However, I find this works much better if there is a gap between studying these ideas strictly in relation to gradient, and then applying them to the equations of linear equations. The application to equations of lines can then serve as a chance to interweave knowledge of parallel and perpendicular gradients with finding the equations of lines:

Find the equations that are (a) parallel to the given equation and (b) perpendicular to the given equation and that pass through the given point.

1 $y = 2x + 3$; (0,1)
2 $y = 1 - x$; (0, 2)
3 $2y = x + 4$; (0, −1)
4 $y + 2x + 5 = 0$; (0, 3)
5 $y = x + 3$; (0, −2)
6 $y = 5 + \frac{1}{2}x$; (0, 2)
7 $3y = 4x + 4$; (0, −1)
8 $y - x + 5 = 0$; (0, 0)
9 $y = 2x + 3$; (1, 1)
10 $y = 1 - x$; (1, 2)
11 $2y = x + 4$; (1, −1)
12 $y + 2x = 5 = 0$; (2, 1)

as well as bringing in further knowledge of coordinates.

Find the equation of the perpendicular bisector of the line segment shown:

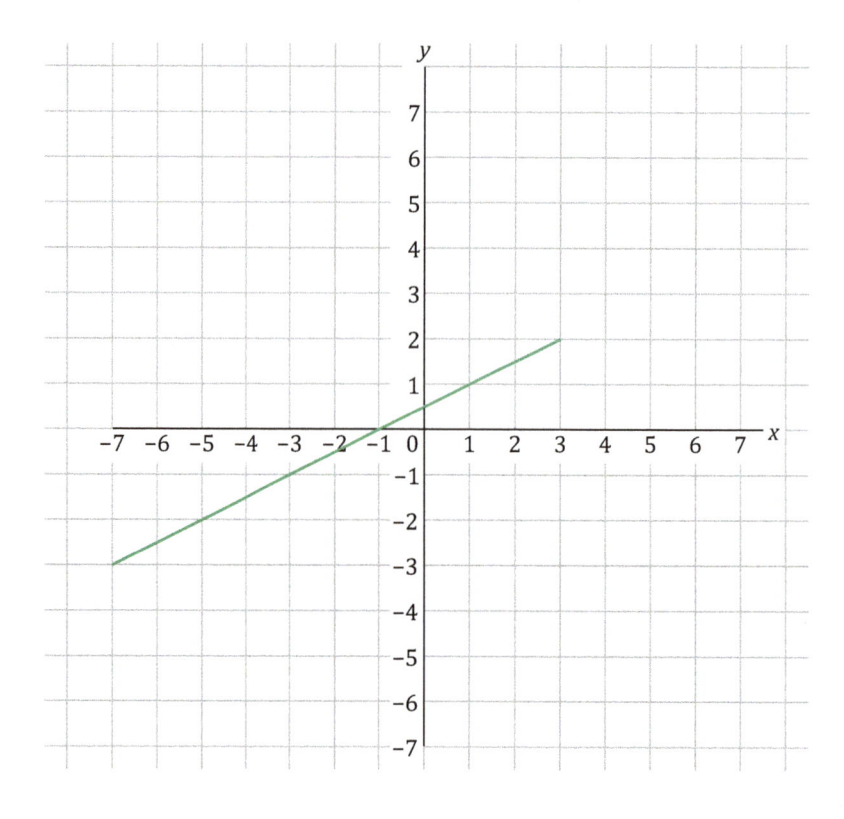

and even interweaving knowledge of things like circle theorems, Pythagoras' theorem and trigonometry:

The points (3,7) and (7, −5) lie on a circle. Find the equation of the radius that bisects the chord.

$\triangle ABC$ has vertices at $A:(1,1)$, $B:(4,4)$, $C:(6,2)$.

a Show that $\triangle ABC$ is a right-angled triangle.

b Find angle ACB.

A triangle is made using lines with equations $y = 2x - 5$, $y = -x + 4$, $y = \frac{1}{2}x - 5$. Find:

a The angle between the lines $y = 2x - 5$ and $y = \frac{1}{2}x - 5$.

b The equation of the angle bisector of the angle between the lines $y = 2x - 5$ and $y = \frac{1}{2}x - 5$.

A particular type of linear graph that we will want to spend time on with pupils is the graph of two variables that are in direct proportion. Pupils should recognise that proportion graphs will be linear graphs that go through the origin. We might begin to explore this by looking at things like conversion graphs:

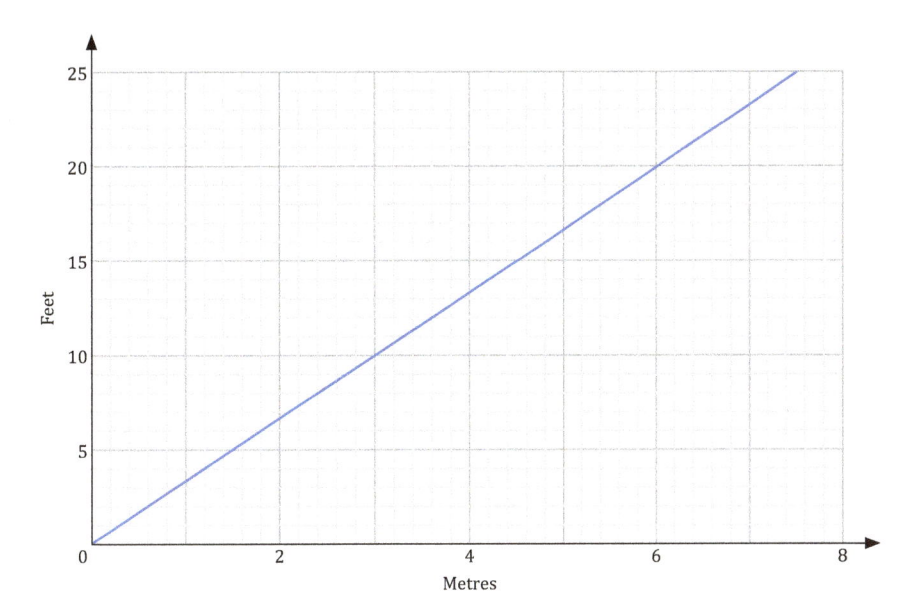

This conversion graph can be used to change between metres and feet.

a Use the conversion graph to change 6 metres to feet.

.... feet

b Use the conversion graph to change 8 feet to metres.

.... metres

Robert jumps 4 metres.

James jumps 12 feet.

c i Who jumps furthest – Robert or James?

ii How did you get your answer?

or currency exchange:

The exchange rate to change pounds(£) into US dollars($) is £1 = $1.50

a   Use this exchange rate to complete the table below.

Pounds(£)	0	1	2	5	10	20	50	100
US dollars ($)	0	1.50		7.50		30		150

b   On the grid, draw a conversion graph for convening between pounds and US dollars.

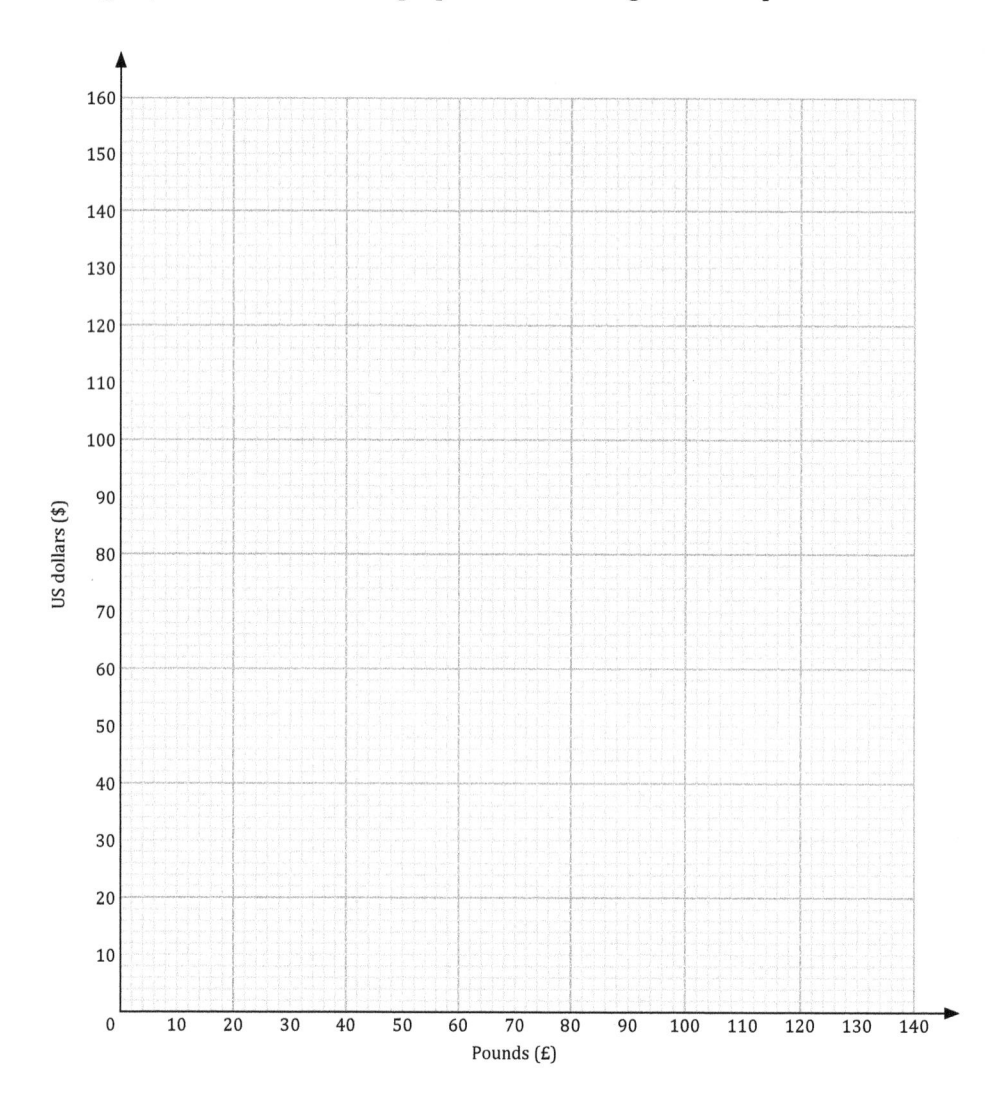

c   Change $100 into pounds(£).

£ ....

We can then look at what these graphs have in common, i.e. that they are straight lines that go through the origin. We can then link this to the common exchange rate, perhaps using the ratio table:

Pounds (£)	US dollars ($)
0	0
1	1.50
5	7.50
20	30
100	150
x	y

× 1.5

This leads to the equation $y = 1.5x$ (in this case), which when compared to the form $y = mx + c$ shows that the graph of such a relationship will pass through the origin (as $c = 0$) and the gradient will be the exchange rate between the two variables. Pupils should be able to reason that, because directly proportional quantities will always have this constant exchange rate, that these things will be true of all graphs of directly proportional variables. We can then follow up with questions designed to prompt pupils to consider how the gradient links to the exchange rate:

2.5 cm = 1 inch. A conversion graph is drawn to convert cm to inches. If inches are on the horizontal axis, find the gradient of the graph.

2.5 cm = 1 inch. A conversion graph is drawn to convert cm to inches. If inches are on the vertical axis, find the gradient of the graph.

Explain how this graph shows that force is proportional to extension.

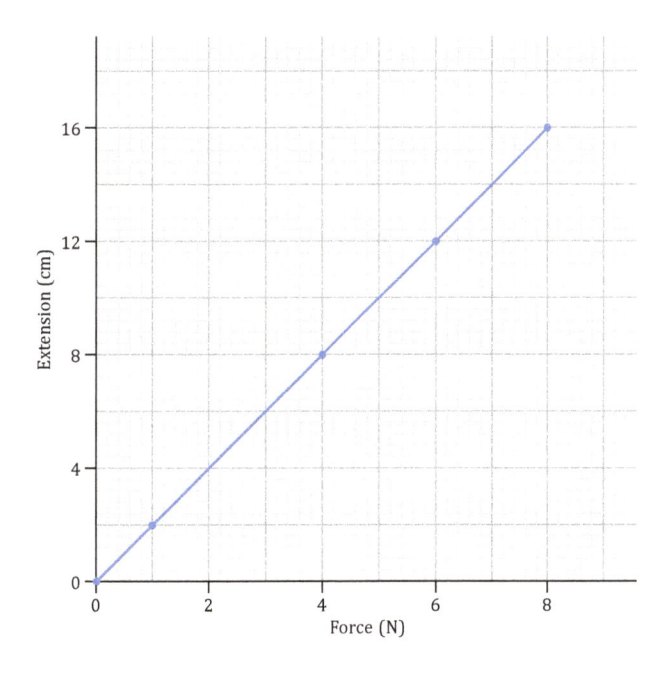

The final thing we will want to explore with pupils is extension of linear equations to looking at linear inequalities. This should start with simple inequalities only involving the variable x:

Represent the inequality $x < 5$ on the axes below.

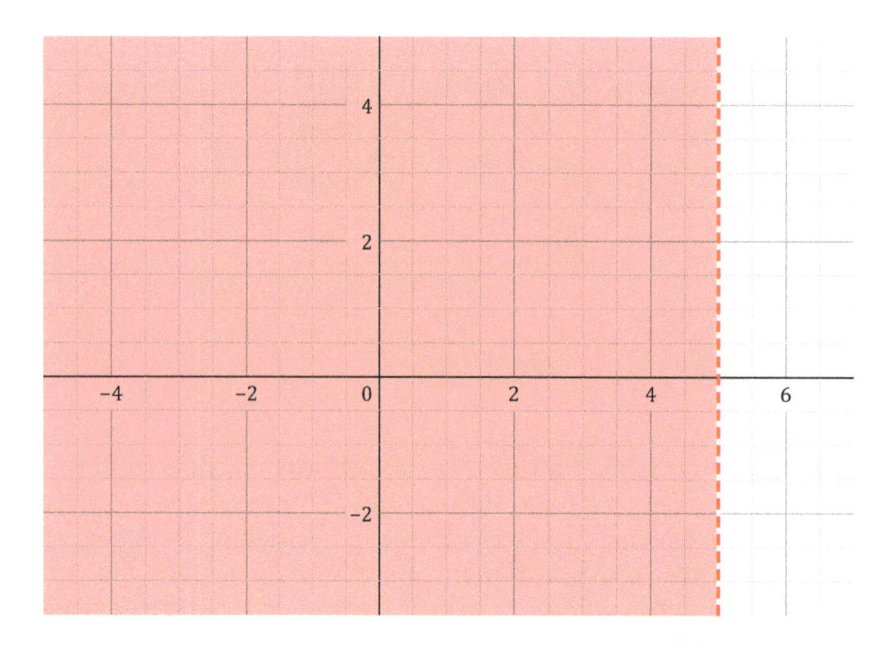

This allows us to make the link to representing this sort of inequality on an axis with representing the same inequality on a number line, linking the dashed line with the open circle and the arrow with the space now that we need to cover two dimensions. We can then remind pupils about different types of inequalities, including 'between' inequalities (making the link between a closed circle and a full line):

Represent the inequality $-3 \leq x < 5$ on the axes below.

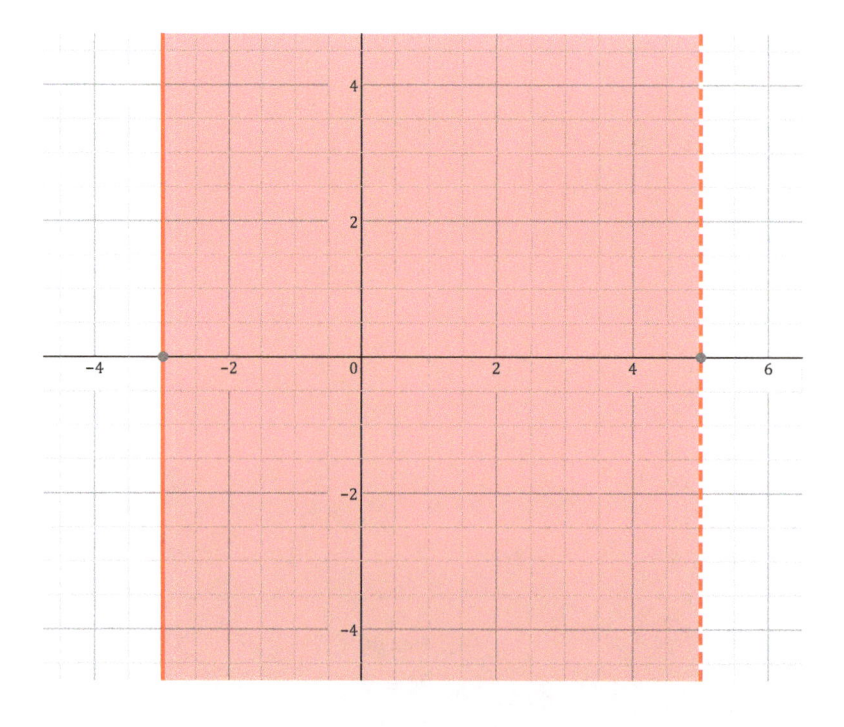

before then prompting pupils to consider what would happen if we switch the variable to y:

Represent the inequality $-2 < y \leq 1$ on the axes below.

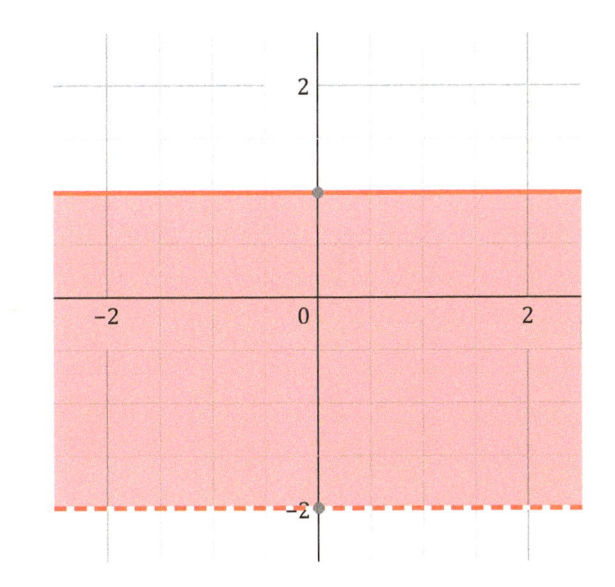

before representing linear inequalities in two variables:

Represent the inequality $y \leq 5 - 3x$ on the axis below.

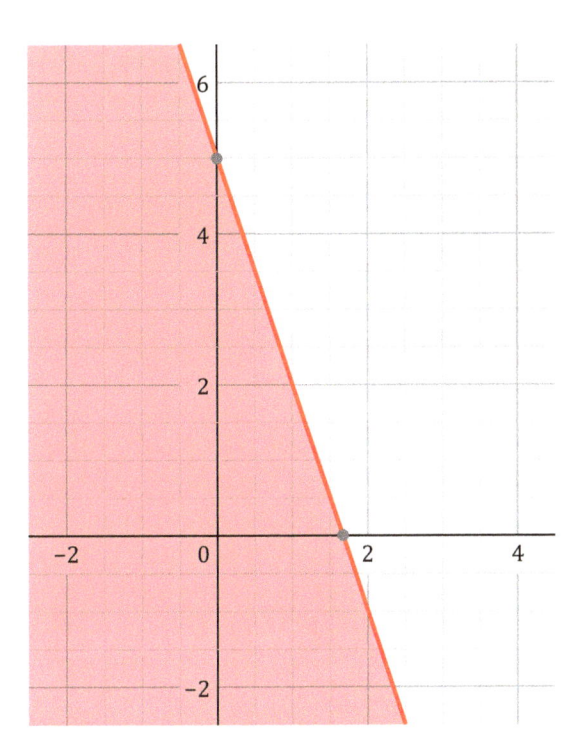

Pupils should understand from earlier work that the boundary line will be plotted as $y = 5 - 3x$, and that this will be a full line rather than a dashed line as the inequality is an inclusive inequality. We then have to concentrate on where to shade: in this case, the points where the y ordinate of any coordinate is less than the y values along the line. We can show this by shading in vertical lines up to the plotted line, so that pupils can see how we are only shading y values up to the line.

Another thing that pupils should understand about graphing inequalities is that the shading is designed to highlight the region that obeys the inequality/inequalities. Whilst there is only one inequality or two parallel inequalities, the best way to draw attention to that region is to shade it in. However, when we have several overlapping inequalities, shading in (at least one at a time) leads to confusion as to what is considered part of the region and what isn't.

Represent the inequalities $y \leq 5 - 3x$, $y > x - 2$ and $x \geq -2$ on the axes below:

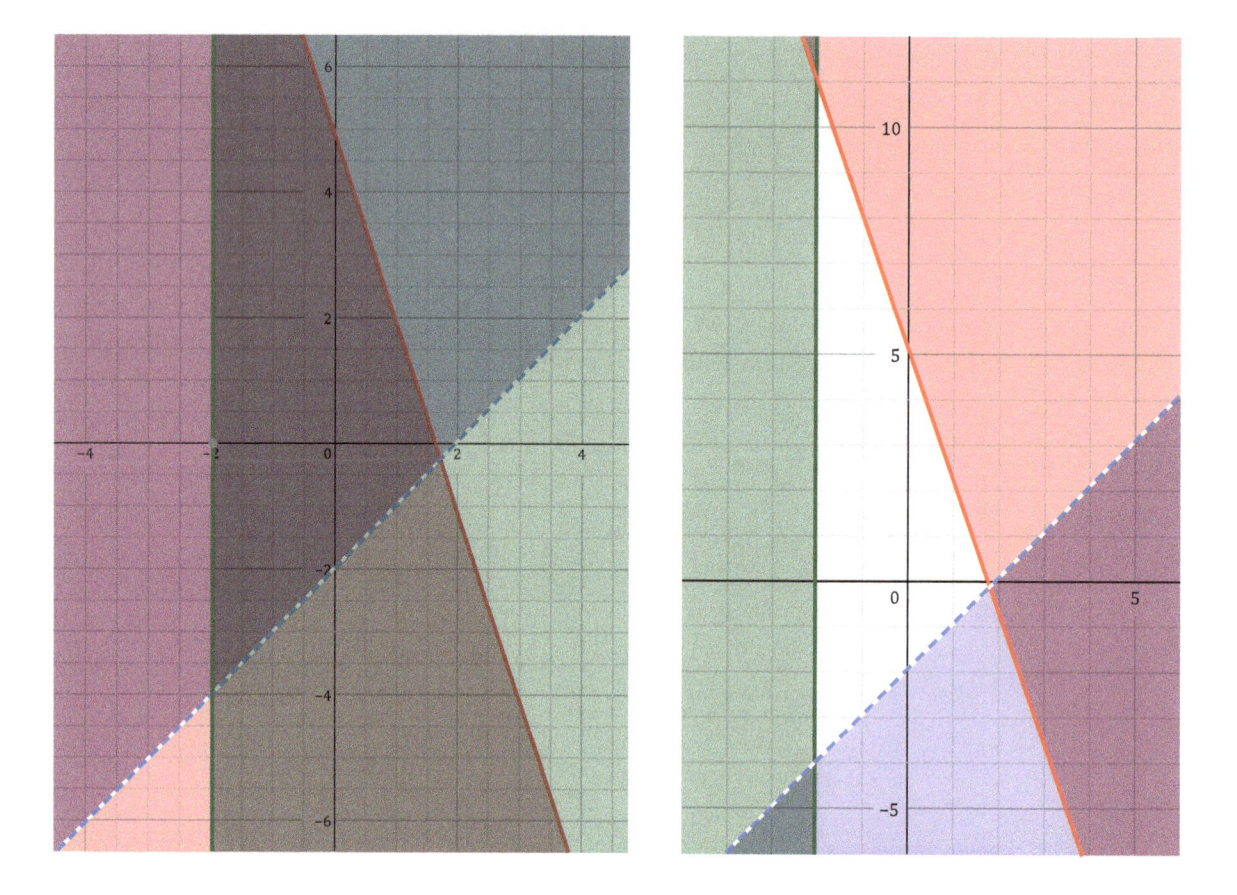

We can see that it is not clear which region actually satisfies all the inequalities. Of course, we could simply draw all the lines and then try and figure out which region it is that satisfies all three inequalities, but the likelihood of mistake is high (plus this is not an approach that can be automated). It is here that pupils need to understand that the best way to draw attention to the region required is to 'shade it out'; that is, as each inequality is plotted we shade the region that is not included in the inequality (this does not affect the lines, as the boundaries will either be included or not either way). This will then leave the feasible region as the only unshaded space in the plane.

A nice activity to include to develop this further is to begin to consider linear programming and integer programming problems. Whilst full linear programming is not explored with pupils until post-16 mathematics, simple problems can be worked on by pupils at school level, such as:

> A company produces two types of gift box, standard and luxury.
>
> Each day, the company produces x standard and y luxury gift boxes. Each day, the company must produce at least 20 of each type and at least 70 in total.
>
> The boxes are produced using three different machines:
> - Machine A must be used for at least 100 minutes each day.
> - Machine B is available for a maximum of 5 hours each day.
> - Machine C is available for a maximum of 8 hours each day.
>
> The time taken to produce a standard box is:
> - 2 minutes on machine A.
> - 3 minutes on machine B.
> - 4 minutes on machine C.
>
> A luxury box requires:
> - 1 minute on machine A.
> - 2 minutes on machine B.
> - 4 minutes on machine C.
>
> Write and plot inequalities to show the constraints on the number of boxes, and the number of minutes required for each machine.

In addition to a detailed examination of linear graphs and functions, pupils will also be exposed to a wide array of non-linear graphs, which is where we now turn our attention.

Concept: non-linear graphs

Prerequisites: Coordinates, graphing/charting, equations.

Linked concepts: Constructions, rearranging formulae, Pythagoras theorem, completing the square.

When it comes to non-linear graphs, there are a huge variety that pupils can work on, but the skills developed will be very similar and so rather than separating out the different types, it may well serve pupils better to introduce them alongside each other. The key things remain the same for all non-linear graphs:

1. We are trying to get a visual sense of the relationship between the variables.
2. We can use the algebraic relationship to generate enough pairs of values that fit the relationship until we can see enough of the picture that we can predict the rest and fill in the gaps.

Pupils can construct tables of values or use pre-drawn tables of values to plot many functions of the form $y = f(x)$:

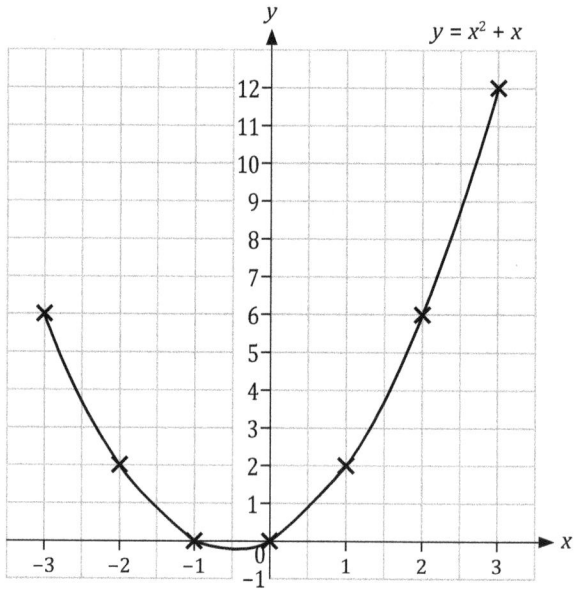

x	−3	−2	−1	0	1	2	3
y	6	2	0	0	2	6	12

When drawing non-linear graphs, pupils should be aware that the graph between the points we plot is definitely not linear, and so we do not join these with straight-line segments.

Pupils will need to work with many different types of non-linear graphs, as they will need to recognise several shapes. There is a nice matching activity on the website VARTHETA that shows the types of non-linear graphs that all pupils will need to study and recognise.[14]

As well as recognising shapes of graphs, pupils should understand how the properties of the function affect the shape of the graph, in particular:

1. that quadratic graphs are U-shaped (parabolic) because squaring positive and negative values of equal magnitude produces the same result.

2. that reciprocal graphs have asymptotes because division by 0 is undefined and we cannot create 0 by division unless we start with 0.

3. that exponential graphs have an asymptote because we cannot create 0 using powers unless we start with 0, and then grows exponentially because of the multiplicative growth factor.

4. how the trigonometric graphs relate to the unit circle:[15]

---

14 VARTHETA, Graph (29 April 2016). Available at: https://vartheta.wordpress.com/2016/04/29/graph/.
15 Online Math Learning, Unit Circle and Trig Graphs (n.d.). Available at: https://www.onlinemathlearning.com/unit-circle-trig-graphs.html.

Charting and graphing

Unit circle and trig graphs

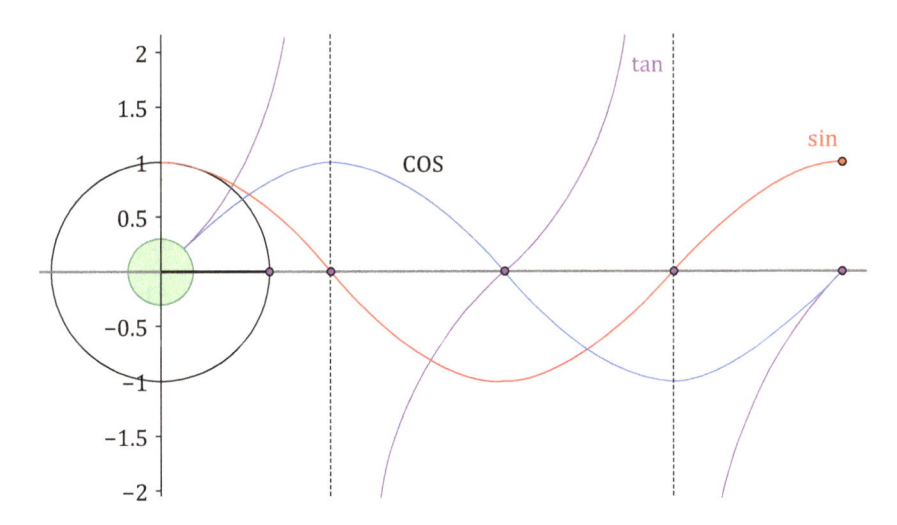

A key idea in recognising and sketching different graph shapes is the extension of the idea of *y*-intercept from linear graphs. This comes in two stages:

1. Recognition that, for any polynomial function $f(x) = c + a_1x + a_2x^2 + \cdots + a_nx^n$ that $f(0) = c$ and so c is the point where the graph of the polynomial crosses the *y*-axis.

2. For any non-polynomial function $y = f(x)$ then if we can find a value for $f(0) = c$, then c is the point where the graph of the function crosses the *y*-axis; but it is not guaranteed that every non-polynomial function will have a *y*-intercept.

We can offer simple questions to help pupils apply this knowledge:

Which equation matches the graph shown?
- $y = x^2 - 4$
- $y = x^2 + 2$
- $y = -x^2 - 4$
- $y = 4 - x^2$
- $y = x^2 - 2$
- $y = 2 - x^2$

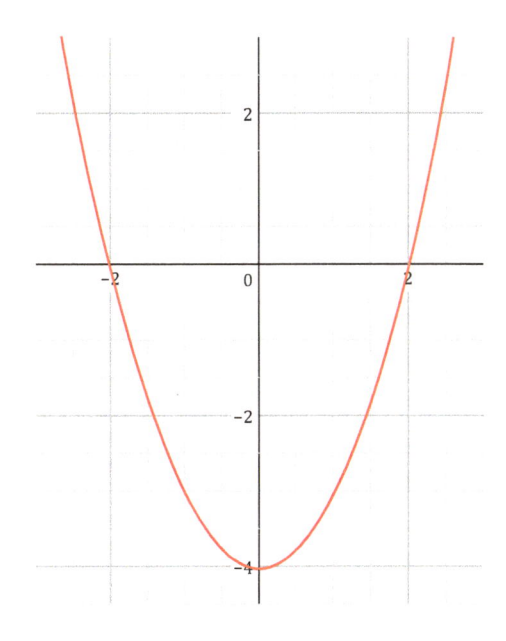

and then potentially stretch this knowledge a little more.

Given that cos 0 = 1, find the *y*-intercept of the following graphs:

a   y = 2 + cos x   c   y = 2 − cos x   e   y = cos x − 2
b   y = 2cos x   d   y = cos² x

Write down an equation involving cos x that would have a *y*-intercept of

a   4   c   0   e   −100
b   −2   d   100

For each of the values above, write down another one. Then write down a peculiar one.

There are several *y*-intercept values that pupils should be familiar with, including:

- sin 0 = 0 and tan 0 = 0
- cos 0 = 1
- $b^0 = 1$ and therefore $A \times b^0 = A$

Of course, in the same way as linear graphs, once we start examining the *y*-intercept, naturally we turn to the *x*-intercepts – which pupils should understand are referred to as 'roots'. For the most part, pupils will have to approximate these from the graphs; however, pupils should still be clear that they are solving *f*(*x*) = 0. Of course, this is an opportunity to bring back other approaches to solving equations that pupils may have previously studied, particularly quadratic equations:

The picture shows the graph of $y = x^2 - 2x - 1$

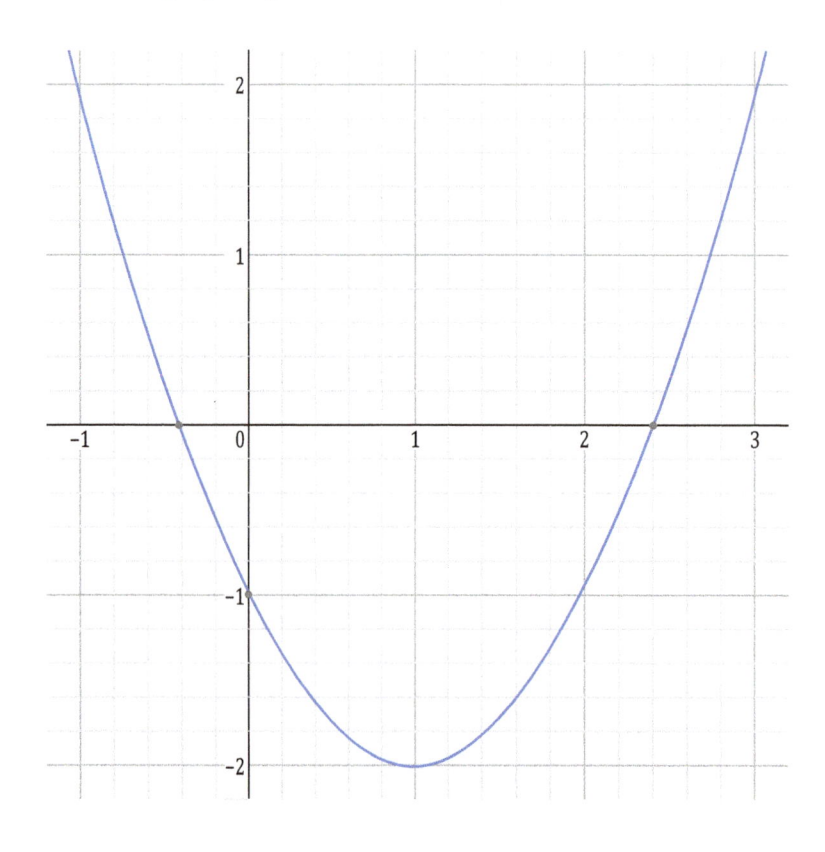

a Use the graph to estimate the solutions to $x^2 - 2x - 1 = 0$.

b Solve the equation $x^2 - 2x - 1 = 0$ using an algebraic approach. Compare your answer to part (a).

and the use of iterative formulae:

The picture shows the graph of $y = x^3 - 3x^2 + 1$

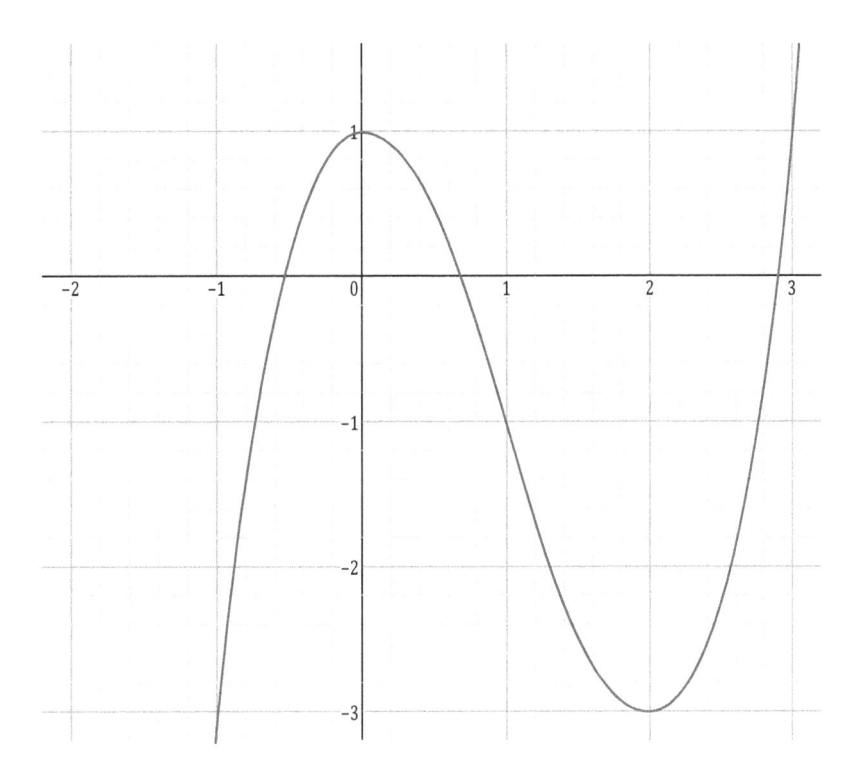

a Use the graph to estimate the roots of $0 = x^3 - 3x^2 + 1$.

b Use the iterative formula $x_{n+1} = \sqrt{-\frac{1}{x_n - 3}}$ to solve the equation $0 = x^3 - 3x^2 + 1$ and verify that your estimate of the root between 0 and 1 is the same correct to 1 decimal place.

As with linear graphs, exploring solutions to $f(x) = 0$ opens up the idea of solving equations graphically more generally. This can be relative simple equations:

The picture shows the graph of $y = x^3 - 3x^2 + 1$.

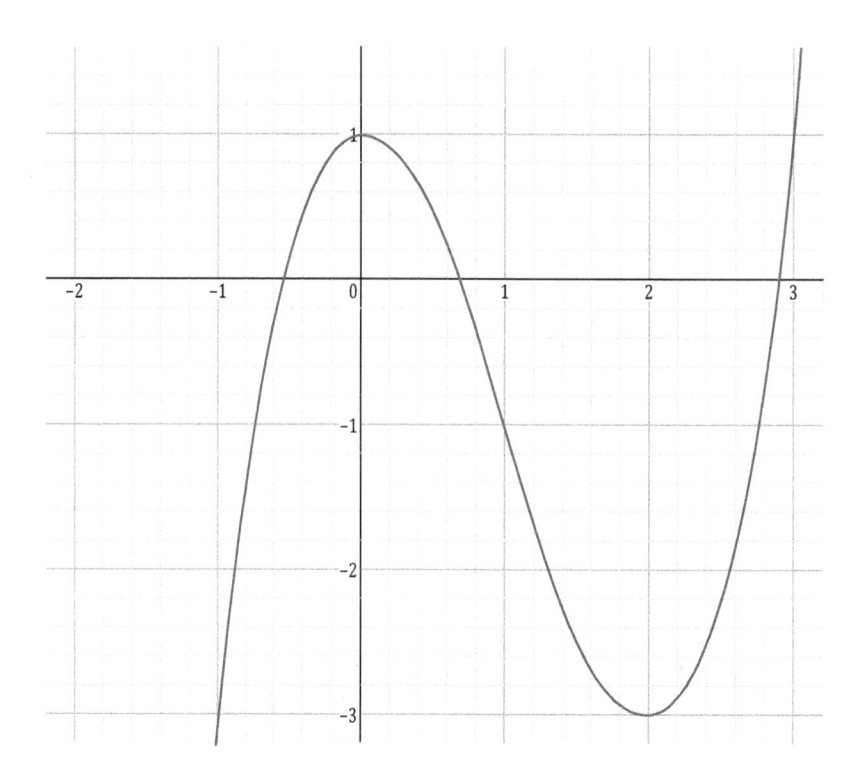

Use the graph to estimate the solution to the equation $x^3 - 3x^2 + 1 = -2$.

or we could ask the same question slightly differently:

The picture shows the graph of $y = x^3 - 3x^2 + 1$.

Use the graph to estimate the solution to the equation $x^3 - 3x^2 + 3 = 0$.

A direct comparison of these two questions is actually a good way to introduce the second type of problem, so pupils recognise that the second type can be solved by manipulating the equation so that the left-hand side of the equation matches the function. This then leads nicely to solution of simultaneous eqautions graphically:

The picture shows the graphs of $y = 3x^2 - 5x + 1$ and $2x + 12y = 5$. Use the graphs to estimate the solutions to the simultaneous equations.

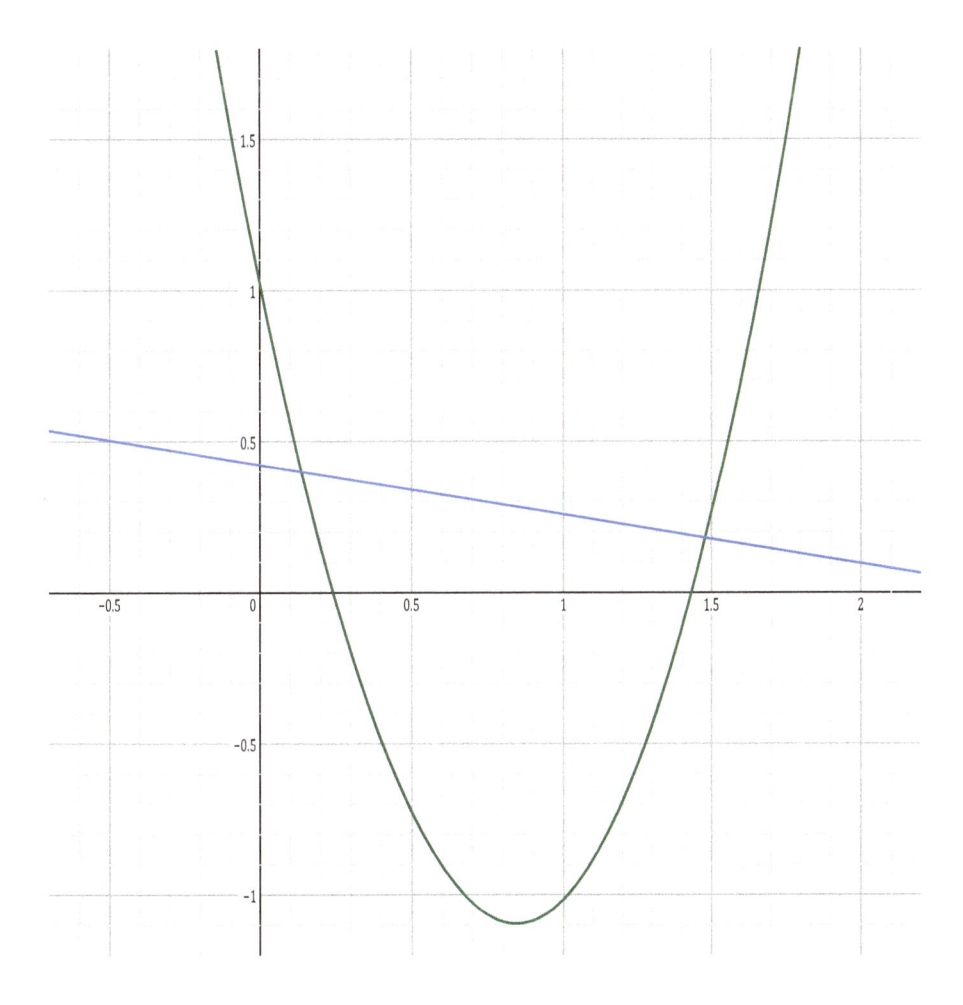

which we can extend further to:

The picture shows the graph of $y = 3x^2 - 5x + 1$. By drawing a suitable line, solve the equations:

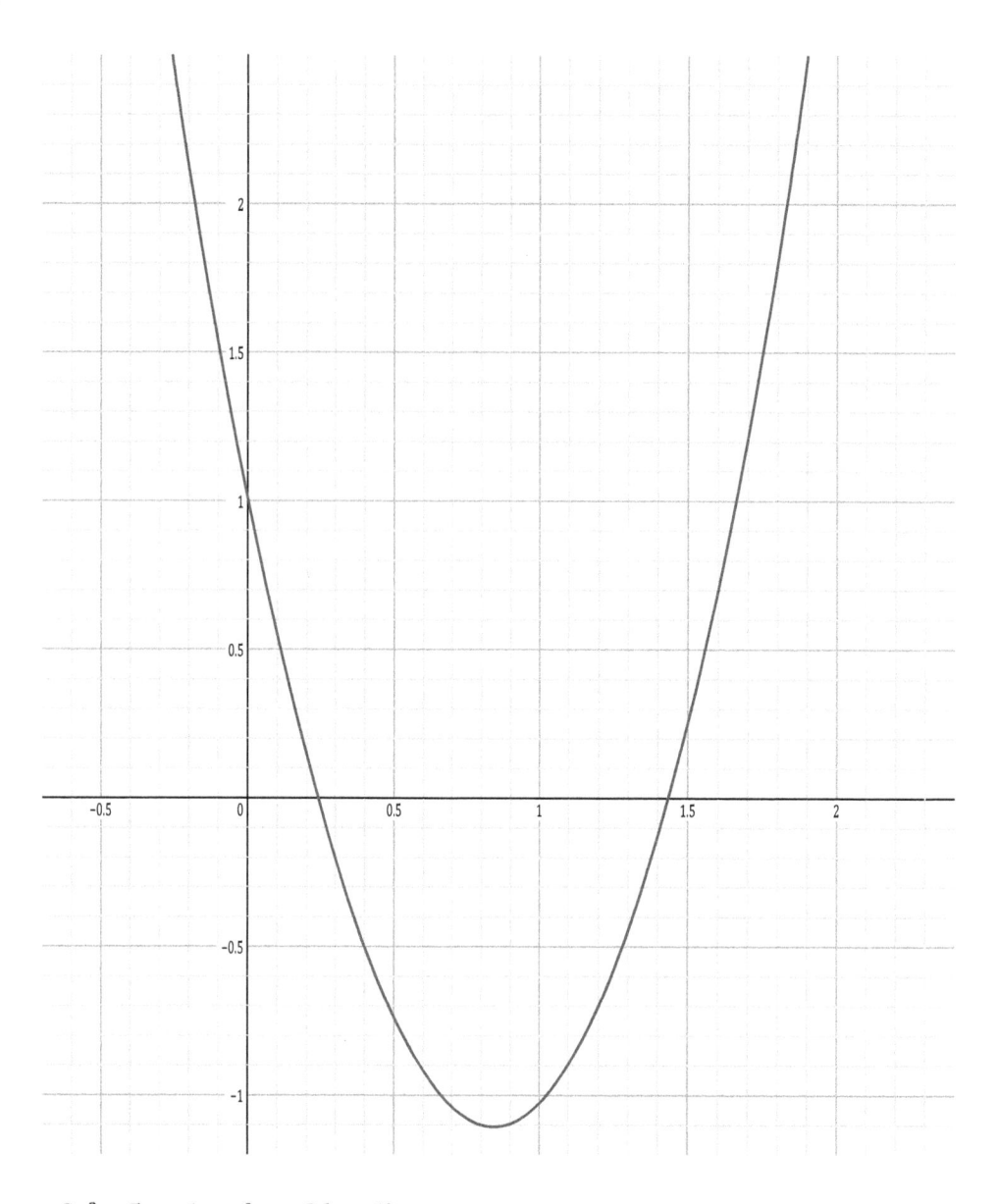

a $y = 3x^2 - 5x + 1$ and $y = 2(x - 1)$

b $y = 3x^2 - 5x + 1$ and $2y - x = 3$

and then even further to:

The picture shows the graph of $y = 3x^2 - 5x + 1$. By drawing a suitable line, solve the equations:

a $3x^2 - 6x + 1 = 0$

b $3x^2 - 3x - 1 = 0$

Pupils should see this as the combination of simultaneous equations with the previous work involving manipulating the equations; for example, (b) above is equivalent to solving the equation $3x^2 - 5x + 1 = 2 - 2x$, which is the same as solving the simultaneous equations $y = 3x^2 - 5x + 1$ and $y = 2 - 2x$.

There are plenty of practical contexts that these graphical skills can be applied to. Chapter 9 from the textbook *Mathematics Standard 1: Cambridge Maths Stage 6* from Cambridge Maths Stage 6 contains a number of practical contexts that can serve as inspiration for offering problems to pupils, particularly if offered in a goal-free format, where we replace each question with a simple 'Write down anything you can about this relationship …'[16]

Whilst the above can apply to pretty much any non-linear graph, there is an aspect of quadratic graphs that we do need to pay specific attention to, namely the turning point. When pupils are introduced to quadratic graphs, and the reasoning behind their parabolic shape, a natural question to ask is how the equation of the line determines the turning point. Pupils will probably have already seen that the expanded form of the quadratic tells us about the y-intercept of the quadratic, and the factorised form of the quadratic tells us about the x-intercepts (if they exist), and so it seems natural that the equation of the graph should also tell us something about the turning point. This is where we can remind pupils about the completed square form (unless pupils spontaneously suggest it). Pupils should already know that any quadratic expression can be written in the form $a(x - b)^2 + c$. We can then reason that the minimum value of this expression is c, and that this occurs when $x = b$ (although we might have to look at some specific examples of this before looking at the general case). Pupils should be offered the opportunity to find the turning point of quadratics with both positive and negative coefficients of x^2.

Find the coordinates of the turning point of the graphs of:

a $x^2 + 6x + 2 = y$ c $y = 2 + 5x - x^2$ e $y = 2x^2 + 10x - 4$

b $y = x^2 + 5x + 2$ d $y = 4 + 10x - 2x^2$ f $4x^2 + 10x - 2 = y$

as well as find equations of graphs that have a given turning point:

$f(x) = x^2 + px + q$. The graph of $y = f(x)$ has a turning point at the coordinate $(3, -5)$. Work out the values of p and q.

Pupils should also recognise that because the turning point of the graph of $y = a(x - b)^2 + c$ is determined solely by the values of b and c, there are infinitely many quadratic graphs that will have a turning point at a given value, with each different equation found for different values of a. The activity below can help prompt pupils to explore this a little more:

Each of the following quadratics has a turning point at $(-1, 2)$. Work out the values of p and q.

a $y = 2x^2 + px + q$ c $y = px^2 + 14x + q$

b $y = 3x^2 + px + q$ d $y = px^2 + qx + 25$

---

16 G. K. Powers, *Mathematics Standard 1: Cambridge Maths Stage 6*. (Sydney: Cambridge Assessment, 2018).

In addition to completing the square, pupils should also recognise that the turning points of a quadratic graph are equidistant between its roots. This allows an alternative approach to finding the turning point:

Part of the graph of $y = (x - p)^2 + q$ is shown. Find the values of p and q.

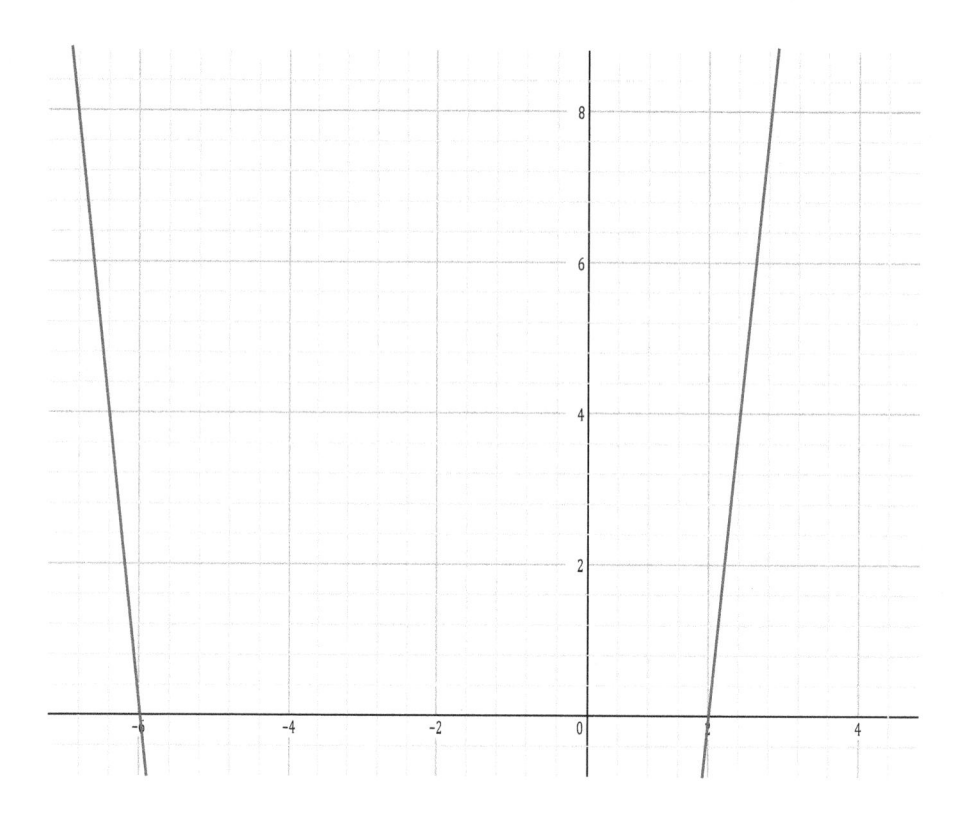

Of course, pupils could just reason that the factorised form of the graph is

$y = (x - 2)(x + 6)$

and hence expand and complete the square; however, we might highlight that the value of p must be -2, giving $y = (x + 2)^2 + q$, and that we can then use any point from the graph to find the value of q, the easiest of which is probably $(2,0)$ giving $0 = (2 + 2)^2 + q$ which is easily solvable to give $q = -16$.

A nice follow-on from this is the link between completed square form and factorised form through the difference of two squares:

$y = (x + 2)^2 - 16$
$y = [(x + 2) + 4][(x + 2) - 4]$
$y = (x + 6)(x - 2)$

A further development we might want to make with the turning point is to highlight to pupils that the turning point isn't simply halfway between the two roots but halfway between any two points of equal height. This gives rise to approaching finding the turning point using partial factorisation:

Find the turning point of the graph of $y = x^2 - 6x + 11$.

This approach works by factorising the first two terms of the quadratic expression:

$y = x(x - 6) + 11$

This implies that when $x = 0$ and $x = 6$, $y = 11$, and so these two points have equal height. This implies that the turning point has an x-ordinate of 3, and substituting in gives a y-ordinate of 2, and so the turning point is (3, 2).

Examination of turning points can also be a starting point to examine how graphs transform: by comparing the equation of a quadratic in completed square form to the equation $y = x^2$ we can see how the turning point, and therefore all other points, have been transformed.

Concept link: transformation and graphs

With pupils having previously been introduced to transformations of points through translation, reflection, rotation and enlargement, it is a lovely link to suggest we examine the effect of these transformations on the equations of different graphs. We can offer pupils different base graphs, and get them to examine the effect on the equation when the graph is transformed in different ways; usually starting with translation:

> The graph of $y = x^2$ is translated using vector $\binom{0}{3}$. What is the equation of the image graph?

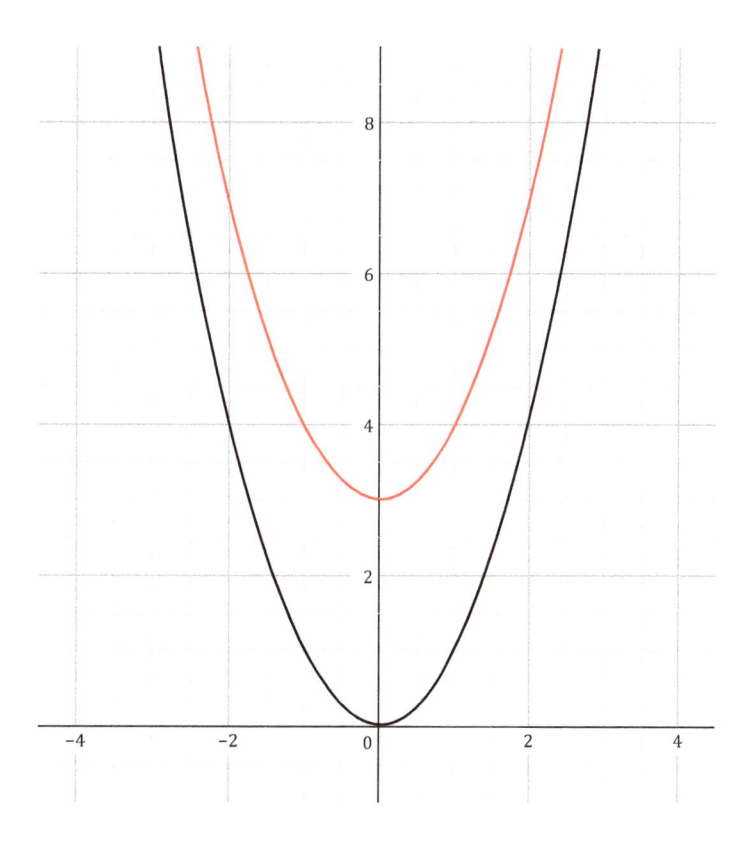

This is probably the easiest transformation to analyse because pupils will already be familiar with y-intercept, and so will see that the translation moved the point from (0, 0) to (0, 3) and hence must have added 3 to the equation, giving $y = x^2 + 3$. Pupils can be offered other graphs to firm up this relationship, and also problems involving equations without the graph:

> The graph of equation $y = x^3 + 3x^2 - 2x - 5$ is translated using vector $\begin{pmatrix} 0 \\ 3 \end{pmatrix}$. What is the equation of the image graph?
>
> Describe the transformation that transforms the graph of the equation $y = 2 + 5 \cos x$ to the graph of the equation $y = 5 \cos x - 4$.

We will also want to offer pupils the opportunity to sketch graphs based on the changed equation:

> The picture below shows the graph of $y = f(x)$. On the same axes, draw the graph of $y = f(x) - 5$

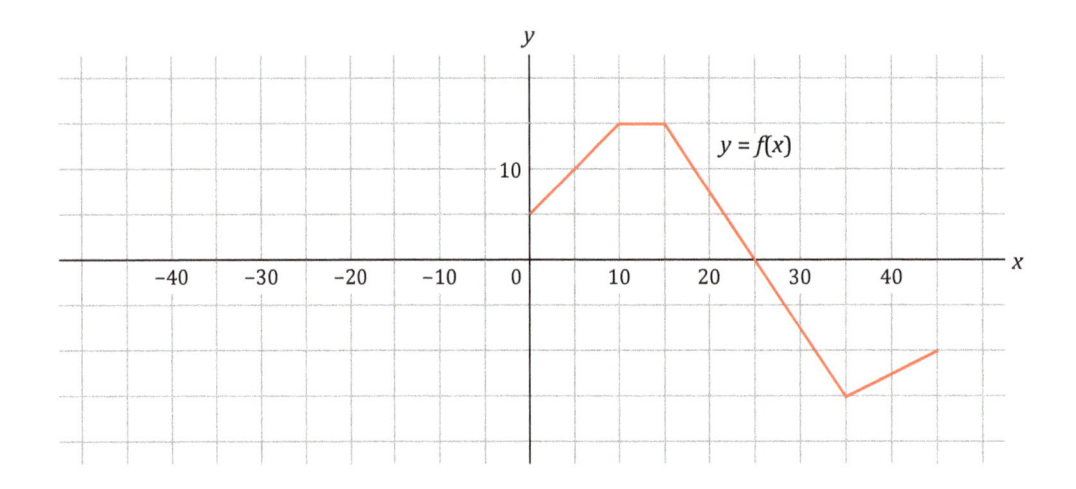

Eventually, we will want to prompt pupils to generalise this, arriving at the idea that a translation of $\begin{pmatrix} 0 \\ a \end{pmatrix}$ results in the equation of $y = f(x)$ becoming $y = f(x) + a$.

Once pupils are comfortable with vertical translation, we will want to move on to horizontal translation. Again, using a base graph is a sensible start point:

> The graph of $y = x^2$ is translated using vector $\begin{pmatrix} 3 \\ 0 \end{pmatrix}$. What is the equation of the image graph?

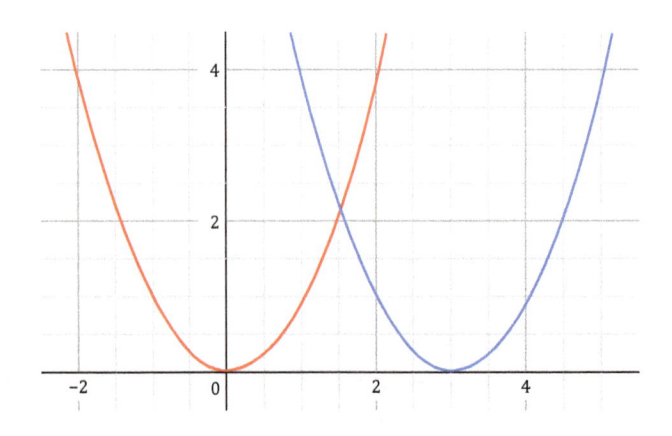

This is often a source of pupil misconception, with pupils very quick to jump to the conclusion that this will be $y = (x + 3)^2$. We need to prompt pupils to consider this more carefully, and in particular to consider the turning point (this is where the completed square form comes into play). If we consider the turning point, then we can see that in order for the turning point to be at (3, 0), we will need the equation to be $y = (x - 3)^2$. We can then go on to justify this with other points with the idea that we need to subtract 3 from a given value of x to produce the same y value as the original function – for example, in the squared function an x value of 2 squares to give a y value of 4. If we want an x value of 5 to now give a y value of 4, then we will need to subtract 3 from the 5 first before squaring, i.e. $(x - 3)^2$.

We will offer pupils similar activities to those previously offered in order to reinforce this relationship:

The graph of equation $y = x^3 + 3x^2 - 2x - 5$ is translated using vector $\binom{3}{0}$. What is the equation of the image graph? Give your answer in expanded form.

Describe the transformation that transforms the graph of the equation $y = 5\cos(x + 2)$ to the graph of the equation $y = 5\cos(x - 4)$.

We will also want to offer pupils the opportunity to sketch graphs based on the changed equation:

The picture below shows the graph of $y = f(x)$. On the same axes, draw the graph of $y = f(x - 5)$.

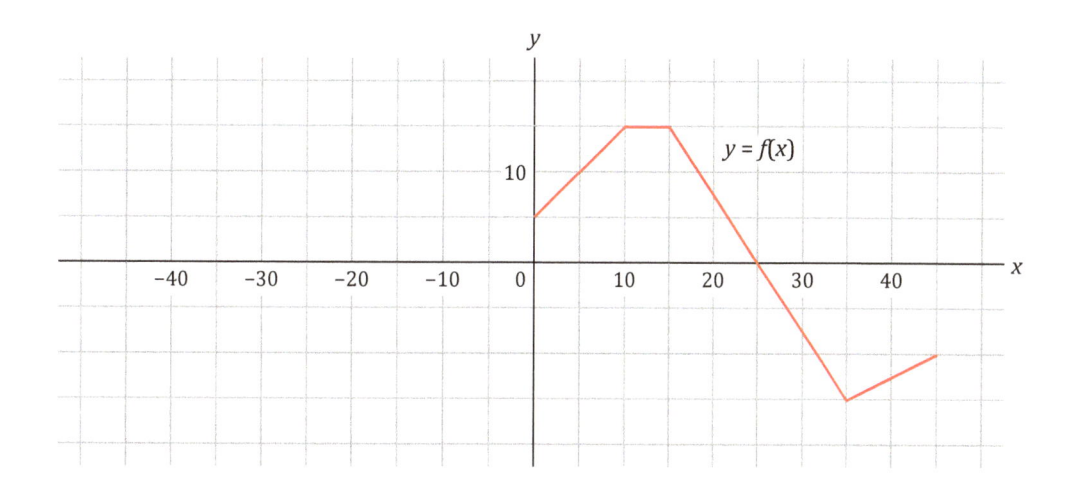

before prompting the same generalisation that a translation of $\binom{a}{0}$ results in the equation of $y = f(x)$ becoming $y = f(x - a)$ and then the further generalisation that a translation of $\binom{a}{b}$ results in $y = f(x)$ becoming $y = f(x - a) + b$; again, the link to the completed square form, with the movement of the turning point of $y = x^2$ compared to $y = (x - a)^2 + b$, is a useful one to highlight to pupils.

Having examined translation, we will then want to turn our attention to reflection and, in particular, reflection in the axes.

The graph of $y = x^2$ is reflected in the x-axis. Work out the equation of the image graph.

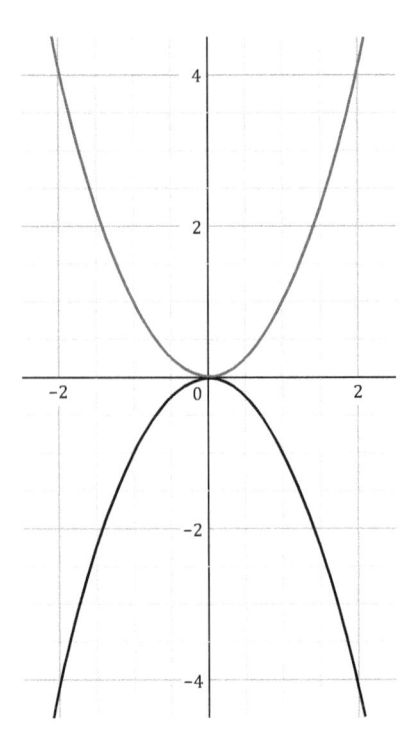

Pupils may well remember that the second graph here is the graph of $y = -x^2$, but we will still want to look at the reasoning behind this being the result of the reflection. We can reason that to reflect a point in the x-axis, we need to make points with a positive y-ordinate have a negative y-ordinate (and vice versa). This means we take the value of the function, and multiply it by −1.

It is important that pupils work with this beyond the base graphs, so that they can apply it to polynomial functions that have a range of signs:

The graph of $y = x^2 - 3x + 2$ is reflected in the x-axis. Write the equation of the image graph in expanded form.

The important thing here is that pupils recognise that the whole expression on the right-hand side needs to be multiplied by −1, i.e. $y = -(x^2 - 3x + 2)$. This, of course, is not in expanded form – we can expand it to give $y = -x^2 + 3x - 2$.

Similarly to looking at translations, we will offer pupils a range of these sorts of activities, such as:

The graph of equation $y = x^3 + 3x^2 - 2x - 5$ is reflected in the x-axis. What is the equation of the image graph? Give your answer in expanded form.

Describe the transformation that transforms the graph of the equation $y = -5 \cos(x + 2)$ to the graph of the equation $y = 5 \cos(x + 2)$.

The picture below shows the graph of $y = f(x)$. On the same axes, draw the graph of $y = f(-x)$.

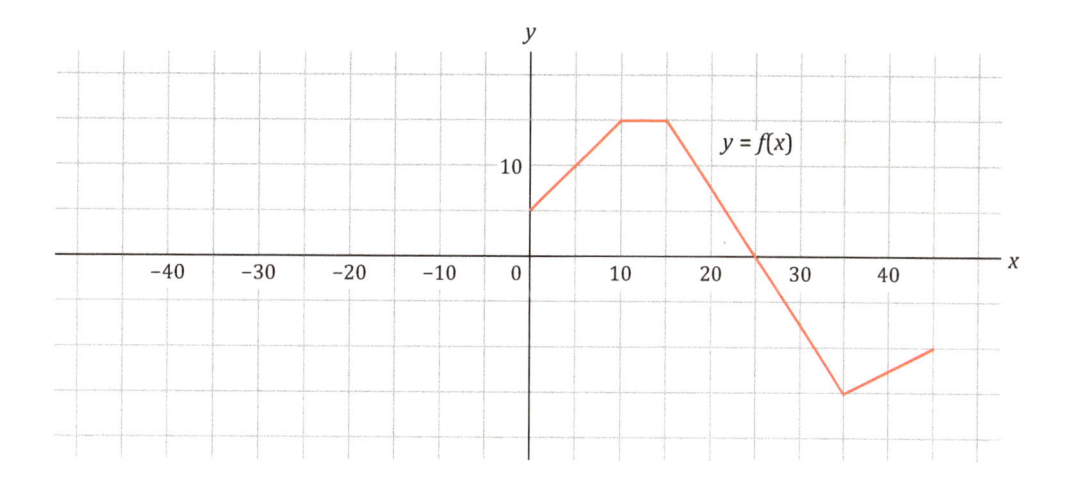

This final question shows the generalisation that we will ultimately want to arrive at with pupils, i.e. that a reflection in the y-axis results in $y = f(x)$ becoming $y = -f(x)$.

After working with reflection in the x-axis, we will want to turn our attention to reflection in the y-axis. In this case the graph of $y = x^2$ is not a good base graph, as it already has a line of symmetry in the y-axis. Similarly, $y = x^3$ is not a good example either, as it looks the same when reflected in either axis. We can discuss this with pupils, and perhaps settle on an equation like $y = (x - 1)^3$ to be the first equation we examine:

The graph of $y = (x - 1)^3$ is reflected in the y-axis. Give the equation of the image graph.

This one is a little harder to reason with, and pupils will likely need significant help in interpreting it. The logic we want pupils to be able to follow here is that to reflect in the y-axis we need the y-ordinate to be unchanged when the x-ordinate takes its negative value. This means we need to change negative x values back to positive values before we evaluate them in order to generate the correct y values. This leads to the equation of the graph being $y = ((-x) - 1)^3$.

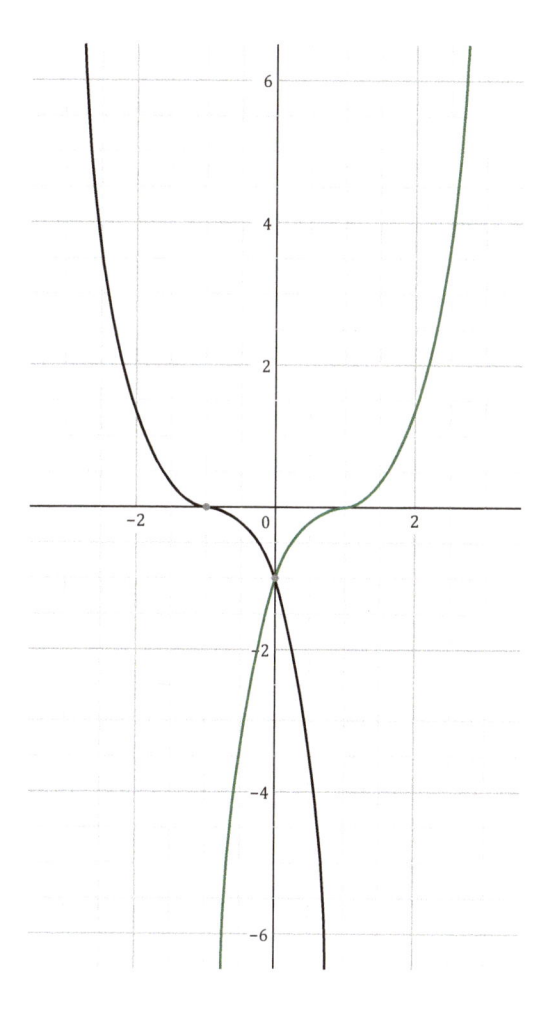

Again, pupils need to work with this in lots of different scenarios:

The graph of equation $y = x^3 + 3x^2 - 2x - 5$ is reflected in the y-axis. What is the equation of the image graph? Give your answer in expanded form.

Describe the transformation that transforms the graph of the equation $y = 5\cos(x + 2)$ to the graph of the equation $y = 5\cos(2 - x)$.

The picture below shows the graph of $y = f(x)$. On the same axes, draw the graph of $y = f(-x)$.

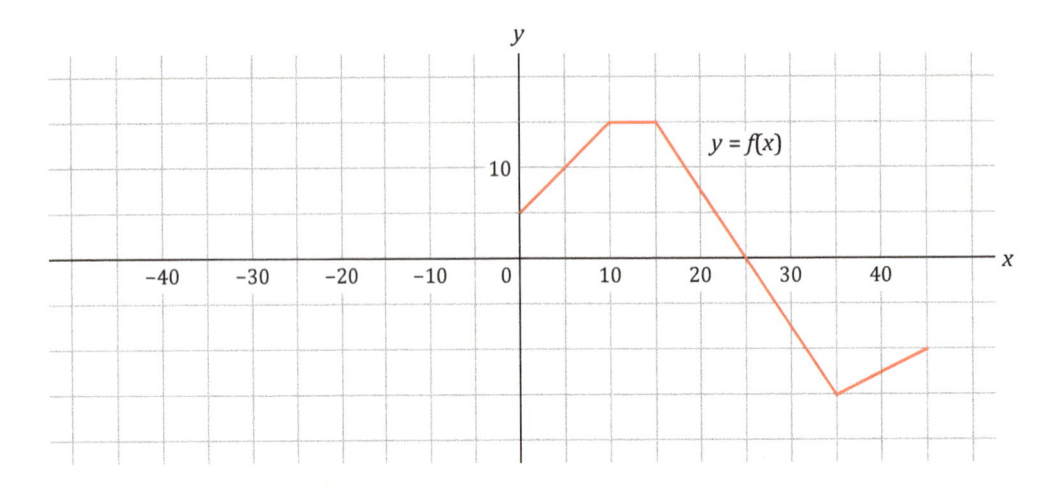

again, with this final question highlighting the generalisation we want to arrive at with pupils; that a reflection in the y-axis results in $y = f(x)$ becoming $y = f(-x)$.

These are all of the transformations of graphs that pupils at school level have to consider; however, there are others we might offer pupils as further things to think about, given what they already know. For example:

- Pupils may be prompted to recall that a rotation of 180° around centre (0, 0) produces the same result as a reflection in the x-axis followed by a reflection in the y-axis (or vice versa).

- Pupils may be able to reason that, as a reflection in the line $y = x$ swaps the values of the x- and y-ordinates, the reflection will transform the equation $y = f(x)$ into $x = f(y)$. This can be particularly nice to link back to quadratics and rearranging formulae through completing the square.

- Pupils may be able to reason that, to enlarge using a scale factor k from centre (0, 0) we will need to make all the y-ordinates k times larger (i.e. $y = kf(x)$) and also make the x-ordinates k times larger (this is harder to reason, but pupils might get as far as figuring out that this is $y = f(\frac{1}{k}x)$ and so putting both together gives $y = kf(\frac{x}{k})$).

There is one graph that we haven't yet mentioned that pupils will need to meet. When we first introduced coordinates, we talked about the opportunity to interweave properties and understanding of shapes. Indeed, one of the key contributions of the Cartesian system was that it allowed the mathematical worlds of geometry and algebra to be combined, so that problems in one world can be transformed into analgolous problems in the other world. So far, beyond straight lines (and therefore all polygons) the shapes we have worked on have been, perhaps, more unfamiliar to pupils (shapes such as parabolas are rarely studied outside of quadratic graphs). It is nice to bring pupils back to more familiar shapes when finishing the school-level journey about graphs, and one of these is the circle.

Concept link: equation of a circle

Before embarking on combining circles with coordinates, we might want to remind pupils about the other shapes they have studied; how they have already been able to create things like triangles, quadrilaterals and other polygons from the straight lines they have previously studied. It might even be worth offering pupils sets of linear equations and asking them to figure out what polygons the lines create. We can then remind pupils of the journey they have previously taken with geometry; first studying line properties, before triangles, quadrilaterals and other polygons, and then finally circles.

The next point of discussion is about what makes a circle a circle. This links to constructions (as do parabolas and other shapes) in that the circle is defined by its constant radius (when we construct a circle, we fix the distance from the point of the compasses to the point of the pencil). So we can look at a circle drawn onto a Cartesian axes (at compulsory school level in England these are limited to circles centred on the origin) and examine the radius:

We have previously seen that, on a Cartesian axes, the length of a line can be found using Pythagoras' theorem. As a circle is defined by the length of this radius, this means any point on the circumference of the circle is r units away from the centre, and so any point on the circumference will have to satisfy the equation $x^2 + y^2 = r^2$.

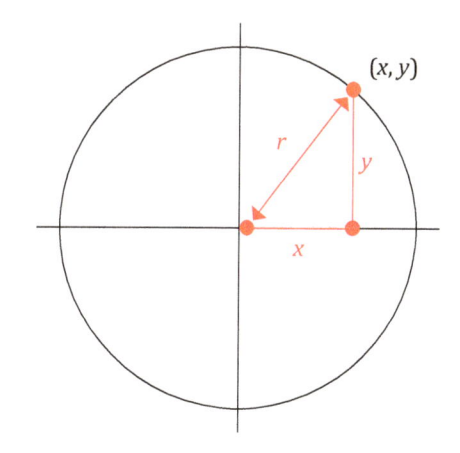

Pupils should have the opportunity to find the equations of different circles:

Write down the equation of a circle, centre (0, 0) with a radius of 9 units.

Write down the equation of the circle below:

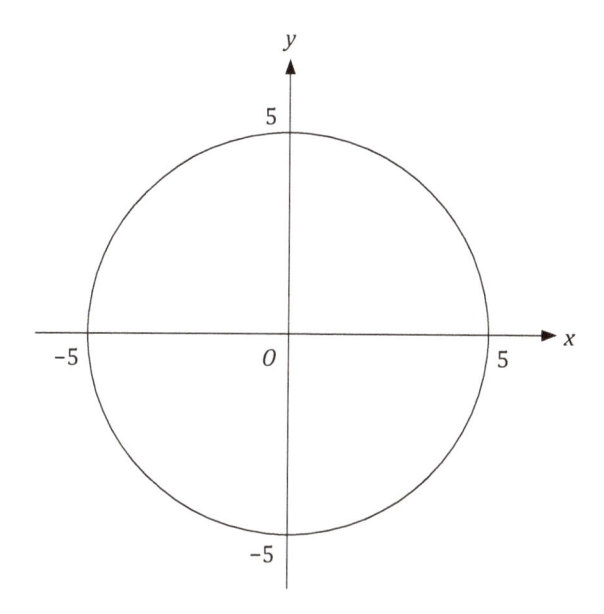

as well as interpreting information from the equation of a circle:

Find the area of the circle with equation $x^2 + y^2 = 40$.

Find the circumference of a circle with equation $x^2 + y^2 = \frac{9}{25}$.

and then interweaving other areas of maths, including circle theorems and simultaneous equation solving:

A circle has equation $x^2 + y^2 = 45$. The line $2y + x = 15$ is a tangent to the circle. Find the point of intersection of the tangent and the circle.

A circle has equation $x^2 + y^2 = 36$. A chord to the circle has equation $y = -\frac{3}{4}x + 4$. Find the equation of the radius that bisects the chord.

A circle with equation $x^2 + y^2 = 25$ has a chord with equation $y = \frac{11x-25}{2}$. Find the points of intersection between the chord and the circle.

A circle with equation $x^2 + y^2 = 169$ goes through points $A = (5, 12)$, $B = (-5, -12)$ and $C = (13, 0)$.

1. Show that AB is a diameter of the circle.
2. State the angle ACB.
3. Hence, or otherwise, find the angle CAB.

This concludes our examination of charting and graphing, its purpose in allowing us to visualise relationships, and the ways in which it can allow interweaving and revisiting of previously studied mathematics. We started the chapter examining charts and graphs that are normally associated with representing data, and we will now finish this work with an examination of the other aspects of data handling.

Chapter 14

Data handling

The study of data is a relatively recent area of mathematics to develop and be taught in schools. Indeed, there are some who think that data handling should not be taught in the mathematics classroom at all but rather in the different social sciences (such as geography, business, etc.) where the need to handle data arises. In saying that, there are a number of links between areas in data handling and other mathematical areas, and so I think there is a definite case for the inclusion of data handling in the mathematics classroom.

Pupils learning about data at school level will, broadly speaking, need to learn about five key areas:

1 Planning – what types of data can be used to investigate situations and how do we make sure we get good data?

2 Collection – how do we gather data?

3 Processing data – how do we take collected data and ensure that it is organised in a way that it can be used?

4 Representation – what graphs and charts might we draw that might give us insight into patterns or trends within the collected data?

5 Analysis and interpretation – what further analysis can we do to help summarise the collected data and how do we go about deciding what this tells us about the situations?

In the past this has been encapsulated in what is called the data handling cycle, which is designed to show how investigations into specific scenarios can be conducted, including how results then feed into new problems:[1]

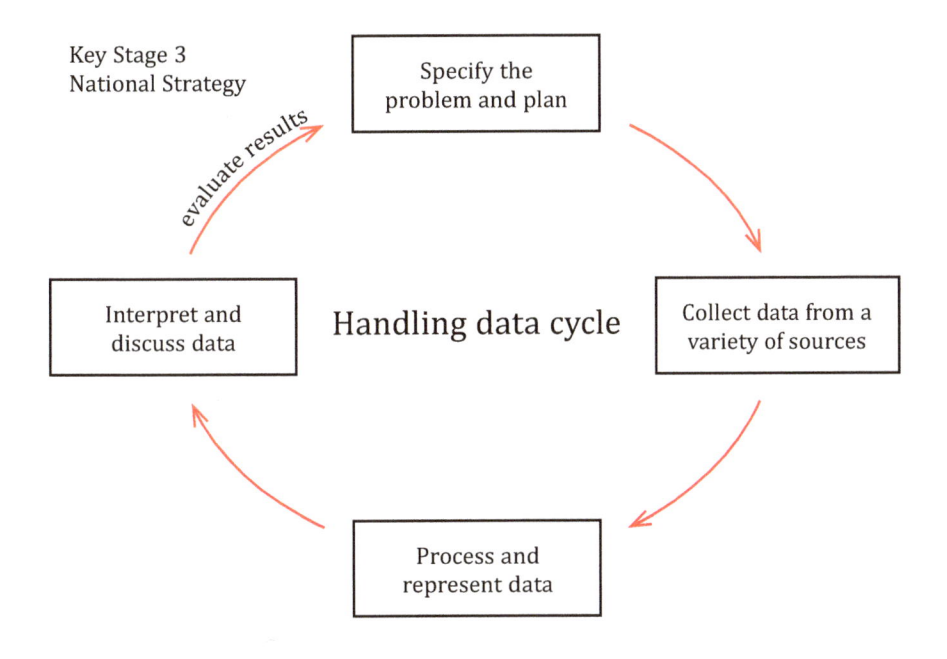

Key Stage 3 National Strategy

Handling data cycle

- Specify the problem and plan
- Collect data from a variety of sources
- Process and represent data
- Interpret and discuss data
- evaluate results

---

[1] STEM Learning, Handling Data Cycle Poster (n.d.). Available at: https://www.stem.org.uk/resources/elibrary/resource/29299/year-eight-handling-data-mini-pack.

We have looked at different representations in the previous chapter, so will cover the other areas in this chapter.

Concept: data planning

Prerequisites: Number.

Linked concepts: Data collection, data processing, data representation, data analysis, proportion, probability.

One of the first questions we should be asking pupils when it comes to data is, 'Where does data even come from?' alongside, 'Why do we need data in the first place?' Pupils might appreciate that, ultimately, data comes from asking people about things or from doing things and recording what happens, and that we do this to try and answer questions about things. We can then use this idea to highlight to pupils that, if we need data to answer a particular question then we have, broadly speaking, two sources:

1. We can come up with a way of getting exactly the data we feel will be useful to answer the question, and then go and get that data first hand.

2. We can look and see if data already exists about the situation that we are asking about, and use this pre-existing data to answer all or part of the question we had.

Both of these have clear advantages and disadvantages that pupils should appreciate. The first obviously allows us to tailor approaches very carefully to cater exactly for the situation we are in and the question(s) we want to answer, the drawback being that this is extra work, time and potentially cost. Pupils should know that this is called **primary data**.

In contrast, the second approach is clearly less expensive in terms of time and probably money, but the data found may not be exactly what is needed, and may also be less reliable as we don't know the situation under which it was collected. Pupils should know that this is called **secondary data.** There are strong links here to primary and secondary sources in history, which may be exploited to support pupils in recognising the difference.

Quickly following this, we will want to be talking with pupils about what sorts of data might be useful in answering different questions, leading to pupils recognising that there are two recognised types of data:

1. Qualitative data – data that describes a quality associated with the subject (this is also called 'categorical data' as it describes a category that the subject falls into).

2. Quantitative data – data that describes a quantity associated with the subject.

Pupils should further be aware that each of these can be split into two further subcategories:

Qualitative data		Quantitative data	
Nominal	Ordinal	Discrete	Continuous
These are names of different categories that have no inherent order, i.e. if you were going to replace them with category numbers 1, 2, 3, etc. then there would be no obvious choice for 1, and having chosen 1 it wouldn't matter which was then 2, 3, etc. Examples include: sex, eye colour, vehicle makes/ models, etc.	These are categories that do have a recognised order, i.e. if you were going to replace them with category numbers 1, 2, 3, etc. then there would be a limited number of possible choices for 1 (less than the total number of categories), and having chosen 1, the category for 2, 3, etc. would automatically follow. Examples include: lettered grades (A, B, C, D, E, F, G or O, E, A, P, D, T); months of the year; Likert agreement scale, etc.	These are numbers that can only assume certain values between the maximum and minimum values of the data. They generally (but not exclusively) arise from situations where people/objects are counted or scored. Examples include: scores rolled on a die; ratings of 1, 2, 3, 4, or 5; numerical grading, number of days absent, shoe size, etc.	These are numbers that can take any value between the maximum and minimum values of the data. They generally (but not exclusively) arise from situations where people/objects are measured. Examples include: height, weight, time taken, percentages (could be discrete – tends to be continuous when calculated over large numbers), etc.

Pupils should work on identifying the types and sources of data in different scenarios:

Scott is researching opinions on uniform in his school. He asks a sample of pupils whether they believe the uniform in the school should be changed. Circle the words that could be used to describe the type and sources of data that Scott collects:

    Primary   Secondary   Categorical   Discrete

    Qualitative   Continuous   Quantitative

as well as creating situations which pull certain types of data from certain sources:

Describe a situation that would lead to the collection of:
1. Primary categorical/qualitative data.
2. Secondary discrete numerical/quantitative data.
3. Primary continuous numerical/quantitative data.
4. Secondary categorical/qualitative data.

5   Primary discrete numerical/quantitative data.

6   Secondary continuous numerical/quantitative data.

My worksheet on *TES* has a selection of questions like this and others that can prompt pupils to think about the different types and sources of data.[2]

A follow-up question we can then prompt pupils to consider is, if collecting primary data, how do we do this in a way that ensures our data tells us the real and whole story. This is the beginning of considering bias in data, and how we make sure that the data is representative of the population. Pupils should consider two potential sources of bias:

1   Bias as a result of who/what we ask/test being limited.

2   Bias as a result of how we ask/carry out the test.

The second of these we will focus on when we look at data collection, but the first is concerned with who or what we sample.

Pupils will need to be introduced to the following terms:

- Population – the entire group of people or objects that we want to answer a question about.
- Sample – a subgroup of the population from which data will be collected.
- Census – when a whole population.

Pupils should see that one way to absolutely assure there is no bias as a result of who/what we ask/test is to ask/test (and get results from) the entire population. This could be giving every person in a school a survey, or testing every item produced from a manufacturing process. However, pupils should also realise that in many cases this will be impracticable, either because the population is too large or because to test every item would leave nothing to use. We can offer pupils the opportunity to reason why we might choose to sample rather than census the whole population:

> A company makes light bulbs.
> The company wants to test that the light bulbs work.
>
> Explain why the company should test a sample and not the whole population.
>
> The manager wants to interview some of the passengers on a trip.
> There are 53 passengers.
>
> Write down one reason why the manager might want to take a sample rather than carry out a census.
>
> A school has 1,000 pupils.
> Pat wants to take a sample of these pupils.
>
> Give one reason why Pat might want to take a sample rather than a census.

---

2   P. Mattock, Types of Data Worksheet, *TES* (20 January 2018). Available at: https://www.tes.com/teaching-resource/types-of-data-worksheet-11816316.

In addition, pupils can work with different scenarios to correctly identify the population sample and identify why a sample might not be suitable. Exercise 1a in the document linked below contains some useful questions to offer pupils (the whole document contains some nice bits to support pupil work on sampling).[3]

This leads nicely into different approaches to sampling. The website Scribbr has an excellent article that showcases different sampling methods, both probabilistic and non-probabilistic in nature.[4] Although pupils are only required to learn about random sampling in any detail, it helps to add context by giving an overview of different sampling methods so that pupils recognise what the alternatives are. There is also a case for asking pupils to work with stratified sampling as a way of interweaving skills around proportion; simple questions like:

Here is a table showing how many students there are at my school:

Year	7	8	9	10	11
No of students	200	240	230	260	252

I want to take a stratified sample of 300 students from the school. How many Year 11 students should I include in my sample?

which can be solved using proportional reasoning strategies, perhaps with the help of a dual number line or ratio table:

Year 11	Total
252	1182
?	300

The main thing that pupils need to understand about random sampling is how difficult it is to achieve true randomness. We might discuss things like the lottery machines that pick out balls as attempts by humans to create randomness, and the difficulties associated with this. One story I always tell is from the early days of my degree in physics (before I changed to mathematics) where we were in a laboratory, having to select straws from a larger group of straws of different lengths (I forget why!). The group I was working with started to simply select straws 'at random' by closing our eyes and picking them out until our professor casually strolled past and asked, 'But aren't you more likely to pick the longer straws?' Of course, this put paid to our choice being 'random' – it clearly wasn't.

The solution to this, which is the one we had to employ in the physics lab, is to use a random number generator; and this is what pupils must learn about random sampling. We might ask them for their approaches to selecting at random first, discussing the different strategies they might suggest (most pupils have never come across a random number generator and so it is unlikely to be suggested). I find introducing pupils to the random number generator on their calculator helpful – most calculators have a random generator that will generate numbers between 0 and 0.999 and most of the newer calculators (at the time of

---

3 See https://studylib.net/doc/25432373/samplingjan06.
4 S. McCombes, An Introduction to Sampling Methods, *Scribbr* (19 September 2019). Available at: https://www.scribbr.com/methodology/sampling-methods/.

writing) will generate a random integer between any two values that are chosen. We might also use the random generator on a spreadsheet to highlight the production of random numbers. Pupils should understand that the only real way to produce a random sample is to number each person or object in the population, and then use a random number generator to generate the required number of values for the size of the sample to be chosen. This can be seen frequently in mark schemes for exam questions involving pupils designing an approach to random sampling. For example, in this question:

5   A school has 1,000 pupils.
     Pat wants to take a sample of these pupils.

5 (b) Briefly describe how Pat could obtain a random sample of the 1,000 pupils.

the mark scheme reads:

5(b)	Number all of the population	B1	oe
	Use random numbers to obtain sample	B1	oe

Similarly, in this question:

In the street there are 80 houses.
Kate wants to sample 20 of these.

6 (c) (i) Briefly explain how she could obtain a random sample of 20 houses.

the mark scheme reads:

6(c)(i)	Obtain random numbers from	B1	calculator/web/etc.
	Select the 20 houses from the numbers obtained	B1	Accept/ignore repeats or values over 80 for this mark
6(c)(ii)	$24 \times \frac{20}{80}$	M1	oe
	6	A1	

(in this case, there is no need to number the houses as they will already be numbered).

Once again the Mathematics Enhancement Programme materials have some nice questions around random sampling[5] – although they are more focused on pupils actually carrying out the sampling process rather than designing it and so need adaptation to focus on this skill. We might also want to discuss the potential drawbacks of a random sample, in particular that we may inadvertently end up with a sample that is not representative of the population, although the chance of this diminishes with larger samples, which should make it clear to pupils why large samples are required (as well as hinting at the links to probability that would be explored post-16).

---

5   CIMT, MEP Y9 Practice Book 9B Chapter 9B (n.d.). Available at: https://cimt.org.uk/projects/mepres/book9/bk9_18.pdf.

Once pupils understand the importance of planning for the sources and types of data, and the importance of making sure the people we choose to answer/the things we choose to test are representative of the population as a whole when we intend to collect primary data, then we can start to consider how we will go about collecting the data that will allow us to answer the question we are setting out to answer in the first place.

Concept: data collection

Prerequisites: Number, types of data.

Linked concepts: Data planning, data processing, data representation, data analysis.

The first thing pupils should appreciate about primary data collection is that the way we collect data depends on:

- the type(s) of data we want to collect.
- the amount of data we want to collect from each subject.

We might wish to start by asking pupils about how they have experienced or witnessed data collection in the past. Pupils might mention people like street canvassers, the national census or other surveys that they or their families may have taken, and so questionnaires are a good place to start a look at data collection.

Although the study of questionnaires is no longer a part of the compulsory school-level curriculum in England, I think there is a strong argument for spending at least some time looking at how they contribute to the data handling process. The study of questionnaires can help reinforce understanding of data types as well as support the development of understanding of how bias can affect data and the importance of what and how we ask in ensuring we get the real and full story from the data. For example, pupils can consider what suitable response sections might look like for questions like:

On which devices do you listen to music more than once per week?

Roughly how many songs do you download each month on average?

Roughly how much time, in hours, do you spend listening to music per week on average?

Considering these sorts of questions can help to reinforce the distinctions between qualitative, discrete and continuous data, and how the type of data affects the sort of responses we might get. In particular, pupils should recognise the importance of covering all the usual options and including an 'Other' option (assuming we cannot cover all the possible options) when collecting categorical data, but that when collecting discrete data we will need either discrete values or suitably structured groups, including a 'More than …' option rather than an 'Other' option. Contrast this with continuous data where we will definitely need groups, and the groups will be structured differently to the discrete groups:

On which devices do you listen to music more than once per week (circle one)?

| Phone | Tablet | TV | Stereo |

Computer   Other (please specify)

Roughly how many songs do you download each month on average (circle one)?

| 0 – 4 | 5 – 9 | 10 – 14 | 15 – 19 | 20 – 24 | 25+ |

Roughly how much time, in hours, do you spend listening to music per week on average (circle one)?

$0 \leq t < 5$ $10 \leq t < 15$ $20 \leq t < 25$

$5 \leq t < 10$ $15 \leq t < 20$ $25 \leq t$

We can also offer pupils examples of poor questions/response sections and look at why they lead to problems in the gathered data:[6]

Comment critically on the following questions. In each case, rewrite the question to show the improvements you have made.

a   Are you young, middle-aged or old?

b   Please select your favourite breakfast cereal from this list:

   Cornflakes ☐   Frosties ☐   Rice Crispies ☐   Bran Flakes ☐

c   How old are you?

   0→5 ☐   7→10 ☐   12+ ☐

d   Do you have any brothers?

   Do you have one brother?

   Do you have more than one brother?

   Do you have at least two brothers?

Pupils should appreciate that a questionnaire-style structure might also be required if testing machines or materials, with spaces to record the results of different tests. In addition, pupils should also appreciate that questionnaires collect quite a reasonable amount of data from/about each subject, which means that it will be difficult and expensive to survey a large number of subjects, both in terms of the initial distribution and collection and the processing and analysis that follows. For example, a questionnaire with 10 questions given to 1,000 people contains 10,000 separate pieces of data that need to be processed. Pupils should realise that this level of data collection and processing will simply be beyond many people/companies, and will only be done when absolutely necessary, even by those that can handle it due to the time and cost implications. In general then, pupils should understand that the primary use of a questionnaire is to gather a lot of information from a relatively small number of people (like a carefully chosen sample) when the depth of insight is required. The question then arises, what if we want a limited amount of data from a lot of subjects – maybe only one or two questions/tests? Clearly, for situations like this, we don't need a full questionnaire. Pupils might suggest just noting these down on a piece of paper, which we can prompt further to get them thinking about organisation of these responses for ease of processing later; and from this is born the idea of the data collection sheet.

In effect, a data collection sheet is simply a table on which we record responses to a question. Having studied questionnaires, pupils should already be familiar with response

---

[6] CIMT, MEP Y8 Practice Book 8B Chapter 20: Questionnaires and Analysis (n.d.). Available at: https://www.cimt.org.uk/projects/mepres/book8/bk8_20.pdf.

sections to questions. Pupils should understand that if we are going to ask a question that we will record through a data collection sheet, then the response section will be the different responses that we can record:

On which devices do you listen to music more than once per week?

Device	Tally	Frequency
Phone		
Tablet		
TV		
Stereo		
Computer		
Other		

Roughly how many songs do you download each month on average?

Number of songs	Tally	Frequency
0–4		
5–9		
10–14		
15–19		
20–24		
25+		

Roughly how much time, in hours, do you spend listing to music per week on average?

Time Spent	Tally	Frequency
$0 \leq t < 5$		
$5 \leq t < 10$		
$10 \leq t < 15$		
$15 \leq t < 20$		
$20 \leq t < 25$		
$25 \leq t$		

Pupils should be introduced to the idea of using tally marks to record responses, including the cross mark to group the results into fives for ease of processing, and then (if pupils haven't already met it) we can introduce pupils to the concept of frequency as a count of all the data in a particular category/group or that has a particular value.

Pupils should have the opportunity to create and use their own data collection sheets. A key part of this is making sure that pupils create suitable groups for grouping both discrete and continuous data, as this is an area that pupils often struggle with.

As well as data collection sheets to collect one item of data, pupils should create data collection sheets designed to collect frequency data about two linked questions. For example:

> Linda is collecting data about the attendance at different classes at her local leisure centre by both adults and children. The classes are swimming, exercise and cycling. Design a data collection sheet for Linda to use.

	Swimming	Exercise	Cycling
Adult			
Child			

Pupils should understand that there is no 'Frequency' column in a table like this; instead, we simply use tally marks in each box. Pupils should practise completing these, as some can find it tricky to keep track of the two criteria at once. We might, however, include a 'Total' for each row/column, leading to an overall total:

	Swimming	Exercise	Cycling	Total
Adult				
Child				
Total				

Once pupils understand the collection of data, we can move on to processing data ready for representation and analysis.

Concept: data processing

Prerequisites: Number, types of data.

Linked concepts: Data planning, data collection, data representation, data analysis, proportion, percentage, probability.

So, we have our completed questionnaires, or have looked up the secondary data, and now what? Rarely can we use the collected data in its **raw** format; typically some measure of processing will be required before data can be represented and/or analysed. Of course, how we process the data will depend on what representation and analysis we intend to complete with the data collected, but we can start by mirroring the collection approaches we saw in the last chapter, starting with tally charts.

Pupils should understand that a tally chart allows for the processing of data in the same way a data collection sheet captures data, in that it can take the responses from a single question on a questionnaire and process them to find out the frequency of each of the responses:

Our Favourite Sports

Sport	Tally	Number of Students
Hockey	卌 I	6
Football	卌	5
Basketball	IIII	4
Gymnastics	II	2

The key thing pupils should recognise here is that there is no 'Other' option in this table; this is the key difference between a tally chart and a data collection sheet. Pupils should understand that because we are using this to process already collected data, we do not need an 'Other' option – we know every choice that was made (assuming the 'Other' on the questionnaire included a 'please specify' part).

A tally chart can also be used for processing data that has been noted down in raw form:

Insect Scavenger Hunt Tally Chart

Insect	Tally	Total
Ladybird	卌 I	6
Ant	卌 卌 III	13
Butterfly	IIII	4

In this case, a pupil either wrote down the list of animals as they saw them, and used the tally chart to count up later, or chose beforehand only to collect data on the number of ladybirds, ants and butterflies they saw. Pupils can practise designing tally charts based on a list of data:

Create a tally chart to process Beth's data.

Beth watches cars go by her window and records these makes:

Rover; Ford; Toyota; Ford; Lada; Ford; Rover; Toyota; Rover; Ford; Toyota; Rover; Ford; Ford; Rover; Toyota; Toyota; Ford; Rover; Ford; Rover; Toyota; Rover; Toyota; Ford; Ford; Toyota; Rover; Lada; Toyota; Ford; Ford; Ford; Ford; Rover; Ford; Toyota; Rover; Ford; Ford; Toyota; Ford; Rover; Toyota; Rover; Ford; Ford; Toyota; Rover; Ford; Ford; Lada; Rover; Ford; Rover; Ford; Toyota; Lada; Rover; Ford; Rover; Ford; Ford; Toyota; Rover; Ford; Rover; Rover; Ford; Toyota.

Pupils can then practise processing through the tally chart. When processing the data, pupils should be taught to take each item of data as it comes, recording with a tally mark and then crossing off the data as it is processed. Some pupils will naturally try and record all of the Rovers, then all of the Fords, then all of the Toyotas and so on. Pupils need to recognise that there is more scope for error in that approach, with missing out or double-counting a data item a significant possibility. If needed, we can also offer pupils separate practice on actually counting up tally marks in order to evaluate frequency. Math Worksheets 4 Kids has an activity that is designed to offer pupils this opportunity to evaluate tally marks.[7]

Pupils should include the use of tally charts to collect discrete numerical data – for example, for processing quiz score data:

Score	Tally	Frequency
1	I	1
2	I	1
3	III	3
4	I	1
5	IIII	4
6	ℍ	5
7	ℍ I	6
8	ℍ	5
9	III	3
10	I	1

---

[7] Math Worksheet 4 Kids, Counting Tally Marks (n.d.). Available at: https://www.mathworksheets4kids.com/tally/reading1.pdf.

as well as for grouped numerical data; both discrete and continuous:

Number of cups of coffee	Tally	Frequency
0–3	II	2
4–7	III	3
8–11	⊮III	8
12–15	III	3
16–19	II	2

Height (cm)	Tally	Frequency
130 < h ≤ 140	III	3
140 < h ≤ 150	⊮II	7
150 < h ≤ 160	⊮IIII	9
160 < h ≤ 170	⊮III	8
170 < h ≤ 180	III	3

This is another excellent opportunity to make sure pupils understand how the grouping structure for discrete and continuous data should be different, and to design groups for both.

Pupils should also have the opportunity to work with two-way tables being used to process data. For example, we could provide pupils with raw data on medal winning from the last Olympic Games and ask them to complete the table below:

	Gold	Silver	Bronze
United States			
China			
Russia			
Great Britain			

Pupils should see that further processing is required in this case, as we do not want to have to be re-evaluating tally marks every time we look at the table, so once we have tallied up the data, we can create a two-way frequency table:

	Gold	Silver	Bronze	Total
United States	46	29	29	104
China	38	27	23	88
Russia	24	26	32	82
Great Britain	29	17	19	65
Total	137	99	103	339

Pupils should notice we have also added a total frequency column and row, which may be useful in representing and/or analysing the data.

In addition to creating two-way tally and frequency tables, partially completed two-way frequency tables are a rich source of reasoning questions that can be used to interweave different skills around number and probability, such as these 'fill in the gaps' activities from JustMaths:[8]

Table A

Students studying a science

	Chemistry	Biology	Physics	Total
Boys	18			47
Girls			19	
Total		21	33	90

Table B

Students studying a language

	German	French	Polish	Total
Girls			9	34
Boys	15			
Total		25	18	60

---

[8] JustMaths, Who Is Right Data Sheet (2012). Available at: https://justmaths.co.uk/wp-content/uploads/2012/12/03-Activity-Who-is-right-data-sheet.pdf.

Table C

Students studying a design and technology subject

	Art	Food	Textiles	Total
Boys	11		15	32
Girls		18		
Total	33			100

Table D

Students studying an English subject

	Language	Literature	Media	Total
Girls		78	20	120
Boys			22	
Total	60		42	238

Table E

Students studying maths

	Applied maths	Statistics	More maths	Total
Girls			20	
Boys		39		167
Total	120		48	282

which has these nice follow-up activities:

How many mistakes?

Four teachers have completed some two-way tables. One of the teachers has made 4 errors, one has made no errors and two have made 1 error. Can you work out the number of errors made by each teacher?

The ICT teacher said:
- the number of boys who study textiles is larger than the number of boys who study physics.
- more boys study English language than girls who study art.
- the number of boys who study food is the same as the number of girls who study biology.
- more boys study Polish than boys study food.

The music teacher said:
- more girls take a design and technology subject than a science subject.
- The number of students studying French is 2 more than the number studying food.
- More boys study English literature than 'more maths'.
- The number of boys studying 'more maths' and girls studying textiles is the same.

The art teacher said:
- more girls study a design and technology subject than boys study an English subject.
- 3 more girls study a maths subject than boys who study an English subject.
- there are 2 more students doing applied maths than girls studying art
- the most popular subject is German.

The English teacher said:
- the most popular individual subject is English literature.
- the total for food and textiles is more than twice the total for art.
- more boys study applied maths than all the students studying design and technology subjects.
- 43 more students study English language than German.

606

Data handling

And these questions from the PixiMaths extension sheet:[9]

300 pupils were asked which their favourite subject was out of maths, English and science. There were equal amounts of boys and girls. Of the 124 that said maths was their favourite, 80 were boys. 60 pupils said English was their favourite. 72 girls said science was their favourite.

1 If I picked a student at random, what is the probability that the student was a girl whose favourite subject was English?

2 Write this as a fraction in its simplest form.

A theatre sells 4,685 tickets to a concert. 3,215 of the tickets are sold to adults. $\frac{3}{5}$ of the adults who have tickets are female. 60% of the children attending the concert are male.

The theatre wants to survey 300 of the people who attend the concert to ask for their opinions on it. They use a stratified sampling technique. Calculate the number of adult males that would be surveyed in the sample.

Linked to two-way frequency tables are other processing tools for data. We have already looked at Venn diagrams, and have seen their relationship to two-way tables:

Smartphone ownership compared to employment status of Year 10 students:

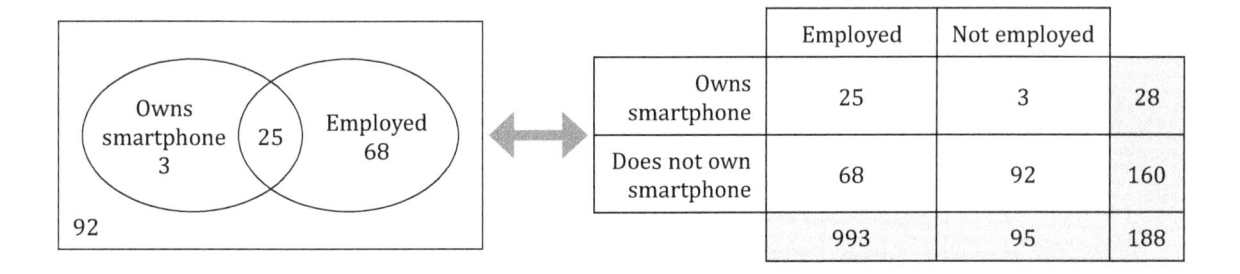

	Employed	Not employed	
Owns smartphone	25	3	28
Does not own smartphone	68	92	160
	993	95	188

A very similar representation is called a Carroll diagram (named after the author Lewis Carroll).

The key difference between a Carroll diagram and a two-way frequency table is that a Carroll diagram sorts and records the actual data via the two attributes, rather than simply counting the frequency of data that had/does not have the attributes. For example:

Sort these numbers into the Carroll diagram

144, 128, 252, 153, 235, 68, 120, 361, 424, 468

	Divisible by 4	Not divisible by 4
Divisible by 9	144 252 468	153 361
Not divisible by 9	128 68 120 424	235

---

9 PixiMaths, Two-Way Tables (n.d.). Available at: https://www.piximaths.co.uk/two-way-tables.

Carroll diagrams are not limited only to sorting numbers. Shapes, labels, any set of objects that has at least two different but not necessarily exclusive attributes can be sorted through a Carroll diagram, which again is also strongly related to a Venn diagram:

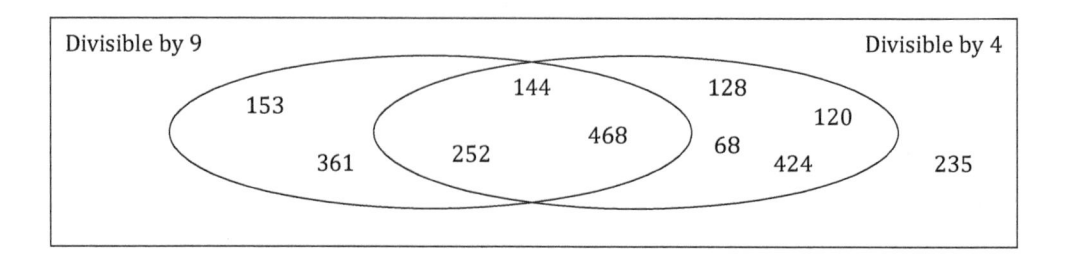

Divisible by 9 — 153, 361, 144, 252, 468 | 128, 68, 120, 424 — Divisible by 4 | 235

In a similar way to how sample spaces and tree diagrams can both be used in the study of probability, we can also represent frequency data that is split into different categories, values or groups using a frequency tree. A frequency tree has the same benefits and drawbacks as a tree diagram for probability, in that we can represent several attributes, but too many categories in an attribute makes the diagram unwieldy:

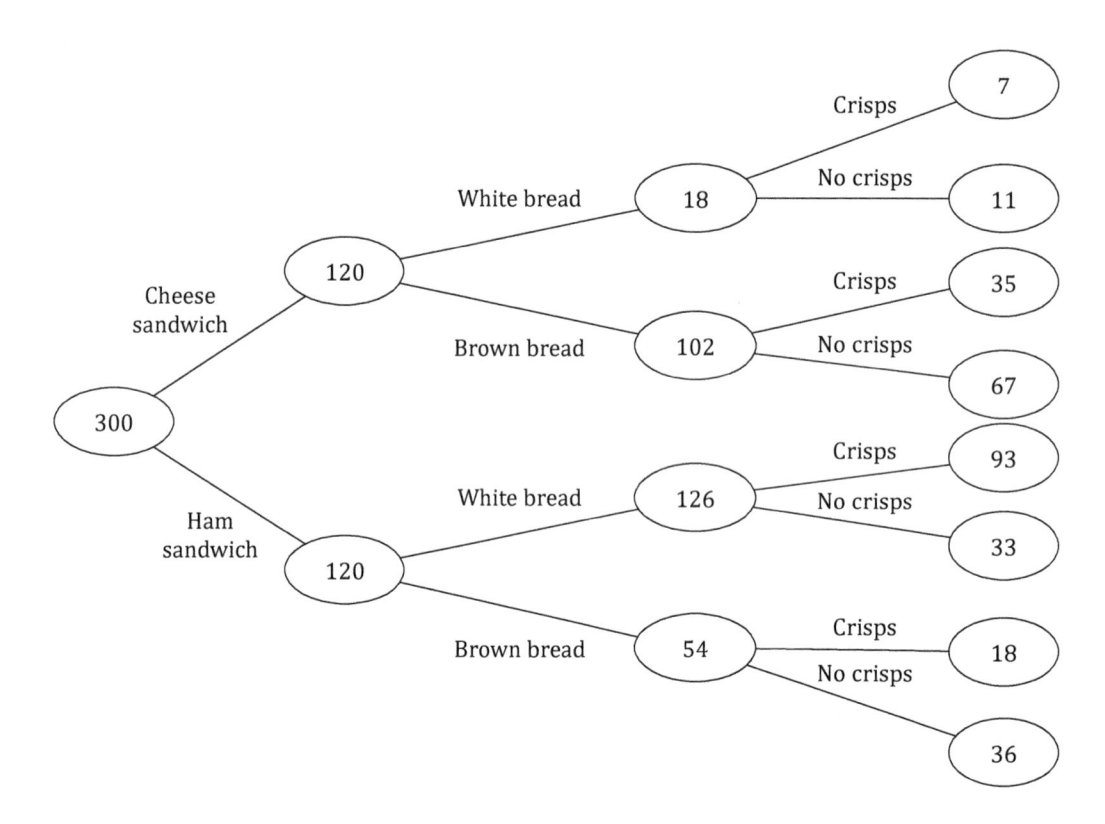

300
- Cheese sandwich: 120
  - White bread: 18
    - Crisps: 7
    - No crisps: 11
  - Brown bread: 102
    - Crisps: 35
    - No crisps: 67
- Ham sandwich: 120
  - White bread: 126
    - Crisps: 93
    - No crisps: 33
  - Brown bread: 54
    - Crisps: 18
    - No crisps: 36

Pupils should have the opportunity to process data through different frequency trees, including simply giving information:

120 people were given 3 minutes to solve a puzzle.

- 45 people who tried to solve the puzzle were under 18 years old.
- 78 people solved the puzzle.
- 32 people aged 18 and over did not solve the puzzle.

Complete the frequency tree using this information.

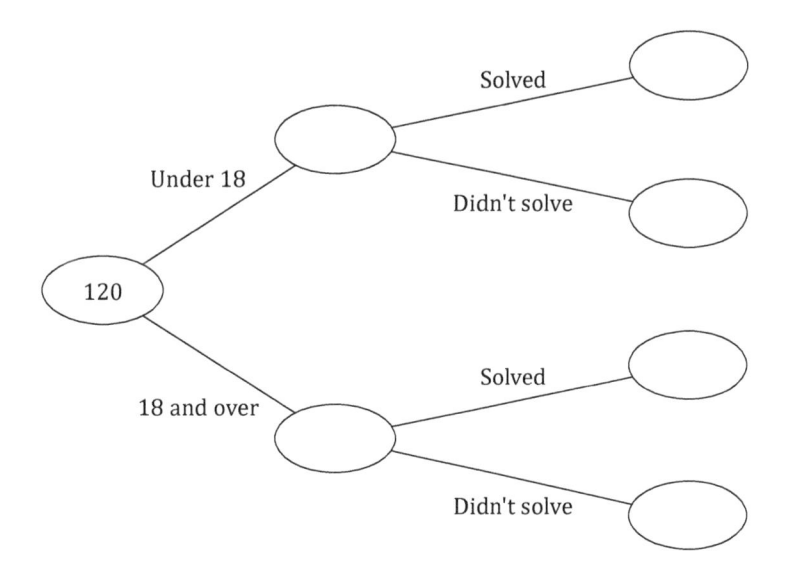

[Frequency tree: 120 branches into "Under 18" (→ Solved / Didn't solve) and "18 and over" (→ Solved / Didn't solve)]

to interweaving work on percentage or ratio:[10]

200 people sat their DVSA driving test over a three-week period.

60% of these had taken 10 or more hours of driving lessons.

Of those with 10 or more hours of driving lessons, 75% passed the test.

Of those with fewer than 10 hours of driving lessons, 60% failed the test.

Complete the frequency tree:

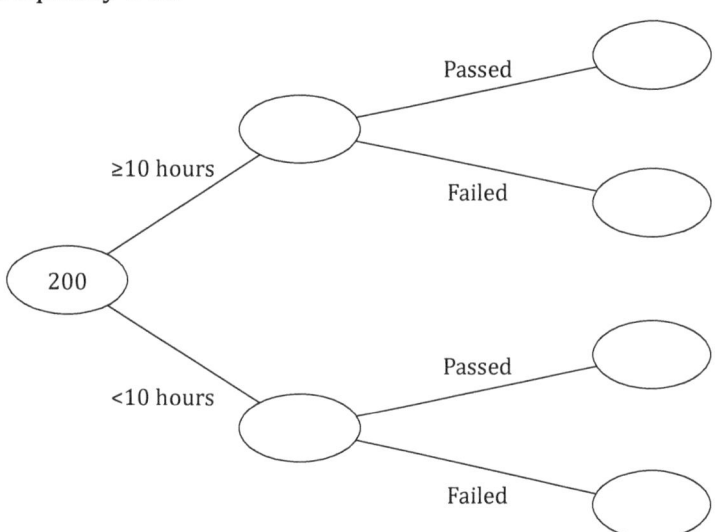

[Frequency tree: 200 branches into "≥10 hours" (→ Passed / Failed) and "<10 hours" (→ Passed / Failed)]

What % of those who passed the test had taken more than 10 hours of driving lessons? Give your answer to 1 d.p.

---

10 D. Steward, Frequency Trees and Percentages, *Median* [blog] (7 December 2019). Available at: https://donsteward.blogspot.com/2019/12/frequency-trees-and-percentages.html.

as well as allowing for reasoning with the information provided:[11]

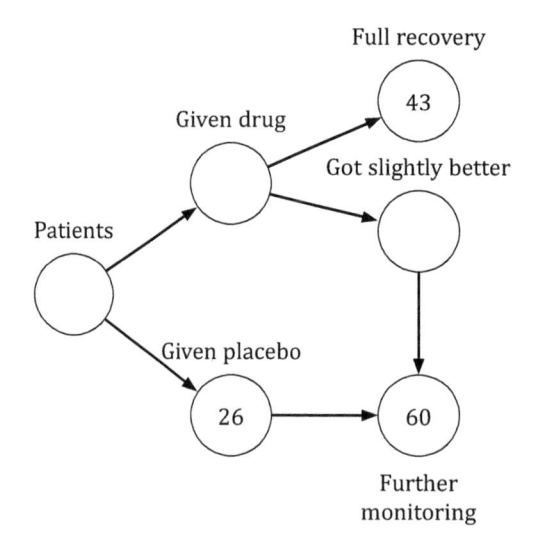

a Complete the frequency tree.

b What is the ratio of patients given drugs to patients given placebos?

c 'The placebos clearly had no effect according to this diagram'. Is this statement true?

A computer game company surveyed 40 players about a game update.
7 adults liked the update. 14 of the 22 children asked liked the update.

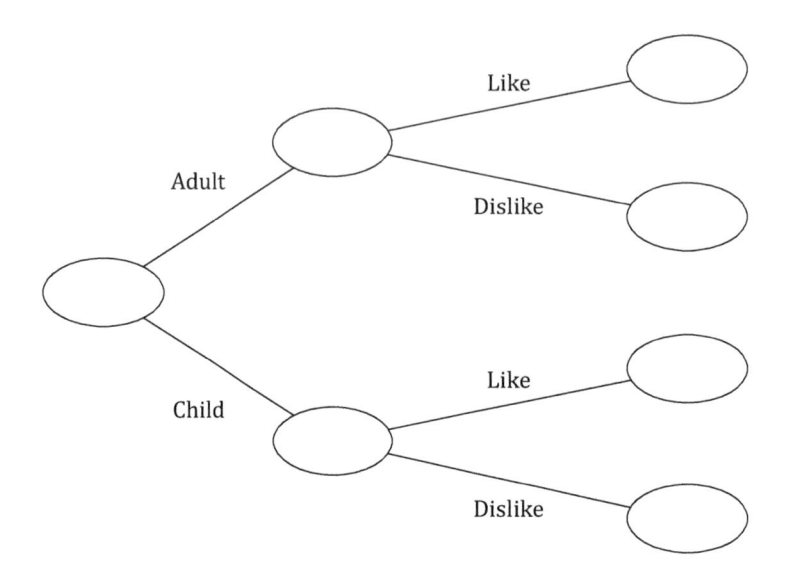

What fraction of the adults disliked the update?

A different technique for processing data that pupils might learn about is the creation of a stem and leaf diagram. Technically, at the time of writing, stem and leaf diagrams have been removed from compulsory school-level mathematics in England (although some exam boards may still use them as a representation of data already processed); however, I still think there is a place for them in pupil learning about data, particularly as they serve both

---

11 Go Teach Maths, Frequency Trees (n.d.). Available at: https://www.goteachmaths.co.uk/frequency-trees/.

as a way of processing and representing data. Pupils can learn about them as a way of being able to 'group' discrete data without losing the individual values that were recorded. Pupils should learn that a stem and leaf diagram separates numerical data into two parts, the 'stem' (which would match to an interval if we were grouping) and then the leaves (which are the remaining digits not involved in the stem). It will be worth showing several examples of these so that pupils understand the structure:

Stem	Leaf
2	3 4 6
3	2 4 6 7 8
4	2 3 3 4 6 7 9
5	0 3 6 7
6	0 3
7	1
8	2 7 9

2 | 3 = 23 years old

Stem	Leaf
13	6 9 9
14	2 3 3 3 3 4
14	6 7 7 8 9
15	1 3 4
15	6 7
16	2 4

Key: 13|6 means 136

3:26|65 represents a time of 3 minutes 26.65 seconds.

Stem	Leaf
3:26	65 87
3:27	51 85 87 94
3:28	46
3:29	08 29 40 43 78
3:30	28 45 46 50 66 78 84
3:31	
3:32	06

In terms of pupils creating stem and leaf diagrams, the most common issues arise from pupils struggling to create suitable stems. Pupils should build up to this, first sorting data into pre-drawn stem and leaf diagrams:[12]

Complete an ordered stem and leaf diagram for the data below:

56 75 62 56 78 67 56 75 73 54 62 53 95 76 87 78 89 78
65 56 76 77 65 78 88 54 51 51 73 62 105 65 79 80 70 70

5	
6	
7	
8	
9	
10	

Key: 9 | 2 represents

Once pupils have worked with pre-drawn stems, we can then offer pupils the opportunity to construct stems for data as a separate exercise. The Beacon Learning Center has a

---

12 S. Gokarakonda,, S2f – Stem and Leaf Diagrams, *Boss Maths* (n.d.). Available at: https://www.bossmaths.com/s2f/.

worksheet on stem and leaf diagrams that includes questions on this;[13] but it is easy enough to take data that pupils would normally be asked to sort into a stem and leaf diagram and ask pupils just to create the stem. In addition, we can offer pupils a blank stem to sort data into; Math Worksheets 4 Kids has a worksheet where the structure of the stem and leaf diagram is pre-drawn, but pupils have to create the stem and then the leaves for themselves.[14]

This can then lead to pupils having to construct the entire stem and leaf diagram from scratch.[15]

Here are the times, in minutes, taken to solve a puzzle.

| 5 | 10 | 15 | 12 | 8 | 7 | 20 | 35 | 24 | 15 |
| 20 | 33 | 15 | 24 | 10 | 8 | 10 | 20 | 16 | 10 |

In the space below, draw a stem and leaf diagram to show these times.

---

13 Beacon Learning Center, Stem and Leaf Plots (2003). Available at: http://www.beaconlearningcenter.com/documents/1600_01.pdf.
14 Math Worksheets 4 Kids, Stem-and-leaf Plots Worksheets (n.d.). Available at: https://www.mathworksheets4kids.com/stem-leaf.php.
15 J. Yusuf, Edexcel GCSE Mathematics (Linear) – 1MA0 Stem & Leaf Diagrams, *Maths Genie* (n.d.). Available at: https://www.mathsgenie.co.uk/resources/49_stem-and-leaf.pdf.

Another nice thing to offer pupils, highlighted by Jo Morgan, is to look at whether data is suitable for the creation of a stem and lead diagram at all. Jo has created a nice activity that provides pupils with different data sets in different formats and asks pupils to choose which would be suitable:[16]

1. Decide which of these data sets could be represented by a stem and leaf diagram.

A. Marks in a science test
56, 56, 5 7, 62, 63, 70, 78, 79, 79, 80, 83, 85, 88, 89, 91, 95, 96, 99, 100, 100

B. Number of siblings of my classmates
1, 1, 1, 1, 2, 0, 5, 4, 1, 1, 2, 2, 3, 0, 0, 1, 2, 1, 1, 1, 3, 0

C Favourite colours
Red
Blue
Red
Red
Yellow
Pink
Purple
Red
Yellow
White
Blue
Red

D. Takings from stalls at the summer fair
£124
£100
£131
£130
£105
£110
£120
£126
£130
£132
£140

E. Heights of my friends

Height (cm)	Frequency
164 • 166	2
166 • 168	5
168-170	4
170 -172	2

F. Time (in seconds) taken to run 100 m
15.3 15.2 15.2 4.3
12.8 15.3 14.4 16.5
16.0 16.6 15.9 15.8
12.5 12.4 18.1 13.8
16.6 15.7 14.2 13.9
13.2 13.4 13.5 14.0

Once pupils understand the structure of a stem and leaf diagram, we can highlight its dual role, both for processing data and also in representing data; in particular, the similar nature to a frequency diagram with the same insight into distribution that this representation offers.

For example, in this stem and leaf diagram pupils should see that, because the leaves are nicely in line, the number of leaves acts like the length of a bar (or the symbols in a pictogram) allowing us to see the distribution of the data over the different 'stem' groups (in this case, a slight positive skew).

Stem	Leaf						
2	3	4	6				
3	2	4	6	7	8		
4	2	3	3	4	6	7	9
5	0	3	6	7			
6	0	3					
7	1						
8	2	7	9				

2 | 3 = 23 years old

---

16 J. Morgan, Long Live Stem and Leaf, *Resourceaholic* [blog] (25 July 2014). Available at: https://www.resourceaholic.com/2014/07/stem-and-leaf.html.

We can interweave knowledge of things like percentages and probability again with stem and leaf diagrams (as with most other processed data), asking questions like, 'What percentage of people are older than 60?' or, 'What is the probability that a person chosen at random is younger than 30?'

Not only does a stem and leaf diagram serve both as a way of processing data and as a representation of data, but because the representation still retains all of the original data values, it is also a representation that allows for relatively straightforward analysis, as we will see.

Concept: data analysis and interpretation

Prerequisites: Number, types of data, addition, subtraction, multiplication, division.

Linked concepts: Data planning, data collection, data processing, data representation, proportion, percentage, probability.

The final step in working with data is analysing the processed and represented data, and then interpreting the findings. This is where we attempt to answer the question that prompted the initial data planning and collection. There are several different aspects of the data we might analyse that might help with interpretation, starting simply with examining the most frequent member of the data set, which pupils should know as the mode.

Subconcept: mode/modal

Pupils should understand mode as the name given to the most frequent item in a set of data. Pupils should be able to identify the mode from a list of data, as well as from many different representations.

Find the mode in each of the following:

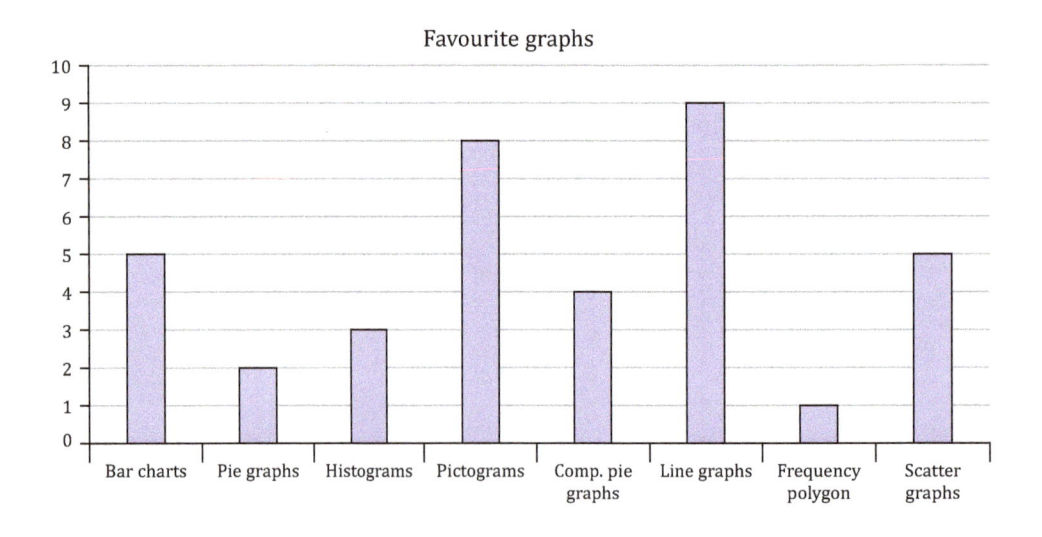

Favourite graphs

Graph type	Count
Bar charts	5
Pie graphs	2
Histograms	3
Pictograms	8
Comp. pie graphs	4
Line graphs	9
Frequency polygon	1
Scatter graphs	5

Favourite sports

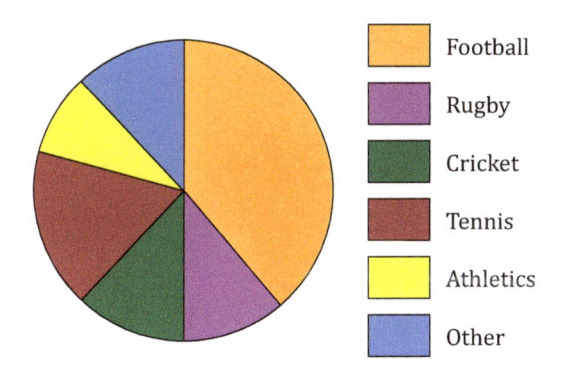

Children absent for a term

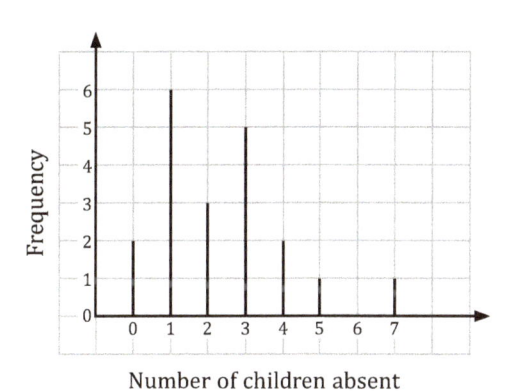

Shoe size

Size	Tally marks	Frequency
4				2
5	ՀԱՄ	5
6						4
7						4
8	ՀԱՄ		6
9	ՀԱՄ ||	7
Total		28

The frequency table is particularly important as pupils will often make mistakes in reading it, meaning they mistake the mode (particularly if mode is introduced as 'most common' rather than 'most frequent'). For example, in the above table, pupils may mistakenly identify 4 as the mode (it appears twice in the frequency column) and also 7 may be misidentified as the mode (it is the largest value in the frequency column).

Pupils should link the idea of mode to that of popularity, recognising that one of the things that mode indicates is most popular selection from a group of options. However, it should also be made clear to pupils that the mode does not indicate that 'most of the data have a particular value; 'most' implies more than half, but clearly, in the case above, much less than half the people have a shoe size of 9. In addition, pupils should be introduced to situations that are bi- or multi-modal, as well as situations where there is no mode (including situations where it might appear there is a mode, but there isn't):

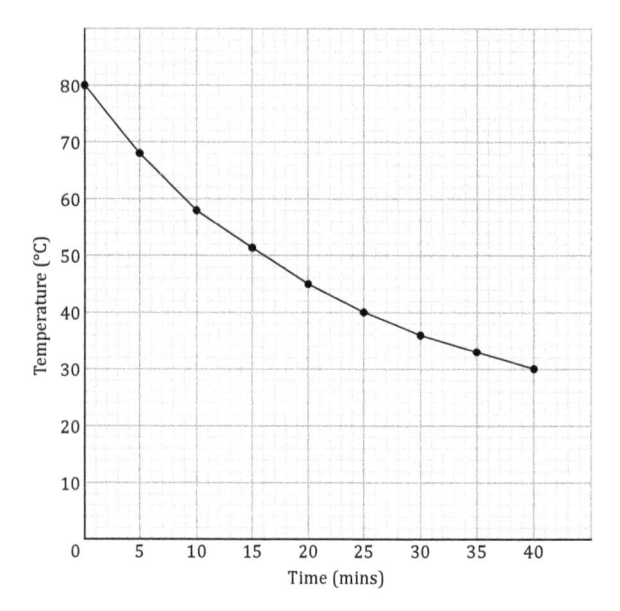

Pupils in this situation may think that 80°C is the mode; whereas there is no mode in this case because each data value is different. This often happens when pupils have identified mode or modal class from frequency diagrams where the physical height of the highest point does indicate mode or modal class.

On the subject of modal class, pupils will need to understand this, and how it is different to mode. A nice way to introduce this is to offer an opportunity for pupils to engage with mistaken reasoning:

The table shows some information about the weights, in kg, of 102 boxes.

Weight of box, w (kg)	Frequency
$0 < w \leq 4$	11
$4 < w \leq 8$	16
$8 < w \leq 12$	29
$12 < w \leq 16$	26
$16 < w \leq 20$	20

Jack is looking at the weight of different boxes in the table. Jack says, 'The mode weight is between 8 and 12 kg.' Explain why Jack is wrong.

This allows us to highlight the difference between 'mode' and 'modal class' as well as making clear that it isn't possible to identify the mode when data are grouped.

Pupils should also identify modal class from representations of grouped data, including frequency diagrams, frequency polygons and histograms. A particular focus should be given to frequency polygons, as it is easy to forget that these are plotted from grouped data. For example, in the frequency polygon below, pupils might mistakenly think the mode is 15 kg, rather than the modal class being 15 to 20 kg.

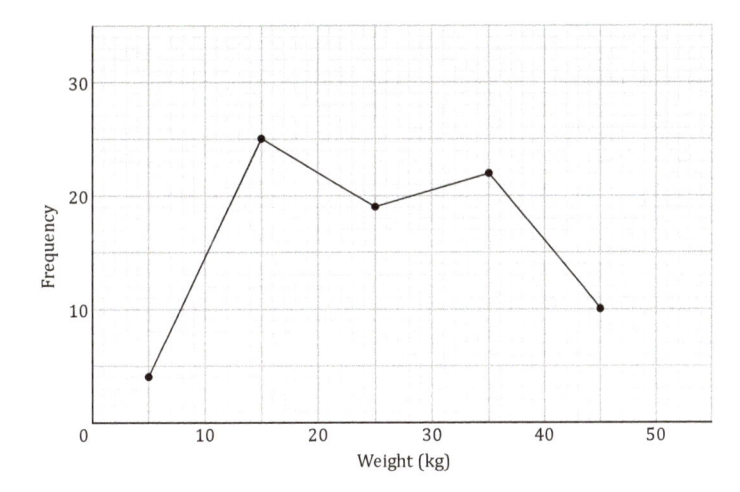

Having examined the idea of 'most frequent', the next idea we will look at is 'middle'.

Subconcept: median

The idea of 'middle' is, perhaps, one that deserves more attention than it might first appear, particularly in its similarity and difference to 'halfway'. A nice way to illustrate this is to examine the question, 'What is half of 5?' and 'Which object is in the middle when 5 objects are arranged in a line?' The difference in the answers to these two questions takes us back to the difference between discrete and continuous: half of 5 being 2.5 considers distance from 0 on a continuous scale, whilst the middle of 5 objects clearly takes the discrete view of the values, with the result being 3 because of the lack of the 'zeroth' object.

Pupils should see the 'median' as synonymous with this idea of 'middle' when values are placed in numerical order. Pupils will start by ordering and identifying the median of small lists with an odd number of values, both with lists ordered from least to greatest value and from greatest to least value, as well as lists that are unordered (and therefore, that pupils have to order). With small lists we should be encouraging direct identification of the middle value, rather than any particular process (which should be possible with single-digit list lengths).

We can then prompt a discussion about a list with an even number of values, asking pupils to suggest potential ideas for how we resolve the situation of not having a single middle value. This will lead to the idea of using the number halfway between the two middle values as the median. Again, this should start with small lists of numbers, where the two middle numbers are close together, so that both the position of the median and its value can be identified by simple number sense and recognition:

Find the median of 10, 12, 17, 11, 14, 20, 21, 11.

When reordered (from least to greatest value) this produces the list 10, 11, 11, 12, 14, 17, 20, 21, which has a (hopefully) clear median of 13. The purpose at this point is for pupils to get a good sense of what median is before introducing any more sophisticated techniques required to find it.

The first of these should be finding a median for a list with an even number of values where the halfway value is not straightforward to identify. Once pupils have a good concept of median in simple cases, we can offer something like this:

Find the median of 66, 67, 72, 93, 100, 101.

Pupils can then consider how we will find the value halfway between 72 and 93. The strategy pupils will generally naturally come up with is to subtract the smaller value from the larger, find half of this difference, and then add this to the smaller (or subtract from the larger). It is worth continuing the discussion here, showing how this approach is equivalent to the more efficient approach of summing the two values and then dividing the sum by 2. Diagrams like the one below may be useful, provided pupils are used to representing numbers as bars:

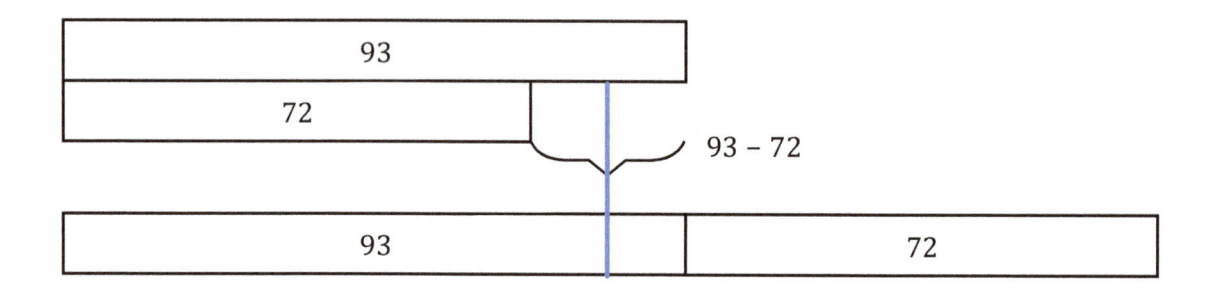

Pupils should work with problems like this; they represent an excellent opportunity to interweave skills around decimal and fraction calculations whilst simultaneously practising calculating median values.

The next step in exploration of median is to expand the size of the list to make it more difficult to identify the position of the median directly, and prompt pupils to have to consider how we can identify the position of the median, again with an odd number of values. It might be worth revisiting the position of median for small lists, to see if pupils can generalise a rule from those things they already know:

Number in list	Median position	Representation
3	2nd	
5	3rd	
7	4th	
9	5th	

As a minimum, pupils should recognise from this that it is not just simply a case of taking the number of values in the list and dividing by 2, but may spot that if they do this and then add $\frac{1}{2}$, this gives the median position. Algebraically, we can then demonstrate that this is equivalent to adding 1 and then dividing by 2: $\frac{n}{2} + \frac{1}{2} = \frac{n+1}{2}$. Alternatively, we might choose to highlight the $\frac{n+1}{2}$ calculation directly, using similar logic to earlier that because we are starting from the 1st object rather than the 0th object, we are wanting to find the halfway point between the 1st and the nth value, and so we use the same calculation of summing and dividing by 2 to find the halfway point.

This is an important thing for pupils to recognise, and it is worth spending time practising with this explicitly. We can start by simply telling pupils how many values there are in the list:

Copy and complete

Number of data points	Position of median
15	
33	
81	
105	
399	
615	
877	

before simply giving lists so that pupils have to count how many values there are. We can then bring in lists with an even number of data points, so that we can discuss with pupils how we interpret having a decimal position – for example, with 64 numbers in a list, the median is in the $\frac{1+64}{2}$ = 32.5th position. Pupils are generally quite accepting of the idea that this is indicating the value halfway between the 32nd and 33rd number in the list, particularly if they are already used to this for lists with an even number of values. Following this, we can offer pupils the opportunity to put all of this together and find the median for relatively large lists of numbers (up to about 30 numbers or so).

Once pupils are comfortable with the idea of finding the median from a reasonably sized list, we can discuss what would happen with very large lists, and the fact that they would be subject to more processing. This is the opportunity to interweave knowledge of how discrete numerical data is processed (or rounded continuous data), focusing on either a stem and leaf diagram or a (grouped) frequency table. Of the two, the better one to explore first is a stem and leaf diagram.

Provided pupils have seen and worked with stem and leaf diagrams before now, we can offer an example and talk about how to identify where the median is, and consequently what the median value is, using the same calculations we have previously used:

As part of their job, taxi drivers record the number of miles they travel each day. A random sample of the mileages recorded by taxi drivers Keith and Asif are summarised in the back-to-back stem and leaf diagram below.

	Keith											Asif					
		8	7	7	4	3	2	1	1	0	18	4	4	5	7		
9	9	8	7	6	5	4	3	3	1	1	19	5	7	8	9	9	
					8	7	4	2	2	0	20	0	2	2	4	4	8
					9	4	3	1	0	0	21	2	3	5	6	6	7	9
							6	4	1	1	22	1	1	2	4	5	5	8
									2	0	23	1	1	3	4	6	6	7	8
									7	1	24	2	4	8	9		
										9	25	4					
									9	3	26						

Key: 0 | 18 | 4 means 180 for Keith and 184 for Asif

In the back-to-back stem and leaf diagram above, identify the median for both Keith and Asif.

Pupils should work with a few different stem and leaf diagrams to find the median, identifying the position of the median value and then counting through the stem and leaf diagram until they identify the middle value. This is invaluable practice for when we then turn our attention to frequency tables.

When it comes to frequency tables, pupils should recognise that the same approaches as we used for finding median from stem and leaf diagrams will continue to be useful. For example:

Number of absent students (i)	Tally	Frequency (f)
0	|||	3
1	卌 |	6
2	卌 ||||	9
3	卌 ||||	9
4	卌 卌	10
5	||	2
6	|	1

1. By counting the number of data values in each row, we can work out the total number of values (in this case, 40).

2. This means we can work out the position of the median using the same calculation as previously ($\frac{1+40}{2}$ = 20.5 = halfway between the 20th and 21st value).

3. We can then count forward (or backwards) through the values until we find the required middle value(s): (in this case, both the 20th and 21st value are both 3).

Some pupils find it useful to examine frequency tables alongside the list of data that would produce the frequency table, so they can see how the process works in parallel to that which they are already familiar with:

0, 0, 0, 1, 1, 1, 1, 1, 1, 2, 2, 2, 2, 2, 2, 2, 2, 3, 3, 3, 3, 3, 3, 3, 3, 3, 3, 4, 4, 4, 4, 4, 4, 4, 4, 4, 4, 5, 5, 6

median = 3

We can also create a 'stem and leaf' style diagram that shows the same data, and allows insight into how the processes for identifying median in a stem and leaf diagram and a frequency table are equivalent:

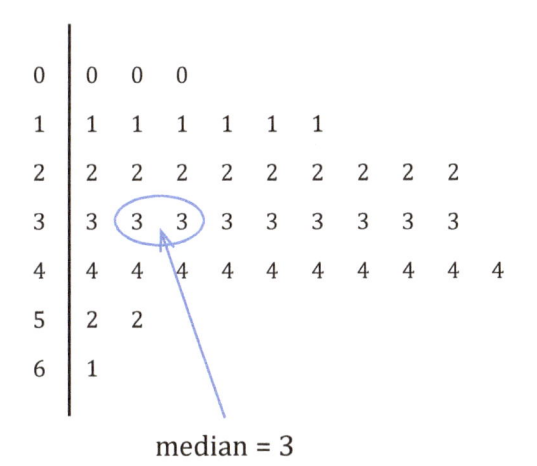

0	0 0 0
1	1 1 1 1 1 1
2	2 2 2 2 2 2 2 2 2
3	3 3 3 3 3 3 3 3 3
4	4 4 4 4 4 4 4 4 4 4
5	2 2
6	1

median = 3

Having examined median for discrete frequency tables, the next natural step is to consider grouped frequency tables. Pupils should recognise that, because the data is grouped, the process outlined above will identify the class that the median is in but will not actually give a value for the median as we do not know what the actual values are. This leads to the conclusion that we will only be able to estimate the median, not identify its true value. We can then introduce pupils to two possible approaches to creating this estimate:

1. The use of a cumulative frequency graph to estimate the median.

2. Using a proportional approach to estimate the median.

With the first approach, pupils should understand the links between cumulative frequency and median, in that working out cumulative frequency leads to knowing the total number of data values, which is the first step in working out the position of the median.

This cumulative frequency graph shows information about the heights of rowers at a rowing club:

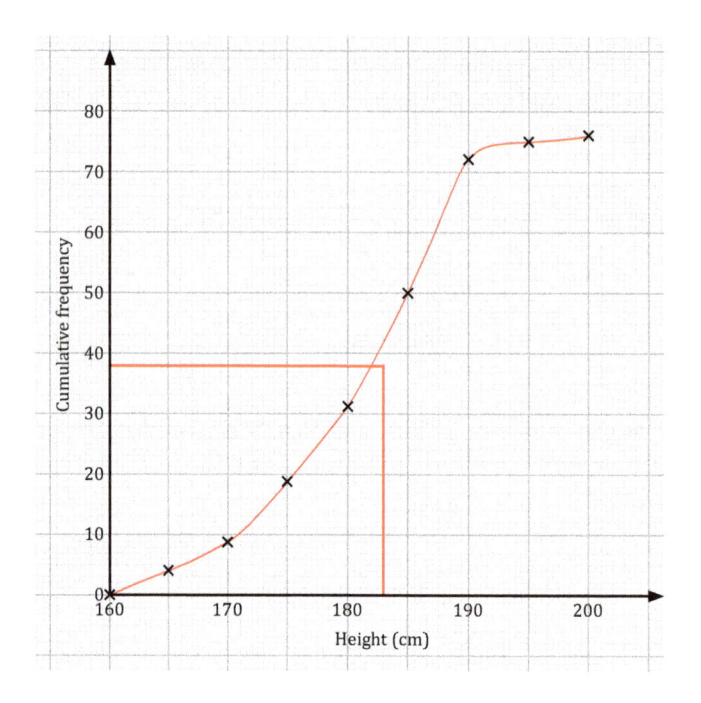

Pupils may (rightly) question why we are now just dividing by 2, rather than adding 1 and then dividing by 2. This is because the scale for cumulative frequency does start at 0, and so we are treating the frequencies as continuous rather than discrete; we are finding the point halfway between 0 and n (76 in this case) rather than between 1 and n.

Pupils should work with different cumulative frequency graphs to estimate the median, and can interweave the creation of cumulative graphs in order to estimate the median, starting with a grouped frequency table, drawing the cumulative frequency graph and then estimating the median.

We can then turn our attention to estimating the median directly from a grouped frequency table. Pupils should already know how to identify the interval that the median is in using the same techniques as for ordinary frequency tables:

Data handling

Weight of box, w (kg)	Frequency
0 < w ≤ 4	11
4 < w ≤ 8	16
8 < w ≤ 12	29
12 < w ≤ 16	26
16 < w ≤ 20	20

1. There are 102 boxes in the table, so the position of the median is $\frac{1+102}{2}$ = 51.5th, i.e. halfway between the 51st and 52nd value.

2. The 51st and 52nd value are both in interval 8 < w ≤ 12, so the median must lie in this interval.

From here we can take it further and look at how far into the interval the median is. In this case, the first 27 boxes are less than 8 kg, so the 51.5th value is a further 24.5 numbers into the 8 to 12 class. We can then use a proportional argument to work out the likely value of the median:

Frequency	Width of class
29	4
24.5	

From here pupils can use their normal proportional strategies to work out how far into the class the median is likely to be (in this case, 3.38 kg) and so a good estimate of the median is 8 + 3.38 = 11.38 kg.

Of course, pupils could approach this from the other end, saying that the median is 4.5 values from the upper end of the 8 to 12 group, leading to being 0.62 kg from the upper end of the class interval, leading to the estimate being 12 − 0.62 = 11.38 kg. Clearly, this is an excellent place to interweave proportional reasoning alongside knowledge and understanding of median.

In addition to the representations examined, pupils should also work with other representations to find the median. In particular, pupils can be offered vertical line graphs and frequency diagrams/polygons or histograms to find the median from; this will generally be recreating the frequency table or grouped frequency table first.

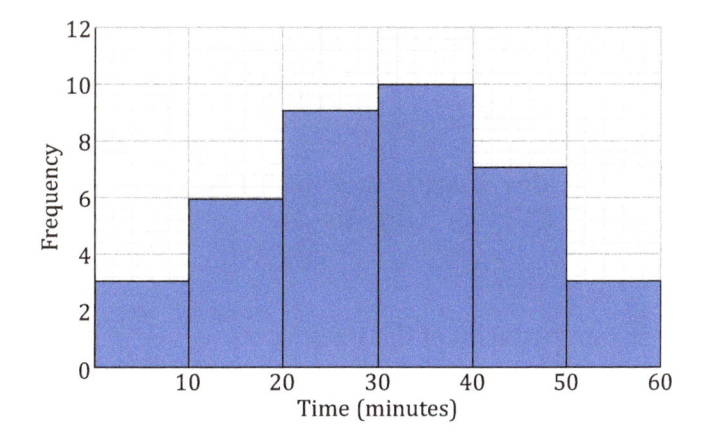

Time, t (minutes)	Frequency
0 ≤ t < 10	3
10 ≤ t < 20	6
20 ≤ t < 30	9
30 ≤ t < 40	10
40 ≤ t < 50	7
50 ≤ t < 60	5

Having examined mode and median, clearly the next idea we will want to examine is mean.

Subconcept: mean

The idea of mean is one that often attracts one of the most ingrained misconceptions across all of the ideas that pupils study. Overwhelmingly, when asked about 'mean' pupils will parrot a line of, 'Add them all up and divide by how many there are'. Not only is this a calculation strategy rather than an insight into what the idea of mean is, it is a calculation strategy that only works in very specific circumstances – namely with a list of raw data. Part of the reason this misconception arises is because, oft times, all of pupils' early experiences of mean are finding mean from raw lists of data, and so this strategy becomes synonymous with the idea.

A much better way to introduce mean to pupils to introduce the idea of 'equalling out'. For example:

Rearrange the squares so that each tower is the same height.

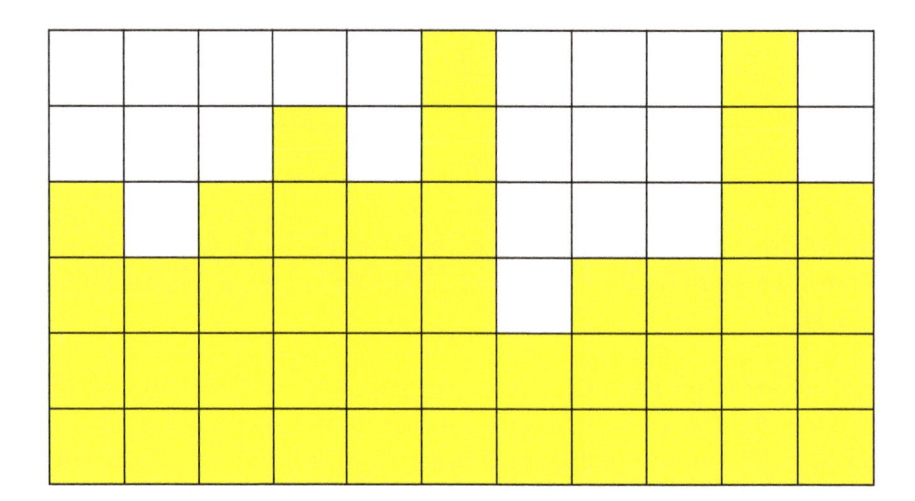

This is something pupils could actually do physically using Multilink cubes or counters rather than just pictorially (or using virtual manipulatives if physical manipulatives aren't available). This is the core idea of 'mean' that we want pupils to have – the idea of equalling out different values.

Pupils should be encouraged to use their own strategies for this, talking about how they are approaching the problem and, importantly, how we can generalise approaches so that we have strategies that can be applied no matter what the numbers or how many numbers there are. This leads to the standard 'find the total and share equally' (a much better phrase than 'add them all up and divide by how many there are').

When pupils are first using this strategy, a good idea is not to start with lists of raw data where pupils have to add to find the total but rather with the total either directly provided:

A list of 8 numbers has a total of 82. Work out the mean of the 8 numbers.

or in scenarios where the total is provided:

Find the mean weight of (a) an apple and (b) a lollipop.

We should also offer pupils the opportunity to manipulate this strategy:

The mean of 8 numbers is 4.2. Work out the total of the 8 numbers.

A list of numbers has a mean of 9 and a total of 117. How many numbers are there?

Only once pupils have a real understanding of the relationship between mean, total, and number of data items, then we can explore combining this with different ways of finding the total. This can include finding the total from a raw list:

Find the mean of 7, 9, 5, 8, 4, 6, 12, 5.

And further developing reasoning and problem-solving approaches with mean:

A list of 5 numbers has a mean of 9. If four of the numbers are 5, 7, 8 and 11, find the fifth number.

A list of 4 numbers has a mean of 35. When we add a fifth number, the mean drops to 32. Find the fifth number.

We can also interweave working with different representations:

Find the mean temperature.

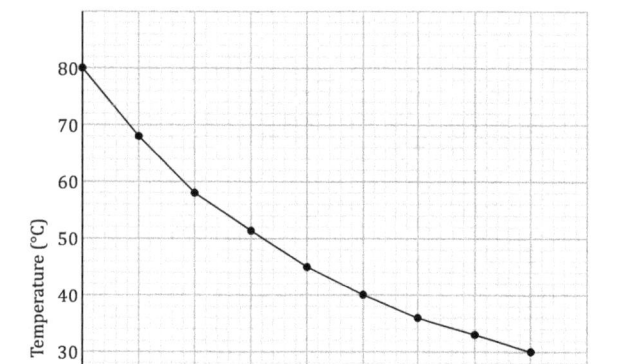

Find the mean percentage.

Stem	Leaf
5	6
6	7, 7, 9
7	2, 4, 7, 7, 8
8	1, 2, 2, 3, 4, 8
9	0, 2, 3, 4

Key: 5|6 = 56%

Including frequency tables:

Find the mean number of absent students.

Number of absent students (i)	Tally	Frequency (f_i)
0	III	3
1	ꟻꟻꟻꟻ I	6
2	ꟻꟻꟻꟻ IIII	9
3	ꟻꟻꟻꟻ IIII	9
4	ꟻꟻꟻꟻ ꟻꟻꟻꟻ	10
5	II	2
6	I	1

This is where pupils who are stuck with an idea of 'add them all up and divide by how many there are' first tend to run into problems – a classic mistake here is for pupils to add up the frequencies and then divide by 7 because there are 7 rows. However, if pupils understand that we are sharing a total, then they can see that the total number of absent students is found by calculating $0 \times 3 + 1 \times 6 + 2 \times 9 + 3 \times 9 + 4 \times 10 + 5 \times 2 + 6 \times 1 = 107$ absences, which will then need to be shared between all of the days recorded (found by summing the frequencies – in this case, 40).

The same logic also helps finding the mean from a vertical line chart:

Find the mean number of times that the teenager is reminded.

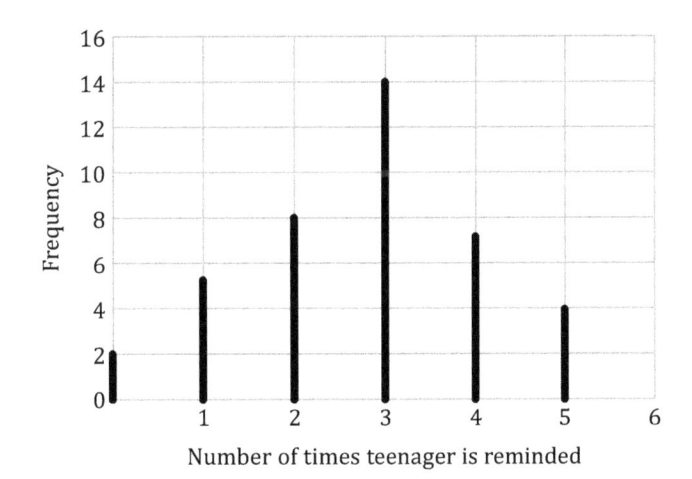

Similarly to learning about median, when it comes to grouped frequency data, pupils should recognise that we won't be able to find the exact value of the mean. However, we can get a reasonable estimate of the mean by assuming that every data value is in the midpoint of the class. For example:

Weight of box, w (kg)	Frequency
$0 < w \leq 4$	11
$4 < w \leq 8$	16
$8 < w \leq 12$	29
$12 < w \leq 16$	26
$16 < w \leq 20$	20

With the weight of these boxes, we want pupils to understand that if we assume that each of the 11 boxes in the 0 to 4 class weighs 2 kg (2 being halfway between 0 and 4) then we can estimate that the total weight is approximately 22 kg for those boxes. In reality, of course, some of those 11 boxes will be less than 2 kg and some will be more, but in effect we are suggesting that these effects will equal out – indeed that the mean of these 11 boxes is 2 kg per box. Pupils should understand that this sort of assumption, applied across all the rows in the grouped frequency table, will allow for an estimate of the total weight, which in turn leads to an estimate of the mean. Pupils may well then understand that this estimate will be better when all classes have a reasonable number of people or objects in, as the mean value being near the midpoint is more likely if there are more values in the class.

Again there are opportunities for reasoning/problem-solving that we can offer to pupils:[17]

Work out the value of a:

Score	Freq
3	1
4	a
5	5
6	2
7	4

Mean score = 5.0

A record of a school survey got torn.

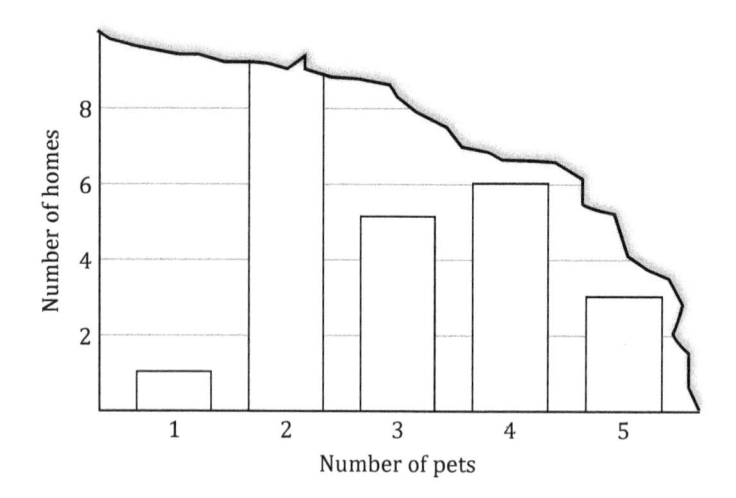

It is known that the mean number of pets per home = 3.

How many homes were there with 2 pets?

This information is about the number of books read by some people in a period of time:

Number of books	Frequency
0 – 4	16
5 – 9	?
10 – 14	20
15 – 19	10

The frequency for the 5–9 group was lost, but the estimated mean was recorded as being 8.5.

Work out the missing frequency.

---

17 D. Steward, Mean of a Frequency Distribution, with Algebra, *Median* [blog] (2 March 2017). Available at: https://donsteward.blogspot.com/2017/03/mean-of-frequency-distribution-with.html.

We can also interweave ideas around upper and lower bounds for measures:

Find the minimum/maximum possible value of the mean weight per box.

Weight of box, w (kg)	Frequency
$0 < w \leq 4$	11
$4 < w \leq 8$	16
$8 < w \leq 12$	29
$12 < w \leq 16$	26
$16 < w \leq 20$	20

And again we can offer different representations for pupils to engage with; frequency polygons are relatively straightforward to access directly, as the frequencies are plotted at the midpoints, so finding the estimated totals for each group is more straightforward:

Find an estimate of the mean weight:

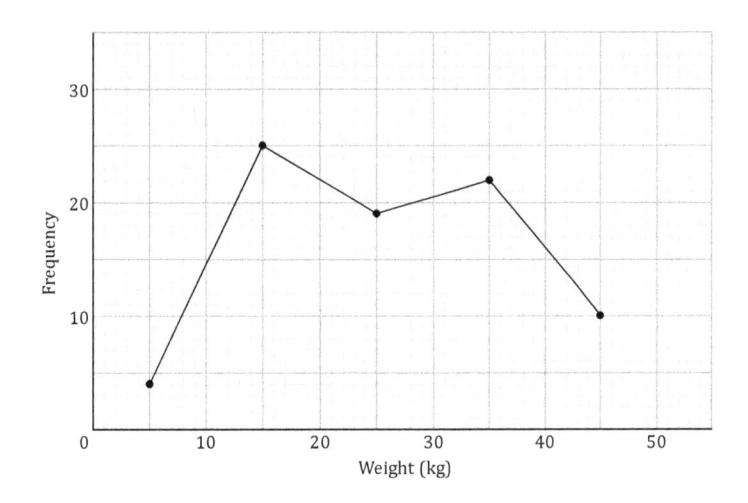

whereas pupils will likely be using cumulative frequency graphs or histograms to basically recreate the frequency table (or at least the normal information contained within it) prior to estimating the mean:

Find an estimate of the mean percentage:

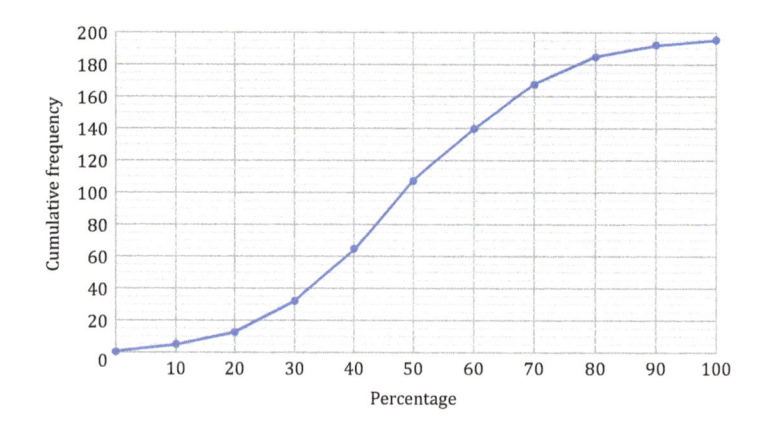

Find an estimate of the mean call length:

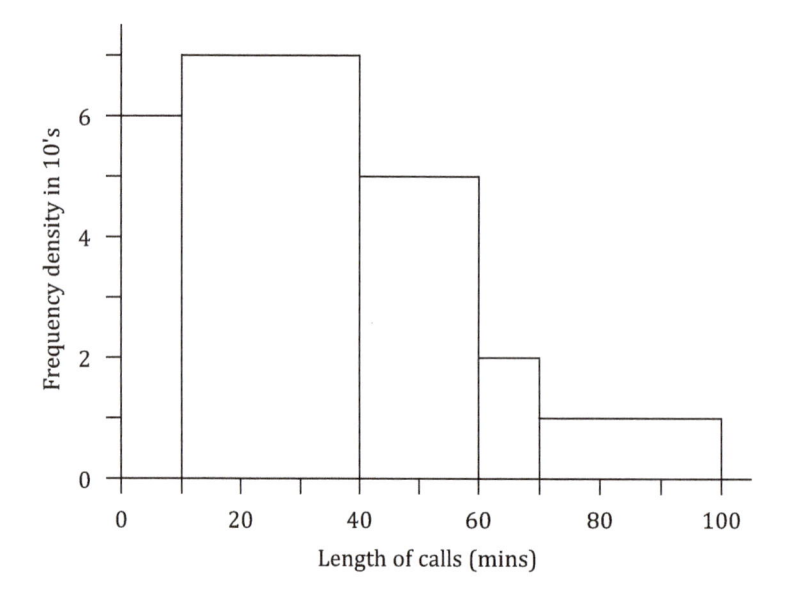

All of these approaches come from the 'total shared' strategy based on 'equalling out' the data values. An alternative but important way of making sense of the mean is as a balance point:

Find the mean of the list 2, 2, 2, 3, 3, 4, 5, 7, 8.

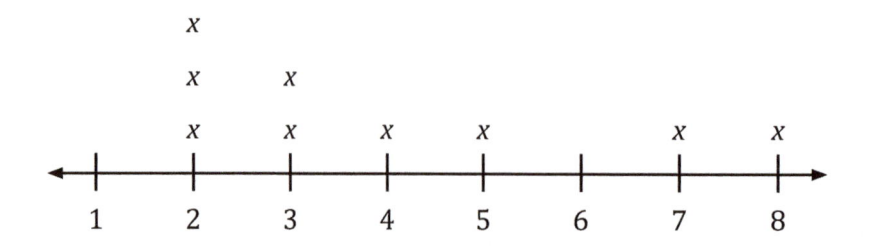

Here we see the numbers represented as on a number line. The follow-up question we can ask pupils is, 'If we placed equal sized weights in each place, where would we have to place a pivot so that the line balanced?' (Alternatively, we could place a weight of 3 at two, a weight of 2 at three, and weights of 1 at 4, 5, 7 and 8.) Pupils should understand that the mean is the point where the pivot would go, and that the distances between the balance point and the points greater than the balance point are equal to the distances between the balance point and the points less than the balance point.

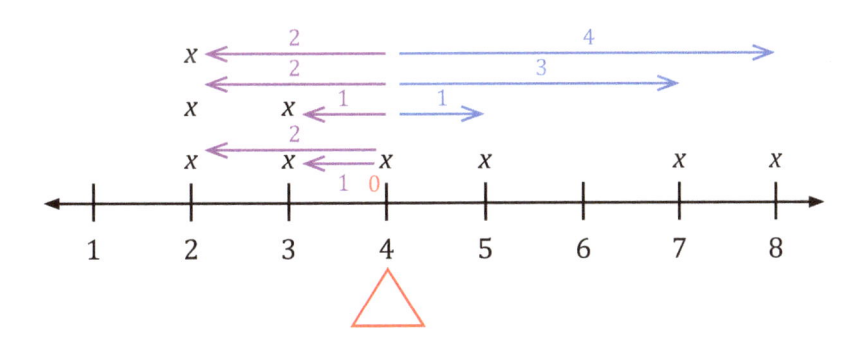

In this case, 2 + 2 + 1 + 2 + 1 = 1 + 3 + 4.

Although the idea of mean as a balance point doesn't automatically seem useful for calculating mean, one aspect of mean that this representation does highlight is the reason why mean is affected by the shape of the distribution:

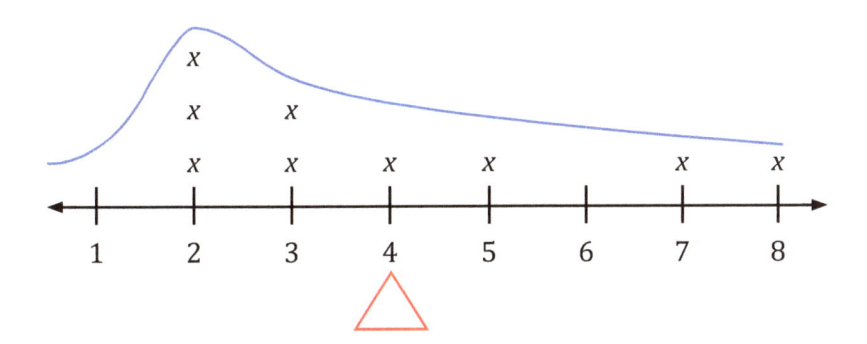

Pupils can use the idea of mean as a balance point, even approximately, to help see how mean is going to relate the other values.

So far we have talked about mode, median and mean, but we have not yet mentioned the idea of average. We will now consider how this idea relates to the other data analysis concepts we have seen so far.

Subconcept: average

There is much debate as to whether mode, median and mean are synonymous with average or not. Personally, I think they probably started out that way, but I think there is a case for them to be considered as concepts in their own right (as they have been laid out above), at least as mathematical ideas. I do accept two arguments, however:

1   The utility of mode, median and mean outside of the concept of average is somewhat lacking; yes, they can be found for lists of numbers (and in the case of mode, items),

but there is little purpose to finding them outside of their usage as an average measure.

2   As average measures, there is still little point in calculating mode, median or mean unless there is a context behind them; a reason for wanting to measure the average of a particular scenario.

That is not to say that I believe the examination of mode, median and mean as separate concepts is completely without merit; there can be insights gained in each idea by studying them outside of any context or link to the idea of average. This being said, the goal with each of these concepts must be to tie them to concept of average.

Although we will want to link average to mode, median and mean, this is not (for me) the best place to start with the study of average. Pupils will almost certainly have pre-conceived notions of 'average' that can be used that will centre around 'normalness' or 'typicality'. We can steer this towards the term we will want pupils to use, which is 'representative'. A good definition for 'average' is a single object or value which is representative of the entire data set, rather than at the extremes. Before we introduce formal measures of average, we can offer pupils questions like the one below to reinforce the idea of 'representative':

What is the average age of the children in this nursery room?

3, 3, 3, 3, 3, 3, 3, 3, 4, 4, 4, 4, 4, 4, 4, 4, 4, 4, 4, 4, 4, 4, 4, 4, 4, 5, 15.

What is the average number of chocolate buttons per packet?

29, 29, 30, 30, 30, 30, 30, 30, 30, 30, 31, 31, 32, 33

Pupils should be quite happy that the average age in the nursery room is around 4, with the 3-year-olds probably reasonably close to turning 4 and the 5-year-old possibly just having turned 5 (the 15-year-old is a child on work experience). Similarly, the average number of buttons is clearly 30 or so.

These informal estimations of average are important, as they can continue to be encouraged to ensure pupils check that their calculated values (once we introduce measures of average) make sense within the context that they are set. They also help to reinforce what we are seeking when we ask about average and set the platform for us to turn our attention to how we might more systematically measure average, leading to the idea of mode, median and mean being suitable ways to measure average (provided pupils have already studied them) dependent on the context. Pupils should be able to quite quickly see how each of the mode, median and mean can act as suitable measures of average, and we can then turn our attention to situations and scenarios where each is more suitable than the other, and the general advantages and drawbacks of each as an average measure. Tristan Jones has produced a table[18] that summarises the advantages and disadvantages nicely.

Pupils should be offered data in different contexts and through different representations and asked to judge which of the three potential measures of average is most suitable for a given situation.

Jim records how many text messages he receives each day for 10 days.

3   0   1   4   1   4   6   1   20   0

---

[18] Tristanjones, Averages (Mode, Median, Mean) GCSE Revision, *TES* (20 January 2015). Available at: https://www.tes.com/teaching-resource/averages-mode-median-mean-gcse-revision-6161872.

a   Write down the mode of the data.

b   Work out the median.

c   What is the mean of the data?

d   Which of these averages better represents the data?

Explain your answer.

Here is the number of goals a hockey team scored in each of 10 matches.

Number of goals	Frequency
2	2
3	3
4	2
5	2
6	1

Find

a   the median

b   the mode

c   the mean

d   which average is most useful in analysing the performance of the team over the 10 matches.

Justify your answer.

As well as choosing suitable averages for different scenarios, we can also offer pupils the opportunity to reason/problem solve with the different average measures:

Three numbers have a mode of 4, a median of 4 and a mean of 3. Work out the three numbers.

Five numbers have mode and median of 2, a mean of 3 and a range of 4 (I know we are still to look at range). Work out the five numbers.

A basketball player has a mean of 36 points after 10 games. After the next game their mean has fallen to 35 points. How many points did they score in their next game?

Understanding 'average' as a representative value for a data set does not, however, give us the whole picture.

Subconcept: range

When we start to analyse performance using average, we might offer pupils a scenario such as:

> The list of numbers below shows the number of strikes scored by two bowlers in their last ten 10-pin bowling games, arranged in numerical order.
>
> Bowler A: 1, 2, 3, 4, 5, 6, 7, 8, 9, 10   Bowler B: 5, 5, 5, 5, 5, 6, 6, 6, 6, 6
>
> Who would you say is the better bowler?

Pupils will invariably highlight bowler B, and will use words like 'consistency' to justify their choice. However, if we look at average performance, both bowlers are identical (the medians and means for both bowlers are 5.5, and there is no mode in either case). So how do we capture and measure this idea that bowler B is more consistent that bowler A? This is where we can introduce pupils to the idea of range, and the use of range to indicate consistency. Pupils can be introduced to range as the difference between the greatest and smallest values in a set of data; and further to the idea that the range gives us a rudimentary measure of consistency – a smaller range indicates a smaller space in which all the data are contained, which indicates more consistent data.

Pupils should calculate range in different scenarios, and again from different representations:

Find the range of temperatures recorded:

Find the range of percentages recorded:

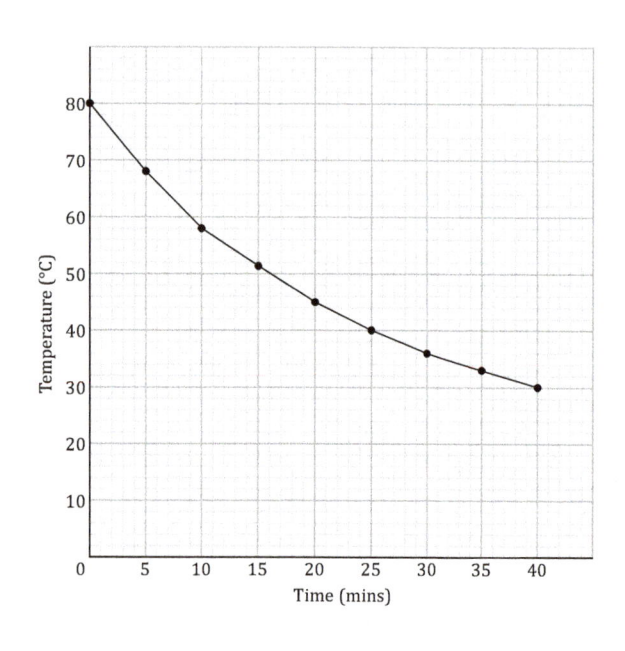

Stem	Leaf
5	6
6	7, 7, 9
7	2, 4, 7, 7, 8
8	1, 2, 2, 3, 4, 8
9	0, 2, 3, 4

Key: 5|6 = 56%

Find the range of goals scored:

Number of goals	Frequency
2	2
3	3
4	2
5	2
6	1

as well as solving the sorts of problems we saw earlier involving use of different average measures and range. However, it is important that 'range' is not conflated with the average measures – range is not a measure of average, and it should be studied sufficiently separately from mode, median and mean so as not to get confused with them.

As pupils study range, one of the things pupils should come to understand is that range is not a particularly good measure of consistency, due to the effect of skew or extreme values. Pupils could be offered scenarios that help make this apparent, such as this tweak on an earlier example:

The list of numbers below shows the number of strikes scored by two bowlers in their last ten 10-pin bowling games arranged in numerical order.

Bowler A: 1, 2, 3, 4, 5, 6, 7, 8, 9, 10   Bowler B: 1, 5, 5, 5, 5, 6, 6, 6, 6, 10

Who would you say is the better bowler?

In this case both bowlers have identical average measures but also identical ranges. Yet it should still be clear to pupils that bowler B is more consistent, except for the one poor game they had, and the one excellent game they had. This sort of scenario can highlight the disadvantage in using the range as a measure of consistency when there are extreme values or when there is skew. We can then introduce an alternative, through looking at quartiles.

Subconcepts: quartiles and interquartile range

Pupils are normally quite receptive to the idea of quartiles – being sufficiently familiar with the language of 'quarters' by this point to understand the relationship. What they may need to be reminded of is the strategy of finding a 'quarter', by finding half of a half. This is synonymous with the approach we take to identifying quartiles for raw data by first identifying the median.

A good place to start with this is with a list of 15 values. This allows for median and the two quartiles to be exact values in the data.

Find the median, lower quartile and upper quartile of this list of values:

$$3, 3, 4, \underset{\text{Lower quartile}}{\textcircled{5}}\ 5, 6, 6, \underset{\text{Median}}{\textcircled{7}}\ 8, 8, 9, \underset{\text{Upper quartile}}{\textcircled{9}}\ 10, 11, 11$$

We can then vary this list (or one similar) to offer pupils the chance to become comfortable with the idea.

Find the median, lower quartile and upper quartile of this list of values:

a   3, 3, 4, 5, 5, 6, 6, 7, 8, 8, 9, 9, 10, 11, 12

b   2, 3, 4, 5, 5, 6, 6, 7, 8, 8, 9, 9, 10, 11, 13

c   3, 4, 5, 5, 6, 6, 7, 8, 8, 9, 9, 10, 11, 12, 12

d   3, 4, 5, 5, 6, 6, 7, 8, 8, 9, 9, 10, 11, 12

e   4, 5, 5, 6, 6, 7, 8, 8, 9, 9, 10, 11, 12

f   4, 5, 5, 6, 6, 7, 8, 8, 9, 9, 10, 11

Pupils should also be given the opportunity to problem-solve with median and interquartile range:

Given the information about each set of data, find a possible missing whole number:

14 17 14 15 18 16 x Median = 15, Lower quartile = 14, Upper quartile = 17.

14 17 14 15 18 16 x Median = 16, Lower quartile = 14, Upper quartile = 18.

14 17 14 15 18 16 x Median = 16, Lower quartile = 14, Upper quartile = 17.

Once pupils understand the idea of quartiles and how to find them, then we can introduce the idea of the interquartile range and how it solves the problem of susceptibility to extreme values/skewing the range. By eliminating the data from the lowest and highest quarter, we are guaranteed to eliminate any extreme values, and then can concentrate on performance around the median (which we can take to be the representative value in this case). Pupils should understand this about interquartile range, as well as understanding that it measures consistency by looking at the spread of the middle 50% of the data: 25% either side of the median. Pupils should then go on from this to use their understanding of median and quartiles to draw box plots (as we saw in Chapter 13).

Once pupils are happy with the idea of finding median and quartiles from raw data, and using these to draw a box plot, then we can offer pupils the opportunity to find the same information from a cumulative frequency diagram:

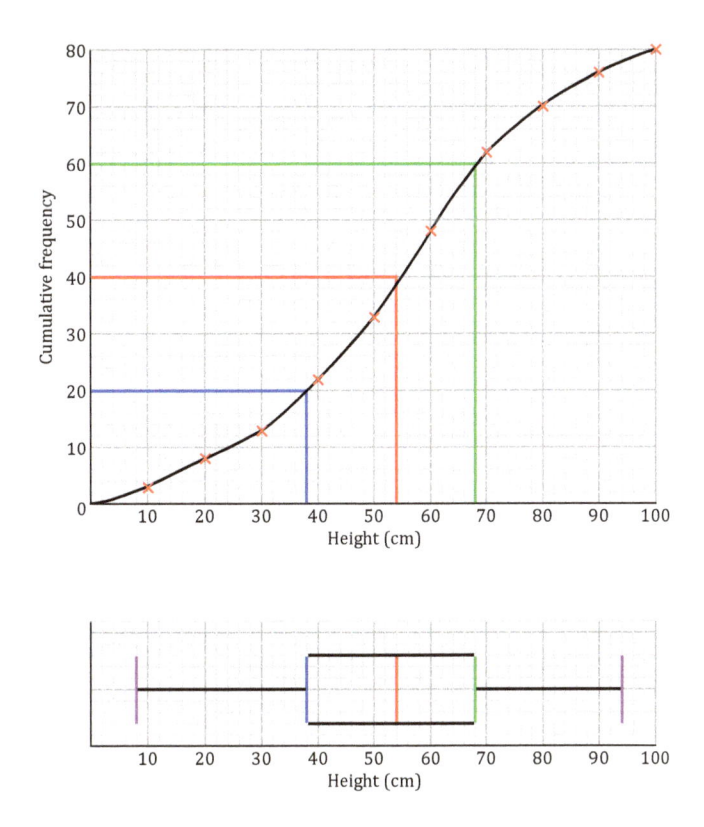

In understanding measures of average and consistency, pupils are developing the tools to compare distributions. When looking at different representations of data in Chapter 13, we looked at the insight into distributions that different charts could give, and now is the time where pupils should recognise what different distributions show and how they compare:

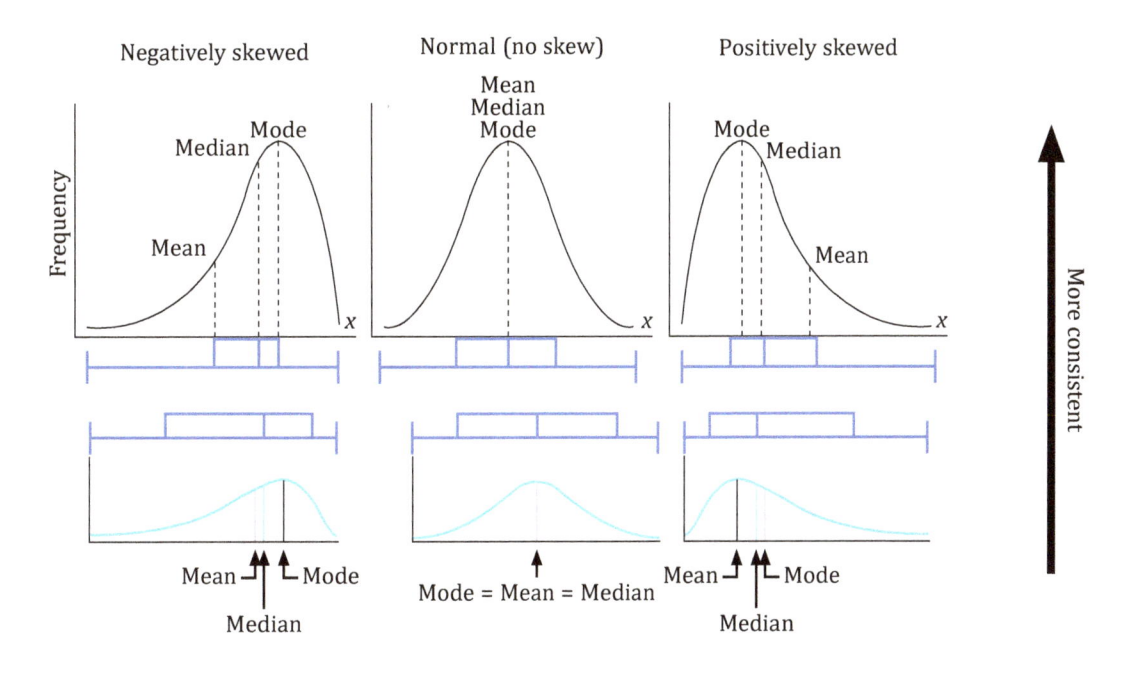

Pupils should learn that when comparing distributions, we tend to look at a suitable average measure, along with a measure of consistency. This might be comparing using summary statistics, such as a calculated mean and range:

| Zeeshan | 33 | 34 | 23 | 36 | 38 | 35 | 29 | 27 | 37 | 28 |
| Saqab | 30 | 33 | 25 | 26 | 30 | 32 | 26 | 27 | 33 | 28 |

Zeeshan and Saqab are cricketers. Above are the number of runs they scored in the last 10 matches.

a   Find the mean and range for each cricketer.

b   Compare their performance as cricketers.

Match the data set to the person, using the clues to help!

Person 1	12	15	20	13	Mean =	Range =
Person 2	13	9	14	12	Mean =	Range =
Person 3	15	10	13	14	Mean =	Range =
Person 4	16	13	11	8	Mean =	Range =
Person 5	12	9	11	12	Mean =	Range =
Person 6	16	15	17	16	Mean =	Range =

Andrea: I was as consistent as Chris, but scored better on average.

Ben: I got the lowest average, but at least I was consistent!

Chris: I had a mean score of 12, and a range of 5.

Danielle: I was the best on average, any way you look at it.

Eva: I scored the same as Chris on average, but wasn't as consistent.

Frank: I got the highest score! Shame I wasn't that good all the time.

or comparing representations:

56 boys and 52 girls took an English test.
The box plots show the distributions of their marks.

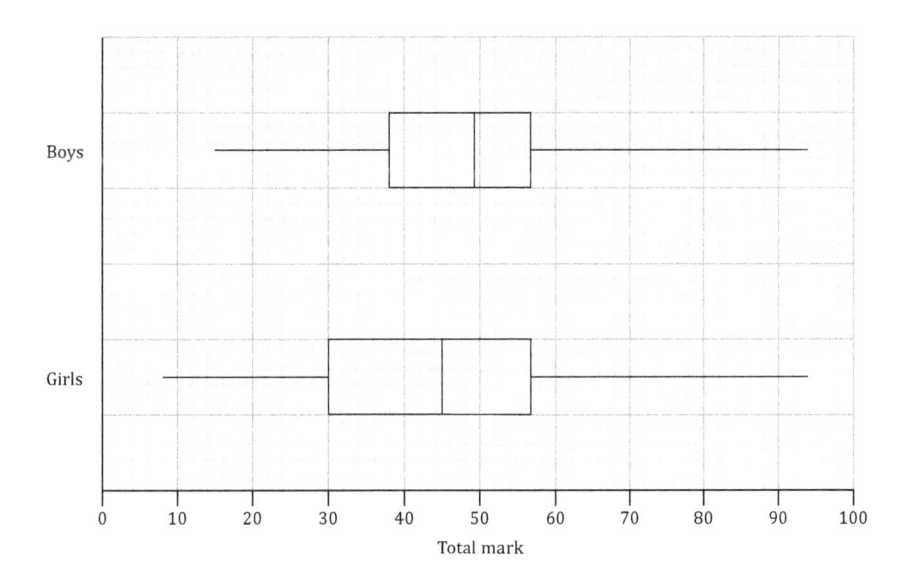

Give two differences between the boys' marks and the girls' marks.

As part of their job, taxi drivers record the number of miles they travel each day. A random sample of the mileages recorded by taxi drivers Keith and Asif are summarised in the back-to-back stem and leaf diagram below.

Keith											Asif							
		8	7	7	4	3	2	1	1	0	18	4	4	5	7			
9	9	8	7	6	5	4	3	3	1	1	19	5	7	8	9	9		
					8	7	4	2	2	0	20	0	2	2	4	4	8	
						9	4	3	1	0	21	2	3	5	6	6	7	9
								6	4	1	22	1	1	2	4	5	5	8
									2	0	23	1	1	3	4	6	6	7	8
									7	1	24	2	4	8	9			
										9	25	4						
									9	3	26							

Key: 0 | 18 | 4 means 180 for Keith and 184 for Asif

Compare the number of miles driven by both Keith and Atif.

And so, this concludes our examination of the concepts that make up compulsory school-level maths. My hope is that this work has helped teachers of mathematics gain insight into some of the connections they may not have appreciated in this past or seen some ways of helping pupils to see those connections they may not have made before. It is my sincere belief that if pupils can see these threads running through their mathematical learning, if they recognise the commonalities in what might have previously been seen as disparate ideas, then we can create a truly coherent curriculum that helps unfold the narrative of school-level maths in a way that will help more pupils learn about mathematics and not just 'to do' some isolated calculations.

Glossary

Algebraic number – A number that is the root of a finite polynomial whose coefficients (including the coefficient of x_0 – the constant term) are all rational numbers.

Area – The space occupied by a flat shape.

Array – Items arranged in rows and/or columns.

Base (place value) – The number of unique digits that are used to build numerals.

Commutative (law) – A property of elements in a set with respect to a given operation where combining the elements in either order produces the same result. For example, with addition of two numbers a and b, $a + b = b + a$.

Continuous – Being in immediate connection or spatial relationship; without cessation.

Dimension – The minimum number of ordinates required to specify a point within the space. For example, a line has one dimension as it only requires a single ordinate – e.g., the numbers on the number line.

Discrete – Defined only for an isolated set of points; apart or detached from others.

Distribution – An arrangement of values of a variable showing their observed or theoretical frequency of occurrence.

Distributive (law) – A property of a set on which two operations are defined (say + and ×) where two elements combined under the first operation $(a + b)$, with the result then combined with a third element under the second operation $(c \times (a + b))$ gives an equivalent result to combining each of the first two elements separately with the third under the second operation $(c \times a, c \times b)$ and then combining the results under the first operation $(c \times a + c \times b)$. In short $c \times (a + b) = c \times a + c \times b$.

Equivalence relation – Any mathematical relation that is reflexive, symmetrical and transitive.

Event (probability) – A set of outcomes of an experiment to which a probability is assigned.

Experiment (probability) – The combination of a number of trials.

Extrapolate/extrapolation – Estimating a value that appears outside of a set of already known data points by extending the known series.

Factorisation – Writing an expression (either numeric or algebraic) as the product of two or more factors.

Fraction family – Each natural number greater than 1 produces a family of fractions when used for the denominator.

Golden Ratio – The ratio $1:\frac{1+\sqrt{5}}{2}$ which is the length of a rectangle of width 1 that if partitioned into a square of length 1 and a smaller rectangle, then the ratio of the width and length of the new rectangle are also $1:\frac{1+\sqrt{5}}{2}$.

Gradient – The measure of steepness of a graph at any point measured by evaluating the vertical change of the graph for a unit horizontal change.

Interpolate/interpolation – Estimating a value that appears within a set of already known data points.

Inverse (number) – A number that, when combined with a given number using a given operation, produces the identity. The most common are the additive inverse (negative), and multiplicative inverse (reciprocal).

Magnitude – The size of a quantity, irrespective of its direction.

Mapping diagram – A diagram that shows how elements in a domain relate to elements in the co-domain.

Numeral – A symbol or mark used to represent a numerical value.

Order – The arrangement of things in relation to each other according to size.

Outcome (probability) – A possible result of an experiment or trial.

Primary data – Data collected for a specific purpose directly from main sources.

Raw data – Data not yet processed or analysed.

Regular (polygon) – A polygon which is both equiangular and equilateral.

Relative frequency – The ratio (usually written as a fraction) of the number of observations in a statistical category to the total number of observations.

Secondary data – Data already collected for a different purpose.

Subject (of a formula) – A variable with coefficient of 1 that appears as a single term expression on one side of the equal sign.

Transcendental number – A number that is not the root of a finite polynomial whose coefficients (including the coefficient of x_0 – the constant term) are all rational numbers.

Trend – A pattern found in time series data used to describe if the data shows an upwards or downwards movement for at least part of the series.

Trial (probability) – A single run of an experiment.

Unitising – To convert, package or organise into one or more units.

Variable – A quantity that can change, usually denoted by a letter in either the Roman or Greek alphabet.

Variation (theory) – The use of carefully structured examples/tasks to emphasise the essential features of a concept by varying the essential and non-essential features to highlight the effect.

Zero-pair – A number paired with its additive inverse so that they sum to zero.

Bibliography

Aldridge, P. (2019) Similar Triangles: Missing Sides, *Variation Theory* (3 May). Available at: https://variationtheory.com/2019/05/03/similar-triangles-calculating-the-length-of-missing-sides/.

AQA (2015) Bridging Units: Resource Pocket 4, Iterative Methods for Solving Equations Numerically. Available at: https://allaboutmaths.aqa.org.uk/attachments/5309.pdf.

Ayalon, M., Watson, A. and Lerman, S. (2017) Students' Conceptualisations of Function Revealed Through Definitions and Examples, *Research in Mathematics Education*, 19(1), 1–19. DOI: 10.1080/14794802.2016.1249397

Beacon Learning Center (2003) Stem and Leaf Plots. Available at: http://www.beaconlearning-center.com/documents/1600_01.pdf.

Bills, C., Bills, L., Mason J. and Watson, A. (2004) *Thinkers: A Collection of Activities to Provoke Mathematical Thinking*. Derby: Association of Teachers of Mathematics, p. 9.

Bogolmony, A. (n.d.) Pythagorean Theorem, *Cut the Knot*. Available at: https://faculty.umb.edu/gary_zabel/Courses/Phil%20281b/Philosophy%20of%20Magic/Arcana/Neoplatonism/Pythagoras/index.shtml.html.

Gokarakonda, S. (n.d.) G2c – Mixed Loci Problems, *Boss Maths*. Available at: https://www.bossmaths.com/g2c/.

Gokarakonda, S. (n.d.) S2f – Stem and Leaf Diagrams, *Boss Maths*. Available at: https://www.bossmaths.com/s2f/.

Brown, M., Hodgen, J. and Küchemann, D. (2016) Learning Experiences Designed to Develop Multiplicative Reasoning: Using Models to Foster Learners' Understanding, *ICCAMS Maths*. Available at: http://iccams-maths.org/wp-content/uploads/2016/01/Brown-Learning-Experiences-Designed-to-Develop-Multiplicative-Reasoning-Using-Models-to-Foster-Learners%E2%80%99-Understanding-1.pdf.

Choy, B. L., Lee, M. Y. and Mizzi, A. (2020) Insights into the Teaching of Gradient from an Exploratory Study of Mathematics Textbooks from Germany, Singapore, and South Korea, *International Electric Journal of Mathematics Education*, 15(3). Available at: https://files.eric.ed.gov/fulltext/EJ1254836.pdf.

Chu96 (2018) Algebraic Vocabulary Match-Up Cards (Term, Expression, Equation, Identity, Formula, Function), *TES* (22 February). Available at: https://www.tes.com/teaching-resource/algebraic-vocabulary-match-up-cards-term-expression-equation-identity-formula-function-11584496.

CIMT (n.d.) MEP Y7 Practice Book 7B, Chapter 21: Probability of One Event. Available at: https://cimt.org.uk/projects/mepres/book7/bk7_21.pdf.

CIMT (n.d.) MEP Y8 Practice Book 8A, Chapter 5: Data Analysis. Available at: https://www.cimt.org.uk/projects/mepres/book8/bk8_5.pdf.

CIMT (n.d.) MEP Y8 Practice Book 8A, Chapter 10: Probability – Two Events. Available at: https://www.cimt.org.uk/projects/mepres/book8/bk8_10.pdf.

CIMT (n.d.) MEP Y8 Practice Book 8B, Chapter 19: Similarity. Available at: https://www.cimt.org.uk/projects/mepres/book8/bk8_19.pdf.

CIMT (n.d.) MEP Y8 Practice Book 8B, Chapter 20: Questionnaires and Analysis. Available at: https://www.cimt.org.uk/projects/mepres/book8/bk8_20.pdf.

CIMT (n.d.) MEP Y9 Practice Book 9A, Chapter 6: Probability. Available at: https://www.cimt.org.uk/projects/mepres/book9/bk9_6.pdf.

CIMT (n.d.) MEP Y9 Practice Book 9B, Chapter 18: Sampling. Available at: https://cimt.org.uk/projects/mepres/book9/bk9_18.pdf.

Cockcroft, W. (1982) *Mathematics Counts: Report of the Committee of Inquiry into the Teaching of Mathematics in Schools under the Chairmanship of Dr W. H. Cockcroft* [Cockcroft Report], p. 71. Available at: http://www.educationengland.org.uk/documents/cockcroft/cockcroft1982.html.

Corbett, J. (2013) Exam Style Questions Histograms, *Corbettmaths*. Available at: https://corbettmaths.com/wp-content/uploads/2013/02/histograms-pdf2.pdf.

Corbett, J. (2015) Exam Style Questions: Lowest Common Multiples Highest Common Factors, *Corbettmaths*. Available at: https://corbettmaths.com/wp-content/uploads/2013/02/lcm-hcf-pdf.pdf.

Corbett, J. (2021) Probability, *Corbettmaths*. Available at: https://corbettmaths.com/wp-content/uploads/2021/03/Probability-2.pdf.

Coward, A. (2021) Distributive Law – Area model and unit counters, *Mr Coward Maths* (22 February). Available at: https://mrcowardmaths.wixsite.com/website/post/distributive-law-area-model-and-unit-counters.

Crypto Corner (n.d.) Cryptography Worksheet – Breaking the Code. Available at: https://crypto.interactive-maths.com/uploads/1/1/3/4/11345755/breaking_the_code.pdf.

Dave314 (2018) Common Mistakes Drawing Axes, *TES*. Available at: https://www.tes.com/teaching-resource/common-mistakesdrawing-axes-11069060.

Department for Education (2013) *Mathematics Programmes of Study: Key Stages 1 and 2 National Curriculum in England.* Ref: DFE-00180-2013. Available at: https://assets.publishing.service.gov.uk/government/uploads/system/uploads/attachment_data/file/335158/PRIMARY_national_curriculum_-_Mathematics_220714.pdf.

Draper, D. (n.d.) Reasoning with Bearings, *Opinions Nobody Asked For*. Available at: https://mrdrapermaths.wordpress.com/2020/02/23/reasoning-with-bearings/.

DrFrostMaths (n.d.) Full Coverage: Vectors. Available at: https://www.drfrostmaths.com/resource.php?rid=341.

eChalk (n.d.) Bearings: Maps and Scale Drawings. Available at: https://www.echalk.co.uk/Maths/bearings/mapReading/bearingsWorksheet.pdf.

Ellis, K. M. (1995) The Monty Hall Problem, *Monty Hall Problem*. Available at: https://www.montyhallproblem.com/.

Errichiello, S. (n.d.) Fraction Division, *Open Middle*. Available at: https://www.openmiddle.com/fraction-division-2/.

Everything2 (2016) Round Half to Even (11 January). Available at: https://everything2.com/title/Round+half+to+even.

Foster, C. (2003) 3.5 Probability, *Foster77*, p. 4. Available at: https://www.foster77.co.uk/3.05%20Probability.pdf.

Galway Maths Grinds (n.d.) Circumcircle and Incircle. Available at: https://galwaymathsgrinds.wordpress.com/maths-topics/circumcircle-and-incircle/.

GINGERSNAPSMATH (2016) The Volume of a Sphere (without Calculus) (24 April). Available at: https://gingersnapsmath.wordpress.com/2016/04/04/the-volume-of-a-sphere-without-calculus/comment-page-1/.

Go Teach Maths (n.d.) Frequency Trees. Available at: https://www.goteachmaths.co.uk/frequency-trees/.

Gray, E. and Tall, D. (1994) Duality, Ambiguity and Flexibility: A Proceptual View of Simple Arithmetic, *Journal for Research in Mathematics Education*, 26(2), 115–141. Available at: https://homepages.warwick.ac.uk/staff/David.Tall/pdfs/dot1994a-gray-jrme.pdf.

Hall, J. (n.d.) Place Value Counters, *MathsBot.com*. Available at: https://mathsbot.com/manipulatives/placeValueCounters.

Hewitt, D. (1996) Mathematical Fluency: The Nature of Practice and the Role of Subordination, *For the Learning of Mathematics*, 16(2), 28–35. Available at: https://flm-journal.org/Articles/233DDDC885A730AB6D45226E38BEF.pdf.

ICCAMS Maths (2013) Mini Ratio Test (Versions A and B). Available at: http://iccams-maths.org/wp-content/uploads/2015/11/MR-2AB-2013z.pdf.

JustMaths (2012) Who Is Right Data Sheet. Available at: https://justmaths.co.uk/wp-content/uploads/2012/12/03-Activity-Who-is-right-data-sheet.pdf.

Kangaroo Maths (2011), Bearings and Scale Drawings. Available at: https://kangaroomaths.co.uk/wp-content/uploads/2019/11/Bearings-and-Scale-Drawing.pdf.

Kaplinsky, R. (n.d.) Dividing Mixed Numbers, *Open Middle*. Available at: https://www.openmiddle.com/dividing-mixed-numbers/.

Koll, H. and Mills, S. (2004) *Year 7: Handling Data: Activities for Teaching Numeracy*. New York: A&C Black Children's & Educational.

Koll, H. and Mills, S. (2004) *Year 9: Measures, Shape and Space: Activities for Teaching Numeracy*. New York: A&C Black Children's & Educational.

Learning Theories (n.d.) Constructivism. Available at: https://www.learning-theories.com/constructivism.html.

Learning Theories (n.d.) Schema Theory. Available at: https://www.learning-theories.org/doku.php?id=learning_theories:schema_theory.

Mason, J., Graham A. and Johnston-Wilder, S. (2005) *Developing Thinking in Algebra*. London: SAGE Publications.

Mason, J. (n.d.) Perimeter and Area: More, Same, Less grid (based on an idea by P. Tsamir and D. Tirosh), *More Same Less*. Available at: https://www.more-same-less.co.uk/grid-collection/Shape?lightbox=comp-k8x2n8zb2__da541e74-d546-4e7d-9053-26507cb6dc35_runtime_dataItem-k8x2n8ze.

Math Worksheets 4 Kids (n.d.) Counting Tally Marks. Available at: https://www.mathworksheets4kids.com/tally/reading1.pdf.

Math Worksheets 4 Kids (n.d.) Stem-and-Leaf Plots Worksheets. Available at: https://www.mathworksheets4kids.com/stem-leaf.php.

Math Worksheets 4 Kids (n.d.) Surface Area of Solids Using Nets. Available at: https://www.mathworksheets4kids.com/surface-area/nets/metric/total-surface-area-1.pdf.

Mattock, P. (2015) Adding and Subtracting with Vectors Matching Cards, *TES* (8 October). Available at: https://www.tes.com/teaching-resource/adding-and-subtracting-with-vectors-matching-cards-11132334.

Mattock, P. (2015) Multiplicative Counting – The Different Types, *Educating Mr Mattock* [blog] (17 August). Available at: https://educatingmrmattock.blogspot.com/2015/08/multiplicative-counting-different-types.html.

Mattock, P. (2015) Vector Proof, *TES* (17 November). Available at: https://www.tes.com/teaching-resource/vector-proof-11138743.

Mattock, P. (2016) Errors in Truncation, *TES* (7 May). Available at: https://www.tes.com/teaching-resource/errors-in-truncation-11271966.

Mattock, P. (2016) Independence, Dependence, Mutually Exclusive or Not?, *TES* (6 November). Available at: https://www.tes.com/teaching-resource/independence-dependence-mutually-exclusive-or-not-11413604.

Mattock, P. (2018) Types of Data Worksheet, *TES* (20 January). Available at: https://www.tes.com/teaching-resource/types-of-data-worksheet-11816316.

Mattock, P. (2021) Rotations on a Triangular Grid, *TES* (12 May). Available at: https://www.tes.com/teaching-resource/rotations-on-a-triangulargrid-12528910.

McCombes, S. (2019) An Introduction to Sampling Methods, *Scribbr* (19 September). Available at: https://www.scribbr.com/methodology/sampling-methods/.

McCourt, M. (2017) A Brief History of Mathematics Education in England, *Emaths* [blog] (29 December). Available at: https://www.emaths.co.uk/index.php/blog/item/a-brief-history-of-mathematics-education-in-england.

MME Revise (n.d.) Loci and Construction Worksheets, Questions and Revision. Available at: https://mathsmadeeasy.co.uk/gcse-maths-revision/loci-and-construction-gcse-revision-and-worksheets/.

Molony, M. (2012) Generating Pythagorean Triples, *Dreamshire* [blog] (14 November). Available at: https://blog.dreamshire.com/generating-pythagorean-triples/.

Morgan, J. (2014) Animations and Simulations, *Resourceaholic* [blog] (7 August). Available at: https://www.resourceaholic.com/2014/08/gifs.html.

Morgan, J. (2014) Long Live Stem and Leaf, *Resourceaholic* [blog] (25 July). Available at: https://www.resourceaholic.com/2014/07/stem-and-leaf.html.

Morgan, J. (2014) Pythagoras' Theorem, *Resourceaholic* [blog] (2 December). Available at: https://www.resourceaholic.com/2014/09/pythagoras.html.

Morgan, J. (2019) *A Compendium of Mathematical Methods.* Woodbridge: John Catt Educational Ltd.

Morgan, J. (2019) Indices in Depth, *Resourceaholic* [blog] (22 December). Available at: https://www.resourceaholic.com/2019/12/indices-in-depth.html.

Morse, D. (2021) Angles in Quadrilaterals (Worksheets with Solutions), *TES* (16 September). Available at: https://www.tes.com/teaching-resource/angles-in-quadrilaterals-worksheets-with-solutions-12208149.

Ms Bello's Math Hub (n.d.) Building Linear Equations. Available at: http://villanovamath.weebly.com/uploads/1/3/7/8/13787526/building_linear_equations.pdf.

Novak, A., Bakogianis, R., Boucher, K., Nolan, J. and Phillips, G. (2009) *Maths Quest 12: Further Mathematics.* London: Jacaranda. Chapter available at: https://www.hawkermaths.com/uploads/7/7/3/8/77386549/bivariate_data_chap_2.pdf.

NPL (n.d.) SI Units: Second (s). Available at: https://www.npl.co.uk/si-units/second.

Nuffield Foundation (2011) Errors. Available at: https://www.nuffieldfoundation.org/sites/default/files/files/FSMA%20Errors%20student(1).pdf.

Nuffield Foundation (2011) Plans. Available at: https://www.nuffieldfoundation.org/sites/default/files/files/FSMA%20Plans%20student.pdf.

Nunes, T. and Bryant, P. (2009) *Key Understandings in Mathematics Learning. Paper 2: Understanding Whole Numbers.* London: Nuffield Foundation, p. 4.

Office for National Statistics (n.d.) Census. Available at: https://www.ons.gov.uk/census#censusdataandbackground.

Oksuz, C. (n.d.) Children's Understanding of Equality and the Equal Symbol, *CIMT*. Available at: https://www.cimt.org.uk/journal/oksuz.pdf.

Online Math Learning (n.d.) Unit Circle and Trig Graphs. Available at: https://www.onlinemathlearning.com/unit-circle-trig-graphs.html.

Pierce, R. (2022) Proportions, *Math Is Fun* (5 June). Available at: https://www.mathsisfun.com/algebra/proportions.html.

PixiMaths (n.d.) Two-Way Tables. Available at: https://www.piximaths.co.uk/two-way-tables.

Prior, J. (2018) Factorising Linear Expressions 1, *Minimally Different* (22 March). Available at: https://minimallydifferent.com/2018/03/22/factorising-linear-expressions-1/.

Reddy, B. (2014) Design Your Own Mastery Curriculum in Maths, *Mr Reddy Maths* [blog] (29 March). Available at: http://mrreddy.com/blog/2014/03/design-your-own-mastery-curriculum-in-maths/.

Resourceaholic (n.d.) Alegraic Expressions 1 Maze. Available at: https://drive.google.com/file/d/0B9L2lYGRiK2bTlVYMUFWZEJCZ3M/view?resourcekey=0C9N92eQ2xf9UWLav_eoW9.

Robbins, N. (2012) Two Opinions on the Usefulness of Pictographs, *Forbes* (12 October). Available at: https://www.forbes.com/sites/naomirobbins/2012/10/10/two-opinions-on-the-usefulness-of-pictographs/?sh=7d9b583623dd.

Ronan, M. (2020) Full Circle, *History Today* (4 April). Available at: https://www.historytoday.com/history-matters/full-circle.

Ross, R. (2017) Eureka! The Archimedes Principle, *Live Science* (2017). Available at: https://www.livescience.com/58839-archimedesprinciple.html.

Rycroft-Smith, L. and Gould, T. (2020) What Does Research Suggest about Teaching and Learning the Equal Sign?, *Cambridge Mathematics Espresso* 34 (November). Available at: https://www.cambridgemaths.org/Images/espresso_34_the_equal_sign.pdf.

Rycroft-Smith, L., Macey, D., Horsman, R. and Gould, T. (2020) What Does Research Suggest about the Development of Proportional Reasoning in Mathematics Learning?, *Cambridge Maths Espresso* 28 (February). Available at: https://www.cambridgemaths.org/Images/espresso_28_proportional_reasoning.pdf.

Siemon, D., Breed, M. and Virgona, J. (2008) From Additive to Multiplicative Thinking – the Big Challenge of the Middle Years, *ResearchGate*. Available at: https://www.researchgate.net/publication/237298794_FROM_ADDITIVE_TO_MULTIPLICATIVE_THINKING_-_THE_BIG_CHALLENGE_OF_THE_MIDDLE_YEARS.

Skemp, R. R. (1976) Relational Understanding and Instrumental Understanding, *Mathematics Teaching*, 77, 20–26. Available at: https://www.lancsngfl.ac.uk/secondary/math/download/file/PDF/Skemp%20Full%20Article.pdf.

Staake, J. (2019) 18 Estimation Activities That Take the Guesswork Out of Teaching Math, *WeAreTeachers* (17 July). Available at: https://www.weareteachers.com/estimation-activities/.

Stack Exchange (2017) Is Pythagoras' Theorem about Distances or Areas?. Available at: https://math.stackexchange.com/questions/2359457/is-pythagoras-theorem-about-distances-or-areas.

Steele, J. (2018) Equations with Arithmetic and Quadratic Sequences, *Median* [blog] (23 May). Available at: https://donsteward.blogspot.com/2018/05/equations-with-arithmetic-and-quadratic.html.

STEM Learning (n.d.) Handling Data Cycle Poster. Available at: https://www.stem.org.uk/resources/elibrary/resource/29299/year-eight-handling-data-mini-pack.

STEM Learning (n.d.) Interpreting Algebraic Expressions A1. Available at: https://www.stem.org.uk/resources/elibrary/resource/26952/interpreting-algebraic-expressions-a1.

STEM Learning (n.d.) Interpreting Frequency Graphs, Cumulative Frequency Graphs, Box and Whisker Plots S6. Available at: https://www.stem.org.uk/resources/elibrary/resource/26994/interpreting-frequency-graphs-cumulative-frequency-graphs-box-and.

STEM Learning (n.d.) Manipulating Surds N11. Available at: https://www.stem.org.uk/resources/elibrary/resource/26731/manipulating-surds-n11.

Steward, D. (2011) Division = Subtraction, *Median* [blog] (27 April). Available at: https://donsteward.blogspot.com/2011/04/division-subtraction.html.

Steward, D. (2011) Fraction Division, *Median* [blog] (24 May). Available at: https://donsteward.blogspot.com/2011/02/fraction-division.html.

Steward, D. (2011) Rectangles on a Grid, *Median* [blog] (16 July). Available at: https://donsteward.blogspot.com/2011/07/rectangles-on-grid.html.

Steward, D. (2011) Relating Charts to Data Sets, *Median* [blog] (20 March). Available at: https://donsteward.blogspot.com/2011/03/relating-charts-to-data-sets.html.

Steward, D. (2011) Temperature Conversion, *Median* [blog] (1 March). Available at: https://donsteward.blogspot.com/2011/03/temperature-conversion.html.

Steward, D. (2012) L-Shaped Perimeters, *Median* [blog] (12 February). Available at: https://donsteward.blogspot.com/2012/02/l-shaped-perimters.html.

Steward, D. (2012) Obloidal Perimeters, *Median* [blog] (22 February). Available at: https://donsteward.blogspot.com/2012/02/obloidal-perimeters.html.

Steward, D. (2012) Similar Pairs, *Median* [blog] (14 September). Available at: https://donsteward.blogspot.com/2012/09/similar-pairs.html.

Steward, D. (2012) Volume of a Pyramid, *Median* [blog] (29 September). Available at: https://donsteward.blogspot.com/2012/09/volume-of-pyramid.html.

Steward, D. (2013) Cone, Sphere, Cylinder, *Median* [blog] (25 July). Available at: https://donsteward.blogspot.com/2013/07/cone-sphere-cylinder.html.

Steward, D. (2013) Cuisenaire Rod Equations, *Median* [blog] (30 March). Available at: https://donsteward.blogspot.com/2013/03/cuisenaire-equations.html?m=0.

Steward, D. (2013) Simultaneous Equation Tasks, *Median* [blog] (14 July). Available at: https://donsteward.blogspot.com/2013/07/simultaneous-equation-tasks.html.

Steward, D. (2013) Sine Rule, *Median* [blog] (19 November). Available at: https://donsteward.blogspot.com/2013/11/sine-rule.html.

Steward, D. (2014) Fractions 'of', *Median* [blog] (17 January). Available at: https://donsteward.blogspot.com/2014/01/fractions-of.html.

Steward, D. (2014) Sum One, Don Steward, *Median* [blog] (22 May). Available at: https://donsteward.blogspot.com/2014/05/sum-one.html?m=0.

Steward, D. (2016) Combined Enlargements, *Median* [blog] (2016). Available at: https://donsteward.blogspot.com/2016/04/combined-enlargements.html.

Steward, D. (2016) Multiplying Mixed Numbers, *Median* [blog] (24 January). Available at: https://donsteward.blogspot.com/2016/01/multiplying-mixed-numbers.html.

Steward, D. (2017) Four Consecutive Numbers, *Median* [blog] (29 April). Available at: https://donsteward.blogspot.com/2017/04/four-consecutive-numbers.html.

Steward, D. (2017) Fraction Addition Denominators Multiples, *Median* [blog] (12 May). Available at: https://donsteward.blogspot.com/2017/05/fraction-addition-denominators-multiples.html.

Steward, D. (2017) Fraction Cancelling, *Median* [blog] (12 May). Available at: https://donsteward.blogspot.com/2017/05/fraction-cancelling.html.

Steward, D. (2017) Mean of a Frequency Distribution, with Algebra, *Median* [blog] (2 March). Available at: https://donsteward.blogspot.com/2017/03/mean-of-frequency-distribution-with.html.

Steward, D. (2017) Rounding to Powers of 10, *Median* [blog] (20 August 2017). Available at: https://donsteward.blogspot.com/2017/08/rounding-to-powers-of-10.html.

Steward, D. (2018) Surface Area and factorizable quadratics, *Median* [blog] (6 December). Available at: https://donsteward.blogspot.com/2018/12/surface-area-and-factorisable.html.

Steward, D. (2019) Division, *Median* [blog] (13 February). Available at: https://donsteward.blogspot.com/2019/02/division.html.

Steward, D. (2019) Frequency Trees and Percentages, *Median* [blog] (7 December). Available at: https://donsteward.blogspot.com/2019/12/frequency-trees-and-percentages.html.

Steward, D. (2019) Simultaneous Equations Generalising 1 (out of 6), *Median* [blog] (20 February). Available at: https://donsteward.blogspot.com/2019/02/simultaneous-equations-generalising-1.html.

Steward, D. (2019) To and Fro, *Median* [blog] (10 July). Available at: https://donsteward.blogspot.com/2019/07/to-and-fro.html.

Story of Mathematics (n.d.) List of Important Mathematicians. Available at: https://www.storyofmathematics.com/mathematicians.html.

Sweller, J. (1988) Cognitive Load During Problem Solving: Effects on Learning, *Cognitive Science* 12. Available at: https://onlinelibrary.wiley.com/doi/pdf/10.1207/s15516709cog1202_4.

teachMathematics (n.d.) Circle Circumference. Available at: https://www.teachmathematics.net/page/11010/around-circles.

Theodore, M. (2022) Similarity Worksheets, *Math-Aids.Com* (16 November). Available at: https://www.math-aids.com/Geometry/Similarity/.

Transfinite (2015) Venn Diagrams Practice Questions + Solutions, *TES* (14 April). Available at: https://www.tes.com/teaching-resource/venn-diagrams-practice-questions-solutions-6330738.

Tristanjones (2015) Averages (Mode, Median, Mean) GCSE Revision, *TES* (20 January). Available at: https://www.tes.com/teaching-resource/averages-mode-median-mean-gcse-revision-6161872.

Tristanjones (2015) Maths GCSE worksheet: Using Angle Facts, *TES* (20 January). Available at: https://www.tes.com/teaching-resource/maths-gcse-worksheet-using-angle-facts-6159350.

VARTHETA (2016) Graph (29 April). Available at: https://vartheta.wordpress.com/2016/04/29/graph/.

Weisstein, E. W. (n.d.) Collatz Problem, *Wolfram MathWorld*. Available at: https://mathworld.wolfram.com/CollatzProblem.html.

Weisstein, E. W. (n.d.) Equality, *Wolfram MathWorld*. Available at: https://mathworld.wolfram.com/Equality.html.

Weisstein, E. W. (n.d.) Euclid's Postulates, *Wolfram MathWorld*. Available at: https://mathworld.wolfram.com/EuclidsPostulates.html.

Wikipedia (2021) Inverse-square law (October 7). Available at: https://en.wikipedia.org/wiki/Inverse-square_law#Occurences.

Wild Maths (n.d.) Rene Descartes and the Fly on the Ceiling. Available at: https://wild.maths.org/ren%C3%A9-descartes-and-fly-ceiling.

Williams, H. J. (2018) Mathematics in the Early Years: What Matters?, *Impact* (12 September). Available at: https://impact.chartered.college/article/mathematics-in-early-years/.

Yusuf, J. (n.d.) Edexcel GCSE Mathematics (Linear) – 1MA0 Stem & Leaf Diagrams, *Maths Genie*. Available at: https://www.mathsgenie.co.uk/resources/49_stem-and-leaf.pdf.

Yusuf, J. (n.d.) GCSE (1–9) Similar Shapes (Area and Volume), *Maths Genie*. Available at: https://www.mathsgenie.co.uk/resources/similarshapes2.pdf.

Ingram Content Group UK Ltd.
Milton Keynes UK
UKHW022353280323
419321UK00007B/30